FORMS OF PRAYER

2008/5768
תשס"ח

I

DAILY, SABBATH
AND OCCASIONAL PRAYERS
EIGHTH EDITION

Published by The Movement for Reform Judaism,
The Sternberg Centre for Judaism
80 East End Road, London N3 2SY

Hardback ISBN 978-0-947884-13-0
Large print extract ISBN 978-0-947884-14-7
Deluxe edition ISBN 978-0-947884-15-4
Compact edition ISBN 978-0-947884-16-1

© Movement for Reform Judaism and the Authors 2008
All rights reserved. No part of this publication may be reproduced or transmitted in any form or by any means or stored in a retrieval system of any nature without prior written permission, except as permitted by law or in accordance with any licence granted by an appropriate reprographic rights organisation. Application for permission for other use of copyright material including permission to reproduce extracts in other published works shall be made to the Publisher. Full acknowledgement of the Publisher and source must be given.

Layout, design, cover logo
and section graphic devices by Marc Michaels.

Some texts used with permission of Davka Corporation, copyright 1995.

Set in Times New Roman and Frank Ruhl.

Printed in The Netherlands by Jongbloed b.v.

Printed on Primapage woodfree paper manufactured
using pulps from sustainable managed forests.

TABLE OF CONTENTS

Table of Contents	iii
Sponsors	vi
Preface	1
Acknowledgements	5
Meditations Before Prayer - Engaging with Prayer	9
Preparation for Prayer	10
The Nature of Prayer	11
The Prayer of the Community	14
Liturgy and Prayer	15
Some Individual Prayers	16
For Moments of Private Prayer	24
Sh'liach Tsibbur - The Worship-Service Leader	26
Daily Morning Service	27
Daily Afternoon Service	61
Daily Evening Service	65
Daily *Amidah*	73
Weekday Torah Service	87
Shabbat Evening Service	95
Shabbat Morning Service	153
Shabbat Torah Service I	235
Shabbat Torah Service II	257
Shabbat Torah Service III	267
Kaddish d'rabanan	270
Additional Service for Shabbat	273
Shabbat Afternoon Service	289
Concluding Prayers and Songs	305
Reflections on the Shabbat Services and Daily Amidah	325
Community Prayers and Passages	349
Prayer of a *Bar Mitsvah*	350
Prayer of a *Bat Mitsvah*	350
A Blessing for Children	351
The Ten Commandments	352
Blessing for Someone Who is Ill	354
Prayers for Healing	355
Thanksgiving for Recovery after Danger (*Gomel*)	355
Marriage Service	356
Sheva B'rachot	358
Thanksgiving Service for Parents (Naming of a Child)	360
Service of Affirmation of the Jewish Faith	363
A Prayer for Committee Meetings	366
A Prayer for Interfaith Meetings	366
A Prayer for International Understanding	366

A Prayer for Responsibility for Justice and the Environment	366
A Prayer for the Release of Captives	366
A Prayer in a Time of War	367
A Prayer in a Time of a Natural Disaster	368
A Liturgy in a Time of Community Threat or Disaster	369
A Prayer for Combating Poverty and Injustice	371
A Prayer for World Peace	372
Calendar of the Year	**373**
Chanukah	374
Tu Bishvat	380
Purim	384
Yom Ha-Shoah - Memorial Service for the Six Million	388
Israel Independence Day - *Yom Ha-Atzma'ut* or *Shabbat Atzma'ut*	394
Tish'ah B'Av	402
Memorial Prayer for Remembrance Shabbat (November)	404
National Holocaust Memorial Day (January)	405
Life Cycle Events	**407**
Blessings for Various Occasions	**408**
Blessings Concerning Food	408
Blessings Concerning Nature	409
Blessings Concerning People	410
Blessings Concerning Events	411
Prayers for Various Life Events	**413**
Prayers for a Journey (including to Israel)	413
A Prayer on Making Aliyah	414
A Prayer on Leaving Home	414
A Prayer for Parents When a Child Leaves Home	415
A Prayer for an Anniversary	416
A Prayer on Retirement	416
A Prayer on the Loss of a Loved One	416
A Prayer during Depression	417
A Prayer for those Responsible for the Care of Others	417
A Prayer about Animal Companions	418
A Prayer during Illness	419
A Prayer on behalf of the Ill	419
A Prayer before Surgery	420
A Prayer During Dangerous Illness (A Deathbed Confession)	420
A Prayer on Behalf of the Terminally Ill	421
Prayers after a Miscarriage or on the Death of an Infant	422
A Prayer in the Home before a Funeral	424
***Yizkor* - Memorial Service**	**426**
Prayers for the stages of mourning	430
At the end of the *Shivah* period	430
At the end of the *Sh'loshim* period	431

v CONTENTS

A Prayer for the *Yahrzeit* (Anniversary of a Death)	431
Prayers on Visiting a Grave	433
Home Services	**435**
Seder Chanukat Ha-Bayit - Service at the Dedication of a Home	436
Seder B'rit Milah - Service at a Circumcision	438
Seder Zeved Ha-Bat - The Precious Gift of a Daughter	440
Night Prayers for Children and Adults	442
Morning Prayers for Children and Adults	444
Shabbat Eve Home Service	446
Kiddush	**451**
Kiddush for Shabbat Eve	451
Kiddush for Shabbat Day	453
***Havdalah* Service**	**457**
The close of Shabbat and *Havdalah*	457
Songs at the Close of Shabbat	460
Blessings Before Meals	462
Thanksgiving After Meals	463
Shorter Forms of Thanksgiving After Meals	481
Thanksgiving After Meals as Songs	485
The Blessings After a Wedding Meal	487
Study Anthology	**489**
The *Siddur*	494
Shabbat Evening Service	504
Shabbat Morning Service	508
Life's Journey	518
Society and Community	548
The Life of the Spirit	572
Passages for Responsive Reading, Study or Meditation	**598**
Psalm Anthology	**609**
Hallel	663
Alternative Second and Third Paragraphs for the *Sh'ma*	**689**
Kaddish Titkabbal	**698**
Sayings of the Fathers	**701**
Notes on Transliteration, Icons and Hebrew	**725**
Glossary and Index	**727**
List of Artists	**741**
List of Illustrations	**743**
Sources of Unnamed Prayers, Meditations and Reflections	**744**
Structure of Shabbat Services	**745**
Song Index	**746**
Permissions and Acknowledgments	**747**
Dedications	**749**
Family Record	**750**

SPONSORS

The following have generously supported the creation and on-going development of this Siddur

Anonymous

Jill and Michael Barrington and family

Leslie and Dee Bergman

Carole and Brian Berman and family

Lillian and Michael Bogod

Sir Michael Burton and family, in loving memory of Corinne

Ruth and Harvey Cohen

Edgware and District Reform Synagogue, in loving memory of
Rabbi Dr Michael Leigh who served the community with devotion

Mike and Fiona Karet Frankl

Ruth, Edward and Andrew Gilbert and family

Jane and Michael Grabiner

Jo and Rick Haller, in memory of their parents

Members of Hendon Reform Synagogue,
in memory of their beloved founder Rabbi Dr Arthur Katz

Patricia and Jerome Karet, לדור ודור

Anonymous

The Kirby family, in memory of Eve and Herbert Kirby

Hilary and James Leek

Colette and Peter Levy, in memory of Harry Lynford

Rhonda and Fraser Marcus

Val and Dolf Mogendorff, in honour of their parents

The family of the late Prof. Alfred Moritz, in his memory

Anonymous

The Moss family Charitable Trust

The family of Lilly Pollock, (née Schindler), in loving memory

The Dr Trevor Rissen Memorial Fund

Joyce and Jeffery Rose

Gerald and Elaina Rothman, in memory of Ann and Syd

Sir Sigmund and Lady Sternberg

The Stone Ashdown Trust

Anonymous

David and Cecilie Stross

Members of West London Synagogue, in loving memory of
Rabbi Hugo Gryn, who cared deeply about the Reform prayerbook

Lana, Debbie, Sara and Ian, in loving memory of Jon Young

Roderick Young and David Mooney, in memory
of Roderick's grandfather Frederick Jessel Benson.

Anonymous

PREFACE

A prayerbook is at the same time the most public and the most private expression of Jewish values and experience. It is the most accessible window into the Jewish soul, but at the same time a witness to the daily struggles that take place within that soul. Liturgies, as they evolve over the centuries, contain the greatest aspirations of a people of faith, yet at the same time the ghostly echoes of old controversies and divisions. Precisely because they are public statements and affirmations, liturgies encapsulate the self-understanding of a given community at a given moment in time. They affirm the inclusion of those who feel themselves part of that community, but whether intentionally or not, may effectively exclude others who do not feel able to join that particular community or that particular form of worship.

Yet while prayerbooks reflect the attitudes of past generations that have formed the community they are also the context, and sometimes the battleground, however well disguised, in which new experiences, views and needs are reflected, tested out or asserted in the public arena. That is why liturgies both unite and divide communities. They are defining texts and events.

At the same time that liturgies provide for collective experiences and expressions, they also offer the possibility of private space and personal meditation in the framework of the liturgical moment. The silences between the words may be as important as the words themselves.

Since liturgies, whatever their content, may accompany people from very early in their lives and acquire special significance at certain times, they become very deeply embedded in our hearts and minds. Even if we are not always aware of this, they represent something eternal, reliable and secure. It has to be said that this is the case even when the texts themselves have little meaning to the person who recites or hears them, either because of the passage of time since their original composition, or because the language is unknown, or because in time the rhythms and cadences have become like a mantra. Yet try to change a word or syllable, a melody or the order of particular prayers that people are used to and enormous emotions are unleashed. It is of little consolation to know that a few years down the line the most radical changes will be equally experienced as if they had been 'eternally there'. At the time of change only the threat and distress may be felt. We underestimate the power and depth of ritual and liturgy at our peril.

But change is at the heart of the value system of Reform Judaism - not change for its own sake, but in order to answer the needs of a community always in transition in a changing world. The 1977 edition of Forms of Prayer was a child of its time. Under the initial chairmanship of Rabbi Dr Werner van der Zyl, and subsequently of Rabbi Hugo Gryn, the prayerbook committee together with the two editors, Rabbi Lionel Blue and Rabbi Jonathan Magonet, spoke for the generation that had experienced the horrors of the Second World War as refugee survivors, and a generation born during and immediately after the war. In addition to addressing what were seen as lacks in the previous edition, the volume had to attempt to create a liturgy after the *Shoah*, the single greatest catastrophe faced by the Jewish people since the destruction of Jerusalem and the beginnings of almost two thousand years of exile from the land, and the miraculous, if ever-threatened, return to the land with the establishment of the State of Israel. For that edition to speak to a new generation, the language had to be made more contemporary, for example replacing the use of Thee and Thou, already archaic in the 1931 edition it was to replace. It became an educational tool providing opportunities to study through responsive readings and a large anthology - it being argued that the *Siddur* was likely to be the only Jewish book owned by members, so that what it contained was crucial in shaping their Jewish knowledge and identity. In these and other areas it pioneered new approaches to liturgy many of which were taken up by other 'progressive' prayerbooks around the world.

This new edition is similarly attempting to address new situations. Already the issue of the equality of men and women, as reflected in the language of the prayerbook, and in the recognition given to women amongst our spiritual ancestors, was noted in the High Holyday volume of 1985 and comprehensively addressed in the Pilgrim Festival Prayerbook of 1995. Lessons learned from the latter have helped to make 'inclusive language' a feature of this new edition.

Whereas in the past one standard service was seen as sufficient for the broad base of a congregation, today many congregations experiment with different types of *minyanim*. Moreover our congregations are quite varied in the mix of traditional and contemporary material, let alone musical styles, which they use. For this reason it was felt that greater flexibility was needed within the service structure, allowing for very different forms of worship. We have tried to meet this need by allowing for and encouraging choices within various sections of the service, so as to provide flexibility within the familiar.

Today we are conscious of a shrinking and aging Jewish population in the United Kingdom, but also of a younger generation that feels detached from congregational life. So the prayerbook needs to be more accessible and welcoming to a wider range of people, both within and beyond our congregations, some of whose Jewish background is often minimal.

<<<

3 PREFACE

Hebrew, such a central aspect of Jewish worship, remains a stumbling block that prevents many fully taking part in religious services, and the bold step has been taken here of transliterating most of the Shabbat services and some home services in the hope that through this encouragement to participate the further step to learning Hebrew will also follow.

The traditional service is expressed in terms of the Jewish people as a collective whole, with our specific values and traditions, our views about God and our relationship to one another. Amidst so much that is stated in terms of 'we' and 'us', it is sometimes difficult to find our individual voice or needs being addressed. The notes that accompany each page, together with a new section on liturgy in the Study Anthology, may go some way to translating the traditional language of prayer into its historical and theological place, but also into more personal understandings. A new section, 'Reflections on the Shabbat Services and Weekday *Amidah*', offers new approaches to addressing the traditional prayers, particularly for people who have questions about their language or affirmations. A *menorah* and page number (🕎*123*) beside a prayer or section indicate where such reflections may be found. Life cycle prayers, as well as a similar section in the Study Anthology, may offer other ways of expressing our own individual voice both within and beyond the service.

Our growing concern with issues like terrorism, the relationship between different religious communities, the environment, poverty and human rights all need to be addressed within the prayer life of the Jewish community. So in addition to prayers for inclusion in appropriate services, to be found in a new section on Public Prayers and Passages, these issues too are addressed in a section of the Study Anthology.

While it is easy now to list the above features of the new *Siddur* as self-evident, each of them has been introduced after much heart-searching and debate within the Editorial Board, the Assembly of Rabbis, and throughout the congregations, since we have conducted a thorough set of trials of different drafts, more so than in any previous edition. People have responded individually and as congregations, and we have tried to take into account a wide range of views and wishes, many of which are inevitably mutually contradictory. Clearly with such a diverse set of congregations, each with a diverse membership, there is no way that all expectations can be met. Yet it is our hope that everyone who expressed an opinion will feel listened to and will recognize places where their influence has been felt. Where their views have not been fully accepted, it is because we have responded to equally strongly felt needs from others and had to make a fine judgment on what to prioritise. In such an enterprise we may have to settle for a holy compromise, but do so in the knowledge that the sacrifice of our own particular opinion has been in order to help many others.

<<<

The desire for a new name for the prayerbook came up relatively early in the process and many names were suggested, most of which have already been used for new prayerbooks of other movements. We first chose the name *Iyyun T'fillah*, 'Devotion in Prayer', because of its presence in the passage within our existing *Siddur* (from *Shabbat* 127a) where it is listed as 'one of the things whose interest we enjoy in this world, while the capital remains for us in the world to come'. The term is not without some controversy, as rabbinic texts understand it either positively, as devotion, or negatively, as attempting to calculate the reward to be obtained from God from our prayers. We felt that these two aspects of the term rightly reflect the tension that is often present within our prayer life, as people struggle to find the holy within a highly secular world. In the end the decision was made to retain the name 'Forms of Prayer', *Seder ha-t'fillot*, from the previous editions. However we have used the term *Iyyun T'fillah*, now translated as 'Engaging with Prayer', as the designation of the page notes, introductions and reflective passages. It is an appropriate term for a Jewish tradition that understands the root meaning of the verb *l'hitpallel*, 'to pray', as meaning to judge, and hence 'to judge oneself', when we stand before God.

The previous edition included illustrations of synagogues, many of which were destroyed in the Second World War, as a memorial to the victims of the *Shoah*. In looking for illustrations for this new edition two ideas were followed. Because of the desire to encourage a greater engagement with Hebrew the aim has been to use Hebrew calligraphy in most cases as the basis of artistic designs. Secondly, in seeking artists, priority was given to those associated with congregations rebuilt or newly created since the war, as a way of looking towards the Jewish future in Europe. We were fortunate in finding artists from Belgium, France, Germany, Holland, Russia, Spain and Switzerland, as well as the UK, Israel and the USA. Of particular help in following the structure of the individual services and the different sections of the book are a series of graphical headings created by Marc Michaels, whose remarkable design skills throughout the *Siddur* have made a complex layout clear and accessible.

It was asked why the traditional first paragraph of the *Amidah* says: 'God of Abraham, God of Isaac and God of Jacob', and not simply 'God of Abraham, Isaac and Jacob'. The answer: that each of the patriarchs had to discover God in his own way, based on the tradition he had inherited but also on his own experience in his own time and place. That is our challenge today - and equally a quest to find the 'God of Sarah, God of Rebecca, God of Rachel and God of Leah'.

It is our hope that this new *Siddur* as a whole will provide both a synagogue resource and a companion in the home, just as the current volume has managed to do for the past thirty years.

Jonathan Magonet, Editor

ACKNOWLEDGEMENTS

This new edition of *Forms of Prayer* is the result of a remarkable collaborative exercise over a seven-year period. The initial idea that a new edition was required to meet the needs of a new generation was welcomed enthusiastically by Rabbi Dr Tony Bayfield as Head of Movement. He offered his own distinctive ideas about what might be required, but having entrusted the task to the editor and his team, stepped back to give the task the freedom needed to evolve with its own dynamic and logic, intervening only towards to end to ensure that certain important opportunities were not overlooked. His trust and support whenever major debates arose within the Movement gave stability and security to the whole enterprise.

The Editorial Board, under the chairmanship of Rabbi Steven Katz, oversaw the entire process. Individual members also contributed specific elements and though its composition varied from time to time because of other commitments the following participated: Rabbis Simon Franses, Paul Freedman, Michael Hilton, Maurice Michaels, Reuven Silverman, Danny Smith, Jacqueline Tabick, Larry Tabick and in addition student rabbi Debbie Young and Dr Helena Miller. Towards the end of the process, a team convened by Rabbi Tony Bayfield, including Rabbis Miriam Bayfield, Howard Cooper, Tony Hammond and Jeffrey Newman, explored and helped produce the Reflective Service materials. The Glossary was prepared by Rabbi Amanda Golby, and the transliteration by Rabbi Larry Tabick. Responsibility for finding music for the *Siddur* was taken by Zoë Jacobs and Rabbis Laura Janner-Klausner and Sybil Sheridan. Throughout the process the Assembly of Rabbis, under the successive chairmanship of Rabbis Sylvia Rothschild, Ian Morris, Maurice Michaels and Jonathan Romain, oversaw all the materials and devoted a number of residential and business sessions to evaluating them, suggesting improvements and agreeing the final contents.

Responsibility for the consultation process for the *Siddur* through its various draft editions, as well as organising the practical arrangements regarding printing, funding, promotion and sales, fell to the *Siddur* Steering Committee under the chairmanship of Rabbi Elaina Rothman, without whose enthusiasm, determination and support the project might never have been realised. The chairs of the two committees together with Jenny Pizer, David Jacobs and the Editor visited congregations throughout the country presenting the materials and fielding questions and concerns in what was a greater consultative process than for any previous edition. Every attempt was made to respond to the written comments, concerns and proposed improvements from numerous individuals and congregations. The members of the Steering Committee included in addition to the above: Dr John Bowden, Jane Cutter,

ACKNOWLEDGMENTS 6

Jon Epstein, Mike Frankl, Andrew Gilbert, Debbie Jacobs, Larry Ross and Robert Shrager. All practical and administrative matters, including researching copyright materials, were undertaken by Sylvia Morris. IT support throughout was undertaken by Marc Ozin. We are sad to record the death of Ian Spinks who undertook the printing of the many early draft versions.

Proofreading of the Hebrew at different stages was undertaken by Rabbis Colin Eimer, Paul Freedman, Amanda Golby, Charles H. Middleburgh, Sammy Pereira, Reuven Silverman, Student Rabbi Yuval Keren, and Dr Annette Boeckler, while the English was examined by Brian Humphreys and Dr John Bowden, to whom additional thanks are due for his practical advice throughout on all matters to do with publishing.

The extraordinary task of creating a layout that could incorporate the Hebrew and English text, transliteration and commentary fell to Marc Michaels without whom the present volume could not have been produced. In addition he designed the numerous section headings, icons and other aids that ensure continuity and ease of use of the services. Each of the sections that make up the *Siddur* went through up to twenty sets of corrections and revisions under his patient guidance and practical care.

Various individuals viewed the contents and made important suggestions and corrections, including Dr Jeremy Schonfield. Pre-eminent amongst them is Dr Eric Friedland, whose knowledge of traditional and progressive Jewish liturgies and sensitivity to the parameters of innovation helped shape the final version.

The artists that we approached were extremely generous in their willingness to offer existing artistic materials and create new ones for the *Siddur*. Their names are recorded in the List of Artists.

The Movement for Reform Judaism is grateful for the considerable care taken by Jongbloed bv in the complex task of printing this *Siddur*.

Jonathan Magonet, Editor

עיון תפלה
Engaging with Prayer

וּקְרָאתֶם אֹתִי וַהֲלַכְתֶּם וְהִתְפַּלַּלְתֶּם אֵלָי וְשָׁמַעְתִּי אֲלֵיכֶם:
וּבִקַּשְׁתֶּם אֹתִי וּמְצָאתֶם כִּי תִדְרְשֻׁנִי בְּכָל־לְבַבְכֶם:
וְנִמְצֵאתִי לָכֶם נְאֻם־יהוה:

When you call Me and come and pray to Me, I will hear you.
When you seek Me, you will find Me,
if you search for Me with all your heart.
I shall let you find Me, says God.

Jeremiah 29: 12-14

The central part of the Shabbat and Daily services, beginning with the *Sh'ma* and its blessings, has a fixed form, the Hebrew term being *keva*, whereas the earlier parts of the service offer greater flexibility. Being 'fixed' there is always the risk that the prayers become mechanical recitations. Rabbinic tradition stressed the need both to concentrate on the meaning of the prayers and to keep them fresh, to read them with *kavvanah*, 'intention'. To aid in this they introduced private meditations and poems. This section provides materials that may aid engaging with prayer, *iyyun tefillah*, meditations that may be read privately before the service begins and opening prayers to set the mood for the individual services.

כוונות
MEDITATIONS BEFORE PRAYER
PREPARATION FOR PRAYER

We should purify our heart before we pray.

Exodus Rabbah

None may stand up to say the *Tefillah* (the statutory prayer, the *Amidah*) save in a sober mood. The pious of old used to wait an hour before they said the *Tefillah*, that they might direct their heart toward God.

Mishnah Berachot 5:1

Our Rabbis taught: we should not stand up to say the *Tefillah* while immersed in sorrow, or idleness, or laughter, or frivolity, or chatter, or idle talk, but only while rejoicing in the performance of some religious act.

Berachot 31a

R. Meir said: Our words should always be few towards God. 'Be not rash with your mouth and let not your heart be hasty to utter a word before God; for God is in heaven, and you upon earth; therefore let your words be few. For a dream comes through a multitude of business; and a fool's voice through a multitude of words' *(Ecclesiastes 5:1-2)*.

Berachot 61a

When you cannot pray with the proper concentration, try your utmost to speak the words in a spirit of belief in their truth.

Nachman of Bratzlav

The Tzanzer was asked by a Chasid: 'What does the Rabbi do before praying?' 'I pray,' was the reply, 'that I may be able to pray properly.'

Chasidic

Rabbi Simon says: When you pray do not make your prayer a fixed formal thing, but an appeal for mercy, a supplication before God.

Sayings of the Fathers 2:18

Those who are about to pray should learn from a common labourer, who sometimes takes a whole day to prepare for a job. A wood-cutter who spends most of the day sharpening the saw and only the last hour cutting the wood, has earned his day's wage.

Mendel of Kotzk

Forget everybody and everything during your worship. Forget yourself and your needs. Forget the people of whom you have need. Then in truth you may worship God.

<<<

When you offer prayer, imagine yourself as one who is newly born; without achievements of which to be proud; without high family descent to make you arrogant. Forget all dignity and self-esteem. Remember only your Maker.

Before the prayers, remember any good qualities you have, or any good deeds which you have performed. This will put life into you and enable you to pray from the heart.

Nachman of Bratzlav

What then is devotion? We must free our heart from all other thoughts and regard ourselves as standing in the presence of God. Therefore, before engaging in prayer, we ought to go aside for a little in order to bring ourselves into a devotional attitude, and then we should pray quietly and with feeling, not like one who carries a weight and goes away. Then after prayer the worshipper ought to sit quiet for a little and then depart.

Maimonides

Let all cry out to God and lift our heart up to God, as if we were hanging by a hair, and a tempest were raging to the very heart of heaven, and we were at a loss for what to do, and there were hardly time to cry out. It is a time when no counsel, indeed, can help us and we have no refuge save to remain in our loneliness and lift our eyes and heart up to God, and cry out to God. And this should be done at all times, for in the world a person is in great danger.

Chasidic

THE NATURE OF PRAYER

We pray for the sake of our soul as we take food for the sake of our body.

Judah Halevi

However, it is essential that you know how to be careful when you make supplication for your needs. God forbid that your intention should be for the gratification of your own desires, for this is self-worship, of which God has no desire, indeed it is abhorrent in God's eyes ... Therefore, when you ask of God your material needs, such as health, riches, peace, and other material perfections, your intention should be that these will help you to serve your Creator, seeing that you cannot properly serve God if you lack the material goods of life, which are God-given aids for the aim you really desire - the improvement of the soul.

Jacob Emden

As the flame clothes the black, sooty clod in a garment of fire, and releases the heat imprisoned therein, even so does prayer clothe us in a garment of holiness, evoke the light and fire implanted within us by our Maker, illumine our whole being, and unify the Lower and the Higher Worlds.

Zohar

The aim of our worship is the purification, enlightenment and uplifting of our inner selves ... Its aim is not simply to stir up the emotions, or to produce fleeting moments of devotion, empty sentimentalism and idle tears, but the cleansing of heart and mind. Life robs us of the correct judgment concerning God, the world, humanity, and Israel, and concerning our own relationship to them all. Leaving the disturbing influences of life, and turning to God, you can find it again through the contemplation that is part of *tefillah* ...

Contemplate afresh our prayers, our divine service as a whole, and see if you do not find it more dignified, meaningful and important than you had ever before imagined.

Samson Raphael Hirsch

Prayer is a brazen act. For it is impossible to stand before God, but brazenly. We all imagine, in one way or another, the greatness of the Creator: How then can we stand in prayer before God? For prayer is a wonder; (its task is) chiefly the assault upon, and the despoiling of, the heavenly order ... We come wishing to despoil the order and do marvels. Therefore we must be shameless in prayer.

Nachman of Bratzlav

Not all tears come before God. Sullen tears, and tears accompanying the petition for vengeance do not ascend on high. But tears of entreaty and penitence, and tears beseeching relief, cleave the very heavens, open the portals and ascend to the Sovereign above all earthly rulers.

Zohar

Prayer is our humble answer to the inconceivable surprise of living.

Abraham Joshua Heschel

We must bear in mind that all such religious acts as reading the *Torah*, praying, and the performance of other precepts, serve exclusively as the means of causing us to occupy and fill our mind with the precepts of God, and free it from worldly business; for we are thus, as it were, in communication with God, and undisturbed by any other thing. If we, however, pray with the motion of our lips, and our face toward the wall, but at the same time think of our business; if we read with our tongue, whilst our heart is occupied with the building of our house, and we do not think of what we are reading; if we perform the commandments only with our limbs, we are like those who are engaged in digging in the ground, or hewing wood in the forest, without reflecting on the nature of these acts, or by whom they are commanded, or what is their object. We must not imagine that in this way we attain the highest perfection; on the contrary, we are then like those in reference to whom Scripture says 'Thou art near in their mouth, and far from their inner life' *(Jeremiah 12: 2)*.

Maimonides

'To serve the Eternal your God with all your heart' *(Deuteronomy 11:13)*. What is a service with the heart? It is prayer.

Ta'anit 2a

We do not even know how we are supposed to pray. All we do is call for help because of the need of the moment. But what the soul intends is spiritual need, only we are not able to express what the soul means. That is why we do not merely ask God to hear our call for help, but also beg the One who knows what is hidden, to hear the silent cry of the soul.

Chasidic

So long as the world moves along accustomed paths, so long as there are no wild catastrophes, we can find sufficient substance for our life by contemplating surface events, theories and movements of society. We can acquire our inner richness from this external kind of 'property'. But this is not the case when life encounters fiery forces of evil and chaos. Then the 'revealed' world begins to totter. Then those who try to sustain themselves only from the surface aspects of existence will suffer terrible impoverishment, begin to stagger, ... then they will feel welling up within themselves a burning thirst for that inner substance and vision which transcends the obvious surfaces of existence and remains unaffected by the world's catastrophes. From such inner sources they will seek the waters of joy which can quicken the dry outer skeleton of existence.

Avraham Isaac Kook

'You are My witnesses,' the Eternal says, 'and I am God.' Rabbi Simeon ben Yochai said: 'If you give witness unto Me, then I am the Eternal. If you are not My witnesses, then I am not the Eternal, as it were.'

Pesikta d'Rav Kahana

In my experience, prayer does not give security or the answer to the problems of the cosmos - at least it never has for me. But though it has not changed the external world to suit my convenience, it has changed me, and I am part of that world. It has not given me security ... but it has given me courage, and helped me cope with the next step ahead.

Lionel Blue

Prayer will not come about by default. It requires education, training, reflection, contemplation. It is not enough to join others; it is necessary to build a sanctuary within.

Abraham Joshua Heschel

For prayer is the language of the heart - needing no measured voice, no spoken tone.

Grace Aguilar

There is one thing in prayer that we all need greatly ... a few minutes each day of peace and quiet with oneself, at least a minute fragment of the day to listen within oneself, attending to the voice of God.

Ellen Littmann

THE PRAYER OF THE COMMUNITY

What are our places of prayer ... but schools of prudence, courage, temperance and justice, of piety, holiness and virtue?

Philo

R. Jose ben Chalafta taught: There are proper times for prayer, as it says, 'As for me, let my prayer come before You at the proper time' *(Psalm 69:14)*. What is a 'proper time'? When the community is at prayer.

Tanchuma

Community prayer is preferable for many reasons. Firstly, the community does not pray for what is hurtful to an individual, whilst the individual sometimes prays for something to the hurt of other individuals, and these pray for something that hurts him; a prayer, however, can be heard only if its object is profitable to the world and in no ways hurtful.

People rarely accomplish their prayer without digression of mind and negligence; we are therefore commanded that we recite the prayers of a community, and if possible in a community of not less than ten people, so that one makes up for the digression or negligence of the other, in order that a perfect prayer, recited with unalloyed devotion, may be made, and its blessing bestowed on the community, each of us receiving our portion.

Judah Halevi

Rav said: Whoever has it in their power to pray on behalf of their neighbour, and fails to do so, is called a sinner.

Berachot

The Baal Shem Tov once refused to enter a certain synagogue because he said it was too full of prayers. Noting his followers' astonishment at his attitude, he explained that so many routine insincere prayers were uttered there that they could not rise to the heavenly throne and stayed on earth, cramming the synagogue full.

Baal Shem Tov

Feel the tribulations of the individual and of the multitude, and implore God to ease their burden.

Nachman of Bratzlav

If we are accustomed to attend synagogue and one day do not go, the Blessed Holy One makes enquiry about us.

Berachot

LITURGY AND PRAYER

Liturgy defines the community that prays.
Prayer is the offering of each individual.

Liturgy affirms the values of that community.
Prayer sets those values on our lips and in our hearts.

Liturgy unites those who share a tradition.
Prayer connects us to all who pray.

Liturgy describes the boundaries of a community.
Prayer locates us within creation as a whole.

Liturgy offers a language for prayer.
Prayer reaches out beyond language.

Liturgy places us within a history.
Prayer opens us to the future.

Liturgy invites our emotions.
Prayer refines our emotions.

Liturgy begins in the world we know.
Prayer suggests worlds to be explored.

Liturgy provides a space in which to pray.
Prayer tests the truth of what we pray.

Liturgy seeks to bring God into the world.
Prayer helps make room for God in our lives.

Liturgy provides security, continuity and certainty.
Prayer disturbs, challenges and confronts.

Liturgy without prayer may become sterile.
Prayer without liturgy may become selfish.

Liturgy is an event. Prayer is a risk.

Liturgy sets limits. Prayer offers space.

Liturgy asserts. Prayer expresses hope.

Liturgy is the motor. Prayer is the fuel.

Liturgy is the vehicle. Prayer is the journey.

Liturgy is the companion. Prayer is the destination.

Jonathan Magonet

SOME INDIVIDUAL PRAYERS

And if I say, 'I will not make mention of God, nor speak any more in God's name,' then there is in my heart as it were a burning fire, shut up in my bones, and I weary myself to hold it in, but cannot.

Jeremiah 20: 9

 I gave orders for my horse to be brought round from the stable. The servant did not understand me. I myself went to the stable, saddled my horse and mounted. In the distance I heard a bugle call, I asked him what this meant. He knew nothing and had heard nothing. At the gate he stopped me, asking, 'Where are you riding to, master?' 'I don't know,' I said, 'only away from here, away from here. Always away from here, only by doing so can I reach my destination.' 'And so you know your destination?' he asked. 'Yes,' I answered, 'didn't I say so? Away-From-Here, that is my destination.' 'You have no provisions with you,' he said. 'I need none,' I said, 'the journey is so long that I must die of hunger if I don't get anything on the way. No provisions can save me. For it is, fortunately, a truly immense journey.'

Franz Kafka

Inscription on the walls of a cellar in Cologne, Germany, where Jews hid from the Nazis:
> I believe in the sun even when it is not shining.
> I believe in love even when feeling it not.
> I believe in God even when God is silent.

Anon

The prayer of a shepherd who 'did not know how to pray':
God of the Universe! It is apparent and known unto You, that if You had sheep and gave them to me to tend, though I take wages for tending from all others, from You I would take nothing, because I love You.

Sefer Chasidim

A favourite saying of the Rabbis of Yavneh was:
> I am God's creature and my fellow is God's creature.
> My work is in the town and his work is in the country.
> I rise early for my work and he rises early for his work.
> Just as he does not presume to do my work,
> so I do not presume to do his work.
> Will you say, I do much and he does little?
> We have learnt: One may do much or one may do little;
> it is all one, provided we direct our heart to heaven.

Berachot 17a

I pray to You O Lord
from all my heart,
O Lord! I pray to You
with fervour and zeal,
for the sufferings of the humiliated,
for the uncertainty of those who wait;
for the non-return of the dead;
for the helplessness of the dying;
for the sadness of the misunderstood;
for those who request in vain;
for all those abused, scorned and disdained;
for the silly, the wicked, the miserable;
for those who hurry in pain
to the nearest physician;
those who return from work
with trembling and anguished hearts to their homes;
for those who are roughly treated and pushed aside,
for those who are hissed on the stage;
for all who are clumsy, ugly, tiresome and dull,
for the weak, the beaten, the oppressed,
for those who cannot find rest
during long sleepless nights;
for those who are afraid of Death;
for those who wait in pharmacies;
for those who have missed the train;
- for all the inhabitants of our earth
and all their pains and troubles,
their worries, sufferings, disappointments,
all their griefs, afflictions, sorrows,
longings, failures, defeats;
for everything which is not joy,
comfort, happiness, bliss ...
Let these shine for ever upon them
with tender love and brightness,
I pray to You O Lord most fervently -
I pray to You O Lord from the depths of my heart.

Juljan Tuwim

Lord, where shall I find You?
High and hidden is Your place.
And where shall I not find You?
The world is full of Your glory.
I have sought Your nearness,
with all my heart I called You
and going out to meet You
I found You coming to meet me.

Judah Halevi

Blessed are You Lord, my God, spirit of the universe, who brought me across the (*Yabok*) bridge of life. When the dim light of my own self will sink and merge within the light which illumines the world and eternity, I shall conclude the order of my days.

In this twilight glow of my life, I stand before the dawn of my new sun with tense consciousness, a man about to die and to live, who feels at one with the universe and eternity, as in the ancient words. 'Hear, Israel, the Lord our God, the Lord is One.' Blessed is the God of life and death, of light and love.

Nachman Syrkin

Lord of the universe, You are doing much to make me desert my faith, but I assure You that, even against the will of the dwellers in heaven, a Jew I am and a Jew I shall remain, and neither the sufferings that You have brought upon me nor that which You will yet bring upon me will be of any avail.

Solomon Ibn Verga

God on high, divine Sovereign, enlighten my soul at all times. Give me, God, true faith, and perfect humility against the world's vanities. Do not give me riches, God, that may make me proud; nor poverty, that may deject me. Give me, God, some help that I may serve You, and life that I may praise You and death that I may find salvation.

Marrano

When all within is dark,
and former friends misprise;
from them I turn to You,
and find love in Your eyes.
When all within is dark,
and I my soul despise;
from me I turn to You,
and find love in Your eyes.

When all Your face is dark,
and Your just angers rise;
from You I turn to You,
and find love in Your eyes.

Israel Abrahams based on Ibn Gabirol

Where I wander - You!
Where I ponder - You!
Only You, You again, always You! You! You! You!
When I am gladdened - You! When I am saddened - You!
Only You, You again, always You! You! You! You!
Sky is You, earth is You!
You above! You below!
In every trend, at every end,
only You, You again, always You! You! You! You!

Levi Yitschak of Berditchev

Good morning, to You, Almighty God,
I, Levi Yitschak son of Sarah of Berditchev,
have come for a judgment against You,
on behalf of Your people Israel.
What do You want of Your people Israel?
Why do You afflict Your people Israel?
The slightest thing and You say,
'Speak to the children of Israel,'
the slightest thing and You turn to the children of Israel,
the slightest thing and You say,
'Tell the children of Israel.'
Our father! There are so many nations in the world,
Persians, Babylonians, Edomites.
The Russians, what do they say?
That their Emperor is the Emperor.
The Germans, what do they say?
That their Empire is the Empire.
And the English, what do they say?
That their Empire is the Empire.
And I, Levi Yitschak son of Sarah of Berditchev, say,
'From this spot I shall not stir,
I shall not stir from this spot,
there must be an end of this,
the exile must end!
Magnified and sanctified be God's great name!'

Levi Yitschak of Berditchev

The needs of Your people Israel are many, but their knowledge is small. May it be Your will, our God and God of our ancestors, to give to every creature what it needs and to every body what it lacks. Blessed is God, for You heard the voice of my supplication. Blessed are You God, who hears prayer.

Yerushalmi

May it be Your will, O Lord, that none foster hatred against us in their heart, and that we foster no hatred in our hearts against any others; that none foster envy of us in their heart, and that we foster no envy in our hearts of any.

Talmud

Your eternal providence has appointed me to watch over the life and health of Your creatures. May the love for my art actuate me at all times; may neither avarice nor miserliness, nor the thirst for glory or for a great reputation engage my mind, for the enemies of truth and philanthropy could easily deceive me and make me forgetful of my lofty aim of doing good to Your children. May I never see in a patient anything but a fellow creature in pain. Grant me strength, time and opportunity always to correct what I have acquired, always to extend its domain, for knowledge is immense and the human spirit can extend indefinitely to enrich itself daily with new requirements.

Today we can discover our errors of yesterday and tomorrow we may obtain new light on what we think ourselves sure of today.

O God, You have appointed me to watch over the life and death of Your creatures. Here I am, ready for my vocation.

Attributed to Maimonides (The Medical Oath)

My Lord and God, I do not desire Your paradise; I do not desire the bliss of the world to come; I desire only You Yourself.

Shneur Zalman of Ladi

When I travel in my coach to teach Torah, give me thought for the mare that carries me, and guard her from my impatience; when I walk through Your woods, may my right foot and my left foot be harmless to the little creatures that move in the grasses; as it is said by the mouth of Your prophet, They shall not hurt nor destroy in all My holy mountain. Amen.

Moshe Hakotun

You were my death;
You I could hold
when all fell away from me.

Paul Celan

Lord, let Your light be only for the day,
and the darkness for the night.
And let my dress, my poor humble dress,
lie quietly over my chair at night.

Let the church-bells be silent,
my neighbour Ivan not ring them at night.
Let the wind not waken the children
out of their sleep at night.

Let the hen sleep on its roost, the horse in the stable
all through the night.
Remove the stone from the middle of the road
that the thief may not stumble at night.

Let heaven be quiet during the night.
Restrain the lightning, silence the thunder,
they should not frighten mothers giving birth
to their babies at night.

And me too protect against fire and water,
protect my poor roof at night.
Let my dress, my poor humble dress
lie quietly over my chair at night.

Nachum Bomze

And yet I pray, for I do not desire to lose the blessed feeling of unity, of communication with You.

Arnold Schoenberg

I do not beg You to reveal to me the secret of Your ways - I could not bear it. But show me one thing; show it to me more clearly and more deeply: show me what this, which is happening at this very moment, means to me, what it demands of me, what You, Lord of the world, are telling me by way of it. Ah, it is not why I suffer, that I wish to know, but only whether I suffer for Your sake.

Levi Yitschak of Berditchev

Anyway, can I pretend I have much choice? I look at myself and see chest, thighs, feet - a head. This strange organization, I know it will die. And inside - something, something, happiness ... 'Thou movest me.' That leaves no choice. Something produces intensity, a holy feeling, as oranges produce orange, as grass green, as birds heat. Some hearts put out more love and some less of it, presumably. Does it signify anything? There are those who say this product of hearts is knowledge ... I couldn't say that, for sure. My face too blind, my mind too limited, my instincts too narrow. But this intensity, doesn't it mean anything? Is it an idiot joy that makes this animal, the most peculiar animal of all, exclaim something? And he thinks this reaction a sign, a proof, of eternity? And he has it in his breast? But I have no arguments to make about it. 'Thou movest me.' 'But what do you want ... ?' 'But that's just it - not a solitary thing. I am pretty well satisfied to be, to be just as it is willed, and for as long as I may remain in occupancy.'

Saul Bellow

I know that in praying something happens, even if there is no one God in the form of a Father or a Mother receiving my prayer. I know that by the act of praying in the desert, out of love (because I wouldn't pray otherwise), something might already be good in myself: a therapy might be taking place. I know that by doing this, I try - I will not necessarily succeed - to affirm and accept something in myself that won't do any harm to anyone, especially to me. The impression that I do something good for myself or my loved ones, that's the calculation. If, through this prayer, I am a little better at reconciliation, and if I give up any calculation because I cannot calculate the incalculable, I can become better.

Jacques Derrida

Kaddish
Let holiness move in us,
let us pay attention to its small voice,
let us see the light in others and honour that light,
remember the dead who paid our way here dearly, dearly,
and remember the unborn for whom we build our houses.
Praise the light that shines before us,
through us, after us.

Marge Piercy

God, take me by Your hand, I shall follow You dutifully, and not resist too much. I shall evade none of the tempests life has in store for me, I shall try to face it all as best I can. But now and then grant me a short respite. I shall never again assume, in my innocence, that any peace that comes my way will be eternal. I shall accept all the inevitable tumult and struggle. I delight in warmth and security, but I shall not rebel if I have to suffer cold, should You so decree. I shall follow wherever Your hand leads me and shall try not to be afraid. I shall try to spread some of my warmth, of my genuine love for others, wherever I go. But we shouldn't boast of our love for others. We cannot be sure that it really exists. I don't want to be anything special, I only want to try to be true to that in me which seeks to fulfil its promise. I sometimes imagine that I long for the seclusion of a nunnery. But I know that I must seek You among people, out in the world.

Etty Hillesum

A Short Dialogue
You and I, dear God,
we both know it,
that Your world was barely ready
when the seventh day
dawned.

So at the time
You relied on Your creation
to help You out.
Oh dear!

Suffering doesn't purify us
and from mistakes we don't become wise,
merely crafty.
- God, You gave us the world as it is
please give us as well
that world-conscience
which was unfortunately not handed over
at the time.

Mascha Kaléko

FOR MOMENTS OF PRIVATE PRAYER

How do I pray?

   My God, I do not know how to pray. I have only the feelings in my heart, the stirrings in my soul, and these impoverished words. Will they suffice this day? Thinking of You, I find my mind wandering, wondering about the journey I have made to reach this moment in time. I think of the burdens I carry and the rewards that have come my way. I remember the joy I have known, and the times when my vision failed. Swept along by the currents of my desires, I am adrift in the midst of life. Your psalmist says 'Be still, and know that I am God'. So still my mind as I wait for You. Teach me to hear the silence - Your voice in me. This is my prayer today, the prayer of one who does not know how to pray. My body is weak, my thoughts distracted, my heart awash with hopes unfulfilled. Let my honesty now be my true devotion to You. Hear me now, in the stillness, and may Your still, small voice echo within and bring my spirit peace.

Howard Cooper

   God, I thank You for this time of prayer, when I become conscious of Your presence, and lay before You my desires, my hopes and my gratitude. This consciousness, this inner certainty of Your presence is my greatest blessing. My life would be empty if I did not have it, if I lost You in the maze of the world, and if I did not return to You from time to time, to be at one with You, certain of Your existence and Your love. It is good that You are with me in all my difficulties and troubles, and that I have in You a friend whose help is sure and whose love never changes.

From Forms of Prayer 1930

I turn towards You, and pray for those I love, who are dearer to me than life. Protect them as a father, and keep them from harm, in body, mind and spirit. Deepen their desire to know Your will, and strengthen them to do it. Help them in their struggle with the world, with selfishness, with laziness, and with forgetfulness of their own souls. Lord, help me as well, so that my own life does not contradict the life I desire for them. Let it serve them as an example, and help them in their struggle for goodness.

I thank You for those who are dear to me, for the privilege of guiding their steps towards You, for the love which binds our hearts together, for its joy, for its solace, and for the strength it gives me in trouble and temptation. Help me to keep that love strong. May no selfishness or misunderstanding weaken it. May it bless me to the end! Amen.

From Forms of Prayer 1930

God, I have not always been true to You in my thoughts. I have doubted Your goodness, Your justice and Your very existence. The pressures of life were too strong, its bitterness more than I could bear. Everything went wrong with my hopes and my plans, and there seemed no way out, no way to turn. I said, 'There is no justice in this life of ours!' Sometimes my own suffering, but still more the suffering of others, strengthened my doubts. 'Why,' I asked, 'does God make His own children suffer? Where is God's love? Where is God's power?' At this point, You almost ceased to exist for me. Your hand would have held me, guided me, comforted me, but I lost touch with You. I should have looked for You more steadily, searched for You more diligently.

Out of my limited experience and my small knowledge, I judged the source of justice, and set my cleverness higher than the ultimate wisdom. I saw only one side of truth - the darkness, not the light. I forgot the smiling face of life and its beauty. I also forgot that the pain of life itself can lead to deeper compassion, and is a teacher of great wisdom. Because I was proud, and claimed to understand what was beyond me, I did not see that human goodness is a token of its Creator's goodness.

Pardon my conceit and my blindness. Help me to greater detachment so that I may see with greater steadiness and calm. Help me to find order in the apparent chaos of human life, and love even in its defeats and trials. Your mercy is always there; You know and feel our pain. Amen.

From Forms of Prayer 1930

SH'LIACH TSIBBUR - THE WORSHIP SERVICE LEADER

To conduct a Jewish worship service is a great privilege and responsibility, an opportunity that is given to few. Whether for a 'professional', for a 'regular congregant' with skills, or for someone asked because 'no one else is available', each of us faces the same challenges:

a worship service belongs to a chain of tradition, yet each worship service is unique;

however familiar it is, we need to review the structure and timing on each occasion;

preparation includes liaising with others who play a part in this particular service;

the clearer we have the flow of the service in our minds, the easier it will be for congregants to participate and follow;

we should respect the *minhag* of those who want what is familiar - and be sensitive and prepare people when introducing something new.

The challenge in a worship service is to be faithful to the liturgy itself, the structure and traditions that have come down to us over the centuries, but at the same time to respect the needs of those who are there, whether to pray or simply to be present. The service should be a 'safe space', one that meets the many different needs that people bring at different times. The words, music and 'choreography' aim to build a collective experience, yet congregants can be helped to find their private space within it, to focus or simply daydream:

through a few moments of stillness, perhaps wrapped in a *tallit*, before the service itself begins;

during the prayer *ribon ha-olamim* which provides a kind of 'spiritual questionnaire';

during the silences, when the second and third paragraphs of the *Sh'ma* are read or at the end of the *Amidah*.

The *Sh'liach Tsibbur* is there for the sake of the service, and not the service for the sake of the *Sh'liach Tsibbur*;

A prayer for the Sh'liach Tsibbur

קַבֵּל Accept my prayer as if it were what it ought to be, wise, eager and worthy of one who is profound and is able to express it, a person whose good nature is known to all.

קַבֵּל תְּפִלָּתִי כִּתְפִלַּת זָקֵן
וְרָגִיל וּפִרְקוֹ נָאֶה וְקוֹלוֹ נָעִים
וּמְעֹרָב בְּדַעַת עִם הַבְּרִיּוֹת:

תפלת שחרית לימות החול
Daily Morning Service

וְאֵרַשְׂתִּיךְ לִי לְעוֹלָם.
וְאֵרַשְׂתִּיךְ לִי בְּצֶדֶק וּבְמִשְׁפָּט וּבְחֶסֶד וּבְרַחֲמִים.
וְאֵרַשְׂתִּיךְ לִי בֶּאֱמוּנָה וְיָדַעַתְּ אֶת יהוה:

I betroth you to Me forever.
I betroth you to Me with integrity and justice, with tenderness and love.
I betroth you to Me with faithfulness
and you will know the Eternal.

Hosea 2: 21-22

The psalmist teaches that 'it is good to give thanks to the Eternal ... to tell of Your love in the morning and Your faithfulness every night' (Psalm 92:2-3). The daily morning service focuses on the renewal of life that is possible each day, as individuals, as part of a living community, of humanity as a whole and of the natural world. This is an expression of God's *chesed*, the 'love' described by the psalmist. That love is reflected in the opening blessings and prayers which describe both our physical and spiritual reality, restored to life after sleep. The wearing of the *tallit* and *tefillin*, during the morning service alone, symbolises our wish to hold on to the spiritual in the midst of the realities and responsibilities of daily life. In the evening prayers, as the day winds down, we reflect on how God's 'faithfulness' has sustained us, however challenged we may have been by what the day has brought.

At the beginning of the day:

מוֹדָה/מוֹדֶה/מוֹדָה I give thanks to You, living and eternal Sovereign, that You have returned my soul to me with compassion - great is Your faithfulness.

On putting on Tsitsit:

בָּרוּךְ Blessed are You, our Living God, Sovereign of the universe, whose commandments make us holy and who commands us concerning the commandment of *Tsitsit* (tassels).

When Tallit and Tefillin are worn, the following are said:
Meditation before putting on the Tallit:

בָּרְכִי Bless the Eternal, my soul! My Living God, how great You are, clothed in majesty and glory, wrapped in light like a robe. You spread out the heavens like a tent.[1]

הִנְנִי I prepare to wrap myself in this *Tallit* to fulfil the command of my Creator. As it is written in the Torah: 'Each generation shall put a tassel on the corners of their clothes.'[2] And just as I cover myself with a robe in this world, so may my soul deserve to be robed in a beautiful robe in the world to come, as in Eden. Amen.

At the beginning of the day:

מוֹדָה/מוֹדֶה אֲנִי לְפָנֶיךָ.
מֶלֶךְ חַי וְקַיָּם.
שֶׁהֶחֱזַרְתָּ בִּי נִשְׁמָתִי בְּחֶמְלָה.
רַבָּה אֱמוּנָתֶךָ:

On putting on Tsitsit:

בָּרוּךְ אַתָּה יהוה אֱלֹהֵינוּ
מֶלֶךְ הָעוֹלָם.
אֲשֶׁר קִדְּשָׁנוּ בְּמִצְוֹתָיו וְצִוָּנוּ
עַל מִצְוַת צִיצִת:

Meditation before putting on the Tallit:

בָּרְכִי נַפְשִׁי אֶת יהוה:
יהוה אֱלֹהַי גָּדַלְתָּ מְאֹד.
הוֹד וְהָדָר לָבָשְׁתָּ:
עֹטֶה־אוֹר כַּשַּׂלְמָה
נוֹטֶה שָׁמַיִם כַּיְרִיעָה:

הִנְנִי מִתְעַטֵּף/מִתְעַטֶּפֶת בְּטַלִּית
שֶׁל־צִיצִת כְּדֵי לְקַיֵּם מִצְוַת
בּוֹרְאִי. כַּכָּתוּב בַּתּוֹרָה. וְעָשׂוּ
לָהֶם צִיצִת עַל כַּנְפֵי בִגְדֵיהֶם
לְדֹרֹתָם: וּכְשֵׁם שֶׁאֲנִי מִתְכַּסֶּה/
מִתְכַּסָּה בְּטַלִּית בָּעוֹלָם הַזֶּה. כֵּן
תִּזְכֶּה נִשְׁמָתִי לְהִתְלַבֵּשׁ בְּטַלִּית
נָאָה לָעוֹלָם הַבָּא בְּגַן עֵדֶן. אָמֵן:

---

[1] Ps 104:1-2.   [2] Num 15:38.

29 DAILY MORNING SERVICE

On putting on the Tallit:

בָּרוּךְ Blessed are You, our Living God, Sovereign of the universe, whose commandments make us holy and who commands us to wrap ourselves in the *Tallit*.

מַה־יָּקָר God,
how precious is Your love!
People take refuge
in the shadow of Your wings.
They feast on the bounty
of Your house,
You let them drink
from the streams of Your pleasures,
for with You is the fountain of life.
In Your light, we see light.
Continue Your love
to those who love You,
and Your faithfulness
to the upright in heart.[1]

On putting on the Tallit:

בָּרוּךְ אַתָּה יהוה אֱלֹהֵינוּ
מֶלֶךְ הָעוֹלָם.
אֲשֶׁר קִדְּשָׁנוּ בְּמִצְוֹתָיו וְצִוָּנוּ
לְהִתְעַטֵּף בַּצִּיצִת:

מַה־יָּקָר חַסְדְּךָ
אֱלֹהִים
וּבְנֵי אָדָם
בְּצֵל כְּנָפֶיךָ יֶחֱסָיוּן:
יִרְוְיֻן מִדֶּשֶׁן בֵּיתֶךָ
וְנַחַל עֲדָנֶיךָ תַשְׁקֵם:
כִּי־עִמְּךָ מְקוֹר חַיִּים
בְּאוֹרְךָ נִרְאֶה־אוֹר:
מְשֹׁךְ חַסְדְּךָ לְיֹדְעֶיךָ
וְצִדְקָתְךָ
לְיִשְׁרֵי־לֵב:

[1] Ps 36:8-11.

Meditation before putting on the Tefillin:

הִנְנִי מְכַוֵּן/מְכַוֶּנֶת בַּהֲנָחַת תְּפִלִּין לְקַיֵּם מִצְוַת בּוֹרְאִי שֶׁצִּוָּנוּ לְהָנִיחַ תְּפִלִּין. כַּכָּתוּב בַּתּוֹרָה. וּקְשַׁרְתָּם לְאוֹת עַל יָדֶךָ וְהָיוּ לְטֹטָפֹת בֵּין עֵינֶיךָ. וְהֵם אַרְבַּע פָּרָשִׁיּוֹת אֵלּוּ. שְׁמַע. וְהָיָה אִם־שָׁמֹעַ. קַדֶּשׁ. וְהָיָה כִּי יְבִיאֲךָ. שֶׁיֵּשׁ בָּהֶם יִחוּדוֹ וְאַחְדוּתוֹ יִתְבָּרַךְ שְׁמוֹ בָּעוֹלָם. וְשֶׁנִּזְכֹּר נִסִּים וְנִפְלָאוֹת שֶׁעָשָׂה עִמָּנוּ בְּהוֹצִיאָנוּ מִמִּצְרָיִם. וַאֲשֶׁר לוֹ הַכֹּחַ וְהַמֶּמְשָׁלָה בָּעֶלְיוֹנִים וּבַתַּחְתּוֹנִים לַעֲשׂוֹת בָּהֶם כִּרְצוֹנוֹ. וְצִוָּנוּ לְהָנִיחַ עַל הַיָּד לְזִכָּרוֹן זְרוֹעוֹ הַנְּטוּיָה. וְשֶׁהִיא נֶגֶד הַלֵּב לְשַׁעְבֵּד בָּזֶה תַּאֲוֹת וּמַחְשְׁבוֹת לִבֵּנוּ לַעֲבוֹדָתוֹ יִתְבָּרַךְ שְׁמוֹ. וְעַל הָרֹאשׁ נֶגֶד הַמֹּחַ שֶׁהַנְּשָׁמָה שֶׁבְּמֹחִי עִם־חוּשַׁי וְכֹחוֹתַי כֻּלָּם יִהְיוּ מְשֻׁעְבָּדִים לַעֲבוֹדָתוֹ יִתְבָּרַךְ שְׁמוֹ. וּמִשֶּׁפַע מִצְוַת תְּפִלִּין יִתְמַשֵּׁךְ עָלַי לִהְיוֹת לִי חַיִּים אֲרֻכִּים וְשֶׁפַע קֹדֶשׁ וּמַחְשָׁבוֹת קְדוֹשׁוֹת בְּלִי הִרְהוּר חֵטְא וְעָוֹן כְּלָל. וְשֶׁלֹּא יְפַתֵּנוּ וְלֹא יִתְגָּרֶה בָּנוּ יֵצֶר הָרָע וְיַנִּיחֵנוּ לַעֲבֹד אֶת־יְהֹוָה כַּאֲשֶׁר עִם־לְבָבֵנוּ. אָמֵן:

Meditation before putting on the Tefillin:

הִנְנִי I now prepare myself to lay *Tefillin* to fulfil the command of my Creator who commanded us to lay *Tefillin,* as it is written in the Torah: 'Hold fast to them as a sign upon your hand and let them be as reminders before your eyes.' And in them are these four sections of the Torah: 'Hear O Israel ...'[1]; 'This will happen ...'[2]; 'Sanctify ...'[3]; 'And when the Eternal shall bring you ...'[4]. They state the uniqueness and unity of God, whose name be blessed. They also record the signs and the wonders that God did for us when bringing us out from Egypt - God, whose power and authority extend over the highest and the lowest, to dealing with them according to the divine plan. God commanded us to lay *Tefillin* on the hand as a reminder of God's 'outstretched arm', and opposite the heart to show in this way that the longings and desires of our heart should be controlled for the service of God, whose name be blessed. And on the head over the brain, showing that the mind that is in my brain, with all my senses and faculties, should be committed to the service of God, whose name be blessed. By keeping the commandment of *Tefillin* may fulfilment in my life increase, together with holiness and holy thought, undisturbed by sin and wrong. Do not let the desire for evil deceive us nor provoke us. Let us be led to serve the Eternal as it is in our hearts to do. Amen.

---

[1] Deut 6:4-9.
[2] Deut 11:13-21.
[3] Ex 13:1-10.
[4] Ex 13:11-16.

31 DAILY MORNING SERVICE

On putting the Tefillin *on the arm:*

בָּרוּךְ Blessed are You, our Living God, Sovereign of the universe, whose commandments make us holy and who commands us to lay *Tefillin*.

On putting the Tefillin *on the head:*

בָּרוּךְ Blessed are You, our Living God, Sovereign of the universe, whose commandments make us holy and who commands us concerning the commandment of *Tefillin*.

בָּרוּךְ Blessed is God's name, whose glorious rule is forever and ever.

As the strap is wound three times round the middle finger:

וְאֵרַשְׂתִּיךְ I betroth you to Me forever.
I betroth you to Me
with integrity and justice,
with tenderness and love.
I betroth you to Me with faithfulness
and you will know the Eternal.[1]

On putting the Tefillin *on the arm:*

בָּרוּךְ אַתָּה יהוה אֱלֹהֵינוּ
מֶלֶךְ הָעוֹלָם. אֲשֶׁר קִדְּשָׁנוּ
בְּמִצְוֹתָיו וְצִוָּנוּ
לְהָנִיחַ תְּפִלִּין:

On putting the Tefillin *on the head:*

בָּרוּךְ אַתָּה יהוה אֱלֹהֵינוּ
מֶלֶךְ הָעוֹלָם. אֲשֶׁר קִדְּשָׁנוּ
בְּמִצְוֹתָיו וְצִוָּנוּ
עַל מִצְוַת תְּפִלִּין:

בָּרוּךְ שֵׁם כְּבוֹד
מַלְכוּתוֹ לְעוֹלָם וָעֶד:

As the strap is wound three times round the middle finger:

וְאֵרַשְׂתִּיךְ לִי לְעוֹלָם.
וְאֵרַשְׂתִּיךְ לִי בְּצֶדֶק וּבְמִשְׁפָּט
וּבְחֶסֶד וּבְרַחֲמִים.
וְאֵרַשְׂתִּיךְ לִי בֶּאֱמוּנָה
וְיָדַעַתְּ אֶת יהוה:

ברכות השחר
THE MORNING BLESSINGS

> The morning blessings reflect on the wonder of awakening each day to life. 'My God the soul you have given me is pure' celebrates the possibility of renewal that each day brings, however challenging the circumstances of our life. The blessings that follow mimic the actions as we open our eyes, dress, move around and relocate ourselves in our physical body and the world around us. Then begins the daily task of seeking meaning and purpose in our lives, examining our values and the quality of our relationships. The blessing to engage in study calls us to look beyond ourselves to the mystery of life itself.

---

[1] Hos 2:21-22.

ACROSS THE THRESHOLD

When in a community:

DIRECTING THE HEART TO GOD

מַה־טֹּבוּ How good are your tents, O Jacob, and your homes, O Israel!

Through the greatness of Your love I enter Your house.
In awe of You I worship before the ark of Your holiness.

God, as I loved the courts of Your temple, and the place where Your glory dwelt, so I still worship and bend low, humble before the Eternal my Maker.

As for me, let my prayer come before You at the proper time.

Answer me God, in the greatness of Your love, for Your deliverance is sure.[1]

מַה־טֹּבוּ אֹהָלֶיךָ
יַעֲקֹב. מִשְׁכְּנֹתֶיךָ יִשְׂרָאֵל:
וַאֲנִי בְּרֹב חַסְדְּךָ אָבוֹא בֵיתֶךָ.
אֶשְׁתַּחֲוֶה אֶל־הֵיכַל־קָדְשְׁךָ
בְּיִרְאָתֶךָ:
יהוה אָהַבְתִּי מְעוֹן בֵּיתֶךָ.
וּמְקוֹם מִשְׁכַּן כְּבוֹדֶךָ:
וַאֲנִי אֶשְׁתַּחֲוֶה וְאֶכְרָעָה.
אֲבָרְכָה לִפְנֵי־יהוה עֹשִׂי:
וַאֲנִי תְפִלָּתִי־לְךָ יהוה עֵת רָצוֹן:
אֱלֹהִים בְּרָב־חַסְדֶּךָ.
עֲנֵנִי בֶּאֱמֶת יִשְׁעֶךָ:

The Yigdal *(page 318) or* Adon Olam *(page 320) or a song may be sung here.*

ENCOUNTERING OURSELVES

In this section we examine our personal life, physical and spiritual, our gifts and our responsibilities.

בָּרוּךְ Blessed are You, our Living God, Sovereign of the universe, who formed human beings in wisdom, creating within them openings and vessels. It is revealed and known before the throne of Your glory that if one of them is opened or one of them closed it would be impossible to remain alive and stand before You. Blessed are You God, who heals all flesh and performs such wonders.

בָּרוּךְ אַתָּה יהוה אֱלֹהֵינוּ מֶלֶךְ
הָעוֹלָם. אֲשֶׁר יָצַר אֶת־הָאָדָם
בְּחָכְמָה. וּבָרָא בוֹ נְקָבִים נְקָבִים.
חֲלוּלִים חֲלוּלִים: גָּלוּי וְיָדוּעַ לִפְנֵי
כִסֵּא כְבוֹדֶךָ שֶׁאִם יִפָּתֵחַ אֶחָד
מֵהֶם. אוֹ יִסָּתֵם אֶחָד מֵהֶם. אִי
אֶפְשַׁר לְהִתְקַיֵּים וְלַעֲמוֹד לְפָנֶיךָ:
בָּרוּךְ אַתָּה יהוה. רוֹפֵא כָל־בָּשָׂר.
וּמַפְלִיא לַעֲשׂוֹת:

---

[1] Num 24:5, Ps 5:8, Ps 26:8, Ps 95:6, Ps 69:14.

DAILY MORNING SERVICE — MORNING BLESSINGS

THE GIFT OF OUR SOUL

My God, the soul
You have given me is pure,
for You created it,
You formed it
and You made it live within me.
You watch over it within me,
but one day
You will take it from me
to everlasting life.
My God and God of
generations before me,
as long as the soul is within me,
I will declare
that You are the power of good deeds,
the Ruler of all creatures,
possessing every soul.
Blessed are You God, giving new life
to our bodies each day.

אֱלֹהַי. נְשָׁמָה שֶׁנָּתַתָּ בִּי
טְהוֹרָה הִיא:
אַתָּה בְרָאתָהּ.
אַתָּה יְצַרְתָּהּ.
אַתָּה נְפַחְתָּהּ בִּי.
וְאַתָּה מְשַׁמְּרָהּ בְּקִרְבִּי.
וְאַתָּה עָתִיד לִטְּלָהּ מִמֶּנִּי
לְחַיֵּי עוֹלָם:
כָּל־זְמַן שֶׁהַנְּשָׁמָה בְקִרְבִּי
מוֹדֶה/מוֹדָה אֲנִי לְפָנֶיךָ
יהוה אֱלֹהַי וֵאלֹהֵי אֲבוֹתַי.
שֶׁאַתָּה הוּא רִבּוֹן כָּל־הַמַּעֲשִׂים.
מוֹשֵׁל בְּכָל־הַבְּרִיּוֹת.
אֲדוֹן כָּל־הַנְּשָׁמוֹת:
בָּרוּךְ אַתָּה יהוה.
הַמַּחֲזִיר נְשָׁמוֹת לַמֵּתִים:

THE GIFT OF BLESSINGS

Blessed are You, our Living
God, Sovereign of the universe, who
has made me in the image of God.

בָּרוּךְ אַתָּה יהוה אֱלֹהֵינוּ מֶלֶךְ
הָעוֹלָם. שֶׁעָשַׂנִי בְּצֶלֶם אֱלֹהִים:

Blessed are You, our Living God,
Sovereign of the universe, who has
not made me a stranger to You.

בָּרוּךְ אַתָּה יהוה אֱלֹהֵינוּ מֶלֶךְ
הָעוֹלָם. שֶׁלֹּא עָשַׂנִי נָכְרִי/נָכְרִיָּה:

Blessed are You, our Living God,
Sovereign of the universe, who has
not enslaved me.

בָּרוּךְ אַתָּה יהוה אֱלֹהֵינוּ מֶלֶךְ
הָעוֹלָם. שֶׁלֹּא עָשַׂנִי עֶבֶד/שִׁפְחָה:

Blessed are You, our Living God,
Sovereign of the universe,
You provide for my every need.

בָּרוּךְ אַתָּה יהוה אֱלֹהֵינוּ מֶלֶךְ
הָעוֹלָם. שֶׁעָשָׂה־לִי כָּל־צָרְכִּי:

Blessed are You, our Living God,
Sovereign of the universe,
You open eyes that cannot see.

בָּרוּךְ אַתָּה יהוה אֱלֹהֵינוּ מֶלֶךְ
הָעוֹלָם. פּוֹקֵחַ עִוְרִים:

ברכות השחר

Blessed are You, our Living God, Sovereign of the universe, You clothe the naked.	בָּרוּךְ אַתָּה יהוה אֱלֹהֵינוּ מֶלֶךְ הָעוֹלָם. מַלְבִּישׁ עֲרֻמִּים:
Blessed are You, our Living God, Sovereign of the universe, You free those who are bound.	בָּרוּךְ אַתָּה יהוה אֱלֹהֵינוּ מֶלֶךְ הָעוֹלָם. מַתִּיר אֲסוּרִים:
Blessed are You, our Living God, Sovereign of the universe, You lift up those bent low.	בָּרוּךְ אַתָּה יהוה אֱלֹהֵינוּ מֶלֶךְ הָעוֹלָם. זוֹקֵף כְּפוּפִים:
Blessed are You, our Living God, Sovereign of the universe, You support our human steps.	בָּרוּךְ אַתָּה יהוה אֱלֹהֵינוּ מֶלֶךְ הָעוֹלָם. הַמֵּכִין מִצְעֲדֵי־גָבֶר:
Blessed are You, our Living God, Sovereign of the universe, You fortify Israel with strength.	בָּרוּךְ אַתָּה יהוה אֱלֹהֵינוּ מֶלֶךְ הָעוֹלָם. אוֹזֵר יִשְׂרָאֵל בִּגְבוּרָה:
Blessed are You, our Living God, Sovereign of the universe, You crown Israel with glory.	בָּרוּךְ אַתָּה יהוה אֱלֹהֵינוּ מֶלֶךְ הָעוֹלָם. עוֹטֵר יִשְׂרָאֵל בְּתִפְאָרָה:
Blessed are You, our Living God, Sovereign of the universe, You give strength to the weary.	בָּרוּךְ אַתָּה יהוה אֱלֹהֵינוּ מֶלֶךְ הָעוֹלָם. הַנּוֹתֵן לַיָּעֵף כֹּחַ:
Blessed are You, our Living God, Sovereign of the universe, You take away sleep from my eyes and slumber from my eyelids.	בָּרוּךְ אַתָּה יהוה אֱלֹהֵינוּ מֶלֶךְ הָעוֹלָם. הַמַּעֲבִיר שֵׁנָה מֵעֵינַי וּתְנוּמָה מֵעַפְעַפָּי:

THE GIFT OF FREEDOM

לְעוֹלָם We should always be in awe of God in private as well as in public; speak the truth aloud and mean it in our heart.

לְעוֹלָם יְהֵא אָדָם יְרֵא שָׁמַיִם בַּסֵּתֶר כְּבַגָּלוּי. וּמוֹדֶה עַל־הָאֱמֶת וְדוֹבֵר אֱמֶת בִּלְבָבוֹ:

35 DAILY MORNING SERVICE — MORNING BLESSINGS

One of the following two passages:

I

יְהִי Our Living God and God of our ancestors, help us to live according to Your teaching and to hold fast to Your commands. Let us not come into the power of sin or wrong-doing, temptation or disgrace. Let no evil within us control us, and keep us far from bad people and bad company. Help us hold fast to the good within us and to good deeds, and bend our will and our desires to serve You. Give us today, and every day, grace, kindness and mercy in Your sight and in the sight of all who regard us, and grant us Your love and kindness. Blessed are You God, inspiring Your people Israel with love and kindness.

יְהִי רָצוֹן מִלְּפָנֶיךָ יהוה אֱלֹהֵינוּ וֵאלֹהֵי אֲבוֹתֵינוּ. שֶׁתַּרְגִּילֵנוּ בְּתוֹרָתֶךָ וְדַבְּקֵנוּ בְּמִצְוֹתֶיךָ. וְאַל תְּבִיאֵנוּ לֹא לִידֵי חֵטְא וְלֹא לִידֵי עֲבֵירָה וְלֹא לִידֵי נִסָּיוֹן וְלֹא לִידֵי בִזָּיוֹן. וְאַל תַּשְׁלֶט־בָּנוּ יֵצֶר הָרָע. וְהַרְחִיקֵנוּ מֵאָדָם רָע וּמֵחָבֵר רָע. וְדַבְּקֵנוּ בְּיֵצֶר הַטּוֹב וּבְמַעֲשִׂים טוֹבִים. וְכֹף אֶת־יִצְרֵנוּ לְהִשְׁתַּעְבֶּד־לָךְ. וּתְנֵנוּ הַיּוֹם וּבְכָל־יוֹם לְחֵן וּלְחֶסֶד וּלְרַחֲמִים בְּעֵינֶיךָ וּבְעֵינֵי כָל־רוֹאֵינוּ. וְתִגְמְלֵנוּ חֲסָדִים טוֹבִים: בָּרוּךְ אַתָּה יהוה. גּוֹמֵל חֲסָדִים טוֹבִים לְעַמּוֹ יִשְׂרָאֵל:

II

יְהִי My Living God and God of my ancestors, may it be Your will to deliver me this day and every day from the arrogance of others and my own arrogance, from bad people, bad companions and bad neighbours, from bad occurrences and destructive forces, from a hard judgment and a hard opponent.

יְהִי רָצוֹן מִלְּפָנֶיךָ יהוה אֱלֹהַי וֵאלֹהֵי אֲבוֹתַי. שֶׁתַּצִּילֵנִי הַיּוֹם וּבְכָל־יוֹם מֵעַזֵּי פָנִים וּמֵעַזּוּת פָּנִים. מֵאָדָם רַע וּמֵחָבֵר רַע וּמִשָּׁכֵן רַע וּמִפֶּגַע רַע וּמִשָּׂטָן הַמַּשְׁחִית. מִדִּין קָשֶׁה וּמִבַּעַל־דִּין קָשֶׁה:

Time may be taken here to reflect on personal concerns and anxieties.

רִבּוֹן Source of existence and of all human strength, we do not rely on our own good deeds but on Your great mercy as we lay our needs before You.
God, hear!
God, pardon!
God, listen and act!
What are we?
What is our life?
What is our love?
What is our justice?
What is our success?
What is our endurance?
What is our power?
Our God, and God of our ancestors, what can we say before You?

הֲלֹא For in Your presence are not the powerful as nothing, the famous as if they had never existed, the learned as if without knowledge, and the intelligent as if without insight? To You most of our actions are pointless and our daily life is shallow. Even our superiority over the animals is nothing. For everything is trivial except the pure soul which must one day give its account and reckoning before the judgment seat of Your glory.

רִבּוֹן הָעוֹלָמִים וַאֲדוֹנֵי הָאֲדוֹנִים. לֹא עַל־צִדְקוֹתֵינוּ אֲנַחְנוּ מַפִּילִים תַּחֲנוּנֵינוּ לְפָנֶיךָ. כִּי עַל־רַחֲמֶיךָ הָרַבִּים:
אֲדֹנָי שְׁמָעָה.
אֲדֹנָי סְלָחָה.
אֲדֹנָי הַקְשִׁיבָה וַעֲשֵׂה:
מַה־אָנוּ.
מֶה־חַיֵּינוּ.
מֶה־חַסְדֵּנוּ.
מַה־צִּדְקוֹתֵינוּ.
מַה־יְשׁוּעָתֵנוּ.
מַה־כֹּחֵנוּ.
מַה־גְּבוּרָתֵנוּ.
מַה־נֹּאמַר לְפָנֶיךָ יהוה אֱלֹהֵינוּ וֵאלֹהֵי אֲבוֹתֵינוּ:

הֲלֹא הַגִּבּוֹרִים כְּאַיִן לְפָנֶיךָ. וְאַנְשֵׁי הַשֵּׁם כְּלֹא הָיוּ. וַחֲכָמִים כִּבְלִי מַדָּע. וּנְבוֹנִים כִּבְלִי הַשְׂכֵּל. כִּי רֹב מַעֲשֵׂינוּ תֹהוּ. וִימֵי חַיֵּינוּ הֶבֶל לְפָנֶיךָ. וּמוֹתַר הָאָדָם מִן הַבְּהֵמָה אָיִן. כִּי הַכֹּל הֶבֶל לְבַד הַנְּשָׁמָה הַטְּהוֹרָה. שֶׁהִיא עֲתִידָה לִתֵּן דִּין וְחֶשְׁבּוֹן לִפְנֵי כִסֵּא כְבוֹדֶךָ:

37 DAILY MORNING SERVICE — MORNING BLESSINGS

אֲבָל Yet we are Your people, the children of Your covenant, the children of Abraham whom You loved, giving him Your promise on Mount Moriah; the descendants of Isaac, bound as an offering on the altar; the congregation of Jacob 'Your son, Your special son'; out of Your love for him and Your delight in him, You changed his name to Israel and Yeshurun. Blessed are You God, You make Your name holy before all.

אֲבָל אֲנַחְנוּ עַמָּךְ. בְּנֵי בְרִיתֶךָ. בְּנֵי אַבְרָהָם אֹהַבְךָ. שֶׁנִּשְׁבַּעְתָּ לּוֹ בְּהַר הַמּוֹרִיָּה. זֶרַע יִצְחָק יְחִידוֹ. שֶׁנֶּעֱקַד עַל גַּבֵּי הַמִּזְבֵּחַ. עֲדַת יַעֲקֹב בִּנְךָ בְּכוֹרֶךָ. שֶׁמֵּאַהֲבָתְךָ שֶׁאָהַבְתָּ אוֹתוֹ. וּמִשִּׂמְחָתְךָ שֶׁשָּׂמַחְתָּ בּוֹ. קָרָאתָ אֶת שְׁמוֹ יִשְׂרָאֵל וִישֻׁרוּן: בָּרוּךְ אַתָּה יהוה מְקַדֵּשׁ אֶת שִׁמְךָ בָּרַבִּים:

THE GIFT OF TORAH

Before study the following blessing is said:

בָּרוּךְ Blessed are You, our Living God, Sovereign of the universe, whose commandments make us holy, and who commands us to devote ourselves to the study of Torah.[1]

בָּרוּךְ אַתָּה יהוה אֱלֹהֵינוּ מֶלֶךְ הָעוֹלָם. אֲשֶׁר קִדְּשָׁנוּ בְּמִצְוֹתָיו. וְצִוָּנוּ לַעֲסוֹק בְּדִבְרֵי תוֹרָה:

The following study passage or an alternative may be inserted here:

אֵלּוּ These are the things whose interest we enjoy in this world, while the capital remains for us in the world to come -
this is what they are:
Respecting one's father and mother,
acts of generosity and love,
coming early to the House of Study, morning and evening,
giving hospitality to strangers,
visiting the sick,
assisting the bride,
escorting the dead,
engaging with prayer,
making peace between companions.
And the study of Torah leads to them all.[2]

אֵלּוּ דְבָרִים שֶׁאָדָם אוֹכֵל פֵּרוֹתֵיהֶם בָּעוֹלָם הַזֶּה וְהַקֶּרֶן קַיֶּמֶת לוֹ לָעוֹלָם הַבָּא. וְאֵלּוּ הֵן: כִּבּוּד אָב וָאֵם.
וּגְמִילוּת חֲסָדִים.
וְהַשְׁכָּמַת בֵּית הַמִּדְרָשׁ שַׁחֲרִית וְעַרְבִית.
וְהַכְנָסַת אוֹרְחִים.
וּבִקּוּר חוֹלִים.
וְהַכְנָסַת כַּלָּה.
וּלְוָיַת הַמֵּת.
וְעִיּוּן תְּפִלָּה.
וַהֲבָאַת שָׁלוֹם בֵּין אָדָם לַחֲבֵרוֹ.
וְתַלְמוּד תּוֹרָה כְּנֶגֶד כֻּלָּם:

---

[1] *Berachot* 11b.   [2] *Mishnah Peah* 1:1 and *Shabbat* 127a.

After study the following blessing may be said:

וְהַעֲרֶב־נָא Our Living God,
make the words of Your Torah
sweet in our mouths,
and in the mouths of Your people,
the family of Israel,
then we and our descendants,
and the descendants of Your people
the family of Israel,
shall all know Your name and study
Your Torah for its own sake.
Blessed are You God,
You teach Torah to your people Israel.[1]

וְהַעֲרֶב־נָא יהוה אֱלֹהֵינוּ
אֶת־דִּבְרֵי תוֹרָתְךָ בְּפִינוּ.
וּבְפִי עַמְּךָ בֵּית יִשְׂרָאֵל.
וְנִהְיֶה אֲנַחְנוּ וְצֶאֱצָאֵינוּ.
וְצֶאֱצָאֵי עַמְּךָ בֵּית יִשְׂרָאֵל.
כֻּלָּנוּ יוֹדְעֵי שְׁמֶךָ.
וְלוֹמְדֵי תוֹרָתְךָ לִשְׁמָהּ:
בָּרוּךְ אַתָּה יהוה.
הַמְלַמֵּד תּוֹרָה לְעַמּוֹ יִשְׂרָאֵל:

PREPARING TO ENCOUNTER GOD

יהוה God **rules**, God has **ruled**,
God **shall rule** forever and ever.

When the rule of God is
acknowledged throughout the earth,
on that day God shall be One, and
known as One.
Save us, our Living God, to
proclaim Your holy name and be
honoured in praising You.
Blessed is the Eternal One, the God
of Israel from everlasting to
everlasting. Let all the people say:
Amen! Praise God!
May all who live praise God.
Hallelujah![2]

יהוה מֶלֶךְ. יהוה מָלָךְ.
יהוה יִמְלֹךְ לְעוֹלָם וָעֶד:
וְהָיָה יהוה לְמֶלֶךְ עַל־כָּל־הָאָרֶץ.
בַּיּוֹם הַהוּא יִהְיֶה יהוה אֶחָד
וּשְׁמוֹ אֶחָד:
הוֹשִׁיעֵנוּ יהוה אֱלֹהֵינוּ. לְהוֹדוֹת
לְשֵׁם קָדְשֶׁךָ לְהִשְׁתַּבֵּחַ בִּתְהִלָּתֶךָ:
בָּרוּךְ יהוה אֱלֹהֵי יִשְׂרָאֵל
מִן־הָעוֹלָם וְעַד הָעוֹלָם. וְאָמַר
כָּל־הָעָם אָמֵן. הַלְלוּיָהּ:
כֹּל הַנְּשָׁמָה תְּהַלֵּל יָהּ.
הַלְלוּיָהּ:

When praying with a community the Mourner's Kaddish may be recited here - page 315.

---

[1] Attributed to Rabbi Yochanan bar Nappacha, third century. *Berachot* 11b.

[2] Zech 14:9, Ps 106:47-48, Ps 150:6.

DAILY MORNING SERVICE — VERSES OF SONG

פסוקי דזמרה
VERSES OF SONG

In this section we consider our personal and communal relationship with God. Between 'Blessed be the One' and 'Praised be Your name forever' (page 53) a selection may be taken from the 'Verses of Song'
Some congregations stand during the recital of **Baruch She'amar.**

THE GIFT OF CREATION

בָּרוּךְ Blessed be the One,
at whose word the world exists.
Blessed be the One,
whose word is deed.
Blessed be the One,
whose command stands firm.
Blessed be the One,
who causes creation.
Blessed be the One,
who has mercy on the earth.
Blessed be the One,
who has mercy on creation.
Blessed be the One, who gives
a good reward to the faithful.
Blessed be the One, who takes away
darkness and brings on light.
Blessed be the One,
who exists before time itself
and endures for eternity.
Blessed be the One in whom there is
no fault and no forgetfulness, who
shows no favour and takes no bribe,
whose ways are righteous
and all of whose deeds are love.
Blessed be the One,
who redeems and rescues.
Blessed be the One,
and blessed be God's name
blessed and remembered
for all eternity.

<<<

בָּרוּךְ שֶׁאָמַר

וְהָיָה הָעוֹלָם: בָּרוּךְ הוּא:
בָּרוּךְ אוֹמֵר וְעוֹשֶׂה:
בָּרוּךְ גּוֹזֵר וּמְקַיֵּם:
בָּרוּךְ עוֹשֶׂה בְרֵאשִׁית:
בָּרוּךְ מְרַחֵם עַל הָאָרֶץ:
בָּרוּךְ מְרַחֵם עַל הַבְּרִיּוֹת:
בָּרוּךְ מְשַׁלֵּם שָׂכָר טוֹב לִירֵאָיו:
בָּרוּךְ מַעֲבִיר אֲפֵלָה וּמֵבִיא אוֹרָה:
בָּרוּךְ אֵל חַי לָעַד וְקַיָּם לָנֶצַח:
בָּרוּךְ שֶׁאֵין לְפָנָיו עַוְלָה
וְלֹא שִׁכְחָה וְלֹא מַשּׂוֹא פָנִים
וְלֹא מִקַּח שֹׁחַד.
צַדִּיק הוּא בְּכָל־דְּרָכָיו
וְחָסִיד בְּכָל־מַעֲשָׂיו:
בָּרוּךְ פּוֹדֶה וּמַצִּיל:
בָּרוּךְ הוּא וּבָרוּךְ שְׁמוֹ.
וּבָרוּךְ זִכְרוֹ לְעוֹלְמֵי עַד:

בָּרוּךְ אַתָּה יהוה אֱלֹהֵינוּ מֶלֶךְ הָעוֹלָם. הַמֶּלֶךְ הַגָּדוֹל וְהַקָּדוֹשׁ. אָב הָרַחֲמָן. מְהֻלָּל בְּפִי עַמּוֹ. מְשֻׁבָּח וּמְפֹאָר בִּלְשׁוֹן כָּל־חֲסִידָיו וַעֲבָדָיו: וּבְשִׁירֵי דָוִד עַבְדְּךָ נְהַלֶּלְךָ יהוה אֱלֹהֵינוּ. בִּשְׁבָחוֹת וּבִזְמִירוֹת נְהוֹדְךָ נְגַדֶּלְךָ נְפָאֶרְךָ וְנַמְלִיכְךָ וְנַזְכִּיר שִׁמְךָ מַלְכֵּנוּ אֱלֹהֵינוּ. יָחִיד חֵי הָעוֹלָמִים. מְשֻׁבָּח וּמְפֹאָר שְׁמוֹ עֲדֵי עַד:
בָּרוּךְ אַתָּה יהוה.
מֶלֶךְ מְהֻלָּל בַּתִּשְׁבָּחוֹת:

בָּרוּךְ Blessed are You, our Living God, Sovereign of the universe, great and holy in power, Source of mercy; praised by Your people; worshipped and glorified by the tongue of all who love and serve You. Therefore we praise You with the psalms of Your servant David; with prayers and songs we declare Your glory, Your greatness, Your splendour, and Your majesty. We proclaim Your name, our Sovereign, our God, who alone is the life of all existence, and whose name is worshipped and glorified forever and ever.
Blessed are You God, the Sovereign praised in all worship.

ק

אמִזְמוֹר לְתוֹדָה
הָרִיעוּ לַיהוה כָּל־הָאָרֶץ:
בעִבְדוּ אֶת־יהוה בְּשִׂמְחָה
בֹּאוּ לְפָנָיו בִּרְנָנָה:
גדְּעוּ כִּי־יהוה הוּא אֱלֹהִים
הוּא עָשָׂנוּ וְלוֹ אֲנַחְנוּ
עַמּוֹ וְצֹאן מַרְעִיתוֹ:
דבֹּאוּ שְׁעָרָיו בְּתוֹדָה
חֲצֵרֹתָיו בִּתְהִלָּה
הוֹדוּ־לוֹ בָּרְכוּ שְׁמוֹ:
הכִּי־טוֹב יהוה לְעוֹלָם חַסְדּוֹ
וְעַד־דֹּר וָדֹר אֱמוּנָתוֹ:

Psalm 100

¹A Psalm of Thanksgiving.
הָרִיעוּ Call out to God all the earth,
²worship the Divine with joy,
come before God with singing.

³Know that the God is Creator,
our Maker to whom we belong,
a people
tended like a flock.

⁴Come into God's gates with thanks,
and courts with praise,
thanking and blessing God's name.

⁵For the Eternal is good,
steadfast in love
and faithful for all generations.

*A selection from the Daily Psalms, Psalms 145 and 150,
or the Song at the Sea (Exodus 15) on page 50 may be included here.*

ON SUNDAY ביום ראשון

Psalm 24   כד

¹David's Psalm.
לַיהוה The earth and its fullness
belong to God,
the world and those who dwell in it,
²for it is the Creator
who set it on the seas
and made it firm upon the depths.
³Who may ascend the mountain of God
and who may stand in that holy place?
⁴Those whose hands are clean,
whose heart is pure,
who have not given up their soul
to worthless things
nor committed themselves to deception.
⁵They shall earn a blessing from the Creator
and be vindicated by God who saves them.
⁶This is a generation that searches for God,
those who seek Your presence
are the family of Jacob
(*selah*).

⁷Gates, lift up your heads!
Be raised, you everlasting doors!
Let the Ruler of glory enter!
⁸"Who is this Ruler of glory?"
God, strong and mighty,
God, mighty in battle!

⁹Gates, lift up your heads!
Rise up you everlasting doors!
Let the Ruler of glory enter!
¹⁰"Who then, is this Ruler of glory?"
The God of all creation,
this One alone is the Ruler of glory
(*selah*)!

ON MONDAY ביום שני

Psalm 48

¹A Song, A Psalm of the Sons of Korach
²גָּדוֹל Great is God and much praised,
in the city of our God,
on God's holy hill.
³The fairest of places,
a joy throughout the earth
is Mount Zion
on the northern side,
the city of the great king.
⁴In her palaces
God is known as a haven.
⁵See, the kings assembled,
they advanced together.
⁶They just saw it
and were astounded,
they panicked and fled;
⁷they were seized with trembling,
writhing as a woman in labour,
⁸just as you shattered
the Tarshish ships
in an easterly gale.
⁹As once we heard, so have we seen
in the city of the God of all creation,
in the city of our God –
may God establish it forever
(*selah*)!
¹⁰We have hoped
for Your steadfast love, O God,
in the midst of Your temple.
¹¹Like Your name, O God,
so is Your praise
to the ends of the earth.
Your right hand
is filled with righteousness.
¹²May Mount Zion be glad,
may the daughters of Judah
come to rejoice
because of Your judgments.

<<<

43 DAILY MORNING SERVICE — VERSES OF SONG

¹³Walk about Zion, go round about her,
number her towers.
¹⁴Mark well in your hearts
her ramparts,
go through her citadels,
that you may tell the next generation
¹⁵that this is God,
our God forever and ever,
who will guide us
even beyond death.

יג סֹבּוּ צִיּוֹן וְהַקִּיפוּהָ
סִפְרוּ מִגְדָּלֶיהָ:
יד שִׁיתוּ לִבְּכֶם לְחֵילָה
פַּסְּגוּ אַרְמְנוֹתֶיהָ
לְמַעַן תְּסַפְּרוּ לְדוֹר אַחֲרוֹן:
טו כִּי זֶה אֱלֹהִים אֱלֹהֵינוּ
עוֹלָם וָעֶד הוּא יְנַהֲגֵנוּ עַל־מוּת:

ON TUESDAY ביום שלישי

Psalm 82   פב

¹A Psalm of Asaph
אֱלֹהִים God stands
in the congregation of the godly,
in the midst of the mighty God judges.

א מִזְמוֹר לְאָסָף
אֱלֹהִים נִצָּב בַּעֲדַת־אֵל
בְּקֶרֶב אֱלֹהִים יִשְׁפֹּט:

²'How long will you judge unjustly,
and show favour to the wicked (*selah*)?
³Do justice for the weak and the orphan,
act rightly for the afflicted
and the destitute!
⁴Rescue the weak and the needy,
save them from the clutches
of the wicked!'
⁵They do not realise,
they do not understand;
they grope in the dark
and the order of the world is shaken.
⁶I said, 'You are godlike beings,
sons of the Highest all of you.
⁷Yet you shall die like men;
princes fall, so shall you.'

⁸God arise, judge the earth!
For You possess all the nations.

ב עַד־מָתַי תִּשְׁפְּטוּ־עָוֶל
וּפְנֵי רְשָׁעִים תִּשְׂאוּ־סֶלָה:
ג שִׁפְטוּ־דַל וְיָתוֹם
עָנִי וָרָשׁ הַצְדִּיקוּ:
ד פַּלְּטוּ־דַל וְאֶבְיוֹן
מִיַּד רְשָׁעִים הַצִּילוּ:
ה לֹא יָדְעוּ וְלֹא יָבִינוּ
בַּחֲשֵׁכָה יִתְהַלָּכוּ
יִמּוֹטוּ כָּל־מוֹסְדֵי אָרֶץ:
ו אֲנִי־אָמַרְתִּי אֱלֹהִים אַתֶּם
וּבְנֵי עֶלְיוֹן כֻּלְּכֶם:
ז אָכֵן כְּאָדָם תְּמוּתוּן
וּכְאַחַד הַשָּׂרִים תִּפֹּלוּ:

ח קוּמָה אֱלֹהִים שָׁפְטָה הָאָרֶץ
כִּי־אַתָּה תִנְחַל בְּכָל־הַגּוֹיִם:

ON WEDNESDAY   ביום רביעי

Psalm 94:1-95:3

¹**אֵל** God of measured justice, Eternal One,
God of measured justice
make Yourself known!
²Arise, Judge of the earth
pay the arrogant their due!
³How long shall the wicked, God,
how long shall the wicked exult?
⁴They are eloquent speaking their deceit,
all who do evil are boasting.
⁵It is Your people, God, whom they crush,
Your very own whom they oppress.
⁶They kill the widow and stranger,
murder the fatherless,
⁷and they boast: 'God does not see,
nor the God of Jacob understand!'
⁸Understand this,
you brutish amongst the people;
fools, when will you gain wisdom!
⁹The One who implants the ear
shall not hear,
who forms the eye shall not see?
¹⁰Who disciplines nations shall not rebuke,
the One who teaches people knowledge?
¹¹God knows human designs,
knows their futility.
¹²Happy are those
You discipline, God,
teaching them Your Torah,
¹³giving calmness in evil days
till the pit be dug for the wicked.
¹⁴For God You will not forsake
Your people, nor abandon Your very own.
¹⁵For justice shall bring back
a righteous state
and all upright in heart shall follow it.

<<<

צד

^אאֵל־נְקָמוֹת יְהוה
אֵל נְקָמוֹת הוֹפִיעַ:
^בהִנָּשֵׂא שֹׁפֵט הָאָרֶץ
הָשֵׁב גְּמוּל עַל־גֵּאִים:
^געַד־מָתַי רְשָׁעִים יְהוה
עַד־מָתַי רְשָׁעִים יַעֲלֹזוּ:
^דיַבִּיעוּ יְדַבְּרוּ עָתָק
יִתְאַמְּרוּ כָּל־פֹּעֲלֵי אָוֶן:
^העַמְּךָ יְהוה יְדַכְּאוּ
וְנַחֲלָתְךָ יְעַנּוּ:
^ואַלְמָנָה וְגֵר יַהֲרֹגוּ
וִיתוֹמִים יְרַצֵּחוּ:
^זוַיֹּאמְרוּ לֹא יִרְאֶה־יָּהּ
וְלֹא־יָבִין אֱלֹהֵי יַעֲקֹב:
^חבִּינוּ בֹּעֲרִים בָּעָם
וּכְסִילִים מָתַי תַּשְׂכִּילוּ:
^טהֲנֹטַע אֹזֶן הֲלֹא יִשְׁמָע
אִם־יֹצֵר עַיִן הֲלֹא יַבִּיט:
^יהֲיֹסֵר גּוֹיִם הֲלֹא יוֹכִיחַ
הַמְלַמֵּד אָדָם דָּעַת:
^{יא}יְהוה יֹדֵעַ מַחְשְׁבוֹת אָדָם
כִּי־הֵמָּה הָבֶל:
^{יב}אַשְׁרֵי הַגֶּבֶר אֲשֶׁר־תְּיַסְּרֶנּוּ יָּהּ
וּמִתּוֹרָתְךָ תְלַמְּדֶנּוּ:
^{יג}לְהַשְׁקִיט לוֹ מִימֵי רָע
עַד יִכָּרֶה לָרָשָׁע שָׁחַת:
^{יד}כִּי לֹא־יִטֹּשׁ יְהוה עַמּוֹ
וְנַחֲלָתוֹ לֹא יַעֲזֹב:
^{טו}כִּי־עַד־צֶדֶק יָשׁוּב מִשְׁפָּט
וְאַחֲרָיו כָּל־יִשְׁרֵי־לֵב:

DAILY MORNING SERVICE — VERSES OF SONG

¹⁶Who will rise up for me
against the wicked,
who will take a stand for me
against those who do evil?
¹⁷If God had not been my help
my soul would soon
have dwelt in silence.
¹⁸When I say 'my foot is slipping',
Your faithful love, God, sustains me.
¹⁹When worries fill my mind,
Your consolations comfort my soul.

²⁰Can the throne of injustice
claim You as a partner,
those who use the law to do harm?
²¹They unite against
the life of the righteous,
condemning the innocent to death.
²²But God is my haven.
My God is my sheltering rock.
²³God will turn their
own violence upon them,
destroy them through their
own wickedness;
our Living God will destroy them.

טז מִי־יָקוּם לִי עִם־מְרֵעִים
מִי־יִתְיַצֵּב לִי עִם־פֹּעֲלֵי אָוֶן:
יז לוּלֵי יְהֹוָה עֶזְרָתָה לִּי
כִּמְעַט שָׁכְנָה דוּמָה נַפְשִׁי:
יח אִם־אָמַרְתִּי מָטָה רַגְלִי
חַסְדְּךָ יְהֹוָה יִסְעָדֵנִי:
יט בְּרֹב שַׂרְעַפַּי בְּקִרְבִּי
תַּנְחוּמֶיךָ יְשַׁעַשְׁעוּ נַפְשִׁי:

כ הַיְחָבְרְךָ כִּסֵּא הַוּוֹת
יֹצֵר עָמָל עֲלֵי־חֹק:
כא יָגוֹדּוּ עַל־נֶפֶשׁ צַדִּיק
וְדָם נָקִי יַרְשִׁיעוּ:
כב וַיְהִי יְהֹוָה לִי לְמִשְׂגָּב
וֵאלֹהַי לְצוּר מַחְסִי:
כג וַיָּשֶׁב עֲלֵיהֶם אֶת־אוֹנָם
וּבְרָעָתָם יַצְמִיתֵם
יַצְמִיתֵם יְהֹוָה אֱלֹהֵינוּ:

Psalm 95 — צה

¹לְכוּ Come let us sing out to the Eternal,
call out to the rock of our safety.
²Let us come before God with thanks,
call out to God with psalms.
³For the Eternal is almighty God,
a mighty ruler
beyond all gods.

א לְכוּ נְרַנְּנָה לַיהֹוָה
נָרִיעָה לְצוּר יִשְׁעֵנוּ:
ב נְקַדְּמָה פָנָיו בְּתוֹדָה
בִּזְמִרוֹת נָרִיעַ לוֹ:
ג כִּי אֵל גָּדוֹל יְהֹוָה
וּמֶלֶךְ גָּדוֹל
עַל־כָּל־אֱלֹהִים:

ON THURSDAY ביום חמישי

Psalm 81

פא לַמְנַצֵּחַ עַל־הַגִּתִּית לְאָסָף:

[1] For the Choirmaster. On the Gittit. Of Asaph.

[2] הַרְנִינוּ Sing joyously to God, our strength,
call out to the God of Jacob.

הַרְנִינוּ לֵאלֹהִים עוּזֵּנוּ
הָרִיעוּ לֵאלֹהֵי יַעֲקֹב:

[3] Take up the song and sound the drum,
the sweet-sounding lyre and harp.

שְׂאוּ־זִמְרָה וּתְנוּ־תֹף
כִּנּוֹר נָעִים עִם־נָבֶל:

[4] Blow the *shofar* on the new moon,
to proclaim the day of our festival.

תִּקְעוּ בַחֹדֶשׁ שׁוֹפָר
בַּכֵּסֶה לְיוֹם חַגֵּנוּ:

[5] For this is a law of Israel,
a decree of the God of Jacob.

כִּי חֹק לְיִשְׂרָאֵל הוּא
מִשְׁפָּט לֵאלֹהֵי יַעֲקֹב:

[6] God imposed it as a decree upon Joseph
when God went forth
over the land of Egypt.
'Then I heard a language
I had not known before':

עֵדוּת בִּיהוֹסֵף שָׂמוֹ
בְּצֵאתוֹ עַל־אֶרֶץ מִצְרָיִם
שְׂפַת לֹא־יָדַעְתִּי אֶשְׁמָע:

[7] 'I relieved Israel's shoulder
from the burden,
his hands were freed from the basket.

הֲסִירוֹתִי מִסֵּבֶל שִׁכְמוֹ
כַּפָּיו מִדּוּד תַּעֲבֹרְנָה:

[8] In distress you called and I rescued you.
I answered you
in the secret place of thunder.
I tested you at the waters of Meribah.
(*selah*)!

בַּצָּרָה קָרָאתָ וָאֲחַלְּצֶךָּ
אֶעֶנְךָ בְּסֵתֶר רַעַם
אֶבְחָנְךָ עַל־מֵי מְרִיבָה
סֶלָה:

[9] Listen, my people,
and I will attest to you:
Israel if you would but listen to me,
[10] there shall be no
strange god amongst you,
nor shall you bow down
before an alien god.

שְׁמַע עַמִּי וְאָעִידָה בָּךְ
יִשְׂרָאֵל אִם־תִּשְׁמַע־לִי:
לֹא־יִהְיֶה בְךָ אֵל זָר
וְלֹא תִשְׁתַּחֲוֶה לְאֵל נֵכָר:

[11] I, the Eternal, am your God,
who brought you out
of the land of Egypt;
open your mouth wide and I will fill it.

אָנֹכִי יהוה אֱלֹהֶיךָ
הַמַּעַלְךָ מֵאֶרֶץ מִצְרָיִם
הַרְחֶב־פִּיךָ וַאֲמַלְאֵהוּ:

<<<

DAILY MORNING SERVICE — VERSES OF SONG

¹²But My people
would not listen to My voice,
and Israel did not desire Me.
¹³So I let them go after their wilful heart;
they follow their own intentions.
¹⁴If only My people would listen to Me,
if Israel would follow My paths.
¹⁵Then I would subdue
their enemies at once,
turn My power against their foes.
¹⁶Those who hate the Eternal shall cower,
their fate sealed forever.
¹⁷But God will feed Israel
with the finest wheat,
I will sate you
with honey from the rock.'

יבוְלֹא־שָׁמַע עַמִּי לְקוֹלִי
וְיִשְׂרָאֵל לֹא־אָבָה לִי:
יגוָאֲשַׁלְּחֵהוּ בִּשְׁרִירוּת לִבָּם
יֵלְכוּ בְּמוֹעֲצוֹתֵיהֶם:
ידלוּ עַמִּי שֹׁמֵעַ לִי
יִשְׂרָאֵל בִּדְרָכַי יְהַלֵּכוּ:
טוכִּמְעַט אוֹיְבֵיהֶם אַכְנִיעַ
וְעַל־צָרֵיהֶם אָשִׁיב יָדִי:
טזמְשַׂנְאֵי יהוה יְכַחֲשׁוּ־לוֹ
וִיהִי עִתָּם לְעוֹלָם:
יזוַיַּאֲכִילֵהוּ מֵחֵלֶב חִטָּה
וּמִצּוּר דְּבַשׁ אַשְׂבִּיעֶךָ:

ON FRIDAY ביום ששי

Psalm 93 צג

¹**יהוה** The Creator reigns
robed in pride,
God is robed in power,
clothed in strength.
So the world was set firm
and cannot be shaken,
²Your throne was set firm long ago,
from eternity You are.

³Almighty, the floods may storm,
the floods may storm aloud,
the floods may storm and thunder.

⁴But even above the roar of great waves,
mighty breakers of the ocean,
supreme is the might of the Creator.

⁵The proofs You give are very sure,
holiness is the mark of Your house,
God, as long as time endures.

איהוה מָלָךְ גֵּאוּת לָבֵשׁ
לָבֵשׁ יהוה עֹז הִתְאַזָּר
אַף־תִּכּוֹן תֵּבֵל בַּל־תִּמּוֹט:
בנָכוֹן כִּסְאֲךָ מֵאָז
מֵעוֹלָם אָתָּה:

גנָשְׂאוּ נְהָרוֹת יהוה
נָשְׂאוּ נְהָרוֹת קוֹלָם
יִשְׂאוּ נְהָרוֹת דָּכְיָם:

דמִקֹּלוֹת מַיִם רַבִּים
אַדִּירִים מִשְׁבְּרֵי־יָם
אַדִּיר בַּמָּרוֹם יהוה:

העֵדֹתֶיךָ נֶאֶמְנוּ מְאֹד
לְבֵיתְךָ נַאֲוָה־קֹדֶשׁ
יהוה לְאֹרֶךְ יָמִים:

After the Daily Psalm, the service continues here.

אַשְׁרֵי Happy are those that live in Your house and can always praise You (*selah*). Happy the people of whom this is true! Happy the people whose God is the Eternal![1]	אַשְׁרֵי יוֹשְׁבֵי בֵיתֶךָ. עוֹד יְהַלְלוּךָ סֶּלָה: אַשְׁרֵי הָעָם שֶׁכָּכָה לּוֹ. אַשְׁרֵי הָעָם שֶׁיהוה אֱלֹהָיו:

Psalm 145

קמה

[1] A Psalm of Praise. David's.	תְּהִלָּה לְדָוִד
אֲרוֹמִמְךָ I will glorify You, God my **Sovereign**, and bless Your name forever and ever. [2] Every day I will bless You and praise Your name forever and ever.	אֲרוֹמִמְךָ אֱלוֹהַי הַמֶּלֶךְ. וַאֲבָרְכָה שִׁמְךָ לְעוֹלָם וָעֶד: בְּכָל־יוֹם אֲבָרְכֶךָּ. וַאֲהַלְלָה שִׁמְךָ לְעוֹלָם וָעֶד:
[3] Great is the Eternal and praised aloud, Your greatness is beyond understanding. [4] One generation shall praise Your deeds to the next and tell of Your mighty acts.	גָּדוֹל יהוה וּמְהֻלָּל מְאֹד. וְלִגְדֻלָּתוֹ אֵין חֵקֶר: דּוֹר לְדוֹר יְשַׁבַּח מַעֲשֶׂיךָ. וּגְבוּרֹתֶיךָ יַגִּידוּ:
[5] The glorious splendour of Your majesty and Your wonders will be my theme. [6] People will speak of the power of Your awesome deeds, and I will describe Your greatness.	הֲדַר כְּבוֹד הוֹדֶךָ. וְדִבְרֵי נִפְלְאֹתֶיךָ אָשִׂיחָה: וֶעֱזוּז נוֹרְאֹתֶיךָ יֹאמֵרוּ. וּגְדֻלָּתְךָ אֲסַפְּרֶנָּה:
[7] They will spread the fame of Your great goodness and sing out loud Your righteousness. [8] Compassionate and merciful is the Eternal, slow to anger, and great in love.	זֵכֶר רַב־טוּבְךָ יַבִּיעוּ. וְצִדְקָתְךָ יְרַנֵּנוּ: חַנּוּן וְרַחוּם יהוה. אֶרֶךְ אַפַּיִם וּגְדָל־חָסֶד:
[9] The Eternal is good to everyone, Your compassion is over all You made. [10] All You made shall praise You, Eternal, and those who love You will bless You.	טוֹב־יהוה לַכֹּל. וְרַחֲמָיו עַל־כָּל־מַעֲשָׂיו: יוֹדוּךָ יהוה כָּל־מַעֲשֶׂיךָ. וַחֲסִידֶיךָ יְבָרְכוּכָה:

<<<

---

[1] Ps 84:5 and 144:15.

49 DAILY MORNING SERVICE — VERSES OF SONG

[11]They shall speak of the glory
of Your **rule**
and talk about Your power,
[12]to let all people know
of Your mighty acts
and the glorious splendour
of Your **rule**.

יאכְּבוֹד מַלְכוּתְךָ יֹאמֵרוּ.
וּגְבוּרָתְךָ יְדַבֵּרוּ:
יבלְהוֹדִיעַ לִבְנֵי הָאָדָם גְּבוּרֹתָיו.
וּכְבוֹד הֲדַר מַלְכוּתוֹ:

[13]Your **rule** is an everlasting **rule**,
Your authority for every generation.
[14]The Eternal supports the falling
and raises all those bent low.

יגמַלְכוּתְךָ מַלְכוּת כָּל־עוֹלָמִים.
וּמֶמְשַׁלְתְּךָ בְּכָל־דֹּר וָדֹר:
ידסוֹמֵךְ יהוה לְכָל־הַנֹּפְלִים.
וְזוֹקֵף לְכָל־הַכְּפוּפִים:

[15]The eyes of all look to You
and You give them food when it is time.
[16]You open Your hand
and satisfy the needs of all living.

טועֵינֵי־כֹל אֵלֶיךָ יְשַׂבֵּרוּ.
וְאַתָּה נוֹתֵן־לָהֶם אֶת־אָכְלָם בְּעִתּוֹ:
טזפּוֹתֵחַ אֶת־יָדֶךָ.
וּמַשְׂבִּיעַ לְכָל־חַי רָצוֹן:

[17]Eternal, You are just
in all Your ways
and loving in all Your deeds.
[18]You are near to all who call You,
to all who call You sincerely.

יזצַדִּיק יהוה בְּכָל־דְּרָכָיו.
וְחָסִיד בְּכָל־מַעֲשָׂיו:
יחקָרוֹב יהוה לְכָל־קֹרְאָיו.
לְכֹל אֲשֶׁר יִקְרָאֻהוּ בֶאֱמֶת:

[19]You fulfil the needs
of those who fear You,
hearing their cry and saving them.
[20]You protect those who love You,
but all the wicked You destroy.

יטרְצוֹן־יְרֵאָיו יַעֲשֶׂה.
וְאֶת־שַׁוְעָתָם יִשְׁמַע וְיוֹשִׁיעֵם:
כשׁוֹמֵר יהוה אֶת־כָּל־אֹהֲבָיו.
וְאֵת כָּל־הָרְשָׁעִים יַשְׁמִיד:

[21]My mouth will speak
the praise of the Eternal
and let all flesh bless
God's holy name forever and ever!

    But we bless God
    now and evermore.
    Praise God![1]

כאתְּהִלַּת יהוה יְדַבֶּר־פִּי.
וִיבָרֵךְ כָּל־בָּשָׂר
שֵׁם קָדְשׁוֹ לְעוֹלָם וָעֶד:
וַאֲנַחְנוּ נְבָרֵךְ יָהּ.
מֵעַתָּה וְעַד־עוֹלָם
הַלְלוּיָהּ:

---

[1] Ps 115:18.

שירת־הים

אָז יָשִׁיר־מֹשֶׁה וּבְנֵי יִשְׂרָאֵל אֶת־הַשִּׁירָה הַזֹּאת לַיהוה וַיֹּאמְרוּ לֵאמֹר אָשִׁירָה לַיהוה כִּי־גָאֹה גָּאָה סוּס וְרֹכְבוֹ רָמָה בַיָּם: עָזִּי וְזִמְרָת יָהּ וַיְהִי־לִי לִישׁוּעָה זֶה אֵלִי וְאַנְוֵהוּ אֱלֹהֵי אָבִי וַאֲרֹמְמֶנְהוּ: יהוה אִישׁ מִלְחָמָה יהוה שְׁמוֹ: מַרְכְּבֹת פַּרְעֹה וְחֵילוֹ יָרָה בַיָּם וּמִבְחַר שָׁלִשָׁיו טֻבְּעוּ בְיַם־סוּף: תְּהֹמֹת יְכַסְיֻמוּ יָרְדוּ בִמְצוֹלֹת כְּמוֹ־אָבֶן: יְמִינְךָ יהוה נֶאְדָּרִי בַּכֹּחַ יְמִינְךָ יהוה תִּרְעַץ אוֹיֵב: וּבְרֹב גְּאוֹנְךָ תַּהֲרֹס קָמֶיךָ תְּשַׁלַּח חֲרֹנְךָ יֹאכְלֵמוֹ כַּקַּשׁ: וּבְרוּחַ אַפֶּיךָ נֶעֶרְמוּ מַיִם נִצְּבוּ כְמוֹ־נֵד נֹזְלִים קָפְאוּ תְהֹמֹת בְּלֶב־יָם: אָמַר אוֹיֵב אֶרְדֹּף אַשִּׂיג אֲחַלֵּק שָׁלָל תִּמְלָאֵמוֹ נַפְשִׁי אָרִיק חַרְבִּי תּוֹרִישֵׁמוֹ יָדִי: נָשַׁפְתָּ בְרוּחֲךָ כִּסָּמוֹ יָם צָלֲלוּ כַּעוֹפֶרֶת בְּמַיִם אַדִּירִים: מִי־כָמֹכָה בָּאֵלִם יהוה מִי כָּמֹכָה נֶאְדָּר בַּקֹּדֶשׁ נוֹרָא תְהִלֹּת עֹשֵׂה־פֶלֶא: נָטִיתָ יְמִינְךָ תִּבְלָעֵמוֹ אָרֶץ: נָחִיתָ בְחַסְדְּךָ עַם־זוּ גָּאָלְתָּ נֵהַלְתָּ בְעָזְּךָ אֶל־נְוֵה קָדְשֶׁךָ: שָׁמְעוּ עַמִּים יִרְגָּזוּן חִיל אָחַז יֹשְׁבֵי פְּלָשֶׁת: אָז נִבְהֲלוּ אַלּוּפֵי אֱדוֹם אֵילֵי מוֹאָב יֹאחֲזֵמוֹ רָעַד נָמֹגוּ כֹּל יֹשְׁבֵי כְנָעַן: תִּפֹּל עֲלֵיהֶם אֵימָתָה וָפַחַד בִּגְדֹל זְרוֹעֲךָ יִדְּמוּ כָּאָבֶן עַד־יַעֲבֹר עַמְּךָ יהוה עַד־יַעֲבֹר עַם־זוּ קָנִיתָ: תְּבִאֵמוֹ וְתִטָּעֵמוֹ בְּהַר נַחֲלָתְךָ מָכוֹן לְשִׁבְתְּךָ פָּעַלְתָּ יהוה מִקְּדָשׁ אֲדֹנָי כּוֹנְנוּ יָדֶיךָ: יהוה יִמְלֹךְ לְעֹלָם וָעֶד:

The Song at the Sea

Then sang Moses and the children of Israel this song to the Almighty:
I will sing to the Almighty who has risen in triumph,
    horse and rider God hurled into the sea.
The Almighty is my strength and song and has become my salvation.
This is my God, whom I will praise, my father's God, whom I will exalt.
    The Almighty is a warrior, so is the Almighty known.

Pharaoh's chariots and army God cast into the sea,
    the pick of his officers are sunk in the sea of reeds.
    The depths cover them,
    they went down to the bottom like a stone.
Your right hand, Almighty, is majestic in power,
Your right hand, Almighty, shatters the enemy.
In the fullness of Your triumph You throw down Your foes.
You unleashed Your anger, it consumed them like chaff.
A blast of Your nostrils and the waters piled high,
    the waves stood up like a wall,
in the heart of the sea the deeps congealed.

The enemy said 'I will chase - overtake!
Divide the spoil! Devour my fill!
Draw my sword! My hand destroy them!'
One puff of Your breath and the waters covered them,
    they sank like lead in the terrible waters.
Who is like You, Almighty, among the gods men worship?
Who, like You, is majestic in holiness,
    awesome in praise, working wonders?

You stretched out Your right hand, the earth swallowed them.
You led with constant love Your ransomed people.
You guided them with Your strength to Your holy place of rest.
    Peoples hear and tremble!
Tremors grip the dwellers in Philistia.
Edom's chieftains are now dismayed.
Shuddering grips Moab's leaders.
All dwellers in Canaan are in turmoil.
Dread and terror fall upon them.
Through the power of Your arm they are still as stone,
    until Your people pass over, Almighty God,
    till the people You have gained pass over.
You will bring them and plant them on the mountain that is Your own,
    the place You have made Your dwelling, God,
the sanctuary, God, prepared by Your own hands.

    God alone shall rule forever and ever.[1]

---
[1] Ex 15:1-18.

קנ

Psalm 150

¹ **הַלְלוּיָהּ** Hallelujah - Praise God!
² Give praise to God in God's holy place,
praise in God's mighty heavens,
³ praise for God's powerful deeds,
praise for God's surpassing greatness.
⁴ Give praise to God with the *shofar* blast;
praise with the lyre and harp,
⁵ praise with drums and dancing,
praise with the lute and pipe.
⁶ Give praise to God
with the clash of cymbals,
praise with the clanging cymbals.
Let everything that has breath
praise God.
Hallelujah - Praise God!

א הַלְלוּיָהּ
ב הַלְלוּ־אֵל בְּקָדְשׁוֹ
הַלְלוּהוּ בִּרְקִיעַ עֻזּוֹ:
ג הַלְלוּהוּ בִגְבוּרֹתָיו
הַלְלוּהוּ כְּרֹב גֻּדְלוֹ:
ד הַלְלוּהוּ בְּתֵקַע שׁוֹפָר
הַלְלוּהוּ בְּנֵבֶל וְכִנּוֹר:
ה הַלְלוּהוּ בְּתֹף וּמָחוֹל
הַלְלוּהוּ בְּמִנִּים וְעוּגָב:
ו הַלְלוּהוּ בְצִלְצְלֵי־שָׁמַע
הַלְלוּהוּ בְּצִלְצְלֵי תְרוּעָה:
כֹּל הַנְּשָׁמָה תְּהַלֵּל יָהּ
הַלְלוּיָהּ:

ALL CREATION PRAISES GOD

וַיְבָרֶךְ Then David blessed the Almighty in the sight of all the congregation, and David said: 'Blessed are You Almighty God, the God of our father Israel from everlasting to everlasting. Yours is the greatness, the power, the splendour, the glory and the majesty, for everything in heaven and earth is Yours. Yours alone is sovereignty and You are exalted supreme over all. Wealth and honour come from You, for You rule over all. In Your hand are strength and might. It is in Your power to give greatness and strength to all. And now, our God, we give You thanks and praise Your glorious name.'¹

וַיְבָרֶךְ דָּוִיד אֶת יהוה לְעֵינֵי כָל־הַקָּהָל. וַיֹּאמֶר דָּוִיד. בָּרוּךְ אַתָּה יהוה אֱלֹהֵי יִשְׂרָאֵל אָבִינוּ מֵעוֹלָם וְעַד־עוֹלָם: לְךָ יהוה הַגְּדֻלָּה וְהַגְּבוּרָה וְהַתִּפְאֶרֶת וְהַנֵּצַח וְהַהוֹד. כִּי כֹל בַּשָּׁמַיִם וּבָאָרֶץ לְךָ יהוה הַמַּמְלָכָה וְהַמִּתְנַשֵּׂא לְכֹל לְרֹאשׁ: וְהָעֹשֶׁר וְהַכָּבוֹד מִלְּפָנֶיךָ וְאַתָּה מוֹשֵׁל בַּכֹּל. וּבְיָדְךָ כֹּחַ וּגְבוּרָה. וּבְיָדְךָ לְגַדֵּל וּלְחַזֵּק לַכֹּל: וְעַתָּה אֱלֹהֵינוּ מוֹדִים אֲנַחְנוּ לָךְ. וּמְהַלְלִים לְשֵׁם תִּפְאַרְתֶּךָ:

<<<

---
¹ I Chron 29:10-13.

53 DAILY MORNING SERVICE — VERSES OF SONG

May the people bless Your glorious name, though it is beyond all blessing and praise. You alone are God; You made the sky, the reaches of space and its countless lights, the earth and everything on it, the seas and everything in them; You give life to them all, and the universe worships You.[1]

וִיבָרְכוּ שֵׁם כְּבֹדֶךָ. וּמְרוֹמַם עַל־כָּל־בְּרָכָה וּתְהִלָּה: אַתָּה הוּא יהוה לְבַדֶּךָ. אַתָּה עָשִׂיתָ אֶת־הַשָּׁמַיִם שְׁמֵי הַשָּׁמַיִם וְכָל־צְבָאָם. הָאָרֶץ וְכָל־אֲשֶׁר עָלֶיהָ. הַיַּמִּים וְכָל־אֲשֶׁר בָּהֶם. וְאַתָּה מְחַיֶּה אֶת־כֻּלָּם. וּצְבָא הַשָּׁמַיִם לְךָ מִשְׁתַּחֲוִים:

בָּרוּךְ Blessed be God forever. Amen and amen.[2]
Blessed be Almighty God, the God of Israel, who alone works wonders. Blessed be the nearness of God's Presence forever, for God's Presence fills all the earth. Amen and amen.[3]

בָּרוּךְ יהוה לְעוֹלָם אָמֵן וְאָמֵן.
בָּרוּךְ יהוה אֱלֹהִים אֱלֹהֵי יִשְׂרָאֵל.
עֹשֵׂה נִפְלָאוֹת לְבַדּוֹ:
וּבָרוּךְ שֵׁם כְּבוֹדוֹ לְעוֹלָם.
וְיִמָּלֵא כְבוֹדוֹ אֶת כָּל־הָאָרֶץ.
אָמֵן וְאָמֵן:

THE DUTY OF PRAISE

יִשְׁתַּבַּח Praised be Your name forever, for You are the God who is the great and holy Sovereign in heaven and on earth. Therefore, our God and God of our ancestors, song and praise, holiness and majesty, blessing and gratitude belong to Your great and holy name forever and ever. From age to age You are God. Blessed are You God, Creator of every living being, the power behind all actions, who chooses songs and psalms, Sovereign, life of all existence.

יִשְׁתַּבַּח שִׁמְךָ לָעַד מַלְכֵּנוּ. הָאֵל הַמֶּלֶךְ הַגָּדוֹל וְהַקָּדוֹשׁ בַּשָּׁמַיִם וּבָאָרֶץ. כִּי לְךָ נָאֶה יהוה אֱלֹהֵינוּ וֵאלֹהֵי אֲבוֹתֵינוּ לְעוֹלָם וָעֶד שִׁיר וּשְׁבָחָה. קְדֻשָּׁה וּמַלְכוּת. בְּרָכוֹת וְהוֹדָאוֹת לְשִׁמְךָ הַגָּדוֹל וְהַקָּדוֹשׁ. וּמֵעוֹלָם וְעַד עוֹלָם אַתָּה אֵל: בָּרוּךְ אַתָּה יהוה. בּוֹרֵא כָּל־הַנְּשָׁמוֹת. רִבּוֹן כָּל־הַמַּעֲשִׂים. הַבּוֹחֵר בְּשִׁירֵי זִמְרָה. מֶלֶךְ חֵי הָעוֹלָמִים:

---

[1] Neh 9:5-6.
[2] Ps 89:53.
[3] Ps 72:18-19.

שמע וברכותיה　　　　　　　　　　תפילת שחרית לימות החול **54**

חֲצִי קַדִּישׁ

Chatsi Kaddish

יִתְגַּדַּל Let us magnify
and let us sanctify in this world
the great name of God
whose will created it.
May God's reign come in your
lifetime, and in your days,
and in the lifetime of the family of
Israel - quickly and speedily
may it come.
Amen.
**May the greatness of God's being
be blessed from eternity to eternity**.
Let us bless and let us extol,
let us tell aloud and let us raise aloft,
let us set on high and let us honour,
let us exalt and
let us praise the Holy One,
whose name is blessed,

who is far beyond any blessing

During the Ten Days of Penitence:
who is far above and beyond any blessing

or song, any honour
or any consolation
that can be spoken of in this world.
Amen.

יִתְגַּדַּל וְיִתְקַדַּשׁ שְׁמֵהּ רַבָּא
בְּעָלְמָא דִּי־בְרָא כִרְעוּתֵהּ:
וְיַמְלִיךְ מַלְכוּתֵהּ
בְּחַיֵּיכוֹן וּבְיוֹמֵיכוֹן
וּבְחַיֵּי דִי־כָל־בֵּית יִשְׂרָאֵל
בַּעֲגָלָא וּבִזְמַן קָרִיב.
וְאִמְרוּ אָמֵן:
יְהֵא שְׁמֵהּ רַבָּא מְבָרַךְ
לְעָלַם וּלְעָלְמֵי עָלְמַיָּא:
יִתְבָּרַךְ וְיִשְׁתַּבַּח וְיִתְפָּאַר
וְיִתְרוֹמַם וְיִתְנַשֵּׂא וְיִתְהַדָּר
וְיִתְעַלֶּה וְיִתְהַלָּל שְׁמֵהּ
דִּי־קֻדְשָׁא. בְּרִיךְ הוּא.

לְעֵלָּא מִן־כָּל־בִּרְכָתָא

During the Ten Days of Penitence:
לְעֵלָּא לְעֵלָּא מִכָּל־בִּרְכָתָא

וְשִׁירָתָא תֻּשְׁבְּחָתָא וְנֶחֱמָתָא
דַּאֲמִירָן בְּעָלְמָא.
וְאִמְרוּ אָמֵן:

שמע וברכותיה
THE *SH'MA* AND ITS BLESSINGS

It is traditional for the Prayer Leader to bow slightly from the waist when saying Bar'chu,
and for the congregation to do likewise when responding,
returning to the upright position when mentioning the name of God.

THE CALL TO COMMUNITY PRAYER

בָּרְכוּ Bless the Living God
whom we are called to bless.

בָּרוּךְ Blessed is the Living
God whom we are called to
bless forever and ever.

בָּרְכוּ אֶת־יְהוָה הַמְבֹרָךְ:

בָּרוּךְ יְהוָה הַמְבֹרָךְ
לְעוֹלָם וָעֶד:

DAILY MORNING SERVICE — THE *SH'MA* AND ITS BLESSINGS

THE CREATOR OF THE UNIVERSE

בָּרוּךְ Blessed are You, our Living God, Sovereign of the universe, who forms light yet creates darkness, who makes peace yet creates all. All things proclaim You, all things honour You, and all say 'None is holy like God!'. The One who gives light to all the world and those who live in it renews in goodness the work of creation day by day. God, how great are Your works; You made them all in wisdom; the earth is full of Your creatures. You are the only Sovereign exalted from the beginning of time, who has been worshipped, praised and glorified since days of old. Everlasting God, in Your great mercy have mercy upon us; Source of our strength, Rock of our protection, Shield of our safety, our true Protector. Blessed are You God, who creates the lights of the universe.

בָּרוּךְ אַתָּה יהוה. אֱלֹהֵינוּ מֶלֶךְ הָעוֹלָם. יוֹצֵר אוֹר וּבוֹרֵא חֹשֶׁךְ. עֹשֶׂה שָׁלוֹם וּבוֹרֵא אֶת הַכֹּל: הַכֹּל יוֹדוּךָ וְהַכֹּל יְשַׁבְּחוּךָ. וְהַכֹּל יֹאמְרוּ אֵין קָדוֹשׁ כַּיהוה: הַמֵּאִיר לָעוֹלָם כֻּלּוֹ וּלְיוֹשְׁבָיו. וּבְטוּבוֹ מְחַדֵּשׁ בְּכָל־יוֹם תָּמִיד מַעֲשֵׂה בְרֵאשִׁית: מָה רַבּוּ מַעֲשֶׂיךָ יהוה. כֻּלָּם בְּחָכְמָה עָשִׂיתָ. מָלְאָה הָאָרֶץ קִנְיָנֶךָ: הַמֶּלֶךְ הַמְרוֹמָם לְבַדּוֹ מֵאָז. הַמְשֻׁבָּח וְהַמְפֹאָר וְהַמִּתְנַשֵּׂא מִימוֹת עוֹלָם: אֱלֹהֵי עוֹלָם. בְּרַחֲמֶיךָ הָרַבִּים רַחֵם עָלֵינוּ. אֲדוֹן עֻזֵּנוּ צוּר מִשְׂגַּבֵּנוּ. מָגֵן יִשְׁעֵנוּ. מִשְׂגָּב בַּעֲדֵנוּ: בָּרוּךְ אַתָּה יהוה יוֹצֵר הַמְּאוֹרוֹת:

GOD'S LOVE FOR ISRAEL

אַהֲבָה With deep love You have loved us, and with great and overflowing tenderness You have taken pity on us. Source of our life and our Sovereign, show us compassion because of Your own greatness, and because of our ancestors who trusted in You, for You taught them rules to live by, to do Your will with their whole heart. Let our eyes see the light of Your teaching and our hearts embrace Your commands. Give us integrity to love You and fear You.

אַהֲבָה רַבָּה אֲהַבְתָּנוּ יהוה אֱלֹהֵינוּ. חֶמְלָה גְדוֹלָה וִיתֵרָה חָמַלְתָּ עָלֵינוּ: אָבִינוּ מַלְכֵּנוּ. בַּעֲבוּר שִׁמְךָ הַגָּדוֹל וּבַעֲבוּר אֲבוֹתֵינוּ שֶׁבָּטְחוּ בָךְ. וַתְּלַמְּדֵם חֻקֵּי חַיִּים לַעֲשׂוֹת רְצוֹנְךָ בְּלֵבָב שָׁלֵם. כֵּן תְּחָנֵּנוּ: הָאֵר עֵינֵינוּ בְּתוֹרָתֶךָ. וְדַבֵּק לִבֵּנוּ בְּמִצְוֹתֶיךָ. וְיַחֵד לְבָבֵנוּ לְאַהֲבָה וּלְיִרְאָה אֶת־שְׁמֶךָ.

<<<

So shall we never lose our self-respect, nor be put to shame, for You are the power which works to save us. You chose us from all peoples and tongues, and in love drew us near to Your own greatness – to honour You, to declare Your unity, and to love You. Blessed are You God, who chooses Your people Israel in love.

לְמַעַן לֹא נֵבוֹשׁ וְלֹא נִכָּלֵם כִּי אֵל פּוֹעֵל יְשׁוּעוֹת אָתָּה. וּבָנוּ בָחַרְתָּ מִכָּל־עַם וְלָשׁוֹן. וְקֵרַבְתָּנוּ מַלְכֵּנוּ לְשִׁמְךָ הַגָּדוֹל בְּאַהֲבָה. לְהוֹדוֹת לְךָ וּלְיַחֶדְךָ וּלְאַהֲבָה אֶת־שְׁמֶךָ: בָּרוּךְ אַתָּה יהוה הַבּוֹחֵר בְּעַמּוֹ יִשְׂרָאֵל בְּאַהֲבָה:

When praying individually it is customary to add here אֵל מֶלֶךְ נֶאֱמָן
el melech ne'eman - *'God, the faithful Sovereign'.*

שְׁמַ**ע** יִשְׂרָאֵל יהוה אֱלֹהֵינוּ יהוה | אֶחָֽ**ד** :

בָּרוּךְ שֵׁם כְּבוֹד מַלְכוּתוֹ לְעוֹלָם וָעֶד:

וְאָהַבְתָּ אֵת יהוה אֱלֹהֶיךָ בְּכָל־לְבָבְךָ וּבְכָל־נַפְשְׁךָ וּבְכָל־מְאֹדֶךָ: וְהָיוּ הַדְּבָרִים הָאֵלֶּה אֲשֶׁר אָנֹכִי מְצַוְּךָ הַיּוֹם עַל־לְבָבֶךָ: וְשִׁנַּנְתָּם לְבָנֶיךָ וְדִבַּרְתָּ בָּם בְּשִׁבְתְּךָ בְּבֵיתֶךָ וּבְלֶכְתְּךָ בַדֶּרֶךְ וּבְשָׁכְבְּךָ וּבְקוּמֶךָ: וּקְשַׁרְתָּם לְאוֹת עַל־יָדֶךָ וְהָיוּ לְטֹטָפֹת בֵּין עֵינֶיךָ: וּכְתַבְתָּם עַל־מְזֻזוֹת בֵּיתֶךָ וּבִשְׁעָרֶיךָ:

GOD IS ONE

שְׁמַע Hear O Israel, the Eternal is our God, the Eternal is One.

בָּרוּךְ Blessed is the knowledge of God's glorious rule forever and ever.

וְאָהַבְתָּ Love the Eternal your God with all your heart, and all your soul, and all your might. These words that I command you today shall be upon your heart. Repeat them to your children, and talk about them when you sit in your home, and when you walk in the street; when you lie down, and when you rise up. Secure them as a sign upon your hand, and let them be as reminders before your eyes. Write them on the doorposts of your home and at your gates.[1]

---

[1] Deut 6:4-9.

57 DAILY MORNING SERVICE — THE *SH'MA* AND ITS BLESSINGS

During the silence the traditional second and third sections of the Sh'ma *may be read, or the alternative Biblical passages on pages 689-697.*

וְהָיָ֗ה אִם־שָׁמֹ֤עַ תִּשְׁמְעוּ֙ אֶל־מִצְוֺתַ֔י אֲשֶׁ֧ר אָנֹכִ֛י מְצַוֶּ֥ה אֶתְכֶ֖ם הַיּ֑וֹם לְאַהֲבָ֞ה אֶת־יְהוָ֤ה אֱלֹהֵיכֶם֙ וּלְעָבְד֔וֹ בְּכָל־לְבַבְכֶ֖ם וּבְכָל־נַפְשְׁכֶֽם׃ וְנָתַתִּ֧י מְטַֽר־אַרְצְכֶ֛ם בְּעִתּ֖וֹ יוֹרֶ֣ה וּמַלְק֑וֹשׁ וְאָסַפְתָּ֣ דְגָנֶ֔ךָ וְתִֽירֹשְׁךָ֖ וְיִצְהָרֶֽךָ׃ וְנָתַתִּ֛י עֵ֥שֶׂב בְּשָׂדְךָ֖ לִבְהֶמְתֶּ֑ךָ וְאָכַלְתָּ֖ וְשָׂבָֽעְתָּ׃ הִשָּֽׁמְר֣וּ לָכֶ֔ם פֶּ֥ן יִפְתֶּ֖ה לְבַבְכֶ֑ם וְסַרְתֶּ֗ם וַעֲבַדְתֶּם֙ אֱלֹהִ֣ים אֲחֵרִ֔ים וְהִשְׁתַּחֲוִיתֶ֖ם לָהֶֽם׃ וְחָרָ֨ה אַף־יְהוָ֜ה בָּכֶ֗ם וְעָצַ֤ר אֶת־הַשָּׁמַ֨יִם֙ וְלֹֽא־יִהְיֶ֣ה מָטָ֔ר וְהָ֣אֲדָמָ֔ה לֹ֥א תִתֵּ֖ן אֶת־יְבוּלָ֑הּ וַאֲבַדְתֶּ֣ם מְהֵרָ֗ה מֵעַל֙ הָאָ֣רֶץ הַטֹּבָ֔ה אֲשֶׁ֥ר יְהוָ֖ה נֹתֵ֥ן לָכֶֽם׃ וְשַׂמְתֶּם֙ אֶת־דְּבָרַ֣י אֵ֔לֶּה עַל־לְבַבְכֶ֖ם וְעַֽל־נַפְשְׁכֶ֑ם וּקְשַׁרְתֶּ֨ם אֹתָ֤ם לְאוֹת֙ עַל־יֶדְכֶ֔ם וְהָי֥וּ לְטוֹטָפֹ֖ת בֵּ֥ין עֵינֵיכֶֽם׃ וְלִמַּדְתֶּ֥ם אֹתָ֛ם אֶת־בְּנֵיכֶ֖ם לְדַבֵּ֣ר בָּ֑ם בְּשִׁבְתְּךָ֤ בְּבֵיתֶ֨ךָ֙ וּבְלֶכְתְּךָ֣ בַדֶּ֔רֶךְ וּֽבְשָׁכְבְּךָ֖ וּבְקוּמֶֽךָ׃ וּכְתַבְתָּ֛ם עַל־מְזוּז֥וֹת בֵּיתֶ֖ךָ וּבִשְׁעָרֶֽיךָ׃ לְמַ֨עַן יִרְבּ֤וּ יְמֵיכֶם֙ וִימֵ֣י בְנֵיכֶ֔ם עַ֚ל הָֽאֲדָמָ֔ה אֲשֶׁ֨ר נִשְׁבַּ֧ע יְהוָ֛ה לַאֲבֹתֵיכֶ֖ם לָתֵ֣ת לָהֶ֑ם כִּימֵ֥י הַשָּׁמַ֖יִם עַל־הָאָֽרֶץ׃

וְהָיָה This will happen if you listen carefully to My commands which I give you today, to love and to serve the Eternal your God with all your heart and all your soul. I shall then give your land rain at the right time, the autumn rain and the spring rain, **so that each one of you can harvest your own grain, wine and oil. I shall also give grass in your fields for your cattle, and you will eat and be satisfied.**
Take care that your heart is not deceived into straying, obeying other gods and worshipping them. God's anger will then blaze out against you. God will shut up the sky. There will be no rain. The land will not produce, and you will quickly be destroyed from the good land which God gives you. So put these words of Mine in your heart and in your soul, and secure them as a sign upon your hand and as reminders before your eyes. Teach them to your children, and talk about them **'when you sit each of you in your home, and when you walk in the street, when you lie down and when you rise up. Write them on the doorposts of your home and at your gates.'**
Then you and your children may live long on the land that God promised to give your ancestors as long as there is a sky over the earth.[1]

---

[1] Deut 11:13-21.

וַיֹּאמֶר יְהֹוָה אֶל־מֹשֶׁה לֵּאמֹר: דַּבֵּר אֶל־בְּנֵי יִשְׂרָאֵל וְאָמַרְתָּ אֲלֵהֶם וְעָשׂוּ לָהֶם צִיצִת עַל־כַּנְפֵי בִגְדֵיהֶם לְדֹרֹתָם וְנָתְנוּ עַל־צִיצִת הַכָּנָף פְּתִיל תְּכֵלֶת: וְהָיָה לָכֶם לְצִיצִת וּרְאִיתֶם אֹתוֹ וּזְכַרְתֶּם אֶת־כָּל־מִצְוֺת יְהֹוָה וַעֲשִׂיתֶם אֹתָם וְלֹא תָתֻרוּ אַחֲרֵי לְבַבְכֶם וְאַחֲרֵי עֵינֵיכֶם אֲשֶׁר־אַתֶּם זֹנִים אַחֲרֵיהֶם: לְמַעַן תִּזְכְּרוּ וַעֲשִׂיתֶם אֶת־כָּל־מִצְוֺתָי וִהְיִיתֶם קְדֹשִׁים לֵאלֹהֵיכֶם: אֲנִי יְהֹוָה אֱלֹהֵיכֶם אֲשֶׁר הוֹצֵאתִי אֶתְכֶם מֵאֶרֶץ מִצְרַיִם לִהְיוֹת לָכֶם לֵאלֹהִים אֲנִי יְהֹוָה אֱלֹהֵיכֶם:

וַיֹּאמֶר The Eternal said to Moses: 'Speak to the children of Israel and tell them that each generation shall put tassels on the corner of their clothes, and put a blue thread on the corner tassel. Then when this tassel catches your eye, you will remember all the commands of the Eternal and do them. Then you will no longer wander after the desires of your heart and your eyes which led you to lust.

Then you will remember all My commands and do them and you will be set apart for your God. I am the Eternal your God Who brought you out of the land of Egypt, to be your own God. I, the Eternal, am your God.'[1]

אֱמֶת וְיַצִּיב וְקַיָּם וּמְקֻבָּל וְטוֹב הַדָּבָר הַזֶּה עָלֵינוּ לְעוֹלָם וָעֶד:

אֱמֶת אֱלֹהֵי עוֹלָם מַלְכֵּנוּ. צוּר יַעֲקֹב מָגֵן יִשְׁעֵנוּ. לְדֹר וָדֹר הוּא קַיָּם. וּמַלְכוּתוֹ וֶאֱמוּנָתוֹ לָעַד קַיָּמֶת.

אֱמֶת שָׁאַתָּה הוּא יְהֹוָה אֱלֹהֵינוּ וֵאלֹהֵי אֲבוֹתֵינוּ. פּוֹדֵנוּ וּמַצִּילֵנוּ מֵעוֹלָם הוּא שְׁמֶךָ. אֵין אֱלֹהִים זוּלָתֶךָ:

אֱמֶת True is Your word forever. It is certain for us, it is firm, accepted and good.

It is true that the Eternal God is our Sovereign; the strength of Jacob, the defender of our safety. God endures from generation to generation. God's rule and faithfulness stand firm forever.

It is true that You are the Faithful One, our God, and God of our ancestors, who rescues and delivers us. So were You ever known. There is no God besides You.

---

[1] Num 15:37-41.

59 DAILY MORNING SERVICE — THE *SH'MA* AND ITS BLESSINGS

עֶזְרַת It is You who always helped our ancestors. In every generation You were the shield and saviour for them and their children after them. Happy indeed are those who hear Your commands, and set Your teaching and Your word upon their hearts.

It is true that You are the first and that You are the last, and besides You we have no Sovereign who rescues and saves us. From Egypt You delivered us, Eternal our God, and redeemed us from the camp of slavery. Moses and Miriam and the children of Israel responded to You in song with great joy, all of them saying:

'God, who is like You among the gods! Who, like You is majestic in holiness, awesome in praises, working wonders?'

On the shore of the sea, those who were rescued sang a new song in Your praise. Together all of them thanked You and proclaimed you as Sovereign:

'God alone will rule forever and ever.'

Rock of Israel, rise up to the aid of Your people Israel. The Creator of all, the Holy One of Israel rescues us. Blessed are You God, who rescues Israel.

עֶזְרַת אֲבוֹתֵינוּ אַתָּה הוּא מֵעוֹלָם. מָגֵן וּמוֹשִׁיעַ לָהֶם וְלִבְנֵיהֶם אַחֲרֵיהֶם בְּכָל־דּוֹר וָדוֹר: אַשְׁרֵי אִישׁ שֶׁיִּשְׁמַע לְמִצְוֹתֶיךָ. וְתוֹרָתְךָ וּדְבָרְךָ יָשִׂים עַל־לִבּוֹ:

אֱמֶת אַתָּה הוּא רִאשׁוֹן וְאַתָּה הוּא אַחֲרוֹן. וּמִבַּלְעָדֶיךָ אֵין לָנוּ מֶלֶךְ גּוֹאֵל וּמוֹשִׁיעַ: מִמִּצְרַיִם גְּאַלְתָּנוּ יהוה אֱלֹהֵינוּ. וּמִבֵּית עֲבָדִים פְּדִיתָנוּ. מֹשֶׁה וּמִרְיָם וּבְנֵי יִשְׂרָאֵל לְךָ עָנוּ שִׁירָה בְּשִׂמְחָה רַבָּה וְאָמְרוּ כֻלָּם:

מִי־כָמֹכָה בָּאֵלִם יהוה. מִי כָּמֹכָה נֶאְדָּר בַּקֹּדֶשׁ. נוֹרָא תְהִלֹּת עֹשֵׂה פֶלֶא:

שִׁירָה חֲדָשָׁה שִׁבְּחוּ גְאוּלִים לְשִׁמְךָ עַל שְׂפַת הַיָּם. יַחַד כֻּלָּם הוֹדוּ וְהִמְלִיכוּ וְאָמְרוּ:

יהוה יִמְלֹךְ לְעוֹלָם וָעֶד:

צוּר יִשְׂרָאֵל. קוּמָה בְּעֶזְרַת יִשְׂרָאֵל. גֹּאֲלֵנוּ יהוה צְבָאוֹת שְׁמוֹ. קְדוֹשׁ יִשְׂרָאֵל: בָּרוּךְ אַתָּה יהוה גָּאַל יִשְׂרָאֵל:

The daily morning service continues with the Amidah *page 73.*

תפלת שחרית לימות החול   שמע וברכותיה

תפלת מנחה לימות החול
Daily Afternoon Service

שחרית מנחה מעריב

קָרוֹב יהוה לְכָל־קֹרְאָיו.

God is near to all who call.

Psalm 145:18

> The timing of each of the daily services has been traditionally ascribed to one of the patriarchs. It says of Abraham that he 'rose up early in the morning' (Gen 22:3), thus instituting the morning prayer. Similarly Jacob arrived at the place where he dreamt of the ladder going to heaven at sunset (Gen 28:11), and instituted the evening prayer. Of Isaac it says that 'he went out to meditate in the field before the evening' (Gen 24:63) and this is understood to refer to the afternoon prayer. Historically this service is timed to replace the afternoon sacrifice that would have taken place in the Temple.
>
> Since the *Sh'ma* refers to speaking of God 'when you lie down and when you rise up' (Deut 6:7), the recital of the *Sh'ma* and its blessings is restricted to the morning and evening services. The afternoon service is largely limited to the recital of psalms and the weekday version of the *Amidah*. This service is sometimes delayed so that it can be combined with the evening service.

The service begins with Psalm 145 on page 48, or another Psalm may be read. Sephardi practice is to read Psalm 67.

Psalm 67 / סז

¹For the Choirmaster. For Strings.
A Psalm. A Song.
²**אֱלֹהִים** May God be gracious to us
and bless us, may God's face
shed its light among us *(selah)*.
³Then Your way will be known on earth,
Your saving power among all nations.

⁴Let the peoples praise You, God,
let all the peoples praise You!
⁵Let the nations be glad
and sing out for joy,
for You will rule the peoples in fairness
and guide the nations of the earth *(selah)*.

⁶Let the peoples praise You, God,
let all the peoples praise You!
⁷The earth has given her harvest,
may God, our God, bless us.
⁸May God bless us
and let the ends of the earth
revere God.

אלַמְנַצֵּחַ בִּנְגִינֹת מִזְמוֹר שִׁיר:
באֱלֹהִים יְחָנֵּנוּ וִיבָרְכֵנוּ
יָאֵר פָּנָיו אִתָּנוּ סֶלָה:
גלָדַעַת בָּאָרֶץ דַּרְכֶּךָ
בְּכָל־גּוֹיִם יְשׁוּעָתֶךָ:

דיוֹדוּךָ עַמִּים אֱלֹהִים
יוֹדוּךָ עַמִּים כֻּלָּם:
היִשְׂמְחוּ וִירַנְּנוּ לְאֻמִּים
כִּי־תִשְׁפֹּט עַמִּים מִישֹׁר
וּלְאֻמִּים בָּאָרֶץ תַּנְחֵם סֶלָה:

ויוֹדוּךָ עַמִּים אֱלֹהִים
יוֹדוּךָ עַמִּים כֻּלָּם:
זאֶרֶץ נָתְנָה יְבוּלָהּ
יְבָרְכֵנוּ אֱלֹהִים אֱלֹהֵינוּ:
חיְבָרְכֵנוּ אֱלֹהִים
וְיִירְאוּ אוֹתוֹ
כָּל־אַפְסֵי־אָרֶץ:

The **Chatsi Kaddish** *may be recited here:*

<<<

63 DAILY AFTERNOON SERVICE

Chatsi Kaddish   חֲצִי קַדִּישׁ

יִתְגַּדַּל Let us magnify
and let us sanctify in this world
the great name of God
whose will created it.
May God's reign come in your
lifetime, and in your days,
and in the lifetime of the family of
Israel - quickly and speedily
may it come.
Amen.
**May the greatness of God's being
be blessed from eternity to eternity**.
Let us bless and let us extol,
let us tell aloud and let us raise aloft,
let us set on high and let us honour,
let us exalt and
let us praise the Holy One,
whose name is blessed,

who is far beyond any blessing

During the Ten Days of Penitence:
 who is far above and beyond any blessing

or song, any honour
or any consolation
that can be spoken of in this world.
Amen.

יִתְגַּדַּל וְיִתְקַדַּשׁ שְׁמֵהּ רַבָּא
בְּעָלְמָא דִּי־בְרָא כִרְעוּתֵהּ:
וְיַמְלִיךְ מַלְכוּתֵהּ
בְּחַיֵּיכוֹן וּבְיוֹמֵיכוֹן
וּבְחַיֵּי דִי־כָל־בֵּית יִשְׂרָאֵל
בַּעֲגָלָא וּבִזְמַן קָרִיב.
וְאִמְרוּ אָמֵן:
יְהֵא שְׁמֵהּ רַבָּא מְבָרַךְ
לְעָלַם וּלְעָלְמֵי עָלְמַיָּא:
יִתְבָּרַךְ וְיִשְׁתַּבַּח וְיִתְפָּאַר
וְיִתְרוֹמַם וְיִתְנַשֵּׂא וְיִתְהַדָּר
וְיִתְעַלֶּה וְיִתְהַלָּל שְׁמֵהּ
דְּקֻדְשָׁא. בְּרִיךְ הוּא.

לְעֵלָא מִן־כָּל־בִּרְכָתָא

During the Ten Days of Penitence:
לְעֵלָא לְעֵלָא מִכָּל־בִּרְכָתָא

וְשִׁירָתָא תֻּשְׁבְּחָתָא וְנֶחֱמָתָא
דַּאֲמִירָן בְּעָלְמָא.
וְאִמְרוּ אָמֵן:

The daily afternoon service continues with the Amidah *page 73.*

64 תפלת מנחה לימות החול

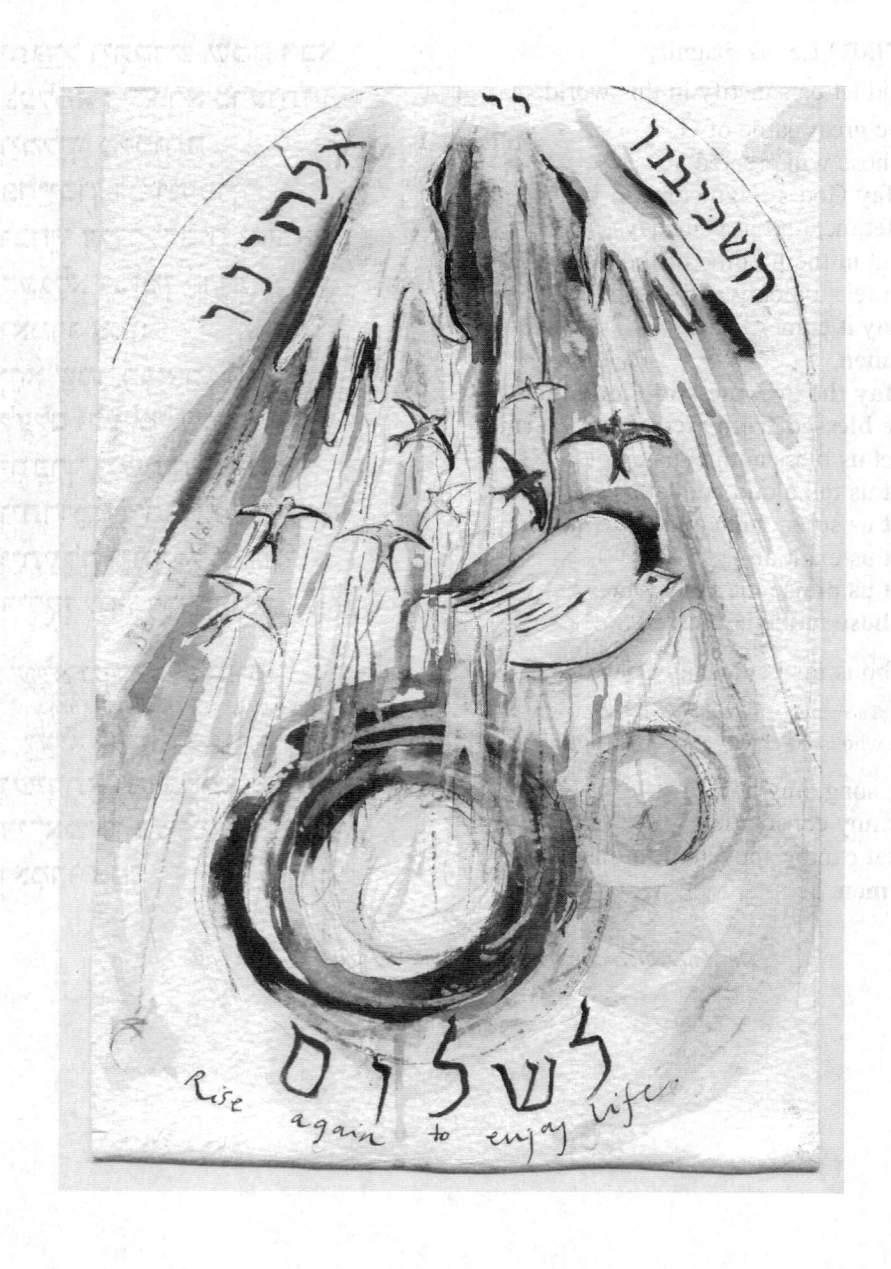

תפלת מעריב לימות החול
Daily Evening Service

הַשְׁכִּיבֵנוּ יהוה אֱלֹהֵינוּ לְשָׁלוֹם וְהַעֲמִידֵנוּ מַלְכֵּנוּ לְחַיִּים.

Cause us to lie down in peace, and rise again to enjoy life.

> The evening service has the same basic structure as that of the morning with its two main sections: the *Sh'ma* with its accompanying blessings, followed by the *Amidah*. The first blessing before the *Sh'ma* in the morning speaks of God as the one who 'creates light'. Similarly the evening blessing follows the theme of God as Creator by focusing on the arrival of the evening, the appearance of the stars and the changing of times and seasons.
>
> Just as in the morning service we think about the restoration of life each day, in the evening there is an additional blessing following the *Sh'ma* which seeks God's protection as we sleep, when we are most vulnerable. The rabbis taught that sleep is one sixtieth part of death, for they thought that the soul was briefly absent, only to be restored to us in the morning. This blessing offers us comfort and hope as we face the darkness of the outer world, but sometimes the darkness we experience within us. It enacts the words of the psalmist: just as it is good to speak of God's love in the morning, so it is good to 'tell of God's faithfulness at night' (Psalm 92:2-3).

Psalm 134 or another Psalm or opening meditation may be read.

Psalm 134 / קלד

שִׁיר הַמַּעֲלוֹת
הִנֵּה בָּרְכוּ אֶת־יְהוָה
כָּל־עַבְדֵי יהוה
הָעֹמְדִים בְּבֵית־יְהוָה בַּלֵּילוֹת:
שְׂאוּ־יְדֵכֶם קֹדֶשׁ
וּבָרְכוּ אֶת־יְהוָה:
יְבָרֶכְךָ יהוה מִצִּיּוֹן
עֹשֵׂה שָׁמַיִם וָאָרֶץ:

¹A Pilgrim Song.
הִנֵּה Come, bless the Eternal,
all who serve the Eternal,
who stand night after night
in the house of the Eternal.
²Raise your hands to the holy place
and bless the Eternal.
³May the Eternal
bless you from Zion,
the maker of heaven and earth.

וְהוּא רַחוּם

יְכַפֵּר עָוֹן וְלֹא יַשְׁחִית
וְהִרְבָּה לְהָשִׁיב אַפּוֹ
וְלֹא יָעִיר כָּל־חֲמָתוֹ:

וְהוּא Being merciful
God forgives sin
and does not destroy.
Many times God turns rage aside
and does not rouse the divine anger.

שמע וברכותיה
THE *SH'MA* AND ITS BLESSINGS

It is traditional for the Prayer Leader to bow slightly from the waist when saying Bar'chu, *and for the congregation to do likewise when responding, returning to the upright position when mentioning the name of God.*

THE CALL TO COMMUNITY PRAYER

בָּרְכוּ אֶת־יְהוָה הַמְבֹרָךְ:

בָּרְכוּ Bless the Living God
whom we are called to bless.

בָּרוּךְ יְהוָה הַמְבֹרָךְ
לְעוֹלָם וָעֶד:

בָּרוּךְ Blessed is the Living
God whom we are called to
bless forever and ever.

DAILY EVENING SERVICE — THE *SH'MA* AND ITS BLESSINGS

THE CREATOR OF THE UNIVERSE

בָּרוּךְ Blessed are You, our Living God, Sovereign of the universe, Whose word brings on the evening twilight; Who opens the gates of dawn with wisdom, and with foresight makes times pass and seasons change. Your plan sets the stars in their courses in the sky, creating day and night, turning light into darkness and darkness into light. You make the day fade away and bring on the night, separating day and night. You are the Ruler of the hosts of heaven. Blessed are You God, who brings on the evening twilight.

בָּרוּךְ אַתָּה יהוה אֱלֹהֵינוּ מֶלֶךְ הָעוֹלָם. אֲשֶׁר בִּדְבָרוֹ מַעֲרִיב עֲרָבִים. בְּחָכְמָה פּוֹתֵחַ שְׁעָרִים. וּבִתְבוּנָה מְשַׁנֶּה עִתִּים. וּמַחֲלִיף אֶת־הַזְּמַנִּים. וּמְסַדֵּר אֶת־הַכּוֹכָבִים בְּמִשְׁמְרוֹתֵיהֶם בָּרָקִיעַ כִּרְצוֹנוֹ: בּוֹרֵא יוֹם וָלָיְלָה. גּוֹלֵל אוֹר מִפְּנֵי חֹשֶׁךְ וְחֹשֶׁךְ מִפְּנֵי אוֹר: הַמַּעֲבִיר יוֹם וּמֵבִיא לָיְלָה. וּמַבְדִּיל בֵּין יוֹם וּבֵין לָיְלָה. יהוה צְבָאוֹת שְׁמוֹ: בָּרוּךְ אַתָּה יהוה. הַמַּעֲרִיב עֲרָבִים:

GOD'S LOVE FOR ISRAEL

אַהֲבַת With everlasting love have You loved Your people the family of Israel. Teaching and practice, duty and justice - these You have taught us. Therefore, our God and Guide, we think upon all this before we sleep and when we wake, and rejoice and delight in Your teaching and its practice forever and ever, for they are our life and the measure of our days. We keep them in mind both day and night. Never take Your love away from us. Blessed are You God, who loves Your people Israel.

אַהֲבַת עוֹלָם בֵּית יִשְׂרָאֵל עַמְּךָ אָהָבְתָּ. תּוֹרָה וּמִצְוֹת חֻקִּים וּמִשְׁפָּטִים אוֹתָנוּ לִמַּדְתָּ: עַל־כֵּן יהוה אֱלֹהֵינוּ. בְּשָׁכְבֵּנוּ וּבְקוּמֵנוּ נָשִׂיחַ בְּחֻקֶּיךָ. וְנִשְׂמַח וְנַעֲלוֹז בְּדִבְרֵי תוֹרָתֶךָ וּמִצְוֹתֶיךָ וְחֻקּוֹתֶיךָ לְעוֹלָם וָעֶד: כִּי הֵם חַיֵּינוּ וְאֹרֶךְ יָמֵינוּ. וּבָהֶם נֶהְגֶּה יוֹמָם וָלָיְלָה. וְאַהֲבָתְךָ אַל־תָּסִיר מִמֶּנּוּ לְעוֹלָמִים: בָּרוּךְ אַתָּה יהוה. אוֹהֵב אֶת־עַמּוֹ יִשְׂרָאֵל:

When praying individually it is customary to add here אֵל מֶלֶךְ נֶאֱמָן
el melech ne'eman - *'God, the faithful Sovereign'.*

שְׁמַע יִשְׂרָאֵל יהוה אֱלֹהֵינוּ יהוה | אֶחָֽד:

בָּרוּךְ שֵׁם כְּבוֹד מַלְכוּתוֹ לְעוֹלָם וָעֶד:

וְאָהַבְתָּ אֵת יהוה אֱלֹהֶיךָ בְּכָל־לְבָבְךָ וּבְכָל־נַפְשְׁךָ וּבְכָל־מְאֹדֶֽךָ: וְהָיוּ הַדְּבָרִים הָאֵלֶּה אֲשֶׁר אָנֹכִי מְצַוְּךָ הַיּוֹם עַל־לְבָבֶֽךָ: וְשִׁנַּנְתָּם לְבָנֶיךָ וְדִבַּרְתָּ בָּם בְּשִׁבְתְּךָ בְּבֵיתֶֽךָ וּבְלֶכְתְּךָ בַדֶּֽרֶךְ וּבְשָׁכְבְּךָ וּבְקוּמֶֽךָ: וּקְשַׁרְתָּם לְאוֹת עַל־יָדֶֽךָ וְהָיוּ לְטֹטָפֹת בֵּין עֵינֶֽיךָ: וּכְתַבְתָּם עַל־מְזֻזוֹת בֵּיתֶֽךָ וּבִשְׁעָרֶֽיךָ:

GOD IS ONE

שְׁמַע Hear O Israel, the Eternal is our God, the Eternal is One.

בָּרוּךְ Blessed is the knowledge of God's glorious rule forever and ever.

וְאָהַבְתָּ Love the Eternal your God with all your heart, and all your soul, and all your might. These words that I command you today shall be upon your heart. Repeat them to your children, and talk about them when you sit in your home, and when you walk in the street; when you lie down, and when you rise up. Secure them as a sign upon your hand, and let them be as reminders before your eyes. Write them on the doorposts of your home and at your gates.[1]

---

[1] Deut 6:4-9.

DAILY EVENING SERVICE — THE *SH'MA* AND ITS BLESSINGS

During the silence the traditional second and third paragraphs of the Sh'ma *may be read, or the alternative Biblical passages on pages 689–697.*

וְהָיָה אִם־שָׁמֹעַ תִּשְׁמְעוּ אֶל־מִצְוֹתַי אֲשֶׁר אָנֹכִי מְצַוֶּה אֶתְכֶם הַיּוֹם לְאַהֲבָה אֶת־יהוה אֱלֹהֵיכֶם וּלְעָבְדוֹ בְּכָל־לְבַבְכֶם וּבְכָל־נַפְשְׁכֶם: וְנָתַתִּי מְטַר־אַרְצְכֶם בְּעִתּוֹ יוֹרֶה וּמַלְקוֹשׁ וְאָסַפְתָּ דְגָנֶךָ וְתִירֹשְׁךָ וְיִצְהָרֶךָ: וְנָתַתִּי עֵשֶׂב בְּשָׂדְךָ לִבְהֶמְתֶּךָ וְאָכַלְתָּ וְשָׂבָעְתָּ:

הִשָּׁמְרוּ לָכֶם פֶּן־יִפְתֶּה לְבַבְכֶם וְסַרְתֶּם וַעֲבַדְתֶּם אֱלֹהִים אֲחֵרִים וְהִשְׁתַּחֲוִיתֶם לָהֶם: וְחָרָה אַף־יהוה בָּכֶם וְעָצַר אֶת־הַשָּׁמַיִם וְלֹא־יִהְיֶה מָטָר וְהָאֲדָמָה לֹא תִתֵּן אֶת־יְבוּלָהּ וַאֲבַדְתֶּם מְהֵרָה מֵעַל הָאָרֶץ הַטֹּבָה אֲשֶׁר יהוה נֹתֵן לָכֶם: וְשַׂמְתֶּם אֶת־דְּבָרַי אֵלֶּה עַל־לְבַבְכֶם וְעַל־נַפְשְׁכֶם וּקְשַׁרְתֶּם אֹתָם לְאוֹת עַל־יֶדְכֶם וְהָיוּ לְטוֹטָפֹת בֵּין עֵינֵיכֶם: וְלִמַּדְתֶּם אֹתָם אֶת־בְּנֵיכֶם לְדַבֵּר בָּם. בְּשִׁבְתְּךָ בְּבֵיתֶךָ וּבְלֶכְתְּךָ בַדֶּרֶךְ וּבְשָׁכְבְּךָ וּבְקוּמֶךָ: וּכְתַבְתָּם עַל־מְזוּזוֹת בֵּיתֶךָ וּבִשְׁעָרֶיךָ:

לְמַעַן יִרְבּוּ יְמֵיכֶם וִימֵי בְנֵיכֶם עַל הָאֲדָמָה אֲשֶׁר נִשְׁבַּע יהוה לַאֲבֹתֵיכֶם לָתֵת לָהֶם כִּימֵי הַשָּׁמַיִם עַל־הָאָרֶץ:

וְהָיָה This will happen if you listen carefully to My commands which I give you today, to love and to serve the Eternal your God with all your heart and all your soul. I shall then give your land rain at the right time, the autumn rain and the spring rain, **so that each one of you can harvest your own grain, wine and oil. I shall also give grass in your fields for your cattle, and you will eat and be satisfied.**

Take care that your heart is not deceived into straying, obeying other gods and worshipping them. God's anger will then blaze out against you. God will shut up the sky. There will be no rain. The land will not produce, and you will quickly be destroyed from the good land which God gives you. So put these words of Mine in your heart and in your soul, and secure them as a sign upon your hand and as reminders before your eyes. Teach them to your children, and talk about them **'when you sit each of you in your home, and when you walk in the street, when you lie down and when you rise up. Write them on the doorposts of your home and at your gates.'**

Then you and your children may live long on the land that God promised to give your ancestors as long as there is a sky over the earth.[1]

---

[1] Deut 11:13-21.

וַיֹּאמֶר The Eternal said to Moses: 'Speak to the children of Israel and tell them that each generation shall put tassels on the corner of their clothes, and put a blue thread on the corner tassel. Then when this tassel catches your eye, you will remember all the commands of the Eternal and do them. Then you will no longer wander after the desires of your heart and your eyes which led you to lust.

Then you will remember all My commands and do them and you will be set apart for your God. I am the Eternal your God Who brought you out of the land of Egypt, to be your own God. I, the Eternal, am your God.'[1]

וַיֹּאמֶר יְהֹוָה אֶל־מֹשֶׁה לֵּאמֹר: דַּבֵּר אֶל־בְּנֵי יִשְׂרָאֵל וְאָמַרְתָּ אֲלֵהֶם וְעָשׂוּ לָהֶם צִיצִת עַל־כַּנְפֵי בִגְדֵיהֶם לְדֹרֹתָם וְנָתְנוּ עַל־צִיצִת הַכָּנָף פְּתִיל תְּכֵלֶת: וְהָיָה לָכֶם לְצִיצִת וּרְאִיתֶם אֹתוֹ וּזְכַרְתֶּם אֶת־כָּל־מִצְוֹת יְהֹוָה וַעֲשִׂיתֶם אֹתָם וְלֹא תָתוּרוּ אַחֲרֵי לְבַבְכֶם וְאַחֲרֵי עֵינֵיכֶם אֲשֶׁר־אַתֶּם זֹנִים אַחֲרֵיהֶם: לְמַעַן תִּזְכְּרוּ וַעֲשִׂיתֶם אֶת־כָּל־מִצְוֹתָי וִהְיִיתֶם קְדֹשִׁים לֵאלֹהֵיכֶם: אֲנִי יְהֹוָה אֱלֹהֵיכֶם אֲשֶׁר הוֹצֵאתִי אֶתְכֶם מֵאֶרֶץ מִצְרַיִם לִהְיוֹת לָכֶם לֵאלֹהִים אֲנִי יְהֹוָה אֱלֹהֵיכֶם:

OUR REDEEMER

אֱמֶת All this is true and firmly held by us, that You are our Living God and no other exists, and that we are Israel, Your people. You perform great deeds beyond research, too wonderful to tell. Your children saw Your power, praised and thanked Your name, and willingly accepted Your rule over them. With great joy Moses and Miriam and the children of Israel answered You in song, all of them saying:
'God, who is like You
among the gods people worship!
Who, like You,
is majestic in holiness,
awesome in praise,
working wonders!'

אֱמֶת וֶאֱמוּנָה

כָּל־זֹאת וְקַיָּם עָלֵינוּ. כִּי הוּא יְהֹוָה אֱלֹהֵינוּ וְאֵין זוּלָתוֹ וַאֲנַחְנוּ יִשְׂרָאֵל עַמּוֹ. הָעֹשֶׂה גְדֹלוֹת עַד־אֵין חֵקֶר וְנִפְלָאוֹת עַד־אֵין מִסְפָּר. וְרָאוּ בָנָיו גְּבוּרָתוֹ שִׁבְּחוּ וְהוֹדוּ לִשְׁמוֹ וּמַלְכוּתוֹ בְּרָצוֹן קִבְּלוּ עֲלֵיהֶם: מֹשֶׁה וּמִרְיָם וּבְנֵי יִשְׂרָאֵל לְךָ עָנוּ שִׁירָה בְּשִׂמְחָה רַבָּה. וְאָמְרוּ כֻלָּם.
מִי־כָמֹכָה בָּאֵלִים יְהֹוָה.
מִי כָּמֹכָה נֶאְדָּר בַּקֹּדֶשׁ
נוֹרָא תְהִלֹּת עֹשֵׂה פֶלֶא:

<<<

---
[1] Num 15:37–41.

71 DAILY EVENING SERVICE — THE *SH'MA* AND ITS BLESSINGS

Our Living God,
Your children saw Your rule
over the Sea of Reeds.
All of them as one
honoured You as Sovereign, saying:
'God shall rule forever and ever!'
And it is prophesied:
'For the Almighty has set Jacob free
and rescued him
from a hand stronger than his own.'[1]
Blessed are You God,
who rescues Israel.

מַלְכוּתְךָ יהוה אֱלֹהֵינוּ
רָאוּ בָנֶיךָ עַל הַיָּם.
יַחַד כֻּלָּם הוֹדוּ וְהִמְלִיכוּ וְאָמְרוּ.
יהוה יִמְלֹךְ לְעוֹלָם וָעֶד:
וְנֶאֱמַר.
כִּי־פָדָה יהוה אֶת־יַעֲקֹב
וּגְאָלוֹ מִיַּד חָזָק מִמֶּנּוּ.
בָּרוּךְ אַתָּה יהוה.
גָּאַל יִשְׂרָאֵל:

GOD'S GIFT OF PEACE AND PROTECTION

הַשְׁכִּיבֵנוּ Source of our life and our Sovereign, cause us to lie down in peace, and rise again to enjoy life. Spread over us the covering of Your peace, guide us with Your good counsel and save us for the sake of Your name. Be a shield about us, turning away every enemy, disease, violence, hunger and sorrow. Remove the temptation that awaits us and the guilt that lies behind us. Shelter us in the shadow of Your wings, for You are a God who guards and protects us, a ruler of mercy and compassion. Guard us when we go out and when we come in, to enjoy life and peace both now and forever. Blessed are You God, guarding Your people Israel forever.

הַשְׁכִּיבֵנוּ יהוה אֱלֹהֵינוּ לְשָׁלוֹם
וְהַעֲמִידֵנוּ מַלְכֵּנוּ לְחַיִּים.
וּפְרוֹשׂ עָלֵינוּ סֻכַּת שְׁלוֹמֶךָ
וְתַקְּנֵנוּ בְּעֵצָה טוֹבָה מִלְּפָנֶיךָ
וְהוֹשִׁיעֵנוּ לְמַעַן שְׁמֶךָ. וְהָגֵן
בַּעֲדֵנוּ וְהָסֵר מֵעָלֵינוּ אוֹיֵב
דֶּבֶר וְחֶרֶב וְרָעָב וְיָגוֹן. וְהָסֵר
שָׂטָן מִלְּפָנֵינוּ וּמֵאַחֲרֵינוּ. וּבְצֵל
כְּנָפֶיךָ תַּסְתִּירֵנוּ כִּי אֵל
שׁוֹמְרֵנוּ וּמַצִּילֵנוּ אָתָּה. כִּי אֵל
מֶלֶךְ חַנּוּן וְרַחוּם אָתָּה. וּשְׁמוֹר
צֵאתֵנוּ וּבוֹאֵנוּ לְחַיִּים וּלְשָׁלוֹם
מֵעַתָּה וְעַד עוֹלָם. בָּרוּךְ אַתָּה
יהוה. שׁוֹמֵר עַמּוֹ יִשְׂרָאֵל לָעַד:

---

[1] Ex 15:11, Ex 15:18, Jer 31:11.

בָּרוּךְ Blessed be God by day. Blessed be God by night. Blessed be God when we lie down. Blessed be God when we rise up. For in Your hands are the souls of the living and the dead. 'In God's hand is the soul of every creature and the soul of human flesh.'[1] 'Within God's hand I lay my soul, You have redeemed me, Eternal God of truth.'[2] Our God who is in heaven, reveal Your unity, establish Your kingdom for all time and rule over us forever and ever.

בָּרוּךְ יהוה בַּיּוֹם. בָּרוּךְ יהוה בַּלָּיְלָה. בָּרוּךְ יהוה בְּשָׁכְבֵנוּ. בָּרוּךְ יהוה בְּקוּמֵנוּ: כִּי בְיָדְךָ נַפְשׁוֹת הַחַיִּים וְהַמֵּתִים: אֲשֶׁר בְּיָדוֹ נֶפֶשׁ כָּל־חָי וְרוּחַ כָּל־בְּשַׂר־אִישׁ: בְּיָדְךָ אַפְקִיד רוּחִי פָּדִיתָה אוֹתִי יהוה אֵל אֱמֶת: אֱלֹהֵינוּ שֶׁבַּשָּׁמַיִם יַחֵד שִׁמְךָ וְקַיֵּם מַלְכוּתְךָ תָּמִיד וּמְלוֹךְ עָלֵינוּ לְעוֹלָם וָעֶד:

The service continues with the Amidah *on page 73*.

---

[1] Job 12:10.   [2] Ps 31:6.

עמידה לימות החול
Daily Amidah 339-344

The daily *Amidah* (literally 'standing'), like the Shabbat and Festival versions, has three opening and three closing blessings. During the weekday there are thirteen intermediate blessings. Originally there were only twelve, making eighteen in all, hence another name for the *Amidah*, the 'eighteen benedictions', *Shemone Esrei*. At a certain stage a thirteenth blessing was introduced, totalling nineteen, but the original name was retained. There are variations in the wording of the traditional versions of this prayer and many were radically reworked within the various Reform traditions, including the 1977 edition of *Forms of Prayer*.

The sequence of intermediate blessings can be understood in a number of ways. In one interpretation, the first three (blessings 4-6) reflect the spiritual needs of the individual (understanding, repentance and spiritual healing); the second three (7-9) our material needs (freedom, health, livelihood); the tenth, the ingathering of the exiles, is the bridge to the third group (11-13), expressing the spiritual needs of a restored nation (justice, punishment of the wicked, reward for the righteous); the final three (14-16) the material needs of the nation (rebuilding of Jerusalem, the coming of the messianic ruler, the acceptance of our prayers). In another version they reflect the programme of stages needed for the historic restoration of the people to the land, the arrival of the messiah coming only at the end after the basis of society has been created.

The *Amidah* was created as a liturgical substitute for the daily sacrifices in the Temple and timed to be recited when they took place - in the morning and afternoon. (Since there was no evening sacrifice, the recital of the *Amidah* in the evening service is said quietly as a private act and, in traditional circles, unlike for the other two daily services, it is not repeated aloud by the *Sh'liach Tsibbur*, the service leader.) A central theme is therefore the return of the nation to its land and the restoration of sovereignty and the Temple worship with its sacrifices. Since prayer has become the normal expression of Jewish worship, without the intercession of priests and sacrifices, this latter desire has been modified by all Reform liturgies, which express more universal hopes.

עמידה לימות החול

Traditionally the Amidah is said whilst standing, beginning with three short steps forward,
a reminder of our entry into the divine presence.
It is customary at the beginning and end of the first paragraph
to bend the knee when saying the word baruch,
to bow from the waist at the second word attah
and to become upright again with the third word, the name of God, Adonai.

אֲדֹנָי שְׂפָתַי תִּפְתָּח וּפִי יַגִּיד תְּהִלָּתֶךָ:

בָּרוּךְ אַתָּה יהוה אֱלֹהֵינוּ
וֵאלֹהֵי אֲבוֹתֵינוּ. וֵאלֹהֵי אִמּוֹתֵינוּ.
אֱלֹהֵי אַבְרָהָם. אֱלֹהֵי שָׂרָה.
אֱלֹהֵי יִצְחָק. אֱלֹהֵי רִבְקָה.
וֵאלֹהֵי יַעֲקֹב. אֱלֹהֵי רָחֵל.
וֵאלֹהֵי לֵאָה.
הָאֵל הַגָּדוֹל הַגִּבּוֹר וְהַנּוֹרָא. אֵל עֶלְיוֹן.
גּוֹמֵל חֲסָדִים טוֹבִים קוֹנֵה הַכֹּל. וְזוֹכֵר חַסְדֵי
אָבוֹת וְאִמָּהוֹת
וּמֵבִיא גוֹאֵל לִבְנֵי בְנֵיהֶם לְמַעַן שְׁמוֹ בְּאַהֲבָה:

During the Ten Days of Penitence add:
זָכְרֵנוּ לְחַיִּים. מֶלֶךְ חָפֵץ בַּחַיִּים.
וְכָתְבֵנוּ בְּסֵפֶר הַחַיִּים. לְמַעַנְךָ אֱלֹהִים חַיִּים:

מֶלֶךְ עוֹזֵר וּמוֹשִׁיעַ וּמָגֵן:
בָּרוּךְ אַתָּה יהוה
מָגֵן אַבְרָהָם פּוֹקֵד שָׂרָה:

אַתָּה גִּבּוֹר לְעוֹלָם אֲדֹנָי. מְחַיֵּה מֵתִים אַתָּה. רַב לְהוֹשִׁיעַ:
In winter מַשִּׁיב הָרוּחַ וּמוֹרִיד הַגֶּשֶׁם:
In summer מוֹרִיד הַטָּל:
מְכַלְכֵּל חַיִּים בְּחֶסֶד. מְחַיֵּה מֵתִים בְּרַחֲמִים רַבִּים. סוֹמֵךְ נוֹפְלִים. וְרוֹפֵא
חוֹלִים. וּמַתִּיר אֲסוּרִים. וּמְקַיֵּם אֱמוּנָתוֹ לִישֵׁנֵי עָפָר: מִי כָמוֹךָ בַּעַל
גְּבוּרוֹת וּמִי דוֹמֶה לָּךְ. מֶלֶךְ מֵמִית וּמְחַיֶּה וּמַצְמִיחַ יְשׁוּעָה:

During the Ten Days of Penitence add:
מִי כָמוֹךָ אַב הָרַחֲמִים. זוֹכֵר יְצוּרָיו לְחַיִּים בְּרַחֲמִים:

וְנֶאֱמָן אַתָּה לְהַחֲיוֹת מֵתִים:
בָּרוּךְ אַתָּה יהוה. מְחַיֵּה הַמֵּתִים:

DAILY *AMIDAH*

אֲדֹנָי My God, open my lips and my mouth shall declare Your praise.[1]

GOD OF HISTORY

בָּרוּךְ Blessed are You, our God, and God of our ancestors,

God of Abraham,	God of Sarah,
God of Isaac,	God of Rebecca,
and God of Jacob,	God of Rachel
	and God of Leah,

the great, the mighty, and the awesome God, God beyond, generous in love and kindness, and possessing all. You remember the good deeds of those before us, and therefore in love bring rescue to the generations, for such is Your being.

> *During the Ten Days of Penitence add:*
> Sovereign Who delights in life, recall us to life and record us in the Book of Life for Your own sake, God of life!

The Sovereign who helps and saves and shields.
Blessed are You God,
who shields Abraham   who remembers Sarah.

GOD OF MIGHT

אַתָּה You are the endless power that renews life beyond death; You are the greatness that saves.

> *In winter months from* Shemini Atzeret *to* Pesach: making the wind blow and the rain fall.
> *In summer months from* Pesach *to* Shemini Atzeret: causing the dew to fall.

You care for the living with love. You renew life beyond death with unending mercy. You support the falling, and heal the sick. You free prisoners, and keep faith with those who sleep in the dust. Who can perform such mighty deeds, and who can compare with You, a Sovereign who brings death and life, and renews salvation?

> *During the Ten Days of Penitence add:*
> Who is like You, source of compassion,
> recalling Your creatures to life in compassion?

You are faithful to renew life beyond death.
Blessed are You God, who renews life beyond death.

---

[1] Ps 51:17.

For a morning or afternoon public service:

GOD OF HOLINESS

נְקַדֵּשׁ We sanctify Your name in the world as they sanctify it in the highest heavens. As it is written by the hand of Your prophet: 'And they called to each other and said:

Holy, holy, holy is the Creator of all, whose glory fills all the earth.'[1]

They cry in answer, 'Blessed…'

Blessed is God's glory, revealed in every place.[2]
From Your place, our Sovereign, shine forth and rule over us, for we wait for You. And in Your holy writing it is said:

The Almighty shall rule forever! Your God, O Zion, for all generations! Praise God![3]

We declare Your greatness to all generations, and to all eternity we proclaim Your holiness. Your praise shall never depart from our mouth, for You are God, the great and holy Sovereign.

Blessed are You, the holy God.

During the Ten Days of Penitence:
the holy Sovereign.

נְקַדֵּשׁ אֶת־שִׁמְךָ בָּעוֹלָם כְּשֵׁם
שֶׁמַּקְדִּישִׁים אוֹתוֹ בִּשְׁמֵי מָרוֹם
כַּכָּתוּב עַל יַד נְבִיאֶךָ. וְקָרָא זֶה
אֶל זֶה וְאָמַר.

קָדוֹשׁ קָדוֹשׁ קָדוֹשׁ יְהוָה צְבָאוֹת.
מְלֹא כָל־הָאָרֶץ כְּבוֹדוֹ.

לְעֻמָּתָם בָּרוּךְ יֹאמֵרוּ.

בָּרוּךְ כְּבוֹד יְהוָה מִמְּקוֹמוֹ.

מִמְּקוֹמְךָ מַלְכֵּנוּ תוֹפִיעַ וְתִמְלוֹךְ
עָלֵינוּ. כִּי מְחַכִּים אֲנַחְנוּ לָךְ.
וּבְדִבְרֵי קָדְשְׁךָ כָּתוּב לֵאמֹר.

יִמְלֹךְ יְהוָה לְעוֹלָם.
אֱלֹהַיִךְ צִיּוֹן לְדֹר וָדֹר הַלְלוּיָהּ.

לְדוֹר וָדוֹר נַגִּיד גָּדְלֶךָ.
וּלְנֵצַח נְצָחִים קְדֻשָּׁתְךָ נַקְדִּישׁ.
וְשִׁבְחֲךָ אֱלֹהֵינוּ מִפִּינוּ לֹא יָמוּשׁ
לְעוֹלָם וָעֶד. כִּי אֵל מֶלֶךְ גָּדוֹל
וְקָדוֹשׁ אָתָּה.

בָּרוּךְ אַתָּה יְהוָה. הָאֵל הַקָּדוֹשׁ:

During the Ten Days of Penitence:
הַמֶּלֶךְ הַקָּדוֹשׁ:

For an evening service or when praying individually:

אַתָּה You are holy
and Your name is holy,
and those who seek holiness
praise You day by day.
Blessed are You, the holy God.

During the Ten Days of Penitence:
the holy Sovereign.

אַתָּה קָדוֹשׁ וְשִׁמְךָ קָדוֹשׁ
וּקְדוֹשִׁים בְּכָל־יוֹם
יְהַלְלוּךָ סֶּלָה:
בָּרוּךְ אַתָּה יְהוָה. הָאֵל הַקָּדוֹשׁ:

During the Ten Days of Penitence:
הַמֶּלֶךְ הַקָּדוֹשׁ:

---

[1] Isa 6:3 [2] Ezek 3:12, [3] Ps 146:10.

DAILY AMIDAH

אַתָּה You favour human beings with knowledge,
and teach mortals understanding.

After Shabbat or a festival ends add:
You have favoured us with intelligence to study Your Torah and taught us to perform the laws You desire, and have made a distinction, our Living God, between the holy and the everyday, between light and darkness, between Israel and other peoples, between the seventh day and the six working days. Source of our life and our Sovereign, make the days before us begin with peace, free from all sin and innocent of all guilt and bound to You in awe. And ...

favour us with the knowledge, understanding and discernment that come from You. Blessed are You God, who favours us with knowledge.

הֲשִׁיבֵנוּ Turn us back to Your teaching, our Creator, and draw us near to Your service, our Sovereign. Bring us back in perfect repentance to Your presence. Blessed are You God, who desires repentance.

סְלַח Forgive us, our Creator, for we have sinned; pardon us, our Sovereign, for we have disobeyed; for You are a God who is good and forgiving. Blessed are You God, who is generous to forgive.

אַתָּה חוֹנֵן לְאָדָם דַּעַת.
וּמְלַמֵּד לֶאֱנוֹשׁ בִּינָה.

אַתָּה חוֹנַנְתָּנוּ לְמַדַּע תּוֹרָתֶךָ וַתְּלַמְּדֵנוּ לַעֲשׂוֹת חֻקֵּי רְצוֹנֶךָ וַתַּבְדֵּל יהוה אֱלֹהֵינוּ בֵּין קֹדֶשׁ לְחוֹל בֵּין אוֹר לְחֹשֶׁךְ בֵּין יִשְׂרָאֵל לָעַמִּים בֵּין יוֹם הַשְּׁבִיעִי לְשֵׁשֶׁת יְמֵי הַמַּעֲשֶׂה: אָבִינוּ מַלְכֵּנוּ הָחֵל עָלֵינוּ הַיָּמִים הַבָּאִים לִקְרָאתֵנוּ לְשָׁלוֹם חֲשׂוּכִים מִכָּל־חֵטְא וּמְנֻקִּים מִכָּל־עָוֹן וּמְדֻבָּקִים בְּיִרְאָתֶךָ. וְ...

חָנֵּנוּ מֵאִתְּךָ דֵּעָה וּבִינָה וְהַשְׂכֵּל.
בָּרוּךְ אַתָּה יהוה. חוֹנֵן הַדָּעַת:

הֲשִׁיבֵנוּ אָבִינוּ לְתוֹרָתֶךָ. וְקָרְבֵנוּ מַלְכֵּנוּ לַעֲבוֹדָתֶךָ. וְהַחֲזִירֵנוּ בִּתְשׁוּבָה שְׁלֵמָה לְפָנֶיךָ. בָּרוּךְ אַתָּה יהוה. הָרוֹצֶה בִּתְשׁוּבָה:

סְלַח לָנוּ אָבִינוּ כִּי חָטָאנוּ. מְחַל לָנוּ מַלְכֵּנוּ כִּי פָשָׁעְנוּ. כִּי אֵל טוֹב וְסַלָּח אָתָּה. בָּרוּךְ אַתָּה יהוה. חַנּוּן הַמַּרְבֶּה לִסְלֹחַ:

אַתָּה חוֹנֵן You favour ...
This first blessing of the daily petitions places a powerful emphasis on the Jewish belief in knowledge and understanding as spiritual paths. *Da'at* is experiential knowledge; *binah* is discernment, the ability to distinguish and discriminate; *haskel* is the power to reason things out.
The language directly echoes the story in Genesis where Adam and Eve have to leave the Garden of Eden having eaten of the 'tree of knowledge'. Instead of understanding this as a 'fall from grace', this knowledge is seen as an act of grace, a gift granted by God, something for 'Adam', for all of humanity.

הֲשִׁיבֵנוּ אָבִינוּ Turn us back ...
With knowledge comes our awareness of our distance from God. We ask to return to the Torah, the teaching of God that is the basis of Jewish self-understanding and wisdom, and to the *avodah*, both the religious 'service' we perform as a community and the spiritual 'work' we need to do on ourselves. The blessing concludes with the affirmation that God desires our *teshuvah*, 'return'.

סְלַח לָנוּ Forgive us ...
The conclusion of the last blessing leads to the realisation that as we seek to return to

78 עמידה לימות החול

רְאֵה Look upon our affliction and defend our cause, and rescue us quickly for the sake of Your name. For You are a mighty redeemer. Blessed are You God, the redeemer of Israel.

רְפָאֵנוּ Heal us, God, and we shall be healed; save us, and we shall be saved; for it is You we praise. Send relief and healing for all our diseases, our sufferings and our wounds;

May it be Your will, our Living God and God of our fathers and mothers, that You send speedily a perfect healing, healing of the spirit and healing of the body, for:
For a woman _____ daughter of _____
For a man _____ son of _____
amongst all who are ill;
for You are a merciful and faithful healer.

Blessed are You God, who heals the sick.

רְאֵה בְעָנְיֵנוּ. וְרִיבָה רִיבֵנוּ. וּגְאָלֵנוּ מְהֵרָה לְמַעַן שְׁמֶךָ. כִּי גּוֹאֵל חָזָק אָתָּה. בָּרוּךְ אַתָּה יהוה. גּוֹאֵל יִשְׂרָאֵל:

רְפָאֵנוּ יהוה וְנֵרָפֵא. הוֹשִׁיעֵנוּ וְנִוָּשֵׁעָה. כִּי תְהִלָּתֵנוּ אָתָּה. וְהַעֲלֵה אֲרוּכָה וּמַרְפֵּא לְכָל־תַּחֲלוּאֵינוּ וּלְכָל־מַכְאוֹבֵינוּ וּלְכָל־מַכּוֹתֵינוּ.

וִיהִי רָצוֹן מִלְּפָנֶיךָ יהוה אֱלֹהֵינוּ וֵאלֹהֵי אֲבוֹתֵינוּ וְאִמּוֹתֵינוּ שֶׁתִּשְׁלַח מְהֵרָה רְפוּאָה שְׁלֵמָה מִן הַשָּׁמַיִם. רְפוּאַת הַנֶּפֶשׁ וּרְפוּאַת הַגּוּף.
לַחוֹלָה _____ בַּת _____
לַחוֹלֶה _____ בֶּן _____
בְּתוֹךְ שְׁאָר הַחוֹלִים.
כִּי אֵל מֶלֶךְ רוֹפֵא רַחֲמָן וְנֶאֱמָן אָתָּה.

בָּרוּךְ אַתָּה יהוה. רוֹפֵא הַחוֹלִים:

God we must change our behaviour. Two terms express this distance from God: *chatanu*, 'we have sinned', a term expressing 'failure', 'a wrong direction', 'missing the target'; and *pashanu*, meaning 'deliberate rebellion' or wrongdoing. If we acknowledge these actions then we can rely on God to accept us in return.

רְאֵה בְעָנְיֵנוּ Look upon our affliction ...
This is the first blessing that speaks of our material well-being. The opening phrase is based on Psalm 25:18 and asks for release from the anxieties and troubles of daily life. The 'redeemer' of the Bible was the family member responsible for releasing others from slavery and ensuring their personal freedom. It is the role played by God at the Exodus from Egypt. This historical act of redemption establishes human rights and human responsibilities as central to the building of society.

רְפָאֵנוּ Heal us ...
The opening of this prayer is based on Jeremiah 17:14 but was changed in the traditional version from the singular form to the plural. Beyond healing it asks for a *yeshua*, 'saving', a new beginning in life after recovery. This blessing offers the opportunity to insert prayers of intercession on behalf of those who are sick, asking for healing for both the body and the spirit.

DAILY AMIDAH

בָּרֵךְ Bless this year, our Living God, and may all that it brings be good for us;

In winter: send dew and rain as a blessing
In summer: send Your blessings

over the face of the earth, bring life-giving water to all the earth, satisfy all the world with Your goodness, and bless our years as good years. Blessed are You God, who blesses the years.

תְּקַע Sound the great horn for our freedom, and raise a banner to restore all of us who experience exile. May the voice of liberty and freedom be heard throughout the four corners of the earth for all its inhabitants, for You are a God who redeems and rescues. Blessed are You God, who sustains Your people Israel.

בָּרֵךְ עָלֵינוּ יהוה אֱלֹהֵינוּ אֶת־הַשָּׁנָה הַזֹּאת וְאֶת־כָּל־מִינֵי תְבוּאָתָהּ לְטוֹבָה.

In winter וְתֵן טַל וּמָטָר לִבְרָכָה
In summer וְתֵן בְּרָכָה

עַל פְּנֵי הָאֲדָמָה. וְרַוֵּה פְּנֵי תֵבֵל. וְשַׂבַּע אֶת הָעוֹלָם כֻּלּוֹ מִטּוּבֶךָ. וּבָרֵךְ שְׁנוֹתֵינוּ כַּשָּׁנִים הַטּוֹבוֹת. בָּרוּךְ אַתָּה יהוה. מְבָרֵךְ הַשָּׁנִים:

תְּקַע בְּשׁוֹפָר גָּדוֹל לְחֵרוּתֵנוּ. וְשָׂא נֵס לְשׁוֹבֵב גָּלִיּוֹתֵינוּ. וְקוֹל דְּרוֹר וִישׁוּעָה יִשָּׁמַע בְּאַרְבַּע כַּנְפוֹת הָאָרֶץ לְכָל־יוֹשְׁבֶיהָ. בָּרוּךְ אַתָּה יהוה. מְקַיֵּם נִדְחֵי עַמּוֹ יִשְׂרָאֵל.

בָּרֵךְ עָלֵינוּ Bless this year ...

Biblical 'blessings' are expressed in terms of prosperity and fruitfulness. Similarly this blessing asks for material and physical sustenance.

Our text is based on the Sephardi version of this blessing used for the winter months. It is particularly apt because of its universal theme requesting that God 'water the surface of the earth and satisfy the entire world with Your goodness'.

But a good harvest alone is not enough without the effective distribution of food to all who need it, which lies within our own area of responsibility.

In one rabbinic view this is the greatest of the blessings within the *Amidah* because it is recited not only on behalf of the Jewish people, or even of humanity as a whole, but on behalf of the entire animal kingdom as well.

תְּקַע בְּשׁוֹפָר Sound the great horn ...

This blessing begins with the call for a *Shofar* blast that symbolises our liberation. It is based on the laws in Leviticus (25:8-13) calling for a jubilee year when all debts are cancelled and all are free to return to their original homes. In the traditional version it becomes a summons to all Jews in exile to return to the land of Israel. Our text is based on a variety of Reform and Liberal versions, but the particular emphasis lies in the idea that the restoration of Israel is to be seen as part of a divine plan for the whole world, based on Isaiah 49:5-6.

'And now, said the Eternal, who formed me from the womb to be His servant, to restore Jacob to him (*l'shovev*) so that Israel be gathered to Him ... And He said, it is too light for you to be my servant to 'raise up' (*l'hakim*) the tribes of Jacob and to bring back the preserved of Israel, for I have made you a light of the nations so that my salvation (*yeshuati*) can be in the utmost part of the earth.'

Our version expresses the hope that all Jews who experience exile, whether

הָשִׁיבָה מִשְׁפַּט־צִדְקָתְךָ בָּעוֹלָם וְהָסֵר מִמֶּנּוּ יָגוֹן וַאֲנָחָה. וּמְלוֹךְ עָלֵינוּ אַתָּה יהוה לְבַדְּךָ בְּחֶסֶד וּבְרַחֲמִים. וְצַדְּקֵנוּ בַּמִּשְׁפָּט. בָּרוּךְ אַתָּה יהוה. מֶלֶךְ אוֹהֵב צְדָקָה וּמִשְׁפָּט.

הָשִׁיבָה Restore Your judgment of righteousness in the world. Turn away from us sorrow and pain, rule over us with love and mercy, and judge us with righteousness. Blessed are You God, the Ruler who loves righteousness and truth.

During the Ten Days of Penitence:
הַמֶּלֶךְ הַמִּשְׁפָּט.

During the Ten Days of Penitence:
the Sovereign of judgment.

וְלַמַּלְשִׁינוּת אַל תְּהִי תִקְוָה וְכָל־ הָרִשְׁעָה כְּרֶגַע תֹּאבֵד. וּמַלְכוּת זָדוֹן תַּעֲבִיר בִּמְהֵרָה בְיָמֵינוּ. בָּרוּךְ אַתָּה יהוה. הַמַּעֲבִיר רִשְׁעָה מִן הָאָרֶץ:

וְלַמַּלְשִׁינוּת And for slander let there be no hope, and may all evil come to nothing, and remove the reign of violence and terror speedily in our days. Blessed are You God, who makes evil pass away from the earth.

הָשִׁיבָה מִשְׁפָּט Restore Your judgement ...
The traditional version of this blessing asks for the restoration of 'our judges as at the first', and it seems to refer to that earlier period of Biblical history when Israel was ruled by judges before there was even a king. So it echoes the Biblical controversy over whether having a human king was right for the Israelite nation, since God was their true king. The blessing affirms that whatever the system of government, the existence of an independent judiciary is essential for maintaining the rule of law and for creating a just society.

Our version speaks more generally about the need to establish justice throughout the world, in the hope that this will help abolish one of the sources of sorrow and pain in the world.

וְלַמַּלְשִׁינוּת And for slander ...
This request for the punishment of 'slanderers' may have been composed during Roman rule, where it would refer to those who had denounced Jews to the Romans. However, another version of the same blessing begins with the word *minim* which seems to refer to sectarian groups. Rather than curse individuals we have followed a rabbinic example and changed the noun from a reference to particular people to the act of slander itself. The request for the removal of a violent regime could be appropriate for any period of human history.

81 DAILY *AMIDAH*

עַל־הַצַּדִּיקִים וְעַל־הַחֲסִידִים וְעַל־הַתְּמִימִים. וְעַל גֵּרֵי הַצֶּדֶק וְעָלֵינוּ. יֶהֱמוּ נָא רַחֲמֶיךָ. יהוה אֱלֹהֵינוּ. וְתֵן שָׂכָר טוֹב לְכָל הַבּוֹטְחִים בְּשִׁמְךָ בֶּאֱמֶת. וְשִׂים חֶלְקֵנוּ עִמָּהֶם לְעוֹלָם. וְלֹא נֵבוֹשׁ כִּי בְךָ בָּטָחְנוּ. בָּרוּךְ אַתָּה יהוה. מִשְׁעָן וּמִבְטָח לַצַּדִּיקִים:

עַל־הַצַּדִּיקִים To the righteous, the pious, and the honest, to those who join us in righteousness, and to us ourselves, be merciful our Living God. Grant a good reward to all who sincerely trust in You. Blessed are You God, the support and safety of the righteous.

וְלִירוּשָׁלַיִם עִירְךָ בְּרַחֲמִים תָּשׁוּב. וְתִשְׁכּוֹן בְּתוֹכָהּ וּבְנֵה אוֹתָהּ כַּאֲשֶׁר דִּבַּרְתָּ. אָז יִקָּרֵא לָהּ עִיר הַצֶּדֶק קִרְיָה נֶאֱמָנָה. וְתָכִין אוֹתָהּ לִמְקוֹם תְּפִלָּה לְכָל־הָעַמִּים. בָּרוּךְ אַתָּה יהוה. בּוֹנֵה יְרוּשָׁלָיִם:

וְלִירוּשָׁלַיִם Turn in mercy to Jerusalem and may Your presence dwell within it. Rebuild it as You have prophesied, then it shall indeed be called 'city of righteousness, faithful city'.[1] Help us establish it as a place worthy of prayer for all peoples. Blessed are You God, who builds Jerusalem.

עַל־הַצַּדִּיקִים To the righteous ...

The traditional version of this blessing includes 'the elders' and 'the remnant of the scribes', suggesting that it was composed to reflect the leadership that survived the Roman destruction of Jerusalem at the time of the full establishment of rabbinic Judaism. In a radically new situation, without priests or kings, learning and the interpretation of Torah provided the authority for the building of the new society. Included also here are 'those who join us in righteousness', a phrase referring to those who convert to Judaism. All are to be equally rewarded by God and never disappointed for trusting in God.

וְלִירוּשָׁלַיִם ... to Jerusalem ...

The traditional version of this blessing calls for the rebuilding of Jerusalem and the establishment of God's presence within it, but also the restoration of 'the throne of David', the monarchy, under a descendant of King David. It is possible that this original blessing was subsequently divided and the following one explores further the appointment of 'an offspring of David'. Our version follows Isaiah (1:26) that Jerusalem needs to be faithful to its title as a 'city of righteousness', and also the prophetic expectation that it become a place where all peoples can worship God (Isa 56:7).

[1] Isa 1:26.

אֶת צֶמַח דָּוִד עַבְדְּךָ מְהֵרָה תַצְמִיחַ. צֶמַח צְדָקָה וּפֶתַח תִּקְוָה. כִּי לִישׁוּעָתְךָ קִוִּינוּ כָּל הַיּוֹם. בָּרוּךְ אַתָּה יהוה. מַצְמִיחַ קֶרֶן יְשׁוּעָה:

אֶת Bring forth soon a new flowering from Your servant David, a flowering of righteousness[1] and a doorway of hope,[2] for we wait and work for Your salvation. Blessed are You God, who makes the power of salvation flourish.

שְׁמַע קוֹלֵנוּ יהוה אֱלֹהֵינוּ אָב הָרַחֲמָן. חוּס וְרַחֵם עָלֵינוּ. וְקַבֵּל בְּרַחֲמִים וּבְרָצוֹן אֶת־תְּפִלָּתֵנוּ. כִּי אֵל שׁוֹמֵעַ תְּפִלּוֹת וְתַחֲנוּנִים אָתָּה. וּמִלְּפָנֶיךָ מַלְכֵּנוּ רֵיקָם אַל תְּשִׁיבֵנוּ. כִּי אַתָּה שׁוֹמֵעַ תְּפִלַּת כָּל־פֶּה. בָּרוּךְ אַתָּה יהוה. שׁוֹמֵעַ תְּפִלָּה:

שְׁמַע Hear our voice, our Living God, source of mercy. Spare us and have pity on us, and receive our prayer with love and favour. For You are a God who listens to our prayers and needs. Our Sovereign, do not turn us away empty from Your presence, for You hear the prayers of all lips. Blessed are You God, who listens to prayers.

אֶת צֶמַח דָּוִד ... a new flowering ... from David ...

Prophetic texts refer to a *tsemach*, a 'sprout', that will arise out of the family of David, a ruler, an 'anointed one' (messiah) who will restore Israel's national status. Jeremiah's prophetic vision of the messianic time says that: In those days and at that time I will cause to sprout up for David a 'sprout of righteousness' and he will perform justice and righteousness in the land (Jeremiah 33:15). We have combined this with a phrase from Hosea 2:17 in which God speaks of the promised land as a *petach tikvah*, a 'door of hope'.

This blessing has been the most contentious one in debates between traditional and progressive Jews since the latter prefer to emphasise the broader Biblical and rabbinic concept of a messianic age rather than the physical person of a messiah, literally 'anointed', a descendant of King David. Since the Biblical term *tsemach* means a 'sprouting' or 'flowering' and is used in early prophetic texts without specific reference to an individual person, we have followed this more general idea, as have other progressive versions, referring to the 'flowering of righteousness'.

שְׁמַע קוֹלֵנוּ Hear our voice ...

The final one of these intermediate blessings invites God to hear all the prayers and petitions that make up the *Amidah*, and respond to them with mercy and compassion. The request that God receive our prayer 'with favour' is understood to express the highest level of spiritual development - where we are so attuned to the divine will that our prayers exactly reflect what God would wish from us and for us.

The traditional version concludes that God hears the prayers of 'Your people Israel'. In line with the broader rabbinic view, and the universal emphasis throughout our version, we conclude that God hears the prayers 'of all people'.

[1] Jer 33:1.
[2] Hos 2:17.

DAILY *AMIDAH*

THANKSGIVING AND PEACE

רְצֵה Our Living God be pleased with Your people Israel and listen to their prayers. In Your great mercy delight in us so that Your presence may rest upon Zion.

רְצֵה יהוה אֱלֹהֵינוּ בְּעַמְּךָ יִשְׂרָאֵל. וְלִתְפִלָּתָם שְׁעֵה. וּבְרַחֲמֶיךָ הָרַבִּים תַּחְפֹּץ בָּנוּ וְתִשְׁרֶה שְׁכִינָתְךָ עַל צִיּוֹן.

On the New Moon and festivals, the following prayers are added, otherwise the service continues on page 84.

אֱלֹהֵינוּ Our God and God of our ancestors, may Your regard and concern for us and our ancestors, for the time of our redemption, for Jerusalem the city of Your holiness, and for all Your people the family of Israel, be close to You and be pleasing to You. Favour us all with freedom and goodness, with grace, love and mercy, on this day of

אֱלֹהֵינוּ וֵאלֹהֵי אֲבוֹתֵינוּ. יַעֲלֶה וְיָבֹא וְיַגִּיעַ וְיֵרָאֶה וְיֵרָצֶה וְיִשָּׁמַע וְיִפָּקֵד וְיִזָּכֵר זִכְרוֹנֵנוּ וּפִקְדּוֹנֵנוּ וְזִכְרוֹן אֲבוֹתֵינוּ וְזִכְרוֹן מָשִׁיחַ בֶּן דָּוִד עַבְדֶּךָ. וְזִכְרוֹן יְרוּשָׁלַיִם עִיר קָדְשֶׁךָ וְזִכְרוֹן כָּל־עַמְּךָ בֵּית יִשְׂרָאֵל לְפָנֶיךָ. לִפְלֵיטָה וּלְטוֹבָה לְחֵן וּלְחֶסֶד וּלְרַחֲמִים לְחַיִּים וּלְשָׁלוֹם בְּיוֹם

(On the New Moon) the New Moon.
(On Pesach) the Feast of Unleavened Bread.
(On Succot) the Feast of Tabernacles.

רֹאשׁ הַחֹדֶשׁ הַזֶּה *On the New Moon*
חַג הַמַּצּוֹת הַזֶּה *On Pesach*
חַג הַסֻּכּוֹת הַזֶּה *On Succot*

Our Living God, remember us for good, *Amen*
bring us Your blessing, *Amen*
and save us for a good life. *Amen*

זָכְרֵנוּ יהוה אֱלֹהֵינוּ בּוֹ לְטוֹבָה אָמֵן
וּפָקְדֵנוּ בוֹ לִבְרָכָה אָמֵן
וְהוֹשִׁיעֵנוּ בוֹ לְחַיִּים טוֹבִים אָמֵן

Spare us and be kind to us according to Your promise of deliverance and mercy. Our eyes are turned towards You, for You are a Sovereign of mercy and compassion.

וּבִדְבַר יְשׁוּעָה וְרַחֲמִים חוּס וְחָנֵּנוּ. כִּי אֵלֶיךָ עֵינֵינוּ. כִּי אֵל מֶלֶךְ חַנּוּן וְרַחוּם אָתָּה.

עמידה לימות החול 84

The service continues here:

וְתֶחֱזֶינָה עֵינֵינוּ בְּשׁוּבְךָ לְצִיּוֹן בְּרַחֲמִים: בָּרוּךְ אַתָּה יהוה, הַמַּחֲזִיר שְׁכִינָתוֹ לְצִיּוֹן.

וְתֶחֱזֶינָה Our eyes look forward to Your return to Zion in mercy! Blessed are You God, ever restoring Your presence to Zion.

It is customary to bow as one recites the opening words of this blessing, rising as we recite the name of God, Adonai *and the list of God's gifts to us.*

מוֹדִים אֲנַחְנוּ לָךְ שָׁאַתָּה הוּא יהוה אֱלֹהֵינוּ וֵאלֹהֵי אֲבוֹתֵינוּ לְעוֹלָם וָעֶד. צוּרֵנוּ צוּר חַיֵּינוּ וּמָגֵן יִשְׁעֵנוּ אַתָּה הוּא: לְדוֹר וָדוֹר נוֹדֶה לְךָ וּנְסַפֵּר תְּהִלָּתֶךָ עַל חַיֵּינוּ הַמְּסוּרִים בְּיָדֶךָ. וְעַל נִשְׁמוֹתֵינוּ הַפְּקוּדוֹת לָךְ. וְעַל נִסֶּיךָ שֶׁבְּכָל־יוֹם עִמָּנוּ. וְעַל נִפְלְאוֹתֶיךָ וְטוֹבוֹתֶיךָ שֶׁבְּכָל־עֵת עֶרֶב וָבֹקֶר וְצָהֳרָיִם: הַטּוֹב כִּי לֹא כָלוּ רַחֲמֶיךָ. הַמְרַחֵם כִּי לֹא תַמּוּ חֲסָדֶיךָ. כִּי מֵעוֹלָם קִוִּינוּ לָךְ.

מוֹדִים We declare with gratitude that You are our God and the God of our ancestors. You are our rock, the rock of our life and the shield that saves us. In every generation we thank You and recount Your praise for our lives held in Your hand, for our souls that are in Your care, and for the signs of Your presence that are with us every day. At every moment, at evening, morning and noon, we experience Your wonders and Your goodness. You are goodness itself, for Your mercy has no end. You are mercy itself, for Your love has no limit. Forever have we put our hope in You.

On Chanukah *add* Al Ha-nissim, *page 374
and on* Purim *add* Al Ha-nissim, *page 384, otherwise continue on the next page:*

85 DAILY *AMIDAH*

Modim *continues here:*

וְעַל כֻּלָּם יִתְבָּרַךְ וְיִתְרוֹמַם וְיִתְנַשֵּׂא תָּמִיד שִׁמְךָ מַלְכֵּנוּ לְעוֹלָם וָעֶד:

During the Ten Days of Penitence add:

וּכְתוֹב לְחַיִּים טוֹבִים כָּל־בְּנֵי בְרִיתֶךָ.

וְכָל־הַחַיִּים יוֹדוּךָ סֶּלָה. וִיהַלְלוּ וִיבָרְכוּ אֶת שִׁמְךָ הַגָּדוֹל בֶּאֱמֶת. הָאֵל יְשׁוּעָתֵנוּ וְעֶזְרָתֵנוּ סֶלָה: בָּרוּךְ אַתָּה יהוה. הַטּוֹב שִׁמְךָ וּלְךָ נָאֶה לְהוֹדוֹת:

וְעַל And for all these things may Your name, our Sovereign, be blessed, exalted and honoured forever and ever.

During the Ten Days of Penitence add:
Record all the children of Your covenant for a good life.

May every living being thank You; may they praise and bless Your great name in truth for You are the God who saves and helps us. Blessed are You God, known as goodness, whom it is right to praise.

For a morning service:

שִׂים שָׁלוֹם טוֹבָה וּבְרָכָה חַיִּים חֵן וָחֶסֶד צְדָקָה וְרַחֲמִים עָלֵינוּ. וּבָרְכֵנוּ אָבִינוּ כֻּלָּנוּ יַחַד בְּאוֹר פָּנֶיךָ. כִּי בְאוֹר פָּנֶיךָ נָתַתָּ לָנוּ יהוה אֱלֹהֵינוּ תּוֹרָה וְחַיִּים. אַהֲבָה וָחֶסֶד. צְדָקָה וְרַחֲמִים. בְּרָכָה וְשָׁלוֹם. וְטוֹב בְּעֵינֶיךָ לְבָרֵךְ אֶת־עַמְּךָ יִשְׂרָאֵל בְּרָב־עֹז וּבְשָׁלוֹם:

שִׂים Grant us peace, goodness and blessing; life, grace and kindness; justice and mercy. Source of our life, bless us all together with the light of Your presence, for in the light of Your presence You give us, our Living God, law and life, love and kindness, justice and mercy, blessing and peace. And in Your eyes it is good to bless Your people Israel with the strength to make peace.

During the Ten Days of Penitence add:

בְּסֵפֶר חַיִּים נִזָּכֵר וְנִכָּתֵב לְפָנֶיךָ אֲנַחְנוּ וְכָל־עַמְּךָ בֵּית יִשְׂרָאֵל לְחַיִּים טוֹבִים וּלְשָׁלוֹם:

בָּרוּךְ אַתָּה יהוה. הַמְבָרֵךְ אֶת עַמּוֹ יִשְׂרָאֵל בַּשָּׁלוֹם:

During the Ten Days of Penitence add:
In Your presence may we and all Your people, the family of Israel, be remembered and recorded in the Book of Life for a good life and for peace.

Blessed are You God, blessing Your people Israel with peace.

For an afternoon or evening service:

שָׁלוֹם Set true peace upon Your people Israel forever. For You are the Source of all peace, and in Your eyes it is good to bless Your people Israel at every time and in every hour with Your peace.

During the Ten Days of Penitence add:
In Your presence may we and all Your people, the family of Israel, be remembered and recorded in the Book of Life for a good life and for peace.

Blessed are You God, blessing Your people Israel with peace.

MEDITATION

אֱלֹהַי My God, keep my tongue from causing harm and my lips from telling lies. Let me be silent if people curse me, my soul still humble and at peace with all. Open my heart to Your teaching, and give me the will to practise it. May the plans and schemes of those who seek my harm come to nothing. May the words of my mouth and the meditation of my heart be acceptable to You, O God, my Rock and my Redeemer.[1]

עֹשֶׂה May the Maker of peace in the highest bring this peace upon us and upon all Israel and upon all the world. Amen.

שָׁלוֹם רָב עַל יִשְׂרָאֵל עַמְּךָ תָּשִׂים לְעוֹלָם. כִּי אַתָּה הוּא מֶלֶךְ אָדוֹן לְכָל־הַשָּׁלוֹם. וְטוֹב בְּעֵינֶיךָ לְבָרֵךְ אֶת עַמְּךָ יִשְׂרָאֵל בְּכָל־עֵת וּבְכָל־שָׁעָה בִּשְׁלוֹמֶךָ.

During the Ten Days of Penitence add:
בְּסֵפֶר חַיִּים נִזָּכֵר וְנִכָּתֵב לְפָנֶיךָ אֲנַחְנוּ וְכָל־עַמְּךָ בֵּית יִשְׂרָאֵל לְחַיִּים טוֹבִים וּלְשָׁלוֹם:

בָּרוּךְ אַתָּה יהוה. הַמְבָרֵךְ אֶת עַמּוֹ יִשְׂרָאֵל בַּשָּׁלוֹם:

אֱלֹהַי נְצוֹר לְשׁוֹנִי מֵרָע. וְשִׂפְתוֹתַי מִדַּבֵּר מִרְמָה. וְלִמְקַלְלַי נַפְשִׁי תִדֹּם. וְנַפְשִׁי כֶּעָפָר לַכֹּל תִּהְיֶה: פְּתַח לִבִּי בְּתוֹרָתֶךָ. וְאַחֲרֵי מִצְוֹתֶיךָ תִּרְדּוֹף נַפְשִׁי. וְכָל־הַקָּמִים עָלַי לְרָעָה מְהֵרָה הָפֵר עֲצָתָם וְקַלְקֵל מַחֲשְׁבוֹתָם: יִהְיוּ לְרָצוֹן אִמְרֵי־פִי. וְהֶגְיוֹן לִבִּי לְפָנֶיךָ. יהוה צוּרִי וְגוֹאֲלִי:

עֹשֶׂה שָׁלוֹם בִּמְרוֹמָיו. הוּא יַעֲשֶׂה שָׁלוֹם עָלֵינוּ וְעַל כָּל־יִשְׂרָאֵל וְעַל־כָּל־הָעוֹלָם. וְאִמְרוּ. אָמֵן:

For a morning service:
On **Rosh Chodesh**, **Chanukah** and **Chol Hamoed** continue with Hallel, page 663.
On a **Monday** or **Thursday** the Torah service may follow here.
Otherwise continue with the Concluding Prayers on page 305.

For an afternoon or evening service continue with the Concluding Prayers on page 305.

---

[1] Ps 19:15.

WEEKDAY TORAH SERVICE

The Chatsi Kaddish *may be included here:*

Chatsi Kaddish   חֲצִי קַדִּישׁ

יִתְגַּדַּל Let us magnify and let us sanctify in this world the great name of God whose will created it. May God's reign come in your lifetime, and in your days, and in the lifetime of the family of Israel - quickly and speedily may it come. **Amen.** **May the greatness of God's being be blessed from eternity to eternity**. Let us bless and let us extol, let us tell aloud and let us raise aloft, let us set on high and let us honour, let us exalt and let us praise the Holy One, **whose name is blessed**, who is far beyond any blessing *During the Ten Days of Penitence:* who is far above and beyond any blessing or song, any honour or any consolation that can be spoken of in this world. **Amen.**	יִתְגַּדַּל וְיִתְקַדַּשׁ שְׁמֵהּ רַבָּא בְּעָלְמָא דִּי־בְרָא כִרְעוּתֵהּ: וְיַמְלִיךְ מַלְכוּתֵהּ בְּחַיֵּיכוֹן וּבְיוֹמֵיכוֹן וּבְחַיֵּי דִי־כָל־בֵּית יִשְׂרָאֵל בַּעֲגָלָא וּבִזְמַן קָרִיב. וְאִמְרוּ אָמֵן: יְהֵא שְׁמֵהּ רַבָּא מְבָרַךְ לְעָלַם וּלְעָלְמֵי עָלְמַיָּא: יִתְבָּרַךְ וְיִשְׁתַּבַּח וְיִתְפָּאַר וְיִתְרוֹמַם וְיִתְנַשֵּׂא וְיִתְהַדָּר וְיִתְעַלֶּה וְיִתְהַלָּל שְׁמֵהּ דְּקֻדְשָׁא. בְּרִיךְ הוּא. לְעֵלָּא מִן־כָּל־בִּרְכָתָא *During the Ten Days of Penitence:* לְעֵלָּא לְעֵלָּא מִכָּל־בִּרְכָתָא וְשִׁירָתָא תֻּשְׁבְּחָתָא וְנֶחָמָתָא דַּאֲמִירָן בְּעָלְמָא. וְאִמְרוּ אָמֵן:

סדר קריאת התורה לימות החול
Weekday Torah Service   345

The reading of the Torah on Monday and Thursday is traditionally ascribed to Ezra the Scribe. These were market days when there were large gatherings which provided the opportunity to teach and expound the Torah in public. A rabbinic parable suggests that just as the children of Israel could not go for three days without water in the wilderness, so one should not go more that three days without Torah, a life-giving source. Only the first section of the reading for the following Shabbat is read, and traditionally only three people are 'called up'.

סדר קריאת התורה לימות החול
WEEKDAY TORAH SERVICE

וַיְהִי Whenever the ark moved forward,
then Moses said:
'Almighty, rise up!
Let Your enemies be scattered,
let those who hate You flee before You!'
For Torah shall come out of Zion
and the word of God from Jerusalem.[1]

גַּדְּלוּ Declare with me the greatness of God,
and let us exalt God's name together.[2]

לְךָ Yours, our Living God,
is the greatness, the power,
the beauty, the victory
and the splendour,
for everything in heaven and earth
is Yours.
Yours is sovereignty
and You are supreme over all.
Exalt the Living God,
and bow down before the footstool
of the Holy One.

Exalt the Living God, and bow down
before the mountain of God's holiness
- for holy is our Living God.[3]

וַיְהִי בִּנְסֹעַ הָאָרֹן
וַיֹּאמֶר מֹשֶׁה:
קוּמָה יהוה וְיָפֻצוּ אֹיְבֶיךָ
וְיָנֻסוּ מְשַׂנְאֶיךָ מִפָּנֶיךָ:
כִּי מִצִּיּוֹן תֵּצֵא תוֹרָה
וּדְבַר־יהוה מִירוּשָׁלָיִם:

גַּדְּלוּ לַיהוה אִתִּי.
וּנְרוֹמְמָה שְׁמוֹ יַחְדָּו:

לְךָ יהוה
הַגְּדֻלָּה וְהַגְּבוּרָה
וְהַתִּפְאֶרֶת וְהַנֵּצַח וְהַהוֹד.
כִּי כֹל בַּשָּׁמַיִם וּבָאָרֶץ.
לְךָ יהוה הַמַּמְלָכָה
וְהַמִּתְנַשֵּׂא לְכֹל לְרֹאשׁ:
רוֹמְמוּ יהוה אֱלֹהֵינוּ
וְהִשְׁתַּחֲווּ לַהֲדֹם רַגְלָיו
קָדוֹשׁ הוּא:
רוֹמְמוּ יהוה אֱלֹהֵינוּ.
וְהִשְׁתַּחֲווּ לְהַר קָדְשׁוֹ.
כִּי קָדוֹשׁ יהוה אֱלֹהֵינוּ:

---

[1] Num 10:35, Is:2:3.
[2] Ps 34:4.
[3] I Chron 29:11, Ps 99:5, Ps 99:9.

89 WEEKDAY TORAH SERVICE

אֵין There is none holy
like the Eternal,
for nothing is like You
and there is no strength like our God.
For who is God besides the Eternal,
and what is strength except our God!
Moses commanded us Torah, the
heritage of the community of Jacob.
It is a tree of life to all who grasp it
and those who hold fast to it
are happy.
Its ways are ways of pleasantness
and all its paths are peace.[1]

אֵין קָדוֹשׁ כַּיהוה כִּי־אֵין בִּלְתֶּךָ.
וְאֵין צוּר כֵּאלֹהֵינוּ:
כִּי מִי אֱלוֹהַּ מִבַּלְעֲדֵי יהוה.
וּמִי צוּר זוּלָתִי אֱלֹהֵינוּ:
תּוֹרָה צִוָּה־לָנוּ מֹשֶׁה.
מוֹרָשָׁה קְהִלַּת יַעֲקֹב:
עֵץ־חַיִּים הִיא לַמַּחֲזִיקִים בָּהּ.
וְתֹמְכֶיהָ מְאֻשָּׁר:
דְּרָכֶיהָ דַרְכֵי־נֹעַם.
וְכָל־נְתִיבוֹתֶיהָ שָׁלוֹם:

שָׁלוֹם There is great peace
for those who love Your Torah,
and for them there is no stumbling.[2]
Give strength to Your people,
bless Your people with peace.[3]
So I call out the name of the One God:
Declare the greatness of our God!
Let everything declare God's power
and the glory of God's Torah.

שָׁלוֹם רָב לְאֹהֲבֵי תוֹרָתֶךָ.
וְאֵין־לָמוֹ מִכְשׁוֹל:
יהוה עֹז לְעַמּוֹ יִתֵּן.
יהוה יְבָרֵךְ אֶת־עַמּוֹ בַשָּׁלוֹם:
כִּי שֵׁם יהוה אֶקְרָא.
הָבוּ גֹדֶל לֵאלֹהֵינוּ:
הַכֹּל תְּנוּ עֹז לֵאלֹהִים.
וּתְנוּ כָבוֹד לַתּוֹרָה:

The Sefer Torah *may be raised here (Sephardi practice):*

וְזֹאת This is the Torah that Moses set
before the children of Israel.
Moses commanded us the Torah,
the heritage of the community of Jacob.
God whose way is perfect,
whose word is proved,
a shield for all who seek refuge.

וְזֹאת הַתּוֹרָה אֲשֶׁר־שָׂם מֹשֶׁה
לִפְנֵי בְּנֵי יִשְׂרָאֵל:
תּוֹרָה צִוָּה־לָנוּ מֹשֶׁה.
מוֹרָשָׁה קְהִלַּת יַעֲקֹב:
הָאֵל תָּמִים דַּרְכּוֹ.
אִמְרַת יהוה צְרוּפָה.
מָגֵן הוּא לְכֹל הַחוֹסִים בּוֹ:

---

[1] I Sam 2:2, Ps 18:32, Deut 33:4, Pr 3:18, Pr 3:17.
[2] Ps 119:165.
[3] Ps 29:11.

Before reading the Torah:

בָּרְכוּ אֶת יהוה הַמְבֹרָךְ:

בָּרְכוּ Bless the One whom we are called to bless.

בָּרוּךְ יהוה הַמְבֹרָךְ לְעוֹלָם וָעֶד:

Blessed is the Living God, whom we are called to bless forever and ever.

בָּרוּךְ אַתָּה יהוה אֱלֹהֵינוּ מֶלֶךְ הָעוֹלָם. אֲשֶׁר בָּחַר־בָּנוּ מִכָּל־הָעַמִּים וְנָתַן־לָנוּ אֶת תּוֹרָתוֹ: בָּרוּךְ אַתָּה יהוה. נוֹתֵן הַתּוֹרָה:

Blessed are You, our Living God, Sovereign of the universe, who chose us from all peoples to give us Your Torah. Blessed are You God, who gives us the Torah.

After reading the Torah:

בָּרוּךְ אַתָּה יהוה אֱלֹהֵינוּ מֶלֶךְ הָעוֹלָם. אֲשֶׁר נָתַן־לָנוּ תּוֹרַת אֱמֶת וְחַיֵּי עוֹלָם נָטַע בְּתוֹכֵנוּ: בָּרוּךְ אַתָּה יהוה. נוֹתֵן הַתּוֹרָה:

בָּרוּךְ Blessed are You, our Living God, Sovereign of the universe, who gave us the teaching of truth and planted eternal life within us. Blessed are You God, who gives us the Torah.

The Sefer Torah may be raised here (Ashkenazi practice):

וְזֹאת הַתּוֹרָה אֲשֶׁר שָׂם מֹשֶׁה לִפְנֵי בְּנֵי יִשְׂרָאֵל. עַל פִּי יהוה בְּיַד מֹשֶׁה:

וְזֹאת This is the Torah that Moses set before the children of Israel, given by God through Moses.

91 WEEKDAY TORAH SERVICE

RETURN OF THE SCROLL

יְהַלְלוּ Praise the Almighty
whose name alone is supreme
and whose majesty
is beyond heaven and earth.
You have restored the honour
of Your people,
the praise of those who love You -
the children of Israel, a people
so close to You.
Praise God!

יְהַלְלוּ אֶת שֵׁם יהוה.
כִּי נִשְׂגָּב שְׁמוֹ לְבַדּוֹ:
הוֹדוֹ עַל אֶרֶץ וְשָׁמָיִם.
וַיָּרֶם קֶרֶן לְעַמּוֹ.
תְּהִלָּה לְכָל־חֲסִידָיו.
לִבְנֵי יִשְׂרָאֵל עַם קְרֹבוֹ.
הַלְלוּיָהּ:

When you call Me & come & pray to Me I will hear. When you seek Me you will find Me if you search for Me with all your heart & know that you find Me

Jeremiah 29: 12-14

כד

Psalm 24

לְדָוִד מִזְמוֹר
לַיהוה הָאָרֶץ וּמְלוֹאָהּ.
תֵּבֵל וְיֹשְׁבֵי בָהּ:
כִּי־הוּא עַל־יַמִּים יְסָדָהּ.
וְעַל־נְהָרוֹת יְכוֹנְנֶהָ:
מִי־יַעֲלֶה בְהַר־יהוה.
וּמִי־יָקוּם בִּמְקוֹם קָדְשׁוֹ:
נְקִי כַפַּיִם וּבַר־לֵבָב.
אֲשֶׁר לֹא־נָשָׂא לַשָּׁוְא נַפְשִׁי.
וְלֹא נִשְׁבַּע לְמִרְמָה:
יִשָּׂא בְרָכָה מֵאֵת יהוה.
וּצְדָקָה מֵאֱלֹהֵי יִשְׁעוֹ:
זֶה דּוֹר דֹּרְשָׁיו.
מְבַקְשֵׁי פָנֶיךָ יַעֲקֹב
סֶלָה:

שְׂאוּ שְׁעָרִים רָאשֵׁיכֶם.
וְהִנָּשְׂאוּ פִּתְחֵי עוֹלָם.
וְיָבוֹא מֶלֶךְ הַכָּבוֹד:
מִי זֶה מֶלֶךְ הַכָּבוֹד.
יהוה עִזּוּז וְגִבּוֹר.
יהוה גִּבּוֹר מִלְחָמָה:

שְׂאוּ שְׁעָרִים רָאשֵׁיכֶם.
וּשְׂאוּ פִּתְחֵי עוֹלָם.
וְיָבֹא מֶלֶךְ הַכָּבוֹד:
מִי הוּא זֶה מֶלֶךְ הַכָּבוֹד.
יהוה צְבָאוֹת.
הוּא מֶלֶךְ הַכָּבוֹד.
סֶלָה:

¹David's Psalm.
לַיהוה The earth and its fullness
belong to God,
the world and those who dwell in it,
²for it is the Creator
who set it on the seas
and made it firm upon the depths.
³Who may ascend the mountain of God
and who may stand in that holy place?
⁴Those whose hands are clean,
whose heart is pure,
who have not given up their soul
to worthless things
nor committed themselves to deception.
⁵They shall earn a blessing from the Creator
and be vindicated by God who saves them.
⁶This is a generation that searches for God,
those who seek Your presence
are the family of Jacob
(*selah*).

⁷Gates, lift up your heads!
Be raised, you everlasting doors!
Let the Ruler of glory enter!
⁸"Who is this Ruler of glory?"
God, strong and mighty,
God, mighty in battle!

⁹Gates, lift up your heads!
Rise up you everlasting doors!
Let the Ruler of glory enter!
¹⁰"Who then, is this Ruler of glory?"
The God of all creation,
this One alone is the Ruler of glory
(*selah*)!

93 WEEKDAY TORAH SERVICE

שְׁכֹן Be present among Your people,
and may Your spirit rest
in Your house of prayer.
For every voice and every tongue
will speak of the glory and majesty of
Your kingdom.
'For I have given you good instruction,
do not forsake My teaching.'[1]

'Turn us back to You, Eternal,
and we shall return;
renew our lives as of old.'[2]

שְׁכֹן יהוה בְּתוֹךְ עַמֶּךָ
וְתָנוּחַ רוּחֲךָ בְּבֵית תְּפִלָּתֶךָ.
כִּי כָל־פֶּה וְכָל־לָשׁוֹן
יִתְּנוּ הוֹד וְהָדָר לְמַלְכוּתֶךָ:
כִּי לֶקַח טוֹב נָתַתִּי לָכֶם.
תּוֹרָתִי אַל תַּעֲזֹבוּ:

הֲשִׁיבֵנוּ יהוה אֵלֶיךָ
וְנָשׁוּבָה.
חַדֵּשׁ יָמֵינוּ כְּקֶדֶם:

Concluding Prayers can be found on page 305.

---

[1] Prov 4:2.   [2] Lam 5:21.

94 סדר קריאת התורה לחול

שמע

תפלת ערבית לשבת
Shabbat Evening Service

לְכָה דוֹדִי לִקְרַאת כַּלָה.
פְּנֵי שַׁבָּת נְקַבְּלָה:

Come, my friend,
to greet the bride,
to welcome in the Shabbat eve.

The form of the Shabbat evening service has evolved over the centuries. The earliest components date back to the Jerusalem Temple. Psalm 93 was the daily Psalm chanted by the Levites in the Temple on 'the sixth day' of the week (Mishnah *Tamid* 7:4). The heading of Psalm 92, 'a Psalm to sing for the Shabbat day', indicates when it was read in the Biblical period. These two Psalms alone introduced the Shabbat in the Sephardi tradition. In Safed in the sixteenth century, mystical circles took up the Talmudic tradition of going into the fields to greet the Shabbat bride. They introduced the reading of six Psalms (95-99, 29), corresponding to the six days of the week. To these they added the song *L'chah dodi*, 'Come my friend, to greet the bride', with its messianic yearnings. We added the *zemirot*, the Shabbat table hymns, in the last edition of *Forms of Prayer,* and *chavurah* groups introduced the singing of the mystical hymn, *yedid nefesh*, 'Beloved of the soul', to set the mood for Shabbat.

BEFORE THE SERVICE BEGINS

Some thoughts to help prepare for the Shabbat Evening Service

'You have six days to labour and do all your work, but the seventh shall be a Shabbat for the Eternal your God' (Exodus 20:9).

We are invited to conduct our lives within God's time. Six days are available to work for our needs, one day is set aside for God. What was once a revolutionary event in the world is now a convention. So we need to rediscover the power and value of Shabbat in every generation, match our lives to this unchanging rhythm.

At Erev Shabbat we mark the transition, as we separate ourselves from the week that is past and shed its burdens and achievements. It is not easy to set them aside. Their demands and their energy still hold us in thrall. Letting go needs time and space and commitment. The stages of our service are there to help us leave one world behind so as to enter into another.

On this journey we join with others. The Opening Prayers belong to our own particular tradition of prayer, study and song. Shared words and voices, familiar and unfamiliar faces, replace the outer world of our individual lives with the inner life of our community.

To help put aside the six days we are leaving behind, we begin with six psalms that open *Kabbalat Shabbat*, the welcoming of the Shabbat. In sequence they convey their own story, drawing us into the world and values of Shabbat.

But on another level, each offers a space within which to think back on the days of the week that is past, to relive them for a moment and then consciously put them aside.

On yet another level we move the centre of our attention from ourselves to outside ourselves, from the ordinary to the sacred, from the mundane to the holy, however we understand it.

---
[1] Ex 20:9.

פתיחה לתפלה
OPENING PRAYERS

For Erev Shabbat ☰326

I

Our Creator, You have made us the masters of Your world, to tend it, to serve it, and to enjoy it. For six days we measure and we build, we count and carry the real and the imagined burdens of our task, the success we earn and the price we pay.

On this, the Shabbat day, give us rest.

For six days, if we are weary or bruised by the world, if we think ourselves giants or cause others pain, there is never a moment to pause, and know what we should really be.

On this, the Shabbat day, give us time.

For six days we are torn between our private greed and the urgent needs of others, between the foolish noises in our ears and the silent prayer of our soul.

On this, the Shabbat day, give us understanding and peace.

Help us, God, to carry these lessons, of rest and time, of understanding and peace, into the six days that lie ahead, to bless us in the working days of our lives.

II

Our God and God of our ancestors, we are all Israel; in Your service we have become old in experience and young in hope. We carry both in the deepest places of our hearts and minds. On this Shabbat day we turn to You with eyes newly open, with hope re-awakened, shrugging off the layers of worry and doubt that have closed about us.

We are all Israel, created by Your promise, raised in Your blessing, fulfilled by Your task, refreshed by the Shabbat of Your love.

We are all Israel, holy by Your word, wise through Your Torah, righteous through Your commands, renewed by the Shabbat of Your rest.

On this Shabbat day keep us; on this Shabbat day remember us; as we keep and remember the Shabbat day, to make it holy.

III

Creator of mercy and blessings, be present in our prayers this Shabbat eve. Shabbat joy follows the working week, and our troubled minds find their comfort and rest. With prayers and thanks we turn to You to make this day holy. Wipe away our sins in Your mercy, and strengthen our work for good. Cleanse us from selfishness, and give us new longing for all that is good and true. Enlighten the darkness that lies within us, and bring a blessing to our homes and to those we love. So may we keep Your covenant forever, for Your help is sure.

May the blessing of this Shabbat come not for ourselves alone but for all. For it is in giving that we find contentment, in serving that we find our true freedom, and in blessing others that we ourselves are blessed. Through us may the promise be fulfilled 'and all the families of the world shall bless themselves by You'.

IV

God of the spirits of all flesh, You are One, always and everywhere the same. We are multi-faceted, ever-changing, volatile. You have set within us instincts that drive us, emotions so that we feel, minds so that we think.

We give thanks for each of them: for our animal nature by which we experience hunger, thirst, and physical sensation; for our emotions of love, fear, joy and righteous indignation; and for our minds with their ability to distinguish between right and wrong, truth and falsehood. Yet these are forces which may pull us in many different directions, producing turmoil and indecision within ourselves, and conflict with others.

On this Shabbat, Your day of rest, help us to find rest and harmony for our inner selves, for our bodies, minds and spirits. Grant us the extra spiritual awareness that Shabbat brings. With this harmony in our heart, we pray that we may bring harmony to Your world, that our unity may mirror Yours.

V

We bless the God who conquers strife, who removes all hatred, and brings harmony to creation. We praise the God we cannot see, who binds together all creatures with unseen threads of service and of love. We honour the Creator who has brought us from ways of cruelty and shown us the ways of kindness. We bend low before the Majesty which teaches us humility and respect for the smallest things in creation. We glorify the Source of peace, for peace is the gate to our perfection, and in perfection is our rest.

God, open our eyes to the beauty of the world and its goodness. Let us be the servants of Your peace which brings all life together: the love of parent and child, the loyalty of friends, and the companionship of animals and people. On this Shabbat day of rest, we know this harmony again and Your presence within it. With all creation we respond in praise, and unify Your name.

VI

'On the seventh day, God finished the work of creation ...' The rabbis asked: *'What was the "work" that God did on the seventh day?'* They taught that God created m'nuchah, *'rest'*.

We turn to You, Creator of work and of rest. We seek to create Shabbat rest in our lives that is more than just an end to the working week. Let us dedicate a day to You alone, setting aside our busy-ness and our ambitions, our anxieties and our control.

May the rituals we take upon ourselves this day give our Shabbat form. May the Torah we study today give our Shabbat meaning. May the companionship we experience today give our Shabbat joy. Support us in all we do to create our Shabbat rest.

For these few precious hours may we experience ourselves once again as creatures in the presence of our Creator. May we celebrate the flow of life about us and within us. May we discover the rhythm of Shabbat and find the joy that comes from Your presence in our lives.

VII

Shabbat

Sometimes I am not ready
to receive you,
but you are already there ...

Sometimes the world, time, rushes by
and you are gone
before I ever noticed you ...

Sometimes everybody stands in front of me
and I cannot see you,
you were there, weren't you?

Sometimes we managed to arrive
together,
you are ready and I am rushed.

Sometimes there is suddenly a deep peace
and intense quiet by candlelight.
I whisper breathlessly: welcome.

Gut Shabbos!!

Sarah (Henriette Verdonk)

---

[1] Gen 2:2.

Some congregations begin the service here:

ACROSS THE THRESHOLD

DIRECTING THE HEART TO GOD

מַה־טֹּבוּ How good are your tents, O Jacob, and your homes, O Israel!

Through the greatness of Your love I enter Your house.
In awe of You I worship before the ark of Your holiness.

God, as I loved the courts of Your temple, and the place where Your glory dwelt, so I still worship and bend low, humble before the Eternal my Maker.

As for me, let my prayer come before You at the proper time.

Answer me God, in the greatness of Your love, for Your deliverance is sure.[1]

מַה־טֹּבוּ אֹהָלֶיךָ
יַעֲקֹב. מִשְׁכְּנֹתֶיךָ יִשְׂרָאֵל:
וַאֲנִי בְּרֹב חַסְדְּךָ אָבוֹא בֵיתֶךָ.
אֶשְׁתַּחֲוֶה אֶל־הֵיכַל־קָדְשְׁךָ
בְּיִרְאָתֶךָ:
יהוה אָהַבְתִּי מְעוֹן בֵּיתֶךָ.
וּמְקוֹם מִשְׁכַּן כְּבוֹדֶךָ:
וַאֲנִי אֶשְׁתַּחֲוֶה וְאֶכְרָעָה.
אֶבְרְכָה לִפְנֵי־יהוה עֹשִׂי:
וַאֲנִי תְפִלָּתִי־לְךָ יהוה עֵת רָצוֹן.
אֱלֹהִים בְּרָב־חַסְדֶּךָ.
עֲנֵנִי בֶּאֱמֶת יִשְׁעֶךָ:

מַה־טֹּבוּ *Mah tovu ohalecha ya'akov, mishk'notecha yisra'el.*
Va'ani b'rov chasd'cha avo veitecha, eshtachaveh el heichal kodsh'cha b'yir'atecha.
Adonai ahavti m'on beitecha, um'kom mishkan k'vodecha.
Va'ani eshtachaveh v'echra'ah, evr'chah lifnei Adonai osi.
Va'ani t'fillati l'cha Adonai eit ratson.
Elohim b'rov chasdecha, aneini be'emet yish'echa.

מַה־טֹּבוּ How good ...

This compilation of Biblical verses takes us on a journey through the different homes we have created in which to meet God: the Tent of Meeting in the wilderness, the holy temple in Jerusalem, the synagogues, houses of God, modest or magnificent, throughout the centuries, where prayers have replaced sacrifices, and nothing and no one is to stand between us and God.

This is a prayer we are invited to recite each time we cross the threshold from the outer world of the everyday to the inner world of the 'house of prayer'.

Three times the Hebrew emphasises *va'ani*, 'I', because with these words we make our own personal journey across time and space in search of 'the greatness of God's love'.

An alternative shorter version evokes the shared role played by patriarchs and matriarchs alike as the founders of the Jewish people.

[1] Num 24:5, Ps 5:8, Ps 26:8, Ps 95:6, Ps 69:14.

SHABBAT EVENING SERVICE — SONGS FOR WELCOMING SHABBAT

An alternative opening:

מַה־טֹּבוּ How good are your tents, O Jacob, and your homes, O Israel!
How good are your tents, O Leah, and your homes, O Rachel!

מַה־טֹּבוּ אֹהָלֶיךָ יַעֲקֹב.
מִשְׁכְּנֹתֶיךָ יִשְׂרָאֵל:
מַה־טֹּבוּ אֹהָלַיִךְ לֵאָה.
מִשְׁכְּנוֹתַיִךְ רָחֵל:

מַה־טֹּבוּ *Mah tovu ohalecha ya'akov, mishk'notecha yisra'el.*
Mah tovu ohalayich le'ah, mishk'notayich rachel.

Some congregations begin here:

שירים לקבלת שבת
SONGS FOR WELCOMING SHABBAT

One or more of the following Shabbat songs on pages 102-110 may be sung:

> The tradition of singing 'table songs' during and after the Friday evening meal goes back to the tenth century. With their mixture of Shabbat themes and often jolly melodies, they help create the unique experience of joy that is central to the Shabbat. We introduced them into the Friday evening service in the last edition of *Forms of Prayer* as a teaching device to help people learn them for their own use at home. The songs themselves reflect traditions that go back to the Talmudic period, to the kabbalistic circles in Safed in the sixteenth century, and to the revival of Hebrew in the twentieth century. They attest to the transformation in our life each week as the Shabbat enters with its opportunity for freedom and rest.

Yom zeh l'yisrael

יוֹם This day for Israel
is light and is joy ...
a Shabbat of rest.

You commanded our ancestors
standing at Sinai
to keep Shabbat and seasons
for all of our years,
to share at our table
the choicest of foods,
a Shabbat of rest. This day ...

Treasure for the hearts of
a wounded people,
for souls that have suffered,
an additional soul,
to soothe away sighs
from a soul that is bound,
a Shabbat of rest. This day...

You have made this the holy,
most blessed of days.
In six days You finished
the work of the worlds,
this day the saddest
find safety and peace,
a Shabbat of rest. This day ...

Isaac Luria

יוֹם זֶה לְיִשְׂרָאֵל
אוֹרָה וְשִׂמְחָה. שַׁבָּת מְנוּחָה:

צִוִּיתָ פִּקּוּדִים בְּמַעֲמַד סִינָי.
שַׁבָּת וּמוֹעֲדִים לִשְׁמֹר בְּכָל־שָׁנַי.
לַעֲרֹךְ לְפָנַי מַשְׂאֵת וַאֲרוּחָה.
שַׁבָּת מְנוּחָה:
יוֹם זֶה....

חֶמְדַּת הַלְּבָבוֹת לְאֻמָּה שְׁבוּרָה.
לִנְפָשׁוֹת נִכְאָבוֹת נְשָׁמָה יְתֵרָה.
לְנֶפֶשׁ מְצֵרָה יָסִיר אֲנָחָה.
שַׁבָּת מְנוּחָה:
יוֹם זֶה....

קִדַּשְׁתָּ בֵּרַכְתָּ אוֹתוֹ מִכָּל־יָמִים.
בְּשֵׁשֶׁת כִּלִּיתָ מְלֶאכֶת עוֹלָמִים.
בּוֹ מָצְאוּ עֲגוּמִים הַשְׁקֵט וּבִטְחָה.
שַׁבָּת מְנוּחָה:
יוֹם זֶה....

יצחק לוריא

יוֹם *Yom zeh l'yisra'el orah v'simchah, shabbat m'nuchah.*
Tsivita pikkudim b'ma'amad sinai, shabbat umo'adim lishmor b'chol shanai,
la'aroch l'fanai mas'eit va'aruchah, shabbat m'nuchah. Yom zeh...
Chemdat ha-l'vavot l'ummah sh'vurah, linfashot nich'avot n'shamah y'teirah,
l'nefesh m'tseirah yasir anachah, shabbat m'nuchah. Yom zeh...
Kiddashta beirachta oto mikkol yamim, b'sheishet killita m'lechet olamim,
bo matz'u agumim hashkeit uvitchah, shabbat m'nuchah. Yom zeh...

יוֹם זֶה לְיִשְׂרָאֵל This day for Israel ...
One of the songs to be sung after the evening meal of Shabbat, the opening letters of each verse together spell *Yitschak*, Isaac, indicating the name of the composer. It is assumed to be *Isaac Luria*, the sixteenth-century kabbalist who lived in Safed.

The Shabbat is more than simply a day of rest, it is a time of 'light and joy', a phrase taken from the Book of Esther, but here applied to Shabbat. For a people embittered by the struggle of life in exile, it offers a taste of freedom. For those worn down by the everyday demands of earning a living or providing for others, it offers the refreshment that comes with an additional Shabbat soul. It is the reward for our ancestors who stood at Mount Sinai and accepted the covenant with God.

103 SHABBAT EVENING SERVICE — SONGS FOR WELCOMING SHABBAT

Yah ribbon

יָהּ Sovereign of the world,
and timeless master,
You rule above all rulers we obey.

Many deeds of Your might,
and Your wonders,
it delights You to display.
Sovereign of the world ...

My praise I bring You,
morning and evening,
God who makes all of
Your creation live;
holy messengers,
each human being, beasts and birds
their form You give.
Sovereign of the world ...

Numberless and powerful
are Your actions.
The proud You teach humility,
the weak You raise.
If our years would be a thousand
we could not express Your praise.
Sovereign of the world ...

יָהּ רִבּוֹן
יָהּ רִבּוֹן עָלַם וְעָלְמַיָּא.
אַנְתְּ הוּא מַלְכָּא מֶלֶךְ מַלְכַיָּא:

עוֹבַד גְּבוּרְתֵּךְ וְתִמְהַיָּא.
שַׁפִּיר קֳדָמָךְ לְהַחֲוָיָה:
יָהּ רִבּוֹן...

שְׁבָחִין אֲסַדֵּר צַפְרָא וְרַמְשָׁא.
לָךְ אֱלָהָא קַדִּישָׁא
דִּי בְרָא כָל־נַפְשָׁא.
עִירִין קַדִּישִׁין וּבְנֵי אֱנָשָׁא.
חֵיוַת בָּרָא וְעוֹפֵי שְׁמַיָּא:
יָהּ רִבּוֹן...

רַבְרְבִין עוֹבְדָיךְ וְתַקִּיפִין.
מָכֵךְ רָמַיָּא זָקֵף כְּפִיפִין.
לוּ יְחֵא גְבַר שְׁנִין אַלְפִין.
לָא יֵעוֹל גְּבוּרְתֵּךְ בְּחֻשְׁבְּנַיָּא:
יָהּ רִבּוֹן...

Israel Najara — ישראל נג'רה

יָהּ *Yah ribbon alam v'almaya, ant hu malka melech malchaya.*
Ovad g'vurteich v'timhaya, shappir kodamach l'hachavayah. Yah ribbon ...
Sh'vachin asaddeir tsafra v'ramsha, lach elaha kaddisha di v'ra chol nafsha,
irin kaddishin uv'nei enasha, cheivat bara v'ofei sh'maya. Yah ribbon ...
Ravr'vin ovdayich v'takkifin, macheich ramayah zakeif k'fifin,
lu y'chei g'var sh'nin alfin, la yei'ol g'vurteich b'chashbanaya. Yah ribbon ...

יָהּ רִבּוֹן Sovereign of the world ...
Composed in Aramaic, the opening letters of the verses, *yod, shin, resh*, indicate the name *Yisrael*, the author being the sixteenth-century poet Israel Najara. It is a hymn of praise to God the Creator of heavenly and earthly beings, of beasts and birds. Were we to live even a thousand years, no human being could adequately express the praise due to God.

Shalom aleichem

שָׁלוֹם עֲלֵיכֶם

שָׁלוֹם עֲלֵיכֶם

מַלְאֲכֵי הַשָּׁרֵת מַלְאֲכֵי עֶלְיוֹן
[מִ]מֶּלֶךְ מַלְכֵי הַמְּלָכִים
הַקָּדוֹשׁ בָּרוּךְ הוּא:

שָׁלוֹם Peace
and welcome to you,
servants of God,
messengers of the Most High,
Ruler above all earthly rulers,
the Holy One of blessing.

בּוֹאֲכֶם לְשָׁלוֹם מַלְאֲכֵי הַשָּׁלוֹם
מַלְאֲכֵי עֶלְיוֹן
[מִ]מֶּלֶךְ מַלְכֵי הַמְּלָכִים
הַקָּדוֹשׁ בָּרוּךְ הוּא:

Enter in peace,
you servants of peace,
messengers of the Most High,
Ruler above all earthly rulers,
the Holy One of blessing.

בָּרְכוּנִי לְשָׁלוֹם מַלְאֲכֵי הַשָּׁלוֹם
מַלְאֲכֵי עֶלְיוֹן
[מִ]מֶּלֶךְ מַלְכֵי הַמְּלָכִים
הַקָּדוֹשׁ בָּרוּךְ הוּא:

Bless me with peace,
you servants of peace,
messengers of the Most High,
Ruler above all earthly rulers,
the Holy One of blessing.

צֵאתְכֶם לְשָׁלוֹם מַלְאֲכֵי הַשָּׁלוֹם
מַלְאֲכֵי עֶלְיוֹן
[מִ]מֶּלֶךְ מַלְכֵי הַמְּלָכִים
הַקָּדוֹשׁ בָּרוּךְ הוּא:

Go forth in peace,
you servants of peace,
messengers of the Most High,
Ruler above all earthly rulers,
the Holy One of blessing.

שָׁלוֹם *Shalom aleichem mal'achei ha-shareit mal'achei elyon*
mimelech malchei ha-m'lachim ha-kadosh baruch hu.
Bo'achem l'shalom mal'achei ha-shalom mal'achei elyon
mimelech malchei ha-m'lachim ha-kadosh baruch hu.
Bar'chuni l'shalom mal'achei ha-shalom mal'achei elyon
mimelech malchei ha-m'lachim ha-kadosh baruch hu.
Tseit'chem l'shalom mal'achei ha-shalom mal'achei elyon
mimelech malchei ha-m'lachim ha-kadosh baruch hu.

שָׁלוֹם עֲלֵיכֶם Peace and welcome to you ...
This song, which first appears in the seventeenth century, is based on a Talmudic legend. When returning home from the synagogue on Friday evening, two angels, a good angel and a bad angel, accompany us. If we find everything prepared for the Shabbat meal, the good angel prays to God that next week's Shabbat will also be like this and the bad angel has to say 'Amen', 'so be it'. But if things are not prepared, the opposite occurs (*Shabbat* 119b). Hence we sing: 'Bless me with peace.'

Though the original text reads *melech*, 'king', the familiar tune to which it is sung and the sense require the extra syllable *mi-melech*, 'from the king'.

105 SHABBAT EVENING SERVICE — SONGS FOR WELCOMING SHABBAT

Shabbat ha-malkah

הַחַמָּה The sun on the treetops
no longer is seen.
Come out, let us
greet the Shabbat, the queen.
See! she descends,
the holy, the blessed,
her messengers with her,
of peace and of rest.
Welcome! welcome the queen!
Welcome! welcome the bride!
Peace be with you,
messengers of peace!

We received the Shabbat
with song and with prayer,
to our homes we bring hearts
filled with gladness to share.
The table is set there,
the candles are bright,
each corner is shining,
the house spreads its light.
Shabbat of peace and blessing,
Shabbat of peace and rest.
Enter in peace,
messengers of peace!

שַׁבָּת הַמַּלְכָּה

הַחַמָּה מֵרֹאשׁ
הָאִילָנוֹת נִסְתַּלְּקָה.
בֹּאוּ וְנֵצֵא לִקְרַאת שַׁבָּת הַמַּלְכָּה:
הִנֵּה הִיא יוֹרֶדֶת.
הַקְּדוֹשָׁה הַבְּרוּכָה.
וְעִמָּהּ מַלְאָכִים.
צְבָא שָׁלוֹם וּמְנוּחָה:
בֹּאִי. בֹּאִי הַמַּלְכָּה:
בֹּאִי. בֹּאִי הַכַּלָּה:
שָׁלוֹם עֲלֵיכֶם מַלְאֲכֵי הַשָּׁלוֹם:

קִבַּלְנוּ פְּנֵי שַׁבָּת בִּרְנָנָה וּתְפִלָּה.
הַבַּיְתָה נָשׁוּבָה בְּלֵב מָלֵא גִילָה:
שָׁם עָרוּךְ הַשֻּׁלְחָן.
הַנֵּרוֹת יָאִירוּ.
כָּל־פִּנּוֹת הַבַּיִת יִזְרְחוּ. יַזְהִירוּ:
שַׁבָּת שָׁלוֹם וּבְרָכָה.
שַׁבָּת שָׁלוֹם וּמְנוּחָה:
בּוֹאֲכֶם לְשָׁלוֹם מַלְאֲכֵי הַשָּׁלוֹם:

Chaim Nachman Bialik — חיים נחמן ביאליק

הַחַמָּה Ha-chammah meirosh ha-ilanot nistall'kah.
Bo'u v'neitsei likrat Shabbat ha-malkah. Hinnei hi yoredet, ha-k'doshah ha-b'ruchah,
v'immah mal'achim tz'va shalom um'nuchah.
Bo'i bo'i ha-malkah. Bo'i bo'i ha-kallah.
Shalom aleichem mal'achei ha-shalom.
Kibbalnu p'nei Shabbat birnanah ut'fillah. Ha-bay'tah nashuvah b'leiv malei gilah.
Sham aruch ha-shulchan ha-neirot ya'iru. Kol pinnot ha-bayit yizrachu yazhiru.
Shabbat shalom uv'racha. Shabbat shalom um'nuchah.
Bo'achem l'shalom mal'achei ha-shalom.

שַׁבָּת הַמַּלְכָּה **The Shabbat Queen ...**
This is the most recent addition to the Shabbat songs, composed by the poet Chaim Nachman Bialik. The familiar phrase *oneg Shabbat*, used today to describe a wide range of Shabbat celebrations, often on Friday evening, was originally coined by Bialik for cultural programmes in Tel Aviv, though based on a phrase in Isaiah 58:13. It echoes the rabbinic and later kabbalistic tradition that we should go outside to greet the Shabbat that comes to us like a bride. Like the song *Shalom Aleichem*, it is also based on the legends of the angels that accompany us homeward from the synagogue on Friday evening.

שירים לקבלת שבת　　　　　　　　　　　　תפלת ערבית לשבת

מפי אל

Mipi Eil

אֵין **None so mighty as our God**
אֵין אַדִּיר כַּאדֹנָי
and none so blessed as Amram's son;
וְאֵין בָּרוּךְ כְּבֶן עַמְרָם.
nothing noble like Torah;
אֵין גְּדוֹלָה כַּתּוֹרָה
none seek its ways like Israel.
וְאֵין דּוֹרְשֶׁיהָ כְּיִשְׂרָאֵל:

   From the mouth of God,
   from the mouth of God
   blessing for all Israel.
   מִפִּי אֵל. מִפִּי אֵל
   יְבֹרַךְ כָּל־יִשְׂרָאֵל:

None so splendid as our God
אֵין הָדוּר כַּאדֹנָי
and none esteemed like Amram's son;
וְאֵין וָתִיק כְּבֶן עַמְרָם.
nothing faultless like Torah;
אֵין זַכָּה כַּתּוֹרָה
none know its ways like Israel.
וְאֵין חֲכָמֶיהָ כְּיִשְׂרָאֵל:

   From the mouth of God ...
   מִפִּי אֵל...

None so perfect as our God
אֵין טָהוֹר כַּאדֹנָי
and none unique like Amram's son;
וְאֵין יָחִיד כְּבֶן עַמְרָם.
nothing awesome like Torah;
אֵין כַּבִּירָה כַּתּוֹרָה
none learn its ways like Israel.
וְאֵין לוֹמְדֶיהָ כְּיִשְׂרָאֵל:

   From the mouth of God ...
   מִפִּי אֵל...

None so regal as our God
אֵין מֶלֶךְ כַּאדֹנָי
none prophesied like Amram's son;
וְאֵין נָבִיא כְּבֶן עַמְרָם.
nothing treasured like Torah;
אֵין סְגֻלָּה כַּתּוֹרָה
none use its ways like Israel.
וְאֵין עוֹסְקֶיהָ כְּיִשְׂרָאֵל:

   From the mouth of God ...
   מִפִּי אֵל...

<<<

מִפִּי אֵל From the mouth of God ...
   This alphabetic poem, of unknown authorship, was originally transmitted orally, and variations exist in both Ashkenazi and Sephardi traditions. The linking together of God (*Adonai*), Moses (*ben Amram*, the son of Amram), the Torah and Israel, and the chorus *mipi eil*, from the mouth of God, relates it to the revelation at Sinai and the festival of *Shavuot*. However, it is sung in both traditions during the *Hakkafot*, the circuits carrying the Torah scrolls, on *Simchat Torah*.

SHABBAT EVENING SERVICE — SONGS FOR WELCOMING SHABBAT

None redeems us as our God	אֵין פּוֹדֶה כַּאדֹנָי
and none is just like Amram's son;	וְאֵין צַדִּיק כְּבֶן עַמְרָם.
nothing holy like Torah;	אֵין קְדוֹשָׁה כַּתּוֹרָה
none praise its ways like Israel.	וְאֵין רוֹמְמֶיהָ כְּיִשְׂרָאֵל:
From the mouth of God ...	מִפִּי אֵל...
None so holy as our God	אֵין קָדוֹשׁ כַּאדֹנָי
and none can teach like Amram's son;	וְאֵין רַבִּי כְּבֶן עַמְרָם.
nothing shelters like Torah;	אֵין שְׁמִירָה כַּתּוֹרָה
none keep its ways like Israel.	וְאֵין תּוֹמְכֶיהָ כְּיִשְׂרָאֵל:
From the mouth of God, from the mouth of God blessing for all Israel.	מִפִּי אֵל. מִפִּי אֵל יְבָרֵךְ כָּל־יִשְׂרָאֵל:

Alphabetic acrostic. Author unknown.

אֵין *Ein addir kadonai, v'ein baruch k'ven amram*
ein g'dolah ka-torah, v'ein dor'sheha k'yisra'el.
Mipi eil mipi eil y'vorach kol yisra'el.

Ein hadur kadonai, v'ein vatik k'ven amram
ein zakkah ka-torah, v'ein chachameha k'yisra'el.
Mipi eil ...

Ein tahor kadonai, v'ein yachid k'ven amram
ein kabbirah ka-torah, v'ein lom'deha k'yisra'el.
Mipi eil ...

Ein melech kadonai, v'ein navi k'ven amram
ein s'gulah ka-torah, v'ein os'keha k'yisra'el.
Mipi eil ...

Ein podeh kadonai, v'ein tsaddik k'ven amram
ein k'dushah ka-torah, v'ein rom'meha k'yisra'el.
Mipi eil ...

Ein kadosh kadonai, v'ein rabbi k'ven amram
ein sh'mirah ka-torah, v'ein tom'cheha k'yisra'el.
Mipi eil mipi eil, y'vorach kol yisra'el.

Tsam'ah nafshi

צָמְאָה נַפְשִׁי

¹צָמְאָה My soul thirsts for God,
the living God.

א צָמְאָה נַפְשִׁי
לֵאלֹהִים לְאֵל חָי.

My heart and flesh sing praise
to the God ever living.

לִבִּי וּבְשָׂרִי יְרַנְּנוּ לְאֵל חָי:

²Our creator is One, who said:
'As I live, none can behold Me
and remain among the living.'
My heart ...

ב אֵל אֶחָד בְּרָאָנִי. וְאָמַר חַי אָנִי.
כִּי לֹא יִרְאַנִי הָאָדָם וָחָי:
לִבִּי ...

³All is made by God's plan,
by God's wisdom and thought,
deeply hidden
from the eyes of the living.
My heart ...

ג בָּרָא כֹל בְּחָכְמָה. בְּעֵצָה וּבִמְזִמָּה.
מְאֹד נֶעֶלְמָה מֵעֵינֵי כָל־חָי:
לִבִּי ...

⁴How can we who are likened to dust
plead our cause?
Truly none can be just
in the world of the living.
My heart ...

ד מִי זֶה יִצְטַדָּק. נִמְשַׁל לְאָבָק דַּק.
אֱמֶת כִּי לֹא יִצְדַּק לְפָנֶיךָ כָל־חָי:
לִבִּי ...

⁵I thank and praise You,
together with all who acclaim You,
for Your hand is ever open
to satisfy all living.

ה עַל כֹּל אֲהוֹדֶךָ. כָּל־פֶּה תְּיַחֲדֶךָ.
פּוֹתֵחַ אֶת־יָדֶךָ. וּמַשְׂבִּיעַ לְכָל־חָי:

My heart and flesh sing praise
to the God ever living.

לִבִּי וּבְשָׂרִי יְרַנְּנוּ לְאֵל חָי:

Abraham ibn Ezra   אברהם אבן־עזרא

¹צָמְאָה *Tsam'ah nafshi leilohim l'eil chai, libbi uv'sari y'ran'nu l'eil chai.*
²*Eil echad b'ra'ani v'amar chai ani, ki lo yir'ani ha-adam vachai. Libbi ...*
³*Bara chol b'chochmah, b'eitsah uvim'zimmah,*
 m'od ne'elmah mei'einei chol chai. Libbi ...
⁴*Mi zeh yitstaddak, nimshal l'avak dak, emet ki lo yitsdak l'fanecha chol chai. Libbi ...*
⁵*Al kol ahodecha, kol peh t'yachadecha, potei'ach et yadecha umasbi'a l'chol chai.*
 Libbi uv'sari y'ran'nu l'eil chai.

צָמְאָה נַפְשִׁי My soul thirsts ...
One of the more solemn of the Shabbat table songs, it is ascribed to the mediaeval Biblical scholar Abraham ibn Ezra, based on the initial letters of each line of the full version. The image of soul, heart and flesh thirsting to be with God is derived from Psalm 63:2. It contains the kabbalistic idea that though God has created the world in wisdom, the ultimate meaning is hidden from human beings.

SHABBAT EVENING SERVICE — SONGS FOR WELCOMING SHABBAT

Some congregations begin the service here:

Y'did nefesh — יְדִיד נֶפֶשׁ

[1] **יְדִיד** Beloved of the soul,
source of mercy,
draw Your servant
to do Your will,
to run to You swift as a hart,
to bow down low
before Your majesty,
finding Your love
sweeter than the honeycomb
and every tempting savour.

[2] Exquisitely beautiful
is the splendour of the world.
My soul pines for Your love.
O God, heal it, I pray You,
by showing it
the delight of Your splendour,
then will it grow strong and be healed
and rejoice evermore.

[3] O mighty One! Manifest Your mercies
and have compassion
upon Your beloved child.
For oh how long
have I been consumed with longing
to behold the triumph of Your might!
These things my heart desires,
take pity and hide not Yourself.

אְיְדִיד נֶפֶשׁ
אַב הָרַחֲמָן
מְשׁוֹךְ עַבְדְּךָ אֶל רְצוֹנֶךָ.
יָרוּץ עַבְדְּךָ כְּמוֹ אַיָּל
יִשְׁתַּחֲוֶה אֶל מוּל הֲדָרֶךָ.
יֶעֱרַב לוֹ יְדִידוֹתֶיךָ
מִנֹּפֶת צוּף וְכָל־טָעַם:

בהָדוּר נָאֶה זִיו הָעוֹלָם
נַפְשִׁי חוֹלַת אַהֲבָתֶךָ.
אָנָּא אֵל נָא רְפָא נָא לָהּ
בְּהַרְאוֹת לָהּ נֹעַם זִיוֶךָ.
אָז תִּתְחַזֵּק וְתִתְרַפֵּא
וְהָיְתָה לָהּ שִׂמְחַת עוֹלָם:

גוָתִיק יֶהֱמוּ נָא רַחֲמֶיךָ
וְחוּסָה נָּא עַל בֵּן אֲהוּבֶךָ.
כִּי זֶה כַּמָּה נִכְסוֹף נִכְסַפְתִּי
לִרְאוֹת בְּתִפְאֶרֶת עֻזֶּךָ.
אֵלֶּה חָמְדָה לִבִּי
וְחוּסָה נָּא וְאַל תִּתְעַלָּם:

<<<

[1] **יְדִיד** Y'did nefesh av ha-rachaman, m'shoch avd'cha el r'tson'cha.
Yaruts avd'cha k'mo ayal, yishtachaveh el mul hadar'cha,
ye'erav lo y'didotecha, minofet tsuf v'chol ta'am.
[2] Hadur na'eh ziv ha-olam, nafshi cholat ahavat'cha.
Anna eil na r'fa na lah, b'har'ot lah no'am ziv'cha.
Az titchazeik v'titrappei, v'hay'tah lah simchat olam.
[3] Vatik yehemu na rachamecha, v'chusah na al bein ahuv'cha,
ki zeh kammah nichsof nichsafti, lir'ot b'tif'eret uzz'cha.
Eilleh cham'dah libbi, v'chusah na v'al tit'alleim

יְדִיד נֶפֶשׁ Beloved of the soul ...

Rabbi Eliezer Azikri composed this poem, strongly based on kabbalistic traditions, in the sixteenth century. The poet who is consumed by longing to be ever closer to his Beloved fills it with expressions of love for God. But his personal desire embraces the hope that the whole world will come to rejoice in the light that comes from God. The acrostic spells out יהוה, God's name.

⁴הִגָּלֵה נָא וּפְרוֹס חֲבִיבִי עָלַי
אֶת־סֻכַּת שְׁלוֹמֶךָ.
תָּאִיר אֶרֶץ מִכְּבוֹדֶךָ
נָגִילָה וְנִשְׂמְחָה בָּךְ.
מַהֵר אֱהוֹב כִּי בָא מוֹעֵד
וְחָנֵּנוּ כִּימֵי עוֹלָם:

⁴Reveal Yourself, O adored One,
and spread over me
the tent of Your peace.
May the earth be illumined
with Your glory
and let us be glad and rejoice in You.
Hasten to show Your love;
and be gracious to us
as in the days gone by.

Eliezer Azikri אליעזר אזקרי

⁴*Higgaleih na uf'ros chavivi alai et sukkat sh'lom'cha.
Ta'ir erets mik'vod'cha, nagilah v'nism'cha bach.
Maheir ehov ki va mo'eid, v'chonneinu kimei olam.*

מזמורים לקבלת שבת
THE PSALMS FOR WELCOMING SHABBAT ☧326

One or more of the following Psalms may be read:

> The mystics of Safed in the sixteenth century created this order of service, beginning with six psalms that, in one interpretation, represent the six days of the week we are leaving behind.
>
> Two of the Psalms, 97 and 99, share with Psalm 93, traditionally read on the eve of Shabbat, the opening words 'The Eternal rules.' They speak of God's rule in the world as already established, justice and righteousness being the 'foundations of God's throne' (Psalm 97:2). In the imagery God is moving closer to us, finally settling in the temple in Jerusalem, God's 'footstool' on earth (Psalm 99:5). But two of the other Psalms, 96 and 98, are expressed as hymns, inviting us to 'Sing to the Eternal a new song'. This invitation is addressed to all the nations of the world in Psalm 96, whereas Psalm 98 focuses on God's loyalty to Israel. It is possible that these two Psalms acted as a kind of sung chorus celebrating the arrival of God described in the other two Psalms, as part of an elaborate liturgy in the temple itself. Together they speak of the enthronement of God in the world, either as an expression of an ongoing reality or of a hope for the future.
>
> Within the service itself this series of Psalms helps us move the centre of our attention from ourselves and the everyday events of the week that is past to beyond ourselves, from the ordinary to the sacred.

SHABBAT EVENING SERVICE — THE PSALMS FOR WELCOMING SHABBAT

Psalm 95

¹ **לְכוּ** Come let us sing out to the Eternal,
call out to the rock of our safety.
² Let us come before God with thanks,
call out to God with psalms.
³ For the Eternal is almighty God,
a mighty ruler
beyond all gods.
⁴ The depths of the earth
are in God's hand
and also the mountain peaks.
⁵ The sea is God's,
it is God who made it,
whose power has shaped the land.
⁶ Come in, let us worship and bend low,
humble before the Eternal our Maker.
⁷ For such is our God
and we are a people God pastures,
a flock in God's hand.
⁸ Today ...
if you would only hear God's voice!

צה
אלְכוּ נְרַנְּנָה לַיהוה
נָרִיעָה לְצוּר יִשְׁעֵנוּ:
בנְקַדְּמָה פָנָיו בְּתוֹדָה
בִּזְמִרוֹת נָרִיעַ לוֹ:
גכִּי אֵל גָּדוֹל יהוה
וּמֶלֶךְ גָּדוֹל
עַל־כָּל־אֱלֹהִים:
דאֲשֶׁר בְּיָדוֹ מֶחְקְרֵי־אָרֶץ
וְתוֹעֲפוֹת הָרִים לוֹ:
האֲשֶׁר־לוֹ הַיָּם וְהוּא עָשָׂהוּ
וְיַבֶּשֶׁת יָדָיו יָצָרוּ:
ובֹּאוּ נִשְׁתַּחֲוֶה וְנִכְרָעָה
נִבְרְכָה לִפְנֵי יהוה עֹשֵׂנוּ:
זכִּי הוּא אֱלֹהֵינוּ
וַאֲנַחְנוּ עַם מַרְעִיתוֹ וְצֹאן יָדוֹ
חהַיּוֹם
אִם־בְּקֹלוֹ תִשְׁמָעוּ:

<<<

¹ **לְכוּ** L'chu n'rann'nah ladonai, nari'ah l'tsur yish'einu.
² N'kadd'mah fanav b'todah, bizmirot nari'a lo.
³ Ki eil gadol Adonai, umelech gadol al kol elohim.
⁴ Asher b'yado mechk'rei arets v'to'afot harim lo.
⁵ Asher lo ha-yam v'hu asahu, v'yabeshet yadav yatsaru.
⁶ Bo'u nishtachaveh v'nichra'ah, nivr'chah lifnei Adonai oseinu.
⁷ Ki hu eloheinu, va'anachnu am mar'ito v'tson yado,
⁸ ha-yom im b'kolo tishma'u.

צה Psalm 95

We turn to God as Creator of the physical world and of ourselves as a people. Yet it ends with a shock, the recollection of past rebellion, and a distancing from God that may last until today. The final word of the Psalm defines the outer world as the opposite of Shabbat, a place without true 'rest'. Reform circles have tended to omit the last section (verses 9-12), preferring to end with the call to listen to God's voice today (verse 8).

Some congregations add verses 9-12:

⁹אַל־תַּקְשׁוּ לְבַבְכֶם כִּמְרִיבָה
כְּיוֹם מַסָּה בַּמִּדְבָּר:
י׳אֲשֶׁר נִסּוּנִי אֲבוֹתֵיכֶם
בְּחָנוּנִי גַּם־רָאוּ פָעֳלִי:
י״אאַרְבָּעִים שָׁנָה אָקוּט בְּדוֹר
וָאֹמַר עַם תֹּעֵי לֵבָב הֵם
וְהֵם לֹא־יָדְעוּ דְרָכָי:
י״באֲשֶׁר־נִשְׁבַּעְתִּי בְאַפִּי
אִם־יְבֹאוּן אֶל־מְנוּחָתִי:

⁹Do not harden your hearts
  as at Meribah,
  as that day at Massah
  in the wilderness.
¹⁰When your ancestors challenged
  Me, tested Me, despite
  having seen all that I had done.
¹¹Forty years I was provoked by
  that generation, thinking
  'A people whose heart confounds
  them, they cannot understand
  My ways.'
¹²That's when I swore
  in My anger 'They will never
  come to the rest I wish for them!'

⁹*Al takshu l'vavchem kimrivah, k'yom massah ba-midbar.*
¹⁰*Asher nissuni avoteichem, b'chanuni gam ra'u fo'oli.*
¹¹*Arba'im shanah akut b'dor, va'omar am to'ei leivav heim,*
  v'heim lo yad'u d'rachai.
¹²*Asher nishba'ti v'api, im y'vo'un el m'nuchati.*

Psalm 96

צו

¹שִׁירוּ **Sing to the Eternal a new song,**
sing to the Eternal all the earth.
²Sing to the Eternal, bless God's name,
proclaim God's salvation day after day.
³Describe God's glory among the nations
and God's wonders among all peoples.

אשִׁירוּ לַיהוה שִׁיר חָדָשׁ
שִׁירוּ לַיהוה כָּל־הָאָרֶץ:
בשִׁירוּ לַיהוה בָּרְכוּ שְׁמוֹ
בַּשְּׂרוּ מִיּוֹם־לְיוֹם יְשׁוּעָתוֹ:
גסַפְּרוּ בַגּוֹיִם כְּבוֹדוֹ
בְּכָל־הָעַמִּים נִפְלְאוֹתָיו:

<<<

צו Psalm 96

The Psalm comes to us with voices from outside our narrow world. All people and faiths are called upon to sing a new song to God. They are invited to admit how limited are the gods they call their own, and in their place to enter the sanctuary we know as our own place to meet God. But why this God amongst so many? Because God is the guarantor of justice, the one value that can mediate the tensions that arise between nations and within them, the universal language we need in an unredeemed world.

Personally we may ask, what was the new song we sang in the week that is past? What did we learn? How did we deal with those about us? What did we give to others?

SHABBAT EVENING SERVICE — THE PSALMS FOR WELCOMING SHABBAT

⁴For great is the Almighty
and praised aloud,
awesome beyond all gods.
⁵For all the peoples' gods
are false gods,
but the Creator has made the heavens.
⁶Splendour and radiance
are in God's presence,
strength and beauty
in God's holy place.

⁷כִּי גָדוֹל יְהוָה וּמְהֻלָּל מְאֹד
נוֹרָא הוּא עַל־כָּל־אֱלֹהִים:
⁵כִּי כָּל־אֱלֹהֵי הָעַמִּים אֱלִילִים
וַיהוָה שָׁמַיִם עָשָׂה:
⁶הוֹד וְהָדָר לְפָנָיו
עֹז וְתִפְאֶרֶת בְּמִקְדָּשׁוֹ:

⁷Give to the Eternal,
you races and peoples,
give to the Eternal
glory and strength.
⁸Give to the Eternal
the glory due to God's name,
bear an offering
and enter God's courts.
⁹Worship the Eternal
in the radiance of holiness,
tremble before God all the earth.
¹⁰Say among the nations
'The Eternal rules!'
The world too is set firm
and cannot be shaken.
God will judge the peoples
with justice.

⁷הָבוּ לַיהוָה מִשְׁפְּחוֹת עַמִּים
הָבוּ לַיהוָה כָּבוֹד וָעֹז:
⁸הָבוּ לַיהוָה כְּבוֹד שְׁמוֹ
שְׂאוּ־מִנְחָה וּבֹאוּ לְחַצְרוֹתָיו:
⁹הִשְׁתַּחֲווּ לַיהוָה בְּהַדְרַת־קֹדֶשׁ
חִילוּ מִפָּנָיו כָּל־הָאָרֶץ:
¹⁰אִמְרוּ בַגּוֹיִם יְהוָה מָלָךְ
אַף־תִּכּוֹן תֵּבֵל בַּל־תִּמּוֹט
יָדִין עַמִּים בְּמֵישָׁרִים:

<<<

¹שִׁירוּ Shiru ladonai shir chadash, shiru ladonai kol ha-arets.
²Shiru ladonai bar'chu sh'mo, bass'ru miyom l'yom y'shu'ato.
³Sapp'ru va-goyim k'vodo, b'chol ha-ammim nifl'otav.
⁴Ki gadol Adonai um'hullal m'od, nora hu al kol elohim.
⁵Ki kol elohei ha-ammim elilim, vadonai shamayim asah.
⁶Hod v'hadar l'fanav, oz v'tif'eret b'mikdasho.

⁷Havu ladonai mishp'chot ammim, havu ladonai kavod va'oz.
⁸Havu ladonai k'vod sh'mo, s'u minchah uvo'u l'chatsrotav.
⁹Hishtachavu ladonai b'hadrat kodesh, chilu mipanav kol ha-arets.
¹⁰Imru va-goyim Adonai malach, af tikkon teiveil bal timmot,
yadin ammim b'meisharim

¹¹יִשְׂמְחוּ הַשָּׁמַיִם וְתָגֵל הָאָרֶץ
יִרְעַם הַיָּם וּמְלֹאוֹ:
¹²יַעֲלֹז שָׂדַי וְכָל־אֲשֶׁר־בּוֹ
אָז יְרַנְּנוּ כָּל־עֲצֵי־יָעַר:
¹³לִפְנֵי יהוה כִּי בָא
כִּי בָא לִשְׁפֹּט הָאָרֶץ
יִשְׁפֹּט־תֵּבֵל בְּצֶדֶק
וְעַמִּים בֶּאֱמוּנָתוֹ:

¹¹Let the heavens rejoice
and the earth delight,
let the sea thunder in its fullness.
¹²Let the field be glad and all within it,
let all trees of the forest sing out
¹³at the presence of the Creator
who comes,
who comes to judge the earth.
God will judge the world
with righteousness
and the peoples with truth.

¹¹Yism'chu ha-shamayim v'tageil ha-arets, yir'am ha-yam um'lo'o.
¹²Ya'aloz sadai v'chol asher bo, az y'rann'nu kol atsei ya'ar.
¹³Lifnei Adonai ki va, ki va lishpot ha-arets
yishpot teiveil b'tsedek, v'ammim be'emunato

צז

ᵃיהוה מָלָךְ תָּגֵל הָאָרֶץ
יִשְׂמְחוּ אִיִּים רַבִּים:
ᵇעָנָן וַעֲרָפֶל סְבִיבָיו
צֶדֶק וּמִשְׁפָּט מְכוֹן כִּסְאוֹ:
ᶜאֵשׁ לְפָנָיו תֵּלֵךְ
וּתְלַהֵט סָבִיב צָרָיו:
ᵈהֵאִירוּ בְרָקָיו תֵּבֵל
רָאֲתָה וַתָּחֵל הָאָרֶץ:
ᵉהָרִים כַּדּוֹנַג נָמַסּוּ
מִלִּפְנֵי יהוה
מִלִּפְנֵי אֲדוֹן
כָּל־הָאָרֶץ:

Psalm 97

¹יהוה The Eternal rules,
let the earth be glad,
let the many isles rejoice!
² Clouds and darkness surround God,
but righteousness and justice
are the foundations of God's throne.
³Fire strides before God,
blazing round all foes.
⁴God's lightning lights up the world,
the earth sees and trembles.
⁵Mountains melt like wax
before the Creator,
before the Sovereign
of all the earth.

<<<

¹יהוה Adonai malach, tageil ha-arets, yism'chu iyim rabbim.
²Anan va'arafel s'vivav, tsedek umishpat m'chon kis'o.
³Eish l'fanav teileich, ut'laheit saviv tsarav.
⁴Hei'iru v'rakav teiveil, ra'attah vatacheil ha-arets.
⁵Harim ka-donag namassu, millifnei Adonai, millifnei adon kol ha-arets.

115 SHABBAT EVENING SERVICE THE PSALMS FOR WELCOMING SHABBAT

⁶The heavens declare
 God's righteousness,
 all peoples see God's glory.
⁷Shame on all those
 who are slaves to an image,
 who puff up their pride with hollow gods.
 False gods, bow down before the One!
⁸Zion heard and rejoiced,
 the daughters of Judah were glad
 because of Your judgments,
 O Eternal.
⁹Because You are the Sovereign,
 supreme over all the earth.
 You are supreme
 beyond all gods.

¹הִגִּידוּ הַשָּׁמַיִם צִדְקוֹ
וְרָאוּ כָל־הָעַמִּים כְּבוֹדוֹ:
²יֵבֹשׁוּ כָּל־עֹבְדֵי פֶסֶל
הַמִּתְהַלְלִים בָּאֱלִילִים
הִשְׁתַּחֲווּ־לוֹ כָּל־אֱלֹהִים:
³שָׁמְעָה וַתִּשְׂמַח צִיּוֹן
וַתָּגֵלְנָה בְּנוֹת יְהוּדָה
לְמַעַן מִשְׁפָּטֶיךָ יהוה:
⁴כִּי־אַתָּה יהוה
עֶלְיוֹן עַל־כָּל־הָאָרֶץ
מְאֹד נַעֲלֵיתָ
עַל־כָּל־אֱלֹהִים:

¹⁰Those who love the Eternal, hate evil.
 God guards the souls
 of those who are faithful,
 saving them from the hand of the wicked.
¹¹A harvest of light
 is sown for the righteous,
 and joy for the constant heart.
¹²You who are righteous,
 rejoice in the Eternal,
 call God's holiness to mind
 with praise!

⁵אֹהֲבֵי יהוה שִׂנְאוּ רָע
שֹׁמֵר נַפְשׁוֹת חֲסִידָיו
מִיַּד רְשָׁעִים יַצִּילֵם:
⁶אוֹר־זָרֻעַ לַצַּדִּיק
וּלְיִשְׁרֵי־לֵב שִׂמְחָה:
⁷שִׂמְחוּ צַדִּיקִים בַּיהוה
וְהוֹדוּ לְזֵכֶר קָדְשׁוֹ:

⁶*Higgidu ha-shamayim tsidko, v'ra'u chol ha-ammim k'vodo.*
⁷*Yeivoshu kol ov'dei fesel, ha-mit-hal'lim ba-elilim, hishtachavu lo kol elohim.*
⁸*Sham'ah vatismach tsiyyon, vatageilnah b'not y'hudah,*
l'ma'an mishpatecha Adonai.
⁹*Ki attah Adonai elyon al kol ha-arets, m'od na'aleita al kol elohim.*
¹⁰*Ohavei Adonai sin'u ra, shomeir nafshot chasidav, miyad r'sha'im yatsileim.*
¹¹*Or zaru'a la-tsaddik, ul'yishrei leiv simchah.*
¹²*Simchu tsaddikim badonai, v'hodu l'zeicher kodsho.*

צז Psalm 97

God is present in the world, present and engaged with the life of nations. But now our own relationship with God begins to emerge, the focus narrows to Zion and the cities of Judah, or literally, the womenfolk, the daughters.

Within Israel two groups are singled out for particular care - those who love God and the 'righteous'. Are these special people alone the few who are to enjoy God's favour? Or are they models, possibilities, aspirations for all of us? They hint at what might one day be possible, a world of light and joy.

Psalm 98

צח

א מִזְמוֹר
שִׁירוּ לַיהוה שִׁיר חָדָשׁ
כִּי־נִפְלָאוֹת עָשָׂה
הוֹשִׁיעָה־לּוֹ יְמִינוֹ
וּזְרוֹעַ קָדְשׁוֹ:
ב הוֹדִיעַ יהוה יְשׁוּעָתוֹ
לְעֵינֵי הַגּוֹיִם גִּלָּה צִדְקָתוֹ:
ג זָכַר חַסְדּוֹ וֶאֱמוּנָתוֹ
לְבֵית יִשְׂרָאֵל
רָאוּ כָל־אַפְסֵי־אָרֶץ
אֵת יְשׁוּעַת אֱלֹהֵינוּ:
ד הָרִיעוּ לַיהוה כָּל־הָאָרֶץ
פִּצְחוּ וְרַנְּנוּ וְזַמֵּרוּ:
ה זַמְּרוּ לַיהוה בְּכִנּוֹר
בְּכִנּוֹר וְקוֹל זִמְרָה:
ו בַּחֲצֹצְרוֹת וְקוֹל שׁוֹפָר
הָרִיעוּ לִפְנֵי הַמֶּלֶךְ יהוה:
ז יִרְעַם הַיָּם וּמְלֹאוֹ
תֵּבֵל וְיֹשְׁבֵי בָהּ:
ח נְהָרוֹת יִמְחֲאוּ־כָף
יַחַד הָרִים יְרַנֵּנוּ:
ט לִפְנֵי יהוה
כִּי בָא לִשְׁפֹּט הָאָרֶץ
יִשְׁפֹּט־תֵּבֵל בְּצֶדֶק
וְעַמִּים בְּמֵישָׁרִים:

¹A Psalm
שִׁירוּ Sing to the Eternal a new song
to the source of wondrous deeds,
whose right hand
and holy arm bring rescue.
²The Almighty has made known
this power to save,
shown righteousness
in the sight of the nations.
³God remembers the divine love,
keeping faith
with the family of Israel.
All the ends of the earth have seen
the power of our God to save.
⁴Call out to the Eternal all the earth,
cheer and sing and play!
⁵Play to the Eternal with the harp,
with the harp
and the voice of music.
⁶With trumpets and the sound of the horn
call out before the Sovereign,
the Eternal.
⁷Let the sea thunder in its fullness,
the world and all who live in it.
⁸Let the rivers clap their hands,
let the mountains sing out as one
⁹at the presence of the Eternal
who comes to judge the earth,
judging the world
with righteousness
and the peoples
with justice.

צח Psalm 98

Again we are invited to sing a new song to God. But the hope expressed in Psalm 96 is now based on experience. Israel saw God's loyalty and power when we left behind us the slavery of Egypt, witnessed by all the nations of the world.

On our personal journey through the week, this is the time to step back and 'count our blessings'. Despite the troubles that may beset us, we should also remember and celebrate the extraordinary gift of life with its 'miracles that are daily with us'. This is an opportunity to remember and value the people we may take for granted till we find ourselves without them, and all that remains is regret for words unsaid.

SHABBAT EVENING SERVICE — THE PSALMS FOR WELCOMING SHABBAT

¹שִׁירוּ *Shiru ladonai shir chadash, ki nifla'ot asah,*
hoshi'ah lo y'mino, uz'ro'a kodsho.
²*Hodi'a Adonai y'shu'ato, l'einei ha-goyim gillah tsidkato.*
³*Zachar chasdo ve'emunato l'veit yisra'el ra'u chol afsei arets eit y'shu'at eloheinu.*
⁴*Hari'u ladonai kol ha-arets, pitschu v'rann'nu v'zameiru.*
⁵*Zamm'ru ladonai b'chinnor, b'chinnor v'kol zimrah.*
⁶*Bachatsots'rot v'kol shofar, hari'u lifnei ha-melech Adonai.*
⁷*Yir'am ha-yam um'lo'o, teiveil v'yosh'vei vah.*
⁸*N'harot yimcha'u chaf, yachad harim y'ranneinu.*
⁹*Lifnei Adonai ki va lishpot ha-arets, yishpot teiveil b'tsedek, v'ammim b'meisharim*

Psalm 99 — צט

¹יהוה The Eternal rules,
let the nations tremble!
God is enthroned in judgment
on the *cherubim*, let the earth shake!
²The Eternal is great in Zion,
high above all peoples.
³They shall praise Your name,
great and awesome.
'Holy is God!'

<<<

איהוה מָלָךְ יִרְגְּזוּ עַמִּים
יֹשֵׁב כְּרוּבִים תָּנוּט הָאָרֶץ:
ביהוה בְּצִיּוֹן גָּדוֹל
וְרָם הוּא עַל־כָּל־הָעַמִּים:
גיוֹדוּ שִׁמְךָ גָּדוֹל וְנוֹרָא
קָדוֹשׁ הוּא:

¹יהוה *Adonai malach, yirg'zu ammim, yosheiv k'ruvim tanut ha-arets.*
²*Adonai b'tsiyyon gadol, v'ram hu al kol ha-ammim.*
³*Yodu shimcha, gadol v'nora, kadosh hu.*

צט Psalm 99
God is enthroned, but not as a distant figure ruling from afar. God is one who responds to those who call, like Moses, Aaron and Samuel in their generations. God, says the psalmist, works with us and through us, but also through a system of guidance and law to support us in our life together. The distance from God threatened in Psalm 95 is now modified. God punishes wrongdoing, but in just measure, and the door remains open for our return. The God who is 'holy', 'other', 'separate', all the meanings of *kadosh*, is not remote, but there to be met in the prayers that we bring.

The fifth day carries with it our anticipation of the Shabbat that lies ahead and a reminder to begin the preparation.

⁴God is strong, a ruler
who loves justice.
It is You who established honesty,
justice and righteousness.
It is You who formed them in Jacob.
⁵Exalt the Eternal, our God,
and bow down before
God's footstool.
'Holy is God!'

⁶Moses and Aaron
were among God's priests,
and Samuel among those
who called on God's name.
They called to the Eternal
who answered them.

⁷In a pillar of cloud God spoke to them.
They kept God's teaching
and the law given to them.

⁸Eternal our God,
You answered them.
To them You were a forgiving God,
though You punished
their wrongdoing.

⁹Exalt the Eternal our God,
bow down before God's holy mountain,
for holy is the Eternal our God.

ד וְעֹז מֶלֶךְ מִשְׁפָּט אָהֵב
אַתָּה כּוֹנַנְתָּ מֵישָׁרִים
מִשְׁפָּט וּצְדָקָה בְּיַעֲקֹב
אַתָּה עָשִׂיתָ:
ה רוֹמְמוּ יהוה אֱלֹהֵינוּ
וְהִשְׁתַּחֲווּ לַהֲדֹם רַגְלָיו
קָדוֹשׁ הוּא:

ו מֹשֶׁה וְאַהֲרֹן בְּכֹהֲנָיו
וּשְׁמוּאֵל בְּקֹרְאֵי שְׁמוֹ
קֹרִאים אֶל־יהוה
וְהוּא יַעֲנֵם:

ז בְּעַמּוּד עָנָן יְדַבֵּר אֲלֵיהֶם
שָׁמְרוּ עֵדֹתָיו וְחֹק נָתַן־לָמוֹ:

ח יהוה אֱלֹהֵינוּ אַתָּה עֲנִיתָם
אֵל נֹשֵׂא הָיִיתָ לָהֶם
וְנֹקֵם עַל־עֲלִילוֹתָם:

ט רוֹמְמוּ יהוה אֱלֹהֵינוּ
וְהִשְׁתַּחֲווּ לְהַר קָדְשׁוֹ
כִּי־קָדוֹשׁ יהוה אֱלֹהֵינוּ:

⁴*V'oz melech mishpat aheiv, attah konanta meisharim
mishpat uts'dakah b'ya'akov attah asita.*
⁵*Rom'mu Adonai eloheinu, v'hishtachavu lahadom raglav, kadosh hu.*
⁶*Mosheh v'aharon b'chohanav ush'mu'eil b'kor'ei sh'mo,
kor'im el Adonai, v'hu ya'aneim.*
⁷*B'ammud anan y'dabbeir aleihem, sham'ru eidotav v'chok natan lamo.*
⁸*Adonai eloheinu attah anitam, eil nosei hayita lahem v'nokeim al alilotam.*
⁹*Rom'mu Adonai eloheinu, v'hishtachavu l'har kodsho, ki kadosh Adonai eloheinu*

SHABBAT EVENING SERVICE — THE PSALMS FOR WELCOMING SHABBAT

Psalm 29

כט

¹A Psalm of David
הָבוּ Give due honour to God, divine beings!
Give due honour to God's awesome power!
²Give the honour that is due to God's name.
Worship God in the beauty of holiness!

³God's voice is over the waters,
present in the thunder's crash.
God rules over stormy waters.

⁴The voice of God is power,
the voice of God is majesty!

⁵The voice of God breaks cedars;
God shatters the cedars of Lebanon,
⁶making them skip like a calf,
Lebanon and Sirion like young oxen.

אמִזְמוֹר לְדָוִד
הָבוּ לַיהוה בְּנֵי אֵלִים
הָבוּ לַיהוה כָּבוֹד וָעֹז׃
בהָבוּ לַיהוה כְּבוֹד שְׁמוֹ
הִשְׁתַּחֲווּ לַיהוה
בְּהַדְרַת־קֹדֶשׁ׃

גקוֹל יהוה עַל־הַמָּיִם
אֵל־הַכָּבוֹד הִרְעִים
יהוה עַל־מַיִם רַבִּים׃
דקוֹל־יהוה בַּכֹּחַ
קוֹל יהוה בֶּהָדָר׃

הקוֹל יהוה שֹׁבֵר אֲרָזִים
וַיְשַׁבֵּר יהוה
אֶת־אַרְזֵי הַלְּבָנוֹן׃
ווַיַּרְקִידֵם כְּמוֹ־עֵגֶל
לְבָנוֹן וְשִׂרְיֹן כְּמוֹ בֶן־רְאֵמִים׃

<<<

¹*Mizmor l'David*
הָבוּ *Havu ladonai b'nei eilim, havu ladonai kavod va'oz.*
²*Havu ladonai k'vod sh'mo, hishtachavu ladonai b'hadrat kodesh.*
³*Kol Adonai al ha-mayim, eil ha-kavod hir'im, Adonai al mayim rabbim.*
⁴*Kol Adonai ba-ko'ach, kol Adonai be-hadar.*
⁵*Kol Adonai shoveir arazim, vay'shabbeir Adonai et arzei ha-l'vanon.*
⁶*Vayarkideim k'mo eigel, l'vanon v'siryon k'mo ven r'eimim.*

כט Psalm 29

We complete the journey back to God. We ended Psalm 99 with God's *kedushah*, 'otherness', 'transcendence'. But the key word that opens and closes Psalm 29 is *kavod*, literally 'weight', the 'heaviness', the 'presence' of God within the world. Where human and divine meet, in the temple, all proclaim God's *kavod*.

The power of that meeting is pictured as a storm, sweeping through the land of Israel from the heights of Lebanon to the Sinai wilderness. Each flash of lightning and thunder is another 'voice' of God. But this power is not destructive, rather it gives us the strength to endure, to hold fast to values and to hope. So the last word of the Psalm, *shalom*, takes us directly into the peace of the Shabbat. The distance from God we experienced at the beginning of the week, 'they will never come to the rest I wish for them', is now set aside. We stand on the threshold, the 'time outside of time' that lies before us, the holiness, the special 'rest', that makes the Shabbat.

⁷God's voice splits the lightning shafts,
God's voice whirls the desert sand,

⁸God whirls the desert of Kadesh.
⁹God's voice makes the wild deer calve,
it strips the forest bare –
while in God's temple
all cry 'Glory!'

¹⁰God was enthroned at the flood;
God is enthroned,
Sovereign forever.
¹¹God give strength to Your people,
God bless Your people
with peace.

׳קוֹל־יהוה חֹצֵב לַהֲבוֹת אֵשׁ:
חקוֹל יהוה יָחִיל מִדְבָּר.
יָחִיל יהוה מִדְבַּר קָדֵשׁ:
טקוֹל יהוה יְחוֹלֵל אַיָּלוֹת
וַיֶּחֱשֹׂף יְעָרוֹת.
וּבְהֵיכָלוֹ
כֻּלּוֹ אֹמֵר כָּבוֹד:
׳יהוה לַמַּבּוּל יָשָׁב
וַיֵּשֶׁב יהוה מֶלֶךְ לְעוֹלָם:
יאיהוה עֹז לְעַמּוֹ יִתֵּן
יהוה יְבָרֵךְ אֶת־עַמּוֹ
בַשָּׁלוֹם:

⁷Kol Adonai chotzeiv lahavot eish.
⁸Kol Adonai yachil midbar, yachil Adonai midbar kadeish.
⁹Kol Adonai y'choleil ayalot vayechesof y'arot, uv'heichalo kullo omeir kavod.
¹⁰Adonai la-mabul yashav, vayeishev Adonai melech l'olam.
¹¹Adonai oz l'ammo yittein, Adonai y'vareich et ammo vashalom.

לכה דודי

L'CHAH DODI

> Early Reformers in the nineteenth century were concerned about certain specific messianic hopes in Jewish liturgy, particularly for the return to the land of Israel, the rebuilding of the temple with its sacrificial cult, and the restoration of the Davidic monarchy. These are central themes in the mystical hymn *L'chah Dodi*. The 1930 edition of *Forms of Prayer* only included the first two and the last verses. In the 1977 edition, verse 5 was added to the Friday evening service, but the full text was included in the song anthology. In this edition we have included the entire text within the service, reflecting the more traditional practice of some congregations within the movement, but indented and coloured those passages which most congregations omit.

SHABBAT EVENING SERVICE — L'CHAH DODI

לְכָה דוֹדִי לִקְרַאת כַּלָּה.
פְּנֵי שַׁבָּת נְקַבְּלָה:

Come, my friend,
to greet the bride,
to welcome in the Shabbat eve.

¹שָׁמוֹר וְזָכוֹר בְּדִבּוּר אֶחָד.
הִשְׁמִיעָנוּ אֵל הַמְּיֻחָד.
יהוה אֶחָד וּשְׁמוֹ אֶחָד.
לְשֵׁם וּלְתִפְאֶרֶת וְלִתְהִלָּה:
לְכָה דוֹדִי...

¹'Observe!', 'Remember!' –
one command,
God made us hear a single phrase.
For God is One, and known as One,
in fame, in glory and in praise.
  Come, my friend …

²לִקְרַאת שַׁבָּת לְכוּ וְנֵלְכָה.
כִּי הִיא מְקוֹר הַבְּרָכָה.
מֵרֹאשׁ מִקֶּדֶם נְסוּכָה.
סוֹף מַעֲשֶׂה בְּמַחֲשָׁבָה תְּחִלָּה:
לְכָה דוֹדִי...

²To greet the Shabbat let us join
for from her endless blessings pour.
First of all creation willed,
the final act, thought long before.
  Come, my friend …

³מִקְדַּשׁ מֶלֶךְ עִיר מְלוּכָה.
קוּמִי צְאִי מִתּוֹךְ הַהֲפֵכָה.
רַב לָךְ שֶׁבֶת בְּעֵמֶק הַבָּכָא.
וְהוּא יַחֲמוֹל עָלַיִךְ חֶמְלָה:
לְכָה דוֹדִי...

³Your royal city, holy place,
rise from the ground
where you have lain;
no more a valley
washed by tears,
for God shall comfort you again.
  Come, my friend …

⁴הִתְנַעֲרִי מֵעָפָר קוּמִי.
לִבְשִׁי בִּגְדֵי תִפְאַרְתֵּךְ עַמִּי:
עַל יַד בֶּן יִשַׁי בֵּית הַלַּחְמִי.
קָרְבָה אֶל נַפְשִׁי גְאָלָה:
לְכָה דוֹדִי...

⁴Shake off the dust as you arise,
my people, don your finest dress!
Through Jesse's son,
of Bethlehem,
release my soul from its distress.
  Come, my friend …

<<<

לְכָה L'chah dodi likrat kallah, p'nei shabbat n'kabb'lah.
¹Shamor v'zachor b'dibbur echad, hishmi'anu eil ha-m'yuchad,
Adonai echad ush'mo echad, l'sheim ul'tif'eret v'lit-hillah. L'chah dodi …
²Likrat shabbat l'chu v'neil'chah, ki hi m'kor ha-b'rachah,
meirosh mikkedem n'suchah, sof ma'aseh b'machashavah t'chillah. L'chah dodi …
[³Mikdash melech ir m'luchah, kumi ts'i mittoch ha-hafeichah,
rav lach shevet b'eimek ha-bacha, v'hu yachamol alayich chemlah. L'chah dodi …
⁴Hitna'ari mei'afar kumi, livshi bigdei tif'arteich ammi,
al yad ben yishai beit ha-lachmi, korvah el nafshi g'alah. L'chah dodi …]

⁵Arouse yourself, arouse yourself,
your light is come, arise and shine!
Awake, awake and pour out songs,
God's glory greets us at this time.
   Come, my friend ...

⁶No more despised
nor put to shame,
why are you bowed,
why so cast down?
My humbled people wait for you,
rebuilt upon your ancient ground.
   Come, my friend ...

⁷Those who would spoil you
shall be spoil.
Your foes will scatter far and wide.
And God will share
with you such joy
as does the bridegroom
with the bride.
   Come, my friend ...

⁸You shall spread out right and left
and worship there our God alone;
through one born
out of Perez' seed,
with joy such as was never known.
   Come, my friend ...

<<<

⁵*Hit'or'ri hit'or'ri, ki va orech kumi ori,*
uri uri shir dabbeiri, k'vod Adonai alayich niglah. L'chah dodi ...
[⁶*Lo teivoshi v'lo tikkal'mi, ma tishtochachi u'ma tehemi,*
bach yechesu aniyei ammi, v'nivn'tah ir al tillah. L'chah dodi ...
⁷*V'hayu limshissah shosayich, v'rachaku kol m'vall'ayich,*
yasis alayich elohayich kimsos chatan al kallah. L'chah dodi ...
⁸*Yamin u'smol tifrotsi v'et Adonai ta'aritsi,*
al yad ish ben partsi, v'nism'cha v'nagilah. L'chah dodi ...]

123 SHABBAT EVENING SERVICE *L'CHAH DODI*

When singing the last verse we rise and turn to face the door to the synagogue.
As we sing the closing words bo'i challah, bo'i challah
we bow to greet the Shabbat queen.

⁹Come in peace and come in joy,
God, your husband,
you, God's pride;
among the faithful
chosen people,
come my bride, come my bride!

⁹בּוֹאִי בְשָׁלוֹם עֲטֶרֶת בַּעְלָהּ.
גַּם בְּשִׂמְחָה וּבְצָהֳלָה.
תּוֹךְ אֱמוּנֵי עַם סְגֻלָּה.
בּוֹאִי כַלָּה. בּוֹאִי כַלָּה:

Come, my friend,
to greet the bride,
to welcome in the Shabbat eve.

לְכָה דוֹדִי לִקְרַאת כַּלָּה.
פְּנֵי שַׁבָּת נְקַבְּלָה:

Shlomo ha-levi Alkabetz   שלמה הלוי אלקבץ

⁹*Bo'i v'shalom ateret ba'lah, gam b'simcha u'vtsoholah,*
toch emunei am s'gullah bo'i challah bo'i challah.
L'chah dodi likrat kallah, p'nei shabbat n'kab'lah.

In some congregations mourners enter at this point and are greeted:

הַמָּקוֹם May the Everpresent
comfort you together with all
those who mourn.

הַמָּקוֹם יְנַחֵם אֶתְכֶם
בְּתוֹךְ שְׁאָר הָאֲבֵלִים:

הַמָּקוֹם *Ha-makom y'nacheim etchem b'toch sh'ar ha-aveilim.*

לְכָה דוֹדִי *L'chah Dodi*
In our imagination we join with the rabbis of Safed who would go into the fields to greet the Shabbat bride. We sing *L'chah dodi* and revisit the millennial dreams, the messianic hopes of our people: the rebuilding of Jerusalem and the temple, the restoration of our people under the leadership of a descendant of King David, a time when we are no longer shamed or bowed down, but instead rejoice in the presence of God. We hold for a moment these visions of generations past, those that remain, those that seem remote. We rise and turn, physically leaving the week that is past behind us. We greet the special time that holds all Jewish hopes and aspirations, past, present and those yet to be dreamed, the Shabbat bride.

Greeting the mourners
The distance between dream and reality is caught for a moment in some traditions when we welcome those in mourning with words of comfort and consolation.

צב

א מִזְמוֹר שִׁיר לְיוֹם הַשַּׁבָּת:

ב טוֹב לְהֹדוֹת לַיהוָה וּלְזַמֵּר לְשִׁמְךָ עֶלְיוֹן:
ג לְהַגִּיד בַּבֹּקֶר חַסְדֶּךָ וֶאֱמוּנָתְךָ בַּלֵּילוֹת:
ד עֲלֵי־עָשׂוֹר וַעֲלֵי־נָבֶל עֲלֵי הִגָּיוֹן בְּכִנּוֹר:
ה כִּי שִׂמַּחְתַּנִי יְהוָה בְּפָעֳלֶךָ בְּמַעֲשֵׂי יָדֶיךָ אֲרַנֵּן:

ו מַה־גָּדְלוּ מַעֲשֶׂיךָ יְהוָה מְאֹד עָמְקוּ מַחְשְׁבֹתֶיךָ:
ז אִישׁ־בַּעַר לֹא יֵדָע וּכְסִיל לֹא־יָבִין אֶת־זֹאת:
ח בִּפְרֹחַ רְשָׁעִים כְּמוֹ עֵשֶׂב וַיָּצִיצוּ כָּל־פֹּעֲלֵי אָוֶן לְהִשָּׁמְדָם עֲדֵי־עַד:

ט וְאַתָּה מָרוֹם לְעֹלָם יְהוָה:

י כִּי הִנֵּה אֹיְבֶיךָ יְהוָה כִּי־הִנֵּה אֹיְבֶיךָ יֹאבֵדוּ יִתְפָּרְדוּ כָּל־פֹּעֲלֵי אָוֶן:
יא וַתָּרֶם כִּרְאֵים קַרְנִי בַּלֹּתִי בְּשֶׁמֶן רַעֲנָן:
יב וַתַּבֵּט עֵינִי בְּשׁוּרָי בַּקָּמִים עָלַי מְרֵעִים תִּשְׁמַעְנָה אָזְנָי:

יג צַדִּיק כַּתָּמָר יִפְרָח כְּאֶרֶז בַּלְּבָנוֹן יִשְׂגֶּה:
יד שְׁתוּלִים בְּבֵית יְהוָה בְּחַצְרוֹת אֱלֹהֵינוּ יַפְרִיחוּ:
טו עוֹד יְנוּבוּן בְּשֵׂיבָה דְּשֵׁנִים וְרַעֲנַנִּים יִהְיוּ:
טז לְהַגִּיד כִּי־יָשָׁר יְהוָה צוּרִי וְלֹא־עַוְלָתָה בּוֹ:

[1] *Mizmor shir l'yom ha-shabbat.*
[2] **טוב** *Tov l'hodot ladonai, ul'zammeir l'shimcha elyon.*
[3] *L'haggid ba-boker chasdecha, ve'emunat'cha ba-leilot.*
[4] *Alei asor va'alei navel, alei higgayon b'chinnor.*
[5] *Ki simmachtani Adonai b'fo'olecha, b'ma'asei yadecha arannein.*
[6] *Mah gad'lu ma'asecha Adonai, m'od am'ku machsh'votecha.*
[7] *Ish ba'ar lo yeida, uch'sil lo yavin et zot.*
[8] *Bifro'ach r'sha'im k'mo eisev, vayatsitsu kol po'alei aven, l'hisham'dam adei ad.*

[9] ***V'attah marom l'olam Adonai.***

[10] *Ki hinnei oy'vecha Adonai, ki hinnei oy'vecha yoveidu yitpar'du kol po'alei aven.*
[11] *Vatarem kir'eim karni balloti b'shemen ra'anan.*
[12] *Vatabbeit eini b'shurai, ba-kamim alai m'rei'im tishma'na oznai.*
[13] *Tsaddik ka-tamar yifrach, k'erez ba-l'vanon yisgeh.*
[14] *Sh'tulim b'veit Adonai, b'chatsrot eloheinu yafrichu.*
[15] *Od y'nuvun b'seivah, d'sheinim v'ra'anannim yihyu.*
[16] *L'haggid ki yashar Adonai, tsuri v'lo avlatah bo.*

Psalm 92

¹ A Psalm to Sing for the Shabbat day.
²טוֹב It is good to give thanks to the Eternal, to praise Your name,
> God beyond all,
³to tell of Your love in the morning and Your faithfulness every night.
⁴With the ten-stringed lute, with the lyre, with the gentle sound of the harp.
⁵For You made me rejoice in Your deeds, O God,
> at the works of Your hand I sing out.

⁶God, how great are Your works, Your thoughts are so very deep.
⁷The stupid do not know this, nor can the foolish understand,
⁸that when the wicked flourish they are only like grass
> and when all who do evil spring up their end is always destruction.

⁹Only You are exalted forever, Eternal.

¹⁰For see Your enemies, God! see how Your enemies shall perish,
> all who do evil shall scatter.
¹¹But You exalted my strength like an ox, anointed me with fresh oil.
¹²My eyes saw the fate of my enemies; and those who rose up to harm me,
> my ears have heard their end.

¹³The righteous shall flourish like the palm tree,
> grow tall like a cedar in Lebanon.
¹⁴Planted in the house of their Maker,
> they shall flourish in the courts of our God,
¹⁵bearing new fruit in old age still full of sap and still green,
¹⁶to declare that the Creator is faithful, my Rock in whom there is no wrong.

צב/צג Psalm 92 and 93

Now firmly within the bounds of Shabbat itself, two Psalms mark the completion of our journey. Both belonged originally to the liturgy of the Temple. Both are composed so that their structure echoes their inner theme: Psalm 92 celebrates God's power over human destructiveness; Psalm 93 God's power over the forces of nature.

צב Psalm 92

The outer framework of the Psalm, verses 1-4 and 12-15, are located in the Temple itself: the music that accompanies the singing of God's praises, morning and evening; the strength and constant renewal of those who stand within God's presence. Between these outer 'walls' that give support to the psalmist, verses 5-7 and 9-11 point to the reality of destructive human forces that flourish (verse 8) in the world, seemingly as plentiful as grass. But in contrast to the righteous who flourish (verse 13) and endure, like a palm tree or cedar, grass soon withers and disappears. At the physical heart of Psalm 92 are four words, literally 'but You, on high, forever, Eternal!', locating God at the 'highest' point in a verse that speaks of God's ultimate power over those who do evil.

Psalm 93

¹ יהוה The Creator reigns
robed in pride,
God is robed in power,
clothed in strength.
So the world was set firm
and cannot be shaken,
² Your throne was set firm long ago,
from eternity You are.

³ Almighty, the floods may storm,
   the floods may storm aloud,
     the floods may storm and thunder.

⁴ But even above the roar of great waves,
   mighty breakers of the ocean,
     supreme is the might of the Creator.

⁵ The proofs You give are very sure,
holiness is the mark of Your house,
God, as long as time endures.

צג

א יהוה מָלָךְ גֵּאוּת לָבֵשׁ
לָבֵשׁ יהוה עֹז הִתְאַזָּר
אַף־תִּכּוֹן תֵּבֵל בַּל־תִּמּוֹט:
ב נָכוֹן כִּסְאֲךָ מֵאָז
מֵעוֹלָם אָתָּה:

ג נָשְׂאוּ נְהָרוֹת יהוה
נָשְׂאוּ נְהָרוֹת קוֹלָם
יִשְׂאוּ נְהָרוֹת דָּכְיָם:

ד מִקֹּלוֹת מַיִם רַבִּים
אַדִּירִים מִשְׁבְּרֵי־יָם
אַדִּיר בַּמָּרוֹם יהוה:

ה עֵדֹתֶיךָ נֶאֶמְנוּ מְאֹד
לְבֵיתְךָ נַאֲוָה־קֹדֶשׁ
יהוה לְאֹרֶךְ יָמִים:

¹ יהוה *Adonai malach gei'ut laveish,*
laveish Adonai, oz hit'azzar
af tikkon teiveil bal timmot.
² *Nachon kis'acha mei'az, mei'olam attah.*
³ *Nas'u n'harot Adonai, nas'u n'harot kolam, yis-u n'harot dochyam.*
⁴ *Mikkolot mayim rabbim addirim mishb'rei yam, addir ba-marom Adonai.*
⁵ *Eidotecha ne'emnu m'od, l'veit'cha na'avah kodesh, Adonai l'orech yamim.*

צג Psalm 93

The Psalm depicts God's ultimate control over nature, enthroned as 'king' in the past and secure for all future time. The outer verses 1-2 and 5 reinforce the idea of stability through their rhythm and the repetition of images of the firm establishment of the physical world, and the trustworthy 'proofs', the laws with which God underpins this stability. This power holds in check the turbulent waters of creation, described at the centre of the Psalm (verses 3-4), where each 'wave' of words, crashes down upon the one before.

With God's rule over humanity and over nature keeping us safe, we are ready to enjoy the freedom and rest promised by Shabbat.

127 SHABBAT EVENING SERVICE   **THE *SH'MA* AND ITS BLESSINGS**

שמע וברכותיה
THE *SH'MA* AND ITS BLESSINGS

> With the *Bar'chu*, the call to worship, the formal part of the service begins. At the heart of the first unit is the *Sh'ma*, 'Hear O Israel …', the central affirmation of Jewish belief: that behind the diversity of nature and of human experience there is a single power, a God who can be known and encountered. The three Biblical passages that make up the '*Sh'ma*', are framed by blessings, two before that reflect on God as Creator of all that exists who has a loving relationship with the Jewish people, and two following, one that celebrates God's engagement in Jewish history and a more private blessing for an untroubled night of rest.

It is traditional for the Prayer Leader to bow slightly from the waist when saying Bar'chu, *and for the congregation to do likewise when responding, returning to the upright position when mentioning the name of God.*

THE CALL TO COMMUNITY PRAYER ♈336

בָּרְכוּ Bless the Living God whom we are called to bless.   בָּרְכוּ אֶת־יהוה הַמְבֹרָךְ:

           בָּרְכוּ *Bar'chu et Adonai ha-m'vorach.*

בָּרוּךְ Blessed is the Living God whom we are called to bless forever and ever.   בָּרוּךְ יהוה הַמְבֹרָךְ לְעוֹלָם וָעֶד:

           בָּרוּךְ *Baruch Adonai ha-m'vorach l'olam va'ed.*

בָּרְכוּ Bless …
The call to 'bless' or 'praise' God marks the next major stage in the service. The individuals who have been preparing themselves, adjusting to the inner world of Jewish worship, now become formally a community. Traditionally, without the presence of a *minyan*, ten adult males, this call to prayer, and some prayers like the mourner's *kaddish*, would not be recited. This is a reminder that all have a shared responsibility for ensuring that the community meets the needs of all its members. Today a *minyan* may be made up in different ways, or even ignored, but this call and its response by the community leads us across another threshold on the journey, outer and inner, towards the divine presence.

THE CREATOR OF THE UNIVERSE ☧ 327

בָּרוּךְ Blessed are You, our God and Creator, Sovereign of the universe, Whose word brings on the evening twilight, Who opens the gates of dawn with wisdom, and with foresight makes times pass and seasons change. Your plan sets the stars in their courses in the sky, creating day and night, turning light into darkness and darkness into light. You make the day fade away and bring on the night, separating day and night. You are the Ruler of the hosts of heaven. Blessed are You God, who brings on the evening twilight.

בָּרוּךְ אַתָּה יהוה אֱלֹהֵינוּ מֶלֶךְ הָעוֹלָם. אֲשֶׁר בִּדְבָרוֹ מַעֲרִיב עֲרָבִים. בְּחָכְמָה פּוֹתֵחַ שְׁעָרִים. וּבִתְבוּנָה מְשַׁנֶּה עִתִּים. וּמַחֲלִיף אֶת־הַזְּמַנִּים. וּמְסַדֵּר אֶת־הַכּוֹכָבִים בְּמִשְׁמְרוֹתֵיהֶם בָּרָקִיעַ כִּרְצוֹנוֹ: בּוֹרֵא יוֹם וָלָיְלָה. גּוֹלֵל אוֹר מִפְּנֵי חֹשֶׁךְ וְחֹשֶׁךְ מִפְּנֵי אוֹר: הַמַּעֲבִיר יוֹם וּמֵבִיא לָיְלָה. וּמַבְדִּיל בֵּין יוֹם וּבֵין לָיְלָה. יהוה צְבָאוֹת שְׁמוֹ: בָּרוּךְ אַתָּה יהוה. הַמַּעֲרִיב עֲרָבִים:

בָּרוּךְ *Baruch attah Adonai eloheinu melech ha-olam, asher bidvaro ma'ariv aravim, b'chochmah potei'ach sh'arim. Uvitvunah m'shanneh ittim, umachalif et ha-z'mannim, um'saddeir et ha-kochavim b'mishm'roteihem baraki'a kirtzono. Borei yom valailah, goleil or mip'nei choshech v'choshech mip'nei or. Hama'avir yom umeivi lailah, umavdil bein yom uvein lailah, Adonai ts'va'ot sh'mo. Baruch attah Adonai, ha-ma'ariv aravim.*

מַעֲרִיב עֲרָבִים
Who brings on the evening twilight ...

This is the first of two blessings leading up to the recital of the *Sh'ma*, 'Hear O Israel ...' Like its morning counterpart (about God who 'creates light'), the blessing acknowledges God as Creator of the universe. The spectacle of the sky at night, the ever-recurring change from light to dark and back again, however we explain this phenomenon, remains an extraordinary pattern of ebb and flow, of concealment and vision, that underpins all of life. For our ancestors, the blaze of light in the skies at night displayed for all to see the battalions of the 'Lord of hosts', or myriads of serving angels, or a supernal light shining through holes in the firmament which covered the earth. This vastness demands that, at least for the duration of the prayer, we mute our human arrogance and acknowledge our collective and individual limitations. But we do not remain cowed or humbled, for the blessing that follows asserts our uniqueness before God.

SHABBAT EVENING SERVICE
THE *SH'MA* AND ITS BLESSINGS

GOD'S LOVE FOR ISRAEL ♦328

אַהֲבַת With everlasting love have You loved Your people the family of Israel. Teaching and practice, duty and justice - these You have taught us. Therefore, our God and Guide, we think upon all this before we sleep and when we wake, and rejoice and delight in Your teaching and its practice forever and ever, for they are our life and the measure of our days. We keep them in mind both day and night. Never take Your love away from us. Blessed are You God, who loves Your people Israel.

אַהֲבַת עוֹלָם בֵּית יִשְׂרָאֵל עַמְּךָ אָהָבְתָּ. תּוֹרָה וּמִצְוֹת חֻקִּים וּמִשְׁפָּטִים אוֹתָנוּ לִמַּדְתָּ: עַל־כֵּן יְהוָֹה אֱלֹהֵינוּ. בְּשָׁכְבֵּנוּ וּבְקוּמֵנוּ נָשִׂיחַ בְּחֻקֶּיךָ. וְנִשְׂמַח וְנַעֲלוֹז בְּדִבְרֵי תוֹרָתֶךָ וּמִצְוֹתֶיךָ וְחֻקּוֹתֶיךָ לְעוֹלָם וָעֶד: כִּי הֵם חַיֵּינוּ וְאֹרֶךְ יָמֵינוּ. וּבָהֶם נֶהְגֶּה יוֹמָם וָלָיְלָה. וְאַהֲבָתְךָ אַל־תָּסִיר מִמֶּנּוּ לְעוֹלָמִים: בָּרוּךְ אַתָּה יְהוָֹה. אוֹהֵב אֶת־עַמּוֹ יִשְׂרָאֵל:

אַהֲבַת *Ahavat olam beit yisra'el amm'cha ahavta, torah umitsvot chukkim umishpatim otanu limmadta. Al kein Adonai eloheinu, b'shochbeinu uv'kumeinu nasi'ach b'chukkecha, v'nismach v'na'aloz b'divrei toratecha umitsvotecha v'chukkotecha l'olam va'ed. Ki heim chayeinu v'orech yameinu, uvahem nehgeh yomam valailah, v'ahavat'cha al tasir mimmennu l'olamim. Baruch attah Adonai, oheiv et ammo yisra'el.*

שמע
SH'MA ♦329

> Traditionally one remains seated during the recital of the *Sh'ma*, though some progressive communities stand so as to give prominence to this affirmation of God's unity. It is a custom to cover the eyes while reciting the first sentence, 'Hear O Israel', as an aid to concentrating on the words. The *dalet*, the final letter of *echad*, 'One', is emphasised because of the danger of misreading the letter as *reish*, which would spell the word *acheir*, 'other'.

אַהֲבַת עוֹלָם *Ahavat olam*
It is the faith and experience of the Jewish people that the God who is the Creator of all holds us in a special regard. The previous blessing signalled the universal power of God, this one centres on our own particular destiny. God's love for us is expressed through the gift of Torah, guidance for our lives, individually and as a people. In the *Sh'ma* that follows we are called to think of God's word 'when you lie down and when you rise up'. Here we assert our willingness to do so, meditating on the Torah, as if a love letter from the beloved, by day and by night.

שמע וברכותיה | תפלת ערבית לשבת

When praying individually it is customary to add here
אֵל מֶלֶךְ נֶאֱמָן *(el melech ne'eman) - 'God, the faithful Sovereign'.*

שְׁמַע יִשְׂרָאֵל יְהוָה אֱלֹהֵינוּ יְהוָה ׀ אֶחָֽד:

Sh'ma Yisra'el, Adonai eloheinu Adonai echad

בָּרוּךְ שֵׁם כְּבוֹד מַלְכוּתוֹ לְעוֹלָם וָעֶד.

Baruch sheim k'vod malchuto l'olam va'ed.

וְאָהַבְתָּ אֵת יְהוָה אֱלֹהֶיךָ בְּכָל־לְבָבְךָ וּבְכָל־נַפְשְׁךָ וּבְכָל־מְאֹדֶֽךָ: וְהָיוּ הַדְּבָרִים הָאֵלֶּה אֲשֶׁר אָנֹכִי מְצַוְּךָ הַיּוֹם עַל־לְבָבֶֽךָ: וְשִׁנַּנְתָּם לְבָנֶיךָ וְדִבַּרְתָּ בָּם בְּשִׁבְתְּךָ בְּבֵיתֶֽךָ וּבְלֶכְתְּךָ בַדֶּֽרֶךְ וּֽבְשָׁכְבְּךָ וּבְקוּמֶֽךָ: וּקְשַׁרְתָּם לְאוֹת עַל־יָדֶֽךָ וְהָיוּ לְטֹטָפֹת בֵּין עֵינֶֽיךָ: וּכְתַבְתָּם עַל־מְזֻזוֹת בֵּיתֶֽךָ וּבִשְׁעָרֶֽיךָ:

וְאָהַבְתָּ *V'ahavta eit Adonai elohecha, b'chol l'vav'cha, uv'chol nafsh'cha uv'chol m'odecha. V'hayu ha-d'varim ha-eilleh asher anochi m'tsav'cha ha-yom al l'vavecha. V'shinnantam l'vanecha, v'dibbarta bam, b'shivt'cha b'veitecha, uv'lecht'cha vaderech uv'shochb'cha uv'kumecha. Uk'shartam l'ot al yadecha, v'hayu l'totafot bein einecha. Uch'tavtam al m'zuzot beitecha uvish'arecha.*

שְׁמַע Hear ...

'Hear' or 'Listen' Israel! In the Bible (Deut 6:4-9) Moses is addressing the Israelites in the wilderness. Here, relocated to the service, we may be addressing each other, or our own inner 'Israel', that part of us which struggles with/for God.

Not a prayer, this and the following passages are examples of texts that we are to study, but also an affirmation of our relationship to God. It is said that 'God is one, but not in number'. This 'unity' of God is at the heart of the Jewish affirmation of faith, but it is no less a mystery. Behind the manifold aspects of life, nature and society, we experience every day a unity that binds all together. That ultimate unity challenges any attempt to elevate any single part of creation above the rest, to worship any ideology, any leader, any idol. The enlarged letter *ayin* at the end of *Sh'ma*, 'Hear!', together with the enlarged *dalet* at the end of *echad*, 'One', spell the word *ed*, 'witness'. By reciting the verse we witness to the existence of God.

In a traditional interpretation by this recital we accept upon ourselves the 'yoke of the kingdom of heaven', taking responsibility for our own life and that of our society.

Baruch sheim k'vod - this doxology, a praise of God, is constructed of Biblical phrases, but is difficult to translate. It emphasises God's rule over the world, and was already recited in the temple. It is recited silently, possibly because it interrupts the text of the *Sh'ma*.

GOD IS ONE

שְׁמַע Hear O Israel, the Eternal is our God, the Eternal is One.

בָּרוּךְ Blessed is the knowledge of God's glorious rule forever and ever.

וְאָהַבְתָּ Love the Eternal your God with all your heart, and all your soul, and all your might. These words that I command you today shall be upon your heart. Repeat them to your children, and talk about them when you sit in your home, and when you walk in the street; when you lie down, and when you rise up. Secure them as a sign upon your hand, and let them be as reminders before your eyes. Write them on the doorposts of your home and at your gates.[1]

V'ahavta et Adonai - in the Biblical world, the *lev*, heart, was the seat of the mind and intellect rather than the emotions. Thus we are called upon to try at all times to understand the meaning and significance of loving God, even when the circumstances make this a challenge. The word *nefesh*, soul, is related to the word for breathing, so it reflects that invisible 'life force' that distinguishes life from death - hence the word can mean 'soul', 'spirit', 'appetite' or 'self'. The *nefesh* can 'leak away' in illness, and be restored on recovery. According to Psalm 19, the Torah itself can 'restore the soul'. Rabbi Akiva understood this love to be self-sacrificing, even to the extent of martyrdom.

'*Me'od*', power, is used to express a great amount of something. In this context it has been understood by Jewish tradition to mean our material wealth that should be dedicated to God as the source of all we possess. What we owe to God, we repay by what we share with others. Thus mind, spirit and material power are to be brought to the service of God.

[1] Deut 6:4-9.

During the silence the traditional second and third paragraphs of the Sh'ma *may be read, or the alternative Biblical passages on pages 689-697.*

וְהָיָ֗ה אִם־שָׁמֹ֤עַ תִּשְׁמְעוּ֙ אֶל־מִצְוֺתַ֔י אֲשֶׁ֧ר אָנֹכִ֛י מְצַוֶּ֥ה אֶתְכֶ֖ם הַיּ֑וֹם לְאַהֲבָ֞ה אֶת־יְהֹוָ֤ה אֱלֹֽהֵיכֶם֙ וּלְעָבְד֔וֹ בְּכָל־לְבַבְכֶ֖ם וּבְכָל־נַפְשְׁכֶֽם: וְנָתַתִּ֧י מְטַֽר־אַרְצְכֶ֛ם בְּעִתּ֖וֹ יוֹרֶ֣ה וּמַלְק֑וֹשׁ וְאָסַפְתָּ֣ דְגָנֶ֔ךָ וְתִֽירֹשְׁךָ֖ וְיִצְהָרֶֽךָ: וְנָתַתִּ֛י עֵ֥שֶׂב בְּשָׂדְךָ֖ לִבְהֶמְתֶּ֑ךָ וְאָכַלְתָּ֖ וְשָׂבָֽעְתָּ: הִשָּֽׁמְר֣וּ לָכֶ֔ם פֶּ֥ן יִפְתֶּ֖ה לְבַבְכֶ֑ם וְסַרְתֶּ֗ם וַעֲבַדְתֶּם֙ אֱלֹהִ֣ים אֲחֵרִ֔ים וְהִשְׁתַּחֲוִיתֶ֖ם לָהֶֽם: וְחָרָ֨ה אַף־יְהֹוָ֜ה בָּכֶ֗ם וְעָצַ֤ר אֶת־הַשָּׁמַ֨יִם֙ וְלֹֽא־יִהְיֶ֣ה מָטָ֔ר וְהָ֣אֲדָמָ֔ה לֹ֥א תִתֵּ֖ן אֶת־יְבוּלָ֑הּ וַאֲבַדְתֶּ֣ם מְהֵרָ֗ה מֵעַל֙ הָאָ֣רֶץ הַטֹּבָ֔ה אֲשֶׁ֥ר יְהֹוָ֖ה נֹתֵ֥ן לָכֶֽם: וְשַׂמְתֶּם֙ אֶת־דְּבָרַ֣י אֵ֔לֶּה עַל־לְבַבְכֶ֖ם וְעַֽל־נַפְשְׁכֶ֑ם וּקְשַׁרְתֶּ֨ם אֹתָ֤ם לְאוֹת֙ עַל־יֶדְכֶ֔ם וְהָי֥וּ לְטוֹטָפֹ֖ת בֵּ֥ין עֵינֵיכֶֽם: וְלִמַּדְתֶּ֥ם אֹתָ֛ם אֶת־בְּנֵיכֶ֖ם לְדַבֵּ֣ר בָּ֑ם בְּשִׁבְתְּךָ֤ בְּבֵיתֶ֨ךָ֙ וּבְלֶכְתְּךָ֣ בַדֶּ֔רֶךְ וּֽבְשָׁכְבְּךָ֖ וּבְקוּמֶֽךָ: וּכְתַבְתָּ֛ם עַל־מְזוּז֥וֹת בֵּיתֶ֖ךָ וּבִשְׁעָרֶֽיךָ: לְמַ֨עַן יִרְבּ֤וּ יְמֵיכֶם֙ וִימֵ֣י בְנֵיכֶ֔ם עַ֚ל הָֽאֲדָמָ֔ה אֲשֶׁ֨ר נִשְׁבַּ֧ע יְהֹוָ֛ה לַאֲבֹתֵיכֶ֖ם לָתֵ֣ת לָהֶ֑ם כִּימֵ֥י הַשָּׁמַ֖יִם עַל־הָאָֽרֶץ:

וְהָיָה This will happen if you listen carefully to My commands which I give you today, to love and to serve the Eternal your God with all your heart and all your soul. I shall then give your land rain at the right time, the autumn rain and the spring rain, **so that each one of you can harvest your own grain, wine and oil. I shall also give grass in your fields for your cattle, and you will eat and be satisfied.**

Take care that your heart is not deceived into straying, obeying other gods and worshipping them. God's anger will then blaze out against you. God will shut up the sky. There will be no rain. The land will not produce, and you will quickly be destroyed from the good land which God gives you. So put these words of Mine in your heart and in your soul, and secure them as a sign upon your hand and as reminders before your eyes. Teach them to your children, and talk about them **'when you sit each of you in your home, and when you walk in the street, when you lie down and when you rise up. Write them on the doorposts of your home and at your gates.'**

Then you and your children may live long on the land that God promised to give your ancestors as long as there is a sky over the earth.[1]

---

[1] Deut 11:13-21.

וְהָיָה *V'hayah im shamo'a tishm'u el mitsvotai asher anochi m'tsaveh etchem ha-yom, l'ahavah et Adonai eloheichem ul'ovdo b'chol l'vavchem uv'chol nafsh'chem. V'natatti m'tar arts'chem b'itto, yoreh umalkosh,* **v'asafta d'ganecha v'tirosh'cha v'yits-harecha.** *V'natatti eisev b'sad'cha livhemtecha, v'achalta v'sava'ta.*
Hisham'ru lachem, pen yifteh l'vavchem, v'sartem va'avadtem elohim acheirim v'hishtachavitem lahem. V'charah af Adonai bachem, v'atsar et ha-shamayim, v'lo yihyeh matar v'ha-adamah lo tittein et y'vulah, va'avadtem m'heirah mei'al ha-arets ha-tovah asher Adonai notein lachem. V'samtem et d'varai eilleh, al l'vavchem v'al nafsh'chem, uk'shartem otam l'ot al yedchem, v'hayu l'totafot bein eineichem. V'limmadtem otam et b'neichem l'dabbeir bam, **b'shivt'cha b'veitecha, uv'lecht'cha va-derech,** *uv'shochb'cha uv'kumecha. Uch'tavtam al m'zuzot beitecha uvisharecha.*
L'ma'an yirbu y'meichem vimei v'neichem, al ha-adamah asher nishba Adonai la'avoteichem lateit lahem, kimei ha-shamayim al ha-arets.

וְהָיָה אִם־שָׁמֹעַ
This will happen if you listen ...
The second paragraph of the *Sh'ma* is mostly addressed to Israel in the plural; obedience of the people as a whole is the condition for bringing the rain. But in two places **(shown in bold)** the individual is addressed ('so that each one of you can harvest ...'; 'when you sit each of you in your home ...') indicating how our personal experience and responsibility are bound up with those of the entire community.

In the traditional view, by reciting this verse we accept upon ourselves the 'yoke of the commandments', our commitment to fulfilling the obligations on the Jewish people as a whole because of our covenant with God.

וַיֹּאמֶר The Eternal said to Moses: 'Speak to the children of Israel and tell them that each generation shall put tassels on the corner of their clothes, and put a blue thread on the corner tassel. Then when this tassel catches your eye, you will remember all the commands of the Eternal and do them. Then you will no longer wander after the desires of your heart and your eyes which led you to lust.

Then you will remember all My commands and do them and you will be set apart for your God. I am the Eternal your God Who brought you out of the land of Egypt, to be your own God. I, the Eternal, am your God.'[1]

וַיֹּאמֶר יְהוָה אֶל־מֹשֶׁה לֵּאמֹר: דַּבֵּר אֶל־בְּנֵי יִשְׂרָאֵל וְאָמַרְתָּ אֲלֵהֶם וְעָשׂוּ לָהֶם צִיצִת עַל־כַּנְפֵי בִגְדֵיהֶם לְדֹרֹתָם וְנָתְנוּ עַל־צִיצִת הַכָּנָף פְּתִיל תְּכֵלֶת: וְהָיָה לָכֶם לְצִיצִת וּרְאִיתֶם אֹתוֹ וּזְכַרְתֶּם אֶת־כָּל־מִצְוֹת יְהוָה וַעֲשִׂיתֶם אֹתָם וְלֹא תָתוּרוּ אַחֲרֵי לְבַבְכֶם וְאַחֲרֵי עֵינֵיכֶם אֲשֶׁר־אַתֶּם זֹנִים אַחֲרֵיהֶם:

לְמַעַן תִּזְכְּרוּ וַעֲשִׂיתֶם אֶת־כָּל־מִצְוֹתָי וִהְיִיתֶם קְדֹשִׁים לֵאלֹהֵיכֶם: אֲנִי יְהוָה אֱלֹהֵיכֶם אֲשֶׁר הוֹצֵאתִי אֶתְכֶם מֵאֶרֶץ מִצְרַיִם לִהְיוֹת לָכֶם לֵאלֹהִים אֲנִי יְהוָה אֱלֹהֵיכֶם:

וַיֹּאמֶר *Vayomer Adonai el mosheh leimor: Dabbeir el b'nei yisra'el v'amarta aleihem, v'asu lahem tsitsit al kanfei vigdeihem l'dorotam, v'nat'nu al tsitsit ha-kanaf p'til t'cheilet. V'hayah lachem l'tsitsit, ur'item oto, uz'chartem et kol mitsvot Adonai, va'asitem otam, v'lo taturu acharei l'vavchem v'acharei eineichem, asher attem zonim achareihem.*
L'ma'an tizk'ru, va'asitem et kol mitsvotai, vih'yitem k'doshim leiloheichem. Ani Adonai eloheichem, asher hotseiti etchem mei'erets mitsrayim, lih'yot lachem leilohim, ani Adonai eloheichem.

וַיֹּאמֶר יהוה The Eternal said ...

This third paragraph of the *Sh'ma* brings the general requirements on the people of Israel as a whole down to our responsibility for our own individual behaviour. Even our very clothing can be used as a symbolic way of remembering God's presence in our lives. It concludes by recalling the exodus from Egypt that introduces the theme of the blessing that follows.

אֱמֶת וֶאֱמוּנָה All this is true ...

This blessing completes the trilogy of blessings that surround the *Sh'ma*. In one interpretation the two that precede it speak of 'Creation', that God is the source of all life, and 'Revelation', that God communicates with humanity, via the Jewish people through the giving of Torah. This third one, which follows, speaks of 'Redemption', that God intervenes in the life of the Jewish people by rescuing us from slavery in the past, and time and time again from other dangers. On another interpretation the first blessing celebrates God's universal concern for all humanity and all of nature, before focusing on God's particular relationship with Israel. Now as we approach the central prayer, the *Amidah*, where we stand before God, we are reassured that God has stood by us in past times of trouble.

[1] Num 15:37-41.

SHABBAT EVENING SERVICE — THE *SH'MA* AND ITS BLESSINGS

OUR REDEEMER

אֱמֶת All this is true and firmly held by us, that You are our Living God and no other exists, and that we are Israel, Your people. You perform great deeds beyond research, too wonderful to tell. Your children saw Your power, praised and thanked Your name, and willingly accepted Your rule over them. With great joy Moses and Miriam and the children of Israel answered You in song, all of them saying:
**'God, who is like You
among the gods people worship!
Who, like You, is majestic in
holiness, awesome in praise,
working wonders!'**
Our Living God
Your children saw Your rule
over the Sea of Reeds.
All of them as one
honoured You as Sovereign, saying:
'God shall rule forever and ever!'
And it is prophesied:
'For the Almighty has set Jacob free
and rescued him
from a hand stronger than his own.'[1]
Blessed are You God,
who rescues Israel.

אֱמֶת וֶאֱמוּנָה
כָּל־זֹאת וְקַיָּם עָלֵינוּ. כִּי הוּא
יהוה אֱלֹהֵינוּ וְאֵין זוּלָתוֹ וַאֲנַחְנוּ
יִשְׂרָאֵל עַמּוֹ. הָעוֹשֶׂה גְדֹלוֹת
עַד־אֵין חֵקֶר וְנִפְלָאוֹת עַד־אֵין
מִסְפָּר. וְרָאוּ בָנָיו גְּבוּרָתוֹ שִׁבְּחוּ
וְהוֹדוּ לִשְׁמוֹ וּמַלְכוּתוֹ בְּרָצוֹן
קִבְּלוּ עֲלֵיהֶם: מֹשֶׁה וּמִרְיָם וּבְנֵי
יִשְׂרָאֵל לְךָ עָנוּ שִׁירָה בְּשִׂמְחָה
רַבָּה. וְאָמְרוּ כֻלָּם.
מִי־כָמֹכָה בָּאֵלִים יהוה.
מִי כָּמֹכָה נֶאְדָּר בַּקֹּדֶשׁ
נוֹרָא תְהִלֹּת עֹשֵׂה פֶלֶא:
מַלְכוּתְךָ יהוה אֱלֹהֵינוּ
רָאוּ בָנֶיךָ עַל הַיָּם.
יַחַד כֻּלָּם הוֹדוּ וְהִמְלִיכוּ וְאָמְרוּ.
יהוה יִמְלֹךְ לְעוֹלָם וָעֶד:
וְנֶאֱמַר. כִּי־פָדָה יהוה אֶת־יַעֲקֹב
וּגְאָלוֹ מִיַּד חָזָק מִמֶּנּוּ.
בָּרוּךְ אַתָּה יהוה.
גָּאַל יִשְׂרָאֵל:

אֱמֶת *Emet ve'emunah kol zot v'kayyam aleinu, ki hu Adonai eloheinu v'ein zulato va'anachnu Yisra'el ammo, ha-oseh g'dolot ad ein cheiker, v'nifla'ot ad ein mispar, v'ra'u vanav g'vurato shib'chu v'hodu lishmo, umalchuto b'ratson kib'lu aleihem, moshe umiryam uv'nei yisra'el l'cha anu shirah b'simchah rabbah, v'am'ru chullam:*
Mi-chamocha ba-eilim Adonai. mi kamocha ned'ar ba-kodesh, nora t'hillot, oseih fele.
*Malchut'cha Adonai eloheinu ra'u vanecha al ha-yam,
yachad kullam hodu v'himlichu v'amaru:*
Adonai yimloch l'olam va'ed.
*V'ne'emar, ki fadah Adonai et ya'akov, ug'alo miyad chazak mimmennu.
Baruch attah Adonai, ga'al yisra'el.*

---

[1] Ex 15:11, Ex 15:18, Jer 31:11.

GOD'S GIFT OF PEACE AND PROTECTION

הַשְׁכִּיבֵנוּ Source of our life and our Sovereign, cause us to lie down in peace, and rise again to enjoy life. Spread over us the covering of Your peace, guide us with Your good counsel and save us for the sake of Your name. Be a shield about us, turning away every enemy, disease, violence, hunger and sorrow. Remove the temptation that awaits us and the guilt that lies behind us. Shelter us in the shadow of Your wings, for You are a God who guards and protects us, a ruler of mercy and compassion. Guard us when we go out and when we come in, to enjoy life and peace both now and forever, and spread over us the shelter of Your peace. Blessed are You God, spreading the shelter of peace over us, over Your people Israel, and over all the world.

הַשְׁכִּיבֵנוּ יהוה אֱלֹהֵינוּ לְשָׁלוֹם וְהַעֲמִידֵנוּ מַלְכֵּנוּ לְחַיִּים. וּפְרוֹשׂ עָלֵינוּ סֻכַּת שְׁלוֹמֶךָ וְתַקְּנֵנוּ בְּעֵצָה טוֹבָה מִלְּפָנֶיךָ וְהוֹשִׁיעֵנוּ לְמַעַן שְׁמֶךָ. וְהָגֵן בַּעֲדֵנוּ וְהָסֵר מֵעָלֵינוּ אוֹיֵב דֶּבֶר וְחֶרֶב וְרָעָב וְיָגוֹן. וְהָסֵר שָׂטָן מִלְּפָנֵינוּ וּמֵאַחֲרֵינוּ. וּבְצֵל כְּנָפֶיךָ תַּסְתִּירֵנוּ כִּי אֵל שׁוֹמְרֵנוּ וּמַצִּילֵנוּ אָתָּה. כִּי אֵל מֶלֶךְ חַנּוּן וְרַחוּם אָתָּה. וּשְׁמוֹר צֵאתֵנוּ וּבוֹאֵנוּ לְחַיִּים וּלְשָׁלוֹם מֵעַתָּה וְעַד עוֹלָם. וּפְרוֹשׂ עָלֵינוּ סֻכַּת שְׁלוֹמֶךָ. בָּרוּךְ אַתָּה יהוה. הַפּוֹרֵשׂ סֻכַּת שָׁלוֹם עָלֵינוּ וְעַל־עַמּוֹ יִשְׂרָאֵל וְעַל־כָּל־הָעוֹלָם:

הַשְׁכִּיבֵנוּ Hashkiveinu Adonai eloheinu l'shalom, v'ha'amideinu malkeinu l'chayyim, uf'ros aleinu sukkat sh'lomecha, v'takk'neinu b'eitsah tovah mill'fanecha, v'hoshi'einu l'ma'an sh'mecha, v'hagein ba'adeinu v'haseir mei'aleinu, oyeiv dever v'cherev v'ra'av v'yagon. V'haseir satan mil'faneinu umei'achareinu, uv'tseil k'nafecha tastireinu, ki eil shom'reinu umatsileinu attah, ki eil melech channun v'rachum attah, ush'mor tseiteinu uvo'einu l'chayyim ul'shalom mei'attah v'ad olam, uf'ros aleinu sukkat sh'lomecha. Baruch attah Adonai, ha-poreis sukkat shalom aleinu v'al ammo yisra'el, v'al kol ha-olam

---

הַשְׁכִּיבֵנוּ Cause us to lie down ...

In the morning service only three 'blessings' surround the *Sh'ma*, but in the evening service this fourth one is added. It is viewed traditionally as a continuation of the theme of the one before, God's protection extended over us at night time as we sleep. But in addition it asks God's help in the face of all the dangers that confront us throughout our life, from illness to natural disasters. It can serve alone as a night time prayer. On weekdays the blessing concludes 'who guards Your people Israel forever'. On Shabbat, the ending is changed as the Shabbat itself is understood to be a 'protection' of Israel. The traditional version concludes 'over Israel and over Jerusalem'. Reform practice has been to universalise this and extend 'God's tabernacle of peace' 'over all the world'.

SHABBAT EVENING SERVICE — THE *SH'MA* AND ITS BLESSINGS

GOD'S GIFT OF PEACE AND PROTECTION

וְשָׁמְרוּ The children of Israel shall keep the Shabbat, observing the Shabbat as a timeless covenant for all generations. It is a sign between Me and the children of Israel forever. For in six days the Creator made heaven and earth and on the seventh day ceased from work and was at rest.[1]

וְשָׁמְרוּ בְנֵי־יִשְׂרָאֵל אֶת־הַשַּׁבָּת לַעֲשׂוֹת אֶת־הַשַּׁבָּת לְדֹרֹתָם בְּרִית עוֹלָם: בֵּינִי וּבֵין בְּנֵי יִשְׂרָאֵל אוֹת הִיא לְעֹלָם כִּי־שֵׁשֶׁת יָמִים עָשָׂה יהוה אֶת־הַשָּׁמַיִם וְאֶת־הָאָרֶץ וּבַיּוֹם הַשְּׁבִיעִי שָׁבַת וַיִּנָּפַשׁ:

וְשָׁמְרוּ *V'sham'ru v'nei yisra'el et ha-shabbat, la'asot et ha-shabbat l'dorotam b'rit olam. Beini uvein b'nei yisra'el ot hi l'olam, ki sheishet yamim asah Adonai et ha-shamayim v'et ha-arets, uva-yom ha-sh'vi'i shavat vayinnafash.*

The service continues with the Chatsi Kaddish *on the following page or the* Amidah *on page 140.*

וְשָׁמְרוּ ... shall keep ...
The special nature of Shabbat is again recalled as we come to the end of this section of the service. Similarly an alternative verse is inserted here on festivals to mark the occasion. The same passage is also inserted into the Shabbat morning *Amidah* and Shabbat morning *Kiddush*. The verse unites the themes of creative activity and rest. It reminds us that the Shabbat requires preparation ahead of time if we are to enjoy the rest that it offers.

[1] Ex 31:16-17.

The Chatsi Kaddish may be read here:

Chatsi Kaddish   חֲצִי קַדִּישׁ

יִתְגַּדַּל Let us magnify
and let us sanctify in this world
the great name of God
whose will created it.
May God's reign come in your
lifetime, and in your days,
and in the lifetime of the family of
Israel - quickly and speedily
may it come.
Amen.
**May the greatness of God's being
be blessed from eternity to eternity.**
Let us bless and let us extol,
let us tell aloud and let us raise aloft,
let us set on high and let us honour,
let us exalt and
let us praise the Holy One,
whose name is blessed,

who is far beyond any blessing

During the Ten Days of Penitence:
  who is far above and beyond any blessing

or song, any honour
or any consolation
that can be spoken of in this world.
Amen.

יִתְגַּדַּל וְיִתְקַדַּשׁ שְׁמֵהּ רַבָּא
בְּעָלְמָא דִּי־בְרָא כִרְעוּתֵהּ:
וְיַמְלִיךְ מַלְכוּתֵהּ
בְּחַיֵּיכוֹן וּבְיוֹמֵיכוֹן
וּבְחַיֵּי דִי־כָל־בֵּית יִשְׂרָאֵל
בַּעֲגָלָא וּבִזְמַן קָרִיב.
וְאִמְרוּ אָמֵן:
יְהֵא שְׁמֵהּ רַבָּא מְבָרַךְ
לְעָלַם וּלְעָלְמֵי עָלְמַיָּא:
יִתְבָּרַךְ וְיִשְׁתַּבַּח וְיִתְפָּאַר
וְיִתְרוֹמַם וְיִתְנַשֵּׂא וְיִתְהַדָּר
וְיִתְעַלֶּה וְיִתְהַלָּל שְׁמֵהּ
דִּי־קֻדְשָׁא. בְּרִיךְ הוּא.

לְעֵלָּא מִן־כָּל־בִּרְכָתָא
During the Ten Days of Penitence:
לְעֵלָּא לְעֵלָּא מִכָּל־בִּרְכָתָא
וְשִׁירָתָא תֻּשְׁבְּחָתָא וְנֶחֱמָתָא
דַּאֲמִירָן בְּעָלְמָא.
וְאִמְרוּ אָמֵן:

יִתְגַּדַּל *Yitgaddal v'yitkaddash sh'meih rabba, b'alma di v'ra chir'uteih, v'yamlich malchuteih, b'chayyeichon uv'yomeichon uv'chayyei di chol beit yisra'el, ba'agala u'vizman kariv, v'imru* **amen.** *Y'hei sh'meih rabba m'varach l'alam ul'almei almaya. Yitbarach v'yishtabbach v'yitpa'ar v'yitromam v'yitnassei, v'yit-haddar v'yit'alleh v'yit-hallal sh'meih di kudsha,* **b'rich hu**, *l'eilla min kol birchata*
  During the Ten Days of Penitence: l'eilla l'eilla mikol birchata
v'shirata, tushb'chata v'nechemata, di amiran b'alma, v'imru **amen.**

חֲצִי קַדִּישׁ *Chatsi Kaddish*
The *Kaddish*, with its praises of God, is used throughout the liturgy to mark the close of particular sections. Here a shortened version prepares us for the *Amidah* that follows immediately after.

SHABBAT EVENING SERVICE

עמידה
AMIDAH 339-344

> Rab Judah said: People should never introduce a petition for their own needs either in the first three or last three blessings of the *Amidah*, but only in the middle [thirteen daily] blessings. Rabbi Hanina said: In the first three we are like a servant who is addressing praises to his master; in the middle ones we are like a servant who is requesting a gift from his master; in the last ones we are like a servant who has received a gift from his master and takes his leave and departs (*Berachot* 34a).
>
> On Shabbat we withhold our petitions, as if giving God a rest, and replace the thirteen middle blessings of the weekday with one in praise of Shabbat rest.

Traditionally the Amidah *is said whilst standing, beginning with three short steps forward,*
a reminder of our entry into the divine presence.
It is customary at the beginning and end of the first paragraph
to bend the knee when saying the word baruch,
to bow from the waist at the second word attah
and to become upright again with the third word, the name of God, Adonai.

אֲדֹנָי שְׂפָתַי תִּפְתָּח וּפִי יַגִּיד תְּהִלָּתֶךָ:

בָּרוּךְ אַתָּה יהוה אֱלֹהֵינוּ
וֵאלֹהֵי אֲבוֹתֵינוּ   וֵאלֹהֵי אִמּוֹתֵינוּ.
אֱלֹהֵי אַבְרָהָם   אֱלֹהֵי שָׂרָה.
אֱלֹהֵי יִצְחָק   אֱלֹהֵי רִבְקָה.
וֵאלֹהֵי יַעֲקֹב   אֱלֹהֵי רָחֵל
וֵאלֹהֵי לֵאָה.
הָאֵל הַגָּדוֹל הַגִּבּוֹר וְהַנּוֹרָא. אֵל עֶלְיוֹן.
גּוֹמֵל חֲסָדִים טוֹבִים קוֹנֵה הַכֹּל. וְזוֹכֵר חַסְדֵי
אָבוֹת   וְאִמָּהוֹת
וּמֵבִיא גוֹאֵל לִבְנֵי בְנֵיהֶם לְמַעַן שְׁמוֹ בְּאַהֲבָה:

During the Ten Days of Penitence add:
זָכְרֵנוּ לְחַיִּים. מֶלֶךְ חָפֵץ בַּחַיִּים.
וְכָתְבֵנוּ בְּסֵפֶר הַחַיִּים. לְמַעֲנָךְ אֱלֹהִים חַיִּים:

מֶלֶךְ עוֹזֵר וּמוֹשִׁיעַ וּמָגֵן:
בָּרוּךְ אַתָּה יהוה
מָגֵן אַבְרָהָם   פּוֹקֵד שָׂרָה:

אֲדֹנָי Adonai s'fatai tiftach ufi yaggid t'hillatecha.

בָּרוּךְ Baruch attah Adonai eloheinu

veilohei avoteinu   veilohei immoteinu.
elohei avraham,   elohei sarah,
elohei yitschak,   elohei rivkah,
veilohei ya'akov,   elohei rachel
                       veilohei le'ah.
Ha'eil ha-gadol, ha-gibbor v'ha-nora, eil elyon,
gomeil chasadim tovim, koneih ha-kol. V'zocheir chasdei
avot   v'immahot
u'meivi go'eil livnei v'neihem l'ma'an sh'mo b'ahavah.
  During the Ten Days of Penitence add: Zochreinu l'chayyim,
  melech chafeits ba-chayyim, v'chotveinu b'seifer ha-chayyim,
  l'ma'ancha elohim chayyim.
Melech ozeir u'moshi'a umagein.
Baruch attah Adonai,
magein avraham   pokeid sarah.

SHABBAT EVENING SERVICE — AMIDAH

אֲדֹנָי My God, open my lips and my mouth shall declare Your praise.[1]

GOD OF HISTORY

בָּרוּךְ Blessed are You, our God, and God of our ancestors,

God of Abraham,	God of Sarah,
God of Isaac,	God of Rebecca,
and God of Jacob,	God of Rachel
	and God of Leah,

the great, the mighty, and the awesome God, God beyond, generous in love and kindness, and possessing all. You remember the good deeds of those before us, and therefore in love bring rescue to the generations, for such is Your being.

During the Ten Days of Penitence add:
Sovereign Who delights in life, recall us to life and record us in the Book of Life for Your own sake, God of life!

The Sovereign who helps and saves and shields.
Blessed are You God,
who shields Abraham   who remembers Sarah.

אֲדֹנָי שְׂפָתַי תִּפְתָּח My God, open my lips ...

This verse, from Psalm 51:17, comes as a personal meditation, 'I', before the *Amidah* itself which is a collective prayer, 'we'. It affirms that I personally feel part of the prayers that the community is about to say. Also it expresses the hope that my prayers are a true expression of my personal relationship with God.

This personal element is matched by the meditation that comes immediately after the close of the *Amidah*, concluding with Psalm 19:15, emphasising the integrity between the words I speak and my inner thoughts.

אָבוֹת Ancestors

The *Amidah*, the 'standing prayer', is known as the 'eighteen blessings', though during the week when the full set are recited, the number was expanded at some time in the past to become nineteen. It opens with the *avot*, the 'patriarchs', to which we add the 'matriarchs', as if we are introducing ourselves as a community to God: 'we are the descendants of that same Abraham, Isaac and Jacob, Sarah, Rebecca, Rachel and Leah, whom You called to Your service'. We list some of God's powers and qualities revealed to different generations in Biblical times. Like the court protocol when addressing a monarch, this introduction makes a formal beginning to the blessings and prayer that follow where we present ourselves and our requests to God.

In our progressive view the tradition has not adequately expressed the equal contribution of women to our understanding and experience of God. God *pakad*, 'visited' ('became directly engaged with'), Sarah (Gen 21:1); God answered the question asked by Rebecca (Gen 25:23); God responded to the prayers of Rachel and Leah (Gen 30). We have included their names and their individual relationship with God.

[1] Ps 51:17.

אַתָּה גִּבּוֹר לְעוֹלָם אֲדֹנָי. מְחַיֵּה מֵתִים אַתָּה. רַב לְהוֹשִׁיעַ:
In winter מַשִּׁיב הָרוּחַ וּמוֹרִיד הַגֶּשֶׁם:
In summer מוֹרִיד הַטָּל:
מְכַלְכֵּל חַיִּים בְּחֶסֶד. מְחַיֵּה מֵתִים בְּרַחֲמִים רַבִּים. סוֹמֵךְ נוֹפְלִים. וְרוֹפֵא חוֹלִים. וּמַתִּיר אֲסוּרִים. וּמְקַיֵּם אֱמוּנָתוֹ לִישֵׁנֵי עָפָר: מִי כָמוֹךָ בַּעַל גְּבוּרוֹת וּמִי דּוֹמֶה לָךְ. מֶלֶךְ מֵמִית וּמְחַיֶּה וּמַצְמִיחַ יְשׁוּעָה:

During the Ten Days of Penitence add:

מִי כָמוֹךָ אַב הָרַחֲמִים. זוֹכֵר יְצוּרָיו לְחַיִּים בְּרַחֲמִים:

וְנֶאֱמָן אַתָּה לְהַחֲיוֹת מֵתִים. בָּרוּךְ אַתָּה יהוה. מְחַיֵּה הַמֵּתִים:

GOD OF MIGHT

אַתָּה You are the endless power that renews life beyond death; You are the greatness that saves.

In winter months from Shemini Atzeret *to* Pesach: making the wind blow and the rain fall.
In summer months from Pesach *to* Shemini Atzeret: causing the dew to fall.

You care for the living with love. You renew life beyond death with unending mercy. You support the falling, and heal the sick. You free prisoners, and keep faith with those who sleep in the dust. Who can perform such mighty deeds, and who can compare with You, a Sovereign who brings death and life, and renews salvation?

During the Ten Days of Penitence add:
Who is like You, source of compassion,
recalling Your creatures to life in compassion.

You are faithful to renew life beyond death.
Blessed are You God, who renews life beyond death.

אַתָּה Attah gibbor l'olam Adonai, mechayyeih meitim attah rav l'hoshi'a.
In winter: Mashiv ha-ru'ach, u'morid ha-gashem. *In summer:* Morid ha-tal.
M'chalkeil chayyim b'chesed, m'chayyeih meitim b'rachamim rabbim, someich noflim, v'rofeih cholim, umattir asurim, um'kayyeim emunato lisheinei afar. Mi chamocha ba'al g'vurot, umi domeh lach, melech meimit um'chayyeh, u'matsmi'ach y'shu'ah.
During the Ten Days of Penitence add:
Mi chamocha av ha-rachamim, zocheir y'tsurav l'chayyim b'rachamim.
V'ne'eman attah l'hachayot meitim. Baruch attah Adonai, m'chayyeih ha-meitim.

גְּבוּרוֹת Powers

Our tradition assumes that life exists for us beyond the grave but without dogmatic views on its form. The repeated phrase that God 'brings the dead to life', or, as we express it, 'gives life beyond death', applies both to awakening daily and to this future existence.

SHABBAT EVENING SERVICE

AMIDAH

One of the following two versions below.
As we recite kadosh kadosh kadosh *some rise on tiptoe,*
as if trying to join with the heavenly beings singing praises to God.

II — GOD OF HOLINESS

וְאַתָּה קָדוֹשׁ יוֹשֵׁב תְּהִלּוֹת יִשְׂרָאֵל׃
קָדוֹשׁ קָדוֹשׁ קָדוֹשׁ יהוה צְבָאוֹת.
מְלֹא כָל־הָאָרֶץ כְּבוֹדוֹ׃
בָּרוּךְ כְּבוֹד־יהוה מִמְּקוֹמוֹ׃
יִמְלֹךְ יהוה לְעוֹלָם
אֱלֹהַיִךְ צִיּוֹן לְדֹר וָדֹר הַלְלוּיָהּ׃
בָּרוּךְ אַתָּה יהוה. הָאֵל הַקָּדוֹשׁ׃

During the Ten Days of Penitence:
הַמֶּֽלֶךְ הַקָּדוֹשׁ׃

וְאַתָּה You are holy,
dwelling in the prayers of Israel.[1]
Holy, holy, holy is the Creator of all,
whose glory fills all the earth.[2]
Blessed is God's glory,
revealed in every place.[3]
The Almighty shall rule forever!
Your God, O Zion, for all
generations! Praise God![4]
Blessed are You, the holy God.

During the Ten Days of Penitence:
the holy Sovereign.[1]

וְאַתָּה *V'attah kadosh yosheiv t'hillot*
yisra'el.
Kadosh kadosh kadosh, Adonai ts'va'ot,
m'lo chol ha-arets k'vodo.
Baruch k'vod Adonai mim'komo.
Yimloch Adonai l'olam,
elohayich tsiyyon,
l'dor vador hal'luyah.
Baruch attah Adonai ha-eil ha-kadosh.

During the Ten Days of Penitence:
ha-melech ha-kadosh.

I

אַתָּה קָדוֹשׁ וְשִׁמְךָ
קָדוֹשׁ וּקְדוֹשִׁים
בְּכָל־יוֹם יְהַלְלוּךָ. סֶּלָה׃
בָּרוּךְ אַתָּה יהוה.
הָאֵל הַקָּדוֹשׁ׃

During the Ten Days of Penitence:
הַמֶּֽלֶךְ הַקָּדוֹשׁ׃

אַתָּה You are holy and
Your name is holy, and
those who seek holiness
praise You day by day.
Blessed are You Eternal,
the holy God.

During the Ten Days of Penitence:
the holy Sovereign.

אַתָּה *Attah kadosh*
v'shimcha kadosh
uk'doshim b'chol yom
y'hal'lucha selah.
Baruch attah Adonai ha-eil
ha-kadosh.

During the Ten Days of Penitence:
ha-melech ha-kadosh.

קְדוּשָׁה **Holiness**
This blessing has many variations: a short statement when said by someone alone, a long series of choral responses for the morning or additional services of Shabbat and festivals.

Its origins lie in the Biblical visions of the heavenly court where semi-divine creatures sing praises to God. We join them in this worship, stringing together phrases from this Biblical experience.

[1] Ps 22:4. [2] Isa 6:3. [3] Ezek 3:12. [4] Ps 146:10.

THE HOLINESS OF THE SHABBAT

אַתָּה **You made the seventh day holy** to Your name, as the end of the creation of heaven and earth. You blessed it above all other days and made it holier above all other times, and so it is written in Your Torah:

אַתָּה קִדַּשְׁתָּ אֶת־יוֹם הַשְּׁבִיעִי לִשְׁמֶךָ: תַּכְלִית מַעֲשֵׂה שָׁמַיִם וָאָרֶץ: וּבֵרַכְתּוֹ מִכָּל־הַיָּמִים. וְקִדַּשְׁתּוֹ מִכָּל־הַזְּמַנִּים וְכֵן כָּתוּב בְּתוֹרָתֶךָ:

אַתָּה *Attah kiddashta et yom ha-shvi'i lishmecha. Tachlit ma'aseih shamayim va'arets. U'veirachto mikkol ha-yamim, v'kiddashto mikkol ha-z'manim, v'chein katuv b'toratecha.*

וַיְכֻלּוּ **Heaven and earth were finished** and all their host. On the seventh day God finished the work that had been done, and ceased on the seventh day from all the work that had been done. God blessed the seventh day, and made it holy, because on it God ceased from all the work of creation that God had done.[1]

וַיְכֻלּוּ הַשָּׁמַיִם וְהָאָרֶץ וְכָל־צְבָאָם: וַיְכַל אֱלֹהִים בַּיּוֹם הַשְּׁבִיעִי מְלַאכְתּוֹ אֲשֶׁר עָשָׂה וַיִּשְׁבֹּת בַּיּוֹם הַשְּׁבִיעִי מִכָּל־מְלַאכְתּוֹ אֲשֶׁר עָשָׂה: וַיְבָרֶךְ אֱלֹהִים אֶת־יוֹם הַשְּׁבִיעִי וַיְקַדֵּשׁ אֹתוֹ כִּי בוֹ שָׁבַת מִכָּל־מְלַאכְתּוֹ אֲשֶׁר־בָּרָא אֱלֹהִים לַעֲשׂוֹת:

וַיְכֻלּוּ *Vay'chulu ha-shamayim v'ha-arets v'chol ts'va'am. Vay'chal elohim ba-yom ha-sh'vi'i m'lachto asher asah, vayishbot ba-yom ha-sh'vi'i mikkol m'lachto asher asah. Vay'varech elohim et yom ha-sh'vi'i vay'kaddesh oto, ki vo shavat mikkol m'lachto, asher bara elohim la'asot.*

אַתָּה קָדוֹשׁ **You are holy ...**

This blessing completes the three opening ones that are recited in every version of the *Amidah*. On weekdays we would now bring our petitions to God, but on Shabbat and festivals we celebrate instead the special nature of the day and express our gratitude for the blessing of rest and peace.

אַתָּה קִדַּשְׁתָּ **You made holy ...**

This summary of the theme of Shabbat, that God sanctified and blessed it, serves to introduce the following Biblical passage.

וַיְכֻלּוּ **... were finished ...**

This passage concludes the creation story at the beginning of the Book of Genesis. By repeating the words for 'work', 'creating' and 'doing' it emphasises the extraordinary complexity of the world and cosmos. All now comes to a halt and stillness, as the seventh day is to be set apart for the special blessing of rest.

[1] Gen 2:1-3.

SHABBAT EVENING SERVICE

AMIDAH

אֱלֹהֵינוּ Our God and God of our ancestors, may our rest be pleasing to You. Make us holy by doing Your commands and let us share in the work of Your Torah. Make us content with Your goodness and let our souls know the joy of Your salvation. Purify our hearts to serve You in truth. In Your love and goodwill let us inherit Your holy Shabbat and may all Israel who seek holiness find in it their rest. Blessed are You God, who makes the Shabbat holy.

אֱלֹהֵינוּ וֵאלֹהֵי אֲבוֹתֵינוּ. רְצֵה־נָא בִמְנוּחָתֵנוּ. קַדְּשֵׁנוּ בְּמִצְוֹתֶיךָ. שִׂים חֶלְקֵנוּ בְּתוֹרָתֶךָ. שַׂבְּעֵנוּ מִטּוּבֶךָ. שַׂמַּח נַפְשֵׁנוּ בִּישׁוּעָתֶךָ. וְטַהֵר לִבֵּנוּ לְעָבְדְּךָ בֶּאֱמֶת. וְהַנְחִילֵנוּ יהוה אֱלֹהֵינוּ בְּאַהֲבָה וּבְרָצוֹן שַׁבַּת קָדְשֶׁךָ. וְיָנוּחוּ בָהּ כָּל־יִשְׂרָאֵל. מְקַדְּשֵׁי שְׁמֶךָ: בָּרוּךְ אַתָּה יהוה. מְקַדֵּשׁ הַשַּׁבָּת:

אֱלֹהֵינוּ *Eloheinu veilohei avoteinu, r'tseih na vimnuchateinu, kadd'sheinu v'mitsvotecha, sim chelkeinu v'toratecha, sab'einu mittuvecha, sammach nafsheinu vishu'atecha, v'taheir libeinu l'ovd'cha be'emet. V'hanchileinu Adonai eloheinu b'ahavah u'v'ratson shabbat kodshecha. V'yanuchu vah kol yisra'el m'kadd'shei sh'mecha. Baruch ata Adonai m'kaddeish ha-shabbat.*

THANKSGIVING AND PEACE

רְצֵה Our Living God be pleased with Your people Israel and listen to their prayers. In Your great mercy delight in us so that Your presence may rest upon Zion.

רְצֵה יהוה אֱלֹהֵינוּ בְּעַמְּךָ יִשְׂרָאֵל. וְלִתְפִלָּתָם שְׁעֵה. וּבְרַחֲמֶיךָ הָרַבִּים תַּחְפֹּץ בָּנוּ וְתַשְׁרֶה שְׁכִינָתְךָ עַל צִיּוֹן.

<<<

רְצֵה *R'tseih Adonai eloheinu b'amm'cha yisra'el, v'litfillatam sh'eih. Uv'rachamecha ha-rabbim tachpots banu, v'tashreh sh'chinat'cha al tsiyyon.*

אֱלֹהֵינוּ Our God ...
Just as God rested so we ask God's blessing on our rest for this day. Let our outer world be secure and let our inner life be dedicated to God's service.

רְצֵה Be pleased ...
This blessing is the first of three closing blessings of the *Amidah*. Just as the opening three followed 'court protocol', on entering the presence of the Sovereign, so we take our leave also in a formal way.

In its earlier forms this blessing called for the restoration of temple sacrifices. This version asks that God accept the prayers we have just recited and find favour with the Jewish people. This hope is to be expressed by our return to the land of Israel, but the physical return should also be accompanied by the tangible presence of God. The passage speaks of 'Zion', the term the psalmists used to describe Jerusalem not just as a political centre but also as a spiritual home for all who wished to encounter God.

On the New Moon and middle days of festivals, a blessing for the special occasion is inserted here.

On the New Moon and festivals, the following prayers are added, otherwise the service continues on page 147.

אֱלֹהֵינוּ Our God and God of our ancestors, may Your regard and concern for us and our ancestors, for the time of our redemption, for Jerusalem the city of Your holiness, and for all Your people the family of Israel, be close to You and be pleasing to You. Favour us all with freedom and goodness, with grace, love and mercy, on this day of

אֱלֹהֵינוּ וֵאלֹהֵי אֲבוֹתֵינוּ. יַעֲלֶה וְיָבֹא וְיַגִּיעַ וְיֵרָאֶה וְיֵרָצֶה וְיִשָּׁמַע וְיִפָּקֵד וְיִזָּכֵר זִכְרוֹנֵנוּ וּפִקְדוֹנֵנוּ וְזִכְרוֹן אֲבוֹתֵינוּ וְזִכְרוֹן מָשִׁיחַ בֶּן דָּוִד עַבְדֶּךָ. וְזִכְרוֹן יְרוּשָׁלַיִם עִיר קָדְשֶׁךָ וְזִכְרוֹן כָּל־עַמְּךָ בֵּית יִשְׂרָאֵל לְפָנֶיךָ. לִפְלֵיטָה וּלְטוֹבָה לְחֵן וּלְחֶסֶד וּלְרַחֲמִים לְחַיִּים וּלְשָׁלוֹם בְּיוֹם

(On the New Moon) the New Moon.
(On Pesach) the Feast of Unleavened Bread.
(On Succot) the Feast of Tabernacles.

רֹאשׁ הַחֹדֶשׁ הַזֶּה *On the New Moon*
חַג הַמַּצּוֹת הַזֶּה *On Pesach*
חַג הַסֻּכּוֹת הַזֶּה *On Succot*

Our Living God, remember us for good, Amen
bring us Your blessing, Amen
and save us for a good life. Amen

זָכְרֵנוּ יהוה אֱלֹהֵינוּ בּוֹ לְטוֹבָה אָמֵן
וּפָקְדֵנוּ בוֹ לִבְרָכָה אָמֵן
וְהוֹשִׁיעֵנוּ בוֹ לְחַיִּים טוֹבִים אָמֵן

Spare us and be kind to us according to Your promise of deliverance and mercy. Our eyes are turned towards You, for You are a Sovereign of mercy and compassion.

וּבִדְבַר יְשׁוּעָה וְרַחֲמִים חוּס וְחָנֵּנוּ. כִּי אֵלֶיךָ עֵינֵינוּ. כִּי אֵל מֶלֶךְ חַנּוּן וְרַחוּם אָתָּה.

אֱלֹהֵינוּ *Eloheinu veilohei avoteinu, ya'aleh v'yavo v'yagi'a v'yeira'eh v'yeiratseh v'yishama v'yippakeid v'yizzacheir zichroneinu ufikdoneinu v'zichron avoteinu v'zichron mashi'ach ben david avdecha, v'zichron y'rushalayim ir kodshecha, v'zichron kol amm'cha beit yisra'el l'fanecha, lifleitah ul'tovah l'chein ul'chesed ul'rachamim, l'chayyim ul'shalom, b'yom (On the New Moon) rosh ha-chodesh ha-zeh (On Pesach) chag ha-matsot ha-zeh (On Succot) chag ha-sukkot ha-zeh*

Zochreinu Adonai eloheinu bo l'tovah Amen
U'fokdeinu vo livracha Amen
V'hoshi'einu vo l'chayyim tovim Amen
Uvidvar y'shua'ah v'rachamim chus v'chonneinu, ki eilecha eineinu, ki eil melech channun v'rachum attah.

147 SHABBAT EVENING SERVICE — AMIDAH

The service continues here:

וְתֶחֱזֶינָה Our eyes look forward to Your return to Zion in mercy! Blessed are You God, ever restoring Your presence to Zion.

וְתֶחֱזֶינָה עֵינֵינוּ בְּשׁוּבְךָ לְצִיּוֹן בְּרַחֲמִים: בָּרוּךְ אַתָּה יהוה. הַמַּחֲזִיר שְׁכִינָתוֹ לְצִיּוֹן.

וְתֶחֱזֶינָה V'techezenah eineinu b'shuv'cha l'tsiyyon b'rachamim. Baruch attah Adonai ha-machazir sh'chinato l'tsiyyon.

It is customary to bow as one recites the opening words of this blessing, rising as we recite the name of God, Adonai *and the list of God's gifts to us.*

מוֹדִים We declare with gratitude that You are our God and the God of our ancestors. You are our rock, the rock of our life and the shield that saves us. In every generation we thank You and recount Your praise for our lives held in Your hand, for our souls that are in Your care, and for the signs of Your presence that are with us every day. At every moment, at evening, morning and noon, we experience Your wonders and Your goodness. You are goodness itself, for Your mercy has no end. You are mercy itself, for Your love has no limit. Forever have we put our hope in You.

מוֹדִים אֲנַחְנוּ לָךְ שָׁאַתָּה הוּא יהוה אֱלֹהֵינוּ וֵאלֹהֵי אֲבוֹתֵינוּ לְעוֹלָם וָעֶד. צוּרֵנוּ צוּר חַיֵּינוּ וּמָגֵן יִשְׁעֵנוּ אַתָּה הוּא: לְדוֹר וָדוֹר נוֹדֶה לְךָ וּנְסַפֵּר תְּהִלָּתֶךָ. עַל חַיֵּינוּ הַמְּסוּרִים בְּיָדֶךָ. וְעַל נִשְׁמוֹתֵינוּ הַפְּקוּדוֹת לָךְ. וְעַל נִסֶּיךָ שֶׁבְּכָל־יוֹם עִמָּנוּ. וְעַל נִפְלְאוֹתֶיךָ וְטוֹבוֹתֶיךָ שֶׁבְּכָל־עֵת עֶרֶב וָבֹקֶר וְצָהֳרָיִם: הַטּוֹב כִּי לֹא כָלוּ רַחֲמֶיךָ. הַמְרַחֵם כִּי לֹא תַמּוּ חֲסָדֶיךָ. כִּי מֵעוֹלָם קִוִּינוּ לָךְ.

<<<

מוֹדִים Modim anachnu lach, she'attah hu Adonai eloheinu veilohei avoteinu l'olam va'ed, tsureinu tsur chayyeinu umagein yish'einu, attah hu. L'dor vador nodeh l'cha un'sappeir t'hillatecha, al chayyeinu ha-m'surim b'yadecha, v'al nishmoteinu ha-p'kudot lach, v'al nissecha sheb'chol yom immanu, v'al nifl'otecha v'tovotecha sheb'chol eit, erev va'voker v'tsohorayim. Ha-tov ki lo chalu rachamecha, ha-m'racheim ki lo tammu chasadecha, ki mei'olam kivvinu lach.

מוֹדִים Gratitude ...

Protocol demands that we express our gratitude when leaving from an audience with the Sovereign. Here we sum up the benefits we have experienced because of our relationship with God. So we are reminded to take nothing in our life for granted, but rather to acknowledge 'the signs of Your presence', the miracles, that are daily with us.

Reference to God's wonders and miracles led to the insertion into this passage of a special prayer for the festival of *Chanukah* to celebrate that miraculous rescue.

On **Chanukah** add *al ha-nissim* on page 374, otherwise continue here:

וְעַל כֻּלָּם יִתְבָּרַךְ וְיִתְרוֹמֵם וְיִתְנַשֵּׂא תָּמִיד שִׁמְךָ מַלְכֵּנוּ לְעוֹלָם וָעֶד:

During the Ten Days of Penitence add:

וּכְתוֹב לְחַיִּים טוֹבִים כָּל־בְּנֵי בְרִיתֶךָ.

וְכֹל־הַחַיִּים יוֹדוּךָ סֶּלָה. וִיהַלְלוּ וִיבָרְכוּ אֶת שִׁמְךָ הַגָּדוֹל בֶּאֱמֶת. הָאֵל יְשׁוּעָתֵנוּ וְעֶזְרָתֵנוּ סֶלָה: בָּרוּךְ אַתָּה יהוה. הַטּוֹב שִׁמְךָ וּלְךָ נָאֶה לְהוֹדוֹת:

וְעַל And for all these things may Your name, our Sovereign, be blessed, exalted and honoured forever and ever.
During the Ten Days of Penitence add:
Record all the children of Your covenant for a good life.
May every living being thank You; may they praise and bless Your great name in truth, for You are the God who saves and helps us. Blessed are You God, known as goodness, whom it is right to praise.

וְעַל V'al kullam yitbarach v'yitromeim v'yitnassei tamid shimcha malkeinu l'olam va'ed.
During the Ten Days of Penitence add: Uch'tov l'chayyim tovim kol b'nei v'ritecha.
V'chol ha-chayyim yoducha selah, vihal'lu vivar'chu et shimcha ha-gadol be'emet, ha-eil y'shu'ateinu v'ezrateinu selah. Baruch attah Adonai, ha-tov shimcha ul'cha na'eh l'hodot.

שָׁלוֹם רָב עַל יִשְׂרָאֵל עַמְּךָ תָּשִׂים לְעוֹלָם. כִּי אַתָּה הוּא מֶלֶךְ אָדוֹן לְכָל־הַשָּׁלוֹם. וְטוֹב בְּעֵינֶיךָ לְבָרֵךְ אֶת עַמְּךָ יִשְׂרָאֵל בְּכָל־עֵת וּבְכָל־שָׁעָה בִּשְׁלוֹמֶךָ.

During the Ten Days of Penitence add:

בְּסֵפֶר חַיִּים נִזָּכֵר וְנִכָּתֵב לְפָנֶיךָ אֲנַחְנוּ וְכָל־עַמְּךָ בֵּית יִשְׂרָאֵל לְחַיִּים טוֹבִים וּלְשָׁלוֹם:

בָּרוּךְ אַתָּה יהוה. הַמְבָרֵךְ אֶת עַמּוֹ יִשְׂרָאֵל בַּשָּׁלוֹם:

שָׁלוֹם Set true peace upon Your people Israel forever. For You are the Source of all peace, and in Your eyes it is good to bless Your people Israel at every time and in every hour with Your peace.

During the Ten Days of Penitence add:
In Your presence may we and all Your people, the family of Israel, be remembered and recorded in the Book of Life for a good life and for peace.

Blessed are You God, blessing Your people Israel with peace.

שָׁלוֹם Shalom rav al Yisra'el amm'cha tasim l'olam, ki attah hu melech adon l'chol ha-shalom, v'tov b'einecha l'vareich et amm'cha Yisra'el b'chol eit uv'chol sha'ah bishlomecha.
During the Ten Days of Penitence: B'seifer chayyim nizzacheir v'nikkateiv l'fanecha, anachnu v'chol amm'cha beit Yisra'el, l'chayyim tovim ul'shalom.
Baruch attah Adonai, ha-m'vareich et ammo Yisra'el ba-shalom.

שָׁלוֹם רָב Set true peace ...
The closing blessing is a request for, and a declaration of, peace. Just as we would want to depart from friends with a word of peace, so do we as we take our leave of the Sovereign.

149 SHABBAT EVENING SERVICE — AMIDAH

MEDITATION

אֱלֹהַי My God, keep my tongue from causing harm and my lips from telling lies. Let me be silent if people curse me, my soul still humble and at peace with all. Open my heart to Your teaching, and give me the will to practise it. May the plans and schemes of those who seek my harm come to nothing.
May the words of my mouth and the meditation of my heart be acceptable to You, O God, my Rock and my Redeemer.[1]

אֱלֹהַי נְצוֹר לְשׁוֹנִי מֵרָע. וְשִׂפְתוֹתַי מִדַּבֵּר מִרְמָה. וְלִמְקַלְלַי נַפְשִׁי תִדֹּם. וְנַפְשִׁי כֶּעָפָר לַכֹּל תִּהְיֶה: פְּתַח לִבִּי בְּתוֹרָתֶךָ. וְאַחֲרֵי מִצְוֹתֶיךָ תִּרְדּוֹף נַפְשִׁי. וְכָל־הַקָּמִים עָלַי לְרָעָה מְהֵרָה הָפֵר עֲצָתָם וְקַלְקֵל מַחְשְׁבוֹתָם: יִהְיוּ לְרָצוֹן אִמְרֵי־פִי. וְהֶגְיוֹן לִבִּי לְפָנֶיךָ. יהוה צוּרִי וְגוֹאֲלִי:

אֱלֹהַי Elohai n'tsor l'shoni meira, v'siftotai middabbeir mirmah, v'limkal'lai nafshi tiddom, v'nafshi ke'afar la-kol tihyeh. P'tach libbi b'toratecha, v'acharei mitsvotecha tirdof nafshi, v'chol ha-kamim alai l'ra'ah, m'heirah hafeir atsatam, v'kalkeil machsh'votam. Yihyu l'ratson imrei fi, v'hegyon libbi l'fanecha, Adonai tsuri v'go'ali.

While reciting Oseh shalom *it is customary to take three steps backwards,
to bow to the left at the words* oseh shalom bimromav,
to the right at hu ya'aseh shalom *and to the centre at* aleinu.

עֹשֶׂה May the Maker of peace in the highest bring this peace upon us and upon all Israel and upon all the world. Amen.

עֹשֶׂה שָׁלוֹם בִּמְרוֹמָיו. הוּא יַעֲשֶׂה שָׁלוֹם עָלֵינוּ וְעַל כָּל־יִשְׂרָאֵל וְעַל־כָּל־הָעוֹלָם. וְאִמְרוּ. אָמֵן:

עֹשֶׂה Oseh shalom bimromav hu ya'aseh shalom aleinu
v'al kol yisra'el v'al kol ha-olam, v'imru Amen.

אֱלֹהַי נְצוֹר My God, keep ...
This private meditation is one of a number included in the Talmud (*Berachot* 16b-17a). It is attributed to Mar bar Ravina (fourth Century CE) At the end of the *Amidah* there is time for private thoughts and prayers, either with or without the words of this passage. It is followed by a quotation from Psalm 19:15 in the first person singular which matches the sentence from Psalm 51 with which we prepared ourselves for the *Amidah*. Now we hope that there is integrity between the thoughts that lie in our hearts and the words that we say aloud.

עֹשֶׂה שָׁלוֹם May the maker of peace ...
Oseh shalom is a rabbinic prayer based on a phrase from Job 25:2 seeking peace at the conclusion of a prayer. It is also found at the end of the *Kaddish*. Various progressive liturgies have made its conclusion more universalistic by adding phrases like 'and upon all dwellers on earth' or 'upon all humanity'.

[1] Ps 19:15.

In some congregations after a silent Amidah,
the following Vay'chulu *and the 'repetition of the* Amidah*' are said.*

וַיְכֻלּוּ Heaven and earth were finished and all their host. On the seventh day God finished the work that had been done, and ceased on the seventh day from all the work that had been done. God blessed the seventh day, and made it holy, because on it God ceased from all the work of creation that God had done.[1]

וַיְכֻלּוּ הַשָּׁמַיִם וְהָאָרֶץ וְכָל־צְבָאָם: וַיְכַל אֱלֹהִים בַּיּוֹם הַשְּׁבִיעִי מְלַאכְתּוֹ אֲשֶׁר עָשָׂה וַיִּשְׁבֹּת בַּיּוֹם הַשְּׁבִיעִי מִכָּל־מְלַאכְתּוֹ אֲשֶׁר עָשָׂה: וַיְבָרֶךְ אֱלֹהִים אֶת־יוֹם הַשְּׁבִיעִי וַיְקַדֵּשׁ אֹתוֹ כִּי בוֹ שָׁבַת מִכָּל־מְלַאכְתּוֹ אֲשֶׁר־בָּרָא אֱלֹהִים לַעֲשׂוֹת:

וַיְכֻלּוּ *Vay'chulu ha-shamayim v'ha-arets v'chol ts'va'am. Vay'chal elohim ba-yom ha-sh'vi'i m'lachto asher asah, vayishbot ba-yom ha-sh'vi'i mikkol m'lachto asher asah. Vay'varech elohim et yom ha-sh'vi'i vay'kaddesh oto, ki vo shavat mikkol m'lachto, asher bara elohim la'asot.*

בָּרוּךְ Blessed are You, our God, and God of our ancestors,

God of Abraham	God of Sarah,
God of Isaac	God of Rebecca,
and God of Jacob,	God of Rachel
	and God of Leah,

the great, the mighty, and the awesome God, God beyond, possessing heaven and earth.

בָּרוּךְ אַתָּה יהוה אֱלֹהֵינוּ וֵאלֹהֵי אֲבוֹתֵינוּ וְאִמּוֹתֵינוּ. אֱלֹהֵי אַבְרָהָם אֱלֹהֵי שָׂרָה. אֱלֹהֵי יִצְחָק אֱלֹהֵי רִבְקָה. וֵאלֹהֵי יַעֲקֹב אֱלֹהֵי רָחֵל וֵאלֹהֵי לֵאָה. הָאֵל הַגָּדוֹל הַגִּבּוֹר וְהַנּוֹרָא. אֵל עֶלְיוֹן. קוֹנֵה שָׁמַיִם וָאָרֶץ:

בָּרוּךְ *Baruch attah Adonai eloheinu veilohei avoteinu v'immoteinu.*
Elohei avraham,   elohei sarah,
elohei yitschak,   elohei rivkah,
veilohei ya'akov,   elohei rachel veilohei le'ah.
Ha'eil ha-gadol, ha-gibbor v'ha-nora, eil elyon, koneih shamayim va'arets.

'Repetition' of the *Amidah*
Traditionally the evening *Amidah* is recited silently by the congregation and not repeated aloud by the prayer leader.

Exceptionally on Shabbat a shortened version of the seven separate blessings may be read, *birkat me-ein sheva.*

[1] Gen 2:1-3.

SHABBAT EVENING SERVICE — AMIDAH

מָגֵן אָבוֹת בִּדְבָרוֹ. מְחַיֵּה מֵתִים בְּמַאֲמָרוֹ. הָאֵל

During the Ten Days of Penitence:
הַמֶּלֶךְ

הַקָּדוֹשׁ שֶׁאֵין כָּמוֹהוּ. הַמֵּנִיחַ לְעַמּוֹ בְּיוֹם שַׁבַּת קָדְשׁוֹ. כִּי בָם רָצָה לְהָנִיחַ לָהֶם: לְפָנָיו נַעֲבוֹד בְּיִרְאָה וָפַחַד. וְנוֹדֶה לִשְׁמוֹ בְּכָל־יוֹם תָּמִיד מֵעֵין הַבְּרָכוֹת. אֵל הַהוֹדָאוֹת אֲדוֹן הַשָּׁלוֹם מְקַדֵּשׁ הַשַּׁבָּת וּמְבָרֵךְ שְׁבִיעִי וּמֵנִיחַ בִּקְדֻשָּׁה לְעַם מְדֻשְּׁנֵי עֹנֶג. זֵכֶר לְמַעֲשֵׂה בְרֵאשִׁית:

מָגֵן You shielded our ancestors through Your word, You give life beyond death through Your speech. Holy God,

During the Ten Days of Penitence:
Holy Sovereign

there is none like You, giving rest to Your people on the holy Shabbat day, for You accepted them, and wished them rest. Before You we will serve with awe and dread and give thanks to You each day, forever drawing from the Source of blessings. God, worthy of gratitude, Source of peace, You make the Shabbat holy and bless the seventh day, giving rest with holiness to a people filled with delight - bringing to mind the act of creation.

מָגֵן Magein avot bidvaro, m'chayyeih meitim b'ma'amaro, ha-eil
During the Ten Days of Penitence: ha-melech
ha-kadosh she'ein kamohu, ha-meini'ach l'ammo b'yom shabbat kodsho, ki vam ratsah l'hani'ach lahem. L'fanav na'avod b'yir'ah vafachad, v'nodeh lishmo b'chol yom tamid, mei'ein ha-b'rachot, eil ha-hoda'ot, adon ha-shalom, m'kaddeish ha-shabbat, um'vareich sh'vi'i, umeini'ach bikdushah l'am m'dush'nei oneg, zeicher l'ma'aseih v'reishit.

<<<

אֱלֹהֵינוּ Our God and God of our ancestors, may our rest be pleasing to You. Make us holy by doing Your commands and let us share in the work of Your Torah. Make us content with Your goodness and let our souls know the joy of Your salvation. Purify our hearts to serve You in truth. In Your love and goodwill let us inherit Your holy Shabbat and may all Israel who seek holiness find in it their rest. Blessed are You God, who makes the Shabbat holy.

אֱלֹהֵינוּ וֵאלֹהֵי אֲבוֹתֵינוּ. רְצֵה־נָא בִמְנוּחָתֵנוּ. קַדְּשֵׁנוּ בְּמִצְוֹתֶיךָ. שִׂים חֶלְקֵנוּ בְּתוֹרָתֶךָ. שַׂבְּעֵנוּ מִטּוּבֶךָ. שַׂמַּח נַפְשֵׁנוּ בִּישׁוּעָתֶךָ. וְטַהֵר לִבֵּנוּ לְעָבְדְּךָ בֶּאֱמֶת. וְהַנְחִילֵנוּ יהוה אֱלֹהֵינוּ בְּאַהֲבָה וּבְרָצוֹן שַׁבַּת קָדְשֶׁךָ. וְיָנוּחוּ בָה כָּל־יִשְׂרָאֵל. מְקַדְּשֵׁי שְׁמֶךָ: בָּרוּךְ אַתָּה יהוה. מְקַדֵּשׁ הַשַּׁבָּת:

אֱלֹהֵינוּ *Eloheinu veilohei avoteinu, r'tseih na vimnuchateinu, kadd'sheinu v'mitsvotecha, sim chelkeinu v'toratecha, sab'einu mittuvecha, sammach nafsheinu vishuatecha, v'taheir libbeinu l'ovd'cha be'emet. V'hanchileinu Adonai eloheinu b'ahavah u'v'ratson shabbat kodshecha. V'yanuchu vah kol yisra'el m'kadd'shei sh'mecha. Baruch ata Adonai m'kaddeish ha-shabbat.*

Kiddush *is on page 451.*

Between **Pesach** *and* **Shavuot** *the* **Omer** *is counted here - see page 308.*
A study passage or address may be included here.

During the Penitential Period from the first day of the month of Elul *until* Shemini Atzeret
Psalm 27 (page 627) may be read here.

The Concluding Prayers for the Evening Service begin on page 309.

תפלת שחרית לשבת
Shabbat Morning Service

אֱלֹהַי נְשָׁמָה שֶׁנָּתַתָּ בִּי טְהוֹרָה הִיא:

My God, the soul You have given me is pure.

> The Shabbat morning service is constructed like the daily morning service with two preparatory sections: the opening 'Morning Blessings', of a personal nature, are followed by the 'Verses of Song', that prepare the community for the formal, 'statutory', part of the service that follows. Introduced by the *bar'chu*, the 'call to prayer', the *Sh'ma* with its blessings opens this section, followed by the *Amidah*, the central 'standing' prayer. Special to Shabbat, and at the heart of the service, is the Torah reading with its accompanying prophetic text, the *Haftarah*. Following the various prayers on behalf of the Jewish people and the community, some congregations include a *Musaf*, 'Additional', *Amidah* in line with the temple practice of offering an additional sacrifice on Shabbat and Festivals. The concluding prayers and songs prepare us for our return to the outer world.

BEFORE THE SERVICE BEGINS

Some thoughts to help prepare for the Shabbat Morning Service

We enter this service bringing with us much of the outer world: the troubles and joys, anxieties and hopes, that accompany our daily life, that are on our mind. The service offers us a different world, one which may give a perspective on our life, or simply time out from the daily round. But to enter it some preparation may help.

As we leave our coats in the hall we shed a part of that outer load. Crossing the threshold into the sanctuary is a further step away and nearer to this new opportunity.

A few moments seated in silence may help compose us. The passages on prayer may ease our way into the formalities of the service.

Donning the *tallit* and reciting its blessing may further close out, however briefly, the outer noise and busy-ness of life.

When about to begin the service itself, it may be appropriate to say aloud, or to oneself, *'hineni'*, 'here I am!'

The first section of the morning service, *Birchot Ha-shachar*, 'the Morning Blessings' is about my personal situation. Though often read in unison, the different passages focus on who I am, my body, my emotions, my spirit, my soul. *Im ein ani li mi li*, 'if I am not for myself, who will be for me?'

But in the next section, *P'sukei D'zimrah*, 'Verses of Song', we join together with all who are present. The focus shifts from my individual self to the community of which I am a part at this particular moment. And we, together, begin to move our attention beyond our individual selves, to God, however we understand such a term: the power of the universe, the mystery of creation, the workings of human consciousness, the beauty of art and nature, the experience of love, the simple awareness that we are not alone and not the centre of the universe. *U'ch'sheani l'atzmi mah ani*, but 'if I am only for myself, what am I?'

With the *Bar'chu*, the Call to Prayer, the formal part of the service begins, and our journey is underway.

Sometimes we can surrender to this world of prayer, sometimes not. Even if it does not always speak to us, our presence may help others find comfort, solace or challenge. That is the value of community and the mystery of a community at prayer.

Welcome!

פתיחה לתפלה
OPENING PRAYERS ♁331

For Shabbat Morning

I The Just Society

Our God and God of our ancestors, we thank You for teaching us how to save each other and ourselves, to give and to receive, and to support each other on life's journey. There is no limit to our ascent, for there is no limit to the goodness we can do. There is no joy we cannot have, for there is no end to giving. There is no height we cannot attain, for we were created to need each other's love and understanding.

      The doors of heaven are open to all. So let us share our blessings and enter in. In the past week we may have denied happiness to others and to ourselves, for selfishness lies in the way, and we can be enemies to our own happiness. Your Shabbat calls us back to the truth. We learn again the way to change hatred into love, and banish bitterness. We know again the strength for good that is in our grasp. We see again the purity of our souls, and Your image shining in us. Blessed are You God, who teaches us to serve each other.

II The Community

God, I come before You surrounded by the members of the community in which I live. I share my happiness with them and it becomes greater. I share my troubles with them and they seem smaller. May I never be too mean to give, nor too proud to receive, for in giving and receiving I discover You, and begin to understand the meaning of life.

Let me not separate myself from the true strength of my community: the experience and wisdom of old people, the hopes of the young, and the examples of care and courage which sustain me. Give me an open heart and an open mind to welcome those who need me, and to receive Your presence in my daily life.

I think of what we could be and the harmony and friendship that could unite us. I think of our loneliness and the friendship that could fill our lives. I think of the good that we could do if we were one in spirit. I know that this is Your will and pray for Your help. May I and those around me find our joy together, and bless You for the power You gave us to help each other.

III The Family of Israel

We are one small part of the family of Israel; together with all other holy communities we turn to God in whom we trust. You are the righteousness our prophets proclaimed and the wisdom our rabbis sought. You are the truth and glory of our history, our strength in all the changes of the world. You led our ancestors to greatness. May You guide us and our children in the days that lie ahead. We bow to You alone, and stand upright before all peoples. By serving You we are free to serve all humanity. Your righteousness unites the family of Israel scattered throughout the world. It speaks to us in every tongue, in every place, to make us the instruments of Your peace. The Guardian of Israel never slumbers and never sleeps. May the One who makes peace and harmony in the highest, bring this peace upon us, and through this people Israel to all the world.

IV Tradition

May my life be one link in a chain of goodness. As I say the prayers of past generations, help me to remember their devotion and faithfulness, their joy and suffering, which are in every word. Holiness is my heritage, may I be worthy of it.

May this tradition live in me and pass from me to generations I shall never know, enriched by the truth that I have found and the good deeds I have done. So may I fulfil my task on earth and receive my blessing.

And when the service ends and the prayers have ceased, help me to bring their spirit into the world in which I live. May I love God above all, and my neighbour as myself, and be a living witness to the truth that never changes.

V Life and Death

God, a mystery surrounds my life. What comes before it and what lies after it are hidden from me. My life is very short, and Your universe is vast. But in the darkness is Your presence, and in the mystery, Your love. My ancestors put their trust in You, and You put goodness in their hearts and peace within their minds. May I be like them and may my reward be like theirs.

In every place, at every time, Your voice speaks within me. It leads me in the way of honesty and charity. It shows me truth and goodness. There are times when it is hard to hear You, and times when it is hard to follow You; and I know this is my loss.

In the quietness of this Shabbat I turn my thoughts to You. Help me to hear Your voice, to find Your image in my soul, and to be at peace.

VI The Future

God, we thank You for Your gift of hope, our strength in times of trouble. Beyond the injustice of our time, its cruelty and its wars, we look forward to a world at peace when people deal kindly with each other, and no one is afraid. Every bad deed delays its coming, every good one brings it nearer. May our lives be Your witness, so that future generations bless us. May the day come, as the prophet taught, when 'the sun of righteousness will rise with healing in its wings'.[1] Help us to pray for it, to wait for it, to work for it and to be worthy of it. Blessed are You God, the Hope of Israel.

VII The Covenants of God

Our God and God of all who live,
You made a covenant with Noah,
to teach us to cherish the earth on which we live.
May we ever be true to Your teaching.

You made a covenant with Abraham,
to teach us that You can be found through many religious paths.
May we ever be true to Your teaching.

You made a covenant with Israel,
to teach us that every people has a special task in this world.
May we ever be true to Your teaching.

You made a covenant with David,
to teach us that everyone can err and fail yet still return to You again.
May we ever be true to Your teaching.

May we be true in our time and place to these covenants of duty
and of love.

VIII Our Heritage

Once, long ago, You came to us in dreams, connecting heaven and earth. You revealed yourself in visions, making wisdom our desire. You showed us Your ways, gave us a purpose for our days. Israel's destiny was assured. Your poets sang of Your glory, rejoicing the heart. Your prophets rebuked and cajoled, restoring hope in troubled times, teaching honesty for all generations. Your rabbis enlightened our eyes, delighting in life, every moment a blessing. Your mystics enlivened our souls, sparking knowledge of You in the depths of our being. All this You have done, and more besides. Gratitude is Your due and in You our faith resides. We hold in trust our sacred task. At this moment, in the quietness of this hour, we realise all we have lost and all we could still regain. Together may we put our hope in You. 'Renew our days, as of old'.

---

[1] Mal 3:20.

IX Our Responsibility

We, the family of Israel, inheritors of a vision, have learned what the Eternal One seeks from us. Is it not to do justly, to love kindness, and to walk humbly with our God? The words are sweet as honey on our tongues. Yet how bitter they can taste when outside us lies a world of poverty and injustice. Let our compassion not become callused, nor our righteousness succumb to despair. O God, give us strength to act in the world, for Your name's sake.

X One Humanity

God of the spirits of all flesh,
You created one human being, so all humanity is one.
You created us in Your image, so all are equal in your sight.

In a world so vast, may all find for themselves a home.
In a world so small, let us make space for one another.
In times of conflict may we help to bring understanding.
In times of bitterness and hate, may we offer healing and love.
When faith erects barriers, may our understanding of You build bridges.
When faith is betrayed or misused, give us courage to seek Your truth.

XI The Gift of Women

May God who remembered Sarah, remember us with blessing.
May God who prophesied to Rebecca, give us vision in our time.
May God who answered Leah, sustain the family of Israel.
May God who heard Rachel, help us in our need.
May God who honoured Shiphra and Puah, support all who resist oppression.
May God who healed Miriam, bring healing to those in pain.
May God who restored Naomi, bring comfort to those who mourn.
May God who guided Abigail, bring wisdom to those in conflict.
May God who responded to Hannah, bring redemption to our world.

159 SHABBAT MORNING SERVICE — OPENING PRAYERS

נִשְׁמַת כָּל חַי תְּבָרֵךְ אֶת שִׁמְךָ

The Breath of Life on every creature shall Bless You God our Creator.

160 תפלת שחרית לשבת

Some congregations begin the service here:

ACROSS THE THRESHOLD

DIRECTING THE HEART TO GOD

מַה־טֹּבוּ How good are your tents,
O Jacob, and your homes, O Israel!

Through the greatness of Your love
I enter Your house.
In awe of You I worship
before the ark of Your holiness.

God, as I loved the courts of Your
temple, and the place where Your
glory dwelt, so I still worship and
bend low, humble before the Eternal
my Maker.

As for me, let my prayer come
before You at the proper time.

Answer me God, in the greatness of
Your love, for Your deliverance
is sure.[1]

מַה־טֹּבוּ אֹהָלֶיךָ
יַעֲקֹב. מִשְׁכְּנֹתֶיךָ יִשְׂרָאֵל:
וַאֲנִי בְּרֹב חַסְדְּךָ אָבוֹא בֵיתֶךָ.
אֶשְׁתַּחֲוֶה אֶל־הֵיכַל־קָדְשְׁךָ
בְּיִרְאָתֶךָ:
יהוה אָהַבְתִּי מְעוֹן בֵּיתֶךָ.
וּמְקוֹם מִשְׁכַּן כְּבוֹדֶךָ:
וַאֲנִי אֶשְׁתַּחֲוֶה וְאֶכְרָעָה.
אֶבְרְכָה לִפְנֵי־יהוה עֹשִׂי:
וַאֲנִי תְפִלָּתִי־לְךָ יהוה עֵת רָצוֹן:
אֱלֹהִים בְּרָב־חַסְדֶּךָ.
עֲנֵנִי בֶּאֱמֶת יִשְׁעֶךָ:

מַה־טֹּבוּ *Mah tovu ohalecha ya'akov, mishk'notecha yisra'el.*
Va'ani b'rov chasd'cha avo veitecha, eshtachaveh el heichal kodsh'cha b'yiratecha.
Adonai ahavti m'on beitecha, um'kom mishkan k'vodecha.
Va'ani eshtachaveh v'echra'ah, evr'chah lifnei Adonai osi.
Va'ani t'fillati l'cha Adonai eit ratson.
Elohim b'rov chasdecha, aneini be'emet yish'echa.

מַה־טֹּבוּ **How good ...**

The first recorded appearance of this passage, traditionally recited on entering the synagogue, is in the Seder Rav Amram Gaon in the ninth century.

The sentence 'How good are your tents, O Jacob...' was said in the Bible by Balaam, a foreign prophet hired to curse the Israelites on their journey through the wilderness. Instead God forced him to bless the people with these opening words. In its Biblical context the 'tents' and 'homes' (literally: 'dwelling places') refer to the encampment in the wilderness, but later tradition interpreted them to refer to 'synagogues' and 'schools'. 'Tents' can also indicate the temporary nature of much of Jewish life in exile, the experience of 'Jacob'; while 'homes' points to a stable messianic future for 'Israel'.

All the Psalm verses that follow are couched in the first person singular except Psalm 95:6, which is in the first person plural. It was modified by the author to fit this liturgical adaptation. The effect is to emphasise how each individual reading it is consciously entering into the world of liturgy and prayer, of community and communion with God.

The alternative version acknowledges the role of both men and women in creating and sustaining Jewish domestic and community life.

[1] Num 24:5, Ps 5:8, Ps 26:8,
Ps 95:6, Ps 69:14.

SHABBAT MORNING SERVICE — MORNING BLESSINGS

An alternative opening:

מַה־טֹּבוּ **How good are your tents, O Jacob,**
and your homes, O Israel!
How good are your tents, O Leah,
and your homes, O Rachel!

מַה־טֹּבוּ אֹהָלֶיךָ יַעֲקֹב.
מִשְׁכְּנֹתֶיךָ יִשְׂרָאֵל:
מַה־טֹּבוּ אֹהָלַיִךְ לֵאָה.
מִשְׁכְּנֹתַיִךְ רָחֵל:

מַה־טֹּבוּ *Mah tovu ohalecha ya'akov, mishk'notecha yisra'el.*
Mah tovu ohalayich le'ah, mishk'notayich rachel.

אם אין לי מי לי
If I am not for myself, who is for me?

Some congregations begin here:

ברכות השחר
MORNING BLESSINGS ☰ 331-335

A selection may be read from the 'Morning Blessings'

The sequence of passages that make up the 'Morning Blessings' were originally recited in the home on awakening, arising and preparing for the day. Their transfer to the synagogue gives them a wider range of meanings, but they retain their private and intimate nature. They allow us to reflect upon our personal situation, our physical and spiritual nature, at this early stage of the service.

The sequence begins with the 'gift of our bodies', a blessing that speaks of the wondrous complexity of our physical being. The next blessing reminds us that as well as our bodies we have a consciousness, an inner life, which we may think of as our 'spirit', 'life force' or 'soul'. The thirteen short blessings that follow enable us to consider the blessings that we have in our lives. The following passages lead us to think about the freedom that we enjoy and the responsibilities that go with this freedom.

Central to our Jewish sense of who we are is the need to study, to seek to understand the world and our place within it. So the next blessing expresses this commitment, and the service offers the opportunity to study a passage that reflects in some way the Torah, the teaching, that we have inherited and that we discover anew each day.

Through these blessings and prayers we have already begun the move away from purely personal concerns to our sense of belonging to a community, so this section of the service leads into the 'Verses of Song' that celebrate our collective existence and relationship to God.

ENCOUNTERING OURSELVES

In this section we examine our personal life,
physical and spiritual, our gifts and our responsibilities.

THE GIFT OF OUR BODY ♦ 332

בָּרוּךְ Blessed are You, our Living God, Sovereign of the universe, who formed human beings in wisdom, creating within them openings and vessels. It is revealed and known before the throne of Your glory that if one of them is opened or one of them closed it would be impossible to remain alive and stand before You.

Blessed are You God, who heals all flesh and performs such wonders.

בָּרוּךְ אַתָּה יהוה אֱלֹהֵינוּ מֶלֶךְ הָעוֹלָם. אֲשֶׁר יָצַר אֶת־הָאָדָם בְּחָכְמָה. וּבָרָא בוֹ נְקָבִים נְקָבִים. חֲלוּלִים חֲלוּלִים: גָּלוּי וְיָדוּעַ לִפְנֵי כִסֵּא כְבוֹדֶךָ שֶׁאִם יִפָּתֵחַ אֶחָד מֵהֶם. אוֹ יִסָּתֵם אֶחָד מֵהֶם. אִי אֶפְשַׁר לְהִתְקַיֵּים וְלַעֲמוֹד לְפָנֶיךָ:

בָּרוּךְ אַתָּה יהוה. רוֹפֵא כָל־בָּשָׂר. וּמַפְלִיא לַעֲשׂוֹת:

בָּרוּךְ *Baruch attah Adonai eloheinu melech ha-olam, asher yatsar et ha-adam b'chochmah, uvara vo n'kavim n'kavim, chalulim chalulim. Galui v'yadu'a lifnei chissei ch'vodecha she'im yippatei'ach echad meihem, o yissateim echad meihem, i efshar l'hitkayyeim v'la'amod l'fanecha.*

Baruch attah Adonai, rofei chol basar, umafli la'asot.

אֲשֶׁר יָצַר אֶת הָאָדָם בְּחָכְמָה
Who formed human beings in wisdom ...
The first of the morning blessings focuses our attention on our physical body and its needs. We thank God for the complexity of our body and the astonishing way in which it functions. The Talmud (*Berachot* 60b) debates how the blessing should end. Rav said 'Who heals the sick', but this would turn the whole world into invalids! Samuel said 'Who performs such wonders'. As a compromise both phrases were used. So in times of good health this blessing is a reminder to take care of our body and be grateful for how it works. It times of illness it may give us courage to seek healing and to pray, but also to accept God's will for circumstances that cannot be changed.

163 SHABBAT MORNING SERVICE — MORNING BLESSINGS

THE GIFT OF OUR SOUL ♱332

אֱלֹהַי My God, the soul
You have given me is pure,
for You created it,
You formed it
and You made it live within me.
You watch over it within me,
but one day
You will take it from me
to everlasting life.

My God and God of
generations before me,
as long as the soul is within me,
I will declare
that You are the power of good deeds,
the Ruler of all creatures,
possessing every soul.

Blessed are You God, giving new life
to our bodies each day.

אֱלֹהַי. נְשָׁמָה שֶׁנָּתַתָּ בִּי
טְהוֹרָה הִיא:
אַתָּה בְרָאתָהּ.
אַתָּה יְצַרְתָּהּ.
אַתָּה נְפַחְתָּהּ בִּי.
וְאַתָּה מְשַׁמְּרָהּ בְּקִרְבִּי.
וְאַתָּה עָתִיד לִטְּלָהּ מִמֶּנִּי
לְחַיֵּי עוֹלָם:
כָּל־זְמַן שֶׁהַנְּשָׁמָה בְקִרְבִּי
מוֹדֶה/מוֹדָה אֲנִי לְפָנֶיךָ
יהוה אֱלֹהַי וֵאלֹהֵי אֲבוֹתַי.
שֶׁאַתָּה הוּא רִבּוֹן כָּל־הַמַּעֲשִׂים.
מוֹשֵׁל בְּכָל־הַבְּרִיּוֹת.
אֲדוֹן כָּל־הַנְּשָׁמוֹת:
בָּרוּךְ אַתָּה יהוה.
הַמַּחֲזִיר נְשָׁמוֹת לַמֵּתִים:

אֱלֹהַי Elohai, n'shamah shennatatta bi t'horah hi.
Attah v'ratah, attah y'tsartah, attah n'fachtah bi,
v'attah m'shamm'rah b'kirbi, v'attah atid litt'lah mimmeni l'chayyei olam.
Kol z'man sheha-n'shamah b'kirbi modeh/modah ani l'fanecha
Adonai elohai veilohei avotai, she'attah hu ribbon kol ha-ma'asim,
mosheil b'chol ha-b'riot, adon kol ha-n'shamot.
Baruch attah Adonai, ha-machazir n'shamot la-meitim.

אֱלֹהַי נְשָׁמָה My God the soul ...
   The text of this blessing appears in the Talmud (*Berachot* 60b). The rabbis taught that sleep was one sixtieth part of death (*Berachot* 57b), and that our souls are restored to us in the morning when we wake up. The act of breathing is evidence of life, and the Hebrew text actually dramatises this.
   In five of the opening sentences the verb ends with the letter *hey* with a dot in it, a so-called *mappik hey*. This indicates that the usually silent letter is to be sounded as we breathe out. Thus we hear the breath being restored to us as we return to the tasks of a new day. A renewed soul offers us the possibility of a new beginning at every stage of our life, whatever has happened to us in the past.

These Morning Blessings were originally recited in the home on waking up, and the phrases correspond to the physical acts - opening the eyes, putting on clothing, stretching, walking. Their transfer to the synagogue has made them less literal and more like metaphors for God's providence. However, some of them can be seen as spelling out our own human responsibilities as God's agents in the world - we are to clothe the naked, to free those who are bound, and so on.

Some progressive liturgies have changed the opening blessings that are expressed in a negative way, for example 'who has not made me a slave', into positive forms, 'who has made me free'. We have retained the traditional formulation in this particular case because of an occurrence in the concentration camps when a rabbi was asked how the inmates could say 'who has not made me a slave' when they were clearly enslaved. His answer was that this blessing was even more important because despite the outer slavery they needed to resist becoming spiritually enslaved.

The first blessing replaces the traditional one recited by men, 'who has not made me a woman', and the woman's equivalent, 'who has made me according to God's will', with the affirmation in the Creation story that we are all made in the image of God. The sequence of blessings moves from the personal, to general statements about God's providence, to those specific to the Jewish people.

THE GIFT OF BLESSINGS

בָּרוּךְ Blessed are You, our Living God, Sovereign of the universe, who has made me in the image of God.

בָּרוּךְ אַתָּה יהוה אֱלֹהֵינוּ מֶלֶךְ הָעוֹלָם. שֶׁעָשַׂנִי בְּצֶלֶם אֱלֹהִים:

Blessed are You, our Living God, Sovereign of the universe, who has not made me a stranger to You.

בָּרוּךְ אַתָּה יהוה אֱלֹהֵינוּ מֶלֶךְ הָעוֹלָם. שֶׁלֹּא עָשַׂנִי נָכְרִי/נָכְרִיָּה:

Blessed are You, our Living God, Sovereign of the universe, who has not enslaved me.

בָּרוּךְ אַתָּה יהוה אֱלֹהֵינוּ מֶלֶךְ הָעוֹלָם. שֶׁלֹּא עָשַׂנִי עֶבֶד/שִׁפְחָה:

Blessed are You, our Living God, Sovereign of the universe,
You provide for my every need.

בָּרוּךְ אַתָּה יהוה אֱלֹהֵינוּ מֶלֶךְ הָעוֹלָם. שֶׁעָשָׂה-לִי כָּל-צָרְכִּי:

Blessed are You, our Living God, Sovereign of the universe,
You open eyes that cannot see.

בָּרוּךְ אַתָּה יהוה אֱלֹהֵינוּ מֶלֶךְ הָעוֹלָם. פּוֹקֵחַ עִוְרִים:

<<<

בָּרוּךְ *Baruch attah Adonai eloheinu melech ha-olam, she'asani b'tselem elohim.*
Baruch attah Adonai eloheinu melech ha-olam, shelo asani nochri/nochriyah.
Baruch attah Adonai eloheinu melech ha-olam, shelo asani aved/shifchah.
Baruch attah Adonai eloheinu melech ha-olam, she'asah li kol tsorki.
Baruch attah Adonai eloheinu melech ha-olam, pokei'ach ivrim.

Blessed are You, our Living God, Sovereign of the universe, You clothe the naked.	בָּרוּךְ אַתָּה יהוה אֱלֹהֵינוּ מֶלֶךְ הָעוֹלָם. מַלְבִּישׁ עֲרֻמִּים:
Blessed are You, our Living God, Sovereign of the universe, You free those who are bound.	בָּרוּךְ אַתָּה יהוה אֱלֹהֵינוּ מֶלֶךְ הָעוֹלָם. מַתִּיר אֲסוּרִים:
Blessed are You, our Living God, Sovereign of the universe, You lift up those bent low.	בָּרוּךְ אַתָּה יהוה אֱלֹהֵינוּ מֶלֶךְ הָעוֹלָם. זוֹקֵף כְּפוּפִים:
Blessed are You, our Living God, Sovereign of the universe, You support our human steps.	בָּרוּךְ אַתָּה יהוה אֱלֹהֵינוּ מֶלֶךְ הָעוֹלָם. הַמֵּכִין מִצְעֲדֵי־גָבֶר:
Blessed are You, our Living God, Sovereign of the universe, You fortify Israel with strength.	בָּרוּךְ אַתָּה יהוה אֱלֹהֵינוּ מֶלֶךְ הָעוֹלָם. אוֹזֵר יִשְׂרָאֵל בִּגְבוּרָה:
Blessed are You, our Living God, Sovereign of the universe, You crown Israel with glory.	בָּרוּךְ אַתָּה יהוה אֱלֹהֵינוּ מֶלֶךְ הָעוֹלָם. עוֹטֵר יִשְׂרָאֵל בְּתִפְאָרָה:
Blessed are You, our Living God, Sovereign of the universe, You give strength to the weary.	בָּרוּךְ אַתָּה יהוה אֱלֹהֵינוּ מֶלֶךְ הָעוֹלָם. הַנּוֹתֵן לַיָּעֵף כֹּחַ:
Blessed are You, our Living God, Sovereign of the universe, You take away sleep from my eyes and slumber from my eyelids.	בָּרוּךְ אַתָּה יהוה אֱלֹהֵינוּ מֶלֶךְ הָעוֹלָם. הַמַּעֲבִיר שֵׁנָה מֵעֵינַי וּתְנוּמָה מֵעַפְעַפָּי:

Baruch attah Adonai eloheinu melech ha-olam, malbish arumim.
Baruch attah Adonai eloheinu melech ha-olam, mattir asurim.
Baruch attah Adonai eloheinu melech ha-olam, zokeif k'fufim.
Baruch attah Adonai eloheinu melech ha-olam, ha-meichin mits'adei gaver.
Baruch attah Adonai eloheinu melech ha-olam, ozeir yisra'el bigvurah.
Baruch attah Adonai eloheinu melech ha-olam, oteir yisra'el b'tif'arah.
Baruch attah Adonai eloheinu melech ha-olam, ha-notein laya'eif ko'ach.
Baruch attah Adonai eloheinu melech ha-olam, ha-ma'avir sheinah mei'einai ut'numah mei'af'appai.

THE GIFT OF FREEDOM

לְעוֹלָם We should always be in awe of God in private as well as in public; speak the truth aloud and mean it in our heart.

יְהִי Our Living God and God of our ancestors, help us to live according to Your teaching and to hold fast to Your commands. Let us not come into the power of sin or wrongdoing, temptation or disgrace. Let no evil within us control us, and keep us far from bad people and bad company. Help us hold fast to the good within us and to good deeds, and bend our will and our desires to serve You. Give us today, and every day, grace, kindness and mercy in Your sight and in the sight of all who regard us, and grant us Your love and kindness. Blessed are You God, inspiring Your people Israel with love and kindness.

לְעוֹלָם יְהֵא אָדָם יְרֵא שָׁמַיִם בַּסֵּתֶר כְּבַגָּלוּי. וּמוֹדֶה עַל־הָאֱמֶת וְדוֹבֵר אֱמֶת בִּלְבָבוֹ:

יְהִי רָצוֹן מִלְּפָנֶיךָ יהוה אֱלֹהֵינוּ וֵאלֹהֵי אֲבוֹתֵינוּ. שֶׁתַּרְגִּילֵנוּ בְּתוֹרָתֶךָ וְדַבְּקֵנוּ בְּמִצְוֹתֶיךָ. וְאַל תְּבִיאֵנוּ לֹא לִידֵי חֵטְא וְלֹא לִידֵי עֲבֵירָה וְלֹא לִידֵי נִסָּיוֹן וְלֹא לִידֵי בִזָּיוֹן. וְאַל תַּשְׁלֶט־בָּנוּ יֵצֶר הָרָע. וְהַרְחִיקֵנוּ מֵאָדָם רָע וּמֵחָבֵר רָע. וְדַבְּקֵנוּ בְּיֵצֶר הַטּוֹב וּבְמַעֲשִׂים טוֹבִים. וְכֹף אֶת־יִצְרֵנוּ לְהִשְׁתַּעְבֶּד־לָךְ. וּתְנֵנוּ הַיּוֹם וּבְכָל־יוֹם לְחֵן וּלְחֶסֶד וּלְרַחֲמִים בְּעֵינֶיךָ וּבְעֵינֵי כָל־רוֹאֵינוּ. וְתִגְמְלֵנוּ חֲסָדִים טוֹבִים: בָּרוּךְ אַתָּה יהוה. גּוֹמֵל חֲסָדִים טוֹבִים לְעַמּוֹ יִשְׂרָאֵל:

לְעוֹלָם *L'olam y'hei adam y'rei shamayim ba-seiter k'va-galui, umodeh al ha-emet, v'doveir emet bilvavo.*

יְהִי *Y'hi ratson mill'fanecha, Adonai eloheinu veilohei avoteinu, shetargileinu b'toratecha v'dabb'keinu b'mitsvotecha, v'al t'vi'einu lo lidei cheit v'lo lidei aveirah, v'lo lidei nissayon v'lo lidei vizzayon, v'al tashlet banu yeitser ha-ra, v'harchikeinu mei'adam ra umeichaveir ra. V'dabb'keinu b'yeitser ha-tov uv'ma'asim tovim, v'chof et yitsreinu l'hishta'bed lach, ut'neinu ha-yom uv'chol yom, l'chein ul'chesed ul'rachamim, b'einecha uv'einei chol ro'einu, v'tigm'leinu chasadim tovim. Baruch attah Adonai, gomeil chasadim tovim l'ammo yisra'el.*

The Gift of Freedom

One of the morning blessings thanks God for not making us a 'slave', a celebration of our freedom as human beings to choose how we conduct our life. The first two passages in this section explore how this freedom is to be used in the service of God, choosing the way of goodness and the affirmation of life.

In the rabbinic view there is a daily struggle within human beings between the 'good inclination', basic to our humanity, and the 'inclination towards evil', a powerful drive within us that needs to be channelled. This drive provides the energy that leads to procreation, human creativity and positive actions in the world (*Genesis Rabbah* 9:7), but unless controlled it becomes destructive. This struggle continues throughout life, but, in the rabbinic view, the teachings and practices of Torah lend support to the 'good inclination'.

SHABBAT MORNING SERVICE — MORNING BLESSINGS

When reading this paragraph it may be helpful to pause after each of the questions (What are we? What is our life? etc.) to take time to consider our personal response:

רִבּוֹן Source of existence and of all human strength, we do not rely on our own good deeds but on Your great mercy as we lay our needs before You.	רִבּוֹן הָעוֹלָמִים וַאֲדוֹנֵי הָאֲדוֹנִים. לֹא עַל־צִדְקוֹתֵינוּ אֲנַחְנוּ מַפִּילִים תַּחֲנוּנֵינוּ לְפָנֶיךָ. כִּי עַל־רַחֲמֶיךָ הָרַבִּים:
God, hear!	אֲדֹנָי שְׁמָעָה.
God, pardon!	אֲדֹנָי סְלָחָה.
God, listen and act![1]	אֲדֹנָי הַקְשִׁיבָה וַעֲשֵׂה:
What are we?	מַה־אָנוּ.
What is our life?	מֶה־חַיֵּינוּ.
What is our love?	מֶה־חַסְדֵּנוּ.
What is our justice?	מַה־צִּדְקוֹתֵינוּ.
What is our success?	מַה־יְּשׁוּעָתֵנוּ.
What is our endurance?	מַה־כֹּחֵנוּ.
What is our power?	מַה־גְּבוּרָתֵנוּ.
Our God, and God of our ancestors, what can we say before You? 🕎333	מַה־נֹּאמַר לְפָנֶיךָ יהוה אֱלֹהֵינוּ וֵאלֹהֵי אֲבוֹתֵינוּ:

רִבּוֹן Ribbon ha-olamim va'adonei ha-adonim, lo al tsidkoteinu anachnu mapilim
tachanuneinu l'fanecha, ki al rachamecha ha-rabbim.
Adonai sh'ma'ah,
Adonai s'lachah,
Adonai hakshivah va'aseih.
Mah anu,
meh chayyeinu,
meh chasdeinu,
mah tsidkoteinu,
mah y'shu'ateinu,
mah kocheinu,
mah g'vurateinu,
mah nomar l'fanecha Adonai eloheinu veilohei avoteinu.

רִבּוֹן הָעוֹלָמִים **Source of existence ...**
Freedom carries with it the responsibility to examine our behaviour and constantly review our values and actions. The first paragraph of *ribbon ha-olamim* contains a questionnaire that explores the nature of our life and how it relates to God.

The prayer quotes from Ecclesiastes with its powerful questioning of the significance of human existence, *hevel*, a mere breath. We follow the Sephardi tradition that ends the paragraph with the affirmation of the significance of each individual soul and the judgment it must one day face.

[1] Dan 9:18-19.

הֲלֹא For in Your presence are not the powerful as nothing, the famous as if they had never existed, the learned as if without knowledge, and the intelligent as if without insight? To You most of our actions are pointless and our daily life is shallow. Even our superiority over the animals is nothing.[1] For everything is trivial except the pure soul which must one day give its account and reckoning before the judgment seat of Your glory.

אֲבָל Yet we are Your people, the children of Your covenant, the children of Abraham whom You loved, giving him Your promise on Mount Moriah; the descendants of Isaac, bound as an offering on the altar; the congregation of Jacob 'Your son, Your special son'; out of Your love for him and Your delight in him, You changed his name to Israel and Yeshurun.[2] Blessed are You God, You make Your name holy before all.

הֲלֹא הַגִּבּוֹרִים כְּאַיִן לְפָנֶיךָ. וְאַנְשֵׁי הַשֵּׁם כְּלֹא הָיוּ. וַחֲכָמִים כִּבְלִי מַדָּע. וּנְבוֹנִים כִּבְלִי הַשְׂכֵּל. כִּי רֹב מַעֲשֵׂינוּ תֹּהוּ. וִימֵי חַיֵּינוּ הֶבֶל לְפָנֶיךָ. וּמוֹתַר הָאָדָם מִן הַבְּהֵמָה אָיִן. כִּי הַכֹּל הָבֶל לְבַד הַנְּשָׁמָה הַטְּהוֹרָה. שֶׁהִיא עֲתִידָה לִתֵּן דִּין וְחֶשְׁבּוֹן לִפְנֵי כִסֵּא כְבוֹדֶךָ:

אֲבָל אֲנַחְנוּ עַמְּךָ. בְּנֵי בְרִיתֶךָ. בְּנֵי אַבְרָהָם אֹהַבְךָ. שֶׁנִּשְׁבַּעְתָּ לּוֹ בְּהַר הַמּוֹרִיָּה. זֶרַע יִצְחָק יְחִידוֹ. שֶׁנֶּעֱקַד עַל גַּבֵּי הַמִּזְבֵּחַ. עֲדַת יַעֲקֹב בִּנְךָ בְּכוֹרֶךָ. שֶׁמֵּאַהֲבָתְךָ שֶׁאָהַבְתָּ אוֹתוֹ. וּמִשִּׂמְחָתְךָ שֶׁשָּׂמַחְתָּ בּוֹ. קָרָאתָ אֶת שְׁמוֹ יִשְׂרָאֵל וִישֻׁרוּן: בָּרוּךְ אַתָּה יהוה מְקַדֵּשׁ אֶת שִׁמְךָ בָּרַבִּים:

הֲלֹא Halo ha-gibborim k'ayin l'fanecha, v'anshei ha-sheim k'lo hayu, vachachamim kivli madda, un'vonim kivli haskeil, ki rov ma'aseinu tohu, vimei chayyeinu hevel l'fanecha, umotar ha-adam min ha-b'heimah ayin, ki ha-kol havel l'vad ha-n'shamah ha-t'horah, shehi atidah littein din v'cheshbon lifnei chissei ch'vodecha.

אֲבָל Aval anachnu amm'cha, b'nei v'ritecha, b'nei avraham ohav'cha, shenishba'ta lo b'har ha-moriyah, zera yitschak y'chido, shene'ekad al gabei ha-mizbei'ach, adat Ya'akov bincha b'chorecha, shemei'ahavat'cha she'ahavta oto, umissimchat'cha shesamachta bo, karata et sh'mo yisra'el vishurun. Baruch attah Adonai m'kaddesh et shim'cha ba-rabbim.

אֲבָל אֲנַחְנוּ עַמְּךָ Yet we are Your people ... This paragraph, which is found in both the Ashkenazi and Sephardi tradition, counters the negative conclusion of human insignificance by affirming that we are God's people, and locates our collective significance through our membership of the Jewish people with its special destiny.

[1] Ecc 3:19.
[2] Yeshurun is a poetic name for Israel, 'the upright one' (Deut 32:15, 33:5,26, Isa 44:2).

169 SHABBAT MORNING SERVICE — MORNING BLESSINGS

THE GIFT OF TORAH

Before study the following blessing is said:

בָּרוּךְ Blessed are You, our Living God, Sovereign of the universe, whose commandments make us holy, and who commands us to devote ourselves to the study of Torah.[1]

בָּרוּךְ אַתָּה יהוה אֱלֹהֵינוּ מֶלֶךְ הָעוֹלָם. אֲשֶׁר קִדְּשָׁנוּ בְּמִצְוֹתָיו. וְצִוָּנוּ לַעֲסוֹק בְּדִבְרֵי תוֹרָה:

בָּרוּךְ *Baruch attah Adonai eloheinu melech ha-olam, asher kidd'shanu b'mitsvotav, v'tsivvanu la'asok b'divrei Torah.*

Instead of the following passage, a study passage (pages 489-597) or a responsive reading (pages 598-608) may be inserted here.

אֵלוּ These are the things whose interest we enjoy in this world, while the capital remains for us in the world to come - this is what they are:
Respecting one's father and mother,
acts of generosity and love,
coming early to the House of Study, morning and evening,
giving hospitality to strangers,
visiting the sick,
assisting the bride,
escorting the dead,
engaging with prayer,
making peace between people.
And the study of Torah leads to them all.[2]

אֵלּוּ דְבָרִים שֶׁאָדָם אוֹכֵל פֵּרוֹתֵיהֶם בָּעוֹלָם הַזֶּה וְהַקֶּרֶן קַיֶּמֶת לוֹ לָעוֹלָם הַבָּא. וְאֵלּוּ הֵן:
כִּבּוּד אָב וָאֵם.
וּגְמִילוּת חֲסָדִים.
וְהַשְׁכָּמַת בֵּית הַמִּדְרָשׁ שַׁחֲרִית וְעַרְבִית.
וְהַכְנָסַת אוֹרְחִים.
וּבִקּוּר חוֹלִים.
וְהַכְנָסַת כַּלָּה.
וּלְוָיַת הַמֵּת.
וְעִיּוּן תְּפִלָּה.
וַהֲבָאַת שָׁלוֹם בֵּין אָדָם לַחֲבֵרוֹ.
וְתַלְמוּד תּוֹרָה כְּנֶגֶד כֻּלָּם:

אֵלּוּ *Eillu d'varim she'adam ocheil peiruteihem ba-olam ha-zeh v'ha-keren kayyemet lo la-olam ha-ba, v'eillu hein.*
Kibbud av va'eim, ug'milut chasadim, v'hashkamat beit ha-midrash shacharit v'arvit, v'hachnasat or'chim, uvikkur cholim, v'hachnasat kallah, ul'vayat ha-meit, **v'iyyun t'fillah**, *vahava'at shalom bein adam lachaveiro, v'talmud torah k'neged kullam.*

---

[1] *Berachot* 11b.   [2] *Mishnah Peah* 1:1 and *Shabbat* 127a.

After study the following blessing may be said:

וְהַעֲרֶב־נָא Our Living God,
make the words of Your Torah
sweet in our mouths,
and in the mouths of Your people,
the family of Israel,
then we and our descendants,
and the descendants of Your people
the family of Israel,
shall all know Your name and study
Your Torah for its own sake.
Blessed are You God,
You teach Torah to Your people Israel.[1]

וְהַעֲרֶב־נָא יהוה אֱלֹהֵינוּ
אֶת־דִּבְרֵי תוֹרָתְךָ בְּפִינוּ.
וּבְפִי עַמְּךָ בֵּית יִשְׂרָאֵל.
וְנִהְיֶה אֲנַחְנוּ וְצֶאֱצָאֵינוּ.
וְצֶאֱצָאֵי עַמְּךָ בֵּית יִשְׂרָאֵל.
כֻּלָּנוּ יוֹדְעֵי שְׁמֶךָ.
וְלוֹמְדֵי תוֹרָתְךָ לִשְׁמָהּ:
בָּרוּךְ אַתָּה יהוה.
הַמְלַמֵּד תּוֹרָה לְעַמּוֹ יִשְׂרָאֵל:

וְהַעֲרֶב־נָא *V'ha'arev na Adonai eloheinu et divrei torat'cha b'finu, uv'fi amm'cha beit yisra'el, v'nih'yeh anachnu v'tse'etsa'einu v'tse'etsa'ei amm'cha beit yisra'el, kullanu yod'ei sh'mecha, v'lom'dei torat'cha lishmah. Baruch attah Adonai, ha-m'lammeid torah l'ammo yisra'el.*

לַעֲסוֹק בְּדִבְרֵי תוֹרָה
To devote ourselves to the study of Torah ...

The last section of the Morning Blessings brings together the individual strands of our personal existence, our membership of the Jewish people and our relationship to God. The seal of that relationship is the Torah that reveals the nature of God and provides guidance for our lives as individuals and within society.

The section consists of an opening and a closing blessing with space between for a study passage. The opening blessing reminds us of the duty to study each day. The closing blessing hopes that the Torah will be sweet in our mouths and in the mouths of those who come after us.

Between these blessings the passage from *Mishnah Peah* 1:1 and *Shabbat* 127a, serves as an example of the Torah we are to study. In this slot we may introduce study material from anywhere within our tradition.

[1] Attributed to Rabbi Yochanan bar Nappacha, third century. *Berachot* 11b.

SHABBAT MORNING SERVICE — MORNING BLESSINGS

PREPARING TO ENCOUNTER GOD

יהוה God **rules**, God has **ruled**, God **shall rule** forever and ever.

When the rule of God is acknowledged throughout the earth, on that day God shall be One, and known as One.
Save us, our Living God, to proclaim Your holy name and be honoured in praising You.
Blessed is the Eternal One, the God of Israel from everlasting to everlasting.
Let all the people say: Amen!
Praise God!
Let everything that has breath praise God.
Hallelujah![1]

יהוה מֶלֶךְ. יהוה מָלָךְ.
יהוה יִמְלֹךְ לְעוֹלָם וָעֶד׃
וְהָיָה יהוה לְמֶלֶךְ עַל־כָּל־הָאָרֶץ.
בַּיּוֹם הַהוּא יִהְיֶה יהוה אֶחָד
וּשְׁמוֹ אֶחָד׃
הוֹשִׁיעֵנוּ יהוה אֱלֹהֵינוּ. לְהֹדוֹת
לְשֵׁם קָדְשֶׁךָ לְהִשְׁתַּבֵּחַ בִּתְהִלָּתֶךָ׃
בָּרוּךְ יהוה אֱלֹהֵי יִשְׂרָאֵל מִן־
הָעוֹלָם וְעַד הָעוֹלָם.
וְאָמַר כָּל־הָעָם אָמֵן.
הַלְלוּיָה׃
כֹּל הַנְּשָׁמָה תְּהַלֵּל יָהּ.
הַלְלוּיָה׃

יהוה *Adonai melech, Adonai malach, Adonai yimloch l'olam va'ed.*
V'hayah Adonai l'melech al kol ha-arets, ba-yom ha-hu yih'yeh ech ad ush'mo echad. Hoshi'einu Adonai eloheinu, l'hodot l'sheim kodshecha l'hishtabei'ach bit'hillatecha. Baruch Adonai elohei yisra'el min ha-olam v'ad ha-olam, v'amar kol ha-am amen, hal'luyah. Kol ha-n'shamah t'halleil yah, hal'luyah.

יהוה מֶלֶךְ God rules ...
The Morning Blessings close with two passages. The sentence 'God rules ...' comes from the Sephardi tradition and points to the tension between the need to affirm the presence of God in our lives today and the messianic hope that one day God's rule will be accepted throughout the world. It helps to mark the transition from our concerns about our individual existence, the theme of the 'morning blessings', to our focus on our community and our relationship with God in the next section, the Verses of Song.

The Book of Psalms is made up of five separate sections, individual 'books', each one concluding with verses in praise of God, a 'doxology'. The Psalm verses here, which mark the end of the 'Morning Blessings' section, are taken from the end of the fourth and final 'books' within the Book of Psalms (106:47-48, 150:6) so that continuity is established between the Bible and the liturgy. Verses from the end of the third and second 'books' within the Book of Psalms are similarly used to mark the end of the Verses of Song section.

[1] Zech 14:9, Ps 106:47-48, Ps 150:6.

But if I am only for myself, what am I? וּכְשֶׁאֲנִי לְעַצְמִי מָה אֲנִי

פְּסוּקֵי דְזִמְרָה
VERSES OF SONG

*In this section we consider our personal and communal relationship with God.
Between 'Blessed be the One' and 'Praised be Your name forever' (page 204)
a selection may be taken from the 'Verses of Song'
Some congregations stand during the recital of* Baruch She'amar.

THE GIFT OF CREATION

בָּרוּךְ Blessed be the One,
at whose word the world exists.
Blessed be the One,
whose word is deed.
Blessed be the One,
whose command stands firm.
Blessed be the One,
who causes creation.
Blessed be the One,
who has mercy on the earth.
Blessed be the One,
who has mercy on creation.
Blessed be the One, who gives
a good reward to the faithful.
Blessed be the One, who takes away
darkness and brings on light.
Blessed be the One,
who exists before time itself
and endures for eternity.
Blessed be the One in whom there is
no fault and no forgetfulness, who
shows no favour and takes no bribe,
whose ways are righteous
and all of whose deeds are love.

בָּרוּךְ שֶׁאָמַר
וְהָיָה הָעוֹלָם: בָּרוּךְ הוּא:
בָּרוּךְ אוֹמֵר וְעוֹשֶׂה:
בָּרוּךְ גּוֹזֵר וּמְקַיֵּם:
בָּרוּךְ עוֹשֶׂה בְרֵאשִׁית:
בָּרוּךְ מְרַחֵם עַל הָאָרֶץ:
בָּרוּךְ מְרַחֵם עַל הַבְּרִיּוֹת:
בָּרוּךְ מְשַׁלֵּם שָׂכָר טוֹב לִירֵאָיו:
בָּרוּךְ מַעֲבִיר אֲפֵלָה וּמֵבִיא אוֹרָה:
בָּרוּךְ אֵל חַי לָעַד וְקַיָּם לָנֶצַח:
בָּרוּךְ שֶׁאֵין לְפָנָיו עַוְלָה
וְלֹא שִׁכְחָה וְלֹא מַשּׂוֹא פָנִים
וְלֹא מִקַּח שֹׁחַד.
צַדִּיק הוּא בְּכָל־דְּרָכָיו
וְחָסִיד בְּכָל־מַעֲשָׂיו:

<<<

173 SHABBAT MORNING SERVICE — VERSES OF SONG

Blessed be the One, who redeems and rescues. Blessed be the One, who gives rest to this people Israel on the holy Shabbat day. Blessed be the One, and blessed be God's name and blessed be the knowledge of God for all eternity.	בָּרוּךְ פּוֹדֶה וּמַצִּיל: בָּרוּךְ הַמַּנְחִיל מְנוּחָה לְעַמּוֹ יִשְׂרָאֵל בְּיוֹם שַׁבַּת קֹדֶשׁ: בָּרוּךְ הוּא וּבָרוּךְ שְׁמוֹ: וּבָרוּךְ זִכְרוֹ לְעוֹלְמֵי עַד:

בָּרוּךְ Baruch she'amar v'hayah ha-olam.
Baruch hu. Baruch omeir v'oseh.
Baruch gozeir um'kayyeim.
Baruch oseh v'reishit.
Baruch m'racheim al ha-arets.
Baruch m'racheim al ha-b'riot.
Baruch m'shaleim sachar tov lirei'av.
Baruch ma'avir afeilah umeivi orah.
Baruch eil chai la'ad v'kayam lanetsach.
Baruch she'ein l'fanav avlah v'lo shich'chah v'lo masso fanim,
v'lo mikkach shochad, tsaddik hu b'chol d'rachav v'chasid b'chol ma'asav.
Baruch podeh umatsil.
Baruch ha-manchil m'nuchah l'ammo yisra'el b'yom shabbat kodesh.
Baruch hu u'varuch sh'mo, uvaruch zichro l'olmei ad.

<<<

בָּרוּךְ שֶׁאָמַר Blessed be the One ...

This passage marks the formal opening of the Verses of Songs. Considered to be of ancient origin, it contains Biblical and Talmudic phrases. As yet another example of the roots of British Reform in the Sephardi tradition, our version contains verses to mark the Shabbat and the phrase 'who takes away darkness and brings on light', which are not to be found in Ashkenazi versions.

The passage locates God at the centre of creation. God spoke and worlds came into existence. Yet this is no God who remains remote from creation, but one who continues to speak, who acts with *rachamim*, translated here as 'mercy' but meaning a deep and abiding love for the earth and all creatures that inhabit it. The world is to be built upon values, and though human beings may fail to live up to them, ultimate justice and integrity lie with God who shows no favour and cannot be bribed.

בָּרוּךְ אַתָּה יהוה אֱלֹהֵינוּ מֶלֶךְ הָעוֹלָם. הַמֶּלֶךְ הַגָּדוֹל וְהַקָּדוֹשׁ. אָב הָרַחֲמָן. מְהֻלָּל בְּפִי עַמּוֹ. מְשֻׁבָּח וּמְפֹאָר בִּלְשׁוֹן כָּל־חֲסִידָיו וַעֲבָדָיו: וּבְשִׁירֵי דָוִד עַבְדְּךָ נְהַלֶּלְךָ יהוה אֱלֹהֵינוּ. בִּשְׁבָחוֹת וּבִזְמִירוֹת נְהוֹדְךָ נְגַדֶּלְךָ נְפָאֶרְךָ וְנַמְלִיכְךָ וְנַזְכִּיר שִׁמְךָ מַלְכֵּנוּ אֱלֹהֵינוּ. יָחִיד חֵי הָעוֹלָמִים. מְשֻׁבָּח וּמְפֹאָר שְׁמוֹ עֲדֵי עַד:
בָּרוּךְ אַתָּה יהוה.
מֶלֶךְ מְהֻלָּל בַּתִּשְׁבָּחוֹת:

בָּרוּךְ Blessed are You, our Living God, Sovereign of the universe, great and holy in power, Source of mercy; praised by Your people; worshipped and glorified by the tongue of all who love and serve You. Therefore we praise You with the psalms of Your servant David; with prayers and songs we declare Your glory, Your greatness, Your splendour, and Your majesty. We proclaim Your name, our Sovereign, our God, who alone is the life of all existence, and whose name is worshipped and glorified forever and ever.
Blessed are You God, the Sovereign praised in all worship.

בָּרוּךְ *Baruch attah Adonai eloheinu melech ha-olam, ha-melech ha-gadol v'ha-kadosh, av ha-rachaman, m'hullal b'fi ammo, m'shubbach um'fo'ar bilshon kol chasidav va'avadav. Uv'shirei david avd'cha n'hallelcha Adonai eloheinu, bishvachot uvizmirot n'hod'cha, n'gaddelcha, n'fa'ercha, v'namlich'cha, v'nazkir shimcha malkeinu eloheinu, yachid chei ha-olamim, m'shubbach um'fo'ar sh'mo adei ad. Baruch attah Adonai, melech m'hullal ba-tishbachot.*

The closing paragraph prepares the way for the Psalms, traditionally ascribed to King David, that are to be a major feature of the coming section.

175 SHABBAT MORNING SERVICE   **VERSES OF SONG**

PSALM 92: THREE CENTRAL VERSES.   Charles Front

THE SHABBAT PSALMS

צב

א מִזְמוֹר שִׁיר לְיוֹם הַשַּׁבָּת:

ב טוֹב לְהֹדוֹת לַיהוה וּלְזַמֵּר לְשִׁמְךָ עֶלְיוֹן:
ג לְהַגִּיד בַּבֹּקֶר חַסְדֶּךָ וֶאֱמוּנָתְךָ בַּלֵּילוֹת:
ד עֲלֵי־עָשׂוֹר וַעֲלֵי־נָבֶל עֲלֵי הִגָּיוֹן בְּכִנּוֹר:
ה כִּי שִׂמַּחְתַּנִי יהוה בְּפָעֳלֶךָ בְּמַעֲשֵׂי יָדֶיךָ אֲרַנֵּן:

ו מַה־גָּדְלוּ מַעֲשֶׂיךָ יהוה מְאֹד עָמְקוּ מַחְשְׁבֹתֶיךָ:
ז אִישׁ־בַּעַר לֹא יֵדָע וּכְסִיל לֹא־יָבִין אֶת־זֹאת:
ח בִּפְרֹחַ רְשָׁעִים כְּמוֹ עֵשֶׂב וַיָּצִיצוּ כָּל־פֹּעֲלֵי אָוֶן לְהִשָּׁמְדָם עֲדֵי־עַד:

ט וְאַתָּה מָרוֹם לְעֹלָם יהוה:

י כִּי הִנֵּה אֹיְבֶיךָ יהוה כִּי־הִנֵּה אֹיְבֶיךָ יֹאבֵדוּ יִתְפָּרְדוּ כָּל־פֹּעֲלֵי אָוֶן:
יא וַתָּרֶם כִּרְאֵים קַרְנִי בַּלֹּתִי בְּשֶׁמֶן רַעֲנָן:
יב וַתַּבֵּט עֵינִי בְּשׁוּרָי בַּקָּמִים עָלַי מְרֵעִים תִּשְׁמַעְנָה אָזְנָי:

יג צַדִּיק כַּתָּמָר יִפְרָח כְּאֶרֶז בַּלְּבָנוֹן יִשְׂגֶּה:
יד שְׁתוּלִים בְּבֵית יהוה בְּחַצְרוֹת אֱלֹהֵינוּ יַפְרִיחוּ:
טו עוֹד יְנוּבוּן בְּשֵׂיבָה דְּשֵׁנִים וְרַעֲנַנִּים יִהְיוּ:
טז לְהַגִּיד כִּי־יָשָׁר יהוה צוּרִי וְלֹא־עַוְלָתָה בּוֹ:

[1] *Mizmor shir l'yom ha-shabbat.*
[2] טוב *Tov l'hodot ladonai, ul'zammeir l'shimcha elyon.*
[3] *L'haggid ba-boker chasdecha, ve'emunat'cha ba-leilot.*
[4] *Alei asor va'alei navel, alei higgayon b'chinnor.*
[5] *Ki simmachtani Adonai b'fo'olecha, b'ma'asei yadecha arannein.*
[6] *Mah gad'lu ma'asecha Adonai m'od am'ku machsh'votecha.*
[7] *Ish ba'ar lo yeida, uch'sil lo yavin et zot.*
[8] *Bifro'ach r'sha'im k'mo eisev vayatsitsu kol po'alei aven l'hisham'dam adei ad.*

[9] *V'attah marom l'olam Adonai.*

[10] *Ki hinnei oy'vecha Adonai, ki hinnei oy'vecha yoveidu yitpar'du kol po'alei aven.*
[11] *Vatarem kir'eim karni balloti b'shemen ra'anan.*
[12] *Vatabbeit eini b'shurai, ba-kamim alai m'rei'im tishma'na oznai.*
[13] *Tsaddik ka-tamar yifrach, k'erez ba-l'vanon yisgeh.*
[14] *Sh'tulim b'veit Adonai, b'chatsrot eloheinu yafrichu.*
[15] *Od y'nuvun b'seivah, d'sheinim v'ra'anannim yihyu.*
[16] *L'haggid ki yashar Adonai, tsuri v'lo avlatah bo.*

SHABBAT MORNING SERVICE — VERSES OF SONG

Psalm 92

¹ A Psalm to Sing for the Shabbat Day.
² טוֹב It is good to give thanks to the Eternal, to praise Your name,
    God beyond all,
³ to tell of Your love in the morning and Your faithfulness every night.
⁴ With the ten-stringed lute, with the lyre, with the gentle sound of the harp.
⁵ For You made me rejoice in Your deeds, O God,
    at the works of Your hand I sing out.

⁶ God, how great are Your works, Your thoughts are so very deep.
⁷ The stupid do not know this, nor can the foolish understand,
⁸ that when the wicked flourish they are only like grass
    and when all who do evil spring up their end is always destruction.

⁹ **Only You are exalted forever, Eternal.**

¹⁰ For see Your enemies, God! see how Your enemies shall perish,
    all who do evil shall scatter.
¹¹ But You exalted my strength like an ox, anointed me with fresh oil.
¹² My eyes saw the fate of my enemies; and those who rose up to harm me,
    my ears have heard their end.

¹³ The righteous shall flourish like the palm tree,
    grow tall like a cedar in Lebanon.
¹⁴ Planted in the house of their Maker,
    they shall flourish in the courts of our God,
¹⁵ bearing new fruit in old age still full of sap and still green,
¹⁶ to declare that the Creator is faithful, my Rock in whom there is no wrong.

צב Psalm 92

The Psalm opens with the choirs and music of the temple and closes with the joy of those privileged to serve God there. But as we move towards the centre of the Psalm a darker theme enters, the difficulty of understanding God's ways, especially when evil seems to grow in the world. However, the wicked who 'flourish like grass' and seem overwhelming in their numbers will scatter and disappear. In contrast the good person, the righteous, though single and alone, is not short-lived like grass, but also 'flourishes', as strong, enduring and fruitful as a palm tree.

The same phrase, 'those who do evil', stands on each side of the central verse of the Psalm. Before it, verse 8, they spring up, but after it, verse 10, they perish and vanish. At the exact geographical centre of the Psalm, as a climax, is a short four-word Hebrew sentence. It describes how God stands eternally above these evildoers, and it is built so that, as a climax, the final triumphant word is the name of God.

Psalm 93

צג

^איהוה מָלָךְ גֵּאוּת לָבֵשׁ
לָבֵשׁ יהוה עֹז הִתְאַזָּר
אַף־תִּכּוֹן תֵּבֵל בַּל־תִּמּוֹט:
^בנָכוֹן כִּסְאֲךָ מֵאָז
מֵעוֹלָם אָתָּה:

^גנָשְׂאוּ נְהָרוֹת יהוה
נָשְׂאוּ נְהָרוֹת קוֹלָם
יִשְׂאוּ נְהָרוֹת דָּכְיָם:

^דמִקֹּלוֹת מַיִם רַבִּים
אַדִּירִים מִשְׁבְּרֵי־יָם
אַדִּיר בַּמָּרוֹם יהוה:

^העֵדֹתֶיךָ נֶאֶמְנוּ מְאֹד
לְבֵיתְךָ נַאֲוָה־קֹדֶשׁ
יהוה לְאֹרֶךְ יָמִים:

¹ יהוה The Creator reigns robed in pride,
God is robed in power,
clothed in strength.
So the world was set firm
and cannot be shaken,
²Your throne was set firm long ago,
from eternity You are.

³Almighty, the floods may storm,
 the floods may storm aloud,
  the floods may storm and thunder.

⁴But even above the roar of great waves,
 mighty breakers of the ocean,
  supreme is the might of the Creator.

⁵The proofs You give are very sure,
holiness is the mark of Your house,
God, as long as time endures.

¹יהוה *Adonai malach gei'ut laveish,*
laveish Adonai, oz hit'azzar
af tikkon teiveil bal timmot.
²*Nachon kis'acha mei'az, mei'olam attah.*
³*Nas'u n'harot Adonai, nas'u n'harot kolam, yis-u n'harot dochyam.*
⁴*Mikkolot mayim rabbim addirim mishb'rei yam, addir ba-marom Adonai.*
⁵*Eidotecha ne'emnu m'od, l'veit'cha na'avah kodesh, Adonai l'orech yamim.*

צג Psalm 93

The second Shabbat Psalm turns back to earlier pre-Biblical traditions about the chaotic waters of creation vying with the gods for power. A reflection of that struggle can be seen in the terrifying power of a storm at sea. In verses 3 and 4, each short phrase 'crashes down' upon the one before it, like waves falling on the shore. In verse 4 the repeated sounds of the letters 'r' and 'm' mimic the thunderous roar of the waves.

But around this constantly moving centre, the opening and closing verses are still and reassuring, like pillars affirming the power of God that guarantees the stability of the foundations of the earth and the eternity of God's rule.

SHABBAT MORNING SERVICE — VERSES OF SONG

PSALMS OF THANKSGIVING AND PRAISE

Psalm 121

¹*A Pilgrim Song*

אֶשָּׂא I lift up my eyes to the hills;
where shall I find my help?
²My help is from God alone,
Maker of heaven and earth.
³God will not allow your foot to slip,
for your Guardian does not slumber.
⁴Know that the Guardian of Israel
never slumbers and never sleeps.
⁵God is your Guardian,
God is your shade at your right hand.
⁶The sun will not strike you by day
nor the moon by night.
⁷God will guard you from all evil,
guarding your soul.
⁸God will guard your going out and your
coming in now and for evermore.

קכא
^אשִׁיר לַמַּעֲלוֹת
אֶשָּׂא עֵינַי אֶל־הֶהָרִים
מֵאַיִן יָבֹא עֶזְרִי:
^בעֶזְרִי מֵעִם יהוה
עֹשֵׂה שָׁמַיִם וָאָרֶץ:
^גאַל־יִתֵּן לַמּוֹט רַגְלֶךָ
אַל־יָנוּם שֹׁמְרֶךָ:
^דהִנֵּה לֹא־יָנוּם וְלֹא יִישָׁן
שׁוֹמֵר יִשְׂרָאֵל:
^היהוה שֹׁמְרֶךָ
יהוה צִלְּךָ עַל־יַד יְמִינֶךָ:
^ויוֹמָם הַשֶּׁמֶשׁ לֹא־יַכֶּכָּה
וְיָרֵחַ בַּלָּיְלָה:
^זיהוה יִשְׁמָרְךָ מִכָּל־רָע
יִשְׁמֹר אֶת־נַפְשֶׁךָ:
^חיהוה יִשְׁמָר־צֵאתְךָ וּבוֹאֶךָ
מֵעַתָּה וְעַד־עוֹלָם:

Shir lama'alot.
¹*אֶשָּׂא Essa einai el he-harim, mei'ayin yavo ezri.*
²*Ezri mei'im Adonai, oseih shamayim va'arets.*
³*Al yittein lammot raglecha, al yanum shom'recha.*
⁴*Hineih lo yanum v'lo yishan shomeir Yisra'el.*
⁵*Adonai shom'recha, Adonai tsill'cha al yad y'minecha.*
⁶*Yomam ha-shemesh lo yakkekkah, v'yarei'ach ba-lailah.*
⁷*Adonai yishmorcha mikkol ra, yishmor et nafshecha.*
⁸*Adonai yishmor tseit'cha uvo'echa, mei'attah v'ad olam.*

קכא Psalm 121

The heading of this Psalm is literally 'a song of ascents' and may refer to the pilgrimage 'up to' Jerusalem, or the words to be sung on climbing the steps to the temple. The repeated phrases (five times the verb for 'guarding') and the way each verse builds on the one before suggest the physical act of rising upwards step by step. Throughout the Psalm the imagery makes us look upwards - to the hills and beyond for help, to God who is the 'maker of heaven and earth', who protects us from dangers that come from the sun and moon above us. The imagery, in part, is military. While the left hand holds a shield and the right-hand a sword, the right side is vulnerable and dependent on one's companion on that side for protection, your 'right hand man'. It is God who protects our vulnerable side.

Psalm 150

¹ **הַלְלוּיָהּ** Hallelujah - Praise God!
Give praise to God in God's holy place,
praise in God's mighty heavens,
²praise for God's powerful deeds,
praise for God's surpassing greatness.
³Give praise to God with the *shofar* blast;
praise with the lyre and harp,
⁴praise with drums and dancing,
praise with the lute and pipe.
⁵Give praise to God
with the clash of cymbals,
praise with the clanging cymbals.
⁶Let everything that has breath
praise God.
Hallelujah - Praise God!

קנ
^אהַלְלוּיָהּ
הַלְלוּ־אֵל בְּקָדְשׁוֹ
הַלְלוּהוּ בִּרְקִיעַ עֻזּוֹ:
^בהַלְלוּהוּ בִגְבוּרֹתָיו
הַלְלוּהוּ כְּרֹב גֻּדְלוֹ:
^גהַלְלוּהוּ בְּתֵקַע שׁוֹפָר
הַלְלוּהוּ בְּנֵבֶל וְכִנּוֹר:
^דהַלְלוּהוּ בְּתֹף וּמָחוֹל
הַלְלוּהוּ בְּמִנִּים וְעוּגָב:
^ההַלְלוּהוּ בְצִלְצְלֵי־שָׁמַע
הַלְלוּהוּ בְּצִלְצְלֵי תְרוּעָה:
^וכֹּל הַנְּשָׁמָה תְּהַלֵּל יָהּ
הַלְלוּיָהּ

¹*Hal'luyah*
Hal'lu eil b'kodsho, hal'luhu birki'a uzzo.
²*Hal'luhu bigvurotav, hal'luhu k'rov gudd'lo.*
³*Hal'luhu b'teika shofar, hal'luhu b'neivel v'chinnor.*
⁴*Hal'luhu b'tof umachol, hal'luhu b'minnim v'ugav.*
⁵*Hal'luhu b'tsilts'lei shama, hal'luhu b'tsilts'lei t'ru'ah.*
⁶*Kol ha-n'shamah t'halleil yah.*
Hal'luyah.

קנ Psalm 150

This Psalm, the last in the Book of Psalms, is a doxology, a hymn of praise to God, a fitting conclusion to the book known as *Sefer Tehillim*, 'the Book of Praises'.

The Jerusalem temple on earth and the heavens, where God was thought to dwell, are linked together through this song. The entire temple orchestra is called upon to play at full volume. It is as if words are no longer sufficient to praise and glorify God, and only pure musical sounds can express the author's wonder and amazement. As befits such a universal theme, it is not the Jewish people alone who are called upon to praise God, but every soul, every living creature that knows God as the source of its existence.

181 SHABBAT MORNING SERVICE   **VERSES OF SONG**

Many of the songs that follow originate as Z'mirot, *table hymns, sung on Shabbat after the midday Shabbat meal.*

פסוקי דזמרה

SONGS IN PRAISE OF GOD AND SHABBAT

Yom shabbaton

¹יוֹם The day of rest
should not be forgotten,
for its memory is a fragrant scent.
On it the dove found ease,
rest too for those failing in strength.
    On it the dove found ease,
    rest too for those failing in strength.

²This day is honoured by the faithful.
Parents and children guard it with care,
engraved on two tablets of stone
by the Source of power,
unfailing in strength.
    On it the dove ...

³All entered a covenant in unity,
'Let us do and obey,' they said as one,
then affirmed together: 'God is one!'
blessed for giving the weary strength.
    On it the dove ...

⁴Holy is the word
from the Mount of teaching
'Remember and keep the seventh day.'
All of its precepts study together,
hold fast and gather your strength.
    On it the dove ...

⁵The people that wandered
like sheep astray
will surely remember
the covenant and oath,
that no harmful thing
should come upon them,
as You swore at the
ending of Noah's flood.
    On it the dove found ease,
    rest too for those failing in strength.

Attributed to Judah Halevi

---

182 תפלת שחרית לשבת

יוֹם שַׁבָּתוֹן

איוֹם שַׁבָּתוֹן אֵין לִשְׁכּוֹחַ.
זִכְרוֹ כְּרֵיחַ הַנִּיחֹחַ.
יוֹנָה מָצְאָה בוֹ מָנוֹחַ.
וְשָׁם יָנוּחוּ יְגִיעֵי כֹחַ:
יוֹנָה מָצְאָה בוֹ מָנוֹחַ.
וְשָׁם יָנוּחוּ יְגִיעֵי כֹחַ:

בהַיּוֹם נִכְבָּד לִבְנֵי אֱמוּנִים.
זְהִירִים לְשָׁמְרוֹ אָבוֹת וּבָנִים.
חָקוּק בִּשְׁנֵי לֻחוֹת אֲבָנִים.
מֵרֹב אוֹנִים וְאַמִּיץ כֹּחַ:
יוֹנָה...

גוּבָאוּ כֻלָּם בִּבְרִית יַחַד.
נַעֲשֶׂה וְנִשְׁמָע אָמְרוּ כְּאֶחָד.
וּפָתְחוּ וְעָנוּ יהוה אֶחָד.
בָּרוּךְ הַנֹּתֵן לַיָּעֵף כֹּחַ:
יוֹנָה...

דדִּבֶּר בְּקָדְשׁוֹ בְּהַר הַמּוֹר.
יוֹם הַשְּׁבִיעִי זָכוֹר וְשָׁמוֹר.
וְכָל־פִּקּוּדָיו יַחַד לִגְמוֹר.
חַזֵּק מָתְנַיִם וְאַמֵּץ כֹּחַ:
יוֹנָה...

ההָעָם אֲשֶׁר נָע כַּצֹּאן תָּעָה.
יִזְכֹּר לְפָקְדוֹ בְּרִית וּשְׁבוּעָה.
לְבַל יַעֲבָר־בָּם מִקְרֵה רָעָה.
כַּאֲשֶׁר נִשְׁבַּעְתָּ עַל מֵי נֹחַ:
יוֹנָה מָצְאָה בוֹ מָנוֹחַ.
וְשָׁם יָנוּחוּ יְגִיעֵי כֹחַ:

יהודה הלוי

SHABBAT MORNING SERVICE — VERSES OF SONG

¹**יוֹם** *Yom shabbaton ein lishko'ach,*
zichro k'rei'ach ha-nicho'ach,
yonah mats'ah vo mano'ach,
v'sham yanuchu y'gi'ei cho'ach.

Yonah mats'ah vo mano'ach,
v'sham yanuchu y'gi'ei cho'ach.

²*Ha-yom nichbad livnei emunim,*
z'hirim l'shomro avot uvanim,
chakuk bishnei luchot avanim,
meirov onim v'ammits ko'ach.
Yonah ...

³*Uva'u chullam bivrit yachad,*
na'aseh v'nishma am'ru k'echad,
ufat'chu v'anu Adonai echad,
Baruch ha-notein la-ya'eif ko'ach.
Yonah...

⁴*Dibbeir b'kodsho b'har ha-mor,*
yom ha-sh'vi'i zachor v'shamor,
v'chol pikkudav yachad ligmor,
chazzeik motnayim v'ammeits ko'ach.
Yonah ...

⁵*Ha-am asher na ka-tson ta'ah,*
yizkor l'fokdo b'rit ush'vu'ah,
l'val ya'avor bam mikreih ra'ah,
ka'asher nishba'ta al mei No'ach.

Yonah mats'ah vo mano'ach,
v'sham yanuchu y'gi'ei cho'ach.

יוֹם שַׁבָּתוֹן The day of rest ...
The 'dove that found ease' is an allusion to the story of Noah's flood. When the flood ended, Noah sent out a dove at seven-day intervals to scout for evidence that the waters had receded. When it could 'not find a resting place' (Gen 8:9) it returned to the ark. But fourteen days later it did not return and the author associates the rest it found with the rest of Shabbat.

The first letters of each verse together spell Yehudah, hence the attribution to Judah Halevi (twelfth-century Spain). The poet links the Shabbat commands given at Sinai with Israel's entry into the covenant with God. Though the people stray, may God not do them harm, just as God had promised Noah never again to destroy the world.

Ki eshmerah Shabbat

כִּי אֶשְׁמְרָה שַׁבָּת

כִּי אֶשְׁמְרָה שַׁבָּת אֵל יִשְׁמְרֵנִי.
אוֹת הִיא לְעוֹלְמֵי עַד בֵּינוֹ וּבֵינִי:

If I keep the Shabbat,
God will keep me,
a sign forever
between God and me.

א אָסוּר מְצֹא חֵפֶץ עֲשׂוֹת דְּרָכִים.
גַּם מִלְדַבֵּר בּוֹ דִּבְרֵי צְרָכִים.
דִּבְרֵי סְחוֹרָה אַף דִּבְרֵי מְלָכִים.
אֶהְגֶּה בְּתוֹרַת אֵל וּתְחַכְּמֵנִי:
אוֹת הִיא...

[1] Forbidden are business
and practical tasks,
even speaking of things
that we need,
or of matters of money
and matters of state;
let me study Torah and grow wise.
A sign ...

ב בּוֹ אֶמְצָא תָּמִיד נֹפֶשׁ לְנַפְשִׁי.
הִנֵּה לְדוֹר רִאשׁוֹן נָתַן קְדוֹשִׁי.
מוֹפֵת בְּתֵת לֶחֶם מִשְׁנֶה בַּשִּׁשִּׁי.
כָּכָה בְּכָל־שִׁשִּׁי יַכְפִּיל מְזוֹנִי:
אוֹת הִיא...

[2] Through Shabbat
I find relief for my soul.
My God gave a sign
to those in the wilderness,
double portions of manna
upon the sixth day.
May my food too
be doubled on each sixth day.
A sign ...

ג רָשַׁם בְּדַת הָאֵל חֹק אֶל סְגָנָיו.
בּוֹ לַעֲרֹךְ לֶחֶם פָּנִים בְּפָנָיו.
עַל כֵּן לְהִתְעַנּוֹת בּוֹ עַל פִּי נְבוֹנָיו.
אָסוּר לְבַד מִיּוֹם כִּפּוּר עֲוֹנִי:
אוֹת הִיא...

[3] Graven in God's law
is a duty of the priests
to set out their bread
in the presence of God.
So our sages
forbade us to fast on that day,
save only on the Atonement Day.
A sign ...

ד הוּא יוֹם מְכֻבָּד הוּא יוֹם תַּעֲנוּגִים.
לֶחֶם וְיַיִן טוֹב בָּשָׂר וְדָגִים.
הַמִּתְאַבְּלִים בּוֹ אָחוֹר נְסוֹגִים.
כִּי יוֹם שְׂמָחוֹת הוּא וּתְשַׂמְּחֵנִי:
אוֹת הִיא...

[4] A day to be honoured,
a day for gladness,
bread and good wine,
the best of all food.
Even the saddest
find their mood changed
for this day is for joy
and makes me rejoice.
A sign ...

SHABBAT MORNING SERVICE — VERSES OF SONG

⁵Whoever misuses it
stands only to lose.
So I cleanse my heart on it
as if with soap.
I will pray to God
Ma'ariv and *Shacharit*,
Musaf and *Minchah*,
and be answered.

A sign forever
between God and me.

מֶחָל מְלָאכָה בּוֹ סוֹפוֹ לְהַכְרִית.
עַל כֵּן אֲכַבֶּס־בּוֹ לִבִּי כְּבֹרִית.
וְאֶתְפַּלְלָה אֶל אֵל עַרְבִית וְשַׁחֲרִית.
מוּסָף וְגַם מִנְחָה הוּא יַעֲנֵנִי:

אוֹת הִיא לְעוֹלְמֵי עַד
בֵּינוֹ וּבֵינִי:

Attributed to Abraham ibn Ezra — אברהם אבן־עזרא

כִּי *Ki eshm'rah Shabbat eil yishm'reini, ot hi l'ol'mei ad beino uveini.*

¹*Asur m'tso cheifets asot d'rachim, gam mill'dabbeir bo divrei ts'rachim,*
Divrei s'chorah af divrei m'lachim, ehgeh b'torat eil ut'chak'meini.

Ot hi l'ol'mei ad beino uveini.

²*Bo emtsa tamid nofesh l'nafshi, hinneih l'dor rishon natan k'doshi,*
Mofeit b'teit lechem mishneh ba-shishi, kachah b'chol shishi yachpil m'zoni.

Ot hi ...

³*Rasham b'dat ha-eil chok el s'ganav, bo la'aroch lechem panim b'fanav,*
Al kein l'hit'annot bo al pi n'vonav, asur l'vad miyyom kippur avoni.

Ot hi ...

⁴*Hu yom m'chubbad, hu yom ta'anugim, lechem v'yayin tov basar v'dagim,*
Ha-mit'abb'lim bo achor n'sogim, ki yom s'machot hu ut'samm'cheini.

Ot hi ...

⁵*Meicheil m'lachah bo sofo l'hachrit, al kein achabes bo libbi k'vorit,*
V'etpall'lah el eil arvit v'shacharit, musaf v'gam minchah hu ya'aneini.

Ot hi l'ol'mei ad beino uveini.

כִּי אֶשְׁמְרָה שַׁבָּת If I keep the Shabbat ...

The initial letters spell the name Abraham, hence the attribution to Abraham ibn Ezra (twelfth-century Spain).

It is not only forbidden to disturb the peace of Shabbat by doing business, even discussion of business topics or politics would ruin the mood.

The focus on the plentiful supply of food for Shabbat matches the theme of a table hymn when we have just eaten, but it is also a reflection of times of real poverty, certainly known by ibn Ezra himself, when there was no guarantee of food on the table for Shabbat. The special refreshment that comes with Shabbat, literally 'a soul for my soul', echoes the view that on Shabbat we receive an extra soul. However, the poet emphasises the meticulous fulfilment of the laws of Shabbat, including attending all four of the services that occur within the day.

D'ror yikra

[1] **דְּרוֹר** God declares freedom
for boy and girl
and guards you
like the apple of the eye.
Your name is pleasant, never to cease.
Rest and be at ease this Shabbat day.

דְּרוֹר יִקְרָא לְבֵן עִם בַּת.
וְיִנְצָרְכֶם כְּמוֹ בָבַת.
נְעִים שִׁמְכֶם וְלֹא יֻשְׁבַּת.
שְׁבוּ וְנוּחוּ בְּיוֹם שַׁבָּת:

[2] Seek out my temple and its hall,
make through me
a sign of Your salvation.
Plant a shoot in my vineyard.
Turn to the cry of my people.

דְּרוֹשׁ נָוִי וְאוּלָמִי.
וְאוֹת יֶשַׁע עֲשֵׂה עִמִּי.
נְטַע שׂוֹרֵק בְּתוֹךְ כַּרְמִי.
שְׁעֵה שַׁוְעַת בְּנֵי עַמִּי:

[3] Tread the wine press in Botzrah,
also in Babylon which grew to power.
Release my foes from angry rage.[1]
Hear my voice on the day I call.

דְּרוֹךְ פּוּרָה בְּתוֹךְ בָּצְרָה.
וְגַם בָּבֶל אֲשֶׁר גָּבְרָה.
נְתוֹשׁ צָרַי מֵאַף וְעֶבְרָה.
שְׁמַע קוֹלִי בְּיוֹם אֶקְרָא:

[4] God bring to the wilderness
mountain myrtle,
acacia, cypress and box tree.
To the bright and to the cautious
give peace that flows as a river.

אֱלֹהִים תֵּן בַּמִּדְבָּר הַר.
הֲדַס שִׁטָּה בְּרוֹשׁ תִּדְהָר.
וְלַמַּזְהִיר וְלַנִּזְהָר.
שְׁלוֹמִים תֵּן כְּמֵי נָהָר:

[5] Passionate God transform my foes,[2]
melting their heart with regret.
Then we will open and fill our mouths,
our tongues singing out to You.

הָשֵׁב קָמַי אֵל קַנָּא.
בְּמוֹג לֵבָב וּבַמְּגִנָּה.
וְנַרְחִיב פֶּה וּנְמַלְּאֶנָּה.
לְשׁוֹנֵנוּ לְךָ רִנָּה:

[6] Know what is wisdom for your soul,
what is a crown for your head
to guard the command
of your Holy One,
to keep your holy Shabbat.

דְּעֵה חָכְמָה לְנַפְשֶׁךָ.
וְהִיא כֶתֶר לְרֹאשֶׁךָ.
נְצוֹר מִצְוַת קְדוֹשֶׁךָ.
שְׁמוֹר שַׁבַּת קָדְשֶׁךָ:

Dunash ben Labrat (amended)   דונש בן־לברט

SHABBAT MORNING SERVICE — VERSES OF SONG

¹דְּרוֹר *D'ror yikra l'vein im bat,*
v'yintsorchem k'mo vavat,
n'im shimchem v'lo yushbat,
sh'vu v'nuchu b'yom shabbat.

²*D'rosh navi v'ulami,*
v'ot yesha aseih immi,
n'sa soreik b'toch karmi,
sh'eih shav'at b'nei ammi.

³*D'roch purah b'toch botsrah,*
v'gam bavel asher gav'rah,
n'tosh tsarai mei'af v'evrah,
sh'ma koli b'yom ekra.

⁴*Elohim tein ba-midbar har,*
hadas shittah b'rosh tidhar,
v'la-mazhir v'la-nizhar,
sh'lomim tein k'mei nahar.

⁵*Hasheiv kamai eil kanna,*
b'mog leivav uva-m'ginnah,
v'narchiv peh un'mall'ennah,
l'shoneinu l'cha rinnah.

⁶*d'eih chochmah l'nafshecha,*
v'hi cheter l'roshecha,
n'tsor mitsvat k'doshecha,
sh'mor shabbat kodshecha.

דְּרוֹר יִקְרָא **God declares freedom...**
The first letters of each line of the first, second, third and final verses spell the name Dunash, indicating that the author is Dunash ben Labrat, tenth-century Fez.

Shabbat offers solace but does not remove the bitterness and anger of an exiled people. The opening call to freedom turns to the wish for the destruction of the nations and powers that destroyed and enslaved the Jewish people. Then in a renewed world, the wilderness will flourish, people will sing God's praises and be able truly to keep Shabbat.

We have modified the violence of two of the verses calling for the destruction of Israel's enemies, asking instead for an end to their hatred and their repentance.

[1] We have amended the Hebrew text from 'smash my foes with angry rage' to 'release my foes from angry rage'.
[2] We have amended the Hebrew text from 'Passionate God tread down my foes' to 'transform my foes'.

Yom zeh m'chubbad

יוֹם זֶה מְכֻבָּד

יוֹם This day is honoured above all days,
for on it rested the Eternal Rock.

יוֹם זֶה מְכֻבָּד מִכָּל־יָמִים
כִּי בוֹ שָׁבַת צוּר עוֹלָמִים:

[1] You have six days
to work for yourselves
but the seventh day is a time for God.
On the Shabbat you are to do no work,
for all was finished in six days.

אֵשֶׁת יָמִים תַּעֲשֶׂה מְלַאכְתֶּךָ.
וְיוֹם הַשְּׁבִיעִי לֵאלֹהֶיךָ.
שַׁבָּת לֹא תַעֲשֶׂה בוֹ מְלָאכָה.
כִּי כֹל עָשָׂה שֵׁשֶׁת יָמִים:

    This day is honoured …

יוֹם זֶה מְכֻבָּד...

[2] It is the first day of holy gatherings
this day of rest, this holy Shabbat day,
so all recite Kiddush over the wine
and seeking wholeness
bless loaves of bread.

רִאשׁוֹן הוּא לְמִקְרָאֵי קֹדֶשׁ.
יוֹם שַׁבָּתוֹן יוֹם שַׁבַּת קֹדֶשׁ.
עַל כֵּן כָּל־אִישׁ בְּיֵינוֹ יְקַדֵּשׁ.
עַל שְׁתֵּי לֶחֶם יִבְצְעוּ תְמִימִים:

    This day is honoured …

יוֹם זֶה מְכֻבָּד...

[3] Eat good food and drink good wine;
to those who cling to God all is given:
clothes to wear, portions of bread,
meat and fish and all tasty foods.

אֱכוֹל מַשְׁמַנִּים שְׁתֵה מַמְתַּקִּים.
כִּי אֵל יִתֵּן לְכָל־בּוֹ דְבֵקִים.
בֶּגֶד לִלְבּוֹשׁ לֶחֶם חֻקִּים.
בָּשָׂר וְדָגִים וְכָל־מַטְעַמִּים:

    This day is honoured …

יוֹם זֶה מְכֻבָּד...

[4] Let nothing be lacking on that day.
Eat, be satisfied and bless the Eternal
your God whom you love,
who has blessed you
amongst all peoples.

לֹא תֶחְסַר כֹּל בּוֹ וְאָכַלְתָּ
וְשָׂבָעְתָּ וּבֵרַכְתָּ אֶת יהוה
אֱלֹהֶיךָ אֲשֶׁר אָהַבְתָּ.
כִּי בֵרַכְךָ מִכָּל־הָעַמִּים:

    This day is honoured …

יוֹם זֶה מְכֻבָּד...

[5] The heavens recite God's glory.
God's grace fills the entire earth.
Recognize all that God has made,
the Rock whose work is perfect.

הַשָּׁמַיִם מְסַפְּרִים כְּבוֹדוֹ.
וְגַם הָאָרֶץ מָלְאָה חַסְדּוֹ.
רְאוּ כִּי כָל־אֵלֶּה עָשְׂתָה יָדוֹ.
כִּי הוּא הַצּוּר פָּעֳלוֹ תָמִים:

This day is honoured above all days,
for on it rested the Eternal Rock.

יוֹם זֶה מְכֻבָּד מִכָּל־יָמִים
כִּי בוֹ שָׁבַת צוּר עוֹלָמִים:

Attributed to Yisrael ha-Ger ישראל הגר

189 SHABBAT MORNING SERVICE   **VERSES OF SONG**

יוֹם *Yom zeh m'chubbad mikkol yamim,*
ki vo shavat tsur olamim.

¹*Sheishet yamim ta'aseh m'lachtecha,*
v'yom ha-sh'vi'i leilohecha,
shabbat lo ta'aseh vo m'lachah,
ki chol asah sheishet yamim.

Yom zeh m'chubbad ...

²*Rishon hu l'mikra'ei kodesh,*
yom shabbaton yom shabbat kodesh,
al kein kol ish b'yeino y'kaddeish,
al shtei lechem yivts'u t'mimim.

Yom zeh m'chubbad ...

³*Echol mashmannim sh'teih mamtakkim,*
ki eil yittein l'chol bo d'veikim,
beged lilbosh lechem chukkim,
basar v'dagim v'chol mat'ammim.

Yom zeh m'chubbad ...

⁴*Lo techsar kol bo v'achalta*
v'sava'ta, uveirachta et Adonai,
elohecha asher ahavta,
ki veirach'cha mikkol ha-ammim.

Yom zeh m'chubbad ...

⁵*Ha-shamayim m'sapp'rim k'vodo,*
v'gam ha-arets mal'ah chasdo,
r'u ki kol eilleh as'tah yado,
ki hu ha-tsur po'olo tamim.

Yom zeh m'chubbad mikkol yamim,
ki vo shavat tsur olamim.

יוֹם זֶה מְכֻבָּד **This day is honoured ...** The initial letters of the verses spell the name Yisrael, and those in the final verse spell *'ha-ger'*, the proselyte, but precisely who this might be is not known.

The poet celebrates the rituals of Shabbat, blessings over wine and bread, the wearing of special clothes. But, as befits a table hymn, he dwells at length on the food and drink, the special meat, fish and desserts to be relished on this day!

Strength and Faithfulness

הָאַדֶּרֶת Strength and faithfulness to the Living One of the universe.	לְחַי עוֹלָמִים:	הָאַדֶּרֶת וְהָאֱמוּנָה
Understanding and blessing …	לְחַי עוֹלָמִים:	הַבִּינָה וְהַבְּרָכָה
Pride and greatness …	לְחַי עוֹלָמִים:	הַגַּאֲוָה וְהַגְּדֻלָּה
Knowledge and speech …	לְחַי עוֹלָמִים:	הַדֵּעָה וְהַדִּבּוּר
Splendour and beauty …	לְחַי עוֹלָמִים:	הַהוֹד וְהֶהָדָר
Meeting and experience …	לְחַי עוֹלָמִים:	הַוַּעַד וְהַוָּתִיקוּת
Purity and radiance …	לְחַי עוֹלָמִים:	הַזָּךְ וְהַזֹּהַר
Strength and wealth …	לְחַי עוֹלָמִים:	הַחַיִל וְהַחֹסֶן
Ritual and purity …	לְחַי עוֹלָמִים:	הַטֶּכֶס וְהַטֹּהַר
Unity and awe …	לְחַי עוֹלָמִים:	הַיִּחוּד וְהַיִּרְאָה
Sovereignty and honour …	לְחַי עוֹלָמִים:	הַכֶּתֶר וְהַכָּבוֹד
Instruction and fascination …	לְחַי עוֹלָמִים:	הַלֶּקַח וְהַלִּבּוּב
Rule and authority …	לְחַי עוֹלָמִים:	הַמְּלוּכָה וְהַמֶּמְשָׁלָה
Wonder and eternity …	לְחַי עוֹלָמִים:	הַנּוֹי וְהַנֶּצַח
Might and elevation …	לְחַי עוֹלָמִים:	הַסִּגּוּי וְהַשֶּׂגֶב
Power and humility …	לְחַי עוֹלָמִים:	הָעֹז וְהָעֲנָוָה
Redemption and distinction …	לְחַי עוֹלָמִים:	הַפְּדוּת וְהַפְּאֵר
Glory and righteousness …	לְחַי עוֹלָמִים:	הַצְּבִי וְהַצֶּדֶק
Acclaim and holiness …	לְחַי עוֹלָמִים:	הַקְּרִיאָה וְהַקְּדֻשָּׁה
Joy and exaltedness …	לְחַי עוֹלָמִים:	הָרֹן וְהָרוֹמֵמוֹת
Song and praise …	לְחַי עוֹלָמִים:	הַשִּׁיר וְהַשֶּׁבַח
Praise and harmony … to the Living One of the universe.	לְחַי עוֹלָמִים:	הַתְּהִלָּה וְהַתִּפְאֶרֶת

From Heichalot Rabbati) היכלות רבתי

SHABBAT MORNING SERVICE — VERSES OF SONG

הָאַדֶּרֶת *Ha-aderet v'ha-emunah l'chai olamim.*
Ha-binah v'ha-b'rachah l'chai olamim.
Ha-ga'avah v'ha-g'dullah l'chai olamim.
Ha-dei'ah v'ha-dibbur l'chai olamim.
Ha-hod v'he-hadar l'chai olamim.
Ha-va'ad v'ha-vatikut l'chai olamim.
Ha-zach v'ha-zohar l'chai olamim.
Ha-chayil v'ha-chosen l'chai olamim.
Ha-teches v'ha-tohar l'chai olamim.
Ha-yichud v'ha-yir'ah l'chai olamim.
Ha-keter v'ha-kavod l'chai olamim.
Ha-lekach v'ha-libbuv l'chai olamim.
Ha-m'luchah v'ha-memshalah l'chai olamim.
Ha-noi v'ha-neitsach l'chai olamim.
Ha-siggui v'ha-segev l'chai olamim.
Ha-oz v'ha-anavah l'chai olamim.
Ha-p'dut v'ha-p'eir l'chai olamim.
Ha-ts'vi v'ha-tsedek l'chai olamim.
Ha-k'ri'ah v'ha-k'dushah l'chai olamim.
Ha-ron v'ha-romeimut l'chai olamim.
Ha-shir v'ha-shevach l'chai olamim.
Ha-t'hillah v'ha-tif'eret l'chai olamim.

הָאַדֶּרֶת וְהָאֱמוּנָה
Strength and faithfulness ...
The source of this hymn is *Heichalot Rabbati*, a sixth-century mystical text. It is a double alphabetical acrostic, each verse listing two attributes of God to which the congregation responds *l'chai olamim,* 'to the Living One of the universe'. From the Middle Ages it was referred to as 'the song of the angels', as the angels were believed to sing it in heaven in praise of God.

Sachaki, sachaki

¹שַׂחֲקִי You may laugh,
laugh at all the dreams
which I, the dreamer, can weave,
because I believe in humanity;
for in you I still believe.

²Yet my soul still yearns for freedom
to no golden calf betrayed.
I still believe in humanity,
so strong is our spirit made.

³Laugh that I still believe in friends
and I yet will find a heart
to share my hope as his own hope,
in my joy and pain take part.

⁴And I believe in the future,
however distant the day,
when nation shall bless each nation
and in peace shall make their way.

⁵My people, too, shall flower again;
generations shall arise,
their fetters of iron cast away,
a new light before their eyes.

Saul Tchernikowsky

שַׂחֲקִי שַׂחֲקִי

אשַׂחֲקִי שַׂחֲקִי עַל הַחֲלוֹמוֹת.
זוּ אֲנִי הַחוֹלֵם שָׂח.
שַׂחֲקִי כִּי בָאָדָם אַאֲמִין.
כִּי עוֹדֶנִּי מַאֲמִין בָּךְ:

בכִּי עוֹד נַפְשִׁי דְּרוֹר שׁוֹאֶפֶת.
לֹא מְכַרְתִּיהָ לְעֵגֶל־פָּז.
כִּי עוֹד אַאֲמִין גַּם בָּאָדָם.
גַּם בְּרוּחוֹ. רוּחַ עָז:

גשַׂחֲקִי כִּי גַם בְּרֵעוּת אַאֲמִין.
אַאֲמִין כִּי עוֹד אֶמְצָא לֵב.
לֵב תִּקְווֹתַי גַּם תִּקְווֹתָיו
יָחוּשׁ אֲשֶׁר יָבִין כְּאֵב:

דאַאֲמִינָה גַם בֶּעָתִיד.
אַף אִם יִרְחַק זֶה הַיּוֹם.
אַךְ בּוֹא יָבוֹא – יִשְׂאוּ שָׁלוֹם
אָז וּבְרָכָה לְאֹם מִלְאֹם:

הּיָשׁוּב יִפְרַח אָז גַּם עַמִּי.
וּבָאָרֶץ יָקוּם דּוֹר.
בַּרְזֶל־כְּבָלָיו יוּסַר מֶנּוּ.
עַיִן־בְּעַיִן יִרְאֶה אוֹר:

שאול טשרניחובסקי

שַׂחֲקִי שַׂחֲקִי You may laugh ...
This poem by Saul Tchernikowsky (1875-1943) was introduced into the liturgy in the last edition of *Forms of Prayer* because of its theme of 'the future'. Born in Russia, he moved to Palestine in 1931. A physician, essayist and translator, particularly of classical Greek literature, he was a major figure in the development of modern Hebrew poetry, but controversial in his almost pagan worship of beauty. He celebrated nature and the joys of human experience. Here he expresses his hope in humanity and the future renewal of the Jewish people.

SHABBAT MORNING SERVICE

VERSES OF SONG

¹**שַׂחֲקִי** *Sachaki sachaki al ha-chalomot, zu ani ha-choleim sach,*
sachaki ki va-adam a'amin, ki odenni ma'amin bach.

²*Ki od nafshi d'ror sho'efet, lo m'chartiha l'eigel paz,*
ki od a'amin gam ba-adam, gam b'rucho, ru'ach az.

³*Sachaki ki gam b'rei'ut a'amin, a'amin ki od emtsa leiv,*
leiv tikvotai gam tikvotav, yachush osher yavin k'eiv.

⁴*A'aminah gam be-atid, af im yirchak zeh ha-yom,*
ach bo yavo - yis'u shalom, az uv'rachah l'om mill'om.

⁵*Yashuv yifrach az gam ammi, uva-arets yakum dor,*
barzel k'valav yusar mennu, ayin b'ayin yir'eh or.

Shachar avakkesh'cha   שַׁחַר אֲבַקֶּשְׁךָ

שַׁחַר Every dawn I seek You
my refuge and might,
set my prayer before You
each morning and night.

שַׁחַר אֲבַקֶּשְׁךָ. צוּרִי וּמִשְׂגַּבִּי.
אֶעֱרוֹךְ לְפָנֶיךָ שַׁחְרִי
וְגַם עַרְבִּי:

Here before Your greatness
I stand so afraid,
for my innermost thoughts
to You are displayed.

לִפְנֵי גְדוּלָּתְךָ אֶעֱמֹד וְאֶבָּהֵל.
כִּי עֵינְךָ תִרְאֶה
כָּל־מַחְשְׁבוֹת לִבִּי:

Whatever can tongue say
or heart hope to be!
What is even the strength
of life within me!

מַה־זֶּה אֲשֶׁר יוּכַל
הַלֵּב וְהַלָּשׁוֹן לַעֲשׂוֹת.
וּמַה כֹּחַ־רוּחִי בְּתוֹךְ קִרְבִּי:

But since everyone's singing
is pleasing to You,
while You give me Your breath
I thank You anew.

הִנֵּה לְךָ תִיטַב זִמְרַת אֱנוֹשׁ.
עַל כֵּן אוֹדְךָ
בְּעוֹד תִּהְיֶה נִשְׁמַת אֱלֹהַּ בִּי:

Solomon ibn Gabirol   שלמה אבן גבירול

שַׁחַר *Shachar avakkesh'cha, tsuri umisgabbi, e'eroch l'fanecha shachari v'gam arbi.*
Lifnei g'dullat'cha e'emod v'ebbaheil, ki ein'cha tir'eh kol machsh'vot libbi.
Mah zeh asher yuchal ha-leiv v'ha-lashon la'asot, umah ko'ach ruchi b'toch kirbi.
Hinneih l'cha titav zimrat enosh, al kein od'cha b'od tih'yeh nishmat elo'ah bi.

שַׁחַר אֲבַקֶּשְׁךָ **Every dawn I seek You ...**
Attributed to Solomon ibn Gabirol (1021-1056), this poem became a regular addition to the morning service, either prior to or within the 'Morning Blessings', in both Ashkenazi and Sephardi traditions. By focusing on the poet's desire to lay his prayer before God it helps create a mood for concentration in prayer.

Anna b'cho'ach

אָנָּא בְּכֹחַ

אָנָּא Release all captives, we beseech You,
Almighty God whose power sets us free;
and hear the glad acclaim of all Your people
who praise and glorify You alone.
Preserve the righteous ones who seek You,
and proclaim Your unity in love;
O guard and bless
with Your abundant goodness
Your people who revere Your name.
You God, who are alone exalted,
turn to us and hear our prayers.

We bless You –
You who know all things hidden.
Your kingdom
is for eternity.

אָנָּא בְּכֹחַ גְּדֻלַּת יְמִינְךָ
תַּתִּיר צְרוּרָה:
קַבֵּל רִנַּת עַמְּךָ
שַׂגְּבֵנוּ טַהֲרֵנוּ נוֹרָא:
נָא גִבּוֹר דּוֹרְשֵׁי יִחוּדְךָ
כְּבָבַת שָׁמְרֵם:
בָּרְכֵם טַהֲרֵם רַחֲמֵי
צִדְקָתְךָ תָּמִיד גָּמְלֵם:
חֲסִין קָדוֹשׁ בְּרוֹב טוּבְךָ
נַהֵל עֲדָתֶךָ:
יָחִיד גֵּאֶה לְעַמְּךָ פְּנֵה
זוֹכְרֵי קְדֻשָּׁתֶךָ:
שַׁוְעָתֵנוּ קַבֵּל וּשְׁמַע צַעֲקָתֵנוּ
יוֹדֵעַ תַּעֲלוּמוֹת:
בָּרוּךְ שֵׁם כְּבוֹד מַלְכוּתוֹ
לְעוֹלָם וָעֶד:

Attributed to Nechunya ben Hakkana נחוניה בן הקנה

אָנָּא *Anna b'cho'ach g'dullat y'min'cha, tattir ts'rurah.*
Kabbeil rinnat amm'cha, sagg'veinu tahareinu nora.
Na gibbor dor'shei yichud'cha, k'vavat shomreim.
Bar'cheim tahareim rachameim tsidkat'cha tamid gomleim,.
Chasin kadosh b'rov tuv'cha, naheil adatecha.
Yachid gei'eh l'amm'cha, p'nei zoch'rei k'dushatecha.
Shav'ateinu kabbeil ush'ma tsa'akateinu, yodei'a ta'alumot.
Baruch sheim k'vod malchuto l'olam va'ed.

אָנָּא בְּכֹחַ Release all captives ...

This kabbalistic prayer is attributed to the second-century Mishnah teacher Nechunya ben Hakkana, though it is probably of a much later date. Made up of seven lines, each with six words, the forty-two words represent the forty-two-letter secret name of God. It contains seven titles for God (*nora* - 'Awesome One'; *gibbor* - 'Mighty One'; *chasin* - 'Almighty'; *kadosh* - 'Holy One'; *yachid* - 'One and Only'; *yodeya ta'alumot* - 'Knower of secrets'). The first letters of the words of the second line spell *k'ra satan*, 'may evil be cut off!' It is found in many locations within the daily liturgy, as well as on Rosh Hashanah and during the counting of the Omer. Scribes are enjoined to recite it with great *kavannah*, devotion and intention, before beginning to write texts of a Torah scroll or other religious document. It is also used as an evening prayer. It is meant to help remove all evil thoughts during prayer.

195 SHABBAT MORNING SERVICE — VERSES OF SONG

שִׁיר הַכָּבוֹד

Shir ha-kavod (selected verses)

אַנְעִים I play sweet psalms
and weave my songs
because for You my spirit longs.
In Your hand's shade my senses yearn
Your secret mysteries to learn.
Your glory, even as I speak
stirs my heart Your love to seek.
And so I tell Your glorious fame,
with songs of love
I praise Your name.
I tell Your glory, never shown,
describing You though still unknown.
Yet through Your prophets
that You taught
a glimpse of majesty is brought.
Your greatness and Your force they told
and showed the power that You hold.
Each age You call, Your word is true.
Seek us, the people seeking You!
Yet who can tell
God's mighty ways
and who can make known
all God's praise.

אַנְעִים זְמִירוֹת וְשִׁירִים אֶאֱרוֹג.
כִּי אֵלֶיךָ נַפְשִׁי תַעֲרוֹג:
נַפְשִׁי חִמְּדָה בְּצֵל יָדֶךָ.
לָדַעַת כָּל־רָז סוֹדֶךָ:
מִדֵּי דַבְּרִי בִּכְבוֹדֶךָ.
הוֹמֶה לִבִּי אֶל דּוֹדֶיךָ:
עַל כֵּן אֲדַבֵּר בְּךָ נִכְבָּדוֹת.
וְשִׁמְךָ אֲכַבֵּד בְּשִׁירֵי יְדִידוֹת:
אֲסַפְּרָה כְבוֹדְךָ וְלֹא רְאִיתִיךָ.
אֲדַמְּךָ אֲכַנְּךָ וְלֹא יְדַעְתִּיךָ:
בְּיַד נְבִיאֶיךָ בְּסוֹד עֲבָדֶיךָ.
דִּמִּיתָ הֲדַר כְּבוֹד הוֹדֶךָ:
גְּדֻלָּתְךָ וּגְבוּרָתֶךָ.
כִּנּוּ לְתֹקֶף פְּעֻלָּתֶךָ:
רֹאשׁ דְּבָרְךָ אֱמֶת.
קוֹרֵא מֵרֹאשׁ דּוֹר וָדוֹר
עַם דּוֹרֶשְׁךָ דְּרוֹשׁ:
מִי יְמַלֵּל גְּבוּרוֹת יהוה
יַשְׁמִיעַ כָּל־תְּהִלָּתוֹ:

Judah he-Chasid — יהודה החסיד

אַנְעִים *An'im z'mirot v'shirim e'erog, ki eilecha nafshi ta'arog.*
Nafshi chimm'dah b'tseil yadecha, lada'at kol raz sodecha.
Middei dabb'ri bichvodecha, homeh libbi el dodecha.
Al kein adabbeir b'cha nichbadot, v'shimcha achabbeid b'shirei y'didot.
Asapp'rah ch'vod'cha v'lo r'iticha, adamm'cha achancha v'lo y'da'ticha.
B'yad n'vi'echa b'sod avadecha, dimmita hadar k'vod hodecha.
G'dullat'cha ug'vuratecha kinnu l'tokef p'ullatecha.
Rosh d'var'cha emet, korei meirosh, dor vador am doreshcha d'rosh.
Mi y'malleil g'vurot Adonai, yashmi'a kol t'hillato.

שִׁיר הַכָּבוֹד **Song of Glory ...**
This poem of longing for nearness to God, often ascribed to Rabbi Judah he-Chasid of Regensburg (d. 1217), is known as the 'Hymn of Glory'. Its recital is usually restricted by some to Shabbat and festivals. The custom arose of a child reading it, to encourage their participation in the service. This was later understood to indicate that such a holy poem should be read by one who had not yet begun to sin. Our version contains the opening verses, one later verse and a concluding addition, Ps 106:2. The full version contains an alphabetic acrostic.

Odeh la-Eil

אוֹדֶה I shall give thanks to God
who tests the heart,
when the morning stars sing together.

אוֹדֶה לָאֵל. לֵבָב חוֹקֵר
בְּרָן־יַחַד כּוֹכְבֵי בֹקֶר:

[1] Attend to the soul:
she is turquoise, agate and jasper.
Her light is like the light of the sun,
   sevenfold the morning's light.

א שִׂימוּ לֵב אֶל הַנְּשָׁמָה.
לְשֶׁם שְׁבוֹ וְאַחְלָמָה:
וְאוֹרָהּ כְּאוֹר הַחַמָּה –
שִׁבְעָתַיִם כְּאוֹר הַבֹּקֶר:

[2] She was hewn from the throne of Glory,
sent to live in a desert land,
to deliver it from fire,
   to shine upon it in the early morning.

ב מִכִּסֵּא כָבוֹד חֻצָּבָה.
לָגוּר בְּאֶרֶץ עֲרָבָה.
לְהַצִּילָהּ מִלֶּהָבָה.
וּלְהַאִירָהּ לִפְנוֹת בֹּקֶר:

[3] Rouse yourself, for every night
your soul goes to heaven
to account for its actions
   before the Maker of
      evening and morning.

ג עוּרוּ נָא. כִּי בְּכָל־לַיְלָה
נִשְׁמַתְכֶם עוֹלָה לְמַעְלָה.
לָתֵת דִּין וְחֶשְׁבּוֹן מִפְעָלָהּ
לְיוֹצֵר עֶרֶב וָבֹקֶר:

[4] The One who is faithful to the task
will return her to you if God so wills.
No one died through God's error –
   and there was evening
      and there was morning.

ד הַנֶּאֱמָן בְּפִקְדוֹנוֹ
יַחֲזִירֶנָּה לוֹ כִּרְצוֹנוֹ:
אִישׁ לֹא גָרַע בַּעֲווֹנוֹ –
וַיְהִי עֶרֶב וַיְהִי בֹקֶר:

[5] Gladden the afflicted one,
the only one, perfect and pure.
If we do not keep our soul alive,
   how will we be worthy
      of the light of morning?

ה וְהַחֲיוּ הָעֲנִיָּה.
יְחִידָה. תַּמָּה וּנְקִיָּה:
וַאֲשֶׁר נַפְשׁוֹ לֹא חִיָּה –
אֵיךְ יִזְכֶּה לְאוֹר הַבֹּקֶר:

Attributed to Rabbi Shemayah רבי שמעיהו

אוֹדֶה לָאֵל I shall give thanks to God ...
This mediaeval poem is recited by some in the morning and as a table hymn on Shabbat. According to custom we have omitted the fourth verse that refers to *tefillin*, that are not worn on Shabbat. It celebrates the rabbinic idea that at night the soul returns to God and it is restored to us in its glory as we awake. It is our task to preserve the soul within us, the source of light.

VERSES OF SONG

אוֹדֶה *Odeh la-Eil, leivav chokeir, b'ron yachad koch'vei voker.*

¹*Simu leiv el ha-n'shamah, leshem sh'vo v'achlamah.*
V'orah k'or ha-chammah – shiv'atayim k'or ha-boker.

²*Mikkisei chavod chutsavah, lagur b'erets aravah,*
L'hatsilah milehavah, ul'ha'irah lifnot boker.

³*Uru na, ki b'chol lailah nishmatchem olah l'ma'lah,*
Lateit din v'cheshbon mif'alah, l'yotseir erev vavoker.

⁴*Ha-ne'eman b'fikdono, yachazirennah lo kirtsono.*
Ish lo gava ba'avono – vay'hi erev vay'hi voker.

⁵*V'hachayu ha-aniyah, y'chidah, tammah un'kiyah.*
Va'asher nafsho lo chiyah – eich yizkeh l'or ha-boker.

ALL CREATION PRAISES GOD

וַיְבָ֫רֶךְ Then David blessed the Almighty in the sight of all the congregation, and David said: 'Blessed are You Almighty God, the God of our father Israel from everlasting to everlasting. Yours is the greatness, the power, the splendour, the glory and the majesty, for everything in heaven and earth is Yours. Yours alone is sovereignty and You are exalted supreme over all. Wealth and honour come from You, for You rule over all. In Your hand are strength and might. It is in Your power to give greatness and strength to all. And now, our God, we give You thanks and praise Your glorious name.'[1] May the people bless Your glorious name, though it is beyond all blessing and praise. You alone are God; You made the sky, the reaches of space and its countless lights, the earth and everything on it, the seas and everything in them; You give life to them all, and the universe worships You.[2]

וַיְבָ֫רֶךְ דָּוִיד אֶת יהוה. לְעֵינֵי כָל־הַקָּהָל. וַיֹּ֫אמֶר דָּוִיד. בָּרוּךְ אַתָּה יהוה אֱלֹהֵי יִשְׂרָאֵל אָבִ֫ינוּ מֵעוֹלָם וְעַד־עוֹלָם: לְךָ יהוה הַגְּדֻלָּה וְהַגְּבוּרָה וְהַתִּפְאֶ֫רֶת וְהַנֵּ֫צַח וְהַהוֹד. כִּי כֹל בַּשָּׁמַ֫יִם וּבָאָ֫רֶץ לְךָ יהוה הַמַּמְלָכָה וְהַמִּתְנַשֵּׂא לְכֹל לְרֹאשׁ: וְהָעֹ֫שֶׁר וְהַכָּבוֹד מִלְּפָנֶ֫יךָ וְאַתָּה מוֹשֵׁל בַּכֹּל. וּבְיָדְךָ כֹּחַ וּגְבוּרָה. וּבְיָדְךָ לְגַדֵּל וּלְחַזֵּק לַכֹּל: וְעַתָּה אֱלֹהֵ֫ינוּ מוֹדִים אֲנַ֫חְנוּ לָךְ. וּמְהַלְלִים לְשֵׁם תִּפְאַרְתֶּ֫ךָ: וִיבָרְכוּ שֵׁם כְּבוֹדֶ֫ךָ. וּמְרוֹמַם עַל־כָּל־בְּרָכָה וּתְהִלָּה: אַתָּה הוּא יהוה לְבַדֶּ֫ךָ. אַתָּה עָשִׂ֫יתָ אֶת־הַשָּׁמַ֫יִם שְׁמֵי הַשָּׁמַ֫יִם וְכָל־צְבָאָם. הָאָ֫רֶץ וְכָל־אֲשֶׁר עָלֶ֫יהָ. הַיַּמִּים וְכָל־אֲשֶׁר בָּהֶם. וְאַתָּה מְחַיֶּה אֶת־כֻּלָּם. וּצְבָא הַשָּׁמַ֫יִם לְךָ מִשְׁתַּחֲוִים:

וַיְבָ֫רֶךְ דָּוִיד Then David blessed ...

This prayer is made up of two Biblical passages, from 1 Chron 29:10-13 and Neh 9:6-11. It introduces the last section of the 'verses of song'. On weekdays it was customary to collect charity when reciting the sentence: 'Wealth and honour come from You, for You rule over all.'

The Book of Chronicles repeats the story of the life of King David but omits the *problematic* issues described in the Book of Samuel. Here David is an ecstatic composer of praises to God, in anticipation of the temple to be built by his son Solomon. The addition from the Book of Nehemiah continues the theme of the whole universe, God's creation, praising the Creator.

Jewish liturgy is God-centred. The act of worship itself is intended to make the presence of God real in the lives of the worshipping community and in the world. To participate is seen as a duty, a task and a joy. It moves the centre of our attention away from ourselves and our regular preoccupations towards something outside of ourselves and greater than ourselves. That change of focus remains a challenge for us today.

[1] I Chron 29:10-13. [2] Neh 9:5-6.

SHABBAT MORNING SERVICE — VERSES OF SONG

וַיְבָרֶךְ *Vay'varech david et Adonai, l'einei kol ha-kahal, vayomer david, baruch attah Adonai elohei yisra'el avinu mei'olam v'ad olam. L'cha Adonai ha-g'dullah v'ha-g'vurah v'ha-tif'eret v'ha-neitsach v'ha-hod, ki chol ba-shamayim uva'arets l'cha Adonai ha-mamlachah v'ha-mitnassei l'chol l'rosh. V'ha-osher v'ha-kavod mill'fanecha, v'attah mosheil ba-kol, uv'yad'cha ko'ach ug'vurah, uv'yad'cha l'gaddeil ul'chazeik la-kol. V'attah eloheinu modim anachnu lach, um'hal'lim l'sheim tif'artecha. Vivar'chu sheim k'vodecha, um'romam al kol b'rachah ut'hillah. Attah hu Adonai l'vaddecha, attah asita et ha-shamayim, sh'mei ha-shamayim v'chol ts'va'am, ha-arets, v'chol asher aleha, ha-yammim v'chol asher bahem, v'attah m'chayeh et kullam, uts'va ha-shamayim l'cha mishtachavim.*

בָּרוּךְ Blessed be God forever.
Amen and amen.
Blessed be Almighty God,
the God of Israel,
who alone works wonders.
Blessed be the nearness
of God's Presence forever,
for God's Presence fills all the earth.
Amen and amen.[1]

בָּרוּךְ יהוה לְעוֹלָם
אָמֵן וְאָמֵן.
בָּרוּךְ יהוה אֱלֹהִים אֱלֹהֵי יִשְׂרָאֵל.
עֹשֵׂה נִפְלָאוֹת לְבַדּוֹ:
וּבָרוּךְ שֵׁם כְּבוֹדוֹ לְעוֹלָם.
וְיִמָּלֵא כְבוֹדוֹ אֶת כָּל־הָאָרֶץ.
אָמֵן וְאָמֵן:

בָּרוּךְ *Baruch Adonai l'olam amen v'amen,
Baruch Adonai elohim elohei yisra'el, oseih nifla'ot l'vaddo.
Uvaruch sheim k'vodo l'olam, v'yimmalei ch'vodo et kol ha-arets, amen v'amen.*

בָּרוּךְ יהוה לְעוֹלָם
Blessed be God forever ...

The Biblical Book of Psalms is divided up into five separate sections, presumably intended to correspond to the five 'Books of Moses', the Torah. The Torah is regarded in Jewish tradition as the direct revelation from God to human beings given through Moses. The second part of the Hebrew Bible, the Prophets, is also understood to be the revealed word of God, but affected by the particular experience and style of the prophet himself. However, the third section of the Hebrew Bible, the 'Writings', beginning with the Psalms, is considered to be made up of books that are inspired by the 'holy spirit', but are far more works of the human imagination. Books like the Psalms and Job represent our human self-revelation to God.

As we noted at the end of the 'Morning Blessings', the conclusion of each of the five 'books' within the Book of Psalms is marked with a couple of verses in praise of God, a 'doxology', and these were also introduced into the morning service to mark the end of the two opening preparatory sections. The texts at the close of the Morning Blessings were taken from Psalm 106:47-48 and Psalm 150:6. Here they are taken from Psalms 89:53 and 72:18-19. Again their presence provides a link between the Psalms, the earliest form of Jewish liturgy, and our own community prayers.

[1] Ps 89:53; 72:18-19.

נִשְׁמַת **The breath of life in every creature** shall bless You, God our Creator, and the spirit of all flesh ever recalls Your beauty and Your greatness. From everlasting to everlasting You are God. Besides You we have no power that can rescue and save us, free and deliver us, and answer and care for us. At all times of trouble and distress there is no ruler who can help and support us but You. God of the first and of the last ages, God of all creatures, acknowledged in every generation, adored in all worship - You guide Your universe with love, and Your creatures with mercy. God neither slumbers nor sleeps, but wakes the sleepers, and rouses the uncaring, restoring life beyond death, healing the sick, giving sight to the unseeing and raising up those bent low. To You alone we declare our gratitude. ♆336

נִשְׁמַת כָּל־חַי תְּבָרֵךְ אֶת־שִׁמְךָ יהוה אֱלֹהֵינוּ. וְרוּחַ כָּל־בָּשָׂר תְּפָאֵר וּתְרוֹמֵם זִכְרְךָ מַלְכֵּנוּ תָּמִיד: מִן הָעוֹלָם וְעַד־הָעוֹלָם אַתָּה אֵל. וּמִבַּלְעָדֶיךָ אֵין לָנוּ מֶלֶךְ גּוֹאֵל וּמוֹשִׁיעַ פּוֹדֶה וּמַצִּיל וְעוֹנֶה וּמְרַחֵם. בְּכָל־עֵת צָרָה וְצוּקָה אֵין לָנוּ מֶלֶךְ עוֹזֵר וְסוֹמֵךְ זוּלָתֶךָ: אֱלֹהֵי הָרִאשׁוֹנִים וְהָאַחֲרוֹנִים. אֱלוֹהַּ כָּל־בְּרִיּוֹת. אֲדוֹן כָּל־תּוֹלָדוֹת. הַמְהֻלָּל בְּכָל־הַתִּשְׁבָּחוֹת. הַמְנַהֵג עוֹלָמוֹ בְּחֶסֶד וּבְרִיּוֹתָיו בְּרַחֲמִים: וַיהוה לֹא יָנוּם וְלֹא יִישָׁן. הַמְעוֹרֵר יְשֵׁנִים וְהַמֵּקִיץ נִרְדָּמִים. מְחַיֶּה מֵתִים וְרוֹפֵא חוֹלִים. פּוֹקֵחַ עִוְרִים וְזוֹקֵף כְּפוּפִים. לְךָ לְבַדְּךָ אֲנַחְנוּ מוֹדִים:

נִשְׁמַת *Nishmat kol chai t'vareich et shimcha Adonai eloheinu, v'ru'ach kol basar t'fa'eir ut'romeim zichr'cha malkeinu tamid. Min ha-olam v'ad ha-olam attah eil, umibal'adecha ein lanu melech go'eil umoshi'a podeh umatsil, v'oneh um'racheim, b'chol eit tsarah v'tsukah, ein lanu melech ozeir v'someich zulatecha. Elohei ha-rishonim v'ha-acharonim, elo'ah kol b'riot, adon kol toladot, ha-m'hullal b'chol ha-tishbachot, ha-m'naheig olamo b'chesed uvri'otav b'rachamim. Vadonai lo yanum v'lo yishan, ha-m'oreir y'sheinim v'ha-meikits nirdamim, m'chayeh meitim v'rofei cholim, pokei'ach ivrim v'zokeif k'fufim, l'cha l'vadd'cha anachnu modim.*

נִשְׁמַת כָּל־חַי
The breath of life in every creature ...

These opening words, 'the breath of life in every creature ...', introduce a long prayer, added to the Morning Service on Shabbat, that continues as far as *Yishtabach*. Of ancient origin, the latter part is ascribed to Rabbi Yochanan as a thanksgiving prayer for rainfall (*Berachot* 59b). Similarly the earlier part is mentioned as part of the conclusion of the Passover *Seder* (*Pesachim* 118a).

The prayer works by the accumulation of words: firstly about the qualities of God, then about our inadequacy in finding enough ways of expressing our gratitude, but finally citing how every organ of speech and every part of ourselves should praise God.

SHABBAT MORNING SERVICE — VERSES OF SONG

וְאִלּוּ If our mouths were full of song as the sea, our tongues with joyful sounds like the roar of its waves, our lips with praise as the outspread sky, our eyes shining like the sun and the moon, our hands stretched out like eagles' wings in the air, our feet as swift as the wild deer; we still could not thank You enough, God our Creator, or bless Your name, our Sovereign, for even one of the thousands upon thousands of the countless good deeds You did for our ancestors and for us.

וְאִלּוּ פִינוּ מָלֵא שִׁירָה כַיָּם.
וּלְשׁוֹנֵנוּ רִנָּה כַּהֲמוֹן גַּלָּיו.
וְשִׂפְתוֹתֵינוּ שֶׁבַח כְּמֶרְחֲבֵי רָקִיעַ.
וְעֵינֵינוּ מְאִירוֹת כַּשֶּׁמֶשׁ וְכַיָּרֵחַ.
וְיָדֵינוּ פְרוּשׂוֹת כְּנִשְׁרֵי שָׁמָיִם.
וְרַגְלֵינוּ קַלּוֹת כָּאַיָּלוֹת.
אֵין אֲנוּ מַסְפִּיקִים
לְהוֹדוֹת לְךָ יהוה אֱלֹהֵינוּ.
וּלְבָרֵךְ אֶת שִׁמְךָ מַלְכֵּנוּ.
עַל אַחַת מֵאֶלֶף אַלְפֵי אֲלָפִים
וְרִבֵּי רְבָבוֹת פְּעָמִים הַטּוֹבוֹת.
שֶׁעָשִׂיתָ עִם־אֲבוֹתֵינוּ וְעִמָּנוּ:

<<<

וְאִלּוּ V'illu finu malei shirah cha-yam, ul'shoneinu rinnah ka-hamon gallav, v'siftoteinu shevach k'merchavei raki'a, v'eineinu m'irot ka-shemesh v'cha-yarei'ach, v'yadeinu f'rusot k'nishrei shamayim, v'ragleinu kallot ka-ayalot, ein anu maspikim l'hodot l'cha Adonai eloheinu, ul'vareich et shimcha malkeinu, al achat mei'elef alfei alafim, v'ribbei r'vavot p'amim ha-tovot, she'asita im avoteinu v'immanu.

Like other parts of the liturgy it also moves from the universal, God as Creator who watches over creation with love and mercy, to the particular acts of rescue and support God has shown to Israel, only to return to the universal at the end. By its emphasis on God as one who 'frees the poor ... and needy' it affirms a value system that it is our responsibility, as God's witnesses and partners, to maintain.

The concluding section, recited only on Shabbat and festivals, begins with *Shochen Ad* (Is 57:15). Those familiar with the Biblical source would have recognised that though it asserts that God's 'dwelling' is far removed from us, yet God is present with those 'whose spirit is crushed', to revive them.

The final sentences, beginning *b'fee yesharim*, contain, in the Sephardi version, a double acrostic naming Isaac and Rebecca. It is not known whether this hints at the name of the author and his wife, or is a playful way of celebrating the patriarch and matriarch.

מִמִּצְרַיִם גְּאַלְתָּנוּ יהוה אֱלֹהֵינוּ.	Our Redeemer,
וּמִבֵּית עֲבָדִים פְּדִיתָנוּ.	You rescued us from Egypt,
	freed us from the camp of slavery.
בְּרָעָב זַנְתָּנוּ.	In times of famine You fed us.
וּבְשָׂבָע כִּלְכַּלְתָּנוּ.	In times of plenty You supported us.
מֵחֶרֶב הִצַּלְתָּנוּ.	From violence You delivered us,
וּמִדֶּבֶר מִלַּטְתָּנוּ.	from plagues You saved us,
וּמֵחֳלָיִם רָעִים וְרַבִּים דִּלִּיתָנוּ:	and from many terrible diseases You rescued us.
עַד הֵנָּה עֲזָרוּנוּ רַחֲמֶיךָ.	Until now Your love has been our help
וְלֹא עֲזָבוּנוּ חֲסָדֶיךָ.	and Your kindness has not left us.
עַל־כֵּן אֵבָרִים שֶׁפִּלַּגְתָּ בָּנוּ.	Therefore the limbs You formed in us,
וְרוּחַ וּנְשָׁמָה שֶׁנָּפַחְתָּ בְּאַפֵּינוּ.	the spirit and soul You breathed into us
וְלָשׁוֹן אֲשֶׁר שַׂמְתָּ בְּפִינוּ.	and the tongue You set in our mouth,
הֵן הֵם יוֹדוּ וִיבָרְכוּ וִישַׁבְּחוּ	ever shall they thank, bless, praise, glorify and sing
וִיפָאֲרוּ וִישׁוֹרְרוּ אֶת־שִׁמְךָ	to Your name,
מַלְכֵּנוּ תָּמִיד:	our Ruler.
כִּי כָל־פֶּה לְךָ יוֹדֶה.	For every mouth shall thank You,
וְכָל־לָשׁוֹן לְךָ תְשַׁבֵּחַ.	every tongue praise You,
וְכָל־עַיִן לְךָ תְצַפֶּה.	every eye look to You,
וְכָל־בֶּרֶךְ לְךָ תִכְרַע.	every knee bend to You
וְכָל־קוֹמָה לְפָנֶיךָ תִשְׁתַּחֲוֶה.	and our pride shall bow low before You.
וְכָל־הַלְּבָבוֹת יִירָאוּךָ.	All hearts shall fear You
וְכָל־קֶרֶב וּכְלָיוֹת יְזַמְּרוּ לִשְׁמֶךָ.	and our innermost being sing praises to Your name,
כַּדָּבָר שֶׁנֶּאֱמַר.	as it is said:

<<<

Mimmitsrayim g'altanu Adonai eloheinu, umibbeit avadim p'ditanu, b'ra'av zantanu, uv'sava kilkaltanu, meicherev hitsaltanu, umiddever millat'tanu, umeicholayim ra'im v'rabbim dillitanu.

Ad heinnah azarunu rachamecha, v'lo azavunu chasadecha, al kein eivarim shepilagta banu, v'ru'ach un'shamah shenafachta b'apeinu, v'lashon asher samta b'finu, hein heim yodu viyvar'chu viyshabb'chu viyfa'aru, viyshor'ru et shimcha malkeinu tamid.

Ki chol peh l'cha yodeh, v'chol lashon l'cha t'shabei'ach, v'chol ayin l'cha titspeh, v'chol berech l'cha tichra, v'chol komah l'fanecha tishtachaveh, v'chol ha-l'vavot yira'ucha, v'chol kerev uch'layot y'zamm'ru lishmecha, ka-davar shene'emar,

SHABBAT MORNING SERVICE — VERSES OF SONG

'All my bones shall say,
God who is like You,
who frees the poor
from those too strong for them,
the poor and needy
from their exploiter?'[1]
Who is like You, who is equal to You,
who can be compared to You,
the great, mighty and awesome God,
transcendent God,
Creator of heaven and earth?

כָּל־עַצְמוֹתַי תֹּאמַרְנָה.
יהוה מִי כָמוֹךָ.
מַצִּיל עָנִי מֵחָזָק מִמֶּנּוּ.
וְעָנִי וְאֶבְיוֹן מִגֹּזְלוֹ:
מִי יִדְמֶה־לָּךְ.
וּמִי יִשְׁוֶה־לָּךְ וּמִי יַעֲרָךְ־לָךְ:
הָאֵל הַגָּדוֹל הַגִּבּוֹר וְהַנּוֹרָא.
אֵל עֶלְיוֹן קֹנֵה שָׁמַיִם וָאָרֶץ:

kol atsmotai tomarna, Adonai mi chamocha, matsil ani meichazak mimennu, v'ani v'evyon miggozlo. Mi yidmeh lach, umi yishveh lach, umi ya'aroch lach. Ha-eil ha-gadol ha-gibbor v'ha-nora, eil elyon, koneih shamayim va'arets.

OUR PRAISE OF GOD

שׁוֹכֵן God is the One
who dwells in eternity,
whose being is high and holy.
So it is written in the Psalms:
'You righteous rejoice in the Eternal!
It is right for honest people to pray.'[2]

שׁוֹכֵן עַד. מָרוֹם וְקָדוֹשׁ שְׁמוֹ:
וְכָתוּב.
רַנְּנוּ צַדִּיקִים בַּיהוה.
לַיְשָׁרִים נָאוָה תְהִלָּה:

By the mouth of the upright
You are exalted,
by the words of the righteous
You are blessed,
by the tongue of the pious
You are honoured,
and among the holy
You are sanctified.

בְּפִי יְשָׁרִים תִּתְרוֹמָם.
וּבְדִבְרֵי צַדִּיקִים תִּתְבָּרַךְ.
וּבִלְשׁוֹן חֲסִידִים תִּתְקַדָּשׁ.
וּבְקֶרֶב קְדוֹשִׁים תִּתְהַלָּל:

שׁוֹכֵן *Shochein ad, marom v'kadosh sh'mo. V'chatuv, rann'nu tsaddikim badonai, la-y'sharim navah t'hillah.*

B'fi y'sharim titromam, uv'divrei tsaddikim titbarach, uvilshon chasidim titkadash, uv'kerev k'doshim tit-hallal.

שׁוֹכֵן עַד ... dwells in eternity ...
The opening words are based on a verse in Isaiah 57:15. At this point in traditional Ashkenazi services the person who leads the Shabbat Morning Service takes over.

בְּפִי יְשָׁרִים By the mouth of the upright ...
The initial letters of the second word in each line make an acrostic spelling the name *Yitschak*, Isaac. Similarly in the Sephardi tradition the third letter in each line spells *Rivkah*, Rebecca. In the Ashkenazi tradition the word order is different and only on Rosh Hashanah and Yom Kippur is it altered so that the name Rebecca appears.

[1] Psalm 35:10   [2] Psalm 33:1.

Traditional authorities differ as to whether or not to stand during Yishtabach, *but it is conventional to stand in anticipation of the* Chatsi Kaddish *and* Bar'chu *that follow it.*

יִשְׁתַּבַּח Praised be Your name forever, for You are the God who is the great and holy Sovereign in heaven and on earth. Therefore, our God and God of our ancestors, song and praise, holiness and majesty, blessing and gratitude belong to Your great and holy name forever and ever. From age to age You are God. Blessed are You God, Creator of every living being, the power behind all actions, who chooses songs and psalms, Sovereign, life of all existence.

יִשְׁתַּבַּח שִׁמְךָ לָעַד מַלְכֵּנוּ. הָאֵל הַמֶּלֶךְ הַגָּדוֹל וְהַקָּדוֹשׁ בַּשָּׁמַיִם וּבָאָרֶץ. כִּי לְךָ נָאֶה יהוה אֱלֹהֵינוּ וֵאלֹהֵי אֲבוֹתֵינוּ לְעוֹלָם וָעֶד שִׁיר וּשְׁבָחָה. קְדֻשָּׁה וּמַלְכוּת. בְּרָכוֹת וְהוֹדָאוֹת לְשִׁמְךָ הַגָּדוֹל וְהַקָּדוֹשׁ. וּמֵעוֹלָם וְעַד עוֹלָם אַתָּה אֵל: בָּרוּךְ אַתָּה יהוה. בּוֹרֵא כָּל־הַנְּשָׁמוֹת. רִבּוֹן כָּל־הַמַּעֲשִׂים. הַבּוֹחֵר בְּשִׁירֵי זִמְרָה. מֶלֶךְ חֵי הָעוֹלָמִים:

יִשְׁתַּבַּח *Yishtabbach shimcha la'ad malkeinu, ha-eil ha-melech ha-gadol v'ha-kadosh ba-shamayim uva'arets, ki l'cha na'eh Adonai eloheinu veilohei avoteinu l'olam va'ed, shir ush'vachah, k'dushah umalchut, b'rachot v'hoda'ot l'shimcha ha-gadol v'ha-kadosh, umei'olam v'ad olam attah eil. Baruch attah Adonai, borei chol ha-n'shamot, ribon kol ha-ma'asim, habocher b'shirei zimrah, melech chei ha-olamim.*

יִשְׁתַּבַּח Praised be Your name forever ...
  This blessing was fixed to mark the conclusion of the section of 'Verses of Song', just as *Baruch She'amar* opened it. Appropriately it asserts that 'song' is a fitting way to praise God. As many as fifteen words in praise of God are included in traditional versions, in line with the courtly mode of praise so common throughout this section.

SHABBAT MORNING SERVICE — VERSES OF SONG

Chatsi Kaddish   חֲצִי קַדִּישׁ

יִתְגַּדַּל Let us magnify and let us sanctify in this world the great name of God whose will created it. May God's reign come in your lifetime, and in your days, and in the lifetime of the family of Israel - quickly and speedily may it come. **Amen.** **May the greatness of God's being be blessed from eternity to eternity.** Let us bless and let us extol, let us tell aloud and let us raise aloft, let us set on high and let us honour, let us exalt and let us praise the Holy One, Whose name is blessed, Who is far beyond any blessing	יִתְגַּדַּל וְיִתְקַדַּשׁ שְׁמֵהּ רַבָּא בְּעָלְמָא דִּי־בְרָא כִרְעוּתֵהּ: וְיַמְלִיךְ מַלְכוּתֵהּ בְּחַיֵּיכוֹן וּבְיוֹמֵיכוֹן וּבְחַיֵּי דִי־כָל־בֵּית יִשְׂרָאֵל בַּעֲגָלָא וּבִזְמַן קָרִיב. וְאִמְרוּ אָמֵן: יְהֵא שְׁמֵהּ רַבָּא מְבָרַךְ לְעָלַם וּלְעָלְמֵי עָלְמַיָּא: יִתְבָּרַךְ וְיִשְׁתַּבַּח וְיִתְפָּאַר וְיִתְרוֹמַם וְיִתְנַשֵּׂא וְיִתְהַדָּר וְיִתְעַלֶּה וְיִתְהַלָּל שְׁמֵהּ דִּי־קֻדְשָׁא. בְּרִיךְ הוּא. לְעֵלָּא מִן־כָּל־בִּרְכָתָא

During the Ten Days of Penitence:
Who is far above and beyond any blessing

During the Ten Days of Penitence:
לְעֵלָּא לְעֵלָּא מִכָּל־בִּרְכָתָא

or song, any honour or any consolation that can be spoken of in this world. **Amen.**	וְשִׁירָתָא תֻּשְׁבְּחָתָא וְנֶחֱמָתָא דִּי־אֲמִירָן בְּעָלְמָא. וְאִמְרוּ אָמֵן:

יִתְגַּדַּל Yitgaddal v'yitkaddash sh'meih rabba, b'alma di v'ra chiruteih, v'yamlich malchuteih, b'chayyeichon uv'yomeichon uv'chayyei di chol beit yisra'el, ba'agala u'vizman kariv, v'imru **amen. Y'hei sh'meih rabba m'varach l'alam ul'almei almaya.** Yitbarach v'yishtabbach v'yitpa'ar v'yitromam v'yitnassei, v'yit-haddar v'yit'alleh v'yit-hallal sh'meih di kudsha, **b'rich hu,** l'eilla min kol birchata
   During the Ten Days of Penitence: l'eilla l'eilla mikol birchata
v'shirata, tushb'chata v'nechemata, di amiran b'alma, v'imru **amen.**

The 'Verses of Song' section has brought about the move from the focus on our individual experience and needs at the beginning of the service to an awareness that we are now part of a community. It is as a formally constituted community, representing the Jewish people, that we approach the next section of the service, beginning with reciting the *Sh'ma* and the blessings, two before and one after, that accompany it. As elsewhere the *Chatsi Kaddish* functions as a service marker, indicating the end of this particular section. With the 'call to prayer', *Bar'chu*, the formal, statutory, part of the service will begin.

שמע וברכותיה
THE SH'MA AND ITS BLESSINGS

It is traditional for the Prayer Leader to bow slightly from the waist when saying Bar'chu, *and for the congregation to do likewise when responding, returning to the upright position when mentioning the name of God.*

THE CALL TO COMMUNITY PRAYER ♦ 336

בָּרְכוּ Bless the Living God whom we are called to bless.

בָּרְכוּ אֶת־יהוה הַמְבֹרָךְ:

בָּרְכוּ *Bar'chu et Adonai ha-m'vorach.*

בָּרוּךְ Blessed is the Living God whom we are called to bless forever and ever.

בָּרוּךְ יהוה הַמְבֹרָךְ לְעוֹלָם וָעֶד:

בָּרוּךְ *Baruch Adonai ha-m'vorach l'olam va'ed.*

בָּרְכוּ Blessed ...

This 'call to prayer' is Biblical in origin (Neh 9:5) and well established in the early rabbinic period (Mishnah *Berachot* 7:3). It marks the point where the statutory part of the liturgy begins after the two preparatory sections, that part required to be recited according to *halachah*, Jewish law. Traditionally, without a *minyan*, a quorum of ten adult males, the *Bar'chu* and other passages were omitted and the service that followed was only an individual, not a community, event. In Progressive circles different views as to the composition of, or requirement for, a *minyan* are found, and the *Bar'chu* is usually recited even if the traditional quorum is not present.

The verb *barach*, which can be translated as 'bless' or 'praise', helps define a special relationship. In the Biblical world God's blessing means fruitfulness and material prosperity for the one who receives it. The word is related to the term for 'knee' and hence 'kneeling'. At this point in the service we are summoned to acknowledge and submit to God who is the source of blessing.

SHABBAT MORNING SERVICE — THE *SH'MA* AND ITS BLESSINGS

THE CREATOR OF THE UNIVERSE ☙ 337

בָּרוּךְ **Blessed are You, our Living God, Sovereign of the universe, who forms light yet creates darkness, who makes peace yet creates all. All things proclaim You, all things honour You, and all say 'None is holy like God!'. The One who gives light to all the world and those who live in it renews in goodness the work of creation day by day. God, how great are Your works; You made them all in wisdom; the earth is full of Your creatures. You are the only Sovereign exalted from the beginning of time, who has been worshipped, praised and glorified since days of old.**

בָּרוּךְ אַתָּה יהוה. אֱלֹהֵינוּ מֶלֶךְ הָעוֹלָם. יוֹצֵר אוֹר וּבוֹרֵא חֹשֶׁךְ. עֹשֶׂה שָׁלוֹם וּבוֹרֵא אֶת הַכֹּל: הַכֹּל יוֹדוּךָ וְהַכֹּל יְשַׁבְּחוּךָ. וְהַכֹּל יֹאמְרוּ אֵין קָדוֹשׁ כַּיהוה: הַמֵּאִיר לָעוֹלָם כֻּלּוֹ וּלְיוֹשְׁבָיו. וּבְטוּבוֹ מְחַדֵּשׁ בְּכָל־יוֹם תָּמִיד מַעֲשֵׂה בְרֵאשִׁית: מָה רַבּוּ מַעֲשֶׂיךָ יהוה. כֻּלָּם בְּחָכְמָה עָשִׂיתָ. מָלְאָה הָאָרֶץ קִנְיָנֶךָ: הַמֶּלֶךְ הַמְרוֹמָם לְבַדּוֹ מֵאָז. הַמְשֻׁבָּח וְהַמְפֹאָר וְהַמִּתְנַשֵּׂא מִימוֹת עוֹלָם:

<<<

בָּרוּךְ *Baruch attah Adonai, eloheinu melech ha-olam, yotseir or uvorei choshech, oseh shalom uvorei et ha-kol. Ha-kol yoducha v'ha-kol y'shabb'chucha, v'ha-kol yomm'ru ein kadosh kadonai. Ha-mei'ir la-olam kullo ul'yosh'vav, uv'tuvo m'chadeish b'chol yom tamid ma'aseih v'reishit. Mah rabbu ma'asecha Adonai, kullam b'chochmah asita, mal'ah ha-arets kinyanecha. Ha-melech ha-m'romam l'vaddo mei'az, ha-m'shubbach v'ha-m'fo'ar v'ha-mitnassei mimot olam.*

יוֹצֵר אוֹר **Who forms light ...**

Like the Bible itself, the statutory part of the service begins with creation, exploring the theme of light, the first thing created by God's word (Gen 1:3). The opening sentence, adapted from Isaiah 45:7, belongs to the rejection of a view, first encountered by the exiles in Babylon, that there exist two gods that struggle with one another, one a god of light and good, the other of darkness and evil. Isaiah asserted that God was a unity, the creator of both light and darkness, the normative Jewish view. The Isaiah verse ended 'and creates evil', but the rabbis substituted the euphemism 'and creates all things', a more reverent expression which better suits the context of prayer (*Berachot* 11a).

By opening the formal part of the liturgy with God as Creator of all that exists, we recognize the larger framework within which our particular destiny as the Jewish people is to be acted out. God will always be greater than any limited understanding we may have.

Some congregations include the piyyut *(poem),* El Adon,
others continue at the bottom of the facing page.

אֵל God, governing all creation,	אֵל אָדוֹן עַל כָּל־הַמַּעֲשִׂים.
blessed by all that draws breath,	בָּרוּךְ וּמְבֹרָךְ בְּפִי כָּל־נְשָׁמָה:
whose greatness and goodness fill the universe,	גָּדְלוֹ וְטוּבוֹ מָלֵא עוֹלָם.
is surrounded by knowledge and wisdom.	דַּעַת וּתְבוּנָה סֹבְבִים אוֹתוֹ:
Holy above all the forces of life,	הַמִּתְגָּאֶה עַל חַיּוֹת הַקֹּדֶשׁ.
glorious beyond every mystic vision,	וְנֶהְדָּר בְּכָבוֹד עַל הַמֶּרְכָּבָה:
purity and integrity stand before Your throne,	זְכוּת וּמִישׁוֹר לִפְנֵי כִסְאוֹ.
love and mercy in the presence of Your glory.	חֶסֶד וְרַחֲמִים לִפְנֵי כְבוֹדוֹ:
Splendid are the lights You created,	טוֹבִים מְאוֹרוֹת שֶׁבָּרָא אֱלֹהֵינוּ.
fashioned with knowledge, wisdom and reason,	יְצָרָם בְּדַעַת בְּבִינָה וּבְהַשְׂכֵּל.
setting within them strength and power	כֹּחַ וּגְבוּרָה נָתַן בָּהֶם.
to govern our world.	לִהְיוֹת מוֹשְׁלִים בְּקֶרֶב תֵּבֵל:
Radiant and glowing with light, their beauty	מְלֵאִים זִיו וּמְפִיקִים נֹגַהּ.
transforms the world.	נָאֶה זִיוָם בְּכָל־הָעוֹלָם.
They rejoice in their rising, exult in their setting,	שְׂמֵחִים בְּצֵאתָם וְשָׂשִׂים בְּבוֹאָם.
fulfilling with wonder the will of their Maker.	עוֹשִׂים בְּאֵימָה רְצוֹן קוֹנָם:
Honour and glory they bring to God's name	פְּאֵר וְכָבוֹד נוֹתְנִים לִשְׁמוֹ.
whose rule they acclaim with exultation and joy.	צָהֳלָה וְרִנָּה לְזֵכֶר מַלְכוּתוֹ:
God called to the sun and it sent out light,	קָרָא לַשֶּׁמֶשׁ וַיִּזְרַח אוֹר.
then looked and fashioned the cycle of the moon.	רָאָה וְהִתְקִין צוּרַת הַלְּבָנָה:
All hosts on high sing praise to God.	שֶׁבַח נוֹתְנִים לוֹ כָּל־צְבָא מָרוֹם.
Worlds unseen give God glory and greatness.	תִּפְאֶרֶת וּגְדֻלָּה שְׂרָפִים וְאוֹפַנִּים וְחַיּוֹת הַקֹּדֶשׁ:

SHABBAT MORNING SERVICE — THE *SH'MA* AND ITS BLESSINGS

אֵל *Eil adon al kol ha-ma'asim,*
baruch um'vorach b'fi kol n'shamah.
Godlo v'tuvo malei olam,
da'at ut'vunah sov'vim oto.
Ha-mitga'eh al chayot ha-kodesh,
v'nehdar b'chavod al ha-merkavah.
Z'chut umishor lifnei chis'o,
chesed v'rachamim lifnei ch'vodo.
Tovim m'orot shebara eloheinu,
y'tsaram b'da'at b'vinah uv'haskeil.
Ko'ach ug'vurah natan bahem,
lihyot mosh'lim b'kerev teiveil.
M'lei'im ziv um'fikim nogah,
na'eh zivam b'chol ha-olam,
s'meichim b'tseitam v'sasim b'vo'am,
osim b'eimah r'tson konam.
P'eir v'chavod not'nim lishmo,
tsoholah v'rinnah l'zeicher malchuto,
kara la-shemesh vayizrach or,
ra'ah v'hitkin tsurat ha-l'vanah.
Shevach not'nim lo kol ts'va marom,
tif'eret ug'dullah s'rafim v'ofannim v'chayot ha-kodesh.

The service continues here:

אֱלֹהֵי Everlasting God, in Your great mercy have mercy upon us; Source of our strength, Rock of our protection, Shield of our safety, our true Protector. Cause a new light to shine upon Zion, and may we all be worthy soon to enjoy its brightness. Blessed are You God, who creates the lights of the universe.

אֱלֹהֵי עוֹלָם. בְּרַחֲמֶיךָ הָרַבִּים
רַחֵם עָלֵינוּ. אֲדוֹן עֻזֵּנוּ צוּר
מִשְׂגַּבֵּנוּ. מָגֵן יִשְׁעֵנוּ. מִשְׂגָּב
בַּעֲדֵנוּ: אוֹר חָדָשׁ עַל־צִיּוֹן
תָּאִיר וְנִזְכֶּה כֻלָּנוּ מְהֵרָה
לְאוֹרוֹ: בָּרוּךְ אַתָּה יהוה
יוֹצֵר הַמְּאוֹרוֹת:

אֱלֹהֵי *Elohei olam, b'rachamecha ha-rabbim racheim aleinu, adon uzzeinu tsur misgabbeinu, magein yish'einu, misgav ba'adeinu. Or chadash al-tsion ta'ir v'nizkeh kullanu m'heirah l'oro. Baruch attah Adonai yotseir ha-m'orot.*

אֵל אָדוֹן God possessing ...
This mediaeval poem is an alphabetic acrostic. Its origin is unknown but it probably belongs to early mystical traditions. It celebrates the purity and compassion of God's rule by focusing on the creation of the sun and moon, the regularity of their cycles and the light that they give to the world. The imagery of light echoes the theme of the opening blessing.

GOD'S LOVE FOR ISRAEL ☰ 338

אַהֲבָה With deep love You have loved us, and with great and overflowing tenderness You have taken pity on us. Source of our life and our Sovereign, show us compassion because of Your own greatness, and because of our ancestors who trusted in You, for You taught them rules to live by, to do Your will with their whole heart. Let our eyes see the light of Your teaching and our hearts embrace Your commands. Give us integrity to love You and fear You. So shall we never lose our self-respect, nor be put to shame, for You are the power which works to save us. You chose us from all peoples and tongues, and in love drew us near to Your own greatness – to honour You, to declare Your unity, and to love You. Blessed are You God, who chooses Your people Israel in love.

אַהֲבָה רַבָּה אֲהַבְתָּנוּ יהוה אֱלֹהֵינוּ. חֶמְלָה גְדוֹלָה וִיתֵרָה חָמַלְתָּ עָלֵינוּ: אָבִינוּ מַלְכֵּנוּ. בַּעֲבוּר שִׁמְךָ הַגָּדוֹל וּבַעֲבוּר אֲבוֹתֵינוּ שֶׁבָּטְחוּ בָךְ. וַתְּלַמְּדֵם חֻקֵּי חַיִּים לַעֲשׂוֹת רְצוֹנְךָ בְּלֵבָב שָׁלֵם. כֵּן תְּחָנֵּנוּ: הָאֵר עֵינֵינוּ בְּתוֹרָתֶךָ. וְדַבֵּק לִבֵּנוּ בְּמִצְוֹתֶיךָ. וְיַחֵד לְבָבֵנוּ לְאַהֲבָה וּלְיִרְאָה אֶת־שְׁמֶךָ. לְמַעַן לֹא נֵבוֹשׁ וְלֹא נִכָּלֵם כִּי אֵל פּוֹעֵל יְשׁוּעוֹת אָתָּה. וּבָנוּ בָחַרְתָּ מִכָּל־עַם וְלָשׁוֹן. וְקֵרַבְתָּנוּ מַלְכֵּנוּ לְשִׁמְךָ הַגָּדוֹל בְּאַהֲבָה. לְהוֹדוֹת לְךָ וּלְיַחֶדְךָ וּלְאַהֲבָה אֶת־שְׁמֶךָ: בָּרוּךְ אַתָּה יהוה הַבּוֹחֵר בְּעַמּוֹ יִשְׂרָאֵל בְּאַהֲבָה:

אַהֲבָה רַבָּה With deep love …

From the universal theme of the previous blessing we focus on the special love God has for the Jewish people. In the Talmud is a debate about two possible openings to the prayer: the version here, *Ahavah Rabbah*, 'with deep love', or the alternative version based on Jeremiah 31:3, *Ahavat Olam*, 'with everlasting love'. We follow the Ashkenazi tradition of using the former for the Morning Service and the latter for the Evening Service.

The love described here is reciprocal and practical. Through the Torah, God's gift to us, we learn the practical expression of our love of God. In the *Sh'ma* we are asked to 'love' God, but in Leviticus 19:14 to 'fear', 'be in awe of', God. In this blessing we seek to unite both emotions.

The blessing refers throughout to the 'name' of God, a rabbinic way to avoid speaking of God directly, itself a reflection of the awe we are to feel.

The end of the blessing speaks of our proclaiming God's unity and loving God which we fulfil, in part, by reciting the *Sh'ma* that follows from which these terms have been taken.

אַהֲבָה *Ahavah rabbah ahavtanu Adonai eloheinu, chemlah g'dolah viteirah chamalta aleinu. Avinu malkeinu, ba'avur shimcha ha-gadol uva'avur avoteinu shebat'chu vach, vat'lamm'deim chukkei chayyim la'asot r'tson'cha b'leivav shaleim, kein t'chonneinu. Ha'eir eineinu b'toratecha, v'dabbeik libbeinu b'mitsvotecha, v'yacheid l'vaveinu l'ahavah ul'yir'ah et sh'mecha, l'ma'an lo neivosh v'lo nikkaleim, ki eil po'eil y'shu'ot attah, uvanu vacharta mikkol am v'lashon, v'keiravtanu malkeinu l'shimcha ha-gadol b'ahavah, l'hodot l'cha ul'yachedcha ul'ahavah et sh'mecha. Baruch attah Adonai ha-bocheir b'ammo yisra'el b'ahavah.*

שמע
SH'MA 338

Traditionally one remains seated during the recital of the *Sh'ma* though some progressive communities stand, so as to give prominence to this affirmation of God's unity. It is a custom to cover the eyes while reciting the first sentence, 'Hear O Israel', as an aid to concentrating on the words. The *dalet*, the final letter of *echad*, 'One', is emphasised because of the danger of misreading the letter as *reish*, which would spell the word *acheir*, 'other'.

When praying individually it is customary to add here אֵל מֶלֶךְ נֶאֱמָן
(el melech ne'eman) - *'God, the faithful Sovereign', whose initial letters spell* Amen.

שְׁמַע יִשְׂרָאֵל יהוה אֱלֹהֵינוּ יהוה ׀ אֶחָד:

Sh'ma yisra'el, Adonai eloheinu Adonai echad

בָּרוּךְ שֵׁם כְּבוֹד מַלְכוּתוֹ לְעוֹלָם וָעֶד:

Baruch sheim k'vod malchuto l'olam va'ed.

וְאָהַבְתָּ אֵת יהוה אֱלֹהֶיךָ בְּכָל־לְבָבְךָ וּבְכָל־נַפְשְׁךָ וּבְכָל־מְאֹדֶךָ: וְהָיוּ הַדְּבָרִים הָאֵלֶּה אֲשֶׁר אָנֹכִי מְצַוְּךָ הַיּוֹם עַל־לְבָבֶךָ: וְשִׁנַּנְתָּם לְבָנֶיךָ וְדִבַּרְתָּ בָּם בְּשִׁבְתְּךָ בְּבֵיתֶךָ וּבְלֶכְתְּךָ בַדֶּרֶךְ וּבְשָׁכְבְּךָ וּבְקוּמֶךָ: וּקְשַׁרְתָּם לְאוֹת עַל־יָדֶךָ וְהָיוּ לְטֹטָפֹת בֵּין עֵינֶיךָ: וּכְתַבְתָּם עַל־מְזֻזוֹת בֵּיתֶךָ וּבִשְׁעָרֶיךָ:

וְאָהַבְתָּ *V'ahavta eit Adonai elohecha, b'chol l'vav'cha, uv'chol nafsh'cha, uv'chol m'odecha. V'hayu ha-d'varim ha-eilleh, asher anochi m'tsav'cha ha-yom al l'vavecha. V'shinnantam l'vanecha, v'dibbarta bam, b'shivt'cha b'veitecha, uv'lecht'cha vaderech, uv'shochb'cha uv'kumecha. Uk'shartam l'ot al yadecha, v'hayu l'totafot bein einecha. Uch'tavtam al m'zuzot beitecha uvisharecha.*

שְׁמַע Hear ...

The opening line of the *Sh'ma* is difficult to translate because of the repetition of the name of God within it. It can be understood as a double affirmation: the Eternal is our God, the Eternal is One. The word 'One' is also open to a variety of senses: that God is unique; is 'one' despite the many ways in which God is experienced; is 'one' in contrast to the many gods of other nations; is the 'one and only' God for Israel.

The recitation of the *Sh'ma* and the Ten Commandments was part of the temple ritual (Mishnah *Tamid* 5:1). However, the latter was dropped from the statutory prayers of the synagogue out of concern that, given such prominence, it would be seen as representing the whole of the Torah.

'The proclamation of the Unity of God is followed by the enunciation of man's duty to love him ... The Unity of God is the basis of the Jewish creed, the Love of God the basis of the Jewish life ... The *Sh'ma* thus enshrines the fundamental *dogma* (Monotheism), the fundamental *duty* (Love), the fundamental *discipline* (Study of the Law [Torah]), and the fundamental *method* (union of 'Letter' and 'Spirit') of the Jewish religion' (*Israel Abrahams*).

GOD IS ONE

שְׁמַע Hear O Israel, the Eternal is our God, the Eternal is One.

בָּרוּךְ Blessed is the knowledge of God's glorious rule forever and ever.

וְאָהַבְתָּ Love the Eternal your God with all your heart, and all your soul, and all your might. These words that I command you today shall be upon your heart. Repeat them to your children, and talk about them when you sit in your home, and when you walk in the street; when you lie down, and when you rise up. Secure them as a sign upon your hand, and let them be as reminders before your eyes. Write them on the doorposts of your home and at your gates.[1]

וְאָהַבְתָּ Love the Eternal ...

בְּכָל־לְבָבְךָ 'With all your heart': The *leiv*, 'heart', is understood in the Bible and rabbinic sources as the centre of the mind and intellect, our conscious way of viewing and understanding the world. The form *l'vav'cha*, with its repetition of the letter *beit*, led the rabbis to suggest that this referred to the two 'drives' or 'inclinations' within human beings, the 'good inclination' and the 'inclination towards evil', and that both these impulses should be harnessed in the love and service of God.

וּבְכָל־נַפְשְׁךָ 'and all your soul': The word *nefesh*, 'soul', has a number of meanings. It is related to the verb for 'breathing', that action that distinguishes the living from the dead. So it can mean the 'life force', or even the 'self'. The rabbis understood its use here to mean the willingness to offer up life itself out of love for God.

וּבְכָל־מְאֹדֶךָ 'and all your might': *M'od* means 'abundance' and hence 'force' or 'might'. Here it is understood to mean that which we own, the possessions that are an extension of ourselves. These too we owe to God and are to use in God's service.

[1] Deut 6:4-9.

During the silence the traditional second and third paragraphs of the Sh'ma *may be read, or the alternative Biblical passages on pages 689-697.*

וְהָיָה אִם־שָׁמֹעַ תִּשְׁמְעוּ אֶל־מִצְוֹתַי אֲשֶׁר אָנֹכִי מְצַוֶּה אֶתְכֶם הַיּוֹם לְאַהֲבָה אֶת־יהוה אֱלֹהֵיכֶם וּלְעָבְדוֹ בְּכָל־לְבַבְכֶם וּבְכָל־נַפְשְׁכֶם: וְנָתַתִּי מְטַר־אַרְצְכֶם בְּעִתּוֹ יוֹרֶה וּמַלְקוֹשׁ וְאָסַפְתָּ דְגָנֶךָ וְתִירֹשְׁךָ וְיִצְהָרֶךָ: וְנָתַתִּי עֵשֶׂב בְּשָׂדְךָ לִבְהֶמְתֶּךָ וְאָכַלְתָּ וְשָׂבָעְתָּ: הִשָּׁמְרוּ לָכֶם פֶּן יִפְתֶּה לְבַבְכֶם וְסַרְתֶּם וַעֲבַדְתֶּם אֱלֹהִים אֲחֵרִים וְהִשְׁתַּחֲוִיתֶם לָהֶם: וְחָרָה אַף־יהוה בָּכֶם וְעָצַר אֶת־הַשָּׁמַיִם וְלֹא־יִהְיֶה מָטָר וְהָאֲדָמָה לֹא תִתֵּן אֶת־יְבוּלָהּ וַאֲבַדְתֶּם מְהֵרָה מֵעַל הָאָרֶץ הַטֹּבָה אֲשֶׁר יהוה נֹתֵן לָכֶם: וְשַׂמְתֶּם אֶת־דְּבָרַי אֵלֶּה עַל־לְבַבְכֶם וְעַל־נַפְשְׁכֶם וּקְשַׁרְתֶּם אֹתָם לְאוֹת עַל־יֶדְכֶם וְהָיוּ לְטוֹטָפֹת בֵּין עֵינֵיכֶם: וְלִמַּדְתֶּם אֹתָם אֶת־בְּנֵיכֶם לְדַבֵּר בָּם בְּשִׁבְתְּךָ בְּבֵיתֶךָ וּבְלֶכְתְּךָ בַדֶּרֶךְ וּבְשָׁכְבְּךָ וּבְקוּמֶךָ: וּכְתַבְתָּם עַל־מְזוּזוֹת בֵּיתֶךָ וּבִשְׁעָרֶיךָ: לְמַעַן יִרְבּוּ יְמֵיכֶם וִימֵי בְנֵיכֶם עַל הָאֲדָמָה אֲשֶׁר נִשְׁבַּע יהוה לַאֲבֹתֵיכֶם לָתֵת לָהֶם כִּימֵי הַשָּׁמַיִם עַל־הָאָרֶץ:

וְהָיָה This will happen if you listen carefully to My commands which I give you today, to love and to serve the Eternal your God with all your heart and all your soul. I shall then give your land rain at the right time, the autumn rain and the spring rain, **so that each one of you can harvest your own grain, wine and oil. I shall also give grass in your fields for your cattle, and you will eat and be satisfied.**
Take care that your heart is not deceived into straying, obeying other gods and worshipping them. God's anger will then blaze out against you. God will shut up the sky. There will be no rain. The land will not produce, and you will quickly be destroyed from the good land which God gives you. So put these words of Mine in your heart and in your soul, and secure them as a sign upon your hand and as reminders before your eyes. Teach them to your children, and talk about them **'when you sit each of you in your home, and when you walk in the street, when you lie down and when you rise up. Write them on the doorposts of your home and at your gates.'**
Then you and your children may live long on the land that God promised to give your ancestors as long as there is a sky over the earth.[1]

---

[1] Deut 11:13-21.

וְהָיָה V'hayah im shamo'a tishm'u el mitsvotai, asher anochi m'tsaveh etchem ha-yom, l'ahavah et Adonai eloheichem ul'ovdo, b'chol l'vavchem uv'chol nafsh'chem. V'natatti m'tar arts'chem b'itto, yoreh umalkosh, **v'asafta d'ganecha v'tirosh'cha v'yits-harecha.** V'natatti eisev b'sad'cha livhemtecha, v'achalta v'sava'ta.
Hisham'ru lachem, pen yifteh l'vavchem, v'sartem va'avadtem elohim acheirim v'hishtachavitem lahem. V'charah af Adonai bachem, v'atsar et ha-shamayim, v'lo yihyeh matar, v'ha-adamah lo tittein et y'vulah, va'avadtem m'heirah mei'al ha-arets ha-tovah, asher Adonai notein lachem. V'samtem et d'varai eilleh al l'vavchem v'al nafsh'chem, uk'shartem otam l'ot al yedchem, v'hayu l'totafot bein eineichem. V'limmadtem otam et b'neichem l'dabbeir bam, **b'shivt'cha b'veitecha, uv'lecht'cha va-derech, uv'shochb'cha uv'kumecha. Uch'tavtam al m'zuzot beitecha uvisharecha.** L'ma'an yirbu y'meichem vimei v'neichem, al ha-adamah asher nishba Adonai la'avoteichem lateit lahem, kimei ha-shamayim al ha-arets.

וְהָיָה אִם־שָׁמֹעַ
This will happen if you listen ...
This passage appears to carry a simple message of reward, for observance of God's commandments, and punishment for setting them aside to serve other gods. Yet this is not how we experience things in life, and the Bible too questions such a reality, notably in the words of the prophet Jeremiah and in the Book of Job. For this reason Reform liturgies have either removed it or offered alternative passages - as on pages 689-697. In retaining it as an option we have drawn attention to the way the passage switches between plural and singular [in bold print] forms of address. It speaks to the nation as a whole, but twice shows the benefit to, and responsibility of, each individual Israelite. Moreover, the Torah includes important laws about how to cultivate and respect the land itself, so that failure to do so could lead to the ecological disaster predicted here.

שמע וברכותיה

וַיֹּאמֶר **וַיֹּאמֶר** The Eternal said to Moses: 'Speak to the children of Israel and tell them that each generation shall put tassels on the corner of their clothes, and put a blue thread on the corner tassel. Then when this tassel catches your eye, you will remember all the commands of the Eternal and do them. Then you will no longer wander after the desires of your heart and your eyes which led you to lust.

Then you will remember all My commands and do them and you will be set apart for your God. I am the Eternal your God Who brought you out of the land of Egypt, to be your own God. I, the Eternal, am your God.'[1]

וַיֹּאמֶר יְהוָה אֶל־מֹשֶׁה לֵּאמֹר: דַּבֵּר אֶל־בְּנֵי יִשְׂרָאֵל וְאָמַרְתָּ אֲלֵהֶם וְעָשׂוּ לָהֶם צִיצִת עַל־כַּנְפֵי בִגְדֵיהֶם לְדֹרֹתָם וְנָתְנוּ עַל־צִיצִת הַכָּנָף פְּתִיל תְּכֵלֶת: וְהָיָה לָכֶם לְצִיצִת וּרְאִיתֶם אֹתוֹ וּזְכַרְתֶּם אֶת־כָּל־מִצְוֹת יְהוָה וַעֲשִׂיתֶם אֹתָם וְלֹא תָתוּרוּ אַחֲרֵי לְבַבְכֶם וְאַחֲרֵי עֵינֵיכֶם אֲשֶׁר־אַתֶּם זֹנִים אַחֲרֵיהֶם:

לְמַעַן תִּזְכְּרוּ וַעֲשִׂיתֶם אֶת־כָּל־מִצְוֹתָי וִהְיִיתֶם קְדֹשִׁים לֵאלֹהֵיכֶם: אֲנִי יְהוָה אֱלֹהֵיכֶם אֲשֶׁר הוֹצֵאתִי אֶתְכֶם מֵאֶרֶץ מִצְרַיִם לִהְיוֹת לָכֶם לֵאלֹהִים אֲנִי יְהוָה אֱלֹהֵיכֶם:

וַיֹּאמֶר *Vayomer Adonai el mosheh leimor: dabbeir el b'nei yisra'el v'amarta aleihem, v'asu lahem tsitsit al kanfei vigdeihem l'dorotam, v'nat'nu al tsitsit ha-kanaf p'til t'cheilet. V'hayah lachem l'tsitsit, ur'item oto, uz'chartem et kol mitsvot Adonai, va'asitem otam, v'lo taturu acharei l'vavchem v'acharei eineichem, asher attem zonim achareihem.*
L'ma'an tizk'ru, va'asitem et kol mitsvotai, vihyitem k'doshim leiloheichem. Ani Adonai eloheichem asher hotseiti etchem mei'erets mitsrayim, lihyot lachem leilohim, ani Adonai eloheichem.

וַיֹּאמֶר יְהוָה And God said ...

Just as the two previous paragraphs have provided tangible symbols of Torah, on our hands, before our eyes, on our homes, so the third paragraph furnishes one for our clothing to remind us of the commandments. The passage concludes with a reference to the Exodus from Egypt, a central theme of Shabbat, which will be further explored in the blessing that follows.

יְהוָה אֱלֹהֵיכֶם אֱמֶת
The Eternal your God is truth

According to a tradition in *Berachot* 14a there should be no pause between the closing words of the third paragraph of the *Sh'ma* and the first word of the blessings that follow, so it is customary to add the word *emet*, 'truth', after *eloheichem*. Some link this to a similar phrase in Jer 10:10, 'The Eternal, God, is true'.

[1] Num 15:37-41.

SHABBAT MORNING SERVICE — THE SH'MA AND ITS BLESSINGS

אֱמֶת True is Your word forever. It is certain for us, it is firm, accepted and good. ☩339

It is true that the Eternal God is our Sovereign; the strength of Jacob, the defender of our safety. God endures from generation to generation. God's rule and faithfulness stand firm forever.
It is true that You are the Faithful One, our God, and God of our ancestors, who rescues and delivers us. So were You ever known. There is no God besides You.

<<<

אֱמֶת וְיַצִּיב וְנָכוֹן וְקַיָּם וּמְקֻבָּל וְטוֹב הַדָּבָר הַזֶּה עָלֵינוּ לְעוֹלָם וָעֶד:
אֱמֶת אֱלֹהֵי עוֹלָם מַלְכֵּנוּ. צוּר יַעֲקֹב מָגֵן יִשְׁעֵנוּ. לְדֹר וָדֹר הוּא קַיָּם. וּמַלְכוּתוֹ וֶאֱמוּנָתוֹ לָעַד קַיֶּמֶת.
אֱמֶת שָׁאַתָּה הוּא יהוה אֱלֹהֵינוּ וֵאלֹהֵי אֲבוֹתֵינוּ. פּוֹדֵנוּ וּמַצִּילֵנוּ מֵעוֹלָם הוּא שְׁמֶךָ. אֵין אֱלֹהִים זוּלָתֶךָ:

אֱמֶת Emet v'yatsiv v'kayyam um'kubbal v'tov ha-davar ha-zeh aleinu l'olam va'ed.
Emet elohei olam malkeinu, tsur ya'akov magein yish'einu, l'dor vador hu kayyam, umalchuto ve'emunato la'ad kayyamet.
Emet she'attah hu Adonai eloheinu veilohei avoteinu, podeinu umatsileinu mei'olam hu sh'mecha, ein elohim zulatecha.

אֱמֶת וְיַצִּיב True and certain ...
This blessing is known as the *ge'ullah*, 'redemption', because of its theme of God as the One who redeems Israel from slavery, physical and spiritual. Its theme picks up the closing of the third paragraph of the *Sh'ma* which speaks of the Exodus from Egyptian slavery.
With its fourfold emphasis on *emet*, 'truth', it is a rare early Jewish declaration of faith, an affirmation of the role God has played in Jewish history. In dark times it would have offered hope and encouragement of rescue and ultimate redemption from the trials of exile.
The blessing is constructed around phrases from the Song at the Sea (Exodus 15) sung by Moses, Miriam and the people after their rescue from Pharaoh's army. It quotes the phrase 'Who is like You ...' (Ex 15:11) which differs slightly in the way the Hebrew is written the two times it appears. *mi-chamocha* links the two words and emphasises the uniqueness of God - who is like You?; *mi kamocha* separates the two words and focuses instead on those that follow, emphasising the special qualities of God, 'Who, like You, is ...'.

שמע וברכותיה

עֶזְרַת It is You who always helped our ancestors. In every generation You were the shield and saviour for them and their children after them. Happy indeed are those who hear Your commands, and set Your teaching and Your word upon their hearts.

It is true that You are the first and that You are the last, and besides You we have no Sovereign who rescues and saves us. From Egypt You delivered us, Eternal our God, and redeemed us from the camp of slavery. Moses and Miriam and the children of Israel responded to You in song with great joy, all of them saying:

'God, who is like You among the gods people worship! Who, like You, is majestic in holiness, awesome in praise, working wonders!'

עֶזְרַת אֲבוֹתֵינוּ אַתָּה הוּא מֵעוֹלָם. מָגֵן וּמוֹשִׁיעַ לָהֶם וְלִבְנֵיהֶם אַחֲרֵיהֶם בְּכָל־דּוֹר וָדוֹר: אַשְׁרֵי אִישׁ שֶׁיִּשְׁמַע לְמִצְוֹתֶיךָ. וְתוֹרָתְךָ וּדְבָרְךָ יָשִׂים עַל־לִבּוֹ:

אֱמֶת אַתָּה הוּא רִאשׁוֹן וְאַתָּה הוּא אַחֲרוֹן. וּמִבַּלְעָדֶיךָ אֵין לָנוּ מֶלֶךְ גּוֹאֵל וּמוֹשִׁיעַ: מִמִּצְרַיִם גְּאַלְתָּנוּ יְהֹוָה אֱלֹהֵינוּ. וּמִבֵּית עֲבָדִים פְּדִיתָנוּ. מֹשֶׁה וּמִרְיָם וּבְנֵי יִשְׂרָאֵל לְךָ עָנוּ שִׁירָה בְּשִׂמְחָה רַבָּה וְאָמְרוּ כֻלָּם:

מִי־כָמֹכָה בָּאֵלִם יְהֹוָה.
מִי כָּמֹכָה נֶאְדָּר בַּקֹּדֶשׁ.
נוֹרָא תְהִלֹּת עֹשֵׂה פֶלֶא:

עֶזְרַת *Ezrat avoteinu attah hu mei'olam, magein umoshi'a lahem v'livneihem achareihem b'chol dor vador. Ashrei ish sheyishma l'mitsvotecha, v'torat'cha ud'var'cha yasim al libbo.*
Emet attah hu rishon v'attah hu acharon, umibbal'adecha ein lanu melech go'eil umoshi'a. Mimmitsrayim g'altanu Adonai eloheinu, umibbeit avadim p'ditanu, mosheh umiryam uv'nei yisra'el l'cha anu shirah b'simchah rabbah v'am'ru chullam.

Mi chamocha ba-eilim Adonai
mi kamocha ne'dar ba-kodesh
nora t'hillot oseih fele.

SHABBAT MORNING SERVICE

THE *SH'MA* AND ITS BLESSINGS

According to the tradition there should be no pause between the closing phrase of the blessing, 'who rescues Israel', and the beginning of the Amidah (page 222).

שִׁירָה On the shore of the sea, those who were rescued sang a new song in Your praise. Together all of them thanked You and proclaimed you as Sovereign:
'God alone will rule forever and ever.'
Rock of Israel, rise up to the aid of Your people Israel. The Creator of all, the Holy One of Israel rescues us. Blessed are You God, who rescues Israel.

שִׁירָה חֲדָשָׁה שִׁבְּחוּ גְאוּלִים לְשִׁמְךָ עַל שְׂפַת הַיָּם. יַחַד כֻּלָּם הוֹדוּ וְהִמְלִיכוּ וְאָמְרוּ:

יהוה יִמְלֹךְ לְעוֹלָם וָעֶד:

צוּר יִשְׂרָאֵל. קוּמָה בְּעֶזְרַת יִשְׂרָאֵל. גֹּאֲלֵנוּ יהוה צְבָאוֹת שְׁמוֹ. קְדוֹשׁ יִשְׂרָאֵל:
בָּרוּךְ אַתָּה יהוה גָּאַל יִשְׂרָאֵל:

שִׁירָה *Shirah chadashah shibb'chu g'ulim l'shimcha al s'fat ha-yam, yachad kullam hodu v'himlichu v'am'ru.*

Adonai yimloch l'olam va'ed.

Tsur yisra'el, kumah b'ezrat yisra'el, go'aleinu Adonai ts'va'ot sh'mo, k'dosh yisra'el. Baruch attah Adonai ga'al yisra'el.

שִׁירָה חֲדָשָׁה **A new song ...**
The closing section of this blessing remains with the theme of the exodus from Egypt and particularly the crossing of the 'Sea of Reeds', following which the Israelites sang a 'new song' in praise of God's saving acts (Ex 15). We have translated the verb *ga'al* as 'rescue', but in a technical sense it means to 'redeem'. In the Biblical world, someone who went into debt could sell his land to another, and, in the most difficult circumstances, sell himself as a slave. But there was an obligation on other members of the family to buy back, to 'redeem', both the land and the man himself so as to preserve the family property and integrity. God is called 'redeemer' in the Book of Exodus because, like a member of the family, God 'buys back' the Israelites from slavery in Egypt.

The 'Song at the Sea' in Ex 15 ends with the phrase quoted here, 'God alone will rule forever and ever'. Because it seems to postpone the rule of God to some point in the future, a passage at the end of the 'Morning Blessings' attempts to make it a present reality and asserts that 'God rules, God has ruled, God shall rule forever and ever'.

אֲדֹנָי שְׂפָתַי תִּפְתָּח וּפִי יַגִּיד תְּהִלָּתֶךָ

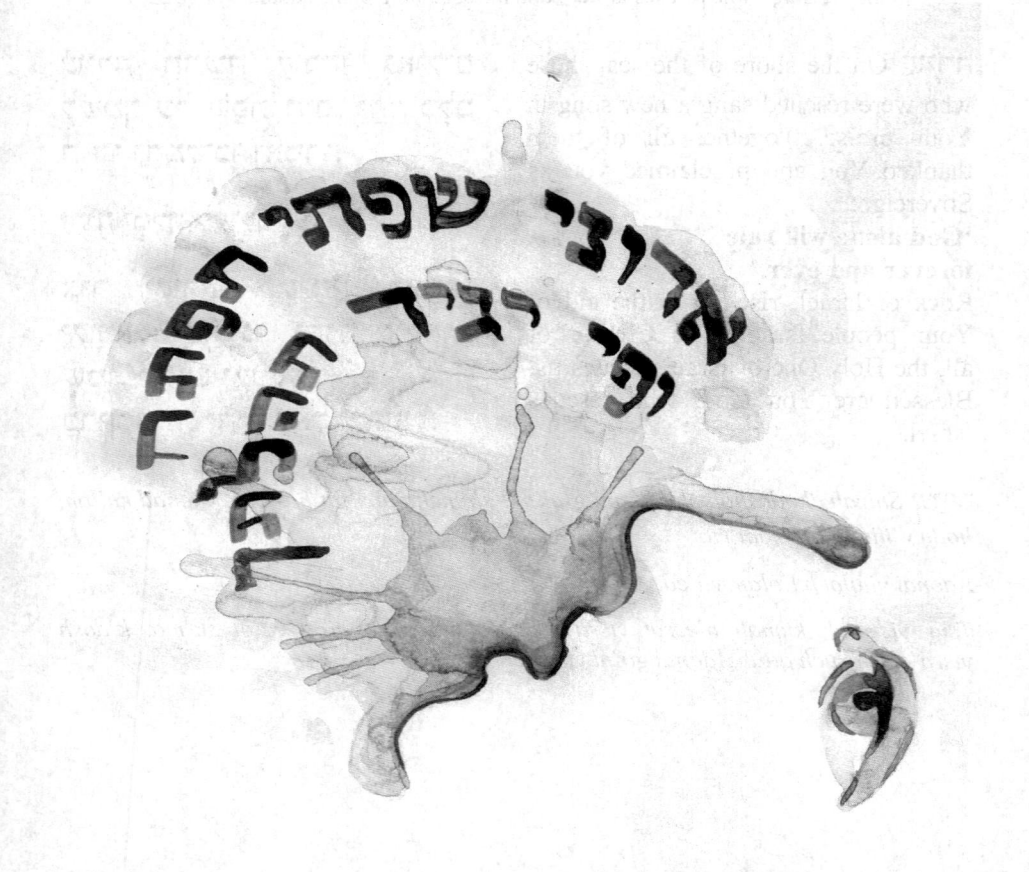

SHABBAT MORNING SERVICE — AMIDAH

עמידה
AMIDAH 339-344

> The *Amidah*, the 'standing prayer', also known as the 'eighteen benedictions', or *ha-tefillah*, '*the* prayer', was instituted by the rabbis as a substitute for the daily sacrifices, and as a way of praying for their restoration. It is constructed on the protocol of a visit to a sovereign. The three opening verses introduce us, acknowledge God's power over us and God's holiness. The closing three reverse the protocol as we, so to speak, leave the royal presence by asking for a favourable response, express our gratitude, and depart with words of peace. Between these opening and closing sections, on weekdays, we bring our petitions; on Shabbat and festivals we bless the special day.
>
> The layout in the first paragraph *avot* allows the community to read the list of patriarchs alone, or followed by the list of the matriarchs, or, by reading across, to link them, or to read the list of matriarchs alone, according to the custom of the community or the particular service

Traditionally the Amidah *is said whilst standing, beginning with three short steps forward,*
a reminder of our entry into the divine presence.
It is customary at the beginning and end of the first paragraph
to bend the knee when saying the word baruch,
to bow from the waist at the second word attah
and to become upright again with the third word, the name of God, Adonai.

תפלת שחרית לשבת

אֲדֹנָי שְׂפָתַי תִּפְתָּח וּפִי יַגִּיד תְּהִלָּתֶךָ:

בָּרוּךְ אַתָּה יהוה אֱלֹהֵינוּ

וֵאלֹהֵי אֲבוֹתֵינוּ וֵאלֹהֵי אִמּוֹתֵינוּ.
אֱלֹהֵי אַבְרָהָם אֱלֹהֵי שָׂרָה.
אֱלֹהֵי יִצְחָק אֱלֹהֵי רִבְקָה.
וֵאלֹהֵי יַעֲקֹב אֱלֹהֵי רָחֵל
וֵאלֹהֵי לֵאָה.
הָאֵל הַגָּדוֹל הַגִּבּוֹר וְהַנּוֹרָא. אֵל עֶלְיוֹן.
גּוֹמֵל חֲסָדִים טוֹבִים קוֹנֵה הַכֹּל. וְזוֹכֵר חַסְדֵי
אָבוֹת וְאִמָּהוֹת
וּמֵבִיא גוֹאֵל לִבְנֵי בְנֵיהֶם לְמַעַן שְׁמוֹ בְּאַהֲבָה:

During the Ten Days of Penitence add:

זָכְרֵנוּ לְחַיִּים. מֶלֶךְ חָפֵץ בַּחַיִּים.
וְכָתְבֵנוּ בְּסֵפֶר הַחַיִּים. לְמַעַנְךָ אֱלֹהִים חַיִּים:

מֶלֶךְ עוֹזֵר וּמוֹשִׁיעַ וּמָגֵן:
בָּרוּךְ אַתָּה יהוה
מָגֵן אַבְרָהָם פּוֹקֵד שָׂרָה:

אֲדֹנָי Adonai s'fatai tiftach ufi yaggid t'hillatecha.

בָּרוּךְ Baruch attah Adonai eloheinu
veilohei avoteinu   veilohei immoteinu.
elohei avraham,   elohei sarah,
elohei yitschak,   elohei rivkah,
veilohei ya'akov,   elohei rachel
                       veilohei le'ah.
Ha'eil ha-gadol, ha-gibbor v'ha-nora, eil elyon,
gomeil chasadim tovim, koneih ha-kol. V'zocheir chasdei
avot   v'immahot
u'meivi go'eil livnei v'neihem l'ma'an sh'mo b'ahavah.
  During the Ten Days of Penitence add: Zochreinu l'chayyim,
  melech chafeits ba-chayyim, v'chotveinu b'seifer ha-chayyim,
  l'ma'ancha elohim chayyim.
Melech ozeir u'moshi'a umagein.
Baruch attah Adonai,
magein avraham   pokeid sarah.

אֲדֹנָי My God, open my lips and my mouth shall declare Your praise.[1]

GOD OF HISTORY
בָּרוּךְ Blessed are You, our God, and God of our ancestors,

God of Abraham,	God of Sarah,
God of Isaac,	God of Rebecca,
and God of Jacob,	God of Rachel
	and God of Leah,

the great, the mighty, and the awesome God, God beyond, generous in love and kindness, and possessing all. You remember the good deeds of those before us, and therefore in love bring rescue to the generations, for such is Your being.

> *During the Ten Days of Penitence add:*
> Sovereign Who delights in life, recall us to life and record us in the Book of Life for Your own sake, God of life!

The Sovereign who helps and saves and shields.
Blessed are You God,
who shields Abraham   who remembers Sarah.

אָבוֹת **Ancestors**

In this opening blessing, *Avot*, 'fathers' or 'ancestors', we establish our identity as the descendants of the patriarchs and matriarchs. The blessing incorporates phrases describing God's qualities from different places in Torah, as if to emphasise the unity of God even though experienced in different ways by different generations - and by us as well.

The word *avot* can mean 'fathers' or 'ancestors'; here we assume the former meaning so have added *immahot*, 'mothers', as they are specifically named.

[1] Psalm 51:1.

אַתָּה גִּבּוֹר לְעוֹלָם אֲדֹנָי. מְחַיֵּה מֵתִים אַתָּה. רַב לְהוֹשִׁיעַ:
In winter מַשִּׁיב הָרוּחַ וּמוֹרִיד הַגָּשֶׁם:
In summer מוֹרִיד הַטָּל:
מְכַלְכֵּל חַיִּים בְּחֶסֶד. מְחַיֵּה מֵתִים בְּרַחֲמִים רַבִּים. סוֹמֵךְ נוֹפְלִים. וְרוֹפֵא חוֹלִים. וּמַתִּיר אֲסוּרִים. וּמְקַיֵּם אֱמוּנָתוֹ לִישֵׁנֵי עָפָר: מִי כָמוֹךָ בַּעַל גְּבוּרוֹת וּמִי דוֹמֶה לָּךְ. מֶלֶךְ מֵמִית וּמְחַיֶּה וּמַצְמִיחַ יְשׁוּעָה:

During the Ten Days of Penitence add:
מִי כָמוֹךָ אַב הָרַחֲמִים. זוֹכֵר יְצוּרָיו לְחַיִּים בְּרַחֲמִים:

וְנֶאֱמָן אַתָּה לְהַחֲיוֹת מֵתִים. בָּרוּךְ אַתָּה יהוה. מְחַיֵּה הַמֵּתִים:

אַתָּה *Attah gibbor l'olam Adonai, mechayyeih meitim attah rav l'hoshi'a.*
In winter: Mashiv ha-ru'ach, u'morid ha-gashem. In summer: Morid ha-tal.
M'chalkeil chayyim b'chesed, m'chayyeih meitim b'rachamim rabbim, someich noflim, v'rofeih cholim, umattir asurim, um'kayyeim emunato lisheinei afar. Mi chamocha ba'al g'vurot, umi domeh lach, melech meimit um'chayyeh, u'matsmi'ach y'shu'ah.
During the Ten Days of Penitence add:
  Mi chamocha av ha-rachamim, zocheir y'tsurav l'chayyim b'rachamim.
V'ne'eman attah l'hachayot meitim. Baruch attah Adonai, m'chayyeih ha-meitim.

An alternative congregational Kedushah *or when praying individually.*

אַתָּה קָדוֹשׁ וְשִׁמְךָ קָדוֹשׁ וּקְדוֹשִׁים בְּכָל־יוֹם יְהַלְלוּךָ סֶּלָה:
בָּרוּךְ אַתָּה יהוה. הָאֵל הַקָּדוֹשׁ:
During the Ten Days of Penitence:
הַמֶּלֶךְ הַקָּדוֹשׁ:

אַתָּה *Attah kadosh v'shimcha kadosh uk'doshim b'chol yom y'hal'lucha sela.*
Baruch attah Adonai ha-eil ha-kadosh.
During the Ten Days of Penitence: **ha-melech ha-kadosh.**

גְּבוּרוֹת **Powers**

The second blessing, *G'vurot*, 'powers', continues the court protocol and describes God's power of life and death over us. Our tradition asserts that the soul continues to exist after death, but arguments have raged over the centuries about the nature of the physical resurrection of the dead at some future, messianic time. It also views each waking day as the restoration of our soul and the beginning of a new life after the partial 'death' of sleep.

The prayer acknowledges that God sustains the living, raises the fallen and heals the sick. As God's witnesses on earth we are also to play our part in this. Human beings are the agency through which God acts.

225 SHABBAT MORNING SERVICE — AMIDAH

GOD OF MIGHT

אַתָּה You are the endless power that renews life beyond death; You are the greatness that saves.

> *In winter months from* Shemini Atzeret *to* Pesach: making the wind blow and the rain fall. *In summer months from* Pesach *to* Shemini Atzeret: causing the dew to fall.

You care for the living with love. You renew life beyond death with unending mercy. You support the falling, and heal the sick. You free prisoners, and keep faith with those who sleep in the dust. Who can perform such mighty deeds, and who can compare with You, a Sovereign who brings death and life, and renews salvation?

> *During the Ten Days of Penitence add:* Who is like You, source of compassion, recalling Your creatures to life in compassion?

You are faithful to renew life beyond death. Blessed are You God, who renews life beyond death.

An alternative congregational Kedushah *or when praying individually.*

GOD OF HOLINESS

אַתָּה You are holy and Your name is holy, and those who seek holiness praise You day by day.

Blessed are You, the holy God.
> *During the Ten Days of Penitence:* **the holy Sovereign.**

קְדֻשַּׁת הַשֵּׁם Kedushat Ha-shem

This third blessing, *k'dushat ha-shem*, 'the sanctification of the name', exists in a variety of forms, depending on whether the worshipper is alone or in a congregation, and on the particular service. The term *kadosh* means 'separate', 'set apart', 'other'.

It is as if in our prayer we are formally acknowledging that God is beyond any way in which we can influence or manipulate the divine will and we are totally dependent on God's mercy. Praying to God is not a magical action with a guaranteed result, a reality that we have to accept even as we prepare to present our petitions before the Sovereign.

עמידה תפלת שחרית לשבת

For public worship:

נְקַדֵּשׁ We sanctify Your name in the world as they sanctify it in the highest heavens. As it is written by the hand of Your prophet: 'And they called to each other and said:

Holy, holy, holy is the Creator of all, whose glory fills all the earth.'[1]

They cry in answer, 'Blessed …'

Blessed is God's glory, revealed in every place.[2]
From Your place, our Sovereign, shine forth and rule over us, for we wait for You. And in Your holy writing it is said:

The Almighty shall rule forever! Your God, O Zion, for all generations! Praise God![3]

We declare Your greatness to all generations, and to all eternity we proclaim Your holiness. Your praise shall never depart from our mouth, for You are God, the great and holy Sovereign.

Blessed are You, the holy God

During the Ten Days of Penitence:
the holy Sovereign.

נְקַדֵּשׁ אֶת־שִׁמְךָ בָּעוֹלָם כְּשֵׁם שֶׁמַּקְדִּישִׁים אוֹתוֹ בִּשְׁמֵי מָרוֹם כַּכָּתוּב עַל יַד נְבִיאֶךָ. וְקָרָא זֶה אֶל זֶה וְאָמַר.

קָדוֹשׁ קָדוֹשׁ קָדוֹשׁ יהוה צְבָאוֹת. מְלֹא כָל־הָאָרֶץ כְּבוֹדוֹ:

לְעֻמָּתָם בָּרוּךְ יֹאמֵרוּ.

בָּרוּךְ כְּבוֹד יהוה מִמְּקוֹמוֹ:

מִמְּקוֹמְךָ מַלְכֵּנוּ תוֹפִיעַ וְתִמְלוֹךְ עָלֵינוּ. כִּי מְחַכִּים אֲנַחְנוּ לָךְ. וּבְדִבְרֵי קָדְשְׁךָ כָּתוּב לֵאמֹר.

יִמְלֹךְ יהוה לְעוֹלָם. אֱלֹהַיִךְ צִיּוֹן לְדֹר וָדֹר הַלְלוּיָהּ:

לְדוֹר וָדוֹר נַגִּיד גָּדְלֶךָ. וּלְנֵצַח נְצָחִים קְדֻשָּׁתְךָ נַקְדִּישׁ. וְשִׁבְחֲךָ אֱלֹהֵינוּ מִפִּינוּ לֹא יָמוּשׁ לְעוֹלָם וָעֶד. כִּי אֵל מֶלֶךְ גָּדוֹל וְקָדוֹשׁ אָתָּה.

בָּרוּךְ אַתָּה יהוה. הָאֵל הַקָּדוֹשׁ:

During the Ten Days of Penitence:
הַמֶּלֶךְ הַקָּדוֹשׁ:

קָדוֹשׁ קָדוֹשׁ קָדוֹשׁ Holy, holy holy …
The prophet Isaiah experienced the awesome nature of God in a vision of heavenly creatures singing God's praises with this sentence (Isa 6:3). The threefold repetition suggests God's unreachable distance from any understanding or contact that we may have with the divine. But the same sentence speaks of God's *kavod*. Related to the root meaning 'weight', it suggests God's tangible 'presence' in this world, in older translations, God's 'glory'. So the verse celebrates the paradox that God is at one and the same time unknowable and distant, but present to be encountered and addressed. There is little we can say *about* God, but we can always speak *to* God.

Our progressive tradition reacted against any literal understanding of 'angels' or other 'heavenly creatures', especially as they developed under the influence of mystical speculations and in folklore. Today we may see such texts as reminders of the limits of our understanding of life, and as a poetic celebration of our ability to imagine, to have visions and to dream.

[1] Isa 6:3 [2] Ezek 3:12, [3] Ps 146:10.

SHABBAT MORNING SERVICE — AMIDAH

נְקַדֵּשׁ *N'kaddeish et shimcha ba-olam k'sheim shemmakdishim oto bishmei marom ka-katuv al yad n'vi'echa v'kara zeh el zeh v'amar.*
Kadosh kadosh kadosh, Adonai ts'va'ot, m'lo chol ha-arets k'vodo.
L'ummatam baruch yomeiru.
Baruch k'vod Adonai mimm'komo.
Mimm'kom'cha malkeinu tofi'a v'timloch aleinu, ki m'chakim anachnu lach, uv'divrei kodsh'cha katuv leimor:
Yimloch Adonai l'olam, elohayich tsiyyon, l'dor vador hal'luyah.
L'dor vador naggid godlecha, ul'neitsach n'tsachim k'dushat'cha nakdish, v'shivchacha eloheinu mippinu lo yamush l'olam va'ed, ki eil melech gadol v'kadosh attah.
Baruch attah Adonai ha-eil ha-kadosh.

During the Ten Days of Penitence: **ha-melech ha-kadosh.**

יִשְׂמַח *Moses rejoiced at the gift of his destiny for You called him a faithful servant. You set a radiance about his head when he stood before You on Mount Sinai, bringing down in his hand the two tablets of stone on which is written the Shabbat command, and so it is written in Your Torah:*

יִשְׂמַח מֹשֶׁה בְּמַתְּנַת חֶלְקוֹ. כִּי עֶבֶד נֶאֱמָן קָרָאתָ לּוֹ. כְּלִיל תִּפְאֶרֶת בְּרֹאשׁוֹ נָתַתָּ. בְּעָמְדוֹ לְפָנֶיךָ עַל הַר סִינַי: וּשְׁנֵי לוּחוֹת אֲבָנִים הוֹרִיד בְּיָדוֹ. וְכָתוּב בָּהֶם שְׁמִירַת שַׁבָּת. וְכֵן כָּתוּב בְּתוֹרָתֶךָ:

יִשְׂמַח *Yismach mosheh b'mattnat chelko, ki eved ne'eman karata lo, k'lil tif'eret b'rosho natatta, b'omdo l'fanecha al har sinai. Ushnei luchot avanim horid b'yado, v'chatuv bahem sh'mirat shabbat, v'chein katuv b'toratecha.*

יִשְׂמַח מֹשֶׁה **Moses rejoiced ...**
This passage introduces the 'fourth', special intermediate blessing for the Shabbat that replaces the petitions of the weekday Amidah. It is also a petition, not for our individual and national needs, but to help us be true to God's will as expressed through the Torah and commandments. It also hints at the true Shabbat rest we will enjoy in the future through God's saving acts.

וְשָׁמְרוּ **The children of Israel shall keep the Shabbat**, observing the Shabbat as a timeless covenant for all generations. It is a sign between Me and the children of Israel forever. For in six days the Creator made heaven and earth and on the seventh day ceased from work and was at rest.[1]

וְשָׁמְרוּ בְנֵי־יִשְׂרָאֵל אֶת־הַשַּׁבָּת לַעֲשׂוֹת אֶת־הַשַּׁבָּת לְדֹרֹתָם בְּרִית עוֹלָם: בֵּינִי וּבֵין בְּנֵי יִשְׂרָאֵל אוֹת הִיא לְעֹלָם כִּי־שֵׁשֶׁת יָמִים עָשָׂה יהוה אֶת־הַשָּׁמַיִם וְאֶת־הָאָרֶץ וּבַיּוֹם הַשְּׁבִיעִי שָׁבַת וַיִּנָּפַשׁ:

וְשָׁמְרוּ *V'sham'ru v'nei yisra'el et ha-shabbat, la'asot et ha-shabbat l'dorotam b'rit olam. Beini uvein b'nei yisra'el ot hi l'olam, ki sheishet yamim asah Adonai et ha-shamayim v'et ha-arets, uva-yom ha-sh'vi'i shavat vayinnafash.*

אֱלֹהֵינוּ **Our God and God of our ancestors**, may our rest be pleasing to You. Make us holy by doing Your commands and let us share in the work of Your Torah. Make us content with Your goodness and let our souls know the joy of Your salvation. Purify our hearts to serve You in truth. In Your love and goodwill let us inherit Your holy Shabbat and may all Israel who seek holiness find in it their rest. Blessed are You God, who makes the Shabbat holy.

אֱלֹהֵינוּ וֵאלֹהֵי אֲבוֹתֵינוּ. רְצֵה־נָא בִמְנוּחָתֵנוּ. קַדְּשֵׁנוּ בְּמִצְוֹתֶיךָ. שִׂים חֶלְקֵנוּ בְּתוֹרָתֶךָ. שַׂבְּעֵנוּ מִטּוּבֶךָ. שַׂמַּח נַפְשֵׁנוּ בִּישׁוּעָתֶךָ. וְטַהֵר לִבֵּנוּ לְעָבְדְּךָ בֶּאֱמֶת. וְהַנְחִילֵנוּ יהוה אֱלֹהֵינוּ בְּאַהֲבָה וּבְרָצוֹן שַׁבַּת קָדְשֶׁךָ. וְיָנוּחוּ בָה כָּל־יִשְׂרָאֵל מְקַדְּשֵׁי שְׁמֶךָ: בָּרוּךְ אַתָּה יהוה. מְקַדֵּשׁ הַשַּׁבָּת:

אֱלֹהֵינוּ *Eloheinu veilohei avoteinu, r'tseih na vimnuchateinu, kadd'sheinu v'mitsvotecha, sim chelkeinu v'toratecha, sab'einu mittuvecha, sammach nafsheinu vishu'atecha, v'taheir libeinu l'ovd'cha b'emet. V'hanchileinu Adonai eloheinu b'ahavah uv'ratson shabbat kodshecha. V'yanuchu vah kol yisra'el m'kadd'shei sh'mecha. Baruch ata Adonai m'kaddeish ha-shabbat.*

אֱלֹהֵינוּ **Our God …**

This is the central blessing of the Shabbat *Amidah*. Rather than petitioning God for our individual and collective needs, as on weekdays, it seeks God's help in enabling us fully to experience in all its aspects the rest, goodness, holiness and security that belong to Shabbat, God's special day.

[1] Ex 31:16-17.

SHABBAT MORNING SERVICE — *AMIDAH*

THANKSGIVING AND PEACE

רְצֵה Our Living God be pleased with Your people Israel and listen to their prayers. In Your great mercy delight in us so that Your presence may rest upon Zion.

רְצֵה יהוה אֱלֹהֵינוּ בְּעַמְּךָ יִשְׂרָאֵל. וְלִתְפִלָּתָם שְׁעֵה. וּבְרַחֲמֶיךָ הָרַבִּים תַּחְפֹּץ בָּנוּ וְתַשְׁרֶה שְׁכִינָתְךָ עַל צִיּוֹן.

<<<

רְצֵה R'tseih Adonai eloheinu b'amm'cha yisra'el, v'litfillatam sh'eih. Uv'rachamecha ha-rabbim tachpots banu v'tashreh sh'chinat'cha al tsiyyon.

On the New Moon and festivals, the prayers on page 230 are added, otherwise the service continues on 231.

רְצֵה Be pleased ...
In its traditional form this blessing, the first of the three closing ones, included a plea for the rebuilding of the temple and the restoration of the sacrificial cult. It has been replaced in virtually all non-Orthodox liturgies with a more general hope that God's presence will be restored to Zion. It also serves as a request that the prayers we have recited will be accepted by God, appropriate to the protocol of taking leave of the Sovereign.

אֱלֹהֵינוּ **Our God and God of our ancestors**, may Your regard and concern for us and our ancestors, for the time of our redemption, for Jerusalem the city of Your holiness, and for all Your people the family of Israel, be close to You and be pleasing to You. Favour us all with freedom and goodness, with grace, love and mercy, on this day of

אֱלֹהֵינוּ וֵאלֹהֵי אֲבוֹתֵינוּ. יַעֲלֶה וְיָבֹא וְיַגִּיעַ וְיֵרָאֶה וְיֵרָצֶה וְיִשָּׁמַע וְיִפָּקֵד וְיִזָּכֵר זִכְרוֹנֵנוּ וּפִקְדוֹנֵנוּ וְזִכְרוֹן אֲבוֹתֵינוּ וְזִכְרוֹן מָשִׁיחַ בֶּן דָּוִד עַבְדֶּךָ. וְזִכְרוֹן יְרוּשָׁלַיִם עִיר קָדְשֶׁךָ וְזִכְרוֹן כָּל־עַמְּךָ בֵּית יִשְׂרָאֵל לְפָנֶיךָ. לִפְלֵיטָה וּלְטוֹבָה לְחֵן וּלְחֶסֶד וּלְרַחֲמִים לְחַיִּים וּלְשָׁלוֹם בְּיוֹם

(On the New Moon) **the New Moon.**   רֹאשׁ הַחֹדֶשׁ הַזֶּה *On the New Moon*
(On Pesach) **the Feast of Unleavened Bread.**   חַג הַמַּצּוֹת הַזֶּה *On Pesach*
(On Succot) **the Feast of Tabernacles.**   חַג הַסֻּכּוֹת הַזֶּה *On Succot*

Our Living God, remember us for good,   *Amen*
bring us Your blessing,   *Amen*
and save us for a good life. *Amen*

זָכְרֵנוּ יְהוָה אֱלֹהֵינוּ בּוֹ לְטוֹבָה אָמֵן
וּפָקְדֵנוּ בוֹ לִבְרָכָה אָמֵן
וְהוֹשִׁיעֵנוּ בוֹ לְחַיִּים טוֹבִים אָמֵן

Spare us and be kind to us according to Your promise of deliverance and mercy. Our eyes are turned towards You, for You are a Sovereign of mercy and compassion.

וּבִדְבַר יְשׁוּעָה וְרַחֲמִים חוּס וְחָנֵּנוּ. כִּי אֵלֶיךָ עֵינֵינוּ. כִּי אֵל מֶלֶךְ חַנּוּן וְרַחוּם אָתָּה.

אֱלֹהֵינוּ *Eloheinu veilohei avoteinu ya'aleh v'yavo v'yagi'a v'yeira'eh v'yeiratseh v'yishama v'yippakeid v'yizzacheir zichroneinu ufikdoneinu, v'zichron avoteinu v'zichron mashi'ach ben david avdecha, v'zichron y'rushalayim ir kodshecha v'zichron kol amm'cha beit yisra'el l'fanecha lifleitah ul'tovah, l'chein ul'chesed ul'rachamim, l'chayyim ul'shalom, b'yom (On the New Moon) Rosh ha-chodesh ha-zeh (On Pesach) Chag ha-matsot ha-zeh (On Succot) Chag ha-sukkot ha-zeh*
Zochreinu Adonai eloheinu bo l'tovah   *Amen*
U'fokdeinu vo livracha   *Amen*
V'hoshi'einu vo l'chayyim tovim   *Amen*
Uvidvar y'shua'ah v'rachamim chus v'chonneinu, ki eilecha eineinu, ki eil melech channun v'rachum attah.

יַעֲלֶה וְיָבֹא **Arise and come …**
This insertion into *r'tseh* allows us to note the special nature of festival occasions. We have retained the traditional Hebrew text, with its reference to 'the anointed son of David Your servant', a reference to the 'messiah' (literally, 'anointed'). We have paraphrased it as 'the time of our redemption', as expressing this messianic hope.

231 SHABBAT MORNING SERVICE — AMIDAH

The service continues here:

וְתֶחֱזֶינָה Our eyes look forward to Your return to Zion in mercy! Blessed are You God, ever restoring Your presence to Zion.

וְתֶחֱזֶינָה עֵינֵינוּ בְּשׁוּבְךָ לְצִיּוֹן בְּרַחֲמִים: בָּרוּךְ אַתָּה יהוה. הַמַּחֲזִיר שְׁכִינָתוֹ לְצִיּוֹן.

וְתֶחֱזֶינָה V'techezenah eineinu b'shuv'cha l'tsiyyon b'rachamim. Baruch attah Adonai ha-machazir sh'chinato l'tsiyyon.

It is customary to bow as one recites the opening words of this blessing, rising as we recite the name of God, Adonai *and the list of God's gifts to us.*

מוֹדִים We declare with gratitude that You are our God and the God of our ancestors. You are our rock, the rock of our life and the shield that saves us. In every generation we thank You and recount Your praise for our lives held in Your hand, for our souls that are in Your care, and for the signs of Your presence that are with us every day. At every moment, at evening, morning and noon, we experience Your wonders and Your goodness. You are goodness itself, for Your mercy has no end. You are mercy itself, for Your love has no limit. Forever have we put our hope in You.

מוֹדִים אֲנַחְנוּ לָךְ שָׁאַתָּה הוּא יהוה אֱלֹהֵינוּ וֵאלֹהֵי אֲבוֹתֵינוּ לְעוֹלָם וָעֶד. צוּרֵנוּ צוּר חַיֵּינוּ וּמָגֵן יִשְׁעֵנוּ אַתָּה הוּא: לְדוֹר וָדוֹר נוֹדֶה לְךָ וּנְסַפֵּר תְּהִלָּתֶךָ עַל חַיֵּינוּ הַמְּסוּרִים בְּיָדֶךָ. וְעַל נִשְׁמוֹתֵינוּ הַפְּקוּדוֹת לָךְ. וְעַל נִסֶּיךָ שֶׁבְּכָל־יוֹם עִמָּנוּ. וְעַל נִפְלְאוֹתֶיךָ וְטוֹבוֹתֶיךָ שֶׁבְּכָל־עֵת עֶרֶב וָבֹקֶר וְצָהֳרָיִם: הַטּוֹב כִּי לֹא כָלוּ רַחֲמֶיךָ. הַמְרַחֵם כִּי לֹא תַמּוּ חֲסָדֶיךָ. כִּי מֵעוֹלָם קִוִּינוּ לָךְ.

מוֹדִים Modim anachnu lach, she'attah hu Adonai eloheinu veilohei avoteinu l'olam va'ed, tsureinu tsur chayyeinu umagein yish'einu attah hu. L'dor vador nodeh l'cha un'sappeir t'hillatecha, al chayyeinu ha-m'surim b'yadecha, v'al nishmoteinu ha-p'kudot lach, v'al nissecha sheb'chol yom immanu, v'al nifl'otecha v'tovotecha sheb'chol eit, erev va'voker v'tsohorayim. Ha-tov ki lo chalu rachamecha, ha-m'racheim ki lo tammu chasadecha, ki mei'olam kivvinu lach.

מוֹדִים Gratitude ...

As befits leaving the presence of the Sovereign, we express our gratitude for the audience, and all the hoped for benefits, in this penultimate blessing. It emphasises something that we too readily take for granted, the miracle of our daily existence and the wonders that surround us at all times.

עמידה | תפלת שחרית לשבת 232

On **Chanukah** add **al ha-nissim** on page 374, otherwise continue here:

וְעַל And for all these things may Your name, our Sovereign, be blessed, exalted and honoured forever and ever.
During the Ten Days of Penitence add: Record all the children of Your covenant for a good life.
May every living being thank You; may they praise and bless Your great name in truth for You are the God who saves and helps us. Blessed are You God, known as goodness, whom it is right to praise.

וְעַל כֻּלָּם יִתְבָּרַךְ וְיִתְרוֹמֵם וְיִתְנַשֵּׂא תָּמִיד שִׁמְךָ מַלְכֵּנוּ לְעוֹלָם וָעֶד:
During the Ten Days of Penitence add:
וּכְתוֹב לְחַיִּים טוֹבִים כָּל־בְּנֵי בְרִיתֶךָ.
וְכֹל־הַחַיִּים יוֹדוּךָ סֶּלָה. וִיהַלְלוּ וִיבָרְכוּ אֶת שִׁמְךָ הַגָּדוֹל בֶּאֱמֶת. הָאֵל יְשׁוּעָתֵנוּ וְעֶזְרָתֵנוּ סֶלָה: בָּרוּךְ אַתָּה יְהוָה. הַטּוֹב שִׁמְךָ וּלְךָ נָאֶה לְהוֹדוֹת:

וְעַל *V'al kullam yitbarach v'yitromeim v'yitnassei tamid shimcha malkeinu l'olam va'ed.*
During the Ten Days of Penitence add: Uch'tov l'chayyim tovim kol b'nei v'ritecha.
V'chol ha-chayyim yoducha selah, vihal'lu vivar'chu et shimcha ha-gadol be'emet, ha-eil y'shu'ateinu v'ezrateinu selah. Baruch attah Adonai, ha-tov shimcha ul'cha na'eh l'hodot.

וּכְתוֹב לְחַיִּים Record for life ...
In a number of places within the *Amidah* there are special insertions for the ten days between *Rosh Hashanah*, the New Year, and *Yom Kippur*, the 'Day for Atonement'. They are based on the imagery of the Book of Life in which is inscribed all that happens to us in the course of the year. On *Rosh Hashanah*, a judgment is made about how we have behaved in the past year, but we have ten days to correct any misdeeds of the past and repair any damaged relationships, before the Book is sealed on *Yom Kippur*.

Two of these insertions appear in the first two blessings of the *Amidah*, and two in the last two blessings. All stress that God delights in life and so ask that we be inscribed in the Book of Life for the coming year. The other addition, in the third blessing of the *Amidah* which speaks of God's holiness, replaces the closing phrase 'the holy God' with 'the holy Sovereign'. This emphasises the view that the New Year is the time when God created the world and now judges it, so God's rule over the entire world should be acknowledged.

שִׂים Grant us peace, goodness and blessing; life, grace and kindness; justice and mercy. Source of our life, bless us all together with the light of Your presence, for in the light of Your presence You give us, our Living God, law and life, love and kindness, justice and mercy, blessing and peace. And in Your eyes it is good to bless Your people Israel with the strength to make peace.

שִׂים שָׁלוֹם טוֹבָה וּבְרָכָה חַיִּים חֵן וָחֶסֶד צְדָקָה וְרַחֲמִים עָלֵינוּ. וּבָרְכֵנוּ אָבִינוּ כֻּלָּנוּ יַחַד בְּאוֹר פָּנֶיךָ. כִּי בְאוֹר פָּנֶיךָ נָתַתָּ לָּנוּ יהוה אֱלֹהֵינוּ תּוֹרָה וְחַיִּים. אַהֲבָה וָחֶסֶד. צְדָקָה וְרַחֲמִים. בְּרָכָה וְשָׁלוֹם. וְטוֹב בְּעֵינֶיךָ לְבָרֵךְ אֶת־עַמְּךָ יִשְׂרָאֵל בְּרָב־עֹז וּבְשָׁלוֹם:

During the Ten Days of Penitence add:
In Your presence may we and all Your people, the family of Israel, be remembered and recorded in the Book of Life for a good life and for peace.

During the Ten Days of Penitence add:
בְּסֵפֶר חַיִּים נִזָּכֵר וְנִכָּתֵב לְפָנֶיךָ אֲנַחְנוּ וְכָל־עַמְּךָ בֵּית יִשְׂרָאֵל לְחַיִּים טוֹבִים וּלְשָׁלוֹם:

Blessed are You God, blessing Your people Israel with peace.

בָּרוּךְ אַתָּה יהוה. הַמְבָרֵךְ אֶת עַמּוֹ יִשְׂרָאֵל בַּשָּׁלוֹם:

שִׂים Sim shalom tovah uv'rachah chayyim chein vachesed, ts'dakah v'rachamim aleinu, uvar'cheinu avinu kullanu yachad b'or panecha, ki v'or panecha natatta lanu Adonai eloheinu torah v'chayyim, ahavah vachesed, ts'dakah v'rachamim, b'rachah v'shalom, v'tov b'einecha l'vareich et amm'cha yisra'el b'rov oz uv'shalom.
During the Ten Days of Penitence add: B'seifer chayyim nizzacheir v'nikkateiv l'fanecha anachnu v'chol amm'cha beit yisra'el, l'chayyim tovim ul'shalom.
Baruch attah Adonai, ha-m'vareich et ammo yisra'el ba-shalom.

שִׂים שָׁלוֹם Grant us peace ...
We depart with words of peace and acknowledge the blessings that come to us through God's favour, beginning with Torah which gives meaning, purpose and direction to life, and concluding with *shalom*, 'wholeness', 'completeness', 'peace'. We have translated two Hebrew phrases, *torah v'chayyim* and *ahavah v'chesed* literally as 'law and life, love and kindness'. Here we follow the Sephardi wording which goes back to the origins of the British Reform movement. However, the Ashkenazi text reads instead *torat chayyim* and *ahavat chesed*, which could be translated as 'guidance for ...' or 'law of life', and 'the love of kindness'. *Chesed* is a difficult word to translate. It means the faithful love and loyalty that exists between people who have made a covenant together, that love and loyalty extending to later generations, even after the original partners to the covenant are no more. It is therefore often translated as 'mercy', 'lovingkindness' or 'compassion', all of which are contained within the word itself. The word is the key to understanding the covenant between God and the Jewish people.

עמידה

MEDITATION

אֱלֹהַי My God, keep my tongue from causing harm and my lips from telling lies. Let me be silent if people curse me, my soul still humble and at peace with all. Open my heart to Your teaching, and give me the will to practise it. May the plans and schemes of those who seek my harm come to nothing. May the words of my mouth and the meditation of my heart be acceptable to You, O God, my Rock and my Redeemer.[1]

אֱלֹהַי נְצוֹר לְשׁוֹנִי מֵרָע. וְשִׂפְתוֹתַי מִדַּבֵּר מִרְמָה. וְלִמְקַלְלַי נַפְשִׁי תִדּוֹם. וְנַפְשִׁי כֶּעָפָר לַכֹּל תִּהְיֶה: פְּתַח לִבִּי בְּתוֹרָתֶךָ. וְאַחֲרֵי מִצְוֹתֶיךָ תִּרְדּוֹף נַפְשִׁי. וְכָל־הַקָּמִים עָלַי לְרָעָה מְהֵרָה הָפֵר עֲצָתָם וְקַלְקֵל מַחֲשְׁבוֹתָם: יִהְיוּ לְרָצוֹן אִמְרֵי־פִי. וְהֶגְיוֹן לִבִּי לְפָנֶיךָ. יְהֹוָה צוּרִי וְגוֹאֲלִי:

אֱלֹהַי Elohai n'tsor l'shoni meira, v'siftotai middabbeir mirmah, v'limkal'lai nafshi tiddom, v'nafshi ke'afar la-kol tihyeh. P'tach libbi b'toratecha, v'acharei mitsvotecha tirdof nafshi, v'chol ha-kamim alai l'ra'ah, m'heirah hafeir atsatam, v'kalkeil machsh'votam. Yihyu l'ratson imrei fi, v'hegyon libbi l'fanecha, Adonai tsuri v'go'ali.

While reciting Oseh Shalom it is customary to take three steps backwards,
to bow to the left at the words oseh shalom bimromav,
to the right at hu ya'aseh shalom and to the centre at aleinu.

עֹשֶׂה May the Maker of peace in the highest bring this peace upon us and upon all Israel and upon all the world. Amen.

עֹשֶׂה שָׁלוֹם בִּמְרוֹמָיו. הוּא יַעֲשֶׂה שָׁלוֹם עָלֵינוּ וְעַל כָּל־יִשְׂרָאֵל וְעַל־כָּל־הָעוֹלָם. וְאִמְרוּ. אָמֵן:

עֹשֶׂה Oseh shalom bimromav hu ya'aseh shalom aleinu
v'al kol yisra'el v'al kol ha-olam, v'imru amen.

On new moon and festivals the service continues with the Hallel on page 663.

אֱלֹהַי נְצוֹר My God, keep ...

This prayer by Mar bar Rabina is recorded in the Talmud (*Berachot* 17a) amongst a number of private prayers composed by individual rabbis. The opening words are based on Psalm 34:14. To the question in the previous verse 'Who is the person who desires life?' comes the answer 'Keep your tongue from causing harm and your lips from telling lies'. Mar invokes God's help and support so that there is integrity between his inner and outer life.

עֹשֶׂה שָׁלוֹם May the Maker of peace ...

The *Amidah* focuses almost exclusively on the needs of the Jewish people as they stand in the presence of God. For this reason the closing sentence, 'May the Maker of peace ...,' mentions Israel alone, but reflects the view that the fate of Israel has significance for the entire world. The peace for which we aspire can only exist if the rest of the world is at peace. Today this universal hope needs a more concrete expression, hence the inclusion of 'and upon all the world'.   [1] Ps 19:15.

SHABBAT MORNING SERVICE — TORAH SERVICE I

סדר קריאת התורה
Torah Service

עֵץ־חַיִּים הִיא לַמַּחֲזִיקִים בָּהּ.

It is a tree of life to all who grasp it.

Proverbs 3:18

One of the following three versions of the Torah Service may be used:

סדר קריאת התורה א'
TORAH SERVICE I

> This traditional Torah Service symbolically re-enacts the events at Mount Sinai when Moses went up the mountain and brought the Torah down to earth, to read it to the assembled people. The passages that are included emphasise the Sovereignty of God. The service is built around two Biblical verses that are set apart from the surrounding ones in the Book of Numbers (10:35-36). The first sentence is effectively a battle-cry that signalled the start of the next stage of the journey of the Israelite encampment through the wilderness - scattering God's enemies before them. The second sentence signalled the next halt and resting place. The Psalm that traditionally accompanies the procession on Shabbat, Psalm 29, also emphasises God's power in the world, like a massive storm sweeping through the land. Other themes are the restoration of Zion and the re-building of Jerusalem.

TORAH SERVICE I

אֵין Almighty God, there is none like You
among the gods people worship,
and no deeds like Yours!
Your dominion is an everlasting dominion.
Your authority is for every generation!
God rules, God has ruled,
God shall rule forever and ever.
God, give strength to Your people
and bless Your people with peace.[1]

אֵין כָּמוֹךָ בָאֱלֹהִים יהוה
וְאֵין כְּמַעֲשֶׂיךָ:
מַלְכוּתְךָ מַלְכוּת כָּל־עֹלָמִים
וּמֶמְשַׁלְתְּךָ בְּכָל־דֹּר וָדֹר:
יהוה מֶלֶךְ יהוה מָלָךְ
יהוה יִמְלֹךְ לְעֹלָם וָעֶד:
יהוה עֹז לְעַמּוֹ יִתֵּן
יהוה יְבָרֵךְ אֶת עַמּוֹ בַשָּׁלוֹם:

אֵין *Ein kamocha va'elohim Adonai, v'ein k'ma'asecha.
Malchut'cha malchut kol olamim, umemshalt'cha b'chol dor vador.
Adonai melech Adonai malach, Adonai yimloch l'olam va'ed.
Adonai oz l'ammo yittein, Adonai y'vareich et ammo va-shalom.*

אָב Source of mercy,
may it please You to be good to Zion,
and build the walls of Jerusalem,
for we trust in You alone,
Ruler and God,
supreme and sublime,
everlasting Sovereign.

אַב הָרַחֲמִים הֵיטִיבָה
בִרְצוֹנְךָ אֶת צִיּוֹן.
תִּבְנֶה חוֹמוֹת יְרוּשָׁלָיִם.
כִּי בְךָ לְבַד בָּטָחְנוּ.
מֶלֶךְ אֵל רָם וְנִשָּׂא
אֲדוֹן עוֹלָמִים:

אָב *Av ha-rachamim, heitivah virtson'cha et tsiyyon, tivneh chomot y'rushalayim,
ki v'cha l'vad batachnu, melech eil ram v'nissa, adon olamim.*

אֵין כָּמוֹךָ There is none like you ...
Many of the following passages were first collected in the *Massechet Soferim*, eighth-century CE, though the full ritual that attends the opening of the ark and the reading from the Torah scroll evolved during the Middle Ages.

If we see the structure of the liturgy up to this point as a symbolic journey to appear before God, God now 'responds' to us through the words of the Torah that we are about to read. The opening verses stress God's uniqueness as Creator and as Sovereign, from before the world existed (*kol olamim*) and throughout human history (*b'chol dor vador*).

[1] Ps 86:8; 145:13; 29:11.

יהוה מֶלֶךְ God rules ...
This is the only verse in this section that is not Biblical, though the individual phrases within it can be found in a variety of Biblical passages. The Song at the Sea (Ex 15:18) concluded that God will rule forever, but, in one interpretation, this seems to locate the rule of God in some distant future. So our sentence asserts that God's rule is in the here and now, just as in the past and in the future.

אַב הָרַחֲמִים Source of mercy ...
Though the revelation came to us at Mount Sinai, Mount Zion became the place where our tradition located God's dwelling on earth. This liturgy, composed in exile,

237 SHABBAT MORNING SERVICE — TORAH SERVICE I

וַיְהִי Whenever the ark moved forward,
then Moses said:
'Almighty, rise up!
Let Your enemies be scattered,
let those who hate You flee before You!'
For Torah shall come out of Zion
and the word of God from Jerusalem.[1]

וַיְהִי בִּנְסֹעַ הָאָרֹן
וַיֹּאמֶר מֹשֶׁה:
קוּמָה יהוה וְיָפֻצוּ אֹיְבֶיךָ
וְיָנֻסוּ מְשַׂנְאֶיךָ מִפָּנֶיךָ:
כִּי מִצִּיּוֹן תֵּצֵא תוֹרָה
וּדְבַר־יהוה מִירוּשָׁלָיִם:

וַיְהִי Vay'hi binso'a ha-aron vayomer mosheh.
Kumah Adonai v'yafutsu oy'vecha v'yanusu m'san'echa mippanecha.
Ki mitsiyon teitsei torah, ud'var Adonai mirushalayim.

בָּרוּךְ Blessed is the One
who in holiness gave Torah to Israel.
Hear O Israel, the Eternal is our God, the
Eternal is One.[2]
Our God is One.
Our Sovereign is great.
Holy is God's name.

בָּרוּךְ שֶׁנָּתַן תּוֹרָה
לְעַמּוֹ יִשְׂרָאֵל בִּקְדֻשָּׁתוֹ:
שְׁמַע יִשְׂרָאֵל יהוה אֱלֹהֵינוּ
יהוה אֶחָד:
אֶחָד אֱלֹהֵינוּ גָּדוֹל אֲדוֹנֵנוּ
קָדוֹשׁ שְׁמוֹ:

During the Ten Days of Penitence read instead:
Holy and awesome is God's name.

During the Ten Days of Penitence read instead:
קָדוֹשׁ וְנוֹרָא שְׁמוֹ:

בָּרוּךְ Baruch shennatan torah l'ammo yisra'el bikdushato.
Sh'ma yisra'el, Adonai eloheinu, Adonai echad.
Echad eloheinu, gadol adoneinu, kadosh sh'mo.
During the Ten Days of Penitence read instead: kadosh v'nora sh'mo.

---

yearns for the return of God's presence to Zion, our spiritual centre, and the restoration of national sovereignty, Jerusalem. Many earlier progressive liturgies have omitted the call for building the walls of Jerusalem because of non-Zionist views. Our hope is that these walls need not be defences to keep people out, but homes within which all inhabitants of Jerusalem may live in security and at peace.

וַיְהִי בִּנְסֹעַ Whenever the ark moved forward ...

This sentence moves us back again to the wilderness wanderings and the words with which each new journey began. It describes the Ark of the Covenant, the symbol of God's presence amongst the people, leading the way, while God removes all obstacles before them. Bringing the scroll down from the ark symbolises the Torah coming to us from Mount Sinai, while the wilderness wanderings are echoed as it is paraded around the congregation. The language is militaristic in tone, in stark contrast to the verse that follows, taken from Isaiah's vision of a time of universal peace when nations will beat their swords into ploughshares. In this new era, Zion, the site of the temple and the final resting place of the ark, becomes the place where a new revelation arises.

בָּרוּךְ שֶׁנָּתַן Blessed is the One who gave ...

With these words we solemnly accept the Torah that has been given to us in the past and symbolically brought into our presence through this service.

---

[1] Num 10:35; Isa 2:3. [2] Deut 6:4.

גַּדְּלוּ Declare with me the greatness of God, and let us exalt God's name together.[1]

גַּדְּלוּ לַיהוה אִתִּי.
וּנְרוֹמְמָה שְׁמוֹ יַחְדָּו:

גַּדְּלוּ *Gadd'lu ladonai itti, un'rom'mah sh'mo yachdav.*

לְךָ Yours, our Living God,
is the greatness, the power,
the beauty, the victory
and the splendour,
for everything in heaven and earth
is Yours.
Yours is sovereignty
and You are supreme over all.
Exalt the Living God, and bow down
before the footstool of the Holy One.
Exalt the Living God, and bow down
before the mountain of God's holiness
- for holy is our Living God.[2]

לְךָ יהוה הַגְּדֻלָּה וְהַגְּבוּרָה
וְהַתִּפְאֶרֶת וְהַנֵּצַח וְהַהוֹד.
כִּי כֹל בַּשָּׁמַיִם וּבָאָרֶץ.
לְךָ יהוה הַמַּמְלָכָה
וְהַמִּתְנַשֵּׂא לְכֹל לְרֹאשׁ:
רוֹמְמוּ יהוה אֱלֹהֵינוּ
וְהִשְׁתַּחֲווּ לַהֲדֹם רַגְלָיו
קָדוֹשׁ הוּא:
רוֹמְמוּ יהוה אֱלֹהֵינוּ.
וְהִשְׁתַּחֲווּ לְהַר קָדְשׁוֹ.
כִּי קָדוֹשׁ יהוה אֱלֹהֵינוּ:

לְךָ *L'cha Adonai ha-g'dullah v'ha-g'vurah v'ha-tif'eret v'ha-neitsach v'ha-hod,
ki chol ba-shamayim uva'arets,
l'cha Adonai ha-mamlachah v'ha-mitnassei l'chol l'rosh.
Rom'mu Adonai eloheinu, v'hishtachavu lahadom raglav, kadosh hu.
Rom'mu Adonai eloheinu, v'hishtachavu l'har kodsho,
ki kadosh Adonai eloheinu.*

גַּדְּלוּ לַיהוה אִתִּי
Declare with me the greatness of God ...
This and the following passages present two key ideas within Jewish tradition: that God is the God of the entire universe and that God has given guidance to humanity through the Torah, with the Jewish people as the agents for that task.

לְךָ יהוה **Yours, our Living God ...**
This hymn of praise to God accompanies the procession with the Torah.

[1] Ps 34:4.
[2] I Chron 29:11; Ps 99:5; Ps 99:9.

239 SHABBAT MORNING SERVICE — TORAH SERVICE I

אֵין There is none holy
like the Eternal,
for nothing is like You
and there is no strength like our God.
For who is God besides the Eternal,
and what is strength except our God!
Moses commanded us Torah, the
heritage of the community of Jacob.
It is a tree of life to all who grasp it
and those who hold fast to it
are happy.
Its ways are ways of pleasantness
and all its paths are peace.[1]

אֵין קָדוֹשׁ כַּיהוה כִּי־אֵין בִּלְתֶּךָ.
וְאֵין צוּר כֵּאלֹהֵינוּ:
כִּי מִי אֱלוֹהַּ מִבַּלְעֲדֵי יהוה.
וּמִי צוּר זוּלָתִי אֱלֹהֵינוּ:
תּוֹרָה צִוָּה־לָנוּ מֹשֶׁה.
מוֹרָשָׁה קְהִלַּת יַעֲקֹב:
עֵץ־חַיִּים הִיא לַמַּחֲזִיקִים בָּהּ.
וְתֹמְכֶיהָ מְאֻשָּׁר:
דְּרָכֶיהָ דַרְכֵי־נֹעַם.
וְכָל־נְתִיבֹתֶיהָ שָׁלוֹם:

אֵין Ein kadosh kadonai ki ein biltecha, v'ein tsur keiloheinu.
Ki mi elo'ah mibbal'adei Adonai, umi tsur zulati eloheinu.
Torah tsivah lanu mosheh, morashah k'hillat ya'akov.
Eits chayyim hi la-machazikim bah, v'tom'cheha m'ushar.
D'racheha darchei no'am, v'chol n'tivoteha shalom.

שָׁלוֹם There is great peace
for those who love Your Torah,
and for them there is no stumbling.
Give strength to Your people,
bless Your people with peace.
So I call out the name of the One God:
Declare the greatness of our God!
Let everything declare God's power
and the glory of God's Torah.[2]

שָׁלוֹם רָב לְאֹהֲבֵי תוֹרָתֶךָ.
וְאֵין־לָמוֹ מִכְשׁוֹל:
יהוה עֹז לְעַמּוֹ יִתֵּן.
יהוה יְבָרֵךְ אֶת־עַמּוֹ בַשָּׁלוֹם:
כִּי שֵׁם יהוה אֶקְרָא.
הָבוּ גֹדֶל לֵאלֹהֵינוּ:
הַכֹּל תְּנוּ עֹז לֵאלֹהִים.
וּתְנוּ כָבוֹד לַתּוֹרָה:

שָׁלוֹם Shalom rav l'ohavei toratecha, v'ein lamo michshol.
Adonai oz l'ammo yittein, Adonai y'vareich et ammo va-shalom.
Ki sheim Adonai ekra, havu godel leiloheinu.
Ha-kol t'nu oz leilohim, ut'nu chavod la-torah.

עֵץ־חַיִּים הִיא It is a tree of life ...
This verse comes from the Book of Proverbs where it actually speaks about *chochmah*, 'wisdom' which in the Biblical world included practical wisdom, acquired through human experience as well as intellectual achievement. By including wisdom here it makes the Torah itself the sustaining 'tree of life', but also allows for all human knowledge, scientific as well as spiritual, to become part of the broadest understanding of God's revelation.

[1] I Sam 2:2; Ps 18:32; Deut 33:4; Pr 3:18,17.
[2] Ps 119:165; 29:11, Deut 32:3.

The Sephardi practice is to raise the Torah scroll here - הַגְבָּהָה *Hagbahah.*
The scroll is elevated to display three columns from the Shabbat reading.

וְזֹאת This is the Torah that Moses set before the children of Israel.
Moses commanded us the Torah, the heritage of the community of Jacob.
God whose way is perfect, whose word is proved, a shield for all who seek refuge.

וְזֹאת הַתּוֹרָה אֲשֶׁר־שָׂם מֹשֶׁה לִפְנֵי בְּנֵי יִשְׂרָאֵל:
תּוֹרָה צִוָּה־לָנוּ מֹשֶׁה.
מוֹרָשָׁה קְהִלַּת יַעֲקֹב:
הָאֵל תָּמִים דַּרְכּוֹ.
אִמְרַת יהוה צְרוּפָה.
מָגֵן הוּא לְכֹל הַחוֹסִים בּוֹ:

וְזֹאת *V'zot ha-torah asher sam mosheh lifnei v'nei yisra'el.*
Torah tsivah lanu mosheh, morashah k'hillat ya'akov.
Ha-eil tamim darko, imrat Adonai ts'rufah,
magein hu l'chol ha-chosim bo.

Before reading the Torah:

בָּרְכוּ Bless the Living God whom we are called to bless.

בָּרְכוּ אֶת יהוה הַמְבֹרָךְ:

בָּרוּךְ Blessed is the Living God, whom we are called to bless forever and ever.

בָּרוּךְ יהוה הַמְבֹרָךְ לְעוֹלָם וָעֶד:

בָּרוּךְ Blessed are You, our Living God, Sovereign of the universe, who chose us from all peoples to give us Your Torah. Blessed are You God, who gives us the Torah.

בָּרוּךְ אַתָּה יהוה אֱלֹהֵינוּ מֶלֶךְ הָעוֹלָם. אֲשֶׁר בָּחַר־בָּנוּ מִכָּל־הָעַמִּים וְנָתַן־לָנוּ אֶת תּוֹרָתוֹ: בָּרוּךְ אַתָּה יהוה. נוֹתֵן הַתּוֹרָה:

בָּרְכוּ *Bar'chu et Adonai ha-m'vorach.*
בָּרוּךְ *Baruch Adonai ha-m'vorach l'olam va'ed.*
בָּרוּךְ *Baruch attah Adonai eloheinu melech ha-olam,*
asher bachar banu mikkol ha-ammim, v'natan lanu et torato.
Baruch attah Adonai, notein ha-torah.

וְזֹאת הַתּוֹרָה **This is the Torah...**
Because Biblical scholarship had cast doubt on the actual historical events, earlier progressive liturgies were uncomfortable with passages that stated that God had literally given the Torah to Moses on Mount Sinai. Today we accept that there are many levels on which to understand this tradition, poetic and symbolic, which provides a central element in our understanding of our relationship with God and the responsibilities it brings to us.

SHABBAT MORNING SERVICE — TORAH SERVICE I

After reading the Torah:

בָּרוּךְ Blessed are You, our Living God, Sovereign of the universe, who gave us the teaching of truth and planted eternal life within us. Blessed are You God, who gives us the Torah.

בָּרוּךְ אַתָּה יהוה אֱלֹהֵינוּ מֶלֶךְ הָעוֹלָם. אֲשֶׁר נָתַן־לָנוּ תּוֹרַת אֱמֶת וְחַיֵּי עוֹלָם נָטַע בְּתוֹכֵנוּ: בָּרוּךְ אַתָּה יהוה. נוֹתֵן הַתּוֹרָה:

בָּרוּךְ *Baruch attah Adonai eloheinu melech ha-olam,*
asher natan lanu torat emet, v'chayei olam nata b'tocheinu.
Baruch attah Adonai, notein ha-torah.

It is customary for someone who has survived a life-threatening experience to be given an aliyah *and to recite the blessing:* Birkat ha-gomel, *to which the congregation responds.*

בָּרוּךְ Blessed are You, our living God, Sovereign of the universe, who shows favour to the undeserving, even to me.

בָּרוּךְ אַתָּה יהוה אֱלֹהֵינוּ מֶלֶךְ הָעוֹלָם הַגּוֹמֵל לְחַיָּבִים טוֹבוֹת שֶׁגְּמָלַנִי כָּל־טוֹב:

The congregation responds:

Amen.
May the One who has shown favour to you, continue to favour you with all that is good.

For a man:
אָמֵן. מִי שֶׁגְּמָלְךָ טוֹב הוּא יִגְמָלְךָ כָּל־טוֹב:

For a woman:
אָמֵן. מִי שֶׁגְּמָלֵךְ טוֹב הוּא יִגְמָלֵךְ כָּל־טוֹב:

בָּרוּךְ *Baruch attah Adonai eloheinu melech ha-olam, ha-gomeil*
l'chayavim tovot sheg'malani kol tov.

The congregation responds for a man:
Amen, mi sheg'malcha tov hu yigmolcha kol tov.
The congregation responds for a woman:
Amen, mi sheg'maleich tov hu yigm'leich kol tov.

The Ashkenazi practice is to raise the Torah *scroll here -* הַגְבָּהָה *Hagbahah.*
The scroll is elevated to display three columns from the scroll reading.

וְזֹאת This is the Torah that Moses set before the children of Israel, given by God through Moses.

וְזֹאת הַתּוֹרָה אֲשֶׁר שָׂם מֹשֶׁה לִפְנֵי בְּנֵי יִשְׂרָאֵל. עַל פִּי יהוה בְּיַד מֹשֶׁה:

וְזֹאת *V'zot ha-torah asher sam mosheh lifnei b'nei yisra'el,*
al pi Adonai b'yad mosheh.

ההפטרה וברכותיה
THE HAFTARAH AND ITS BLESSINGS

The Haftarah is traditionally taken from the second part of the Hebrew Bible, *nevi'im*, 'prophets', which includes the books from Joshua to the twelve 'Minor Prophets'. The passage is often selected because of some connection with the Torah reading of that particular Shabbat, though the exact reason for including it is not known. It is suggested that it was included when the Romans forbade the reading of the Torah and this was substituted as a reminder of the Torah text. However some *Haftarot* are chosen to reflect the time of the year: in the three weeks before *Tisha b'Av*, the fast commemorating the destruction of both temples, we read prophetic words of warning from Jeremiah and Isaiah. But from the Shabbat following this date we read seven weekly passages of comfort and consolation which 'strengthen' us as we prepare for *Rosh Hashanah*. special readings also precede *Purim* and *Pesach*.

In our Reform tradition we sometimes take passages from the third section of the Hebrew Bible, the *K'tuvim*, 'Writings', where they make an appropriate comment on the Torah reading itself, in which case we read the blessings on page 245.

Before reading the Haftarah:

בָּרוּךְ Blessed are You, our Living God, Sovereign of the universe, who chose good prophets and was pleased by their words for they were spoken in truth. Blessed are You God, for You chose the Torah, Moses Your servant, Israel Your people and the true and righteous prophets.

בָּרוּךְ אַתָּה יהוה אֱלֹהֵינוּ מֶלֶךְ הָעוֹלָם. אֲשֶׁר בָּחַר בִּנְבִיאִים טוֹבִים וְרָצָה בְדִבְרֵיהֶם הַנֶּאֱמָרִים בֶּאֱמֶת: בָּרוּךְ אַתָּה יהוה. הַבּוֹחֵר בַּתּוֹרָה וּבְמֹשֶׁה עַבְדּוֹ וּבְיִשְׂרָאֵל עַמּוֹ וּבִנְבִיאֵי הָאֱמֶת וָצֶדֶק:

בָּרוּךְ *Baruch attah Adonai eloheinu melech ha-olam, asher bachar binvi'im tovim, v'ratsah v'divreihem ha-ne'emarim be'emet. Baruch attah Adonai, ha-bocheir ba-torah, uv'mosheh avdo, uv'yisra'el ammo, uvinvi'ei ha-emet vatsedek.*

SHABBAT MORNING SERVICE — TORAH SERVICE I

After reading the Haftarah, some congregations include the following blessings. Most begin with al ha-torah, *the final paragraph on page 244.*

בָּרוּךְ אַתָּה יהוה אֱלֹהֵינוּ מֶלֶךְ הָעוֹלָם. צוּר כָּל־הָעוֹלָמִים. צַדִּיק בְּכָל־הַדּוֹרוֹת. הָאֵל הַנֶּאֱמָן הָאוֹמֵר וְעֹשֶׂה הַמְדַבֵּר וּמְקַיֵּם שֶׁכָּל־דְּבָרָיו אֱמֶת וָצֶדֶק: נֶאֱמָן אַתָּה הוּא יהוה אֱלֹהֵינוּ וְנֶאֱמָנִים דְּבָרֶיךָ וְדָבָר אֶחָד מִדְּבָרֶיךָ אָחוֹר לֹא יָשׁוּב רֵיקָם כִּי אֵל מֶלֶךְ נֶאֱמָן וְרַחֲמָן אָתָּה: בָּרוּךְ אַתָּה יהוה. הָאֵל הַנֶּאֱמָן בְּכָל־דְּבָרָיו:

בָּרוּךְ Blessed are You, our Living God, Sovereign of the universe, Rock of all ages, righteous in all generations, trustworthy in what You say and do, speaking and fulfilling Your word, for all Your words are true and just. You are faithful, our Living God, and Your words are reliable, and no single word of Yours returns to You empty, for You are the Sovereign God, faithful and merciful. Blessed are You God, on whose words we can rely.

בָּרוּךְ Baruch attah Adonai eloheinu melech ha-olam, tsur kol ha-olamim, tsaddik b'chol ha-dorot, ha-eil ha-ne'eman, ha-omeir v'oseh, ha-m'dabbeir um'kayyeim, she'kol d'varav emet vatsedek. Ne'eman attah hu Adonai eloheinu v'ne'emanim d'varecha, v'davar echad midd'varecha achor lo yashuv reikam, ki eil melech ne'eman v'rachaman attah. Baruch attah Adonai, ha-eil ha-ne'eman b'chol d'varav.

רַחֵם עַל צִיּוֹן כִּי הִיא בֵּית חַיֵּינוּ וְלַעֲלוּבַת נֶפֶשׁ תּוֹשִׁיעַ בִּמְהֵרָה בְיָמֵינוּ: בָּרוּךְ אַתָּה יהוה. מְשַׂמֵּחַ צִיּוֹן בְּבָנֶיהָ:

רַחֵם Have mercy on Zion for it is the home of our life, and to all those humbled in spirit bring rescue speedily in our days. Blessed are You God, who makes Zion rejoice in her children.

<<<

רַחֵם Racheim al tsiyyon ki hi beit chayyeinu, v'la'aluvat nefesh toshi'a bimheirah v'yameinu. Baruch attah Adonai, m'sammei'ach tsiyyon b'vaneha.

שַׂמְּחֵנוּ Our Living God, bring us joy through Elijah the prophet, and the establishing of the just rule of the house of David, Your anointed one; may he come speedily and make our hearts rejoice. May no destructive powers occupy his throne and let no others usurp his glory, for You swore to him in Your holy name that his light would not be extinguished forever. Blessed are You God, shield of David.

שַׂמְּחֵנוּ יהוה אֱלֹהֵינוּ בְּאֵלִיָּהוּ הַנָּבִיא עַבְדֶּךָ וּבְמַלְכוּת בֵּית דָּוִד מְשִׁיחֶךָ. בִּמְהֵרָה יָבֹא וְיָגֵל לִבֵּנוּ. עַל כִּסְאוֹ לֹא יֵשֵׁב זָר. וְלֹא יִנְחֲלוּ עוֹד אֲחֵרִים אֶת כְּבוֹדוֹ כִּי בְשֵׁם קָדְשְׁךָ נִשְׁבַּעְתָּ לוֹ שֶׁלֹּא יִכְבֶּה נֵרוֹ לְעוֹלָם וָעֶד: בָּרוּךְ אַתָּה יהוה. מָגֵן דָּוִד:

שַׂמְּחֵנוּ Samm'cheinu Adonai eloheinu, b'eiliyahu ha-navi avdecha, uv'malchut beit david m'shichecha, bimheirah yavo v'yageil libbeinu, al kis'o lo yeishev zar, v'lo yinchalu od acheirim et k'vodo, ki v'sheim kodsh'cha nishba'ta lo shello yichbeh neiro l'olam va'ed. Baruch attah Adonai, magein david.

Most congregations begin the blessings after the Haftarah here:

עַל For the Torah, for the service, for the prophets and for this Shabbat day which You gave us, our Living God, for holiness and rest, for glory and beauty - for all these, God our Creator, we thank and bless You. May Your name be blessed by the mouth of all living forever and ever. Blessed are You God, who makes the Shabbat holy.

עַל הַתּוֹרָה וְעַל הָעֲבוֹדָה וְעַל הַנְּבִיאִים וְעַל יוֹם הַשַּׁבָּת הַזֶּה שֶׁנָּתַתָּ לָּנוּ יהוה אֱלֹהֵינוּ לִקְדֻשָּׁה וְלִמְנוּחָה לְכָבוֹד וּלְתִפְאָרֶת. עַל הַכֹּל יהוה אֱלֹהֵינוּ אֲנַחְנוּ מוֹדִים לָךְ וּמְבָרְכִים אוֹתָךְ. יִתְבָּרַךְ שִׁמְךָ בְּפִי כָּל־חַי תָּמִיד לְעוֹלָם וָעֶד: בָּרוּךְ אַתָּה יהוה. מְקַדֵּשׁ הַשַּׁבָּת:

עַל Al ha-torah, v'al ha-avodah, v'al ha-n'vi'im v'al yom ha-shabbat ha-zeh, shennatatta lanu, Adonai eloheinu likdushah v'limnuchah, l'chavod ul'tif'aret, al ha-kol Adonai eloheinu, anachnu modim lach, um'var'chim otach, yitbarach shimcha b'fi chol chai tamid l'olam va'ed. Baruch attah Adonai, m'kaddeish ha-shabbat.

SHABBAT MORNING SERVICE — TORAH SERVICE I

If the Haftarah is taken from the K'tuvim, 'Writings', the following blessing may be said:

בָּרוּךְ Blessed are You, our Living God, Sovereign of the universe, Your holy spirit rested on those who revered You, and You were pleased with their words for they were written in truth. Blessed are You God, for You chose the Torah, Moses Your servant, Israel Your people and words that were true and righteous.

בָּרוּךְ אַתָּה יהוה אֱלֹהֵינוּ מֶלֶךְ הָעוֹלָם. שֶׁהִנִּיחַ אֶת־רוּחַ הַקֹּדֶשׁ עַל יְרֵאָיו. וְרָצָה בְדִבְרֵיהֶם הַכְּתוּבִים בֶּאֱמֶת: בָּרוּךְ אַתָּה יהוה. הַבּוֹחֵר בַּתּוֹרָה וּבְמֹשֶׁה עַבְדּוֹ. וּבְיִשְׂרָאֵל עַמּוֹ. וּבְדִבְרֵי אֱמֶת וָצֶדֶק:

בָּרוּךְ *Baruch attah Adonai eloheinu melech ha-olam, she-hinni'ach et ru'ach ha-kodesh al y'rei'av, v'ratsah v'divreihem ha-k'tuvim be'emet. Baruch attah Adonai, ha-bocheir ba-torah uv'mosheh avdo, uv'yisra'el ammo, uv'divrei emet va-tsedek.*

After reading from the K'tuvim, 'Writings', the following may be said:

בָּרוּךְ For the Torah, for the service, for the writers of wisdom and for this Shabbat day which You gave us, our Living God, for holiness and rest, for glory and beauty - for all these, God our Creator, we thank and bless You. May Your name be blessed by the mouth of all living forever and ever. Blessed are You God, who makes the Shabbat holy.

עַל הַתּוֹרָה. וְעַל הָעֲבוֹדָה. וְעַל כֹּתְבֵי חָכְמָה. וְעַל יוֹם הַשַּׁבָּת הַזֶּה. שֶׁנָּתַתָּ לָּנוּ. יהוה אֱלֹהֵינוּ. לִקְדֻשָּׁה וְלִמְנוּחָה. לְכָבוֹד וּלְתִפְאָרֶת. עַל הַכֹּל יהוה אֱלֹהֵינוּ אֲנַחְנוּ מוֹדִים לָךְ וּמְבָרְכִים אוֹתָךְ. יִתְבָּרַךְ שִׁמְךָ בְּפִי כָּל־חַי תָּמִיד לְעוֹלָם וָעֶד: בָּרוּךְ אַתָּה יהוה. מְקַדֵּשׁ הַשַּׁבָּת:

בָּרוּךְ *Al ha-torah, v'al ha-avodah, v'al kotvei chochmah, v'al yom ha-shabbat ha-zeh, shennatatta lanu, Adonai eloheinu, likdushah v'limnuchah, l'chavod ul'tif'aret. Al ha-kol, Adonai eloheinu, anachnu modim lach, um'var'chim otach, yitbarach shimcha b'fi chol chai tamid l'olam va'ed. Baruch attah Adonai, m'kaddeish ha-shabbat.*

סדר קריאת התורה · תפלת שחרית לשבת · 246

*The following shorter prayer (I) may be read
or some of the prayers (II) which follow.*

THE PRAYERS OF THE COMMUNITY

I

Our God, whose dominion is everlasting, we ask you to bless

our Sovereign Lady Queen Elizabeth,

and to guide the government of this country. Help us to be good citizens, working together for justice and peace at home and abroad. Bless this holy community and all holy communities, and support the life and work of all who labour for their welfare.

Our God and God of our ancestors, we ask Your blessing on the State of Israel and all who live there. Give wisdom and understanding to its leaders, and friendship and compassion to the people, so that there may be lasting peace on its borders and in its homes. Soon may Your promise be fulfilled: 'for Torah shall come out of Zion and the word of God from Jerusalem'.

We ask You to listen to our prayers and look on us kindly, supporting those who are troubled, consoling the bereaved, sending relief to those in pain or anxiety.

As You blessed our fathers Abraham, Isaac and Jacob and our mothers Sarah, Rebecca, Rachel and Leah, bless our own congregation, all other congregations gathered in prayer, and everyone who responds to the needs of the community.

May such be the Divine will. And let us say Amen.

*On the Shabbat preceding the New Moon
the service continues on page 250, otherwise on page 251:*

II

FOR THE SOVEREIGN

May God whose dominion is an everlasting dominion bless

Our Sovereign Lady, Queen Elizabeth.

May God give wisdom to the government of this country, to all who lead it and to all who have responsibility for its safety and its welfare. May God give us all the strength to do our duty, and the love to do it well, so that justice and kindness may dwell in our land. May God's peace be in our hearts, so that every community of our nation may meet in understanding and respect, united by love of goodness, and keeping far from violence and strife. Together may we work for peace and justice among all nations, and may we and our children live in peace. So may this kingdom find its honour and greatness in the work of redemption, and the building of God's realm here on earth. May such be the Divine will. And let us say Amen.

247 SHABBAT MORNING SERVICE — TORAH SERVICE I

FOR THE STATE OF ISRAEL

אֱלֹהֵינוּ Our God and God of the generations, we ask Your blessing upon the State of Israel and all who dwell in it. Send Your light and Your truth to the leaders of the people, and guide them with wisdom and understanding, so that peace and tranquillity may reign on its borders and in its homes. May the spirit of friendship and understanding remove all fears and heal all wounds. There, may mercy and truth come together for the good of all, so that Your promise is fulfilled: 'for Torah shall come out of Zion and the word of God from Jerusalem.' Amen.

אֱלֹהֵינוּ וֵאלֹהֵי כָּל־הַדּוֹרוֹת שְׁלַח־נָא בִּרְכָתְךָ עַל מְדִינַת יִשְׂרָאֵל וְעַל־כָּל־יוֹשְׁבֶיהָ: שְׁלַח־נָא אוֹרְךָ וַאֲמִתְּךָ לְמַנְהִיגֵי־הָעָם וְהַדְרִיכֵם בְּחָכְמָה וּבִתְבוּנָה כְּדֵי שֶׁיִּשְׂרוֹר שָׁלוֹם בִּגְבוּלוֹתֶיהָ וְשַׁלְוָה בְּבָתֶּיהָ: רוּחַ־אַחֲוָה וַהֲבָנָה הֲדָדִית תְּרַפֵּא כָּל־פֶּצַע וְחַבּוּרָה: תִּקְוַת־עַמָּהּ וַעֲבוֹדַת־בָּנֶיהָ תַּגְשֶׁמְנָה אֶת־חֲזוֹן הַנְּבִיאִים. כִּי מִצִּיּוֹן תֵּצֵא תוֹרָה וּדְבַר־יהוה מִירוּשָׁלָיִם. אָמֵן:

FOR CONSOLATION

אַב Source of mercy, whose all-embracing love is our refuge and our hope, support with tenderness the sorrowing hearts among us. Comfort them with the knowledge that they will be united with those who are dear to them in eternal blessedness. Give them faith and courage and acceptance of Your will. Amen.

אַב הָרַחֲמִים חֲמָל־נָא וְחוּס־נָא עַל הָאֲבֵלִים בְּקִרְבֵּנוּ: נַחֵם אוֹתָם בְּחַסְדְּךָ הַגָּדוֹל חַזְּקֵם בְּתִקְוַת אַלְמָוֶת לַחֲזוֹת בְּנֹעַם בִּרְכוּתֶיךָ בְּחַיֵּי־הַנֶּצַח: יְקַבְּלוּ בִהַכְנָעָה אֶת־מוּסָרְךָ וְיַעֲשׂוּ רְצוֹנְךָ כִּרְצוֹנָם. אָמֵן:

FOR HEALING

אֵל God, may it please You to send healing to those who are in pain or in anxiety. Be their refuge through their time of trial. Make them secure in the knowledge that they will never be forgotten by You, for You are the shield of all who trust in You. Amen.

אֵל מֶלֶךְ נֶאֱמָן הָרוֹפֵא לִשְׁבוּרֵי לֵב וּמְחַבֵּשׁ לְעַצְּבוֹתָם שְׁלַח רְפוּאָה שְׁלֵמָה לְחוֹלֵי עַמֶּךָ: יֵדְעוּ כֻלָּם כִּי זִכְרוֹנָם לְפָנֶיךָ תָּמִיד וְאַתָּה הוּא מָגֵן וּמוֹשִׁיעַ לְכָל הַחוֹסִים בָּךְ. אָמֵן:

FOR THE CONGREGATION

מִי May God who blessed our ancestors, Abraham, Isaac and Jacob, Sarah, Rebecca, Rachel, Leah, bless this holy community with all other holy communities; them, their families and all they have. Bless those who come together to maintain synagogues for prayer, and those who come to pray in them; those who provide Shabbat candles, and wine for *Kiddush* and *Havdalah*; those who share their food with strangers, give charity to the poor, and devote themselves to the needs of society in a true spirit.

May the Sovereign of all worlds bless you and consider you worthy; listen to your prayers and free and release you from all trouble and anxiety. May the kindness of the Merciful One support you and protect you, spreading over you the shelter of peace and planting among you enduring love and kinship, peace and friendship.
May the God of your ancestors increase you and bless you according to the Divine promise. May such be God's will. And let us say Amen.

מִי שֶׁבֵּרַךְ אֲבוֹתֵינוּ אַבְרָהָם יִצְחָק וְיַעֲקֹב וְאִמּוֹתֵינוּ שָׂרָה רִבְקָה רָחֵל וְלֵאָה הוּא יְבָרֵךְ אֶת־כָּל־הַקָּהָל הַקָּדוֹשׁ הַזֶּה עִם כָּל־קְהִלּוֹת הַקֹּדֶשׁ. הֵם וּבְנֵיהֶם וּבְנוֹתֵיהֶם. וְכָל־אֲשֶׁר לָהֶם. וּמִי שֶׁמְּיַחֲדִים בָּתֵּי כְנֵסִיּוֹת לִתְפִלָּה. וּמִי שֶׁבָּאִים בְּתוֹכָם לְהִתְפַּלֵּל. וּמִי שֶׁנּוֹתְנִים נֵר לַמָּאוֹר וְיַיִן לְקִדּוּשׁ וּלְהַבְדָּלָה וּפַת לָאוֹרְחִים וּצְדָקָה לָעֲנִיִּים. וְכָל־מִי שֶׁעוֹסְקִים בְּצָרְכֵי צִבּוּר בֶּאֱמוּנָה:

מֶלֶךְ עוֹלָמִים יְבָרֵךְ אֶתְכֶם וִיזַכֶּה אֶתְכֶם וְיִשְׁמַע קוֹל תְּפִלּוֹתֵיכֶם. וְיִפְדֶּה וְיַצִּיל אֶתְכֶם מִכָּל־צָרָה וְצוּקָה. וְחֶסֶד יהוה יְהִי בְּסַעְדְּכֶם וְיָגֵן בַּעַדְכֶם. וְיִפְרֹשׂ סֻכַּת שְׁלוֹמוֹ עֲלֵיכֶם וְיִטַּע בֵּינֵיכֶם אַהֲבָה וְאַחְוָה שָׁלוֹם וְרֵעוּת לְעוֹלָם:
יהוה אֱלֹהֵי אֲבוֹתֵיכֶם וְאִמּוֹתֵיכֶם יֹסֵף עֲלֵיכֶם כָּכֶם אֶלֶף פְּעָמִים וִיבָרֵךְ אֶתְכֶם כַּאֲשֶׁר דִּבֶּר־לָכֶם. וְכֵן יְהִי רָצוֹן. וְנֹאמַר אָמֵן:

On appropriate occasions a prayer for International Understanding (I),
for Interfaith Understanding (II),
or for Responsibility for Justice and the Environment (III), may be read here.

I

PRAYER FOR INTERNATIONAL UNDERSTANDING

M'kor ha-shalom, Source of peace, be with those who guide the destinies of the world so that an end may come to boasting and vainglory, and the reign of arrogance dwindle in our time. Give them the courage to speak the truth and the humility to listen. Help us all to put the good of our fellow human beings above our own ambitions, and the truth which does not profit us above the lie which does. So may we stand upright, freed from the burden of fear and the weight of suspicion, learning to trust each other.

Help each one of us to bring our own offering of understanding, and our own sacrifice for peace, so that we are at peace with ourselves and live in peace with those around us. Then in tranquillity may we all go forward to build Your realm in the world, until the earth shall be filled with Your knowledge as the waters cover the sea. Amen.

II

PRAYER FOR INTERFAITH UNDERSTANDING

God of all creation, we stand in awe before You, impelled by visions of human harmony. We are children of many traditions - inheritors of shared wisdom and tragic misunderstanding, of proud hopes and humble successes. Now it is time for us to meet - in memory and truth, in courage and trust, in love and promise.

In that which we share, let us see the common prayer of humanity; where we differ, let us wonder at human freedom; in our unity and our differences, let us know the uniqueness that is God.

May our courage match our convictions, and our integrity match our hope.
May our faith in You bring us closer to each other.
May our meeting with past and present bring blessing for the future. Amen.

III

PRAYER FOR RESPONSIBILITY FOR JUSTICE AND THE ENVIRONMENT

We, the family of Israel, live in a world where fears hold our hearts hostage, terror clutches the soul, and real foes or imagined enemies can invade our daily lives. We know how easily our loving-kindness melts away, our sense of justice goes into eclipse. Yet our security comes from You. Let our openness and commitment to the world help transform its future so that we and our children may live in peace. O God, give us courage to face the dangers we see with hope undiminished, for Your name's sake.

We, the family of Israel, carry a sacred responsibility for this our fragile planet, the glory of Your creation. You have made us stewards of the land, protectors of the seas and guardians of the air we breathe. Let us not poison our destiny with selfishness or presumption. Let us draw deep from the living waters of Torah, humbly devoted to respect for all Your creatures and reverence for all Your creation. Let our actions each day help repair Your world, for this is our holy task. O God, help us remember that we are guests in the world, for Your name's sake.

On the Shabbat preceding the New Moon, the following is said:

יְהִי רָצוֹן מִלְּפָנֶיךָ יהוה אֱלֹהֵינוּ וֵאלֹהֵי אֲבוֹתֵינוּ שֶׁתְּחַדֵּשׁ עָלֵינוּ אֶת־הַחֹדֶשׁ הַזֶּה לְטוֹבָה וְלִבְרָכָה. וְתִתֶּן־לָנוּ חַיִּים אֲרֻכִּים. חַיִּים שֶׁל־שָׁלוֹם. חַיִּים שֶׁל־טוֹבָה. חַיִּים שֶׁל־בְּרָכָה. חַיִּים שֶׁל־פַּרְנָסָה. חַיִּים שֶׁל־חִלּוּץ עֲצָמוֹת. חַיִּים שֶׁיֵּשׁ בָּהֶם יִרְאַת שָׁמַיִם וְיִרְאַת חֵטְא: חַיִּים שֶׁאֵין בָּהֶם בּוּשָׁה וּכְלִמָּה. חַיִּים שֶׁל־עֹשֶׁר וְכָבוֹד. חַיִּים שֶׁל אַהֲבַת תּוֹרָה וְיִרְאַת שָׁמַיִם. חַיִּים שֶׁיִּמָּלְאוּ מִשְׁאֲלוֹת לִבֵּנוּ לְטוֹבָה. אָמֵן:

יְהִי Our God, and God of our ancestors, may it be Your will that the new moon come to us for goodness and blessing. May the new month bring us a life of fulfilment and peace, a life of goodness and blessing; a life of sustenance and health; a life filled with awe of God and fear of sin; a life without self-reproach and shame; a life of wealth and honour; a life marked by love of Your teaching and awe of God, when the desires of our hearts may be fulfilled for good. Amen.

יְהִי *Y'hi ratson mill'fanecha Adonai eloheinu v'elohei avoteinu shet'chaddeish aleinu et ha-chodesh ha-zeh l'tovah v'livrachah, v'tittein lanu chayyim aruchim, chayyim shel shalom, chayyim shel tovah, chayyim shel b'rachah, chayyim shel parnasah, chayyim shel chilluts atsamot, chayyim sheyeish bahem yir'at shamayim v'yir'at cheit, chayyim she'ein bahem bushah uch'limmah, chayyim shel osher v'chavod, chayyim shel ahavat torah v'yir'at shamayim, chayyim sheyimmal'u mish'alot libbeinu l'tovah. Amen.*

251 SHABBAT MORNING SERVICE — TORAH SERVICE I

The new moon of _____
will be on _____

רֹאשׁ חֹדֶשׁ _____
יִהְיֶה בְּיוֹם _____

May it come to us and to all Israel for good.

הַבָּא עָלֵינוּ וְעַל כָּל־יִשְׂרָאֵל לְטוֹבָה:

May the Holy One, who is blessed, bring us and all this people, the family of Israel, a new month of life and peace, of happiness and joy, of achievement and consolation. And let us say Amen.

יְחַדְּשֵׁהוּ הַקָּדוֹשׁ בָּרוּךְ הוּא עָלֵינוּ וְעַל כָּל־עַמּוֹ בֵּית יִשְׂרָאֵל לְחַיִּים וּלְשָׁלוֹם. לְשָׂשׂוֹן וּלְשִׂמְחָה. לִישׁוּעָה וּלְנֶחָמָה. וְנֹאמַר אָמֵן.

*Rosh chodesh _____ yihyeh b'yom _____
ha-ba aleinu v'al kol yisra'el l'tovah.
Y'chadd'sheihu ha-kadosh baruch hu aleinu v'al kol ammo beit yisra'el
l'chayyim ul'shalom, l'sason ul'simchah, lishu'ah ul'nechamah, v'nomar amen.*

The service continues here: 🐟

RETURN OF THE SCROLL

יְהַלְלוּ Praise the Almighty
whose name alone is supreme
and whose majesty
is beyond heaven and earth.
You have restored the honour
of Your people,
the praise of those who love You –
the children of Israel, a people
so close to You.
Praise God![1]

יְהַלְלוּ אֶת שֵׁם יהוה.
כִּי נִשְׂגָּב שְׁמוֹ לְבַדּוֹ.
הוֹדוֹ עַל אֶרֶץ וְשָׁמָיִם.
וַיָּרֶם קֶרֶן לְעַמּוֹ.
תְּהִלָּה לְכָל־חֲסִידָיו.
לִבְנֵי יִשְׂרָאֵל עַם קְרוֹבוֹ.
הַלְלוּיָהּ:

*יְהַלְלוּ Y'hal'lu et sheim Adonai, ki nisgav sh'mo l'vaddo.
Hodo al erets v'shamayim, vayarem keren l'ammo, t'hillah l'chol chasidav,
livnei yisra'el am k'rovo, hal'luyah.*

---

[1] Ps 148:13-14.

One of the following Psalms:

כט

Psalm 29

‏^א מִזְמוֹר לְדָוִד
הָבוּ לַיהוה בְּנֵי אֵלִים
הָבוּ לַיהוה כָּבוֹד וָעֹז:
‏^ב הָבוּ לַיהוה כְּבוֹד שְׁמוֹ
הִשְׁתַּחֲווּ לַיהוה
בְּהַדְרַת־קֹדֶשׁ:
‏^ג קוֹל יהוה עַל־הַמָּיִם
אֵל־הַכָּבוֹד הִרְעִים
יהוה עַל־מַיִם רַבִּים:
‏^ד קוֹל־יהוה בַּכֹּחַ
קוֹל יהוה בֶּהָדָר:
‏^ה קוֹל יהוה שֹׁבֵר אֲרָזִים
וַיְשַׁבֵּר יהוה
אֶת־אַרְזֵי הַלְּבָנוֹן:
‏^ו וַיַּרְקִידֵם כְּמוֹ־עֵגֶל
לְבָנוֹן וְשִׂרְיֹן כְּמוֹ בֶן־רְאֵמִים:
‏^ז קוֹל־יהוה חֹצֵב לַהֲבוֹת אֵשׁ:
‏^ח קוֹל יהוה יָחִיל מִדְבָּר.
יָחִיל יהוה מִדְבַּר קָדֵשׁ:
‏^ט קוֹל יהוה יְחוֹלֵל אַיָּלוֹת
וַיֶּחֱשֹׂף יְעָרוֹת.
וּבְהֵיכָלוֹ כֻּלּוֹ אֹמֵר כָּבוֹד:
‏^י יהוה לַמַּבּוּל יָשָׁב
וַיֵּשֶׁב יהוה מֶלֶךְ לְעוֹלָם:
‏^{יא} יהוה עֹז לְעַמּוֹ יִתֵּן
יהוה יְבָרֵךְ אֶת־עַמּוֹ בַשָּׁלוֹם:

‏¹A Psalm of David
הָבוּ Give due honour to God,
divine beings!
Give due honour to
God's awesome power.
‏²Give the honour
that is due to God's name.
Worship God in the beauty of holiness.
‏³God's voice is over the waters,
present in the thunder's crash.
God rules over stormy waters.
‏⁴The voice of God is power!
The voice of God is majesty!
‏⁵The voice of God breaks the cedars;
God shatters the cedars of Lebanon,
‏⁶making them skip like a calf,
Lebanon and Sirion like young oxen.
‏⁷God's voice
splits the lightning shafts,
‏⁸God's voice whirls the desert sand,
God whirls the desert of Kadesh.
‏⁹God's voice
makes the wild deer calve,
it strips the forest bare –
While in God's temple
all cry 'Glory!'
‏¹⁰God was enthroned at the flood;
God is enthroned,
Sovereign forever.
‏¹¹God give strength to Your people,
bless Your people with peace.

^{1}*Mizmor l'david*

הָבוּ Havu ladonai b'nei eilim,
havu ladonai kavod va'oz.
^{2}Havu ladonai k'vod sh'mo,
hishtachavu ladonai b'hadrat kodesh.
^{3}Kol Adonai al ha-mayim, eil ha-kavod hir'im,
Adonai al mayim rabbim.
^{4}Kol Adonai ba-ko'ach,
kol Adonai be-hadar.
^{5}Kol Adonai shoveir arazim,
vay'shabbeir Adonai et arzei ha-l'vanon.
^{6}Vayarkideim k'mo eigel,
l'vanon v'siryon k'mo ven r'eimim.
^{7}Kol Adonai chotzeiv lahavot eish.
^{8}Kol Adonai yachil midbar,
yachil Adonai midbar kadeish.
^{9}Kol Adonai y'choleil ayalot,
vayechesof y'arot uv'heichalo kullo omeir kavod.
^{10}Adonai la-mabul yashav,
vayeishev Adonai melech l'olam.
^{11}Adonai oz l'ammo yittein,
Adonai y'vareich et ammo vashalom.

כט Psalm 29

This Psalm is traditionally used on Shabbat, whereas on those weekdays when the Torah is read, Psalm 24 is recited.

The eighteen mentions of the name of God in this Psalm were traditionally seen as hinting at the eighteen blessings contained in the *Amidah*.

The 'divine beings' of the opening (verses 1-2), literally 'sons of gods', or 'powerful ones', may refer to heavenly creatures that surround God's throne in early, pre-biblical mythology. In verse 9 they are linked to the worshippers in the temple, as both proclaim God's *kavod*, literally 'weightiness', God's presence in and engagement with the world.

Psalm 24

כ

לְדָוִד מִזְמוֹר

[1] David's Psalm.

לַיהוה The earth and its fullness
belong to God,
the world and those who dwell in it,
[2] for it is the Creator
who set it on the seas
and made it firm upon the depths.
[3] Who may ascend the mountain of God
and who may stand in that holy place?
[4] Those whose hands are clean,
whose heart is pure,
who have not given up their soul
to worthless things
nor committed themselves to deception.
[5] They shall earn a blessing from the Creator
and be vindicated by God who saves them.
[6] This is a generation that searches for God,
those who seek Your presence
are the family of Jacob
(selah).

לַיהוה הָאָרֶץ וּמְלוֹאָהּ.
תֵּבֵל וְיֹשְׁבֵי בָהּ:
כִּי־הוּא עַל־יַמִּים יְסָדָהּ.
וְעַל־נְהָרוֹת יְכוֹנְנֶהָ:
מִי־יַעֲלֶה בְהַר־יהוה.
וּמִי־יָקוּם בִּמְקוֹם קָדְשׁוֹ:
נְקִי כַפַּיִם וּבַר־לֵבָב.
אֲשֶׁר לֹא־נָשָׂא לַשָּׁוְא נַפְשִׁי.
וְלֹא נִשְׁבַּע לְמִרְמָה:
יִשָּׂא בְרָכָה מֵאֵת יהוה.
וּצְדָקָה מֵאֱלֹהֵי יִשְׁעוֹ:
זֶה דּוֹר דּוֹרְשָׁיו.
מְבַקְשֵׁי פָנֶיךָ יַעֲקֹב
סֶלָה:

[7] Gates, lift up your heads!
Be raised, you everlasting doors!
Let the Ruler of glory enter!
[8] "Who is this Ruler of glory?"
God, strong and mighty,
God, mighty in battle!

שְׂאוּ שְׁעָרִים רָאשֵׁיכֶם.
וְהִנָּשְׂאוּ פִּתְחֵי עוֹלָם.
וְיָבוֹא מֶלֶךְ הַכָּבוֹד:
מִי זֶה מֶלֶךְ הַכָּבוֹד.
יהוה עִזּוּז וְגִבּוֹר.
יהוה גִּבּוֹר מִלְחָמָה:

[9] Gates, lift up your heads!
Rise up you everlasting doors!
Let the Ruler of glory enter!
[10] "Who then, is this Ruler of glory?"
The God of all creation,
this One alone is the Ruler of glory
(selah)!

שְׂאוּ שְׁעָרִים רָאשֵׁיכֶם.
וּשְׂאוּ פִּתְחֵי עוֹלָם.
וְיָבֹא מֶלֶךְ הַכָּבוֹד:
מִי הוּא זֶה מֶלֶךְ הַכָּבוֹד.
יהוה צְבָאוֹת.
הוּא מֶלֶךְ הַכָּבוֹד.
סֶלָה:

^{1}*L'david mizmor.*
לַיהוָה *Ladonai ha-arets um'lo'ah,*
teiveil v'yosh'vei vah.
^{2}*Ki hu al yammim y'sadah,*
v'al n'harot y'chon'neha.
^{3}*Mi ya'aleh v'har Adonai,*
umi yakum bimkom kodsho.
^{4}*N'ki chappayim uvar leivav,*
asher lo nasa la-shav nafsho,
v'lo nishba l'mirmah.
^{5}*Yissa v'rachah mei'eit Adonai,*
uts'dakah mei'elohei yish'o.
^{6}*Zeh dor dor'shav,*
m'vak'shei fanecha ya'akov, selah.

^{7}*S'u sh'arim rasheichem,*
v'hinnas'u pitchei olam,
v'yavo melech ha-kavod.
^{8}*Mi zeh melech ha-kavod,*
Adonai izzuz v'gibbor,
Adonai gibbor milchamah.

^{9}*S'u sh'arim rasheichem,*
us'u pitchei olam,
v'yavo melech ha-kavod.
^{10}*Mi hu zeh melech ha-kavod,*
Adonai ts'va'ot,
hu melech ha-kavod, selah.

כד **Psalm 24**

This Psalm, traditionally recited on those weekdays when the Torah is read, belongs to the ritual of entering the temple. Those who wish to do so are challenged to examine the purity of their actions and intentions. Verse 6 identifies us with the patriarch Jacob, as part of the succession of generations who seek God's face. Since the text is unclear, others amend it to read 'O God of Jacob'.

The repeated closing section, verses 7-8, 9-10, suggest that the first description of God as a mighty warlike figure is not acceptable for admission to the temple, so a second broader description, as the 'God of all creation', is required. (King David was not allowed to build the temple because his hands had shed blood [I Chron 22:8]). Rabbinic legend has the doors of the newly built temple refusing to admit Solomon until he had mentioned his father David (*Midrash* Psalms 24:10).

סדר קריאת התורה א' | תפלת שחרית לשבת

RETURN OF ISRAEL

One of the following two paragraphs:

I

וּבִנְחֹה And when the ark rested
Moses used to say:
'Return, God,
to the countless
thousands of Israel.'
Rise up to Your place of rest,
You and the ark of Your strength!
Your priests will be clothed
in righteousness
and those who love You
will shout for joy.
For the sake of Your servant David,
do not turn away
the face of Your anointed.
'For I have given you good instruction,
do not forsake My teaching.'
It is a tree of life to all who grasp it
and those who hold fast to it are happy.
Its ways are ways of pleasantness
and all its paths are peace.[1]

וּבְנֻחֹה יֹאמַר:
שׁוּבָה יהוה רִבְבוֹת
אַלְפֵי יִשְׂרָאֵל:
קוּמָה יהוה לִמְנוּחָתֶךָ.
אַתָּה וַאֲרוֹן עֻזֶּךָ:
כֹּהֲנֶיךָ יִלְבְּשׁוּ־צֶדֶק
וַחֲסִידֶיךָ יְרַנֵּנוּ:
בַּעֲבוּר דָּוִד עַבְדֶּךָ.
אַל־תָּשֵׁב פְּנֵי מְשִׁיחֶךָ:
כִּי לֶקַח טוֹב נָתַתִּי לָכֶם.
תּוֹרָתִי אַל־תַּעֲזֹבוּ:
עֵץ־חַיִּים הִיא לַמַּחֲזִיקִים בָּהּ.
וְתֹמְכֶיהָ מְאֻשָּׁר:
דְּרָכֶיהָ דַרְכֵי־נֹעַם.
וְכָל־נְתִיבוֹתֶיהָ שָׁלוֹם:

וּבִנְחֹה Uv'nucho yomar, shuvah Adonai riv'vot alfei yisra'el.
Kumah Adonai limnuchatecha, attah va'aron uzzecha.
Kohanecha yilb'shu tsedek vachasidecha y'ranneinu.
Ba'avur david avdecha, al tasheiv p'nei m'shichecha.
Ki lekach tov natati lachem, torati al ta'azovu.
Eits chayyim hi la-machazikim bah, v'tom'cheha m'ushar.
D'racheha darchei no'am, v'chol n'tivoteha shalom.

וּבִנְחֹה יֹאמַר/שְׁכֹן
And when the Ark rested/Be present ...
    Just as the Torah service began with the imagery of the ark moving forward during the wandering in the wilderness, so we close with the related verse from the Book of Numbers that speaks of the ark resting at the end of each stage of the journey. It was King David who brought the ark into Jerusalem to the site that would later become the temple, and so his memory is evoked here together with the encouragement that the teachings of the Torah become a central part of our lives.

    The alternative passage (the Sephardi equivalent) focuses more on our present situation of Jewish houses of prayer throughout the world and the hope that God's presence can be found here.
    Both passages conclude with the penultimate verse from the Book of Lamentations which commemorates the destruction of Jerusalem by the Babylonians and the beginning of the exile. Yet it points to the hope of restoration, to the renewal of our relationship with God as fruitful and fulfilling as ever in the past.

[1] Num 10:36; Ps 132:8-10; Prov 4:2; 3:18,17.

II

שְׁכֹן Be present among Your people,
and may Your spirit rest
in Your house of prayer.
For every voice and every tongue
will speak of the glory and majesty of
Your kingdom.
'For I have given you good instruction,
do not forsake My teaching.' [1]

שְׁכֹן יהוה בְּתוֹךְ עַמֶּךָ
וְתָנוּחַ רוּחֲךָ בְּבֵית תְּפִלָּתֶךָ.
כִּי כָל־פֶּה וְכָל־לָשׁוֹן
יִתְּנוּ הוֹד וְהָדָר לְמַלְכוּתֶךָ:
כִּי לֶקַח טוֹב נָתַתִּי לָכֶם.
תּוֹרָתִי אַל תַּעֲזֹבוּ:

שְׁכֹן *Sh'chon Adonai b'toch ammecha
v'tanu'ach ruchacha b'veit t'fillatecha,
Ki chol peh v'chol lashon yitt'nu hod v'hadar l'malchutecha.
Ki lekach tov natati lachem, torati al ta'azovu.*

הֲשִׁיבֵנוּ Turn us back to You,
Eternal, and we shall return;
renew our lives as of old. [2]

הֲשִׁיבֵנוּ יהוה אֵלֶיךָ וְנָשׁוּבָה.
חַדֵּשׁ יָמֵינוּ כְּקֶדֶם:

הֲשִׁיבֵנוּ *Hashiveinu Adonai eilecha v'nashuvah, chaddeish yameinu k'kedem.*

Where Musaf *is recited continue on page 275 or 278,
otherwise the service continues on page 306.*

סדר קריאת התורה ב׳
TORAH SERVICE II

The traditional Torah Service is built around the revelation at Sinai, but is based on the triumphal march of the Israelites through the wilderness. This alternative version focuses more directly on the revelation of the Torah and the covenant between God and Israel. Central to these ideas are the way the Torah revives and nourishes those who accept it, and supports our striving for justice in the world.

---

[1] Prov 4:2.   [2] Lam 5:21.

TORAH SERVICE II

Taking out the Scroll(s)

הַקְהֵל Gather the people together, men and women and children, and the stranger who lives with you, that they may learn and revere the Eternal your God.[1]

הַקְהֵל אֶת־הָעָם הָאֲנָשִׁים וְהַנָּשִׁים וְהַטַּף וְגֵרְךָ אֲשֶׁר בִּשְׁעָרֶיךָ לְמַעַן יִשְׁמְעוּ וּלְמַעַן יִלְמְדוּ וְיָרְאוּ אֶת־יְהוָֹה אֱלֹהֵיכֶם:

הַקְהֵל *Hakheil et ha-am, ha-anashim v'ha-nashim v'ha-taf, v'ger'cha asher bish'arecha, l'ma'an yishm'u ul'ma'an yilm'du, v'yar'u et Adonai eloheichem.*

תּוֹרַת The Torah of the Eternal is perfect,
reviving the soul.
The testimony of the Eternal is sure,
making wise the simple.
The duties of the Eternal are right,
rejoicing the heart.
The commandment of the Eternal is clear,
enlightening the eyes.
The fear of the Eternal is pure,
enduring forever.
The judgments of the Eternal are true,
all of them just.[2]

תּוֹרַת יְהוָֹה תְּמִימָה
מְשִׁיבַת נָפֶשׁ
עֵדוּת יְהוָֹה נֶאֱמָנָה
מַחְכִּימַת פֶּתִי:
פִּקּוּדֵי יְהוָֹה יְשָׁרִים
מְשַׂמְּחֵי־לֵב
מִצְוַת יְהוָֹה בָּרָה
מְאִירַת עֵינָיִם:
יִרְאַת יְהוָֹה טְהוֹרָה
עוֹמֶדֶת לָעַד
מִשְׁפְּטֵי־יְהוָֹה אֱמֶת
צָדְקוּ יַחְדָּו:

תּוֹרַת *Torat Adonai t'mimah, m'shivat nafesh*
Eidut Adonai ne'emanah, machkimat peti.
Pikkudei Adonai y'sharim, m'samm'chei leiv
Mitsvat Adonai barah, m'irat einayim.
Yir'at Adonai t'horah, omedet la'ad
Mishp'tei Adonai emet, tsad'ku yachdav.

---

[1] Deut 31:12. [2] Ps 19:8-10.

259 SHABBAT MORNING SERVICE — TORAH SERVICE II

בָּרוּךְ Blessed is the One who
in holiness gave Torah to Israel.
Hear O Israel, God alone is our God,
One God alone.
Our God is One. Our Sovereign is great.
Holy is God's name.

בָּרוּךְ שֶׁנָּתַן תּוֹרָה
לְעַמּוֹ יִשְׂרָאֵל בִּקְדֻשָּׁתוֹ:
שְׁמַע יִשְׂרָאֵל יהוה אֱלֹהֵינוּ
יהוה אֶחָד:
אֶחָד אֱלֹהֵינוּ גָּדוֹל אֲדוֹנֵנוּ
קָדוֹשׁ שְׁמוֹ:

Declare with me the greatness of God,
and let us exalt God's name together.[1]

גַּדְּלוּ לַיהוה אִתִּי.
וּנְרוֹמְמָה שְׁמוֹ יַחְדָּו:

בָּרוּךְ *Baruch shennatan torah l'ammo yisra'el bikdushato.*
Sh'ma yisra'el, Adonai eloheinu Adonai echad.
Echad eloheinu, gadol adoneinu, kadosh sh'mo.

Gad'lu ladonai itti, un'rom'mah sh'mo yachdav.

Procession - one of the following two passages may be sung:

I

טוֹב It is good to give thanks to the Eternal,
to praise Your name, God beyond all,
to tell of Your love in the morning
and Your faithfulness every night.
With the ten-stringed lute, with the lyre,
with the gentle sound of the harp.
For You made me rejoice
in Your deeds, O God,
at the works of Your hand I sing out.[2]

טוֹב לְהֹדוֹת לַיהוה
וּלְזַמֵּר לְשִׁמְךָ עֶלְיוֹן:
לְהַגִּיד בַּבֹּקֶר חַסְדֶּךָ
וֶאֱמוּנָתְךָ בַּלֵּילוֹת:
עֲלֵי־עָשׂוֹר וַעֲלֵי־נָבֶל
עֲלֵי הִגָּיוֹן בְּכִנּוֹר:
כִּי שִׂמַּחְתַּנִי יהוה בְּפָעֳלֶךָ
בְּמַעֲשֵׂי יָדֶיךָ אֲרַנֵּן:

טוֹב *Tov l'hodot ladonai, ul'zammeir l'shimcha elyon.*
L'haggid ba-boker chasdecha, ve'emunat'cha ba-leilot.
Alei asor va'alei navel, alei higgayon b'chinnor.
Ki simmachtani Adonai b'fo'olecha, b'ma'asei yadecha arannein.

---

[1] Ps 34:4.   [2] Ps 92:2-5.

II

צַדִּיק The righteous shall flourish like the palm tree, grow tall like a cedar in Lebanon. Planted in the house of their Maker they shall flourish in the courts of our God, bearing new fruit in old age still full of sap and still green, to declare that the Creator is faithful my Rock in Whom there is no wrong.[1]

צַדִּיק כַּתָּמָר יִפְרָח
כְּאֶרֶז בַּלְּבָנוֹן יִשְׂגֶּה:
שְׁתוּלִים בְּבֵית יהוה
בְּחַצְרוֹת אֱלֹהֵינוּ יַפְרִיחוּ:
עוֹד יְנוּבוּן בְּשֵׂיבָה
דְּשֵׁנִים וְרַעֲנַנִּים יִהְיוּ:
לְהַגִּיד כִּי־יָשָׁר יהוה
צוּרִי וְלֹא־עַוְלָתָה בּוֹ:

צַדִּיק Tsaddik ka-tamar yifrach, k'erez ba-l'vanon yisgeh.
Sh'tulim b'veit Adonai, b'chatsrot eloheinu yafrichu.
Od y'nuvun b'seivah, d'sheinim v'ra'ananim yihyu.
L'haggid ki yashar Adonai, tsuri v'lo avlatah bo.

During G'lilah:

הוֹי Come all who are thirsty,
come to the water,
and if you have no money,
come and buy and eat:
buy wine and milk
with no money and no price.
Why spend money for what is not bread
and your labour without satisfaction?
Listen and come to Me,
hear and your soul shall live.
Seek God who is there to be found,
call out for God is near.

הוֹי כָּל־צָמֵא לְכוּ לַמַּיִם
וַאֲשֶׁר אֵין־לוֹ כָּסֶף
לְכוּ שִׁבְרוּ וֶאֱכֹלוּ
וּלְכוּ שִׁבְרוּ בְּלוֹא־כֶסֶף
וּבְלוֹא מְחִיר יַיִן וְחָלָב:
לָמָּה תִשְׁקְלוּ־כֶסֶף בְּלוֹא־לֶחֶם
וִיגִיעֲכֶם בְּלוֹא לְשָׂבְעָה
הַטּוּ אָזְנְכֶם וּלְכוּ אֵלַי
שִׁמְעוּ וּתְחִי נַפְשְׁכֶם:
דִּרְשׁוּ יהוה בְּהִמָּצְאוֹ
קְרָאֻהוּ בִּהְיוֹתוֹ קָרוֹב:

<<<

הוֹי Hoi kol tsamei l'chu la-mayim, va'asher ein lo kasef, l'chu shivru ve'echolu,
ul'chu shivru b'lo chesef, uv'lo m'chir yayin v'chalav.
Lamah tishk'lu chesef b'lo lechem, vigi'achem b'lo l'sov'ah, hattu ozn'chem ul'chu
eilai, shim'u ut'chi nafsh'chem. Dirshu Adonai b'himats'o, k'ra'uhu bihyoto karov.

---

[1] Ps 92:13-16.

Let the wicked forsake their way	יַעֲזֹב רָשָׁע דַּרְכּוֹ
and those who plot harm their thoughts,	וְאִישׁ אָוֶן מַחְשְׁבֹתָיו
let them turn back to the Merciful One	וְיָשֹׁב אֶל־יהוה
who will take pity on them,	וִירַחֲמֵהוּ
to our God who is generous to forgive.	וְאֶל־אֱלֹהֵינוּ כִּי־יַרְבֶּה לִסְלוֹחַ:
God has said:	כֹּה אָמַר יהוה
Care for justice and do what is right,	שִׁמְרוּ מִשְׁפָּט וַעֲשׂוּ צְדָקָה
for My salvation is about to come	כִּי־קְרוֹבָה יְשׁוּעָתִי לָבוֹא
and My righteousness to appear.	וְצִדְקָתִי לְהִגָּלוֹת:
Happy are those who do this	אַשְׁרֵי אֱנוֹשׁ יַעֲשֶׂה־זֹּאת
and all who grasp it,	וּבֶן־אָדָם יַחֲזִיק בָּהּ
caring for the Shabbat	שֹׁמֵר שַׁבָּת מֵחַלְּלוֹ
without dishonouring it,	
and keeping far from doing evil.[1]	וְשֹׁמֵר יָדוֹ מֵעֲשׂוֹת כָּל־רָע:

Ya'azov rasha darko, v'ish aven machsh'votav,
v'yashov el Adonai virachameihu, v'el eloheinu ki yarbeh lislo'ach.
Ko amar Adonai, shimru mishpat va'asu ts'dakah,
ki k'rovah y'shu'ati lavo, v'tsidkati l'higgalot.
Ashrei enosh ya'aseh zot, uven adam yachazik bah, shomeir shabbat meichall'lo,
v'shomeir yado me'asot kol ra.

Lifting the Scroll:

כִּי For this is the covenant	כִּי זֹאת הַבְּרִית
which I will make with Israel:	אֲשֶׁר אֶכְרֹת אֶת־בֵּית יִשְׂרָאֵל
I will set my Torah within them	נָתַתִּי אֶת־תּוֹרָתִי בְּקִרְבָּם
and write it on their hearts.	וְעַל־לִבָּם אֶכְתֲּבֶנָּה
I shall be their God	וְהָיִיתִי לָהֶם לֵאלֹהִים
and they will be My people;	וְהֵמָּה יִהְיוּ־לִי לְעָם:
All of them will know Me.[2]	כִּי־כוּלָּם יֵדְעוּ אוֹתִי:

כִּי *Ki zot ha-b'rit asher echrot et beit yisra'el,*
natatti et torati b'kirbam, v'al libbam echtavennah,
v'hayiti lahem leilohim, v'heimah yihyu li l'am.
Ki chullam yeid'u oti.

---

[1] Isa 55:1-3,6-7;56:1-2.   [2] Jer 31:33-34.

Before reading the Torah:

בָּרְכוּ אֶת יהוה הַמְבֹרָךְ:

בָּרְכוּ Bless the Living God whom we are called to bless.

בָּרוּךְ יהוה הַמְבֹרָךְ לְעוֹלָם וָעֶד:

בָּרוּךְ Blessed is the Living God, whom we are called to bless forever and ever.

בָּרוּךְ אַתָּה יהוה אֱלֹהֵינוּ מֶלֶךְ הָעוֹלָם. אֲשֶׁר בָּחַר־בָּנוּ מִכָּל־הָעַמִּים וְנָתַן־לָנוּ אֶת תּוֹרָתוֹ: בָּרוּךְ אַתָּה יהוה. נוֹתֵן הַתּוֹרָה:

בָּרוּךְ Blessed are You, our Living God, Sovereign of the universe, who chose us from all peoples to give us Your Torah. Blessed are You God, who gives us the Torah.

בָּרְכוּ *Bar'chu et Adonai ha-m'vorach.*
בָּרוּךְ *Baruch Adonai ha-m'vorach l'olam va'ed.*
בָּרוּךְ *Baruch attah Adonai eloheinu melech ha-olam, asher bachar banu mikkol ha-ammim, v'natan lanu et torato. Baruch attah Adonai, notein ha-torah.*

After reading the Torah:

בָּרוּךְ אַתָּה יהוה אֱלֹהֵינוּ מֶלֶךְ הָעוֹלָם. אֲשֶׁר נָתַן־לָנוּ תּוֹרַת אֱמֶת וְחַיֵּי עוֹלָם נָטַע בְּתוֹכֵנוּ: בָּרוּךְ אַתָּה יהוה. נוֹתֵן הַתּוֹרָה:

בָּרוּךְ Blessed are You, our Living God, Sovereign of the universe, who gave us the teaching of truth and planted eternal life within us. Blessed are You God, who gives us the Torah.

בָּרוּךְ *Baruch attah Adonai eloheinu melech ha-olam, asher natan lanu torat emet v'chayyei olam nata b'tocheinu. Baruch attah Adonai, notein ha-torah.*

SHABBAT MORNING SERVICE — TORAH SERVICE II

Following the Torah reading:

לֹא This Book of the Torah shall not depart from your mouth; but you shall meditate on it day and night.[1]

לֹא־יָמוּשׁ סֵפֶר הַתּוֹרָה הַזֶּה מִפִּיךָ וְהָגִיתָ בּוֹ יוֹמָם וָלָיְלָה:

לֹא *Lo yamush seifer ha-torah ha-zeh mippicha, v'hagita bo yomam valaylah.*

Before reading the Haftarah:

בָּרוּךְ Blessed are You, our Living God, Sovereign of the universe, who chose good prophets and was pleased by their words, for they were spoken in truth. Blessed are You God, for You chose the Torah, Moses Your servant, Israel Your people and the true and righteous prophets.

בָּרוּךְ אַתָּה יהוה אֱלֹהֵינוּ מֶלֶךְ הָעוֹלָם. אֲשֶׁר בָּחַר בִּנְבִיאִים טוֹבִים וְרָצָה בְדִבְרֵיהֶם הַנֶּאֱמָרִים בֶּאֱמֶת: בָּרוּךְ אַתָּה יהוה. הַבּוֹחֵר בַּתּוֹרָה וּבְמֹשֶׁה עַבְדּוֹ וּבְיִשְׂרָאֵל עַמּוֹ וּבִנְבִיאֵי הָאֱמֶת וָצֶדֶק:

בָּרוּךְ *Baruch attah Adonai eloheinu melech ha-olam, asher bachar binvi'im tovim, v'ratsah v'divreihem ha-ne'emarim be'emet. Baruch attah Adonai, ha-bocheir ba-torah, uv'mosheh avdo, uv'yisra'el ammo, uvinvi'ei ha-emet vatsedek.*

After reading the Haftarah:

עַל For the Torah, for the service, for the prophets and for this Shabbat day which You gave us, our Living God, for holiness and rest, for glory and beauty - for all these, God our Creator, we thank and bless You. May Your name be blessed by the mouth of all living forever and ever. Blessed are You God, who makes the Shabbat holy.

עַל הַתּוֹרָה וְעַל הָעֲבוֹדָה וְעַל הַנְּבִיאִים וְעַל יוֹם הַשַּׁבָּת הַזֶּה שֶׁנָּתַתָּ לָּנוּ יהוה אֱלֹהֵינוּ לִקְדֻשָּׁה וְלִמְנוּחָה לְכָבוֹד וּלְתִפְאָרֶת. עַל הַכֹּל יהוה אֱלֹהֵינוּ אֲנַחְנוּ מוֹדִים לָךְ וּמְבָרְכִים אוֹתָךְ. יִתְבָּרַךְ שִׁמְךָ בְּפִי כָּל־חַי תָּמִיד לְעוֹלָם וָעֶד: בָּרוּךְ אַתָּה יהוה. מְקַדֵּשׁ הַשַּׁבָּת:

עַל *Al ha-torah v'al ha-avodah, v'al ha-n'vi'im, v'al yom ha-shabbat ha-zeh, shennatatta lanu, Adonai eloheinu, likdushah v'limnuchah, l'chavod ul'tif'aret, al ha-kol Adonai eloheinu, anachnu modim lach um'var'chim otach, yitbarach shimcha b'fi chol chai tamid l'olam va'ed. Baruch attah Adonai, m'kaddeish ha-shabbat.*

---

[1] Jos 1:8.

The prayers for the community can be found on pages 246-251.
The procession is introduced with:

אַשְׁרֵי Happy are those whose path is blameless, | אַשְׁרֵי תְמִימֵי־דָרֶךְ
who walk in the way of God's Torah. | הַהֹלְכִים בְּתוֹרַת יהוה׃
Happy are those who keep God's testimonies, | אַשְׁרֵי נֹצְרֵי עֵדֹתָיו
and who seek God with their whole heart.[1] | בְּכָל־לֵב יִדְרְשׁוּהוּ׃

אַשְׁרֵי Ashrei t'mimei darech, ha-hol'chim b'torat Adonai.
Ashrei nots'rei eidotav, b'chol leiv yidr'shuhu.

One of the following:

I

Psalm 150 — **קנ**

[1]**הַלְלוּיָהּ** Hallelujah - Praise God! | הַלְלוּיָהּ
Give praise to God in God's holy place, | הַלְלוּ־אֵל בְּקָדְשׁוֹ
praise in God's mighty heavens, | הַלְלוּהוּ בִּרְקִיעַ עֻזּוֹ׃
[2]praise for God's powerful deeds, | הַלְלוּהוּ בִגְבוּרֹתָיו
praise for God's surpassing greatness. | הַלְלוּהוּ כְּרֹב גֻּדְלוֹ׃
[3]Give praise to God with the *shofar* blast; | הַלְלוּהוּ בְּתֵקַע שׁוֹפָר
praise with the lyre and harp, | הַלְלוּהוּ בְּנֵבֶל וְכִנּוֹר׃
[4]praise with drums and dancing, | הַלְלוּהוּ בְּתֹף וּמָחוֹל
praise with the lute and pipe. | הַלְלוּהוּ בְּמִנִּים וְעוּגָב׃
[5]Give praise to God | הַלְלוּהוּ בְצִלְצְלֵי־שָׁמַע
with the clash of cymbals, | הַלְלוּהוּ בְּצִלְצְלֵי תְרוּעָה׃
praise with the clanging cymbals. |
[6]Let everything that has breath | כֹּל הַנְּשָׁמָה תְּהַלֵּל יָהּ
praise God. |
Hallelujah - Praise God! | הַלְלוּיָהּ

[1]**הַלְלוּיָהּ** Hal'luyah
Hal'lu eil b'kodsho, hal'luhu birki'a uzzo.
[2]Hal'luhu bigvurotav, hal'luhu k'rov guddlo.
[3]Hal'luhu b'teika shofar, hal'luhu b'neivel v'chinnor.
[4]Hal'luhu b'tof umachol, hal'luhu b'minnim v'ugav.
[5]Hal'luhu b'tsilts'lei shama, hal'luhu b'tsilts'lei t'ru'ah.
[6]Kol ha-n'shamah t'halleil yah.
Hal'luyah.

---
[1] Ps 119:1-2.

SHABBAT MORNING SERVICE — TORAH SERVICE II

II

רַנְּנוּ Sing out to God, you who are just,
such praise is right for upright people.
Give thanks to God on the harp,
playing on the ten-stringed lute.
Sing to God a song that is new,
play it aloud with shouts of joy.
For God's word is honest,
and all God's works can be trusted.[1]

רַנְּנוּ צַדִּיקִים בַּיהוה
לַיְשָׁרִים נָאוָה תְהִלָּה:
הוֹדוּ לַיהוה בְּכִנּוֹר
בְּנֵבֶל עָשׂוֹר זַמְּרוּ־לוֹ:
שִׁירוּ לוֹ שִׁיר חָדָשׁ
הֵיטִיבוּ נַגֵּן בִּתְרוּעָה:
כִּי־יָשָׁר דְּבַר־יהוה
וְכָל־מַעֲשֵׂהוּ בֶּאֱמוּנָה:

> רַנְּנוּ *Rann'nu tsaddikim badonai, la-y'sharim navah t'hillah.*
> *Hodu ladonai b'chinnor, b'neivel asor zamm'ru lo.*
> *Shiru lo shir chadash, heitivu naggein bitru'ah.*
> *Ki yashar d'var Adonai, v'chol ma'aseihu be'emunah.*

Return of the Scroll(s) to the ark:

שׁוּבָה Return to us, God! How long?
And relent concerning Your servants.
May the favour of the Eternal
our God be upon us,
to support us in the work we do,
And support the work we do.
For this commandment
which I place upon you today
is not too wonderful for you
nor too remote.
For it is something very near to you,
it is in your mouth
and in your heart to do it.[2]

שׁוּבָה יהוה עַד־מָתָי
וְהִנָּחֵם עַל־עֲבָדֶיךָ:
וִיהִי נֹעַם אֲדֹנָי אֱלֹהֵינוּ עָלֵינוּ
וּמַעֲשֵׂה יָדֵינוּ כּוֹנְנָה עָלֵינוּ
וּמַעֲשֵׂה יָדֵינוּ כּוֹנְנֵהוּ:
כִּי הַמִּצְוָה הַזֹּאת
אֲשֶׁר אָנֹכִי מְצַוְּךָ הַיּוֹם
לֹא־נִפְלֵאת הִיא מִמְּךָ
וְלֹא־רְחֹקָה הִיא:
כִּי־קָרוֹב אֵלֶיךָ הַדָּבָר מְאֹד
בְּפִיךָ וּבִלְבָבְךָ לַעֲשֹׂתוֹ:

> שׁוּבָה *Shuvah Adonai, ad matai, v'hinnacheim al avadecha.*
> *Vihi no'am Adonai eloheinu aleinu,*
> *Uma'aseih yadeinu kon'nah aleinu,*
> *Uma'aseih yadeinu kon'neihu.*
> *Ki ha-mitsvah ha-zot asher anochi m'tsav'cha ha-yom,*
> *Lo nifleit hi mimm'cha, v'lo r'chokah hi.*
> *Ki karov eilecha ha-davar m'od, b'ficha uvilvav'cha la'asoto.*

---

[1] Ps 33:1-4.   [2] Ps 90:13,17; Deut 30:11,14.

הֲשִׁיבֵ֨נוּ Turn us back to You, Eternal, and we shall return; renew our lives as of old.[1]

הֲשִׁיבֵ֨נוּ יְהֹוָה אֵלֶ֨יךָ וְֽנָשׁ֔וּבָה. חַדֵּ֥שׁ יָמֵ֖ינוּ כְּקֶֽדֶם:

הֲשִׁיבֵ֨נוּ *Hashiveinu Adonai eilecha v'nashuvah, chaddeish yameinu k'kedem.*

Where Musaf *is recited continue on page 275 or 278, otherwise the service continues on page 306.*

---

[1] Lam 5:21.

267 SHABBAT MORNING SERVICE — TORAH SERVICE III

על שלשה דברים
העולם עומד
על
התורה העבודה גמילות חסדים

סדר קריאת התורה ג'
TORAH SERVICE III

This third service uses a minimum of ritual so that time can be devoted to studying the Torah text itself or related material. The passages selected to accompany it emphasise the tradition, Biblical and rabbinic, of studying the Torah in public.

If the Torah passage is not read from a scroll, but instead from a printed text, the blessings before and after the reading are not recited.

TORAH SERVICE III

One of the following passages:

עַל Civilisation is based
on three things -
on Torah,
on service
and on loving deeds.[1]

עַל־שְׁלֹשָׁה דְבָרִים
הָעוֹלָם עוֹמֵד:
עַל הַתּוֹרָה
וְעַל הָעֲבוֹדָה
וְעַל גְּמִילוּת חֲסָדִים:

עַל *Al sh'loshah d'varim ha-olam omeid.*
Al ha-torah, v'al ha-avodah, v'al g'milut chasadim.

וְהָאֵר Enlighten our eyes in Your Torah.
Attach our heart to Your commandments.
Unite our hearts to love
and revere Your name
so that we may never be put to shame.

וְהָאֵר עֵינֵינוּ בְּתוֹרָתֶךָ
וְדַבֵּק לִבֵּנוּ בְּמִצְוֹתֶיךָ
וְיַחֵד לְבָבֵנוּ לְאַהֲבָה
וּלְיִרְאָה אֶת־שְׁמֶךָ
שֶׁלֹּא נֵבוֹשׁ וְלֹא נִכָּלֵם
וְלֹא נִכָּשֵׁל לְעוֹלָם וָעֶד:

וְהָאֵר *V'ha'eir eineinu b'toratecha, v'dabbeik libbeinu b'mitsvotecha,*
v'yacheid l'vaveinu l'ahavah, ul'yir'ah et sh'mecha,
shello neivosh v'lo nikkaleim, v'lo nikkasheil l'olam va'ed.

The Scroll is undressed:

וְהַלְוִיִּם While the people remained in their places, the Levites taught them the Torah. They read in the book of the Torah of God, clearly, giving the sense, so that the people understood the reading.[2]

וְהַלְוִיִּם מְבִינִים אֶת־הָעָם לַתּוֹרָה
וְהָעָם עַל־עָמְדָם:
וַיִּקְרְאוּ בַסֵּפֶר בְּתוֹרַת הָאֱלֹהִים
מְפֹרָשׁ וְשׂוֹם שֶׂכֶל וַיָּבִינוּ בַּמִּקְרָא:

וְהַלְוִיִּם *V'ha-l'vi'im m'vinim et ha-am la-torah, v'ha-am al omdam.*
Vayikr'u va-seifer b'torat ha-elohim m'forash, v'som sechel vayavinu ba-mikra.

---

[1] *Pirke Avot* 1:2.   [2] Neh 8:7-8.

SHABBAT MORNING SERVICE — TORAH SERVICE III

*If there is no Torah Scroll, and the passage is read from a book,
the blessings below are omitted.*

Before reading the Torah:

בָּרְכוּ Bless the Living God whom we are called to bless.

בָּרְכוּ אֶת יהוה הַמְבֹרָךְ:

בָּרוּךְ Blessed is the Living God, whom we are called to bless forever and ever.

בָּרוּךְ יהוה הַמְבֹרָךְ לְעוֹלָם וָעֶד:

בָּרוּךְ Blessed are You, our Living God, Sovereign of the universe, who chose us from all peoples to give us Your Torah. Blessed are You God, who gives us the Torah.

בָּרוּךְ אַתָּה יהוה אֱלֹהֵינוּ מֶלֶךְ הָעוֹלָם. אֲשֶׁר בָּחַר־בָּנוּ מִכָּל־הָעַמִּים וְנָתַן־לָנוּ אֶת תּוֹרָתוֹ: בָּרוּךְ אַתָּה יהוה. נוֹתֵן הַתּוֹרָה:

בָּרְכוּ *Bar'chu et Adonai ha-m'vorach.*
בָּרוּךְ *Baruch Adonai ha-m'vorach l'olam va'ed.*
בָּרוּךְ *Baruch attah Adonai eloheinu melech ha-olam,
asher bachar banu mikkol ha-ammim, v'natan lanu et torato.
Baruch attah Adonai, notein ha-torah.*

After reading the Torah:

בָּרוּךְ Blessed are You, our Living God, Sovereign of the universe, who gave us the teaching of truth and planted eternal life within us. Blessed are You God, who gives us the Torah.

בָּרוּךְ אַתָּה יהוה אֱלֹהֵינוּ מֶלֶךְ הָעוֹלָם. אֲשֶׁר נָתַן־לָנוּ תּוֹרַת אֱמֶת וְחַיֵּי עוֹלָם נָטַע בְּתוֹכֵנוּ: בָּרוּךְ אַתָּה יהוה. נוֹתֵן הַתּוֹרָה:

בָּרוּךְ *Baruch attah Adonai eloheinu melech ha-olam,
asher natan lanu torat emet v'chayyei olam nata b'tocheinu.
Baruch attah Adonai, notein ha-torah.*

*If the Haftarah is read, the blessings can be found on pages 242-245.
The prayers for the community can be found on pages 246-251.*

The Scroll is dressed:

וְכֹהֵן גָּדוֹל עוֹמֵד וּמְקַבֵּל וְקוֹרֵא... וְגוֹלֵל אֶת הַתּוֹרָה וּמַנִּיחָהּ בְּחֵיקוֹ וְאוֹמֵר. יוֹתֵר מִמַּה שֶּׁקָּרִיתִי לִפְנֵיכֶם כָּתוּב כָּאן:

וְכֹהֵן In the temple, the High Priest would stand and receive the Torah and read ... Then he would roll the Torah scroll and embracing it proclaim: 'More than what I have read to you is written here.'[1]

וְכֹהֵן V'chohein gadol omeid um'kabbeil v'korei...
v'goleil et ha-torah umannichah b'cheiko v'omeir:
Yoteir mimmah shekkariti lifneichem katuv kan.

קדיש דרבנן

יִתְגַּדַּל וְיִתְקַדַּשׁ שְׁמֵהּ רַבָּא
בְּעָלְמָא דִּי־בְרָא כִרְעוּתֵהּ:
וְיַמְלִיךְ מַלְכוּתֵהּ
בְּחַיֵּיכוֹן וּבְיוֹמֵיכוֹן
וּבְחַיֵּי דִי־כָל־בֵּית יִשְׂרָאֵל
בַּעֲגָלָא וּבִזְמַן קָרִיב.
וְאִמְרוּ אָמֵן:
יְהֵא שְׁמֵהּ רַבָּא מְבָרַךְ
לְעָלַם וּלְעָלְמֵי עָלְמַיָּא:
יִתְבָּרַךְ וְיִשְׁתַּבַּח וְיִתְפָּאַר
וְיִתְרוֹמַם וְיִתְנַשֵּׂא וְיִתְהַדָּר
וְיִתְעַלֶּה וְיִתְהַלָּל
שְׁמֵהּ דִּי־קֻדְשָׁא.
בְּרִיךְ הוּא:

Kaddish d'rabanan

יִתְגַּדַּל Let us magnify and
let us sanctify in this world
the great name of God
whose will created it.
May God's reign come in your
lifetime, and in your days,
and in the lifetime of the family of
Israel - quickly and speedily
may it come. Amen.
**May the greatness of God's being
be blessed from eternity to eternity.**
Let us bless and let us extol,
let us tell aloud and let us raise aloft,
let us set on high and let us honour,
let us exalt and
let us praise the Holy One,
whose name is blessed,

<<<

יִתְגַּדַּל *Yitgaddal v'yitkaddash sh'meih rabba, b'alma di v'ra chiruteih, v'yamlich malchuteih, b'chayyeichon uv'yomeichon uv'chayyei di chol beit yisra'el, ba'agala u'vizman kariv, v'imru amen.* **Y'hei sh'meih rabba m'varach l'alam ul'almei almaya.** *Yitbarach v'yishtabbach v'yitpa'ar v'yitromam v'yitnassei, v'yit-haddar v'yit'alleh v'yit-hallal, sh'meih di kudsha,* **b'rich hu,**

---

[1] Mishnah *Sotah* 7:7.

271 SHABBAT MORNING SERVICE — TORAH SERVICE III

who is far beyond any blessing	לְעֵלָא מִן־כָּל־בִּרְכָתָא
During the Ten Days of Penitence:	*During the Ten Days of Penitence:*
who is far above and beyond any blessing	לְעֵלָא לְעֵלָא מִכָּל־בִּרְכָתָא
or song, any honour	וְשִׁירָתָא תֻּשְׁבְּחָתָא וְנֶחֱמָתָא
or any consolation	דִּי־אֲמִירָן בְּעָלְמָא.
that can be spoken of in this world.	
Amen.	וְאִמְרוּ אָמֵן:
For Israel and for the rabbis,	עַל יִשְׂרָאֵל וְעַל רַבָּנָן
for their pupils,	וְעַל תַּלְמִידֵיהוֹן
and the pupils of their pupils,	וְעַל כָּל־תַּלְמִידֵי תַלְמִידֵיהוֹן
who devote themselves	וְעַל כָּל־מָן דִּי עָסְקִין בְּאוֹרַיְתָא
to the study of Torah,	דִּי בְאַתְרָא הָדֵן
in this place and every other place;	
let there be for them and for you	וְדִי בְּכָל־אֲתַר וַאֲתַר יְהֵא לְהוֹן
great peace and favour,	וּלְכוֹן שְׁלָמָא רַבָּא חִנָּא וְחִסְדָּא
love and mercy,	וְרַחֲמִין וְחַיִּין אֲרִיכִין וּמְזוֹנָא
a life of fulfilment	רְוִיחָא וּפֻרְקָנָא
and of plenty, and redemption	
from their father who is in heaven.	מִן־קֳדָם אֲבוּהוֹן דִּי בִשְׁמַיָּא.
Amen.	וְאִמְרוּ אָמֵן:
May great peace from heaven and	יְהֵא שְׁלָמָא רַבָּא מִן שְׁמַיָּא
the gift of life be granted to us	וְחַיִּים עָלֵינוּ וְעַל־כָּל־יִשְׂרָאֵל.
and to all the family of Israel.	
Amen.	וְאִמְרוּ אָמֵן:
May the Maker of peace	עֹשֶׂה שָׁלוֹם בִּמְרוֹמָיו
in the highest bring this peace	הוּא יַעֲשֶׂה שָׁלוֹם
upon us and upon all Israel	עָלֵינוּ וְעַל כָּל־יִשְׂרָאֵל
and upon all the world.	וְעַל־כָּל־הָעוֹלָם.
Amen.	וְאִמְרוּ אָמֵן:

l'eilla min kol birchata
During the Ten Days of Penitence: l'eilla l'eilla mikol birchata
v'shirata, tushb'chata v'nechemata, di amiran b'alma, v'imru **amen**.
Al yisra'el, v'al rabbanan, v'al talmideihon, v'al kol talmidei talmideihon, v'al kol man di askin b'orayta di b'atra hadein v'di b'chol atar v'atar, y'hei l'hon ul'chon, sh'lama rabba, chinna v'chisda, v'rachamin v'chayyin arichin, um'zona r'vicha ufarkana, min kodam avuhon di vishmaya, v'imru **amen**.
Y'hei sh'lama rabba min sh'maya, v'chayyim aleinu v'al kol yisra'el, v'imru **amen**.
Oseh shalom bimromav, hu ya'aseh shalom aleinu v'al kol yisra'el, *v'al kol ha-olam,* v'imru **amen**.

Following the study, the Torah service may be concluded with the following:

עַל Civilisation is preserved by three things: by truth, by justice and by peace.[1]

עַל־שְׁלֹשָׁה דְבָרִים הָעוֹלָם קַיָּם: עַל־הָאֱמֶת וְעַל־הַדִּין וְעַל־הַשָּׁלוֹם:

עַל *Al sh'loshah d'varim ha-olam kayam.*
Al ha-emet, v'al ha-din, v'al ha-shalom.

Where Musaf is recited continue on page 275 or 278, otherwise the service continues on page 306.

---

[1] Pirke Avot 1:18.

מוסף לשבת
Additional Service for Shabbat ♦346

אֲרֶשֶׁת שְׂפָתֵינוּ
וְהֶגְיוֹן לִבֵּנוּ
כְּקׇרְבָּנוֹת

The prayers of our lips
and the meditation of our heart
replace the sacrifices of old.

On Shabbat and festivals an additional (*musaf*) sacrifice was made in the temple, and when the temple was destroyed and the *Amidah* was instituted, an additional recitation was arranged to coincide with the sacrifice. Some, but not all of the early Reformers, with their rejection of the sacrificial cult and dislike of what they considered to be unnecessary repetitions, omitted the *Musaf* service. In making it an option for this prayer book we have changed the desire for the restoration of the temple cult of the central blessing, emphasising instead how prayer has replaced animal sacrifice and expressing the universal hope that all people can meet in prayer in a restored Jerusalem.

We provide a short version of the *Musaf Amidah* for those who wish to retain a symbolic reminiscence of it, and a full version. If the latter is used, the earlier part of the service will need to be shortened.

חֲצִי קַדִּישׁ
Chatsi Kaddish

יִתְגַּדַּל Let us magnify
and let us sanctify in this world
the great name of God
whose will created it.
May God's reign come in your
lifetime, and in your days,
and in the lifetime of the family of
Israel - quickly and speedily
may it come.
**Amen.
May the greatness of God's being
be blessed from eternity to eternity.**
Let us bless and let us extol,
let us tell aloud and let us raise aloft,
let us set on high and let us honour,
let us exalt and
let us praise the Holy One,
Whose name is blessed,
Who is far beyond any blessing

During the Ten Days of Penitence:
Who is far above and beyond any blessing

or song, any honour
or any consolation
that can be spoken of in this world.
Amen.

יִתְגַּדַּל וְיִתְקַדַּשׁ שְׁמֵהּ רַבָּא
בְּעָלְמָא דִּי־בְרָא כִרְעוּתֵהּ:
וְיַמְלִיךְ מַלְכוּתֵהּ
בְּחַיֵּיכוֹן וּבְיוֹמֵיכוֹן
וּבְחַיֵּי דִי־כָל־בֵּית יִשְׂרָאֵל
בַּעֲגָלָא וּבִזְמַן קָרִיב.
וְאִמְרוּ אָמֵן:
יְהֵא שְׁמֵהּ רַבָּא מְבָרַךְ
לְעָלַם וּלְעָלְמֵי עָלְמַיָּא:
יִתְבָּרַךְ וְיִשְׁתַּבַּח וְיִתְפָּאַר
וְיִתְרוֹמַם וְיִתְנַשֵּׂא וְיִתְהַדָּר
וְיִתְעַלֶּה וְיִתְהַלָּל שְׁמֵהּ דִּי־קֻדְשָׁא.
בְּרִיךְ הוּא.
לְעֵלָּא מִן־כָּל־בִּרְכָתָא

During the Ten Days of Penitence:
לְעֵלָּא לְעֵלָּא מִכָּל־בִּרְכָתָא

וְשִׁירָתָא תֻּשְׁבְּחָתָא וְנֶחֱמָתָא
דַּאֲמִירָן בְּעָלְמָא.
וְאִמְרוּ אָמֵן:

יִתְגַּדַּל Yitgaddal v'yitkaddash sh'meih rabba, b'alma di v'ra chiruteih, v'yamlich malchuteih, b'chayyeichon uv'yomeichon uv'chayyei di chol beit yisra'el, ba'agala u'vizman kariv, v'imru **amen**. **Y'hei sh'meih rabba m'varach l'alam ul'almei almaya**. Yitbarach v'yishtabbach v'yitpa'ar v'yitromam v'yitnassei, v'yit-haddar v'yit'alleh v'yit-hallal sh'meih di kudsha, **b'rich hu**, l'eilla min kol birchata
During the Ten Days of Penitence: l'eilla l'eilla mikol birchata
v'shirata, tushb'chata v'nechemata, di amiran b'alma, v'imru **amen**.

275 SHABBAT ADDITIONAL SERVICE — AMIDAH I

One of the following:

I A SHORTER FORM OF MUSAF AMIDAH

אֲדֹנָי שְׂפָתַי תִּפְתָּח וּפִי יַגִּיד תְּהִלָּתֶךָ:

בָּרוּךְ אַתָּה יהוה אֱלֹהֵינוּ
וֵאלֹהֵי אֲבוֹתֵינוּ   וֵאלֹהֵי אִמּוֹתֵינוּ.
אֱלֹהֵי אַבְרָהָם,   אֱלֹהֵי שָׂרָה.
אֱלֹהֵי יִצְחָק,   אֱלֹהֵי רִבְקָה.
וֵאלֹהֵי יַעֲקֹב,   אֱלֹהֵי רָחֵל
                         וֵאלֹהֵי לֵאָה.
הָאֵל הַגָּדוֹל הַגִּבּוֹר וְהַנּוֹרָא. אֵל עֶלְיוֹן קוֹנֵה בְרַחֲמָיו שָׁמַיִם וָאָרֶץ: מָגֵן אָבוֹת בִּדְבָרוֹ. מְחַיֵּה מֵתִים בְּמַאֲמָרוֹ. הָאֵל הַקָּדוֹשׁ:

During the Ten Days of Penitence:

הַמֶּלֶךְ הַקָּדוֹשׁ:

אֲדֹנָי My God, open my lips and my mouth shall declare Your praise.[1]

בָּרוּךְ Blessed are You, our God, and God of our ancestors,
God of Abraham,   God of Sarah,
God of Isaac,   God of Rebecca,
and God of Jacob,   God of Rachel
                        and God of Leah,
the great, the mighty, and the awesome God, God beyond, shaping both heaven and earth with love and care; whose message was the defence of our ancestors, and whose word brings the dead to life, the Holy God.

During the Ten Days of Penitence: **the holy Sovereign.**

אֲדֹנָי Adonai s'fatai tiftach ufi yaggid t'hillatecha.

בָּרוּךְ Baruch attah Adonai eloheinu
veilohei avoteinu   veilohei immoteinu.
elohei avraham,   elohei sarah,
elohei yitschak,   elohei rivkah,
veilohei ya'akov,   elohei rachel
                        veilohei le'ah.
Ha'eil ha-gadol, ha-gibbor v'ha-nora, eil elyon, koneh v'rachamav shamayim va'arets. Magein avot bidvaro, m'chayyeih meitim b'ma'amaro, ha-eil ha-kadosh.

During the Ten Days of Penitence: ha-melech ha-kadosh.

---
[1] Ps 51:1.

מֵאָז חָרַב מִקְדָשֵׁנוּ וְגָלִינוּ מֵאַרְצֵנוּ הָיוּ אֲרֶשֶׁת שְׂפָתֵינוּ וְהֶגְיוֹן לִבֵּנוּ כְּקָרְבָּנוֹת שֶׁהִקְרִיבוּ לְפָנֶיךָ אֲבוֹתֵינוּ כַּכָּתוּב עַל־יַד נְבִיאֶךָ. הִנֵּה שְׁמֹעַ מִזֶּבַח טוֹב לְהַקְשִׁיב מֵחֵלֶב אֵילִים: יְהִי רָצוֹן מִלְּפָנֶיךָ יהוה אֱלֹהֵינוּ שֶׁנִּרְאֶה בְּיָמֵינוּ שָׁלוֹם בֵּין כָּל־בְּנֵי אַבְרָהָם וְשָׁלוֹם בְּצִיּוֹן וְשַׁלְוָה בִּירוּשָׁלַיִם וְתָכִין בְּתוֹכָהּ מְקוֹם־תְּפִלָּה לְכָל־הָעַמִּים:

מֵאָז Since our temple was destroyed and we were exiled from our land, the prayer of our lips and the meditation of our heart have become like the sacrifices that our ancestors brought before You, as it is prophesied: 'Behold! Listening is better than sacrifices, obeying than the fat of rams.'[1] May it be Your will, our Living God, that we witness in our day peace amongst all the descendants of Abraham, peace in Zion and tranquillity in Jerusalem, a place of prayer for all peoples.

מֵאָז Mei'az chareiv mikdasheinu, v'galinu mei'artseinu, hayu areshet s'fateinu v'hegyon libbeinu k'korbanot shehikrivu l'fanecha avoteinu, ka-katuv al yad n'vi'echa, hinneih sh'mo'a mizzevach tov, l'hakshiv meicheilev eilim. Y'hi ratson mill'fanecha Adonai eloheinu, shennir'eh b'yameinu shalom bein kol b'nei avraham v'shalom b'tsiyyon v'shalvah birushalayim, v'tachin b'tochah m'kom t'fillah l'chol ha-ammim.

רְצֵה יהוה אֱלֹהֵינוּ בְּעַמְּךָ יִשְׂרָאֵל. וְלִתְפִלָּתָם שְׁעֵה: מוֹדִים אֲנַחְנוּ לָךְ עַל כָּל־הַטּוֹבוֹת שֶׁעָשִׂיתָ עִמָּנוּ וְעִם אֲבוֹתֵינוּ. וְאִם אָמַרְנוּ מָטָה רַגְלֵנוּ חַסְדְּךָ יהוה יִסְעָדֵנוּ: שִׂים שָׁלוֹם טוֹבָה וּבְרָכָה עָלֵינוּ: בָּרוּךְ אַתָּה יהוה. הַמְבָרֵךְ אֶת עַמּוֹ יִשְׂרָאֵל בַּשָּׁלוֹם:

רְצֵה Be pleased with Your people Israel and listen to their prayers. We thank You for all the goodness You have done for our ancestors and for us. When we admitted 'Our foot has stumbled,' then Your love supported us. Grant us peace, goodness and blessing. Blessed are You God, blessing Your people with peace.

רְצֵה R'tsei Adonai eloheinu b'amm'cha yisra'el, v'lit'fillatam sh'eih. Modim anachnu lach, al kol ha-tovot she'asita immanu v'im avoteinu, v'im amarnu matah ragleinu, chasd'cha Adonai yisadeinu. Sim shalom tovah uv'rachah aleinu. Baruch attah Adonai, ha-m'vareich et ammo yisra'el ba-shalom.

---

[1] I Sam 15:22.

277 SHABBAT ADDITIONAL SERVICE

AMIDAH I

עֹשֶׂה May the Maker of peace in the highest bring this peace upon us and upon all Israel and upon all the world. Amen.

עֹשֶׂה שָׁלוֹם בִּמְרוֹמָיו. הוּא יַעֲשֶׂה שָׁלוֹם עָלֵינוּ וְעַל כָּל־יִשְׂרָאֵל וְעַל־כָּל־הָעוֹלָם. וְאִמְרוּ. אָמֵן:

עֹשֶׂה *Oseh shalom bimromav hu ya'aseh shalom aleinu v'al kol yisra'el v'al kol ha-olam, v'imru amen.*

The service continues with the Concluding Prayers on page 306.

אֲדֹנָי שְׂפָתַי תִּפְתָּח וּפִי יַגִּיד תְּהִלָּתֶךָ:

בָּרוּךְ אַתָּה יהוה אֱלֹהֵינוּ
וֵאלֹהֵי אֲבוֹתֵינוּ   וֵאלֹהֵי אִמּוֹתֵינוּ.
אֱלֹהֵי אַבְרָהָם   אֱלֹהֵי שָׂרָה.
אֱלֹהֵי יִצְחָק   אֱלֹהֵי רִבְקָה.
וֵאלֹהֵי יַעֲקֹב   אֱלֹהֵי רָחֵל
                          וֵאלֹהֵי לֵאָה.
הָאֵל הַגָּדוֹל הַגִּבּוֹר וְהַנּוֹרָא. אֵל עֶלְיוֹן.
גּוֹמֵל חֲסָדִים טוֹבִים קוֹנֵה הַכֹּל. וְזוֹכֵר חַסְדֵי
אָבוֹת   וְאִמָּהוֹת
וּמֵבִיא גּוֹאֵל לִבְנֵי בְנֵיהֶם לְמַעַן שְׁמוֹ בְּאַהֲבָה:

During the Ten Days of Penitence add:
זָכְרֵנוּ לְחַיִּים. מֶלֶךְ חָפֵץ בַּחַיִּים.
וְכָתְבֵנוּ בְּסֵפֶר הַחַיִּים. לְמַעַנְךָ אֱלֹהִים חַיִּים:

מֶלֶךְ עוֹזֵר וּמוֹשִׁיעַ וּמָגֵן:
בָּרוּךְ אַתָּה יהוה
מָגֵן אַבְרָהָם   פּוֹקֵד שָׂרָה:

אֲדֹנָי *Adonai s'fatai tiftach ufi yaggid t'hillatecha.*

בָּרוּךְ *Baruch attah Adonai eloheinu*
veilohei avoteinu   veilohei immoteinu.
elohei avraham,   elohei sarah,
elohei yitschak,   elohei rivkah,
veilohei ya'akov,   elohei rachel
                          veilohei le'ah.
Ha'eil ha-gadol, ha-gibbor v'ha-nora, eil elyon,
gomeil chasadim tovim, koneih ha-kol. V'zocheir chasdei
avot   v'immahot
u'meivi go'eil livnei v'neihem l'ma'an sh'mo b'ahavah.
  During the Ten Days of Penitence add: Zochreinu l'chayyim,
  melech chafeits ba-chayyim, v'chotveinu b'seifer ha-chayyim,
  l'ma'ancha elohim chayyim.
Melech ozeir u'moshi'a umagein.
Baruch attah Adonai,
magein avraham   pokeid sarah.

II *A FULLER FORM OF* MUSAF AMIDAH

אֲדֹנָי My God, open my lips and my mouth shall declare Your praise.[1]

GOD OF HISTORY

בָּרוּךְ Blessed are You, our God, and God of our ancestors,

God of Abraham,	God of Sarah,
God of Isaac,	God of Rebecca,
and God of Jacob,	God of Rachel
	and God of Leah,

the great, the mighty, and the awesome God, God beyond, generous in love and kindness, and possessing all. You remember the good deeds of those before us, and therefore in love bring rescue to the generations, for such is Your being.

> *During the Ten Days of Penitence add:*
> Sovereign Who delights in life, recall us to life and record us in the Book of Life for Your own sake, God of life!

The Sovereign who helps and saves and shields.
Blessed are You God,
who shields Abraham   who remembers Sarah.

---

[1] Ps 51:17.

אַתָּה גִּבּוֹר לְעוֹלָם אֲדֹנָי. מְחַיֵּה מֵתִים אַתָּה. רַב לְהוֹשִׁיעַ:
In winter מַשִּׁיב הָרוּחַ וּמוֹרִיד הַגֶּשֶׁם:
In summer מוֹרִיד הַטָּל:
מְכַלְכֵּל חַיִּים בְּחֶסֶד. מְחַיֵּה מֵתִים בְּרַחֲמִים רַבִּים. סוֹמֵךְ נוֹפְלִים. וְרוֹפֵא חוֹלִים. וּמַתִּיר אֲסוּרִים. וּמְקַיֵּם אֱמוּנָתוֹ לִישֵׁנֵי עָפָר: מִי כָמוֹךָ בַּעַל גְּבוּרוֹת וּמִי דּוֹמֶה לָּךְ. מֶלֶךְ מֵמִית וּמְחַיֶּה וּמַצְמִיחַ יְשׁוּעָה:

During the Ten Days of Penitence add:
מִי כָמוֹךָ אַב הָרַחֲמִים. זוֹכֵר יְצוּרָיו לְחַיִּים בְּרַחֲמִים:

וְנֶאֱמָן אַתָּה לְהַחֲיוֹת מֵתִים. בָּרוּךְ אַתָּה יהוה. מְחַיֵּה הַמֵּתִים:

GOD OF MIGHT

אַתָּה You are the endless power that renews life beyond death; You are the greatness that saves.

> In winter months from Shemini Atzeret to Pesach: making the wind blow and the rain fall. In summer months from Pesach to Shemini Atzeret: causing the dew to fall.

You care for the living with love. You renew life beyond death with unending mercy. You support the falling, and heal the sick. You free prisoners, and keep faith with those who sleep in the dust. Who can perform such mighty deeds, and who can compare with You, a Sovereign who brings death and life, and renews salvation?

> During the Ten Days of Penitence add: Who is like You, source of compassion, recalling Your creatures to life in compassion?

You are faithful to renew life beyond death. Blessed are You God, who renews life beyond death.

אַתָּה *Attah gibbor l'olam Adonai, mechayyeih meitim attah rav l'hoshi'a.*
> *In winter:* Mashiv ha-ru'ach, u'morid ha-gashem. *In summer:* Morid ha-tal.

M'chalkeil chayyim b'chesed, m'chayyeih meitim b'rachamim rabbim, someich noflim, v'rofeih cholim, umattir asurim, um'kayyeim emunato lisheinei afar. Mi chamocha ba'al g'vurot, umi domeh lach, melech meimit um'chayyeh, u'matsmi'ach y'shu'ah.

> *During the Ten Days of Penitence add:*
> Mi chamocha av ha-rachamim, zocheir y'tsurav l'chayyim b'rachamim.

V'ne'eman attah l'hachayot meitim. Baruch attah Adonai, m'chayyeih ha-meitim.

SHABBAT ADDITIONAL SERVICE — AMIDAH II

GOD OF HOLINESS

נַעֲרִיצְךָ We worship and sanctify You as they sanctify You in the highest heavens. As it is written by the hand of Your prophet, 'And they called to each other and said:

Holy, holy, holy is the Creator of all, whose glory fills all the earth.'[1]

God's glory fills the universe. Your servants ask each other, 'Where is the place of Your glory?' They cry in answer, 'Blessed …'

Blessed is God's glory, revealed in every place.[2]
May You turn from Your place in mercy, and be gracious to the people who in love declare Your unity twice each day, evening and morning, with the words of the *Sh'ma* …

Hear O Israel, God alone is our God, One God alone.[3]

Our God is One, our source of life, our Sovereign, our deliverer who will repeat to us in mercy, in the presence of all living, the promise to be your God.

נַעֲרִיצְךָ וְנַקְדִּישְׁךָ כְּשֵׁם שֶׁמַּקְדִּישִׁים אוֹתוֹ בִּשְׁמֵי מָרוֹם. כַּכָּתוּב עַל יַד נְבִיאֶךָ. וְקָרָא זֶה אֶל זֶה וְאָמַר.

קָדוֹשׁ קָדוֹשׁ קָדוֹשׁ יהוה צְבָאוֹת. מְלֹא כָל־הָאָרֶץ כְּבוֹדוֹ:

כְּבוֹדוֹ מָלֵא עוֹלָם מְשָׁרְתָיו שׁוֹאֲלִים זֶה לָזֶה אַיֵּה מְקוֹם כְּבוֹדוֹ. לְעֻמָּתָם בָּרוּךְ יֹאמֵרוּ:

בָּרוּךְ כְּבוֹד יהוה מִמְּקוֹמוֹ:

מִמְּקוֹמוֹ הוּא יִפֶן בְּרַחֲמִים וְיָחוֹן עַם הַמְיַחֲדִים שְׁמוֹ עֶרֶב וָבֹקֶר בְּכָל־יוֹם תָּמִיד פַּעֲמַיִם בְּאַהֲבָה שְׁמַע אוֹמְרִים:

שְׁמַע יִשְׂרָאֵל יהוה אֱלֹהֵינוּ יהוה אֶחָד:

אֶחָד הוּא אֱלֹהֵינוּ הוּא אָבִינוּ הוּא מַלְכֵּנוּ הוּא מוֹשִׁיעֵנוּ. וְהוּא יַשְׁמִיעֵנוּ בְּרַחֲמָיו שֵׁנִית לְעֵינֵי כָּל־חַי לִהְיוֹת לָכֶם לֵאלֹהִים:

<<<

נַעֲרִיצְךָ Na'arits'cha v'nakdish'cha k'sheim shemakdishim oto bishmei marom, ka-katuv al yad n'vi'echa, v'kara zeh el zeh v'amar.
Kadosh kadosh kadosh, Adonai ts'va'ot, m'lo chol ha-arets k'vodo.
K'vodo malei olam, m'shar'tav sho'alim zeh la-zeh: ayeih m'kom k'vodo, l'ummatam baruch yomeiru.
Baruch k'vod Adonai mimm'komo.
Mimm'komo hu yifen b'rachamim, v'yachon am ha-m'yachadim sh'mo, erev vavoker b'chol yom tamid, pa'amayim b'ahavah, sh'ma om'rim.
Sh'ma yisra'el, Adonai eloheinu, Adonai echad.
Echad hu eloheinu, hu avinu, hu malkeinu, hu moshi'einu, v'hu yashmi'einu b'rachamav sheinit l'einei kol chai, lihyot lachem leilohim.

---

[1] Is 6:3.
[2] Ezek 3:12.
[3] Deut 6:4.

I am your God, the Eternal!⁴

אֲנִי יהוה אֱלֹהֵיכֶם:

And in Your holy writing it is said:

וּבְדִבְרֵי קָדְשְׁךָ כָּתוּב לֵאמֹר:

The Almighty shall rule forever! Your God, O Zion, for all generations! Praise God!⁵

יִמְלֹךְ יהוה לְעוֹלָם. אֱלֹהַיִךְ צִיּוֹן לְדֹר וָדֹר הַלְלוּיָהּ:

We declare Your greatness to all generations, and to all eternity we proclaim Your holiness. Your praise shall never depart from our mouth, for You are God, the great and holy Sovereign.

לְדוֹר וָדוֹר נַגִּיד גָּדְלֶךָ. וּלְנֵצַח נְצָחִים קְדֻשָּׁתְךָ נַקְדִּישׁ. וְשִׁבְחֲךָ אֱלֹהֵינוּ מִפִּינוּ לֹא יָמוּשׁ לְעוֹלָם וָעֶד. כִּי אֵל מֶלֶךְ גָּדוֹל וְקָדוֹשׁ אָתָּה.

Blessed are You, the holy God
During the Ten Days of Penitence:
the holy Sovereign.¹

בָּרוּךְ אַתָּה יהוה. הָאֵל הַקָּדוֹשׁ:
During the Ten Days of Penitence:
הַמֶּלֶךְ הַקָּדוֹשׁ:

Ani Adonai eloheichem.
Uv'divrei kodsh'cha katuv leimor.
Yimloch Adonai l'olam, elohayich tsiyyon l'dor vador hal'luyah.
L'dor vador naggid godlecha, ul'neitsach n'tsachim k'dushat'cha nakdish, v'shivchacha eloheinu mipinu lo yamush l'olam va'ed, ki eil melech gadol v'kadosh attah.
Baruch attah Adonai ha-eil ha-kadosh.
   During the Ten Days of Penitence: **ha-melech ha-kadosh.**

---

⁴ Num 15:41. ⁵ Ps 146:10.

HOLINESS OF SHABBAT

תִּכַּנְתָּ You established the Shabbat, accepted its sacrifices, commanding its practices and offerings. Those who delight in it will inherit eternal honour, those who taste it earn eternal life and those who love its teachings have chosen greatness. But since our temple was destroyed and we were exiled from our land, the prayer of our lips and the meditation of our heart have become like the sacrifices that our ancestors brought before You, as it is prophesied: 'Behold! Listening is better than sacrifices, obeying than the fat of rams.'[1] And it is written: 'The sacrifices of God are a broken spirit; a heart that is broken and crushed, God, You will not despise.'[2] May it be Your will, our Living God, that we witness in our day peace amongst all the descendants of Abraham, peace in Zion and tranquility in Jerusalem, a place of prayer for all peoples.

תִּכַּנְתָּ שַׁבָּת רָצִיתָ קָרְבְּנוֹתֶיהָ.
צִוִּיתָ פֵּרוּשֶׁיהָ עִם סִדּוּרֵי נְסָכֶיהָ.
מְעַנְגֶּיהָ לְעוֹלָם כָּבוֹד יִנְחָלוּ.
טוֹעֲמֶיהָ חַיִּים זָכוּ. וְגַם הָאוֹהֲבִים דְּבָרֶיהָ גְּדֻלָּה בָּחָרוּ:
וּמֵאָז חָרַב מִקְדָּשֵׁנוּ וְגָלִינוּ מֵאַרְצֵנוּ הָיוּ אֲרֶשֶׁת שְׂפָתֵינוּ וְהֶגְיוֹן לִבֵּנוּ כְּקָרְבָּנוֹת שֶׁהִקְרִיבוּ לְפָנֶיךָ אֲבוֹתֵינוּ כַּכָּתוּב עַל־יַד נְבִיאֶךָ. הִנֵּה שְׁמֹעַ מִזֶּבַח טוֹב לְהַקְשִׁיב מֵחֵלֶב אֵילִים: וְכָתוּב. זִבְחֵי אֱלֹהִים רוּחַ נִשְׁבָּרָה. לֵב נִשְׁבָּר וְנִדְכֶּה אֱלֹהִים לֹא תִבְזֶה:
יְהִי רָצוֹן לְפָנֶיךָ יהוה אֱלֹהֵינוּ שֶׁנִּרְאֶה בְיָמֵינוּ שָׁלוֹם בֵּין כָּל־בְּנֵי אַבְרָהָם וְשָׁלוֹם בְּצִיּוֹן וְשַׁלְוָה בִּירוּשָׁלַיִם וְתָכִין בְּתוֹכָהּ מְקוֹם־תְּפִלָּה לְכָל־הָעַמִּים:

תִּכַּנְתָּ Tikkanta shabbat ratsita korb'noteha, tsivita peirusheha im siddurei n'sacheha, m'ann'geha l'olam kavod yinchalu, to'ameha chayyim zachu, v'gam ha-ohavim d'vareha g'dullah bacharu. Umei'az chareiv mikdasheinu, v'galinu mei'artseinu, hayu areshet s'fateinu v'hegyon libbeinu k'korbanot shehikrivu l'fanecha avoteinu, kakatuv al yad n'vi'echa, hinneih sh'mo'a mizzevach tov, l'hakshiv meichelev eilim. V'chatuv, zivchei elohim ru'ach nishbarah, leiv nishbar v'nidkeh elohim lo tivzeh. Y'hi ratson l'fanecha Adonai eloheinu shennir'eh b'yameinu shalom bein kol b'nei avraham, v'shalom b'tsiyyon v'shalvah birushalayim, v'tachin b'tochah m'kom t'fillah l'chol ha-ammim.

תִּכַּנְתָּ You established ...
Rather than seeking to restore temple sacrifice, this version based on texts of the Israel Reform movement and our additions expresses a universal hope.

[1] I Sam 15:22.
[2] Ps 51:19.

יִשְׂמְחוּ בְמַלְכוּתְךָ שׁוֹמְרֵי שַׁבָּת וְקוֹרְאֵי עֹנֶג: עַם מְקַדְּשֵׁי שְׁבִיעִי. כֻּלָּם יִשְׂבְּעוּ וְיִתְעַנְּגוּ מִטּוּבֶךָ. וּבַשְּׁבִיעִי רָצִיתָ בּוֹ וְקִדַּשְׁתּוֹ. חֶמְדַּת יָמִים אוֹתוֹ קָרָאתָ. זֵכֶר לְמַעֲשֵׂה בְרֵאשִׁית:

יִשְׂמְחוּ May all who keep the Shabbat and call it a delight rejoice in Your rule. May all who make it holy find serenity and delight in Your goodness. For You Yourself desired the seventh day and made it holy, proclaiming it the most precious of days, recalling the work of creation.

יִשְׂמְחוּ Yism'chu v'malchut'cha, shom'rei shabbat v'kor'ei oneg. Am m'kadd'shei sh'vi'i, kullam yisb'u v'yit'ann'gu mittuvecha. Uva-sh'v'i ratsita bo v'kiddashto, chemdat yamim oto karata, zeicher l'ma'aseih v'reishit.

אֱלֹהֵינוּ וֵאלֹהֵי אֲבוֹתֵינוּ. רְצֵה־נָא בִמְנוּחָתֵנוּ. קַדְּשֵׁנוּ בְּמִצְוֹתֶיךָ. שִׂים חֶלְקֵנוּ בְּתוֹרָתֶךָ. שַׂבְּעֵנוּ מִטּוּבֶךָ. שַׂמַּח נַפְשֵׁנוּ בִּישׁוּעָתֶךָ. וְטַהֵר לִבֵּנוּ לְעָבְדְּךָ בֶּאֱמֶת. וְהַנְחִילֵנוּ יְהֹוָה אֱלֹהֵינוּ בְּאַהֲבָה וּבְרָצוֹן שַׁבַּת קָדְשֶׁךָ. וְיָנוּחוּ בָה כָּל־יִשְׂרָאֵל. מְקַדְּשֵׁי שְׁמֶךָ: בָּרוּךְ אַתָּה יְהֹוָה. מְקַדֵּשׁ הַשַּׁבָּת:

אֱלֹהֵינוּ Our God and God of our ancestors, may our rest be pleasing to You. Make us holy by doing Your commands and let us share in the work of Your Torah. Make us content with Your goodness and let our souls know the joy of Your salvation. Purify our hearts to serve You in truth. In Your love and goodwill let us inherit Your holy Shabbat and may all Israel who seek holiness find in it their rest. Blessed are You God, Who makes the Shabbat holy.

אֱלֹהֵינוּ Eloheinu veilohei avoteinu, r'tseih na vimnuchateinu, kadd'sheinu v'mitsvotecha, sim chelkeinu v'toratecha, sabb'einu mittuvecha, sammach nafsheinu vishu'atecha, v'taheir libbeinu l'ovd'cha b'emet. V'hanchileinu Adonai eloheinu b'ahavah uv'ratson shabbat kodshecha. V'yanuchu vah kol yisra'el m'kadd'shei sh'mecha. Baruch ata Adonai m'kaddeish ha-shabbat.

THANKSGIVING AND PEACE

רְצֵה יְהֹוָה אֱלֹהֵינוּ בְּעַמְּךָ יִשְׂרָאֵל. וְלִתְפִלָּתָם שְׁעֵה. וּבְרַחֲמֶיךָ הָרַבִּים תֶּחְפֹּץ בָּנוּ וְתִשְׁרֶה שְׁכִינָתְךָ עַל צִיּוֹן.

רְצֵה Our Living God be pleased with Your people Israel and listen to their prayers. In Your great mercy delight in us so that Your presence may rest upon Zion.

<<<

רְצֵה R'tseih Adonai eloheinu b'amm'cha yisra'el, v'litfillatam sh'eih. U'v'rachamecha ha-rabbim tachpots banu, v'tashreh sh'chinat'cha al tsiyyon.

SHABBAT ADDITIONAL SERVICE

AMIDAH II

On the New Moon and festivals the prayers on page 230 are added here:

וְתֶחֱזֶינָה Our eyes look forward to Your return to Zion in mercy! Blessed are You God, ever restoring Your presence to Zion.

וְתֶחֱזֶינָה עֵינֵינוּ בְּשׁוּבְךָ לְצִיּוֹן בְּרַחֲמִים: בָּרוּךְ אַתָּה יהוה. הַמַּחֲזִיר שְׁכִינָתוֹ לְצִיּוֹן.

וְתֶחֱזֶינָה *V'techezena eineinu b'shuv'cha l'tsiyyon b'rachamim. Baruch attah Adonai ha-machazir sh'chinato l'tsiyyon.*

It is customary to bow as one recites the opening words of this blessing, rising as we recite the name of God, Adonai *and the list of God's gifts to us.*

מוֹדִים We declare with gratitude that You are our God and the God of our ancestors. You are our rock, the rock of our life and the shield that saves us. In every generation we thank You and recount Your praise for our lives held in Your hand, for our souls that are in Your care, and for the signs of Your presence that are with us every day. At every moment, at evening, morning and noon, we experience Your wonders and Your goodness. You are goodness itself, for Your mercy has no end. You are mercy itself, for Your love has no limit. Forever have we put our hope in You.

מוֹדִים אֲנַחְנוּ לָךְ שָׁאַתָּה הוּא יהוה אֱלֹהֵינוּ וֵאלֹהֵי אֲבוֹתֵינוּ לְעוֹלָם וָעֶד. צוּרֵנוּ צוּר חַיֵּינוּ וּמָגֵן יִשְׁעֵנוּ אַתָּה הוּא: לְדוֹר וָדוֹר נוֹדֶה לְךָ וּנְסַפֵּר תְּהִלָּתֶךָ עַל חַיֵּינוּ הַמְּסוּרִים בְּיָדֶךָ. וְעַל נִשְׁמוֹתֵינוּ הַפְּקוּדוֹת לָךְ. וְעַל נִסֶּיךָ שֶׁבְּכָל־יוֹם עִמָּנוּ. וְעַל נִפְלְאוֹתֶיךָ וְטוֹבוֹתֶיךָ שֶׁבְּכָל־עֵת עֶרֶב וָבֹקֶר וְצָהֳרָיִם: הַטּוֹב כִּי לֹא כָלוּ רַחֲמֶיךָ. הַמְרַחֵם כִּי לֹא תַמּוּ חֲסָדֶיךָ. כִּי מֵעוֹלָם קִוִּינוּ לָךְ.

<<<

מוֹדִים *Modim anachnu lach, she'attah hu Adonai eloheinu veilohei avoteinu l'olam va'ed, tsureinu tsur chayyeinu umagein yish'einu attah hu. L'dor vador nodeh l'cha un'sappeir t'hillatecha al chayyeinu ha-m'surim b'yadecha, v'al nishmoteinu ha-p'kudot lach, v'al nissecha shebb'chol yom immanu, v'al nifl'otecha v'tovotecha sheb'chol eit, erev vavoker v'tsohorayim. Ha-tov ki lo chalu rachamecha, ha-m'racheim ki lo tammu chasadecha, ki mei'olam kivvinu lach.*

On Chanukah add al ha-nissim on page 374, otherwise continue here:

וְעַל And for all these things may Your name, our Sovereign, be blessed, exalted and honoured forever and ever.

וְעַל כֻּלָּם יִתְבָּרַךְ וְיִתְרוֹמֵם וְיִתְנַשֵּׂא תָּמִיד שִׁמְךָ מַלְכֵּנוּ לְעוֹלָם וָעֶד:

During the Ten Days of Penitence add:
Record all the children of Your covenant for a good life.

During the Ten Days of Penitence add:
וּכְתוֹב לְחַיִּים טוֹבִים כָּל־בְּנֵי בְרִיתֶךָ.

May every living being thank You; may they praise and bless Your great name in truth for You are the God who saves and helps us. Blessed are You God, known as goodness, whom it is right to praise.

וְכָל־הַחַיִּים יוֹדוּךָ סֶּלָה. וִיהַלְלוּ וִיבָרְכוּ אֶת שִׁמְךָ הַגָּדוֹל בֶּאֱמֶת. הָאֵל יְשׁוּעָתֵנוּ וְעֶזְרָתֵנוּ סֶלָה: בָּרוּךְ אַתָּה יהוה. הַטּוֹב שִׁמְךָ וּלְךָ נָאֶה לְהוֹדוֹת:

וְעַל *V'al kullam yitbarach v'yitromeim v'yitnassei tamid shimcha malkeinu l'olam va'ed.*
During the Ten Days of Penitence add: Uch'tov l'chayyim tovim kol b'nei v'ritecha.
V'chol ha-chayyim yoducha selah, vihal'lu vivar'chu et shimcha ha-gadol be'emet, ha-eil y'shu'ateinu v'ezrateinu selah. Baruch attah Adonai, ha-tov shimcha ul'cha na'eh l'hodot.

אֱלֹהֵינוּ Our God and God of our ancestors, bless us with the threefold blessing written in the Torah by Moses Your servant, spoken by the mouth of Aaron and his sons, the priests of Your holy people.

אֱלֹהֵינוּ וֵאלֹהֵי אֲבוֹתֵינוּ. בָּרְכֵנוּ בַבְּרָכָה הַמְשֻׁלֶּשֶׁת בַּתּוֹרָה הַכְּתוּבָה עַל יְדֵי מֹשֶׁה עַבְדֶּךָ. הָאֲמוּרָה מִפִּי אַהֲרֹן וּבָנָיו כֹּהֲנִים עַם קְדוֹשֶׁךָ. כָּאָמוּר.

May God bless you and keep you.
May this be God's will!

יְבָרֶכְךָ יהוה וְיִשְׁמְרֶךָ.
כֵּן יְהִי רָצוֹן

May God's face shine upon you and be gracious to you.
May this be God's will!

יָאֵר יהוה פָּנָיו אֵלֶיךָ וִיחֻנֶּךָּ.
כֵּן יְהִי רָצוֹן

May God's face turn towards you and give You peace.
May this be God's will!

יִשָּׂא יהוה פָּנָיו אֵלֶיךָ וְיָשֵׂם לְךָ שָׁלוֹם.
כֵּן יְהִי רָצוֹן

אֱלֹהֵינוּ *Eloheinu veilohei avoteinu, bar'cheinu va-b'rachah ha-m'shulleshet ba-torah ha-k'tuvah al y'dei mosheh avdecha, ha-amurah mippi aharon uvanav kohanim am k'doshecha, ka'amur:*
Y'varech'cha Adonai v'yishm'recha. Kein y'hi ratson.
Ya'eir Adonai panav eilecha vichunneka. Kein y'hi ratson.
Yissa Adonai panav eilecha, v'yaseim l'cha shalom. Kein y'hi ratson.

SHABBAT ADDITIONAL SERVICE — AMIDAH II

שִׂים Grant us peace, goodness and blessing; life, grace and kindness; justice and mercy. Source of our life, bless us all together with the light of Your presence, for in the light of Your presence You give us, our Living God, law and life, love and kindness, justice and mercy, blessing and peace. And in Your eyes it is good to bless Your people Israel with the strength to make peace.

During the Ten Days of Penitence add:
In Your presence may we and all Your people, the family of Israel, be remembered and recorded in the Book of Life for a good life and for peace.

Blessed are You God, blessing Your people Israel with peace.

שִׂים שָׁלוֹם טוֹבָה וּבְרָכָה חַיִּים חֵן וָחֶסֶד צְדָקָה וְרַחֲמִים עָלֵינוּ. וּבָרְכֵנוּ אָבִינוּ כֻּלָּנוּ יַחַד בְּאוֹר פָּנֶיךָ. כִּי בְאוֹר פָּנֶיךָ נָתַתָּ לָּנוּ יהוה אֱלֹהֵינוּ תּוֹרָה וְחַיִּים. אַהֲבָה וָחֶסֶד. צְדָקָה וְרַחֲמִים. בְּרָכָה וְשָׁלוֹם. וְטוֹב בְּעֵינֶיךָ לְבָרֵךְ אֶת־עַמְּךָ יִשְׂרָאֵל בְּרָב־עֹז וּבְשָׁלוֹם:

During the Ten Days of Penitence add:
בְּסֵפֶר חַיִּים נִזָּכֵר וְנִכָּתֵב לְפָנֶיךָ אֲנַחְנוּ וְכָל־עַמְּךָ בֵּית יִשְׂרָאֵל לְחַיִּים טוֹבִים וּלְשָׁלוֹם:

בָּרוּךְ אַתָּה יהוה. הַמְבָרֵךְ אֶת עַמּוֹ יִשְׂרָאֵל בַּשָּׁלוֹם:

שִׂים Sim shalom tovah uv'rachah, chayyim chein vachesed, ts'dakah v'rachamim aleinu, uvar'cheinu avinu kullanu yachad b'or panecha, ki v'or panecha natatta lanu Adonai eloheinu, torah v'chayyim, ahavah vachesed, ts'dakah v'rachamim, b'rachah v'shalom, v'tov b'einecha l'vareich et amm'cha yisra'el b'rov oz uv'shalom.

During the Ten Days of Penitence add: B'seifer chayyim nizzacheir v'nikkateiv l'fanecha anachnu v'chol amm'cha beit yisra'el, l'chayyim tovim ul'shalom.

Baruch attah Adonai, ha-m'vareich et ammo yisra'el ba-shalom.

MEDITATION

אֱלֹהַי My God, keep my tongue from causing harm and my lips from telling lies. Let me be silent if people curse me, my soul still humble and at peace with all. Open my heart to Your teaching, and give me the will to practise it. May the plans and schemes of those who seek my harm come to nothing.
May the words of my mouth and the meditation of my heart be acceptable to You, O God, my Rock and my Redeemer.[1]

אֱלֹהַי נְצוֹר לְשׁוֹנִי מֵרָע. וּשְׂפָתוֹתַי מִדַּבֵּר מִרְמָה. וְלִמְקַלְלַי נַפְשִׁי תִדֹּם. וְנַפְשִׁי כֶּעָפָר לַכֹּל תִּהְיֶה: פְּתַח לִבִּי בְּתוֹרָתֶךָ. וְאַחֲרֵי מִצְוֺתֶיךָ תִּרְדּוֹף נַפְשִׁי. וְכָל־הַקָּמִים עָלַי לְרָעָה מְהֵרָה הָפֵר עֲצָתָם וְקַלְקֵל מַחְשְׁבוֹתָם: יִהְיוּ לְרָצוֹן אִמְרֵי־פִי. וְהֶגְיוֹן לִבִּי לְפָנֶיךָ. יהוה צוּרִי וְגוֹאֲלִי:

אֱלֹהַי Elohai n'tsor l'shoni meira, v'siftotai middabbeir mirmah, v'limkal'lai nafshi tiddom, v'nafshi ke'afar la-kol tihyeh. P'tach libbi b'toratecha, v'acharei mitsvotecha tirdof nafshi, v'chol ha-kamim alai l'ra'ah, m'heirah hafeir atsatam, v'kalkeil machsh'votam. Yihyu l'ratson imrei fi, v'hegyon libbi l'fanecha, Adonai tsuri v'go'ali.

עֹשֶׂה May the Maker of peace in the highest bring this peace upon us and upon all Israel and upon all the world. Amen.

עֹשֶׂה שָׁלוֹם בִּמְרוֹמָיו. הוּא יַעֲשֶׂה שָׁלוֹם עָלֵינוּ וְעַל כָּל־יִשְׂרָאֵל וְעַל־כָּל־הָעוֹלָם. וְאִמְרוּ. אָמֵן:

עֹשֶׂה Oseh shalom bimromav hu ya'aseh shalom aleinu v'al kol yisra'el v'al kol ha-olam, v'imru Amen.

The service continues with the Concluding Prayers on page 306.

---

[1] Ps 19:15.

תפלת מנחה לשבת
Shabbat Afternoon Service

וַאֲנִי תְפִלָּתִי־לְךָ יהוה עֵת רָצוֹן:
אֱלֹהִים בְּרָב־חַסְדֶּךָ · עֲנֵנִי בֶּאֱמֶת יִשְׁעֶךָ:

As for me, let my prayer come before You at the proper time.
Answer me God, in the greatness of Your love, for Your deliverance is sure.

Psalm 69:14

The *Minchah* service on *Shabbat* reflects two major themes of the *Shabbat*: that of rest itself and the anticipation of a messianic time when there will be the universal peace and harmony symbolised by *Shabbat* rest. The introduction to the *Torah* service expresses the hope that our prayers 'at the proper time' will help bring this period. The insertion in the *Amidah* prayer begins with the affirmation that 'You are One and Your name is One' as if the time had already been reached that the prophet Zechariah spoke of, and which we recite daily at the end of the second paragraph of the *Aleinu* prayer: 'On that day the Eternal shall be One, and known as One' (Zech 14:9). The passage goes on to celebrate all the different dimensions associated with this rest: 'rest given freely in love, true and faithful rest, peaceful, tranquil rest, quiet and secure, the perfect rest that You desire'.

The service begins with Psalm 145 which can be found on page 48.

וּבָא לְצִיּוֹן גּוֹאֵל. וּלְשָׁבֵי פֶשַׁע בְּיַעֲקֹב. נְאֻם יהוה: וַאֲנִי זֹאת בְּרִיתִי אוֹתָם אָמַר יהוה. רוּחִי אֲשֶׁר עָלֶיךָ. וּדְבָרַי אֲשֶׁר שַׂמְתִּי בְּפִיךָ לֹא יָמוּשׁוּ מִפִּיךָ. וּמִפִּי זַרְעֲךָ. וּמִפִּי זֶרַע זַרְעֲךָ. אָמַר יהוה. מֵעַתָּה וְעַד עוֹלָם:

בָּא A redeemer shall come to Zion and to those in Jacob who turn from wrong, says the Eternal. As for Me, this is My covenant which I make with them, says the Eternal. My spirit which is upon you and My words which I have put in your mouth will never leave your mouth, nor the mouth of your children nor the mouth of your children's children.[1]

TRUSTING IN GOD

בָּרוּךְ אֱלֹהֵינוּ. שֶׁבְּרָאָנוּ לִכְבוֹדוֹ. וְנָתַן לָנוּ תּוֹרַת אֱמֶת. וְחַיֵּי עוֹלָם נָטַע בְּתוֹכֵנוּ: הוּא יִפְתַּח לִבֵּנוּ בְּתוֹרָתוֹ וְיָשֵׂם בְּלִבֵּנוּ אַהֲבָתוֹ וְיִרְאָתוֹ. וְלַעֲשׂוֹת רְצוֹנוֹ וּלְעָבְדוֹ בְּלֵבָב שָׁלֵם. לְמַעַן לֹא נִיגַע לָרִיק. וְלֹא נֵלֵד לַבֶּהָלָה: יְהִי רָצוֹן מִלְּפָנֶיךָ. יהוה אֱלֹהֵינוּ וֵאלֹהֵי אֲבוֹתֵינוּ. שֶׁנִּשְׁמֹר חֻקֶּיךָ בָּעוֹלָם הַזֶּה. וְנִזְכֶּה וְנִחְיֶה וְנִרְאֶה וְנִירַשׁ טוֹבָה וּבְרָכָה. לִשְׁנֵי יְמוֹת הַמָּשִׁיחַ. וּלְחַיֵּי הָעוֹלָם הַבָּא: וְיִבְטְחוּ בְךָ יוֹדְעֵי שְׁמֶךָ. כִּי לֹא־עָזַבְתָּ דֹּרְשֶׁיךָ יהוה:

בָּרוּךְ Blessed is our God. You created us for Your own sake. May You open our hearts to Your teaching and set both the love and awe of You within them, so that we do not wear ourselves away for nothing only to produce confusion. Our Living God, and God of generations past, help us to keep to Your commands in this world today, so that we earn the right to life, and inherit the goodness and blessing of the messianic days and the life of the world to come.
'Those who truly know You put their trust in You, for You never abandon those who seek You.'[2]

יהוה חָפֵץ לְמַעַן צִדְקוֹ. יַגְדִּיל תּוֹרָה וְיַאְדִּיר:

'Desiring righteousness
the Living God
made Torah great and powerful.'[3]

---

[1] Isa 59:20-21.
[2] Ps 9:11.

[3] Isa 42:21.

SHABBAT AFTERNOON SERVICE — TORAH SERVICE

The **Chatsi Kaddish** *may be recited here:*

Chatsi Kaddish / חֲצִי קַדִּישׁ

יִתְגַּדַּל Let us magnify
and let us sanctify in this world
the great name of God
whose will created it.
May God's reign come in your
lifetime, and in your days,
and in the lifetime of the family of
Israel - quickly and speedily
may it come.
Amen.
**May the greatness of God's being
be blessed from eternity to eternity.**
Let us bless and let us extol,
let us tell aloud and let us raise aloft,
let us set on high and let us honour,
let us exalt and
let us praise the Holy One,
whose name is blessed,

who is far beyond any blessing

During the Ten Days of Penitence:
  who is far above and beyond any blessing

or song, any honour
or any consolation
that can be spoken of in this world.
Amen.

יִתְגַּדַּל וְיִתְקַדַּשׁ שְׁמֵהּ רַבָּא
בְּעָלְמָא דִּי־בְרָא כִרְעוּתֵהּ:
וְיַמְלִיךְ מַלְכוּתֵהּ
בְּחַיֵּיכוֹן וּבְיוֹמֵיכוֹן
וּבְחַיֵּי דִי־כָל־בֵּית יִשְׂרָאֵל
בַּעֲגָלָא וּבִזְמַן קָרִיב.
וְאִמְרוּ אָמֵן:
יְהֵא שְׁמֵהּ רַבָּא מְבָרַךְ
לְעָלַם וּלְעָלְמֵי עָלְמַיָּא:
יִתְבָּרַךְ וְיִשְׁתַּבַּח וְיִתְפָּאַר
וְיִתְרוֹמַם וְיִתְנַשֵּׂא וְיִתְהַדָּר
וְיִתְעַלֶּה וְיִתְהַלָּל שְׁמֵהּ
דִּי־קֻדְשָׁא. בְּרִיךְ הוּא.

לְעֵלָּא מִן־כָּל־בִּרְכָתָא

During the Ten Days of Penitence:
לְעֵלָּא לְעֵלָּא מִכָּל־בִּרְכָתָא

וְשִׁירָתָא תֻּשְׁבְּחָתָא וְנֶחֱמָתָא
דַּאֲמִירָן בְּעָלְמָא.
וְאִמְרוּ אָמֵן:

סדר קריאת התורה
TORAH SERVICE 345

According to the *Talmud* (*Baba Kama* 82a) the reading of an extract from the Torah portion from the following week was to enable those to hear it who could not otherwise do so on the Monday or Thursday, market days on which a passage was read during the service, because of their business activities. An extract is read but there is no accompanying Haftarah reading. Just as the morning began with a reading from the Torah to set the Shabbat apart, so it is appropriate to have another reading at the end of the day to help carry the spirit and learning of Shabbat into the working week.

סדר קריאת התורה
TORAH SERVICE

וַאֲנִי תְפִלָּתִי־לְךָ יהוה עֵת רָצוֹן
אֱלֹהִים בְּרָב־חַסְדֶּךָ.
עֲנֵנִי בֶּאֱמֶת יִשְׁעֶךָ:

וַאֲנִי As for me, let my prayer
come before You at the proper time.
Answer me God,
in the greatness of Your love,
for Your deliverance is sure.[1]

וַיְהִי בִּנְסֹעַ הָאָרֹן
וַיֹּאמֶר מֹשֶׁה:
קוּמָה יהוה וְיָפֻצוּ אֹיְבֶיךָ
וְיָנֻסוּ מְשַׂנְאֶיךָ מִפָּנֶיךָ:
כִּי מִצִּיּוֹן תֵּצֵא תוֹרָה
וּדְבַר־יהוה מִירוּשָׁלָיִם:

וַיְהִי Whenever the ark moved forward,
then Moses said:
'Almighty, rise up!
Let Your enemies be scattered,
let those who hate You flee before You!'
For Torah shall come out of Zion
and the word of God from Jerusalem.[2]

גַּדְּלוּ לַיהוה אִתִּי.
וּנְרוֹמְמָה שְׁמוֹ יַחְדָּו:

גַּדְּלוּ Declare with me the greatness of God,
and let us exalt God's name together.[3]

לְךָ יהוה הַגְּדֻלָּה
וְהַגְּבוּרָה
וְהַתִּפְאֶרֶת וְהַנֵּצַח וְהַהוֹד.
כִּי כֹל בַּשָּׁמַיִם וּבָאָרֶץ.
לְךָ יהוה הַמַּמְלָכָה
וְהַמִּתְנַשֵּׂא לְכֹל לְרֹאשׁ:
רוֹמְמוּ יהוה אֱלֹהֵינוּ
וְהִשְׁתַּחֲווּ לַהֲדֹם רַגְלָיו
קָדוֹשׁ הוּא:
רוֹמְמוּ יהוה אֱלֹהֵינוּ.
וְהִשְׁתַּחֲווּ לְהַר קָדְשׁוֹ.
כִּי קָדוֹשׁ יהוה אֱלֹהֵינוּ:

לְךָ Yours, our Living God,
is the greatness, the power,
the beauty, the victory
and the splendour,
for everything in heaven and earth
is Yours.
Yours is sovereignty
and You are supreme over all.
Exalt the Living God, and bow down
before the footstool of the Holy One.
Exalt the Living God, and bow down
before the mountain of God's holiness
- for holy is our Living God.[4]

---

[1] Ps 69:14.
[2] Num 10:35, Is 2:3.
[3] Ps 34:4.
[4] I Chron 29:11, Ps 99:5, Ps 99:9.

293 SHABBAT AFTERNOON SERVICE — TORAH SERVICE

אָב Source of mercy, have mercy on a people You have always sustained, remembering the covenant with our ancestors and rescuing our lives from evil times. May You restrain our own impulse to do harm. Through Your grace help us survive and respond to our need for safety and compassion.

אָב הָרַחֲמִים. הוּא יְרַחֵם עַם עֲמוּסִים. וְיִזְכֹּר בְּרִית אֵיתָנִים. וְיַצִּיל נַפְשׁוֹתֵינוּ מִן הַשָּׁעוֹת הָרָעוֹת. וְיִגְעַר בְּיֵצֶר הָרָע מִן הַנְּשׂוּאִים. וְיָחֹן אוֹתָנוּ לִפְלֵיטַת עוֹלָמִים. וִימַלֵּא מִשְׁאֲלוֹתֵינוּ בְּמִדָּה טוֹבָה יְשׁוּעָה וְרַחֲמִים:

Machzor Vitry מחזור ותרי

וְתִגָּלֶה May Your sovereignty be revealed to us soon. Show Your love to us and to the remnant of Your people Israel, with grace and faithfulness, with compassion and favour.

וְתִגָּלֶה וְתֵרָאֶה מַלְכוּתוֹ עָלֵינוּ בִּזְמַן קָרוֹב. וְיָחֹן פְּלֵטָתֵנוּ וּפְלֵטַת עַמּוֹ בֵּית יִשְׂרָאֵל לְחֵן וּלְחֶסֶד לְרַחֲמִים וּלְרָצוֹן וְנֹאמַר אָמֵן:

Let everything declare God's power and the glory of God's Torah!

הַכֹּל תְּנוּ עֹז לֵאלֹהִים וּתְנוּ כָבוֹד לַתּוֹרָה:

Before reading the Torah:

בָּרְכוּ Bless the Living God whom we are called to bless.

בָּרְכוּ אֶת יהוה הַמְבֹרָךְ:

בָּרוּךְ Blessed is the Living God, whom we are called to bless forever and ever.

בָּרוּךְ יהוה הַמְבֹרָךְ לְעוֹלָם וָעֶד:

בָּרוּךְ Blessed are You, our Living God, Sovereign of the universe, who chose us from all peoples to give us Your Torah. Blessed are You God, who gives us the Torah.

בָּרוּךְ אַתָּה יהוה אֱלֹהֵינוּ מֶלֶךְ הָעוֹלָם. אֲשֶׁר בָּחַר־בָּנוּ מִכָּל־הָעַמִּים וְנָתַן־לָנוּ אֶת תּוֹרָתוֹ: בָּרוּךְ אַתָּה יהוה נוֹתֵן הַתּוֹרָה:

After reading the Torah:

בָּרוּךְ אַתָּה יהוה אֱלֹהֵינוּ מֶלֶךְ הָעוֹלָם. אֲשֶׁר נָתַן־לָנוּ תּוֹרַת אֱמֶת וְחַיֵּי עוֹלָם נָטַע בְּתוֹכֵנוּ: בָּרוּךְ אַתָּה יהוה. נוֹתֵן הַתּוֹרָה:

בָּרוּךְ Blessed are You, our Living God, Sovereign of the universe, who gave us the teaching of truth and planted eternal life within us. Blessed are You God, who gives us the Torah.

וְזֹאת הַתּוֹרָה אֲשֶׁר שָׂם מֹשֶׁה לִפְנֵי בְּנֵי יִשְׂרָאֵל. עַל פִּי יהוה בְּיַד מֹשֶׁה:

וְזֹאת This is the Torah that Moses set before the children of Israel, given by God through Moses.

RETURN OF THE SCROLL

יְהַלְלוּ אֶת שֵׁם יהוה.
כִּי נִשְׂגָּב שְׁמוֹ לְבַדּוֹ:
הוֹדוֹ עַל אֶרֶץ וְשָׁמָיִם.
וַיָּרֶם קֶרֶן לְעַמּוֹ.
תְּהִלָּה לְכָל־חֲסִידָיו.
לִבְנֵי יִשְׂרָאֵל עַם קְרֹבוֹ.
הַלְלוּיָהּ:

יְהַלְלוּ Praise the Almighty
whose name alone is supreme
and whose majesty
is beyond heaven and earth.
You have restored the honour
of Your people,
the praise of those who love You -
the children of Israel, a people
so close to You.
Praise God![1]

Psalm 24 can be found on page 254.

וּבְנֻחֹה יֹאמַר:
שׁוּבָה יהוה רִבְבוֹת אַלְפֵי יִשְׂרָאֵל:
קוּמָה יהוה לִמְנוּחָתֶךָ.
אַתָּה וַאֲרוֹן עֻזֶּךָ:
כֹּהֲנֶיךָ יִלְבְּשׁוּ־צֶדֶק
וַחֲסִידֶיךָ יְרַנֵּנוּ:
בַּעֲבוּר דָּוִד עַבְדֶּךָ.
אַל־תָּשֵׁב פְּנֵי מְשִׁיחֶךָ:

וּבְנֻחֹה And when the ark rested
Moses used to say:
'Return, God, to the countless
thousands of Israel.'
Rise up to Your place of rest,
You and the ark of Your strength!
Your priests will be clothed
in righteousness
and those who love You
will shout for joy.
For the sake of Your servant David,
do not turn away the face of Your anointed.[2]

---

[1] Ps 148:13-14.   [2] Num 10:36, Ps 132:8-10.

295 **SHABBAT AFTERNOON SERVICE** **TORAH SERVICE**

'For I have given you
good instruction,
do not forsake My teaching.'
It is a tree of life
to all who grasp it
and those who hold fast to it are happy.
Its ways are ways of pleasantness
and all its paths are peace.[1]

כִּי לֶקַח טוֹב נָתַתִּי לָכֶם.
תּוֹרָתִי אַל תַּעֲזֹֽבוּ:
עֵץ־חַיִּים הִיא לַמַּחֲזִיקִים בָּהּ.
וְתֹמְכֶֽיהָ מְאֻשָּׁר:
דְּרָכֶֽיהָ דַרְכֵי־נֹֽעַם.
וְכָל־נְתִיבוֹתֶֽיהָ שָׁלוֹם:

הֲשִׁיבֵֽנוּ Turn us back to You,
Eternal, and we shall return;
renew our lives as of old.[2]

הֲשִׁיבֵֽנוּ יהוה אֵלֶֽיךָ וְנָשֽׁוּבָה.
חַדֵּשׁ יָמֵֽינוּ כְּקֶֽדֶם:

The Chatsi Kaddish may be recited here:

Chatsi Kaddish חֲצִי קַדִּישׁ

יִתְגַּדַּל Let us magnify
and let us sanctify in this world
the great name of God
whose will created it.
May God's reign come in your
lifetime, and in your days,
and in the lifetime of the family of
Israel - quickly and speedily
may it come.
Amen.
**May the greatness of God's being
be blessed from eternity to eternity**.
Let us bless and let us extol,
let us tell aloud and let us raise aloft,
let us set on high and let us honour,
let us exalt and
let us praise the Holy One,
whose name is blessed,

who is far beyond any blessing

During the Ten Days of Penitence:
who is far above and beyond any blessing

or song, any honour
or any consolation
that can be spoken of in this world.
Amen.

יִתְגַּדַּל וְיִתְקַדַּשׁ שְׁמֵהּ רַבָּא
בְּעָלְמָא דִּי־בְרָא כִרְעוּתֵהּ:
וְיַמְלִיךְ מַלְכוּתֵהּ
בְּחַיֵּיכוֹן וּבְיוֹמֵיכוֹן
וּבְחַיֵּי דִי־כָל־בֵּית יִשְׂרָאֵל
בַּעֲגָלָא וּבִזְמַן קָרִיב.
וְאִמְרוּ אָמֵן:
יְהֵא שְׁמֵהּ רַבָּא מְבָרַךְ
לְעָלַם וּלְעָלְמֵי עָלְמַיָּא:
יִתְבָּרַךְ וְיִשְׁתַּבַּח וְיִתְפָּאַר
וְיִתְרוֹמַם וְיִתְנַשֵּׂא וְיִתְהַדָּר
וְיִתְעַלֶּה וְיִתְהַלָּל שְׁמֵהּ
דְּקֻדְשָׁא. בְּרִיךְ הוּא.

לְעֵֽלָּא מִן־כָּל־בִּרְכָתָא

During the Ten Days of Penitence:
לְעֵֽלָּא לְעֵֽלָּא מִכָּל־בִּרְכָתָא

וְשִׁירָתָא תֻּשְׁבְּחָתָא וְנֶחֱמָתָא
דַּאֲמִירָן בְּעָלְמָא.
וְאִמְרוּ אָמֵן:

---

[1] Pr 4:2, Pr 3:18, Pr 3:17, Lam 5:2.   [2] Lam 5:21.

עמידה למנחה לשבת
SHABBAT AFTERNOON *AMIDAH*

אֲדֹנָי שְׂפָתַי תִּפְתָּח וּפִי יַגִּיד תְּהִלָּתֶךָ:

בָּרוּךְ אַתָּה יהוה אֱלֹהֵינוּ
וֵאלֹהֵי אֲבוֹתֵינוּ. וֵאלֹהֵי אִמּוֹתֵינוּ.
אֱלֹהֵי אַבְרָהָם. אֱלֹהֵי שָׂרָה.
אֱלֹהֵי יִצְחָק. אֱלֹהֵי רִבְקָה.
וֵאלֹהֵי יַעֲקֹב. אֱלֹהֵי רָחֵל.
וֵאלֹהֵי לֵאָה.
הָאֵל הַגָּדוֹל הַגִּבּוֹר וְהַנּוֹרָא. אֵל עֶלְיוֹן.
גּוֹמֵל חֲסָדִים טוֹבִים קוֹנֵה הַכֹּל. וְזוֹכֵר חַסְדֵי
אָבוֹת וְאִמָּהוֹת
וּמֵבִיא גוֹאֵל לִבְנֵי בְנֵיהֶם לְמַעַן שְׁמוֹ בְּאַהֲבָה:

During the Ten Days of Penitence add:
זָכְרֵנוּ לְחַיִּים. מֶלֶךְ חָפֵץ בַּחַיִּים.
וְכָתְבֵנוּ בְּסֵפֶר הַחַיִּים. לְמַעַנְךָ אֱלֹהִים חַיִּים:

מֶלֶךְ עוֹזֵר וּמוֹשִׁיעַ וּמָגֵן:
בָּרוּךְ אַתָּה יהוה
מָגֵן אַבְרָהָם פּוֹקֵד שָׂרָה:

אַתָּה גִּבּוֹר לְעוֹלָם אֲדֹנָי. מְחַיֵּה מֵתִים אַתָּה. רַב לְהוֹשִׁיעַ:
In winter מַשִּׁיב הָרוּחַ וּמוֹרִיד הַגָּשֶׁם:
In summer מוֹרִיד הַטָּל:
מְכַלְכֵּל חַיִּים בְּחֶסֶד. מְחַיֵּה מֵתִים בְּרַחֲמִים רַבִּים. סוֹמֵךְ נוֹפְלִים. וְרוֹפֵא חוֹלִים. וּמַתִּיר אֲסוּרִים. וּמְקַיֵּם אֱמוּנָתוֹ לִישֵׁנֵי עָפָר: מִי כָמוֹךָ בַּעַל גְּבוּרוֹת וּמִי דּוֹמֶה לָּךְ. מֶלֶךְ מֵמִית וּמְחַיֶּה וּמַצְמִיחַ יְשׁוּעָה:
During the Ten Days of Penitence add:
מִי כָמוֹךָ אַב הָרַחֲמִים. זוֹכֵר יְצוּרָיו לְחַיִּים בְּרַחֲמִים:
וְנֶאֱמָן אַתָּה לְהַחֲיוֹת מֵתִים:
בָּרוּךְ אַתָּה יהוה. מְחַיֵּה הַמֵּתִים:

SHABBAT AFTERNOON SERVICE

אֲדֹנָי My God, open my lips and my mouth shall declare Your praise.[1]

GOD OF HISTORY

בָּרוּךְ Blessed are You, our God, and God of our ancestors,

God of Abraham,	God of Sarah,
God of Isaac,	God of Rebecca,
and God of Jacob,	God of Rachel
	and God of Leah,

the great, the mighty, and the awesome God, God beyond, generous in love and kindness, and possessing all. You remember the good deeds of those before us, and therefore in love bring rescue to the generations, for such is Your being.

> *During the Ten Days of Penitence add:*
> Sovereign Who delights in life, recall us to life and record us in the Book of Life for Your own sake, God of life!

The Sovereign who helps and saves and shields.
Blessed are You God,
who shields Abraham   who remembers Sarah.

GOD OF MIGHT

אַתָּה You are the endless power that renews life beyond death; You are the greatness that saves.

> *In winter months from* Shemini Atzeret *to* Pesach: making the wind blow and the rain fall.
> *In summer months from* Pesach *to* Shemini Atzeret: causing the dew to fall.

You care for the living with love. You renew life beyond death with unending mercy. You support the falling, and heal the sick. You free prisoners, and keep faith with those who sleep in the dust. Who can perform such mighty deeds, and who can compare with You, a Sovereign who brings death and life, and renews salvation?

> *During the Ten Days of Penitence add:*
> Who is like You, source of compassion,
> recalling Your creatures to life in compassion?

You are faithful to renew life beyond death.
Blessed are You God, who renews life beyond death.

---

[1] Psalm 51:17.

GOD OF HOLINESS

נְקַדֵּשׁ We sanctify Your name in the world as they sanctify it in the highest heavens. As it is written by the hand of Your prophet: 'And they called to each other and said:

נְקַדֵּשׁ אֶת־שִׁמְךָ בָּעוֹלָם כְּשֵׁם שֶׁמַּקְדִּישִׁים אוֹתוֹ בִּשְׁמֵי מָרוֹם כַּכָּתוּב עַל יַד נְבִיאֶךָ. וְקָרָא זֶה אֶל זֶה וְאָמַר.

Holy, holy, holy is the Creator of all, whose glory fills all the earth.'[1]

קָדוֹשׁ קָדוֹשׁ קָדוֹשׁ יהוה צְבָאוֹת. מְלֹא כָל־הָאָרֶץ כְּבוֹדוֹ:

They cry in answer, 'Blessed …'

לְעֻמָּתָם בָּרוּךְ יֹאמֵרוּ.

Blessed is God's glory, revealed in every place.[2]

בָּרוּךְ כְּבוֹד יהוה מִמְּקוֹמוֹ:

From Your place, our Sovereign, shine forth and rule over us, for we wait for You. And in Your holy writing it is said:

מִמְּקוֹמְךָ מַלְכֵּנוּ תוֹפִיעַ וְתִמְלוֹךְ עָלֵינוּ. כִּי מְחַכִּים אֲנַחְנוּ לָךְ. וּבְדִבְרֵי קָדְשְׁךָ כָּתוּב לֵאמֹר.

The Almighty shall rule forever! Your God, O Zion, for all generations! Praise God![3]

יִמְלֹךְ יהוה לְעוֹלָם. אֱלֹהַיִךְ צִיּוֹן לְדֹר וָדֹר הַלְלוּיָהּ:

We declare Your greatness to all generations, and to all eternity we proclaim Your holiness. Your praise shall never depart from our mouth, for You are God, the great and holy Sovereign.

לְדוֹר וָדוֹר נַגִּיד גָּדְלֶךָ. וּלְנֵצַח נְצָחִים קְדֻשָּׁתְךָ נַקְדִּישׁ. וְשִׁבְחֲךָ אֱלֹהֵינוּ מִפִּינוּ לֹא יָמוּשׁ לְעוֹלָם וָעֶד. כִּי אֵל מֶלֶךְ גָּדוֹל וְקָדוֹשׁ אָתָּה.

Blessed are You, the holy God

בָּרוּךְ אַתָּה יהוה. הָאֵל הַקָּדוֹשׁ:

During the Ten Days of Penitence:
the holy Sovereign.

During the Ten Days of Penitence:
הַמֶּלֶךְ הַקָּדוֹשׁ:

---

[1] Isa 6:3.
[2] Ez 3:12.
[3] Ps 146:10.

299 SHABBAT AFTERNOON SERVICE — AMIDAH

אַתָּה You are One and Your name is One, and who is like Your people Israel, a nation unique on the earth? A splendid greatness, a crown of salvation is the day of rest and holiness You gave to Your people. Abraham was glad, Isaac rejoiced, Jacob and his sons rested on it. Rest given freely in love, true and faithful rest, peaceful, tranquil rest, quiet and secure - the perfect rest that You desire. May Your children realise and know that their rest comes from You, and through their rest they make Your name holy.

אַתָּה אֶחָד וְשִׁמְךָ אֶחָד. וּמִי כְּעַמְּךָ יִשְׂרָאֵל גּוֹי אֶחָד בָּאָרֶץ: תִּפְאֶרֶת גְּדֻלָּה וַעֲטֶרֶת יְשׁוּעָה. יוֹם מְנוּחָה וּקְדֻשָּׁה לְעַמְּךָ נָתָתָּ: אַבְרָהָם יָגֵל. יִצְחָק יְרַנֵּן. יַעֲקֹב וּבָנָיו יָנוּחוּ בוֹ. מְנוּחַת אַהֲבָה וּנְדָבָה. מְנוּחַת אֱמֶת וֶאֱמוּנָה. מְנוּחַת שָׁלוֹם וְשַׁלְוָה וְהַשְׁקֵט וָבֶטַח. מְנוּחָה שְׁלֵמָה שֶׁאַתָּה רוֹצֶה בָּהּ: יַכִּירוּ בָנֶיךָ וְיֵדְעוּ כִּי מֵאִתְּךָ הִיא מְנוּחָתָם. וְעַל מְנוּחָתָם יַקְדִּישׁוּ אֶת שְׁמֶךָ:

אֱלֹהֵינוּ Our God and God of our ancestors, may our rest be pleasing to You. Make us holy by doing Your commands and let us share in the work of Your Torah. Make us content with Your goodness and let our souls know the joy of Your salvation. Purify our hearts to serve You in truth. In Your love and goodwill let us inherit Your holy Shabbat and may all Israel who seek holiness find in it their rest. Blessed are You God, who makes the Shabbat holy.

אֱלֹהֵינוּ וֵאלֹהֵי אֲבוֹתֵינוּ. רְצֵה־נָא בִמְנוּחָתֵנוּ. קַדְּשֵׁנוּ בְּמִצְוֹתֶיךָ. שִׂים חֶלְקֵנוּ בְּתוֹרָתֶךָ. שַׂבְּעֵנוּ מִטּוּבֶךָ. שַׂמַּח נַפְשֵׁנוּ בִּישׁוּעָתֶךָ. וְטַהֵר לִבֵּנוּ לְעָבְדְּךָ בֶּאֱמֶת. וְהַנְחִילֵנוּ יהוה אֱלֹהֵינוּ בְּאַהֲבָה וּבְרָצוֹן שַׁבַּת קָדְשֶׁךָ. וְיָנוּחוּ בָה כָּל־יִשְׂרָאֵל מְקַדְּשֵׁי שְׁמֶךָ: בָּרוּךְ אַתָּה יהוה. מְקַדֵּשׁ הַשַּׁבָּת:

THANKSGIVING AND PEACE

רְצֵה Our Living God be pleased with Your people Israel and listen to their prayers. In Your great mercy delight in us so that Your presence may rest upon Zion.

רְצֵה יהוה אֱלֹהֵינוּ בְּעַמְּךָ יִשְׂרָאֵל. וְלִתְפִלָּתָם שְׁעֵה. וּבְרַחֲמֶיךָ הָרַבִּים תַּחְפֹּץ בָּנוּ וְתַשְׁרֶה שְׁכִינָתְךָ עַל צִיּוֹן

On the New Moon and festivals, the prayers on page 230 are added, otherwise the service continues here:

וְתֶחֱזֶינָה עֵינֵינוּ בְּשׁוּבְךָ לְצִיּוֹן בְּרַחֲמִים: בָּרוּךְ אַתָּה יהוה. הַמַּחֲזִיר שְׁכִינָתוֹ לְצִיּוֹן.

וְתֶחֱזֶינָה Our eyes look forward to Your return to Zion in mercy! Blessed are You God, ever restoring Your presence to Zion.

מוֹדִים אֲנַחְנוּ לָךְ שָׁאַתָּה הוּא יהוה אֱלֹהֵינוּ וֵאלֹהֵי אֲבוֹתֵינוּ לְעוֹלָם וָעֶד. צוּרֵנוּ צוּר חַיֵּינוּ וּמָגֵן יִשְׁעֵנוּ אַתָּה הוּא: לְדוֹר וָדוֹר נוֹדֶה לְךָ וּנְסַפֵּר תְּהִלָּתֶךָ. עַל חַיֵּינוּ הַמְּסוּרִים בְּיָדֶךָ. וְעַל נִשְׁמוֹתֵינוּ הַפְּקוּדוֹת לָךְ. וְעַל נִסֶּיךָ שֶׁבְּכָל־יוֹם עִמָּנוּ. וְעַל נִפְלְאוֹתֶיךָ וְטוֹבוֹתֶיךָ שֶׁבְּכָל־עֵת עֶרֶב וָבֹקֶר וְצָהֳרָיִם: הַטּוֹב כִּי לֹא כָלוּ רַחֲמֶיךָ. הַמְרַחֵם כִּי לֹא תַמּוּ חֲסָדֶיךָ. כִּי מֵעוֹלָם קִוִּינוּ לָךְ.

מוֹדִים We declare with gratitude that You are our God and the God of our ancestors. You are our rock, the rock of our life and the shield that saves us. In every generation we thank You and recount Your praise for our lives held in Your hand, for our souls that are in Your care, and for the signs of Your presence that are with us every day. At every moment, at evening, morning and noon, we experience Your wonders and Your goodness. You are goodness itself, for Your mercy has no end. You are mercy itself, for Your love has no limit. Forever have we put our hope in You.

On Chanukah add al ha-nissim on page 374, otherwise continue here:

וְעַל כֻּלָּם יִתְבָּרַךְ וְיִתְרוֹמַם וְיִתְנַשֵּׂא תָּמִיד שִׁמְךָ מַלְכֵּנוּ לְעוֹלָם וָעֶד:

וְעַל And for all these things may Your name, our Sovereign, be blessed, exalted and honoured forever and ever.

During the Ten Days of Penitence add:
וּכְתוֹב לְחַיִּים טוֹבִים כָּל־בְּנֵי בְרִיתֶךָ.

During the Ten Days of Penitence add:
Record all the children of Your covenant for a good life.

וְכֹל־הַחַיִּים יוֹדוּךָ סֶּלָה. וִיהַלְלוּ וִיבָרְכוּ אֶת שִׁמְךָ הַגָּדוֹל בֶּאֱמֶת. הָאֵל יְשׁוּעָתֵנוּ וְעֶזְרָתֵנוּ סֶלָה. בָּרוּךְ אַתָּה יהוה. הַטּוֹב שִׁמְךָ וּלְךָ נָאֶה לְהוֹדוֹת:

May every living being thank You; may they praise and bless Your great name in truth, for You are the God who saves and helps us. Blessed are You God, known as goodness, whom it is right to praise.

SHABBAT AFTERNOON SERVICE

שָׁלוֹם Set true peace upon Your people Israel forever. For You are the Source of all peace, and in Your eyes it is good to bless Your people Israel at every time and in every hour with Your peace.

During the Ten Days of Penitence add:
In Your presence may we and all Your people, the family of Israel, be remembered and recorded in the Book of Life for a good life and for peace.

Blessed are You God, blessing Your people Israel with peace.

שָׁלוֹם רָב עַל יִשְׂרָאֵל עַמְּךָ תָּשִׂים לְעוֹלָם. כִּי אַתָּה הוּא מֶלֶךְ אָדוֹן לְכָל־הַשָּׁלוֹם. וְטוֹב בְּעֵינֶיךָ לְבָרֵךְ אֶת עַמְּךָ יִשְׂרָאֵל בְּכָל־עֵת וּבְכָל־שָׁעָה בִּשְׁלוֹמֶךָ.

During the Ten Days of Penitence add:
בְּסֵפֶר חַיִּים נִזָּכֵר וְנִכָּתֵב לְפָנֶיךָ אֲנַחְנוּ וְכָל־עַמְּךָ בֵּית יִשְׂרָאֵל לְחַיִּים טוֹבִים וּלְשָׁלוֹם:

בָּרוּךְ אַתָּה יהוה. הַמְבָרֵךְ אֶת עַמּוֹ יִשְׂרָאֵל בַּשָּׁלוֹם:

MEDITATION

אֱלֹהַי My God, keep my tongue from causing harm and my lips from telling lies. Let me be silent if people curse me, my soul still humble and at peace with all. Open my heart to Your teaching, and give me the will to practise it. May the plans and schemes of those who seek my harm come to nothing.
May the words of my mouth and the meditation of my heart be acceptable to You, O God, my Rock and my Redeemer.[1]

אֱלֹהַי נְצוֹר לְשׁוֹנִי מֵרָע. וְשִׂפְתוֹתַי מִדַּבֵּר מִרְמָה. וְלִמְקַלְלַי נַפְשִׁי תִדֹּם. וְנַפְשִׁי כֶּעָפָר לַכֹּל תִּהְיֶה: פְּתַח לִבִּי בְּתוֹרָתֶךָ. וְאַחֲרֵי מִצְוֹתֶיךָ תִּרְדּוֹף נַפְשִׁי. וְכָל־הַקָּמִים עָלַי לְרָעָה מְהֵרָה הָפֵר עֲצָתָם וְקַלְקֵל מַחְשְׁבוֹתָם: יִהְיוּ לְרָצוֹן אִמְרֵי־פִי. וְהֶגְיוֹן לִבִּי לְפָנֶיךָ. יהוה צוּרִי וְגוֹאֲלִי:

עֹשֶׂה May the Maker of peace in the highest bring this peace upon us and upon all Israel and upon all the world. Amen.

עֹשֶׂה שָׁלוֹם בִּמְרוֹמָיו. הוּא יַעֲשֶׂה שָׁלוֹם עָלֵינוּ וְעַל כָּל־יִשְׂרָאֵל וְעַל־כָּל־הָעוֹלָם. וְאִמְרוּ. אָמֵן:

The service continues with one or more songs or psalms expressing messianic hopes.

---

[1] Ps 19:15.

Y'did Nefesh

יְדִיד נֶפֶשׁ

Y'did Nefesh can be found on page 109.

Mah yafeh ha-yom

מַה יָפֶה הַיוֹם

מַה How beautiful is this day.
A Sabbath of peace.

מַה יָפֶה הַיוֹם
שַׁבָּת שָׁלוֹם

Psalm 23

כג

[1] A psalm of David

ᵃ מִזְמוֹר לְדָוִד

יהוה God is my shepherd,
I shall not want.

יהוה רֹעִי לֹא אֶחְסָר:

[2] In green fields God lets me lie,
leading me by quiet streams,
restoring my soul.

ᵇ בִּנְאוֹת דֶּשֶׁא יַרְבִּיצֵנִי
עַל־מֵי מְנֻחוֹת יְנַהֲלֵנִי:
נַפְשִׁי יְשׁוֹבֵב

[3] God guides me in paths of truth
for such is God's name.

ᶜ יַנְחֵנִי בְמַעְגְּלֵי־צֶדֶק
לְמַעַן שְׁמוֹ:

[4] Though I walk through
the valley of the shadow of death
I fear no harm
for You are beside me;
Your rod and staff
they comfort me.

ᵈ גַּם כִּי־אֵלֵךְ בְּגֵיא צַלְמָוֶת
לֹא־אִירָא רָע
כִּי־אַתָּה עִמָּדִי
שִׁבְטְךָ וּמִשְׁעַנְתֶּךָ הֵמָּה יְנַחֲמֻנִי:

[5] You spread a table before me
in front of my enemies.
You soothe my head with oil;
my cup runs over.

ᵉ תַּעֲרֹךְ לְפָנַי שֻׁלְחָן נֶגֶד צֹרְרָי
דִּשַּׁנְתָּ בַשֶּׁמֶן רֹאשִׁי כּוֹסִי רְוָיָה:

[6] Surely goodness and mercy seek me
all the days of my life
and I shall dwell
in the house of God forever.

ᶠ אַךְ טוֹב וָחֶסֶד יִרְדְּפוּנִי
כָּל־יְמֵי חַיָּי
וְשַׁבְתִּי בְּבֵית־יהוה לְאֹרֶךְ יָמִים:

SHABBAT AFTERNOON SERVICE

Eli Eli

אֵלִי O God, my God,
I pray that these things never end,
the sand and the sea,
the rush of the water,
the crash of the heavens,
our human prayer.

Hannah Sennesh חנה סנש

אֵלִי אֵלִי
שֶׁלֹא יִגָּמֵר לְעוֹלָם
הַחוֹל וְהַיָּם
רִשְׁרוּשׁ שֶׁל הַמַּיִם
בְּרַק הַשָּׁמַיִם
תְּפִלַּת הָאָדָם:

כִּי For My house shall be called
a house of prayer for all peoples.[1]

כִּי בֵיתִי בֵּית־תְּפִלָּה
יִקָּרֵא לְכָל־הָעַמִּים:

Psalm 121

קכא

[1] *A Pilgrim Song*

אֶשָּׂא I lift up my eyes to the hills;
where shall I find my help?
[2] My help is from God alone,
Maker of heaven and earth.
[3] God will not allow your foot to slip,
for your Guardian does not slumber.
[4] Know that the Guardian of Israel
never slumbers and never sleeps.
[5] God is your Guardian,
God is your shade at your right hand.
[6] The sun will not strike you by day
nor the moon by night.
[7] God will guard you from all evil,
guarding your soul.
[8] God will guard your going out and your
coming in now and for evermore.

שִׁיר לַמַּעֲלוֹת
אֶשָּׂא עֵינַי אֶל־הֶהָרִים
מֵאַיִן יָבֹא עֶזְרִי:
עֶזְרִי מֵעִם יהוה
עֹשֵׂה שָׁמַיִם וָאָרֶץ:
אַל־יִתֵּן לַמּוֹט רַגְלֶךָ
אַל־יָנוּם שֹׁמְרֶךָ:
הִנֵּה לֹא־יָנוּם וְלֹא יִישָׁן
שׁוֹמֵר יִשְׂרָאֵל:
יהוה שֹׁמְרֶךָ
יהוה צִלְּךָ עַל־יַד יְמִינֶךָ:
יוֹמָם הַשֶּׁמֶשׁ לֹא־יַכֶּכָּה
וְיָרֵחַ בַּלָּיְלָה:
יהוה יִשְׁמָרְךָ מִכָּל־רָע
יִשְׁמֹר אֶת־נַפְשֶׁךָ:
יהוה יִשְׁמָר־צֵאתְךָ וּבוֹאֶךָ
מֵעַתָּה וְעַד־עוֹלָם:

---

[1] Isa 56:7.

Psalm 128

¹*A Pilgrim Song*

אַשְׁרֵי Happy are those
who fear the Eternal,
who walk in God's ways.
²When you eat the product of your hands
happy shall you be
and it shall go well with you;
³your wife, like a fruitful vine,
in the heart of your house;
your children,
like shoots of the olive tree,
around your table.
⁴Surely this is how they are blessed
who fear the Eternal.
⁵May the Eternal
bless you from Zion!
May you see the good of Jerusalem
all the days of your life.
⁶May you see
your children's children!
Peace upon Israel!

קכח

^אשִׁיר הַמַּעֲלוֹת
אַשְׁרֵי כָּל־יְרֵא יהוה
הַהֹלֵךְ בִּדְרָכָיו:
^ביְגִיעַ כַּפֶּיךָ כִּי תֹאכֵל
אַשְׁרֶיךָ וְטוֹב לָךְ:
^גאֶשְׁתְּךָ כְּגֶפֶן פֹּרִיָּה
בְּיַרְכְּתֵי בֵיתֶךָ
בָּנֶיךָ כִּשְׁתִלֵי זֵיתִים
סָבִיב לְשֻׁלְחָנֶךָ:
^דהִנֵּה כִי־כֵן יְבֹרַךְ גָּבֶר
יְרֵא יהוה:
^היְבָרֶכְךָ יהוה מִצִּיּוֹן
וּרְאֵה בְּטוּב יְרוּשָׁלָיִם
כֹּל יְמֵי חַיֶּיךָ:
^ווּרְאֵה־בָנִים לְבָנֶיךָ
שָׁלוֹם עַל־יִשְׂרָאֵל:

Passages from the Sayings of the Fathers may be read here, pages 701-724.

Concluding prayers can be found on pages 306-324.

סיום התפלה
Concluding Prayers and Songs

עָלֵינוּ לְשַׁבֵּחַ לַאֲדוֹן הַכֹּל.

It is our duty to praise the Ruler of all.

> There is no traditional term for the closing part of the service, though certain elements including the *Aleinu* prayer, the mourner's *Kaddish* and a closing song are standard.
>
> This part of the service serves a number of purposes. It retraces and reverses the journey represented by our service. At the beginning we moved from the outside world to the special 'space' of the synagogue, community and service. When the formal prayers began with the *Bar'chu*, the first blessing also spoke of this outside world to which we belong, speaking of God as Creator of the world and all peoples. Only then, with the second blessing, did we move on to God's particular relationship with the Jewish people.
>
> At the *Amidah* we stood in the presence of God and, on Shabbat and certain weekdays, received the words of Torah. Now we sum up our responsibility and task as the Jewish people (the first paragraph of the *Aleinu*) but then our hopes for the rest of the world (the second paragraph). The *Kaddish*, though given special significance for mourners, also expresses these messianic hopes.
>
> Having set aside the outside world when we entered the synagogue and service, this concluding section also prepares us for our return to that outside world and the many realities that await us.

סיום התפלה

וְאִם לֹא עַכְשָׁיו אֵימָתַי
And if not now, when?

The Shabbat *morning service continues here. All other morning and afternoon services continue with Aleinu on page 310 or 312. For additions to the evening services during the Penitential Season and during the Counting of the* Omer, *see page 308.*

אֵין כֵּאלֹהֵינוּ. אֵין כַּאדוֹנֵינוּ.
אֵין כְּמַלְכֵּנוּ. אֵין כְּמוֹשִׁיעֵנוּ:

אֵין There is none like our God;
there is none like our Lord;
there is none like our Sovereign;
there is none like our Saviour.

מִי כֵאלֹהֵינוּ. מִי כַאדוֹנֵינוּ.
מִי כְמַלְכֵּנוּ. מִי כְמוֹשִׁיעֵנוּ:

Who is like our God;
who is like our Lord;
who is like our Sovereign;
who is like our Saviour?

נוֹדֶה לֵאלֹהֵינוּ. נוֹדֶה לַאדוֹנֵינוּ.
נוֹדֶה לְמַלְכֵּנוּ. נוֹדֶה לְמוֹשִׁיעֵנוּ:

We give thanks to our God;
we give thanks to our Lord;
we give thanks to our Sovereign;
we give thanks to our Saviour.

בָּרוּךְ אֱלֹהֵינוּ. בָּרוּךְ אֲדוֹנֵינוּ.
בָּרוּךְ מַלְכֵּנוּ. בָּרוּךְ מוֹשִׁיעֵנוּ:

Blessed is our God;
blessed is our Lord;
blessed is our Sovereign;
blessed is our Saviour.

אַתָּה הוּא אֱלֹהֵינוּ.
אַתָּה הוּא אֲדוֹנֵינוּ.
אַתָּה הוּא מַלְכֵּנוּ.
אַתָּה הוּא מוֹשִׁיעֵנוּ:

You are our God;
You are our Lord;
You are our Sovereign;
You are our Saviour.

אֵין *Ein keiloheinu, ein kadoneinu, ein k'malkeinu, ein k'moshi'einu.*
Mi cheiloheinu, mi chadoneinu, mi ch'malkeinu, mi ch'moshi'einu.
Nodeh leiloheinu, nodeh ladoneinu, nodeh l'malkeinu, nodeh l'moshi'einu.
Baruch eloheinu, baruch adoneinu, baruch malkeinu, baruch moshi'einu.
Attah hu eloheinu, attah hu adoneinu, attah hu malkeinu, attah hu moshi'einu.

אֵין כֵּאלֹהֵינוּ There is none like our God ...
This popular ancient hymn is located after the *Musaf* service in both Ashkenazi and Sephardi traditions. The initial letters of the first three verses spell Amen and the last two verses begin *baruch, attah*, 'blessed are You'. It may have been originally located at the close of the Shabbat as a way of bidding farewell to Shabbat, just as we greeted the Shabbat bride at the beginning.

Ladino Version of Ein Keloheinu

Non komo muestro Dio
Non komo muestro Senyor
Non komo muestro Re
Non komo muestro Salvador.

Ken komo muestro Dio
Ken komo muestro Senyor
Ken komo muestro Re
Ken komo muestro Salvador.

Loaremos a muestro Dio
Loaremos a muestro Senyor
Loaremos a muestro Re
Loaremos a muestro Salvador.

Bendicho muestro Dio
Bendicho muestro Senyor
Bendicho muestro Re
Bendicho muestro Salvador.

Tu sos muestro Dio
Tu sos muestro Senyor
Tu sos muestro Re
Tu sos muestro Salvador.

During the Penitential Period, from the first day of the month of Elul *until* Shemini Atzeret, *Psalm 27 (page 627) may be read here.*

> During the *Omer* period, forty-nine days between *Pesach*, starting on the evening of the second day, and *Shavuot*, it is customary to count the *Omer*. This is an echo of the practice in Biblical times of marking the beginning of the grain harvest by bringing a measure, an Omer, of barley to the temple where it was waved by the priest. *Shavuot*, seven weeks later, marked the beginning of the wheat harvest. After the destruction of the temple and the loss of the land of Israel the tradition of counting these days was maintained.
>
> The practice consists of reciting a blessing and then numbering the specific day according to the formula indicated below.

Readings for each day of the Omer *period can be found in*
Forms of Prayer II Prayers for the Pilgrim Festivals, pages 655-718.

ספירת העמר
COUNTING THE *OMER*

בָּרוּךְ Blessed are You, our Living God, Sovereign of the universe, whose commandments make us holy and who commands us to count the Omer.

בָּרוּךְ אַתָּה יהוה אֱלֹהֵינוּ מֶלֶךְ הָעוֹלָם אֲשֶׁר קִדְּשָׁנוּ בְּמִצְוֹתָיו וְצִוָּנוּ עַל סְפִירַת הָעֹמֶר:

בָּרוּךְ *Baruch attah Adonai eloheinu melech ha-olam,*
asher kidd'shanu b'mitsvotav v'tsivanu al s'firat ha-omer.

הַיּוֹם This is the _____ day of the *Omer*.

הַיּוֹם _____ יָמִים לָעֹמֶר:

After the first week:
הַיּוֹם This is the _____ day, making _____ week(s) and _____ days of the *Omer*.

הַיּוֹם _____ יָמִים
שֶׁהֵם _____ שָׁבוּעוֹת
וְ _____ יָמִים לָעֹמֶר:

From the eleventh night:
הַיּוֹם This is the _____ day, making _____ week(s) and _____ days of the *Omer*.

הַיּוֹם _____ יוֹם
שֶׁהֵם _____ שָׁבוּעוֹת
וְ _____ יָמִים לָעֹמֶר:

הַיּוֹם *Hayom* _____ *yamim la-omer.*

After the first week: הַיּוֹם *Hayom* _____ *yamim la-omer,*
shehem _____ *shavuot v'* _____ *yamim la-omer.*

After the first week: הַיּוֹם *Hayom* _____ *yom la-omer,*
shehem _____ *shavuot v'* _____ *yamim la-omer.*

309 CONCLUDING PRAYERS AND SONGS   *ALEINU*

עָלֵינוּ

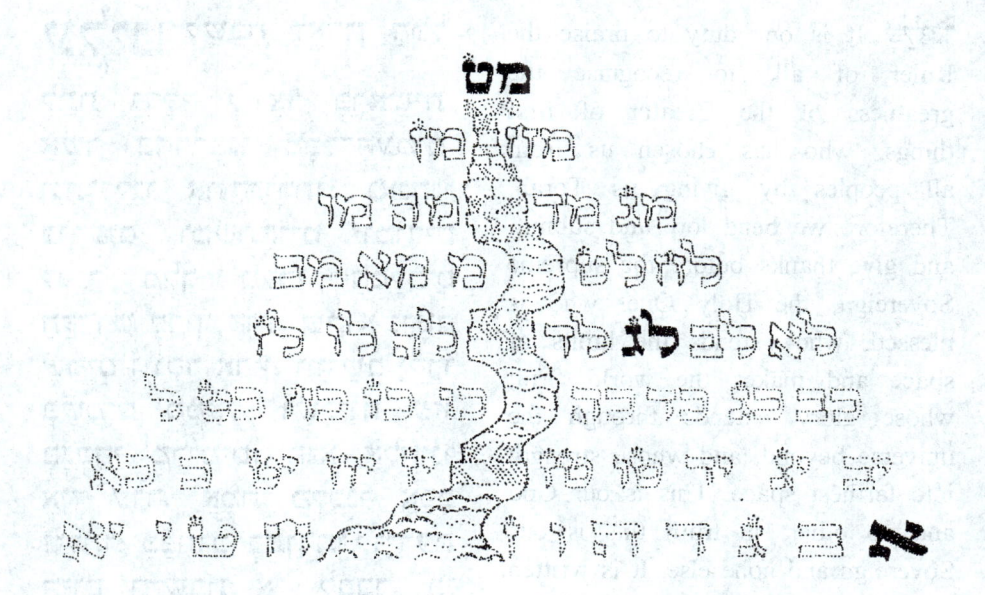

ALEINU

> The *Aleinu* prayer originated in the *Rosh Hashanah Musaf*, 'Additional' Service, where it introduces a section on *Malchuyot*, God's Sovereignty. It consists of two paragraphs and marks the final stage of the service as we prepare to move away from the world of prayer into the life outside. We have focused intensively on our identity as the Jewish people and our special relationship with God, the theme of the first paragraph. Now as we reunite with other people we try to understand our relationship with them as well, the theme of the second paragraph.
>
> We provide two versions of the prayer: *I*, a slight variation on the form that has been in use in most editions of *Forms of Prayer* since 1841, and *II*, an amended version reflecting changes introduced in progressive liturgies in Israel and the USA.

עלינו

One of the following two versions of the Aleinu/Al ken n'kaveh:

I BUILDING THE KINGDOM OF GOD: THE DUTY OF ISRAEL ⟨346⟩

עָלֵינוּ It is our duty to praise the Ruler of all, to recognise the greatness of the Creator of first things, who has chosen us from all peoples by giving us Torah. Therefore we bend low and submit, and give thanks before the supreme Sovereign, the Holy One, who is blessed, who extends the limits of space and makes the world firm; whose glory extends through the universe beyond, and whose strength into farthest space. This is our God and no other; in truth this is our Sovereign and none else. It is written in God's Torah: 'Realise this today and take it to heart; that God is Sovereign in the heavens above and on the earth beneath; no other exists.'[1]

עָלֵינוּ לְשַׁבֵּחַ לַאֲדוֹן הַכֹּל. לָתֵת גְּדֻלָּה לְיוֹצֵר בְּרֵאשִׁית. אֲשֶׁר בָּחַר־בָּנוּ מִכָּל־הָעַמִּים. וְנָתַן־לָנוּ אֶת־תּוֹרָתוֹ: וַאֲנַחְנוּ כּוֹרְעִים וּמִשְׁתַּחֲוִים וּמוֹדִים לִפְנֵי מֶלֶךְ מַלְכֵי הַמְּלָכִים הַקָּדוֹשׁ בָּרוּךְ הוּא: שֶׁהוּא נוֹטֶה שָׁמַיִם וְיוֹסֵד אָרֶץ. וּמוֹשַׁב יְקָרוֹ בַּשָּׁמַיִם מִמַּעַל. וּשְׁכִינַת עֻזּוֹ בְּגָבְהֵי מְרוֹמִים: הוּא אֱלֹהֵינוּ אֵין עוֹד. אֱמֶת מַלְכֵּנוּ אֶפֶס זוּלָתוֹ: כַּכָּתוּב בְּתוֹרָתוֹ. וְיָדַעְתָּ הַיּוֹם וַהֲשֵׁבֹתָ אֶל לְבָבֶךָ. כִּי יהוה הוּא הָאֱלֹהִים בַּשָּׁמַיִם מִמַּעַל וְעַל הָאָרֶץ מִתָּחַת אֵין עוֹד:

עָלֵינוּ Aleinu l'shabbei'ach la'adon ha-kol, lateit g'dullah l'yotseir b'reishit, asher bachar banu mikkol ha-ammim, v'natan lanu et torato, va'anachnu kor'im umishtachavim umodim, lifnei melech malchei ha-m'lachim, ha-kadosh baruch hu, shehu noteh shamayim v'yoseid arets, umoshav y'karo ba-shamayim mimma'al ush'chinat uzzo b'govhei m'romim. Hu eloheinu, ein od, emet malkeinu, efes zulato, ka-katuv b'torato: V'yadata ha-yom vahasheivota el l'vavecha, ki Adonai hu ha-elohim bashamayim mimma'al v'al ha-arets mittachat ein od.

עָלֵינוּ **It is our ...**

The first paragraph defines our task to be witnesses to God, and to make God's presence known and celebrated in the world. Earlier versions expressed the need to do this by contrasting us with other peoples and faiths, who are viewed negatively as idol-worshippers. Some of these phrases were censored by surrounding authorities or by Jewish self-censorship. One of them, 'who has not made us like the nations of the earth', is a potentially dangerous denial of our own capability to behave badly as individual Jews or as a nation when we have power over others. We have replaced them with another classical Jewish teaching that by giving us the Torah, God has offered us a special role in the world.

[1] Deut 4:39.

311 CONCLUDING PRAYERS AND SONGS — ALEINU

THE HOPE FOR HUMANITY ☰ 347

עַל־כֵּן **Therefore, Almighty God, we put our hope in You.** Soon let us witness the glory of Your power; when the worship of material things shall pass away from the earth, and prejudice and superstition shall at last be cut off; when the world will be set right by the rule of God, and all humanity shall speak out in Your name, and all the wicked of the earth shall turn to You. Then all who inhabit this world shall meet in understanding, and shall know that to You alone each one shall submit, and pledge themselves in every tongue. In Your presence, Almighty God, they shall bow down and be humble, honouring the glory of Your being. All shall accept the duty of building Your kingdom, so that Your reign of goodness shall come soon and last forever. For Yours alone is the true kingdom, and only the glory of Your rule endures forever. So it is written in Your Torah: 'The Eternal shall rule forever and ever.' So it is prophesied: 'The Eternal shall be Sovereign over all the earth. On that day the Eternal shall be One, and known as One.'[1]

עַל־כֵּן נְקַוֶּה לְךָ יהוה אֱלֹהֵינוּ לִרְאוֹת מְהֵרָה בְּתִפְאֶרֶת עֻזֶּךָ. לְהַעֲבִיר גִּלּוּלִים מִן הָאָרֶץ וְהָאֱלִילִים כָּרוֹת יִכָּרֵתוּן. לְתַקֵּן עוֹלָם בְּמַלְכוּת שַׁדַּי. וְכָל־בְּנֵי בָשָׂר יִקְרְאוּ בִשְׁמֶךָ. לְהַפְנוֹת אֵלֶיךָ כָּל־רִשְׁעֵי אָרֶץ: יַכִּירוּ וְיֵדְעוּ כָּל־יוֹשְׁבֵי תֵבֵל כִּי לְךָ תִּכְרַע כָּל־בֶּרֶךְ. תִּשָּׁבַע כָּל־לָשׁוֹן: לְפָנֶיךָ יהוה אֱלֹהֵינוּ יִכְרְעוּ וְיִפֹּלוּ. וְלִכְבוֹד שִׁמְךָ יְקָר יִתֵּנוּ. וִיקַבְּלוּ כֻלָּם אֶת־עוֹל מַלְכוּתֶךָ. וְתִמְלֹךְ עֲלֵיהֶם מְהֵרָה לְעוֹלָם וָעֶד. כִּי הַמַּלְכוּת שֶׁלְּךָ הִיא וּלְעוֹלְמֵי עַד תִּמְלוֹךְ בְּכָבוֹד: כַּכָּתוּב בְּתוֹרָתֶךָ. יהוה יִמְלֹךְ לְעוֹלָם וָעֶד: וְנֶאֱמַר. וְהָיָה יהוה לְמֶלֶךְ עַל־כָּל־הָאָרֶץ. בַּיּוֹם הַהוּא יִהְיֶה יהוה אֶחָד וּשְׁמוֹ אֶחָד:

עַל־כֵּן *Al kein n'kavveh l'cha Adonai eloheinu lir'ot m'heirah b'tif'eret uzzecha, l'ha'avir gillulim min ha-arets, v'ha-elilim karot yikkareitun, l'takkein olam b'malchut shaddai, v'chol b'nei vasar yikr'u vishmecha, l'hafnot eilecha kol rish'ei arets. Yakiru v'yeid'u kol yosh'vei teiveil, ki l'cha tichra kol berech tishava kol lashon. L'fanecha Adonai eloheinu, yichr'u v'yippolu, v'lichvod shimcha y'kar yitteinu, vikabb'lu chullam et ol malchutecha, v'timloch aleihem m'heirah l'olam va'ed, ki ha-malchut shell'cha hi, ul'ol'mei ad timloch b'chavod, ka-katuv b'toratecha: Adonai yimloch l'olam va'ed. V'ne'emar: v'hayah Adonai l'melech al kol ha-arets, ba-yom ha-hu yihyeh Adonai echad ush'mo echad.*

עַל־כֵּן נְקַוֶּה **Therefore we put our hope ...**
The second complementary paragraph reminds us just as forcibly that we are not alone in the world, nor are we the only ones addressed by God. This traditional version sees all nations as turning to Israel's God when all forms of idolatry vanish from the earth in the longed-for messianic time. We have interpreted the Hebrew terms *elilim* and *gillulim*, diminutive words of contempt for idols, as 'the worship of material things' and as 'prejudice and superstition'.

[1] Ex 15:18; Zech 14:9.

II BUILDING THE KINGDOM OF GOD: THE DUTY OF ISRAEL ♇346

עָלֵינוּ It is our duty to praise the Ruler of all, to recognise the greatness of the Creator of first things, who has given us the Torah of truth, and planted eternal life within us. For all the peoples walk in the name of their gods, but we walk in the name of the Eternal our God forever and ever; who extends the limits of space and makes the world firm, whose glory extends through the universe beyond, and whose strength into farthest space. This is our God and no other; in truth this is our Sovereign and none else. It is written in God's Torah: 'It is you that God took and brought out of the fiery furnace of Egypt, to be God's own people as at this very day.'[1]

עָלֵינוּ לְשַׁבֵּחַ לַאֲדוֹן הַכֹּל. לָתֵת גְּדֻלָּה לְיוֹצֵר בְּרֵאשִׁית: אֲשֶׁר נָתַן לָנוּ תּוֹרַת אֱמֶת. וְחַיֵּי עוֹלָם נָטַע בְּתוֹכֵנוּ. כִּי כָל־הָעַמִּים יֵלְכוּ אִישׁ בְּשֵׁם אֱלֹהָיו וַאֲנַחְנוּ נֵלֵךְ בְּשֵׁם־יְהֹוָה אֱלֹהֵינוּ לְעוֹלָם וָעֶד: שֶׁהוּא נוֹטֶה שָׁמַיִם וְיוֹסֵד אָרֶץ. וּמוֹשַׁב יְקָרוֹ בַּשָּׁמַיִם מִמַּעַל. וּשְׁכִינַת עֻזּוֹ בְּגָבְהֵי מְרוֹמִים: הוּא אֱלֹהֵינוּ אֵין עוֹד. אֱמֶת מַלְכֵּנוּ אֶפֶס זוּלָתוֹ: כַּכָּתוּב בְּתוֹרָתוֹ. וְאֶתְכֶם לָקַח יְהֹוָה וַיּוֹצֵא אֶתְכֶם מִכּוּר הַבַּרְזֶל מִמִּצְרָיִם לִהְיוֹת לוֹ לְעַם נַחֲלָה כַּיּוֹם הַזֶּה:

עָלֵינוּ Aleinu l'shabbei'ach la'adon ha-kol lateit g'dullah l'yotseir b'reishit, asher natan lanu torat emet, v'chayyei olam nata b'tocheinu, ki kol ha-amim yeil'chu ish b'sheim elohav, va'anachnu neileich b'sheim Adonai eloheinu l'olam va'ed, shehu noteh shamayim v'yoseid arets, umoshav y'karo bashamayim mimma'al ush'chinat uzzo b'govhei m'romim. Hu eloheinu, ein od, emet malkeinu, efes zulato, ka-katuv b'torato: V'etchem lakach Adonai vayotsei etchem mikur ha-barzel mimitsrayim lih'yot lo l'am nachalah ka-yom ha-zeh.

עָלֵינוּ *It is our ...*
In this version, while asserting our distinctive role as the recipients of God's Torah, we acknowledge that 'all peoples walk in the name of their god', the words of the prophet Micah (4:5).

[1] Deut 4:20.

313 CONCLUDING PRAYERS AND SONGS — ALEINU

THE HOPE FOR HUMANITY ☰ 347

עַל־כֵּן Therefore, Almighty God, we put our hope in You. Soon let us witness the glory of Your power; when the worship of material things shall pass away from the earth, and prejudice and superstition shall at last be cut off; when the world will be set right by the rule of God, and all humanity shall speak out in Your name, and all the wicked of the earth shall turn to You. Then all who inhabit this world shall meet in understanding, and shall know that we are all partners in the repairing of Your world. For Yours alone is the true kingdom, and only the glory of Your rule endures forever.
So it is written in Your Torah:
'The Eternal shall rule forever and ever.'
So it is prophesied:
'The Eternal shall be Sovereign over all the earth. On that day the Eternal shall be One, and known as One.'[1]

עַל־כֵּן נְקַוֶּה לְךָ יהוה אֱלֹהֵינוּ לִרְאוֹת מְהֵרָה בְּתִפְאֶרֶת עֻזֶּךָ. לְהַעֲבִיר גִּלּוּלִים מִן הָאָרֶץ וְהָאֱלִילִים כָּרוֹת יִכָּרֵתוּן: לְתַקֵּן עוֹלָם בְּמַלְכוּת שַׁדַּי. וְכָל־בְּנֵי בָשָׂר יִקְרְאוּ בִשְׁמֶךָ. לְהַפְנוֹת אֵלֶיךָ כָּל־רִשְׁעֵי אָרֶץ: יַכִּירוּ וְיֵדְעוּ כָּל־יוֹשְׁבֵי תֵבֵל כִּי שֻׁתָּפִים כֻּלָּנוּ בְּתִקּוּן עוֹלָמֶךָ. כִּי הַמַּלְכוּת שֶׁלְּךָ הִיא וּלְעוֹלְמֵי עַד תִּמְלֹךְ בְּכָבוֹד: כַּכָּתוּב בְּתוֹרָתֶךָ. יהוה יִמְלֹךְ לְעֹלָם וָעֶד: וְנֶאֱמַר. וְהָיָה יהוה לְמֶלֶךְ עַל־כָּל־הָאָרֶץ. בַּיּוֹם הַהוּא יִהְיֶה יהוה אֶחָד וּשְׁמוֹ אֶחָד:

עַל־כֵּן Al kein n'kavveh l'cha Adonai eloheinu lir'ot m'heirah b'tif'eret uzzecha, l'ha'avir gillulim min ha-arets, v'ha-elilim karot yikareitun, l'takkein olam b'malchut shaddai v'chol b'nei vasar yikr'u vishmecha, l'hafnot eilecha kol rish'ei arets. Yakiru v'yeid'u kol yosh'vei teiveil, ki shuttafim kullanu b'tikkun olamecha, ki ha-malchut shell'cha hi, ul'ol'mei ad timloch b'chavod, ka-katuv b'toratecha: Adonai yimloch l'olam va'ed. V'ne'emar: v'hayah Adonai l'melech al kol ha-arets, ba-yom ha-hu yihyeh Adonai echad ush'mo echad.

עַל־כֵּן נְקַוֶּה **Therefore we put our hope ...**
Rather than insist that all peoples will eventually come to worship Israel's God, as in the traditional version, we express here the hope that all will acknowledge our shared responsibility, each in our own particular way, as partners in *tikkun olam*, in 'repairing the world'. 'Every people is a question which God addresses to humanity; and every people, from its place, with its special talents and possibilities must answer for its own sake and for the sake of humanity' (*Leo Baeck*).

[1] Ex 15:18; Zech 14:9.

One of the following prayers may be read before reciting the Kaddish:

I

On this Shabbat, as our week's work is ended, and we enjoy a brief time of rest, we think of those whose life's work is done, and have gone to their eternal rest. We think especially now of those who died at this time in years past.

We face the mysteries of life and death and eternal life. We put our trust in God whom we have never trusted enough. *Harachaman*, may we inherit a day that shall be wholly a Shabbat and rest in life everlasting.

We pray for the coming of God's kingdom in the words of the *Kaddish* …

II

We live our life, yet hardly know its nature, for from a mystery we come and to this mystery we return. The death of those close to our hearts grieves and humbles us. It reminds us that we all must die, like grass that grows in the morning, that grows so fresh in the morning, and in the evening fades and dies. So we end our years like a sigh.

Let us think of those who died at this time in years past.

How can we accept the reality of death? By remembering the goodness of our loved ones, and by shaping our lives after their example. For the memory of the righteous is truly a blessing, and an inspiration for all our days. May our lives be always worthy of their memory.

III

The souls of the righteous are in the hands of God and no harm shall come to them.

God, source of compassion, You give life, in which joys and sorrows are mingled, and send death with its promise of eternal peace.

(We mourn this week the deaths of ...
May You comfort their families and all who mourn for them. May God who is full of compassion, whose presence is over us, cover them in the shelter of Your wings forever and bind their souls into the gathering of life.)

We remember at this time all those who once shared with us the joys and challenges of life, but who are with us no longer. May their souls shine like the brightness of the heavens. We thank You for all You gave them during their lives.

(We think especially of those who died at this time in years past ...)

Zichronam livrachah - may the memory of their love and guidance be a source of enduring blessing. In loving memory we sanctify Your name and say:

When the Kaddish *is recited by the mourners the congregation responds throughout at* Amen *and* b'rich hu *as well as reciting the sentence beginning:* y'hei sh'meih rabba ...

Before reciting the concluding sentence, oseh shalom, *as previously at the end of the* Amidah, *it is a custom to take three steps backwards, to bow to the left at the words* oseh shalom bimromav, *to the right at* hu ya'aseh shalom *and to the centre at* aleinu.

קדיש יתום
MOURNERS' KADDISH

קדיש

יִתְגַּדַּל Let us magnify and let us sanctify in this world the great name of God whose will created it. May God's reign come in your lifetime, and in your days, and in the lifetime of the family of Israel - quickly and speedily may it come. **Amen.** **May the greatness of God's being be blessed from eternity to eternity.** Let us bless and let us extol, let us tell aloud and let us raise aloft, let us set on high and let us honour, let us exalt and let us praise the Holy One, **whose name is blessed,**	יִתְגַּדַּל וְיִתְקַדַּשׁ שְׁמֵהּ רַבָּא בְּעָלְמָא דִּי־בְרָא כִרְעוּתֵהּ: וְיַמְלִיךְ מַלְכוּתֵהּ בְּחַיֵּיכוֹן וּבְיוֹמֵיכוֹן וּבְחַיֵּי דִי־כָל־בֵּית יִשְׂרָאֵל בַּעֲגָלָא וּבִזְמַן קָרִיב. וְאִמְרוּ אָמֵן: יְהֵא שְׁמֵהּ רַבָּא מְבָרַךְ לְעָלַם וּלְעָלְמֵי עָלְמַיָּא: יִתְבָּרַךְ וְיִשְׁתַּבַּח וְיִתְפָּאַר וְיִתְרוֹמַם וְיִתְנַשֵּׂא וְיִתְהַדָּר וְיִתְעַלֶּה וְיִתְהַלָּל שְׁמֵהּ דִּי־קֻדְשָׁא. בְּרִיךְ הוּא.
who is far beyond any blessing or song,	לְעֵלָּא מִן־כָּל־בִּרְכָתָא
During the Ten Days of Penitence: who is far above and beyond any blessing	*During the Ten Days of Penitence:* לְעֵלָּא לְעֵלָּא מִכָּל־בִּרְכָתָא
any honour or any consolation that can be spoken of in this world. **Amen.**	וְשִׁירָתָא תֻּשְׁבְּחָתָא וְנֶחֱמָתָא דִּי־אֲמִירָן בְּעָלְמָא. וְאִמְרוּ אָמֵן:
May great peace from heaven and the gift of life be granted to us and to all the family of Israel. **Amen.** May the Maker of peace in the highest bring this peace upon us and upon all Israel and upon all the world. **Amen.**	יְהֵא שְׁלָמָא רַבָּא מִן שְׁמַיָּא וְחַיִּים עָלֵינוּ וְעַל־כָּל־יִשְׂרָאֵל. וְאִמְרוּ אָמֵן: עֹשֶׂה שָׁלוֹם בִּמְרוֹמָיו הוּא יַעֲשֶׂה שָׁלוֹם עָלֵינוּ וְעַל כָּל־יִשְׂרָאֵל וְעַל־כָּל־הָעוֹלָם. וְאִמְרוּ אָמֵן:

קַדִּישׁ יָתוֹם Mourners' *Kaddish*

The *Kaddish*, composed in Aramaic, in its various forms is a hymn of praise to God that is used to mark the conclusion of different sections of the service. At the end of the service it is customary for mourners to recite it during the period of mourning after the death of a relative and on the anniversary of that death. In some congregations it is the custom, following the

CONCLUDING PREYERS AND SONGS — KADDISH

יִתְגַּדַּל *Yitgaddal v'yitkaddash sh'meih rabba,*
b'alma di v'ra chiruteih,
v'yamlich malchuteih,
b'chayyeichon uv'yomeichon
uv'chayyei di chol beit yisra'el,
ba'agala u'vizman kariv,
v'imru **amen.**
Y'hei sh'meih rabba m'varach,
l'alam ul'almei almaya.
Yitbarach v'yishtabbach v'yitpa'ar
v'yitromam v'yitnassei v'yit-haddar
v'yit'alleh v'yit-hallal,
sh'meih di kudsha,
b'rich hu,
l'eilla min kol birchata
  During the Ten Days of Penitence:
  l'eilla l'eilla mikol birchata
v'shirata tushb'chata v'nechemata,
di amiran b'alma,
v'imru **amen.**
Y'hei sh'lama rabba min sh'maya,
v'chayyim aleinu v'al kol yisra'el,
v'imru **amen.**
Oseh shalom bimromav,
hu ya'aseh shalom
aleinu v'al kol yisra'el,
  v'al kol ha-olam,
v'imru **amen.**

---

tradition, for the mourners alone to recite it; in others the entire congregation recites it, taking on this responsibility of behalf of those, like victims of the *Shoah*, who have no survivors to recite it.

During the High Holydays the word *l'eilla*, 'above', in the third paragraph, is repeated as God is understood to ascend to the judgment seat.

סיום התפלה

One of the following concluding hymns or another song:

יִגְדַּל We praise the living God, the One Whom we adore, who is outside the bounds of space and time;	יִגְדַּל אֱלֹהִים חַי וְיִשְׁתַּבַּח. נִמְצָא וְאֵין עֵת אֶל־מְצִיאוּתוֹ:
Who is unique, alone and far beyond compare, outside all limitations we define;	אֶחָד וְאֵין יָחִיד כְּיִחוּדוֹ. נֶעְלָם וְגַם אֵין סוֹף לְאַחְדוּתוֹ:
Who has no human frame, no human shape or form; alone the source of holiness and awe.	אֵין לוֹ דְמוּת הַגּוּף וְאֵינוֹ גוּף. לֹא נַעֲרוֹךְ אֵלָיו קְדֻשָּׁתוֹ:
When not a single form appeared within the world, God was the first where nothing was before.	קַדְמוֹן לְכָל־דָּבָר אֲשֶׁר נִבְרָא. רִאשׁוֹן וְאֵין רֵאשִׁית לְרֵאשִׁיתוֹ:
Such is the Sovereign power that rules the universe, each creature knows it lives in God's domain.	הִנּוֹ אֲדוֹן עוֹלָם. לְכָל־נוֹצָר יוֹרֶה גְדֻלָּתוֹ וּמַלְכוּתוֹ:
But through a special grace the prophets learned God's will, those chosen ones who guide our journeying.	שֶׁפַע נְבוּאָתוֹ נְתָנוֹ. אֶל־אַנְשֵׁי סְגֻלָּתוֹ וְתִפְאַרְתּוֹ:

<<<

יִגְדַּל *Yigdal elohim chai v'yishtabach, nimtsa v'ein eit el m'tsi'uto.*
Echad v'ein yachid k'yichudo, ne'lam v'gam ein sof l'achduto.
Ein lo d'mut ha-guf v'eino guf, lo na'aroch eilav k'dushato.
Kadmon l'chol davar asher nivra, rishon v'ein reishit l'reishito.
Hinno adon olam l'chol notsar yoreh g'dulato umalchuto.
Shefa n'vu'ato n'tano, el anshei s'gullato v'tif'arto.

יִגְדַּל *Yigdal*

The hymn *Yigdal* is based on the thirteen principles of faith expressed by Moses Maimonides (1135-1204). They represent issues that he felt needed to be addressed in his time, partly because of internal debates within Judaism, partly to distinguish it from the views of the surrounding Islamic culture. This version may have been composed in the fourteenth century by the judge Daniel ben Yehudah of Rome. The poem is not included in some traditional prayer books as it was felt wrong to reduce the 613 *mitsvot* to any formulaic list. The conclusion 'These thirteen ...' is a Sephardic addition.

We have understood the line that God 'brings evil (punishment) upon evil-doers according to their evil' in line with Psalm 1, that evil leads to its own disaster.

319 CONCLUDING PRAYERS AND SONGS

No prophet has there been since Moses was our guide, who knew the Living God and came so close.	לֹא קָם בְּיִשְׂרָאֵל כְּמֹשֶׁה עוֹד נָבִיא. וּמַבִּיט אֶל־תְּמוּנָתוֹ:
God gave to Israel truth by which to lead our lives taught by the faithful prophet that God chose.	תּוֹרַת אֱמֶת נָתַן לְעַמּוֹ אֵל. עַל יַד נְבִיאוֹ נֶאֱמַן בֵּיתוֹ:
God will never change the teaching we received nor ever put another in its place.	לֹא יַחֲלִיף הָאֵל וְלֹא יָמִיר דָּתוֹ לְעוֹלָמִים לְזוּלָתוֹ:
God watches and can see the secrets in our hearts, before each deed foresees its final ways.	צוֹפֶה וְיוֹדֵעַ סְתָרֵינוּ. מַבִּיט לְסוֹף דָּבָר בְּקַדְמוּתוֹ:
Whoever loves good deeds rejoices in God's love, but evil leads to evil which destroys.	גּוֹמֵל לְאִישׁ חָסִיד כְּמִפְעָלוֹ. נוֹתֵן לְרָשָׁע רָע כְּרִשְׁעָתוֹ:
And at the end of days, an anointed one will come redeeming those who wait for God to save.	יִשְׁלַח לְקֵץ יָמִים מְשִׁיחֵנוּ. לִפְדּוֹת מְחַכֵּי קֵץ יְשׁוּעָתוֹ:
Life beyond all death, God gives with greatest love. We bless for evermore God's glorious name.	מֵתִים יְחַיֶּה אֵל בְּרוֹב חַסְדּוֹ. בָּרוּךְ עֲדֵי עַד שֵׁם תְּהִלָּתוֹ:
These thirteen play a part in Israel's faith in God, the principles derived from God's Torah.	אֵלֶּה שְׁלֹשׁ עֶשְׂרֵה לְעִקָּרִים. הִנָּם יְסוֹד דַּת אֵל וְתוֹרָתוֹ:

*Lo kam b'yisra'el k'mosheh od navi, umabbit el t'munato.
Torat emet natan l'ammo eil, al yad n'vi'o ne'eman beito.
Lo yachalif ha-eil v'lo yamir dato, l'olamim l'zulato.
Tsofeh v'yodei'a s'tareinu, mabbit l'sof davar b'kadmuto.
Gomeil l'ish chasid k'mif'alo, notein l'rasha ra k'rish'ato.
Yishlach l'keits yamim m'shicheinu, lifdot m'chakkei keits y'shu'ato.
Meitim y'chayeh eil b'rov chasdo, baruch adei ad sheim t'hillato.*

*Eilleh sh'losh esreih l'ikkarim,
Hinnam y'sod dat eil v'torato.*

סיום התפלה

אֲדוֹן עוֹלָם אֲשֶׁר מָלַךְ, בְּטֶרֶם כָּל־יְצִיר נִבְרָא:
לְעֵת נַעֲשָׂה בְחֶפְצוֹ כֹּל, אֲזַי מֶלֶךְ שְׁמוֹ נִקְרָא:
וְאַחֲרֵי כִּכְלוֹת הַכֹּל, לְבַדּוֹ יִמְלוֹךְ נוֹרָא:
וְהוּא הָיָה. וְהוּא הֹוֶה. וְהוּא יִהְיֶה בְּתִפְאָרָה:
וְהוּא אֶחָד וְאֵין שֵׁנִי, לְהַמְשִׁיל לוֹ לְהַחְבִּירָה:
בְּלִי רֵאשִׁית בְּלִי תַכְלִית, וְלוֹ הָעֹז וְהַמִּשְׂרָה:
וְהוּא אֵלִי וְחַי גּוֹאֲלִי, וְצוּר חֶבְלִי בְּיוֹם צָרָה:
וְהוּא נִסִּי וּמָנוּסִי, מְנָת כּוֹסִי בְּיוֹם אֶקְרָא:
בְּיָדוֹ אַפְקִיד רוּחִי, בְּעֵת אִישַׁן וְאָעִירָה:
וְעִם רוּחִי גְוִיָּתִי. אֲדֹנָי לִי וְלֹא אִירָא:

אֲדוֹן Eternal God who ruled alone
before creation of all forms,
at whose desire all began
and as the Sovereign was proclaimed.

Who, after everything shall end
alone, in awe, will ever reign,
who was and is for evermore,
the glory that will never change.

Unique and One, no other is
to be compared, to stand beside,
neither before, nor following,
alone the source
of power and might.

This is my God, who saves my life,
the rock I grasp in deep despair,
the flag I wave, the place I hide,
who shares my cup the day I call.

In my Maker's hand I lay my soul
both when I sleep
and when I wake,
and with my soul my body too,
my God is close, I shall not fear.

321 CONCLUDING PRAYERS AND SONGS — BLESSINGS

אֲדוֹן *Adon olam asher malach, b'terem kol y'tsir nivra.*
L'eit na'asah k'cheftso kol, azai melech sh'mo nikra.

V'acharei kichlot ha-kol, l'vaddo yimloch nora.
V'hu hayah v'hu hoveh, v'hu yihyeh b'tif'arah.

V'hu echad v'ein sheini, l'hamshil lo l'hachbirah.
B'li reishit b'li tachlit, v'lo ha-oz v'ha-misrah.

V'hu eili v'chai go'ali, v'tsur chevli b'yom tsarah.
V'hu nissi umanusi, m'nat kosi b'yom ekra.

B'yado afkid ruchi, b'eit ishan v'a'irah.
V'im ruchi g'vi'ati, Adonai li v'lo ira.

CONCLUDING BLESSINGS

It is a Reform tradition to conclude the service with a blessing, often the Biblical priestly blessing (Num 6:24-26), traditionally recited within the service by those who have the family tradition of being *cohanim*, descended from a priestly family. The one who recites the blessing invokes God to bestow it, as the Biblical text makes clear: 'They shall place My name upon the children of Israel and I will bless them.' It is appropriate to conclude the service with a word of blessing as we prepare to depart, just as we entered quoting the blessing of Balaam.

We have provided a number of alternative blessings from traditional sources to suit the particular occasion.

אֲדוֹן עוֹלָם *Adon Olam*

Like *Yigdal*, this hymn expresses a series of Jewish beliefs in a simple and memorable form. It has been incorporated into the morning service since the fifteenth century, but the authorship has been credited to a number of figures of the Gaonic period, between the seventh and eleventh centuries.

God existed before and beyond time; is apart from the world, 'transcendent', yet is engaged with human beings, 'immanent', and near when they call. The closing sentence suggests that it might have been intended as a night prayer.

For an explanation of the enlarged final letters see the commentary on page 517.

I

יְבָרֶכְךָ **May God bless you and keep you.**
May God's face shine upon you
and be gracious to you.
May God's face turn towards you
and give you peace.[1]

יְבָרֶכְךָ יהוה וְיִשְׁמְרֶךָ.
יָאֵר יהוה פָּנָיו אֵלֶיךָ וִיחֻנֶּךָּ.
יִשָּׂא יהוה פָּנָיו אֵלֶיךָ
וְיָשֵׂם לְךָ שָׁלוֹם:

> יְבָרֶכְךָ *Y'varech'cha Adonai v'yishm'recha.*
> *Ya'eir Adonai panav eilecha vichunnekka.*
> *Yissa Adonai panav eilecha, v'yaseim l'cha shalom.*

II

יְבָרְכֵנוּ **May God bless us and keep us.**
May God's face shine upon us
and be gracious to us.
May God's face turn towards us
and give us peace.[2]

יְבָרְכֵנוּ יהוה וְיִשְׁמְרֵנוּ.
יָאֵר יהוה פָּנָיו אֵלֵינוּ וִיחֻנֵּנוּ.
יִשָּׂא יהוה פָּנָיו אֵלֵינוּ
וְיָשֵׂם לָנוּ שָׁלוֹם:

> יְבָרְכֵנוּ *Y'var'cheinu Adonai v'yishm'reinu.*
> *Ya'eir Adonai panav eileinu vichunneinu.*
> *Yissa Adonai panav eileinu v'yaseim lanu shalom.*

III

יְהִי **May it be God's will**
that the divine presence
rest upon the work of your hands.[3]

יְהִי רָצוֹן שֶׁתִּשְׁרֶה שְׁכִינָה
בְּמַעֲשֵׂה יְדֵיכֶם:

> יְהִי *Y'hi ratson shetishreh sh'chinah b'ma'aseih y'deichem.*

IV

בָּרוּךְ **Blessed shall you be in the city,**
and blessed shall you be in the field.
Blessed shall you be when you come in,
and blessed shall you be when you go out.[4]

בָּרוּךְ אַתָּה בָּעִיר.
וּבָרוּךְ אַתָּה בַּשָּׂדֶה:
בָּרוּךְ אַתָּה בְּבֹאֶךָ.
וּבָרוּךְ אַתָּה בְּצֵאתֶךָ:

> בָּרוּךְ *Baruch attah ba-ir, uvaruch attah ba-sadeh.*
> *Baruch attah b'vo'echa, uvaruch attah b'tseitecha.*

---

[1] Num 6:24-26.
[2] Based on Num 6:24-26.
[3] Rashi on Ex 39:43.
[4] Deut 28:3,6.

323 CONCLUDING PRAYERS AND SONGS — BLESSINGS

V

יהוה May the Eternal God guard your going out and your coming in, now and forever.[1]

יהוה יִשְׁמָר־צֵאתְךָ וּבוֹאֶךָ
מֵעַתָּה וְעַד־עוֹלָם:

יהוה Adonai yishmor tseit'cha uvo'echa, mei'atta v'ad olam.

VI

יהוה God, give strength to Your people, bless Your people with peace.[2]

יהוה עֹז לְעַמּוֹ יִתֵּן
יהוה יְבָרֵךְ אֶת עַמּוֹ בַשָּׁלוֹם:

יהוה Adonai oz l'ammo yittein, Adonai y'vareich et ammo va-shalom.

VII

מַלְכָּא May the Sovereign of the universe extend your lives, increase your days and add to your years.

May you be saved from all trouble and delivered from all mishap. May the Master of heaven be your help at all times and in every season.[3]

מַלְכָּא דִי־עָלְמָא יְבָרֵךְ יַתְכוֹן
יַפִישׁ חַיֵּיכוֹן וְיַשְׂגֵּא יוֹמֵיכוֹן
וְיִתֵּן אַרְכָה לִשְׁנֵיכוֹן:
וְתִתְפָּרְקוּן וְתִשְׁתֵּיזְבוּן מִן
כָּל־עָקָא וּמִן כָּל־מַרְעִין
בִּישִׁין: מָרָן דִי־בִשְׁמַיָּא
יְהֵא בְסַעְדְּכוֹן כָּל־זְמַן וְעִדָּן:

מַלְכָּא Malka di alma y'vareich yatchon, yafish chayyeichon, v'yasgei yomeichon v'yittein archa lishneichon. V'titpar'kun v'tishteiz'vun min kol aka, umin kol mar'in bishin. Maran di vishmaya y'hei b'sa'd'chon, kol z'man v'iddan.

---

[1] Ps 121:8.
[2] Ps 29:11.
[3] The conclusion of the traditional Aramaic congregational prayer *Yekum purkan* (seventh century).

VIII

יְבָרֶכְכָה May God bless you with all that is good, and guard you from all that is harmful. May God enlighten your heart with the wisdom of life and give you understanding of many worlds. May God in faithful love offer you enduring peace.[1]

יְבָרֶכְכָה בְּכוֹל טוֹב.
וְיִשְׁמוֹרְכָה מִכּוֹל רָע.
וְיָאִיר לְבְּכָה בְּשֶׂכֶל חַיִּים.
וִיחוֹנְכָה בְּדַעַת עוֹלָמִים.
וְיִשָּׂא פְּנֵי חֲסָדָיו לְכָה
לְשָׁלוֹם עוֹלָמִים:

Y'varech'chah b'chol tov, v'yishmor'chah mikkol ra, v'ya'ir libb'chah b'seichel chayyim, v'yachon'chah b'da'at olamim, v'yissa p'nei chasadav, l'chah lishlom olamim.

IX

בְּרוּכִים Just as you were blessed when you entered,
May you be blessed as you depart.[2]

בְּרוּכִים אַתֶּם בְּבֹאֲכֶם
וּבְרוּכִים אַתֶּם בְּצֵאתְכֶם:

B'ruchim attem b'vo'achem, uv'ruchim attem b'tseit'chem.

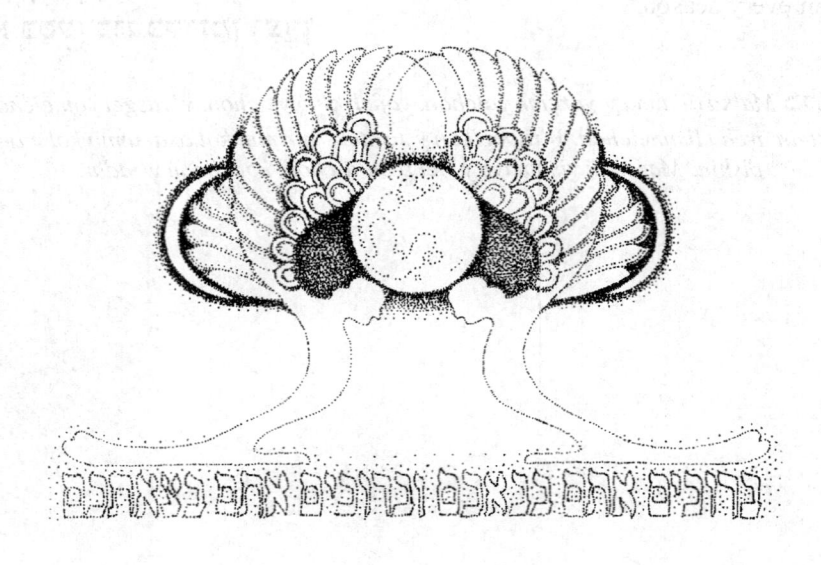

---

[1] From the Dead Sea Scrolls, *Megillat Ha-Serachim* 2:2f.

[2] Based on Deut 28:6.

Reflections on the Shabbat Services and the Daily *Amidah*

> The modern western world has had a profound impact on all who live within it. While our Jewish prayers speak to the personal experiences of our lives, from birth to death, through love and loss, in suffering and in joy, as individuals and as part of the Jewish people, much of the language and many of the assumptions belong to a very different understanding of the world, the universe and God. The following materials are intended to raise some of the questions we bring to the prayers we recite or offer another way of expressing the ideas and hopes they contain. The passages may be used alone or together, for private or public reading, as alternative 'reflections' on the traditional prayers. Further reflections on the themes of the service can be found in the Study Anthology.

REFLECTIONS ON THE EREV SHABBAT SERVICE

As we welcome Shabbat in song, we encounter the God of much of our liturgy - Sovereign of the world, Timeless Master, Ruler above all rulers, Almighty. For some, such a powerful and triumphant God may seem remote and inaccessible. It may be helpful to remember that 'Israel' means 'one who struggles with God' and reflect on our long and time-honoured tradition of questioning and challenging.

Meditation

This is how it ends. The week is winding down. Tired limbs and minds wait for rest. What is done is done, for good or ill. What has gone has gone, though it lingers with us still. The achievements and disappointments of the week live on, but soon will fade from memory. New challenges, fears and hopes will take their place. But not just yet...

We are at the threshold. It is time to recall - then let go of - what we have done and what we have failed to do, the gains and mistakes we've made, our satisfactions and discontents. We stand at the threshold. We pause for a moment, to catch the last gasps and glimmers of the week that has passed ...

And now it is time. Time to enter into the timeless, time for Shabbat, time for a glimpse of the world to come. We let go of the week that has passed and make space, and time, for something new to enter in.

This is how it ends. And this is how we begin again: let our lives be renewed at this sacred time, when the end and the beginning become One.

Kabbalat Shabbat - Welcoming Shabbat

From *Sabbath in the Kibbutz*

Mother Sabbath lays white cloths upon the tables
and lights the candles with an unseen hand -
she has gathered her children from their six days of labour
to a family meal.

Light falls on the tables, shadows lurk round walls -
there is shadow in wrinkles, light on sunburnt arms;
and shirts gleam white around shoulders and necks,
like prayer-shawls ...

There are eyes here have delved into unstudied futures,
and eyes that have filled with trembling or joy -
and someone furtively feels sorrow in her soul -
and her tear heals ...

Light is sown on the table. It rises and grows:
as eyes meet eyes, new sparks are born.
the shadows have fled from the wall, where pass the white hands
of unseen Mother Sabbath.

Mother Sabbath! Do you hear the pounding of hearts
and the silence of lips this night on the Jordan?
They thirst for prayer. Spread your hands over this bread
and bless them.

Bless the faithful, the sowers of light in the fields of all peoples -
and put the world's joy into hearts longing for companionship.
More will yet come, all to sit together like companions
at the Sabbath of rest ...

Ma'ariv Aravim - Who brings on the evening twilight

Sunset Prayer

I'll let you in on a secret
about how one should pray the sunset prayer.
It's like a juicy bit of praying,
like strolling on grass.
Nobody's chasing you, nobody hurries you.
You walk towards your Creator
with gifts in pure, empty hands.
The words are golden, their meaning is transparent,
it's as though you're saying them for the first time.

If you don't catch on
that you should feel a little elevated,
you're not saying the sunset prayer.
The tune is sheer simplicity,
you're just lending a helping hand
to the sinking day.
It's a heavy responsibility.
You take a created day
and you slip it
into the archive of life,
where all our lived-out days are lying together.

<<<

The day is departing with a quiet kiss.
It lies open at your feet
while you stand saying the blessings.
You can't create anything yourself, but you
can lead the day to its end and see
clearly the smile of its going down.

See how whole it all is,
not diminished for a second,
how you age with the days
that keep dawning,
how you bring your lived-out day
as a gift to eternity.

Ahavat Olam - With Everlasting Love

God is loving. There are so many ways to love. There is erotic love - passionate, searing, erratic. There is virtuous love - ongoing, nurturing, morally rooted. There is parental love - protective, demanding, guiding even in its anger.

Sometimes love is unilateral; sometimes it is dialogic. Sometimes love is sacrificial; sometimes it is commanding, imperial. Sometimes love is open, articulated clearly; sometimes it is hidden, veiled ...

Love is the affirmation of the other, given and received in wholeness. And forgiveness. Love is the presence of moral truth and goodness. Love is also the commitment to lead a life dedicated to truth and goodness. It is the stubborn perseverance on the way, no matter what the obstacle, the temptation, the sin.

Love is not smooth. It wrenches, it drags one along, it demands. And love frustrates; it causes deep anger. How does one love one's parent without superimposing that image on the child? How does one love one's child who rebels forcefully? How does one love the dying other?

Love is exclusive, dedicated to special persons in special ways. And love is inclusive, reaching out to an-other, seeking to embrace the stranger.

Love does not tolerate injustice; it impels one to action. Love forces one from security and lethargy into the world of the impersonal and evil. Love demands confrontation, risk, and danger; not foolhardiness but courage.

Because it is many and varied, love is contradictory. Love is not monolithic. It cannot be rationalised into a coherent whole, into a system or a single theology. Love is much more complex than its metaphors.

God loves all humanity, and individual human beings, in all these ways - as human beings love others and seek to be loved, in all these ways.

REFLECTIONS   EREV SHABBAT SERVICE

Sh'ma

We stumble through the *Sh'ma*
beginning together well, then stumbling.
At home in the sounds, then stalling through syllables
and groping for meanings.
Sh'ma! hear, listen, understand!
Commanded, commanding our sisters and brothers of Israel
Yisrael - 'wrestler with God'!

'*Adonai*' - my Master, '*Eloheinu*'- our God...
I cover my eyes with my hand, I shade myself
from all influences whether confident or faltering
and I listen, I try to hear
as I pronounce the name which is no name
'*Adonai*' I don't know, don't deny
'*Echad*' - the One, the One in all, in which all resides.

You shall love, you tell me.
Love who? Or what? Who and what are you?
With my hand on my heart, or my eyes, do I know?
With all my faculties, heart, mind, soul, might;
no partial love is this, not from part of me,
nor for what I'm partial to.
A love for the All in my life,
all of it: good, bad and indifferent.

'These words that I command you.'
Now I hear you say 'I', speaking directly,
commanding me from millennia past
yet you say '*ha-yom*' - today
calling to me in my here and now.

These words that I stumble through,
all that I wrestle with, you say 'shall be upon your heart'.
They beat my heart, they thump my breast, my brow, my ears.
And they shall be? Is that a promise?
If I hear, if I listen, if I understand.
And if I don't? If I love?

'And you shall repeat them to your children
and talk about them ...'
Children I love, home I love, walking, lying down, rising up.
If I love will I hear and understand?

<<<

If I am to tie them for a sign upon my hand
and let them be as reminders before my eyes,
when I take away my hand from my eyes and open them,
I would like it all to be One,
the good, the bad, and the indifferent,
the doubts, the confusion, the not knowing
all to be, just be there in the here and now
when I arise and when I lie down,
so that at the beginning and the end of the day
and at the end of all my days
the command is there forever to love,
calling from the doorposts of my mind
and opening out from the gates of my heart.

Amidah

A short Amidah
They say we're supposed to be in a palace.
So we bow and take certain steps
as the prescribed supplication
drops from our lips.
But what do we really know
of castles and kings?
My kitchen faucet constantly leaks
and the kids' faces
usually need cleaning.
If a door opened to a real palace,
I'd probably forget
and carry in a load of groceries.

No, the door we stand in front of
when the *Amidah* begins is silence.
And when we open it
and step through,
we arrive in our hearts.
Mine's not a fancy place,
no jewels, no throne,
certainly not fit for a king.
But in that small chamber,
for just a few moments on Sabbath,
God and I can roll up our sleeves,
put some schnapps out on the table,
sit down together, and finally talk.
That's palace enough for me.

Reflections on the Concluding Prayers begin on page 346.

REFLECTIONS ON THE SHABBAT MORNING SERVICE

Meditation

    This is the beginning. Almost anything can happen. We each bring with us the concerns of our daily lives, our hopes and fears. And as we move through the service, a multitude of feelings and thoughts will jostle for space within us. We may feel uplifted or distracted, bored or inspired, moved or indifferent - and perhaps all of these at different moments. We may lose ourselves in the words and melodies, then find ourselves again. We may leave this service unaffected by its opportunities, having missed our way. Or we may leave it refreshed and with spirits revived. There is no knowing in advance. Will a new insight arrive? A renewal of resolve be granted? A deeper understanding emerge? A restoration of hope? A moment of blessing? There is a mystery to our lives here on earth. As we open ourselves in prayer, we await what will unfold ...

    Let this journey we now begin offer us signposts along the way, glimpses of meaning, glimmers of purpose and belief. Let us find strength and renewal as we venture along - alone with ourselves, together with one another, alone and together with You.

Birchot Ha-shachar - Morning Blessings

    Teach me, God, to pray, to praise
    the splendour of ripe fruit, the wonder of a wrinkled leaf,
    the freedom to see, to feel to breathe,
    to know, to hope, and even to know grief.

    Teach my lips blessing, song, and praise
    when You renew Your time each night, each dawn,
    so that my days will not repeat my yesterdays,
    to save my life from mere routine of all days gone.

The Gift of our Body

We all have a body, so we are supposed to know what it is and what it means to have one, but when we talk or read about it, it seems as if we came from different planets ...

The body can be seen as a vessel of good and evil, or as a temple; it can be seen as a prison, or as a guesthouse of the soul; as a source of aesthetic and sensual delight, or as a despicable bag of flesh; as something that needs to be punished and starved, to neglect and hide, or as something to admire, to adorn and to take care of. It can be seen as a wild animal that needs to be tamed, or it can be perceived as a passive erotic object. Our bodies can be thought of as the essence of our individuality or, on the contrary, not at all our most essential part. They can be viewed as material things that we may manipulate, dissect and control, or as spiritual gateways ...

The body is itself the 'Golden Gate', because it is the memory-house of all the good and bad experiences we ever had and at the same time the treasure-house of knowledge, understanding and wisdom. Through it we can shape our lives in this and in the future world. It is up to us to make use of all its possibilities, both the physical and the spiritual, in an undivided cooperation and concord.

The Gift of our Soul

We talk of the soul but doubt its existence. Our lives are crowded in by the daily dramas and troubles that occupy our thoughts. Wearied and bruised by the world, our worries are legion - about our health, our work, our finances, our family, our future. We face loss and bereavement, disabilities and downfalls. These do not change. They do not go away. The messiness of life is all around us, confounding our hopes, our cheerfulness, our belief in goodness, our wish that there is a meaning to it all. And then we look up and out beyond our immediate concerns - and the horrors of the world stare back at us, diminishing our fragile faith. We are dismayed by the realities we see and distressed by the difficulties we may face. And where is the soul when we need it most?

The soul, antidote to oblivion, lives within us, waiting, hoping to be discovered anew. So we are told. The spirit that animates all being lives within us, offering us its promise of renewal. So it is said.

We may doubt its existence but the spark of God within is never extinguished until the day of our death. We creatures of flesh and blood have been gifted an essence we can never hold or grasp. It is part of every moment of our lives, yet always slipping out of sight. Beyond our questions and our fears it secures us in the world and makes our world secure.

What are we?

Body and mind, feelings and spirit. This is where we start. One life, our life, here and now. As blood pulses through our veins, our heart beats out the hours and days. And our bodies speak the mundane majesty of human life on earth. As neurones fire through the myriad pathways of our brain, a maze of thoughts spark in our skulls. And our minds declare the baffling glory of human life on earth. As the fabric of feelings spins on the loom of our lives, we sense a pattern emerging: love and loss, hurt and healing, sadness, joy, pain and pleasure. And the emotional strands that texture us all witness to the consoling grandeur of human life on earth.

And as we contemplate our own unique physical, mental and emotional life, do we not glimpse another truth about ourselves? Something we cannot grasp, cannot name, though names we have aplenty? Soul, spirit, Self, the spark of God within - how can mere words reveal the essence of ourselves? We are more than we can ever know, a mystery through and through.

What is our life?

We are one link in the great chain of being. Carbon atoms from the very beginning of time are in our every breath - the universe is imprinted within our flesh and blood. Strangely and wondrously wrought, we reflect the image of God, or so it is said. What meaning does this have? What meaning can we make? Adrift within the unyielding flow of time we struggle to understand our lives, our own small place in the larger scheme of things. Yet nobody like us has ever been, nor will ever be again. The mystery of creation is mirrored in ourselves.

What is our love?

We who may never have been loved enough, how many fellow human beings can we truly love? Only a few, to be sure. To the rest we lend a smile, at best. Our incompetence in love is humbling. Our love can be strong, passionate at times, but there are limits, and these we know too well. Yet love is a spiritual drama on which the world depends. So give us the strength to love a little more, and fear a little less. Love is more than a feeling - it prompts us to act, to give, to share. And as we move towards the other, we are unmasked, and see how much we care.

What is our justice?

'Justice, justice, you shall pursue ...'[1] This, we sense, is what it is all about. The Torah's daunting vision haunts the imagination. What can we do that makes a difference? Lives of poverty, humiliation, degradation and fear - and we are summoned to respond, to 'clothe the naked, free those who are bound, lift up those bent low'.

How much effort does it take to live the vision of a better world? Each one of us is called to task. The Torah's humble, lofty dream is in our hands. Let it not slip though our fingers as we sit and wait. May we find the courage to live the prophet's truth: 'Let justice roll down like waters, and righteousness like a mighty stream …'[1]

What is our success?

How much faith do we put in things that cannot last? The transience of life is hard to bear, when all that is solid melts into air. Or that's how it seems. We measure success by things that pass, when in our hearts we know that fame and fortune wither on the vine. We are hard-pressed to treasure what it is that really counts. Yet so much of what we need is present here and now: the richness of life unfolding, in all its dense abundance, humming its glory, whispering its secrets as we quietly attend. It's ours to hold, embrace, enjoy - before we have to let it go. For now, it's all we need.

What is our endurance?

How often our wishes come to nothing, our hopes are dashed, and restlessness is all we seem to know. We try so hard and fail so often. Help us to fail better. Help us not to succumb to the weariness of life. Life's blessings are a fragile gift, beyond our own control. This is difficult to remember, harder still to appreciate with our unquiet minds. Yet we frail creatures have an inner strength, a fortitude of spirit that quickens our resolve. We can recover our zest for life. We can learn to dream again. For we have courage and endurance grafted to our souls. Help us discover it once more, help us uncover the treasure that lies within.

What is our power?

We are the heirs of a great and gifted nation, inheritors of riches that cannot be counted. We are the descendants of a people who wrestled with the divine in order to discover the secrets of our life on earth. We are a people who have known tragedy and glory - and have survived both. We are the recipients of a wisdom as deep as the ocean, as broad as the heavens, as precious as life itself. And we have been entrusted with a task and a destiny that we have never abandoned. This is a miracle, we speak of it with awe. Hesitantly, defiantly, we remain committed to the fulfillment of our impossible task: the repair of the world, and the redemption of the One who was and is and will be, hidden in creation, hidden in us, waiting to be made whole again. 'On that day the Eternal will become One again, and known as One.'[2]

<<<

---

[1] Amos 5:24. [2] Zech 14:9.

What can we say before You?

You see how we try to reach with words what matters most. And how we fail. You see how we try to address in words the wonder and distress our world contains. And how little we can really say. Yet from time to time a word, a phrase, a sentence resonates with life, and meaning, as we glimpse some deeper knowledge - and know that we are not alone. Help us appreciate these moments. And when our words do fail, let silence take their place. Not the empty silence that our minds may fear, but the full, rich silence in which our soul's contentment lies. May this silence comfort us and sustain us, for it is filled with Your being. 'Be still, and know that I am God.'[1]

P'sukei D'zimra - Songs of Praise

I

There are those who sing the song of their own soul, and in their soul they find everything, full spiritual satisfaction.

And there are those who sing the song of the people. For they do not find the circle of their private soul wide enough, and so go beyond it, reaching for more powerful heights. And they unite themselves with the soul of the community of Israel, sing its songs, suffer with its sorrows and are delighted by its hopes ...

And there are those whose soul lifts beyond the limitations of Israel, to sing the song of humanity. Their spirit expands to include the glory of the human image and its dreams ...

And there are those who lift beyond this level, until they become one with all creation and all creatures, and all the worlds. And with all of them they sing a song ...

And there are those who rise together with the bundle of all these songs. All of them sing out, each gives meaning and life to the other.

And this completeness is the song of holiness, the song of God, the song of Israel ...

II

> *Everyone Sang*
> Everyone suddenly burst out singing;
> and I was filled with such delight
> as prisoned birds must find in freedom
> winging wildly across the white
> orchards and dark green fields; on; on; and out of sight.
>
> Everyone's voice was suddenly lifted,
> and beauty came like the setting sun.
> My heart was shaken with tears, and horror
> drifted away ... O but every one
> was a bird; and the song was wordless; the singing will
> never be done.

---

[1] Ps 46:10.

Nishmat kol chai - The breath of life in every creature

The breath of life is in me now, I speak the words in wonder. I sense the mystery in every breath, treasure each moment as if it were my own: life is fragile, precious, hanging by the threads with which each one of us is bound to boundless life eternal. The miracle of life on earth, of anything at all! And we the creatures conscious of the power that animates it all, the spirit suffusing all that is and was and all that is to come. We call the mystery God, the One who is, and declare our gratitude for what sustains our souls as we savour our indebtedness to life. Yet every breath we take reminds us: our power is limited and our span of days is fixed. Transient and mortal as we are, still we add our grace notes to the melodies we hear hymning their glory in our ear. For we are held within a greater rhythm that echoes through our lives.

When the tides of history threaten to sweep us away, or tragedy seeks to undermine our faith, we recall the journey our people made, and make anew each day. From slavery to freedom, constraints to liberation - we trace our journey over and again, renewing our purpose with humble confidence and hope. For we are not alone, each one of us is held within a larger, grander scheme, brimming with significance. No words of ours can speak of all we owe - yet still our hearts and mouths resound with sheer delight and thankfulness. The breath of life is in me now, no words of mine can ever speak the wonder of it all.

Bar'chu - The Call to Prayer

Baruch - 'Blessed'. If I say 'blessed', where are the bending knees, the *birkayim* that inhabit the root of this word? And where is the inner pool of water, the *b'reichah* from which all blessings flow? Where is the energy, the surge of power that is exchanged between the blesser and the blessed? Where the love that lies behind the gift of blessing? How many words will I need to convey them, when they all dwell together in this simple *baruch*? A word of fullness beyond belief, of giving, loving, and submitting all at once.

Yotzer Or - Who forms light

I

'The heavens declare the glory of God,'[1] but the heavens have expanded beyond anything our ancestors could imagine, and for many God no longer sits above them enthroned in glory.

'Day pours out speech to day.'[2] The Psalmist saw the words of Torah emblazoned across the night sky; we see the traces of expanding galaxies, exploding suns, collapsing stars, cosmic debris, ancient before our earth came into being, before it knew the tread of human steps.

In the past, we crafted poetry, in awe of the light that illumines the world; now we craft experiments and compose equations, seeking enlightenment in a different kind of language to express a different kind of awe.

Yet we too stand before the mystery of creation itself, and light still becomes darkness and darkness light.

By reciting a blessing we address the inexpressible, boundless and awesome wonder that is creation, and the light that sustains life on earth.

בָּרוּךְ Blessed are You God, בָּרוּךְ אַתָּה יהוה יוֹצֵר הַמְּאוֹרוֹת:
who creates the lights of the universe.

II
A reflection on creation

We are in the middle of the greatest of all cultural revolutions: one that is being carried through in silence by the astrophysicists. The layperson (and we are all laypeople, with the exception of about 1,000 specialists in the world) can only accept the vastness of the new celestial bodies, suppress fresh shudders, keep quiet and reflect ...

We are alone. If we have interlocutors, they are so far away that, barring unforeseeable turns of events, we shall never talk to them; in spite of this, some years ago we sent them a pathetic message. Every year that passes leaves us more alone. Not only are we not the centre of the universe, but the universe is not made for human beings; it is hostile, violent, alien. In the sky there are no Elysian fields, only matter and light, distorted, compressed, dilated and rarefied to a degree that eludes our senses and our language. Every year that passes, while earthly matters grow ever more convoluted, the challenge of the cosmos grows keener and more bitter: the heavens are not simple, but neither are they impermeable to our minds - they are waiting to be deciphered.

Human misery has another face, one imprinted with nobility; maybe we exist by chance, perhaps we are the sole instance of intelligence in the universe, certain, we are immeasurably small, weak and alone, but if the human mind has conceived Black Holes, and dares to speculate on what happened in the first moments of creation, why should it not know how to conquer fear, poverty and grief?

---

[1] Ps 19:2. [2] Ps 19:3.

Ahavah Rabbah - With great love

We are a people apart. We define ourselves this way yet passionately debate the boundaries of belonging and what it means to 'dwell alone'.

Our particular destiny as Israel was shaped long ago: by a call to journey to a distant land; by a promise to be numbered as the stars of the heavens; by a task to witness in the world to the God of justice and love.

We have been faithful to that call, both in times of worldly success and in the bitterness of suffering and death; sometimes we responded with fervour, at other times with reluctance. Yet always we have listened for that voice that called and calls, for a love reaching out to us across time, as we sought to become another link in the chain that connects us to our destiny.

If we are chosen, then all are chosen - as families, tribes or peoples - each of us charged with finding our special task, our unique gift to human hopes and dreams.

We are called to proclaim the unity of God; to reflect that all-embracing love in whatever way we can; and reflect on it for as long as we choose to be chosen.

בָּרוּךְ Blessed are You God,
who chooses Your people Israel in love.

בָּרוּךְ אַתָּה יהוה
הַבּוֹחֵר בְּעַמּוֹ יִשְׂרָאֵל בְּאַהֲבָה:

Sh'ma - Hear O Israel

'Pay attention, Israel': the daily call to attentiveness does not cease - not even on Shabbat, the day of rest. Morning and evening, day in, day out, the call to remain attentive reminds us of Israel's task. To pay attention to the One who was, is and will be.

We struggle to hear God's voice amidst the clamour of the world and the restlessness of our minds. How can we learn to pay attention to the Eternal when we feel surrounded by discord and discontent? If we are to be devoted to attentiveness - even on Shabbat - then it cannot be yet another activity to fit into a crowded day. For paying attention is about *being* rather than doing.

Being with ourselves - our innermost thoughts, our deeper feelings, our bodies' desires and needs, honouring the uniqueness of who we are.

Being with others - our family, friends, community, honouring our shared humanity.

Being with *Adonai Eloheinu* - the eternal energy that animates existence, the spirit of all life that flows in us and between us.

'Pay attention, Israel': we are in the presence of a stillness to which we belong. The silence at the heart of all being. The silence which is Being. Do *not be afraid, for the spirit of all being is with you*. Its presence accompanies you at every moment of the journey, from Egypt to your promised land - and through the wilderness between.

<<<

339 REFLECTIONS — AMIDAH

Emet v'yatsiv - True is Your word

Emet, 'truth', is not an abstract truth, a theoretical ordering of the universe, a system of belief that explains it all, that demands our loyalty and consent.

Emet, 'truth', and '*emunah*', 'trust', belong to the world of experience, affirmed by generations past, but to be tested out in our own lives. Both derive from the word '*amen*', that which is 'firm', 'secure', on which we can rely, which we 'affirm' when we say the word aloud.

In what way is it true that God's word is eternal?

In what way is it true that God is the source of our strength through the ages?

In what way is it true that God rescues and delivers us?

In what way is it true that God is the first and the last, that God alone delivered us, and delivers us each day, from slavery to freedom?

Every generation has its doubts when faced with its own challenges and pain, and our liturgy invites such questions. The assurances of the past give us hope, but do not remove the task of seeking our own answers in our own time and place.

'Religion offers answers without obliterating the questions. They become blunted and will not attack you with the same ferocity. But without them the answer would dry up and wither away. The question is a great religious act; it helps you live great religious truth.'

בָּרוּךְ Blessed are You God, who rescues Israel.   בָּרוּךְ אַתָּה יְהֹוָה גָּאַל יִשְׂרָאֵל׃

REFLECTIONS ON THE *AMIDAH* - SHABBAT AND DAILY

Avot - Ancestors

We speak of 'the God of our ancestors', remembering how each of them had to discover, in their generation, the place of the divine in their lives. They inherited names and qualities of God, 'great, mighty and awesome', but tested them against their own experience and understanding. Some things they took on trust, but maintained the right to question and to doubt. We too both affirm and question as we seek meaning and purpose in our lives. May we do so with the same integrity as generations past, we who bless and are blessed.

בָּרוּךְ אַתָּה יהוה מָגֵן אַבְרָהָם וּפוֹקֵד שָׂרָה׃

G'vurot - Powers

Our life is subject to forces beyond our control, our death is seldom ours to determine. We wonder what rules our lives - is it fate, or chance or the will of the divine? What exist before life or beyond death are mysteries we address through faith or speculation, with hesitation or hope. Yet in this lifetime, 'to support the fallen, to heal the sick, to loose the bound', these are part of our calling, to act as if all depended on us. May we accept this power and this responsibility, we who bless and are blessed.

בָּרוּךְ אַתָּה יהוה. מְחַיֵּה הַמֵּתִים:

Kedushat ha-shem - Holiness

At the limits of our understanding 'holiness', 'k'dushah', speaks of the vastness and complexity of the universe we inhabit. We personalise the forces within it, guided by our human perception and imagination. Yet our minds constantly venture beyond. We extend our knowledge and creativity into farthest and innermost space. May we always be in wonder and awe before the known and unknown worlds about us and within us, we who bless and are blessed.

בָּרוּךְ אַתָּה יהוה. הָאֵל הַקָּדוֹשׁ:

FOR SHABBAT

R'tseih na vimnuchateinu - May our rest be pleasing to You

We celebrate this weekly opportunity to pause, rest, and take stock; to cease the busy-ness that wears us down; to set aside, if only for a short while, the problems that pursue us during the working week and so appreciate each other's presence in our lives. May we enjoy this different rhythm, these different values, and this place of safety and renewal, time out of time, we who bless and are blessed.

בָּרוּךְ אַתָּה יהוה. מְקַדֵּשׁ הַשַּׁבָּת:

FOR A WEEKDAY

Attah chonein l'adam da'at - You favour human beings with knowledge

Our mind is our glory, to think, perceive, discern; to investigate what we do not yet understand, evaluate what we experience, envisage the consequences of what we do; to imagine, to dream and to know. May we use these gifts not to harm but to heal, not to destroy but to create, for ourselves and for our world, we who bless and are blessed.

בָּרוּךְ אַתָּה יְהֹוָה. חוֹנֵן הַדָּעַת:

Hashiveinu avinu l'toratecha - Turn us back to Your teaching, our Creator

On our journey through life we make many choices and sometimes lose our way. We wander from the path we are to follow, '*Torah*', 'teaching', and from the work we are called to do, '*Avodah*', 'service'. Yet however far we stray, there is always the chance to return, to change our stance or the direction we face. May we always learn from our experience, and feel able to begin our journey anew, we who bless and are blessed.

בָּרוּךְ אַתָּה יהוה. הָרוֹצֶה בִּתְשׁוּבָה:

S'lach lanu avinu ki chatanu - Forgive us, our Creator, for we have sinned

We do not always see what is around us, the mistakes we make, the people we hurt, the damage we do. Sometimes we fail in what we should do and 'sin', and often we deny the consequences of our acts and 'transgress'. With knowledge comes pain and shame, but also the possibility of repairing, of reconciliation, to be forgiven and forgive ourselves, we who bless and are blessed.

בָּרוּךְ אַתָּה יהוה. חַנּוּן הַמַּרְבֶּה לִסְלֹחַ:

R'ei v'onyeinu - Look upon our affliction

We cannot live in this world without encountering suffering and hurt, from failures within, from violence without. This we share with all humanity, but we are also bound up with the fate of our people Israel, we who are vulnerable in our weakness and in our power. We hope for strength for the struggle, for release from all that limits, brutalises or diminishes us as a people, we who bless and are blessed.

בָּרוּךְ אַתָּה יהוה. גּוֹאֵל יִשְׂרָאֵל:

Refa'einu adonai v'neirafei - Heal us, God, and we shall be healed

We ask for '*refuah*', for 'healing', for we are aware that our bodies, minds and spirit are frail. We ask for '*yeshua*', for 'rescue', for we know that we carry wounds and scars as a people. All this affects how we see ourselves and the world around us. So the healing we seek is both private and shared, for ourselves, for those we care for and love, for the Jewish people, and for a world that is torn, wounded and scarred, we who bless and are blessed.

בָּרוּךְ אַתָּה יהוה. רוֹפֵא הַחוֹלִים:

Bareich aleinu ... et ha-shanah ha-zot - **Bless this year**

When we pray for something we become responsible for helping it come to pass. So, when we ask for blessing on the earth, for the rain in its season, for harvests and fruitfulness, we make a commitment to protect our planet, not to pollute it or harm the living creatures with which we share it, but to live in harmony with nature. Like Adam and Eve in the Garden of Eden, we are charged 'to serve it and to guard it', for that is part of our task, we who bless and are blessed.

בָּרוּךְ אַתָּה יהוה. מְבָרֵךְ הַשָּׁנִים:

T'ka b'shofar gadol l'cheiruteinu - **Sound the great horn for our freedom**

The hardest pains to bear are those inflicted on us by fellow human beings. The bitterest burden to endure is to be enslaved to others - by poverty or politics or the cruelty of those with power. Yet we are responsible for each other. The prophet Isaiah calls us 'to break every yoke and free those who are bound'.[1] May our courage match our conviction, we who bless and are blessed.

בָּרוּךְ אַתָּה יהוה. מְקַיֵּם נִדְחֵי עַמּוֹ יִשְׂרָאֵל:

Hashiva mishpat tsidkat'cha - **Restore Your judgment of righteousness**

For human society to survive we need '*tsedek*', that which is right, true and just. The bond that holds us together we call '*chesed*', abiding love, respect and care. Our task is to bring about '*mishpat*', the justice that binds these values together, the harmony we seek to find or restore, we who bless and are blessed.

בָּרוּךְ אַתָּה יהוה. מֶלֶךְ אוֹהֵב צְדָקָה וּמִשְׁפָּט:

V'la-malshinut al t'hi tikvah - **And for slander let there be no hope**

How deep is the bitterness of betrayal, how seductive is righteous anger, how easy it is to hate the many for the crimes of a few, how unwelcome the plea for moderation, how challenging the call to forgive. May we only hate the acts that cause harm, and leave open the hope that those who perform them may change, we who bless and are blessed.

בָּרוּךְ אַתָּה יהוה. הַמַּעֲבִיר רִשְׁעָה מִן־הָאָרֶץ:

---

[1] Is 58:6.

Al ha-tsadikim - To the righteous

Remembering the righteous, the pious and the honest, those who stand beside us in need and those who join us in faith, we absorb their values and teachings. May the good in others always move us to find the good within ourselves, we who bless and are blessed.

בָּרוּךְ אַתָּה יהוה. מִשְׁעָן וּמִבְטָח לַצַּדִּיקִים:

V'lirushalayim ir'cha b'rachamim tashuv - Turn in mercy to Jerusalem

A place is not holy. Only the deeds committed within it, or in its name, may become holy. No holiness is guaranteed to last, but must be earned anew in each generation. We are custodians of the holiness of Jerusalem, together with all who look to it for inspiration or hope. May we never mistake its outer stones for the inner spirit it represents. May we never betray the quest for holiness, we who bless and are blessed.

בָּרוּךְ אַתָּה יהוה. בּוֹנֵה יְרוּשָׁלָיִם:

Et tsemach david - Bring forth a new flowering from Your servant David

One human being alone was created, and our hope remains to become again one human society. Faith in great leaders, revolutions that promise to transform in an instant, the slow evolution of human society - we have tried them all and know the dangers and disappointments. We have also taught about the spark of the 'messiah', the anointed one, concealed in each of us, and the unique contribution we can make. All the calculated times have passed, yet still we wait and labour and dream of that time yet to come, we who bless and are blessed.

בָּרוּךְ אַתָּה יהוה. מַצְמִיחַ קֶרֶן יְשׁוּעָה:

Sh'ma koleinu - Hear our voice

As we are called to hear that voice that summons us to our task as Israel, so we also call out to be heard. We seek compassion for our failures, understanding for our inadequacies, respect for our achievements. We try to ask only for what we need to continue our journey and our task, and to recognise the next step we are to take. In the fire, the wind and the tremors that shake our world and shape our lives, we hope that our still, small voice may be heard, we who bless and are blessed.

בָּרוּךְ אַתָּה יהוה. שׁוֹמֵעַ תְּפִלָּה:

CONCLUSION OF THE *AMIDAH*

R'tsei - Acceptance

We are each of us alone, yet bound to others as part of our human heritage and by virtue of our human nature. We build community because we need one another. So we must share our concerns and take responsibility for our life together. Our actions have effects, immediate and distant, foreseeable and beyond anything we can imagine. Yet our task is to try to build harmony within human society and within the natural world around us. May what we do, and strive to do, be acceptable, we who bless and are blessed.

בָּרוּךְ אַתָּה יהוה. הַמַּחֲזִיר שְׁכִינָתוֹ לְצִיּוֹן.

Modim - Thanksgiving

Before the sorrows and joys of life; before love that sustains us and loss that cuts to the heart; before successes and failures that teach us; before past wisdom and traditions that inform us; before creativity that enlarges and enriches us; before poverty, disease and suffering that challenge us to act; before pain that humanises us and generosity that ennobles us; before beauty that leaves us breathless and harmonies that enchant us; before all these and the sheer wonder of life let us offer thanks, we who bless and are blessed.

בָּרוּךְ אַתָּה יהוה. הַטּוֹב שִׁמְךָ וּלְךָ נָאֶה לְהוֹדוֹת:

Shalom - Peace

We long for shalom, 'wholeness, 'completeness', and 'peace'. Yet peace, we learn, is something to which we can only aspire. Moses, our teacher, went '*towards* peace'[1] - for we never attain it while life still awaits us. There is always another journey, another goal, another task; always something to repair in a fractured world: a relationship that needs to be healed; an injustice to be corrected; a conflict to be transformed. May all our paths be in search of peace, we who bless and are blessed.

בָּרוּךְ אַתָּה יהוה. הַמְבָרֵךְ אֶת עַמּוֹ יִשְׂרָאֵל בַּשָּׁלוֹם:

---

[1] Ex 4:18.

TORAH SERVICE

I

To the Book of Deuteronomy, Torah is the life and good which is set before us as an alternative to death and evil; at the same time it is Israel's wisdom and understanding in the eyes of the nations.

To the Prophet it is the water for which all people thirst, the bread for which they starve - which is yet dispensed without silver or price.

To the Psalmist it is the light in which he sees light, and the spiritual sustenance whose taste is sweeter than honey and the drippings of the honeycomb.

To a Rabbi of ancient days it is a living text to be delved into further and further, since all things are in it; something over which one may grow grey and old, never stirring from its contemplation, knowing that one can have no better pursuit or rule.

To mediaeval Jews in their ghettos it is, by the testimony of a folk-song, a treasure better than all worldly goods.

To the Jew of modernity, Torah remains a revelation in general, not in detail; in its directions though not necessarily in each step. It has authority because it gives so full a report of what they found out when they applied their heads and hearts to the deepest questions of human existence.

To all generations of Jews from Isaiah on, it is the word of God destined in the end to regenerate humanity and society.

II

It is exceedingly difficult, if not impossible, to account for the lofty teachings of the Hebrew prophets, the civilizing influence of the great Law of Moses, the history of a small people who found God and brought Him to mankind, the Sinaitic revelation itself and the spiritual power these books continue to exercise over men's souls, unless Israel really met with God and recorded in immortal language the meaning of that encounter. We can be sceptical of individual details in the Bible. We can dwell on the numerous parallels with Egyptian, Babylonian and Assyrian mores. We can point out the striking resemblances between Hebrew poetry in the Bible and Canaanite hymns in praise of the pagan gods. We are forced to recognise, to a degree quite beyond the imagination of our ancestors, the human element in the Biblical record. What cannot be seriously doubted is the 'something else' which has ensured that this and no other collection of books has become the sacred Scripture of a large proportion of humanity; that there are living Jews who regard themselves as the heirs to the Bible and no living Babylonians, Canaanites and Assyrians; that there is a Voice which speaks here in promise of great vision, of dreams of world peace, of holiness, justice and mercy, of freedom and the unique worth of each individual as a child of God ...

MUSAF - ADDITIONAL SERVICE

When the temple stood in Jerusalem we marked the special nature of Shabbat in the most reverential way we knew, by an additional sacrifice to God.

When the temple fell we replaced the sacrifice of bulls with the offering of words. Temple, land, nation and king, these were the pillars of that society, so we prayed for the restoration of that distantly remembered world.

Time has modified these hopes. We live in many lands and again in the land of Israel. A restored temple and its sacrifices still express the religious hopes of a few, but for most of us our religious vision has moved on. We form new images of future hope, knowing that messianic pretenders to the throne of King David have come and gone, often leaving disaster in their wake.

Today the unity of the Jewish people is part of the quest for the unity of humanity. The fate of our promised land is bound to the fate of the earth as a whole.

The *Musaf* service invites us to a new hope for Jerusalem, symbol of reconciliation and the healing of wounds. With the Psalmist we pray: Seek the peace of Jerusalem![1] With the prophet we say: 'My house shall be called a house of prayer for all peoples.'[2]

CONCLUDING PRAYERS

Aleinu - Our task as Israel

All is movement, change, light, growth, decay, return - and we submit to the power that makes it so. We name this power 'the One who is' and wait to see what will evolve. Within this sacred drama we the people Israel wrestle with our mission. We must embody holiness in our deeds, enact our vision, for we are emblems of the eternal. We realise this today and take it to heart: divinity is around us and within us. This is the truth we bear and the truth we carry into the days ahead.

> To open eyes when others close them
> to hear when others do not wish to listen
> to look when others turn away
> to seek to understand when others give up
> to rouse oneself when others accept
> to continue the struggle even when one is not the strongest
> to cry out when others keep silent
> to be a Jew
> it is that
> it is first of all that
> and further
> to live when others are dead
> and to remember when others have forgotten.

---

[1]. Ps 122:6.   [1]. Isa 56:7.

Al Kein N'kavveh - **Our hope for humanity**

We look to the future with hope. So many dreams have faded in the accusing light of day, so many visions of better times have turned into nightmares and blood. We have been disappointed too often. And yet still we hope. We hope for transformation: for societies where prejudice and superstition, fear and unrest give way to fullness of life, and the humble recognition of our common humanity. We are in this together. We need each other and we need to affirm our hope. For goodness is real, and justice is possible, and life on earth can be enhanced by those filled with an awareness of the eternal and a knowledge of their own transience. We are guests, passing through. With patience, resilience and courage we can leave this world a little better for our having been here. This is our hope, this is our security: in the light of eternity we have a significance we cannot measure. Moment by moment we build 'God's kingdom'. Our world is in the process of being repaired, through us and within us. This is our redemption. We look to the future with hope.

And then all that has divided us will merge
And then compassion will be wedded to power
And then softness will come to a world that is harsh and unkind
And then both men and women will be gentle
And then both women and men will be strong
And then no person will be subject to another's will
And then all will be rich and free and varied
And then the greed of some will give way to the needs of many
And then all will care for the sick and the weak and the old
And then all will nourish the young
And then all will cherish life's creatures
And then all will live in harmony with one another and the Earth
And then everywhere will be called Eden once again.

KADDISH

I
Meditation

Yitgadal, v'yitkadash sh'mei rabba ... The old words stir memories: of those now long gone, or those more recently departed. So many have left us. Parents ... friends ... family ... community ... those we loved and those we could never love enough. And we, the survivors, reflect awhile as the ancient text is read anew. This is the prayer for those no longer with us. And as we pause, we hear the euphemisms we use: 'gone', 'departed', 'left us', 'no longer with us'. We hesitate to name the unavoidable truth that underpins our life. Yet the end of life is a destination all must one day reach, a fate we can never overcome, a destiny not to be denied. Now we recall another truth, that often slips from view: this Kaddish prayer never mentions death. Instead, defying our fears, it extols life, reveres the Giver of life, the Sustainer of life, and celebrates the origin and terminus of life. It offers us a saving, larger view. It overwhelms our doubts, persuades us - if only for a moment - that every day is holy, that all of life is precious, that peace and wholeness are the highest values to which we can aspire, here in this world, where we exist awesomely, defiantly, alive. 'Let us magnify and let us sanctify the wondrous nature of all being …'

II

Look around us, search above us, below, behind.
We stand in a great web of being joined together.
Let us praise, let us love the life we are lent
passing through us in the body of Israel
and our own bodies, let's say Amen.

Time flows through us like water.
The past and the dead speak through us.
We breathe out our children's children, blessing.

Blessed is the earth from which we grow,
blessed the life we are lent,
blessed the ones who teach us,
blessed the ones we teach,
blessed is the word that cannot say the glory
that shines through us and remains to shine
flowing past distant suns on the way to forever.
Let's say Amen.

Blessed is light, blessed is darkness,
but blessed above all else is peace
which bears the fruits of knowledge
on strong branches, let's say Amen.

Peace that bears joy into the world,
peace that enables love, peace over Israel,
everywhere, blessed and holy is peace, let's say Amen.

Community Prayers and Passages

הכנסת
תפלה
מדרש

Contents

Prayer of a *Bar Mitsvah*	350
Prayer of a *Bat Mitsvah*	350
A Blessing for Children	351
The Ten Commandments	352
Blessing for Someone Who is Ill	354
Prayers for Healing	355
Thanksgiving for Recovery after Danger (*Gomel*)	355
Marriage Service	356
Sheva B'rachot	358
Thanksgiving Service for Parents (Naming of a Child)	360
Service of Affirmation of the Jewish Faith	363
A Prayer for Committee Meetings	366
A Prayer for Interfaith Meetings	366
A Prayer for International Understanding	366
A Prayer for Responsibility for Justice and the Environment	366
A Prayer for the Release of Captives	367
A Prayer in a Time of War	367
A Prayer in a Time of a Natural Disaster	368
A Liturgy in a Time of Community Threat or Disaster	369
A Prayer for Combating Poverty and Injustice	371
A Prayer for World Peace	372

PRAYER OF A *BAR MITSVAH*

In the presence of my teachers, the leaders and the members of this holy congregation, I now prepare to take upon myself the duties which are binding on all the family of Israel. I ask their help in the years that lie ahead to strengthen my loyalty and devotion so that I may grow in charity and good deeds. I think also of those who have gone before me, who through all the troubles of the world preserved this heritage of holiness and goodness, so that I should enter into it now.

May I be a true *Bar Mitsvah*, a son of the commandment, taking my place in the community of Israel, accepting its responsibilities, rejoicing in its blessing. May I be a witness to the living God and to God's goodness, and to the tradition that lives within me.

I remember all those who have helped me reach this time. I give thanks for the love and care of my family, the patience and instruction of my teachers, and the support and companionship of my friends.

In the Torah I have read the word of God. With God's help may I go on to fulfil it in my life. Amen.

שְׁמַע יִשְׂרָאֵל יהוה אֱלֹהֵינוּ יהוה | אֶחָד:

שְׁמַע Hear O Israel, the Eternal is our God, the Eternal is One.

PRAYER OF A *BAT MITSVAH*

In the presence of my teachers, the leaders and the members of this holy congregation, I now prepare to take upon myself the duties which are binding on all the family of Israel. I ask their help in the years that lie ahead to strengthen my loyalty and devotion so that I may grow in charity and good deeds. I think also of those who have gone before me, who through all the troubles of the world preserved this heritage of holiness and goodness, so that I should enter into it now.

May I be a true *Bat Mitsvah*, a daughter of the commandment, taking my place in the community of Israel, accepting its responsibilities, rejoicing in its blessing. May I be a witness to the living God and to God's goodness, and to the tradition that lives within me.

I remember all those who have helped me reach this time. I give thanks for the love and care of my family, the patience and instruction of my teachers, and the support and companionship of my friends.

In the Torah I have read the word of God. With God's help may I go on to fulfil it in my life. Amen.

שְׁמַע יִשְׂרָאֵל יהוה אֱלֹהֵינוּ יהוה | אֶחָד:

שְׁמַע Hear O Israel, the Eternal is our God, the Eternal is One.

The following blessing may be used privately or as part of a bar/bat-mitsvah *service.*

A BLESSING FOR CHILDREN

עוֹלָמְךָ May you live
to see your world fulfilled,
may your destiny be for worlds
still to come,
and may you trust in generations
past and yet to be,
may your heart be filled with intuition
and your words be filled with insight.
May songs of praise
ever be upon your tongue
and your vision be in a straight path
before you.
May your eyes shine
with the light of holy words
and your face reflect
the brightness of the heavens.
May your lips speak wisdom
and your fulfillment be in righteousness
even as you ever yearn to hear words
of the Holy Ancient One.

עוֹלָמְךָ תִּרְאֶה בְחַיֶּיךָ
וְאַחֲרִיתְךָ לְחַיֵּי הָעוֹלָם הַבָּא
וְתִקְוָתְךָ לְדוֹר דּוֹרִים
לִבְּךָ יֶהְגֶּה תְבוּנָה
פִּיךָ יְדַבֵּר חָכְמוֹת
וּלְשׁוֹנְךָ יַרְחִישׁ רְנָנוֹת
עַפְעַפֶּיךָ יְיַשִּׁירוּ נֶגְדְּךָ
עֵינֶיךָ יָאִירוּ בִּמְאוֹר
תּוֹרָה וּפָנֶיךָ יַזְהִירוּ
כְּזוֹהַר הָרָקִיעַ
שִׂפְתוֹתֶיךָ יַבִּיעוּ דַעַת
וְכִלְיוֹתֶיךָ תַּעֲלוֹזְנָה מֵישָׁרִים
וּפְעָמֶיךָ יָרוּצוּ לִשְׁמוֹעַ דִּבְרֵי
עַתִּיק יוֹמִין:

Berachot 17a   ברכות יז

עשרת הדברות

וַיְדַבֵּר אֱלֹהִים אֵת כָּל־הַדְּבָרִים הָאֵלֶּה לֵאמֹר:

א אָנֹכִי יהוה אֱלֹהֶיךָ אֲשֶׁר הוֹצֵאתִיךָ מֵאֶרֶץ מִצְרַיִם מִבֵּית עֲבָדִים:

ב לֹא־יִהְיֶה לְךָ אֱלֹהִים אֲחֵרִים עַל־פָּנָי: לֹא־תַעֲשֶׂה לְךָ פֶסֶל וְכָל־תְּמוּנָה אֲשֶׁר בַּשָּׁמַיִם מִמַּעַל וַאֲשֶׁר בָּאָרֶץ מִתַּחַת וַאֲשֶׁר בַּמַּיִם מִתַּחַת לָאָרֶץ: לֹא־תִשְׁתַּחֲוֶה לָהֶם וְלֹא תָעָבְדֵם כִּי אָנֹכִי יהוה אֱלֹהֶיךָ אֵל קַנָּא פֹּקֵד עֲוֹן אָבֹת עַל־בָּנִים עַל־שִׁלֵּשִׁים וְעַל־רִבֵּעִים לְשֹׂנְאָי: וְעֹשֶׂה חֶסֶד לַאֲלָפִים לְאֹהֲבַי וּלְשֹׁמְרֵי מִצְוֹתָי:

ג לֹא תִשָּׂא אֶת־שֵׁם־יהוה אֱלֹהֶיךָ לַשָּׁוְא כִּי לֹא יְנַקֶּה יהוה אֵת אֲשֶׁר־יִשָּׂא אֶת־שְׁמוֹ לַשָּׁוְא:

ד זָכוֹר אֶת־יוֹם הַשַּׁבָּת לְקַדְּשׁוֹ: שֵׁשֶׁת יָמִים תַּעֲבֹד וְעָשִׂיתָ כָּל־מְלַאכְתֶּךָ: וְיוֹם הַשְּׁבִיעִי שַׁבָּת לַיהוה אֱלֹהֶיךָ לֹא־תַעֲשֶׂה כָל־מְלָאכָה אַתָּה וּבִנְךָ וּבִתֶּךָ עַבְדְּךָ וַאֲמָתְךָ וּבְהֶמְתֶּךָ וְגֵרְךָ אֲשֶׁר בִּשְׁעָרֶיךָ: כִּי שֵׁשֶׁת־יָמִים עָשָׂה יהוה אֶת־הַשָּׁמַיִם וְאֶת־הָאָרֶץ אֶת־הַיָּם וְאֶת־כָּל־אֲשֶׁר־בָּם וַיָּנַח בַּיּוֹם הַשְּׁבִיעִי עַל־כֵּן בֵּרַךְ יהוה אֶת־יוֹם הַשַּׁבָּת וַיְקַדְּשֵׁהוּ:

ה כַּבֵּד אֶת־אָבִיךָ וְאֶת־אִמֶּךָ לְמַעַן יַאֲרִכוּן יָמֶיךָ עַל הָאֲדָמָה אֲשֶׁר־יהוה אֱלֹהֶיךָ נֹתֵן לָךְ:

ו לֹא תִרְצָח

ז לֹא תִנְאָף

ח לֹא תִגְנֹב

ט לֹא־תַעֲנֶה בְרֵעֲךָ עֵד שָׁקֶר:

י לֹא תַחְמֹד בֵּית רֵעֶךָ. לֹא־תַחְמֹד אֵשֶׁת רֵעֶךָ וְעַבְדּוֹ וַאֲמָתוֹ וְשׁוֹרוֹ וַחֲמֹרוֹ וְכֹל אֲשֶׁר לְרֵעֶךָ:

שָׁמוֹר אֶת־יוֹם הַשַּׁבָּת לְקַדְּשׁוֹ כַּאֲשֶׁר צִוְּךָ יהוה אֱלֹהֶיךָ: שֵׁשֶׁת יָמִים תַּעֲבֹד וְעָשִׂיתָ כָּל־מְלַאכְתֶּךָ: וְיוֹם הַשְּׁבִיעִי שַׁבָּת לַיהוה אֱלֹהֶיךָ לֹא־תַעֲשֶׂה כָל־מְלָאכָה אַתָּה וּבִנְךָ־וּבִתֶּךָ וְעַבְדְּךָ־וַאֲמָתֶךָ וְשׁוֹרְךָ וַחֲמֹרְךָ וְכָל־

Observe the Sabbath day and keep it holy as the Eternal your God commanded you. You have six days to labour and do all your work, but the seventh shall be a Sabbath for the Eternal your God. That day you shall do no work, neither you, nor your son, nor your daughter, nor your servant, man or woman, nor your ox nor your ass, nor any of

THE TEN COMMANDMENTS

וַיְדַבֵּר Then God spoke all these words:

1. I am the Eternal your God who brought you out of the land of Egypt, out of the camp of slavery.
2. You shall have no other gods but Me. You shall not make yourself an idol in the likeness of anything which is in the sky above or on the earth below, or in the deeps under the earth. You shall not worship them nor serve them, for I the Eternal your God am a demanding God, burdening the children down to the third and fourth generations with their fathers' guilt, if they hate Me, but showing kindness to thousands of generations if they should love Me, and keep My commands.
3. You shall not use the name of the Eternal your God falsely, for the Eternal will not excuse anyone who uses the divine name falsely.
4. Remember the Sabbath day and keep it holy. You have six days to labour and do all your work. But the seventh shall be a Sabbath for the Eternal your God. That day you shall do no work, neither you, nor your son, nor your daughter, nor your servant, man or woman, nor your cattle, nor the stranger who lives in your home. For in six days the Eternal made heaven and earth, the seas and all that is in them, and rested on the seventh day. Therefore, God blessed the Sabbath day and made it holy.
5. Respect your father and your mother so that the days of your life be fulfilled on the land which the Eternal your God gives you.
6. You shall not murder.
7. You shall not commit adultery.
8. You shall not steal.
9. You shall not give false evidence against your neighbour.
10. You shall not covet your neighbour's house, you shall not covet your neighbour's wife, nor his servant, man or woman, nor his ox, nor his ass, nor anything that is your neighbour's.[1]

---

your animals, nor the stranger who lives in your home; so that those who serve you, men and women, shall rest like you. Remember you served as slaves in the land of Egypt and from there the Eternal your God brought you out with a mighty hand and outstretched arm. Therefore the Eternal your God commanded you to keep the Sabbath day. (Deut 5:12-15)

בְּהֶמְתֶּךָ וְגֵרְךָ אֲשֶׁר בִּשְׁעָרֶיךָ לְמַעַן יָנוּחַ עַבְדְּךָ וַאֲמָתְךָ כָּמוֹךָ: וְזָכַרְתָּ כִּי עֶבֶד הָיִיתָ בְּאֶרֶץ מִצְרַיִם וַיֹּצִאֲךָ יהוה אֱלֹהֶיךָ מִשָּׁם בְּיָד חֲזָקָה וּבִזְרֹעַ נְטוּיָה עַל־כֵּן צִוְּךָ יהוה אֱלֹהֶיךָ לַעֲשׂוֹת אֶת־יוֹם הַשַּׁבָּת:

[1] Ex 20:1-14.

מי שברך לחולה
BLESSING FOR SOMEONE WHO IS ILL

For a man

מִי May the One who blessed our ancestors Abraham, Isaac and Jacob, bless _____ son of _____ who is ill. Please heal him. In the fullness of Your compassion for him restore and revive him and send him speedily a perfect healing amidst those of Israel who are ill, healing of the soul and of the body. Now, speedily and soon.
And let us say: Amen.

מִי שֶׁבֵּרַךְ אֲבוֹתֵינוּ אַבְרָהָם יִצְחָק וְיַעֲקֹב הוּא יְבָרֵךְ אֶת־הַחוֹלֶה בֶּן _____ אָנָא רְפָא נָא לוֹ. הַמָּלֵא נָא רַחֲמִים עָלָיו לְהַחֲלִימוֹ וּלְהַחֲיוֹתוֹ וְשָׁלַח לוֹ בִּמְהֵרָה רְפוּאָה שְׁלֵמָה בְּתוֹךְ שְׁאָר חוֹלֵי יִשְׂרָאֵל רְפוּאַת הַנֶּפֶשׁ וּרְפוּאַת הַגּוּף. הַשְׁתָּא בַּעֲגָלָא וּבִזְמַן קָרִיב. וְנֹאמַר אָמֵן:

For a woman

מִי May the One who blessed our ancestors Sarah, Rebecca, Rachel and Leah, bless _____ daughter of _____ who is ill. Please heal her. In the fullness of Your compassion for her restore and revive her and send her speedily a perfect healing amidst those of Israel who are ill, healing of the soul and of the body. Now, speedily and soon.
And let us say: Amen.

מִי שֶׁבֵּרַךְ אִמּוֹתֵינוּ שָׂרָה רִבְקָה רָחֵל וְלֵאָה הוּא יְבָרֵךְ אֶת־הַחוֹלָה _____ בַּת _____ אָנָא רְפָא נָא לָהּ. הַמָּלֵא נָא רַחֲמִים עָלֶיהָ לְהַחֲלִימָהּ וּלְהַחֲיוֹתָהּ וְשָׁלַח לָהּ בִּמְהֵרָה רְפוּאָה שְׁלֵמָה בְּתוֹךְ שְׁאָר חוֹלֵי יִשְׂרָאֵל רְפוּאַת הַנֶּפֶשׁ וּרְפוּאַת הַגּוּף. הַשְׁתָּא בַּעֲגָלָא וּבִזְמַן קָרִיב. וְנֹאמַר אָמֵן:

PRAYERS FOR HEALING

I

Hillel said, 'Do not separate yourself from the community.'[1]

At times when we feel our most vulnerable we need the physical and emotional strength that our community can provide.

We now leave a silence in which to name out loud or in our hearts those who need our care and our love.

We pray that the warmth of God's light envelops those who need its power. We join our prayers with the prayers of all who love them. Give them renewed comfort and courage.

בָּרוּךְ Blessed are You God, who heals the sick.

בָּרוּךְ אַתָּה יהוה. רוֹפֵא הַחוֹלִים:

II

מִי May the source of strength,
Who blessed the ones before us,
help us find the courage to make our
lives a blessing
and let us say: Amen.

מִי שֶׁבֵּרַךְ אֲבוֹתֵינוּ
מְקוֹר הַבְּרָכָה לְאִמּוֹתֵינוּ

מִי Mi sheberach avoteinu,
M'kor hab'racha l'immoteinu

מִי Bless those in need of healing
with *r'fuah sh'leimah*,
the renewal of body,
the renewal of spirit,
and let us say: Amen.

מִי שֶׁבֵּרַךְ אִמּוֹתֵינוּ
מְקוֹר הַבְּרָכָה לַאֲבוֹתֵינוּ

מִי Mi sheberach immoteinu,
M'kor hab'racha la-avoteinu

THANKSGIVING FOR
RECOVERY AFTER DANGER (*Gomel*)
(*See Page 241*)

---

[1] *Pirke Avot 2:4.*

סדר קדושין ונשואין
MARRIAGE SERVICE

Psalm 84 can be found on page 649.
Psalm 100 can be found on page 40.

One of the following prayers:

I

God, at the quietness of this time, and in the holiness of this place, give Your blessing to Your children. You have given them youth with its hopes and love with its dreams. May these come true through their faith in each other and their trust in You. Let them be devoted to each other, and as the years go by, teach them how great is the joy that comes from sharing, and how deep the love that grows with giving. May Your presence dwell among them in the warmth of their love, in the kindness of their home, and in their charity for others.

II

God, who taught men and women to help and serve each other in marriage, and lead each other into happiness, bless this covenant of affection, these promises of truth. Protect and care for the bridegroom and bride as they go through life together. May they be loving companions, secure in their devotion which deepens with the passing years. In their respect and honour for each other may they find their peace, and in their affection and tenderness their happiness. May Your presence be in their home and in their hearts.

III

God, we stand before Your holiness, and in quietness thank You for bringing us to this time. May Your love protect _____ and _____ who ask You to bless them. They ask it not for themselves alone but for each other, and for their life together, for in Your blessing is loyalty and devotion, love and trust. Be with them so that they may know true happiness and bring joy to all who love them. Let them honour You, and so bring honour to themselves. Blessed are You, who teaches us the way to happiness.

בָּרוּךְ Blessed are You, our Living God, Sovereign of the universe, who creates the fruit of the vine.

בָּרוּךְ אַתָּה יהוה אֱלֹהֵינוּ מֶלֶךְ הָעוֹלָם. בּוֹרֵא פְּרִי הַגָּפֶן:

357 COMMUNITY PRAYERS AND PASSAGES **MARRIAGE SERVICE**

בָּרוּךְ Blessed are You, our Living God, Sovereign of the universe, whose commands make us holy and who makes Your people Israel holy by the ceremony of the *chuppah* and the sanctity of marriage.

בָּרוּךְ אַתָּה יהוה. אֱלֹהֵינוּ מֶלֶךְ הָעוֹלָם. אֲשֶׁר קִדְּשָׁנוּ בְּמִצְוֹתָיו וּמְקַדֵּשׁ עַמּוֹ יִשְׂרָאֵל עַל יְדֵי חֻפָּה וְקִדּוּשִׁין:

Do you _____ enter into this holy covenant of affection and truth to take _____ to be your wife in the sight of God and the world?
And do you faithfully promise to be a true and devoted husband to her?

Do you _____ enter into this holy covenant of affection and truth to take _____ to be your husband in the sight of God and the world?
And do you faithfully promise to be a true and devoted wife to him?

הֲרֵי By this ring you are married to me in holiness according to the law of Moses and Israel.

הֲרֵי אַתְּ מְקֻדֶּשֶׁת לִי בְּטַבַּעַת זוֹ כְּדַת מֹשֶׁה וְיִשְׂרָאֵל:

הֲרֵי And you are married to me in holiness according to the law of Moses and Israel.

הֲרֵי אַתָּה מְקֻדָּשׁ לִי כְּדַת מֹשֶׁה וְיִשְׂרָאֵל:

שבע ברכות
THE *SHEVA B'RACHOT* (SEVEN BLESSINGS)

בָּרוּךְ Blessed are You, our Living God, Sovereign of the universe, who creates the fruit of the vine.

בָּרוּךְ אַתָּה יהוה אֱלֹהֵינוּ מֶלֶךְ הָעוֹלָם. בּוֹרֵא פְּרִי הַגָּפֶן:

בָּרוּךְ Blessed are You, our Living God, Sovereign of the universe, who created everything for the divine glory.

בָּרוּךְ אַתָּה יהוה אֱלֹהֵינוּ מֶלֶךְ הָעוֹלָם. שֶׁהַכֹּל בָּרָא לִכְבוֹדוֹ:

בָּרוּךְ Blessed are You, our Living God, Sovereign of the universe, who forms human beings.

בָּרוּךְ אַתָּה יהוה אֱלֹהֵינוּ מֶלֶךְ הָעוֹלָם. יוֹצֵר הָאָדָם:

בָּרוּךְ Blessed are You, our Living God, Sovereign of the universe, who formed human beings in the divine image, to be like God, to imitate and to resemble God, and prepared from human beings and for human beings a constant sharing and renewal. Blessed are You God, who forms human beings.

בָּרוּךְ אַתָּה יהוה אֱלֹהֵינוּ מֶלֶךְ הָעוֹלָם. אֲשֶׁר יָצַר אֶת הָאָדָם בְּצַלְמוֹ. בְּצֶלֶם דְּמוּת תַּבְנִיתוֹ. וְהִתְקִין לוֹ מִמֶּנּוּ בִּנְיַן עֲדֵי עַד: בָּרוּךְ אַתָּה יהוה. יוֹצֵר הָאָדָם:

שׂוֹשׂ Let Zion, deprived of her young, rise up again and cry out for joy as her children are gathered around her in happiness. Blessed are You God, who gives joy to Zion through her children.

שׂוֹשׂ תָּשִׂישׂ וְתָגֵל הָעֲקָרָה בְּקִבּוּץ בָּנֶיהָ לְתוֹכָהּ בְּשִׂמְחָה: בָּרוּךְ אַתָּה יהוה. מְשַׂמֵּחַ צִיּוֹן בְּבָנֶיהָ:

שַׂמֵּחַ Give these companions in love, great happiness, the happiness of Your creatures in Eden long ago. May Your children be worthy to create a Jewish home, that honours You and honours them. Blessed are You God, who rejoices the bridegroom and the bride.

שַׂמֵּחַ תְּשַׂמַּח רֵעִים הָאֲהוּבִים כְּשַׂמֵּחֲךָ יְצִירְךָ בְּגַן עֵדֶן מִקֶּדֶם. יִזְכּוּ בָנֶיךָ הָאֵלֶּה לִבְנוֹת בַּיִת בְּיִשְׂרָאֵל לִכְבוֹד שְׁמֶךָ: בָּרוּךְ אַתָּה יהוה. מְשַׂמֵּחַ חָתָן וְכַלָּה:

359 COMMUNITY PRAYERS AND PASSAGES — SEVEN BLESSINGS

בָּרוּךְ Blessed are You, our Living God, Sovereign of the universe, who created joy and happiness, bride and bridegroom, mirth, celebration, pleasure and delight, love and companionship, peace and friendship. Soon, our Living God, may the sound of happiness and rejoicing be heard in the towns of Judah and in the streets of Jerusalem, the voice of the bridegroom and the voice of the bride. Blessed are You God, who causes the bridegroom to rejoice with the bride.

בָּרוּךְ אַתָּה יהוה אֱלֹהֵינוּ מֶלֶךְ הָעוֹלָם. אֲשֶׁר בָּרָא שָׂשׂוֹן וְשִׂמְחָה. חָתָן וְכַלָּה. גִּילָה רִנָּה דִּיצָה וְחֶדְוָה. אַהֲבָה וְאַחֲוָה. וְשָׁלוֹם וְרֵעוּת: מְהֵרָה יהוה אֱלֹהֵינוּ יִשָּׁמַע בְּעָרֵי יְהוּדָה וּבְחֻצוֹת יְרוּשָׁלָיִם קוֹל שָׂשׂוֹן וְקוֹל שִׂמְחָה קוֹל חָתָן וְקוֹל כַּלָּה: בָּרוּךְ אַתָּה יהוה. מְשַׂמֵּחַ חָתָן עִם הַכַּלָּה:

בָּרוּךְ Baruch attah Adonai eloheinu melech ha-olam, borei p'ri ha-gafen.

בָּרוּךְ Baruch attah Adonai eloheinu melech ha-olam, sheha-kol bara lichvodo.

בָּרוּךְ Baruch attah Adonai eloheinu melech ha-olam, yotseir ha-adam.

בָּרוּךְ Baruch attah Adonai eloheinu melech ha-olam,
asher yatsar et ha-adam b'tsalmo,
b'tselem d'mut tavnito, v'hitkin lo mimmenu binyan adei ad.
Baruch attah Adonai, yotseir ha-adam.

שׂוֹשׂ Sos tasis v'tageil ha-akarah b'kibbuts baneha l'tochah b'simchah.
Baruch attah Adonai, m'sammei'ach tsiyyon b'vaneha.

שַׂמֵּחַ Sammei'ach t'sammach rei'im ha-ahuvim
k'sammeichacha y'tsir'cha b'gan eiden mikkedem,
yizku vaneha ha'eileh livnot bayit b'yisra'el lichvod sh'mecha.
Baruch attah Adonai, m'sammei'ach chatan v'chalah.

בָּרוּךְ Baruch attah Adonai eloheinu melech ha-olam,
asher bara sason v'simchah, chatan v'chalah,
gilah rinnah ditsah v'chedvah
ahavah v'achavah, v'shalom v'rei'ut.
M'heirah Adonai eloheinu yishama b'arei y'hudah uv'chutsot y'rushalayim
kol sason v'kol simchah kol chatan v'kol kalah.
Baruch attah Adonai, m'sammei'ach chatan im ha-kalah

Psalm 150 can be found on page 52.

THANKSGIVING SERVICE FOR PARENTS
(NAMING OF A CHILD)

אָהַבְתִּי I love my Maker who hears my voice, my pleading, whose ear is turned towards me, therefore I pray throughout my days. Merciful is the Eternal and just, our God has compassion. Return, my soul, to your rest, for your Maker has been generous to you. What can I return to my Maker for all the kindness shown me? I will fulfil my promises to the Eternal in the presence of godly people. To You I offer the offering of gratitude and call on the name of the Eternal. Praise God![1]	אָהַבְתִּי כִּי־יִשְׁמַע יהוה אֶת קוֹלִי תַּחֲנוּנָי: כִּי־הִטָּה אָזְנוֹ לִי וּבְיָמַי אֶקְרָא: חַנּוּן יהוה וְצַדִּיק. וֵאלֹהֵינוּ מְרַחֵם: שׁוּבִי נַפְשִׁי לִמְנוּחָיְכִי כִּי־יהוה גָּמַל עָלָיְכִי: מָה־אָשִׁיב לַיהוה כָּל־תַּגְמוּלוֹהִי עָלָי: נְדָרַי לַיהוה אֲשַׁלֵּם. נֶגְדָה־נָּא לְכָל עַמּוֹ: לְךָ אֶזְבַּח זֶבַח תּוֹדָה וּבְשֵׁם יהוה אֶקְרָא: הַלְלוּיָהּ:

The Mother's Prayer
Creator of all human beings and source of life, through Your great love I enter Your house to thank You and to bless Your name. You have given me the joy of creation, which supported me in my weakness, and comforted me in my anxiety. Your mercy has restored me. I thank You for my life and for the life of my child, for You renew the wonder of creation.

The Parent's Prayer (including for an adopted child)
Creator of all human beings, and source of all life, through Your great love I enter Your house to thank You and to bless Your name. I give You thanks for You have given me this opportunity and responsibility. I turn to You in awe because You have put Your trust in Me. I bless You for the love which binds me to my child; and for the wonder of creation which You have renewed within my heart.

---

[1] From Ps. 116.

The Parent or Grandparent continues here for a boy
As he grows in body and in mind, may the teaching of truth be found on his lips and the love of justice in his heart. May he be a blessing to those around him and bring honour to Israel in the sight of all.

The Parent continues here for a boy
God, be with me and my family; may our love for our child draw us even more closely together in helpfulness and in trust.
Teach us to carry on through our child the heritage of Israel, so that its tradition of wisdom and holiness may never cease.
Now in love we comfort him; may he comfort us in future years.

The Parent or Grandparent continues here for a girl
As she grows in body and in mind, may the teaching of truth be found on her lips and the love of justice in her heart. May she be a blessing to those around her and bring honour to Israel in the sight of all.

The Parent continues here for a girl
God, be with me and my family; may our love for our child draw us even more closely together in helpfulness and in trust.
Teach us to carry on through our child the heritage of Israel, so that its tradition of wisdom and holiness may never cease.
Now in love we comfort her; may she comfort us in future years.

Prayer by the Rabbi
Creator of love and compassion, accept the thanksgiving of this mother in Israel. May her spirit lifted to You now in humble gratitude be ever directed to You for help and strength. May all who help raise this child be guided by Your wisdom, giving examples in their lives of Your care and understanding. May the light of love fill their home, and Your blessing be upon them and all who are dear to them.

For a boy

מִי May the One who blessed our ancestors Abraham, Isaac and Jacob, bless this child, who shall be known in Israel as _____ son of _____. God, grant him life and health of body and mind. May he grow with Torah, to Chuppah and to good deeds. Make him a constant joy to his family, a blessing to all who know him, an honour to Israel and to God's holy name.

מִי שֶׁבֵּרַךְ אֲבוֹתֵינוּ אַבְרָהָם יִצְחָק וְיַעֲקֹב הוּא יְבָרֵךְ אֶת־הַיֶּלֶד הַזֶּה וְיִקָּרֵא שְׁמוֹ בְּיִשְׂרָאֵל _____ בֶּן _____ וְיִתֵּן לוֹ אֱלֹהִים חַיִּים אֲרֻכִּים וַחֲלוּץ־עֲצָמוֹת. יִגְדַּל לְתוֹרָה וּלְחֻפָּה וּלְמַעֲשִׂים טוֹבִים. תִּשְׂמַח בּוֹ מִשְׁפַּחְתּוֹ. וִיהִי בְרָכָה לְכָל־מַכִּירָיו וְכָבוֹד לְיִשְׂרָאֵל וּלְשֵׁם־קָדְשׁוֹ.

For a girl

מִי May the One who blessed our ancestors Sarah, Rebecca, Rachel and Leah, bless this child, who shall be known in Israel as _____ daughter of _____. God, grant her life and health of body and mind. May she grow with Torah, to Chuppah and to good deeds. Make her a constant joy to her family, a blessing to all who know her, an honour to Israel and to God's holy name.

מִי שֶׁבֵּרַךְ אִמּוֹתֵינוּ שָׂרָה רִבְקָה רָחֵל וְלֵאָה הוּא יְבָרֵךְ אֶת־הַיַּלְדָּה הַזֹּאת וְיִקָּרֵא שְׁמָהּ בְּיִשְׂרָאֵל _____ בַּת _____ וְיִתֵּן לָהּ אֱלֹהִים חַיִּים אֲרֻכִּים וַחֲלוּץ־עֲצָמוֹת. תִּגְדַּל לְתוֹרָה וּלְחֻפָּה וּלְמַעֲשִׂים טוֹבִים. תִּשְׂמַח בָּהּ מִשְׁפַּחְתָּהּ. וּתְהִי בְרָכָה לְכָל־מַכִּירֶיהָ וְכָבוֹד לְיִשְׂרָאֵל וּלְשֵׁם־קָדְשׁוֹ.

A concluding blessing may be added here.

---

[1] From Ps. 116.

SERVICE OF AFFIRMATION OF THE JEWISH FAITH

Psalm 15 (page 620) or Psalm 121 (page 179) may be read or chanted.

Prayer by the Rabbi for a man

    Almighty God, we welcome into our community our brother _____ whose name shall be called in Israel _____ son of _____. Care for him and hear his prayer, for he has chosen to serve You. May Your image in him be a light for him and for us. May his love for You and Your teaching grow stronger as the years increase. May he be a loyal member of the community of Israel, gaining respect for it in the eyes of the world, and so helping people to righteousness and truth.

    He has declared his trust in You, the one and only God, who has formed the souls of all people and in whose love they are equal. He has declared his belief in You, who judges people by their righteousness alone, and whom all may approach through prayer and integrity. On Your love and mercy he relies.

    Keep this knowledge alive within him. May his devotion to Judaism and his love for the family of Israel grow from strength to strength. In sorrow may this be his comfort; in weakness may this be his strength; in all the changes and chances of life may it bring him joy. Filled with awe and trust, he has come to live under the shelter of Your wings. God of Israel, be his refuge and his shield for evermore.

יְשַׁלֵּם May God reward you for your work, and may you find fulfillment with the Eternal God of Israel under whose wings you have taken refuge.[1]

יְשַׁלֵּם יהוה פָּעֳלֵךְ וּתְהִי מַשְׂכֻּרְתֵּךְ שְׁלֵמָה מֵעִם יהוה אֱלֹהֵי יִשְׂרָאֵל אֲשֶׁר־בָּאת לַחֲסוֹת תַּחַת־כְּנָפָיו:

---

[1] Based on Ruth 2:12.

Prayer by the Rabbi for a woman

Almighty God, we welcome into our community our sister _____ whose name shall be called in Israel _____ daughter of _____. Care for her and hear her prayer, for she has chosen to serve You. May Your image in her be a light for her and for us. May her love for You and Your teaching grow stronger as the years increase. May she be a loyal member of the community of Israel, gaining respect for it in the eyes of the world, and so helping people to righteousness and truth.

She has declared her trust in You, the one and only God, who has formed the souls of all people and in whose love they are equal. She has declared her belief in You, who judges people by their righteousness alone, and whom all may approach through prayer and integrity. On Your love and mercy she relies.

Keep this knowledge alive within her. May her devotion to Judaism and her love for the family of Israel grow from strength to strength. In sorrow may this be her comfort; in weakness may this be her strength; in all the changes and chances of life may it bring her joy. Filled with awe and trust, she has come to live under the shelter of Your wings. God of Israel, be her refuge and her shield for evermore.

יְשַׁלֵּם May God reward you for your work, and may you find fulfillment with the Eternal God of Israel under whose wings you have taken refuge.[1]

יְשַׁלֵּם יהוה פָּעֳלֵךְ וּתְהִי מַשְׂכֻּרְתֵּךְ שְׁלֵמָה מֵעִם יהוה אֱלֹהֵי יִשְׂרָאֵל אֲשֶׁר־בָּאת לַחֲסוֹת תַּחַת־כְּנָפָיו:

Rabbi or congregation:

וַתֹּאמֶר Ruth said:
'Do not entreat me to leave you,
or to return from following after you.
For wherever you go, I will go.
Wherever you lodge, I will lodge.
Your people shall be my people,
and your God my God.
Where you die, I will die,
and there will I be buried.'[2]

וַתֹּאמֶר רוּת
אַל־תִּפְגְּעִי־בִי לְעָזְבֵךְ
לָשׁוּב מֵאַחֲרָיִךְ
כִּי אֶל־אֲשֶׁר תֵּלְכִי אֵלֵךְ
וּבַאֲשֶׁר תָּלִינִי אָלִין
עַמֵּךְ עַמִּי
וֵאלֹהַיִךְ אֱלֹהָי:
בַּאֲשֶׁר תָּמוּתִי אָמוּת
וְשָׁם אֶקָּבֵר:

---

[1] Ruth 2:12.   [2] Ruth 1:16-17.

To be recited by the ger tzedek

My God, accept the offering of my heart at this solemn time. I have chosen to enter the family of Israel. I stand in Your presence as a member of Your people and ask for Your blessing. Help me to follow the teachings of Judaism, to live a Jewish life and to be part of Israel's destiny. Give me the strength and courage to share its dangers and difficulties as well as its responsibilities and opportunities. I thank You for this moment and all the future offers me. Be the light which guides me through my life. May my words and actions earn Your blessing; may they bring honour to Israel; may they make Your name holy in the world.

שְׁמַע יִשְׂרָאֵל יהוה אֱלֹהֵינוּ יהוה | אֶחָד:

שְׁמַע Hear O Israel, the Eternal is our God, the Eternal is One.

וְאָהַבְתָּ Love the Eternal your God with all your heart, and all your soul, and all your might.

וְאָהַבְתָּ אֵת יהוה אֱלֹהֶיךָ
בְּכָל־לְבָבְךָ וּבְכָל־נַפְשְׁךָ
וּבְכָל־מְאֹדֶךָ:

A concluding blessing may be added here.

PRAYER FOR COMMITTEE MEETINGS

Let us come together in God's name and prepare to do God's will.

May Your presence dwell among us, drawing us to serve You and Your creatures with justice and with love. Let us listen to each other with respect, and treat each other with wisdom and generosity, so that we witness to the Creator we serve, and justify Your choice of us.

May none of our controversies rise up like those of Korach, from ambition and self-seeking.[1] Let them only be for the sake of heaven, like those of Hillel and Shammai. May our eyes be open to see Your greatness in the smallest things we do.

Through our faithfulness may the cause of goodness prosper in the world.

וִיהִי May the favour of the Creator, our God, be upon us to support us in the work we do.

וִיהִי נֹעַם אֲדֹנָי אֱלֹהֵינוּ עָלֵינוּ וּמַעֲשֵׂה יָדֵינוּ כּוֹנְנָה עָלֵינוּ׃

וּמַעֲשֵׂה May God support the work we do.[2]

וּמַעֲשֵׂה יָדֵינוּ כּוֹנְנֵהוּ׃

A PRAYER FOR INTERNATIONAL UNDERSTANDING
(See page 249)

A PRAYER FOR INTERFAITH UNDERSTANDING *(See page 249)*

A PRAYER FOR RESPONSIBILITY FOR JUSTICE AND THE ENVIRONMENT *(See page 250)*

A PRAYER FOR THE RELEASE OF CAPTIVES

> The Torah states that the kidnapping of another human being is as serious a crime as murder.[3] The commandment to set a captive free, *pidyon sh'vuyim*, together with the commandment of *pikkuach nefesh*, 'the saving of human life', are so important that they override the laws of Shabbat.[4]

---

[1] Num 16.
[2] Ps 90:17.
[3] Ex 21:16.
[4] Yoma 85a, Shabbat 132a.

God, our redeemer, who set us free from the slavery of Egypt, we turn to You to release all hostages and captives, all who are enslaved to others. We pray now in particular for _____. May you be with him / her / them at this time of trial. Give wisdom and strength to those who work for his / her / their release and bring about a speedy end to this suffering. May you support the families and friends who can only watch and wait in fear and anxiety. Help us know what we too can do when prayers alone are not enough.

בָּרוּךְ Blessed are You, our Living God, Sovereign of the universe, whose commandments make us holy and who commands us concerning the freeing of captives.

בָּרוּךְ אַתָּה יהוה אֱלֹהֵינוּ מֶלֶךְ הָעוֹלָם. אֲשֶׁר קִדְּשָׁנוּ בְּמִצְוֹתָיו וְצִוָּנוּ עַל פִּדְיוֹן שְׁבוּיִים:

A PRAYER IN A TIME OF WAR

At this time of conflict we turn to You, God, as the Creator of all human beings, each of us made in Your image, each of us equal in Your sight. Our sages have taught, whoever takes a single human life, it is as if they have destroyed an entire world.[1]

They also taught, in that hour when the Egyptians drowned in the Sea of Reeds, the angels wished to sing a song of praise before God. But God rebuked them saying, My children are drowning in the sea, would you utter a song before Me in honour of that!?[2]

Be with Your children of all nations and religions, and give them strength and courage in this time of uncertainty and fear. Any war claims its victims on all sides. Have mercy on them and bring this conflict speedily to an end, so that its casualties may be few and damage light; so that acts of violence and bloodshed may be replaced with words and acts of conciliation. Shelter under Your care those who perish and show compassion to those who mourn for them. For those injured in body or mind, bring a perfect healing, so that their lives are not destroyed.

עֹשֶׂה May the One who brings peace in the highest, bring peace to us and to all Israel and to the whole world and let us say, Amen.

עֹשֶׂה שָׁלוֹם בִּמְרוֹמָיו. הוּא יַעֲשֶׂה שָׁלוֹם עָלֵינוּ וְעַל כָּל־יִשְׂרָאֵל וְעַל־כָּל־הָעוֹלָם. וְאִמְרוּ. אָמֵן:

---

[1] *Avot d'Rabbi Natan* 31.   [2] *Megillah* 10b.

A PRAYER IN A TIME OF A NATURAL DISASTER

Eternal One, our Rock and our Refuge, You are the source of our trust and our salvation. To You we turn with thoughts and prayers for those whose lives were lost ...

We think of those who died, of those who lost all that was precious and dear to them, family, friends, homes and possessions, of those whose lives are now blighted with loss, suffering, disease and poverty and who cry out to You: 'Save me, O God; I am weary with my crying; my throat is parched, my eyes grow dim.'[1]

O God, do not be far from those who cry out to You: guide us in all that we undertake on their behalf. As You support the needy when they call, may we respond with generosity and compassion; as You have pity on the weak and the poor, so may we help save the lives of those in danger, alleviate their suffering and bring hope and help to all those who have survived and must rebuild their lives.

You are our God; in You shall be our faithfulness and steadfast love, for You are our God and the Rock of our salvation.

עד So long as the earth endures, seedtime and harvest, cold and heat, summer and winter, day and night, shall not cease.[2]

עֹד כָּל־יְמֵי הָאָרֶץ זֶרַע וְקָצִיר וְקֹר וָחֹם וְקַיִץ וָחֹרֶף וְיוֹם וָלַיְלָה לֹא יִשְׁבֹּתוּ:

---

[1] Ps 69:2,4.   [2] Gen 8:22.

A LITURGY IN A TIME OF COMMUNITY THREAT OR DISASTER

'If no rain has fallen on a city, or if it has suffered pestilence or destruction, that city fasts and sounds the *Shofar*. They stand up in prayer and send an elder, well versed in prayer before the Ark, so that he may pray wholeheartedly. He recites before them twenty-four blessings, the eighteen blessings of the daily *Amidah* to which are added six more.'[1]

The following passages and blessings may be recited responsively and the Shofar *sounded.*

רָעָב If there be a famine in the land or there be pestilence ... or the enemy be at the gates ... then everyone of the people of Israel should bring their prayer and petition ... and raise their hands towards this house, the temple.[2]

רָעָב כִּי־יִהְיֶה בָאָרֶץ דֶּבֶר כִּי־יִהְיֶה ... כִּי יָצַר־לוֹ אֹיְבוֹ בְּאֶרֶץ שְׁעָרָיו ... כָּל־תְּפִלָּה כָל־תְּחִנָּה אֲשֶׁר תִהְיֶה לְכָל־הָאָדָם לְכֹל עַמְּךָ יִשְׂרָאֵל ... וּפָרַשׂ כַּפָּיו אֶל־הַבַּיִת הַזֶּה:

מִי May God who answered our ancestors at the crossing of the Sea of Reeds, may God answer you and hear your cry this day. Blessed are You, our living God, who remembers things forgotten.

מִי שֶׁעָנָה אֶת־אֲבוֹתֵינוּ עַל יַם סוּף הוּא יַעֲנֶה אֶתְכֶם וְיִשְׁמַע בְּקוֹל צַעֲקַתְכֶם הַיּוֹם הַזֶּה. בָּרוּךְ אַתָּה יהוה זוֹכֵר הַנִּשְׁכָּחוֹת:

אֲשֶׁר The word of God that came to Jeremiah concerning the drought ... O hope of Israel, and our Saviour in times of trouble, why should You be as a stranger in the land![3]

אֲשֶׁר הָיָה דְבַר־יְהֹוָה אֶל־יִרְמְיָהוּ עַל־דִּבְרֵי הַבַּצָּרוֹת ... מִקְוֵה יִשְׂרָאֵל מוֹשִׁיעוֹ בְּעֵת צָרָה לָמָּה תִהְיֶה כְּגֵר בָּאָרֶץ:

מִי May God who answered Joshua at Gilgal answer you and hearken to the voice of your crying this day. Blessed are You, our Living God, who hears the sound of the *Shofar*.

מִי שֶׁעָנָה אֶת־יְהוֹשֻׁעַ בַּגִּלְגָּל הוּא יַעֲנֶה אֶתְכֶם וְיִשְׁמַע בְּקוֹל צַעֲקַתְכֶם הַיּוֹם הַזֶּה. בָּרוּךְ אַתָּה יהוה שׁוֹמֵעַ תְּרוּעָה:

אֲשֶׁר In my distress
I cried out to God, who answered me.[4]

אֶל־יְהֹוָה בַּצָּרָתָה לִּי קָרָאתִי וַיַּעֲנֵנִי:

<<<

---

[1] Based on Mishnah *Ta'anit* 3:2; 2:1,2-4.
[2] From I Kings 8:37-38.
[3] From Jer 14:1,8.
[4] Ps 120:1.

IN A TIME OF DISASTER — COMMUNITY PRAYERS AND PASSAGES — 370

מִי שֶׁעָנָה אֶת־שְׁמוּאֵל בַּמִּצְפָּה הוּא יַעֲנֶה אֶתְכֶם וְיִשְׁמַע בְּקוֹל צַעֲקַתְכֶם הַיּוֹם הַזֶּה. בָּרוּךְ אַתָּה יהוה שׁוֹמֵעַ צְעָקָה:

מִי May God who answered Samuel at Mizpeh answer you and hearken to the voice of your crying this day. Blessed are You, our Living God, who hears those who cry out.

אֶשָּׂא עֵינַי אֶל־הֶהָרִים מֵאַיִן יָבֹא עֶזְרִי:

אֶשָּׂא I lift up my eyes to the hills; where shall I find my help?[1]

מִי שֶׁעָנָה אֶת־אֵלִיָּהוּ בְּהַר הַכַּרְמֶל הוּא יַעֲנֶה אֶתְכֶם וְיִשְׁמַע בְּקוֹל צַעֲקַתְכֶם הַיּוֹם הַזֶּה. בָּרוּךְ אַתָּה יהוה שׁוֹמֵעַ תְּפִלָּה:

מִי May God who answered Elijah on Mount Carmel answer you and hearken to the voice of your crying this day. Blessed are You, our Living God, who hears prayer.

מִמַּעֲמַקִּים קְרָאתִיךָ יהוה: אֲדֹנָי שִׁמְעָה בְקוֹלִי תִּהְיֶינָה אָזְנֶיךָ קַשֻּׁבוֹת לְקוֹל תַּחֲנוּנָי:

מִמַּעֲמַקִּים Out of the depths I called to You God, God, hear my voice. Let Your ears listen to the voice of my pleading.[2]

מִי שֶׁעָנָה אֶת־יוֹנָה מִמְּעֵי הַדָּגָה הוּא יַעֲנֶה אֶתְכֶם וְיִשְׁמַע בְּקוֹל צַעֲקַתְכֶם הַיּוֹם הַזֶּה. בָּרוּךְ אַתָּה יהוה הָעוֹנֶה בְּעֵת צָרָה:

מִי May God who answered Jonah in the belly of the fish answer you and hearken to the voice of your crying this day. Blessed are You, our Living God, who answers in times of trouble.

תְּפִלָּה לְעָנִי כִי־יַעֲטֹף וְלִפְנֵי יהוה יִשְׁפֹּךְ שִׂיחוֹ:

תְּפִלָּה The prayer of the afflicted when they are overwhelmed and pour out their thoughts to God.[3]

מִי שֶׁעָנָה אֶת־דָּוִד וְאֶת שְׁלֹמֹה בְנוֹ בִּירוּשָׁלַיִם הוּא יַעֲנֶה אֶתְכֶם וְיִשְׁמַע בְּקוֹל צַעֲקַתְכֶם הַיּוֹם הַזֶּה. בָּרוּךְ אַתָּה יהוה הַמְרַחֵם עַל הָאָרֶץ:

מִי May God who answered David and his son Solomon in Jerusalem answer you and hearken to the voice of your crying this day. Blessed are You, our Living God, who has compassion on the world.

---

[1] Ps 121:1.
[2] Ps 130:1-2.
[3] Ps 102:1.

A PRAYER FOR COMBATING POVERTY AND INJUSTICE

In the quietness of this hour, and amidst the comfort of our lives, we recall the wisdom of old: 'Happy are those who care for the poor.'[1]

When we are tempted to turn away from the poverty and injustice of the world, renew in us the faith of former times and the task You have entrusted to us: 'Do not sell out the poor for a pair of shoes.'[2] Although disease and violence, hunger and sorrow tarnish our world and impoverish our humanity, help us not to respond with indifference or despair. We can do more than we imagine, for we are made in Your image. Let callousness give way to compassion, and a passion for justice encompass us, as we strive to repair this fractured world, one step at a time. Renew our vision of how empathy, generosity, and the work of our hands can bring hope to others and honour to You. Through us let the Psalmist's hope be fulfilled: 'God will champion the cause of the poor, do justice to those in need.'[3]

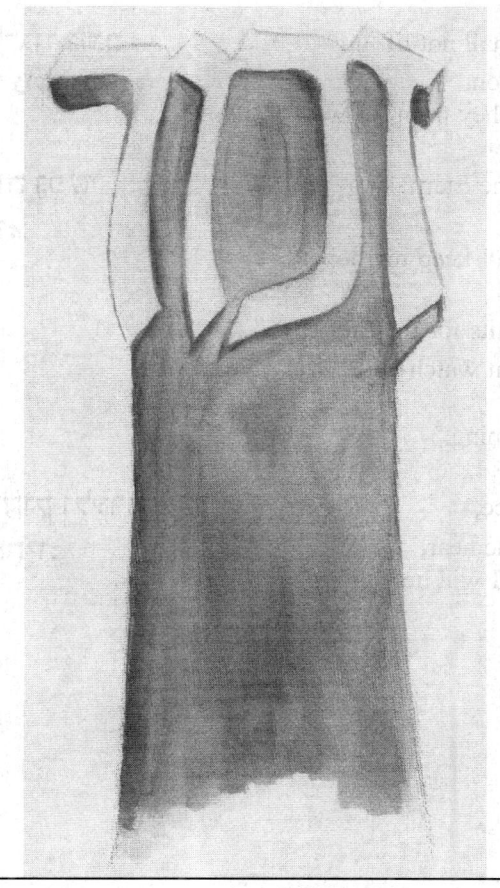

---

[1] Ps 41:1.
[2] Amos 2:6.
[3] Ps 140:13.

A PRAYER FOR WORLD PEACE

Eternal God, whose presence is over all of us, help us through our prayers and our deeds to be able to build trust in our world. We ask You to spread Your shelter of peace over all dwellers on earth, over all lands and peoples affected by war or fear of war, bringing calm to conflict and peace of mind to all who live in fear. We ask You to grant safety to those who guard and those who watch, and skill to those who must take difficult decisions, so that they be always guided by the need to avoid harm to the innocent. May we in our days learn to overcome prejudice and anger, hatred and fear, so that we may learn to live side by side in peace and harmony. May Your Divine presence, Your light and Your love shine down upon our troubled world, comforting the bereaved, helping the wounded, soothing all pain, enabling us to raise our spirits of hope and understanding, so that in our lifetime we shall be able to know how good and how pleasant it is for brothers and sisters to dwell together.

לֹא Then nation shall not lift up
sword against nation;
never again shall they train for war.[1]

לֹא־יִשָּׂא גוֹי אֶל־גּוֹי חֶרֶב
וְלֹא־יִלְמְדוּ עוֹד מִלְחָמָה׃

קִוִּיתִי I wait for the Eternal,
my soul waits,
and in God's word I keep my hope.[2]

קִוִּיתִי יהוה קִוְּתָה נַפְשִׁי
וְלִדְבָרוֹ הוֹחָלְתִּי׃

נַפְשִׁי My soul waits for the Eternal
more than they that watch
for the morning
watch for the morning.[3]

נַפְשִׁי לַאדֹנָי
מִשֹּׁמְרִים לַבֹּקֶר
שֹׁמְרִים לַבֹּקֶר׃

שָׁלוֹם Peace, peace,
to the far and to the near,'
says the Eternal, 'I will heal them.[4]

שָׁלוֹם שָׁלוֹם לָרָחוֹק וְלַקָּרוֹב
אָמַר יהוה וּרְפָאתִיו׃

---

[1] Is 2:4. [2] Ps 130:5.
[3] Ps 130:6. [4] Isa 57:19.

Calendar of the Year

תשרי חשון כסלו טבת
שבט אדר ניסן אייר
סיון תמוז אב אלול

Contents
Chanukah — 374
Tu Bishvat — 380
Purim — 384
Yom Ha-Shoah - Memorial Service for the Six Million — 388
Israel Independence Day - *Yom Ha-Atzma'ut* or *Shabbat Atzma'ut* — 394
Tish'ah B'Av — 402
Memorial Prayer for Remembrance Shabbat (November) — 404
National Holocaust Memorial Day (January) — 405

חנוכה
CHANUKAH

On Chanukah the following prayer, Al ha-nissim, *'for the wonders', is inserted in the* Amidah.

עַל הַנִּסִּים We thank You for the wonders, the victories and the marvellous and consoling deeds You performed for our ancestors, in those days at this season. In the days of Mattathias, the Hasmonean, the son of Yochanan the priest, and his sons and Hannah and her sons, when the kingdom of Antiochus rose up against Your people Israel to make them forget Your teaching, then You in Your great mercy stood up for them in their hour of need. You heard their plea. You judged their cause. You delivered the strong into the hands of the weak, and the many into the hands of the few. You made Your name great and holy in Your world, and gave a great victory to Your people Israel as at this day. Afterwards Your children entered the inner sanctuary of Your house, they cleared the temple, and lit the lamps in Your holy courts. Then they appointed eight days of dedication to thank and honour Your great name.

עַל הַנִּסִּים. וְעַל הַתְּשׁוּעוֹת. וְעַל הַנִּפְלָאוֹת. וְעַל הַנֶּחָמוֹת שֶׁעָשִׂיתָ לַאֲבוֹתֵינוּ בַּיָּמִים הָהֵם וּבַזְּמַן הַזֶּה: בִּימֵי מַתִּתְיָהוּ בֶּן יוֹחָנָן הַחַשְׁמוֹנַאי וּבָנָיו וְחַנָּה וּבָנֶיהָ. כְּשֶׁעָמְדָה מַלְכוּת אַנְטִיוֹכוֹס עַל עַמְּךָ יִשְׂרָאֵל לְהַשְׁכִּיחָם תּוֹרָתֶךָ: וְאַתָּה בְּרַחֲמֶיךָ הָרַבִּים עָמַדְתָּ לָהֶם בְּעֵת צָרָתָם. רַבְתָּ אֶת־רִיבָם. דַּנְתָּ אֶת־דִּינָם. מָסַרְתָּ גִּבּוֹרִים בְּיַד חַלָּשִׁים. וְרַבִּים בְּיַד מְעַטִּים. וּלְךָ עָשִׂיתָ שֵׁם גָּדוֹל וְקָדוֹשׁ בְּעוֹלָמֶךָ. וּלְעַמְּךָ יִשְׂרָאֵל עָשִׂיתָ תְּשׁוּעָה גְדוֹלָה כְּהַיּוֹם הַזֶּה: וְאַחֲרֵי־כֵן בָּאוּ בָנֶיךָ לִדְבִיר בֵּיתֶךָ. וּפִנּוּ אֶת־הֵיכָלֶךָ. וְהִדְלִיקוּ נֵרוֹת בְּחַצְרוֹת קָדְשֶׁךָ. וְקָבְעוּ שְׁמוֹנַת יְמֵי חֲנֻכָּה לְהוֹדוֹת וּלְהַלֵּל לְשִׁמְךָ הַגָּדוֹל:

עַל הַנִּסִּים **For the heroic acts...**

This traditional insertion for the festival of *Chanukah* focuses on the rebellion of the Maccabees against Antiochus IV and the liberation of Jerusalem and the purification of the temple in 165 BCE. The Books of the Maccabees are not included in the Jewish Biblical canon, and references in the Talmud are restricted to the miracle of the oil that burned for eight days (*Shabbat* 21b).

This reflects a conflict between the founders of the rabbinic movement and the royal priestly families that descended from the Maccabees. We have added the other legend of that period preserved in the Talmud (*Gittin* 57b) and in II Macc 7, Hannah and her seven sons who chose martyrdom rather than worshipping the Greek gods.

CHANUKAH

עַל הַנִּסִּים *Al ha-nissim, v'al ha-t'shu'ot v'al ha-nifla'ot, v'al ha-nechamot she'asita la'avoteinu ba-yamim ha-heim uva-z'man ha-zeh. Bimei mattityahu ben yochanan ha-chashmonai uvanav, v'channah u'vaneha, k'she'amdah malchut antiyochos al amm'cha yisra'el l'hashkicham toratecha. V'attah b'rachmecha ha-rabbim amadta lahem b'eit tsaratam, ravta et rivam, danta et dinam, masarta gibborim b'yad challashim, v'rabbim b'yad m'attim, ul'cha asita sheim gadol v'kadosh b'olamecha, ul'amm'cha yisra'el asita t'shu'ah g'dolah k'ha-yom ha-zeh. V'acharei chein ba'u vanecha lidvir beitecha, ufinnu et heichalecha, v'hidliku neirot b'chatsrot kodshecha, v'kav'u sh'monat y'mei chanukah l'hodot ul'halleil l'shimcha ha-gadol.*

Before lighting the Chanukiah

בָּרוּךְ Blessed are You, our Living God, Sovereign of the universe, whose commandments make us holy, and who commands us to kindle the lights of *Chanukah*.

בָּרוּךְ אַתָּה יהוה אֱלֹהֵינוּ מֶלֶךְ הָעוֹלָם. אֲשֶׁר קִדְּשָׁנוּ בְּמִצְוֹתָיו. וְצִוָּנוּ לְהַדְלִיק נֵר שֶׁל חֲנֻכָּה:

בָּרוּךְ *Baruch attah Adonai eloheinu melech ha-olam, asher kidd'shanu b'mitsvotav, v'tsivvanu l'hadlik neir shel chanukah.*

בָּרוּךְ Blessed are You, our Living God, Sovereign of the universe, who did wonders for our ancestors in those days at this season.

בָּרוּךְ אַתָּה יהוה אֱלֹהֵינוּ מֶלֶךְ הָעוֹלָם. שֶׁעָשָׂה נִסִּים לַאֲבוֹתֵינוּ בַּיָּמִים הָהֵם וּבַזְּמַן הַזֶּה:

בָּרוּךְ *Baruch attah Adonai eloheinu melech ha-olam, she'asah nissim la'avoteinu ba-yamim ha-heim uva-z'man ha-zeh.*

On the first night add

בָּרוּךְ Blessed are You, our Living God, Sovereign of the universe, who has kept us alive and supported us and brought us to this season.

בָּרוּךְ אַתָּה יהוה אֱלֹהֵינוּ מֶלֶךְ הָעוֹלָם. שֶׁהֶחֱיָנוּ וְקִיְּמָנוּ וְהִגִּיעָנוּ לַזְּמַן הַזֶּה:

בָּרוּךְ *Baruch attah Adonai eloheinu melech ha-olam, shehecheyanu v'kiy'manu v'higgi'anu la-z'man ha-zeh.*

חנוכה

After lighting the Chanukiah

הַנֵּרוֹת We kindle these lights to commemorate the wonders, the victories and the marvellous and consoling deeds which You performed for our ancestors through Your holy priests in those days at this season. During all the eight days of *Chanukah* these lights are holy and we are not permitted to make use of them, but only to see them in order to thank Your name for the wonders, the victories and the marvellous deeds.

הַנֵּרוֹת הַלָּלוּ אָנוּ מַדְלִיקִים עַל הַנִּסִּים וְעַל הַתְּשׁוּעוֹת וְעַל הַנִּפְלָאוֹת וְעַל הַנֶּחָמוֹת שֶׁעָשִׂיתָ לַאֲבוֹתֵינוּ בַּיָּמִים הָהֵם וּבַזְּמַן הַזֶּה עַל יְדֵי כֹּהֲנֶיךָ הַקְּדוֹשִׁים. וְכָל־שְׁמֹנַת יְמֵי חֲנוּכָה הַנֵּרוֹת הַלָּלוּ קֹדֶשׁ וְאֵין לָנוּ רְשׁוּת לְהִשְׁתַּמֵּשׁ בָּהֶם אֶלָּא לִרְאוֹתָם בִּלְבָד. כְּדֵי לְהוֹדוֹת לְשִׁמְךָ עַל־נִסֶּיךָ וְעַל־יְשׁוּעָתֶךָ וְעַל־נִפְלְאוֹתֶיךָ:

הַנֵּרוֹת Ha-neirot hallalu anu madlikim al ha-nissim v'al ha-t'shu'ot v'al ha-nifla'ot v'al ha-nechamot she'asita la'avoteinu ba-yamim ha-heim uva-z'man ha-zeh, al y'dei kohanecha ha-k'doshim, v'chol sh'monat y'mei chanukah ha-neirot hallalu kodesh, v'ein lanu r'shut l'hishtameish ba-hem, ella lir'otam bilvad, k'dei l'hodot l'shimcha al nissecha v'al y-shu'atecha v'al nifl'otecha.

Ma'oz Tsur   מָעוֹז צוּר

מָעוֹז Fortress, rock who sets me free,
how fine it is to sing Your praise.
When my house of prayer shall be,
our offerings of thanks we'll raise.
the time You end all slaughter,[1]
enemies shall falter.
I'll complete
a song to greet
and dedicate the altar.

מָעוֹז צוּר יְשׁוּעָתִי
לְךָ נָאֶה לְשַׁבֵּחַ
תִּכּוֹן בֵּית תְּפִלָּתִי
וְשָׁם תּוֹדָה נְזַבֵּחַ
לְעֵת תַּשְׁבִּית מַטְבֵּחַ
מִצָּר הַמְנַבֵּחַ
אָז אֶגְמוֹר
בְּשִׁיר מִזְמוֹר
חֲנֻכַּת הַמִּזְבֵּחַ:

מָעוֹז Ma'oz tsur y'shu'ati l'cha na'eh l'shabei'ach,
Tikkon beit t'fillati v'sham todah n'zabei'ach,
L'eit tashbit matbei'ach mitsar ha-m'nabei'ach,
Az egmor b'shir mizmor
Chanukat ha-mizbei'ach.

<<<

---

[1] The original text read 'When You have prepared a slaughter for the blaspheming foe', but we have followed the minor amendment suggested by Chief Rabbi J.H.Hertz to read 'the time you end all slaughter'.

How my soul was filled with strife,	רָעוֹת שָׂבְעָה נַפְשִׁי.
sorrow robbed my strength from me.	בְּיָגוֹן כֹּחִי כָלָה
Bitter hardship ruled my life,	חַיַּי מֵרְרוּ בְּקוֹשִׁי
bound by Egypt's slavery.	בְּשִׁעְבּוּד מַלְכוּת עֶגְלָה
You let Your mighty hand show,	וּבְיָדוֹ הַגְּדוֹלָה
to help Your chosen people go.	הוֹצִיא אֶת־הַסְּגֻלָּה
Pharaoh's power,	חֵיל פַּרְעֹה
his finest flower,	וְכָל־זַרְעוֹ
sank into the depths below.	יָרְדוּ כְּאֶבֶן מְצוּלָה:
Brought to God's own holy place	דְּבִיר קָדְשׁוֹ הֱבִיאַנִי
even there no peace I found.	וְגַם שָׁם לֹא שָׁקַטְתִּי
Sent to exile in disgrace,	וּבָא נוֹגֵשׂ וְהִגְלַנִי
to other gods I still felt bound.	כִּי זָרִים עָבַדְתִּי
I drank the wine of madness,	וְיֵין רַעַל מָסַכְתִּי
seventy years of sadness.	כִּמְעַט שֶׁעָבַרְתִּי
Babylon fell;	קֵץ בָּבֶל
Zerubavel[1]	זְרֻבָּבֶל
brought salvation's gladness.	לְקֵץ שִׁבְעִים נוֹשָׁעְתִּי:

Ra'ot sav'ah nafshi, b'yagon kochi chalah,
Chayyai meir'ru b'kushi b'shi'bud malchut eglah,
Uv'yado ha-g'dolah hotsi et ha-s'gullah,
Cheil par'o v'chol zar'o
Yar'du k'even m'tsulah.

D'vir kodsho hevi'ani v'gam sham lo shakatti,
Uva nogeis v'higlani ki zarim avadti,
V'yein ra'al masachti kim'at she'avarti,
Keits bavel z'rubavel
L'keits shiv'im nosha'ti.

<<<

---

[1] Governor of the returned exiles from Babylon.

Haman of the Agag clan	כְּרֹת קוֹמַת בְּרוֹשׁ בִּקֵּשׁ
sought to make our leader fall,	אֲגָגִי בֶּן־הַמְּדָתָא
but was trapped by his own plan	וְנִהְיָתָה לּוֹ לְמוֹקֵשׁ
and his pride was made to stall.	וְגַאֲוָתוֹ נִשְׁבָּתָה
Mordechai You defended,	רֹאשׁ יְמִינִי נִשֵּׂאתָ
Haman's name was ended.	וְאוֹיֵב שְׁמוֹ מָחִיתָ
One by one	רֹב בָּנָיו
You slew each son	וְקִנְיָנָיו
from a tree suspended.	עַל הָעֵץ תָּלִיתָ:
When the Greeks were gathered round	יְוָנִים נִקְבְּצוּ עָלַי
in the Maccabean days,	אֲזַי בִּימֵי חַשְׁמַנִּים
broke my towers to the ground,	וּפָרְצוּ חוֹמוֹת מִגְדָּלַי
spoilt the oil used for Your praise.	וְטִמְּאוּ כָּל־הַשְּׁמָנִים
Your sign guided our fate,	וּמִנּוֹתַר קַנְקַנִּים
one day's oil lasted for eight.	נַעֲשָׂה נֵס לַשּׁוֹשַׁנִּים
Our wise men	בְּנֵי בִינָה
established then	יְמֵי שְׁמוֹנָה
this festival we celebrate.	קָבְעוּ שִׁיר וּרְנָנִים:

Attributed to Mordechai, an unknown author, thirteenth century.

K'rot komat b'rosh bikkeish agagi ben ha-m'data,
V'nihyatah lo l'mokeish v'ga'avato nishbatah,
Rosh y'mini nisseita v'oyeiv sh'mo machita,
Rov banav v'kinyanav
Al ha-eits talita.

Y'vanim nikb'tsu alai azai bimei chashmannim,
Ufar'tsu chomot migdalai v'timm'u kol ha-sh'manim,
Uminnotar kankanim na'asah neis l'shoshannim,
B'nei vinah y'mei sh'monah
Kav'u shir ur'nanim.

OTHER SONGS FOR *CHANUKAH*

Mi Y'malleil

מִי Who can relate
the heroic deeds of Israel,
who can count them?
Behold, in every generation
a hero has arisen,
a saviour of the people.

Listen! in those days at this season
the Maccabi saved and rescued.
And in our days
all the people of Israel
will unite, arise and be redeemed.

מִי יְמַלֵּל
מִי יְמַלֵּל גְּבוּרוֹת יִשְׂרָאֵל
אוֹתָן מִי יִמְנֶה
הֵן בְּכָל־דּוֹר יָקוּם הַגִּבּוֹר
גּוֹאֵל הָעָם:
שְׁמַע. בַּיָּמִים הָהֵם בַּזְּמַן הַזֶּה
מַכַּבִּי מוֹשִׁיעַ וּפוֹדֶה:
וּבְיָמֵינוּ כָּל־עַם יִשְׂרָאֵל
יִתְאַחֵד יָקוּם לְהִגָּאֵל:

Menashe Rabina

Mi Y'malleil

מִי Mi y'malleil g'vurot yisra'eil otan mi yimneh,
Hein b'chol dor yakum ha-gibbor go'eil ha-am.
Sh'ma, ba-yamim ha-heim ba-z'man ha-zeh makkabbi moshi'a ufodeh,
Uv'yameinu kol am yisra'eil yitacheid yakum l'higga'eil.

Chanukah

בָּאנוּ We come to drive away darkness,
in our hands are light and fire.
Each one is a small light,
and all of us are a mighty light.
Away with darkness,
away with blackness!
Away before light.

חֲנֻכָּה
בָּאנוּ חֹשֶׁךְ לְגָרֵשׁ
בְּיָדֵנוּ אוֹר וָאֵשׁ:
כָּל־אֶחָד הוּא אוֹר קָטָן
וְכֻלָּנוּ אוֹר אֵיתָן:
סוּרָה חֹשֶׁךְ הָלְאָה שְׁחוֹר
סוּרָה מִפְּנֵי הָאוֹר:

Sarah Levy

Chanukah

בָּאנוּ Banu choshech l'gareish,
B'yadeinu or va'eish.
Kol echad hu or katan,
V'chullanu or eitan.
Surah choshech hal'ah sh'chor,
Surah mip'nei ha-or.

טו בשבט
TU BISHVAT

> This minor festival occurs on the 15th day of the month of *Sh'vat*. It marks the beginning of spring in the land of Israel. In the rabbinic period it was designated as one of four 'new years' that served different fiscal purposes, including providing 'tithes' of produce to support the priesthood (*Mishnah Rosh Hashanah* 1:1). As the 'New Year for Trees' it is marked in the Diaspora by eating special fruits. In Israel it has been celebrated by tree-planting ceremonies, and this gives us an opportunity to do the same in the Diaspora and consider our ecological responsibilities. The following verses, passages and songs may be used in combination with such a ceremony.

I

וַיֹּאמֶר God said: 'Let the earth sprout vegetation: seed-bearing plants, fruit trees of every kind on earth that bear fruit with the seed in it.' And it was so. The earth brought forth vegetation: seed-bearing plants of every kind, and trees of every kind bearing fruit with the seed in it. And God saw that it was good.[1]

וַיֹּאמֶר אֱלֹהִים תַּדְשֵׁא הָאָרֶץ דֶּשֶׁא עֵשֶׂב מַזְרִיעַ זֶרַע עֵץ פְּרִי עֹשֶׂה פְּרִי לְמִינוֹ אֲשֶׁר זַרְעוֹ־בוֹ עַל־הָאָרֶץ וַיְהִי־כֵן: וַתּוֹצֵא הָאָרֶץ דֶּשֶׁא עֵשֶׂב מַזְרִיעַ זֶרַע לְמִינֵהוּ וְעֵץ עֹשֶׂה־פְּרִי אֲשֶׁר זַרְעוֹ־בוֹ לְמִינֵהוּ וַיַּרְא אֱלֹהִים כִּי־טוֹב:

II

כִּי־תָצוּר When you besiege a city for a long time in order to capture it, you shall not destroy its trees, wielding an axe against them. You may eat of them but not cut them down, for the tree of the field is human life.[2]

כִּי־תָצוּר אֶל־עִיר יָמִים רַבִּים לְהִלָּחֵם עָלֶיהָ לְתָפְשָׂהּ לֹא־תַשְׁחִית אֶת־עֵצָהּ לִנְדֹּחַ עָלָיו גַּרְזֶן כִּי מִמֶּנּוּ תֹאכֵל וְאֹתוֹ לֹא תִכְרֹת כִּי הָאָדָם עֵץ הַשָּׂדֶה...:

---

[1] Gen 1:11-12.
[2] Deut 20:19. Though this may be the sense of the closing part of the sentence, the exact meaning is unclear. Nevertheless the rabbinic prohibition on the wasteful use of human resources and needless destruction is based on this verse.

III

וְעַל־הַנַּחַל All kinds of trees for food will grow on both banks of the stream. Their leaves will not wither nor their fruit fail. They will yield new fruit each month, for their waters come from a holy place. Their fruit will provide food and their leaves healing.[1]

וְעַל־הַנַּחַל יַעֲלֶה עַל־שְׂפָתוֹ מִזֶּה וּמִזֶּה כָּל־עֵץ־מַאֲכָל לֹא־יִבּוֹל עָלֵהוּ וְלֹא־יִתֹּם פִּרְיוֹ לָחֳדָשָׁיו יְבַכֵּר כִּי מֵימָיו מִן־הַמִּקְדָּשׁ הֵמָּה יוֹצְאִים וְהָיָה פִרְיוֹ לְמַאֲכָל וְעָלֵהוּ לִתְרוּפָה׃

IV

What is the reason for *Tu Bishvat*? Said Rabbi Elazar in the name of Rabbi Oshaya: 'It is because most of the rains have passed.' Rashi comments: 'Since most of the winter's days have passed, now is the time for taking root, the sap ascends the trees, and fruit ripens from this moment on.'[2]

V

Once while Honi Ha-Ma'agal was walking along the road he saw a man plant a carob tree. Choni asked, how many years will it be before this tree bears fruit? The man answered that it would take seventy years. Choni asked, do you expect to live that length of time and eat of its fruit? The man answered, I found a fruitful world because of what my ancestors planted for me. So I will do the same for my children.[3]

VI

And God planted a garden in Eden, in the east: and there God put the man whom God had formed. Out of the ground God the Creator made to grow every tree that is pleasant to the sight and good for food, the tree of life also in the midst of the garden, and the tree of the knowledge of good and evil.[4]

VII

God led Adam and Eve around the Garden of Eden and said, 'Look at My works. See how beautiful they are, how excellent! For your sake I created them all. See to it that you do not spoil or destroy My world - for if you do, there will be no one to repair it after you.'[5]

If a tree is planted

On this *Tu Bishvat*, we plant this tree as a symbol of regeneration of life in the world. May the planting of trees and the proper care of our world bring hope to all who are affected by drought or famine, by war or by climate change. May peace be as abundant on earth as the trees of the woods and the flowers of the fields, and let us say Amen.

---

[1] Ezek 47:12.
[2] *Rosh Hashanah* 14a.
[3] *Ta'anit* 23a.
[4] Gen 2:8-9.
[5] Ecclesiastes Rabbah 7:13.

ט״ו בשבט — CALENDAR OF THE YEAR

On planting a tree

בָּרוּךְ Blessed are You, our Living God, Sovereign of the universe, for the tree and its fruit.

בָּרוּךְ אַתָּה יהוה אֱלֹהֵינוּ מֶלֶךְ הָעוֹלָם. עַל הָעֵץ וְעַל פְּרִי הָעֵץ:

בָּרוּךְ Blessed are You, our Living God, Sovereign of the universe, who has kept us alive and supported us and brought us to this season.

בָּרוּךְ אַתָּה יהוה אֱלֹהֵינוּ מֶלֶךְ הָעוֹלָם. שֶׁהֶחֱיָנוּ וְקִיְּמָנוּ וְהִגִּיעָנוּ לַזְּמַן הַזֶּה:

SONGS FOR *TU BISHVAT*

צַדִּיק The righteous shall flourish like the palm tree grow tall like a cedar in Lebanon.

צַדִּיק כַּתָּמָר יִפְרָח כְּאֶרֶז בַּלְּבָנוֹן יִשְׂגֶּה:

צַדִּיק *Tsaddik ka-tamar yifrach, k'erez ba-l'vanon yisgeh.*

Tu Bishvat

הַשְּׁקֵדִיָּה The almond tree blossoms and a golden sun does shine. Birds from every rooftop announce the festive time:
  Tu Bishvat is here -
  the festival of trees.

ט״ו בִּשְׁבָט
הַשְּׁקֵדִיָּה פּוֹרַחַת.
וְשֶׁמֶשׁ פָּז זוֹרַחַת:
צִפֳּרִים מֵרֹאשׁ כָּל־גָּג
מְבַשְּׂרוֹת אֶת־בֹּא הֶחָג:
ט״ו בִּשְׁבָט הִגִּיעַ חַג הָאִילָנוֹת:

The land cries out:
the planting time has come!
Let everyone take a sapling.
Let us go to dig and plant.
  Tu Bishvat is here -
  the festival of trees.

הָאָרֶץ מְשַׁוַּעַת.
הִגִּיעַ עֵת לָטַעַת:
כָּל־אֶחָד יִקַּח לוֹ עֵץ.
בְּאֵתִים נֵצֵא חוּצָה:
ט״ו בִּשְׁבָט הִגִּיעַ חַג הָאִילָנוֹת:

Let us plant each mountain and hill from Dan to Be'er Sheva and we shall again possess our land - the land of olives, oil and honey.
  Tu Bishvat is here -
  the festival of trees.

נִטַּע כָּל־הַר וָגֶבַע.
מִדָּן וְעַד בְּאֵר־שֶׁבַע:
וְאַרְצֵנוּ שׁוּב נִירַשׁ.
אֶרֶץ זַיִת יִצְהָר וּדְבַשׁ:
ט״ו בִּשְׁבָט הִגִּיעַ חַג הָאִילָנוֹת:

הַשְּׁקֵדִיָּה *Ha-sh'keidiyyah porachat, v'shemesh paz zorachat.*
Tsipporim meirosh kol gag m'vass'rot et bo he-chag.
Tu bishvat higi'a chag ha-ilanot.

Ha-arets m'shavva'at, higgi'a eit lata'at.
Kol echad yikkach lo eits, b'ittim neitsei chotseits.
Tu bishvat higi'a chag ha-ilanot.

Nitta kol har vageva, middan v'ad b'eir sheva.
V'artseinu shuv nirash, erets zeit yitshar ud'vash.
Tu bishvat higi'a chag ha-ilanot.

פורים
PURIM

On Purim *the following prayer,* Al ha-nissim, *'for the wonders', is inserted in the* Amidah.

עַל הַנִּסִּים We thank You for the wonders, the victories and the marvellous and consoling deeds You performed for our ancestors, in those days at this season. In the days of Mordechai and Esther, in Shushan the capital, when the wicked Haman rose up against them, he sought to destroy, kill and exterminate all the Jews, both young and old, little children and women, on one day, and plunder their possessions. (That is the thirteenth day of the twelfth month, which is the month of Adar.) Then You, in Your great mercy, upset his plan and overthrew his design, and made his acts recoil upon his own head. And You performed a wonder and a marvel for them, therefore we thank Your great name.

עַל הַנִּסִּים. וְעַל הַתְּשׁוּעוֹת. וְעַל הַנִּפְלָאוֹת. וְעַל הַנֶּחָמוֹת שֶׁעָשִׂיתָ לַאֲבוֹתֵינוּ בַּיָּמִים הָהֵם וּבַזְּמַן הַזֶּה: בִּימֵי מָרְדְּכַי וְאֶסְתֵּר בְּשׁוּשַׁן הַבִּירָה. כְּשֶׁעָמַד עֲלֵיהֶם הָמָן הָרָשָׁע. בִּקֵּשׁ לְהַשְׁמִיד לַהֲרוֹג וּלְאַבֵּד אֶת־כָּל־הַיְּהוּדִים. מִנַּעַר וְעַד־זָקֵן טַף וְנָשִׁים בְּיוֹם אֶחָד. בִּשְׁלֹשָׁה עָשָׂר לְחֹדֶשׁ שְׁנֵים־עָשָׂר הוּא חֹדֶשׁ אֲדָר. וּשְׁלָלָם לָבוֹז: וְאַתָּה בְּרַחֲמֶיךָ הָרַבִּים הֵפַרְתָּ אֶת־עֲצָתוֹ. וְקִלְקַלְתָּ אֶת־מַחֲשַׁבְתּוֹ. וַהֲשֵׁבוֹתָ לּוֹ גְמוּלוֹ בְרֹאשׁוֹ: וְעָשִׂיתָ עִמָּהֶם נֵס וָפֶלֶא. וְנוֹדֶה לְשִׁמְךָ הַגָּדוֹל:

עַל הַנִּסִּים *Al ha-nissim, v'al ha-t'shu'ot v'al ha-nifla'ot, v'al ha-nechamot she'asita la'avoteinu ba-yamim ha-heim uva-z'man ha-zeh. Bimei mord'chai v'esteir b'shushan ha-birah, k'she'amad aleihem haman ha-rasha, bikkeish l'hashmid laharog ul'abeid et kol ha-y'hudim, mina'ar v'ad zakein taf v'nashim b'yom echad, bishloshah asar l'chodesh shneim asar, hu chodesh adar, ush'lalam lavoz. V'attah b'rachamecha ha-rabbim heifarta et atsato, v'kilkalta et machashavto, vahasheivota lo g'mulo v'rosho. V'asita imahem neis vafele, v'nodeh l'shimcha ha-gadol.*

PURIM

Before reading the Scroll of Esther

בָּרוּךְ Blessed are You, our Living God, Sovereign of the universe, whose commandments make us holy, and who commands us to read the Scroll of Esther.

בָּרוּךְ אַתָּה יהוה אֱלֹהֵינוּ מֶלֶךְ הָעוֹלָם. אֲשֶׁר קִדְּשָׁנוּ בְּמִצְוֹתָיו. וְצִוָּנוּ עַל מִקְרָא מְגִלָּה:

בָּרוּךְ Baruch attah Adonai eloheinu melech ha-olam, asher kidd'shanu b'mitsvotav, v'tsivvanu al mikra m'gillah.

בָּרוּךְ Blessed are You, our Living God, Sovereign of the universe, who did wonders for our ancestors in those days at this season.

בָּרוּךְ אַתָּה יהוה אֱלֹהֵינוּ מֶלֶךְ הָעוֹלָם. שֶׁעָשָׂה נִסִּים לַאֲבוֹתֵינוּ בַּיָּמִים הָהֵם וּבַזְּמַן הַזֶּה:

בָּרוּךְ Baruch attah Adonai eloheinu melech ha-olam, she'asah nissim la'avoteinu ba-yamim ha-heim uva-z'man ha-zeh.

בָּרוּךְ Blessed are You, our Living God, Sovereign of the universe, who has kept us alive and supported us and brought us to this season.

בָּרוּךְ אַתָּה יהוה אֱלֹהֵינוּ מֶלֶךְ הָעוֹלָם. שֶׁהֶחֱיָנוּ וְקִיְּמָנוּ וְהִגִּיעָנוּ לַזְּמַן הַזֶּה:

בָּרוּךְ Baruch attah Adonai eloheinu melech ha-olam, shehecheyanu v'kiy'manu v'higgi'anu la-z'man ha-zeh.

After reading the Scroll of Esther

בָּרוּךְ Blessed are You, our Living God, Sovereign of the universe, who heard our plea and judged our cause. You are the One who has always saved us, our hope in every generation. May those who trust in You never be ashamed or humiliated. Blessed are You God, the Power that saves us.

בָּרוּךְ אַתָּה יהוה אֱלֹהֵינוּ מֶלֶךְ הָעוֹלָם. הָרָב אֶת־רִיבֵנוּ וְהַדָּן אֶת־דִּינֵנוּ. תְּשׁוּעָתֵנוּ הָיִיתָ לָנֶצַח וְתִקְוָתֵנוּ בְּכָל־דּוֹר וָדוֹר. לֹא־יֵבוֹשׁוּ וְלֹא־יִכָּלְמוּ לָנֶצַח כָּל־הַחוֹסִים בָּךְ: בָּרוּךְ אַתָּה יהוה. הָאֵל הַמּוֹשִׁיעַ:

בָּרוּךְ Baruch attah Adonai eloheinu melech ha-olam, ha-rav et riveinu, v'ha-dan et dineinu, t'shu'ateinu hayita la-netsach, v'tikvateinu b'chol dor vador, lo yeivoshu v'lo yikkal'mu la-netsach kol ha-chosim bach. Baruch attah Adonai, ha-eil ha-moshi'a.

SONGS FOR *PURIM*

שׁוֹשַׁנַּת The Jews of Shushan, the flower of Jacob, were joyful and glad when all of them saw Mordechai clothed in the royal purple. You have always been the One who saved them, and their hope in every generation, to make known that all who hope in You shall never be disappointed, nor shall any be humiliated who put their trust in You.

שׁוֹשַׁנַּת יַעֲקֹב צָהֲלָה
וְשָׂמֵחָה בִּרְאוֹתָם יַחַד תְּכֵלֶת
מָרְדְּכָי: תְּשׁוּעָתָם הָיִיתָ
לָנֶצַח וְתִקְוָתָם בְּכָל־דּוֹר
וָדוֹר: לְהוֹדִיעַ שֶׁכָּל־קֹוֶיךָ
לֹא יֵבשׁוּ וְלֹא יִכָּלְמוּ לָנֶצַח
כָּל־הַחוֹסִים בָּךְ:

שׁוֹשַׁנַּת Shoshannat ya'akov tsahalah v'sameichah, birotam yachad t'cheilet mord'chai. T'shu'atam hayita la-netsach, v'tikvatam b'chol dor vador. L'hodi'a shekkol kovecha lo yeivoshu v'lo yikkal'mu la-netsach kol ha-chosim bach.

Chag Purim

חַג The festival of *Purim*
is a great festival for the Jews.
Masks, rattles, songs and dances.
Come let us make a noise:
Rash, rash, rash,
with rattles.

חַג פּוּרִים
חַג פּוּרִים. חַג גָּדוֹל לַיְּהוּדִים:
מַסֵּכוֹת רַעֲשָׁנִים
זְמִירוֹת וְרִקּוּדִים:
הָבָה נַרְעִישָׁה רַשׁ רַשׁ רַשׁ.
בְּרַעֲשָׁנִים:

Chasidic

חַג Chag purim, chag gadol la-y'hudim.
Masseichot ra'ashanim z'mirot v'rikkudim.
Havah nar'isha rash rash rash.
Ba-ra'ashanim.

Ani Purim

אֲנִי My name is *Purim* and I come
good fun and frolic bringing.
Just once a year I visit you
to cheer you with my singing.
La, la, la ...

אֲנִי פּוּרִים
אֲנִי פּוּרִים
שָׂמֵחַ וּמְבַדֵּחַ
הֲלֹא רַק פַּעַם בַּשָּׁנָה
אָבוֹא לְהִתְאָרֵחַ:

Hurrah *Purim*, hurrah *Purim*,
we love your merry drumming;
and if we had our way, *Purim*,
each month you would be coming!
La, la, la ...

הֵידָד פּוּרִים
הַכּוּ בְּתֹף וּמְצִלְתַּיִם
הוֹי מִי יִתֵּן וּבָא פּוּרִים
לְחֹדֶשׁ לָחֳדָשַׁיִם:

Oh, Mister *Purim*, tell us why
we see you only yearly.
Please make it once or twice a week
because we love you dearly.
La, la, la …

רַב פּוּרִים
אֱמֹר נָא לִי מַדּוּעַ
מַדּוּעַ לֹא יָחוּל פּוּרִים
פַּעֲמַיִם בְּשָׁבוּעַ:

אֲנִי *Ani purim samei'ach um'vaddei'ach*
Halo rak pa'am ba-shanah avo l'hitarei'ach.

Heidad purim haku b'tof um'tsiltayim
Hoi mi yittein uva purim l'chodesh l'chodshayim.

Rav purim emor na li madu'a
Madu'a lo yachul purim pa'amayim b'shavu'a.

Ze Ha-yom

זֶה Today is *Purim*,
how fine and how good.
Let us sing songs and rejoice
without end.
Rejoice, Mordecai, rejoice.
Please forget the troubles.
We will never forget this wonder.
Let us sing a song,
for in the city of Shushan
Haman the Agagite is dead.

זֶה הַיּוֹם
זֶה הַיּוֹם יוֹם פּוּרִים
מַה נָּעִים וּמַה טּוֹב.
זְמִירוֹת נְזַמֵּרָה
וְנִשְׂמַח עַד אֵין סוֹף:
שְׂמַח מָרְדְּכַי
שְׂמַח הַצָּרוֹת נָא שְׁכַח:
לָנֶצַח לֹא נִשְׁכַּח הַנֵּס:
הוֹי שִׁירוּ נָא שִׁיר.
כִּי בְּשׁוּשַׁן הָעִיר
הָמָן הָאֲגָגִי מֵת:

זֶה *Zeh ha-yom yom purim, mah na'im umah tov,*
Z'mirot n'zammeirah, v'nismach ad ein sof.
S'mach mord'chai s'mach, ha-tsarot na sh'chach.
La-netsach lo nishkach ha-neis.
Hoi shiru na shir, ki shushan ha-ir
Haman ha-agagi meit.

יום השואה
YOM HA-SHOAH
MEMORIAL SERVICE FOR THE SIX MILLION

*In some congregations memorial candles are lit.
Some or all of the following materials may be used in compiling a memorial service.*

We remember our six million dead, who died when violence ruled the world and evil dwelt on earth. We remember those we knew, and those whose very name is lost.

We mourn for all that died with them; their goodness and their wisdom, which could have saved the world and healed so many wounds. We mourn for the genius and the wit that died, the learning and the laughter that were lost. The world has become a poorer place and our hearts become cold as we think of the splendour that might have been.

We stand in gratitude for their example of decency and goodness. They are like candles which shine out from the darkness of those years, and in their light we know what goodness is - and evil.

We salute those men and women who were not Jews, who had the courage to stand outside the mob and suffer with us. They, too, are Your witnesses, a source of hope when we despair.

May such times never come again, and may their sacrifice not be in vain. In our daily fight against cruelty and prejudice, against tyranny and persecution, their memory gives us strength and leads us on.

In silence we remember those who sanctified Your name on earth.

PASSAGES FOR REFLECTION

I

I stand in awe before the memory of the *K'doshim* (the holy ones) who walked into the gas chambers with the *Ani Ma'amin* - I believe - on their lips. How dare I question, if they did not question? I believe because they believed. And I stand in awe before the *K'doshim*, before the memory of the untold suffering of innocent human beings who walked to the gas chambers without faith, because what was imposed upon them was more than man can endure. They could not believe any more - and now I do not know how to believe because I understand so well their disbelief. In fact, I find it easier to understand the loss of faith in the 'Kz' (concentration camps) than the faith preserved and affirmed. The faith affirmed was superhuman; the loss of faith - in the circumstances - human. Since I am only human, what is human is nearer to me than is the superhuman. The faith is holy; but so are the disbelief and the religious rebellion of the concentration camps holy. The disbelief was not intellectual, but faith crushed, shattered, pulverized. And faith murdered a millionfold is holy disbelief. Those who were not there, and yet readily accept the Holocaust as the will of God that must not be questioned, desecrate the holy disbelief of those whose faith was murdered. And those who were not there and yet join with self-assurance the ranks of the disbelievers, desecrate the holy faith of the believers ...

We are not Job and we dare not speak and respond as if we were. We are only Job's brother. We must believe, because our brother Job believed; and we must question, because our brother Job so often could not believe any more. This is not a comfortable situation; but is our condition in this era after the Holocaust.

Eliezer Berkovits

II

We have been pointedly reminded that we are in hiding, that we are Jews in chains, chained to one spot, without any rights, but with a thousand duties. We Jews mustn't show our feelings, must be brave and strong, must accept all inconveniences and not grumble, must do what is within our power and trust in God. Sometime this terrible war will be over. Surely the time will come when we are people again, and not just Jews.

Who has inflicted this upon us? Who has made us Jews different from all other people? Who has allowed us to suffer so terribly up till now? It is God that has made us as we are, but it will be God, too, who will raise us up again. If we bear all this suffering and if there are still Jews left when it is over, then Jews, instead of being doomed, will be held up as an example. Who knows, it might even be our religion from which the world and all peoples learn good, and for that reason and that reason only do we have to suffer now.

Let us remain aware of our task and not grumble, a solution will come, God has never deserted our people. Right through the ages there have been Jews, through all the ages they have had to suffer, but it has made them strong too; the weak fall, but the strong will remain and never go under!

If God lets me live, I shall attain more than my mother ever has done, I shall not remain insignificant, I shall work in the world and for mankind!

And now I know that first and foremost I shall require courage and cheerfulness!

Anne Frank

III

With the full weight of the authority granted to me as your Rabbi, I command you to leave me here. You must flee and save yourselves! Take heed of your bodies and your souls. Do not place your lives in danger unnecessarily because of the lightning bolt that strikes from without, but do not think for one fleeting instant that you must sacrifice your lives for inner spiritual matters. I beseech and adjure you to remember always those of our people who fell at the hands of the murderers. It is not for man to judge which one of them shall be a saint and which not. Everyone slaughtered by the wicked ones is to be judged a saint.

My dear students, always remember the Nehardea of Lithuania, the Yeshiva of Slabodka. And when the world returns again to stability and quiet, never become weary of teaching the glories, the wisdom, the Torah and the *Musar* of Lithuania, the beautiful and ethical life which Jews lived here. Do not become embittered by wailing and tears. Speak of these matters with calmness and serenity, as did our holy Sages in the Midrash, *Lamentations Rabbati*. And do as our holy Sages have done - pour forth your words and cast them into letters. This will be the greatest retribution which you can wreak upon these wicked ones. Despite the raging wrath of our foes the holy souls of your brothers and sisters will then remain alive. These evil ones schemed to blot out their names from the face of the earth; but a man cannot destroy letters. For words have wings; they mount up to the heavenly heights and they endure for eternity.

Rabbi Nachum Yanchiker - the last Musar talk delivered in the Slabodka Musar-Yeshiva, Kovno, moments before the German invasion.

IV

Our Jewish people is sent from God into history as 'blessed', 'from God blessed', which means, wherever one steps in every life situation, bestow blessing, goodness and faithfulness - humility before God's selflessness, whose devotion-full love for his creatures maintains the world. To establish these pillars of the world was and is Israel's task. Men and women, women and men have undertaken this work with the same Jewish faithfulness. This ideal also serves our testing Theresienstadt work. We are God's servants and as such we are moving from earthly to heavenly spheres. May all our work, which we have tried to perform as God's servants, be a blessing for Israel's future and humanity.

Regina Jonas

V

Two contradictory emotions governed much of my inner life: That I was innocent and that I was abandoned. They came to a head during my first *Yom Kippur* in the camps. We knew the date and like many others I fasted and created a little hiding place for myself among stacks of insulation boards. I spent most of the usual working day there - at first reciting bits of remembered liturgy, even singing the *Kol Nidre*, asking for God's forgiveness for promises made and not kept. But eventually I dissolved into crying. I must have sobbed for hours. Never before, nor since, have I cried with such intensity. And then I seemed to be granted a curious inner peace. Something of it is still with me. I believe God was also crying. And I understand a bit of the revelation that is implicit in Auschwitz. It is about man and his idols. God - the God of Abraham - could not abandon me. Only I could abandon God. I would like you to understand that in that builder's yard, on that Day of Atonement, I found God. But not the God I had childishly clung to until those jet streams dissolved over Auschwitz.

Hugo Gryn

כָּל This whole world
is a narrow bridge
- but the essential thing
is never to be afraid.

כָּל־הָעוֹלָם כֻּלּוֹ
גֶּשֶׁר צַר מְאֹד.
וְהָעִקָּר לֹא לְפַחֵד כְּלָל:

Nachman of Bratslav

כָּל *Kol ha-olam kullo gesher tsar m'od, v'ha-ikkar lo l'facheid k'lal.*

אֵלִי O God, my God,
I pray that these things never end,
the sand and the sea,
the rush of the water,
the crash of the heavens,
each human prayer.

אֵלִי אֵלִי
שֶׁלֹּא יִגָּמֵר לְעוֹלָם
הַחוֹל וְהַיָּם
רִשְׁרוּשׁ שֶׁל הַמַּיִם
בְּרַק הַשָּׁמַיִם
תְּפִלַּת הָאָדָם:

Hannah Senesh

אֵלִי *Eli, eli, shelo yiggameir l'olam*
Ha-chol v'ha-yam
Rishrush shel ha-mayim
B'rak ha-shamayim
T'fillat ha-adam.

יום השואה

אֲנִי I believe with perfect faith

in the coming of the Messiah

and even if he delay,

I will wait for Him.

אֲנִי מַאֲמִין בֶּאֱמוּנָה שְׁלֵמָה
בְּבִיאַת הַמָּשִׁיחַ.
וְאַף עַל־פִּי שֶׁיִּתְמַהְמֵהַּ
עִם כָּל־זֶה אֲחַכֶּה־לּוֹ
בְּכָל־יוֹם שֶׁיָּבֹא:

אֲנִי *Ani ma'amin b'emunah shelemah b'viat ha-mashiach.*
V'af al-pi sheyitmahmei'ah im kol zeh achakkeh lo b'chol yom sheyavo.

We must never lose our courage
in the fight,
though skies of lead
turn days of sunshine into night.
Because the hour for which
we've yearned will yet arrive,
and our marching steps
will thunder: we survive!

From land of palm trees
to the land of distant snow,
we have come
with our deep sorrow and our woe.
And everywhere
our blood was innocently shed,
our fighting spirits
will again avenge our dead.

The golden rays of morning sun
will dry our tears,
dispelling bitter agony
of yesteryears.
But if the sun and dawn
with us will be delayed -
then let this song ring out
the call to you instead.

<<<

Zog Nit Keynmol!
Zog nit keynmol
az du geyst dem letstn veg,
Chotsh himlen blayene
farshteln bloye teg,
Kumen vet noch undzer
oysgebenkte sho,
S'vet a poyk ton undzer trot -
mir zaynen do!

Fun grinem palmen-land
biz vaytn land fun shney,
Mir kumen on mit undzer payn,
mit undzer vey,
Un vu gefaln s'iz a shprits
fun undzer blut,
Shprotsn vet dort undzer gvure,
undzer mut.

S'vet di morgn-zun bagildn
undz dem haynt,
Un der nechtn vet farshvindn
mitn faynt,
Nor oyb farzamen vet di zun
un der kayor -
Vi a parol zol geyn des lid
fun dor tsu dor.

Not lead, but blood inscribed
this song which now we sing,
it's not a carolling of birds
upon the wing,
but a people midst
the crashing fires of hell,
sang this song and fought
courageous till it fell!

So we must never lose our courage
in the fight,
though skies of lead
turn days of sunshine into night.
Because the hour for which
we've yearned will yet arrive,
and our marching steps
will thunder: we survive!

Dos lid geshribn iz
mit blut un nit mit blay,
S'iz nit kayn lidl
fun a foygl oyf der fray,
Dos hot a folk tsvishn falndike vent,
Dos lid gezungen
mit naganes in di hent.

To zog nit keynmol
az du geyst dem letstn veg,
Chotsh himlen blayene
farshteln bloye teg,
Kumen vet noch undzer
oysgebenkte sho,
S'vet a poyk ton undzer trot –
mir zaynen do!

Hirsch Glick

אֵל God full of compassion whose presence is over us, may the souls of our six million dead who have gone to their everlasting home with the holy and pure on high who shine as the lights of heaven find the safety and rest denied them on earth beneath the shelter of Your presence. Source of mercy, cover them in the shelter of Your wings forever, and bind their souls into the gathering of life. It is God who is their heritage. May they be at peace in their place of rest. Amen.

אֵל מָלֵא רַחֲמִים שׁוֹכֵן בַּמְּרוֹמִים הַמְצֵא מְנוּחָה נְכוֹנָה תַּחַת כַּנְפֵי הַשְּׁכִינָה בְּמַעֲלוֹת קְדוֹשִׁים וּטְהוֹרִים כְּזֹהַר הָרָקִיעַ מַזְהִירִים לְנִשְׁמוֹת שִׁשָּׁה מִלְיוֹן אַחֵינוּ וְאַחְיוֹתֵינוּ שֶׁמֵּתוּ עַל־קִדּוּשׁ הַשֵּׁם. יָנוּחוּ בְּשַׁלְוָה וּבְשָׁלוֹם שֶׁלֹּא יָדְעוּ בְחַיֵּיהֶם. אָנָּא בַּעַל הָרַחֲמִים הַסְתִּירֵם בְּסֵתֶר כְּנָפֶיךָ לְעוֹלָמִים וּצְרוֹר בִּצְרוֹר הַחַיִּים אֶת־נִשְׁמָתָם: יהוה הוּא נַחֲלָתָם וְיָנוּחוּ בְשָׁלוֹם עַל מִשְׁכָּבָם וְנֹאמַר אָמֵן:

אֵל *Eil malei rachamim, shochein ba-m'romim, hamtsei m'nuchah n'chonah tachat kanfei ha-sh'chinah, b'ma'alot k'doshim ut'horim, k'zohar ha-raki'a mazhirim l'nishmot shishah milyon acheinu v'achyoteinu shemeitu al kiddush ha-shem. Yanuchu va-shalvah uva-shalom, shelo yad'u b'chayyeihem. Anna ba'al ha-rachamim, hastireim b'seiter k'nafecha l'olamim, uts'ror bitsror ha-chayyim et nishmatam. Adonai hu nachalatam, v'yanuchu v'shalom al mishkavam, v'nomar amen.*

The *Kaddish* is on page 316.

יום העצמאות
ISRAEL INDEPENDENCE DAY
YOM HA-ATZMA'UT
OR
SHABBAT ATZMA'UT

Some or all of the following materials may be used in compiling a service for Yom Ha-Atzma'ut or the preceding Shabbat.

The day before Yom Ha'Atzma'ut, *Israel Independence Day, is* Yom Ha-Zikkaron, *the Day of Remembrance for those who fell during the creation of the State of Israel and in defence of its existence. In remembrance of their sacrifice we begin our service with the memorial prayer.*

אֵל God full of compassion whose presence is over us, may the souls of those who gave their lives to rebuild the land, and in times of disaster gave new hope to Your people Israel, and those of the armed forces of Israel who gave their lives in the defence of the nation, find safety and rest with the holy and pure on high who shine as the lights of heaven, beneath the shelter of Your presence. Source of mercy, cover them in the shelter of Your wings forever, and bind their souls into the gathering of life. It is God who is their heritage. May they be at peace in their place of rest. Amen.

אֵל מָלֵא רַחֲמִים שׁוֹכֵן בַּמְּרוֹמִים הַמְצֵא מְנוּחָה נְכוֹנָה תַּחַת כַּנְפֵי הַשְּׁכִינָה בְּמַעֲלוֹת קְדוֹשִׁים וּטְהוֹרִים כְּזֹהַר הָרָקִיעַ מַזְהִרִים לְנִשְׁמוֹת אֵלֶה שֶׁהִקְרִיבוּ אֶת־חַיֵּיהֶם עַל הֲקָמַת מְדִינַת יִשְׂרָאֵל וּבְעֵת צָרָה נָטְעוּ תִקְוָה חֲדָשָׁה בְּלֵב עַמְּךָ יִשְׂרָאֵל וְלִנְשְׁמוֹת חַיָּלֵי צְבָא הֲגָנָה לְיִשְׂרָאֵל אֲשֶׁר מָסְרוּ נַפְשָׁם עַל הֲגָנַת הַמְּדִינָה. אָנָּא בַּעַל הָרַחֲמִים הַסְתִּירֵם בְּסֵתֶר כְּנָפֶיךָ לְעוֹלָמִים וּצְרוֹר בִּצְרוֹר הַחַיִּים אֶת־נִשְׁמָתָם: יהוה הוּא נַחֲלָתָם וְיָנוּחוּ בְשָׁלוֹם עַל מִשְׁכָּבָם וְנֹאמַר אָמֵן:

אֵל Eil malei rachamim, shochein ba-m'romim, hamtsei m'nuchah n'chonah tachat kanfei ha-sh'chinah, b'ma'alot k'doshim ut'horim, k'zohar ha-raki'a mazhirim l'nishmot eilu shehikrivu et chayyeihem al hakamat ha-m'dinah, uv'eit tsarah nat'u tikvah chadashah b'leiv amm'cha yisra'el, ul'nishmot chayyalei ts'vah haganah l'yisra'el, asher mas'ru nafsham al haganat ha-m'dinah. Anna ba'al ha-rachamim, hastireim b'seiter k'nafecha l'olamim, uts'ror bitsror ha-chayyim et nishmatam. Adonai hu nachalatam, v'yanuchu v'shalom al mishkavam, v'nomar amen.

The Kaddish is on page 316.

From the Declaration of Independence 1948

Accordingly we, the members of the National Council, representing the Jewish people in the State of Israel and the Zionist Movement, have assembled on the day of the termination of the British Mandate for Palestine, and, by virtue of our natural and historic right and of the resolution of the United Nations, do hereby proclaim the establishment of a Jewish State in the Land of Israel - the State of Israel.

The State of Israel will be open to Jewish immigration and the ingathering of exiles. It will devote itself to developing the land for the good of all its inhabitants. It will rest upon foundations of liberty, justice and peace as envisioned by the prophets of Israel. It will maintain complete equality of social and political rights for all its citizens, without distinction of creed, race or sex. It will guarantee freedom of religion and conscience, of language, education and culture. It will safeguard the Holy Places of all religions. It will be loyal to the principles of the United Nations Charter.

Even amidst the violent attacks launched against us for months past, we call upon the sons of the Arab people dwelling in Israel to keep the peace and to play their part in building the State on the basis of full and equal citizenship and due representation in all its institutions, provisional and permanent.

We extend the hand of peace and good-neighbourliness to all the states around us and to their peoples, and we call upon them to co-operate in mutual helpfulness with the independent Jewish nation in its land. The State of Israel is prepared to make its contribution in a concerted effort for the advancement of the entire Middle East.

We call upon the Jewish people throughout the Diaspora to join forces with us in immigration and construction, and to be at our right hand in the great endeavour to fulfil the age-old longing for the redemption of Israel.

With trust in Almighty God, we set our hands in witness to this Proclamation, at this session of the Provisional Council of State, on the soil of the homeland, in the city of Tel Aviv, this Sabbath Eve, the fifth of Iyar, 5708, the fourteenth of May 1948.

The Half-Hallel *may be recited, pages 663-674.*

CALENDAR OF THE YEAR

One or more of the following prayers may be read.

I

אֱלֹהֵינוּ Our God in heaven, Rock of Israel and our Redeemer, bless the State of Israel, the first flowering of our redemption. Shelter it under the wings of your faithful love and send Your light and Your truth to its leaders and policy makers and guide them with good counsel that comes from You. Strengthen the hands of those who defend the land and grant them deliverance and grant peace to the land and lasting joy to all its inhabitants.

אֱלֹהֵינוּ שֶׁבַּשָּׁמַיִם צוּר יִשְׂרָאֵל וְגוֹאֲלוֹ בָּרֵךְ אֶת מְדִינַת יִשְׂרָאֵל רֵאשִׁית צְמִיחַת גְּאֻלָּתֵנוּ: הָגֵן עָלֶיהָ בְּאֶבְרַת חַסְדֶּךָ וּפְרוֹס עָלֶיהָ סֻכַּת שְׁלוֹמֶךָ. וּשְׁלַח אוֹרְךָ וַאֲמִתְּךָ לְרָאשֶׁיהָ וְיוֹעֲצֶיהָ וְתַקְּנֵם בְּעֵצָה טוֹבָה מִלְּפָנֶיךָ: חַזֵּק אֶת יְדֵי מְגִנֵּי הָאָרֶץ וְהַנְחִילֵם יְשׁוּעָה וְנָתַתָּ שָׁלוֹם בָּאָרֶץ וְשִׂמְחַת עוֹלָם לְכָל־יוֹשְׁבֶיהָ:

II

Eternal God, whose presence is over all of us, help us through our prayers and our deeds to be able to build trust between us and our enemies. We ask You to spread Your shelter of peace over the State of Israel, granting safety to those who guard and those who watch, giving skill to those who negotiate, so that the peoples of Israel and Palestine may come to a closer understanding of each other. Help them to overcome prejudice and anger, hatred and fear, so that they may learn to live side by side in peace and harmony. May Your Divine presence, Your light and Your love shine down upon these troubled souls, comforting the bereaved, healing and soothing all pain, enabling them to raise their spirits of hope and understanding, so that in our lifetime we shall be able to know how good and how pleasant it is for brothers and sisters to dwell together.[1]

הִנֵּה מַה־טּוֹב וּמַה־נָּעִים שֶׁבֶת אַחִים גַּם־יָחַד:

I wait for the Eternal, my soul waits, and in God's word I keep my hope.[2]

קִוִּיתִי יהוה קִוְּתָה נַפְשִׁי וְלִדְבָרוֹ הוֹחָלְתִּי:

---

[1] Ps 133:1.   [2] Ps 130:5.

III

God of Abraham, God of Sarah and God of Hagar, God of Isaac and God of Ishmael, God of the twelve sons of Jacob and God of the twelve sons of Ishmael, God of the spirits of all human beings, we turn to You for guidance. We are all Your children, descendants of Abraham, entrusted with Your blessing: 'through you shall all the peoples of the earth be blessed.'

We have failed You and each other.
We face each other across barriers
of misunderstanding and mistrust,
of hatred and fear.
Where there is injustice, let there be justice.
Where there are wounds, let there be healing.
Where there is pain, let there be relief.
Where there is violence, let there be negotiation.
Where there is singlemindedness, let there be compromise.
Where there is bitterness, let there be forgiveness.
Where there is humiliation, let there be honour.
Where there is contempt, let there be respect.
Where there is guilt, let there be repentance.
Where there is death, let there be life.
Where there is hatred, let there be love.
Where there is war, let there be peace.

Psalm 122 (page 675) or Psalm 126 (page 464) may be recited.

יְבָרֶכְךָ May God bless you from Zion. May you see the welfare of Jerusalem all the days of your life. May you see your children's children. May there be peace for Israel.[1]	יְבָרֶכְךָ יהוה מִצִּיּוֹן וּרְאֵה בְּטוּב יְרוּשָׁלָיִם כֹּל יְמֵי חַיֶּיךָ: וּרְאֵה־בָנִים לְבָנֶיךָ שָׁלוֹם עַל־יִשְׂרָאֵל:

---

[1] Ps 128:5-6.

CALENDAR OF THE YEAR   יום העצמאות

Yerushalayim shel zahav

ירוּשָׁלַיִם שֶׁל זָהָב

אֲוִיר The mountain air is as clear as wine,
and the smell of the pine tree
is carried on the evening breeze
with the sound of bells.
The city is imprisoned
in a sleep of tree and stone,
the city which dwells alone
and in its heart a wall.

אֲוִיר הָרִים צָלוּל כַּיַּיִן
וְרֵיחַ אֳרָנִים
נִשָּׂא בְּרוּחַ הָעַרְבַּיִם
עִם קוֹל פַּעֲמוֹנִים:
וּבְתַרְדֵּמַת אִילָן וָאֶבֶן
שְׁבוּיָה בַּחֲלוֹמָהּ.
הָעִיר אֲשֶׁר בָּדָד יוֹשֶׁבֶת
וּבְלִבָּהּ חוֹמָה:

   Jerusalem of gold,
   of copper and of light,
   I am a harp
   for all your songs.

ירוּשָׁלַיִם שֶׁל זָהָב
וְשֶׁל נְחוֹשֶׁת וְשֶׁל אוֹר
הֲלֹא לְכָל־שִׁירַיִךְ
אֲנִי כִּנּוֹר:

We have returned to the water cisterns, to
the market and the squares.
A *shofar* is heard on the temple Mount
in the Old City.
In the caves in the rocks
a thousand windows gleam.
Let us once again descend
to the Dead Sea by way of Jericho

חָזַרְנוּ אֶל בּוֹרוֹת הַמַּיִם
לַשּׁוּק וְלַכִּכָּר:
שׁוֹפָר קוֹרֵא בְּהַר הַבַּיִת
בָּעִיר הָעַתִּיקָה:
וּבַמְּעָרוֹת אֲשֶׁר בַּסֶּלַע
אַלְפֵי שְׁמָשׁוֹת זוֹרְחוֹת:
נָשׁוּב נֵרֵד אֶל יָם הַמֶּלַח
בְּדֶרֶךְ יְרִיחוֹ:

   Jerusalem of gold ...

ירוּשָׁלַיִם שֶׁל זָהָב ...

But when I come today
to sing to you and to crown you,
I am less than the least of your children
and the last of your poets,
for your name burns the lips
like the kiss of a seraph.
If I forget you, O Jerusalem,
which is all gold.

אַךְ בְּבוֹאִי הַיּוֹם לָשִׁיר לָךְ
וְלָךְ לִקְשֹׁר כְּתָרִים:
קָטֹנְתִּי מִצְּעִיר בָּנַיִךְ
וּמֵאַחֲרוֹן הַמְשׁוֹרְרִים.
כִּי שְׁמֵךְ צוֹרֵב אֶת־הַשְּׂפָתַיִם
כִּנְשִׁיקַת שָׂרָף:
אִם אֶשְׁכָּחֵךְ יְרוּשָׁלַיִם
אֲשֶׁר כֻּלָּהּ זָהָב:

   Jerusalem of gold ...

ירוּשָׁלַיִם שֶׁל זָהָב ...

Naomi Shemer

אֲוִיר *Avir harim tsalul ka-yayin v'rei'ach oranim.*
Nissa b'ru'ach ha-arbayim im kol pa'amonim.
Uv'tardeimat ilan va'even sh'vuyah bachalomah.
Ha'ir asher badad yoshevet uv'libba chomah.
Y'rushalayim shel zahav v'shel n'choshet v'shel or,
Halo l'chol shirayich ani kinnor.

Chazarnu el borot ha-mayim la-shuk v'la-kikar.
Shofar korei b'har ha-bayit ba-ir ha-atikah.
Uvam'arot asher ba-sella' alfei sh'mashot zor'chot.
Nashuv neireid el yam ha-melach b'derech y'richo.
Y'rushalayim shel zahav v'shel n'choshet v'shel or,
Halo l'chol shirayich ani kinnor.

Ach b'vo'i ha-yom lashir lach v'lach likshor k'tarim.
Katonti mits'ir banayich umei'acharon ha-m'shor'rim.
Ki sh'meich tsoreiv et ha-s'fatayim kinshikat saraf.
Im eshkacheich y'rushalayim asher kullah zahav.
Y'rushalayim shel zahav v'shel n'choshet v'shel or,
Halo l'chol shirayich ani kinnor.

Od yavo shalom aleinu	עוֹד יָבוֹא שָׁלוֹם עָלֵינוּ
עוֹד Peace will come to us,	עוֹד יָבוֹא שָׁלוֹם עָלֵינוּ
peace will yet come to us,	וְעַל כֻּלָּם:
Peace will come to us, and everyone.	סַלָאם.
Salaam,	
peace for us and for all the world,	עָלֵינוּ וְעַל־כָּל־הָעוֹלָם.
peace, peace.	סַלָאם סַלָאם:

Moshe ben Ari

עוֹד *Od yavo shalom aleinu, od yavo shalom aleinu,*
od yavo shalom aleinu, v'al kulam.
Salaam, aleinu v'al kol ha-olam, salaam, salaam.
Salaam, aleinu v'al kol ha-olam, salaam, salaam.
Od yavo shalom aleinu, od yavo shalom aleinu, od yavo shalom aleinu, v'al kulam.

יום העצמאות

Hatikvah

As long as a Jewish soul
still yearns in the innermost heart,
and eyes turn eastward
gazing towards Zion,
then our hope is not lost,
the hope of two thousand years
- to be a free people in our land,
the land of Zion and Jerusalem.

הַתִּקְוָה

כֹּל עוֹד בַּלֵּבָב פְּנִימָה
נֶפֶשׁ יְהוּדִי הוֹמִיָּה
וּלְפַאֲתֵי מִזְרָח קָדִימָה
עַיִן לְצִיּוֹן צוֹפִיָּה
עוֹד לֹא אָבְדָה תִּקְוָתֵנוּ
הַתִּקְוָה שְׁנוֹת אַלְפַּיִם
לִהְיוֹת עַם חָפְשִׁי בְּאַרְצֵנוּ
בְּאֶרֶץ צִיּוֹן וִירוּשָׁלָיִם:

Hatikvah

Kol od ba-leivav p'nimah
Nefesh y'hudi homiyyah.
Ul'fa'atei mizrach kadimah
Ayin l'tsiyyon tsofiyah.
Od lo av'dah tikvateinu,
Hatikvah sh'not alpayim,
Lihyot am chofshi b'artseinu
B'erets tsiyyon virushalayim.

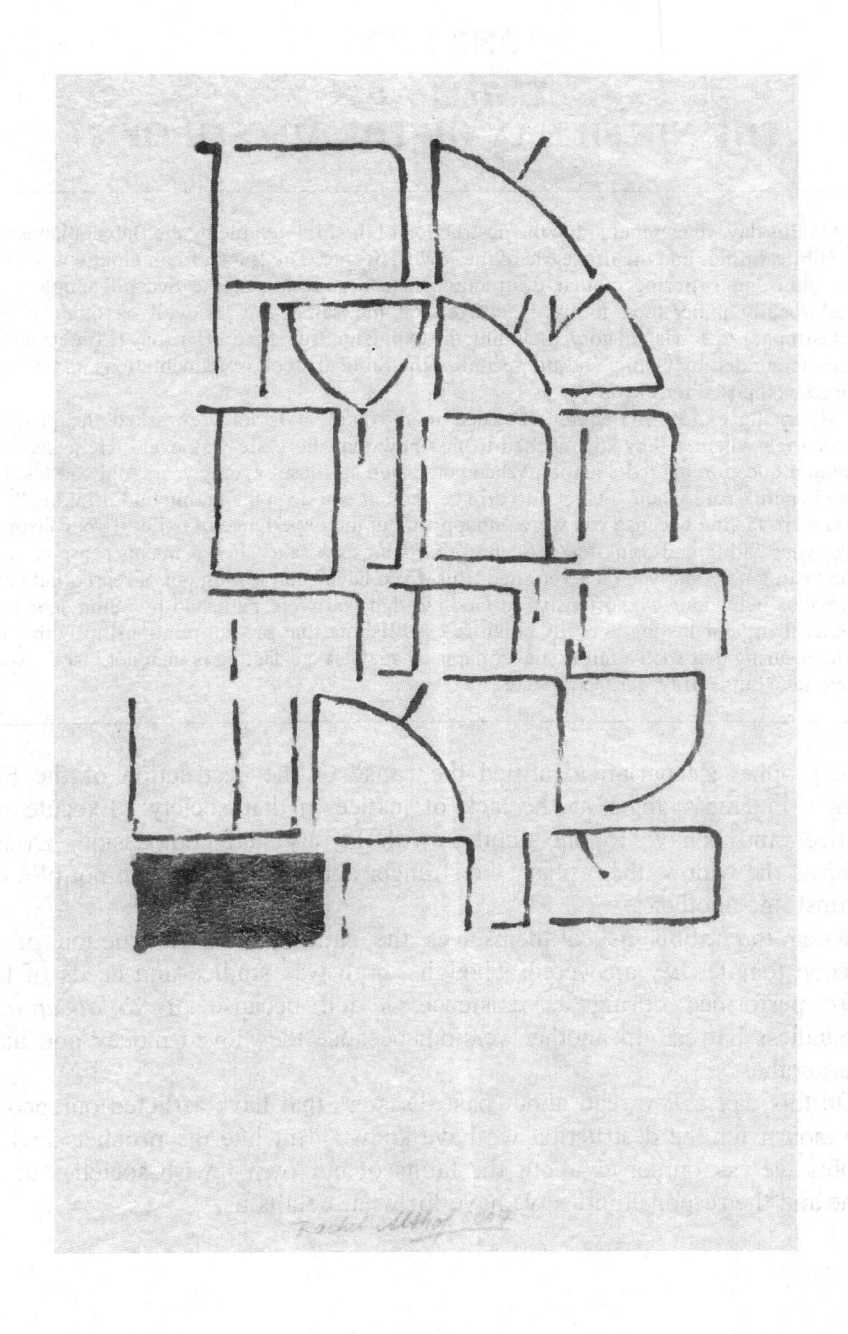

401 CALENDAR OF THE YEAR ISRAEL INDEPENDENCE DAY

תשעה באב
TISH'AH B'AV
THE NINTH DAY OF THE MONTH OF *AV*

On this day we commemorate the destruction of the First temple by the Babylonian army in Biblical times and the first exile of the Jewish people. The Book of Lamentations recalls the pain and suffering of that destruction. The destruction of the Second temple was traditionally understood to have occurred on the same day, as well as other major catastrophes in Jewish history, including the expulsion from Spain. The day is traditionally commemorated by fasting and the recital of the biblical Book of Lamentations and *Kinot*, dirges composed for the day.

When the exiles in Babylon returned to the land of Israel they asked the prophet Zechariah whether they still needed to fast now that the exile was over. He asked the counter question in God's name: 'When you fasted all these seventy years, did you fast for My benefit? And when you eat and drink, who but you does the eating and drinking?'[1] If you were fasting because you were unhappy about the experience of exile; if your fasting, like your eating and drinking, was purely for your own sake, then it makes sense to stop the fasting now that you have returned. But if you have been fasting out of regret that your previous behaviour was offensive to God, so that you were punished by being sent into exile, then your fasting is really about re-establishing that broken relationship with God and ensuring that such a failure never happens again. Your fasting is then not just for your own sake but is truly 'for God's sake'.

The prophet Zechariah identified the cause of the destruction of the First temple in God's anger at the lack of justice in that society: 'Execute true justice, and behave to one another with loyalty and compassion. Do not oppress the widow, the orphan, the stranger and the poor, and do not plot evil against one another.'[2]

When the rabbis asked themselves the cause of the destruction of the Second temple they answered: Though Torah was studied and deeds of love were performed during its existence, it fell because of *sin'at chinam*, groundless hatred.[3] In another version: because they loved money and hated one another.[4]

On this day as we read about past disasters that have afflicted our people, we mourn for the destruction we have known. But like the prophets and the rabbis we ask ourselves about the faults of our own Jewish societies in our time and the responsibilities we have for what befalls us.

---

[1] Zech 7:5-6.
[2] Zech 7:9-10.
[3] *Yoma* 9b.
[4] *Tosefta Menachot* 13:22.

אֵיכָה Ah! how lonely lies the city
once great with people;
once great among the nations,
is now become like a widow;
once a princess among the states,
is now enslaved.
Bitterly she weeps at night,
her cheek wet with tears.
There is none to comfort her
of all her allies.
All her neighbours
betrayed her;
they became her foes.[1]

אֵיכָה יָשְׁבָה בָדָד הָעִיר
רַבָּתִי עָם
הָיְתָה כְּאַלְמָנָה
רַבָּתִי בַגּוֹיִם
שָׂרָתִי בַּמְּדִינוֹת הָיְתָה לָמַס:
בָּכוֹ תִבְכֶּה בַּלַּיְלָה
וְדִמְעָתָהּ עַל לֶחֱיָהּ
אֵין־לָהּ מְנַחֵם מִכָּל־אֹהֲבֶיהָ
כָּל־רֵעֶיהָ בָּגְדוּ בָהּ
הָיוּ לָהּ לְאֹיְבִים:

A selection of appropriate readings may be included here.

אַתָּה But You, God,
are enthroned forever,
Your throne endures through the ages.
Why have You forgotten us utterly,
forsaken us for all time?
Turn us back to You, God,
and we shall return;
renew our lives as of old.[2]

אַתָּה יהוה לְעוֹלָם תֵּשֵׁב
כִּסְאֲךָ לְדֹר וָדוֹר:
לָמָּה לָנֶצַח תִּשְׁכָּחֵנוּ
תַּעַזְבֵנוּ לְאֹרֶךְ יָמִים:
הֲשִׁיבֵנוּ יהוה אֵלֶיךָ וְנָשׁוּבָה
חַדֵּשׁ יָמֵינוּ כְּקֶדֶם:

---

[1] Lam 1:2.   [2] Lam 5:19-21.

MEMORIAL PRAYER
FOR REMEMBRANCE SHABBAT (November)

'To everything there is a season, A time for everything under the sun: A time to be born, and a time to die, A time to seek and a time to lose.'[1]

This is the time to remember. November 11th was Armistice Day in 1918, the end of the war they called 'the war to end wars'. It did not end war. Countless other conflicts have happened since then, and many still die in war in our time. We remember at this time all who gave their lives in the service of our country, especially those who served in the two world wars, those who died, that we might be free; those who died, so we could live on. There were many who had the strength to stand up to evil, protecting others from its consequences. Their example is still our defence and our shelter.

Together
'They shall grow not old, as we that are left grow old. Age shall not weary them, nor the years condemn. At the going down of the sun and in the morning. We will remember them. We will remember them.'

Laurence Binyon

When you go home, tell them of us, and say, for your tomorrow, we gave our today.[2]

Kohima Epitaph

אֵל God full of compassion whose presence is over us, may the souls of our brothers and sisters who gave their lives in war find safety and rest with the holy and pure on high who shine as the lights of heaven, beneath the shelter of Your presence. Source of mercy, cover them in the shelter of Your wings forever, and bind their souls into the gathering of life. It is God who is their heritage. May they be at peace in their place of rest. Amen.

אֵל מָלֵא רַחֲמִים שׁוֹכֵן בַּמְּרוֹמִים. הַמְצֵא מְנוּחָה נְכוֹנָה תַּחַת כַּנְפֵי הַשְּׁכִינָה. בְּמַעֲלוֹת קְדוֹשִׁים וּטְהוֹרִים. כְּזֹהַר הָרָקִיעַ מַזְהִירִים אֶת־נִשְׁמוֹת אַחֵינוּ וַאֲחִיוֹתֵינוּ שֶׁנָּפְלוּ בְּמִלְחָמָה וְהָלְכוּ לְעוֹלָמָם. אָנָּא בַּעַל הָרַחֲמִים הַסְתִּירֵם בְּסֵתֶר כְּנָפֶךָ לְעוֹלָמִים. וּצְרוֹר בִּצְרוֹר הַחַיִּים אֶת־נִשְׁמוֹתָם. יְהֹוָה הוּא נַחֲלָתָם וְיָנוּחוּ בְּשָׁלוֹם עַל מִשְׁכָּבָם וְנֹאמַר אָמֵן:

The Kaddish is on page 316.

---

[1] Ecc 3:1-2,6.
[2] The Kohima Epitaph is the memorial to the men of the British Second Division who fell in the Battle of Kohima in 1944. It is based on an epitaph written during the First World War by John Maxwell Edmonds (1875-1958).

NATIONAL HOLOCAUST MEMORIAL DAY (January)

וַיֹּאמֶר Cain spoke to Abel his brother, and when they were in the field, Cain rose up against Abel his brother and killed him. God said to Cain: 'Where is Abel your brother?' He replied: 'I do not know. Am I my brother's keeper?' God said: 'What have you done? The voice of your brother's blood is crying out to Me from the ground.'[1]

וַיֹּאמֶר קַיִן אֶל־הֶבֶל אָחִיו וַיְהִי בִּהְיוֹתָם בַּשָּׂדֶה וַיָּקָם קַיִן אֶל־הֶבֶל אָחִיו וַיַּהַרְגֵהוּ: וַיֹּאמֶר יהוה אֶל־קַיִן אֵי הֶבֶל אָחִיךָ וַיֹּאמֶר לֹא יָדַעְתִּי הֲשֹׁמֵר אָחִי אָנֹכִי: וַיֹּאמֶר מֶה עָשִׂיתָ קוֹל דְּמֵי אָחִיךָ צֹעֲקִים אֵלַי מִן־הָאֲדָמָה:

The first murder recorded in the Bible occurs before there is any division between tribes, races, nations and creeds. Cain and Abel are brothers, the first children of the first human couple, yet needless hatred leads to the violent death of one, the victim, and exile and suffering for the other, the perpetrator. Since that moment the earth has had reason to cry out each day at the blood that has been shed.

Despite our own history of suffering as victims of prejudice and hatred, nothing prepared us for the horror of the Nazi genocide, the deliberate, systematic, cunning and brutal attempt to wipe the Jewish people from the face of the earth. The pain of the loss of one third of our people is deeply embedded in our hearts, our minds and our souls. Vainly we hoped that such an atrocity could never be visited again on another people. Yet still daily we learn of new horrors, justified by perverse reasoning, conducted with ever more efficient weapons or with brutal slaughter. Each such destruction is unique to those who endure it; each generates new potentials for revenge and an escalation of the horror.

This day we join with people throughout the land in calling for an end to such brutality, to murder in the name of tribe, race, nation or creed. We know that good intentions, or prayers alone are not enough to stop the slaughter. We pledge our support for the United Nations and all agencies that work for international understanding, for conflict resolution, management or transformation. We affirm our commitment to interfaith dialogue and combating racial prejudice here in our neighbourhood and wherever a Jewish voice is present. As our tradition has taught us, we acknowledge that within ourselves too are the seeds of violence against others, so that we too must take responsibility for actions carried out in our name.

<<<

---

[1] Gen 4:8-10.

Together

God of Cain, God of Abel, help us work for a time when such horrors cease from the earth; when violence is no longer acceptable to solve conflicts; when no conditions exist to warrant acts of brutality and terror. May our small contribution, as individuals and as a community, together with all people of good will, help bring this about. And let us say: Amen.

לֹא־יִשָּׂא Nation shall not lift up sword against nation. Never again shall they train for war.[1]

לֹא־יִשָּׂא גוֹי אֶל־גּוֹי חֶרֶב
וְלֹא־יִלְמְדוּ עוֹד מִלְחָמָה:

---

[1] Isa 2:4.

Life Cycle Events

Contents
Blessings for Various Occasions **408**
   Blessings Concerning Food   408
   Blessings Concerning Nature   409
   Blessings Concerning People   410
   Blessings Concerning Events   411
Prayers for Various Life Events **413**
   Prayers for a Journey (including to Israel)   413
   A Prayer on Making *Aliyah*   414
   A Prayer on Leaving Home   414
   A Prayer for Parents When a Child Leaves Home   415
   A Prayer for an Anniversary   416
   A Prayer on Retirement   416
   A Prayer on the Loss of a Loved One   416
   A Prayer during Depression   417
   A Prayer for those Responsible for the Care of Others   417
   A Prayer about Animal Companions   418
   A Prayer during Illness   419
   A Prayer on behalf of the Ill   419
   A Prayer before Surgery   420
   A Prayer during Dangerous Illness (A Deathbed Confession)   420
   A Prayer on behalf of the Terminally Ill   421
   Prayers after a Miscarriage or on the Death of an Infant   422
   A Prayer in the Home before a Funeral   424
***Yizkor* - Memorial Service** **426**
Prayers for the stages of mourning   430
      At the end of the *Shivah* period   430
      At the end of the *Sh'loshim* period   431
A Prayer for the *Yahrzeit* (Anniversary of a Death)   431
Prayers on Visiting a Grave   433

BLESSINGS FOR VARIOUS OCCASIONS

BLESSINGS CONCERNING FOOD

Washing the hands before a meal

בָּרוּךְ Blessed are You, our Living God, Sovereign of the universe, whose commands make us holy and who commands us concerning washing the hands.

בָּרוּךְ אַתָּה יהוה אֱלֹהֵינוּ מֶלֶךְ הָעוֹלָם. אֲשֶׁר קִדְּשָׁנוּ בְּמִצְוֹתָיו וְצִוָּנוּ עַל נְטִילַת יָדָיִם:

For wine

בָּרוּךְ Blessed are You, our Living God, Sovereign of the universe, who creates the fruit of the vine.

בָּרוּךְ אַתָּה יהוה אֱלֹהֵינוּ מֶלֶךְ הָעוֹלָם. בּוֹרֵא פְּרִי הַגָּפֶן:

For bread

בָּרוּךְ Blessed are You, our Living God, Sovereign of the universe, who brings forth food out of the earth.

בָּרוּךְ אַתָּה יהוה אֱלֹהֵינוּ מֶלֶךְ הָעוֹלָם. הַמּוֹצִיא לֶחֶם מִן הָאָרֶץ:

For cake and pastry

בָּרוּךְ Blessed are You, our Living God, Sovereign of the universe, who creates different kinds of food.

בָּרוּךְ אַתָּה יהוה אֱלֹהֵינוּ מֶלֶךְ הָעוֹלָם. בּוֹרֵא מִינֵי מְזוֹנוֹת:

For fruits which grow on trees

בָּרוּךְ Blessed are You, our Living God, Sovereign of the universe, who creates the fruit of the trees.

בָּרוּךְ אַתָּה יהוה אֱלֹהֵינוּ מֶלֶךְ הָעוֹלָם. בּוֹרֵא פְּרִי הָעֵץ:

For vegetables

בָּרוּךְ Blessed are You, our Living God, Sovereign of the universe, who creates the fruit of the earth.

בָּרוּךְ אַתָּה יהוה אֱלֹהֵינוּ מֶלֶךְ הָעוֹלָם. בּוֹרֵא פְּרִי הָאֲדָמָה:

For all other food

בָּרוּךְ Blessed are You, our Living God, Sovereign of the universe, by whose word all things exist.

בָּרוּךְ אַתָּה יהוה אֱלֹהֵינוּ מֶלֶךְ הָעוֹלָם. שֶׁהַכֹּל נִהְיָה בִּדְבָרוֹ:

409 LIFE CYCLE EVENTS — BLESSINGS FOR VARIOUS OCCASIONS

After eating any food except bread

בָּרוּךְ Blessed are You, our Living God, Sovereign of the universe, who creates many living things and their needs, with all that You created to keep each one of them alive. Blessed are You, the life of all existence.

בָּרוּךְ אַתָּה יהוה אֱלֹהֵינוּ מֶלֶךְ הָעוֹלָם. בּוֹרֵא נְפָשׁוֹת רַבּוֹת וְחֶסְרוֹנָן. עַל כָּל־מַה־שֶּׁבָּרָאתָ לְהַחֲיוֹת בָּהֶם נֶפֶשׁ כָּל־חָי. בָּרוּךְ חֵי הָעוֹלָמִים:

BLESSINGS CONCERNING NATURE

On smelling flowers

בָּרוּךְ Blessed are You, our Living God, Sovereign of the universe, who creates fragrant plants.

בָּרוּךְ אַתָּה יהוה אֱלֹהֵינוּ מֶלֶךְ הָעוֹלָם. בּוֹרֵא עִשְׂבוֹת בְּשָׂמִים:

On smelling spices

בָּרוּךְ Blessed are You, our Living God, Sovereign of the universe, who creates different kinds of spices.

בָּרוּךְ אַתָּה יהוה אֱלֹהֵינוּ מֶלֶךְ הָעוֹלָם. בּוֹרֵא מִינֵי בְשָׂמִים:

On smelling perfumes

בָּרוּךְ Blessed are You, our Living God, Sovereign of the universe, who creates sweet smelling oil.

בָּרוּךְ אַתָּה יהוה אֱלֹהֵינוּ מֶלֶךְ הָעוֹלָם. בּוֹרֵא שֶׁמֶן עָרֵב:

On seeing the wonders of nature

בָּרוּךְ Blessed are You, our Living God, Sovereign of the universe, who performs the work of creation.

בָּרוּךְ אַתָּה יהוה אֱלֹהֵינוּ מֶלֶךְ הָעוֹלָם. עֹשֵׂה מַעֲשֵׂה בְרֵאשִׁית:

On hearing thunder

בָּרוּךְ Blessed are You, our Living God, Sovereign of the universe, whose strength and power fill the world.

בָּרוּךְ אַתָּה יהוה אֱלֹהֵינוּ מֶלֶךְ הָעוֹלָם. שֶׁכֹּחוֹ וּגְבוּרָתוֹ מָלֵא עוֹלָם:

On seeing a rainbow

בָּרוּךְ Blessed are You, our Living God, Sovereign of the universe, You remember Your covenant and are faithful to it, and keep Your promise.[1]

בָּרוּךְ אַתָּה יהוה אֱלֹהֵינוּ מֶלֶךְ הָעוֹלָם. זוֹכֵר הַבְּרִית וְנֶאֱמָן בִּבְרִיתוֹ וְקַיָּם בְּמַאֲמָרוֹ:

---

[1] Based on God's covenant with Noah never again to bring a flood to destroy the earth,

Gen 9:8-17.

BLESSINGS FOR VARIOUS OCCASIONS　　　LIFE CYCLE EVENTS **410**

On seeing the sea

בָּרוּךְ Blessed are You, our Living God, Sovereign of the universe, who made the great sea.

בָּרוּךְ אַתָּה יהוה אֱלֹהֵינוּ מֶלֶךְ הָעוֹלָם. שֶׁעָשָׂה אֶת־הַיָּם הַגָּדוֹל:

On seeing the beauties of nature

בָּרוּךְ Blessed are You, our Living God, Sovereign of the universe, who have such as these in Your world.

בָּרוּךְ אַתָּה יהוה אֱלֹהֵינוּ מֶלֶךְ הָעוֹלָם. שֶׁכָּכָה לוֹ בְּעוֹלָמוֹ:

On seeing trees in blossom
for the first time in the year

בָּרוּךְ Blessed are You, our Living God, Sovereign of the universe, You have not made Your world lack for anything, and have created in it fine creatures and trees to give pleasure to humankind.

בָּרוּךְ אַתָּה יהוה אֱלֹהֵינוּ מֶלֶךְ הָעוֹלָם. שֶׁלֹּא חִסֵּר בְּעוֹלָמוֹ דָּבָר. וּבָרָא בוֹ בְּרִיּוֹת טוֹבוֹת וְאִילָנוֹת טוֹבִים לְהַנּוֹת בָּהֶם בְּנֵי אָדָם:

BLESSINGS CONCERNING PEOPLE

On seeing people of unusual appearance

בָּרוּךְ Blessed are You, our Living God, Sovereign of the universe, who varies the forms of creation.

בָּרוּךְ אַתָּה יהוה אֱלֹהֵינוּ מֶלֶךְ הָעוֹלָם. מְשַׁנֶּה הַבְּרִיּוֹת:

On seeing monarchs and rulers

בָּרוּךְ Blessed are You, our Living God, Sovereign of the universe, You have given of Your glory to flesh and blood.

בָּרוּךְ אַתָּה יהוה אֱלֹהֵינוּ מֶלֶךְ הָעוֹלָם. שֶׁנָּתַן מִכְּבוֹדוֹ לְבָשָׂר וָדָם:

On seeing people with religious knowledge and wisdom

בָּרוּךְ Blessed are You, our Living God, Sovereign of the universe, You have given a share of Your wisdom to those in awe of You.

בָּרוּךְ אַתָּה יהוה אֱלֹהֵינוּ מֶלֶךְ הָעוֹלָם. שֶׁחָלַק מֵחָכְמָתוֹ לִירֵאָיו:

On seeing people
with great secular learning

בָּרוּךְ Blessed are You, our Living God, Sovereign of the universe, You have given of Your wisdom to flesh and blood.

בָּרוּךְ אַתָּה יהוה אֱלֹהֵינוּ מֶלֶךְ הָעוֹלָם. שֶׁנָּתַן מֵחָכְמָתוֹ לְבָשָׂר וָדָם:

BLESSINGS CONCERNING EVENTS

On fixing a mezuzah
בָּרוּךְ Blessed are You, our Living God, Sovereign of the universe, whose commands make us holy, and commands us to fix the *mezuzah*.

בָּרוּךְ אַתָּה יהוה אֱלֹהֵינוּ מֶלֶךְ הָעוֹלָם. אֲשֶׁר קִדְּשָׁנוּ בְּמִצְוֹתָיו וְצִוָּנוּ לִקְבּוֹעַ מְזוּזָה:

On tasting new fruits, on moving into a new home and on wearing new clothes[1]
בָּרוּךְ Blessed are You, our Living God, Sovereign of the universe, who has kept us alive and supported us and brought us to this season.

בָּרוּךְ אַתָּה יהוה אֱלֹהֵינוּ מֶלֶךְ הָעוֹלָם. שֶׁהֶחֱיָנוּ וְקִיְּמָנוּ וְהִגִּיעָנוּ לַזְּמַן הַזֶּה:

On hearing bad news
בָּרוּךְ Blessed are You, our Living God, Sovereign of the universe, the true judge.

בָּרוּךְ אַתָּה יהוה אֱלֹהֵינוּ מֶלֶךְ הָעוֹלָם. דַּיַּן הָאֱמֶת:

On hearing news which is good for you and for others
בָּרוּךְ Blessed are You, our Living God, Sovereign of the universe, who is good and does good.

בָּרוּךְ אַתָּה יהוה אֱלֹהֵינוּ מֶלֶךְ הָעוֹלָם. הַטּוֹב וְהַמֵּטִיב:

On seeing one who has recovered from serious illness
בְּרִיךְ Blessed is the All-merciful, Sovereign of the universe, who has restored you to us and not to the dust.

בְּרִיךְ רַחֲמָנָא מַלְכָּא דְעָלְמָא דִּי יַהֲבָךְ לָן וְלָא יַהֲבָךְ לְעַפְרָא:

On seeing synagogues which remain after a destruction
בָּרוּךְ Blessed are You, our Living God, Sovereign of the universe, who 'preserves the portion of the vulnerable'.[2]

בָּרוּךְ אַתָּה יהוה אֱלֹהֵינוּ מֶלֶךְ הָעוֹלָם. מַצִּיב גְּבוּל אַלְמָנָה:

---

[1] The exception is on leather shoes or garments as they have cost an animal its life.

[2] Prov 15:25.

LIFE CYCLE EVENTS 412

Before using the mikveh

בָּרוּךְ Blessed are You, our Living God, Sovereign of the universe, whose commands make us holy and who commands us concerning ritual immersion.

בָּרוּךְ אַתָּה יהוה אֱלֹהֵינוּ מֶלֶךְ הָעוֹלָם. אֲשֶׁר קִדְּשָׁנוּ בְּמִצְוֹתָיו וְצִוָּנוּ עַל הַטְּבִילָה:

On seeing a place
where a wonderful thing happened to you

בָּרוּךְ Blessed are You, our Living God, Sovereign of the universe, who performed a wonderful thing for me at this place.

בָּרוּךְ אַתָּה יהוה אֱלֹהֵינוּ מֶלֶךְ הָעוֹלָם. שֶׁעָשָׂה לִי נֵס בַּמָּקוֹם הַזֶּה:

PRAYERS FOR VARIOUS LIFE EVENTS

PRAYERS FOR A JOURNEY
(INCLUDING TO ISRAEL)

I

May God who called our ancestors Abraham and Sarah to journey into the unknown, and guarded them, and blessed them, protect me/us too and bless my/our journey. May Your confidence support me/us as I/we set out, may Your spirit be with me/us on the way, and may You lead me/us back to my/our home in peace. Those I/we love, I/we commend to Your care. You are with them, I/we shall not fear. As for myself/ourselves, may Your presence be my/our companion, so that blessing comes to me/us, and to everyone I/we meet.

בָּרוּךְ Blessed are You, our Living God, whose presence journeys with Your people.

בָּרוּךְ אַתָּה יהוה שְׁשְׁכִינָתְךָ
נוֹסַעַת עִם עַמֶּךָ:

II

יְהִי May it be Your will, our Living God, and God of our ancestors, that You lead us towards peace and direct our footsteps towards peace, that You guide us towards peace and lead us to our desired destination - to life, joy and peace. May You rescue us from all dangers on the way, from enemies and ambush, robbers and wild animals; from all kinds of disasters that come into this world. May You send blessing on everything we do, and give us grace favour and mercy in Your sight and in the sight of all who regard us. Hear the voice of our prayer, for You are a God who listens to supplication and prayer. Blessed are You God, who listens to prayer.

יְהִי רָצוֹן מִלְּפָנֶיךָ יהוה אֱלֹהֵינוּ
וֵאלֹהֵי אֲבוֹתֵינוּ שֶׁתּוֹלִיכֵנוּ
לְשָׁלוֹם וְתַצְעִידֵנוּ לְשָׁלוֹם
וְתַדְרִיכֵנוּ לְשָׁלוֹם וְתַנְחֵנוּ
אֶל־מְחוֹז חֶפְצֵנוּ לְחַיִּים וּלְשִׂמְחָה
וּלְשָׁלוֹם. וְתַצִּילֵנוּ מִכַּף כָּל־אוֹיֵב
וְלִסְטִים וְחַיּוֹת רָעוֹת בַּדֶּרֶךְ
וּמִכָּל־מִינֵי פֻּרְעָנִיּוֹת הַמִּתְרַגְּשׁוֹת
וּבָאוֹת לָעוֹלָם. וְתִשְׁלַח בְּרָכָה
בְּכָל־מַעֲשֵׂה יָדֵינוּ וְתִתְּנֵנוּ לְחֵן
וּלְחֶסֶד וּלְרַחֲמִים בְּעֵינֶיךָ וּבְעֵינֵי
כָל־רוֹאֵינוּ וְתִשְׁמַע קוֹל תַּחֲנוּנֵנוּ
כִּי אֵל שׁוֹמֵעַ תְּפִלָּה וְתַחֲנוּן אָתָּה:
בָּרוּךְ אַתָּה יהוה שׁוֹמֵעַ תְּפִלָּה:

Those travelling to Israel may add:

May God bless us from Zion, so that we see the welfare of Jerusalem all the days of our life.[1]

יְבָרְכֵנוּ יהוה מִצִּיּוֹן וּרְאֵה בְּטוּב
יְרוּשָׁלָיִם כֹּל יְמֵי חַיֵּינוּ:

---
[1] Based on Ps 128:5.

A PRAYER ON MAKING *ALIYAH*

לִבִּי 'My heart is in the East
and I am at the edge of the West.'

לִבִּי בְמִזְרָח
וְאָנֹכִי בְּסוֹף מַעֲרָב:

Judah Halevi

Here I am, ready to perform the command of my Creator, to settle in the land of Israel as countless generations before me.
May I face with courage the challenges that lie ahead.
May my dreams prove to be realistic, and my anxieties without foundation.
May I value the best of what the country of my birth and upbringing has given me, and bring these gifts to my new home.
May I make my own contribution to the land and to the life of the Jewish people.

The congregation responds

יְבָרֶכְךָ May God bless you from Zion,
so that you see the welfare of Jerusalem
all the days of your life.[1]

יְבָרֶכְךָ יהוה מִצִּיּוֹן
וּרְאֵה בְּטוּב יְרוּשָׁלָיִם
כֹּל יְמֵי חַיֶּיךָ:

A PRAYER ON LEAVING HOME

אֲדֹנָי God, You have been our home
from age to age.[2]

אֲדֹנָי מָעוֹן אַתָּה הָיִיתָ לָּנוּ
בְּדֹר וָדֹר:

My own home is both a place where I live and a state of mind. It contains so many memories of the different stages of my life. Good times and difficult times are mingled together. I have been through so many changes since my childhood, so many emotional ups and downs with my family. Now it is time to move on and begin a different kind of life and a new set of responsibilities.
I look back with gratitude for what has been given me. The ties with family and friends accompany me. I look forward with excitement and anticipation. Help me find my own way at the beginning of this journey in search of a new place for myself in the world, a new home.

וִיהִי May the favour of the Creator,
our God, be with me,
to support me in the task before me,
and support whatever I do.[3]

וִיהִי נֹעַם אֲדֹנָי אֱלֹהֵינוּ עָלֵינוּ
וּמַעֲשֵׂה יָדֵינוּ כּוֹנְנָה עָלֵינוּ
וּמַעֲשֵׂה יָדֵינוּ כּוֹנְנֵהוּ:

---

[1] Ps 128:5.
[2] Ps 90:2.
[3] Adapted from Ps 90:17.

A PRAYER FOR PARENTS WHEN A CHILD LEAVES HOME

To everything there is a season, and a time for every purpose under heaven.
A time to embrace and a time to refrain from embracing.
A time to keep hold and a time to let go.[1]

I know that it is never easy to let go. A child grows, becomes more independent and leaves home to begin a new stage of life. This is natural and right, and a moment to celebrate, even if tinged with a sense of loss.

God of Abraham and Sarah, help me as I face the changes this moment brings, and nurture the new relationship that will grow between us.

God of Isaac and Rebecca, may the best of what I have given be fruitful; may the right path lie open ahead.

God of Jacob, Rachel and Leah, be with my child, who is no longer a child, on this journey; guard and guide the life that now begins.

For a boy:
Be there for him,
as I/we tried to be there when needed.

וּשְׁמוֹר Guard his going out
and his coming in,
from now on and forever.

וְיִשְׁמוֹר צֵאתוֹ
וּבוֹאוֹ
מֵעַתָּה וְעַד עוֹלָם:

For a girl:
Be there for her,
as I/we tried to be there when needed.

וּשְׁמוֹר Guard her going out
and her coming in,
from now on and forever.

וְיִשְׁמוֹר צֵאתָהּ
וּבוֹאָהּ
מֵעַתָּה וְעַד עוֹלָם:

יְבָרֶכְךָ May God bless you and keep you.
May God's face shine upon you
and be gracious to you.
May God's face turn towards you
and give you peace.

יְבָרֶכְךָ יהוה וְיִשְׁמְרֶךָ.
יָאֵר יהוה פָּנָיו אֵלֶיךָ וִיחֻנֶּךָּ.
יִשָּׂא יהוה פָּנָיו אֵלֶיךָ
וְיָשֵׂם לְךָ שָׁלוֹם:

---

[1] Ecc 3:1,5,6.

A PRAYER FOR AN ANNIVERSARY

God, who makes times pass and seasons change, You appointed for our people festivals of gladness and seasons of joy, for our remembrance is always before You. On this day I come before You with my private memories, and thank You for my own experience, and for companionship and love. Whatever the future brings may this day always renew my spirit, giving me happiness on my journey through life. My heart is grateful for the kindness You have shown me. Bless me also in the years that lie ahead.

A PRAYER ON RETIREMENT

God of the spirits of all living creatures, You alone understand the many changes we meet in the course of our life on earth.

As I pass from one active stage to another I turn to You, grateful for what I have achieved, anticipating all that still lies before me.

Let no regrets about the past or anxieties about the future overwhelm me. Let me not be complacent or resigned, as if my life was already completed.

'The soul You have given me is pure' and is renewed within me each waking day. May I also find renewal each day as I enter yet another stage and face once again the mystery of what lies before me.

May I not become a burden to others, but accept and welcome help when I need it. May I keep friendships of the past and find new ones in the life ahead. May I gain strength from those I love, and be able to give to them in return.

יְהִיוּ May these my words,   יִהְיוּ לְרָצוֹן אִמְרֵי־פִי.
and these hopes in my heart,   וְהֶגְיוֹן לִבִּי לְפָנֶיךָ.
be acceptable to You,
O God, my Rock and my Redeemer.[1]   יהוה צוּרִי וְגֹאֲלִי:

A PRAYER ON THE LOSS OF A LOVED ONE

God, I turn to You, weighed down by the loss of _____ who has been so central to my life. I know with my mind that the price we pay for loving someone is the pain of parting and loss. But this knowledge brings no comfort to my heart. I feel abandoned and alone.

I turn to You for help and for strength. What has gone will never return. My memories may sustain me, but You alone can heal the sadness that overwhelms me.

Like the psalmist, 'I lift up my eyes to the hills' and ask, 'from where will I find my help?' I pray that in time I too can say, 'my help comes from the Living God'.[2] For now I can only ask that You are near me, that You hear my words and the inner cry I bring to You.

---

[1] Ps 19:15.   [2] Ps 121:1-2.

A PRAYER DURING DEPRESSION

מִמַּעֲמַקִּים Out of the depths I call to You, my Living God.
God, listen to my voice.
Let Your ears hear the sound of my pleading.[1]

מִמַּעֲמַקִּים קְרָאתִיךָ יהוה:
אֲדֹנָי שִׁמְעָה בְקוֹלִי
תִּהְיֶינָה אָזְנֶיךָ קַשֻּׁבוֹת
לְקוֹל תַּחֲנוּנָי:

   Source of Mercy, help me at this time of need. My soul is full of anguish and my spirit full of disquiet and terror. I see the world as though through a darkened glass. I cannot connect with anyone, not even those I am close to. Even the tender reaching out of friendship or love fills me with a sense of loss and sadness. Why does everything appear so distant from me? What is the path that lies ahead? Why am I so afraid of what will become of me? Show me Your tenderness, forgiving God. Help me to open myself to Your presence; pour Your spirit into my soul that I may gain the patience for this journey to continue. May I put my trust in You, and understand soon that I, too, am Your creation, formed in Your image and worthy to receive Your love and goodness. Amen.

יהוה God is my light and my safety, whom shall I fear?
God is the strength of my life, of whom shall I be afraid?[2]

יהוה אוֹרִי וְיִשְׁעִי מִמִּי אִירָא
יהוה מָעוֹז חַיַּי מִמִּי אֶפְחָד:

A PRAYER FOR THOSE RESPONSIBLE FOR THE CARE OF OTHERS

   Av ha'rachaman, Source of Mercy and Compassion, You have given me the task of caring for another human being. Give me the strength to do my duty, the patience to do it well, and the support I need for my own well-being.
   Give me the wisdom to understand my own limitations, the courage to accept them and to seek whatever help I may also need.
   When the burden seems too great for me, may Your love sustain me.
   In good times and in bad, may I never forget that we are all created in Your image.

עֶזְרִי My Carer is the Living God, Creator of heaven and earth.[3]

עֶזְרִי מֵעִם יהוה
עֹשֵׂה שָׁמַיִם וָאָרֶץ:

---

[1] Ps 130:1-2.
[2] Ps 27:1.
[3] Ps 121:2.

PRAYERS ABOUT ANIMAL COMPANIONS

וַיֹּאמֶר And God spoke to Noah and his children with him, saying: I establish My covenant with you and your offspring to come, and with every living thing that is with you - birds, cattle and every living thing on the earth with you, everything that comes out of the ark, every living thing on the earth.[1]

וַיֹּאמֶר אֱלֹהִים אֶל־נֹחַ וְאֶל־בָּנָיו אִתּוֹ לֵאמֹר: וַאֲנִי הִנְנִי מֵקִים אֶת־בְּרִיתִי אִתְּכֶם וְאֶת־זַרְעֲכֶם אַחֲרֵיכֶם: וְאֵת כָּל־נֶפֶשׁ הַחַיָּה אֲשֶׁר אִתְּכֶם בָּעוֹף בַּבְּהֵמָה וּבְכָל־חַיַּת הָאָרֶץ אִתְּכֶם מִכֹּל יֹצְאֵי הַתֵּבָה לְכֹל חַיַּת הָאָרֶץ:

On acquiring a pet:
Eternal God, grant us many years of happiness and companionship with _____ who has joined our family/will be part of our home. May _____ presence bring us joy and may we be ever attentive to his/her needs and aware of our own responsibilities.

בָּרוּךְ Blessed are You, our Living God, Sovereign of the universe, whose world contains such beauty.

בָּרוּךְ אַתָּה יהוה אֱלֹהֵינוּ מֶלֶךְ הָעוֹלָם שֶׁכָּכָה לוֹ בְּעוֹלָמוֹ:

בָּרוּךְ Blessed are You, our Living God, Sovereign of the universe, who has kept us alive and supported us and brought us to this happy day.

בָּרוּךְ אַתָּה יהוה אֱלֹהֵינוּ מֶלֶךְ הָעוֹלָם שֶׁהֶחֱיָנוּ וְקִיְּמָנוּ וְהִגִּיעָנוּ לַזְּמַן הַזֶּה:

On the death of a pet:
O God, we mourn the passing of our beloved _____ who has entered the life of everlasting peace. We give thanks for the years of loyalty and companionship that we have enjoyed, and all the moments of happiness which we have shared. We shall always cherish memories of the time we spent together and through us _____ will continue to live in our hearts.

*Words of consolation
on the loss of an animal companion:*

הַמָּקוֹם May the Everpresent restore to you what you have lost.[2]

הַמָּקוֹם
יְמַלֵּא לְךָ חֶסְרוֹנָךְ

---

[1] Gen 9:8-10.   [2] *Berachot* 16b.

A PRAYER DURING ILLNESS

In my illness God, I turn to You, for I am Your creation. Your strength and courage are in my spirit, and Your powers of healing are within my body. May it be Your will to restore me to health.

In my illness I have learnt what is great and what is small. I know how dependent I am upon You. My own pain and anxiety have been my teachers. May I never forget this precious knowledge when I am well again.

Comfort me, God, and shelter me in Your love. Heal me and I shall be healed, save me and I shall be saved.

בָּרוּךְ Blessed are You, our Living God,   בָּרוּךְ אַתָּה יהוה
the faithful and merciful healer.   רוֹפֵא נֶאֱמָן וְרַחֲמָן:

A PRAYER ON BEHALF OF THE ILL

For a man:
God, I pray for _____ in his illness. May it be Your will to renew his strength and bring him back to good health. Renew his spirit also and free him from anxiety, for You watch over his body and his soul.

Though I cannot share his pain, help me to bring him good cheer and comfort. Give us the joy of helping each other through all the fortunes of life.

For a woman:
God, I pray for _____ in her illness. May it be Your will to renew her strength and bring her back to good health. Renew her spirit also and free her from anxiety, for You watch over her body and her soul.

Though I cannot share her pain, help me to bring her good cheer and comfort. Give us the joy of helping each other through all the fortunes of life.

בָּרוּךְ Blessed are You, our Living God,   בָּרוּךְ אַתָּה יהוה
the faithful and merciful healer.   רוֹפֵא נֶאֱמָן וְרַחֲמָן:

A PRAYER BEFORE SURGERY

Before my operation I turn to You, because You are always beside me.
You created the healing powers of my body and the strength and courage of my spirit. They are Your gifts to carry me from fear to confidence.
Yours are the wonders of science and the marvels of creation. I thank You for the wisdom of my doctors, the skill of my surgeon's hands and the devotion of my nurses. They are Your helpers in the work of healing. They comfort me.
God, I am Your child whom You created. Lead me gently into sleep and waken me to health. In Your love I trust.

A PRAYER DURING DANGEROUS ILLNESS
(A DEATHBED CONFESSION)

As a child turns to a parent, I turn to You, my God who created me. You are the source of my life and death, may it be Your will to heal me and keep me in life. But if it is time for me to go forward, through death to life everlasting, give me courage and trust to ease my journey.
I regret the hurts I have caused and the mistakes I have made. Forgive my sins, and my soul will be pure as it returns to You. Protect those I love whom I leave behind, for their lives are in Your care. Through Your mercy we shall come together in the gathering of life. In Your hand I lay my soul, when I sleep and when I wake, and with my soul my body too. You are with me, I shall not fear.

יהוה God **rules**, God has **ruled**, God **shall rule** forever and ever.	יהוה מֶלֶךְ. יהוה מָלָךְ. יהוה יִמְלֹךְ לְעוֹלָם וָעֶד:
בָּרוּךְ Blessed is the knowledge of God's glorious rule forever and ever.	בָּרוּךְ שֵׁם כְּבוֹד מַלְכוּתוֹ לְעוֹלָם וָעֶד:
יהוה The Eternal alone is our God.	יהוה הוּא הָאֱלֹהִים:

שְׁמַע יִשְׂרָאֵל יהוה אֱלֹהֵינוּ יהוה | אֶחָד:

שְׁמַע Hear O Israel, the Eternal is our God, the Eternal is One.

יהוה *Adonai melech. Adonai malach. Adonai yimloch l'olam va'ed.*

בָּרוּךְ *Baruch sheim k'vod malchuto l'olam va'ed.*

יהוה *Adonai hu ha-elohim.*

שְׁמַע *Sh'ma yisra'el Adonai eloheinu Adonai echad.*

A PRAYER ON BEHALF OF THE TERMINALLY ILL

For a man:

   I pray to You for _____ who approaches the frontiers of this life. You are the source of life and death and his fate is in Your hands. Heal his body and restore him to life, if this is Your will. If it is not, be with him and give him courage to conquer pain, and hope to overcome fear. Lead him forwards in peace from this world into the life that has no end, supported by his own good deeds, and accompanied by love.

To be added by someone who is close:

   Help me, too, and teach me that though we may part now, we shall come together once again in the gathering of life.

בְּיָדְךָ His soul is in Your hand,	בְּיָדְךָ אַפְקִיד רוּחוֹ
and with his soul, his body too.	וְעִם רוּחוֹ גְוִיָתוֹ.
You are with him, I shall not fear.	יהוה לוֹ וְלֹא אִירָא:

For a woman:

   I pray to You for _____ who approaches the frontiers of this life. You are the source of life and death and her fate is in Your hands. Heal her body and restore her to life, if this is Your will. If it is not, be with her and give her courage to conquer pain, and hope to overcome fear. Lead her forwards in peace from this world into the life that has no end, supported by her own good deeds, and accompanied by love.

To be added by someone who is close:

   Help me, too, and teach me that though we may part now, we shall come together once again in the gathering of life.

בְּיָדְךָ Her soul is in Your hand,	בְּיָדְךָ אַפְקִיד רוּחָהּ
and with her soul, her body too.	וְעִם רוּחָהּ גְוִיָתָהּ.
You are with her, I shall not fear.	יהוה לָהּ וְלֹא אִירָא:

PRAYERS AFTER A MISCARRIAGE
OR ON THE DEATH OF AN INFANT

Whether alone or in the presence of friends, a memorial candle may be lit. Any of the following passages may be said:

I light this candle [in memory of my unborn child]/[in the name of _____] whose soul has returned to God before we could properly know you.

As this candle burns, so too you shone for us. As this candle flickers, so too your life was fragile. As this candle will end, so too your life has ended. Yet we knew of your existence, your light showed us a different landscape, and we will never forget what we have seen because you were, for so short a time, part of this our world. May your soul be bound up in the bonds of eternal life, in the mesh of all who have lived and all who will ever live.

El malei rachamim
God, full of mercy
Mercy-full
Womb-full
Creator of all
El malei rachamim
I am emptied and hollowed
created not in Your image at this moment
empty of mercy, bereft of life
angry and hurt.
The only child around is me.
El malei rachamim
shelter me under Your wings
protect me and grant me perfect rest
as I say goodbye to my child
who has gone to eternity.
El malei rachamim
Tachat kanfei ha-sh'chinah
under the wings of the *Sh'chinah* I allow my words to flow
and my cry will rend the heavens
and accompany my child
Shehal'cha l'olamah
who has gone to eternity.

Eternal One our God,
for a time You gave us the hope of new life,
placed in us the expectation of new awakening.
Now, in Your wisdom,
You have taken that hope from us,
have delayed for reasons known only to You,
the arrival of that new soul into our world.

Eternal One, we thank You still
for the hope You gave us,
and pray that You may renew in us that hope in time to come.
Though the pain of our disappointment is real and deep,
we acknowledge still that You are our God;
You renew Life beyond Death,
You give, and take away,
You hold all our souls in the palm of Your hand.

May it be Your will that we shall be strengthened
both by our hopes and by our disappointments
and learn to love, the more deeply, that which we have.
Blessed are You, Eternal One,
who shares the sorrow of
Your creation.

A PRAYER IN THE HOME BEFORE A FUNERAL

For a man:

God of mercy and compassion, be with us as we gather in this house, the home of our dear one who has gone forward to life everlasting. We remember all his goodness. May his memory be a blessing.

Help us to remember that the soul does not die. Our dear one has gone to that eternal home which You have prepared for us when our life on earth is done, and our time here is ended. Open the gates of mercy for him. May he enter into everlasting peace. In Your light we see beyond the frontiers of death to the life that has no end.

This house was built by human hands, but we shall come together in a home where we shall never part, surrounded by Your presence. Amen.

For a woman:

God of mercy and compassion, be with us as we gather in this house, the home of our dear one who has gone forward to life everlasting. We remember all her goodness. May her memory be a blessing.

Help us to remember that the soul does not die. Our dear one has gone to that eternal home which You have prepared for us when our life on earth is done, and our time here is ended. Open the gates of mercy for her. May she enter into everlasting peace. In Your light we see beyond the frontiers of death to the life that has no end.

This house was built by human hands, but we shall come together in a home where we shall never part, surrounded by Your presence. Amen.

Psalm 23 (page 302).

Psalm 91 — צא

¹יֹשֵׁב בְּסֵתֶר עֶלְיוֹן
בְּצֵל שַׁדַּי יִתְלוֹנָן:
²אֹמַר לַיהוה
מַחְסִי וּמְצוּדָתִי
אֱלֹהַי אֶבְטַח־בּוֹ:
³כִּי הוּא יַצִּילְךָ מִפַּח יָקוּשׁ
מִדֶּבֶר הַוּוֹת:

¹יֵשֵׁב The one who dwells
in the mystery of the Most High
rests in the shadow of the Almighty.
²Therefore I say
that the Eternal is my shelter,
my fortress, my God in whom I trust!
³For God rescues you
from the hunter's trap,
from a death that is final destruction.

<<<

⁴God's strength covers you,
you find shelter
beneath God's wings.
God's truth surrounds and shields you.
⁵Do not fear the terror of the night,
nor the sharp blows that fly by day,
⁶the disease that walks in darkness,
the sickness that destroys at noon.
⁷Though a thousand
fall at your side,
ten thousand
at your right hand,
no harm can come to you.
⁸Just look with your eyes
and see the results of wickedness.
⁹Because you say
'the Eternal is my refuge',
and make the Most High
your dwelling,
¹⁰no evil shall come upon you,
no blow shall come near your house.
¹¹For God commands messengers
to watch over you,
to keep you in all your ways.
¹²They bear you in their hands
lest your feet stumble on a stone.
¹³Through terror and venom
you will find your way,
you will crush down
new fears and evil.
¹⁴'Those who cling to me in love,
I set free,
I protect them for they know my being.
¹⁵When they call Me I answer them.
I will be with them in trouble.
I will rescue them
and bring them honour.
¹⁶I give them the span of their life,
then I show them My salvation.'

ד בְּאֶבְרָתוֹ יָסֶךְ לָךְ
וְתַחַת כְּנָפָיו תֶּחְסֶה
צִנָּה וְסֹחֵרָה אֲמִתּוֹ:
ה לֹא־תִירָא מִפַּחַד לָיְלָה
מֵחֵץ יָעוּף יוֹמָם:
ו מִדֶּבֶר בָּאֹפֶל יַהֲלֹךְ
מִקֶּטֶב יָשׁוּד צָהֳרָיִם:
ז יִפֹּל מִצִּדְּךָ אֶלֶף
וּרְבָבָה מִימִינֶךָ
אֵלֶיךָ לֹא יִגָּשׁ:
ח רַק בְּעֵינֶיךָ תַבִּיט
וְשִׁלֻּמַת רְשָׁעִים תִּרְאֶה:
ט כִּי־אַתָּה יְהֹוָה מַחְסִי עֶלְיוֹן
שַׂמְתָּ מְעוֹנֶךָ:
י לֹא־תְאֻנֶּה אֵלֶיךָ רָעָה
וְנֶגַע לֹא־יִקְרַב בְּאָהֳלֶךָ:
יא כִּי מַלְאָכָיו יְצַוֶּה־לָּךְ
לִשְׁמָרְךָ בְּכָל־דְּרָכֶיךָ:
יב עַל־כַּפַּיִם יִשָּׂאוּנְךָ
פֶּן־תִּגֹּף בָּאֶבֶן רַגְלֶךָ:
יג עַל־שַׁחַל וָפֶתֶן תִּדְרֹךְ
תִּרְמֹס כְּפִיר וְתַנִּין:
יד כִּי בִי חָשַׁק וַאֲפַלְּטֵהוּ
אֲשַׂגְּבֵהוּ כִּי־יָדַע שְׁמִי:
טו יִקְרָאֵנִי וְאֶעֱנֵהוּ
עִמּוֹ אָנֹכִי בְּצָרָה
אֲחַלְּצֵהוּ וַאֲכַבְּדֵהוּ:
טז אֹרֶךְ יָמִים אַשְׂבִּיעֵהוּ
וְאַרְאֵהוּ בִּישׁוּעָתִי:

יזכור
MEMORIAL SERVICE

The souls of the righteous are in the hands of God, and no harm shall touch them. In the eyes of the ignorant they appeared to die, and their going seemed to be their hurt. But they are at peace, and their hope is full of immortality. Their chastening was slight compared to the great good they shall receive. God has put them to the test and proved them worthy to be with God.

Wisdom of Solomon 3: 1-5

Psalm 23 (page 302) and Psalm 103 (page 656).

Eternal God, source of all being and fountain of life, what can we say to You, for You see and know all things. In Your wisdom You formed the universe and in Your love You provide for all Your creatures. What can we do but acknowledge Your power, accept Your gifts with gratitude, and according to Your will, give You back Your own.

Eternal God, source of all being, may the light of Your presence shine on us as we gather here, our hearts bowed down by the loss of _____ whom You have gathered to Yourself. Accept in Your great mercy the earthly life which has now ended and shelter with Your tender care this soul that is so precious to our hearts.

For a man

We thank You for all that was gentle and noble in his life. Through his name inspire us with strength and light. Help us to use our grief itself for acts of service and of love.

Eternal God, help us to realise more and more that time and space are not the measure of all things. Though our eyes do not see, teach us to understand that the soul of our dear one is not cut off. Love and truth are stronger than the grave. Just as our affection and the memory of the good he did unite us with him at this time, so may our trust in You lift us to the vision of the life that knows no death.

For a woman

We thank You for all that was gentle and noble in her life. Through her name inspire us with strength and light. Help us to use our grief itself for acts of service and of love.

Eternal God, help us to realise more and more that time and space are not the measure of all things. Though our eyes do not see, teach us to understand that the soul of our dear one is not cut off. Love and truth are stronger than the grave. Just as our affection and the memory of the good she did unite us with her at this time, so may our trust in You lift us to the vision of the life that knows no death.

427 LIFE CYCLE EVENTS — MEMORIAL SERVICE

God of our strength, in our weakness help us; in our sorrow comfort us; in our confusion guide us. Without You our lives are diminished; with You there is fullness of life for evermore.

May the words of our mouths and the meditations of our hearts be acceptable to You, God, our Rock and our Redeemer.

For a man

אֵל God full of compassion whose presence is over us, grant perfect rest beneath the shelter of Your presence with the holy and pure on high who shine as the lights of heaven, to _____ who has gone to his everlasting home. Source of mercy, cover him in the shelter of Your wings forever, and bind his soul into the gathering of life. It is God who is his heritage. May he be at peace in his place of rest. Amen.

For a woman

אֵל God full of compassion whose presence is over us, grant perfect rest beneath the shelter of Your presence with the holy and pure on high who shine as the lights of heaven, to _____ who has gone to her everlasting home. Source of mercy, cover her in the shelter of Your wings forever, and bind her soul into the gathering of life. It is God who is her heritage. May she be at peace in her place of rest. Amen.

For a man

אֵל מָלֵא רַחֲמִים
שׁוֹכֵן בַּמְּרוֹמִים. הַמְצֵא מְנוּחָה
נְכוֹנָה תַּחַת כַּנְפֵי הַשְּׁכִינָה. בְּמַעֲלוֹת
קְדוֹשִׁים וּטְהוֹרִים. כְּזֹהַר הָרָקִיעַ
מַזְהִירִים אֶת־נִשְׁמַת _____
שֶׁהָלַךְ לְעוֹלָמוֹ. אָנָּא בַּעַל הָרַחֲמִים
הַסְתִּירֵהוּ בְּסֵתֶר כְּנָפֶיךָ לְעוֹלָמִים.
וּצְרוֹר בִּצְרוֹר הַחַיִּים אֶת־נִשְׁמָתוֹ.
יהוה הוּא נַחֲלָתוֹ וְיָנוּחַ בְּשָׁלוֹם עַל
מִשְׁכָּבוֹ. וְנֹאמַר אָמֵן:

For a woman

אֵל מָלֵא רַחֲמִים
שׁוֹכֵן בַּמְּרוֹמִים. הַמְצֵא מְנוּחָה
נְכוֹנָה תַּחַת כַּנְפֵי הַשְּׁכִינָה. בְּמַעֲלוֹת
קְדוֹשִׁים וּטְהוֹרִים. כְּזֹהַר הָרָקִיעַ
מַזְהִירִים אֶת־נִשְׁמַת _____
שֶׁהָלְכָה לְעוֹלָמָהּ. אָנָּא בַּעַל הָרַחֲמִים
הַסְתִּירֶהָ בְּסֵתֶר כְּנָפֶיךָ לְעוֹלָמִים.
וּצְרוֹר בִּצְרוֹר הַחַיִּים אֶת־נִשְׁמָתָהּ.
יהוה הוּא נַחֲלָתָהּ וְתָנוּחַ בְּשָׁלוֹם עַל
מִשְׁכָּבָהּ. וְנֹאמַר אָמֵן:

יזכור   LIFE CYCLE EVENTS **428**

יִתְגַּדַּל Let us magnify
and let us sanctify in this world
the great name of God
whose will created it.
May God's reign come in your
lifetime, and in your days,
and in the lifetime of the family of
Israel - quickly and speedily
may it come.
Amen.
**May the greatness of God's being
be blessed from eternity to eternity.**
Let us bless and let us extol,
let us tell aloud and let us raise aloft,
let us set on high and let us honour,
let us exalt and
let us praise the Holy One,
whose name is blessed,

who is far beyond any blessing or song,

During the Ten Days of Penitence:
  who is far above and beyond any blessing

any honour
or any consolation
that can be spoken of in this world.
Amen.

May great peace from heaven and
the gift of life be granted to us
and to all the family of Israel.
Amen.
May the Maker of peace
in the highest bring this peace
upon us and upon all Israel
  and upon all the world.
Amen.

יִתְגַּדַּל וְיִתְקַדַּשׁ שְׁמֵהּ רַבָּא
בְּעָלְמָא דִּי־בְרָא כִרְעוּתֵהּ:
וְיַמְלִיךְ מַלְכוּתֵהּ
בְּחַיֵּיכוֹן וּבְיוֹמֵיכוֹן
וּבְחַיֵּי דִי־כָל־בֵּית יִשְׂרָאֵל
בַּעֲגָלָא וּבִזְמַן קָרִיב.
וְאִמְרוּ אָמֵן:
יְהֵא שְׁמֵהּ רַבָּא מְבָרַךְ
לְעָלַם וּלְעָלְמֵי עָלְמַיָּא:
יִתְבָּרַךְ וְיִשְׁתַּבַּח וְיִתְפָּאַר
וְיִתְרוֹמַם וְיִתְנַשֵּׂא וְיִתְהַדָּר
וְיִתְעַלֶּה וְיִתְהַלָּל
שְׁמֵהּ דִּי־קֻדְשָׁא.
בְּרִיךְ הוּא.

לְעֵלָּא מִן־כָּל־בִּרְכָתָא
During the Ten Days of Penitence:
לְעֵלָּא לְעֵלָּא מִכָּל־בִּרְכָתָא
וְשִׁירָתָא תֻּשְׁבְּחָתָא וְנֶחֱמָתָא
דַּאֲמִירָן בְּעָלְמָא.
וְאִמְרוּ אָמֵן:
יְהֵא שְׁלָמָא רַבָּא מִן שְׁמַיָּא
וְחַיִּים עָלֵינוּ וְעַל־כָּל־יִשְׂרָאֵל.
וְאִמְרוּ אָמֵן:
עֹשֶׂה שָׁלוֹם בִּמְרוֹמָיו
הוּא יַעֲשֶׂה שָׁלוֹם
עָלֵינוּ וְעַל כָּל־יִשְׂרָאֵל
וְעַל־כָּל־הָעוֹלָם.
וְאִמְרוּ אָמֵן:

יִתְגַּדַּל *Yitgaddal v'yitkaddash sh'meih rabba*

b'alma di v'ra chiruteih,
v'yamlich malchuteih
b'chayyeichon uv'yomeichon
uv'chayyei di chol beit yisra'el
ba'agala u'vizman kariv,
v'imru **amen.**
Y'hei sh'meih rabba m'varach
l'alam ul'almei almaya.
Yitbarach v'yishtabbach v'yitpa'ar
v'yitromam v'yitnassei v'yit-haddar
v'yit'alleh v'yit-hallal
sh'meih di kudsha,
b'rich hu,
l'eilla min kol birchata
   During the Ten Days of Penitence:
   l'eilla l'eilla mikol birchata
v'shirata tushb'chata v'nechemata
di amiran b'alma,
v'imru **amen.**
Y'hei sh'lama rabba min sh'maya,
v'chayyim aleinu v'al kol yisra'el,
v'imru **amen.**
Oseh shalom bimromav
hu ya'aseh shalom
aleinu v'al kol yisra'el,
   v'al kol ha-olam,
v'imru **amen.**

PRAYERS FOR THE STAGES OF MOURNING

> Mourning Customs and Traditions
>
> Traditionally Jews mourn for their immediate family and spouse/partner, but may take on mourning for others. Immediately after the death, before the burial, the period called *aninut* is not yet technically 'mourning' and one may undertake all necessary arrangements for the burial. Following the funeral the first seven days (*shivah*) of mourning begin. A memorial candle is lit in the home. Daily prayers are recited in the home. Mourners are encouraged to stay home during this period and refrain from ordinary pursuits and occupations. However, formal mourning is suspended on Shabbat and mourners are encouraged to attend synagogue. No special ceremonies mark the end of the *shivah* period, though it is customary to go for a short walk to symbolise the return to daily life.
>
> The third phase of mourning is *sh'loshim*, the thirty days after the funeral, when the mourner returns to normal activities but should refrain from entertainments. In Israel the tombstone is erected at the end of this period, but in the Diaspora it is delayed till the end of the year.
>
> The fourth phase lasts till the end of eleven months during which *Kaddish* continues to be recited daily. Subsequently *Kaddish* is recited on the Hebrew anniversary of the death, the *Yahrzeit*. *Kaddish* may be recited by converts for their non-Jewish family.

AT THE END OF THE *SHIVAH* PERIOD

The mourner says:

The period of formal mourning is ended, and it is time to return to normal activities and daily life. Grief is not ended, but little by little, may my memories bring me comfort and hope bring consolation.

כְּאִישׁ 'As a mother comforts her child, so will I comfort You,' says the Living God.[1]	כְּאִישׁ אֲשֶׁר אִמּוֹ תְּנַחֲמֶנּוּ כֵּן אָנֹכִי אֲנַחֶמְכֶם:

Those present say:

הַמָּקוֹם May God comfort you together with all those who mourn.	הַמָּקוֹם יְנַחֵם אֶתְכֶם בְּתוֹךְ שְׁאָר הָאֲבֵלִים:

---

[1] Isa 66:13.

AT THE END OF THE *SH'LOSHIM* PERIOD

The mourner says:
   God, as my life returns to its normal course, an absence remains where once _____ was present. May the beauty of his/her life shine forever and may my life bring honour to his/her memory.

Psalm 23 (page 302) may be read.

A PRAYER FOR THE *YAHRZEIT*
(Anniversary of a Death)

For a woman:
   Today I remember with love _____ who has gone to everlasting life, and I honour her memory. As this light burns pure and clear, so may the enduring memory of her goodness shine in my heart and strengthen me, God, to do Your will. Amen.

On lighting the Yahrzeit *candle say:*

זֵכֶר 'The memory of the righteous is as a blessing.'[1]

זֵכֶר צַדֶּקֶת
לִבְרָכָה:

God full of compassion whose presence is over us, grant perfect rest beneath the shelter of Your presence with the holy and pure on high who shine as the lights of heaven, to _____ who has gone to her everlasting home. Source of mercy, cover her in the shelter of Your wings forever, and bind her soul into the gathering of life. It is God who is her heritage. May she be at peace in her place of rest. Amen.

אֵל מָלֵא רַחֲמִים
שׁוֹכֵן בַּמְּרוֹמִים הַמְצֵא מְנוּחָה נְכוֹנָה תַּחַת כַּנְפֵי הַשְּׁכִינָה בְּמַעֲלוֹת קְדוֹשִׁים וּטְהוֹרִים כְּזֹהַר הָרָקִיעַ מַזְהִירִים אֶת־נִשְׁמַת _____ שֶׁהָלְכָה לְעוֹלָמָהּ: אָנָּא בַּעַל הָרַחֲמִים הַסְתִּירֶהָ בְּסֵתֶר כְּנָפֶיךָ לְעוֹלָמִים וּצְרוֹר בִּצְרוֹר הַחַיִּים אֶת־נִשְׁמָתָהּ: יהוה הוּא נַחֲלָתָהּ וְתָנוּחַ בְּשָׁלוֹם עַל מִשְׁכָּבָהּ וְנֹאמַר אָמֵן:

The Kaddish *(page 428) is recited here.*

---

[1] Prov 10:7.

For a man:

Today I remember with love _____ who has gone to everlasting life, and I honour his memory. As this light burns pure and clear, so may the enduring memory of his goodness shine in my heart and strengthen me, God, to do Your will. Amen.

On lighting the Yahrzeit *candle say:*

זֵכֶר 'The memory of the righteous is as a blessing.'[1]

זֵכֶר צַדִּיק לִבְרָכָה:

God full of compassion whose presence is over us, grant perfect rest beneath the shelter of Your presence with the holy and pure on high who shine as the lights of heaven, to _____ who has gone to his everlasting home. Source of mercy, cover him in the shelter of Your wings forever, and bind his soul into the gathering of life. It is God who is his heritage. May he be at peace in his place of rest. Amen.

אֵל מָלֵא רַחֲמִים שׁוֹכֵן בַּמְּרוֹמִים הַמְצֵא מְנוּחָה נְכוֹנָה תַּחַת כַּנְפֵי הַשְּׁכִינָה בְּמַעֲלוֹת קְדוֹשִׁים וּטְהוֹרִים כְּזוֹהַר הָרָקִיעַ מַזְהִרִים אֶת־נִשְׁמַת _____ שֶׁהָלַךְ לְעוֹלָמוֹ: אָנָּא בַּעַל הָרַחֲמִים הַסְתִּירֵהוּ בְּסֵתֶר כְּנָפֶיךָ לְעוֹלָמִים וּצְרוֹר בִּצְרוֹר הַחַיִּים אֶת־נִשְׁמָתוֹ: יהוה הוּא נַחֲלָתוֹ וְיָנוּחַ בְּשָׁלוֹם עַל מִשְׁכָּבוֹ וְנֹאמַר אָמֵן:

The Kaddish *(page 428) is recited here.*

---

[1] Prov 10:7.

PRAYERS ON VISITING A GRAVE

Psalm 23 (page 302) may be read.

For a man

In the quietness of this place I think of _____ with the love and understanding that still join us together. I remember his goodness and the blessings I received through him. His memory is precious to me and is always with me.

May his memory continue to strengthen me and guide me. Because life is short, let me fill it with acts of goodness, let me be broader in my sympathies, and purer in my motives.

For a woman

In the quietness of this place I think of _____ with the love and understanding that still join us together. I remember her goodness and the blessings I received through her. Her memory is precious to me and is always with me.

May her memory continue to strengthen me and guide me. Because life is short, let me fill it with acts of goodness, let me be broader in my sympathies, and purer in my motives.

Continue here:

Help me to learn the meaning and value of life. Help me to know that goodness is not in vain, and that the grave is not the end.

As the heavens are high above the earth, so are Your ways beyond our understanding. Yet Your love surrounds Your children to protect them, for with You are light and comfort and peace. Amen.

The memorial prayer, el malei rachamim, *'God full of compassion',* for a man can be found on page 427, and for a woman on page 427. The Kaddish can be found on page 428.

עֹשֶׂה May the One
who makes peace in the highest
bring this peace
upon us and upon all Israel.
Amen.

עֹשֶׂה שָׁלוֹם בִּמְרוֹמָיו.
הוּא יַעֲשֶׂה שָׁלוֹם.
עָלֵינוּ וְעַל כָּל־יִשְׂרָאֵל.
וְאִמְרוּ אָמֵן:

Home Services

Contents
Seder Chanukat Ha-Bayit - Service at the Dedication of a Home ... 436
Seder B'rit Milah - Service at a Circumcision ... 438
Seder Zeved Ha-bat - The Precious Gift of a Daughter ... 440
Night Prayers for Children and Adults ... 442
Morning Prayers for Children and Adults ... 444
Shabbat Eve Home Service ... 446
Kiddush for Shabbat Eve ... 452
Kiddush for Shabbat Day ... 454
The close of Shabbat and *Havdalah* ... 458
Songs at the Close of Shabbat ... 460
Blessing before meals ... 462
Thanksgiving after meals ... 464
   Shorter Forms of Thanksgiving After Meals ... 481
   Thanksgiving After Meals as Songs ... 485
   The Blessings After a Wedding Meal ... 487

סדר חנוכת הבית
SEDER CHANUKAT HA-BAYIT
SERVICE AT THE DEDICATION OF A HOME

אִם 'Unless God builds the house, its builders toil in vain.'[1]

אִם־יהוה לֹא־יִבְנֶה בַיִת
שָׁוְא עָמְלוּ בוֹנָיו בּוֹ:

We fix the *mezuzah* to the doorpost of this home to fulfil the command of our Creator and to remind ourselves and all who enter that we should love God with all our heart and all our soul and all our might.

We ask God's blessing on this home and all who live in it. May its doors be open to those in need and its rooms be filled with kindness. May love dwell within its walls, and joy shine from its windows. May God's peace protect it and God's presence never leave it.

שְׁמַע יִשְׂרָאֵל יהוה אֱלֹהֵינוּ יהוה | אֶחָד:

בָּרוּךְ שֵׁם כְּבוֹד מַלְכוּתוֹ לְעוֹלָם וָעֶד:

וְאָהַבְתָּ אֵת יהוה אֱלֹהֶיךָ בְּכָל־לְבָבְךָ וּבְכָל־נַפְשְׁךָ וּבְכָל־מְאֹדֶךָ:
וְהָיוּ הַדְּבָרִים הָאֵלֶּה אֲשֶׁר אָנֹכִי מְצַוְּךָ הַיּוֹם עַל־לְבָבֶךָ: וְשִׁנַּנְתָּם
לְבָנֶיךָ וְדִבַּרְתָּ בָּם בְּשִׁבְתְּךָ בְּבֵיתֶךָ וּבְלֶכְתְּךָ בַדֶּרֶךְ וּבְשָׁכְבְּךָ
וּבְקוּמֶךָ: וּקְשַׁרְתָּם לְאוֹת עַל־יָדֶךָ וְהָיוּ לְטֹטָפֹת בֵּין עֵינֶיךָ:
וּכְתַבְתָּם עַל־מְזֻזוֹת בֵּיתֶךָ וּבִשְׁעָרֶיךָ:

שְׁמַע Hear O Israel, the Eternal is our God, the Eternal is One.

בָּרוּךְ Blessed is the knowledge of God's glorious rule forever and ever.

וְאָהַבְתָּ Love the Eternal your God with all your heart, and all your soul, and all your might. These words that I command you today shall be upon your heart. Repeat them to your children, and talk about them when you sit in your home, and when you walk in the street; when you lie down, and when you rise up. Secure them as a sign upon your hand, and let them be as reminders before your eyes. Write them on the doorposts of your home and at your gates.[2]

---

[1] Ps 127:1.   [2] Deut 6:4-9.

DEDICATION AT A HOME

On affixing the mezuzah

בָּרוּךְ Blessed are You, our Living God, Sovereign of the universe, whose commandments make us holy and who commands us to fix the *mezuzah*.

בָּרוּךְ אַתָּה יהוה אֱלֹהֵינוּ מֶלֶךְ הָעוֹלָם. אֲשֶׁר קִדְּשָׁנוּ בְּמִצְוֹתָיו וְצִוָּנוּ לִקְבּוֹעַ מְזוּזָה:

In this gate,
  may there come no sorrow.
In this dwelling,
  may there come no trouble.
Through this door,
  may there come no panic.
In this area,
  may there come no conflicts.
In this place,
  may there be blessing and peace.

בְּזֶה הַשַּׁעַר   לֹא יָבוֹא צַעַר:
בְּזֹאת הַדִּירָה   לֹא תָבוֹא צָרָה:
בְּזֹאת הַדֶּלֶת   לֹא תָבוֹא בֶּהָלָה:
בְּזֹאת הַמַּחְלָקָה   לֹא תָבוֹא מַחֲלוֹקֶת:
בְּזֶה הַמָּקוֹם   תְּהִי בְרָכָה וְשָׁלוֹם:

בָּרוּךְ Blessed are You, our Living God, Sovereign of the universe, who has kept us alive and supported us and brought us to this season.

בָּרוּךְ אַתָּה יהוה אֱלֹהֵינוּ מֶלֶךְ הָעוֹלָם. שֶׁהֶחֱיָנוּ וְקִיְּמָנוּ וְהִגִּיעָנוּ לַזְּמַן הַזֶּה:

סדר ברית מילה
SEDER B'RIT MILAH
SERVICE AT A CIRCUMCISION

בָּרוּךְ Blessed be the one who comes in the name of God.
You are blessed by God, maker of heaven and earth.

בָּרוּךְ הַבָּא בְּשֵׁם יהוה:

בְּרוּכִים אַתֶּם לַיהוה עֹשֵׂה שָׁמַיִם וָאָרֶץ:

The parent says

בָּרוּךְ I am ready to fulfil the commandment to circumcise my son, as the Creator has commanded us for it is written in the Torah: 'And God said to Abraham, You shall keep My covenant, you and your children after you throughout their generations. This is My covenant which you shall keep, between Me and you and your children after you; every male among you shall be circumcised.'[1]
And it is also written in the Torah: 'The Eternal your God shall circumcise your heart, and the heart of your children, to Love the Eternal your God, with all your heart and with all your soul, that you may live.'[2]

הִנְנִי מוּכָן לְקַיֵּם מִצְוַת עֲשֵׂה שֶׁצִּוָּנוּ הַבּוֹרֵא יִתְבָּרַךְ לָמוּל אֶת־בְּנִי. כַּכָּתוּב בַּתּוֹרָה. וַיֹּאמֶר אֱלֹהִים אֶל־אַבְרָהָם וְאַתָּה אֶת־בְּרִיתִי תִשְׁמֹר אַתָּה וְזַרְעֲךָ אַחֲרֶיךָ לְדֹרֹתָם: זֹאת בְּרִיתִי אֲשֶׁר תִּשְׁמְרוּ בֵּינִי וּבֵינֵיכֶם וּבֵין זַרְעֲךָ אַחֲרֶיךָ הִמּוֹל לָכֶם כָּל־זָכָר:

וְנֶאֱמַר. וּמָל יהוה אֱלֹהֶיךָ אֶת־לְבָבְךָ וְאֶת־לְבַב זַרְעֶךָ לְאַהֲבָה אֶת־יהוה אֱלֹהֶיךָ בְּכָל־לְבָבְךָ וּבְכָל־נַפְשְׁךָ לְמַעַן חַיֶּיךָ:

The Mohel *says*

זֶה This is the chair of Elijah.
May he be remembered for good.

זֶה הַכִּסֵּא שֶׁל אֵלִיָּהוּ זָכוּר לַטּוֹב:

בָּרוּךְ Blessed are You, our Living God, Sovereign of the universe, whose commandments make us holy and who commands us concerning circumcision.

בָּרוּךְ אַתָּה יהוה אֱלֹהֵינוּ מֶלֶךְ הָעוֹלָם. אֲשֶׁר קִדְּשָׁנוּ בְּמִצְוֹתָיו וְצִוָּנוּ עַל הַמִּילָה:

---

[1] Gen 17:9-10.   [2] Deut 30:6.

SERVICE AT A CIRCUMCISION

The parent says

בָּרוּךְ Blessed are You, our Living God, Sovereign of the universe, whose commandments make us holy and who commands us to bring our sons into the covenant of our father, Abraham.

בָּרוּךְ אַתָּה יהוה אֱלֹהֵינוּ מֶלֶךְ הָעוֹלָם. אֲשֶׁר קִדְּשָׁנוּ בְּמִצְוֹתָיו וְצִוָּנוּ לְהַכְנִיסוֹ בִּבְרִיתוֹ שֶׁל אַבְרָהָם אָבִינוּ:

בָּרוּךְ Blessed are You, our Living God, Sovereign of the universe, who has kept us alive and supported us and brought us to this season.

בָּרוּךְ אַתָּה יהוה אֱלֹהֵינוּ מֶלֶךְ הָעוֹלָם. שֶׁהֶחֱיָנוּ וְקִיְּמָנוּ וְהִגִּיעָנוּ לַזְּמַן הַזֶּה:

All present reply

כְּשֵׁם Just as he has entered into the covenant, so may he also enter into the blessings of Torah, of marriage and of good deeds.

כְּשֵׁם שֶׁנִּכְנַס לַבְּרִית כֵּן יִכָּנֵס לַתּוֹרָה וּלְחֻפָּה וּלְמַעֲשִׂים טוֹבִים:

The Mohel *or Rabbi says*

בָּרוּךְ Blessed are You, our Living God, Sovereign of the universe, who creates the fruit of the vine.

בָּרוּךְ אַתָּה יהוה אֱלֹהֵינוּ מֶלֶךְ הָעוֹלָם. בּוֹרֵא פְּרִי הַגָּפֶן:

אֱלֹהֵינוּ Our God and God of our ancestors, support this child, and may his name be called in Israel _____ son of _____. May his father and mother rejoice in him. With love and wisdom may they teach him the meaning of the covenant which he has entered today, so that he may practise righteousness, seeking truth and walking in the ways of peace. May this young child grow into adulthood as a blessing to his family, the family of Israel and the family of humankind. Just as he has entered into the covenant, so may he also enter into the blessings of Torah, of *chuppah* and of good deeds.

אֱלֹהֵינוּ וֵאלֹהֵי אֲבוֹתֵינוּ. קַיֵּם אֶת־הַיֶּלֶד הַזֶּה וְיִקָּרֵא שְׁמוֹ בְּיִשְׂרָאֵל _____ בֶּן _____: יִשְׂמְחוּ בוֹ אָבִיו וְאִמּוֹ וִילַמְּדוּהוּ בְּאַהֲבָה וּבְחָכְמָה אֶת־פֵּשֶׁר־הַבְּרִית הַזֹּאת אֲשֶׁר נִכְנַס בָּהּ הַיּוֹם. לְמַעַן יִרְדּוֹף צֶדֶק וֶאֱמֶת וְיֵלֵךְ בְּדַרְכֵי־שָׁלוֹם. יִגְדַּל הַיֶּלֶד הַזֶּה לְהָבִיא בְּרָכָה עַל־מִשְׁפַּחְתּוֹ וְעַל־בֵּית־יִשְׂרָאֵל וְעַל־כָּל־מִשְׁפְּחוֹת־הָאֲדָמָה. כְּשֵׁם שֶׁנִּכְנַס לַבְּרִית כֵּן יִכָּנֵס לַתּוֹרָה וּלְחֻפָּה וּלְמַעֲשִׂים טוֹבִים:

May God bless you and keep you.
May God's face shine upon you
and be gracious to you.
May God's face turn towards you
and give you peace.

יְבָרֶכְךָ יהוה וְיִשְׁמְרֶךָ.
יָאֵר יהוה פָּנָיו אֵלֶיךָ וִיחֻנֶּךָּ.
יִשָּׂא יהוה פָּנָיו אֵלֶיךָ
וְיָשֵׂם לְךָ שָׁלוֹם:

סדר זבד הבת
SEDER ZEVED HA-BAT
THE PRECIOUS GIFT OF A DAUGHTER[1]

Those who are present say

בָּרוּךְ Blessed be she
who comes in the name of God.

בְּרוּכָה הַבָּאָה בְּשֵׁם יהוה:

The leader says

רָנִּי Shout for joy, Daughter Zion,
rejoice and be glad with all your heart,
Daughter Jerusalem,[2]
for we asked for life from God
who has given a new soul
into our midst.
O my dove, in the cranny of the rocks,
hidden by the cliff,
let me see your face,
let me hear your voice, for your voice
is sweet and your face is fair.[3]
They blessed Rebecca and said to her:
'You are our sister, may you grow
into thousands of myriads.'[4]

רָנִּי בַּת־צִיּוֹן. שִׂמְחִי וְעָלְזִי
בְּכָל־לֵב בַּת יְרוּשָׁלָיִם:
חַיִּים שָׁאֲלוּ מֵאֵת יהוה.
נֶפֶשׁ חֲדָשָׁה נָתַן בְּקִרְבֵּנוּ:
יוֹנָתִי בְּחַגְוֵי הַסֶּלַע בְּסֵתֶר
הַמַּדְרֵגָה הַרְאִינִי אֶת־מַרְאַיִךְ
הַשְׁמִיעִינִי אֶת־קוֹלֵךְ כִּי־קוֹלֵךְ
עָרֵב וּמַרְאֵיךְ נָאוֶה:
וַיְבָרֲכוּ אֶת־רִבְקָה וַיֹּאמְרוּ לָהּ
אֲחוֹתֵנוּ אַתְּ הֲיִי לְאַלְפֵי רְבָבָה:

The leader says the blessing over wine

בָּרוּךְ Blessed are You, our Living
God, Sovereign of the universe, who
creates the fruit of the vine.

בָּרוּךְ אַתָּה יהוה אֱלֹהֵינוּ מֶלֶךְ
הָעוֹלָם. בּוֹרֵא פְּרִי הַגָּפֶן:

בָּרוּךְ Blessed are You, our Living
God, Sovereign of the universe, who
has kept us alive and supported us
and brought us to this season.

בָּרוּךְ אַתָּה יהוה אֱלֹהֵינוּ מֶלֶךְ
הָעוֹלָם. שֶׁהֶחֱיָנוּ וְקִיְּמָנוּ וְהִגִּיעָנוּ
לַזְּמַן הַזֶּה:

---

[1] A naming ceremony for a daughter, based on Sephardi tradition.
[2] Zeph 3:14.
[3] Shir 2:14.
[4] Gen 24:60.

THE PRECIOUS GIFT OF A DAUGHTER

The leader says

מִי May the One who blessed our ancestors Sarah, Rebecca, Rachel and Leah, and Miriam the prophetess, and Abigail and Esther the Queen, bless this beloved girl. May her name be called in Israel, _____ daughter of _____. May she grow up with health, peace and tranquillity.

מִי שֶׁבֵּרַךְ אִמּוֹתֵינוּ שָׂרָה וְרִבְקָה רָחֵל וְלֵאָה וּמִרְיָם הַנְּבִיאָה וַאֲבִגַיִל וְאֶסְתֵּר הַמַּלְכָּה הוּא יְבָרֵךְ אֶת הַיַּלְדָּה הַנְּעִימָה הַזֹּאת. וְיִקָּרֵא שְׁמָהּ בְּיִשְׂרָאֵל _____ בַּת _____. וִיגַדְּלֶהָ בִּבְרִיאוּת שָׁלוֹם וּמְנוּחָה:

יְשִׂימָה May God make her a joy to her parents and a blessing to all her people, and may she grow with Torah, and to *chuppah* and to good deeds.

יְשִׂימָה אֱלֹהִים שִׂמְחָה לְהוֹרֶיהָ וּבְרָכָה לְכָל עַמָּהּ וְתִגְדַּל לַתּוֹרָה וּלְחֻפָּה וּלְמַעֲשִׂים טוֹבִים:

One of the following forms of the Priestly Blessing may be used.

I

May God bless you and keep you.
May God's face shine upon you
and be gracious to you.
May God's face turn towards you
and give you peace.

יְבָרֶכְךָ יהוה וְיִשְׁמְרֶךָ.
יָאֵר יהוה פָּנָיו אֵלֶיךָ וִיחֻנֶּךָּ.
יִשָּׂא יהוה פָּנָיו אֵלֶיךָ
וְיָשֵׂם לְךָ שָׁלוֹם:

II

May God bless you and keep you.
May God's face shine upon you
and be gracious to you.
May God's face turn towards you
and give you peace.

יְבָרֶכֵךְ יהוה וְיִשְׁמְרֵךְ.
יָאֵר יהוה פָּנָיו אֵלַיִךְ וִיחֻנֵּךְ.
יִשָּׂא יהוה פָּנָיו אֵלַיִךְ
וְיָשֵׂם לָךְ שָׁלוֹם:

NIGHT PRAYERS FOR CHILDREN AND ADULTS

Any of these passages can be used together with the first lines of the Sh'ma
and with any personal prayers.

הַשְׁכִּיבֵנִי God, may I sleep in peace and wake up to a good life.
Cover me with the shelter of Your peace and protect me because You are good.

הַשְׁכִּיבֵנִי יהוה לְשָׁלוֹם.
וְהַעֲמִידֵנִי לְחַיִּים טוֹבִים.
וּפְרוֹשׂ עָלַי סֻכַּת שְׁלוֹמֶךָ.
וְשָׁמְרֵנִי לְמַעַן שְׁמֶךָ:

הִנֵּה Know that the Guardian of Israel never slumbers and never sleeps.

הִנֵּה לֹא יָנוּם וְלֹא יִישָׁן שׁוֹמֵר יִשְׂרָאֵל:

בָּרוּךְ Blessed are You, our Living God, who makes the bands of sleep fall upon my eyes and slumber upon my eyelids.

בָּרוּךְ אַתָּה יהוה אֱלֹהֵינוּ מֶלֶךְ הָעוֹלָם הַמַּפִּיל חֶבְלֵי שֵׁנָה עַל־עֵינָי וּתְנוּמָה עַל־עַפְעַפָּי:

וִיהִי May it be Your will, my God and God of my ancestors, that you allow me to lie down in peace and rise again in peace.
May neither concerns of the daytime nor bad or troubling dreams disturb my rest.
For You are the one who gives light to the apple of the eye.
Blessed are You, God, You light up the whole world with Your presence.

וִיהִי רָצוֹן מִלְּפָנֶיךָ יהוה אֱלֹהַי וֵאלֹהֵי אֲבוֹתַי שֶׁתַּשְׁכִּיבֵנִי לְשָׁלוֹם וְתַעֲמִידֵנִי לְשָׁלוֹם:
וְאַל יְבַהֲלוּנִי רַעְיוֹנַי וַחֲלוֹמוֹת רָעִים וְהִרְהוּרִים רָעִים:
כִּי אַתָּה הַמֵּאִיר לְאִישׁוֹן בַּת־עָיִן:
בָּרוּךְ אַתָּה יהוה הַמֵּאִיר לָעוֹלָם כֻּלּוֹ בִּכְבוֹדוֹ:

יהוה God will guard your going out and your coming in, now and for evermore.

יהוה יִשְׁמָר־צֵאתְךָ וּבוֹאֶךָ מֵעַתָּה וְעַד עוֹלָם:

NIGHT PRAYERS

שְׁמַ**ע** יִשְׂרָאֵל יהוה אֱלֹהֵינוּ יהוה | אֶחָ**ד**׃

שְׁמַע Hear O Israel, the Eternal is our God, the Eternal is One.

וְאָהַבְתָּ Love the Eternal your God with all your heart, and all your soul, and all your might.

וְאָהַבְתָּ אֵת יהוה אֱלֹהֶיךָ
בְּכָל־לְבָבְךָ וּבְכָל־נַפְשְׁךָ
וּבְכָל־מְאֹדֶךָ׃

בְּיָדוֹ Within God's hand I lay my soul
both when I sleep
and when I wake,
and with my soul my body too,
my God is close I shall not fear.

בְּיָדוֹ אַפְקִיד רוּחִי.
בְּעֵת אִישָׁן וְאָעִירָה׃
וְעִם רוּחִי גְוִיָּתִי.
אֲדֹנָי לִי וְלֹא אִירָא׃

בָּרוּךְ Blessed be God by day;
blessed be God by night.
Blessed be God when we lie down;
blessed be God when we rise up.

בָּרוּךְ יהוה בַּיוֹם.
בָּרוּךְ יהוה בַּלָּיְלָה.
בָּרוּךְ יהוה בְּשָׁכְבֵנוּ.
בָּרוּךְ יהוה בְּקוּמֵנוּ׃

בְּשֵׁם In the name of the Living God of Israel, may *Michael*, the protection of God, be at my right hand; and *Gabriel*, the power of God, at my left; before me *Uriel*, the light of God; behind me *Raphael*, the healing of God; and above my head *Shechinat El*, the presence of God.

בְּשֵׁם יהוה אֱלֹהֵי יִשְׂרָאֵל
מִימִינִי מִיכָאֵל. וּמִשְּׂמֹאלִי
גַּבְרִיאֵל. וּמִלְּפָנַי אוּרִיאֵל.
וּמֵאֲחוֹרַי רְפָאֵל. וְעַל רֹאשִׁי
שְׁכִינַת אֵל׃

MORNING PRAYERS FOR CHILDREN AND ADULTS

Any of these passages can be used together with the first lines of the Sh'ma and with any personal prayers.

מוֹדָה/מוֹדֶה/מוֹדָה I thank You, living and eternal Sovereign, that You have returned my soul to me, with compassion - great is Your faithfulness.

מוֹדָה/מוֹדֶה/מוֹדָה אֲנִי לְפָנֶיךָ מֶלֶךְ חַי וְקַיָּם שֶׁהֶחֱזַרְתָּ בִּי נִשְׁמָתִי בְּחֶמְלָה. רַבָּה אֱמוּנָתֶךָ:

בָּרוּךְ Blessed are You, our Living God, Sovereign of the universe, You take away sleep from my eyes and slumber from my eyelids.

בָּרוּךְ אַתָּה יהוה אֱלֹהֵינוּ מֶלֶךְ הָעוֹלָם. הַמַּעֲבִיר שֵׁנָה מֵעֵינַי וּתְנוּמָה מֵעַפְעַפָּי:

יהוה God is my shepherd,
I shall not want.
In green fields God lets me lie,
leading me by quiet streams.
Surely goodness and mercy seek me
all the days of my life
and I shall dwell
in the house of God
forever.

יהוה רֹעִי לֹא אֶחְסָר:
בִּנְאוֹת דֶּשֶׁא יַרְבִּיצֵנִי
עַל־מֵי מְנֻחוֹת יְנַהֲלֵנִי:
אַךְ טוֹב וָחֶסֶד יִרְדְּפוּנִי
כָּל־יְמֵי חַיָּי
וְשַׁבְתִּי בְּבֵית־יהוה
לְאֹרֶךְ יָמִים:

לְעוֹלָם We should always be in awe of God in private as well as in public; speak the truth aloud and mean it in our heart.

לְעוֹלָם יְהֵא אָדָם יְרֵא שָׁמַיִם בַּסֵּתֶר כְּבַגָּלוּי. וּמוֹדֶה עַל־הָאֱמֶת וְדוֹבֵר אֱמֶת בִּלְבָבוֹ:

שְׁמַע יִשְׂרָאֵל יהוה אֱלֹהֵינוּ יהוה | אֶחָד:

שְׁמַע Hear O Israel, the Eternal is our God, the Eternal is One.

וְאָהַבְתָּ Love the Eternal your God with all your heart, and all your soul, and all your might.

וְאָהַבְתָּ אֵת יהוה אֱלֹהֶיךָ בְּכָל־לְבָבְךָ וּבְכָל־נַפְשְׁךָ וּבְכָל־מְאֹדֶךָ:

HOME SERVICES — MORNING PRAYERS

אֱלֹהַי My God,
keep my tongue from causing harm
and my lips from telling lies.

אֱלֹהַי נְצוֹר לְשׁוֹנִי מֵרָע.
וְשִׂפְתוֹתַי מִדַּבֵּר מִרְמָה:

פְּתַח Open my heart to your teachings
and help me to do them.

פְּתַח לִבִּי בְּתוֹרָתֶךָ.
וְאַחֲרֵי מִצְוֹתֶיךָ תִּרְדּוֹף נַפְשִׁי:

יִהְיוּ May the words I speak aloud and
the thoughts that lie within my heart
always please You God, who gives me
strength and saves me.

יִהְיוּ לְרָצוֹן אִמְרֵי־פִי.
וְהֶגְיוֹן לִבִּי לְפָנֶיךָ.
יהוה צוּרִי וְגֹאֲלִי:

וְגָר The wolf shall live with the lamb,
the leopard lie down with the kid,
the calf and the young lion
shall feed together,
and a little child shall lead them.
They shall not hurt nor destroy
in all My holy mountain.

וְגָר זְאֵב עִם־כֶּבֶשׂ
וְנָמֵר עִם־גְּדִי יִרְבָּץ
וְעֵגֶל וּכְפִיר וּמְרִיא יַחְדָּו
וְנַעַר קָטֹן נֹהֵג בָּם:
לֹא־יָרֵעוּ וְלֹא־יַשְׁחִיתוּ
בְּכָל־הַר קָדְשִׁי:

שְׁמַע יִשְׂרָאֵל

SHABBAT EVE HOME SERVICE

One or more of the following meditations may be read.

I

לְהַדְלִיק To light candles
in all the worlds - that is Shabbat.
To light Shabbat candles
is a soul-leap
pregnant with potential
into a splendid sea,
in the mystery
of the fire of sunset.
Lighting the candles transforms
my room into a river of light,
my heart
sets in an emerald waterfall.

לְהַדְלִיק נֵרוֹת בְּכָל־הָעוֹלָמוֹת
זוֹהִי שַׁבָּת:
לְהַדְלִיק נֵרוֹת־שַׁבָּת
זוֹהִי קְפִיצַת־נֶפֶשׁ הָרַת נִצוֹרוֹת
לְיָם נֶהְדָּר. שֶׁיֵּשׁ בָּהּ מִסְתּוֹרִין
שֶׁל אֵשׁ־הַשְּׁקִיעָה:
בְּהַדְלִיקִי הַנֵּרוֹת יֵהָפֵךְ
חַדְרִי לִנְהַר דִּי־נוּר.
בְּאַשְׁדּוֹת בָּרֶקֶת שׁוֹקֵעַ לִבִּי:

Zelda

II

God, I prepare to honour the Sabbath, keeping faith with You and the generations that have gone before. I cast away any hatred or bitterness that lingers from the week that is past so that my spirit may be at rest, and I can truly speak Your name. I see those about me in the light of the Sabbath candles as You want me to see them, and thank You for family and friendship, loyalty and love. I make *kiddush,* and receive the gift of happiness, the peace that comes from holiness, the joy that comes from giving. As I eat the bread, I remember all I owe to others, and look forward to that great Sabbath when all shall find their joy and peace.

III

Riboyne shel oylem, may the mitsvah of my lighting the candles be accepted as equivalent to the mitsvah of the High Priest when he lit the candles in the precious temple. As his observance was accepted, so may mine be accepted. 'Your words are a candle at my feet and a light for my path'[1] means that Your words are a candle at my feet so that all my children may walk in God's path, and may the mitsvah of my candle-lighting be accepted so that my children's eyes may be illumined by the precious holy Torah ...

Sore bas Toyvim (17th Century)

---

[1] Ps 119:105.

IV

Shabbat Alone

Two candles, one person.
I welcome this Shabbat alone
and join myself to the community of Israel.
One candle for me.
One candle for my people.
Together and alone
we share our heritage,
our future,
our yearning
for the peace of Shabbat.

After lighting the candles

בָּרוּךְ Blessed are You, our Living God, Sovereign of the universe, whose commandments make us holy, and who commands us to light the Sabbath candles.

בָּרוּךְ אַתָּה יהוה אֱלֹהֵינוּ מֶלֶךְ הָעוֹלָם. אֲשֶׁר קִדְּשָׁנוּ בְּמִצְוֹתָיו. וְצִוָּנוּ לְהַדְלִיק נֵר שֶׁל שַׁבָּת:

אֵל God of might, light of the world, bless us with a perfect blessing in Your presence. Enlighten our eyes with Your light and Your truth, just as we light the Sabbath candles before You, and so make a spirit of trust and love dwell in our homes. Guide us with the light of Your presence, for in Your light we see light. Send Your blessing to every home of Israel and to the whole world, and set peace and eternal blessing upon them. Amen.

אֵל שַׁדַּי אוֹר־הָעוֹלָם. בָּרְכֵנִי בִּבְרָכָה שְׁלֵמָה מִלְּפָנֶיךָ: רְצֵה־נָא וְהָאֵר אֶת־עֵינֵינוּ בְּאוֹרֶךָ וּבַאֲמִתֶּךָ כְּמוֹ שֶׁהִדְלַקְנוּ לְפָנֶיךָ אֶת־נֵרוֹת הַשַּׁבָּת. וְהַשְׁכֵּן בִּנְאוֹתֵינוּ רוּחַ אֱמוּנִים וְאַהֲבָה: הַדְרִיכֵנוּ בְּאוֹר פָּנֶיךָ וּבְאוֹרְךָ נִרְאֶה אוֹר: שְׁלַח־נָא אֶת־בִּרְכָתְךָ לְכָל־בֵּית בְּיִשְׂרָאֵל וּבָעוֹלָם כֻּלּוֹ וְתֵן שָׁלוֹם וְשִׂמְחַת עוֹלָם עַל רֹאשָׁם. אָמֵן:

ערב שבת   HOME SERVICES **448**

Shalom aleichem   שָׁלוֹם עֲלֵיכֶם

שָׁלוֹם Peace   **שָׁלוֹם עֲלֵיכֶם**
and welcome to you,   מַלְאֲכֵי הַשָּׁרֵת מַלְאֲכֵי עֶלְיוֹן
servants of God,   [מִ]מֶּלֶךְ מַלְכֵי הַמְּלָכִים
messengers of the Most High,
Ruler above all earthly rulers,   הַקָּדוֹשׁ בָּרוּךְ הוּא:
the Holy One of blessing.

Enter in peace,   בּוֹאֲכֶם לְשָׁלוֹם מַלְאֲכֵי הַשָּׁלוֹם
you servants of peace,   מַלְאֲכֵי עֶלְיוֹן
messengers of the Most High,   [מִ]מֶּלֶךְ מַלְכֵי הַמְּלָכִים
Ruler above all earthly rulers,
the Holy One of blessing.   הַקָּדוֹשׁ בָּרוּךְ הוּא:

Bless me with peace,   בָּרְכוּנִי לְשָׁלוֹם מַלְאֲכֵי הַשָּׁלוֹם
you servants of peace,   מַלְאֲכֵי עֶלְיוֹן
messengers of the Most High,   [מִ]מֶּלֶךְ מַלְכֵי הַמְּלָכִים
Ruler above all earthly rulers,
the Holy One of blessing.   הַקָּדוֹשׁ בָּרוּךְ הוּא:

Go forth in peace,   צֵאתְכֶם לְשָׁלוֹם מַלְאֲכֵי הַשָּׁלוֹם
you servants of peace,   מַלְאֲכֵי עֶלְיוֹן
messengers of the Most High,   [מִ]מֶּלֶךְ מַלְכֵי הַמְּלָכִים
Ruler above all earthly rulers,
the Holy One of blessing.   הַקָּדוֹשׁ בָּרוּךְ הוּא:

HOME SERVICES — SHABBAT EVE

To a woman

אֵשֶׁת חַיִל
אֵשֶׁת חַיִל מִי יִמְצָא וְרָחֹק מִפְּנִינִים מִכְרָהּ:
בָּטַח בָּהּ לֵב בַּעְלָהּ וְשָׁלָל לֹא יֶחְסָר:
גְּמָלַתְהוּ טוֹב וְלֹא־רָע כֹּל יְמֵי חַיֶּיהָ:
כַּפָּהּ פָּרְשָׂה לֶעָנִי וְיָדֶיהָ שִׁלְּחָה לָאֶבְיוֹן:
עוֹז־וְהָדָר לְבוּשָׁהּ וַתִּשְׂחַק לְיוֹם אַחֲרוֹן:
פִּיהָ פָּתְחָה בְחָכְמָה וְתוֹרַת־חֶסֶד עַל־לְשׁוֹנָהּ:
צוֹפִיָּה הֲלִיכוֹת בֵּיתָהּ וְלֶחֶם עַצְלוּת לֹא תֹאכֵל:
קָמוּ בָנֶיהָ וַיְאַשְּׁרוּהָ בַּעְלָהּ וַיְהַלְלָהּ:
רַבּוֹת בָּנוֹת עָשׂוּ חָיִל וְאַתְּ עָלִית עַל־כֻּלָּנָה:
שֶׁקֶר הַחֵן וְהֶבֶל הַיֹּפִי אִשָּׁה יִרְאַת־יהוה הִיא תִתְהַלָּל:
תְּנוּ־לָהּ מִפְּרִי יָדֶיהָ וִיהַלְלוּהָ בַשְּׁעָרִים מַעֲשֶׂיהָ:

Eshet Chayil

אֵשֶׁת A woman of worth, who can find her,
for she is more precious than rubies.
Her husband trusts her in his heart
and has no loss by it.
Every day of her life
she does him good, not harm.
Her hand is held out open to the poor,
reaching out to those in need.
She is clothed in strength and dignity,
serene before the time to come.
When she speaks, it is with wisdom
and on her tongue is the guidance of love.
She looks after her home with care,
and does not idle away her time.
Her children stand up and honour her,
and her husband sings her praises.
'Many a woman has done splendid deeds,
but you surpass them all.'
Charm deceives and beauty fades,
so praise the woman who honours God.
Give her honour for the work of her hands,
and her own good deeds will praise her in public.[1]

---

[1] From Prov 31.

ערב שבת   HOME SERVICES 450

To a man

אַשְׁרֵי Happy is the man
who does not follow
the advice of the wicked,
nor take his stand
on the sinner's road,
nor sit at ease among the scornful.
But his delight
is in the teaching of the Eternal,
reflecting on God's teaching
day and night.
He is like a tree
planted by streams of water.
It gives its fruit in its season,
its leaf never fades.
Everything he does shall prosper.[1]

אַשְׁרֵי־הָאִישׁ
אֲשֶׁר לֹא הָלַךְ בַּעֲצַת רְשָׁעִים
וּבְדֶרֶךְ חַטָּאִים לֹא עָמָד
וּבְמוֹשַׁב לֵצִים לֹא יָשָׁב:
כִּי אִם־בְּתוֹרַת יהוה חֶפְצוֹ
וּבְתוֹרָתוֹ יֶהְגֶּה יוֹמָם וָלָיְלָה:
וְהָיָה כְּעֵץ שָׁתוּל
עַל־פַּלְגֵי מָיִם
אֲשֶׁר פִּרְיוֹ יִתֵּן בְּעִתּוֹ
וְעָלֵהוּ לֹא יִבּוֹל
וְכֹל אֲשֶׁר־יַעֲשֶׂה יַצְלִיחַ:

Blessing the children

For boys

יְשִׂמְךָ May God make you like
Ephraim and Manasseh.

יְשִׂמְךָ אֱלֹהִים
כְּאֶפְרַיִם וְכִמְנַשֶּׁה

For girls

יְשִׂמֵךְ May God make you like
Sarah, Rebecca, Rachel and Leah.

יְשִׂמֵךְ אֱלֹהִים
כְּשָׂרָה רִבְקָה רָחֵל וְלֵאָה

May God bless you and keep you.
May God's face shine upon you
and be gracious to you.
May God's face turn towards you
and give you peace.

יְבָרֶכְךָ יהוה וְיִשְׁמְרֶךָ.
יָאֵר יהוה פָּנָיו אֵלֶיךָ וִיחֻנֶּךָּ.
יִשָּׂא יהוה פָּנָיו אֵלֶיךָ
וְיָשֵׂם לְךָ שָׁלוֹם:

---

[1] From Ps 1.

קדוש
Kiddush

סדר קדוש לליל שבת
KIDDUSH FOR SHABBAT EVE

The 'sanctification of the day', *Kiddush ha-yom*, belongs in the home services for Friday night, but from early times it was also recited in the synagogue where travellers would stay, and also to enable those who were unskilled in the recital to participate.

The opening paragraph, from Genesis 2:1-3, sets the context of the end of the story of creation and God's setting aside of the seventh day for rest. Wine as a symbol of joy is a fitting choice to welcome the special nature of Shabbat. The second blessing, for the day, with variations for festival occasions, notes the dual themes of Shabbat, creation and the exodus from Egypt. We celebrate both the physical and the spiritual freedom that are the essence of the day.

The blessing over the wine and the day, which are considered a single unit, precede the blessing of the bread, the two loaves coinciding with the double portion of manna that appeared for the Shabbat during the wilderness period. However, according to the Talmud, since wheat is mentioned before the vine in the listing of the seven plants to be found in Israel (Deuteronomy 8:8), the blessing over bread should really take precedence (*Berachot* 41a). That is why the bread is covered while the blessing over wine is recited, as if it was not present. Though a curious gesture, it deals with the serious problem of reconciling two conflicting priorities and the need to find wherever possible a suitable compromise that respects both.

סדר קדוש לליל שבת

וַיְכֻלּוּ הַשָּׁמַיִם וְהָאָרֶץ וְכָל־צְבָאָם: וַיְכַל אֱלֹהִים בַּיּוֹם הַשְּׁבִיעִי מְלַאכְתּוֹ אֲשֶׁר עָשָׂה וַיִּשְׁבֹּת בַּיּוֹם הַשְּׁבִיעִי מִכָּל־מְלַאכְתּוֹ אֲשֶׁר עָשָׂה: וַיְבָרֶךְ אֱלֹהִים אֶת־יוֹם הַשְּׁבִיעִי וַיְקַדֵּשׁ אֹתוֹ כִּי בוֹ שָׁבַת מִכָּל־מְלַאכְתּוֹ אֲשֶׁר־בָּרָא אֱלֹהִים לַעֲשׂוֹת:

וַיְכֻלּוּ Heaven and earth were finished and all their host. On the seventh day God finished the work that had been done, and ceased on the seventh day from all the work that had been done. God blessed the seventh day, and made it holy, resting on it from all the work of creation that God had done.[1]

וַיְכֻלּוּ Vay'chulu ha-shamayim v'ha-arets v'chol ts'va'am. Vay'chal elohim ba-yom ha-sh'vi'i, m'lachto asher asah, vayishbot ba-yom ha-sh'vi'i mikkol m'lachto asher asah. Vay'varech elohim et yom ha-sh'vi'i vay'kaddesh oto, ki vo shavat mikkol m'lachto, asher bara elohim la'asot.

ברכת יין

בָּרוּךְ אַתָּה יְהוָֹה אֱלֹהֵינוּ מֶלֶךְ הָעוֹלָם. בּוֹרֵא פְּרִי הַגָּפֶן:

Blessing for wine

בָּרוּךְ Blessed are You, our Living God, Sovereign of the universe, who creates the fruit of the vine.

בָּרוּךְ Baruch attah Adonai eloheinu melech ha-olam, borei p'ri ha-gafen.

ברכת היום

בָּרוּךְ אַתָּה יְהוָֹה אֱלֹהֵינוּ מֶלֶךְ הָעוֹלָם. אֲשֶׁר קִדְּשָׁנוּ בְּמִצְוֹתָיו וְרָצָה בָנוּ. וְשַׁבַּת קָדְשׁוֹ בְּאַהֲבָה וּבְרָצוֹן הִנְחִילָנוּ. זִכָּרוֹן לְמַעֲשֵׂה בְרֵאשִׁית. כִּי הוּא יוֹם תְּחִלָּה לְמִקְרָאֵי קֹדֶשׁ. זֵכֶר לִיצִיאַת מִצְרָיִם: כִּי בָנוּ בָחַרְתָּ וְאוֹתָנוּ קִדַּשְׁתָּ מִכָּל־הָעַמִּים. וְשַׁבַּת קָדְשְׁךָ בְּאַהֲבָה וּבְרָצוֹן הִנְחַלְתָּנוּ: בָּרוּךְ אַתָּה יְהוָֹה. מְקַדֵּשׁ הַשַּׁבָּת:

Blessing for the day

בָּרוּךְ Blessed are You, our Living God, Sovereign of the universe, whose commands make us holy, and who delights in us. Willingly and with love You give us Your holy Shabbat to inherit, for it recalls the act of creation. This is the first day of holy gatherings, a reminder of the exodus from Egypt. Because You chose us to be holy among all peoples, willingly and with love You gave us Your holy Shabbat to inherit. Blessed are You God, who makes the Shabbat holy.

---

[1] Genesis 2: 1-3.

בָּרוּךְ *Baruch attah Adonai eloheinu melech ha-olam, asher kidd'shanu b'mitsvotav v'ratsah vanu, v'shabbat kodsho b'ahavah uv'ratson hinchilanu, zikkaron l'ma'aseih v'reishit, ki hu yom t'chillah l'mikra'ei kodesh, zeicher litsi'at mitsrayim, ki vanu vacharta v'otanu kiddashta mikkol ha-ammim, v'shabbat kodsh'cha b'ahavah uv'ratson hinchaltanu. Baruch attah Adonai, m'kaddeish ha-shabbat.*

After washing the hands

בָּרוּךְ Blessed are You, our Living God, Sovereign of the universe, whose commands make us holy and who commands us concerning washing the hands.

אחרי הרחיצה

בָּרוּךְ אַתָּה יהוה אֱלֹהֵינוּ מֶלֶךְ הָעוֹלָם. אֲשֶׁר קִדְּשָׁנוּ בְּמִצְוֹתָיו וְצִוָּנוּ עַל נְטִילַת יָדָיִם:

בָּרוּךְ *Baruch attah Adonai eloheinu melech ha-olam, asher kidd'shanu b'mitsvotav, v'tsivvanu al n'tilat yadayim.*

Blessing for bread

בָּרוּךְ Blessed are You, our Living God, Sovereign of the universe, who brings forth food out of the earth.

המוציא

בָּרוּךְ אַתָּה יהוה אֱלֹהֵינוּ מֶלֶךְ הָעוֹלָם. הַמּוֹצִיא לֶחֶם מִן הָאָרֶץ:

בָּרוּךְ *Baruch attah Adonai eloheinu melech ha-olam, ha-motzi lechem min ha-arets.*

קדושא רבא לשבת
K'DUSHA RABBA L'SHABBAT
KIDDUSH FOR SHABBAT DAY

The *Kiddush* for the morning of the Shabbat consisted originally simply of the blessing over the wine without the second paragraph recited on the Shabbat Eve. Yet it bore the name *K'dusha Rabba*, 'the great *Kiddush*', to give it greater significance. Only later was it adorned with the two Biblical passages, from Exodus 31 and from the Exodus version of the Ten Commandments (Exodus 20:8-11). Whereas the texts read in the evening also include the theme of the exodus from Egypt and freedom, both morning passages refer only to the theme of creation and rest which we are experiencing at this time.

קדוש רבא לשבת

וְשָׁמְרוּ The children of Israel shall keep the Shabbat, observing the Shabbat as a timeless covenant for all generations. It is a sign between Me and the children of Israel forever. For in six days the Creator made heaven and earth and on the seventh day ceased from work and was at rest.[1]

וְשָׁמְרוּ בְנֵי־יִשְׂרָאֵל אֶת־הַשַּׁבָּת לַעֲשׂוֹת אֶת־הַשַּׁבָּת לְדֹרֹתָם בְּרִית עוֹלָם: בֵּינִי וּבֵין בְּנֵי יִשְׂרָאֵל אוֹת הִיא לְעֹלָם כִּי־שֵׁשֶׁת יָמִים עָשָׂה יהוה אֶת־הַשָּׁמַיִם וְאֶת־הָאָרֶץ וּבַיּוֹם הַשְּׁבִיעִי שָׁבַת וַיִּנָּפַשׁ:

וְשָׁמְרוּ V'sham'ru v'nei yisra'el et ha-shabbat, la'asot et ha-shabbat l'dorotam b'rit olam. Beini uvein b'nei yisra'el ot hi l'olam, ki sheishet yamim asah Adonai et ha-shamayim v'et ha-arets, uva-yom ha-sh'vi'i shavat vayinnafash.

זָכוֹר Remember the Shabbat day and keep it holy. You have six days to labour and do all your work, but the seventh shall be a Shabbat for the Eternal your God. That day you shall do no work - neither you, nor your son, nor your daughter, nor your servant, man or woman, nor your cattle, nor the stranger who lives in your home. For in six days the Creator made heaven and earth, the seas and all that is in them, and rested on the seventh day. Therefore, God blessed the Shabbat day and made it holy.[2]

זָכוֹר אֶת־יוֹם הַשַּׁבָּת לְקַדְּשׁוֹ: שֵׁשֶׁת יָמִים תַּעֲבֹד וְעָשִׂיתָ כָּל־מְלַאכְתֶּךָ: וְיוֹם הַשְּׁבִיעִי שַׁבָּת לַיהוה אֱלֹהֶיךָ לֹא־תַעֲשֶׂה כָל־מְלָאכָה אַתָּה וּבִנְךָ וּבִתֶּךָ עַבְדְּךָ וַאֲמָתְךָ וּבְהֶמְתֶּךָ וְגֵרְךָ אֲשֶׁר בִּשְׁעָרֶיךָ: כִּי שֵׁשֶׁת־יָמִים עָשָׂה יהוה אֶת־הַשָּׁמַיִם וְאֶת־הָאָרֶץ אֶת־הַיָּם וְאֶת־כָּל־אֲשֶׁר־בָּם וַיָּנַח בַּיּוֹם הַשְּׁבִיעִי עַל־כֵּן בֵּרַךְ יהוה אֶת־יוֹם הַשַּׁבָּת וַיְקַדְּשֵׁהוּ:

זָכוֹר Zachor et yom ha-shabbat l'kadd'sho. Sheishet yamim ta'avod v'asita kol m'lachtecha. V'yom ha-sh'vi'i shabbat ladonai elohecha, lo ta'aseh chol m'lachah, atah uvincha uvittecha, avd'cha va'amat'cha uv'hemtecha, v'geir'cha asher bish'arecha. Ki sheishet yamim asah Adonai et ha-shamayim v'et ha-arets, et ha-yam v'et kol asher bam, vayyanach ba-yom ha-sh'vi'i; al kein beirach Adonai et yom ha-shabbat vay'kadd'sheihu.

---

[1] Exodus 31: 16-17.   [2] Exodus 20: 8-11.

KIDDUSH FOR SHABBAT DAY

Blessing for wine

בְּרָכַת יין

בָּרוּךְ Blessed are You, our Living God, Sovereign of the universe, who creates the fruit of the vine.

בָּרוּךְ אַתָּה יהוה אֱלֹהֵינוּ מֶלֶךְ הָעוֹלָם. בּוֹרֵא פְּרִי הַגֶּפֶן:

בָּרוּךְ Baruch attah Adonai eloheinu melech ha-olam, borei p'ri ha-gafen.

After washing the hands

אחרי הרחיצה

בָּרוּךְ Blessed are You, our Living God, Sovereign of the universe, whose commands make us holy and who commands us concerning washing the hands.

בָּרוּךְ אַתָּה יהוה אֱלֹהֵינוּ מֶלֶךְ הָעוֹלָם. אֲשֶׁר קִדְּשָׁנוּ בְּמִצְוֹתָיו וְצִוָּנוּ עַל נְטִילַת יָדָיִם:

בָּרוּךְ Baruch attah Adonai eloheinu melech ha-olam, asher kidd'shanu b'mitsvotav v'tsivvanu al n'tilat yadayim.

Blessing for bread

המוציא

בָּרוּךְ Blessed are You, our Living God, Sovereign of the universe, who brings forth food out of the earth.

בָּרוּךְ אַתָּה יהוה אֱלֹהֵינוּ מֶלֶךְ הָעוֹלָם. הַמּוֹצִיא לֶחֶם מִן הָאָרֶץ:

בָּרוּךְ Baruch attah Adonai eloheinu melech ha-olam, ha-motzi lechem min ha-arets.

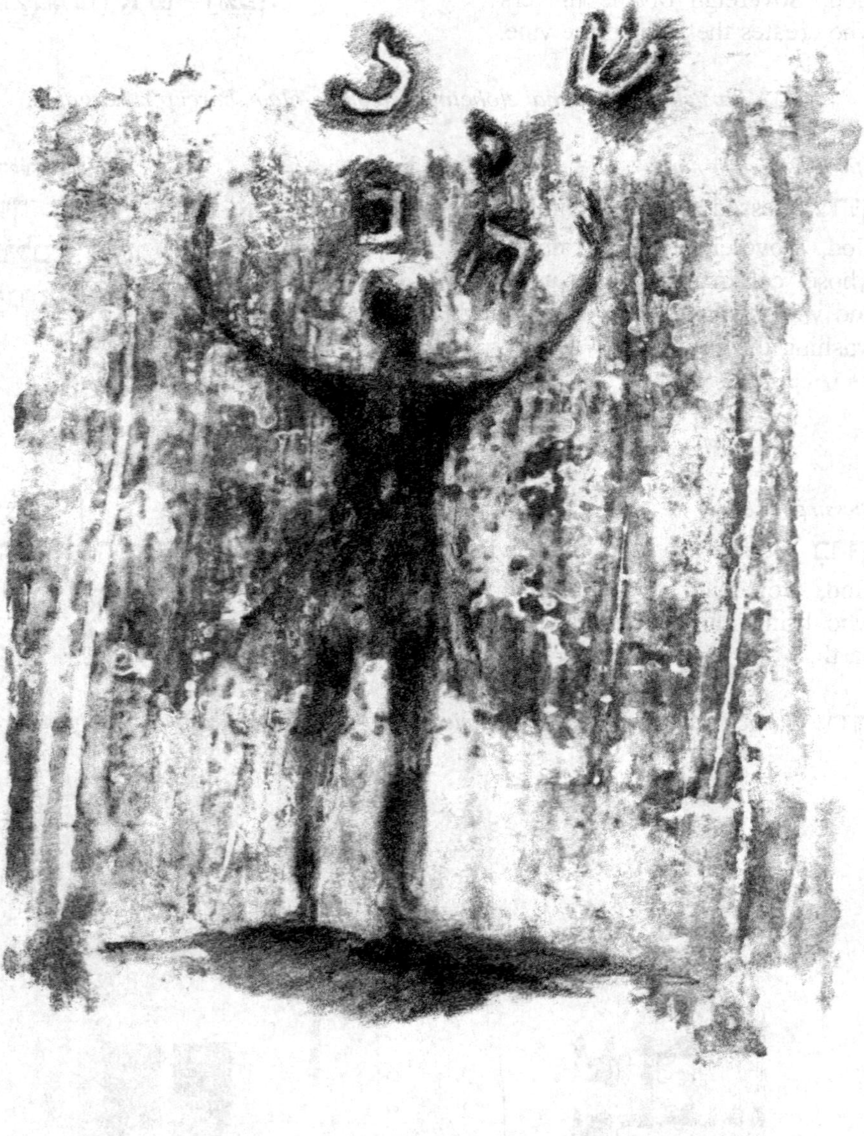

סדר הבדלה
Havdalah Service

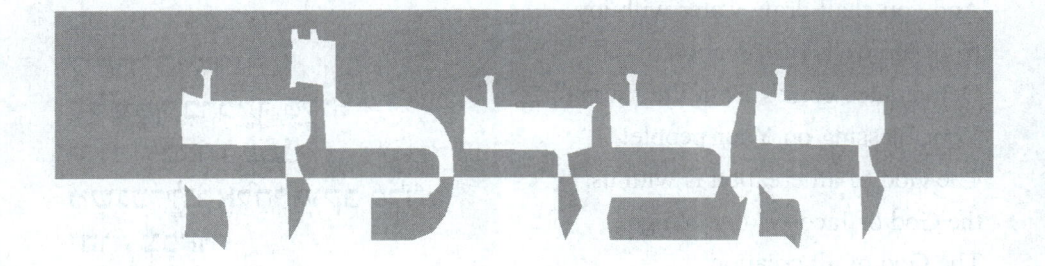

וּשְׁאַבְתֶּם מַיִם בְּשָׂשׂוֹן מִמַּעַיְנֵי הַיְשׁוּעָה:

'You shall draw water with joy from the wells of salvation'

Isaiah 12:3

סדר הבדלה
HAVDALAH

We welcomed the Shabbat by lighting candles and drinking wine. The same two symbolic actions are part of the ceremony of *Havdalah*, literally 'separation', with which we mark the close of the Shabbat. Yet their meaning is different. The candles of Shabbat eve symbolise the light of the Shabbat itself, but also serve the practical task of providing light for the night when no new 'fire' is to be created. So lighting the *Havdalah* candle is a forceful reminder that the working week has now begun. This candle, with its many woven threads, is then extinguished, making it clear that the Shabbat is truly over. Similarly, the wine of erev Shabbat is actually drunk and is a symbol of joy as it accompanies the meal. But the wine of *Havdalah* is spilled to help extinguish the candle, and merely tasted. Only the third blessing brings a new element. The third of our senses is evoked by the blessing over spices, the most ephemeral of all, our sense of smell. Yet this is to carry the 'scent' of the Shabbat into our daily lives.

The opening prayer carries with it the messianic hopes associated with the ending of Shabbat. It consists entirely of quotations, with one exception. To the passage from Esther (8:13), 'The Jews had light and joy, gladness and honour', is added the simple wish, 'so may it be with us!'

The theme of 'separations', distinctions, echoes the stages of the creation of the world, beginning with the creation of light. But now as we re-enter the working week we are confronted with the divisions all about us that the Shabbat has helped us set aside for a brief time, divisions and conflicts that we are invited to help to heal. We are asked to acknowledge the difference between what is *kodesh*, 'holy', 'separate', 'special', and what is 'ordinary' and 'mundane', all within our world that is not yet 'holy'

סדר הבדלה

הִנֵּה See how God is my salvation!	הִנֵּה אֵל יְשׁוּעָתִי
I trust and shall not fear,	אֶבְטַח וְלֹא אֶפְחָד.
for God the Eternal	כִּי עָזִּי וְזִמְרָת יָהּ יהוה
is my strength and song,	וַיְהִי לִי לִישׁוּעָה:
and has become my salvation!	וּשְׁאַבְתֶּם מַיִם בְּשָׂשׂוֹן
And you shall draw water with joy	מִמַּעַיְנֵי הַיְשׁוּעָה:
from the wells of salvation.	לַיהוה הַיְשׁוּעָה
Deliverance comes from the Eternal;	עַל עַמְּךָ בִרְכָתֶךָ סֶּלָה:
Your blessing on Your people!	יהוה צְבָאוֹת עִמָּנוּ
The God of all creation is with us,	מִשְׂגָּב־לָנוּ אֱלֹהֵי יַעֲקֹב סֶלָה:
the God of Jacob is our refuge.	יהוה צְבָאוֹת
The God of all creation,	אַשְׁרֵי אָדָם בֹּטֵחַ בָּךְ:
happy the person who trusts in You.	יהוה הוֹשִׁיעָה
God, deliver us;	הַמֶּלֶךְ יַעֲנֵנוּ בְיוֹם קָרְאֵנוּ:
Sovereign, answer us	לַיְּהוּדִים הָיְתָה
on the day we call.	אוֹרָה וְשִׂמְחָה
The Jews had light and joy,	וְשָׂשׂוֹן וִיקָר:
gladness and honour	כֵּן תִּהְיֶה לָּנוּ:
- so may it be with us!	כּוֹס יְשׁוּעוֹת אֶשָּׂא
I lift the cup of salvation	וּבְשֵׁם יהוה אֶקְרָא:
and call in the name of God.[1]	

הִנֵּה Hinneih eil y'shu'ati evtach v'lo efchad, ki ozzi v'zimrat yah Adonai vay'hi li lishu'ah. Ush'avtem mayim b'sason mima'y'nei ha-y'shu'ah. Ladonai ha-y'shu'ah al amm'cha virchatecha selah. Adonai ts'va'ot immanu misgav lanu elohei ya'akov selah. Adonai ts'va'ot ashrei adam botei'ach bach. Adonai hoshi'ah ha-melech ya'aneinu v'yom kor'einu. La-y'hudim hay'tah orah v'simchah v'sason vikar, kein tihyeh lanu. Kos y'shu'ot essa uv'sheim Adonai ekra.

---

[1] Isa 12:2-3; Ps 3:9; 46:8,12; 84:13; 20:10; Est 8:16; Ps 116:13.

HAVDALAH SERVICE

Raising the cup of wine

בָּרוּךְ Blessed are You, our Living God, Sovereign of the universe, who creates the fruit of the vine.

בָּרוּךְ אַתָּה יהוה אֱלֹהֵינוּ מֶלֶךְ הָעוֹלָם. בּוֹרֵא פְּרִי הַגָּפֶן:

בָּרוּךְ Baruch attah Adonai eloheinu melech ha-olam, borei p'ri ha-gafen.

Taking the spice box

בָּרוּךְ Blessed are You, our Living God, Sovereign of the universe, who creates different kinds of spices.

בָּרוּךְ אַתָּה יהוה אֱלֹהֵינוּ מֶלֶךְ הָעוֹלָם. בּוֹרֵא מִינֵי בְשָׂמִים:

בָּרוּךְ Baruch attah Adonai eloheinu melech ha-olam, borei minei v'samim.

Spreading the hands to the light

בָּרוּךְ Blessed are You, our Living God, Sovereign of the universe, who creates the lights of the fire.

בָּרוּךְ אַתָּה יהוה אֱלֹהֵינוּ מֶלֶךְ הָעוֹלָם. בּוֹרֵא מְאוֹרֵי הָאֵשׁ:

בָּרוּךְ Baruch attah Adonai eloheinu melech ha-olam, borei m'orei ha-eish.

בָּרוּךְ Blessed are You, our Living God, Sovereign of the universe, who makes distinctions between the holy and the everyday, between light and darkness, between Israel and other peoples, between the seventh day and the six working days. Blessed are You God, who distinguishes between the holy and the everyday.

בָּרוּךְ אַתָּה יהוה אֱלֹהֵינוּ מֶלֶךְ הָעוֹלָם. הַמַּבְדִּיל בֵּין קֹדֶשׁ לְחוֹל. בֵּין אוֹר לְחֹשֶׁךְ. בֵּין יִשְׂרָאֵל לָעַמִּים. בֵּין יוֹם הַשְּׁבִיעִי לְשֵׁשֶׁת יְמֵי הַמַּעֲשֶׂה: בָּרוּךְ אַתָּה יהוה הַמַּבְדִּיל בֵּין קֹדֶשׁ לְחוֹל:

בָּרוּךְ Baruch attah Adonai eloheinu melech ha-olam, ha-mavdil bein kodesh l'chol bein or l'choshech bein yisra'el la-ammim, bein yom ha-sh'vi'i l'sheishet y'mei ha-ma'aseh. Baruch attah Adonai ha-mavdil bein kodesh l'chol.

זמירות למוצאי שבת
SONGS AT THE CLOSE OF SHABBAT

הַמַּבְדִּיל בֵּין קֹדֶשׁ לְחוֹל.
חַטֹּאתֵינוּ יִמְחוֹל.
זַרְעֵנוּ וְכַסְפֵּנוּ יַרְבֶּה
כַחוֹל. וְכַכּוֹכָבִים בַּלָּיְלָה:

May the One
who divides holy from profane
pardon our sins,
increase our offspring and our fortune
as the sand
and as the stars at night.

יוֹם פָּנָה כְּצֵל תֹּמֶר.
אֶקְרָא לָאֵל עָלַי גֹּמֵר.
אָמַר שׁוֹמֵר.
אָתָא בֹקֶר וְגַם־לָיְלָה:

As day turns, like the palm-tree's shade,
I call on God to complete for me
that day of which
the watchman says
'Morning will come, though it still be night!'

הַעְתֵּר נוֹרָא וְאָיוֹם.
אֲשַׁוֵּעַ תְּנָה פִדְיוֹם.
בְּנֶשֶׁף בְּעֶרֶב יוֹם.
בְּאִישׁוֹן לָיְלָה:

Be moved, awesome and wondrous God!
I cry to You to grant redemption,
at sunset, the evening of the day,
in the darkness of the night.

נַחְנוּ בְיָדְךָ כַּחֹמֶר.
סְלַח נָא עַל קַל וָחֹמֶר.
יוֹם לְיוֹם יַבִּיעַ אֹמֶר.
וְלַיְלָה לְּלָיְלָה:

We are like clay in Your hands;
forgive our sins, light and grave,
as day pours out Your word to day,
and night to night.

הַמַּבְדִּיל בֵּין קֹדֶשׁ לְחוֹל.
חַטֹּאתֵינוּ יִמְחוֹל.
זַרְעֵנוּ וְכַסְפֵּנוּ יַרְבֶּה
כַחוֹל. וְכַכּוֹכָבִים בַּלָּיְלָה:

May the One
who divides holy from profane
pardon our sins,
increase our offspring and our fortune
as the sand
and as the stars at night.

הַמַּבְדִּיל *Ha-mavdil bein kodesh l'chol, chattoteinu yimchol,*
zar'einu v'chaspeinu yarbeh ka-chol, v'cha-kochavim ba-lailah.
Yom panah k'tseil tomer, ekra la-eil alai gomer,
amar shomeir, ata voker v'gam lailah.
Hei'ateir nora v'ayom, ashavvei'a t'nah fidyom,
b'neshef b'erev yom, b'ishon lailah.
Nachnu v'yad'cha ka-chomer, s'lach na al kal vachomer,
yom l'yom yabbi'a omer, v'lailah l'lailah.
Ha-mavdil bein kodesh l'chol, chattoteinu yimchol,
zar'einu v'chaspeinu yarbeh ka-chol, v'cha-kochavim ba-lailah.

SONGS AT THE CLOSE OF SHABBAT

אֵלִיָּֽהוּ הַנָּבִיא.
אֵלִיָּֽהוּ הַתִּשְׁבִּי.
אֵלִיָּֽהוּ הַגִּלְעָדִי.

אֵלִיָּֽהוּ Elijah the prophet,
Elijah the Tishbite,
Elijah the man of Gilead

בִּמְהֵרָה יָבֹא אֵלֵֽינוּ
עִם מָשִֽׁיחַ בֶּן־דָּוִד:

- may he come to us soon,
with the Messiah, son of David.

אֵלִיָּֽהוּ *Eliyahu ha-navi, eliyahu ha-tishbi, eliyahu ha-gil'adi,
bimheirah yavo eileinu im mashi'ach ben david.*

Some add:

מִרְיָם הַנְּבִיאָה.
עֹז וְזִמְרָה בְּיָדָהּ:
מִרְיָם תִּרְקֹד אִתָּֽנוּ
לְהַגְדִּיל זִמְרַת עוֹלָם:
מִרְיָם תִּרְקֹד אִתָּֽנוּ
לְתַקֵּן אֶת הָעוֹלָם:

מִרְיָם Miriam the prophetess,
strength and song are in her hand.
Miriam will dance with us
to strengthen the song of the world.
Miriam will dance with us
to repair the world.

בִּמְהֵרָה בְיָמֵֽינוּ הִיא תְּבִיאֵֽנוּ
אֶל מֵי הַיְשׁוּעָה:

Soon, in our time, may she bring us
to the waters of redemption.

Leila Gal Berner

מִרְיָם *Mir'yam ha-n'vi'ah, oz v'zimrah b'yadah.
Mir'yam tirkod ittanu l'hagdil zimrat olam.
Mir'yam tirkod ittanu l'takkein et ha-olam.
Bimheirah v'yameinu hi t'vi'einu el mei ha-y'shu'ah.*

שָׁבֽוּעַ טוֹב:

A good week.

Shavua Tov.

הַחַמָּה מֵרֹאשׁ הָאִילָנוֹת נִסְתַּלְּקָה.	**הַחַמָּה** The sun at the treetops no longer is seen,
בּוֹאוּ וּנְלַוֶּה אֶת־שַׁבָּת הַמַּלְכָּה.	come let us accompany the Sabbath Queen.
צֵאתֵךְ לְשָׁלוֹם הַקְּדוֹשָׁה. הַזַּכָּה.	Depart in peace, the holy, the pure,
דְּעִי שֵׁשֶׁת יָמִים אֶל־שׁוּבֵךְ נְחַכֶּה:	know that for six days we await your return.
כֵּן לַשַּׁבָּת הַבָּאָה.	Yes, for next Sabbath!
כֵּן לַשַּׁבָּת הַבָּאָה.	Yes, for next Sabbath!
צֵאתְכֶם לְשָׁלוֹם מַלְאֲכֵי הַשָּׁלוֹם:	Depart in peace, messengers of peace.
חיים נחמן ביאליק	*Chaim Nachman Bialik*

הַחַמָּה *Ha-chammah meirosh ha-ilanot nistall'kah,*
bo'u un'lavveh et shabbat ha-malkah,
tseiteich l'shalom ha-k'doshah, ha-zakkah,
d'i sheishet yamim el shuveich n'chakkeh.
Kein la-shabbat ha-ba'ah,
kein la-shabbat ha-ba'ah,
tseit'chem l'shalom mal'achei ha-shalom.

ברכות לפני סעודה
BLESSINGS BEFORE MEALS

אחרי הרחיצה	*After washing the hands*
בָּרוּךְ אַתָּה יהוה אֱלֹהֵינוּ מֶלֶךְ הָעוֹלָם. אֲשֶׁר קִדְּשָׁנוּ בְּמִצְוֹתָיו וְצִוָּנוּ עַל נְטִילַת יָדָיִם:	**בָּרוּךְ** Blessed are You, our Living God, Sovereign of the universe, whose commands make us holy and who commands us concerning washing the hands.

בָּרוּךְ *Baruch attah Adonai eloheinu melech ha-olam,*
asher kidd'shanu b'mitsvotav v'tsivvanu al n'tilat yadayim.

המוציא	*Blessing for bread*
בָּרוּךְ אַתָּה יהוה אֱלֹהֵינוּ מֶלֶךְ הָעוֹלָם. הַמּוֹצִיא לֶחֶם מִן הָאָרֶץ:	**בָּרוּךְ** Blessed are You, our Living God, Sovereign of the universe, who brings forth food out of the earth.

בָּרוּךְ *Baruch attah Adonai eloheinu melech ha-olam, ha-motzi lechem min ha-arets.*

ברכת המזון
Thanksgiving After Meals

Judaism speaks of a three-way connection between God, human beings and the world. There is no act which cannot be lifted out of the realm of the ordinary and mundane and given a dimension of holiness: in the kitchen and the dining-room as much as in prayer or study. The family table is the altar of the small sanctuary, where hospitality can be practised and eating can be something more than the mere intake of food. Through the act of blessing before and after meals we can acknowledge the source of our sustenance in God and so become more aware of ourselves and our place in the universe of creation.

The basic Thanksgiving after Meals can be seen in the shorter form (III) on pages 482 - 483. The first two paragraphs, traditionally, were instituted by Moses and Joshua - that is to say they are seen as having great antiquity and authority. The third is a messianic vision of Jerusalem. The fourth was instituted after the Bar Kochba revolt in 135 CE, the last military attempt at Jewish independence under the Romans. The four paragraphs indicate four primary Jewish teachings:

'who gives food to all' is a reminder that as God's agents we are duty-bound to ensure that all are fed.

'for the land and for the food' speaks of the need to care for the earth that yields so much and is abused so easily.

'who builds Jerusalem' reminds us that concern with what we eat and how we eat is part of our responsibility in the building of God's kingdom.

'who does good to all' speaks of the need to be sensitive to the quality of the lives of the creatures we eat and the manner of their deaths.

On Shabbat and joyful days Psalm 126 is sung.

קכו

Psalm 126

¹שִׁיר הַמַּעֲלוֹת
בְּשׁוּב יהוה אֶת־שִׁיבַת צִיּוֹן
הָיִינוּ כְּחֹלְמִים:
²אָז יִמָּלֵא שְׂחוֹק פִּינוּ
וּלְשׁוֹנֵנוּ רִנָּה

אָז יֹאמְרוּ בַגּוֹיִם
הִגְדִּיל יהוה לַעֲשׂוֹת עִם־אֵלֶּה:
³הִגְדִּיל יהוה לַעֲשׂוֹת עִמָּנוּ
הָיִינוּ שְׂמֵחִים:

⁴שׁוּבָה יהוה אֶת־שְׁבִיתֵנוּ
כַּאֲפִיקִים בַּנֶּגֶב:
⁵הַזֹּרְעִים בְּדִמְעָה
בְּרִנָּה יִקְצֹרוּ:

⁶הָלוֹךְ יֵלֵךְ וּבָכֹה
נֹשֵׂא מֶשֶׁךְ־הַזָּרַע
בֹּא־יָבֹא בְרִנָּה
נֹשֵׂא אֲלֻמֹּתָיו:

¹שִׁיר **A pilgrim song.**
When God brought back
the captives to Zion
we felt as if in a dream.
²Then our mouths
were filled with laughter,
and our tongues with song.

Even among the nations they said:
'What great things
God has done with them!'
³Indeed God has done
great things with us!
How we rejoiced!

⁴God, bring back those
who cannot return,
like streams in a dry land;
⁵that those who sow in tears
may reap in joy.

⁶Whoever goes out weeping
carrying seed to sow;
shall come back singing
carrying sheaves.

¹שִׁיר *Shir ha-ma'alot. B'shuv Adonai et shivat tsiyyon hayinu k'chol'mim.*
²*Az y'malei s'chok pinu ul'shoneinu rinnah.*
Az yom'ru va-goyim higdil Adonai la'asot im eileh.
³*Higdil Adonai la'asot immanu hayinu s'meichim.*
⁴*Shuvah Adonai et sh'viteinu ka'afikim ba-negev.*
⁵*Ha-zor'im b'dim'ah b'rinnah yiktsoru.*
⁶*Haloch yeileich uvachoh nosei meshech ha-zara'
bo yavo v'rinnah nosei alumotav.*

<<<

465 THANKSGIVING AFTER MEALS

Some add the following verses:

My mouth will speak the praise of the Eternal and let all flesh bless God's holy name forever and ever![1]	תְּהִלַּת יהוה יְדַבֶּר פִּי. וִיבָרֵךְ כָּל־בָּשָׂר שֵׁם קָדְשׁוֹ לְעוֹלָם וָעֶד:
For we bless God now and evermore. Praise God![2]	וַאֲנַחְנוּ נְבָרֵךְ יָהּ מֵעַתָּה וְעַד־עוֹלָם הַלְלוּיָהּ:
Give thanks to God who is good, whose love is everlasting.[3]	הוֹדוּ לַיהוה כִּי טוֹב כִּי לְעוֹלָם חַסְדּוֹ:
Who can describe the mighty deeds of God, or utter all God's praise?[4]	מִי יְמַלֵּל גְּבוּרוֹת יהוה. יַשְׁמִיעַ כָּל־תְּהִלָּתוֹ:

T'hillat Adonai y'dabeir pi, vivareich kol basar sheim kodsho l'olam va'ed.
Va'anachnu n'vareich yah, mei'atah v'ad olam, hall'luyah.
Hodu ladonai ki tov, ki l'olam chasdo.
Mi y'malleil g'vurot Adonai, yashmia kol t'hillato.

---

[1] Ps 145:21.
[2] Ps 115:18.
[3] Ps 118:1.
[2] Ps 106:2.

466 ברכת המזון

The leader	*The leader*
חֲבֵרַי Friends, let us bless.	חֲבֵרַי נְבָרֵךְ:
All reply	*All reply*
יְהִי Blessed be the name of the Creator from now and forever.	יְהִי שֵׁם יהוה מְבֹרָךְ מֵעַתָּה וְעַד עוֹלָם:
	The leader
יְהִי Blessed be the name of the Creator from now and forever. With your permission, friends, let us bless (our God[1]) the One whose food we have eaten.	יְהִי שֵׁם יהוה מְבֹרָךְ מֵעַתָּה וְעַד עוֹלָם: בִּרְשׁוּת חֲבֵרַי. נְבָרֵךְ (אֱלֹהֵינוּ) שֶׁאָכַלְנוּ מִשֶּׁלּוֹ:
All reply	*All reply*
בָּרוּךְ Blessed be (our God) the One whose food we have eaten, and through whose goodness we live.	בָּרוּךְ (אֱלֹהֵינוּ) שֶׁאָכַלְנוּ מִשֶּׁלּוֹ וּבְטוּבוֹ חָיִינוּ.
The leader	*The leader*
בָּרוּךְ Blessed be (our God) the One whose food we have eaten, and through whose goodness we live. Blessed be God, and blessed be God's name.	בָּרוּךְ (אֱלֹהֵינוּ) שֶׁאָכַלְנוּ מִשֶּׁלּוֹ וּבְטוּבוֹ חָיִינוּ. בָּרוּךְ הוּא וּבָרוּךְ שְׁמוֹ:

The leader
חֲבֵרַי Chaveirai n'vareich.

All reply
יְהִי Y'hi sheim Adonai m'vorach mei'attah v'ad olam.

The leader
יְהִי Y'hi sheim Adonai m'vorach mei'attah v'ad olam.
Birshut chaveirai, n'vareich (eloheinu) she'achalnu mishelo.

All reply
בָּרוּךְ Baruch (eloheinu) she'achalnu mishelo uv'tuvo chayinu.

The leader
בָּרוּךְ Baruch (eloheinu) she'achalnu mishelo uv'tuvo chayinu.
Baruch hu uvaruch sh'mo.

---

[1]In a community setting, we add 'our God'/ אֱלֹהֵינוּ to each of these responses.

THANKSGIVING AFTER MEALS

בָּרוּךְ Blessed are You, our Living God, Sovereign of the universe. You feed the whole world through Your goodness, with grace, kindness and mercy. You make it possible for all to have food, for Your love is forever. Through Your great goodness food has never failed us, and may we never fail to share food for the sake of Your great reputation; for You feed and provide for all and do good to all, and make us the agents through whom all Your creatures may have food. Blessed are You God, providing enough food for all.

בָּרוּךְ אַתָּה יהוה אֱלֹהֵינוּ מֶלֶךְ הָעוֹלָם. הַזָּן אֶת־הָעוֹלָם כֻּלּוֹ בְּטוּבוֹ בְּחֵן בְּחֶסֶד וּבְרַחֲמִים. הוּא נוֹתֵן לֶחֶם לְכָל־בָּשָׂר. כִּי לְעוֹלָם חַסְדּוֹ: וּבְטוּבוֹ הַגָּדוֹל תָּמִיד לֹא־חָסַר לָנוּ. וְאַל יֶחְסַר־לָנוּ מָזוֹן לְעוֹלָם וָעֶד בַּעֲבוּר שְׁמוֹ הַגָּדוֹל. כִּי הוּא זָן וּמְפַרְנֵס לַכֹּל וּמֵטִיב לַכֹּל וּמֵכִין מָזוֹן לְכָל־בְּרִיּוֹתָיו אֲשֶׁר בָּרָא: בָּרוּךְ אַתָּה יהוה. הַזָּן אֶת הַכֹּל:

בָּרוּךְ *Baruch attah Adonai eloheinu melech ha-olam, ha-zan et ha-olam kullo b'tuvo b'chein b'chesed uv'rachamim, hu notein lechem l'chol basar ki l'olam chasdo. Uv'tuvo ha-gadol tamid lo chasar lanu, v'al yechsar lanu mazon l'olam va'ed ba'avur sh'mo ha-gadol, ki hu zan um'farneis la-kol umeitiv la-kol umeichin mazon l'chol b'ri'otav asher bara. Baruch attah Adonai ha-zan et ha-kol.*

נוֹדֶה **We thank You, our Living God,** for giving our ancestors the heritage of a desirable, good and ample land, for bringing us out of the land of Egypt, redeeming us from the camp of slavery, and for Your covenant that You sealed in our flesh and in our hearts, and for Your Torah that You taught us, and for the laws of life You helped us understand, and for the life, grace and love You graciously gave us, and the food that you provide to support us always, everyday, every hour and every moment.

נוֹדֶה לְךָ יהוה אֱלֹהֵינוּ עַל שֶׁהִנְחַלְתָּ לַאֲבוֹתֵינוּ אֶרֶץ חֶמְדָּה טוֹבָה וּרְחָבָה. וְעַל שֶׁהוֹצֵאתָנוּ יהוה אֱלֹהֵינוּ מֵאֶרֶץ מִצְרָיִם. וּפְדִיתָנוּ מִבֵּית עֲבָדִים. וְעַל בְּרִיתְךָ שֶׁחָתַמְתָּ בִּבְשָׂרֵנוּ וּבְלִבָּבֵנוּ. וְעַל תּוֹרָתְךָ שֶׁלִּמַּדְתָּנוּ. וְעַל חֻקֶּיךָ שֶׁהוֹדַעְתָּנוּ. וְעַל חַיִּים חֵן וָחֶסֶד שֶׁחוֹנַנְתָּנוּ. וְעַל אֲכִילַת מָזוֹן שָׁאַתָּה זָן וּמְפַרְנֵס אוֹתָנוּ תָּמִיד בְּכָל־יוֹם וּבְכָל־עֵת וּבְכָל־שָׁעָה:

נוֹדֶה *Nodeh l'cha Adonai eloheinu al shehinchalta la'avoteinu erets chemdah tovah ur'chavah, v'al she'hotseitanu Adonai eloheinu mei'erets mitsrayim, uf'ditanu mibbeit avadim, v'al b'rit'cha shechatamta bivsareinu uvilvaveinu, v'al torat'cha shelimmadtanu, v'al chukkecha shehoda'tanu, v'al chayyim chein vachesed shechonantanu, v'al achilat mazon sha'attah zan um'farneis otanu tamid b'chol yom uv'chol eit uv'chol sha'ah.*

On Chanukah and Purim continue below,
otherwise continue on page 471.

On Chanukah and Purim add:
עַל **We thank You** for the wonders, the heroic acts, the victories and the marvellous and consoling deeds You performed for our ancestors, in those days at this season.

On Chanukah and Purim add:
עַל הַנִּסִּים. וְעַל הַגְּבוּרוֹת. וְעַל הַתְּשׁוּעוֹת. וְעַל הַנִּפְלָאוֹת. וְעַל הַנֶּחָמוֹת שֶׁעָשִׂיתָ לַאֲבוֹתֵינוּ בַּיָּמִים הָהֵם וּבַזְּמַן הַזֶּה.

On Chanukah and Purim add:
עַל *Al ha-nissim v'al ha-g'vurot, v'al ha-t'shu'ot v'al ha-nifla'ot, v'al ha-nechamot she'asita la'avoteinu ba-yamim ha-heim uva-z'man ha-zeh.*

469 THANKSGIVING AFTER MEALS

On **Chanukah:**

בִּימֵי In the days of Mattathias, the Hasmonean, the son of Yochanan the priest, and his sons and Hannah and her sons, when the kingdom of Antiochus rose up against Your people Israel to make them forget Your teaching, then You in Your great mercy stood up for them in their hour of need. You heard their plea. You judged their cause. You delivered the strong into the hands of the weak, and the many into the hands of the few. You made Your name great and holy in Your world, and gave a great victory to Your people Israel as at this day. Afterwards Your children entered the inner sanctuary of Your house, they cleared the temple, and lit the lamps in Your holy courts. Then they appointed eight days of dedication to thank and honour Your great name.

On Chanukah:

בִּימֵי מַתִּתְיָהוּ בֶּן יוֹחָנָן הַחַשְׁמוֹנַאי וּבָנָיו וְחַנָּה וּבָנֶיהָ. כְּשֶׁעָמְדָה מַלְכוּת אַנְטִיוֹכוֹס עַל עַמְּךָ יִשְׂרָאֵל לְהַשְׁכִּיחָם תּוֹרָתֶךָ: וְאַתָּה בְּרַחֲמֶיךָ הָרַבִּים עָמַדְתָּ לָהֶם בְּעֵת צָרָתָם. רַבְתָּ אֶת־רִיבָם. דַּנְתָּ אֶת־דִּינָם. מָסַרְתָּ גִּבּוֹרִים בְּיַד חַלָּשִׁים. וְרַבִּים בְּיַד מְעַטִּים. וּלְךָ עָשִׂיתָ שֵׁם גָּדוֹל וְקָדוֹשׁ בְּעוֹלָמֶךָ. וּלְעַמְּךָ יִשְׂרָאֵל עָשִׂיתָ תְּשׁוּעָה גְדוֹלָה כְּהַיּוֹם הַזֶּה: וְאַחֲרֵי־כֵן בָּאוּ בָנֶיךָ לִדְבִיר בֵּיתֶךָ. וּפִנּוּ אֶת־הֵיכָלֶךָ. וְהִדְלִיקוּ נֵרוֹת בְּחַצְרוֹת קָדְשֶׁךָ. וְקָבְעוּ שְׁמוֹנַת יְמֵי חֲנֻכָּה לְהוֹדוֹת וּלְהַלֵּל לְשִׁמְךָ הַגָּדוֹל:

On Chanukah:

בִּימֵי *Bimei mattityahu ben yochanan ha-chashmonai uvanav, v'channah uvaneha, k'she'am'dah malchut antiyochos al amm'cha yisra'el l'hashkicham toratecha. V'attah b'rachmecha ha-rabbim amadta lahem b'eit tsaratam, ravta et rivam, danta et dinam, masarta gibborim b'yad challashim, v'rabbim b'yad m'attim, ul'cha asita sheim gadol v'kadosh b'olamecha, ul'amm'cha yisra'el asita t'shu'ah g'dolah k'ha-yom ha-zeh. V'acharei chein ba'u vanecha lidvir beitecha, ufinnu et heichalecha, v'hidliku neirot b'chatsrot kodshecha, v'kav'u sh'monat y'mei chanukah l'hodot ul'halleil l'shimcha ha-gadol.*

470 ברכת המזון

On Purim:

בִּימֵי In the days of Mordechai and Esther, in Shushan the capital, when the wicked Haman rose up against them, he sought to destroy, kill and exterminate all the Jews, both young and old, little children and women, on one day, and plunder their possessions. (That is on the thirteenth day of the twelfth month, which is the month of Adar.) Then You, in Your great mercy, upset his plan and overthrew his design, and made his acts recoil upon his own head. And You performed a wonder and a marvel for them therefore we thank Your great name.

On Purim:

בִּימֵי מָרְדְּכַי וְאֶסְתֵּר בְּשׁוּשַׁן הַבִּירָה. כְּשֶׁעָמַד עֲלֵיהֶם הָמָן הָרָשָׁע. בִּקֵּשׁ לְהַשְׁמִיד לַהֲרֹג וּלְאַבֵּד אֶת־כָּל־הַיְּהוּדִים. מִנַּעַר וְעַד־זָקֵן טַף וְנָשִׁים בְּיוֹם אֶחָד. בִּשְׁלוֹשָׁה עָשָׂר לְחֹדֶשׁ שְׁנֵים־עָשָׂר. הוּא חֹדֶשׁ אֲדָר. וּשְׁלָלָם לָבוֹז: וְאַתָּה בְּרַחֲמֶיךָ הָרַבִּים הֵפַרְתָּ אֶת עֲצָתוֹ. וְקִלְקַלְתָּ אֶת מַחֲשַׁבְתּוֹ. וַהֲשֵׁבוֹתָ לּוֹ גְּמוּלוֹ בְּרֹאשׁוֹ: וְעָשִׂיתָ עִמָּהֶם נֵס וָפֶלֶא. וְנוֹדֶה לְשִׁמְךָ הַגָּדוֹל:

On Purim:

בִּימֵי Bimei mordechai v'ester b'shushan ha-birah, k'she'amad aleihem haman ha-rasha, bikkeish l'hashmid laharog ul'abbeid et kol ha-y'hudim, minna'ar v'ad zakein taf v'nashim b'yom echad, bishloshah asar l'chodesh adar, ush'lalam lavoz. V'attah b'rachamecha ha-rabbim heifarta et atsato, v'kilkalta et machashavto, vahasheivota lo g'mulo b'rosho. V'asita immahem neis vafele, v'nodeh l'shimcha ha-gadol.

471 THANKSGIVING AFTER MEALS

וְעַל And for all this, our Living God, we thank and bless You; may Your name be blessed in the mouth of all living always and at all times, as it is written in the Torah: 'And you shall eat and be satisfied and bless the Eternal your God for the good land which God has given you'.[1] Blessed are You God, for the land and for the food.

וְעַל הַכֹּל יהוה אֱלֹהֵינוּ אֲנַחְנוּ מוֹדִים לָךְ וּמְבָרְכִים אוֹתָךְ. יִתְבָּרַךְ שִׁמְךָ בְּפִי כָּל־חַי תָּמִיד לְעוֹלָם וָעֶד: כַּכָּתוּב. וְאָכַלְתָּ וְשָׂבָעְתָּ וּבֵרַכְתָּ אֶת־יהוה אֱלֹהֶיךָ עַל־הָאָרֶץ הַטֹּבָה אֲשֶׁר נָתַן־לָךְ. בָּרוּךְ אַתָּה יהוה. עַל־הָאָרֶץ וְעַל־הַמָּזוֹן:

וְעַל V'al ha-kol Adonai eloheinu anachnu modim lach um'var'chim otach, yitbarach shimcha b'fi kol chai tamid l'olam va'ed. Ka-katuv, v'achalta v'sava'ta uveirachta et Adonai elohecha al ha-arets ha-tovah asher natan lach. Baruch attah Adonai, al ha-arets v'al ha-mazon.

רַחֵם Our Living God, be merciful to Israel Your people, to Jerusalem Your city, and to Zion where Your glory appeared, and bring the reign of goodness promised in the name of the house of David, when all shall worship together in the place dedicated to Your holy name. Our God, giver of life, be our shepherd and feed us, provide for us, sustain us and support us, and relieve us speedily from all our troubles. Let us never be in need of the charity of others nor their loans, but dependent on Your hand alone which is full, open, holy and ample; so shall we never lose our self-respect nor be put to shame.

רַחֵם יהוה אֱלֹהֵינוּ עַל־יִשְׂרָאֵל עַמֶּךָ. וְעַל יְרוּשָׁלַיִם עִירֶךָ. וְעַל צִיּוֹן מִשְׁכַּן כְּבוֹדֶךָ. וְעַל מַלְכוּת בֵּית דָּוִד מְשִׁיחֶךָ. וְעַל הַבַּיִת הַגָּדוֹל וְהַקָּדוֹשׁ שֶׁנִּקְרָא שִׁמְךָ עָלָיו: אֱלֹהֵינוּ אָבִינוּ רְעֵנוּ זוּנֵנוּ פַּרְנְסֵנוּ וְכַלְכְּלֵנוּ וְהַרְוִיחֵנוּ וְהַרְוַח־לָנוּ יהוה אֱלֹהֵינוּ מְהֵרָה מִכָּל־צָרוֹתֵינוּ: וְנָא אַל תַּצְרִיכֵנוּ יהוה אֱלֹהֵינוּ. לֹא לִידֵי מַתְּנַת בָּשָׂר וָדָם וְלֹא לִידֵי הַלְוָאָתָם. כִּי אִם לְיָדְךָ הַמְּלֵאָה הַפְּתוּחָה הַקְּדוֹשָׁה וְהָרְחָבָה. שֶׁלֹּא נֵבוֹשׁ וְלֹא נִכָּלֵם לְעוֹלָם וָעֶד:

רַחֵם Racheim Adonai eloheinu al yisra'el ammecha, v'al y'rushalayim irecha, v'al tsiyyon mishkan k'vodecha, v'al malchut beit david m'shichecha, v'al ha-bayit ha-gadol v'ha-kadosh shenikra shimcha alav. Eloheinu avinu r'einu zuneinu parn'seinu v'chalk'leinu v'harvicheinu v'harvach lanu Adonai eloheinu m'heirah mikkol tsaroteinu. V'na al tatsricheinu Adonai eloheinu, lo lidei matnat basar vadam v'lo lidei halva'atam, ki im l'yad'cha ha-m'lei'ah ha-p'tuchah ha-k'doshah v'ha-r'chavah, she'lo neivosh v'lo nikkaleim l'olam va'ed.

[1.] Deut. 8:10.

ברכת המזון 472

On Shabbat add:

רְצֵה Our Living God, strengthen us by Your commandments and by the commandment of the seventh day, this great and holy Sabbath; for You this day is a great and holy one to cease from work and be at rest according to Your will in love. Give us rest so that there shall be no trouble, grief or crying on our day of rest; and show us the consolation of Zion, Your city, and the building of Jerusalem, city of Your holiness, for You are the source of salvation and consolation.

On Shabbat add:

רְצֵה וְהַחֲלִיצֵנוּ יהוה אֱלֹהֵינוּ בְּמִצְוֹתֶיךָ וּבְמִצְוַת יוֹם הַשְּׁבִיעִי הַשַּׁבָּת הַגָּדוֹל וְהַקָּדוֹשׁ הַזֶּה. כִּי יוֹם זֶה גָּדוֹל וְקָדוֹשׁ הוּא לְפָנֶיךָ. לִשְׁבָּת־בּוֹ וְלָנוּחַ בּוֹ בְּאַהֲבָה כְּמִצְוַת רְצוֹנֶךָ. וּבִרְצוֹנְךָ הָנִיחַ לָנוּ יהוה אֱלֹהֵינוּ שֶׁלֹּא תְהִי צָרָה וְיָגוֹן וַאֲנָחָה בְּיוֹם מְנוּחָתֵנוּ. וְהַרְאֵנוּ יהוה אֱלֹהֵינוּ בְּנֶחָמַת צִיּוֹן עִירֶךָ. וּבְבִנְיַן יְרוּשָׁלַיִם עִיר קָדְשֶׁךָ. כִּי אַתָּה הוּא בַּעַל הַיְשׁוּעוֹת וּבַעַל הַנֶּחָמוֹת:

On Shabbat add:

רְצֵה R'tseih v'hachalitseinu Adonai eloheinu b'mitsvotecha uv'mitsvat yom ha-sh'vi'i ha-shabbat ha-gadol v'ha-kadosh ha-zeh, ki yom zeh gadol v'kadosh hu l'fanecha, lishbot bo v'lanu'ach bo b'ahavah k'mitsvat r'tsonecha, uvirtson'cha hani'ach lanu Adonai eloheinu shello t'hi tsarah v'yagon va'anacha b'yom m'nuchateinu, v'har'einu Adonai eloheinu b'nechemat tsiyyon irecha, uv'vinyan y'rushalayim ir kodshecha, ki attah hu ba'al ha-y'shu'ot uva'al ha-nechamot.

On New Moon and festivals add:

אֱלֹהֵינוּ Our God and God of our ancestors, may Your regard and concern for us and our ancestors, for the time of our redemption, for Jerusalem the city of Your holiness, and for all Your people the family of Israel, be close to You and be pleasing to You. Favour us all with freedom and goodness, with grace, love and mercy, on this day of ...

On New Moon and festivals add:

אֱלֹהֵינוּ וֵאלֹהֵי אֲבוֹתֵינוּ. יַעֲלֶה וְיָבֹא וְיַגִּיעַ וְיֵרָאֶה וְיֵרָצֶה וְיִשָּׁמַע וְיִפָּקֵד וְיִזָּכֵר זִכְרוֹנֵנוּ וּפִקְדוֹנֵנוּ וְזִכְרוֹן אֲבוֹתֵינוּ וְזִכְרוֹן מָשִׁיחַ בֶּן דָּוִד עַבְדֶּךָ. וְזִכְרוֹן יְרוּשָׁלַיִם עִיר קָדְשֶׁךָ וְזִכְרוֹן כָּל־עַמְּךָ בֵּית יִשְׂרָאֵל לְפָנֶיךָ. לִפְלֵיטָה וּלְטוֹבָה לְחֵן וּלְחֶסֶד וּלְרַחֲמִים לְחַיִּים וּלְשָׁלוֹם בְּיוֹם...

On New Moon and festivals add:

אֱלֹהֵינוּ Eloheinu veilohei avoteinu ya'aleh v'yavo v'yagi'a v'yeira'eh v'yeiratseh v'yishama vayippakeid vayizzacheir zichroneinu ufikdoneinu, v'zichron avoteinu v'zichron mashi'ach ben david avdecha, v'zichron y'rushalayim ir kodshecha v'zichron kol amm'cha beit yisra'el l'fanecha lifleitah u'l'tovah l'chein ul'chesed u'l'rachamim, l'chayyim ul'shalom, b'yom...

473 THANKSGIVING AFTER MEALS

(On the New Moon)
the New Moon
(On Pesach)
the Festival of Unleavened Bread
(On Shavuot)
the Festival of Weeks
(On the New Year)
Remembrance
(On Sukkot)
the Festival of Tabernacles
(On Shemini Atseret)
the Festival of Completion

On the New Moon
רֹאשׁ הַחֹדֶשׁ הַזֶּה
On Pesach
חַג הַמַּצּוֹת הַזֶּה
On Shavuot
חַג הַשָּׁבֻעוֹת הַזֶּה
On the New Year
הַזִּכָּרוֹן הַזֶּה
On Sukkot
חַג הַסֻּכּוֹת הַזֶּה
On Shemini Atseret
הַשְּׁמִינִי חַג הָעֲצֶרֶת הַזֶּה

(On the New Moon) *Rosh ha-chodesh ha-zeh*
(On Pesach) *Chag ha-matsot ha-zeh*
(On Shavuot) *Chag ha-shavuot ha-zeh*
(On Rosh Hashanah) *ha-zikkaron ha-zeh*
(On Sukkot) *Chag ha-sukkot ha-zeh*
(On Shemini Atseret) *Hashmini chag ha-atseret ha-zeh*

זָכְרֵנוּ Our Living God,
remember us for good,   Amen
bring us Your blessing,   Amen
and save us
for a good life   Amen
Spare us and be kind to us according to Your promise of deliverance and mercy. Our eyes are turned towards You, for You are a Sovereign of mercy and compassion.

זָכְרֵנוּ יהוה אֱלֹהֵינוּ בּוֹ לְטוֹבָה אָמֵן
וּפָקְדֵנוּ בּוֹ לִבְרָכָה אָמֵן
וְהוֹשִׁיעֵנוּ בּוֹ לְחַיִּים טוֹבִים אָמֵן
וּבִדְבַר יְשׁוּעָה וְרַחֲמִים חוּס וְחָנֵּנוּ. כִּי אֵלֶיךָ עֵינֵינוּ. כִּי אֵל מֶלֶךְ חַנּוּן וְרַחוּם אָתָּה.

זָכְרֵנוּ *Zochreinu Adonai eloheinu bo l'tovah*   Amen
U'fokdeinu vo livracha   Amen
V'hoshi'einu vo l'chayyim tovim   Amen
Uvidvar y'shua'ah v'rachamim chus v'chonneinu ki eilecha eineinu ki eil melech channun v'rachum attah.

וּבְנֵה יְרוּשָׁלַיִם

עִיר הַקֹּדֶשׁ בִּמְהֵרָה בְיָמֵינוּ:
בָּרוּךְ אַתָּה יהוה.
בּוֹנֶה בְרַחֲמָיו יְרוּשָׁלָיִם. אָמֵן

וּבְנֵה And build Jerusalem,
as a city that can truly be called holy,
soon in our days.
Blessed are You God.
Help us build Jerusalem,
true to Your compassion. Amen.

וּבְנֵה Uv'neih y'rushalayim ir ha-kodesh bimheirah v'yameinu.
Baruch attah Adonai boneh v'rachamav y'rushalayim, Amen.

בָּרוּךְ אַתָּה יהוה אֱלֹהֵינוּ מֶלֶךְ הָעוֹלָם. הָאֵל אָבִינוּ מַלְכֵּנוּ אַדִּירֵנוּ בּוֹרְאֵנוּ גּוֹאֲלֵנוּ יוֹצְרֵנוּ קְדוֹשֵׁנוּ קְדוֹשׁ יַעֲקֹב. רוֹעֵנוּ רוֹעֵה יִשְׂרָאֵל. הַמֶּלֶךְ הַטּוֹב וְהַמֵּטִיב לַכֹּל שֶׁבְּכָל־יוֹם וָיוֹם הוּא הֵטִיב. הוּא מֵטִיב. הוּא יֵיטִיב לָנוּ: הוּא גְמָלָנוּ. הוּא גוֹמְלֵנוּ. הוּא יִגְמְלֵנוּ לָעַד. לְחֵן וּלְחֶסֶד וּלְרַחֲמִים וּלְרֶוַח הַצָּלָה וְהַצְלָחָה בְּרָכָה וִישׁוּעָה. נֶחָמָה פַּרְנָסָה וְכַלְכָּלָה. וְרַחֲמִים וְחַיִּים וְשָׁלוֹם וְכָל־טוֹב. וּמִכָּל־טוּב לְעוֹלָם אַל יְחַסְּרֵנוּ:

בָּרוּךְ Blessed are You, our Living God, Sovereign of the universe; the God who is our parent, our Sovereign, our source of power, our creator, our redeemer, our maker, our Holy One, the Holy One of Jacob; our shepherd, the shepherd of Israel, the good Sovereign who does good to all. Every day You have done good, do good and will do good for us. Generously You have provided for us, You do provide for us and always will provide for us grace, kindness, mercy and relief, deliverance and prosperity, blessing and salvation, consolation, provision and support, mercy, life, peace and all good. Let us never be in want of any goodness.

בָּרוּךְ Baruch attah Adonai eloheinu melech ha-olam, ha-eil avinu malkeinu adireinu bor'einu go'aleinu yots'reinu k'dosheinu k'dosh ya'akov, ro'einu ro'eih yisra'el, ha-melech ha-tov v'ha-meitiv lakol sheb'chol yom vayom hu heitiv hu meitiv hu yeitiv lanu. Hu g'malanu, hu gom'leinu, hu yigm'leinu la'ad, l'chein ul'chesed ul'rachamim ul'revach ha-tsalah v'hatslachah b'rachah vishu'ah, nechamah parnasah v'chalkalah, v'rachamim v'chayyim v'shalom v'chol tov, umikkol tuv l'olam al y'chass'reinu.

475 THANKSGIVING AFTER MEALS

הָרַחֲמָן The **All-merciful**, may You rule over us forever and ever.	הָרַחֲמָן הוּא יִמְלוֹךְ עָלֵינוּ לְעוֹלָם וָעֶד:
The **All-merciful**, may You be blessed in heaven and on earth.	הָרַחֲמָן. הוּא יִתְבָּרַךְ בַּשָּׁמַיִם וּבָאָרֶץ:
The **All-merciful**, may You be praised through all generations, glorified among us for eternity, and honoured among us forever.	הָרַחֲמָן. הוּא יִשְׁתַּבַּח לְדוֹר דּוֹרִים. וְיִתְפָּאַר בָּנוּ לָעַד וּלְנֵצַח נְצָחִים. וְיִתְהַדַּר בָּנוּ לָעַד וּלְעוֹלְמֵי עוֹלָמִים:
The **All-merciful**, may You give us an honourable livelihood.	הָרַחֲמָן. הוּא יְפַרְנְסֵנוּ בְּכָבוֹד:
The **All-merciful**, may You break off any yoke from our neck, and lead us with uprightness to our land.	הָרַחֲמָן. הוּא יִשְׁבּוֹר עֻלֵּנוּ מֵעַל צַוָּארֵנוּ. וְהוּא יוֹלִיכֵנוּ קוֹמְמִיּוּת לְאַרְצֵנוּ:
The **All-merciful**, may You send a plentiful blessing on this house, and on this table at which we have eaten.	הָרַחֲמָן. הוּא יִשְׁלַח לָנוּ בְּרָכָה מְרֻבָּה בַּבַּיִת הַזֶּה. וְעַל שֻׁלְחָן זֶה שֶׁאָכַלְנוּ עָלָיו:
The **All-merciful**, may You send us Elijah the prophet - may he be remembered for good! - who will bring us good news of salvation and comfort.	הָרַחֲמָן. הוּא יִשְׁלַח לָנוּ אֶת אֵלִיָּהוּ הַנָּבִיא זָכוּר לַטּוֹב. וִיבַשֶּׂר־לָנוּ בְּשׂוֹרוֹת טוֹבוֹת יְשׁוּעוֹת וְנֶחָמוֹת:

הָרַחֲמָן *Ha-rachaman, hu yimloch aleinu l'olam va'ed.*
Ha-rachaman, hu yitbarach ba-shamayim uva-arets.
Ha-rachaman, hu yishtabbach l'dor dorim,
v'yitpa'ar banu la'ad ul'neitsach n'tsachim,
v'yit-hadar banu la'ad ul'ol'mei olamim.
Ha-rachaman, hu y'farn'seinu b'chavod.
Ha-rachaman, hu yishbor ulleinu mei'al tsavareinu,
v'hu yolicheinu kom'miyut l'artseinu.
Ha-rachaman, hu yishlach lanu b'rachah m'rubbah ba-bayit ha-zeh,
v'al shulchan zeh she'achalnu alav.
Ha-rachaman, hu yishlach lanu et eliyahu ha-navi zachur la-tov,
vivasser lanu b'sorot tovot y'shu'ot v'nechamot.

הָרַחֲמָן. הוּא יְבָרֵךְ (אֶת־בַּעַל הַבַּיִת הַזֶּה. וְאֶת־בַּעֲלַת הַבַּיִת הַזֶּה. אוֹתָם וְאֶת־כָּל־אֲשֶׁר לָהֶם. וְ) אֶת־כָּל־הַמְסֻבִּין כָּאן. אוֹתָנוּ וְאֶת־כָּל־אֲשֶׁר לָנוּ. כְּמוֹ שֶׁנִּתְבָּרְכוּ אִמּוֹתֵינוּ שָׂרָה רִבְקָה רָחֵל וְלֵאָה. הֵיטִיב. טֹבַת. טוֹב. טוֹב. וּכְמוֹ שֶׁנִּתְבָּרְכוּ אֲבוֹתֵינוּ. אַבְרָהָם יִצְחָק וְיַעֲקֹב. בַּכֹּל. מִכֹּל. כֹּל. כֵּן יְבָרֵךְ אוֹתָנוּ כֻּלָּנוּ יַחַד. בִּבְרָכָה שְׁלֵמָה. וְנֹאמַר אָמֵן:

The **All-merciful**, may You bless (the master of this house, the mistress of this house, them and all that is theirs and) all who are seated here, us and all that is ours, as our mothers Sarah, Rebecca, Rachel and Leah were each of them blessed with 'good'[1] and as our fathers Abraham, Isaac and Jacob were each of them blessed with 'everything',[2] so may You bless all of us together with a perfect blessing. Amen.

Ha-rachaman, hu y'vareich [et ba'al ha-bayit ha-zeh, v'et ba'alat ha-bayit ha-zeh, otam v'et kol asher lahem, v'] et kol ha-m'subbin kan, otanu v'et kol asher lanu, k'mo shenitbar'chu immoteinu, sarah, rivkah, rachel v'le'ah heitiv tovat tov tov, uch'mo shenitbar'chu avoteinu, avraham, yitschak v'ya'akov, ba-kol, mikkol, kol, kein y'vareich otanu kullanu yachad, bivrachah sh'leimah, v'nomar amen.

בַּמָּרוֹם יְלַמְּדוּ עֲלֵיהֶם וְעָלֵינוּ זְכוּת שֶׁתְּהִי לְמִשְׁמֶרֶת שָׁלוֹם. וְנִשָּׂא בְרָכָה מֵאֵת יהוה וּצְדָקָה מֵאֱלֹהֵי יִשְׁעֵנוּ. וְנִמְצָא חֵן וְשֵׂכֶל טוֹב בְּעֵינֵי אֱלֹהִים וְאָדָם:

בַּמָּרוֹם On high may they plead for them and for us, so that we merit a lasting peace, and may gain a blessing from the Creator, and vindication from the God of our salvation. May we find grace and understanding in the sight of God and all people.

בַּמָּרוֹם *Ba-marom y'lamm'du aleihem v'aleinu z'chut shet'hi l'mishmeret shalom, v'nissa v'rachah mei'eit Adonai uts'dakah mei'elohei yisheinu, v'nimtsa chein v'seichel tov b'einei elohim v'adam.*

---

[1]. Gen 12:16; 24:16; 29:19; 30:20.   [2]. Gen 24:1; 27:33; 33:11.

477 THANKSGIVING AFTER MEALS

On Shabbat add:
The **All-merciful**, may You let us inherit a day that shall be wholly a Sabbath and rest in life everlasting.

On New Moon add:
The **All-merciful**, may You renew to us this month for goodness and blessing.

On festivals add:
The **All-merciful**, may You let us inherit a day that shall be wholly good.

On the New Year add:
The **All-merciful**, may You renew to us this year for goodness and blessing.

For Israel:
The **All-merciful**, may You bless the State of Israel and all who live there.

The **All-merciful**, may you create a bond of friendship between the descendants of Sarah and the descendants of Hagar.

On Shabbat add:
הָרַחֲמָן. הוּא יַנְחִילֵנוּ יוֹם שֶׁכֻּלּוֹ שַׁבָּת וּמְנוּחָה לְחַיֵּי הָעוֹלָמִים:

On New Moon add:
הָרַחֲמָן. הוּא יְחַדֵּשׁ עָלֵינוּ אֶת הַחֹדֶשׁ הַזֶּה לְטוֹבָה וְלִבְרָכָה:

On festivals add:
הָרַחֲמָן. הוּא יַנְחִילֵנוּ יוֹם שֶׁכֻּלּוֹ טוֹב:

On the New Year add:
הָרַחֲמָן. הוּא יְחַדֵּשׁ עָלֵינוּ אֶת הַשָּׁנָה הַזֹּאת לְטוֹבָה וְלִבְרָכָה:

For Israel:
הָרַחֲמָן. הוּא יְבָרֵךְ אֶת מְדִינַת יִשְׂרָאֵל וְאֶת־כָּל־יוֹשְׁבֶיהָ:

הָרַחֲמָן הוּא יִתֵּן אַחֲוָה בֵּין בְּנֵי שָׂרָה וּבֵין בְּנֵי הָגָר:

On Shabbat add:
Ha-rachaman, hu yanchileinu yom shekullo shabbat um'nuchah l'chayyei ha-olamim.

On New Moon add:
Ha-rachaman, hu y'chadeish aleinu et ha-chodesh ha-zeh l'tovah v'livrachah.

On festivals add:
Ha-rachaman, hu yanchileinu yom shekullo tov.

On the New Year add:
Ha-rachaman, hu y'chadeish aleinu et ha-shanah ha-zot l'tovah v'livrachah.

For Israel:
Ha-rachaman, hu y'vareich et m'dinat yisra'el v'et kol yosh'veha.

Ha-rachaman, hu yittein achavah bein b'nei sarah uvein b'nei hagar.

For people in need:
The **All-merciful**, may You bless all
those who are in distress
and bring them
out of darkness into the light.

*Personal petitions may be
added at this point:*
The **All-merciful** ...

הָרַחֲמָן The **All-merciful**, may You
make us worthy of the messianic days
and the life of the world to come.

For people in need:
הָרַחֲמָן. הוּא יְבָרֵךְ
אֶת־כָּל־בְּנֵי־אָדָם
הַנְּתוּנִים בַּצָּרָה
וְיוֹצִיאֵם מֵאֲפֵלָה לְאוֹרָה:

הָרַחֲמָן ...

הָרַחֲמָן. הוּא יְזַכֵּנוּ לִימוֹת
הַמָּשִׁיחַ וּלְחַיֵּי הָעוֹלָם הַבָּא:

*Ha-rachaman, hu y'varech et kol b'nei adam, han'tunim batsarah,
v'yotsi'eim mei'afeilah l'orah.*

Personal petitions may be added at this point:
Ha-rachaman...

הָרַחֲמָן *Ha-rachaman, hu y'zakkeinu limot ha-mashi'ach
ul'chayyei ha-olam ha-ba.*

On Shabbat and festivals:
מִגְדּוֹל God is a tower of strength to
the earthly king, (*On weekdays:* מַגְדִּיל
God gives great salvation to the
earthly king,) and shows love
and kindness to God's anointed,
to David and his seed forever.[1]

On Shabbat and festivals:
מִגְדּוֹל
(*On weekdays:* מַגְדִּיל)
יְשׁוּעוֹת מַלְכּוֹ.
וְעֹשֶׂה חֶסֶד לִמְשִׁיחוֹ
לְדָוִד וּלְזַרְעוֹ עַד עוֹלָם:

On Shabbat and festivals:
מִגְדּוֹל *Migdol*
On weekdays: מַגְדִּיל *Magdil*
y'shu'ot malko, v'oseh chesed limshicho l'david ul'zar'o ad olam.

---

[1] Two versions of this verse appear in the Bible, in Psalms 18:51 and II Samuel 22:51, the former begins with *magdil* and the latter with *migdol*. It is possible that an abbreviated note beside the Psalms verse read: 'in Second Samuel בש״ב we find "*migdol*"', but this abbreviation was misread to mean 'on Shabbat', בשבת, hence the variation between Shabbat and weekdays.

479 THANKSGIVING AFTER MEALS

עֹשֶׂה May the One
who makes peace in the highest
bring this peace
upon us and upon all Israel,
and upon all the world. Amen.

עֹשֶׂה שָׁלוֹם בִּמְרוֹמָיו.
הוּא יַעֲשֶׂה שָׁלוֹם.
עָלֵינוּ וְעַל כָּל־יִשְׂרָאֵל
וְעַל כָּל־הָעוֹלָם. וְאִמְרוּ אָמֵן:

*עֹשֶׂה Oseh shalom bimromav hu ya'aseh shalom
aleinu v'al kol ysra'el, v'al kol ha'olam, v'imru amen.*

One of the following concluding passages:

I

יְראוּ Be in awe of God, You who seek holiness, for those who fear God lack nothing. Young lions may be in want and hungry, but those who seek God lack no good thing. Give thanks to the Living God who is good, whose love is everlasting. You open up Your hand and satisfy the needs of all living beings. Blessed is the one who trusts in God and whose trust is God alone.

> I was young and have grown old and was never willing to see the innocent forsaken and their children begging for bread.

יהוה God give strength to Your people, and bless Your people with peace.[1]

יְראוּ אֶת יהוה קְדוֹשָׁיו כִּי אֵין
מַחְסוֹר לִירֵאָיו: כְּפִירִים רָשׁוּ
וְרָעֵבוּ וְדוֹרְשֵׁי יהוה לֹא יַחְסְרוּ
כָל־טוֹב: הוֹדוּ לַיהוה כִּי טוֹב כִּי
לְעוֹלָם חַסְדּוֹ: פּוֹתֵחַ אֶת־יָדֶךָ
וּמַשְׂבִּיעַ לְכָל־חַי רָצוֹן: בָּרוּךְ
הַגֶּבֶר אֲשֶׁר יִבְטַח בַּיהוה וְהָיָה
יהוה מִבְטַחוֹ:

נַעַר הָיִיתִי גַּם זָקַנְתִּי וְלֹא רָאִיתִי
צַדִּיק נֶעֱזָב וְזַרְעוֹ מְבַקֶּשׁ לָחֶם:

יהוה עֹז לְעַמּוֹ יִתֵּן יהוה יְבָרֵךְ
אֶת עַמּוֹ בַשָּׁלוֹם:

I

יְראוּ Y'ru et Adonai k'doshav ki ein machsor lirei'av. K'firim rashu v'ra'eivu v'dor'shei Adonai lo yachs'ru chol tov. Hodu ladonai ki tov ki l'olam chasdo. Potei'ach et yadecha umasbi'a l'chol chai ratson. Baruch ha-gever asher yivtach badonai v'hayah Adonai mivtacho.

(Na'ar hayiti gam zakanti v'lo ra'iti tsaddik ne'ezav v'zar'o m'vakkeish lachem.)

יהוה Adonai oz l'ammo yittein, Adonai y'vareich et ammo va-shalom.

---

[1] Ps 34:10-11, 118:1, 145:16, Jer 17:7, Ps 37:25, Ps 29:11.

נַעַר הָיִיתִי I was young
This Psalm verse literally states that 'I have never seen the righteous (or innocent) forsaken', an affirmation of faith in God's ultimate providence. Nevertheless there is a custom to recite it quietly lest it offend anyone present who has suffered, and after the *Shoah* and the death of millions of innocents, it can no longer be said lightly or naively. We have retained it in smaller print to remind us that it is a problematic sentiment and have translated it as an assertion of our responsibility not to be bystanders when the innocent suffer.

II

אָכַלְנוּ We have eaten and been satisfied. May we not turn aside from the needs of others, nor ignore their cry for food. Open our eyes and our hearts and our hands so that we may share Your gifts, and help to remove hunger and want from our world.

יהוה God give strength to Your people, and bless Your people with peace.

אָכַלְנוּ וְשָׂבָעְנוּ. אַל־נָא נִתְעַלֵּם מִצָּרְכֵי־רֵעֵנוּ וְאַל־תֵּאָטַמְנָה אָזְנֵינוּ מִצַּעֲקָתָם לְמָזוֹן: פְּקַח אֶת־עֵינֵינוּ וּפְתַח אֶת־לְבָבֵנוּ וְאֶת־יָדֵינוּ וְנִתְחַלְּקָה בְּמַתְּנוֹתֶיךָ לְמַעַן חִסּוּל־הָרָעָב וְהַמַּחְסוֹר מֵעוֹלָמֵנוּ:

יהוה עֹז לְעַמּוֹ יִתֵּן
יהוה יְבָרֵךְ אֶת עַמּוֹ בַשָּׁלוֹם:

II

אָכַלְנוּ *Achalnu v'sava'nu, al na nit'alleim mitsorchei rei'einu v'al tei'atamnah ozneinu mitsa'akatam l'mazon. P'kach eineinu uf'tach l'vaveinu v'yadeinu v'nitchall'kah b'matnotecha l'ma'an chissul ha-ra'av v'ha-machsor mei'olameinu.*

יהוה *Adonai oz l'ammo yittein, Adonai y'vareich et ammo va-shalom.*

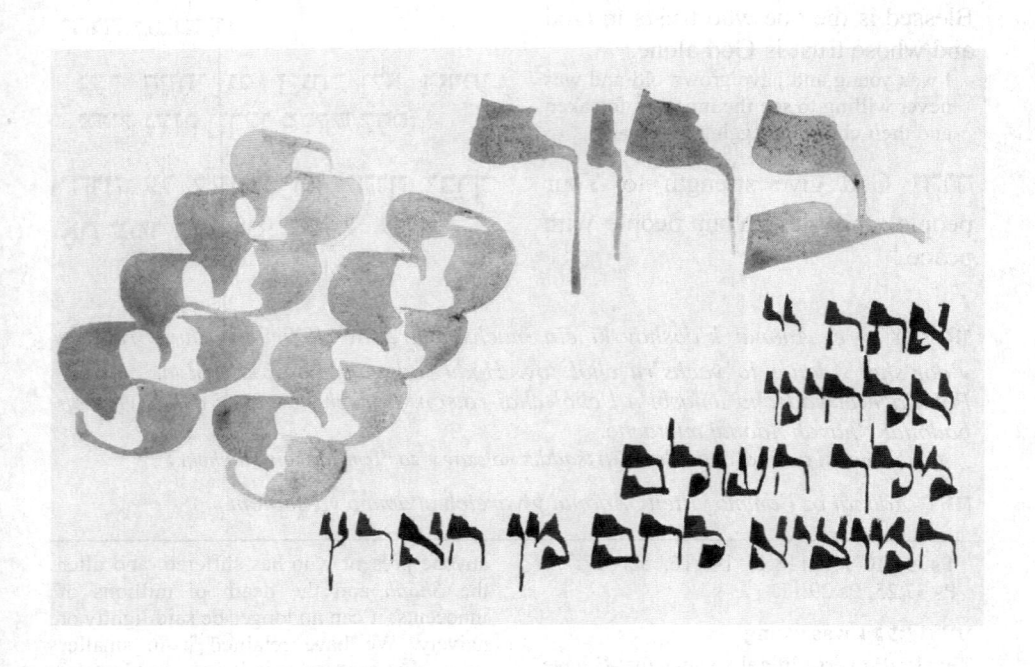

481 THANKSGIVING AFTER MEALS

גרסאות קצרות לברכת המזון
SHORTER FORMS OF THANKSGIVING AFTER MEALS

I

מַה **May what we have eaten satisfy us,**
what we have drunk refresh us,
and what we have left be for a blessing.
For it is written:
'So he set it before them,
and they ate and some was left over,
as the Eternal had said.'[1]
You are blessed by the Eternal,
maker of heaven and earth.
Blessed is the one
who trusts in the Eternal,
putting confidence in God.
God give strength to Your people,
and bless Your people with peace.

מַה שֶּׁאָכַלְנוּ יִהְיֶה לְשָׂבְעָה.
וּמַה שֶּׁשָּׁתִינוּ יִהְיֶה לְרְוָיָה.
וּמַה שֶּׁהוֹתַרְנוּ יִהְיֶה לִבְרָכָה.
כְּדִכְתִיב. וַיִּתֵּן לִפְנֵיהֶם:
וַיֹּאכְלוּ וַיּוֹתִרוּ כִּדְבַר יהוה:
בְּרוּכִים אַתֶּם לַיהוה.
עֹשֵׂה שָׁמַיִם וָאָרֶץ:
בָּרוּךְ הַגֶּבֶר
אֲשֶׁר יִבְטַח בַּיהוה.
וְהָיָה יהוה מִבְטַחוֹ:
יהוה עֹז לְעַמּוֹ יִתֵּן
יהוה יְבָרֵךְ אֶת עַמּוֹ בַשָּׁלוֹם:

I

מַה *Mah she'achalnu yihyeh l'sov'ah, umah sheshatinu yihyeh lirvayah, umah shehotarnu yihyeh livrachah, k'dichtiv, vayittein lifneihem, vayoch'lu vayotiru kidvar Adonai. B'ruchim attem ladonai, oseih shamayim va'arets. Baruch ha-gever asher yivtach badonai v'hayah Adonai mivtacho. Adonai oz l'ammo yittein, Adonai y'vareich et ammo va-shalom.*

II

בְּרִיךְ **Blessed be the Merciful One,**
Sovereign of the universe,
the owner of this bread.[2]

בְּרִיךְ רַחֲמָנָא מַלְכָּא דְעָלְמָא
מָרֵיהּ דְּהַאי פִּיתָּא:

II

בְּרִיךְ *B'rich rachamana malka d'alma mareih d'hai pitta.*

[1.] II Kings 4:44.   [2] *Berachot* 40b.

III

בָּרוּךְ **Blessed** are You, our Living God, Sovereign of the universe. You feed the whole world through Your goodness, with grace, kindness and mercy. You make it possible for all to have food, for Your love is forever. Through Your great goodness food has never failed us, and may we never fail to share food for the sake of Your great reputation; for You feed and provide for all and do good to all, and make us the agents through whom all Your creatures may have food. Blessed are You God, providing enough food for all.

בָּרוּךְ אַתָּה יהוה אֱלֹהֵינוּ מֶלֶךְ הָעוֹלָם. הַזָּן אֶת־הָעוֹלָם כֻּלּוֹ בְּטוּבוֹ בְּחֵן בְּחֶסֶד וּבְרַחֲמִים. הוּא נוֹתֵן לֶחֶם לְכָל־בָּשָׂר. כִּי לְעוֹלָם חַסְדּוֹ: וּבְטוּבוֹ הַגָּדוֹל תָּמִיד לֹא־חָסַר לָנוּ. וְאַל יֶחְסַר־לָנוּ מָזוֹן לְעוֹלָם וָעֶד בַּעֲבוּר שְׁמוֹ הַגָּדוֹל. כִּי הוּא זָן וּמְפַרְנֵס לַכֹּל וּמֵטִיב לַכֹּל וּמֵכִין מָזוֹן לְכָל־בְּרִיּוֹתָיו אֲשֶׁר בָּרָא: בָּרוּךְ אַתָּה יהוה. הַזָּן אֶת הַכֹּל:

III

בָּרוּךְ *Baruch attah Adonai eloheinu melech ha-olam, ha-zan et ha-olam kullo b'tuvo b'chein b'chesed uv'rachamim, hu notein lechem l'chol basar ki l'olam chasdo. Uv'tuvo ha-gadol tamid lo chasar lanu, v'al yechsar lanu mazon l'olam va'ed ba'avur sh'mo ha-gadol, ki hu zan um'farneis la-kol umeitiv la-kol umeichin mazon l'chol b'ri'otav asher bara. Baruch attah Adonai ha-zan et ha-kol.*

נוֹדֶה **We thank You**, our Living God, for giving our ancestors the heritage of a desirable, good and ample land, covenant and Torah, and food to satisfy, as it is written in the Torah: 'And you shall eat and be satisfied and bless the Eternal your God for the good land which God has given you'. Blessed are You God, for the land and for the food.

נוֹדֶה לְךָ יהוה אֱלֹהֵינוּ עַל שֶׁהִנְחַלְתָּ לַאֲבוֹתֵינוּ אֶרֶץ חֶמְדָּה טוֹבָה וּרְחָבָה. בְּרִית וְתוֹרָה. וְלֶחֶם לְשׂוֹבַע. כַּכָּתוּב. וְאָכַלְתָּ וְשָׂבָעְתָּ וּבֵרַכְתָּ אֶת־יהוה אֱלֹהֶיךָ עַל־הָאָרֶץ הַטֹּבָה אֲשֶׁר נָתַן־לָךְ. בָּרוּךְ אַתָּה יהוה. עַל־הָאָרֶץ וְעַל־הַמָּזוֹן:

נוֹדֶה *Nodeh l'cha Adonai eloheinu al shehinchalta la'avoteinu erets chemdah tovah ur'chavah, b'rit v'torah, v'lechem l'sova, ka-katuv, v'achalta v'sava'ta uveirachta et Adonai elohecha al ha-arets ha-tovah asher natan lach. Baruch attah Adonai, al ha-arets v'al ha-mazon.*

THANKSGIVING AFTER MEALS

רַחֵם **Our Living God, be merciful** to Israel Your people, to Jerusalem Your city, and to Zion where Your glory appeared. And build Jerusalem, as a city that can truly be called holy, soon in our days. Blessed are You God. Help us build Jerusalem, true to Your compassion. Amen.

רַחֵם יהוה אֱלֹהֵינוּ עַל־יִשְׂרָאֵל עַמֶּךָ. וְעַל יְרוּשָׁלַיִם עִירֶךָ. וְעַל צִיּוֹן מִשְׁכַּן כְּבוֹדֶךָ. וּבְנֵה יְרוּשָׁלַיִם עִיר הַקֹּדֶשׁ בִּמְהֵרָה בְיָמֵינוּ: בָּרוּךְ אַתָּה יהוה. בּוֹנֵה בְרַחֲמָיו יְרוּשָׁלָיִם. אָמֵן

רַחֵם *Racheim Adonai eloheinu al yisra'el ammecha, v'al y'rushalayim irecha, v'al tsiyyon mishkan k'vodecha, uv'neih y'rushalayim ir ha-kodesh bimheirah v'yameinu. Baruch attah Adonai boneh v'rachamav y'rushalayim, amen.*

בָּרוּךְ **Blessed** are You, our Living God, Sovereign of the universe; the good Sovereign who does good to all. Every day You have done good, do good and will do good for us.

בָּרוּךְ אַתָּה יהוה אֱלֹהֵינוּ מֶלֶךְ הָעוֹלָם. הַמֶּלֶךְ הַטּוֹב וְהַמֵּטִיב לַכֹּל שֶׁבְּכָל־יוֹם וָיוֹם הוּא הֵטִיב. הוּא מֵטִיב. הוּא יֵיטִיב לָנוּ:

בָּרוּךְ *Baruch attah Adonai eloheinu melech ha-olam, ha-melech ha-tov v'ha-meitiv la-kol sheb'chol yom vayom hu heitiv hu meitiv hu yeitiv lanu.*

הָרַחֲמָן **The All-merciful**, may You bless all who are seated here, us and all that is ours.

הָרַחֲמָן. הוּא יְבָרֵךְ אֶת־כָּל־הַמְסֻבִּין כָּאן.

הָרַחֲמָן **The All-merciful**, may You make us worthy of the messianic days and the life of the world to come.

הָרַחֲמָן. הוּא יְזַכֵּנוּ לִימוֹת הַמָּשִׁיחַ וּלְחַיֵּי הָעוֹלָם הַבָּא:

הָרַחֲמָן *Ha-rachaman, hu y'vareich et kol ha-m'subbin kan.*

הָרַחֲמָן *Ha-rachaman, hu y'zakkeinu limot ha-mashi'ach ul'chayei ha-olam ha-ba.*

ברכת המזון 484

On Shabbat and festivals:
מִגְדּוֹל God is a tower of strength to the earthly king, (*On weekdays:* God gives great salvation to the earthly king,) and shows love and kindness to God's anointed, to David and his seed forever.

On Shabbat and festivals:
מִגְדּוֹל
(*On weekdays:* מַגְדִּיל)
יְשׁוּעוֹת מַלְכּוֹ.
וְעֹשֶׂה חֶסֶד לִמְשִׁיחוֹ לְדָוִד
וּלְזַרְעוֹ עַד עוֹלָם:

On Shabbat and festivals:
מִגְדּוֹל Migdol
On weekdays: מַגְדִּיל Magdil
y'shu'ot malko, v'oseh chesed limshicho l'david ul'zar'o ad olam.

עֹשֶׂה May the One who makes peace in the highest bring this peace upon us and upon all Israel, and upon all the world. Amen.

עֹשֶׂה שָׁלוֹם בִּמְרוֹמָיו.
הוּא יַעֲשֶׂה שָׁלוֹם
עָלֵינוּ וְעַל כָּל־יִשְׂרָאֵל
וְעַל כָּל־הָעוֹלָם. וְאִמְרוּ אָמֵן:

עֹשֶׂה Oseh shalom bimromav hu ya'aseh shalom
aleinu v'al kol ysra'el, v'al kol ha'olam, v'imru amen.

יהוה God give strength to Your people, and bless Your people with peace.

יהוה עֹז לְעַמּוֹ יִתֵּן
יהוה יְבָרֵךְ אֶת עַמּוֹ בַשָּׁלוֹם:

יהוה Adonai oz l'ammo yittein, Adonai y'vareich et ammo va-shalom.

ברכת המזון בשירים
THANKSGIVING AFTER MEALS AS SONGS

I Bendigamos

Bendigamos al Altisimo,
al Senyor que nos crió;
démosle agradecimiento
por los bienes que nos dió.

Alabado sea su Santo Nombre
porque siempre nos apiadó;
load al Senyor que es bueno,
que para siempre su merced.

Bendigamos al Altisimo
por su Ley primeramente,
que liga a nuestra raza
con el cielo continuamente.

Bendigamos al Altisimo
por el pan segundamente,
y también por los manjares
que comimos juntamente.

Pues comimos alegremente,
su merced nunca nos faltó.
Load al Senyor que es bueno,
que para siempre su merced.

Bendita sea la casa esta,
el hogar de su presencia,
donde guardamos su fiesta
con alegria y permanencia.

Alabado sea su Santo Nombre
porque siempre nos apiadó.
Hodu ladonai ki tov
ki l'olam hasdo.

Let us bless the Most High
the Lord who has created us;
let us offer praises
for the good that we are given.

Exalted be the Holy Name
who always is our help;
praise the Lord who is good,
whose mercy endures forever.

Let us bless the Most High,
primarily for the Torah
that links our people
perpetually with heaven.

Let us bless the Most High,
secondarily for this bread
and for all these foods
that we eat together.

Therefore let us eat happily,
lacking nothing in Your mercy.
Praise the Lord who is good,
whose mercy endures forever.

Blessed be this house,
the hearth of Your presence,
where we keep the festivals
happily and faithfully.

Exalted be the Holy Name
who is ever our help.
Praise the Lord who is good
whose mercy endures forever.

II

צוּר Rock by whose gift we eat,
bless God, my faithful ones,
for we have been satisfied
and food is left over,
as was the word of God.

צוּר מִשֶּׁלּוֹ אָכַלְנוּ.
בָּרְכוּ אֱמוּנַי.
שָׂבַעְנוּ וְהוֹתַרְנוּ.
כִּדְבַר יהוה:

God feeds all the world,
our shepherd, our father.
We have eaten Your bread,
we have drunk of Your wine,
now therefore we thank You
and praise with our mouths;
we say and we sing
none is holy as God.

הַזָּן אֶת־עוֹלָמוֹ.
רוֹעֵנוּ אָבִינוּ.
אָכַלְנוּ אֶת־לַחְמוֹ.
וְיֵינוֹ שָׁתִינוּ.
עַל־כֵּן נוֹדֶה לִשְׁמוֹ.
וּנְהַלְלוֹ בְּפִינוּ.
אָמַרְנוּ וְעָנִינוּ
אֵין־קָדוֹשׁ כַּיהוה:

Rock by whose gift we eat,
bless God, my faithful ones,
for we have been satisfied
and food is left over,
as was the word of God.

צוּר מִשֶּׁלּוֹ אָכַלְנוּ.
בָּרְכוּ אֱמוּנַי.
שָׂבַעְנוּ וְהוֹתַרְנוּ.
כִּדְבַר יהוה:

With song and thanksgiving
let us now bless our God
for the plentiful land
which our ancestors received.
God has given us food
for our bodies and souls.
God's mercy protects us,
ever true is our God.

בְּשִׁיר וְקוֹל תּוֹדָה.
נְבָרֵךְ אֱלֹהֵינוּ.
עַל אֶרֶץ חֶמְדָּה.
שֶׁהִנְחִיל לַאֲבוֹתֵינוּ.
מָזוֹן וְצֵידָה.
הִשְׂבִּיעַ לְנַפְשֵׁנוּ.
חַסְדּוֹ גָּבַר עָלֵינוּ.
וֶאֱמֶת יהוה:

Rock by whose gift we eat,
bless God, my faithful ones,
for we have been satisfied
and food is left over,
as was the word of God.

צוּר מִשֶּׁלּוֹ אָכַלְנוּ.
בָּרְכוּ אֱמוּנַי.
שָׂבַעְנוּ וְהוֹתַרְנוּ.
כִּדְבַר יהוה:

487 THANKSGIVING AFTER MEALS

צוּר *Tsur mishello achalnu, bar'chu emunai, sava'nu v'hotarnu, kidvar Adonai.*

Ha-zan et olamo, ro'einu avinu, achalnu et lachmo, v'yeino shatinu, al kein nodeh lishmo, un'hal'lo b'finu, amarnu v'aninu ein kadosh kadonai.

Tsur mishello achalnu, bar'chu emunai, sava'nu v'hotarnu, kidvar Adonai.

B'shir v'kol todah, n'vareich eloheinu, al erets chemdah, shehinchil la'avoteinu, mazon v'tseidah, hisbi'a l'nafsheinu, chasdo gavar aleinu, ve'emet Adonai.

Tsur mishello achalnu, bar'chu emunai, sava'nu v'hotarnu, kidvar Adonai.

הברכות אחרי סעודת חתונה
THE BLESSINGS AFTER A WEDDING MEAL

Following **Shir Ha-ma'alot**, *the following form is used:*

The leader	*The leader*
חֲבֵרַי Friends, let us bless.	חֲבֵרַי נְבָרֵךְ:
All reply	*All reply*
יְהִי Blessed be the name of the Creator from now and forever.	יְהִי שֵׁם יהוה מְבֹרָךְ מֵעַתָּה וְעַד עוֹלָם:
The leader	*The leader*
יְהִי Blessed be the name of the Creator from now and forever.	יְהִי שֵׁם יהוה מְבֹרָךְ מֵעַתָּה וְעַד עוֹלָם:
דְּוַי Sweep away sadness and anger. Then even the silent will burst out in song. Guide us in the paths of righteousness. Accept the blessing of the descendants of Yeshurun.[1]	דְּוַי הָסֵר וְגַם חָרוֹן. וְאָז אִלֵּם בְּשִׁיר יָרוֹן. נְחֵנוּ בְּמַעְגְּלֵי צֶדֶק. שְׁעֵה בִּרְכַּת בְּנֵי יְשֻׁרוּן:

Dunash ben Labrat

<<<

The leader:
חֲבֵרַי *Chaveirai n'vareich.*

All reply:
יְהִי *Y'hi sheim Adonai m'vorach mei'attah v'ad olam.*

The leader:
יְהִי *Y'hi sheim Adonai m'vorach mei'attah v'ad olam.*
דְּוַי *D'vai haseir v'gam charon, v'az illeim b'shir yaron, N'cheinu b'ma'g'lei tsedek, sh'eih birkat b'nei Yeshurun.*

---

[1] Yeshurun is a poetic name for Israel, 'the upright one' (Deut 13:15, 33:5, Isa 44:2).

488 ברכת המזון

בִּרְשׁוּת With your permission, friends,
let us bless our God in whose abode
is joy and whose food we have eaten.

בִּרְשׁוּת חֲבֵרַי נְבָרֵךְ אֱלֹהֵינוּ
שֶׁהַשִּׂמְחָה בִּמְעוֹנוֹ.
וְשֶׁאָכַלְנוּ מִשֶּׁלּוֹ:

All reply
בָּרוּךְ Blessed is our God
in whose abode is joy
and whose food
we have eaten.

All reply
בָּרוּךְ אֱלֹהֵינוּ שֶׁהַשִּׂמְחָה
בִּמְעוֹנוֹ.
וְשֶׁאָכַלְנוּ מִשֶּׁלּוֹ
וּבְטוּבוֹ חָיִינוּ:

The leader
בָּרוּךְ Blessed is our God
in whose abode is joy
and whose food
we have eaten.
Blessed be God,
and blessed be God's name.

The leader
בָּרוּךְ אֱלֹהֵינוּ
שֶׁהַשִּׂמְחָה בִּמְעוֹנוֹ.
וְשֶׁאָכַלְנוּ מִשֶּׁלּוֹ
וּבְטוּבוֹ חָיִינוּ:
בָּרוּךְ הוּא וּבָרוּךְ שְׁמוֹ:

בִּרְשׁוּת *Birshut chaveirai n'vareich eloheinu sheha-simchah vim'ono,*
v'she'achalnu mishello.

All reply:
בָּרוּךְ *Baruch eloheinu sheha-simchah vim'ono,*
v'she'achalnu mishello uv'tuvo chayinu.

The leader:
בָּרוּךְ *Baruch eloheinu sheha-simchah vim'ono,*
v'she'achalnu mishello uv'tuvo chayinu.
Baruch hu uvaruch sh'mo.

Continue with Thanksgiving After Meals page 467.

At the conclusion a cup of wine is poured
and the Seven Blessings are recited (page 358)
though the first blessing (borei p'ri ha-gafen) is recited last.

Study Anthology

TABLE OF CONTENTS

Transliterations within passages taken from other sources appear as they do in the original.

THE *SIDDUR*

The History and Structure of the Daily Service	494
The Journey Through the Palace - A Meditation on the Structure of the Liturgy	494
Opening Prayers	494
Birchot Ha-Shachar, the Morning Blessings	495
Pesukei D'zimra, Verses of Song	495
The *Sh'ma* and its Blessings	495
The *Amidah*	497
The Torah Service	498
Musaf, Additional Service for Shabbat	499
Concluding Prayers	500
Blessing	502
On Entering the Synagogue - *Mah Tovu*	502

SHABBAT EVENING SERVICE

Song of Songs	504
L'cha Dodi	504
L'cha Dodi - Traditions	505
L'cha Dodi - Commentary	505
Six Psalms	506
Psalm 95	506
Psalm 96	507
Ahavat Olam - God's Love for Israel	507
Ma'ariv Aravim - Commentary	508

<<<

SHABBAT MORNING SERVICE

Baruch She'amar	508
Bar'chu	508
El Adon	509
The Opening of the *Sh'ma*	509
The Second Paragraph of the *Sh'ma*	510
Emet V'emunah	510
Amidah - Insertions in the Second Blessing	511
Amidah - Second Blessing - *G'vurot*	512
Amidah - Second Blessing - *Matsmi'ach y'shu'ah.*	512
Amidah - Seventeenth Blessing - *R'tseih*	512
Amidah - Eighteenth Blessing - *Modim*	513
Amidah - Eighteenth Blessing - *Al nissecha sheb'chol yom immanu*	513
The Reading from the Torah	514
The Torah Blessings	515
Before the Reading	515
After the Reading	515
	515
Closing Prayers	
Aleinu	515
The *Kaddish* - History, forms and practice	515
The *Kaddish* - Commentary	516
Adon Olam	517

LIFE'S JOURNEY

Life's Journey	518
Laws of Life	519
On Reality	520
On Ownership	520
The Golden Mean	520
Changes	521
Responsibility	522
Relationships	522
On Judging Others	523
On Earning Love	524
Parents and Children	524
Children and Prayer	526
Bar/Bat Mitsvah	526
Mikveh	526
The Wedding	527

On Marriage	529
On the Death of an Infant	530
On Loss	531
On Bereavement	532
On Suffering	533
On Survival	535
On Hope	536
On Illness	536
On Recovery	538
On Aging	539
Talking to My Grandfather	540
On Dying	542
A Meditation on Death	543
Yahrzeit	544
Relapse 28 May 1998	546
Only Us	547

SOCIETY AND COMMUNITY

The Mysteries of Life	548
Love of Neighbour	548
Visiting the Sick - *Bikkur Cholim*	549
Freedom of Speech	550
On Prejudice	550
Hatred and Forgiveness	551
Community	552
Abuse of Religion	553
Social Justice	553
Social Responsibility	554
Ts'dakah	556
The Challenge of Civilisation	556
Heart and Brain	557
Good and Evil	557
Environment	558
On Hunting	558
On Pluralism	559
On Interfaith Dialogue	559
Hospitality	561
The Jewish People	561
The Jewish People - Who Belongs?	562
Power and Powerlessness	564

<<<

Israel	565
Jerusalem	566
In a Time of War	566
A Meditation for *Yom Ha-Zikaron*	568
On Peace	569

THE LIFE OF THE SPIRIT

God	572
Messiah	573
Images of God	574
Study	575
Torah	575
Halachah and *Aggadah*	577
Truth	578
Known and Unknown	578
Talmud Study	578
Ritual Life	579
The World of Shabbat	579
Shabbat Peace and Harmony	580
Business Permitted on Shabbat	581
Prayer	581
Why Prayer	584
Prayer and Healing	585
The *Siddur*	585
Sh'liach Tsibbur - Service Leader	586
Public Worship	586
Honesty in Prayer	587
The Journey of Prayer	587
Custom - *Minhag*	589
Tradition and Change	589
The Religious Quest	590
The Religious Challenge	590
The Imitation of God	590
A Meditation on Psalm 23	592
Escape	593
Fear and Awe of God	593
Daily Sins	593
On Faith	594
Faithfulness	594
The Limits of Faith	595
Faith and Reality	596
The Fanatic	597
Silence	597

PASSAGES FOR RESPONSIVE READING, STUDY OR MEDITATION

On the Laws of Life	598
On the Challenges of Life	599
On God's Promises for the Future	600
On the Messianic Age	601
On Our Duties	602
On Our Responsibilities	603
On the Individual	604
On the Family	605
On the Community	606
On Civilisation	607
On God and Israel	608

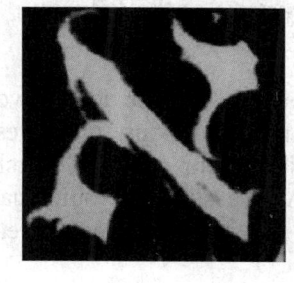

THE *SIDDUR*

The History and Structure of the Daily Service

The core of the daily morning service consists of two elements that were originally independent of one another, but since the third century CE are inextricably bound together. The first element is the *Sh'ma*, 'Hear O Israel', (Deuteronomy 6:4-9, 11:13-21; Numbers 15:37-41) and the blessings (*berachot*) that bracket it, that describe in poetic language the belief in Creation, Revelation and Redemption. The second element is the main prayer of the Synagogue, called the 'Eighteen Benedictions' because it consisted originally of eighteen blessings ... Parts of it go back to the time of the Jerusalem temple. The sequence of the eighteen blessings and their content, though not the specific wording, were fixed under the aegis of Rabban Gamaliel II at the end of the first and beginning of the second century CE. The wording remained fluid for a long time until two versions crystallised out, one Palestinian and one Babylonian. All today's liturgies follow the Babylonian version of the 'eighteen benedictions' (actually nineteen due to a later addition, though the name has been retained). The first three and the last three provide the frame for the main prayer on Shabbat and Festivals. However, on those days the thirteen middle blessings drop out and are replaced by a single one, the 'sanctification of the day'. (On the New Year's Day in the *Musaf* service [i.e. the 'additional' service] two further blessings are added.) The evening service is like the morning one, including the *Sh'ma* with its blessings and the Eighteen Benedictions, though the blessings around the *Sh'ma* have a different wording, for example focusing on the sunset. At a later period the 'Call to Prayer' (Bless the Living God whom we are called to bless!) was added.

Jakob J. Petuchowski

The Journey through the Palace
- A Meditation on the Structure of the Liturgy

Opening Prayers

We have crossed a threshold. Outside is the world with its rhythms and cadences, commonplaces and disruptions, pressures and concerns. We carry them with us into this building, our place of worship, but hope to see them here in a different light. As we shed our outer garments some part of that outer world recedes. New and familiar faces greet us, other possibilities of sharing and learning.

These moments are important for what is to follow. Are we greeted or left alone? Who conducts us or accompanies us through the next open door? Are we welcome here, or a stranger, or one who welcomes others? Who is at home in this place and who is a guest, who guards it and who invites?

We cross another threshold, from the entrance into the sanctuary. We are carried along by each other's energy, tales briefly told, greetings and glances exchanged. We find our place, familiar or unfamiliar, and wrap ourselves in the stillness we will need for the outer and the inner journey before us. Almost unnoticed, and without words, our prayer has begun.

Birchot Ha-Shachar, the Morning Blessings

Time stops, loops back upon itself and we return to the beginning of the day, or start it anew. We will read the 'morning blessings'.

'Where does the soul go when we sleep?' asked the rabbis. Sleep is one sixtieth part of death, they taught. The soul departs but returns each morning and as we awake, we are truly reborn. The first blessings of the day, to be said as we arise from our bed, are now transferred to the synagogue. So we experience and celebrate our physical and spiritual reawakening. We remind ourselves of the wonder of the endless possibilities of each new beginning, and the mystery of who we are. We live!

Pesukei D'zimra, Verses of Song

We enter the sanctuary alone. We are joined by others, but are not yet a community. We look around for those we know as we ease our way into the service. We discover our voices, recognise melodies, familiar and unfamiliar sounds. We begin to focus together on what lies ahead.

Song opens channels to those about us. Praise of God, in all its diversity, is the unifying theme. Through words with or without music, or music with or without words, we make a first, tentative sharing with one another. We discover again the familiar and feel our way into the language and routine, the forms, traditional and new, that will sustain us on the journey ahead. Yet still as individuals, still tentative, we prepare for the encounter before us with God, together.

The *Sh'ma* and its blessings

We are a delegation of the Jewish people visiting the palace of the Sovereign. Before the gate we stand to attention, face the same direction, smarten up, wait in anticipation.

Our delegated representative announces our presence and calls us to order: 'Bless the One whom we are called to bless.'

For the first time as a community, as Israel, we respond: 'Blessed is the Living God, whom we are called to bless forever and ever.'

We enter the first chamber of the Palace, the blessing called *yotzeir or*, 'Who forms light'.

We share this reception area with others. As we look around we experience the light of creation.

The walls dazzle, as stars and planets whirl about us. A change of perspective and the earth lies before us, lush, green and white and blue. Look closer and we see it swarming with every form of life. Step back and we are aware that we are not alone in this chamber. Other delegations of Jews are here in all their diversity, each intent, each acknowledging, however reluctantly, the presence of the others. But looking further the chamber becomes ever more crowded, people of every race and colour, of every known faith and every private belief. For this chamber is the first blessing that will lead us to the *Sh'ma*, the blessing that celebrates creation in all its beauty, diversity and energy. It evokes light and darkness, peace but also all that is not peace.

Though overwhelmed at first by this richness, we are not merely tourists in God's world. Impatiently we move on. Our visit to the palace of the Sovereign has purpose. Through the endlessly changing movement about us we glimpse our next goal, a small door marked simply with our name, Israel. Other doors mark the names of every other community that is assembled here, but this door is for us alone. Our eyes meet. We are ready to cross the next threshold, from this world we share with all to the private arena of our own particular task. For our ties to the Sovereign are ancient and special. We are drawn as petitioners, but also as lover and beloved, towards the Presence. We pass through the door into the second chamber, the second blessing, *Ahavah Rabbah*, 'with deep love', God's love for Israel.

This smaller room accommodates itself to our number. Here we prepare ourselves for the encounter ahead. We remember the love that has bound us to God over time: a patient love, tested in fire, renewed across generations, at once fragile and demanding. This love that comes to us is passionate, jealous, burning, yearning for our love in return. Yet we have been faithful, after our own restless fashion. Our presence now, however tentative and uncertain, is the proof. We, this generation, this community, this small sample of the Jewish people, will now affirm with heart, soul and might that God is One.

Up to this moment we have talked or chanted or sung together in unison or in harmony. But before we can encounter the Sovereign one more action is needed to make us, for however brief a moment, into a true community. Now is the time to speak to one another, talking to the Israel beside us and to the Israel within us. Just as God is One, so are we 'one people on earth'. One, not in conformity, but one despite our diversity. For we are not puppets but people, each of us unique, unique in who we are and in what we may become together.

So in the privacy of this chamber we recite the *Sh'ma*, affirm to one another that together we take on the yoke of the reign of God and the yoke of the covenant and all it demands of us.

The door at the end of the room opens into the corridor that leads to the throne room.

We anticipate the moment to come and need further reassurance, for who can know what will happen when we stand before the Sovereign? So this first blessing after the paragraphs of the *Sh'ma, emet v'yatziv*, 'true is Your word forever', is there to reassure us. Has not God helped and supported us in the past? Remember our birth as a people, passing through the waters that divided, redeeming us from slavery and separating us from the enemy behind and their bitter fate. It is as if the walls depict those moments and others, reminding us how far we have come, leading us on to the final door, the last threshold before the Presence we now must encounter.

The *Amidah*

The door opens directly into the throne room, and no words may interrupt our passage. We have penetrated to the deepest chamber of the palace and stand before our God. From now on all that we say will be the collective word of all Israel, the 'we' who address God, united with generations past and present. Yet for just one instant our individuality asserts itself. As if under our breath, we give our private assent to the words we are about to say. If God will open *my* lips, then *my* mouth can indeed speak God's praises.

The moment passes and the protocol of the court takes over, to see us through the first awkward moments till we gain the confidence to speak our own words. Standing in respect, bowing as appropriate, we introduce ourselves. We are the extended family of Abraham and his descendants. We have known You through many names and titles, 'great, mighty and revered', 'God beyond'. Ambassadors of the people of Israel, we present to You our credentials.

As is required in the presence of a Sovereign, we next address God's power of life and death over us. Yet You are a generous ruler, for You sustain all the living, support those who fall and heal those who are sick.

But this does not even begin to describe Your power or the seemingly unbridgeable distance between us. For You are *kadosh*, other, remote, beyond, yet at the same time Your *kavod*, Your 'weight', Your presence, fills the world about us. And there are other worlds and dimensions beyond our grasp that know You and serve You, so all we can do is imitate as best we can their adoration.

These first three paragraphs of the 'standing prayer' help us across another threshold into intimate contact with the Sovereign. Now is our opportunity to be heard. Were this a weekday we would indeed bring our petitions and requests before the Sovereign, the urgent hopes and demands of our people: for knowledge and forgiveness, for good harvests and for health, for advocacy on our behalf in the world and for the restoration of so much of our national life that was lost. But today is Shabbat and this litany of requests is silenced, as we honour God's rest on this day. Nor should we underestimate the price we pay for this holding back, if not now or for us at this moment, then for others whose need to tell God of our pain, our distress, is urgent. Silence may be the deepest sacrifice we offer for the sake of Shabbat peace.

Protocol will also provide the formality we need as we withdraw and prepare to depart. Just as the first three blessings ushered us in, so the last three will usher us out. May our prayers and petitions be acceptable. We bow as we express our gratitude for having been heard. We part with words of peace and the hope for peace on our lips.

We should leave, but as if reluctant to depart we are granted a few moments for our private hopes and wishes. Even in the midst of such formality there is room for silence in the presence of God. With song the silence and the spell is broken.

We should depart at once and prepare to take our leave from the palace. But Shabbat offers space and time for another possibility. The silence of God may be broken. And if no new word breaks the silence, then we can listen instead to the eternal word of God, the Torah, and try to find within it the message for today and now.

The Torah Service

The word of God comes to us and for a brief period the walls of the palace disappear and we stand under an open sky. The reading of the Torah was once a simple act, with only a blessing to be recited before and after. But layers of tradition have accumulated around it.

We stand in an arid landscape, in the encampment of the Israelites on their journey through the wilderness. We enclose our reading within that wider framework: 'Whenever the ark moved forward, then Moses said ...', 'And when the ark rested, Moses used to say ...' (Num 10:35-36). But between these moments we stand again at Mt. Sinai. As once Moses went up the mountain, so we go up to the ark to bring down the Torah into the midst of the community. Indeed we parade it, offering it to all who are present to affirm their personal relationship to it.

When the word comes to us we must do our best to ensure that it comes in its exactness. The one who reads carries a great responsibility, so it is shared with those who stand beside the reader, correcting and supporting where necessary. The word of God is precious and rare, so these are moments of tension and expectation.

One by one we share in the task ascending in turn, our *aliyah*, on behalf of the community as a whole. Tradition tells us that whatever the needs of the community at that particular time, the answer can be discerned in the words of Torah that are read on that Shabbat. So this is a climactic moment of the service. It is our privilege and challenge to hear what is said and seek to find within and behind the words the special meaning for here and now. We listen through the ears of our teachers of the past, but must also bring the best understanding of our own that we can offer. We join ourselves in our small way with the chain of tradition.

But there is also a tradition that the portion that we are honoured to hear when we are called to the Torah contains a special message for us alone. Again the 'I' and the 'we' meet at the very heart of our worship.

As if such a tension cannot be long sustained, other layers of materials have been added: a word from the prophets, the haftarah, blessings to be bestowed on us, on our community, on our country, on our State. While the Torah is in our midst it is as if it supports our petitions and hopes.

But the Torah must return, leaving behind the words that work within us. 'Just as the rain and snow descend from the sky and do not return there until they have watered the earth, so that it gives birth and flourishes, giving seed to the sower and bread to the eater, so is My word which comes from My mouth; it will not return to Me empty but will do that which I desire and succeed in that purpose for which I sent it' (Isa 55:10-11).

As the doors of the ark close, the wilderness recedes, the walls of the palace close in and we prepare to take our leave. One small detour through our history may still detain us.

Musaf, Additional Service for Shabbat

Having entered so far into the palace of the Sovereign, we are tempted to stay, to learn more, to explore other corridors and turnings and chambers. One door remains open for those who wish to remain a little longer. It leads into a place the complete opposite of the wilderness we visited when we read the Torah. For Jewish life exists between two poles that pull at us, homeland and exile, Zion and Sinai. We have just visited Sinai; now, for a few moments, we can look upon what was once the centre of our religious life, the Temple in Jerusalem.

On Shabbat in those ancient times an extra sacrifice marked the special nature of this day. Now an extra reading of the *Amidah* offers a ghostly reminiscence of how things once were. Yet to look back is also to look forward in anticipation and hope of restoration. But what is it we wish to see restored? An identical past reproduced before our eyes is still not what it once was; too much time and experience have changed our understanding of who we are, how we see the world and what God expects from us. So perhaps we should not remember the Temple and its animal sacrifices, for there is also a price to be paid for living in a remembered or imagined past. Yet we must also know where we come from, what forces shaped us, if we are to be their master and not their victim. So when we revisit the Temple, let our own imagination and hope shape its contours and its content.

This additional service once focused alone on ourselves, on our relationship with God and the tragedy when our failures estranged us from the source of our life. But now is the time to see Zion and the Temple as the prophets sometimes glimpsed them, as a place of prayer for all peoples, where others may join themselves to God's service and as a source of hope for all who inhabit this earth. We linger for a moment, then close another door and begin the journey back into the world.

Concluding Prayers

Leaving the palace is in some ways a reversal of the journey we have undertaken. We have been close to the Sovereign, enjoying the sense of belonging, of a special relationship that is our own unique privilege. Departing carries with it a sense of loss, of things unsaid, hopes unexpressed, possibilities unexplored. And outside, awaiting us, is a very different world to which we are about to return. It is a world in which we must act out our own particular destiny amidst the destiny of many others, each in their own way looking for the meaning and purpose of their lives. We will be scattered amongst their multitudes, trying to retain what we can of all we have experienced on our journey. But we know that we share with them all that is human, all vulnerabilities and aspirations. So our departure must prepare us to take again our place in that world to which we are returning.

The first chamber we enter is disturbing. We meet up again with those other delegations we saw long ago when we entered the palace. As is not unexpected, the silence and awe that we shared at that time have given way to argument and debate. For this chamber represents the first paragraph of the *Aleinu* prayer - 'it is our duty to praise the Ruler of all …' With these words we seek to define our special relationship with God and our unique calling. Inevitably, to do so, we must compare ourselves with others, and here the arguments begin. Because in that world outside to which we return, what we say and do is under scrutiny. Once we needed to be careful because others could be offended by our words, and when they had power over us could abuse that power if they so wished. Sometimes we censored our own feelings, in anticipation of what others might think. Now there are those who would celebrate our relative freedom by finding the strongest possible expression of that which separates us from others by diminishing their own beliefs. And yet others would argue that to assert our uniqueness in a world of many peoples and faiths does not require the denigration of others but a recognition of our diversity as itself a gift of God. 'Each of us is a question posed by God to humanity as a whole.'

The debate will not be stilled, and we will choose the words that suit our time and the temperament of our own particular community. We leave the chamber strengthened in our identity and confirmed in our special task to be God's witnesses in the world to which we will shortly return.

But more is demanded of us, and the last chamber we enter brings us forcibly back into the reality of what awaits us. For we are back in that first chamber we entered, where all of nature and all of humanity is gathered, waiting to visit the Sovereign. But now we see it through different eyes. Where once we saw only the magnificence of creation, now we see the harsh reality of human conflict and struggle, the possibility of mutual support and collaboration and the tragedy of bloodshed and wars. Now we must find the words that define our own hopes for the entire world, no longer isolated to our own particular circle.

The second paragraph of the *Aleinu*, *Al kein n'kavveh*, 'Therefore, Almighty God, we put our hope in You ...', confronts the turbulence and chaos of a world in need of healing and repair, of mutual understanding and of some kind of peace. We can take comfort from the words of the prophets that one day this harmony will come about under the rule of God, but their words are also a challenge to us to do what we can to help bring about such a time. That is our universal hope and that is our particular task.

We will leave the palace a different community from the one that entered. Some will have experienced the journey in the terms described above; others will have understood it in different ways. It is clearly a journey inwards and outwards. The picture we have explored belongs to the regal structure that our liturgy has bequeathed to us from an earlier time of all-powerful kings and hierarchies. That is no longer our experience of the world, so the journey may instead be an inner one, into chambers within us where we look to find our spirit or soul. Other images still may guide us, but some of the landmarks may help us anchor our search in the forms and guidelines of our tradition. The journey itself is what matters.

Before leaving we need a formal closure for this experience. So we turn, as we have done before along the way, to a prayer of extraordinary power, all the stronger for its rhythmic repetitions of words not even in Hebrew but Aramaic. The *Kaddish* is a formula for praising God, used to mark the end of a section of liturgy in an age before prayer books were available. It has accompanied us throughout our visit to the palace as we crossed a number of thresholds, reminding us that we have just completed a distinct part of our journey. But over time it has taken on additional meanings and now, in this final version, is associated with personal memories of those who have died, and the need to memorialise them alongside those we never knew but who belonged to the community of our people, and even those who were not Jews but who accompanied us in some significant way in our lives.

We began our journey when our delegated representative called upon us to 'Bless the One whom we are called to bless'. Now, as is fitting, we bring our journey to a close by doing just that, acknowledging at the same time that God is 'far beyond any blessing or song, any honour or any consolation that can be spoken of in this world'. But that is the paradox of our task, and resolving it is one of the challenges before us on our truly immense journey.

Jonathan Magonet

Blessing

For the formal service the form of the *berachah*, 'blessing', was chosen which then became the classical form of Jewish prayer. A 'blessing' is a prayer that begins with 'Blessed are You, Eternal ...' and/or ends with a sentence with the words 'Blessed are You, Eternal ...' The actual content may be a petition or a word in praise of God.

Jakob J. Petuchowski

The rabbis noted an apparent contradiction between two Biblical verses: Psalm 24:1, 'The earth and its fullness belong to God, the world and those who dwell in it.' and Psalm 115:16, 'Heaven is the heaven of God, who has given the earth to human beings.' Their solution? The former applies before one recites a blessing, and the latter after. A blessing before eating does not make the food 'holy', but rather 'secular'; by acknowledging its source in God, we are allowed to remove it from the 'heavenly' domain and use it for our own 'earthly' benefit.

Jonathan Magonet

On Entering the Synagogue - *Mah Tovu*

'How Good Are Your Tents ...'

The *Mah Tovu*, recited on entering the synagogue, is a compilation of five biblical verses (Numbers 24:5; Psalm 5:8, Psalm 26:8, Psalm 95:6, Psalm 69:14) by an unknown editor. Unlike the majority of Jewish prayers, this composition is in the singular; indeed the verse from Psalm 95 has been transposed into the singular form from the plural. It explains the prayer relationship between the Jew, as worshipper, and God, whose loving kindness is emphasised. The petitioner arrives at and progresses through the doors of the synagogue into the traditional mode and position of prayer, and looks ultimately to God for an answer.

Symbolically the passage also progresses through the places of worship from the Tent of Meeting in the wilderness, through the Sanctuary and Temples, to the synagogue of today. In each of these places the glory of God resides.

The first verse, from the Biblical story of Balaam, is unique in taking the words of a gentile prophet and incorporating them into the liturgy. The second verse contains ten words and was used to count those present to ensure a *minyan*, it being forbidden to count people by numbers but acceptable to use the words of a verse instead.

Maurice Michaels

'For Your deliverance is sure'

An old Yiddish comment on this verse says that often we do not know what is really good for us, and we pray for things that are really inappropriate. A story, from the Midrash, is told of two rich businessmen: each loaded a ship at the quayside in preparation to setting out over the seas. On the quay, one broke his foot, became ill, and could not go. He bewailed his fate, as the other one set off. After a while the news came that the other ship had sunk with all hands. The first merchant then praised God for having broken his foot. What he thought was a misfortune turned out to be his deliverance. Therefore we have to pray that God answers us with true deliverance, that God satisfies our real needs and not merely our desires.

Larry Tabick

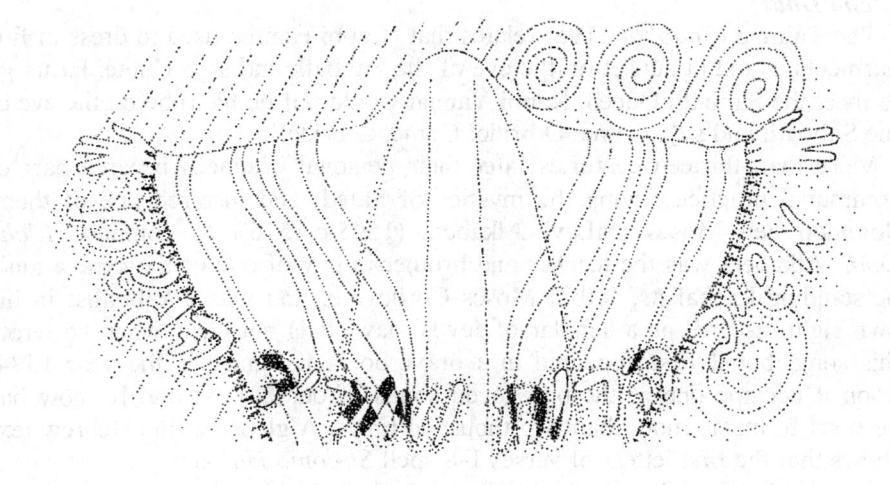

תפלת ערבית לשבת
SHABBAT EVENING SERVICE

Song of Songs
Some communities chant the entire Song of Songs during the Friday evening service, but when time is short they recite four verses instead, 1:2, 4:16, 2:8, 5:1. According to Rabbi Isaiah Horowitz (1565?-1630) in *siddur Sha'ar Ha-shamayim*, these verses were chosen to fulfil the prophecy of the Book of Isaiah (58:14): 'Then I will let You eat of the inheritance of Jacob, your father.' In Hebrew, the opening letters of these verses spell *Ya'akov*, Jacob.

Larry Tabick

L'cha Dodi
The Talmud (*Shabbat* 119a) relates that 'Rabbi Hanina used to dress in fine garments, stand at sunset on the eve of the Sabbath and say: Come, let us go to meet the Sabbath Queen. Rabbi Yannai would put on his robe on the eve of the Sabbath and say: Come, O bride! Come, O bride!'

More than thirteen centuries later their personal practices became part of communal practice among the mystics of Safed, and inspired one of them, Solomon ben Moses HaLevi Alkabetz (1505-c.1576), to compose *L'cha Dodi*. Alkabetz was the teacher and brother-in-law of one of the generation's outstanding kabbalists, Rabbi Moses Cordovero, and was a kabbalist in his own right, as well as a scholar of Jewish law. It is not clear when he wrote this song, but it first appeared in a prayerbook in Venice in the year 1584. Soon it became one of the best loved songs of our liturgy, and by now has been set to music more than two thousand times. A glance at the Hebrew text shows that the first letters of verses 1-8 spell *Sh'lomo HaLevi*.

As a kabbalist, Alkabetz was well acquainted with the idea that a given text might contain many layers of meaning, and constructed *L'cha Dodi* with that in mind. Accordingly it may be understood at a personal, national or mystical level. The redemption of the people from exile is, at one and the same time, the redemption of the *Sh'chinah*, the 'feminine' presence of God, from her exile in the material world. The Sabbath is both symbolic of that and a foretaste of it.

In the chorus we might wish to think of ourselves as encouraging each other ('my friend') to greet the Sabbath bride, or, more mystically, we are fostering the union between the *Sh'chinah*, God's 'feminine' receptivity, with the Holy One, blessed be He, God's 'masculine' energies. From their union, of which human sexuality is only a pale reflection, emerges peace and harmony in the spiritual, emotional and, ultimately, material realms.

Larry Tabick

L'cha Dodi - Traditions

In traditional congregations and some Reform ones, the community stands for the last verse and turns to face the door - in commemoration, some say, of that original Friday afternoon walk outdoors by the kabbalists of Safed; others see it as standing to greet the Shabbat Queen.

In some congregations, mourners during *shivah* wait outside the synagogue proper until *L'cha Dodi* has been sung. As they enter, everybody says the 'greeting' to mourners, 'May the Everpresent comfort you together with all the mourners of Zion and Jerusalem.' Perhaps having them wait outside is in recognition of the fact that while public acts of mourning are not permitted on Shabbat, mourners are not in the right frame of mind to participate in the joyfulness of *L'cha Dodi*. It also serves the purpose of identifying to/for the community those who have been recently bereaved.

Colin Eimer

L'cha Dodi - Commentary

L'cha Dodi stands at the gateway to Shabbat, a portal into eternity. It is the song of transition as we move from the working week into the boundlessness of our day of rest, as we glide from time into timelessness.

The poet greets the community - 'my friend' - with unfettered familiarity. Each soul of Israel is welcomed, invited to the gathering of joy which is the wedding between God and the *Shechinah*; the marriage of the unknowable with intimate knowing. But the bride is also Shabbat itself, and the marriage between God and Shabbat is about to be consummated. We are the witnesses - and participants - in a sacred drama. Each member of the community of Israel has a part to play. As we stand at the threshold we rehearse our roles.

We stand again at Sinai (verse 1), recalling the revelation of God's being: 'Observe Shabbat and keep it holy' (Deut. 5:12), 'Remember Shabbat and keep it holy' (Exodus 20:4). The community of Israel hears the voice of the One who is, and it echoes within us. Voice and echo, call and response: on Shabbat all are One.

Where did it all begin, this wondrous journey of Israel? Back in time, before there was time, we picture a divine moment of conception (verse 2): there will be waves and particles, movement and rest, motion and stasis, activity and Shabbat. The duality of being unfolding within Being - and we are participants in the sacred narrative of life. Revelation, preceded by Creation: on Shabbat all are One.

And where does it lead, this sacred story through which we enact our destiny? Our destination is - redemption (verse 3), 'God's glory' made manifest to us, and through us. 'Arise and shine' - the always postponed future redemption is here and now. Creation, Revelation, Redemption: on Shabbat all are One.

The marriage between God and the *Shechinah*, God and Shabbat, is also a marriage between God and the community of Israel: the 'faithful, chosen people' (Verse 4). As we enter Shabbat, God enters us. God's desire meets our desire. **And we are One.**

Howard Cooper

Six Psalms

A series of six Psalms (Psalms 95-99 and 29) commences the Erev Shabbat Service and together with *L'cha Dodi* and Psalms 92 and 93 forms *Kabbalat Shabbat*, the 'receiving of the Shabbat'. The six Psalms and the hymn were introduced into the service by the kabbalists of Safed in the middle of the sixteenth century. The custom of reciting the six Psalms is ascribed to Rabbi Moses Cordovero (1522-1570), the latter two Psalms being a part of the service much earlier. The six Psalms give praise to God as Creator and Saviour transcendent and immanent, Sovereign and Judge, God of history and of the present. As Shabbat begins, these Psalms symbolise the six working days of the week. There is also the view that they replace the six *shofar* blasts that, in the days of the Temple, were blown at regular intervals on Friday afternoon to herald the commencement of the Shabbat. The last of these Psalms, Psalm 29 (the only one of the six recited in the Sephardi tradition), has a special symbolic significance according to the *Talmud*, in that it is associated with the *Amidah* (*Berachot 28b*). It is said to be the basis of the *Amidah*, which daily has eighteen blessings (according to the traditional name, though nineteen in practice) and seven on Shabbat, as the Psalm mentions the name of God eighteen times and seven times refers to the 'voice of God' (*Midrash* Psalms *29:2*).

Maurice Michaels

Psalm 95

We begin, conventionally, with the sound of our own voices: singing, calling out, offering thanks, ventriloquizing the words of our faith (verses 1-2). There is security here, the safe familiarity of tradition, the hymns and melodies of old resounding within us once again. What gives us such cause to rejoice? The elemental energy of creation: valleys and mountains, oceans and continents, a planet formed by a guiding force more powerful than the world can conceive (verses 3-5). These middle verses of the Psalm remove us from the scene. In the presence of the mystery of creation, we are as nothing. When we re-emerge in the poem (verse 6), it is with a sense of ourselves, a humility in the face of the divine architecture of the natural world, aeons in the making. In awe we recognise our insignificance, and as we recall our smallness we glimpse beneath the veil of creation: the One who is the animating energy behind the natural world is also the One 'who made *us*'.

We too are created - and we are the only part of creation that knows itself to be part of creation. The Jewish people are bound up with this vision: we are fragile, dependent human beings with eternity written into our souls. But how can we hear the eternal voice within us? Through our songs and Psalms, and words hallowed by tradition? The psalmist subverts our expectations: we began with our own voices sounding out, but we end with our voices stilled. We are here to listen. To hear eternity now - 'today' - you will need to learn how to listen, to pay attention, *sh'ma* (verse 8, last word). What will we hear? What will be revealed in the quietness, when the sound of our voices ceases to fill the space? Nothing - except the mystery of the One who sustains the world and ourselves within it.

Howard Cooper

Psalm 96

The opening of the Psalm speaks of three groups: verse 1, Sing to the Eternal *all the earth*; verse 3, Declare among *the nations* ... [and] among *the peoples*. Are these terms simply synonyms or do they mean different things? In the second half of the Psalm we come across the same words in the same order: verse 9, Tremble before God *all the earth*; verse 10, Say among *the nations* ... God will judge *the peoples*. In verse 7, at the centre of the poem, the poet calls out not simply to the earth or the nations, but to the 'families of nations'. The poet recognises God's transcendence and universalism in the enormous picture of creation, like some dramatic backdrop to the Psalm, but he is not content with seeing the earth as composed of disparate nations. At the centre of the Psalm stands this phrase *mishp'chot amim*, 'families of peoples', unifying creation.

At the beginning of the Psalm we are scattered and disparate, disconnected one from another throughout the earth. We are individuals, who then become nations ... But as peoples begin to understand something of the connection between different nations or faiths or faces, we move on to becoming a people, and then a family of peoples, completely connected, recognising the common parenthood and grandeur of God, a common brotherhood and sisterhood. It is in this connectedness and with this mutual recognition that God will judge us with righteousness and truth ... This pivotal phrase 'families of peoples' unifies creation in its great moral purpose.

Alexandra Wright

Ahavat Olam - God's love for Israel

The Mishnah (*Berakhot* 1:4) ordains: 'In the morning two blessings are said before the *Sh'ma* and one after; in the evening two are said before and two after.' The 'second' blessing before the *Sh'ma* in both morning and evening describes God's special love for Israel. The opening phrase *ahavat olam*, 'With everlasting love', is taken from Jeremiah 31:3. The prophet offers consolation to his suffering people: 'With an everlasting love I have loved you, so I have continued my faithfulness to you.' The blessing, which reminds God of this prophetic promise, is composed to introduce the *Sh'ma*, so it explains that we think of God's love 'before we sleep and when we wake', the two times of day when the *Sh'ma* is recited.

The blessings move from God as Creator of the universe to God's special love for Israel as shown through the giving of Torah. 'What kind of God would put us into this world and not give us some kind of guidance for living in it?!' (Shmuel Sperber). The revelation of Torah respects the fact that we are not simply puppets obedient to the will of a master, but free to choose our path. If God's love is '*olam*', 'forever', then we will meditate on and rejoice in Torah and commandments '*l'olam*', 'forever', for they are the basis of our lives. Yet the end of the blessing seems to reflect an anxiety about that unique relationship with God and hence a prayer: 'Do not take Your love away from us '*l'olam*', 'forever'. The Sephardi tradition phrases it as a statement: 'Your love shall not depart from us forever.'

Jonathan Magonet

Ma'ariv Aravim - Commentary

There is more depth in this prayer than merely blessing God for being the eternal timekeeper. It addresses the One who with wisdom 'opens gates', as the Hebrew laconically states. In our lives we are plunged into darkness and back into light. The *Ma'ariv* prayer affirms that there is understanding or foresight behind it all and we seek meaning in the changes.

The Friday evening *Ma'ariv* prayer takes us back from the threshold of the seventh day of the week to the first day of Creation. At the very beginning of the creation of light and the division between light and darkness a '*havdalah*' is made. As we welcome Shabbat we are encouraged to make our own separation between our day of rest and the workaday week.

Reuven Silverman

'By whose word the evenings fall.' The word plays a central role in the Jewish imagination. Our liturgy fantasises that God brings on evening each night by saying 'evening!' Thus we repeat each day the original act of Creation that took place by means of the divine word. It is only because we affirm a God who so values language that we feel ourselves able to use words in prayer. Our word, perhaps like God's, gives expression to a depth that goes beyond language, but that can be shared only through the symbolic power of speech.

Levi Weiman-Kelman

תפלת שחרית לשבת
SHABBAT MORNING SERVICE

Baruch She'amar

Baruch She'amar is the introductory prayer to *P'sukey D'Zimra* (Verses of Song). This section of the service was often sung in its entirety. In the Middle Ages the prayer leader would chant *Baruch She'amar*, emphasising the joy the Jew found in praising 'the Sovereign praised in all worship'. In Prague every synagogue had a singing group called *M'zamrei Baruch She'amar*, and the tombstones of deceased members were marked '*M'zamrei B'sh*'.

Steven Katz

Bar'chu

Bar'chu is the official summoning of the congregation to prayer, which can be traced back to the times of the Temple. The Prayer Leader would utter the first line and the people responded with the second line.

The importance of the *Bar'chu*, like that of the *Kedushah*, the third blessing of the *Amidah*, the *Kaddish*, and the reading of the Torah, is confirmed by the traditional requirement of a *minyan* if they are to be read in the service.

Steven Katz

El Adon

'*El Adon*' is an anonymous alphabetical *piyyut* (hymn) of 22 verses, with a regular metre of four accents to the line. The first two verses contain five words each, corresponding to the ten utterances with which God created the world; the last two verses contain six words each, corresponding to the twelve signs of the zodiac. It is attributed to the eighth-century theosophical mystics '*Yordei Merkavah*' (the Riders on the Chariot), mystics who based their speculations on the vision of Ezekiel (chapters 1,10).

There are both theological and astrological elements in the poem. The theological approach would be based on Genesis 1:14-18, where God is described as creating 'lights in the sky' with specific tasks, e.g. to provide light for night and day, or to stand watch in specific posts to which God assigns them, i.e. they have no power or initiative of their own, but just obey the Divine orders. This is a direct attack on any belief in the stars as having any autonomous power or influence. The astrological approach in contrast ascribes certain power and influence to stars, planets or other heavenly bodies, power beyond what are accepted natural phenomena such as heat and light from the sun, or tidal pull from the moon. This poem refers to such heavenly beings and powers as existing, even if God is then assigned greater power and glory. The hymn is inserted on Shabbat and Festival mornings in both Ashkenazi and Sephardi traditions into the *Yotzer*, the first of the two blessings that lead to the *Sh'ma*, appropriate to its theme of God's creation of the world.

Walter Rothschild

The Opening of the *Sh'ma*

Twice daily, we pray 'Hear O Israel, the Eternal is our God the Eternal is One'. We learn from our tradition that the principle of a Jewish hope of universality and global humanity is contained in this Biblical verse. Indeed, the first line of the *Sh'ma* does not say 'Hear O Israel, the Eternal is our God', full stop. We do not stop with particularism, omitting the universal vision that 'God is One'. But equally true, we learn that one is not permitted to say 'Hear O Israel, the Eternal is One', full stop, omitting 'the Eternal is our God' and therefore bypassing particularism in order to reach to the universal.

The Jewish view of the universal dream passes through the acceptance of our particular relationship with God, through the particularities of our history. It is only if we accept who we are, with all our specificities, that we can then reach out to the universal message of our tradition.

Ploni Almoni

The Second Paragraph of the *Sh'ma*

V'hayah im shamoa. 'This will happen if you listen carefully' (Deuteronomy 11:13-21).

This paragraph has been an integral part of the *Sh'ma* for 2000 years or more, but it presented difficulties for our Reform predecessors. Based on their understanding of modern scientific knowledge, they could not see the truth of the teaching embedded here, that our moral and spiritual attitudes are closely bound up with the environment. They were also troubled by the notion of a wrathful, punishing God.

Developments that began in the field of nuclear physics, but which have extended throughout the sciences, now confirm what mystics of all traditions have long recognised: we cannot separate ourselves from that which we observe or from the world around us. The universe is precisely that: a 'uni-verse', a single, wondrous, interconnected entity. We are part of it; it flows through us, and all our actions, prayers and thoughts reverberate through it, and rebound back upon us for good or for ill. Our ancestors of Biblical times expressed their appreciation of this truth through the image of a God who rewards the righteous and punishes the wicked. We may feel uncomfortable with the image, but its underlying truth remains valid.

One of the ways in which the interconnectedness of All is made manifest, this passage teaches, is that Jewish possession of the Promised Land is not a matter of inheritance, but is conditional upon the maintenance of high moral and spiritual standards. May not the same be said of human possession of the Earth?

Larry Tabick

The Torah posits that the land is entrusted to the Children of Israel only if the Jewish people live up to the standards enunciated in the Torah: to practise morality, pursue justice, and to obey certain agricultural rules ... The link that the Jews have with the Land of Israel is therefore contractual rather than organic.

Yakov M. Rabkin

Emet V'emunah

The ultimate image of rescue from mortal danger in our tradition is the safe crossing of the 'Sea of Reeds' and the destruction of the pursuing Egyptian army. It is celebrated in the Bible by the 'Song at the Sea' (Exodus 15:1-18), two verses of which, 11 and 18, form the climax of this prayer. In Exodus the 'song' is first sung by Moses and the children of Israel, then Miriam leads the women in a dance, repeating the words of the song.

<<<

We have introduced Miriam's role into the text of this prayer, as have a number of modern liturgies. Her role in Israelite history is emphasised in the following Talmudic passage: Three good leaders arose for Israel, Moses, Aaron and Miriam, and for their sake three good things were conferred on Israel, the well, the cloud and the manna [that accompanied the Israelites in the wilderness] ... When Miriam died the well disappeared, for the Bible records immediately after the account of her death 'and there was no water for the congregation' (*Ta'anit* 9a).

Whilst Moses carried the externals - of the Voice speaking at Sinai and of the Commands of the Legislator, and Aaron carried the externals of the Priesthood - its dress, its Tabernacle, its rituals; Miriam carried the internalised meaning - the joy expressed in song, the love expressed through her righteous acts and the milk, the sustenance expressed as the never-failing, sweet waters of the well that was hers, that was her.

Tony Bayfield

Amidah - Insertions in the Second Blessing
'Making the wind to blow and the rain to fall'
The insertion of this phrase during the summer months is recorded in the Mishnah (*Berachot* 5:2, *Ta'anit* 1:1) as one of the 'powers' of God. The phrase 'causing the dew to fall' is a Sephardi tradition. Including both enables us to relate ourselves to the seasons in the land of Israel.

Jonathan Magonet

Once Rabbi ordained a fast (at a time of drought) but no rain came. The leader of the prayers went down before him to the *bimah* and recited 'making the wind to blow' - and the wind blew, 'and the rain to fall' - and the rain fell. Rabbi asked him, 'What good deeds do you fulfil?' He answered, 'I live in a city that is poor and they have no wine for *kiddush* and *havdalah*. So I go out of my way to bring wine for *kiddush* and *havdalah* so that they can fulfil their religious duty.'

Rav happened to visit a certain place (where there was a drought). He declared a fast but the rain did not fall. The leader of the prayers went down before him to the *bimah* and recited 'making the wind to blow' - and the wind blew; 'and the rain to fall' - and the rain fell. Rav asked him 'What is your occupation?' He replied 'I am a teacher of Torah to children. I teach the children of the poor as well as the children of the rich; and if any are too poor to pay I take no fee. I have a little pond with fish, and if there is any child who is reluctant to study, I bribe him with them and send for him and appease him until he comes and studies.'

Ta'anit 24a

Amidah - Second Blessing - *G'vurot*

'You sustain the living with *hesed*, give life to the dead with great compassion.' The entire blessing is in the present, a series of participles that help us to see the verb behind the noun. *Someich noflim* means not only 'Supporter of the Fallen' but also 'supporting the fallen', showing that the action goes on forever. The same has to be said of 'sustaining the living': God continually sustains the living; God is always the sustainer of life. But then the same must be said of *m'chayeih ha-meitim* as well. Y-H-W-H is forever 'giving life to the dead'! The blessing does not refer to a great resurrection of the future, as it is often read, but rather to a constant ongoing process, one that exists throughout both nature and history, transcending its obvious seeming untruth regarding individual human lives. Yes, death is final, and it is our task to accept that fact. But we need also to see how the dead are born again in the ongoing generations of their families, how human generations are like the seasons of the year, the sprouting of seeds, the cycles of fertilization and pollination, and all the other wonderful intricacies through which life is passed on. Life is far more miraculous than any 'mere' resurrection of the dead. In each moment God gives and bestows life in more ways than we can ever imagine. Who are we, Israel, a people reborn in this generation from the ashes of death and destruction, if not one of God's witnesses to this truth?

Arthur Green

Amidah - Second Blessing - *Matsmi'ach y'shu'ah*

'You cause salvation to grow.' The [verbal] root usually refers to vegetation. The phrase sounds like: 'You make salvation grow like a vegetable'. That's the way it should be. The Kotsker found a verse that says, 'May truth grow from the ground.' Truth won't come out of heaven, he taught. It rather has to spring up from the earth, deeply rooted in the soil of human experience, concrete earthly reality. The same is true of salvation. For too long we waited for it to float down, fully grown, from the heavens. In our day we have learned that the only bits of salvation we find are the results of our own human labours. It is in the efforts of people to bring about salvation that we also come to see the hidden hand of God, ever working to bring that salvation nearer, through us and within us.

Arthur Green

Amidah - Seventeenth Blessing - *R'tseih*

I always find the word *r'tseih* in prayer to be a particularly poignant one. It is the imperative of the verb 'to want'. 'Want us, O Lord!' 'Desire us!' Offended by the passionate demand of those terms, we settle for the quieter 'accept'.

Arthur Green

Amidah - Eighteenth Blessing - *Modim*

According to Midrash, this prayer, the penultimate in the *Amidah*, was first sung by the chorus of angels round God's throne when the first sacrifices were offered in the Temple built by King Solomon. More likely, but less poetically, Lawrence Hoffman suggests that 'following the daily offerings in the Temple, the people present would prostrate themselves as a token of their gratitude, mixed with acknowledgement of God's reality. That act became a blessing in its own right.' While the content of the blessing was fixed by the Talmudic period, the actual words varied from place to place. Even in the fourteenth century, a wandering Spanish scholar commented on the fact that wherever he went, the text for the *Amidah* varied. Local variations gradually ceased with the advent of printing.

The twin ideas of acknowledging that we need to give thanks and that what God has created is fundamentally good, for God is good, are the foundation of religion and prayer. It tells us in the Talmud (*Berachot* 34a) that like servants who are obliged to thank their master, so we are required to thank God for all that is provided for us each day, indeed each minute of our lives. As we are told in the prayer, 'Your miracles are with us every day …' True worship depends on us recognising the ordinary things around us, our food, our relationships, the environment, as daily miracles that must waken in us the obligation to give thanks.

The way we offer this prayer is clearly choreographed by the rabbis (*Berachot* 34a). We should bow from the waist at the first word, *Modim*, and then straighten up again at the word Eternal One, *Adonai*, 'for the Eternal One upholds the fallen'. Again at the conclusion of the prayer, we should bow, this time from the knees, at the word *'Baruch'*, blessed, again rising at the mention of God's name, *Adonai*.

As this is the prayer where we acknowledge all that God provides for us, so at *Chanukah* and *Purim* it is here that we add the extra paragraphs, the *Al Ha-nissim*, in which we thank God for helping us survive those difficult and dangerous times.

Jacqueline Tabick

Amidah - Eighteenth Blessing - *Al nissecha sheb'chol yom immanu* - 'For Your miracles that are with us daily'

Here the concept of 'miracle' is renewed and transformed for us. If 'miracles' were with us only occasionally, we might think the word referred specifically to such triumphs of the 'special-effects' department as the plagues in Egypt or the splitting of the Reed Sea. These, as everyone knows, are difficult for us moderns. But 'miracles … with us daily'? And parallel, in the next phrase, to 'goodly wonders, evening, morning, and noon'?

<<<

These are hardly the suspension of nature; they refer rather to the miraculous qualities of nature itself. We thank God here for such miracles as breathing and seeing, our health and the growth of our children, gifts of love and kindness, and all the rest. Each of these, and every moment in which they exist, is truly the supreme miracle. We thank God mostly for the greatest gift of all: our ability to see the miraculous within the everyday.

Arthur Green

The Reading from the Torah

There is a complex etiquette employed in traditional synagogues as to who is called up to the reading of the Torah. During a daily morning service on a Monday or a Thursday when the Torah is read (a relic of ancient custom in Babylon when these were market days), or on *Rosh Chodesh*, three men would be summoned to the reading; on a Festival, five, on a Shabbat, seven, plus a 'closing reader', known as *'maftir'*. When the Torah is read during a Shabbat *Minchah* (afternoon) service, only one section is read and therefore usually only one person is called up.

The traditional priority sequence calls first a *Cohen*, then a *Levi* second, in memory of the distinguished tasks these groups had to perform in the Temple ritual. After these comes the turn of *Israel*, the rest of the people. Priority might then be given based on life events, such as someone whose wife had just had a child, someone just returned from a journey who wished to express thanks through an additional prayer (in Yiddish to *'bentsch gomel'*), or a visiting preacher, or someone with an anniversary to mark or a *bar mitsvah*, or someone about to be married (in Yiddish an *'aufruf'*, literally an 'up-calling'). You would be called by your Hebrew name and usually the designation 'second' (*sheni*), 'third' (*shelishi*), 'fourth' (*revii*), etc, as appropriate.

When called you ascended to the *Bimah* and stood at the right side of the person who was reading. You came up by the shorter route from your seat and went down again via the longer route - to express eagerness to come and reluctance to leave! It became a custom to touch the *sefer torah* with the fringe of your *tallit* and kiss it to show respect and to mark the section you were honouring. You then recited the blessings before the reading and subsequently the blessing after the reading, and then stood on the left-hand side of the reader whilst the next person was called up. When his section had been concluded you would receive a blessing, a *misheberach*, and return to your seat shaking hands with all the communal dignitaries on the way.

In Reform synagogues some of these traditions have been retained and others not. We make no distinction for *Cohen* or *Levi*; women may also be called up. The Hebrew name may include both the father's and mother's names. Because we read a shorter section fewer people may be called up - three verses is the minimum number to be read.

Walter Rothschild

The Torah Blessings
Before the Reading

The opening call and response are the same as those used to start the main part of the service. They call the people's attention and remind them that it is time to hear God's word.

God is described as having 'chosen us from all peoples', in that God gave us the Torah. This is the basic element of the 'chosenness'. By giving us a set of rules and a national history God chose us and makes us different from the rest of the peoples that this God also created. Judaism does not portray other peoples as somehow diabolic - they are also divine, also God's creation, and may each have been chosen for some special task or quality. Our task and quality is defined by having been given the Torah. In the closing blessing the verb for 'give' is in the present tense. The giving of Torah is still going on, it was not a single, finite event. God is giving the Torah all the time.

The blessing refers at first to God giving us 'His' Torah, but at the end God gives us 'the' Torah. God's version was given then at Sinai, but now we must understand it for ourselves and make it 'our' Torah.

After the Reading

The second blessing stresses that the Torah which has just been read is the 'true Torah' or 'the Torah of truth' - it validates what has just been read. It adds that God has 'planted eternal life in our midst'. This could refer to the Torah itself, for in the Torah there are morals, ethics, destinies and a relationship with the Creator that needs constantly working on. It could also mean that when we learn and apply the Torah we acquire or deserve the gift of 'eternal life' in the form of existence after death.

Significantly the second blessing also closes with the phrase 'who is giving us God's Torah' - for it goes on still.

Walter Rothschild

Closing Prayers
Aleinu

The *Aleinu* is recited at the conclusion of all evening, morning and afternoon services. It is attributed by some scholars to the Babylonian sage Rav and its origins lie in the Rosh Hashanah *Musaf* (Additional) service where it introduces the '*Malchuyot*' section (extolling God's sovereignty over the world), not becoming a daily prayer until the thirteenth century. Early British Reform prayerbooks omitted the second paragraph in accordance with general Sephardi custom.

The first paragraph is quite explicit in emphasising the particularistic element of Judaism, while the second paragraph broadens our horizons with the loftiest of universalistic sentiments. Both aspects, the particularistic and the universalistic, are integral components of Judaism.

Steven Katz

<<<

The *Kaddish* - History, forms and practice.

The words of the *Kaddish* are an amalgam of Aramaic, the language of Babylon, and Hebrew, and its origins rest in the *Beth Ha-midrash*, the House of Study, where it was recited during the Talmudic period by the teacher at the end of his discourse. The *Kaddish* is first mentioned as part of the synagogue service in *Massechet Soferim* and by the Geonic period, ninth century, it had become a statutory synagogue prayer to be recited in the presence of a *minyan*.

The mourner's *Kaddish* holds a special place in the Jewish heart. Initially it was recited at the end of a study text given in a house of mourning after the death of a learned person. Later, in order not to bring shame on the unlearned, the practice of honouring the memory of the learned was extended to include everyone. The earliest reference to the *Kaddish* recited by all mourners is attributed to the thirteenth century rabbi, Isaac ben Moses of Vienna.

There are five different texts of the *Kaddish*: 1. *Chatsi-Kaddish* (Half-*Kaddish*), recited between sections of the liturgy. 2. *Kaddish Titkabbal*, recited at the end of the *Selichot* service and at the conclusion of the *Neilah* Service on *Yom Kippur*. 3. *Kaddish Yatom* (orphan's *Kaddish*), recited by the mourner for the first eleven months of mourning and at each *Yahrzeit* (anniversary) and also each *Yizkor* (memorial) service on Jewish Festivals. 4. *Kaddish D'rabbanan* (the teachers' *Kaddish*) recited by mourners after the study of rabbinic texts. 5. *Kaddish Le'ithadeta* (*Kaddish* of Renewal) sometimes recited after burial.

Steven Katz

The *Kaddish* - Commentary.

The *Kaddish* makes no mention of death. Instead the words emphasise God's majesty, magnificence and sanctity. The very heart of the *Kaddish* is the congregational response 'May His great name be blessed'. It is around this response, rooted in Daniel 2:20, that the entire *Kaddish* evolved. Leon Wieseltier gives voice to the resonating impact of the *Kaddish* through the centuries. 'I stood in the ashes of fury and spoke the sentences of praise. Was the voice my voice? It was no longer the effusion of woe. Magnified, I said. Sanctified, I said. I looked below me, I looked around me. With my own eyes, I saw magnificence.'

Why is the mourner, whose heart is filled with pain, urged to praise God? With the words of the *Kaddish*, mourners praise God for life, above all for the life and love shared with their lost loved one. The *Kaddish* puts death into perspective through sanctifying life and praising the Source of life, God.

Steven Katz

In traditional services the *Kaddish* in one or another of its forms occurs so frequently that the originators of Reform felt not only that it lengthened the service unduly but also that the frequent repetition tended to make it almost meaningless. It was therefore excised altogether from the Reform liturgy except for its use by mourners, and even here attempts were made to use it in a Hebrew translation rather than its Aramaic form ... Recently the *Kaddish*, usually in the *Hatzi-Kaddish* form, has been optionally reinserted in various places; the extent to which we readopt it must essentially be a matter of taste, but where we do so we should do it in full knowledge of its traditional use and functions.

Alfred Moritz

Adon Olam

Adon Olam is a complex poem with hidden messages. One such message is encoded in the final letters of each line. The first three lines end with the letter *heh*, the next three with the letter *alef*, and the last four alternately with *heh* and *alef*. If the *heh* stands for the Tetragrammaton, the four-letter name of God, and the *alef* for *Elohim*, then this song unites the divine qualities represented by these divine names. In rabbinic thought the Tetragrammaton denotes God's mercy and *Elohim* God's severity, to which may be attributed happy and saddening experiences respectively. Read in this way, the poem can be read as a commentary on the first line of the *Sh'ma*, which challenges us to understand the unity of experience by juxtaposing these names and informing us that they are one.

Jeremy Schonfield

LIFE'S JOURNEY

Life's Journey

O my soul, set your mind on the highway, the way on which you have walked. For all came from the dust, and indeed shall return to the dust. Every thing that was created and fashioned has an end and a goal, to return to the earth from which it was taken. Life and death are brothers, they dwell together; they are joined to one another; they cling together, so that they cannot be separated. They are joined together by the two ends of a frail bridge over which all created beings travel. Life is the entrance and death the exit. Life builds and death demolishes; life sows and death reaps; life plants and death uproots; life joins together and death separates; life links together and death scatters. So please understand and see that the cup will also pass to you, and you shall soon go from the lodging place which is on the way, when time and chance happen to you, and you return to your eternal home. On that day you shall delight in your work and take your reward for the work in which you laboured in this world, whether it be good or bad.

Bachya Ibn Pakuda

In this world, a person should traverse and negotiate all the holy books and learn them all in order to travel everywhere. Just as the wealthy travel all over the world, spending enormous sums on their journeys, so that they can later say that they have travelled widely; just as the wealthy boast and say, 'I have been in Warsaw, and so on' - similarly should a person in this world be in all the holy places of the Torah so that in the world-to-come he will be able to boast that he has been everywhere - that is, in all the holy books.

Nachman of Bratslav

Self-satisfaction is the opiate of fools. Self-fulfilment is a myth which the noble mind must find degrading. All that is creative in man stems from a seed of endless discontent. New insight begins when satisfaction comes to an end, when all that has been said, seen or done looks like a distortion.

A.J.Heschel

Laws of Life

People are known by three things: by their cup, by their pocket and by their anger. (Some say: by their laughter.)

Eruvin 65b

This epigram by Rabbi Ilai, who lived in Tiberias in the third century, loses something in the translation. It is actually a pun on three Hebrew words *kos* (cup), *kis* (purse or pocket) and *ka'as* (anger).

Days are scrolls: write on them what you want to be remembered.

Bachya

One thing acquired through pain is better for us than one hundred things easily acquired.

Midrash

One cannot say to the Angel of Death:
'I wish to arrange my affairs before I die.'

Midrash

What should we do that we may live? Destroy our self.

Tamid

For us, earth is a prison all our days,
so I say this truth to the fool,
you rush around - but the sky is all around you,
arise and get out if you can!

Shmuel Hanagid

Are birds free of the chains of the skyways?

Bob Dylan

If you spit in the air, it will land on your face.

Ecclesiastes Rabbah 7:21

Everyone must have two pockets, so that we can reach into the one or the other, according to our needs. In our right pocket are to be the words 'For my sake was the world created,' and in our left 'I am dust and ashes.'

Rabbi Bunam of Pzhysha

Those who think they can live without others are mistaken. Those who think others cannot live without them are more mistaken.

Chasidic

Question: Our sages say, 'And there is not a thing that has not its place.' And so people too have their place. Then why do people sometimes feel so crowded?
Answer: Because each wants to occupy the place of the other.

Chasidic

On Reality
We are afraid of things that cannot harm us, and we know it. And we long for things that cannot help us, and we know it. But actually it is something within us that we are afraid of, and it is something within us that we long for.

Chasidic

In a dream we live seventy years and discover, on awakening, that it was a quarter of an hour. In our life, which passes as a dream, we live seventy years, and then we waken to a greater understanding which shows us that it was a quarter of an hour.

Chasidic

On Ownership
We are held responsible for everything we receive in this world, and our children are responsible too. The fact is nothing belongs to us, everything is God's and whatever we received we received only on credit and God will exact payment for it. This may be compared to someone who entered a city and found no one there. He walked into a house and there found a table set with all kinds of food and drink. So he began to eat and drink, thinking, 'I deserve all of this, all of it is mine, I shall do with it what I please.' He did not even notice that the owners were watching him from the side! He will yet have to pay for everything he ate and drank, for he is in a spot from which he will not be able to escape.

Jonah Ibn Janach

The Golden Mean
The divine law does not impose asceticism upon us. Rather it prefers that we keep to the golden mean and give to every mental and physical faculty its appropriate share, without giving too much to one faculty and too little to another. Thus, someone who is inclined to lust decreases his thinking faculty; and on the other hand, someone who is inclined to abstinence decreases some other faculty. Fasting for a long period is no act of piety for someone whose appetites are weak, whose faculties are feeble and whose body is thin; instead he should pamper his body. Nor is decreasing your wealth an act of piety, if you happen to have earned it in a lawful way without trouble, and owning it does not keep you from studying and performing good deeds, especially if you have dependants and children and your desire is to spend money for the sake of God - better that such a person should amass wealth.

As a general rule, our Torah, the teaching of God, is divided into fear, love and joy, by each of which you may draw near to God.

Judah Halevi

You might say, since jealousy, passion and love of honour can bring disaster on us we should therefore go to the opposite extreme and say: 'I will avoid meat and wine or marriage or a beautiful house or fashionable clothes ...' This is an unacceptable way and forbidden! Whoever follows such a way is a sinner! ... Are there not enough prohibitions in the Torah that you go looking for extra ones?!

Maimonides, Mishneh Torah, Deut 3:1,2

Samuel said: 'Keen scholar! Don't delay your eating or your drinking, for this world which we are destined to leave is like a wedding.' Rab said to Rab Hamnuna: 'My son, if you have the means, enjoy yourself. For there is no pleasure when you're in the grave, and death does not delay. And if you say to yourself "I will leave a sum to my children", in the grave who is going to thank you for it! People are like the grass of the field, some blossom and some fade.'

Eruvin 54a

The pleasures of eating are the most immediate and intense. But is there any experience that is so shortlived and limited? For it only lasts for as long as the food enters the gullet, and by the time it reaches the stomach its memory is forgotten as if it had never been. And if we eat enough, whether fatted capons or simple bread, we are satisfied.

Moreover, if we consider all the many illnesses that we could suffer from gorging ourselves, and not least the feeling of oppressive heaviness and the gases that dull our minds, how much more should we be concerned about eating. For all these reasons, we should not seek enjoyment in this, for the good we derive is not really good and the evils are evil indeed!

Moses Hayyim Luzzatto

Changes

Shadow-love and shadow-kisses,
life of shadows, wondrous strange!
Shall all hours be sweet as this is,
silly darling, safe from change?

All things that we clasp and cherish,
pass like dreams we may not keep.
Human hearts forget and perish,
human eyes must fall asleep.

Heinrich Heine

Responsibility

Responsibility is the recognised obligation to care for another being, who is at risk in his/her vulnerability and thus is a matter of concern to us ... What will happen to him/her if I show no interest in his/her fate? The more impenetrable the answer, the clearer is the responsibility.

Hans Jonas

'Go through the city, through Jerusalem, and put a mark upon the foreheads of the men who sigh and groan over all the abominations that are committed in it' (Ezekiel 9:4).

The Holy One said to the angel Gabriel: Go mark the foreheads of the righteous with an X of ink so that the angels of death do not harm them, and the foreheads of the wicked with an X of blood so that the angels of death do harm them. Hearing that, Justice spoke up and said: 'Lord of the Universe, what is the difference between them?' God answered: 'These are the wholly righteous and those the wholly wicked.' Justice replied: 'Lord of the Universe, they could have protested but did not.' Said God: 'But I know that even if they had protested no one would have listened to them.' Said Justice: 'Lord of the Universe, You knew it, but did they?'

Shabbat 55a

Nothing is harder and nothing builds more character than to find oneself in open opposition to one's time and to say aloud: 'No!'

Kurt Tucholsky

Relationships

Friendliness is not the abolishing of distance but the bringing of distance to life.

Walter Benjamin

Just as the water reflects one's face, so does one's heart reflect other human hearts.

Proverbs 27:1

Do good to all men, evil to none; do good even to the non-Jew in the street, even to an enemy who has pursued you with relentless hate. If you have an opportunity for revenge, do not avail yourselves of it, but load your adversary with favours ... If your foe is seeking your hurt you may prevent him, but you must not injure him beyond the point of making him powerless to harm you. If an opportunity offers of serving him, thank God for the chance, and though he has done you the most fearful wrongs, forget the injuries you have sustained at his hands. Make yourselves wings like eagles to succour him, and refrain from reminding him by a word of his former conduct.

Israel Lipschuetz of Danzig

Jewish life celebrates our humanity ... the humanity of a people who have not had an easy or placid relationship with God, but who have a loving, questioning, doubting, struggling, sometimes even tormented relationship with God, with Judaism, even with life itself.

Judaism understands deep in its soul that the most profound of all relationships are relationships of struggle and growth. Our relationships with our parents, with our lovers, with our children, and with our closest friends are not always easy ones. But ... they are the relationships through which we grow ... they are the relationships that ultimately transform us.

Daniel Gordis

We should not invite our neighbours to eat at our table if we know quite well that the invitation will be refused. We should not pretend to give them a present knowing full well that they will not accept it. And the same applies to whenever we do similar things, saying one thing with our mouth and meaning something different in our heart, showing our neighbours that we intend to honour them but not really meaning it deep in our heart. Our mouth and heart should be as one and we should train our lips to speak honestly, our spirit to be one of integrity and our heart pure.

Kitzur Shulchan Aruch

On Judging Others

Hillel was a great teacher of Torah. I love Hillel's saying that you should never judge a person until you are in his or her shoes. I have often felt judged by people who look at me and think I am retarded because I can't speak or move the way most people can. Hillel probably didn't know anyone who had autism but his teachings are very meaningful to me because I love Torah just as he did, and it is very comforting to know that great Jews like Hillel have taught about me without even knowing me. I learn from him that I also need to be more patient with people and try to see their perspective before I make negative judgments about them.

Jacob Artson (aged 11)

Respect an old man who has lost his learning through no fault of his own. The fragments of the Tablets broken by Moses were kept in the Ark of the Covenant alongside the new ones.

Judah bar Ilai

The Lesson of the Kindertransport
When Nazi said '*Du bist ein Untermensch*'
When stranger said 'You will be my servant'
When synagogue said 'You are an inconvenience'
When child in school of 1941 said 'Go home, German pig'
I felt a no-one

But it was not to me, individually;
it was from the circumstance of prejudice,
it was from the System
that the words were spoken.   Yet I felt a no-one

When *Mutti* said 'Go, and go on living'
When headmaster said 'Come, learn and be a teacher'
When husband said 'You are my beloved'
When children said 'You are our best Mummy'
When friend said
'With guts you have done it' I felt a some-one

Now it was to me, the individual;
to my own personhood
that the words were spoken.   And I felt a some-one

No-one, some-one
it is our humanity that says it
each to another.

Ingeborg Bower

On Earning Love

To love somebody is not just a strong feeling - it is a decision, it is a judgment, it is a promise. If love were only a feeling, there would be no basis for the promise to love each other forever. A feeling comes and it may go. How can I judge that it will stay forever, when my act does not involve judgment and decision?

Erich Fromm

Parents and Children

The child must be seen as a foreigner who does not understand the language of the street plan, who is ignorant of the laws and customs. Occasionally he likes to go sightseeing on his own; and when up against some difficulty, asks for information and advice. Wanted - a guide to answer questions politely.

Janusz Korczak

Mein Yingele - My Little Son

    I have a little boy,
    a fine little son,
    when I see him, it seems to me
    I own the whole world.
    But I seldom see him,
    my little son, when he is awake.
    I always meet him when he sleeps.
    I only see him at night.
    My work drives me out early
    and makes me come home late.
    Strange to me is my own flesh and blood.
    Strange to me the look of my child.
    When I come home shattered,
    wrapped up in darkness,
    then my pale wife tells me
    how nicely our child plays,
    how sweetly he chatters, how cleverly he asks:
    'O mother, good mother,
    when will he bring me a penny
    my good, good father?'
    I listen and yes, it must,
    yes, yes, it must happen!
    Father love blazes up in me.
    My child, I must see him.
    I must stand by his cot
    and see and hear and look.
    A dream stirs his lips:
    'O where is daddy?'
    I kiss the little blue eyes.
    They open, O child!
    They see me
    and quickly they close.
    There stands your father, dearest,
    there you have a penny!
    A dream stirs his lips;
    'O where is daddy?'
    I become sad and oppressed,
    bitterly I think,
    when you finally wake, my child,
    you won't find me anymore.

Morris Rosenfeld

Children and Prayer

It must be the task of all religious education once again to teach the child to pray. It is of course obvious that this must be undertaken primarily in the parental home. Mothers who are concerned that their children should have a religious education must pray with their children daily, whether in Hebrew or in their native tongue. But there is one essential element in this: the inner approach to prayer and the personal relationship. The familiar approach to God must already be expressed in prayer at a very early age ... There is one thing in prayer that we all need so greatly and which children can already learn: a few minutes each day of peace and quiet with oneself, at least a minute fragment of the day to listen within oneself, attending to the voice of God.

Ellen Littmann

Bar/Bat Mitsvah

The *Bar/Bat Mitsvah* rite of passage can open up a world of meaning to the youngster. Meaning in their studying, in their choice of vocation or profession, in their talent for living. They must be taught through precept and conduct that being a Jew is to be enlarged, that their horizons are expanded beyond the shrivelling shopping malls. They must be taught to respect themselves as children of prophets who gave the world, Western and Eastern civilisations, the idea of a God who cares for the weak and is angry with the callous and cries with the dispossessed. They are children of a community who in the eighteenth century supported one out of three Jews in Germany, Italy and England. They must be taught the moral vocabulary of our tradition: *zedakah, rahmanut, gemilut chasadim, hachnasat kallah, tamhui, linat hatzedek, moshav zekenim, beith yetomim* - the Jewish semantics of meaningful living: charity, compassion, loving kindness, dowering the bride, soup kitchens, homes for the aged, the orphans, the poor.

The *Bar* and *Bat Mitsvah* has in our times become a major event in the lifecycle of Jews. It can become a sacred event, a significant transition from childhood to mature Jewish adulthood.

Harold M. Schulweis

Mikveh

Mikveh in the context of *niddah* (menstruation) remains, for me, an outdated ritual derived from an elaborate rabbinic complex of laws of menstrual purity. Like so many Jewish laws they evolved to deal with a particular set of socio-cultural circumstances very different to our own. That is not to say that contemporary women necessarily feel constrained or oppressed by this archaic ritual cycle ... If one feels empowered by an activity then this liberating sensation becomes more important than the circumstances surrounding it ...

<<<

Focusing on the symbolism of water, immersion and spiritual transformation, groups of women are creating new practices involving *mikveh* to mark important events in their lives. *Mikveh* is incorporated into ways of marking the birth of a baby girl, for divorce, for infertility, for *bat mitsvah* and for the onset of menstruation/menopause.

Female lifecycle events used largely to pass by without formal communal response. Naming ceremonies for baby girls and *b'not mitsvah* have come a long way in redressing this balance, but there is potential to make these events even more relevant and related to an individual's experience. Twelve/thirteen is undoubtedly an important time in the development of both boys and girls. For teenage girls in particular, the onset of menstruation coincides with a relentless subjection to unattainable standards of beauty. *Bat mitsvah* publicly addresses an individual's coming of age, and an accepting of the responsibilities of adulthood in both family and communal settings. But for a teenage girl, coming to terms with the consequences of her new adult status, a personal ceremony such as *mikveh* might help ease this transition. Immersion has the symbolic potential to integrate the physical with the spiritual and to celebrate the individual in her unique body. What better way to affirm a girl's personal commitment to her cultural heritage whilst acknowledging the sanctity of her body?

Anouska Salida

The Wedding
The *B'deken* - veiling

Genesis 24:65 relates that when Rebecca first set eyes on Isaac she immediately veiled herself. The *b'deken*, the 'veiling', is usually a private ceremony before the public proceedings in which the bride and groom take their first look at each other that day, and traditionally the groom veils the bride, mirroring the Genesis story.

The veil also teaches that 'the glory of the princess is the interior' of a person, the inner qualities of soul and character are more important.

Similarly, a Jewish groom sometimes wears a *kittel*, a white robe symbolising purity and forgiveness, which can be worn in synagogue on some holidays and at home during the Passover *seder*. It can also be used as a burial shroud, so wearing it at the wedding humbles the groom and reminds him that all the attention will pass and that he is merely mortal.

The *Chuppah* - wedding canopy

The *chuppah* may be a reminder of ancient Israelite tent-life or may symbolise the house into which the newlyweds entered at the end of the engagement period. The *chuppah's* simplicity invites the couple to be wealthy, not rich, to seek elegance rather than luxury, and refinement rather than fashion.

The *chuppah* also sets the couple apart, establishing an island of serenity.

Circling

Jewish brides sometimes circle the groom three or seven times. The original custom may well have its origins in superstition, since demons cannot break circles, and odd numbers are similarly repellent. Others suggest that the number three echoes Hosea 2:21-22 where the word 'betroth' comes three times, while the number seven has great significance, for example the Shabbat as the seventh day.

A possible practice today is for bride and groom to circle each other three times and complete the seven by circling together. This would be a physical manifestation of Genesis 2:24 which states that 'a man shall leave his father and mother and cleave to his wife and they shall be one flesh'. A circle is drawn with the beloved at the centre and with the parents and family as the new periphery. But the circle is open expressing that the marriage, while exclusive and inviolable, is not a closed system, and that the new family is part of a new community.

The *Ketubah* - marriage document

Traditionally the *ketubah* described the legal obligations of the husband to the wife but not of the wife to the husband. Today the *ketubah* may mirror some of the traditional legal language but reflect the equal obligations of husband and wife.

Breaking the Glass

Several reasons are suggested for the custom of breaking a glass at the end of the ceremony, in which the underlying purpose is always the creation of noise.

Two talmudic stories tell of rabbis whose wedding guests became too boisterous, and who therefore brought before them a precious cup or glass and shattered it, reminding them of the need to moralise pleasure and temper emotions.

In the fourteenth century, it was suggested that the custom reminds us of the destruction of the Temple. As such, the custom of shouting '*mazal tov*' immediately after the act is not a celebration of the breaking of the glass, but of the completion of the ceremony. The Talmud says (*Sotah* 2a) that joining two people in marriage is as difficult as splitting the sea - the breaking of the glass celebrates the making of a new home and all its wonderful challenges.

Yichud - union, privacy

After the ceremony the couple move off to a separate room for *yichud*. There, privacy guarded by witnesses, they may break their day's fast if that has been their practice, and spend the first few moments of married life together in peace.

Neil and Jenny Amswych

On Marriage

A Roman matron asked Rabbi Jose ben Chalafta, 'How many days did it take God to create the world?' 'Six days,' he replied. 'And what has God been doing ever since?' 'Making marriages.' 'And is that all God does?' asked the woman. 'I could do as much myself! I have men slaves and women slaves. In one hour I could marry them all.' 'Though it may appear easy in your eyes,' said the Rabbi, 'yet every marriage means as much to God as the splitting of the Reed Sea.'

What did the woman do when Rabbi Jose was gone? She took a thousand men slaves and a thousand women slaves, placed them in two rows, and said: 'Let this one take that one, let this one take that one' - and in a single night she married them all. The next morning the women came to the house of their mistress. One had a cracked skull, another a bruised eye, a third a broken arm. 'What happened?' she asked. And each one replied: 'I will not live with this one - I will not live with that one ...'

Then the woman sent for Rabbi Jose, and said to him: 'There is no God like your God, and your Torah is beautiful and praiseworthy, for you were in the right.' And he replied: 'Did I not say that though a good marriage may seem an easy thing in your eyes, to God it means as much work as the miracle of the splitting of the Reed Sea?'

Genesis Rabbah 68:4

To relate is to sacrifice, and though no one would deny their need to relate, we all do deny our need to sacrifice. We want it all. When we don't get it all, we describe the circumstances with words like 'adapting - making do - learning to live with - copping out - stuck - trapped - etc, etc.' and what we are really talking about is our inability to give up something we can't have, under circumstances where it is unavoidable. All we can really do is be conscious of sacrifice or blind to it, but it lays there under the surface no matter what our attitude to it is. Our reluctance to look under the surface, and the endless social phenomenon of marriage and divorce, seem to be rooted in the desire to return to the Garden, where no sacrifice was required. Well, we were expelled from the Garden and it was destroyed. We now live in the world that God filled with suffering, and our striving for wholeness is tied to the world and the people in it. If we are to survive with the heritage of suffering we must do so by lessening it as God suggested, by utilizing and developing the bond between man and woman so two can bear the pain which otherwise one must bear alone. If we can't go backward, and we can't, then we must go forward in lessened suffering, willingly sacrificing what we cannot have and being content with what we can.

Abraham Barzeli

Love, according to the Torah, should express itself in a commitment to sustain one's partner, to provide security for one's partner and to act in a loving and pleasure-giving fashion. *She'er*, food, becomes a symbol for all sustenance, and without satisfying one's needs for sustenance, all protestations of caring become a mockery. *Keshut*, clothing, is emblematic of physical security, something we also need as a bedrock on which to build our lives. Love cannot survive without sustenance and security.

The last category, *onah*, is the most intriguing. Rabbinic tradition, as well as the Septuagint, Peshitta and Targums, translate *onah* as conjugal rights. That reading is unique among all ancient law codes, mandating a healthy and loving sexuality as a necessary component of an adult love relationship ...

The Torah points the way to a love that is grounded both in the body and in the spirit, a coming together of two people in their wholeness, both physical and emotional.

Bradley Shavit Artson

On the Death of an Infant
Lost Without Trace
When you were born
  - my little boy, just like a doll -
I soared to the stars
but you only stayed two weeks,
then the skies turned black
the lid was hammered down
all trace of you, gone ...
where to, I never knew.
There was no formality, no funeral,
no rabbi. You were not quite kosher,
they said. No time for the ritual snip
to mark you one of the tribe.
You went unsung, but not unmourned.
I still cry, decades on,
that I don't know where you lie.
How I wish I'd buried you under a headstone
and kicked the tradition into an unmarked grave.

Joan Gordon

On Loss

Several of our friends have commented on how well Rita and I seem to be bearing the loss of our beloved son, and I thought it might be of help to others to know some of the thoughts which crowd our minds in these difficult hours.

I find little consolation in the notion of a heavenly Kingdom where our souls will meet, though I do not dismiss such an event as being beyond possibility. Nor do I derive comfort from the belief that God so loved Andy that He drew our son to Himself. I find no meaning in this tragedy and this is perhaps the only comfort. Were I to believe there was justice in such an affliction, even a justice I do not understand, I think it would drive me mad.

An event such as this happens by chance, because death is as much part of the divine scheme as life. Sorrow is as intrinsic to human existence as joy.

It is neither philosophic acumen nor intensity of faith which enables us to keep functioning. Rather it is the life force which continues to assert itself within us. Friendship, fresh adventure, laughter are extremely important now. The miracle of Jewish survival in the face of the many horrors which have dogged us through the centuries was an appetite for life under almost any conditions. It is this same craving for existence which makes Rita and me wish to continue, and allows us to relish the days and experiences and friendships we may yet be privileged to know.

Jay R. Brickman

I once had a letter from a distraught wife, begging me to tell her how she could stop her husband snoring. 'Sometimes,' she wrote, 'I feel like putting a pillow over his face!'

I offered a few suggestions and then, a year or so later, she wrote again, telling me her beloved husband had died. 'What wouldn't I give now,' she said, 'to have him beside me in bed, snoring …'

Marjorie Proops

A king once owned a large, beautiful, pure diamond of which he was justly proud, for it had no equal anywhere. One day, the diamond accidentally sustained a deep scratch. The king called in the most skilled diamond cutters and offered them a great reward if they could remove the imperfection from his treasured jewel. But none could repair the blemish. The king was sorely distressed.

After some time a gifted jeweller came to the king and promised to make the rare diamond even more beautiful than it had been before the mishap. The king was impressed by his confidence and entrusted his precious stone to his care. And the man kept his word.

With superb artistry he engraved a lovely rosebud around the imperfection and he used the scratch to make the stem.

The Dubner Maggid

The Journey
Your hand, warm, dry, inert
is clasped in mine, clammy despite the heat.
A gadget holds your tongue in place
a loud, unrhythmic snore dominates;
lying on your side, despite your tan
you have changed into an old, old man
a stranger, yet every pore familiar.
Nurse offers me a soapy razor
I shrink back and shake my head ...
Does he know anything?
My throat is dry, voice cracked ...
He may hear you, we don't know ...
My roots stir; I ask for a rabbi
he sways and prays in the accustomed chant
I do not understand but am comforted.
Can you hear it? Will it ease your journey?
When we are alone I whisper
in my dry tight voice, what you mean to me.
There is no response, only the rasping snore.
I do not hear you go. The room is suddenly quiet
yet full of whispers, not to disturb you.
I kiss you that last goodbye
smell the decay under the newly-shaven skin
wonder how far I shall travel without you.

Joan Gordon

On Bereavement

The caring instinct towards both the dying and the living is the one thing which helps counter the extreme loneliness which threatens to swamp you at such a time.

The Jewish mourning rituals are particularly helpful in this respect. For they help connect the mourner with both the living and the dead in a way which brings both consolation and healing.

The *shivah* enables you to float through that first strange week in a kind of protected bubble. The whole set-up makes you feel cared for: the visitors who battle through heavy traffic to attend evening prayers, or who bring home-made cakes or a ready-roasted chicken, or who just sit and listen.

All this kindness, by definition, repeatedly connects the mourner with other people. It prevents you from retreating into your own, solitary pain.

Above all, what it does is enable you to focus upon the departed soul with more intensity than you have ever done in the past or will probably ever do again. This forges the first link in a new and very different chain of connection.

<<<

There is comfort in this, as there is - surprisingly - in the various restrictions on behaviour that tradition enjoins for the prescribed eleven months of mourning, and which are relaxed to some extent after the first thirty-day period has passed.

For these restrictions, and the period of time that they mark, provide a structure to hang on to, a scaffolding that furnishes a sense of order and of continuity that are in themselves both a crutch and a set of benchmarks that help you come to terms with your loss.

And both the restrictions and the ritual of saying *Kaddish* provide the impression of a continuing connection with the one who is mourned. It is like a long, slow, metaphorical letting-go - or maybe, a gradual induction into a new normality.

Melanie Phillips

Does it comfort the adult bereaved to know that their dead help to grow something, that something remains as seed in the ground, in the universe, in other people, in the bereaved himself? Do adults - like children - have a heightened awareness of new life, of creation, when they have to face death? Does it comfort the bereaved to know that death and birth are part of the continuing cycle of life - transitory and eternal?

There is no growth without pain and conflict; there is no loss which cannot lead to gain. Although this interconnection is what life is all about, it is difficult for the newly bereaved to accept. Only slowly may he who has been in touch with death through the loss of a significant person regain touch with life. A life which may bring new growth through the acceptance of death and pain and loss, and thus become truly a new life, a rebirth.

Lily Pincus

On Suffering

'People are born to trouble as surely as sparks fly upward.'

Job 5:7

'Not to know suffering means not to be a human being.'

Genesis Rabbah 92:1

Rava said: If people experience much suffering, they should examine their deeds. If this shows they have sinned in some way, they should repent. If this examination reveals nothing, then they should attribute their sufferings to their neglect of study of the Torah. If this is still not the case, then they should know that their sufferings are 'afflictions of love', as it is written, 'Everyone in whom God delights, He crushes with sufferings' (Isaiah 53:10).

Berachot 5a

Rabbi Hiyya bar Abba became ill. Rabbi Yohanan went in to him. He said to him: 'Is suffering dear to to you?' He answered him: 'Neither it, nor its reward.' He said to him: 'Give me your hand.' He gave him his hand and raised (healed) him.

Rabbi Yohanan became ill. Rabbi Hanina went in to him. He said to him: 'Is suffering dear to you?' He answered him: 'Neither it, nor its reward.' He said to him: 'Give me your hand.' He gave him his hand and raised (healed) him.

And why? Let Rabbi Yohanan raise himself!

They say, 'One who is imprisoned does not release himself from prison.'

Berachot 5b

It was much later that I really understood the meaning of suffering. It can have a meaning if it changes you for the better. As I learnt from Martin Buber, the Hasidim say there are two forms of suffering: one has a positive influence and the other a negative. How do you tell the difference? Suffering from God teaches you something, and suffering from evil drags you down. Of course, at the time of suffering you don't see this.

One of the greatest things it can teach us is a greater understanding of other human beings. It is so basic that it shakes you to your soul and therefore it shows you yourself and the reality of 'self' in other people - it opens your eyes to the reality of other human beings which you would never otherwise understand. Because of this you can come to understand even your oppressors somehow. I don't say we have to learn understanding in this way, but it is one of the positive results of suffering.

Yehudah Bacon

The truth is that the world is full of woes. There is no one who really possesses this world. Even the greatest magnates and princes do not truly possess this world, because their days are filled with upsets and pain, with disturbances and sadness, and every one has his own particular woe.

Nachman of Bratslav

A man once came to Rabbi Mendel of Kotzk to pour out his bitter heart. His wife had died in childbirth leaving him with seven young children including the newly-born infant. He had other woes too and did not know where to turn.

Rabbi Mendel listened to him, but while listening the Rabbi kept his eyes lowered. After a moment of deep meditation Rabbi Mendel raised his head, looked straight into the eyes of the petitioner and said: 'I am not equal to the task of consoling you after such cruel suffering. Only the true Master of mercy is equal to that. Turn to Him.'

Mendel of Kotzk

The Talmud states in *Hagigah 5b* that we may apply the verse 'Strength and rejoicing are in God's place' (1 Chronicles 16:27) to God's outer chambers, but in God's inner chambers God grieves and weeps for the sufferings of Israel ... So that one who pushes in and comes close to God by means of studying Torah, weeps together with God, and studies Torah with God. Just this makes the difference: the weeping, the pain, which a person undergoes by himself, alone, may have the effect of breaking him, of bringing him down, so that he is incapable of doing anything. But the weeping which a person does together with God - that strengthens him. He weeps - and is strengthened; he is broken - but finds courage to study and teach.

Kalonymus Kalman Shapiro

Whenever one is confronted with an inescapable, unavoidable situation, whenever one has to face a fate which cannot be changed, e.g. an incurable disease, such as an incurable cancer; just then one is given a last chance to actualize the highest value, to fulfil the deepest meaning, the meaning of suffering. For what matters above all is the attitude we take towards suffering, the attitude in which we take our suffering upon ourselves.

Viktor Frankl

On Survival

When I was a student I hitchhiked back from my first term at University to visit my parents. I arrived home as they were going out to a party. They took me to a house full of people aged in their thirties and forties who were drinking cups of tea, and chatting about mortgages and house prices, rewiring and children's education. I was eighteen, long-haired and bearded. No one was talking about the meaning of life or the overthrow of political tyranny! It was all about plumbing and the cost of school uniforms. Rabbi Hugo Gryn was also there. He came to me as I sat in a corner. He asked me, 'What do you think of the party?' I said, 'Nice people, but it is a little boring.'

'Don't you know who these people are?' asked Hugo. 'No,' I replied.

'These are the people your parents looked after following the war; every one of them has a story. Ask your parents.'

I asked my parents. During the war they had a home for *Kindertransport* children, and after the war they looked after children from the camps. This party was a reunion. My mother told me about them: 'Twenty years ago that woman was a child who could never be left alone because she was suicidal, while that man over there had to sleep alone, because he screamed so much throughout the night that he kept everyone else awake.'

These people had all been through the most profound physical and psychological difficulties when they were children; and now they were here, and the fact that they could discuss schools and homes was extraordinary. These ordinary people were moral giants. They were keeping the story alive. They were living life and living it well.

Daniel Smith

On Hope

During these years I have met people who have been weakened from constant disappointments. They continually create new hopes for themselves, and as a result they betray themselves. Others live in the world of illusions, hastily and incessantly building and rebuilding their world in order to prevent real life from ultimately destroying it.

What then is the solution? The only answer is to find the meaning of your current life. It's best if you are left with only one hope - the hope of remaining yourself no matter what happens. Don't fear, don't believe, and don't hope. Don't believe words from the outside; believe your own heart. Believe in that meaning which was revealed to you in this life, and hope that you will succeed in guarding it.

Anatholy Sharansky

On Illness
Adventure

Being operated on for the first time at forty-five
was one of my adventures.
Ordered to remove all dentures,
I laughed; wheeled in on a stretcher, I smiled -
knowing that I would be wheeled out alive;
that, compared to certain others, I had the health of a child.
For several days, since harvesting notes
is one of my professions,
I let myself swarm with anecdotes
and impressions
so that I could feel genuinely richer coming out,
despite the bill, than I had been
when going in.
There was, it is true, some pain to grumble about,
and for a while I was forbidden to drive,
but all in all
being operated on for the first time at forty-five
was what you might call a ball.
It was what you might call a ball, except
for the undertone, usually at night, that crept
in through the slats of the door
from other rooms along my floor
whose occupants were mostly older
than forty-five (though one of them was scarcely half),
and had been opened in more important places
than the left shoulder,
and did not laugh
about dentures, and had no smiles on their faces,
so pale, so thin,
when the stretchers wheeled them in.

Aaron Kramer

Prayer for a Cure for Cancer
We are sometimes mistaken
when we fear that which is big,
Godzilla, King Kong,
Asteroid, Armageddon,
at least we can see it when it comes,
    We are sometimes mistaken
    when we fear that which is big.
    Change, birth,
        death, love
at least we can throw our arms wide around it.

God of big things
God of great deeds,
God of the drama of the Exodus,
the parting of the seas,
the fire on the mountain,
    the creation out of nothing
we are wonderstruck by You,
dazzled by big things.

But are You not also the God of the small,
    God of the turning leaf,
    God of the grain of sand,
    God of the passing shadow,
    God of the rotting fruit on the window sill?

    I address You now
    as God of the small,
because sometimes we are mistaken when we fear that which is big,
when that which is most frightening of all is small,
the size of a melanomic cell,

the size of a metastatic pinpoint

the size of a grapefruit

growing where there is no tree

<<<

That immutable danger,
that makes us victims of our own soft tissue, lymphnodes and blood,
that devastating fear
that stalks us out of passing shadows,
out of the mist of pesticide,
tar, benzene, p.c.b. toxicities,
out of the glow of gamma-rays, x-rays, ultraviolet rays, aluminium foil,
out of silicone, the tobacco, the skin of an apple,
the high saturated fats, the low fibre,
the vegetable hair dyes,
out of nothing.
    Out of nothing
You are good at that God,
Creation out of nothing.

I pray to You now, God of small things,
God of miracles-barely-perceived by the naked, mortal eye,
I pray to you now, God of small things
for a spontaneous global remission.
for erasure of that word that lurks darkly behind our words.

When Moses' sister was struck,
Moses spoke five small words to You.
He said:
El na refa na lah,
God please heal her, please.
You answered and You healed her.

El na refa na lah.
El na refa na lah.

Zoe Klein

On Recovery

On Friday, since all was going well, I was permitted to spend a night at home. The whole family gathered to welcome me - it was Sabbath Eve. The next morning, I went to the synagogue with my father and brothers, and we were all called up together for the reading of the law. And this was an inexpressible experience; for behind my family I felt embraced by a community and, behind this, by the beauty of old traditions, and, behind this, by the ultimate, eternal joy of the law. The portion was from Genesis, near the beginning, most appropriate to a man who felt reborn; for shortly before, on *Simchat Torah* - The Rejoicing of the Law - the year-long reading of the law had come to its end, and restarted, and the *shofar* had been blown, followed by a great cry: 'Now the world is new created.'

<<<

The service, the ceremonies, the Bible stories, now made sense - in a way which they had never fully or truly done before. A pantheistic feeling had infused the past month, the feeling that the world was God's gift, to be thanked for back to God. Now, within the religious ceremonies and stories, I found a true parable of my own experience and condition - the experience of affliction and redemption, darkness and light, death and rebirth - the 'pilgrimage' which fortune, or my injury, had forced upon me. Now, as never before, I found relevance in the scriptural symbols and stories. I felt that my own story had the shape of such a universal existential experience, the journey of a soul into the underworld and back, a spiritual drama - on a neurological basis.

Oliver Sachs

On Aging
It is forbidden to be old!

Nachman of Bratslav

Prophecy
As I'm no longer young in life
and there seem to me not
so many pleasures to look forward to
how fortunate to be free
to write of cars and wars, truths and eras,
throw away old useless
ties and pants that don't fit. (January 9, 1985)

Allen Ginsberg

The tusks that clashed in mighty brawls
of mastodons are billiard balls.

The sword of Charlemagne the Just
is ferric oxide, known as rust.

The grizzly bear whose potent hug
was feared by all is now a rug.

Great Caesar's bust is on the shelf,
and I don't feel so well myself!

Arthur Guiterman

I am not among those who disdain instant coffee; we drink it most mornings. Not quite as good as the real thing, but the instant variety is a fair approximation. Its main advantage, of course, is the time it saves - this is important in the morning. I use a heaped teaspoonful for each cup of rapidly boiling water.

At night I use a Melior coffeemaker. I measure two cups of water into an adjacent kettle and while this is heating, I set the coffeemaker on a cold burner, place a filter in the top, creasing one edge so that it stays open. I measure two tablespoons of coffee beans into the electric grinder and turn it on for ten seconds. Then I turn on the burner under the coffeemaker and pour in the water. The process makes an excellent cup of coffee, and in the evening, one has time. The Japanese tea ceremony takes longer. We should derive gratification not only from the product of our acts but from the procedure.

The saving of time is essential in one's early years because so much needs to be accomplished: schooling, gaining a livelihood, raising a family. Older people have a problem with too much time. One technique for dealing with this new challenge is to discard all instant food preparation. Inscribe the words, 'Cook from Scratch', on the kitchen wall. As a first step I recommend the Melior coffeemaker. Later on, if time is still a problem, one might consider mastering the Japanese tea ceremony.

Jay R. Brickman

The way is so beautiful - says the child
The way is so difficult - says the youngster
The way is so long - says the adult
The old one sat beside the way to rest.

The sinking sun bathes his white hair in gold and red
The grass at his feet shines with the dew of evening.
The last bird of the day sings above him:
Do you remember how beautiful it was, how long the way?

Leah Goldberg

Talking to My Grandfather

I was trying to reach my grandfather this morning.
I needed to talk to him.
He would have been 99 on September twelfth.

Nothing was working.
I thought I could do it
by remembering the arrangement of his kitchen
and putting him across from me at the table

where he used to read his racing forms
for the harmless two-dollar bets
he liked to place now and again,
but I had no luck.
After I failed with that trick,
all I could come up with, by way of comparison, was:
it was like fiddling with the TV antenna
and still not getting a picture without shadows
no matter which way you turned it or angled the rabbit ears.

Then I tried to remember
the smell of work boots and gloves in his store,
hoping from there I would see him standing at the cash register
and slipping me a quarter to play the pinball machines down the block,
but that didn't happen either.

I needed to talk to him,
and tell him I missed him,
and how was business?
and did he still have a cold?
and did the optometrist get him his new glasses yet?
and did he want me to come over
to watch the wrestling matches with him
so we could cheer or boo when the champ -
Gorgeous George in those days -
threw the other guy half-way across the ring
or got all bent up in a vicious hammer lock?

I even tried imagining how huge and quiet his old Hudson was,
(picturing the old cars was always a sure stimulus in the past,)
and I would be sitting as straight as I could in the back
so I could reach the windows to see outside
while he got behind the wheel
to take me up the hill to the nice fish place
where, in my mother's absence,
(she had stayed behind for some reason or another,)
he would let me use as much ketchup as I wanted
on the French fries
because that was one of the ways he spoiled me.
But, for the third time, I had no luck,
which, as I write this, seems so wrong,
because I just wanted to talk to him
and see how he was doing.

<<<

But, as the writing of poems has its way
of sometimes resembling love,
which, in this case at least,
is also exactly the way life operates -
at the beginning, in the middle,
and sometimes even towards the end of love and of life,
you still might not know how it's going to turn out -
I see just at this moment I had this need to stay in touch
because there were two questions I had to ask,
maybe during the commercials between the wrestling matches:
Is there some form of happiness after you die?
and Was the Talmud right when it said dying
is as simple and painless as pulling a hair out of a cup of milk?

Danny Siegel

On Dying

When I was a small boy, and even into my early teens, my grandmother prayed in the synagogue on the High Holy days. As difficult as the five-block pilgrimage became, she would somehow manage it, negotiating cracked areas in the Bronx pavement with her worn prayer book held very snugly under one armpit lest she sin by letting it fall to the ground. I would take her there. How I regret every murmur of complaint, how I wish I was not sometimes - no, not sometimes, but often - ashamed of being seen with this black-kerchiefed, shuffling remnant of a shtetl culture that was all but gone even as she stubbornly refused to join it in the grave. Everyone else's grandparents seemed so much younger, they spoke English, and they were independent - mine was a reminder not only of the lost world of Eastern European Jewry but of my own turbulent conflict about the load of emotional detritus I nowadays euphemistically call my heritage.

...

About five years before her death, Bubbeh could no longer make the long walk to the synagogue, even with both grandsons to help her. Relying largely on her still-intact long-term memory, she recited the liturgy at home, sitting by the open window as she had done every Saturday morning during all the years I knew her. After a few years, even that became too much. She could barely see the sentences and her memory for the prayers learned in her youth was giving out. Finally, she stopped praying altogether.

By the time Bubbeh stopped praying, she had stopped virtually everything else as well. Her food intake had become minimal - she spent most of each day seated quietly at her window, and she spoke sometimes of death. And yet she had no disease. I'm sure some eager physician might have pointed out her chronic cardiac failure and added to it the probability that there was an element of atherosclerosis, and perhaps he would have prescribed some

digitalis. To me, that would have been like dignifying the degeneration of her joints by calling it osteoarthritis. Of course it was arthritis, and of course she was in chronic failure, but only because her pinions and springs were giving way under the weight of the years. She had never been sick a day in her life.
...

   Mankind cannot afford to destroy the balance - the economy, if you will - by tinkering with one of its most essential elements. For plants and animals, renewal requires that death precede it so that the weary may be replaced by the vigorous. That is what is meant by the cycles of nature. There is nothing pathological or sick about the sequence - in fact, it is the antithesis of sick. To call a natural process by the name of a disease is the first step in the attempt to cure and thereby thwart it. To thwart it is the first step towards thwarting the continuation of exactly that which we try to preserve, which is, after all, the order and system of our universe.

And so, Bubbeh had to die, as you and I will one day have to die.

Sherwin B. Nuland

A Meditation on Death
What ends, what begins?
   Someone has died. What has happened? Nothing, perhaps, and perhaps everything. Only a few hours' grief, perhaps, or months: and then everything will be calm once more and life will go on as before. Or perhaps something that once looked like an indivisible whole will be torn into a thousand shreds, perhaps a life will suddenly lose all the meaning that was once dreamed into it; or perhaps sterile longings will blossom into new strength. Something is collapsing, perhaps, or perhaps something else is being built; perhaps neither of the two is happening and perhaps both. Who knows? Who can tell?

What does it mean?
   Someone has died. And the survivors are faced with the painful forever fruitless question of the eternal distance, the unbridgeable void between one human being and another. Nothing remains that they might cling to, for the illusion of understanding another person is fed only by the renewed miracles, the anticipated surprises of constant companionship; these alone are capable of giving something like reality to illusion, which is directionless - like air. The sense of belonging together is kept alive only by continuity, and once this is destroyed, even the past disappears; everything one person may know about another is only expectation, only potentiality, only wish or fear, acquiring reality only as a result of what happens later; and this reality, too, dissolves straightaway into potentialities. Every rupture - unless it is a conscious ending, something which severs all the threads of the past from real life and ties them together in order to give them final and complete form, the static form of a finished work of art - every rupture not only cuts off the future for all eternity, but also destroys the entire past ...

<<<

The questions.
   The questions pile up, the doubts come down and the lost possibilities whirl around in a mad witches' dance. Everything whirls, everything else - dream and life, wish and reality, fear and truth, the lying denial of pain and the courageous confrontation of sadness. What is left? What is sure in this life of ours? Where is the place, however bleak and bare, however remote from all beauty and richness, where a man may strike solid roots? Where is there anything that does not trickle away like sand between one's fingers just when one would wish to lift that thing out of the formless mass of life and hold it fast, if only for a brief moment? Where is the dividing line between dream and reality, the 'I' of the world, deep meaning and fleeting impression?

Georg Lukács

Yahrzeit
I Am Older Now: A Yahrzeit Candle Lit at Home
The *yahrzeit* candle is different
announcing neither Sabbath nor festival.
No benediction recited
no song sung
no psalm mandated.

Before this unlit candle
without a quorum, I stand
unstruck match in my hand.

It is less distant now
the remembrance ritual of parents deceased
I am older now
closer to their age than before.
I am older now
their aches in my body
their white hairs beneath my shaved skin
their wrinkles creased into my face.

It is less distant now
this ritual
once made me think of them
now makes me think of me.
Once it recalled relationships to them
now it ponders on my children's relationship to me.
Once I wondered what to remember of them
now I ask what my children remember of me
what smile, what grimace
what stories they will tell their children of me.

<<<

It is less distant now.
How would I be remembered?
How would I be mourned?
Will they come to the synagogue
light a candle
recite the *Kaddish*?
It is less distant now.
Once *yahrzeit* was about parents deceased
now it is of children alive
Once it was about a distant past
now it is about tomorrow.

Harold M. Schulweis

Relapse 28 May 1998

I wanted to write this book as an inspiration to others, to show that while being diagnosed with a life-threatening disease is unbelievably traumatic and painful, there are positives and you can beat it if you put your mind to it. This is the first time that I have lost the intuitive belief that I'm going to be OK. When I was first diagnosed I philosophised about death but I never truly believed I was going to die. I remember saying at the time that if I was to die (which I wasn't but if I was) I know I will have led a full and active life and on the whole a very happy one, short though it may be. In the last 22 years I have managed to live in 3 countries, met dozens of fascinating people, been able to do the type of work that I believe in (although lucrative - it wasn't!), built up a beautiful set of friends and have very close, loving relationships with my family. But perhaps most importantly I have finally got to the stage where I like the person that I have become. I remember also saying that wasn't it crazy that all this time, money, faith and effort was being placed in getting me better, really only putting off the inevitable that everyone has to face at some point.

I watched the Dutch film 'Antonia's Line' at the time which is about an old lady on her death bed looking at her life and it often refers to the 'miracle of death'. At first I felt uneasy with the expression. I guess few of us can really deal with the word 'death', let alone celebrate its meaning. But as I thought about it more, it made more and more sense. If we can talk about the miracle of birth, why not talk about the miracle of death? We don't know where we come from when we enter this world but we enter seemingly fairly untraumatised from where we have come from (although I know there are many who disagree with that last statement) and we go back to what seems like to us now, with our very limited minds and imaginations, an oblivion. I personally believe that the human soul is far too beautiful and complex to just be destroyed. I believe that in some way or another it lives on but our imaginations are simply incapable of imagining how and we'll only find out when we get there.

So here I am at the darkest hour of this whole ordeal. I've gone through so much treatment and it has all failed. My only hope is a new treatment that only 12 people have tried and only two of them have had CML in blast crises. I'm walking a tightrope. I'm balancing for dear life. My options are death or miraculous cure, either way at least it is going to be dramatic.

<<<

When I was first told about the relapse I decided I was going to bin the idea of writing a book. I thought that maybe I would continue to write it as my own private outlet but that it would never see the light of day. When I was first diagnosed I desperately needed to meet people who had been through this and come out the other side. I wanted this book to provide that hope to others and now I cannot guarantee it. Maybe my intuitive belief that everything will be alright will come back, maybe it won't, maybe nobody will want to publish this book so it won't be an issue but I've decided to carry on writing it in the hope that it will be published because I want to be informative about treatments which of course doctors can explain but they don't know what it feels like; I want to show that alongside the agony one is also exposed to the greatest of human warmth and emotion, whether it be your sister or a vague acquaintance; I want to show that your mind is a very valuable tool and that you can use it in ways you never thought possible; I want to say that somehow, no matter what the outcome, things work out for the best even if it is not initially obvious.

This was the last entry by Karen Morris and was written a few days after she suffered a relapse. Karen deteriorated rapidly and passed away on 18 September 1998. The Karen Morris Memorial Trust was set up in June 1999 to continue her fundraising initiative and in an attempt to find some meaning in her last sentence.

Only Us
Only us. That's all-of-us. All there is, is an us
until there isn't an us. Maybe it'll be one-of-us that
goes, or some-of-us, or in the end the all-of-us who
were once here. So, all that we've got is either us, or
not-us. Nothing in-between. Or out-there. It's an
us-for-a-while, then a not-us. In our case there was
one-kind-of-us, one kind of a way of being us, and
now, with one less of us, there's another-kind-of-us.
When that hurts I'm better with the me, when it's in
some kind of us, even if it roars with being a new-us.

Michael Rosen

SOCIETY AND COMMUNITY

The Mysteries of Life
The rabbis taught that seven things are hidden from us, and these are they:
> The day of death.
> The day of consolation.
> The extent of the judgment.
> Nobody knows what is in the heart of their neighbour.
> Nobody knows how they are to earn their living,
> nor when the Kingdom of David will be restored (the messianic time),
> nor when the reign of evil will cease.
>
> Pesachim 54b

Love of Neighbour
Whatever I want for myself, I want the same for that other person. And whatever I do not want for myself or my friends I do not want for that other person. This is the meaning of God's words: 'You shall love the other as yourself' (Lev 19:18).

Maimonides, Sefer ha-mitzvot, Positive Commandment 206

Every single person is required to say: For my sake the world was created.

Mishnah Sanhedrin, end of chapter 4

Judaism demands that we consider the honour of our neighbour as sacred as our own. It therefore prohibits the derogation of our neighbour through evil gossip or hurting him through mockery and shame. Judaism demands that we respect the religious convictions of others. It therefore prohibits any derogation or disrespect of religious customs and symbols of people of other faiths.

Prayerbook of Berlin Liberal Synagogue

Rabbi Dostai, son of Rabbi Yannai, explained: If a person gives even a '*perutah*', a small coin, to someone who is poor, that person deserves to experience the presence of God, as it says: Through just actions I will see Your face, when I awake I am filled with the vision of You (*Psalm 17:15*).

Baba Batra 10a

So thus says the Eternal: If you produce something precious out of what is worthless, then you will speak for Me.

Jeremiah 15:19

'Do not rob a poor person because that person is poor' (Proverbs 22:22). Our rabbis have taught: What is this verse really speaking about? If the person is really poor, what could we possibly be robbing? Rather, the verse must be speaking about the gifts that belong to the poor that the Torah expects us to give to the poor: the gleanings, the forgotten sheaves of grain, the corners of the field, and the poor person's tithe. The Holy One gave a warning that we should not rob poor people of these gifts which rightfully belong to them because they are poor. It is enough for them that they have to endure poverty. Is it not enough that the wealthy are comfortable, and the poor are in distress? Yet they would steal from the poor that which God has given to them (by not observing the mitzvah of giving charity)!

Numbers Rabbah 5:2

The Torah demands that we seek what is best for our fellows: not by repressing our hatred or rejection of them, nor by loving them out of a sense of duty, for this is no genuine love. We should simply love our neighbour as we love ourselves. We do not love ourselves because we are human beings, but our self-love comes to us naturally without any calculations, or limits, or aims. It would never occur to someone to say: 'I have already fulfilled my obligation towards myself!' - The same way we should love our fellows naturally and spontaneously, with joy and pleasure, without limits, purposes or rationalisations.

Israel Salanter

Visiting the sick - *Bikkur Cholim*

We should not neglect to invoke Divine compassion on every sick person we visit. If we spent time with the sick but forgot to pray for Divine compassion, we have not fulfilled the *mitzvah* completely ... We may pray for the sick in any language we wish since we are addressing our words directly to the *Shechinah* (the presence of God) which is at the side of the patient ... We should say: 'May the All-present have mercy upon you among the sick ones of Israel.' For Sabbath the formula is: 'It is Sabbath, to cry out is forbidden. But the cure will come speedily, and God's mercies are many. Have a peaceful Sabbath.'

Chafetz Chaim

Once a disciple of Rabbi Akiba became ill and no one visited him. Rabbi Akiba, however, entered the sick man's room, arranged that it be swept and cleaned, placed the pillow in order, and the like. All this assisted the recovery of the disciple.

He exclaimed: 'O Master, you have revived me!'

When Rabbi Akiba departed, he said: 'Whosoever neglects to visit a friendless, sick person is as if he has shed his blood.'

Nedarim 40a

Freedom of Speech

Even if what someone says is directed against your religion or faith, do not tell them not to speak or suppress their words. Otherwise there will be no clarification in religion. In fact, you should tell such people to say whatever they want ... and not give them the excuse that they would have said more if they had been given the opportunity ...

My views are the opposite of what some people think. They believe that when it is forbidden to speak against religion, religion is strengthened ... But this is simply not so. By suppressing the opinions of those who are opposed to religion, you actually undermine religion and weaken it. It is far better to go looking for them and study them ... For anyone of character who wants to wrestle with someone else and show their own strength will be eager to make sure that their opponent has every advantage so as to show off their own real powers ... But what strength do you show when you forbid your opponents to defend themselves and fight against you?!

Judah Loewe ben Bezalel, the Maharal of Prague

Governments which suppress freedom of speech ... act like children who shut their eyes in order not to be seen.

Ludwig Boerne

Freedom is absolutely necessary for progress in science and the liberal arts. Not only is freedom of thought and speech compatible with piety and the peace of the State, but it cannot be withheld without destroying at the same time both the peace of the State and piety itself.

Baruch Spinoza

On Prejudice

There is nothing inevitable about human prejudice. There is no biological gene which stipulates that groups should harbour distrust against 'others'. If there is pessimism, it is because the conditions which have created the movement of populations are exactly those which politicians can exploit by using nationalist messages to appeal to popular insecurities.

On the other hand, these conditions also create other possibilities. Instead of fear of 'otherness', there is the possibility of celebrating difference. Few political leaders have the courage to welcome immigration as a positive force in the contemporary world. Far from being a social problem to be avoided, immigration can be seen as a benefit which contains the possibility of cultural innovation. Culture should not be seen as something static, which is threatened by exposure to difference; instead it could be argued that culture stagnates if excluded from difference.

<<<

Thus, groups which bring together people from different religions can symbolise a more hopeful future. The precondition is not that groups should come together in order to learn about 'the other', as if the other were an interesting anthropological specimen. Instead, there should be a willingness to accept that, in learning from others, oneself changes. What might have seemed alien becomes familiar - and that otherness, which has been learnt, becomes part of oneself. This is the very condition which terrifies the authoritarian personality - the acceptance of one's own otherness. However, this acceptance is all the more pressing if tolerance is to prevail over the psychological forces of bigotry; and if understanding, acceptance and hope are to conquer fear.

Michael Billig

Racism is the precursor, the forerunner, the first diseased step towards the death of decency ...
Those who attack racism of any sort do not create racism - racists do that.

Greville Janner

Hatred and Forgiveness

My personal temperament is not inclined to hatred. I regard it as bestial, crude, and prefer on the contrary that my actions and thoughts, as far as possible, should be the product of reason; therefore I have never cultivated within myself hatred as a desire for revenge, or as a desire to inflict suffering on my real or presumed enemy, or as a private vendetta. Even less do I accept hatred as directed collectively at an ethnic group, for example, all the Germans; if I accepted it, I would feel that I was following the precepts of Nazism, which was founded precisely on national and racial hatred ...

All the same I would not want my abstaining from explicit judgement to be confused with an indiscriminate pardon. No, I have not forgiven any of the culprits, nor am I willing to forgive a single one of them, unless he has shown (with deeds, not words, and not too long afterward) that he has become conscious of the crimes and errors of Italian and foreign Fascism and is determined to condemn them, uproot them, from his conscience and from that of others. Only in this case am I, a non-Christian, prepared to follow the Jewish and Christian precept of forgiving my enemy, because an enemy who has seen the error of his ways ceases to be an enemy.

Primo Levi

Community

The Baal Shem Tov used to spend many hours praying. Many of his followers would leave because they became hungry or tired, but some would remain until the Baal Shem had completed his prayers. One day all of his disciples left him alone to pray and that day he finished very quickly. When they returned they asked him, 'Why did you finish so quickly?' In response he related a parable.

'One day there were many people near a tree but only one person could see the beautiful bird in the tree. In order to touch that bird, the man had to stand each person one on top of the other's shoulders, and only then could he reach the bird's nest.'

When I stand, *siddur* in my hand, surrounded by the members of my community, I stand on the shoulders of generations of Jews before me. I gather spiritual strength and breadth as I embrace and express the joys, fears, doubts, hopes and affirmations which psalmists, talmudists, mystics poured out before the Eternal.

When I stand, *siddur* in my hand, surrounded by the members of my community, I stand on the shoulders of those around me today as together we pour out psalms, pray prayers and sing songs. I know that around me are others who, like me, seek to add spiritual breadth, height and depth to their lives. Their faith, their voices, their presence helps me to climb.

Sometimes in the privacy of my own space and time I pray my own prayers and sing my own songs, but I finish so quickly. We need each other's shoulders, the shoulders of the Jewish past and the Jewish present, a *siddur* and a *kehillah*, a prayer book and a community, to give us spiritual strength. Perhaps the Messiah is waiting until he sees us carrying each other on our shoulders.'

Steven Katz

The Jewish ideal is a sacred community ... A Talmudic adage urges, *tafasta m'rubah lo tafasta*. 'If you reach too far, you capture nothing.' The successful beginning, then, is hardly a mission statement announcing the need to find God in an instant, or even a day, or a month or a year. Sacred community begins with a modest but firm commitment to the project of our generation: to transcend ethnicity and seek out the holy in such things as the ways we think, the blessings we say, the truths we discover, and the homes we have or seek to find. Jewish spirituality is not just real. It is reasonable and it is deep. And it beckons us now more than ever to return home to find it.

Lawrence A. Hoffman

Abuse of Religion

Ambition and unscrupulousness have grown so powerful that religion is thought to consist not so much in respecting the writings of the Holy Spirit as in defending human commentaries, so that religion is no longer identified with charity, but with spreading discord and propagating insensate hatred disguised under the name of zeal for the Lord, and eager ardour ...

Every result of their diseased imagination they attribute to the Holy Spirit, and strive to defend with the utmost zeal and passion; for it is an observed fact that men employ their reason to defend conclusions arrived at by reason, but conclusions arrived at by the passions are defended by the passions.

Baruch Spinoza

Social Justice

'Justice, justice shall you pursue ...' (Deut 16:20). The plain sense of the repetition is that we should be just both in what we say and in what we do. When people are just in their words, it is a sure sign that they are also just in their deeds. It also teaches: the means you use in the pursuit of justice must themselves be just. Those who study and teach Torah, observe and practise it, but, when they are able to protest against injustice, fail to do so, are included among those of whom Scripture says: 'Cursed be those who do not uphold the words of this Torah.'

Bachya ben Asher

One can always find warm hearts who in a glow of emotion would like to make the whole world happy but who have never attempted the sober experiment of bringing a real blessing to a single human being. It is easy to revel enthusiastically in one's love of man, but it is more difficult to do good to someone solely because he is a human being. When we are approached by a human being demanding his right, we cannot replace definite ethical action by mere vague goodwill.

Leo Baeck

The Crimes of the People of Sodom

There were four judges in Sodom, Shakrai, Shakurai, Zayyafi and Mazle Dina ... If someone wounded his neighbour they would say to the victim: 'Give him a fee for bleeding you.' Whoever crossed on the ferry had to pay four *zuzim*, but someone who crossed through the water had to pay eight *zuzim*. Once a certain fuller came there. They said to him: 'Give us four *zuzim* for the ferry.' 'But,' he said, 'I crossed through the water.' 'Then you have to give us eight *zuzim*!' He refused so they assaulted him. He went to the judge who ordered: 'Give them a fee for bleeding you and the eight *zuzim* for crossing through the water.' Eliezer, Abraham's servant, happened to be visiting Sodom and was attacked. When he went before the judge he was ordered to pay his attackers a fee for bleeding him. So Eliezer took a stone and hit the judge! 'What was that for!' demanded the judge. Said Eliezer: 'The fee you now owe me (for bleeding you) pay to the man who attacked me!'

They also had beds on which travellers slept. If the guest was too long they shortened him by cutting off his feet. If too short, they stretched him! When Eliezer, Abraham's servant, came along he escaped by saying that he had made a vow since the day of his mother's death never to sleep on a bed.

If a poor man came to Sodom every resident gave him a *denar* with his name on it. But they would never sell him any food. When he starved to death they all came and collected their coins.

They had another agreement amongst themselves that whoever invited a stranger to a meal would be stripped of his garments. When Eliezer came there, a banquet was in progress, but they gave him nothing to eat. So he went and sat down next to someone at the end of the table. They asked him: 'Who invited you here?' So he turned to the man next to him and said: 'You invited me.' The man was scared that he would be stripped of his garments, so he grabbed them and fled. And Eliezer repeated this with each of the Sodomites till they had all left and he ate the whole meal.

Based on Sanhedrin 109b

Social Responsibility

The more deeply immersed I became in the thinking of the prophets, the more powerfully it became clear to me what the lives of the prophets sought to convey: that morally speaking there is no limit to the concern one must feel for the suffering of human beings. It also became clear to me that in regard to cruelties committed in the name of a free society, some are guilty, while all are responsible.

Abraham Joshua Heschel

We can never divorce ourselves from our obligations to combat racism wherever it may exist, from working for fairer asylum and immigration legislation and from teaching our children that they have and will increasingly have a responsibility to develop a more just and harmonious multiracial society ...

It is of paramount importance that we ... examine our own attitudes and behaviour and the ways in which these can result in discrimination, either consciously or unconsciously. Too often we labour under the misconception that because we have suffered and to some extent continue to suffer discrimination, we cannot ourselves be guilty of its practice. For some of us this will not be an easy task, for it requires a profound philosophical shift from seeing ourselves as victims only (a self-concept deeply and for good reason embedded in many of us) to a new self-concept which encompasses both victim and perpetrator.

Edie Friedman

Injustice, poverty, slavery, ignorance - these may be cured by reform and revolution. But men do not live only by fighting evils. They live by positive goals, individual and collective, a vast variety of them, seldom predictable, at times incompatible. It is from intense preoccupation with these ends ... that the best moments come in the lives of individuals and people.

Isaiah Berlin

'A man should concern himself more that he not injure others than that he not be injured.' For when a man tries to keep a watch that his fist not injure others, by that very act he enthrones in the world the God of truth and righteousness and adds power to the kingdom of justice; and it is precisely this power which will defend him against injury by others. ... When a man constantly portrays to himself scenes of terror, when he asserts that everyone wants to obliterate him and that he can rely only on the power of his own fist, by this he denies the kingdom of truth and justice and enthrones the power of the fist. And since the fist is by nature poor at making distinctions, in the end defence and attack become reversed: instead of defending himself by means of the fist, such a man becomes himself the assailant and destroyer of others. Hence, like begetting like, others repay him in kind, and so the earth is filled with violence and oppression.

Aaron Samuel Tamaret

Ts'dakah
There are eight degrees in the giving of charity, one higher than the other:
   Those who give grudgingly, reluctantly, or with regret.
   Those who give less than they should, but give graciously.
   Those who give what they should, but only after they are asked.
   Those who give before they are asked.
   Those who give without knowing to whom they give,
   although the recipient knows the identity of the donor.
   Those who give without making their identity known.
   Those who give without knowing to whom they give,
   and the recipients not knowing from whom they receive.
   Those who help others to support themselves by a gift, or a loan,
   or by finding employment for them,
   thus helping them to become self-supporting.

Maimonides

More than the householder does for the beggar, the beggar does for the householder.

Leviticus Rabbah

From each according to his abilities, to each according to his needs.

Karl Marx

The Challenge of Civilisation
According to a rabbinic commentary on the building of the Tower of Babel (Genesis 11), if somebody fell and died, nobody paid any attention to it. However if a brick fell, then they would sit and cry and say, 'whenever shall we erect another one in its place.' (*Pirke de Rabbi Eliezer 24*). The Tower of Babel instantly demonstrates towards which principles the city built on the political and animal nature of human beings tends: the crushing of the individual by the collectivity; mass civilisation ... depersonalisation: the work does not stop when a worker gets crushed, but the entire project fails when, by accident, a brick is dropped.

...

The unenviable duty of 'Jerusalem' is to stand against the Babel-like illusion in democratic cities. It is to remember always the limit and the tragic consequence of that limit - between a charter and its practise, between a Declaration of the Rights of Man and its actualisation.

André Neher

In the years before the Great War ... it was not yet a matter of indifference whether a man lived or died. When someone was expunged from the lists of the living, someone else did not immediately step up to take his place, but a gap was left to show where he had been, and those who knew the man who had died or disappeared, well or even less well, fell silent whenever they saw the gap. When a fire happened to consume a particular dwelling in a row of dwellings, the site of the conflagration remained for a long time afterwards. For masons and bricklayers worked slowly and thoughtfully, and when they walked past the ruins, neighbours and passers-by alike recalled the form and the walls of the house that had once stood there. That's how it was then! Everything that grew took long to grow; and everything that ended took a long time to be forgotten. Everything that existed left behind traces of itself, and people then lived by their memories, just as we nowadays live by our capacity to forget, quickly and comprehensively.

Joseph Roth

Heart and Brain

The feeling of pity is one of the sources of human kindness. Pity for the fate of our fellow men, for the misery around us, for the suffering of human beings, stirs our emotions by the resonance of sympathy. Our own attachments to life and people, the ties which bind us to the outside world, awaken our emotional response to the struggle and suffering outside ourselves. But there is also another entirely different source of human kindness. It is the detached feeling of duty based on aloof, clear reasoning. Good, clear thinking leads to kindness and loyalty because this is what makes life simpler, fuller, richer, diminishes friction and unhappiness in our environment and therefore also in our lives. A sound social attitude, helpfulness, friendliness, kindness may come from both these different sources: to express it anatomically, from heart and brain.

Leopold Infeld

Good and Evil

In an important, little appreciated, and utterly tragic principle regulating the structure of nearly all complex systems, building up must be accomplished step by tiny step, whereas destruction need occupy but an instant. I have called this phenomenon The Great Asymmetry (with uppercase letters to emphasize the sad generality). Ten thousand acts of kindness done by thousands of people, and slowly building trust and harmony over many years, can be undone by one destructive act of a skilled and committed psychopath. Thus, even if the *effects* of kindness and evil balance out in the course of history, The Great Asymmetry guarantees that the *numbers* of kind and evil people could hardly differ more, for thousands of good souls overwhelm each perpetrator of darkness.

Stephen Jay Gould

Environment

When a tree that bears fruit is cut down its moan goes from one end of the world to the other, yet no sound is heard.

Pirke de Rabbi Eliezer 34

The quality of urban air compared to the air in the deserts and forests is like thick and turbulent water compared to pure and light water. And this is because in the cities with their tall buildings and narrow roads, the pollution that comes from their residents, their waste, their corpses, and offal from their cattle, and the stench of their adulterated food, make their entire air malodorous, turbulent, reeking and thick, and the winds become accordingly so, although no one is aware of it.

And since there is no way out, because we grow up in cities and become used to them, we can at least choose a city with an open horizon ... And if you have no choice, and you cannot move out of the city, try at least to live in a suburb created to the northeast. Let the house be tall and the court wide enough to permit the northern wind and the sun to come through, because the sun thins out the pollution of the air, and makes it light and pure.

Moses Maimonides

We should contemplate the Natural World not as disconnected observers but as active participants. We are part of Nature, but unlike the rest of the animal kingdom we alone have the ability to save it, or to do it irreparable damage.

Animals and birds, reptiles and fish, and myriads of insects offer us opportunities for wonder, amusement, inspiration and the purest joy. Those who share creation with us should be counted as precious to us as ourselves, for without their presence our own existence would be immeasurably the poorer.

So let us treasure Nature, the inspiration of so much dignity, beauty and poetry, and let us honour and cherish the Earth which provides a home for us all.

Charles H. Middleburgh

On Hunting

We find in the Torah that only fierce characters like Nimrod or Esau are known as hunters, never Abraham, Isaac and Jacob or their descendants. Rabbi Weil (quoted by *Rema, Orach Chayyim* 223) has already pointed out that the usual blessing on donning new clothes should not be recited when putting on a fur coat. Such a blessing might make it appear that killing animals is not only accepted but considered desirable, which goes against the verse 'God's tender mercies are over all God's works' (Psalm 145:9).

It is true that Rabbi Moses Isserles (who commented on the major codification of Jewish law, the *Shulchan Aruch*) remarks that the reason given is weak. But it is only weak because the fact of putting on the fur coat does not necessarily imply that the owner directly caused the killing. The fur may be of animals who died a natural death. And he agrees with the decision of Rabbi Weil. But I cannot understand how a Jew could even dream of killing animals merely for the pleasure of hunting, when he has no immediate need for the bodies of the creatures ...

It is only true when these wild animals are found in places inhabited by people so that they are a menace to society. It is certainly not a worthy act to hunt them in their own haunts. It is, instead, something governed by lust. There is one exception made in the case of someone who earns a living from hunting by selling the furs or skins. The animal world is under the rule of human beings to provide for their needs. So it makes no difference whether we take the life of clean animals for food, or kill unclean animals for their skins and furs. But when the act is not based on any such consideration, it is simply an act of cruelty!

Ezekiel Landau

On Pluralism

We have benedictions for all occasions - on seeing the ocean, a rainbow, the blossoming of trees, an electrical storm. And on beholding a Jewish audience, the Talmud prescribes a special benediction: 'Blessed is He who discerns secrets, for the mind of each is different from the other.' It is a blessing in praise of God, who creates diversity in our world, and rejoices in different minds, perceptions, judgments, visages. It is a blessing over Jewish pluralism.

The benediction is easier said than lived. It is one thing to acknowledge the pluralism among us, it is another to acknowledge it as a blessing. It is one thing to love Jews because we share a common fate, it is another to love Jews who hold different theologies, different modes of ritual and religious practice, different politics. Religious and ethnic parties have entered a stage on the brink of sectarianism, denominationalism, schismatic movements. The signs of aggravating incivility abound. A small Jewish world is made smaller yet by factionalism with impenetrable *mechitzot* (partitions).

Harold M. Schulweis

On Interfaith Dialogue

All these activities of Jesus the Christian, and the Ishmaelite (Muhammad) who came after him, are for the purpose of paving the way for the true King Messiah, and preparing the entire world to worship God together, as it is written (Zephaniah 3:9): 'For then I will change the nations to a pure language, so that they may call in the name of God and serve God together.'

Maimonides, Laws of Kings 11:4

Why, then, does the world make so little progress? One reason is that ancient hatreds and rivalries are allowed to deflect people from the problems of the present. Political and religious ideologies perpetuate hatred at the same time as they preach peace and love ... Religions harbour vast destructive forces.

Yet at the same time they have a vast potentiality for good ... How do we harness the good which is in religions at the same time as ensuring that the bad which is in them does not take over? This is precisely the role of dialogue, and it demands openness and often painful self-criticism. When we talk together, the presence of the other makes us turn back to the sources of our faiths and rediscover the seminal, constructive elements within them, elements the faithful may have marginalized. In looking together at the world we encounter a common responsibility and hence a common mission. In the light of nuclear threat and environmental hazard our common mission turns out to be far more urgent than the narrow, individual missions directed against one another, aimed at propagating some particular formulation of religious faith.

There are, within all our political and religious groupings, those who put doctrine before the needs of people, who talk of love and concern but who see others only as potential converts to their own way of thinking. These are the sort of people who, centuries ago, turned the Middle Ages into a byword for obscurantism and intolerance. Even now they are ready to head us back along the same path to an age made still darker by abuse of the powerful gifts of modern science and technology. Jews and Christians together must resist this and offer a more enlightened leadership ... The intelligent articulation in the contemporary context of the richness of our own traditions is the building block we bring to the reconstruction of the world.

Norman Solomon

In the past the different faiths have defined themselves in contradistinction and in opposition to one another. Today we need to define ourselves in relationship to one another.

Jonathan Magonet

Hospitality

Abraham offers us a model of reaching out beyond social divides; of breaking through the barrier of alienation. This model in a word is 'hospitality to' - a quality all of our traditions, Judaism, Christianity and Islam, associate with Abraham. Genesis 18:1 describes Abraham as 'sitting at the entry to his tent in the heat of the day' looking for wayfarers to offer hospitality, when 'he lifts up his eyes and sees and behold three men are standing before him'. A chasidic master raised the question why these angels are referred to as just 'men', especially when the next chapter of Genesis begins with the words 'and the two *angels* came to Sodom ... and Lot saw them and got up to meet them ...' The rabbi's answer was that there was no need for the angels to reveal themselves as such, for Abraham saw the angel in every person.

David Rosen

The Jewish People

Now the Eternal said to Abram: 'Go out from your country, and from your family and your father's house, to the land that I will show you. And I will make a great nation of you, and I will bless you and make your name great; and be you a blessing ... and all the families of the earth shall be blessed in you.'

Genesis 12:1-3

Every people is a question which God addresses to humanity; and every people, from its place, with its special talents and possibilities, must answer for its own sake and for the sake of humanity ... This people Israel developed and grew in one millennium and formed the question that rests within it. It has kept arising ever again, through rebirths, in new epochs, for more than two millennia now. Through its prophets, its poets, its teachers, its righteous ones, Israel was able to learn how to listen to the question which God addressed to it. Its question proved, in Israel's experience, to be the deepest of all questions which live within and from humanity. This people's hope is, therefore, the greatest of all hopes; it is the great expectation to which the way of all ways leads. The iniquity of this people is, therefore, deeper iniquity than any other. And offences against this people signify more than other offences. Both need 'God's reconciliation'. This people is 'a covenant for the nations', a law for the peoples.

Leo Baeck

To be a Jew is an act of the strenuous mind as it stands before the fakeries and lying seductions of the world, saying no and no again as they parade by in all their allure.

Cynthia Ozick

I am a Jew because, born of Israel and having lost her, I have felt her live again in me, more living than myself.

I am a Jew because, born of Israel and having regained her, I wish her to live after me, more living than in myself.

I am a Jew because the faith of Israel demands of me no abdication of the mind.

I am a Jew because the faith of Israel requires of me all the devotion of my heart.

I am a Jew because in every place where suffering weeps, the Jew weeps.

I am a Jew because at every time when despair cries out, the Jew hopes.

I am a Jew because the word of Israel is the oldest and the newest.

I am a Jew because the promise of Israel is the universal promise.

I am a Jew because, for Israel, the world is not yet completed; men are completing it.

I am a Jew because above all the nations and Israel, Israel places man and his unity.

I am a Jew because above man, image of the divine Unity, Israel places the divine Unity and its divinity.

Edmond Fleg

The Jewish People - Who Belongs?

Diversity is legitimate so long as each Jewish group keeps the well-being of the entire Jewish people in mind. We are all limbs on one body. As the rabbis saw it, 'all Israel are comrades'.

So long as we understand that our Jewish self-interest requires us to care for, and to be involved in, the defence and love of all Jews, our particular understanding of how to be Jewish or what Judaism may mean can only enrich our larger Jewish community.

Bradley Shavit Artson

Maimonides' reply to a proselyte who asked if he could say the prayers which began: 'Our God and God of *our* fathers ...'

Pronounce all prayers as they are written and do not change anything. Your prayers and blessings should be the same as that of any other Israelite, regardless of whether you pray in private or conduct the service. The explanation is as follows: Abraham, our father, taught mankind the true belief and the unity of God, repudiating idolatry; through him many of his own household and also others were guided 'to keep the way of the Eternal, to do righteousness and justice'. Thus he who becomes a proselyte and confesses the unity of God, as taught in the Torah, is a disciple of Abraham, our father. Such persons are of his household ...

<<<

You should therefore pray: 'Our God and God of our fathers', for Abraham is also *your* father. In no respect is there a difference between us and you. Do not think little of your origin: we are descended from Abraham, Isaac and Jacob, but your descent is from the Creator, for in the words of Isaiah: 'One shall say "I am the Lord's"; and another shall call himself by the name of Jacob.'

Maimonides

Bilhah's Prayer
Oh Lord I pray You, hear my prayer.

Given of Laban to Rachel and loaned by Rachel to Jacob,
I am Bilhah, unloved bondswoman of the well-beloved wife,
vessel of Jacob's seed.

Blessed are You, Eternal our God, Sovereign of the universe,
who frees those who are bound.

'Where you go I shall go,' Ruth's bond of love, freely given.
Mine were fetters attached without attachment,
binding me without consent to go where they go,
bearing children and hardship.
My path, robbed of choice to choose,
did it not lead to You as surely as theirs?

Blessed are You, Eternal our God, Sovereign of the universe,
who makes firm the steps of the strong.

In the night we waited for the Eternal or for Esau, Zilpah,
I and our children shivering with the fear more than with the cold.
In the morning You sheltered Jacob, saving him, and us with him.
Were we not of ourselves as courageous and as worthy as him?
Though we lacked swords with which to defend ourselves and family and
status to shield us surely we were no less Your children and Your charge.

Blessed are You, Eternal our God, Sovereign of the universe,
the support and safety of the righteous.

When Reuben lay with me, without love, without passion, without compassion, taking me not as a woman but as a symbol of his power and his inheritance, I was bowed low not in supplication and humility but in humiliation. Though punishment was done to him, no justice was done for me.

<<<

Blessed are You, Eternal our God, Sovereign of the universe,
who rules through justice.

In the centuries since I am silenced, forgotten.
My suffering not to be spoken or explained,
an embarrassment to my children. Oh God I pray You hear my prayer.
Let my words come forth that I may speak justice.
For while I am mute all mouths cannot praise You.

Lord, open my lips and my mouth shall declare Your praise.

Lawrence Becker

Power and Powerlessness

From Biblical times to the present day, the Jews have wandered the uncertain terrain between power and powerlessness, never quite achieving the power necessary to guarantee long-term security, but equally avoiding, with a number of disastrous exceptions, the abyss of absolute impotence. They developed the consummate political art of living with uncertainty and insecurity; their long survival owes much to this extraordinary achievement; Jews today must struggle to come to terms with this history in the light of their present power, to see both past and present through a realistic lens, neither inflating their power nor exaggerating their powerlessness. The lessons this history can teach are necessary for their own continued existence and are equally relevant to the continued existence of mankind.

David Biale

Israel

What ought to be the moral restraints and ethical sensitivities of a Jewish state? We have inherited many wonderful and inspiring moral insights in the pages of our traditional sources. These ideas, however, were enunciated and transmitted when Jews were powerless, and it is always easy to those without power to be idealistic and moral. What, however, is to happen now that we Jews have power? Will it be used wisely and moderately?

This very issue is reflected in an incident in which an Israeli soldier named David was involved. His unit had just completed morning exercises in the Jericho region, and was breaking for lunch. Those finished eating had thrown their garbage in a nearby receptacle, and as often happens, a Bedouin had begun rummaging through the remains. David then took the remainder of his meal, walked over to the Arab, and gave him the food. Upon returning to his group, one of his fellow soldiers turned to him and said: 'You know, David, I think that I would be afraid to go into battle with you. I'm not sure you would know when to start shooting.' David looked at him and replied: 'You know, I'm not sure I'd want to go into battle with you. I'm afraid you wouldn't know when to stop shooting!'

That response is as important a part of the Zionist message as any. The Jewish state must be strong, but also compassionate; its soldiers must be brave, but also humane. Without these qualities, Zionism and Israeli society at large would lose much credibility and legitimacy - first and foremost in our own eyes, we the citizens of this country.

Lee Levine

As for the Land of Israel, the Torah posits that the land is entrusted to the Children of Israel only if the Jewish people live up to the standards enunciated in the Torah: to practice morality, pursue justice, and to obey certain agricultural rules. The nature of our relationship to the Land of Israel is therefore different from that of other nations in their respective motherlands. Unlike the images common in other cultures, Israel is not a mother who would welcome her son whatever his misdeeds. Rather, Israel is portrayed as a bride who can reject her partner (or even, as in Leviticus 18:28, a land that can 'vomit its inhabitants') if she disapproves of his behaviour ... The link that the Jews have with the Land of Israel is therefore contractual rather than organic.

Yakov M. Rabkin

Jerusalem

Jerusalem is a port city on the shore of eternity.
The Temple Mount is a huge ship, a magnificent
luxury liner. From the portholes of her Western Wall
cheerful saints look out, travellers. Hasidim on the pier
wave goodbye, shout hooray, hooray, bon voyage! She is
always arriving, always sailing away. And the fences and the piers
and the policemen and the flags and the high masts of churches
and mosques and the smokestacks of synagogues and the boats
of psalms of praise and the mountain waves. The shofar blows:
another one has just left. Yom Kippur sailors in white uniforms
climb among ladders and ropes of well-tested prayers.
And the commerce and the gates and the golden domes:
Jerusalem is the Venice of God.

Yehudah Amichai

In a Time of War

Despite the explicit Torah commandment to wage war, we are enjoined to have mercy on the enemy, too, and not to kill even in wartime, except when self-defence is imperative for conquest and victory, and not to harm a non-combatant population. It is certainly forbidden to harm women and children who are not taking part in the war. Except for those obligatory wars that we were explicitly commanded by the Torah to wage in antiquity, in which 'you shall not let a soul remain alive', because the enemies too behaved savagely in those times, and therefore the Torah has taken a severe line against them ... one must not learn from them, heaven forbid, about other wars and our own time ... We are commanded by the Torah to follow in the ways [of God] and to have compassion for God's creatures, as it is written: 'God's mercy is upon all God's works' (Psalm 145:9).

Shlomo Goren

Break of Day in the Trenches
    The darkness crumbles away -
    It is the same old Druid Time as ever.
    Only a live thing leaps my hand -
    A queer sardonic rat -
    As I pull the parapet's poppy
    To stick behind my ear.
    Droll rat, they would shoot you if they knew
    Your cosmopolitan sympathies.
    Now you have touched this English hand
    You will do the same to a German -
    Soon, no doubt, if it be your pleasure
    To cross the sleeping green between.
    It seems you inwardly grin as you pass
    Strong eyes, fine limbs, haughty athletes
    Less chanced than you for life,
    Bonds to the whims of murder,
    Sprawled in the bowels of the earth,
    The torn fields of France.
    What do you see in our eyes
    At the shrieking iron and flame
    Hurled through still heavens?
    What quaver - what heart aghast?
    Poppies whose roots are in man's veins
    Drop, and are ever dropping:
    But mine in my ear is safe,
    Just a little white with the dust.

                                               Isaac Rosenberg

At first war seems like a beautiful woman,
every man desires to play with her.
But in the end it is like a repulsive hag,
all her lovers weep and sicken.

                                             Shmuel Hanagid

A Meditation for *Yom Ha-Zikaron*

Song of David
Look at the skies David \ look \ blue \ Shabbat \ transparent are the skies \ bluish gray \ on the Sabbath day \ for God has finished \ let's sit \ here \ on the sand dune \ and let our eyes behold \ the skies \ the sand \ and the eye is full of sand \ right and left \ let's look \ smoke a cigarette \ we'll look at the silence \ (a bird did not chirp) \ we'll look \ look at the skies \ David \ look at the skies \ airplanes \ one plane \ David \ a second plane \ David \ and a third \ and a fourth David \ look how beautiful \ how elegant \ silvery \ circling \ circles in the air \ plane following plane \ how handsome \ raise your eyes David and see \ waving their wings \ the planes \ circling and waving \ at one another's tail \ David \ now they're declining \ declining \ circling and declining \ look David \ so low \ grazing sand \ the planes \ now the pilot in his canopy \ and the second and the third and the fourth \ David \ now we are hidden under the shelter of their wings \ look David \ look \ fire in their wings \ fire \ look \ fire is coming down from heaven \ fire \ fire \ fire from heaven \ towards you David \ towards me \ fire is sent \ get up and run \ David \ get up and run \ get up and run \ look David \ here is the machine-gun \ here's mine \ lie on your back \ David \ lie down \ gun-barrels to heaven \ gun barrels to heaven \ pull David \ pull \ I'm pulling \ fire from heaven \ machine-gun fire \ fire to fire in the air \ here they are circling \ again \ circling \ one and two and a third and a fourth \ circling \ fire in their wings \ fire and thunder \ in their wings \ squeeze the trigger \ David \ squeeze \ don't let go \ we won't let go \ fire rises to heaven \ fire comes down \ heaven and earth \ down comes the fire \ heaven have mercy \ have mercy He who abides in highest heavens \ fire touches fire \ behold the pilot's eyes \ behold my eyes in his \ now his wings catch fire \ we've hit David \ we've hit \ don't let go \ we won't let go \ we've hit \ David \ we did not hit \ now the thunder \ behold flow streams of fire \ fire consumes fire \ the fire is in us \ behold the sand is in the air \ behold you land \ David \ land \ upon me \ you land \ David \ rise David \ rise \ you're heavy David \ rise \ David \ and squeeze the trigger \ roll yourself off

<<<

me \ David \ David \ David \ rise Man Greatly Beloved \ your head is filled with dewy lights \ your locks with the dewdrops of the night \ your body all openings and cavities \ cavities and holes \ your body is heavy upon me \ rise I said \ rise I said \ right now \ rise \ please David \ pray awaken \ wake I beseech thee \ pray stand \ pray rise up \ pray rise \ David \ rise \ right now \ we'll listen to the silence \ look at the skies \ bluish gray \ fire on the Sabbath day \ for the Lord has ended \ we'll listen to the silence \ David \ it's so quiet here \ and hot \ October and hot \ hot blood \ hot blood \ my fingers in your holes \ to keep your blood from streaming \ from overflowing \ lest your bowels be troubled for us \ lest you perish \ David \ lest you cease \ Our Father our King act for the sake of those who went into fire \ for those who went into fire, beheading and strangling \ act \ for those asleep in the dust \ act \ right now \ act \ act I said \ act \ act with us for thy name \ to increase our days \ act \ act now \ right now \ act \ the sand bubbles \ the fire is lofty \ the wind \ the wind \ clouds no more \ rain no more \ wind no more \ blood \ no more

Tamir Lahav Radlemesser (translated from the Hebrew by Irit Sela)

On Peace

We have failed to fight for right, for justice, for goodness; as a result we must fight against wrong, against injustice, against evil. We have failed to offer sacrifices on the altar of peace; now we must offer sacrifices on the altar of war.

Abraham Joshua Heschel

Schpil-she mir a Lidele in Jiddisch
    Play me a little song in Yiddish,
    one that brings joy
    and no nasty surprises.
    One that all people can understand,
    great and small,
    for it must go from mouth to mouth.
        Play, play, musicians
        you know already what I mean and what I want!
        Play, play me a song,
        play a tune with heart and feelings.

<<<

A song without sighing and tears.
Play it so that all can hear it,
so that all can see: I'm alive and I can still sing!
more sweetly and better than before.
    Play...

Play me the song of peace,
of true peace and not just a dream
that all peoples, great and small,
must understand each other
behave with each other without war or strife.
    Play...

Let us sing, sing the song together,
like good friends, like children of one mother.
The only thing I desire
is that it ring out free and true,
a song that is my own and for all peoples.
    Play...

I.Kotliar

I, May I Rest in Peace

I, may I rest in peace - I, who am still living, say,
may I have peace in the rest of my life.
I want peace right now while I'm still alive.
I don't want to wait like that pious man who wished for one leg
of the golden chair of Paradise, I want a four legged chair
right here, a plain wooden chair. I want the rest of my peace now.
I have lived out my life in wars of every kind: battles without
and within, close combat, face-to-face, the face always
my own, my lover-face, my enemy-face.
Wars with the old weapons - sticks and stones, blunt axe, words,
dull ripping knife, love and hate,
and wars with newfangled weapons - machine gun, missile,
words, land mines exploding, love and hate.
I don't want to fulfil my parents' prophesy that life is war.
I want peace with all my body and all my soul.
Rest me in peace.

Yehudah Amichai

May the will come from You
to annul wars and the shedding of blood from the universe,
and to extend a peace, great and wondrous, in the universe.
Nor again shall one people raise the sword against another
and they shall learn war no more.
But let all the residents of earth recognize and know the innermost truth:
that we are not come into this world for quarrel and division,
nor for hate and jealousy, contrariness and bloodshed;
but we are come into this world
to recognize and know You,
may You be blessed forever.
And let Your glory fill all our wits and minds, knowledge and hearts;
and may I be a chariot for the presence of Your divinity.
May I not again depart from holiness as much as a hairsbreadth.
May I not think one extraneous thought.
But may I ever cling to You and to Your sacred Torah,
until I be worthy to introduce others into the
knowledge of the truth of Your divinity.
To announce to all people Your power,
and the honour of the glory of Your kingdom.

Nachman of Bratslav

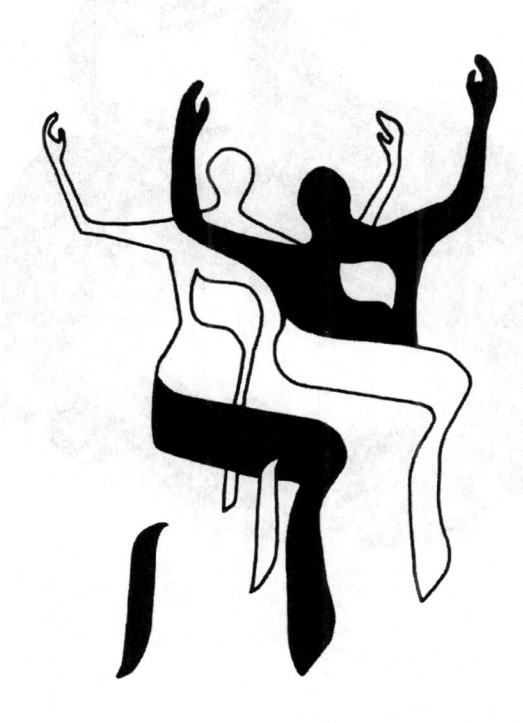

THE LIFE OF THE SPIRIT

God

For the spiritually authentic person, God is real, not a label we brazenly attach to our own wishes and opinions. God is out there, but through a miracle of divine communication, God's words move from out there to in here, and after a struggle, God's will becomes our will. We will have integrated God's perspective into our own thinking, and achieved integrity. It is the struggle, the feeling that God's demands are at least a little bit unwelcome, that gives us reason to believe that the voice inside our head is God's voice, or God's voice speaking as our voice, and not merely our own. And when the struggle is over, it is the sense that God's voice has become our voice, God's will has been integrated into our will, which lets us know we have won the prize of integrity.

Harold Kushner

Thus says the Eternal, Let not the wise man glory in his wisdom, neither let the mighty man glory in his might, let not the rich man glory in his riches, but let him that glories glory in this, that he understands and knows Me, that I am the Eternal who acts with love, justice and righteousness in the earth, for in these things I delight, says the Eternal.

Jeremiah 9:22-23

Messiah

Rabbi Joshua came upon the prophet Elijah as he was standing at the entrance of Rabbi Simeon ben Yochai's cave.

He asked him: 'When is the Messiah coming?'

The other replied: 'Go and ask him yourself.'

'Where shall I find him?'

'Before the gates of Rome.'

'By what sign shall I know him?'

'He is sitting among poor people covered with wounds. The others unbind all their wounds at once, and then bind them up again. But he unbinds one wound at a time, and then binds it up again straightaway. He tells himself: "Perhaps I shall be needed (to appear as the Messiah) - and I must not take time and be late!"'

So he went and found him and said: 'Peace be with you, my master and teacher!'

He answered him: 'Peace be with you, son of Levi!'

Then he asked him: 'When are you coming, master?'

He answered him: 'Today!'

Thereupon he returned to Elijah and said to him: 'He has deceived me, he has indeed deceived me! He told me, "Today I am coming!" and he has not come.'

But the other said to him: 'This is what he told you, "Today - if you would only hear His voice"' *(Psalm 95: 7).*

Sanhedrin 98a

I believe with perfect faith in the coming of the Messiah; and, though he tarry, I will wait daily for his coming.

Maimonides

Rabbi Yochanan ben Zakkai used to say: If there be a plant in your hand when they say to you 'Behold the Messiah!' go and plant the plant, and afterwards go out to greet him.

Avot d'Rabbi Natan

All the calculated ends have already passed, and it now depends entirely on repentance and good deeds.

Sanhedrin

In the days of the Messiah, the Holy One will execute the urge to evil. The righteous, to whom it will then seem as an enormous mountain, will weep and say: 'How did we conquer such a height?' The wicked, to whom it will look like a hair, will weep and say: 'Why did we not overcome it?'

Judah bar Ilai

Images of God

Images of God as fountain, source, wellspring, or ground of life and being remind us that God loves and befriends us as one who brings forth all being and sustains it in existence ...

Images of God as rock, tree of life, light, darkness, and myriad other metaphors drawn from nature, teach us the intrinsic value of this wider web of being in which we dwell. The God who is the ground of being is present and imaged forth in all beings, so that every aspect of creation shows us another face of God ...

This God is male/female lover, friend, companion, co-creator, the one who, seeing what is best in us, lures us to be the most we can become. This God is ground and source of all life, creating, holding, sustaining the great web of existence and, as part of, the human companions who labour to make the *world* a home for the divine presence.

Judith Plaskow

Summoned by God to personal responsibility, my piety expresses itself as a personal activism that finds its motive and standard in my being privileged to serve God as a covenantal partner. Who this God of all humankind might be must yet be explored but one thing may already be said: I am one of those who no longer has such confidence in the human self as to say 'God' and merely mean humanity extended.

Eugene B. Borowitz

To believe in God maturely, intelligently, is to believe that reality did not just 'happen', that it is no accident, no pointless interplay of matter and energy. It is to insist rather that things, including man's life, make sense, that they add up to something. It is to hold that the universe, physical and moral, is a cosmos, not an anarchy ... meaningful rather than mad, because it is the manifestation of a creating, sustaining, animating, design-lending Spirit, a Mind-will, or to use the oldest, most familiar and best word, a God.

Milton Steinberg

Study

Since the House of Shammai declare unclean and the House of Hillel clean, this one prohibits and that one permits, how, then can I learn Torah? All the words have been given by a single shepherd. So make yourself a heart of many rooms and bring into it the words of the House of Shammai and the words of the House of Hillel.

Tosefta Sotah 7:12

A scholar takes precedence over a king of Israel, for if a scholar dies no one can replace him, while if a king dies, all Israel is eligible for kingship.

Horayot 13a

The Holy One gave the Torah to Israel like wheat from which to derive fine flour, or like flax from which to make a garment.

Seder Eliyahu Zuta 2

In the quest for truth, he who thinks he has finished is finished.

Mendel of Kotsk

Teach your tongue to say: 'I don't know.'

Berachot 4a

Whoever feels, after many trials, that the soul within him can find repose only when it is occupied with the mysteries of the Torah, should know that for this has he been destined.

May no obstacle in the world, fleshly or even spiritual, confuse or turn him from the pursuit of the fountain of his life, his true fulfilment.

And it is well for him to know that not only his own self-fulfilment and salvation wait upon the satisfaction of this tendency within him... The saving of society and the perfecting of the world also depend upon it. For a soul fulfilled helps to fulfil the world. True thoughts, when they flow without hindrance into any one of the corners of life, bless all of life.

But should he abandon his search, and wander about seeking water from wells which are not really his, then, though he draw water as much as the ocean, and take from streams in every part of the earth, yet will he not find peace. For like a bird who has wandered from his nest, so is the person who wanders from his place.

Abraham Issac Kook

Torah

The Torah of Moses does not include philosophical theories, or logical investigations, or proofs involving high inquiries. For human success is above Reason and beyond Nature.

Abravanel

Once there was a king who had only one daughter, whom another king married. When the latter wished to return to his country and take his wife with him, the father said, 'My daughter whom I have given to you in marriage is my only child. My love for her is great. I cannot depart from her. Yet I cannot ask you not to take her to your realm. It is now her proper home. Permit me this one request. To whatever distant place you take her now to live, always have a chamber ready for me that I may dwell with you and with her, for I can never consider really leaving my daughter.' So God said to Israel: 'I have given you the Torah from which I cannot really part. I cannot tell you not to receive it in love. Yet, I request only this. Wherever you go with it, make Me a house wherein I may sojourn.' As it is written, 'Let them make Me a sanctuary so that I may dwell among them' (Exodus 25:8).

Exodus Rabbah 33:1

The words of the Torah are not given as clear-cut decisions. For with every word which the blessed Holy One spoke to Moses, God offered him forty-nine arguments by which a thing may be proven clean, and forty-nine other arguments by which the same thing may be proven unclean. When Moses asked 'Master of the Universe, in what way shall we discern the true law?' God replied 'The majority is to be followed (Exodus 23:21), that is to say, when a majority says it is unclean, it is unclean; when a majority says it is clean, it is clean.'

Midrash on Psalms 12:4

The law of God cannot be perfect so as to be adequate for all times, because the ever new details of human relations, their customs and their acts are too numerous to be embraced in a book. Therefore, Moses was given orally certain general principles, only briefly alluded to in the Torah, by means of which the wise men in every generation may work out the details as they appear.

Joseph Albo, Sefer Ikkarim 3:23

The Torah was not given to the angels. It was given to human beings who possess intelligence. God gave us the Torah according to the ability of the human mind to decide, even though it may not be the [ultimate] truth, but rather true according to the conclusions of the human mind.

Aryeh Leib Heller

When Moses descended from Mount Sinai he held in his arms the tablets of stone engraved by the finger of the blessed Holy One. And such was the virtue of the inscription, that it was not Moses who carried the tablets, but the tablets which carried Moses. But when he neared the mountain's base and caught his first glimpse of the Golden Calf, when God's words and the idol were brought into confrontation with each other, a wonder ensued. The sacred letters detached themselves from the stone in which they had been inscribed and vanished into thin air. Moses was left holding a blank, inert thing, too heavy for him. It is not true, the sages assert, that Moses threw the tablets on the earth, so shattering them. The fact is that he had to let them go or be crushed. The lettered stone which had carried Moses was, once letterless, too much for him to bear. It is not difficult to discern what the ancient rabbis are trying to say in their parable: given knowledge and insight, Judaism sustains the Jew; without them, it is a crushing burden, too heavy for even the strongest to withstand.

Milton Steinberg

Halachah and *Aggadah*

Halachah represents the strength to shape one's life according to a fixed pattern; it is a form-giving force. *Aggadah* is the expression of man's ceaseless striving, which often defies all limitations. *Halachah* is the rationalisation and schematisation of living; it defines, specifies, sets measure and limit, placing life into an exact system. *Aggadah* deals with man's ineffable relations to God, to other men, and to the world. *Halachah* deals with details, with each commandment separately, *aggadah* with the whole of life, with the totality of religious life. *Halachah* deals with the law, *aggadah* with the meaning of the law. *Halachah* deals with subjects that can be expressed literally; *aggadah* introduces us to a realm which lies beyond the range of expression. *Halachah* teaches us how to perform common acts; *aggadah* tells us how to participate in the eternal drama. *Halachah* gives us knowledge; *aggadah* exaltation. *Halachah* prescribes, *aggadah* suggests; *halachah* decrees, *aggadah* inspires; *halachah* is definite, *aggadah* is allusive.

To maintain that the essence of Judaism consists exclusively of *halachah* is as erroneous as to maintain that the essence of Judaism consists exclusively of *aggadah*.

The interrelationship of *halachah and aggadah* is the very heart of Judaism. *Halachah* without *aggadah* is dead, *aggadah* without *halachah* is wild.

Abraham Joshua Heschel

Truth
The Torah does not oblige us to believe absurdities.

Joseph Albo

The central issue is not Truth in terms of a doctrine, but veracity, honesty, or sincerity in terms of personal existence. ... The Baal Shem quoted the Psalm, 'Truth shall spring out of the earth' (85:12), and asked, 'surely it must be easy to find Truth?' 'Indeed it is easy,' he continued, 'but no one wants to bend down. No one is willing to stoop to pick up a little truth.'

Abraham Joshua Heschel

Reason is an inadequate tool for the comprehension of ultimate reality, but it is the only tool we have for distinguishing faith from credulity, true religion from superstition, enthusiasm from fanaticism.

Louis Jacobs

Religion offers answers without obliterating the questions. They become blunted and will not attack you with the same ferocity. But without them the answer would dry up and wither away. The question is a great religious act; it helps you live great religious truth.

Shmuel Sperber

Known and Unknown
For myself, I like a universe that includes much that is unknown and, at the same time, much that is knowable. A universe in which everything is known would be static and dull, as boring as the heaven of some weak-minded theologians. A universe that is unknowable is no fit place for a thinking being. The ideal universe for us is one very much like the universe we inhabit. And I would guess that this is not really much of a coincidence.

Carl Sagan

Talmud Study
Study Talmud! There are lots of unscientific texts in the world, but you'd be hard-pressed to find a less scientific one than the Talmud. Still, I am quite serious about my recommendation. To study Talmud is to study reading. The Talmud is the ultimate challenge to close readers. Whether you do the thing right and study for a decade or merely skim the surface for a year or two, you cannot emerge from Talmud study without a transformed understanding of how to squeeze, distil, coax, urge, cajole, boil or otherwise extract meaning from a text.

David Gelernter

Ritual Life

Traditional ritual seems mysterious, inexplicable, non-rational. We sense something unsophisticated, almost embarrassing ... But we are also more complicated and less rational beings than we often want to admit. There are moments in our lives when we desperately wish to be moved ...

While the American Jewish edifices in which many Jews grew up allowed them to *think* about Jewish issues, they later discovered that they could think without the synagogue, the rabbi... or even their tradition. ... But Western culture and our newly diluted Judaism never satisfied our need to feel, to touch the transcendent in the world. So many of us, when we want to express that which goes beyond the mind and beyond reason, hark back to tradition out of the sense that maybe, if we are fortunate, returning to tradition will allow us to feel.

Daniel Gordis

Unfree people are horrified by the suggestion of accepting a daily discipline. Confusing inner control with external tyranny, they prefer caprice to self-restraint. They would rather have ideals than norms, hopes than directions, faith than forms. But the goal and the way cannot long endure in separation. The days of the week, the food that we eat, the holidays of the year, the deeds that we do - these are the frontiers of faith. Unless the outer life expresses the inner world, piety stagnates and intention decays.

Abraham Joshua Heschel

If you weary in the service of God, it means you are carrying other burdens, not that of the yoke of heaven.

Dubner Maggid

The World of Shabbat

Six days he has worked and attended to all his affairs; now, on the seventh, he rests. Six days he has uttered the many useful and useless things the workday demanded of him, but on the seventh he obeys the command of the prophet; he lets his tongue rest from the talk of every day, and learns to be silent, to *listen*. And this sanctifying of the day of rest by listening to God's voice in silence must be shared by all members of his house. It must not be fretted by the voice of command. The man-servant and the maid-servant must also rest; and it is even said that just for the sake of their rest the day of rest was instituted, for when rest has penetrated to them, then all the house is, indeed, freed from the noise and chatter of the weekday, and redeemed to rest.

Franz Rosenzweig

We have a basic problem with the concept of Shabbat as total rest - because this is physically impossible for us! We cannot just 'switch off'. We cannot not eat or drink, animals also need to be fed and watered, cows need to be milked. If it is cold, our bodies desire warmth; if it is hot, our bodies desire shade or wind or some other means of cooling. We use machines nowadays which function constantly - but the mere act of opening a door can trip a switch which - automatically - changes the status of a piece of that machine from 'inactive' to 'active'. Some activities can be avoided, and some can be limited to a necessary minimum - but the reason why there is such a vast amount of Law about Shabbat is simply that the term 'necessary minimum' needs somehow to be defined - perhaps differently in different climates or centuries or societies. We have to walk - but how far? We have to carry, even if only carrying a piece of clothing from the cupboard or carrying a cup to the table. So what can we carry, and where? Is there a difference between 'public' and 'private' areas, and how can we define these? In the Mishnah 39 separate activities are listed and defined.

Walter Rothschild

The world of Shabbat is totally different from the weekday universe: there is no work to do, no deprivation. On Shabbat, there is neither anxiety nor bad news. Since such a world does not yet exist in space, it is first created in time, on the seventh day of the week. Jews travel through time in order to enter a perfect world for a night and a day. The goal is to create a reality so complete and absorbing that these time travellers are caught up in its values and renewed. The Shabbat is the foretaste of the messianic redemption. But even as this enclave of perfection is carved out in the realm of time, the world goes on as usual in the realm of surrounding space. This is why Shabbat needs a community in order to be credible. By an act of will, the community creates this sacred time and space, and agrees to live by its rules.

Irving Greenberg

Shabbat Peace and Harmony

The goal of man is to live again in peace and harmony with his fellow men, with animals, with the soil. But this new harmony is different from that in paradise. It can now be obtained only if man develops fully in order to become truly human, by knowing the truth and doing justly, by developing his power of reason to a point which frees him from the bondage of man and of irrational passions ... On the Sabbath, in the state of rest, man anticipates the state of human freedom that will be fulfilled eventually, when the Messiah will come. The relationship of man and nature and of man and man is one of harmony, peace and non-interference. Where work is a symbol of conflict and disharmony, rest is an expression of dignity, peace and freedom ... That is why the Sabbath commandment is at one time motivated by God's *rest* and at the other by the liberation from Egypt. Both mean the same and interpret each other: rest is freedom.

Erich Fromm

A simple vegetable meal on Shabbat in a home where there is love between husband, wife and children is better than a fatted ox in a home where there is hatred. A man should not plan to honour Shabbat with delicacies while he knows that he will quarrel with his wife, or father, or mother. Whether it be Shabbat or festival - 'Better a dry morsel and quietness therewith, than a house full of feasting with strife' *(Proverbs 17:1)*. One should honour Shabbat by having no strife thereon.

Yehudah HeChasid

There are objects in life higher than success. The Sabbath, with its exhortation to the worship of God and the doing of kindly deeds, reminds us week by week of these higher objects. It prevents us reducing our life to the level of a machine. The gathered experience of mankind, that the break in the routine of work one day in seven will heighten the value of the very work itself, is not lightly to be put aside. The Sabbath is one of the glories of our humanity. For if to labour is noble, of our own free will to pause in that labour which may lead to success, to money, or to fame, may be nobler still. To dedicate one day a week to rest and to God, this is the prerogative and privilege of man alone. It is an ordinance which we may rightly call Divine.

C. G. Montefiore

Business Permitted on Shabbat
Rabbi Chisda and Rabbi Hamnuna said that it is permissible to make plans for good deeds on the Sabbath; and Rabbi Elazar said that one may arrange about alms to the poor on Sabbath. Rabbi Yochanan said: One may transact business which has to do with the saving of life or with public health on Sabbath, and one may go to synagogue to discuss public affairs on Sabbath. Rabbi Jonathan said: One may even go to theatres and circuses on Sabbath for such a purpose. And in the school of Manasseh it was said that one may talk about the future marriage of one's children on Sabbath, or about the children's education, or about teaching them a handicraft, for the Scripture forbids 'your business', but *God's* business is permitted.

Shabbat

Prayer
There is more to prayer than feelings ... but any form of prayer that excludes the real and necessary expression of feelings will ultimately fail in transforming our lives. And it will alienate those of us whose primary connection to the world is emotional.

Shefa Gold

The treasure is where you're standing.
I just had to tell you...
Though your gaze is fixed on distant shores,
and though you're scanning the sky madly for that one
miracle that will tuck your doubts to bed
and kiss them away.
You're looking for the one that will clinch it, aren't you?
Well, you're looking too far ... 'cause,
the miracle is where you're standing.
Miracles are commonplace.
They can walk in broad daylight,
and not be recognized.
But rare ... oh so rare is the one who can step up to that
imposter-ordinaire and rip away the mask and say to
each and every day in its disguise,
'Aha! This here and now is miracle and I wasn't fooled
for a minute.'
The miracle is where you're standing,
but who would think to dig beneath the soil of his own
complaint.

Shefa Gold

There is nothing that induces one to love the creator and to enjoy God's love more than the voice raised in an extended tune.

Sefer Hasidim

Supermarket Prayer
    Last week in the supermarket
    at an unlikely hour
    I saw a woman I know.
    She tried to avoid me
    pretended not to remember me
    but I had unwittingly trapped her
    blocked escape in the tuna fish aisle.

    I just wanted to say hello
    my cruelty was inadvertent
    but up close I saw
    her hair was in disarray
    and dirty, her face
    without its careful mask
    of lipstick, blusher, shadow.
    She was wearing a ratty old jacket
    the discard of her husband
    or perhaps her teenaged son.

<<<

Nine thirty, on a Tuesday morning,
dressed like that -
suddenly I knew she was out of work
and ashamed.   And coming undone
there in the tuna fish aisle.

I tried as best I could
to help her cover her nakedness
but all that day and the next
she haunted me.
How strange, I thought,
how strange and how sad
that she should feel threatened, judged,
shamed by me.

The rabbis say
when you bring colour to someone's face
it's as if you shed their blood.
Forgive me.
May you be restored to your full self
soon, speedily, in our day.
And let us say amen.

Merle Feld

Singles

Singles gather together
    like religious Jews on Yom Kippur,
fervently praying for contact
    with the 'other'.

'May my make-up not run,
    don't let me act the fool,
let my conversation be witty,
    may my breath be fresh
and my deodorant last.
    Help us, O Lord, Make contact
with the "other".'

    True prayers and hopes
are not uttered in Temple;
    they're offered at crises
in parties and bars.

Norman Lipson

Why Prayer

A frequently asked question is why God needs prayer. To this, the tradition offers two distinct answers. The first is quite simply that God needs prayer to the extent that He needs (or, better, wishes) to have communication with His creations. Judaism presupposes that God cares for and wishes to relate to human beings. For that reason alone prayer is important.

The second answer is that God does not truly 'need' prayer, human beings do. It makes no difference to God's 'self-conception' that I praise or glorify Him. The difference to my self-conception, on the other hand, is profound. I am reminded of my station and task in this world. For a moment it strikes me anew that my life is a gift, tenuous, fleeting, and that I owe the granting of that gift to God. Exalting God brings home to me my limitations, often hard to recall in a world where human endeavour had done so much, achieved so stupendously.

This explains the rabbinic regulation concerning bowing during the *Amidah*, the central prayer of the Jewish worship service. A regular worshipper bows at the beginning and end of two of the benedictions. A high priest bows at the beginning of each of the eighteen blessings, and a king remains bowed for the entire prayer (*Berachot* 34a,b). The greater the temptation to pride, the more one must be humbled. The greater the position we attain in this world, the more we need to recall that each of us is human, each of us needs guidance and mercy.

David Wolpe

I consider prayer to be indispensable to our growth as spiritual creatures, but I see no easy solution in the offing that would convert the masses to its practice. How could it be otherwise? Prayer is, after all, not only a means to self-transcendence. It is one of the very goals of human development. For it is only in prayer that men and women deliberately acknowledge the limits of their creatureliness, the greatness of their creative gifts, and the responsibility that they have as a result of these two features of their nature. Men and women will dispute among themselves about whether their prayers fall upon a listening ear or whether they are a form of introspection or meditation. But both one who turns to 'God' and one who seeks one's better self are united in the realization of their dependence on one another and on a reality into which all creatures are born and whose origin and ultimate fate neither can ever know. In prayer, humans accept with gratitude what they are and what they have. It is their way of proclaiming with humility the values by which they propose to live. It is the opening of their minds and hearts to the voices of experience and integrity that, from time to time, call upon them to retreat from their overbearing certainties. The task of spiritually alert Jews is to bring together under one roof of worshipful search and dedication men and women who have different visions of God, humankind, and the universe but who are united by their love of Israel and of their fellow human beings.

Jack Cohen

Often we present Reform Judaism as being the Judaism that is in tune with the modern world. That is only part of the truth. For the further the world moves from religious values, the further each of us has to journey to get back to them. Living a religious life in an open society becomes ever harder.

But above all of this Reform Judaism has to mean a Judaism where we care for each other. I have worked in a congregation and seen the pain of redundancy, the shadow cast by cancer, the grief caused by death. There is not one of us untouched by pain and grief. We look to our tradition, our faith, for healing and calm. Prayer can be a way of finding God for those who have lost their spiritual life, a way of recovering a path through the world, and above all, a way of relieving loneliness at lonely times.

Michael Hilton

Prayer and Healing

Healing does not always mean that the illness is cured, however much we might want that to be the case. The reality is that we may not get well, or even better. When we say prayers for healing, we must at the same time acknowledge that complete health may not come. Healing can mean that illness is removed, but it can also mean that deeper self-understanding is gained ...

A sixteenth-century Japanese potter would never allow his apprentices to discard a cracked pot. He would say, 'Honour the workings of chance in your creation.' He would often instruct them to outline the cracks with tracings of gold. So too illness, or other 'cracks' in our souls or bodies, although unwanted and sources of pain, can be honoured as teachers for us. It is not God that can teach us these lessons. In order to gain greater understanding of ourselves in relation to our illness or suffering, it is we who must do the work to open our hearts or minds.

Marcia Plumb

The *Siddur*

There is a persistent belief that the Jewish prayer book is monolithic in its structure and content. It is assumed that the prayer book was composed by divinely inspired men and that its text is therefore sacred and immutable. The assumption that the traditional prayer book has a definitive form which has remained fixed and unaltered to this day led Rabbi Judah He-Hasid and his mediaeval school of mystics to search the text of the prayers for divine mysteries in the same way that the kabbalists searched the biblical text for divine secrets. These mystics counted the words and even the letters of the prayers, hoping to decipher their esoteric implications. But these assumptions of the mystics were unfounded. The prayer book has never been uniform in content. Even before it was committed to writing there were already a number of well-defined versions with variant readings.

Abraham Millgram

Sh'liach Tsibbur - *Service Leader*

Think of the *sh'liach tsibbur* as a conductor on a train. In fact, a train is a good metaphor for a worship service. Everyone on the train is headed down the track in the same direction. Yet while they are on the train, the passengers don't all do the same thing at the same moment. Some stand, some sit, some walk around. Traditional Jewish worship allows each worshipper to proceed at an individual pace. The leader is responsible for directing the collective flow of the service; he or she lets the worshipper know where the *service* is but not necessarily where the *worshipper* is in the service. Related to this metaphor, consider the *sh'liach tsibbur* as a *moreh derekh*, a tour guide, who takes the congregation on a path that ultimately may bring them closer to God. Jewish worship does many things to make that path more accessible: we follow a set order in the service. We return to familiar melodies. We even travel in a group. Yet the experienced *sh'liach tsibbur* knows that for all our intentions the journey is an uncertain endeavour, and we travellers who have joined the trip may be at very different points in our lives.

Jeffrey Summit

Public Worship

The effectiveness of public worship depends not upon one thing, but upon two. It depends not only upon the abstract appropriateness of the service, but also upon the power of the worshipper to respond to its appeal. You may modernise the prayerbook as much as you please; you may remove all its anachronisms, its supplications for the restoration of the sacrificial rite, its petitions for Zion, its 'anthropomorphisms', but you will not thereby ensure prayerful feeling. This only the worshipper himself can supply; and he can supply it only if he bear the elements of it in his own breast - in his faith in the Unseen, and his desire to surrender himself to the Unseen. It is because people forget this fundamental truth that so many unmerited accusations are brought against our public worship. They condemn the service when they ought rather to blame themselves. They leave the synagogue unrefreshed, unhelped - to use their own expressions, irritated, alienated. But they do not see that much of this failure is chargeable to their own lack of devoutness, their own want of spiritual preparedness, on a frame of mind, cold, sceptical, irresponsive, which would suffice to make even the ideal service uninspiring and barren ... Public worship ... can give us back only what we bring to it.

Morris Joseph

Honesty in Prayer

Firstly, we must be honest in prayer. The great temptation is to be conventional, to mouth platitudes for the things for which we know we ought to pray. But the truth is that often no one would be more shocked than we should our prayers be granted. We may pray for the giving up of some habit without the slightest intention of doing so. We may pray for some virtue or quality without any real desire to possess it. We may pray to be made into a certain kind of person when the last thing that we in fact want is to be changed, when we are very well content to be as we are. This is lying to God. We should not pray unless it is with our whole hearts. There should be in our prayers an astringent personal honesty, for God knows the secrets of our hearts, and God knows when we are merely asking for blessings which we have no real desire to receive.

A second rule of prayer follows naturally from this: we must be very definite in prayer. It is not enough to ask God's forgiveness because we are wretched and miserable sinners. That is far too easy and, paradoxical though it may sound, far too comfortable. We must name and confess our actual sins to God. It is not enough vaguely to thank God for all His gifts: we must specifically name the gifts. It is not enough simply to ask God to make us good. We must ask for the particular things in which we know that we are lacking and which we know that we need. Herein lies the great difficulty of prayer. There can be no real prayer without self-examination. This is why the Hebrew word for prayer, *le-hitpallel*, is in the reflexive tense. Coming from a root word *palal* meaning to judge, prayer in Hebrew really means to judge oneself. And believe me, to judge oneself is difficult, exhausting and, above all, humiliating. Many of us spend our life running away rather than facing ourselves. One of the main reasons why our prayers are not what they should be is because so few people will face the stern discipline of self-examination in the presence of God on which prayer is based. Prayer and self-examination go hand in hand.

P. Selvin Goldberg

The Journey of Prayer

Fortunately we do not have to create our own religion from scratch. A great tradition has already mapped out the way. There are many conveyances - prayers, symbols, meditations, to name only a few. For those who find difficulties in prayer I would suggest - don't pray too much. A prayer is not judged by its length nor a service by the number of pages. The absence of words - a short silence - might help. If conversational prayer does not come easily, since it implies a faith in the existence of another Being which has not yet already been experienced, the more subjective 'meditational' form of prayer may be used.

Perhaps the repetitious character of Jewish prayer makes it appear difficult. This characteristic is understandable. One prays in a relationship of love, and to people in love the same phrases are never exhausted. To the outsider they may be platitudes, to the insider they are not. Many people (including some great rabbis) have often felt that too many words act as a barrier to God rather than a medium to God. In that case reduce the words! If you can only feel deeply the sense of one word alone - and it is a word like '*baruch*' or '*hesed*' - then you have got to the heart of the matter.

Certain exercises can be made. Look around at the people sitting next to you in a bus or café, and try to see them in the light of the newly found knowledge as souls (immortal at that). It will take some time to get adjusted to the new religious spectacles. Another exercise! Try and think of the liturgy not as poetry but as having the precision of a legal document. Certain shocks may occur (I suggest the prayer *elohai neshamah* at the beginning of the morning service).

Many people have a romantic view of prayer. They assume that, without any preparation on their part, they can commune with the Almighty at 11 a.m. sharp every Shabbat. But prayer though it does not involve expertise does involve effort. To pray one must concentrate and have some preparatory quiet. Five minutes' 'tuning in' before a service begins frequently makes all the difference.

These are then some tips. It will not go completely smoothly. There are always wrong detours, blank periods, and moments of 'fed-upness'. These in their way are necessary. Too smooth a way leads often to too smooth a religion. Moreover one only appreciates what has been acquired by effort. There was an old Yiddish phrase that means 'nothing produces nothing'. In religion too there is a law of returns. What one puts in one gets out - usually no more and no less.

Is all this worthwhile? Here one has to trust. Those who have made the journey to the interior have brought back reports that nothing can equal the worth of its peace and its radiance. In any case something does make us go to synagogue, something does make us join in the prayers, something does in an obscure way push us on. What is this something? Perhaps it is the soul trying to break through the artificial barriers and come home.

Lionel Blue

Custom - *Minhag*

Custom is lovable in a way that law is not. Custom is so unpristine. It has fingerprints all over it. It asserts the reality of practices against the ideality of principles ... You can destroy objects, you cannot destroy geometry. But you cannot touch or taste geometry.

'At home, we used to ...': there was never a holiday in our household when my father or my mother did not begin a sentence with those words, and describe the manner in which the occasions were observed in their corner of the Carpathians in the 1930s, before the apocalypse ... They boasted about the vanished usages, as if to say: See how much there was! Custom ... lives in the individuals and the communities that practise it, it dies with them too ... The preservation of custom ... is a moral imperative. My parents taught me this ... When, on the eve of Passover, I chop apples and walnuts and cinnamon with wine precisely as my parents, and their parents, chopped them, I mark the defeat of our enemies. In our kitchen, empires fall again.

Leon Wieseltier

Tradition and Change

When the Baal Shem Tov had a difficult task before him, he would go to a certain place in the woods, light a fire and meditate in prayer - and what he had set out to perform was done.

When a generation later the Maggid of Meseritz was faced with the same task he would go to the same place in the woods and say: 'We can no longer light the fire, but we can still speak the prayers' - and what he wanted done became reality.

Again a generation later Rabbi Moshe-Leib of Sassov had to perform this task. And he too went into the woods and said: 'We can no longer light a fire, nor do we know the secret meditations belonging to the prayer, but we do know the place in the woods - and that must be sufficient' - and sufficient it was.

But when another generation had passed and Rabbi Israel of Rishin was called upon to perform the task, he sat in his golden chair in his castle and said: 'We cannot light the fire, we cannot speak the prayers, we do not know the place, but we can tell the story of how it was done.' And the story which he told had the same effect as the actions of the other three.

Gershom Scholem quoting S.J.Agnon

You can say if you will that this profound little anecdote symbolises the decay of a great movement. You can also say that it reflects the transformation of all its values, a transformation so profound that in the end all that remained of the mystery was the tale. That is the position in which we find ourselves today, or in which Jewish mysticism finds itself. The story is not ended, it has not yet become history, and the secret life it holds can break out tomorrow in you or in me. Under what aspect this invisible stream of Jewish mysticism will again come to the surface we cannot tell.

Gershom Scholem

The Religious Quest

He who seeks God can do no other than to persist in his quest to the last, to keep on inquiring, struggling, challenging. He will not be granted tranquillity of soul. But if it be given him to renew the forces of his being day by day and constantly to be among the seekers, the rebellious - that is the crown of his life and the height of his desire.

Judah L. Magnes

Relationships develop, often unpredictably; Judaism's conception of how Jews come to know God is very similar. It is not certainty that Jews seek; Jewish life is about searching for God's sheltering nearness, a sense of God's presence, a glimpse of God's love. It is not an even, easy, or predictable road, but it is open to believers and doubters alike.

Daniel Gordis

Rabbi Baer of Radoschitz once said to his teacher, the rabbi of Lublin: 'Show me one general way to the service of God.' The zaddik replied: 'It is impossible to tell people what way they should take. For one way to serve God is through the teachings, another through prayer, another through fasting, and still another through eating. Everyone should carefully observe what way their heart draws them to, and then choose their way with all their strength.' God does not say: 'This way leads to Me and that does not,' but God says, 'Whatever you do may be a way to Me, provided you do it in such a manner that it leads you to Me.'

Martin Buber

The Religious Challenge

There are two hells, one of fire and one of snow. The hell of fire is for people who burn with the passion for lust and transgression. But the hell of snow is the penalty for demoralization. People are filled with regrets. Demoralization is the greatest obstacle to returning to God. People think that they have sinned so much that repentance won't help them. They give up all hope of drawing close to God. The hell of these people is cold and bitter: the hell of snow. Don't become cold in your pursuit of the Torah and of God's commandments. 'She is not afraid of the snow for her household, for all her household are clothed with scarlet' (Proverbs 31:21).

Nachman of Bratslav

The Imitation of God

A human being's nature is radically different from God's, but human beings are capable of approaching God's actions, God's love, God's mercy, God's justice.

Maimonides

God is holy, holiness is synonymous with ethics, the ethical must be spelled out in a detailed code of concrete practice and that code of practice is Jewish law. Law is reflective of the will of God, the will of God is ethical, and acting in the image of God means responding to the ethical nature of God through *mitsvot*, commandments, through *halakhah*, Jewish law.

There are passionate debates all around the Jewish world today about who 'created' the ever-developing code of law, God or human beings, about its authority, about its hermeneutics, about how its dynamism was maintained, about the need to create a new kind of law more subtle and open to individual response and choice but that, though enormously important, doesn't affect my central point. God, holiness, ethics, justice, *mitsvot*, *halakhah* must be one.

Tony Bayfield

A Meditation on Psalm 23

My poem is dedicated to the Shepherd of old who in our literature still reigns supreme in a pastoral, semi-romantic setting. But this scenery has now almost been replaced by technology, computer science and machinery: they can protect and guide, but never lead and comfort. It is God behind the shepherd's mask whose nearness we seek.

> Lord of all creations,
> abide with us.
> Be our shepherd
> protect green meadows from the might of grey cities:
> fruit of the field for hungry people
> clean water for thirst of the poor.
> Let us rest on green grass
> listen to the gentle sounds of springs
> shield us from noise of the world
> guide us to the path of the righteous!
> We share with You, O Lord, Your name *Tzaddik,* righteous.
> Protect us from heat and strife!
> Shield us from the shadows:
> *Pachad leyla* - terror by night,
> *Tzalamut* - black darkness,
> *Tzalmavet* - the valley of the shadow.
> Be not afraid of death - nor the fear of it!
> Fear not the evil done *to* you
> but the evil done *by* you.
> Fear the Eye that sees and the Ear that hears!
> Invisible God be beside us!
> You prepare a table for me
> set a place for my enemy
> so that we shall be friends.
> Come all who are hungry!
> Eat with us: *Friends* of the past,
> *friends* today.
> You anoint our head with oil,
> our cups are full to the brim.
> Now we are as kings at our very own table.
> Turn around, my friends, who follows us?
> Pharaoh's soldiers, crusaders, Nazis?
> No: Goodness and Mercy - joy and grace.
> Let us enter into Your gates, O God, with thanksgiving.
> For we shall dwell in Your house
> as long as we shall live.

Jan Fuchs

Escape

In literature and folklore, the significance and the fascination of golems - from Rabbi Loew's to Victor Frankenstein's - lay in their soullessness, in their tireless inhuman strength, in their metaphorical association with overweening human ambition, and in the frightening ease with which they passed beyond the control of their horrified and admiring creators. But it seemed... that none of these ... were among the true reasons that impelled men, time after time, to hazard the making of golems. The shaping of a golem ... was a gesture of hope, offered against hope, in a time of desperation. It was the expression of a yearning that a few magic words and an artful hand might produce something - one poor, dumb, powerful thing - exempt from the crushing strictures, from the ills, cruelties, and inevitable failures of the greater Creation. It was the voicing of a vain wish, when you got down to it, to escape. To slip ... free of the entangling chain of reality and the straitjacket of physical laws. Harry Houdini had roamed the Palladiums and Hippodromes of the world encumbered by an entire cargo-hold of crates and boxes, stuffed with chains, iron hardware, brightly painted flats and hokum, animated all the while only by this same desire, never fulfilled: truly to escape, if only for one instant; to poke his head through the borders of this world, with its harsh physics, into the mysterious spirit world that lay beyond.

Michael Chabon

Fear and Awe of God

Rabbi Samuel went to Rome at a time when the queen lost her bracelet. He happened to find it. Meanwhile a crier went around the kingdom announcing: 'Whoever brings back the queen's bracelet within thirty days will receive a great reward. But if the bracelet is found on him after the thirty days, his head will be cut off!' Rabbi Samuel did not return it within the thirty days, but a day later brought it back to the queen. She asked him: 'Weren't you in the kingdom?' He replied: 'Yes.' 'So did you not hear the proclamation?' He answered: 'Yes.' She asked: 'What did the crier say?' He told her the crier's words. So she asked: 'Then why did you not return it within thirty days?' He replied: 'So that you would not say that I feared *you*, but I returned it because I feared God.' 'Blessed be the God of the Jews!' she said.

Yerushalmi Baba Metzia

Daily Sins

There are three sins that no one can escape on any given day: sinful thoughts; the presumption that God must answer our prayers, and the 'dust of slander'.

Baba Batra 164b

On Faith

Faith does not spring out of nothing. It comes with the discovery of the holy dimension of our existence ...

Faith does not detach man from thinking, it does not suspend reason. It is opposed not to knowledge but to indifferent aloofness to the essence of living.

Faith means to hold small things great, to take light matters seriously, to distinguish the common and the passing from the aspect of the lasting ...

Faith is a dynamic, personal act, flowing between the heart of man and the love of God ...

Faith is the insight that life is not a self-maintaining, private affair, not a chaos of whims and instincts, but an aspiration, a way, not a refuge.

Faith is real only when it is not one-sided but reciprocal. Man can rely on God, if God can rely on man.

Abraham Joshua Heschel

Learn, with the whole of your ability to learn, all that you can of *'devekut'* (communion with God). Learn in the place where you are, within the circumstances, complexities, joys and sorrows in which you find yourself, learn *through* these involvements, to understand - with heart, not head - the meanings that emanate from them. No one can take this task from you. No one else can do this work for you. Faith speaks to you and me, and it relies on the experience of those greater than us. The world is not blind, is not meaningless. Redemption awaits us just behind the curtain. It is not given to an individual man to draw this curtain aside and bring about the redemption. But he isn't compelled to sit and wait, without doing anything. It is given to him to be a *partner* in the act of redemption. By a man's opening in himself the inner sources through which flows and rises the light of redemption for the individual, in keeping with his ability to receive it, the kingdom of heaven grows and increases in the world. And the active hope of many individuals will bring the total redemption nearer. That is the hope of Israel.

Shmuel Hugo Bergman

Faithfulness

Often, when he came to visit, my grandfather would bring me a present. These were never the sorts of things that other people brought, dolls and books and stuffed animals. My dolls and stuffed animals have been gone for more than half a century, but many of my grandfather's gifts are with me still.

Once he brought me a little paper cup. I looked inside it expecting something special. It was full of dirt. I was not allowed to play with dirt. Disappointed, I told him this. He smiled at me fondly. Turning, he picked up the little teapot from my dolls' tea set and took me to the kitchen where he filled it with water. Back in the nursery, he put the teacup on the windowsill and handed me the teapot. 'If you promise to put some water in the cup every day, something may happen,' he told me.

At the time, I was four years old and my nursery was on the sixth floor of an apartment building in Manhattan. This whole thing made no sense to me at all. I looked at him dubiously. He nodded with encouragement. 'Every day, *Neshume-le*,' he told me.

And so I promised. At first, curious to see what would happen, I did not mind doing this. But as the days went by and nothing changed, it got harder and harder to remember to put water in the cup. After a week, I asked my grandfather if it was time to stop yet. Shaking his head no, he said, 'Every day, *Neshume-le*.' The second week was even harder, and I became resentful of my promise to put water in the cup. When my grandfather came again, I tried to give it back to him but he refused to take it, saying simply, 'Every day, *Neshume-le*.' By the third week, I began to forget to put water in the cup. Often I would remember only after I had been put to bed and would have to get out of bed and water it in the dark. But I did not miss a single day. And one morning, there were two little green leaves that had not been there the night before.

I was completely astonished. Day by day they got bigger. I could not wait to tell my grandfather, certain that he would be as surprised as I was. But of course he was not. Carefully he explained to me that life is everywhere, hidden in the most ordinary and unlikely places. I was delighted. 'And all it needs is water, Grandpa?' I asked him. Gently he touched me on the top of my head. 'No, *Neshume-le*,' he said, 'all it needs is your faithfulness.'

Rachel Naomi Remen

The Limits of Faith

Few things have done more harm than the belief on the part of individuals and groups (or tribes or states or nations or churches) that he or she or they are in *sole* possession of the truth ... It is a terrible and dangerous arrogance to believe that you alone are right: have a magical eye which sees *the* truth; and that others cannot be right if they disagree. This makes one certain that there is *one* goal and only one for one's nation or church or the whole of humanity, and that it is worth any amount of suffering (particularly on the part of other people) if only the goal is attained - 'through an ocean of blood to the Kingdom of Love' (or something like this) said Robespierre: and Hitler, Lenin, Stalin, and I daresay leaders in the religious wars of Christian v. Muslim or Catholics v. Protestants sincerely believed this: the belief that there is one and only one true answer to the central questions which have agonized mankind and that one has it oneself – or one's Leader has it - was responsible for the oceans of blood: But no Kingdom of Love sprang from it - or could ...

Isaiah Berlin

Faith and Reality

Whenever I left home, *Re'ach* [my dog] stood tense and tragic on the stairs. As the door closed, her world came to an end. When I returned, she bounded down the stairs, ecstatic beyond reason. She threw me to the ground, stood on my chest, and licked my face in a flamboyant orgy of joy. Now this drama occurred whether I went to Berlin or Rome for two weeks, or to get a newspaper round the corner for two minutes.

'Doesn't she ever learn,' I complained to the vet, 'that nothing is going to happen to me? I always come back.' Patiently he explained, 'Don't you realize she is only an animal? What is real to her is what lies within her senses, what she can touch, see, and smell, especially smell. When you walk out of that door, you walk out of the orbit of her senses, and you have ceased to exist. You have died and she is bereaved. And when you come back, suddenly she can hear you, see you, smell you again. You have become alive again.'

I understood now why she was so emotional. If I experienced the death and resurrection of my nearest and dearest several times a day, I would also have a rocky ride through life.

I brooded over this a long time, and remembered a line from the Psalms, that we humans are only a little higher than the animals, and just a little lower than the angels. Because we are only a little higher than the animals, what is real to us is what we can sense, our furniture, our friends, our pay checks, our cars, our homes. But because we are also a little lower than the angels, we are the first creatures in the evolutionary chain who can give reality to what is outside our senses, like a soul, or conscience, or God. Our hold on such see-through spiritual 'things' is weak, for all our animal instincts go against it. We cannot see them, so can they be there? Does a God really exist? After all, we can't touch God. Are we deluding ourselves about religion and spiritual experience? To believe in the reality of what cannot be sensed stretches us to the limit and beyond the limit of our animal nature.

Many times we fall back, exhausted from the mental and imaginative effort it requires. What is not sense turns into nonsense and is dismissed. And then we face the opposite dilemma. Without this flimsy see-through stuff, our lives lose whatever grandeur or glory they possess. It is 'nothing', yet we lean on it in tough times. It does not give us security but it does give us courage. This 'no-thing' supports us. This is part of common experience.

Lionel Blue

The Fanatic

The fanatic longs to accelerate the advent of the kingdom, to have it come before its time. He seeks to capture the kingdom forcibly at the point which the searchlight of his prayer shows him as the next one but which never is closer than next-but-one. His prayer and his love wither for him and so in the end he himself has also withdrawn from the moment, full of grace, which awaited his deed like everyone else's. He has delayed the advent of the kingdom which he wanted to accelerate. Thus only the prayer that is offered at the proper time will not delay the advent of the kingdom of heaven.

Franz Rosenzweig

Silence

Rabbi Abin said: When Jacob of the village of Neboria was in Tyre he interpreted the phrase in the Psalms 'Praise is silence for You, O God' (Psalm 65:2) as meaning: Silence is the height of all praises of God. For God is like a jewel without price; however high you appraise it, still you undervalue it.

Midrash Psalms 19:2

Years ago a piano recital in a famous concert hall in the States premiered a strange composition: the pianist raised his hands over the keyboard, sat immobile for three minutes, then lowered his hands and got up to bow and receive his applause. The composer explained as follows to those puzzled by the silence of his new composition: 'Music is composed of two elements: notes and rests. Bach, Mozart and Beethoven have written music made up entirely of notes, so I composed one piece entirely of rests.' I don't suppose any of us would want to sit through a concert of such works, but the composer was making an important statement about the nature of all music; silences can be as important as the sounds.

Shamai Kanter

Few of us would associate 'silence' with a Jewish service. Surely a Shabbat service is filled with noise, with words and music, with people coming and going - really very noisy in fact? And all this is true of course. But beyond the noise, behind the words there is a great pool of silence. Think of a seashore with great waves breaking on it; beyond the waves - the sea is calm. The service, the peripheral noise, is the breakers on the shore; beyond is a sea of silence which only we, individually, can reach, but we must go through the surf to get there. And if we do get to the silence beyond we will find that it is infinite, deep - a place where we might meet God or come face to face with ourselves. For it is the silence that dwells on the very edge of our experience. Rarely are we able to make it through the breakers to the silence beyond but when we have been there we return changed; for we realise that the soul needs silence just as much as the mind needs the stimulation of the world and its noise.

Elaina Rothman

PASSAGES FOR RESPONSIVE READING, STUDY OR MEDITATION

ON THE LAWS OF LIFE

Let us learn the laws of life and the ways of peace.
    O humanity, God has told you what is good and what the Eternal asks of you. Is it not to do justice, to love mercy, and to walk humbly with your God!
Micah 6: 8

Let us learn that the more we give, the more we have.
    Giving changes a person's impulse to cruelty into kindness of heart. This is the chief service of giving.
Nachman of Bratslav

Let us learn that in order to change the world, we must also change ourselves.
    Those whom you strengthen in their service to God will love you. The way to strengthen them is to love them.
Nachman of Bratslav

Let us learn to accept our human limitations.
    It is of great advantage that we shall know our place, and not imagine that the whole universe exists for us alone.
Maimonides

Let us learn to accept our human responsibility.
    Everyone in Israel should know and consider that they are unique in the world ... and that they are called upon to fulfil their particular task.
Chasidic

Let us learn that within each problem we meet, God has set an answer.
    There is no stumbling block one cannot push aside, for the stumbling-block is only there for the sake of the will, and there actually are no stumbling-blocks save in the spirit.
Chasidic

Let us learn that love is a giving and not a taking.
    If love depends on some selfish cause, when the cause disappears, love disappears; but if love does not depend on a selfish cause, it will never disappear.
Sayings of the Fathers

ON THE CHALLENGES OF LIFE

Let us learn to see more than outward things, and to trust God's voice within us.
> Prefer the truth and right by which you seem to lose to the falsehood and wrong by which you seem to gain.
> *Maimonides*

Let us learn to have the courage to stand alone and walk before God.
> Let us do good deeds and then ask Torah from God. Let us do righteous and fitting deeds, and then ask wisdom from God. Let us take the way of humility, and then ask understanding from God.
> *Seder Eliyahu Rabbah*

Let us learn that we have the right to do the work,
but the results are in God's hand.
> One may do much or one may do little; it is all one, provided we direct our heart to heaven.
> *Berachot*

Let us learn that it is not for us to complete the work,
but neither may we desist from it.
> Do God's will as if it were your will so that God may do your will as if it were God's will.
> *Sayings of the Fathers*

Let us learn that this world is not the measure of all things.
> Plan for this world as if you were to live forever; plan for the world to come as if you were to die tomorrow.
> *Ibn Gabirol*

Let us learn to see in every ending a new beginning.
> The world is like a corridor to the world to come. Prepare yourself in the corridor so that you may enter the inner chamber.
> *Sayings of the Fathers*

Let us learn to consider the mystery of life and death.
> One hour of repentance and good deeds in this world is better than all the life of the world to come; and one hour of calmness of spirit in the world to come is better than all the life of this world.
> *Sayings of the Fathers*

ON GOD'S PROMISES FOR THE FUTURE

I am God of might, walk before Me and be perfect.
Genesis 17:1

Do not think meanly of yourself and do not despair of perfection.
Maimonides

*I will restore honest language to the nations, so that all may speak
in God's name, and serve God together with one mind.*
Zephaniah 3:9

I call heaven and earth to witness that whether it be Jew or non-Jew, man or woman, free or enslaved - only according to their deeds does the spirit of God rest upon them.
Seder Eliyahu Rabbah

*No longer will we teach our neighbour or those near to us saying:
'Know the Eternal'. All of them will know Me.*
Based on Jeremiah 31:34

Take care of your own soul and of another person's body but not of your own body and of another person's soul.
Mendel of Kotzk

*At that time I will bring you in, and at that time I will gather you.
I will give you praise and renown among all the peoples of the earth,
when I turn your captivity before your eyes.*
Zephaniah 3:20

The world will be freer by our liberty, richer by our wealth, greater by our greatness.
Theodor Herzl

*Nation shall not lift up sword against nation,
never again shall they train for war.*
Micah 4:3

In God's eyes the person stands high who makes peace between people - between husband and wife, between parents and children, between management and labour, between neighbour and neighbour. But they stand highest who establish peace among the nations.
Talmud

601 PASSAGES FOR RESPONSIVE READING, STUDY OR MEDITATION

ON THE MESSIANIC AGE

The wolf shall live with the lamb,
the leopard lie down with the kid,
the calf and young lion shall feed together,
and a little child shall lead them.

Isaiah 11:6

See My works, how fine and excellent they are. All that I created, I created for you. Think upon this, and do not desolate and corrupt My world, for if you corrupt it, there is no one to set it right after you.

Ecclesiastes Rabbah

A shoot shall grow from the broken tree of Jesse,
and a branch shall spring from its roots.
The spirit of God shall rest upon him,
the spirit of wisdom and understanding.

Isaiah 11:1-2

No duty is more sacred than for us to cherish that spark of the Messiah in our soul and save it from extinction.

Nachman of Bratslav

Who can endure the day of his coming?
Who can stand firm when he appears?
He shall sit as a refiner and purifier of silver,
and he shall purify the sons of Levi,
and purge them as gold and silver.

Malachi 3:2-3

The world is judged by the majority of its people, and individuals are judged by the majority of their deeds. Happy are those who perform a good deed: that may tip the scales for them and the world.

Kiddushin

It shall be said in that day:
This is our God for whom we waited to save us;
this is the God for whom we waited,
we will be glad and rejoice in God's salvation.

Isaiah 25:9

May God's kingdom come in your lifetime, and in your days, and in the lifetime of all the family of Israel - quickly and speedily may it come.

Kaddish

ON OUR DUTIES

We are asked to befriend and honour the old, for we too shall grow old.
> You shall rise in the presence of grey hairs, give honour to the aged, and fear your God. I am the Eternal.
> *Leviticus 19:32*

We are asked to share the anxieties of others, for God hears them.
> Closed in by troubles I called on the Eternal who answered me and set me free.
> *Psalm 118:5*

We are asked to rule other creatures as we would have God rule over us.
> It is forbidden to harm any living creature. It is one's duty to save any living creature from pain.
> *Kitzur Shulchan Aruch*

We are asked to overcome our prejudice,
for we have been, and are, the victim of prejudice.
> Are not you and the Ethiopians all the same to Me, children of Israel? - It is the Eternal who speaks.
> *Amos 9:7*

We are asked to visit the sick, for our bodies too are frail.
> We should pay attention to the needs of the sick, to care for them, give them pleasure and pray for mercy for them.
> *Kitzur Shulchan Aruch*

We are asked to support the disabled,
for some are disabled in body and some in spirit.
> You shall not treat the deaf with contempt, nor make the blind stumble.
> *Leviticus 19:14*

We are asked to love all people whether they be Jew or non-Jew.
> Love your neighbour, and love the stranger, as you love yourself. I am the Eternal.
> *Leviticus 19: 18, 34*

ON OUR RESPONSIBILITIES

We are asked to help the poor
because our ancestors ate the bread of poverty.
> Happy are those who care for the poor. God will help them in their time of need.
>
> *Psalm 41:2*

We are asked to welcome the stranger,
for we have been homeless many times.
> Share your food with the hungry; bring the homeless into your home.
>
> *Isaiah 58:7*

We are asked to protect the weak, for we, too,
are weak and pray for God's protection.
> Rob not the poor because they are poor, nor use the law to crush the weak.
>
> *Proverbs 22:22*

We are asked to transform enmity,
for we are often our own worst enemy.
> Who is mighty among the mighty? Those who control their passion and make their enemy their friend.
>
> *Avot d'Rabbi Natan*

We are asked to understand those who are sick in mind,
for who among us knows all reality?
> Hold no people insignificant and nothing improbable, for there are none that do not have their hour and no thing that does not have its place.
>
> *Sayings of the Fathers*

We are asked to seek out the lonely,
for this is the meaning of community.
> You stand this day all of you before the Lord, all of you are pledges one for the other.
>
> *Tanchuma*

We are asked to strengthen ourselves,
for the task God has given us needs all the strength we possess.
> Love the Eternal, your God, with all your heart and all your soul and all your might.
>
> *Deuteronomy 6:5*

ON THE INDIVIDUAL

They are free who serve God by serving others.
> Others gain authority over you if you possess a will distinct from God's will.
>
> *Nachman of Bratslav*

They are happy who are at peace with themselves.
> To begin with oneself, but not to end with oneself;
> to start from oneself, but not to aim at oneself;
> to comprehend oneself, but not to be preoccupied with oneself.
>
> *Martin Buber*

They are beloved who give and accept friendship.
> A faithful friend is a life-giving medicine, and those who fear God will find one. Whoever fears God makes true friends, for as people are, so are their friends.
>
> *Ecclesiasticus*

They are generous who rejoice in the fortune of their neighbour.
> It is only right that we desire our neighbour's wellbeing, that we look with goodwill on the fortune of our neighbour and that our neighbour's honour be as dear to us as our own; for we and our neighbour are one.
>
> *Moses Cordovero*

They are righteous who accept the duties of power.
> We are held responsible for the sins of our family, or of our community, or even of all peoples, when we fail to use our influence for the correction of wrongs.
>
> *Shabbat*

They are humble who serve the community in which they pray.
> Prayers for the community come before those for ourselves, and those who set its claims above their private interests are especially acceptable to God.
>
> *Josephus*

ON THE FAMILY

May we have the strength to build our home with patience and with love.
　　Everyone has in their life a beautiful day when they find love without care and trouble. But when this day is past, you earn love, as you earn bread, by the sweat of the brow.
　　　　　　　　　　　　　　　　　　　　　　　　　Ludwig Boerne

May we fulfil our duty to respect our parents.
　　What is the honour due to parents? To provide them with food, drink, with clothing and cover, to bring them home and take them out, to provide for their needs and to do so with a cheerful face.
　　　　　　　　　　　　　　　　　　　　　　　　Kitzur Shutchan Aruch

May we know the joy of bringing up children with care.
　　Whoever brings up a righteous child is like one who never dies.
　　　　　　　　　　　　　　　　　　　　　　　　　　　　　Rashi

May we understand the dimensions of family life.
　　In the end Jewish families have to confront the spiritual dimension of Jewish identity.
　　　　　　　　　　　　　　　　　　　　　　　　　Howard Cooper

May we be comforted for all the ways in which we fail.
　　Of all the love that parents have in their hearts to give to their children - how much of it is lost! ... How many leave their children too early, either taken by death or because of divorce or other family pain! What happens to all that lost love?
　　　　　　　　　　　　　　　　　　　　　　　　　Arthur Green

May we have the courage to face the breakdown of family life.
　　Any relationship breakdown is a site of broken dreams and lost hopes. It is a place of bereavement that needs careful handling, so that the bruised souls of the two individuals can be healed a little.
　　　　　　　　　　　　　　　　　　　　　　　　　Helen Freeman

ON THE COMMUNITY

A community is a place where all are welcome.
> No two individuals are alike, and each one of us is infinitely precious. And so the community is not simply the sum of its individual members: it is what happens when persons meet and share and live with one another.
>
> Elizabeth Tikvah Sarah

A community offers support in times of need, of illness or of loss.
> When one visits the sick ... we are there to give practical help ... to offer companionship and, above all, to pray for the well-being and restoration to health of the patient.
>
> Jonathan Wittenberg

A community teaches us respect for one another.
> Accept upon yourself the yoke of the kingdom of heaven, and correct one another in the fear of heaven, and deal with one another in charity.
>
> Sifre

A community is open to all who wish to be Jews.
> Even more critical is our attitude to the children of non-Jewish mothers and Jewish fathers ... They have a right to their Jewish heritage and we should help them gain access to it.
>
> Jonathan Romain

A community calls us to commitment and action.
> There is little point in praying that the sorrowing may be comforted and the lonely cheered unless we ourselves set out to bring comfort and cheer to the sad and the neglected in our own sphere.
>
> P. Selvin Goldberg

A community accepts its responsibilities within our society and our world.
> To disregard issues of war and peace, of our treatment of the environment, of racial and religious oppression, is to disregard the very core of how Judaism conceives of religion.
>
> Tony Bayfield

ON CIVILISATION

We are called to take our full responsibility in the world.
> What should we do to be of use in the world ... ? We should devote time to public affairs and to the public welfare.
>
> Leviticus Rabbah

We are called to bring hope into the society in which we live.
> Seek the peace of the city to which I have carried you, and pray to the Eternal for it. For on its peace your own peace depends.
>
> Jeremiah 29: 7

We are called to be alert to the needs of others.
> If people become poor, do not let them fall. They are like a load resting on a wall: one person can hold it and prevent it from falling, but once it has fallen to the ground, five people cannot raise it up again.
>
> Sifra

We are called to fight for the rights of all.
> If refugees live among us, we must guarantee that they have the same rights that we do ... And if other minority communities live among us, then we must work to safeguard justice for them.
>
> Deborah Kahn-Harris

We are called to share with others in the healing of the world.
> Jews are few in number and need to work in concert with others who care equally about the future of our planet. Survival is a collective responsibility.
>
> Hillel Avidan

We are called to become partners with God in creation.
> The world through which the committed Jew moves ... is a place of moral chaos into which the Jew strives to bring order and purpose, even as God brought physical order out of the chaotic deep.
>
> Fred Morgan

We are called to share our blessings with the whole of creation.
> You shall be a blessing ... and in you shall all the families of the earth be blessed.
>
> Genesis 12: 2-3

ON GOD AND ISRAEL

We are Your people and You are our God.
　　When is God exalted in heaven?
　　When God's people are one band on earth.
　　　　　　　　　　　　　　　　　Leviticus Rabbah

We are Your children and You are our parent.
　　When you act like children of God,
　　then you deserve to be called God's children.
　　　　　　　　　　　　　　　　　Kiddushin

We are Your servants and You are our master.
　　To serve God is perfect freedom,
　　and to worship God the soul's purest happiness.
　　　　　　　　　　　　　　　　　Union Prayer Book

We are Your community and You are our portion.
　　When we are at one with the community our prayer becomes unselfish.
　　　　　　　　　　　　　　　　　Moses Chasid

We are Your inheritance and You are our destiny.
　　Moses commanded us Torah, the heritage of the community of Jacob.
　　　　　　　　　　　　　　　　　Deuteronomy 33:4

We are Your flock and You are our shepherd.
　　God who scattered Israel will gather them,
　　and guard them as shepherds guard their flocks.
　　　　　　　　　　　　　　　　　Jeremiah 31: 10

We are Your vineyard and You are our keeper.
　　As the vine will receive no graft from another tree,
　　so the community of Israel accepts no master but God.
　　　　　　　　　　　　　　　　　Zohar

We are Your work and You are our creator.
　　Everyone who acts in justice and truth
　　is a partner with God in the work of creation.
　　　　　　　　　　　　　　　　　Mechilta

We are Your beloved and You are our friend.
　　I have loved you with an everlasting love,
　　and so I stretch My faithful care upon you.
　　　　　　　　　　　　　　　　　Jeremiah 31: 3

We are Your very own and You are our nearest.
　　If you obey My voice and keep My covenant ...
　　you shall be for me a kingdom of priests and a holy nation.
　　　　　　　　　　　　　　　　　Exodus 19:5-6

We are Your people and You are our Sovereign.
　　Accept the yoke of the kingdom of heaven,
　　and practise love and kindness to one another.
　　　　　　　　　　　　　　　　　Sifre

We are Your acknowledged people and You are our acknowledged God.
　　It is our duty to praise the God of all,
　　to recognise the greatness of the Creator of first things.
　　　　　　　　　　　　　　　　　Aleinu Prayer

תהלים
Psalm Anthology

The Book of Psalms probably had its origin in collections of 'hymns' and 'poems' used as part of the worship in the Jerusalem Temple, alongside sacrifices and other ritual acts. Some are designed for a major performance, with musical instruments and choirs, but others belong to more private situations, like thanksgiving, perhaps after recovery from illness or danger. However, other kinds of material, wisdom poems, thoughts about exile, inner religious debates, were included to make up the collection in the Bible. In this form they are available both for community worship and individual meditation or prayer. They are arranged as five collections (Psalms 1-41, 42-72, 73-89, 90-106, 107-150), probably as a deliberate parallel to the 'Five Books of Moses'.

As in earlier editions of *Forms of Prayer* we have included a selection of psalms that may be used within weekly, Shabbat or festival services, but also ones that lend themselves to private reading or contemplation. In addition to indicating the content of each of the psalms, we have provided a list of themes that may be helpful in particular circumstances.

DESCRIPTION OF THE PSALMS

1.	The way of the righteous and the way of the wicked	613
3.	Confidence under persecution	614
4.	Confidence in God	615
8.	Humanity's place in creation	616
11.	Reliance on God's judgment in persecution	617
12.	Truth in a world of lies	618
14.	God looks down on the corruption in the world	619
15.	Who may dwell with God	620
16.	Happiness and trust	621
19.	The universe and Torah, witnesses to God	622
20.	A prayer before battle	624
23.	God is my shepherd	302
24.	Greeting the universal ruler at the Temple doors	41,92,254
25.	The prayer of a humble person. An alphabetic psalm	625
27.	Trust triumphs over fear. A Psalm read daily during the Penitential Period	627
29.	God in the storm	119,252
30.	Thanksgiving after danger	628
36.	The inner conflict between good and evil	630
37.	The problem of the prosperity of the wicked An alphabetic psalm	631
40.	A prayer for God's help	632
42/43.	The lament of an exile	634/636
46.	God, the nation's fortress	636
48.	Celebrating Zion and Jerusalem	42
51.	The repentant sinner	638
57.	God, the refuge in danger	640
62.	Safety is from God alone	641
63.	Longing for God in the wilderness	643
67.	A harvest hymn for all peoples	62
71.	A prayer in old age	644
73.	Someone's faith is tested	646
77.	Hope in God after national disaster	648
81.	God's actions in Israel's history	46
82.	Against corrupt authority	43
84.	The pilgrim's song of joy	649
85.	Past captivity and future peace	651
86.	Thoughts in troubled times	652
90.	The shortness of life	655
91.	In the shelter of God's wings	424
92.	The Shabbat psalm	176
93.	God reigns	47,126,178

<<<

94.	An appeal for God's justice to be seen	44
95.	Israel sings out to God	111
96.	All peoples worship God	112
97.	The creation worships God	114
98.	A new song to God	116
99.	God, the holy ruler	117
100.	Calling the earth to the service of God	40
103.	Rejoicing in God's compassion	656
104.	The glory of God's creation	658
112.	The success of the righteous person. An alphabetic psalm	661
113.	In praise of God who raises the poor. *Hallel*	665
114.	The Exodus. *Hallel*	666
115.	God and the false gods. *Hallel*	667
116.	Personal thanks for a new lease of life. *Hallel*	669
117.	All nations praise God. *Hallel*	671
118.	National thanksgiving. *Hallel*	671
121.	I lift my eyes to the hills	179,303
122.	Jerusalem. A pilgrim's song	675
124.	Deliverance after a national crisis	676
125.	Unshakeable trust	676
126.	Song of the returning exiles	464
127.	Unless God builds the house	677
128.	The happiness of the pious	304
130.	Out of the depths. Repentance	678
131.	Humility	678
133.	Brotherhood and unity	679
134.	A night hymn in the Temple	66
137.	By the waters of Babylon	679
138.	Thanking God	680
139.	God knows everything about me	681
143.	A prayer in time of distress	682
145.	Glory to God the ruler	48
146.	Praise to God the helper	684
147.	God maintains Israel and the world	685
148.	All creation praises God	686
150.	Hallelujah!	52,180,264

תהלים **612**

PSALMS TO TURN TO

All of us, according to what we are, are able to find ourselves within the Book of Psalms, and earn repentance through reading the psalms.

Nachman of Bratslav

Life's Journey
For a sleepless night 4
The miracle of life 139
Worries about livelihood 23, 62
Depressed or sad 30, 42, 43
When life is severely disrupted 34, 46, 57, 77, 86, 121, 138
When feeling abandoned 4, 23, 27
Facing old age 71, 90
The end of life 91

Society and Community
Anger at the wickedness of people 36, 37, 49, 73
Despairing at the wrongs in society 14
Anxiety about danger from others 3, 17, 43 57, 72
God's justice 11, 12, 82
Jews under threat 20, 124, 137
Jewish experience and hope 85, 122, 124, 126, 147
How society should be 133
In the synagogue 27, 63, 73, 84, 96, 122
God and nature 19, 104, 148
God's blessing in the world 67, 103

The Life of the Spirit
When studying Torah 1, 19
On keeping our integrity 15, 24, 112
When feeling uplifted 8, 19, 24, 47
Doubts about faith 1, 19, 25, 37, 143
After doing wrong 25, 51, 130
On regret and repentance 40, 51, 90
Needing God's help 27, 91, 121, 130
Seeking God 63, 127
Trusting God 16, 23, 62, 84, 125, 128, 131,146
Wishing to pray 51
At home with God 84, 103

Psalm 1

[1] **אַשְׁרֵי** Happy is the one
who does not follow
the advice of the wicked,
nor take a stand on the sinner's road,
nor sit at ease among the scornful.
[2] But whose delight
is in God's teaching,
reflecting on God's teaching
day and night.

[3] Such a one is like a tree
planted by streams of water.
It gives its fruit in its season,
its leaf never fades.
Everything it does shall prosper.

[4] It is not like this with the wicked,
for they are like chaff
blown by the wind.
[5] Therefore the wicked shall
not withstand the judgment,
nor sinners stand
in the company of the just.

[6] For God watches
over the way of the just,
but the way of the wicked is doomed.

א

[1] אַשְׁרֵי־הָאִישׁ
אֲשֶׁר לֹא הָלַךְ בַּעֲצַת רְשָׁעִים
וּבְדֶרֶךְ חַטָּאִים לֹא עָמָד
וּבְמוֹשַׁב לֵצִים לֹא יָשָׁב:
[2] כִּי אִם בְּתוֹרַת יהוה חֶפְצוֹ
וּבְתוֹרָתוֹ יֶהְגֶּה יוֹמָם וָלָיְלָה:

[3] וְהָיָה כְּעֵץ שָׁתוּל עַל־פַּלְגֵי מָיִם
אֲשֶׁר פִּרְיוֹ יִתֵּן בְּעִתּוֹ
וְעָלֵהוּ לֹא־יִבּוֹל
וְכֹל אֲשֶׁר־יַעֲשֶׂה יַצְלִיחַ:

[4] לֹא־כֵן הָרְשָׁעִים כִּי אִם־כַּמֹּץ
אֲשֶׁר־תִּדְּפֶנּוּ רוּחַ:
[5] עַל־כֵּן לֹא־יָקֻמוּ רְשָׁעִים בַּמִּשְׁפָּט
וְחַטָּאִים בַּעֲדַת צַדִּיקִים:

[6] כִּי־יוֹדֵעַ יהוה דֶּרֶךְ צַדִּיקִים
וְדֶרֶךְ רְשָׁעִים תֹּאבֵד:

Psalm 3

¹A Psalm of David, when he fled
from Absalom his son.
²יהוה O God, how many are
closing in on me,
how many are rising against me,
³how many are saying about my life;
'No help for you in God!'
(selah).

⁴But God,
You are the shield about me,
You are my glory,
You hold my head up high.
⁵I cry aloud, I call to my Protector,
You answer me
from Your holy mountain
(selah).

⁶Now I can lie down and sleep,
and then awake, for God upholds me.
⁷I need not fear the thousands of people
surrounding me,
ranged against me.

⁸O God, rise up! My God, save me!
For You struck all my enemies
in the face,
shattered the teeth of the wicked!

⁹Deliverance comes from God.
Your blessing on Your people
(selah)!

ג

א מִזְמוֹר לְדָוִד בְּבָרְחוֹ
מִפְּנֵי אַבְשָׁלוֹם בְּנוֹ:
ב יְהוָה מָה־רַבּוּ צָרָי
רַבִּים קָמִים עָלָי:
ג רַבִּים אֹמְרִים לְנַפְשִׁי
אֵין יְשׁוּעָתָה לּוֹ בֵאלֹהִים
סֶלָה:

ד וְאַתָּה יְהוָה מָגֵן בַּעֲדִי
כְּבוֹדִי
וּמֵרִים רֹאשִׁי:
ה קוֹלִי אֶל־יְהוָה אֶקְרָא
וַיַּעֲנֵנִי מֵהַר קָדְשׁוֹ
סֶלָה:

ו אֲנִי שָׁכַבְתִּי וָאִישָׁנָה
הֱקִיצוֹתִי כִּי יְהוָה יִסְמְכֵנִי:
ז לֹא־אִירָא מֵרִבְבוֹת עָם
אֲשֶׁר סָבִיב שָׁתוּ עָלָי:

ח קוּמָה יְהוָה הוֹשִׁיעֵנִי אֱלֹהַי
כִּי־הִכִּיתָ אֶת־כָּל־אֹיְבַי לֶחִי
שִׁנֵּי רְשָׁעִים שִׁבַּרְתָּ:

ט לַיהוָה הַיְשׁוּעָה
עַל־עַמְּךָ בִרְכָתֶךָ
סֶלָה:

Psalm 4

¹For the Choirmaster. With string music.
A Psalm of David.
²בְּקָרְאִי When I call, answer me,
God of justice!
You set me free when troubles close me in.
Show me Your favour and hear my prayer!

³People!
how long will you put my glory to shame?
What you love is illusion,
what you seek is a lie
(selah).

⁴But know this!
God has set apart the faithful.
God hears whenever I call.
⁵Tremble and do not sin!
Search your heart
as you lie in bed and be still
(selah).

⁶Let justice be your offering,
and trust in God.

⁷'Who can bring us happiness?'
many people say.
'God, show us the light of Your face!'

⁸You put in my heart a greater joy
than theirs, for all the abundance
of their corn and wine.

⁹In peace I lie down
and fall asleep,
for, God,
You alone let me live in safety.

ד
א לַמְנַצֵּחַ בִּנְגִינוֹת מִזְמוֹר לְדָוִד:
ב בְּקָרְאִי עֲנֵנִי
אֱלֹהֵי צִדְקִי
בַּצָּר הִרְחַבְתָּ לִּי
חָנֵּנִי וּשְׁמַע תְּפִלָּתִי:

ג בְּנֵי־אִישׁ
עַד־מֶה כְבוֹדִי לִכְלִמָּה
תֶּאֱהָבוּן רִיק
תְּבַקְשׁוּ כָזָב
סֶלָה:

ד וּדְעוּ
כִּי־הִפְלָה יהוה חָסִיד לוֹ
יהוה יִשְׁמַע בְּקָרְאִי אֵלָיו:
ה רִגְזוּ וְאַל־תֶּחֱטָאוּ
אִמְרוּ בִלְבַבְכֶם
עַל־מִשְׁכַּבְכֶם וְדֹמּוּ
סֶלָה:

ו זִבְחוּ זִבְחֵי־צֶדֶק
וּבִטְחוּ אֶל־יהוה:

ז רַבִּים אֹמְרִים
מִי־יַרְאֵנוּ טוֹב
נְסָה־עָלֵינוּ אוֹר פָּנֶיךָ יהוה:

ח נָתַתָּה שִׂמְחָה בְלִבִּי
מֵעֵת דְּגָנָם וְתִירוֹשָׁם רָבּוּ:

ט בְּשָׁלוֹם יַחְדָּו
אֶשְׁכְּבָה וְאִישָׁן
כִּי־אַתָּה יהוה
לְבָדָד לָבֶטַח תּוֹשִׁיבֵנִי:

ח

אלַמְנַצֵּחַ עַל־הַגִּתִּית
מִזְמוֹר לְדָוִד:
ביְהוָה אֲדֹנֵינוּ מָה־אַדִּיר שִׁמְךָ בְּכָל־הָאָרֶץ אֲשֶׁר־תְּנָה הוֹדְךָ עַל־הַשָּׁמָיִם:
גמִפִּי עוֹלְלִים וְיֹנְקִים יִסַּדְתָּ עֹז לְמַעַן צוֹרְרֶיךָ לְהַשְׁבִּית אוֹיֵב וּמִתְנַקֵּם:
דכִּי־אֶרְאֶה שָׁמֶיךָ מַעֲשֵׂי אֶצְבְּעֹתֶיךָ יָרֵחַ וְכוֹכָבִים אֲשֶׁר כּוֹנָנְתָּה:
המָה־אֱנוֹשׁ כִּי־תִזְכְּרֶנּוּ
וּבֶן־אָדָם כִּי תִפְקְדֶנּוּ:
ווַתְּחַסְּרֵהוּ מְּעַט מֵאֱלֹהִים
וְכָבוֹד וְהָדָר תְּעַטְּרֵהוּ:
זתַּמְשִׁילֵהוּ בְּמַעֲשֵׂי יָדֶיךָ
כֹּל שַׁתָּה תַחַת־רַגְלָיו:
חצֹנֶה וַאֲלָפִים כֻּלָּם
וְגַם בַּהֲמוֹת שָׂדָי:
טצִפּוֹר שָׁמַיִם וּדְגֵי הַיָּם
עֹבֵר אָרְחוֹת יַמִּים:
ייְהוָה אֲדֹנֵינוּ מָה־אַדִּיר שִׁמְךָ בְּכָל־הָאָרֶץ:

Psalm 8

[1] For the Choirmaster. Upon the *gittit*.
A Psalm of David.
[2] **יהוה** God, our Creator, how glorious is Your name in all the earth!
Your majesty is proclaimed beyond the heavens.
[3] In the mouths of children and babes in arms You placed strength,
to rebuke Your foes, silencing enmity and vengeance.
[4] When I look up at Your heavens, the work of Your hands,
the moon and the stars You set in place,
[5] what is humanity that You should remember it,
or mortal beings that You should care for them?
[6] Yet You have made them little less than divine,
and crowned them with glory and splendour.
[7] You gave them power over the works of Your hands,
You put all things beneath their feet.
[8] Sheep and cattle, all of them,
also the beasts of the field,
[9] the birds of the air, and the fish of the sea,
that make their way through the oceans.
[10] God, our Creator, how glorious is Your name in all the earth!

Psalm 11

יא

[1] For the Choirmaster. David's.
בַּיהוָה In God I have taken shelter!
How can you say to me,
'Fly back like a bird to your mountain!'

[2] See how the wicked
are bending the bow,
fitting their arrow to the string,
to shoot at honest people
from the shadows.

[3] When the foundations are undermined,
what can the righteous do!

[4] God is in the holy temple,
God whose throne is in heaven,
whose eyes can see!
whose gaze searches all human beings!

[5] God may test the just,
but the wicked and the lover of violence,
God hates,

[6] raining coals of fire and brimstone
on the wicked;
from their cup
they shall drink a burning wind.

[7] God is just and loves justice,
the upright shall see God's face!

א לַמְנַצֵּחַ לְדָוִד
בַּיהוָה חָסִיתִי
אֵיךְ תֹּאמְרוּ לְנַפְשִׁי
נוּדִי הַרְכֶם צִפּוֹר:

ב כִּי הִנֵּה הָרְשָׁעִים
יִדְרְכוּן קֶשֶׁת
כּוֹנְנוּ חִצָּם עַל־יֶתֶר
לִירוֹת בְּמוֹ־אֹפֶל
לְיִשְׁרֵי־לֵב:

ג כִּי הַשָּׁתוֹת יֵהָרֵסוּן
צַדִּיק מַה־פָּעָל:

ד יְהוָה בְּהֵיכַל קָדְשׁוֹ
יְהוָה בַּשָּׁמַיִם כִּסְאוֹ
עֵינָיו יֶחֱזוּ
עַפְעַפָּיו יִבְחֲנוּ בְּנֵי אָדָם:

ה יְהוָה צַדִּיק יִבְחָן
וְרָשָׁע וְאֹהֵב חָמָס
שָׂנְאָה נַפְשׁוֹ:

ו יַמְטֵר עַל־רְשָׁעִים
פַּחִים אֵשׁ וְגָפְרִית
וְרוּחַ זִלְעָפוֹת
מְנָת כּוֹסָם:

ז כִּי־צַדִּיק יְהוָה צְדָקוֹת אָהֵב
יָשָׁר יֶחֱזוּ פָנֵימוֹ:

Psalm 12

יב

א לַמְנַצֵּחַ עַל־הַשְּׁמִינִית מִזְמוֹר לְדָוִד

[1] For the Choirmaster. On the *sheminit*. A Psalm of David.

ב הוֹשִׁיעָה יהוה כִּי־גָמַר חָסִיד כִּי־פַסּוּ אֱמוּנִים מִבְּנֵי אָדָם:

[2] הוֹשִׁיעָה Save us, God,
for the pious are no more
and the faithful have vanished
from the human race.

ג שָׁוְא יְדַבְּרוּ אִישׁ אֶת־רֵעֵהוּ שְׂפַת חֲלָקוֹת בְּלֵב וָלֵב יְדַבֵּרוּ:

[3] People lie to one another,
they speak with flattering lips
and with false hearts.

ד יַכְרֵת יהוה כָּל־שִׂפְתֵי חֲלָקוֹת לָשׁוֹן מְדַבֶּרֶת גְּדֹלוֹת:

[4] May God cut off all flattering lips
and tongues that speak
high-sounding words

ה אֲשֶׁר אָמְרוּ לִלְשֹׁנֵנוּ נַגְבִּיר שְׂפָתֵינוּ אִתָּנוּ מִי אָדוֹן לָנוּ:

[5] saying, 'We shall strengthen our tongue,
our lips are our own;
who can be our master!'

ו מִשֹּׁד עֲנִיִּים מֵאֶנְקַת אֶבְיוֹנִים עַתָּה אָקוּם יֹאמַר יהוה אָשִׁית בְּיֵשַׁע יָפִיחַ לוֹ:

[6] 'Because of the oppression of the poor,
and the groaning of the needy,
now I shall arise,' says God,
'and make them secure
though they are despised.'

ז אִמְרוֹת יהוה אֲמָרוֹת טְהֹרוֹת כֶּסֶף צָרוּף בַּעֲלִיל לָאָרֶץ מְזֻקָּק שִׁבְעָתָיִם:

[7] God's words are pure words,
silver from the furnace,
poured into a mould,
seven times refined.

ח אַתָּה־יהוה תִּשְׁמְרֵם תִּצְּרֶנּוּ מִן־הַדּוֹר זוּ לְעוֹלָם:

[8] It is You, God,
who will guard the oppressed,
and ever protect us from this generation.

ט סָבִיב רְשָׁעִים יִתְהַלָּכוּן כְּרֻם זֻלּוּת לִבְנֵי אָדָם:

[9] The wicked go about on every side,
and the worthless are prized by people
everywhere.

Psalm 14

¹For the Choirmaster. David's.
אָמַר Fools say in their heart,
'There is no God!'
People deal corruptly, they are depraved,
none of them does good.

²God looks down from heaven
on every person alive,
to see if there is anyone who understands,
who searches for God.

³All of them have fallen away,
they have gone rotten together.
None of them does good, not even one!
⁴Are they so ignorant,
all of those who do evil,
devouring my people as they devour food,
never mentioning God?

⁵But look how they tremble with fear,
for God is on the side of the just.
⁶You may mock the hope of the poor,
but God is their protection.

⁷If only Israel's help
would come from Zion,
when God brings this people home!
What joy for Jacob!
What happiness for Israel!

יד

אלַמְנַצֵּחַ לְדָוִד
אָמַר נָבָל בְּלִבּוֹ אֵין אֱלֹהִים
הִשְׁחִיתוּ הִתְעִיבוּ עֲלִילָה
אֵין עֹשֵׂה־טוֹב:

ביְהוָה מִשָּׁמַיִם הִשְׁקִיף
עַל־בְּנֵי־אָדָם
לִרְאוֹת הֲיֵשׁ מַשְׂכִּיל
דֹּרֵשׁ אֶת־אֱלֹהִים:

גהַכֹּל סָר יַחְדָּו נֶאֱלָחוּ
אֵין עֹשֵׂה־טוֹב אֵין גַּם־אֶחָד:
דהֲלֹא יָדְעוּ כָּל־פֹּעֲלֵי אָוֶן
אֹכְלֵי עַמִּי אָכְלוּ לֶחֶם
יְהוָה לֹא קָרָאוּ:

השָׁם פָּחֲדוּ פָחַד
כִּי־אֱלֹהִים בְּדוֹר צַדִּיק:
ועֲצַת־עָנִי תָבִישׁוּ
כִּי יְהוָה מַחְסֵהוּ:

זמִי־יִתֵּן מִצִּיּוֹן
יְשׁוּעַת יִשְׂרָאֵל
בְּשׁוּב יְהוָה שְׁבוּת עַמּוֹ
יָגֵל יַעֲקֹב יִשְׂמַח יִשְׂרָאֵל:

Psalm 15

[1] A Psalm of David.
יהוה God, who may live in Your tent,
who may dwell
on the mountain of Your holiness?
[2] Those who follow integrity
and do what is right
and speak the truth in their heart.
[3] No malice is on their tongue,
they never do wrong to others,
cast no discredit on their neighbour.
[4] The worthless are rejected in their eyes,
but they honour those who fear God.
They swear to their own hurt,
but do not retract.
[5] They lend no money for unfair gain
and take no bribe
against the innocent.
Such people will never be shaken.

טו

א מִזְמוֹר לְדָוִד
יְהֹוָה מִי־יָגוּר בְּאָהֳלֶךָ
מִי־יִשְׁכֹּן בְּהַר קָדְשֶׁךָ:
ב הוֹלֵךְ תָּמִים וּפֹעֵל צֶדֶק
וְדֹבֵר אֱמֶת בִּלְבָבוֹ:
ג לֹא־רָגַל עַל־לְשֹׁנוֹ
לֹא־עָשָׂה לְרֵעֵהוּ רָעָה
וְחֶרְפָּה לֹא־נָשָׂא עַל־קְרֹבוֹ:
ד נִבְזֶה בְּעֵינָיו נִמְאָס
וְאֶת־יִרְאֵי יְהֹוָה יְכַבֵּד
נִשְׁבַּע לְהָרַע וְלֹא יָמִר:
ה כַּסְפּוֹ לֹא־נָתַן בְּנֶשֶׁךְ
וְשֹׁחַד עַל־נָקִי לֹא־לָקָח
עֹשֵׂה־אֵלֶּה לֹא יִמּוֹט לְעוֹלָם:

621 PSALM ANTHOLOGY

Psalm 16

[טז]

¹A *michtam* of David.
שָׁמְרֵנִי Keep me, God,
  for in You I found refuge.
²I said to the Source of life,
  'You are my God,
  my happiness lies in You alone.'

³All my desire is to be among
  the holy ones of the land,
  them and the noble-hearted.
⁴Sorrows increase
  for those who follow another god;
  never will I pour out
  their offerings of blood,
  never will I bring their names to my lips.

⁵God, my share of the heritage, my cup,
  it is You who keep my fate secure.
⁶The lines have fallen for me
  in pleasant places;
  a wonderful heritage is mine.

⁷I will bless God who gives me counsel,
  even at night my inner self instructs me.
⁸I keep God before me always;
  with God at my right hand
  I cannot be shaken.

⁹So my heart is glad,
  and my soul rejoices,
  even my body shall rest in safety,
¹⁰for You will not abandon
  my soul in death,
  nor let Your faithful know corruption.

¹¹You will show me the path of life,
  the fullness of joy in Your presence,
  everlasting happiness
  at Your right hand.

ᵃמִכְתָּם לְדָוִד
שָׁמְרֵנִי אֵל כִּי־חָסִיתִי בָךְ:
אָמַרְתְּ לַיהוה אֲדֹנָי אָתָּה
טוֹבָתִי בַּל־עָלֶיךָ:
לִקְדוֹשִׁים אֲשֶׁר־בָּאָרֶץ הֵמָּה
וְאַדִּירֵי כָּל־חֶפְצִי־בָם:
יִרְבּוּ עַצְּבוֹתָם אַחֵר מָהָרוּ
בַּל־אַסִּיךְ נִסְכֵּיהֶם מִדָּם
וּבַל־אֶשָּׂא אֶת־שְׁמוֹתָם
עַל־שְׂפָתָי:

יהוה מְנָת־חֶלְקִי וְכוֹסִי
אַתָּה תּוֹמִיךְ גּוֹרָלִי:
ᵛחֲבָלִים נָפְלוּ־לִי בַּנְּעִמִים
אַף־נַחֲלָת שָׁפְרָה עָלָי:

ᵎאֲבָרֵךְ אֶת־יהוה אֲשֶׁר יְעָצָנִי
אַף־לֵילוֹת יִסְּרוּנִי כִלְיוֹתָי:
ᴴשִׁוִּיתִי יהוה לְנֶגְדִּי תָמִיד
כִּי מִימִינִי בַּל־אֶמּוֹט:

ᵗלָכֵן שָׂמַח לִבִּי וַיָּגֶל כְּבוֹדִי
אַף־בְּשָׂרִי יִשְׁכֹּן לָבֶטַח:
ᵎכִּי לֹא־תַעֲזֹב נַפְשִׁי לִשְׁאוֹל
לֹא־תִתֵּן חֲסִידְךָ
לִרְאוֹת שָׁחַת:

ᵃתּוֹדִיעֵנִי אֹרַח חַיִּים
שֹׂבַע שְׂמָחוֹת אֶת־פָּנֶיךָ
נְעִמוֹת בִּימִינְךָ נֶצַח:

יט

א לַמְנַצֵּחַ מִזְמוֹר לְדָוִד:
ב הַשָּׁמַיִם מְסַפְּרִים כְּבוֹד־אֵל
וּמַעֲשֵׂה יָדָיו מַגִּיד הָרָקִיעַ:
ג יוֹם לְיוֹם יַבִּיעַ אֹמֶר וְלַיְלָה לְּלַיְלָה יְחַוֶּה־דָּעַת:
ד אֵין־אֹמֶר וְאֵין דְּבָרִים בְּלִי נִשְׁמָע קוֹלָם:

ה בְּכָל־הָאָרֶץ יָצָא קַוָּם וּבִקְצֵה תֵבֵל מִלֵּיהֶם
לַשֶּׁמֶשׁ שָׂם־אֹהֶל בָּהֶם:
ו וְהוּא כְּחָתָן יֹצֵא מֵחֻפָּתוֹ יָשִׂישׂ כְּגִבּוֹר לָרוּץ אֹרַח:
ז מִקְצֵה הַשָּׁמַיִם מוֹצָאוֹ וּתְקוּפָתוֹ עַל־קְצוֹתָם
וְאֵין נִסְתָּר מֵחַמָּתוֹ:

ח תּוֹרַת יהוה תְּמִימָה מְשִׁיבַת נָפֶשׁ
עֵדוּת יהוה נֶאֱמָנָה מַחְכִּימַת פֶּתִי:
ט פִּקּוּדֵי יהוה יְשָׁרִים מְשַׂמְּחֵי־לֵב
מִצְוַת יהוה בָּרָה מְאִירַת עֵינָיִם:
י יִרְאַת יהוה טְהוֹרָה עוֹמֶדֶת לָעַד
מִשְׁפְּטֵי־יהוה אֱמֶת צָדְקוּ יַחְדָּו:

יא הַנֶּחֱמָדִים מִזָּהָב וּמִפַּז רָב
וּמְתוּקִים מִדְּבַשׁ וְנֹפֶת צוּפִים:
יב גַּם־עַבְדְּךָ נִזְהָר בָּהֶם בְּשָׁמְרָם עֵקֶב רָב:

יג שְׁגִיאוֹת מִי־יָבִין מִנִּסְתָּרוֹת נַקֵּנִי:
יד גַּם מִזֵּדִים חֲשֹׂךְ עַבְדֶּךָ אַל־יִמְשְׁלוּ־בִי
אָז אֵיתָם וְנִקֵּיתִי מִפֶּשַׁע רָב:

טו יִהְיוּ לְרָצוֹן אִמְרֵי־פִי וְהֶגְיוֹן לִבִּי לְפָנֶיךָ
יהוה צוּרִי וְגֹאֲלִי:

Psalm 19

¹For the Choirmaster. A Psalm of David.
²הַשָּׁמַיִם Heaven declares the glory of God
 and the sky reveals the work of God's hands.
³Each day pours out speech to the other
 and night to night passes on the knowledge.

⁴No speech at all! There are no words! Their sound cannot be heard!
⁵And yet their scope extends through all the earth
 and their message to the end of the world.
 In it God set a tent for the sun;
⁶it is like a bridegroom coming from his bridal chamber,
 like a champion who rejoices in running a race.
⁷At one end of heaven is the rising of the sun and its course to the other end;
 nothing can escape from its heat.

> ⁸The teaching of God is perfect, restoring the soul.
>
> The evidence of God can be trusted, making wise the simple.
>
> ⁹The duties of God are right, rejoicing the heart.
>
> The command of God is clear, enlightening the eyes.
>
> ¹⁰The fear of God is pure, standing forever.
>
> The judgments of God are true, all of them just.

¹¹They are more to be desired than gold, even the finest gold.
 They are even sweeter than the honey as it drips from the honeycomb.
¹²Through them Your servant is warned, in keeping them much follows.

¹³Who can detect their own failings, cleanse me from hidden faults.
¹⁴Preserve Your servant from sins of pride, do not let them control me!
 Then I shall be blameless, innocent of grave sin.

¹⁵May the words of my mouth and the meditation of my heart
 be acceptable to You,
 O God, my rock and my redeemer.

Psalm 20

כ

לַמְנַצֵּחַ מִזְמוֹר לְדָוִד:

[1] For the Choirmaster. A Psalm of David.

[2] יַעַנְךָ May God answer you
on the day of trouble,
may the name of Jacob's God protect you,
[3] sending you help from the sanctuary,
giving you support from Zion.

יַעַנְךָ יְהוָה בְּיוֹם צָרָה
יְשַׂגֶּבְךָ שֵׁם אֱלֹהֵי יַעֲקֹב:
יִשְׁלַח־עֶזְרְךָ מִקֹּדֶשׁ
וּמִצִּיּוֹן יִסְעָדֶךָּ:

[4] May God remember
all you have sacrificed,
and accept your offerings
(*selah*),
[5] giving you your heart's desire,
and making all your plans succeed.

יִזְכֹּר כָּל־מִנְחֹתֶךָ
וְעוֹלָתְךָ יְדַשְּׁנֶה
סֶלָה:
יִתֶּן־לְךָ כִלְבָבֶךָ
וְכָל־עֲצָתְךָ יְמַלֵּא:

[6] We shout for joy at your victory,
and in God's name
we plant our banners.
'May God grant all you ask!'

נְרַנְּנָה בִּישׁוּעָתֶךָ
וּבְשֵׁם־אֱלֹהֵינוּ נִדְגֹּל
יְמַלֵּא יְהוָה כָּל־מִשְׁאֲלוֹתֶיךָ:

[7] Now I know that God
saves the anointed one,
answering from God's holy heaven,
with the mighty victories
of God's right hand.

עַתָּה יָדַעְתִּי
כִּי הוֹשִׁיעַ יְהוָה מְשִׁיחוֹ
יַעֲנֵהוּ מִשְּׁמֵי קָדְשׁוֹ
בִּגְבֻרוֹת יֵשַׁע יְמִינוֹ:

[8] Some trust in chariots,
and some in horses,
but we
proclaim the name of the Eternal our God.
[9] They crumple and fall!
But we
rise up and stand firm.

אֵלֶּה בָרֶכֶב וְאֵלֶּה בַסּוּסִים
וַאֲנַחְנוּ
בְּשֵׁם־יְהוָה אֱלֹהֵינוּ נַזְכִּיר:
הֵמָּה כָּרְעוּ וְנָפָלוּ
וַאֲנַחְנוּ
קַּמְנוּ וַנִּתְעוֹדָד:

[10] Save us God!
May Your power answer us
on the day we call!

יְהוָה הוֹשִׁיעָה
הַמֶּלֶךְ יַעֲנֵנוּ בְיוֹם־קָרְאֵנוּ:

Psalm 23 can be found on page 302.
Psalm 24 can be found on page 41.

625 PSALM ANTHOLOGY

Psalm 25

¹David's.

אֵלֶיךָ God, I set my hope on You.

²My God, I put my trust in You,
let me not be put to shame,
do not let my enemies triumph over me.

³No, those who hope in You
are never shamed;
ashamed are traitors without a cause.

⁴God, let me know Your ways,
teach me Your paths.

⁵Guide me in Your truth and teach me,
for You, God, are my help,
for You alone I wait all day long.

⁶Remember Your compassion God,
and Your mercies,
for they have existed since ages past.

⁷Do not remember the sins of my youth
and my wrongdoing,
but remember me in love,
for the sake of Your righteousness, God.

⁸God is good and upright,
showing the way to sinners,

⁹guiding the humble in justice,
teaching the humble God's way.

¹⁰All God's paths are mercy and truth
for those faithful
to God's covenant and will.

כה

אׇ לְדָוִד
אֵלֶיךָ יהוה נַפְשִׁי אֶשָּׂא׃

בׇּ אֱלֹהַי בְּךָ בָטַחְתִּי
אַל־אֵבוֹשָׁה
אַל־יַעַלְצוּ אֹיְבַי לִי׃

גׇּ גַּם כׇּל־קוֶֹיךָ
לֹא יֵבֹשׁוּ
יֵבֹשׁוּ הַבּוֹגְדִים רֵיקָם׃

דׇּ דְּרָכֶיךָ יהוה הוֹדִיעֵנִי
אֹרְחוֹתֶיךָ לַמְּדֵנִי׃

הׇ הַדְרִיכֵנִי בַאֲמִתֶּךָ וְלַמְּדֵנִי
כִּי־אַתָּה אֱלֹהֵי יִשְׁעִי
אוֹתְךָ קִוִּיתִי כׇּל־הַיּוֹם׃

וׇ זְכֹר־רַחֲמֶיךָ יהוה
וַחֲסָדֶיךָ
כִּי מֵעוֹלָם הֵמָּה׃

זׇ חַטֹּאות נְעוּרַי
וּפְשָׁעַי אַל־תִּזְכֹּר
כְּחַסְדְּךָ זְכׇר־לִי־אַתָּה
לְמַעַן טוּבְךָ יהוה׃

חׇ טוֹב־וְיָשָׁר יהוה עַל־כֵּן
יוֹרֶה חַטָּאִים בַּדָּרֶךְ׃

טׇ יַדְרֵךְ עֲנָוִים בַּמִּשְׁפָּט
וִילַמֵּד עֲנָוִים דַּרְכּוֹ׃

יׇ כׇּל־אׇרְחוֹת יהוה
חֶסֶד וֶאֱמֶת
לְנֹצְרֵי בְרִיתוֹ וְעֵדֹתָיו׃

<<<

¹¹God, for the sake of Your name, 　forgive my guilt, 　pardon my iniquity for it is great.	לְמַעַן־שִׁמְךָ יְהֹוָה וְסָלַחְתָּ לַעֲוֺנִי כִּי רַב־הוּא:
¹²Those who fear God 　are shown the way they should choose. ¹³Their soul shall live in goodness 　and their children inherit the land. ¹⁴God's hidden purpose is kept for them, 　God's covenant gives them knowledge.	מִי־זֶה הָאִישׁ יְרֵא יְהֹוָה יוֹרֶנּוּ בְּדֶרֶךְ יִבְחָר: נַפְשׁוֹ בְּטוֹב תָּלִין וְזַרְעוֹ יִירַשׁ אָרֶץ: סוֹד יְהֹוָה לִירֵאָיו וּבְרִיתוֹ לְהוֹדִיעָם:
¹⁵My eyes look always to God, 　who releases my foot from the snare. ¹⁶Turn to me and take pity on me 　for I am lonely and poor. ¹⁷The sorrows of my heart have increased, 　release me from my distress. ¹⁸See my misery and pain, 　and take away all my sins.	עֵינַי תָּמִיד אֶל־יְהֹוָה כִּי הוּא־יוֹצִיא מֵרֶשֶׁת רַגְלָי: פְּנֵה־אֵלַי וְחָנֵּנִי כִּי־יָחִיד וְעָנִי אָנִי: צָרוֹת לְבָבִי הִרְחִיבוּ מִמְּצוּקוֹתַי הוֹצִיאֵנִי: רְאֵה־עָנְיִי וַעֲמָלִי וְשָׂא לְכָל־חַטֹּאותָי:
¹⁹See my enemies, how many they are, 　and how violently they hate me. ²⁰Guard my soul and deliver me; 　I fear no shame for I shelter in You. ²¹Innocence and integrity shall preserve me 　because I waited for You.	רְאֵה־אוֹיְבַי כִּי־רָבּוּ וְשִׂנְאַת חָמָס שְׂנֵאוּנִי: שָׁמְרָה נַפְשִׁי וְהַצִּילֵנִי אַל־אֵבוֹשׁ כִּי־חָסִיתִי בָךְ: תֹּם־וָיֹשֶׁר יִצְּרוּנִי כִּי קִוִּיתִיךָ:
²²God, redeem Israel 　from all our troubles!	פְּדֵה־אֱלֹהִים אֶת־יִשְׂרָאֵל מִכֹּל צָרוֹתָיו:

627 PSALM ANTHOLOGY

Psalm 27

כז

¹David's.

יהוה God is my light and my safety
whom shall I fear?
God is the strength of my life
of whom shall I be afraid?
²When evil people come to attack me
to eat up my flesh,
it is my oppressors and enemies
who stumble and fall.
³Even if an army camped against me
my heart would not fear.
Even if war broke out against me,
even then I would trust.

⁴One thing I ask of God,
that only do I seek:
to live in Your house
all the days of my life,
Your comforting presence before me,
praying each morning
in Your temple.

⁵For God's shelter protects me
in times of trouble,
God's tent concealing me,
lifting me to safety on a rock.
⁶So now my head is held up high
above my enemies around me
and I offer inside God's tent
an offering of triumph,
singing psalms of joy.

⁷God, hear my voice when I call!
Take pity on me, and answer me!
⁸Of You my heart has said,
'Seek My face!'
God, it is Your face I seek,

אלְדָוִד
יְהוָה אוֹרִי וְיִשְׁעִי מִמִּי אִירָא
יְהוָה מָעוֹז חַיַּי מִמִּי אֶפְחָד:
בבִּקְרֹב עָלַי מְרֵעִים
לֶאֱכֹל אֶת־בְּשָׂרִי
צָרַי וְאֹיְבַי לִי
הֵמָּה כָּשְׁלוּ וְנָפָלוּ:
גאִם־תַּחֲנֶה עָלַי מַחֲנֶה
לֹא־יִירָא לִבִּי
אִם־תָּקוּם עָלַי מִלְחָמָה
בְּזֹאת אֲנִי בוֹטֵחַ:

דאַחַת שָׁאַלְתִּי מֵאֵת־יְהוָה
אוֹתָהּ אֲבַקֵּשׁ
שִׁבְתִּי בְּבֵית־יְהוָה
כָּל־יְמֵי חַיַּי
לַחֲזוֹת בְּנֹעַם־יְהוָה
וּלְבַקֵּר בְּהֵיכָלוֹ:

הכִּי יִצְפְּנֵנִי בְּסֻכֹּה
בְּיוֹם רָעָה
יַסְתִּרֵנִי בְּסֵתֶר אָהֳלוֹ
בְּצוּר יְרוֹמְמֵנִי:
ווְעַתָּה יָרוּם רֹאשִׁי
עַל־אֹיְבַי סְבִיבוֹתַי
וְאֶזְבְּחָה בְאָהֳלוֹ זִבְחֵי תְרוּעָה
אָשִׁירָה וַאֲזַמְּרָה לַיהוָה:

זשְׁמַע־יְהוָה קוֹלִי אֶקְרָא
וְחָנֵּנִי וַעֲנֵנִי:
חלְךָ אָמַר לִבִּי בַּקְּשׁוּ פָנָי
אֶת־פָּנֶיךָ יְהוָה אֲבַקֵּשׁ:

<<<

⁹Do not hide Your face from me.
Do not turn away Your servant in anger,
You have been my help.
Never leave me, never desert me,
God of my safety.
¹⁰Even if my father and mother desert me,
God will care for me still.

¹¹God, direct me in Your way,
lead me in the path of integrity,
for people lie in wait for me.
¹²Do not put me in the power of my foes;
the false witnesses,
who pant for violence,
are rising up against me.

¹³So I trusted - to see God's goodness
in the land of the living.
¹⁴Wait for God!
Be strong
and let your heart take courage!
Wait for God!

ט אַל־תַּסְתֵּר פָּנֶיךָ מִמֶּנִּי
אַל־תַּט בְּאַף עַבְדֶּךָ
עֶזְרָתִי הָיִיתָ אַל־תִּטְּשֵׁנִי
וְאַל־תַּעַזְבֵנִי אֱלֹהֵי יִשְׁעִי:
י כִּי־אָבִי וְאִמִּי עֲזָבוּנִי
וַיהוה יַאַסְפֵנִי:

יא הוֹרֵנִי יהוה דַּרְכֶּךָ וּנְחֵנִי
בְּאֹרַח מִישׁוֹר
לְמַעַן שׁוֹרְרָי:
יב אַל־תִּתְּנֵנִי בְּנֶפֶשׁ צָרָי
כִּי קָמוּ־בִי עֵדֵי־שֶׁקֶר
וִיפֵחַ חָמָס:

יג לוּלֵא הֶאֱמַנְתִּי לִרְאוֹת
בְּטוּב־יהוה בְּאֶרֶץ חַיִּים:
יד קַוֵּה אֶל־יהוה
חֲזַק וְיַאֲמֵץ לִבֶּךָ
וְקַוֵּה אֶל־יהוה:

Psalm 29 can be found on page 119.

Psalm 30

¹A Psalm. A Song for the Dedication
of the House. David's.
²**אֲרוֹמִמְךָ** I exalt You, God,
for You raised me up,
and did not let my enemies gloat over me.
³My God, my Protector,
I cried out to You and You healed me.
⁴God, You brought up my soul from below,
You kept me alive,
stopped me sinking into the grave.

ל
א מִזְמוֹר שִׁיר חֲנֻכַּת הַבַּיִת לְדָוִד
ב אֲרוֹמִמְךָ יהוה כִּי דִלִּיתָנִי
וְלֹא־שִׂמַּחְתָּ אֹיְבַי לִי:
ג יהוה אֱלֹהָי
שִׁוַּעְתִּי אֵלֶיךָ וַתִּרְפָּאֵנִי:
ד יהוה הֶעֱלִיתָ מִן־שְׁאוֹל
נַפְשִׁי
חִיִּיתַנִי מִיָּרְדִי־בוֹר:

<<<

⁵Sing psalms to God, you who love God
  and give thanks
  as you remember God's holy ways:
⁶anger that lasts but a moment,
  favour that lasts a lifetime.
  Tears may linger at evening,
  but in the morning comes joy.

⁷I, too, once said in my success,
  'I shall never slip.'
⁸God, Your favour
  set me on a mountain stronghold -
  but then You hid Your face,
  and I was in terror.

⁹To You, God, I call,
  from my God I ask pity.
¹⁰"What profit is there
  in shedding my blood,
  if I go down to the grave?
  Can the dust praise You?
  Can it proclaim Your truth?

¹¹Hear me, God, and take pity on me!
  God, be my helper!

¹²You turned my mourning into dancing;
  You stripped off my sackcloth,
  and wrapped me in joy.
¹³So my soul sings Your psalms,
  silent no longer;
  my God, my Protector,
  I praise You
  forever and ever.

זַמְּרוּ לַיהוה חֲסִידָיו
וְהוֹדוּ לְזֵכֶר קָדְשׁוֹ:
כִּי רֶגַע בְּאַפּוֹ חַיִּים בִּרְצוֹנוֹ
בָּעֶרֶב יָלִין בֶּכִי
וְלַבֹּקֶר רִנָּה:

וַאֲנִי אָמַרְתִּי בְשַׁלְוִי
בַּל־אֶמּוֹט לְעוֹלָם:
יהוה בִּרְצוֹנְךָ
הֶעֱמַדְתָּה לְהַרְרִי עֹז
הִסְתַּרְתָּ פָנֶיךָ הָיִיתִי נִבְהָל:

אֵלֶיךָ יהוה אֶקְרָא
וְאֶל־אֲדֹנָי אֶתְחַנָּן:
מַה־בֶּצַע בְּדָמִי בְּרִדְתִּי
אֶל־שָׁחַת
הֲיוֹדְךָ עָפָר הֲיַגִּיד אֲמִתֶּךָ:

שְׁמַע־יהוה וְחָנֵּנִי
יהוה הֱיֵה־עֹזֵר לִי:

הָפַכְתָּ מִסְפְּדִי לְמָחוֹל לִי
פִּתַּחְתָּ שַׂקִּי
וַתְּאַזְּרֵנִי שִׂמְחָה:
לְמַעַן יְזַמֶּרְךָ כָבוֹד
וְלֹא יִדֹּם
יהוה אֱלֹהַי לְעוֹלָם אוֹדֶךָּ:

Psalm 36

לו

¹For the Choirmaster.
For God's Servant. David's.

א לַמְנַצֵּחַ לְעֶבֶד־יהוה לְדָוִד

²**נְאֻם־פֶּשַׁע** Sin speaks to sinners,
deep in the heart;
there is no dread of God
before their eyes.

ב נְאֻם־פֶּשַׁע לָרָשָׁע בְּקֶרֶב לִבִּי
אֵין־פַּחַד אֱלֹהִים לְנֶגֶד עֵינָיו:

³It flatters them too much
in their own eyes
to detect and hate their guilt.
⁴The words of their mouth
become mischief and deceit,
the urge for wisdom and goodness
has gone.

ג כִּי־הֶחֱלִיק אֵלָיו בְּעֵינָיו
לִמְצֹא עֲוֺנוֹ לִשְׂנֹא:
ד דִּבְרֵי־פִיו
אָוֶן וּמִרְמָה
חָדַל לְהַשְׂכִּיל לְהֵיטִיב:

⁵They think up mischief
as they lie in bed.
They are set on a way that is not good.
They do not reject evil.

ה אָוֶן יַחְשֹׁב עַל־מִשְׁכָּבוֹ
יִתְיַצֵּב עַל־דֶּרֶךְ לֹא־טוֹב
רָע לֹא יִמְאָס:

⁶God, Your love reaches to heaven,
Your faithfulness up to the skies.
⁷Your righteousness
is like the mighty mountains,
Your judgments like the great deep.
God, You save man and beast!

ו יהוה בְּהַשָּׁמַיִם חַסְדֶּךָ
אֱמוּנָתְךָ עַד־שְׁחָקִים:
ז צִדְקָתְךָ כְּהַרְרֵי־אֵל
מִשְׁפָּטֶיךָ תְּהוֹם רַבָּה
אָדָם וּבְהֵמָה תוֹשִׁיעַ יהוה:

⁸God, How precious is Your love!
All mortals find refuge
in the shadow of Your wings.
⁹They feast on the bounty of Your house,
and drink from the stream
of Your pleasures,
¹⁰for with You is the fountain of life.
In Your light, we see light.

ח מַה־יָּקָר חַסְדְּךָ אֱלֹהִים
וּבְנֵי אָדָם בְּצֵל כְּנָפֶיךָ יֶחֱסָיוּן:
ט יִרְוְיֻן מִדֶּשֶׁן בֵּיתֶךָ
וְנַחַל עֲדָנֶיךָ תַשְׁקֵם:
י כִּי־עִמְּךָ מְקוֹר חַיִּים
בְּאוֹרְךָ נִרְאֶה־אוֹר:

¹¹Continue Your love to those who love You,
and Your faithfulness to the upright in heart.
¹²Do not let the foot of the proud crush me,
nor the hand of the wicked drive me away.

יא מְשֹׁךְ חַסְדְּךָ לְיֹדְעֶיךָ
וְצִדְקָתְךָ לְיִשְׁרֵי־לֵב:
יב אַל־תְּבוֹאֵנִי רֶגֶל גַּאֲוָה
וְיַד־רְשָׁעִים אַל־תְּנִדֵנִי:

¹³The workers of iniquity have fallen,
there they lie; flung down,
they cannot rise again.

יג שָׁם נָפְלוּ פֹּעֲלֵי אָוֶן
דֹּחוּ וְלֹא־יָכְלוּ קוּם:

Psalm 37 (1-11)

¹David's.
אַל־תִּתְחַר Do not worry
because of the wicked.
Do not envy those who do wrong,
²for like the grass they quickly wither,
like the green of the field
they fade away.

³Trust in God and do good,
live in the land, and keep faith.
⁴Find your delight in God,
who will give you
your heart's desires.

⁵Commit your way to God,
rely on God who will act,
⁶bringing your righteousness to light
and your integrity
into the light of noon.

⁷Be still before God, and wait patiently,
do not fret about those
who push for success,
who carry out their schemes.
⁸Cease from anger, leave your rage.
Do not fret - it only leads to wrong.
⁹For those who do wrong
will be cut off,
but those who wait for God
shall inherit the earth.

¹⁰A little while longer -
and the wicked are no more.
Search for their place -
nothing is there!
¹¹But the humble shall inherit the earth,
delighting in abundant peace.

לז (א–יא)

אְלְדָוִד
אַל־תִּתְחַר בַּמְּרֵעִים
אַל־תְּקַנֵּא בְּעֹשֵׂי עַוְלָה:
בכִּי כֶחָצִיר מְהֵרָה יִמָּלוּ
וּכְיֶרֶק דֶּשֶׁא יִבּוֹלוּן:

גבְּטַח בַּיהוה וַעֲשֵׂה־טוֹב
שְׁכָן־אֶרֶץ וּרְעֵה אֱמוּנָה:
דוְהִתְעַנַּג עַל־יהוה
וְיִתֶּן־לְךָ מִשְׁאֲלֹת לִבֶּךָ:

הגּוֹל עַל־יהוה דַּרְכֶּךָ
וּבְטַח עָלָיו וְהוּא יַעֲשֶׂה:
ווְהוֹצִיא כָאוֹר צִדְקֶךָ
וּמִשְׁפָּטֶךָ כַּצָּהֳרָיִם:

זדּוֹם לַיהוה וְהִתְחוֹלֵל לוֹ
אַל־תִּתְחַר בְּמַצְלִיחַ דַּרְכּוֹ
בְּאִישׁ עֹשֶׂה מְזִמּוֹת:
חהֶרֶף מֵאַף וַעֲזֹב חֵמָה
אַל־תִּתְחַר אַךְ־לְהָרֵעַ:
טכִּי־מְרֵעִים יִכָּרֵתוּן
וְקוֵֹי יהוה הֵמָּה
יִירְשׁוּ־אָרֶץ:

יוְעוֹד מְעַט וְאֵין רָשָׁע
וְהִתְבּוֹנַנְתָּ עַל־מְקוֹמוֹ וְאֵינֶנּוּ:
יאוַעֲנָוִים יִירְשׁוּ־אָרֶץ
וְהִתְעַנְּגוּ עַל־רֹב שָׁלוֹם:

Psalm 40

מ

לַמְנַצֵּחַ לְדָוִד מִזְמוֹר

[1] For the Choirmaster. David's Psalm.

[2] קַוֹּה I waited and hoped for God
who bent down to me,
who heard my cry for help,

קַוֹּה קִוִּיתִי יהוה
וַיֵּט אֵלַי וַיִּשְׁמַע שַׁוְעָתִי:

[3] pulling me out of a quaking pit,
out of clinging mud.
Then God set my foot upon a rock
and steadied my steps,

וַיַּעֲלֵנִי מִבּוֹר שָׁאוֹן
מִטִּיט הַיָּוֵן
וַיָּקֶם עַל־סֶלַע רַגְלַי
כּוֹנֵן אֲשֻׁרָי:

[4] setting a new song in my mouth,
praising our God.
Many shall see and fear,
and trust in God.

וַיִּתֵּן בְּפִי שִׁיר חָדָשׁ
תְּהִלָּה לֵאלֹהֵינוּ
יִרְאוּ רַבִּים וְיִירָאוּ
וְיִבְטְחוּ בַּיהוָה:

[5] Happy are they
who have put their trust in God,
who have not turned to the arrogant,
to those who rely on a lie.

אַשְׁרֵי הַגֶּבֶר
אֲשֶׁר־שָׂם יְהוָה מִבְטַחוֹ
וְלֹא־פָנָה אֶל־רְהָבִים
וְשָׂטֵי כָזָב:

[6] You have done so many things, my God,
so many wonderful things –
made so many plans for us –
You have no equal!
If I proclaim and speak of them
they are more than can be told.

רַבּוֹת עָשִׂיתָ אַתָּה
יְהוָה אֱלֹהַי
נִפְלְאֹתֶיךָ וּמַחְשְׁבֹתֶיךָ אֵלֵינוּ
אֵין עֲרֹךְ אֵלֶיךָ
אַגִּידָה וַאֲדַבֵּרָה
עָצְמוּ מִסַּפֵּר:

[7] You did not want sacrifices
and offerings
– instead You opened my ears!
You asked for no burnt or sin offerings –
[8] therefore I said:
'See! I have come with a scroll
of a book
written about myself.

זֶבַח וּמִנְחָה לֹא־חָפַצְתָּ
אָזְנַיִם כָּרִיתָ לִּי
עוֹלָה וַחֲטָאָה לֹא שָׁאָלְתָּ:
אָז אָמַרְתִּי
הִנֵּה־בָאתִי בִּמְגִלַּת־סֵפֶר
כָּתוּב עָלָי:

[9] To do Your will, God,
has been my desire,
with Your teaching
in the depths of my being.'

לַעֲשׂוֹת רְצוֹנְךָ
אֱלֹהַי חָפָצְתִּי
וְתוֹרָתְךָ בְּתוֹךְ מֵעָי:

<<<

633 PSALM ANTHOLOGY

¹⁰I have preached justice
in the great congregation,
I have not curbed my lips
as You know, God!
¹¹I did not hide Your righteousness
in my heart
but I declared Your
faithfulness and Your salvation;
I never concealed
Your love and Your truth
in the great congregation.

¹²But You, God, will not withhold
Your mercy from me,
Your love and Your truth
will always preserve me.

¹³More evils have gathered around me
than I can count.
My sins have closed in on me
so that I can hardly see -
for they are more
than the hairs of my head,
my courage fails me.

¹⁴God, may it be Your will to deliver me.
God, come quickly to my aid!

¹⁵Let them be
ashamed and humbled together,
those who seek my life to destroy it.
Sweep them away in confusion
who delight in my harm!
¹⁶Let them be appalled
by their shame,
for taunting me and jeering.

<<<

י בִּשַּׂרְתִּי צֶדֶק בְּקָהָל רָב
הִנֵּה שְׂפָתַי לֹא אֶכְלָא יהוה
אַתָּה יָדָעְתָּ:
יא צִדְקָתְךָ לֹא־כִסִּיתִי
בְּתוֹךְ לִבִּי
אֱמוּנָתְךָ וּתְשׁוּעָתְךָ אָמָרְתִּי
לֹא־כִחַדְתִּי חַסְדְּךָ וַאֲמִתְּךָ
לְקָהָל רָב:

יב אַתָּה יהוה לֹא־תִכְלָא
רַחֲמֶיךָ מִמֶּנִּי
חַסְדְּךָ וַאֲמִתְּךָ תָּמִיד יִצְּרוּנִי:

יג כִּי אָפְפוּ־עָלַי רָעוֹת
עַד־אֵין מִסְפָּר
הִשִּׂיגוּנִי עֲוֹנֹתַי
וְלֹא־יָכֹלְתִּי לִרְאוֹת
עָצְמוּ מִשַּׂעֲרוֹת רֹאשִׁי
וְלִבִּי עֲזָבָנִי:

יד רְצֵה־יהוה לְהַצִּילֵנִי
יהוה לְעֶזְרָתִי חוּשָׁה:

טו יֵבֹשׁוּ וְיַחְפְּרוּ יַחַד
מְבַקְשֵׁי נַפְשִׁי לִסְפּוֹתָהּ
יִסֹּגוּ אָחוֹר וְיִכָּלְמוּ
חֲפֵצֵי רָעָתִי:
טז יָשֹׁמּוּ עַל־עֵקֶב בָּשְׁתָּם
הָאֹמְרִים לִי הֶאָח הֶאָח:

¹⁷Let there be joy and gladness
for all who seek You.
Let those who love Your salvation
always have cause to say,
'God is great!'
¹⁸As for me, poor and in need,
may God think of me.
You are my help, my deliverer.
My God, do not delay!

Psalm 42

¹For the Choirmaster.
A Poem of the Sons of Korach.
²כְּאַיָּל As a deer longs
for running streams,
so my soul longs for You, my God.
³My soul thirsts for God,
the living God.
'When shall I come and appear
before God?'
⁴My tears have been my food,
by day and night,
as all day long they say to me,
'Where is your God?'

<<<

PSALM ANTHOLOGY

⁵These things I remember,
as I pour out my soul -
how I would pass by
with the throng,
leading them to the house of God,
with voices raised
in joy and praise,
the noise of celebration.
⁶Why are you cast down my soul,
and why do you moan within me?
Hope in God! I praise You still,
for Your saving presence.

⁷My God,
when my soul is cast down
within me, I think of You,
from the land of Jordan,
and the Hermons,
from the hill of Mitzar.
⁸Deep calls to deep
in the roar of Your cataracts.
All Your waves and breakers
swept over me.

⁹By day God's faithful love
will appear,
God's song stay with me at night,
a prayer to the God of my life.
¹⁰I will say to God, my rock,
'Why have You forgotten me?
Why must I go about mournfully,
oppressed by the enemy?'
¹¹My enemies taunt me,
as if crushing my bones,
as all day long they ask me,
'Where is your God?'

¹²Why are you cast down my soul,
and why do you moan within me?
Hope in God!
I praise You still,
my own salvation, and my God.

ה אֵ֤לֶּה אֶזְכְּרָ֨ה
וְאֶשְׁפְּכָ֬ה עָלַ֨י ׀ נַפְשִׁ֗י
כִּ֤י אֶֽעֱבֹ֨ר ׀ בַּסָּ֗ךְ אֶדַּדֵּ֥ם
עַד־בֵּ֥ית אֱלֹהִ֑ים
בְּקֽוֹל־רִנָּ֥ה וְ֝תוֹדָ֗ה הָמ֥וֹן חוֹגֵֽג׃
ו מַה־תִּשְׁתּ֬וֹחֲחִ֨י ׀ נַפְשִׁי֮
וַתֶּהֱמִ֪י עָ֫לָ֥י
הוֹחִ֣ילִי לֵֽ֭אלֹהִים כִּי־ע֥וֹד אוֹדֶ֗נּוּ
יְשׁוּע֥וֹת פָּנָֽיו׃

ז אֱֽלֹהַ֗י
עָלַי֮ נַפְשִׁ֪י תִשְׁתּ֫וֹחָ֥ח
עַל־כֵּ֗ן אֶ֭זְכָּרְךָ מֵאֶ֣רֶץ יַרְדֵּ֑ן
וְ֝חֶרְמוֹנִ֗ים מֵהַ֥ר מִצְעָֽר׃
ח תְּהֽוֹם־אֶל־תְּה֣וֹם ק֭וֹרֵא
לְק֣וֹל צִנּוֹרֶ֑יךָ
כָּֽל־מִשְׁבָּרֶ֥יךָ וְ֝גַלֶּ֗יךָ עָלַ֥י עָבָֽרוּ׃

ט יוֹמָ֤ם ׀ יְצַוֶּ֬ה יְהוָ֨ה ׀ חַסְדּ֗וֹ
וּ֭בַלַּיְלָה שִׁירֹ֣ה עִמִּ֑י
תְּ֝פִלָּ֗ה לְאֵ֣ל חַיָּֽי׃
י אוֹמְרָ֤ה ׀ לְאֵ֥ל סַלְעִי֮
לָמָ֪ה שְׁכַ֫חְתָּ֥נִי
לָֽמָּה־קֹדֵ֥ר אֵלֵ֗ךְ בְּלַ֣חַץ אוֹיֵֽב׃
יא בְּרֶ֤צַח ׀ בְּֽעַצְמוֹתַ֗י חֵרְפ֥וּנִי צוֹרְרָ֑י
בְּאָמְרָ֖ם אֵלַ֥י כָּל־הַ֝יּ֗וֹם
אַיֵּ֥ה אֱלֹהֶֽיךָ׃

יב מַה־תִּשְׁתּ֬וֹחֲחִ֨י ׀ נַפְשִׁי֮
וּֽמַה־תֶּהֱמִ֪י עָ֫לָ֥י
הוֹחִ֣ילִי לֵֽ֭אלֹהִים כִּי־ע֣וֹד אוֹדֶ֑נּוּ
יְשׁוּעֹ֥ת פָּ֝נַ֗י וֵֽאלֹהָֽי׃

Psalm 43

¹ שָׁפְטֵנִי God be my judge,
and plead my cause
against a nation with no mercy,
from people of deceit
and lies deliver me!
² Since You are the God of my strength
why have You rejected me?
Why do I walk alone, mourning,
oppressed by the enemy?
³ Send out Your light and Your truth
- may they guide me!
Let them bring me to Your holy mountain
and to Your dwelling places.
⁴ Then I shall come to the altar of God,
the God of joy, my delight,
and I shall praise You with the harp,
O God, my God.
⁵ Why are you cast down my soul,
and why do you moan within me?
Hope in God!
I praise You still,
my own salvation, and my God.

Psalm 46

¹ For the Choirmaster. Of the Sons of Korach.
Upon *alamot*. A Song.
² אֱלֹהִים God is our refuge and strength,
an ever-present help in trouble.
³ Therefore we shall not fear
though the earth is changed
and the mountains
fall into the depths of the sea;

מג
א שָׁפְטֵנִי אֱלֹהִים
וְרִיבָה רִיבִי
מִגּוֹי לֹא־חָסִיד
מֵאִישׁ־מִרְמָה
וְעַוְלָה תְפַלְּטֵנִי:
ב כִּי־אַתָּה אֱלֹהֵי מָעוּזִּי
לָמָה זְנַחְתָּנִי
לָמָּה־קֹדֵר אֶתְהַלֵּךְ
בְּלַחַץ אוֹיֵב:
ג שְׁלַח־אוֹרְךָ וַאֲמִתְּךָ
הֵמָּה יַנְחוּנִי
יְבִיאוּנִי אֶל־הַר־קָדְשְׁךָ
וְאֶל־מִשְׁכְּנוֹתֶיךָ:
ד וְאָבוֹאָה אֶל־מִזְבַּח אֱלֹהִים
אֶל־אֵל שִׂמְחַת גִּילִי
וְאוֹדְךָ בְכִנּוֹר
אֱלֹהִים אֱלֹהָי:
ה מַה־תִּשְׁתּוֹחֲחִי נַפְשִׁי
וּמַה־תֶּהֱמִי עָלָי
הוֹחִילִי לֵאלֹהִים
כִּי־עוֹד אוֹדֶנּוּ
יְשׁוּעֹת פָּנַי וֵאלֹהָי:

מו
א לַמְנַצֵּחַ לִבְנֵי־קֹרַח
עַל־עֲלָמוֹת שִׁיר
ב אֱלֹהִים לָנוּ מַחֲסֶה וָעֹז
עֶזְרָה בְצָרוֹת נִמְצָא מְאֹד:
ג עַל־כֵּן לֹא־נִירָא
בְּהָמִיר אָרֶץ
וּבְמוֹט הָרִים בְּלֵב יַמִּים:

⁴even though its waters roar and foam,
though the mountains shake as they swell
(*selah*).

⁵There is a river whose waters give joy
to the city of God,
the holy place of the presence of God.
⁶God is within, it cannot be shaken.
God will help it at the dawning of the day.
⁷Nations are in tumult, kingdoms totter;
God speaks out, the earth melts away.

⁸The God of all creation is with us,
the God of Jacob is our refuge
(*selah*).

⁹Come and consider what God has done,
astonishing things on earth:
¹⁰making wars end throughout the earth,
breaking the bow, snapping the spear,
burning the chariots with fire.
¹¹'Be still and know
that I am God,
supreme among the nations,
supreme on earth!'

¹²The God of all creation is with us.
the God of Jacob is our refuge
(*selah*).

Psalm 48 can be found on page 42.

נא (א–יט)

אלַמְנַצֵּחַ מִזְמוֹר לְדָוִד:
בבְּבוֹא־אֵלָיו נָתָן הַנָּבִיא כַּאֲשֶׁר־בָּא אֶל־בַּת־שָׁבַע:
גחָנֵּנִי אֱלֹהִים כְּחַסְדֶּךָ כְּרֹב רַחֲמֶיךָ מְחֵה פְשָׁעָי:
דהֶרֶב כַּבְּסֵנִי מֵעֲוֹנִי וּמֵחַטָּאתִי טַהֲרֵנִי:
הכִּי־פְשָׁעַי אֲנִי אֵדָע וְחַטָּאתִי נֶגְדִּי תָמִיד:
ולְךָ לְבַדְּךָ חָטָאתִי וְהָרַע בְּעֵינֶיךָ עָשִׂיתִי
לְמַעַן תִּצְדַּק בְּדָבְרֶךָ תִּזְכֶּה בְשָׁפְטֶךָ:

זהֵן־בְּעָווֹן חוֹלָלְתִּי וּבְחֵטְא יֶחֱמַתְנִי אִמִּי:
חהֵן־אֱמֶת חָפַצְתָּ בַטֻּחוֹת וּבְסָתֻם חָכְמָה תוֹדִיעֵנִי:

טתְּחַטְּאֵנִי בְאֵזוֹב וְאֶטְהָר תְּכַבְּסֵנִי וּמִשֶּׁלֶג אַלְבִּין:
תַּשְׁמִיעֵנִי שָׂשׂוֹן וְשִׂמְחָה תָּגֵלְנָה עֲצָמוֹת דִּכִּיתָ:
יאהַסְתֵּר פָּנֶיךָ מֵחֲטָאָי וְכָל־עֲוֹנֹתַי מְחֵה:

יבלֵב טָהוֹר בְּרָא־לִי אֱלֹהִים וְרוּחַ נָכוֹן חַדֵּשׁ בְּקִרְבִּי:
יגאַל־תַּשְׁלִיכֵנִי מִלְּפָנֶיךָ וְרוּחַ קָדְשְׁךָ אַל־תִּקַּח מִמֶּנִּי:
ידהָשִׁיבָה לִּי שְׂשׂוֹן יִשְׁעֶךָ וְרוּחַ נְדִיבָה תִסְמְכֵנִי:
טואֲלַמְּדָה פֹשְׁעִים דְּרָכֶיךָ וְחַטָּאִים אֵלֶיךָ יָשׁוּבוּ:
טזהַצִּילֵנִי מִדָּמִים אֱלֹהִים אֱלֹהֵי תְּשׁוּעָתִי תְּרַנֵּן לְשׁוֹנִי צִדְקָתֶךָ:

יזאֲדֹנָי שְׂפָתַי תִּפְתָּח וּפִי יַגִּיד תְּהִלָּתֶךָ:

יחכִּי לֹא־תַחְפֹּץ זֶבַח וְאֶתֵּנָה עוֹלָה לֹא תִרְצֶה:
יטזִבְחֵי אֱלֹהִים רוּחַ נִשְׁבָּרָה לֵב־נִשְׁבָּר וְנִדְכֶּה אֱלֹהִים לֹא תִבְזֶה:

Psalm 51 (1-19)

¹For the Choirmaster. A Psalm of David
²when Nathan the prophet came to him after he had been with Bathsheba.

³חָנֵּנִי Be kind to me, God, in Your mercy,
in Your great compassion blot out my misdeeds.
⁴Wash me free from my guilt and cleanse me from my sin.
⁵For my misdeeds I know too well and my sin is always before me.
⁶Against You, You only, have I sinned, and done what is evil in Your sight.
Therefore, You are just in Your sentence, and right in Your judgment.

⁷Even if I was born through a guilty act,
or my mother conceived me in sin,
⁸the truth is still what You desire within me,
and in my inmost heart You show me wisdom.

⁹Purify me with hyssop, and I shall be clean,
wash me, and I shall be whiter than snow.
¹⁰Let me hear joy and gladness, so that the bones You crushed dance again.
¹¹Turn Your gaze away from my sins and blot out all my guilt.

¹²Create a pure heart for me, God, and put a firm and steadfast spirit in me.
¹³Do not cast me away from Your presence,
nor take Your holy spirit from me.
¹⁴Give me back the joy of Your salvation and let a willing spirit uphold me.
¹⁵Then I will teach transgressors the way so that sinners may return to You.
¹⁶Keep me from bloodshed, O God. You are the God who saves me.
My tongue shall ring out Your justice.

¹⁷My God, open my lips and my mouth shall declare Your praise.

¹⁸For You desire no sacrifice, or I would give it,
burnt offerings You do not want.
¹⁹God's sacrifices are a humbled spirit, a broken and a contrite heart
You will not despise.

Psalm 57

נז

א לַמְנַצֵּחַ אַל־תַּשְׁחֵת לְדָוִד מִכְתָּם
בְּבָרְחוֹ מִפְּנֵי־שָׁאוּל בַּמְּעָרָה׃

¹ For the Choirmaster. To the Tune 'Do not destroy'. David's *michtam* when he fled from Saul, in the cave.

ב חָנֵּנִי אֱלֹהִים חָנֵּנִי
כִּי בְךָ חָסָיָה נַפְשִׁי
וּבְצֵל־כְּנָפֶיךָ אֶחְסֶה
עַד יַעֲבֹר הַוּוֹת׃

² **חָנֵּנִי** Take pity on me God, take pity,
for in You my soul has taken refuge.
I take refuge in the shadow of Your wings
until the storms are past.

ג אֶקְרָא לֵאלֹהִים עֶלְיוֹן
לָאֵל גֹּמֵר עָלָי׃
ד יִשְׁלַח מִשָּׁמַיִם וְיוֹשִׁיעֵנִי
חֵרֵף שֹׁאֲפִי סֶלָה
יִשְׁלַח אֱלֹהִים חַסְדּוֹ וַאֲמִתּוֹ׃

³ I call to God, the highest,
to God who has a purpose for me,
⁴ who will send from heaven and save me
from the taunts of my persecutor (*selah*).
God will send divine faithful love.

ה נַפְשִׁי בְּתוֹךְ לְבָאִם
אֶשְׁכְּבָה לֹהֲטִים
בְּנֵי־אָדָם שִׁנֵּיהֶם
חֲנִית וְחִצִּים
וּלְשׁוֹנָם חֶרֶב חַדָּה׃

⁵ My soul is in the midst of lions,
I lie down among those ablaze with hatred,
people whose teeth
are spears and arrows,
whose tongue is a sharp sword.

ו רוּמָה עַל־הַשָּׁמַיִם
אֱלֹהִים
עַל כָּל־הָאָרֶץ כְּבוֹדֶךָ׃

⁶ God, show Yourself exalted
beyond the heavens,
Your glory over all the earth.

ז רֶשֶׁת הֵכִינוּ לִפְעָמַי
כָּפַף נַפְשִׁי
כָּרוּ לְפָנַי שִׁיחָה
נָפְלוּ בְתוֹכָהּ
סֶלָה׃

⁷ They set a trap for my steps,
my soul was bowed down.
They dug a pit before me,
they fell into it themselves
(*selah*).

ח נָכוֹן לִבִּי
אֱלֹהִים נָכוֹן לִבִּי
אָשִׁירָה וַאֲזַמֵּרָה׃

⁸ Firm is my heart,
O God, firm is my heart.
I shall sing and play music.

<<<

PSALM ANTHOLOGY

⁹Awake my glory!	ט עוּרָה כְבוֹדִי
Awake lyre and harp!	עוּרָה הַנֵּבֶל וְכִנּוֹר
I will awake the dawn.	אָעִירָה שָּׁחַר:
¹⁰I will thank You, my God,	י אוֹדְךָ בָעַמִּים אֲדֹנָי
among the peoples,	אֲזַמֶּרְךָ בַּלְאֻמִּים:
and praise You among the nations.	
¹¹For Your love is great,	יא כִּי־גָדֹל עַד־שָׁמַיִם חַסְדֶּךָ
reaching up to heaven,	וְעַד־שְׁחָקִים אֲמִתֶּךָ:
and Your faithfulness up to the skies.	
¹²God, show Yourself,	יב רוּמָה עַל־שָׁמַיִם
exalted beyond the heavens,	אֱלֹהִים
Your glory over all the earth.	עַל כָּל־הָאָרֶץ כְּבוֹדֶךָ:

Psalm 62

סב

¹For the Choirmaster. Setting by Yedutun. A Psalm of David.	א לַמְנַצֵּחַ עַל־יְדוּתוּן מִזְמוֹר לְדָוִד
²**אַךְ** Only in God do I find rest for my soul,	ב אַךְ אֶל־אֱלֹהִים דּוּמִיָּה נַפְשִׁי
from there comes my safety.	מִמֶּנּוּ יְשׁוּעָתִי:
³Only God is my rock and my safety,	ג אַךְ־הוּא צוּרִי וִישׁוּעָתִי
my fortress so that I never fall.	מִשְׂגַּבִּי לֹא־אֶמּוֹט רַבָּה:
⁴How long will you threaten a man,	ד עַד־אָנָה תְּהוֹתְתוּ עַל־אִישׁ
all of you trying to destroy him,	תְּרָצְּחוּ כֻלְּכֶם
like a wall already tottering,	כְּקִיר נָטוּי גָּדֵר הַדְּחוּיָה:
a toppling rampart!	

<<<

⁵They only scheme to throw him
off his height,
they delight in deceit;
they bless him with their mouth,
but inwardly they curse him
(*selah*).

⁶Only in God find your rest, my soul,
for from there comes my hope.
⁷Only God is my rock and my safety,
my fortress so that I never fall.

⁸My safety, my honour, depend on God,
the rock of my strength
- my shelter is in God.
⁹Rely on God, people, at all times!
Pour out your hearts before God,
the only true shelter for us
(*selah*)!

¹⁰The 'common man' is only an empty wind,
the 'superman' a tiny speck.
Put them in the scales together
- they go up,
lighter even than an empty wind.

¹¹Put no trust in extortion,
no empty hopes in robbery.
Though wealth breeds wealth,
keep your heart detached.

¹²One thing God has said
- twice I have learnt it -
that 'strength depends on God'
¹³and 'My God,
faithful love is Yours'
for You repay each of us
according to what we do.

⁵אַךְ מִשְּׂאֵתוֹ יָעֲצוּ לְהַדִּיחַ
יִרְצוּ כָזָב
בְּפִיו יְבָרֵכוּ
וּבְקִרְבָּם יְקַלְלוּ־
סֶלָה׃

⁶אַךְ לֵאלֹהִים דּוֹמִי נַפְשִׁי
כִּי־מִמֶּנּוּ תִּקְוָתִי׃
⁷אַךְ־הוּא צוּרִי וִישׁוּעָתִי
מִשְׂגַּבִּי לֹא אֶמּוֹט׃

⁸עַל־אֱלֹהִים יִשְׁעִי וּכְבוֹדִי
צוּר־עֻזִּי מַחְסִי בֵּאלֹהִים׃
⁹בִּטְחוּ בוֹ בְכָל־עֵת עָם
שִׁפְכוּ־לְפָנָיו לְבַבְכֶם
אֱלֹהִים מַחֲסֶה־לָּנוּ
סֶלָה׃

¹⁰אַךְ הֶבֶל בְּנֵי־אָדָם
כָּזָב בְּנֵי אִישׁ
בְּמֹאזְנַיִם לַעֲלוֹת הֵמָּה
מֵהֶבֶל יָחַד׃

¹¹אַל־תִּבְטְחוּ בְעֹשֶׁק
וּבְגָזֵל אַל־תֶּהְבָּלוּ
חַיִל כִּי־יָנוּב אַל־תָּשִׁיתוּ לֵב׃

¹²אַחַת דִּבֶּר אֱלֹהִים
שְׁתַּיִם־זוּ שָׁמָעְתִּי
כִּי עֹז לֵאלֹהִים׃
¹³וּלְךָ־אֲדֹנָי חָסֶד
כִּי־אַתָּה תְשַׁלֵּם
לְאִישׁ כְּמַעֲשֵׂהוּ׃

PSALM ANTHOLOGY

Psalm 63 (1-9)

[1] A Psalm of David when he was in the desert of Judah.
[2] **אֱלֹהִים** God, You are my God,
with longing do I seek You.
My soul is thirsty for You,
my flesh is pining for You
in a dry and weary land
where there is no water.

[3] So I looked for You
in the holy place,
to see Your power and glory.
[4] Because Your love is better than life,
my lips shall praise You.
[5] So I bless You as long as I live,
in Your name
I raise my hands in prayer.

[6] My soul is satisfied as at a feast,
my lips sing out Your praise.
[7] I remember You on my bed,
and think of You
through the night,
[8] for You have been my help,
and in the shadow of Your wings
I sing for joy.

[9] My soul clings to You,
Your right hand supports Me.

סג (א–ט)

אמִזְמוֹר לְדָוִד בִּהְיוֹתוֹ
בְּמִדְבַּר יְהוּדָה
באֱלֹהִים אֵלִי אַתָּה אֲשַׁחֲרֶךָּ
צָמְאָה לְךָ נַפְשִׁי
כָּמַהּ לְךָ בְשָׂרִי
בְּאֶרֶץ־צִיָּה וְעָיֵף בְּלִי־מָיִם:

גכֵּן בַּקֹּדֶשׁ חֲזִיתִךָ
לִרְאוֹת עֻזְּךָ וּכְבוֹדֶךָ:
דכִּי־טוֹב חַסְדְּךָ מֵחַיִּים
שְׂפָתַי יְשַׁבְּחוּנְךָ:
הכֵּן אֲבָרֶכְךָ בְחַיָּי
בְּשִׁמְךָ אֶשָּׂא כַפָּי:

וכְּמוֹ חֵלֶב וָדֶשֶׁן תִּשְׂבַּע נַפְשִׁי
וְשִׂפְתֵי רְנָנוֹת יְהַלֶּל־פִּי:
זאִם־זְכַרְתִּיךָ עַל־יְצוּעָי
בְּאַשְׁמֻרוֹת אֶהְגֶּה־בָּךְ:
חכִּי־הָיִיתָ עֶזְרָתָה לִּי
וּבְצֵל כְּנָפֶיךָ אֲרַנֵּן:

טדָּבְקָה נַפְשִׁי אַחֲרֶיךָ
בִּי תָּמְכָה יְמִינֶךָ

Psalm 67 can be found on page 62.

Psalm 71

¹**בְּךָ־יְהוָה** My God,
in You I have taken refuge,
let me never be ashamed.
²In Your justice, rescue me and free me,
listen to me and save me.
³Be my sheltering rock,
where I may always come,
which You prepared
for my safety –
You are my rock and my fortress!

⁴My God,
rescue me from the hand of the wicked,
from the power of the unjust
and the ruthless.
⁵God, You are my hope, the Living God
I trusted since my childhood.
⁶Since my birth I have relied upon You,
for You delivered me
from my mother's womb –
I praise You always.

⁷My life has been a mystery to many,
but You are my strong refuge.
⁸My mouth shall be filled
with Your praise and Your glory
all day long.
⁹Do not reject me in old age;
when my strength is feeble,
do not abandon me.
¹⁰My enemies are plotting against me,
those who watch me
take counsel together,
¹¹saying, 'God has forsaken him,
let us follow him, and catch him,
for no-one comes to his rescue.'

¹²God, do not stay so far from me,
my God, hurry to help me.
¹³Let those who seek my life
be ashamed and destroyed.
Let those who try to harm me
be covered with shame and confusion.

<<<

עא

א בְּךָ־יְהוָה חָסִיתִי
אַל־אֵבוֹשָׁה לְעוֹלָם:
ב בְּצִדְקָתְךָ תַּצִּילֵנִי וּתְפַלְּטֵנִי
הַטֵּה־אֵלַי אָזְנְךָ וְהוֹשִׁיעֵנִי:
ג הֱיֵה לִי לְצוּר מָעוֹן
לָבוֹא תָּמִיד
צִוִּיתָ לְהוֹשִׁיעֵנִי
כִּי־סַלְעִי וּמְצוּדָתִי אָתָּה:
ד אֱלֹהַי פַּלְּטֵנִי מִיַּד רָשָׁע
מִכַּף מְעַוֵּל וְחוֹמֵץ:
ה כִּי־אַתָּה תִקְוָתִי אֲדֹנָי יְהוִה
מִבְטַחִי מִנְּעוּרָי:
ו עָלֶיךָ נִסְמַכְתִּי מִבֶּטֶן
מִמְּעֵי אִמִּי אַתָּה גוֹזִי
בְּךָ תְהִלָּתִי תָמִיד:
ז כְּמוֹפֵת הָיִיתִי לְרַבִּים
וְאַתָּה מַחֲסִי־עֹז:
ח יִמָּלֵא פִי תְּהִלָּתֶךָ
כָּל־הַיּוֹם תִּפְאַרְתֶּךָ:
ט אַל־תַּשְׁלִיכֵנִי לְעֵת זִקְנָה
כִּכְלוֹת כֹּחִי אַל־תַּעַזְבֵנִי:
י כִּי־אָמְרוּ אוֹיְבַי לִי
וְשֹׁמְרֵי נַפְשִׁי נוֹעֲצוּ יַחְדָּו:
יא לֵאמֹר אֱלֹהִים עֲזָבוֹ
רִדְפוּ וְתִפְשׂוּהוּ
כִּי אֵין מַצִּיל:
יב אֱלֹהִים אַל־תִּרְחַק מִמֶּנִּי
אֱלֹהַי לְעֶזְרָתִי חוּשָׁה:
יג יֵבֹשׁוּ יִכְלוּ שֹׂטְנֵי נַפְשִׁי
יַעֲטוּ חֶרְפָּה וּכְלִמָּה
מְבַקְשֵׁי רָעָתִי:

645 PSALM ANTHOLOGY

¹⁴But I shall always hope
and praise You more and more.
¹⁵My lips will speak
of Your righteousness
and Your salvation
all day long,
though it is more than I can understand.

¹⁶I shall tell of Your mighty deeds,
Lord God, declaring Your righteousness,
Yours alone.
¹⁷God, You have taught me
since my youth, and even now
I still proclaim Your wonders.

¹⁸Now that I am old and grey,
do not abandon me, God,
until I have told the next generation
of Your outstretched arm,
of Your might to all who come after.

¹⁹Your righteousness, O God,
extends to heaven.
You have done great things.
God, there is no one like You.
²⁰You have shown me
many bitter troubles,
but You will revive me again
and raise me up again
from the depths of the earth.
²¹You will make me
greater than ever
and comfort me again.

²²And I will praise You on the lyre
for Your truth, my God.
On my harp I will play to You,
Holy One of Israel.
²³When I sing for You
my lips will rejoice.
So will my soul
which You have redeemed.
²⁴My tongue will speak of Your
righteousness all day long -
for shamed and disgraced
are those who try to hurt me.

יד וַאֲנִי תָּמִיד אֲיַחֵל
וְהוֹסַפְתִּי עַל־כָּל־תְּהִלָּתֶךָ:
טו פִּי יְסַפֵּר צִדְקָתֶךָ
כָּל־הַיּוֹם תְּשׁוּעָתֶךָ
כִּי לֹא יָדַעְתִּי סְפֹרוֹת:

טז אָבוֹא בִּגְבֻרוֹת אֲדֹנָי יֱהֹוִה
אַזְכִּיר צִדְקָתְךָ לְבַדֶּךָ:
יז אֱלֹהִים לִמַּדְתַּנִי מִנְּעוּרָי
וְעַד־הֵנָּה אַגִּיד נִפְלְאוֹתֶיךָ:

יח וְגַם עַד־זִקְנָה וְשֵׂיבָה
אֱלֹהִים אַל־תַּעַזְבֵנִי
עַד־אַגִּיד זְרוֹעֲךָ לְדוֹר
לְכָל־יָבוֹא גְּבוּרָתֶךָ:

יט וְצִדְקָתְךָ אֱלֹהִים עַד־מָרוֹם
אֲשֶׁר־עָשִׂיתָ גְדֹלוֹת
אֱלֹהִים מִי כָמוֹךָ:
כ אֲשֶׁר הִרְאִיתַנִי צָרוֹת
רַבּוֹת וְרָעוֹת
תָּשׁוּב תְּחַיֵּינִי
וּמִתְּהֹמוֹת הָאָרֶץ
תָּשׁוּב תַּעֲלֵנִי:
כא תֶּרֶב גְּדֻלָּתִי וְתִסֹּב תְּנַחֲמֵנִי:

כב גַּם־אֲנִי אוֹדְךָ בִכְלִי־נֶבֶל
אֲמִתְּךָ אֱלֹהָי אֲזַמְּרָה לְךָ בְכִנּוֹר
קְדוֹשׁ יִשְׂרָאֵל:
כג תְּרַנֵּנָּה שְׂפָתַי כִּי אֲזַמְּרָה־לָּךְ
וְנַפְשִׁי אֲשֶׁר פָּדִיתָ:
כד גַּם־לְשׁוֹנִי כָּל־הַיּוֹם
תֶּהְגֶּה צִדְקָתֶךָ
כִּי־בֹשׁוּ כִי־חָפְרוּ
מְבַקְשֵׁי רָעָתִי:

Psalm 73

עג

¹A Psalm of Asaph.
אַךְ How good is God to Israel!
to those who are pure in heart!

מִזְמוֹר לְאָסָף
אַךְ טוֹב לְיִשְׂרָאֵל אֱלֹהִים
לְבָרֵי לֵבָב:

²Yet my foot came close to stumbling,
my footsteps almost slipped.

וַאֲנִי כִּמְעַט נָטָיוּ רַגְלָי
כְּאַיִן שֻׁפְּכוּ אֲשֻׁרָי:

³For I was envious of the arrogant
when I saw the case of the wicked.

כִּי־קִנֵּאתִי בַּהוֹלְלִים
שְׁלוֹם רְשָׁעִים אֶרְאֶה:

⁴No anguished death for them,
their bodies are perfectly sound.

כִּי אֵין חַרְצֻבּוֹת לְמוֹתָם
וּבָרִיא אוּלָם:

⁵They are not burdened like other mortals,
nor stricken like honest people.

בַּעֲמַל אֱנוֹשׁ אֵינֵמוֹ
וְעִם־אָדָם לֹא יְנֻגָּעוּ:

⁶Pride is their chain of honour,
they clothe themselves in violence.

לָכֵן עֲנָקַתְמוֹ גַאֲוָה
יַעֲטָף־שִׁית חָמָס לָמוֹ:

⁷Their eyes bulge out of fatness,
the insolence in their hearts overflows.

יָצָא מֵחֵלֶב עֵינֵמוֹ
עָבְרוּ מַשְׂכִּיּוֹת לֵבָב:

⁸They scoff and talk of evil,
planning oppression from above.

יָמִיקוּ וִידַבְּרוּ בְרָע
עֹשֶׁק מִמָּרוֹם יְדַבֵּרוּ:

⁹They set their mouth against the very heavens
and their tongue struts through the earth.

שַׁתּוּ בַשָּׁמַיִם פִּיהֶם
וּלְשׁוֹנָם תִּהֲלַךְ בָּאָרֶץ:

¹⁰So God's people turn towards them
drinking in their words to the full.

לָכֵן יָשׁוּב עַמּוֹ הֲלֹם
וּמֵי מָלֵא יִמָּצוּ לָמוֹ:

¹¹And they say: 'How can God know?
Does the Most High take notice?

וְאָמְרוּ אֵיכָה יָדַע־אֵל
וְיֵשׁ דֵּעָה בְעֶלְיוֹן:

¹²Look! Such are the wicked,
always at ease and growing in power!'

הִנֵּה־אֵלֶּה רְשָׁעִים
וְשַׁלְוֵי עוֹלָם הִשְׂגּוּ־חָיִל:

¹³How useless it seemed to cleanse my heart
and wash my hands in innocence!

אַךְ־רִיק זִכִּיתִי לְבָבִי
וָאֶרְחַץ בְּנִקָּיוֹן כַּפָּי:

¹⁴For I was stricken all the day long,
tormented morning after morning.

וָאֱהִי נָגוּעַ כָּל־הַיּוֹם
וְתוֹכַחְתִּי לַבְּקָרִים:

<<<

¹⁵Yet if I had said: 'I will tell this aloud!'
I would have betrayed
a generation of Your children.
¹⁶But the more I tried to understand it,
this burden was always before my eyes.

¹⁷Then I came into God's holy place
and realised their final end.
¹⁸You set them on a slippery path,
hurl them into utter ruin.
¹⁹One moment
and they will be a desolation,
completely engulfed in terrors.
²⁰God, like a dream
to one suddenly awake,
You shake off these phantoms
when You arise!

²¹How bitter was my heart
and sharp the pain within me.
²²For I was stupid
and did not understand,
behaving like an animal before You.

²³Yet I am always with You.
You have grasped me by the hand.
²⁴You will guide me
with Your counsel
and afterwards receive me in glory.
²⁵Whom have I in heaven
but You?
Beside You,
I desire nothing on earth.
²⁶My flesh and heart may fail
but God is the rock of my heart
and my portion forever.

²⁷For those who go far from You perish,
You destroy all who betray Your trust.
²⁸But for me,
the nearness of God is my good.
I have made the Lord God my refuge
that I might tell of all Your works.

טו אִם־אָמַרְתִּי אֲסַפְּרָה כְמוֹ
הִנֵּה דוֹר בָּנֶיךָ בָגָדְתִּי:
טז וָאֲחַשְּׁבָה לָדַעַת זֹאת
עָמָל הוּא בְעֵינָי:

יז עַד־אָבוֹא אֶל־מִקְדְּשֵׁי־אֵל
אָבִינָה לְאַחֲרִיתָם:
יח אַךְ בַּחֲלָקוֹת תָּשִׁית לָמוֹ
הִפַּלְתָּם לְמַשּׁוּאוֹת:
יט אֵיךְ הָיוּ לְשַׁמָּה כְרָגַע
סָפוּ תַמּוּ מִן־בַּלָּהוֹת:
כ כַּחֲלוֹם מֵהָקִיץ אֲדֹנָי
בָּעִיר צַלְמָם תִּבְזֶה:

כא כִּי־יִתְחַמֵּץ לְבָבִי
וְכִלְיוֹתַי אֶשְׁתּוֹנָן:
כב וַאֲנִי־בַעַר וְלֹא אֵדָע
בְּהֵמוֹת הָיִיתִי עִמָּךְ:

כג וַאֲנִי תָמִיד עִמָּךְ
אָחַזְתָּ בְּיַד־יְמִינִי:
כד בַּעֲצָתְךָ תַנְחֵנִי
וְאַחַר כָּבוֹד תִּקָּחֵנִי:
כה מִי־לִי בַשָּׁמָיִם
וְעִמְּךָ לֹא־חָפַצְתִּי בָאָרֶץ:
כו כָּלָה שְׁאֵרִי וּלְבָבִי
צוּר־לְבָבִי
וְחֶלְקִי אֱלֹהִים לְעוֹלָם:

כז כִּי־הִנֵּה רְחֵקֶיךָ יֹאבֵדוּ
הִצְמַתָּה כָּל־זוֹנֶה מִמֶּךָּ:
כח וַאֲנִי קִרֲבַת אֱלֹהִים לִי־טוֹב
שַׁתִּי בַּאדֹנָי יְהוִה מַחְסִי
לְסַפֵּר כָּל־מַלְאֲכוֹתֶיךָ:

Psalm 77

[1] For the Choirmaster. Setting by Yedutun. Asaph's Psalm.
[2] קוֹלִי I cried aloud to God, I shouted out,
I cried aloud to God, who heard me.
[3] In the day of my distress
I searched for God.
My hand was stretched out all night long,
my soul refused all comfort.
[4] I moaned
when I remembered God;
as I lay thinking, my spirit sank
(selah).

[5] You stopped me closing my eyes,
so disturbed
that I could not speak.
[6] I thought over days long past,
the years of former times.
[7] I remembered
my old song of happiness in the night.
I prayed in my heart,
and my spirit asked this question:

[8] 'Will God reject us forever
and show us favour no more?
[9] Has God's love vanished to nothing?
Is the promise
made to all generations finished,
[10] God's mercy forgotten,
God's compassion
shut in by anger'
(selah)?

[11] But then I said,
'This is my weakness,
does the right hand
of the Most High change?'
[12] I remember the deeds of God,
I remember Your wonders of old.
[13] I think over all Your works
and ponder all You have done.

<<<

עז

א לַמְנַצֵּחַ עַל־יְדוּתוּן לְאָסָף מִזְמוֹר
ב קוֹלִי אֶל־אֱלֹהִים וְאֶצְעָקָה
קוֹלִי אֶל־אֱלֹהִים וְהַאֲזִין אֵלָי:
ג בְּיוֹם צָרָתִי אֲדֹנָי דָּרָשְׁתִּי
יָדִי לַיְלָה נִגְּרָה
וְלֹא תָפוּג מֵאֲנָה הִנָּחֵם נַפְשִׁי:
ד אֶזְכְּרָה אֱלֹהִים וְאֶהֱמָיָה
אָשִׂיחָה וְתִתְעַטֵּף רוּחִי
סֶלָה:

ה אָחַזְתָּ שְׁמֻרוֹת עֵינָי
נִפְעַמְתִּי וְלֹא אֲדַבֵּר:
ו חִשַּׁבְתִּי יָמִים מִקֶּדֶם
שְׁנוֹת עוֹלָמִים:
ז אֶזְכְּרָה נְגִינָתִי בַּלָּיְלָה
עִם־לְבָבִי אָשִׂיחָה
וַיְחַפֵּשׂ רוּחִי:

ח הַלְעוֹלָמִים יִזְנַח אֲדֹנָי
וְלֹא־יֹסִיף לִרְצוֹת עוֹד:
ט הֶאָפֵס לָנֶצַח חַסְדּוֹ
גָּמַר אֹמֶר לְדֹר וָדֹר:
י הֲשָׁכַח חַנּוֹת אֵל
אִם־קָפַץ בְּאַף רַחֲמָיו
סֶלָה:

יא וָאֹמַר חַלּוֹתִי הִיא
שְׁנוֹת יְמִין עֶלְיוֹן:
יב אֶזְכּוֹר מַעַלְלֵי־יָהּ
כִּי־אֶזְכְּרָה מִקֶּדֶם פִּלְאֶךָ:
יג וְהָגִיתִי בְכָל־פָּעֳלֶךָ
וּבַעֲלִילוֹתֶיךָ אָשִׂיחָה:

¹⁴God,
Your way leads through holiness;
what power is as great as God!
¹⁵You are the God who does wonders,
You showed Your power
 among the peoples.
¹⁶You redeemed, with arm outstretched,
the children of Jacob and Joseph
(*selah*).

¹⁷Then the waters saw You,
 O God,
the waters saw You and whirled about,
 they trembled to their depths.
¹⁸The clouds poured out rain,
 the skies thundered,
Your shafts flashed down.
¹⁹The roar
 of Your thunder rolled by,
Your lightning
 lit up the world,
the earth trembled and shook.

²⁰Your way was through the sea,
Your path through mighty water,
but Your steps could not be known.

²¹You led Your people like a flock
by the hand of Moses and Aaron.

יד אֱלֹהִים בַּקֹּדֶשׁ דַּרְכֶּךָ
מִי־אֵל גָּדוֹל כֵּאלֹהִים:
טו אַתָּה הָאֵל עֹשֵׂה פֶלֶא
הוֹדַעְתָּ בָעַמִּים עֻזֶּךָ:
טז גָּאַלְתָּ בִּזְרוֹעַ עַמֶּךָ
בְּנֵי־יַעֲקֹב וְיוֹסֵף
סֶלָה:

יז רָאוּךָ מַּיִם אֱלֹהִים
רָאוּךָ מַּיִם יָחִילוּ
אַף יִרְגְּזוּ תְהֹמוֹת:
יח זֹרְמוּ מַיִם עָבוֹת
קוֹל נָתְנוּ שְׁחָקִים
אַף־חֲצָצֶיךָ יִתְהַלָּכוּ:
יט קוֹל רַעַמְךָ בַּגַּלְגַּל
הֵאִירוּ בְרָקִים תֵּבֵל
רָגְזָה וַתִּרְעַשׁ הָאָרֶץ:

כ בַּיָּם דַּרְכֶּךָ
וּשְׁבִילְךָ בְּמַיִם רַבִּים
וְעִקְּבוֹתֶיךָ לֹא נֹדָעוּ:

כא נָחִיתָ כַצֹּאן עַמֶּךָ
בְּיַד־מֹשֶׁה וְאַהֲרֹן:

Psalm 81 can be found on page 46.
Psalm 82 can be found on page 43.

פד

Psalm 84

¹For the Choirmaster. Upon the Gittit.
For the Sons of Korach. A Psalm
²How lovely where
 Your presence dwells
 Creator of all.
³My soul is longing, pining
 for the courts of the Eternal.
My heart and my flesh sing out
 to the Living God.

א לַמְנַצֵּחַ עַל־הַגִּתִּית
לִבְנֵי־קֹרַח מִזְמוֹר:
ב מַה־יְּדִידוֹת מִשְׁכְּנוֹתֶיךָ
יְהוָה צְבָאוֹת:
ג נִכְסְפָה וְגַם־כָּלְתָה
נַפְשִׁי לְחַצְרוֹת יְהוָה
לִבִּי וּבְשָׂרִי יְרַנְּנוּ אֶל־אֵל חָי:

⁴Even a sparrow finds a home
and a swallow her own nest
in which to lay her young –
such are Your altars,
Creator of all,
my Ruler and my God.

⁵Happy are those who live in Your house
and can always praise You (*selah*).
⁶Happy the pilgrim inspired by You,
they journey to You
in their heart.
⁷They pass through the dry sad valley
and make it seem a place of springs,
as if the early rain
covered it with blessings.
⁸They go from strength to strength
to appear before God in Zion.

⁹Eternal God of creation,
hear my prayer,
listen,
God of Jacob (*selah*).
¹⁰God, our shield, look
and watch over Your anointed.
¹¹For one day in Your courts
is better than a thousand elsewhere.
I would rather stand at the doorway
of the house of my God
than live at ease
in the tents of the wicked.

¹²For the Living God
is a sun and a shield,
the Eternal gives favour and glory,
never withholding goodness
from those who walk in integrity
¹³Creator of all,
happy are they
who trust in You.

ד גַּם־צִפּוֹר מָצְאָה בַיִת
וּדְרוֹר קֵן לָהּ
אֲשֶׁר־שָׁתָה אֶפְרֹחֶיהָ
אֶת־מִזְבְּחוֹתֶיךָ יהוה צְבָאוֹת
מַלְכִּי וֵאלֹהָי:

ה אַשְׁרֵי יוֹשְׁבֵי בֵיתֶךָ
עוֹד יְהַלְלוּךָ סֶּלָה:
ו אַשְׁרֵי אָדָם עוֹז־לוֹ־בָךְ
מְסִלּוֹת בִּלְבָבָם:
ז עֹבְרֵי בְּעֵמֶק הַבָּכָא מַעְיָן
יְשִׁיתוּהוּ גַּם־בְּרָכוֹת
יַעְטֶה מוֹרֶה:
ח יֵלְכוּ מֵחַיִל אֶל־חָיִל
יֵרָאֶה אֶל־אֱלֹהִים בְּצִיּוֹן:

ט יהוה אֱלֹהִים צְבָאוֹת
שִׁמְעָה תְפִלָּתִי
הַאֲזִינָה אֱלֹהֵי יַעֲקֹב סֶלָה:
י מָגִנֵּנוּ רְאֵה אֱלֹהִים
וְהַבֵּט פְּנֵי מְשִׁיחֶךָ:
יא כִּי טוֹב־יוֹם בַּחֲצֵרֶיךָ
מֵאָלֶף
בָּחַרְתִּי הִסְתּוֹפֵף בְּבֵית אֱלֹהַי
מִדּוּר בְּאָהֳלֵי־רֶשַׁע:

יב כִּי שֶׁמֶשׁ וּמָגֵן יהוה אֱלֹהִים
חֵן וְכָבוֹד יִתֵּן יהוה
לֹא־יִמְנַע טוֹב
לַהֹלְכִים בְּתָמִים:
יג יהוה צְבָאוֹת
אַשְׁרֵי אָדָם בֹּטֵחַ בָּךְ:

Psalm 85

¹For the Choirmaster. For the Sons of Korach. A Psalm.
²רָצִיתָ God, You have shown favour
to Your land,
You reversed the captivity of Jacob.
³You forgave the guilt of Your people,
You covered all their sins.   (selah)
⁴You retracted all Your anger,
You turned away
from Your bitter rage.

⁵Bring us back, O God, our saviour,
and cancel Your indignation against us.
⁶Will You be angry with us forever,
prolonging Your anger
to all generations?
⁷Will You not bring us back to life
so that Your people
may rejoice in You!
⁸God, show us Your mercy
and grant us Your salvation.

⁹I will hear what God,
the Merciful One, has to say
for God means peace
for this people,
for all those who love God,
if they renounce their folly.
¹⁰God's help is near to the faithful,
so that glory
may dwell in our land.

¹¹Mercy and truth have met together,
righteousness and peace
have kissed each other.
¹²Truth springs up from the earth
and righteousness looks down from heaven.

¹³Yes, God gives what is good
and our land
shall give its harvest.
¹⁴Righteousness shall go before,
making a way for God's footsteps.

פה

א לַמְנַצֵּחַ לִבְנֵי־קֹרַח מִזְמוֹר
ב רָצִיתָ יהוה אַרְצֶךָ
שַׁבְתָּ שְׁבִית יַעֲקֹב:
ג נָשָׂאתָ עֲוֹן עַמֶּךָ
כִּסִּיתָ כָל־חַטָּאתָם סֶלָה:
ד אָסַפְתָּ כָל־עֶבְרָתֶךָ
הֱשִׁיבוֹתָ מֵחֲרוֹן אַפֶּךָ:

ה שׁוּבֵנוּ אֱלֹהֵי יִשְׁעֵנוּ
וְהָפֵר כַּעַסְךָ עִמָּנוּ:
ו הַלְעוֹלָם תֶּאֱנַף־בָּנוּ
תִּמְשֹׁךְ אַפְּךָ לְדֹר וָדֹר:
ז הֲלֹא־אַתָּה תָּשׁוּב תְּחַיֵּנוּ
וְעַמְּךָ יִשְׂמְחוּ־בָךְ:
ח הַרְאֵנוּ יהוה חַסְדֶּךָ
וְיֶשְׁעֲךָ תִּתֶּן־לָנוּ:

ט אֶשְׁמְעָה מַה־יְדַבֵּר
הָאֵל יהוה
כִּי יְדַבֵּר שָׁלוֹם אֶל־עַמּוֹ
וְאֶל־חֲסִידָיו
וְאַל־יָשׁוּבוּ לְכִסְלָה:
י אַךְ קָרוֹב לִירֵאָיו יִשְׁעוֹ
לִשְׁכֹּן כָּבוֹד בְּאַרְצֵנוּ:

יא חֶסֶד־וֶאֱמֶת נִפְגָּשׁוּ
צֶדֶק וְשָׁלוֹם נָשָׁקוּ:
יב אֱמֶת מֵאֶרֶץ תִּצְמָח
וְצֶדֶק מִשָּׁמַיִם נִשְׁקָף:

יג גַּם־יהוה יִתֵּן הַטּוֹב
וְאַרְצֵנוּ תִּתֵּן יְבוּלָהּ:
יד צֶדֶק לְפָנָיו יְהַלֵּךְ
וְיָשֵׂם לְדֶרֶךְ פְּעָמָיו:

Psalm 86

פו

תְּפִלָּה לְדָוִד
הַטֵּה יהוה אָזְנְךָ עֲנֵנִי
כִּי־עָנִי וְאֶבְיוֹן אָנִי:
שָׁמְרָה נַפְשִׁי כִּי־חָסִיד אָנִי
הוֹשַׁע עַבְדְּךָ אַתָּה אֱלֹהַי
הַבּוֹטֵחַ אֵלֶיךָ:

חָנֵּנִי אֲדֹנָי
כִּי־אֵלֶיךָ אֶקְרָא כָּל־הַיּוֹם:
שַׂמֵּחַ נֶפֶשׁ עַבְדֶּךָ
כִּי אֵלֶיךָ אֲדֹנָי נַפְשִׁי אֶשָּׂא:

כִּי־אַתָּה אֲדֹנָי טוֹב וְסַלָּח
וְרַב־חֶסֶד לְכָל־קֹרְאֶיךָ:
הַאֲזִינָה יהוה תְּפִלָּתִי
וְהַקְשִׁיבָה בְּקוֹל תַּחֲנוּנוֹתָי:

בְּיוֹם צָרָתִי אֶקְרָאֶךָּ
כִּי תַעֲנֵנִי:
אֵין־כָּמוֹךָ בָאֱלֹהִים אֲדֹנָי
וְאֵין כְּמַעֲשֶׂיךָ:

כָּל־גּוֹיִם אֲשֶׁר עָשִׂיתָ
יָבוֹאוּ וְיִשְׁתַּחֲווּ לְפָנֶיךָ
אֲדֹנָי וִיכַבְּדוּ לִשְׁמֶךָ:
כִּי־גָדוֹל אַתָּה
וְעֹשֵׂה נִפְלָאוֹת
אַתָּה אֱלֹהִים לְבַדֶּךָ:

¹A Prayer of David.
הַטֵּה God, turn Your ear to me!
Answer me!
For I am poor and in need.
²Guard my soul, for I am devoted to You.
You are my God, save Your servant
who trusts in You.

³God be gracious to me,
for I cry to You all day long.
⁴Rejoice the soul of Your servant,
for God, I put my hope in You.

⁵God, You are good and forgiving,
full of mercy to all who call upon You.
⁶God, listen to my prayer,
and hear my voice when I plead.

⁷In my day of distress I call to You,
for You will answer me.
⁸God, there is no power like You,
no deeds like Yours!

⁹All the nations that You made
shall come and worship before You,
God, and glorify Your name.
¹⁰For You are great
and do such wonders,
You, God, only You.

<<<

¹¹Show me, God, Your way
  so that I may walk in Your truth.
  Give my heart integrity
  to revere Your name.
¹²Then I will thank You,
  my Living God,
  with all my heart
  and glorify Your name forever.
¹³Your love for me has been so great
  that You rescued me
  from the lower world.

¹⁴O God, proud men rise against me,
  a violent mob, who seek my life,
  people to whom You mean nothing.
¹⁵But You are the Lord,
  the God of mercy and compassion,
  slow to anger,
  ever loving and ever true.

¹⁶Turn to me, God,
  and be gracious to me.
  Give Your strength to Your servant.
  Rescue the child of a woman
  who served You.
¹⁷Show me a sign of Your goodness,
  let my enemies see it
  and be ashamed.
  Because You, God,
  have been my help and my comfort.

א הוֹרֵנִי יְהוָה דַּרְכֶּךָ
אֲהַלֵּךְ בַּאֲמִתֶּךָ
יַחֵד לְבָבִי לְיִרְאָה שְׁמֶךָ:
ב אוֹדְךָ אֲדֹנָי אֱלֹהַי
בְּכָל־לְבָבִי
וַאֲכַבְּדָה שִׁמְךָ לְעוֹלָם:
ג כִּי־חַסְדְּךָ גָּדוֹל עָלָי
וְהִצַּלְתָּ נַפְשִׁי מִשְּׁאוֹל תַּחְתִּיָּה:

ד אֱלֹהִים זֵדִים קָמוּ עָלַי
וַעֲדַת עָרִיצִים בִּקְשׁוּ נַפְשִׁי
וְלֹא שָׂמוּךָ לְנֶגְדָּם:
ה וְאַתָּה אֲדֹנָי אֵל־רַחוּם וְחַנּוּן
אֶרֶךְ אַפַּיִם וְרַב־חֶסֶד וֶאֱמֶת:

ו פְּנֵה אֵלַי וְחָנֵּנִי
תְּנָה־עֻזְּךָ לְעַבְדֶּךָ
וְהוֹשִׁיעָה לְבֶן־אֲמָתֶךָ:
ז עֲשֵׂה־עִמִּי אוֹת לְטוֹבָה
וְיִרְאוּ שֹׂנְאַי וְיֵבֹשׁוּ
כִּי־אַתָּה יְהוָה
עֲזַרְתַּנִי וְנִחַמְתָּנִי:

צ

א תְּפִלָּה לְמֹשֶׁה אִישׁ־הָאֱלֹהִים
אֲדֹנָי מָעוֹן אַתָּה הָיִיתָ לָּנוּ בְּדֹר וָדֹר:
ב בְּטֶרֶם הָרִים יֻלָּדוּ וַתְּחוֹלֵל אֶרֶץ וְתֵבֵל
וּמֵעוֹלָם עַד־עוֹלָם אַתָּה אֵל:

ג תָּשֵׁב אֱנוֹשׁ עַד־דַּכָּא וַתֹּאמֶר שׁוּבוּ בְנֵי־אָדָם:
ד כִּי אֶלֶף שָׁנִים בְּעֵינֶיךָ כְּיוֹם אֶתְמוֹל כִּי יַעֲבֹר
וְאַשְׁמוּרָה בַלָּיְלָה:
ה זְרַמְתָּם שֵׁנָה יִהְיוּ בַּבֹּקֶר כֶּחָצִיר יַחֲלֹף:
ו בַּבֹּקֶר יָצִיץ וְחָלָף לָעֶרֶב יְמוֹלֵל וְיָבֵשׁ:
ז כִּי־כָלִינוּ בְאַפֶּךָ וּבַחֲמָתְךָ נִבְהָלְנוּ:
ח שַׁתָּה עֲוֺנֹתֵינוּ לְנֶגְדֶּךָ עֲלֻמֵנוּ לִמְאוֹר פָּנֶיךָ:
ט כִּי כָל־יָמֵינוּ פָּנוּ בְעֶבְרָתֶךָ כִּלִּינוּ שָׁנֵינוּ כְמוֹ־הֶגֶה:

י יְמֵי שְׁנוֹתֵינוּ בָהֶם שִׁבְעִים שָׁנָה וְאִם בִּגְבוּרֹת שְׁמוֹנִים שָׁנָה
וְרָהְבָּם עָמָל וָאָוֶן כִּי־גָז חִישׁ וַנָּעֻפָה:
יא מִי־יוֹדֵעַ עֹז אַפֶּךָ וּכְיִרְאָתְךָ עֶבְרָתֶךָ:
יב לִמְנוֹת יָמֵינוּ כֵּן הוֹדַע וְנָבִא לְבַב חָכְמָה:

יג שׁוּבָה יְהֹוָה עַד־מָתָי וְהִנָּחֵם עַל־עֲבָדֶיךָ:
יד שַׂבְּעֵנוּ בַבֹּקֶר חַסְדֶּךָ וּנְרַנְּנָה וְנִשְׂמְחָה בְּכָל־יָמֵינוּ:
טו שַׂמְּחֵנוּ כִּימוֹת עִנִּיתָנוּ שְׁנוֹת רָאִינוּ רָעָה:
טז יֵרָאֶה אֶל־עֲבָדֶיךָ פָעֳלֶךָ וַהֲדָרְךָ עַל־בְּנֵיהֶם:

יז וִיהִי נֹעַם אֲדֹנָי אֱלֹהֵינוּ עָלֵינוּ
וּמַעֲשֵׂה יָדֵינוּ כּוֹנְנָה עָלֵינוּ וּמַעֲשֵׂה יָדֵינוּ כּוֹנְנֵהוּ:

Psalm 91 can be found on page 424.

Psalm 92 can be found on page 124.

Psalm 93 can be found on page 47.

Psalm 94 can be found on page 44.

Psalm 95 can be found on page 111.

Psalm 90

[1] A Prayer of Moses, the Man of God.
אֲדֹנָי Our Creator, You have been our home from age to age.
Before the mountains were born,
[2] before You brought the earth and world to birth,
You were God from eternity, and will be forever.

[3] You turn human beings back to dust
yet You say: 'Children of Adam, turn back to Me!'
[4] For You a thousand years are like a yesterday gone by,
a passing hour in the night.
[5] You sweep people away, they are frail as sleep;
like grass that grows in the morning,
[6] that grows so fresh in the morning, and in the evening fades and dies.
[7] We are burnt up by Your anger and dismayed by Your wrath.
[8] You lay bare our sins before You,
our secret sins in the light of Your presence.
[9] Our days pass away in Your anger, so we end our years like a sigh.

[10] For us, our lives can reach seventy years, eighty years with strength,
and they are troubled with grief and emptiness,
but this is soon over and then we move on.
[11] Who knows the power of Your anger and fears the strength of Your wrath!
[12] So show us how to spend our time and acquire a heart of wisdom.

[13] God, turn back to us! How long till You take pity on Your servants?
[14] Fill the morning of our life with Your love to be glad and sing all our days.
[15] Give us happiness to match our sadness,
for times when we knew misfortune.
[16] Let the meaning of Your work be clear to Your servants
and Your glory to their children.

[17] May the favour of the Creator our God be upon us
to support us in the work we do, and support the work we do.

Psalm 96 can be found on page 112.
Psalm 97 can be found on page 114.
Psalm 98 can be found on page 116.
Psalm 99 can be found on page 117.
Psalm 100 can be found on page 40.

Psalm 103

¹David's.

בָּרְכִי Bless God, my soul,
all that is in me
bless God's holy name!
²Bless God, my soul,
and forget none of God's kind deeds.

³The One who pardons all your deceit,
who heals all your suffering,
⁴who redeems your life
from the pit of death,
who surrounds you with
love and compassion,
⁵who fills your old age with goodness,
renewing your youth like an eagle.

⁶God does what is right,
does justice to all the oppressed.
⁷God's ways were made known to Moses,
God's great acts
to the children of Israel.

⁸Tender and compassionate
is the Merciful One,
slow to anger and full of love.
⁹Not for all time does God accuse,
not forever remain angry,
¹⁰not as our failings deserve
has God dealt with us,
not treated us as our deceit required.
¹¹As high as the sky over the earth,
so great is God's love over the faithful;
¹²as far as the east from the west,
so far has God taken
our misdeeds from us.

<<<

קג

א לְדָוִד
בָּרְכִי נַפְשִׁי אֶת־יְהוָה
וְכָל־קְרָבַי אֶת־שֵׁם קָדְשׁוֹ:
ב בָּרְכִי נַפְשִׁי אֶת־יְהוָה
וְאַל־תִּשְׁכְּחִי כָּל־גְּמוּלָיו:
ג הַסֹּלֵחַ לְכָל־עֲוֹנֵכִי
הָרֹפֵא לְכָל־תַּחֲלֻאָיְכִי:
ד הַגּוֹאֵל מִשַּׁחַת חַיָּיְכִי
הַמְעַטְּרֵכִי חֶסֶד וְרַחֲמִים:
ה הַמַּשְׂבִּיעַ בַּטּוֹב עֶדְיֵךְ
תִּתְחַדֵּשׁ כַּנֶּשֶׁר נְעוּרָיְכִי:
ו עֹשֵׂה צְדָקוֹת יְהוָה
וּמִשְׁפָּטִים לְכָל־עֲשׁוּקִים:
ז יוֹדִיעַ דְּרָכָיו לְמֹשֶׁה
לִבְנֵי יִשְׂרָאֵל עֲלִילוֹתָיו:
ח רַחוּם וְחַנּוּן יְהוָה
אֶרֶךְ אַפַּיִם וְרַב־חָסֶד:
ט לֹא־לָנֶצַח יָרִיב
וְלֹא לְעוֹלָם יִטּוֹר:
לֹא כַחֲטָאֵינוּ עָשָׂה לָנוּ
וְלֹא כַעֲוֹנֹתֵינוּ גָּמַל עָלֵינוּ:
יא כִּי כִגְבֹהַּ שָׁמַיִם עַל־הָאָרֶץ
גָּבַר חַסְדּוֹ עַל־יְרֵאָיו:
יב כִּרְחֹק מִזְרָח מִמַּעֲרָב
הִרְחִיק מִמֶּנּוּ אֶת־פְּשָׁעֵינוּ:

¹³As a father is tender to his children,
  so the Merciful One
  is tender to the faithful;
¹⁴for it is God who knows our nature,
  remembers that we are dust.
¹⁵Frail mortals,
  their days are like the grass,
  they blossom like a flower in the field;
¹⁶but the breeze passes over it
  and it is gone
  and its place knows it no more.

¹⁷But the love of the Merciful One
  lasts forever and ever
  for those who are faithful,
  showing loyalty to the children's children
¹⁸of those who keep God's covenant,
  bearing God's laws in their mind,
  to do them.

¹⁹God's throne
  is set firm in heaven
  and God's rule is over all.
²⁰Bless God, You messengers,
  the mighty in strength
  who perform God's word,
  obedient to God's command!
²¹Bless God, all creatures,
  servants who do God's will!
²²Bless God, all creations,
  in all the places
  of God's dominion!

Bless God, my soul!

יג כְּרַחֵם אָב עַל־בָּנִים
רִחַם יְהוָה עַל־יְרֵאָיו:
יד כִּי הוּא יָדַע יִצְרֵנוּ
זָכוּר כִּי־עָפָר אֲנָחְנוּ:
טו אֱנוֹשׁ כֶּחָצִיר יָמָיו
כְּצִיץ הַשָּׂדֶה כֵּן יָצִיץ:
טז כִּי רוּחַ עָבְרָה־בּוֹ וְאֵינֶנּוּ
וְלֹא־יַכִּירֶנּוּ עוֹד מְקוֹמוֹ:

יז וְחֶסֶד יְהוָה מֵעוֹלָם וְעַד־עוֹלָם
עַל־יְרֵאָיו
וְצִדְקָתוֹ לִבְנֵי בָנִים:
יח לְשֹׁמְרֵי בְרִיתוֹ
וּלְזֹכְרֵי פִקֻּדָיו לַעֲשׂוֹתָם:

יט יְהוָה בַּשָּׁמַיִם הֵכִין כִּסְאוֹ
וּמַלְכוּתוֹ בַּכֹּל מָשָׁלָה:
כ בָּרְכוּ יְהוָה מַלְאָכָיו
גִּבֹּרֵי כֹחַ עֹשֵׂי דְבָרוֹ
לִשְׁמֹעַ בְּקוֹל דְּבָרוֹ:
כא בָּרְכוּ יְהוָה כָּל־צְבָאָיו
מְשָׁרְתָיו עֹשֵׂי רְצוֹנוֹ:
כב בָּרְכוּ יְהוָה כָּל־מַעֲשָׂיו
בְּכָל־מְקֹמוֹת מֶמְשַׁלְתּוֹ

בָּרְכִי נַפְשִׁי אֶת־יְהוָה:

Psalm 104

¹ בָּרְכִי Bless God, my soul!
My Living God,
  how great You are,
    clothed in majesty and glory,
² wrapped in light like a robe.
You spread out the heavens
  like a tent,
³ building on the waters
  Your place on high,
using the clouds as a chariot,
  moving on the wings of the wind.
⁴ You make the winds Your messengers.
  flashing fire Your servants.

⁵ You set the earth on its foundations,
  unshakeable forever.
⁶ You covered it with the ocean
  like a robe,
  the waters overflowing the mountains.
⁷ At Your rebuke the waters fled,
  at the sound of Your thunder
    they rushed away.
⁸ The mountains rose, the valleys sank
to the very place You fixed for them.
⁹ You set a boundary
  they should not cross,
  nor return to cover the earth.
¹⁰ You make springs
  flow in the valleys,
  running between the hills.
¹¹ They give water
  to the beasts of the field,
  the wild asses quench their thirst.
¹² Birds of the air nest beside them,
  singing among the branches.

<<<

קד

^א בָּרֲכִי נַפְשִׁי אֶת־יְהֹוָה
יְהֹוָה אֱלֹהַי גָּדַלְתָּ מְּאֹד
הוֹד וְהָדָר לָבָשְׁתָּ׃
^ב עֹטֶה־אוֹר כַּשַּׂלְמָה
נוֹטֶה שָׁמַיִם כַּיְרִיעָה׃
^ג הַמְקָרֶה בַמַּיִם עֲלִיּוֹתָיו
הַשָּׂם־עָבִים רְכוּבוֹ
הַמְהַלֵּךְ עַל־כַּנְפֵי־רוּחַ׃
^ד עֹשֶׂה מַלְאָכָיו רוּחוֹת
מְשָׁרְתָיו אֵשׁ לֹהֵט׃

^ה יָסַד־אֶרֶץ עַל־מְכוֹנֶיהָ
בַּל־תִּמּוֹט עוֹלָם וָעֶד׃
^ו תְּהוֹם כַּלְּבוּשׁ כִּסִּיתוֹ
עַל־הָרִים יַעַמְדוּ־מָיִם׃
^ז מִן־גַּעֲרָתְךָ יְנוּסוּן
מִן־קוֹל רַעַמְךָ יֵחָפֵזוּן׃
^ח יַעֲלוּ הָרִים יֵרְדוּ בְקָעוֹת
אֶל־מְקוֹם זֶה יָסַדְתָּ לָהֶם׃
^ט גְּבוּל־שַׂמְתָּ בַּל־יַעֲבֹרוּן
בַּל־יְשׁוּבוּן לְכַסּוֹת הָאָרֶץ׃
^י הַמְשַׁלֵּחַ מַעְיָנִים בַּנְּחָלִים
בֵּין הָרִים יְהַלֵּכוּן׃
^{יא} יַשְׁקוּ כָּל־חַיְתוֹ שָׂדָי
יִשְׁבְּרוּ פְרָאִים צְמָאָם׃
^{יב} עֲלֵיהֶם עוֹף־הַשָּׁמַיִם יִשְׁכּוֹן
מִבֵּין עֳפָאיִם יִתְּנוּ־קוֹל׃

659 PSALM ANTHOLOGY

¹³You send rain
on the mountains from above,
the earth is full
of the fruit of Your works.
¹⁴You make grass grow for the cattle,
plants for human labour
to bring forth bread from the earth;
¹⁵and wine
to gladden people's hearts,
oil to freshen their faces,
bread to sustain their hearts.

¹⁶God's trees drink their fill,
the cedars of Lebanon God planted.
¹⁷The birds build their nest in them
and storks make the fir trees their home.
¹⁸The high mountains
are for the wild goats,
badgers hide in the rocks.

¹⁹You make the moon
mark the seasons,
the sun knows where to set.
²⁰You make the darkness and it is night,
and creatures of the forest creep out.
²¹The young lions
roar for their prey,
seeking their food from God.
²²The sun rises, they steal away,
returning to rest in their dens.
²³People go out to their tasks
and to their labour
until evening.

<<<

יג מַשְׁקֶה הָרִים מֵעֲלִיּוֹתָיו
מִפְּרִי מַעֲשֶׂיךָ תִּשְׂבַּע הָאָרֶץ:
יד מַצְמִיחַ חָצִיר לַבְּהֵמָה
וְעֵשֶׂב לַעֲבֹדַת הָאָדָם
לְהוֹצִיא לֶחֶם מִן־הָאָרֶץ:
טו וְיַיִן יְשַׂמַּח לְבַב־אֱנוֹשׁ
לְהַצְהִיל פָּנִים מִשָּׁמֶן
וְלֶחֶם לְבַב־אֱנוֹשׁ יִסְעָד:

טז יִשְׂבְּעוּ עֲצֵי יְהוָה
אַרְזֵי לְבָנוֹן אֲשֶׁר נָטָע:
יז אֲשֶׁר־שָׁם צִפֳּרִים יְקַנֵּנוּ
חֲסִידָה בְּרוֹשִׁים בֵּיתָהּ:
יח הָרִים הַגְּבֹהִים לַיְּעֵלִים
סְלָעִים מַחְסֶה לַשְׁפַנִּים:

יט עָשָׂה יָרֵחַ לְמוֹעֲדִים
שֶׁמֶשׁ יָדַע מְבוֹאוֹ:
כ תָּשֶׁת־חֹשֶׁךְ וִיהִי לָיְלָה
בּוֹ־תִרְמֹשׂ כָּל־חַיְתוֹ־יָעַר:
כא הַכְּפִירִים שֹׁאֲגִים לַטָּרֶף
וּלְבַקֵּשׁ מֵאֵל אָכְלָם:
כב תִּזְרַח הַשֶּׁמֶשׁ יֵאָסֵפוּן
וְאֶל־מְעוֹנֹתָם יִרְבָּצוּן:
כג יֵצֵא אָדָם לְפָעֳלוֹ
וְלַעֲבֹדָתוֹ עֲדֵי־עָרֶב:

²⁴God, how great are Your works,
You made them all in wisdom;
the earth is full of Your creatures.
²⁵This vast expanse of ocean!
There go swarms
of creeping creatures,
all forms of life,
great and small!
²⁶There the ships make their way,
the sea monsters
You formed to play with –
²⁷all of them depend on You
to give them food
when it is needed.
²⁸You give it to them – they gather it.
You open Your hand – they eat their fill.
²⁹You hide Your face – they vanish.
You take back Your spirit –
they die
and return to their dust.
³⁰You give breath –
they are created,
and You renew the face of the earth.

³¹May God's glory endure forever.
May God rejoice in all creation.
³²God scans the earth and it trembles,
touches the mountains
and they pour out smoke.

³³I will sing to God as long as I live.
I will sing my God's praises
as long as I exist.
³⁴May my thoughts give pleasure,
for I rejoice in God.
³⁵May sinners vanish from the earth
and the wicked
be no more.

Bless God, my soul!
Praise God!

660 תהלים

כד מָה־רַבּוּ מַעֲשֶׂיךָ יְהוָה
כֻּלָּם בְּחָכְמָה עָשִׂיתָ
מָלְאָה הָאָרֶץ קִנְיָנֶךָ:
כה זֶה ׀ הַיָּם גָּדוֹל וּרְחַב יָדָיִם
שָׁם־רֶמֶשׂ וְאֵין מִסְפָּר
חַיּוֹת קְטַנּוֹת עִם־גְּדֹלוֹת:
כו שָׁם אֳנִיּוֹת יְהַלֵּכוּן
לִוְיָתָן זֶה־יָצַרְתָּ לְשַׂחֶק־בּוֹ:
כז כֻּלָּם אֵלֶיךָ יְשַׂבֵּרוּן לָתֵת
אָכְלָם בְּעִתּוֹ:
כח תִּתֵּן לָהֶם יִלְקֹטוּן
תִּפְתַּח יָדְךָ יִשְׂבְּעוּן טוֹב:
כט תַּסְתִּיר פָּנֶיךָ יִבָּהֵלוּן
תֹּסֵף רוּחָם יִגְוָעוּן
וְאֶל־עֲפָרָם יְשׁוּבוּן:
ל תְּשַׁלַּח רוּחֲךָ יִבָּרֵאוּן
וּתְחַדֵּשׁ פְּנֵי אֲדָמָה:

לא יְהִי כְבוֹד יְהוָה לְעוֹלָם
יִשְׂמַח יְהוָה בְּמַעֲשָׂיו:
לב הַמַּבִּיט לָאָרֶץ וַתִּרְעָד
יִגַּע בֶּהָרִים וְיֶעֱשָׁנוּ:

לג אָשִׁירָה לַיהוָה בְּחַיָּי
אֲזַמְּרָה לֵאלֹהַי בְּעוֹדִי:
לד יֶעֱרַב עָלָיו שִׂיחִי
אָנֹכִי אֶשְׂמַח בַּיהוָה:
לה יִתַּמּוּ חַטָּאִים ׀ מִן־הָאָרֶץ
וּרְשָׁעִים ׀ עוֹד אֵינָם

בָּרֲכִי נַפְשִׁי אֶת־יְהוָה
הַלְלוּיָהּ:

Psalm 112

¹הַלְלוּיָהּ Praise God!
Happy are those who revere God,
who take great joy
in God's commands.
²Their children
will be powerful on earth,
an upright generation are well blessed.
³Wealth and prosperity
are in their houses,
their righteous deeds stand firm forever.
⁴They are a light in darkness
for the upright,
they are generous, merciful and just.
⁵It is good when people are generous
and lend
and conduct their affairs with honour.
⁶For the righteous
will never waver
and will be remembered forever.
⁷They do not fear bad news,
their hearts are firm,
they trust in God.
⁸Their hearts are steadfast,
they do not fear,
for they will see the downfall of their foes.
⁹They are open-hearted,
they give to the poor;
their righteousness stands firm forever,
their heads held high with honour.
¹⁰The evil man sees
and his anger rises,
he grinds his teeth
and melts away.

קיב
^אהַלְלוּיָהּ
אַשְׁרֵי־אִישׁ יָרֵא אֶת־יְהוָה
בְּמִצְוֺתָיו חָפֵץ מְאֹד:
^בגִּבּוֹר בָּאָרֶץ יִהְיֶה זַרְעוֹ
דּוֹר יְשָׁרִים יְבֹרָךְ:
^גהוֹן־וָעֹשֶׁר בְּבֵיתוֹ
וְצִדְקָתוֹ עֹמֶדֶת לָעַד:
^דזָרַח בַּחֹשֶׁךְ אוֹר לַיְשָׁרִים
חַנּוּן וְרַחוּם וְצַדִּיק:
^הטוֹב־אִישׁ חוֹנֵן וּמַלְוֶה
יְכַלְכֵּל דְּבָרָיו בְּמִשְׁפָּט:
^וכִּי־לְעוֹלָם לֹא יִמּוֹט
לְזֵכֶר עוֹלָם יִהְיֶה צַדִּיק:
^זמִשְּׁמוּעָה רָעָה לֹא יִירָא
נָכוֹן לִבּוֹ בָּטֻחַ בַּיהוָה:
^חסָמוּךְ לִבּוֹ לֹא יִירָא
עַד אֲשֶׁר־יִרְאֶה בְצָרָיו:
^טפִּזַּר נָתַן לָאֶבְיוֹנִים
צִדְקָתוֹ עֹמֶדֶת לָעַד
קַרְנוֹ תָּרוּם בְּכָבוֹד:
^ירָשָׁע יִרְאֶה וְכָעָס
שִׁנָּיו יַחֲרֹק וְנָמָס
תַּאֲוַת רְשָׁעִים תֹּאבֵד:

תהלים 662

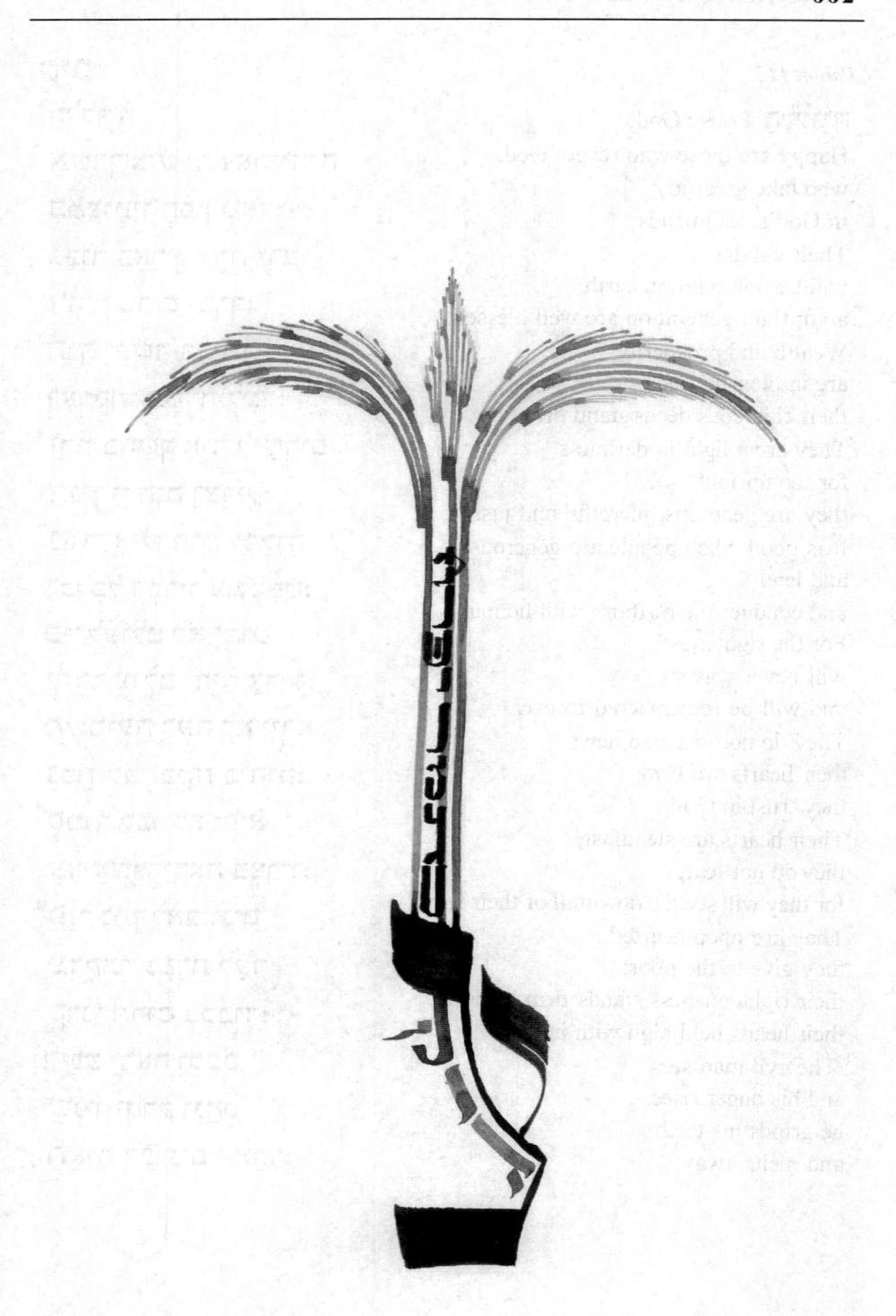

סדר הלל

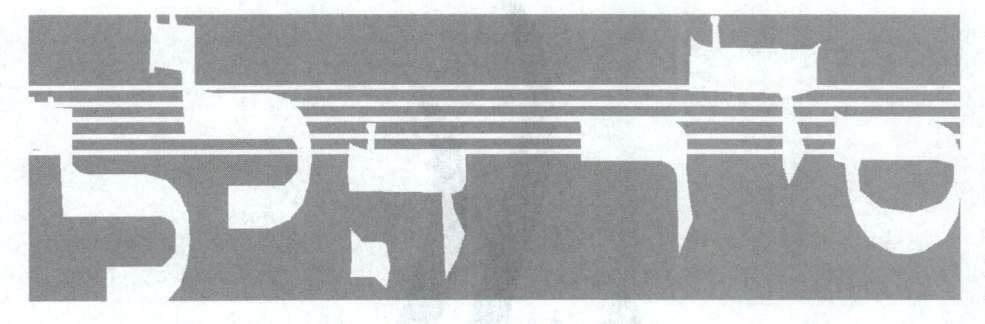

Hallel

הוֹדוּ לַיהוה כִּי טוֹב כִּי לְעוֹלָם חַסְדּוֹ:

Give thanks to God who is good, whose love is everlasting.

Psalm 118:1

סדר הלל
HALLEL

The *Hallel* (more strictly the 'Egyptian *Hallel*', to distinguish this set of Psalms from others also known by this title) comprises Psalms 113-118. The Rabbis of the Talmud (*Pesachim* 117a) ordained that we recite these psalms when we are so immediately aware of God's active presence in the life of our people that we are compelled to sing God's praises. Pre-eminent among these moments is the Exodus from Egypt so the *Hallel* is recited among other times at the three festivals associated with the miracle of Exodus. Foremost among these festivals is *Pesach*, when the slavery of the people was transformed miraculously into freedom.

The *Hallel* is intimately associated with the Exodus, yet the Exodus is not mentioned until the second psalm in the series, Psalm 114: 'When Israel came out of Egypt.' The key to the *Hallel* is at the very beginning of the first psalm in the series, Psalm 113, 'Servants of the Eternal, praise the name of the Eternal!' In Egypt the Jewish people were not 'servants of the Eternal' but 'slaves to Pharaoh'. The recital of the *Hallel*, particularly at the *Pesach Seder*, concerns our personal exodus from a Jewish childhood to a Jewish adulthood, from servitude to service.

Like songs everywhere and in every age, these songs are designed to release us from the strictures of the everyday and encourage us to soar freely in the inner space of our imagination. They lead us from the 'narrowness' (*metzar*) which was Egyptian (*mitzrayim*) bondage to the 'unbounded space' (*merchav*) which is presented as God's response to our cries for help in moments of distress (Psalm 118:5). But the efficacy of the *Hallel* is dependent on trust: only when 'God is my strength and song' can it be said, 'God is there to save me' (Psalm 118:13-14). In this way, the *Hallel* demonstrates in itself the paradoxical and demanding character of freedom. It is only meaningful to us if we allow it to be.

הַלְלוּיָהּ

Before reciting the Hallel

בָּרוּךְ Blessed are You, our Living God, Sovereign of the universe, whose commandments make us holy who commands us to read the *Hallel*,[1] the psalms of joy.

בָּרוּךְ אַתָּה יהוה אֱלֹהֵינוּ מֶלֶךְ הָעוֹלָם אֲשֶׁר קִדְּשָׁנוּ בְּמִצְוֹתָיו וְצִוָּנוּ לִקְרוֹא אֶת־הַהַלֵּל:

בָּרוּךְ *Baruch attah Adonai eloheinu melech ha-olam, asher kidd'shanu b'mitsvotav v'tsivvanu likro et ha-halleil.*

---

[1] The Hallel (Psalms 113-118) is recited after the *Amidah* of the morning service on the Pilgrim Festivals and on *Chanukah* and *Rosh Chodesh*, the New Moon. On *Rosh Chodesh* and the last six days of *Pesach* two passages are omitted as indicated below.

Psalm 113

הַלְלוּיָהּ Praise God!

Servants of the Eternal,
praise the name of the Eternal!
²May the name of the Eternal be blessed
now and evermore.
³From the rising of the sun to its setting
praised be the name of the Eternal.
⁴High above all nations is the Almighty,
whose glory is beyond the heavens.

⁵Who is like our Living God,
who lives so far beyond,
⁶who dwells so close within
to watch the heavens and the earth?
⁷Who raises the weak from the dust,
lifts the poor from the dirt
⁸to set them with the noble,
with the noble of God's people.
⁹who gives the childless wife a home
as the happy mother of children.

Praise God!

קיג

ᵃהַלְלוּיָהּ
הַלְלוּ עַבְדֵי יהוה
הַלְלוּ אֶת שֵׁם יהוה:
ᵇיְהִי שֵׁם יהוה מְבֹרָךְ
מֵעַתָּה וְעַד־עוֹלָם:
ᶜמִמִּזְרַח שֶׁמֶשׁ עַד מְבוֹאוֹ
מְהֻלָּל שֵׁם יהוה:
ᵈרָם עַל־כָּל־גּוֹיִם יהוה
עַל הַשָּׁמַיִם כְּבוֹדוֹ:

ᵉמִי כַּיהוה אֱלֹהֵינוּ
הַמַּגְבִּיהִי לָשָׁבֶת:
ᶠהַמַּשְׁפִּילִי לִרְאוֹת
בַּשָּׁמַיִם וּבָאָרֶץ:
ᵍמְקִימִי מֵעָפָר דָּל
מֵאַשְׁפֹּת יָרִים אֶבְיוֹן:
ʰלְהוֹשִׁיבִי עִם נְדִיבִים
עִם נְדִיבֵי עַמּוֹ:
ⁱמוֹשִׁיבִי עֲקֶרֶת הַבַּיִת
אֵם הַבָּנִים שְׂמֵחָה
הַלְלוּיָהּ:

הַלְלוּיָהּ¹ Hal'luyah.
Hal'lu avdei Adonai, hal'lu et sheim Adonai.
²Y'hi sheim Adonai m'vorach mei'attah v'ad olam.
³Mimmizrach shemesh ad m'vo'o m'hullal sheim Adonai.
⁴Ram al kol goyim Adonai, al ha-shamayim k'vodo.
⁵Mi kadonai eloheinu ha-magbihi lashavet.
⁶Ha-mashpili lir'ot ba-shamayim uva'arets.
⁷M'kimi mei'afar dal, mei'ashpot yarim evyon.
⁸L'hoshivi im n'divim, im n'divei ammo.
⁹Moshivi akeret ha-bayit eim ha-banim s'meichah.
Hal'luyah.

סדר הלל

Psalm 114

קיד

¹**בְּצֵאת** When Israel came out of Egypt,
the family of Jacob
from a people of foreign tongue,
²then Judah became God's holy place,
Israel were those God ruled.

^אבְּצֵאת יִשְׂרָאֵל מִמִּצְרָיִם
בֵּית יַעֲקֹב מֵעַם לֹעֵז:
^בהָיְתָה יְהוּדָה לְקָדְשׁוֹ
יִשְׂרָאֵל מַמְשְׁלוֹתָיו:

³The sea saw it and ran away,
Jordan turned back its course,
⁴the mountains skipped like rams,
the hills like young lambs.

^גהַיָּם רָאָה וַיָּנֹס
הַיַּרְדֵּן יִסֹּב לְאָחוֹר:
^דהֶהָרִים רָקְדוּ כְאֵילִים
גְּבָעוֹת כִּבְנֵי צֹאן:

⁵Sea! why do you run away,
Jordan! why turn back your course,
⁶mountains, why do you skip like rams,
hills like young lambs?

^המַה לְּךָ הַיָּם כִּי תָנוּס
הַיַּרְדֵּן תִּסֹּב לְאָחוֹר:
^והֶהָרִים תִּרְקְדוּ כְאֵילִים
גְּבָעוֹת כִּבְנֵי צֹאן:

⁷Earth, tremble before the Mighty One,
before the God of Jacob,
⁸who turns the rock into a pool,
the flint into a spring of water.

^זמִלִּפְנֵי אָדוֹן חוּלִי אָרֶץ
מִלִּפְנֵי אֱלוֹהַּ יַעֲקֹב:
^חהַהֹפְכִי הַצּוּר אֲגַם מָיִם
חַלָּמִישׁ לְמַעְיְנוֹ מָיִם:

¹בְּצֵאת *B'tseit yisra'el mimitsrayim, beit ya'akov mei'am lo'eiz.*
²*Hay'tah y'hudah l'kodsho, yisra'el mamsh'lotav.*
³*Ha-yam ra'ah vayanos, ha-yardein yissov l'achor.*
⁴*He-harim rak'du ch'eilim, g'va'ot kivnei tson.*
⁵*Mah l'cha ha-yam ki tanus, ha-yardein tissov l'achor.*
⁶*He-harim tirk'du ch'eilim, g'va'ot kivnei tson.*
⁷*Millifnei adon chuli arets, millifnei elo'ah ya'akov.*
⁸*Ha-hofchi ha-tsur agam mayim, challamish l'ma'y'no mayim.*

667 PSALM ANTHOLOGY — HALLEL

On Rosh Chodesh *and during the last six days of* Pesach *omit from* lo lanu *(Psalm 115:1) down to the final* ezram umaginam hu *(Psalm 115:11).*

Psalm 115 — קטו

¹**לֹא** Not to us, Eternal, not to us,
but to Your name give glory,
for the sake of Your love
and Your truth.

²Why do the nations ask:
'Where is their God?'

³Our God is in heaven,
all that God desires comes to pass.

⁴But their idols are silver and gold,
the work of human hands.

⁵They have a mouth,
but do not speak,
they have eyes, but do not see.

⁶They have ears, but do not hear,
they have a nose, but do not smell.

⁷With their hands they do not feel,
with their feet they do not walk,
they make no sound in their throat.

⁸Their makers shall
become like them,
so do all who trust in them.

¹לֹא *Lo lanu Adonai, lo lanu,*
ki l'shimcha tein kavod, al chasd'cha al amittecha.
²*Lamah yom'ru ha-goyim ayeih na eloheihem.*
³*Veiloheinu va-shamayim, kol asher chafeits asah.*
⁴*Atsabeihem kesef v'zahav, ma'aseih y'dei adam.*
⁵*Peh lahem v'lo y'dabeiru, einayim lahem v'lo yir'u.*
⁶*Oznayim lahem v'lo yishma'u, af lahem v'lo y'richun.*
⁷*Y'deihem v'lo y'mishun, ragleihem v'lo y'halleichu, lo yehgu bigronam.*
⁸*K'mohem yihyu oseihem, kol asher botei'ach bahem.*

<<<

¹לֹא לָנוּ יְהוָה לֹא לָנוּ
כִּי־לְשִׁמְךָ תֵּן כָּבוֹד
עַל חַסְדְּךָ עַל אֲמִתֶּךָ:

²לָמָּה יֹאמְרוּ הַגּוֹיִם
אַיֵּה נָא אֱלֹהֵיהֶם:

³וֵאלֹהֵינוּ בַשָּׁמָיִם
כֹּל אֲשֶׁר חָפֵץ עָשָׂה:

⁴עֲצַבֵּיהֶם כֶּסֶף וְזָהָב
מַעֲשֵׂה יְדֵי אָדָם:

⁵פֶּה לָהֶם וְלֹא יְדַבֵּרוּ
עֵינַיִם לָהֶם וְלֹא יִרְאוּ:

⁶אָזְנַיִם לָהֶם וְלֹא יִשְׁמָעוּ
אַף לָהֶם וְלֹא יְרִיחוּן:

⁷יְדֵיהֶם וְלֹא יְמִישׁוּן
רַגְלֵיהֶם וְלֹא יְהַלֵּכוּ
לֹא יֶהְגּוּ בִּגְרוֹנָם:

⁸כְּמוֹהֶם יִהְיוּ עֹשֵׂיהֶם
כֹּל אֲשֶׁר בֹּטֵחַ בָּהֶם:

[9] Israel, trust in the Eternal	ט יִשְׂרָאֵל בְּטַח בַּיהוה
- 'who is their help and their shield'.	עֶזְרָם וּמָגִנָּם הוּא:
[10] House of Aaron, trust in the Eternal	י בֵּית אַהֲרֹן בִּטְחוּ בַיהוה
- 'who is their help and their shield'.	עֶזְרָם וּמָגִנָּם הוּא:
[11] All who fear God, trust in the Eternal	יא יִרְאֵי יהוה בִּטְחוּ בַיהוה
- 'who is their help and their shield'.	עֶזְרָם וּמָגִנָּם הוּא:

[9] *Yisra'el b'tach badonai, ezram umaginnam hu.*
[10] *Beit aharon bitchu vadonai, ezram umaginnam hu.*
[11] *Yir'ei Adonai bitchu vadonai, ezram umaginnam hu.*

All Festivals (including Rosh Chodesh *and the last six days of* Pesach*) continue here.*

[12] God remembers us to bless us,	יב יהוה זְכָרָנוּ יְבָרֵךְ
blessing the house of Israel,	יְבָרֵךְ אֶת בֵּית יִשְׂרָאֵל
blessing the house of Aaron,	יְבָרֵךְ אֶת בֵּית אַהֲרֹן:
[13] blessing all God-fearing people,	יג יְבָרֵךְ יִרְאֵי יהוה
small and great alike!	הַקְּטַנִּים עִם הַגְּדֹלִים:
[14] May the Eternal increase you,	יד יֹסֵף יהוה עֲלֵיכֶם
you and your children.	עֲלֵיכֶם וְעַל בְּנֵיכֶם:
[15] You are blessed by God,	טו בְּרוּכִים אַתֶּם לַיהוה
by the Maker of heaven and earth -	עֹשֵׂה שָׁמַיִם וָאָרֶץ:
[16] heaven is the heaven of God	טז הַשָּׁמַיִם שָׁמַיִם לַיהוה
who gave the earth for human beings.	וְהָאָרֶץ נָתַן לִבְנֵי אָדָם:
[17] The dead do not praise God,	יז לֹא הַמֵּתִים יְהַלְלוּ יָהּ
nor all who go down into silence,	וְלֹא כָּל יֹרְדֵי דוּמָה
[18] but we bless God	יח וַאֲנַחְנוּ נְבָרֵךְ יָהּ
now and evermore.	מֵעַתָּה וְעַד עוֹלָם
Praise God!	הַלְלוּיָהּ:

[12] *Adonai z'charanu y'vareich, y'vareich et beit yisra'el, y'vareich et beit aharon.*
[13] *Y'vareich yir'ei Adonai, ha-k'tannim im ha-g'dolim.*
[14] *Yoseif Adonai aleichem, aleichem v'al b'neichem.*
[15] *B'ruchim attem ladonai, oseih shamayim va'arets.*
[16] *Ha-shamayim shamayim ladonai, v'ha-arets natan livnei adam.*
[17] *Lo ha-meitim y'hal'luyah, v'lo kol yor'dei dumah.*
[18] *Va'anachnu n'vareich yah mei'attah v'ad olam. Hal'luyah.*

669 PSALM ANTHOLOGY   **HALLEL**

On Rosh Chodesh *and during the last six days of* Pesach, *omit the first section of Psalm 116 (verses 1-11) and continue with* ma ashiv *(verse 12).*

Psalm 116   קטז

¹אָהַבְתִּי I love my Maker
who hears my voice, my pleading,
²whose ear is turned towards me,
therefore I pray all my days.

³The pangs of death
drew tight around me,
the horrors of the grave
took hold of me,
I found sorrow and grief;
⁴then I called
on the name of the Eternal:
'God, rescue my soul!'
⁵Merciful is the Eternal and just,
our God has compassion,
⁶protecting simple people,
saving me when I was weak.

⁷Return, my soul, to your rest,
for your Maker
has been generous to you.
⁸You rescued my soul from death,
my eye from tears
and my foot from stumbling.
⁹I shall journey
in the presence of my Maker
through the lands of the living.

¹אָהַבְתִּי Ahavti ki yishma Adonai et koli tachanunai.
²Ki hittah ozno li, uv'yamai ekra.
³Afafuni chevlei mavet, um'tsarei sh'ol m'tsa'uni, tsarah v'yagon emtsa.
⁴Uv'sheim Adonai ekra, anna Adonai mall'tah nafshi.
⁵Channun Adonai v'tsaddik, veiloheinu m'racheim.
⁶Shomeir p'ta'im Adonai, dalloti v'li y'hoshi'a.
⁷Shuvi nafshi limnuchaichi, ki Adonai gamal alaichi.
⁸Ki chillatsta nafshi mimmavet, et eini min dim'ah, et ragli middechi.
⁹Et-halleich lifnei Adonai b'artsot ha-chayim.

<<<

¹⁰I trust,
although when I spoke out,
I was deeply depressed.
¹¹I said in my panic:
'Everybody lies!'

הֶאֱמַנְתִּי כִּי אֲדַבֵּר
אֲנִי עָנִיתִי מְאֹד:
^{יא}אֲנִי אָמַרְתִּי בְחָפְזִי
כָּל־הָאָדָם כֹּזֵב:

¹⁰*He'emanti ki adabbeir, ani aniti m'od.*
¹¹*Ani amarti v'chofzi, kol ha-adam kozeiv.*

All Festivals, including Rosh Chodesh *and the last six days of* Pesach, *continue here.*

¹²What can I return to my Maker
for all the kindness shown me?
¹³I will lift up the cup of salvation
and call on the name of the Eternal.
¹⁴I will fulfil my promises to the Eternal
in the presence of godly people.

¹⁵Precious in the sight of our Creator
are those who die, devoted to God.
¹⁶Because I am Your servant, God,
I am Your servant,
the child of a woman who served You,
You freed me from my bonds.
¹⁷To You I offer the offering of gratitude
and call on the name of the Eternal.
¹⁸I will fulfil my promises to the Eternal
in the presence of all God's people,
¹⁹in the courts of the house of the Eternal,
in your midst, Jerusalem!

Praise God!

^{יב}מָה־אָשִׁיב לַיהוה
כָּל־תַּגְמוּלוֹהִי עָלָי:
^{יג}כּוֹס־יְשׁוּעוֹת אֶשָּׂא
וּבְשֵׁם יהוה אֶקְרָא:
^{יד}נְדָרַי לַיהוה אֲשַׁלֵּם
נֶגְדָה־נָּא לְכָל־עַמּוֹ:

^{טו}יָקָר בְּעֵינֵי יהוה
הַמָּוְתָה לַחֲסִידָיו:
^{טז}אָנָּה יהוה כִּי־אֲנִי עַבְדֶּךָ
אֲנִי־עַבְדְּךָ בֶּן־אֲמָתֶךָ
פִּתַּחְתָּ לְמוֹסֵרָי:
^{יז}לְךָ־אֶזְבַּח זֶבַח תּוֹדָה
וּבְשֵׁם יהוה אֶקְרָא:
^{יח}נְדָרַי לַיהוה אֲשַׁלֵּם
נֶגְדָה־נָּא לְכָל־עַמּוֹ:
^{יט}בְּחַצְרוֹת בֵּית יהוה
בְּתוֹכֵכִי יְרוּשָׁלָיִם
הַלְלוּיָהּ:

¹²*Mah ashiv ladonai kol tagmulohi alai.*
¹³*Kos y'shu'ot essa, uv'sheim Adonai ekra.*
¹⁴*N'darai ladonai ashalleim, negdah na l'chol ammo.*
¹⁵*Yakar b'einei Adonai ha-mav'tah lachasidav.*
¹⁶*Anna Adonai ki ani avdecha, ani avd'cha ben amatecha, pitachta l'moseirai.*
¹⁷*L'cha ezbach zevach todah, uv'sheim Adonai ekra.*
¹⁸*N'darai ladonai ashalleim, negdah na l'chol ammo.*
¹⁹*B'chatsrot beit Adonai, b'tocheichi yerushalayim.*
Hal'luyah.

Psalm 117

קיז

¹הַלְלוּ Praise the Creator, all nations,
glorify God, all peoples!
²Whose love for us is strong,
whose truth is eternal.

אהַלְלוּ אֶת יהוה כָּל־גּוֹיִם
שַׁבְּחוּהוּ כָּל־הָאֻמִּים:
בכִּי גָבַר עָלֵינוּ חַסְדּוֹ
וֶאֱמֶת יהוה לְעוֹלָם

Praise God!

הַלְלוּיָהּ:

¹הַלְלוּ *Hal'lu et Adonai kol goyim, shabb'chuhu kol ha-ummim.*
²*Ki gavar aleinu chasdo, ve'emet Adonai l'olam.*
Hal'luyah.

Psalm 118

קיח

¹הוֹדוּ Give thanks to God who is good,
whose love is everlasting.
²Let Israel now say:
'whose love is everlasting.'
³Let the house of Aaron now say:
'whose love is everlasting.'
⁴Let all who fear God now say:
'whose love is everlasting.'
⁵Closed in by troubles
I called on the Eternal,
who answered me and set me free.
⁶The Eternal is for me, I shall not fear.
What can people do to me?
⁷The Eternal is for me,
my source of help,
so I confront those who hate me!

אהוֹדוּ לַיהוה כִּי־טוֹב
כִּי לְעוֹלָם חַסְדּוֹ:
ביֹאמַר־נָא יִשְׂרָאֵל
כִּי לְעוֹלָם חַסְדּוֹ:
גיֹאמְרוּ־נָא בֵית־אַהֲרֹן
כִּי לְעוֹלָם חַסְדּוֹ:
דיֹאמְרוּ־נָא יִרְאֵי יהוה
כִּי לְעוֹלָם חַסְדּוֹ:
המִן הַמֵּצַר קָרָאתִי יָּהּ
עָנָנִי בַמֶּרְחָב יָהּ:
ויהוה לִי לֹא אִירָא
מַה יַּעֲשֶׂה לִי אָדָם:
זיהוה לִי בְּעֹזְרָי
וַאֲנִי אֶרְאֶה בְשֹׂנְאָי:

¹הוֹדוּ *Hodu ladonai ki tov, ki l'olam chasdo.*
²*Yomar na yisra'el, ki l'olam chasdo.*
³*Yom'ru na veit Aharon, ki l'olam chasdo.*
⁴*Yom'ru na yir'ei Adonai, ki l'olam chasdo.*
⁵*Min ha-meitsar karati yah, anani vamerchav yah.*
⁶*Adonai li lo ira, mah ya'aseh li adam.*
⁷*Adonai li b'ozrai, va'ani er'eh v'son'ai.*

<<<

[8] It is better to trust in the Eternal than to rely on people.	ח טוֹב לַחֲסוֹת בַּיהוה מִבְּטֹחַ בָּאָדָם:
[9] It is better to trust in the Eternal than to rely on leaders.	ט טוֹב לַחֲסוֹת בַּיהוה מִבְּטֹחַ בִּנְדִיבִים:
[10] All nations surrounded me - but by the name of the Eternal I cut them down.	י כָּל־גּוֹיִם סְבָבוּנִי בְּשֵׁם יהוה כִּי אֲמִילַם:
[11] They swarmed and surrounded me - but by the name of the Eternal I cut them down.	יא סַבּוּנִי גַם־סְבָבוּנִי בְּשֵׁם יהוה כִּי אֲמִילַם:
[12] They swarmed around me like bees, they were quenched like a fire among thorns - but by the name of the Eternal I cut them down.	יב סַבּוּנִי כִדְבֹרִים דֹּעֲכוּ כְּאֵשׁ קוֹצִים בְּשֵׁם יהוה כִּי אֲמִילַם:
[13] You pressed me so that I nearly fell, but the Eternal helped me.	יג דָּחֹה דְחִיתַנִי לִנְפֹּל וַיהוה עֲזָרָנִי:
[14] God is my strength and song, Always there to save me.	יד עָזִּי וְזִמְרָת יָהּ וַיְהִי־לִי לִישׁוּעָה:
[15] Shouts of joy and triumph are in the tents of the just:	טו קוֹל רִנָּה וִישׁוּעָה בְּאָהֳלֵי צַדִּיקִים
'God's right hand works mightily!	יְמִין יהוה עֹשָׂה חָיִל:
[16] God's right hand is raised! God's right hand works mightily!'	טז יְמִין יהוה רוֹמֵמָה יְמִין יהוה עֹשָׂה חָיִל:

[8] Tov lachasot badonai mib'to'ach ba-adam.
[9] Tov lachasot badonai mib'to'ach bindivim.
[10] Kol goyim s'vavuni b'sheim Adonai ki amilam.
[11] Sabbuni gam s'vavuni b'sheim Adonai ki amilam.
[12] Sabbuni chidvorim, do'achu k'eish kotsim, b'sheim Adonai ki amilam.
[13] Dacho d'chitani linpol, vadonai azarani.
[14] Ozzi v'zimrat yah vay'hi li lishu'ah.
[15] Kol rinnah viyshu'ah b'oholei tsaddikim, y'min Adonai osah chayil.
[16] Y'min Adonai rommeimah, y'min Adonai osah chayil.

<<<

¹⁷I shall not die, but live and declare the acts of God. ¹⁸God has taught me sharply but has not surrendered me to death. ¹⁹Open the gates of justice for me, I shall enter them and thank the Eternal.	יזלֹא־אָמוּת כִּי־אֶחְיֶה וַאֲסַפֵּר מַעֲשֵׂי יָהּ: יחיַסֹּר יִסְּרַנִּי יָהּ וְלַמָּוֶת לֹא נְתָנָנִי: יטפִּתְחוּ־לִי שַׁעֲרֵי־צֶדֶק אָבֹא בָם אוֹדֶה יָהּ:
²⁰This is the gate of the Eternal, the just may enter in. ²¹I thank You, for You answered me, it was You who saved me.	כזֶה־הַשַּׁעַר לַיהוה צַדִּיקִים יָבֹאוּ בוֹ: כאאוֹדְךָ כִּי עֲנִיתָנִי וַתְּהִי־לִי לִישׁוּעָה:
²²A stone the builders rejected has become the corner-stone itself. ²³Through God this came about, this wonder to our eyes. ²⁴This is the day God has made, let us be glad and rejoice on it.	כבאֶבֶן מָאֲסוּ הַבּוֹנִים הָיְתָה לְרֹאשׁ פִּנָּה: כגמֵאֵת יהוה הָיְתָה זֹּאת הִיא נִפְלָאת בְּעֵינֵינוּ: כדזֶה־הַיּוֹם עָשָׂה יהוה נָגִילָה וְנִשְׂמְחָה בוֹ:

²⁵God, we beseech You,
    save us now!
God, we beseech You,
    let us prosper now!
	כהאָנָּא יהוה הוֹשִׁיעָה נָּא:
	אָנָּא יהוה הַצְלִיחָה נָּא:

²⁶Blessed is the one who comes in God's name, we bless you from the house of God.	כובָּרוּךְ הַבָּא בְּשֵׁם יהוה בֵּרַכְנוּכֶם מִבֵּית יהוה:

¹⁷*Lo amut ki echyeh, va'asapeir ma'asei yah.*
¹⁸*Yassor yiss'ranni yah, v'la-mavet lo n'tanani.*
¹⁹*Pitchu li sha'arei tsedek, avo vam, odeh yah.*
²⁰*Zeh ha-sha'ar ladonai, tsaddikim yavo'u vo.*
²¹*Od'cha ki anitani, vatt'hi li lishu'ah.*
²²*Even ma'asu ha-bonim hay'tah l'rosh pinnah.*
²³*Mei'eit Adonai hay'tah zot, hi niflat b'eineinu.*
²⁴*Zeh ha-yom asah Adonai, nagilah v'nism'chah vo.*
²⁵*Anna Adonai hoshi'ah na. Anna Adonai hatslichah na.*
²⁶*Baruch ha-ba b'sheim Adonai, beirachnuchem mibbeit Adonai.*

²⁷God is the Creator who gives us light.
(Form the procession with the branches
up to the horns of the altar.)
²⁸You are my God and I thank You.
My God, I praise You!

²⁹Thank the Eternal, who is good,
whose love is everlasting.

כז אֵל יהוה וַיָּאֶר לָנוּ
אִסְרוּ־חַג בַּעֲבֹתִים
עַד־קַרְנוֹת הַמִּזְבֵּחַ:
כח אֵלִי אַתָּה וְאוֹדֶךָּ
אֱלֹהַי אֲרוֹמְמֶךָּ:

כט הוֹדוּ לַיהוה כִּי טוֹב
כִּי לְעוֹלָם חַסְדּוֹ:

²⁷Eil Adonai vaya'eir lanu, isru chag ba'avotim ad karnot ha-mizbei'ach.
²⁸Eili attah v'odeka, elohai arom'meka.
²⁹Hodu ladonai ki tov, ki l'olam chasdo.

After the Hallel, *the following blessing may be said.*

יְהַלְלוּךָ Our Living God, all Your works shall praise You; and all who love You, the righteous who do Your will, and all Your people, the family of Israel, shall thank You with joyful song; and bless and praise and sanctify You, accepting You as our Sovereign. It is good to thank You and it is right to sing to Your name, for You are God from everlasting to everlasting. Blessed are You God, the Sovereign praised in all worship.

יְהַלְלוּךָ יהוה אֱלֹהֵינוּ כָּל־מַעֲשֶׂיךָ.
וַחֲסִידֶיךָ צַדִּיקִים עוֹשֵׂי רְצוֹנֶךָ
וְכָל־עַמְּךָ בֵּית יִשְׂרָאֵל בְּרִנָּה יוֹדוּ
וִיבָרְכוּ וִישַׁבְּחוּ וִיפָאֲרוּ וִירוֹמְמוּ
וְיַעֲרִיצוּ וְיַקְדִּישׁוּ וְיַמְלִיכוּ אֶת־
שִׁמְךָ מַלְכֵּנוּ. כִּי לְךָ טוֹב לְהוֹדוֹת
וּלְשִׁמְךָ נָאֶה לְזַמֵּר כִּי מֵעוֹלָם וְעַד
עוֹלָם אַתָּה אֵל: בָּרוּךְ אַתָּה יהוה
מֶלֶךְ מְהֻלָּל בַּתִּשְׁבָּחוֹת:

¹**יְהַלְלוּךָ** Y'hal'lucha Adonai eloheinu kol ma'asecha, vachasidecha tsaddikim osei r'tsonecha, v'chol amm'cha beit yisra'el, b'rinnah yodu vivar'chu vishabb'chu vifa'aru virom'mu v'ya'aritsu v'yakdishu v'yamlichu et shimcha malkeinu, ki l'cha tov l'hodot, ul'shimcha na'eh l'zammeir, ki mei'olam v'ad olam attah eil. Baruch attah Adonai melech m'hullal ba-tishbachot.

Psalm 121 can be found on page 179.

PSALM ANTHOLOGY

Psalm 122

¹A Pilgrim Song. David's
שָׂמַחְתִּיI rejoiced
when they said to me:
'Let us go to the house of the Eternal!'
²And now our feet are standing
inside your gates, O Jerusalem!

³Jerusalem rebuilt!
As a city
where all are united together.
⁴Here the tribes came up,
the tribes of the Eternal
- for it is a mark of Israel
to thank the name
of the Eternal.
⁵There were
the seats of justice,
the thrones
of the house of David.
⁶Pray for the peace of Jerusalem,
may those
who love you prosper.
⁷Peace be within your walls,
tranquillity inside your homes.

⁸For the sake
of my brothers and friends
I call out, 'Peace be with you!'
⁹For the sake
of the house of the Eternal our God,
I will seek your good.

קכב

א שִׁיר הַמַּעֲלוֹת לְדָוִד
שָׂמַחְתִּי בְּאֹמְרִים לִי
בֵּית יהוה נֵלֵךְ:
ב עֹמְדוֹת הָיוּ רַגְלֵינוּ
בִּשְׁעָרַיִךְ יְרוּשָׁלָיִם:

ג יְרוּשָׁלַיִם הַבְּנוּיָה
כְּעִיר שֶׁחֻבְּרָה־לָּהּ יַחְדָּו:
ד שֶׁשָּׁם עָלוּ שְׁבָטִים
שִׁבְטֵי־יָהּ
עֵדוּת לְיִשְׂרָאֵל
לְהֹדוֹת לְשֵׁם יהוה:
ה כִּי שָׁמָּה יָשְׁבוּ
כִסְאוֹת לְמִשְׁפָּט
כִּסְאוֹת לְבֵית דָּוִד:
ו שַׁאֲלוּ שְׁלוֹם יְרוּשָׁלָיִם
יִשְׁלָיוּ אֹהֲבָיִךְ:
ז יְהִי־שָׁלוֹם בְּחֵילֵךְ
שַׁלְוָה בְּאַרְמְנוֹתָיִךְ:

ח לְמַעַן־אַחַי וְרֵעָי
אֲדַבְּרָה־נָּא שָׁלוֹם בָּךְ:
ט לְמַעַן בֵּית־יהוה אֱלֹהֵינוּ
אֲבַקְשָׁה טוֹב לָךְ:

Psalm 124 — קכד

שִׁיר הַמַּעֲלוֹת לְדָוִד
לוּלֵי יהוה שֶׁהָיָה לָנוּ
יֹאמַר־נָא יִשְׂרָאֵל:
לוּלֵי יהוה שֶׁהָיָה לָנוּ
בְּקוּם עָלֵינוּ אָדָם:
אֲזַי חַיִּים בְּלָעוּנוּ
בַּחֲרוֹת אַפָּם בָּנוּ:
אֲזַי הַמַּיִם שְׁטָפוּנוּ
נַחְלָה עָבַר עַל־נַפְשֵׁנוּ:
אֲזַי עָבַר עַל־נַפְשֵׁנוּ
הַמַּיִם הַזֵּידוֹנִים:
בָּרוּךְ יהוה שֶׁלֹּא נְתָנָנוּ
טֶרֶף לְשִׁנֵּיהֶם:
נַפְשֵׁנוּ כְּצִפּוֹר
נִמְלְטָה מִפַּח יוֹקְשִׁים
הַפַּח נִשְׁבָּר
וַאֲנַחְנוּ נִמְלָטְנוּ:
עֶזְרֵנוּ בְּשֵׁם יהוה עֹשֵׂה
שָׁמַיִם וָאָרֶץ:

¹A Pilgrim Song. David's.
לוּלֵי 'If God had not been for us,'
 - let Israel repeat it,
²'If God had not been for us,
 when people rose up against us,
³they would have swallowed us up alive
 in their burning rage at us;
⁴the waters would have overwhelmed us,
 a torrent sweeping over our souls;
⁵they would have swept away our lives,
 the high and mighty waters!'

⁶Blessed is God
 who did not make us a prey to their teeth.
⁷Our soul is like a bird
 that escaped from the fowlers' trap.
 The trap itself is smashed
 and we have escaped.
⁸Our help is in God's name,
 the maker of heaven and earth.

Psalm 125 — קכה

שִׁיר הַמַּעֲלוֹת
הַבֹּטְחִים בַּיהוה כְּהַר־צִיּוֹן
לֹא־יִמּוֹט לְעוֹלָם יֵשֵׁב:
יְרוּשָׁלִַם הָרִים סָבִיב לָהּ
וַיהוה סָבִיב לְעַמּוֹ
מֵעַתָּה וְעַד־עוֹלָם:
כִּי לֹא יָנוּחַ שֵׁבֶט הָרֶשַׁע
עַל גּוֹרַל הַצַּדִּיקִים
לְמַעַן לֹא־יִשְׁלְחוּ הַצַּדִּיקִים
בְּעַוְלָתָה יְדֵיהֶם:

¹A Pilgrim Song.
הַבֹּטְחִים Those who trust in God
 are like Mount Zion,
 unshakeable, enduring forever.
²Jerusalem!
 surrounded by mountains,
 just as God surrounds this people
 now and forever.
³For the rod of the wicked
 shall not rest
 on the heritage of the righteous.
 So the righteous shall not put
 their hand to injustice.

<<<

677 PSALM ANTHOLOGY

⁴God, do good to the good,
to those with honest hearts.
⁵But opportunists
who turn to crooked ways,
God will send them away
with those who do evil.

        Peace upon Israel!

הֵיטִיבָה יהוה לַטּוֹבִים
וְלִישָׁרִים בְּלִבּוֹתָם:
וְהַמַּטִּים עֲקַלְקַלּוֹתָם
יוֹלִיכֵם יהוה
אֶת־פֹּעֲלֵי הָאָוֶן
שָׁלוֹם עַל־יִשְׂרָאֵל:

Psalm 126 can be found on page 464.

Psalm 127

¹A Pilgrim Song. Solomon's.
אִם Unless God builds the house,
its builders toil in vain.
Unless God guards the city
the sentry keeps watch in vain.

²It is vain for you to rise up early,
or to sit up late,
toiling for the bread you eat,
for it comes
to those God loves while they sleep.

³Children are a gift of God,
a reward, the fruit of the womb.
⁴Like arrows in the hand of a fighter
are the children of one's youth.

⁵Happy are they
who have filled their quiver with them.
Such people shall not be put to shame
when they confront their enemies at the gate.

קכז

שִׁיר הַמַּעֲלוֹת לִשְׁלֹמֹה
אִם־יהוה לֹא־יִבְנֶה בַיִת
שָׁוְא עָמְלוּ בוֹנָיו בּוֹ
אִם־יהוה לֹא־יִשְׁמָר־עִיר
שָׁוְא שָׁקַד שׁוֹמֵר:
שָׁוְא לָכֶם מַשְׁכִּימֵי קוּם
מְאַחֲרֵי־שֶׁבֶת
אֹכְלֵי לֶחֶם הָעֲצָבִים
כֵּן יִתֵּן
לִידִידוֹ שֵׁנָא:
הִנֵּה נַחֲלַת יהוה בָּנִים
שָׂכָר פְּרִי הַבָּטֶן:
כְּחִצִּים בְּיַד־גִּבּוֹר
כֵּן בְּנֵי הַנְּעוּרִים:
אַשְׁרֵי הַגֶּבֶר אֲשֶׁר מִלֵּא
אֶת־אַשְׁפָּתוֹ מֵהֶם
לֹא יֵבֹשׁוּ כִּי־יְדַבְּרוּ
אֶת־אוֹיְבִים בַּשָּׁעַר:

Psalm 128 can be found on page 304.

Psalm 130

¹A Pilgrim Song.
מִמַּעֲמַקִּים Out of the depths
I called to You, God,
²God, hear my voice.
Let Your ears listen
to the voice of my pleading.

³God, if You should mark sins,
O God, who could stand?
⁴But with You there is forgiveness,
for this You are held in awe.

⁵I hope in God, my soul has hope,
and for God's word I wait.
⁶My soul waits for God
more than watchmen for the morning,
watching for the morning.

⁷Israel, hope in God,
for with God is constant love,
and great power to redeem.

⁸It is God who redeems Israel
from all their sins.

Psalm 131

¹A Pilgrim Song. David's.
יהוה O God, my heart is not proud,
my eyes are not ambitious.
I am not busy with things too great
or too wonderful for me.

²Have I not set my soul
in quietness and peace;
like a child at its mother's breast,
my soul is like a weaned child.

³O Israel, hope in God
now and forever!

קל

אשִׁיר הַמַּעֲלוֹת
מִמַּעֲמַקִּים קְרָאתִיךָ יהוה:
באֲדֹנָי שִׁמְעָה בְקוֹלִי
תִּהְיֶינָה אָזְנֶיךָ קַשֻּׁבוֹת
לְקוֹל תַּחֲנוּנָי:

גאִם־עֲוֹנוֹת תִּשְׁמָר־יָהּ
אֲדֹנָי מִי יַעֲמֹד:
דכִּי־עִמְּךָ הַסְּלִיחָה לְמַעַן תִּוָּרֵא:

הקִוִּיתִי יהוה קִוְּתָה נַפְשִׁי
וְלִדְבָרוֹ הוֹחָלְתִּי:
ונַפְשִׁי לַאדֹנָי
מִשֹּׁמְרִים לַבֹּקֶר שֹׁמְרִים לַבֹּקֶר:

זיַחֵל יִשְׂרָאֵל אֶל־יהוה
כִּי־עִם־יהוה הַחֶסֶד
וְהַרְבֵּה עִמּוֹ פְדוּת:

חוְהוּא יִפְדֶּה אֶת־יִשְׂרָאֵל
מִכֹּל עֲוֹנֹתָיו:

קלא

אשִׁיר הַמַּעֲלוֹת לְדָוִד
יהוה לֹא־גָבַהּ לִבִּי וְלֹא־רָמוּ עֵינַי
וְלֹא־הִלַּכְתִּי בִּגְדֹלוֹת
וּבְנִפְלָאוֹת מִמֶּנִּי:

באִם־לֹא שִׁוִּיתִי וְדוֹמַמְתִּי נַפְשִׁי
כְּגָמֻל עֲלֵי אִמּוֹ
כַּגָּמֻל עָלַי נַפְשִׁי:

גיַחֵל יִשְׂרָאֵל אֶל־יהוה
מֵעַתָּה וְעַד־עוֹלָם:

PSALM ANTHOLOGY

Psalm 133

¹A Pilgrim Song. David's.
הִנֵּה How good it is
and how pleasant
when brothers live in unity together.

²It is like precious oil on the head,
running down upon the beard,
running down from Aaron's beard
upon the collar of his robes.

³It is like the dew of Hermon,
falling on the hills of Zion
where God proclaimed the blessing,
life forever!

קלג

אשִׁיר הַמַּעֲלוֹת לְדָוִד
הִנֵּה מַה־טּוֹב וּמַה־נָּעִים
שֶׁבֶת אַחִים גַּם־יָחַד:

בכְּשֶׁמֶן הַטּוֹב עַל־הָרֹאשׁ
יֹרֵד עַל־הַזָּקָן
זְקַן־אַהֲרֹן שֶׁיֹּרֵד עַל־פִּי מִדּוֹתָיו:

גכְּטַל־חֶרְמוֹן
שֶׁיֹּרֵד עַל־הַרְרֵי צִיּוֹן
כִּי שָׁם צִוָּה יְהוָה אֶת־הַבְּרָכָה
חַיִּים עַד־הָעוֹלָם:

Psalm 134 can be found on page 66.

Psalm 137 (1-6)

¹עַל By the rivers of Babylon
there we sat. Yes, we wept
as we remembered Zion.
²There upon the willows
we hung up our harps.

³For it was there our captors
asked for songs,
our tormentors for joy:
'Sing us one of the songs of Zion!'
⁴How could we sing God's song
in a strange land!

⁵If I forget you, O Jerusalem,
let my right hand
forget its cunning.
⁶Let my tongue
stick to the roof of my mouth,
if I do not remember you,
if I do not put Jerusalem
above my highest joy.

קלז (א-ו)

אעַל־נַהֲרוֹת בָּבֶל שָׁם יָשַׁבְנוּ
גַּם־בָּכִינוּ בְּזָכְרֵנוּ אֶת־צִיּוֹן:
בעַל־עֲרָבִים בְּתוֹכָהּ
תָּלִינוּ כִּנֹּרוֹתֵינוּ:

גכִּי שָׁם שְׁאֵלוּנוּ שׁוֹבֵינוּ דִּבְרֵי־שִׁיר
וְתוֹלָלֵינוּ שִׂמְחָה
שִׁירוּ לָנוּ מִשִּׁיר צִיּוֹן:
דאֵיךְ נָשִׁיר אֶת־שִׁיר־יְהוָה
עַל אַדְמַת נֵכָר:

האִם־אֶשְׁכָּחֵךְ יְרוּשָׁלִָם
תִּשְׁכַּח יְמִינִי:
ותִּדְבַּק־לְשׁוֹנִי לְחִכִּי
אִם־לֹא אֶזְכְּרֵכִי
אִם־לֹא אַעֲלֶה אֶת־יְרוּשָׁלִַם
עַל רֹאשׁ שִׂמְחָתִי:

קלח

אָלְדָוִד
אוֹדְךָ בְכָל־לִבִּי
נֶגֶד אֱלֹהִים אֲזַמְּרֶךָּ:
בּאֶשְׁתַּחֲוֶה אֶל־הֵיכַל קָדְשְׁךָ
וְאוֹדֶה אֶת־שְׁמֶךָ
עַל־חַסְדְּךָ וְעַל־אֲמִתֶּךָ
כִּי־הִגְדַּלְתָּ
עַל־כָּל־שִׁמְךָ אִמְרָתֶךָ:
גבְּיוֹם קָרָאתִי וַתַּעֲנֵנִי
תַּרְהִבֵנִי בְנַפְשִׁי עֹז:

דיוֹדוּךָ יְהֹוָה כָּל־מַלְכֵי־אָרֶץ
כִּי שָׁמְעוּ אִמְרֵי־פִיךָ:
הוְיָשִׁירוּ בְּדַרְכֵי יְהֹוָה
כִּי גָדוֹל כְּבוֹד יְהֹוָה:

וכִּי־רָם יְהֹוָה וְשָׁפָל יִרְאֶה
וְגָבֹהַּ מִמֶּרְחָק יְיֵדָע:
זאִם־אֵלֵךְ בְּקֶרֶב צָרָה
תְּחַיֵּנִי
עַל אַף אֹיְבַי תִּשְׁלַח יָדֶךָ
וְתוֹשִׁיעֵנִי יְמִינֶךָ:

חיְהֹוָה יִגְמֹר בַּעֲדִי
יְהֹוָה חַסְדְּךָ לְעוֹלָם
מַעֲשֵׂי יָדֶיךָ אַל־תֶּרֶף:

Psalm 138
¹David's.
אוֹדְךָ I thank You, God, with all my heart.
In the presence of the mighty
I sing Your praise.
²I bow down
towards the temple of Your holiness,
I give thanks to Your name
for Your loyalty and love
because it is Your nature
to exceed Your promise.
³In the day I called,
You answered me
and increased the strength of my soul.

⁴All the kings on earth
give thanks to You,
for they have heard
the words of Your mouth.
⁵They sing of God's ways:
'Great is the glory of God!'

⁶Though raised on high,
God regards the lowly,
but marks the haughty from afar.
⁷Though I walk in the midst of sorrow
You keep me alive.
You set Your hand
against the wrath of my enemies
and Your right hand saves me.

⁸God's purpose for me will be fulfilled.
God, Your love endures forever,
do not abandon
the work of Your hands!

PSALM ANTHOLOGY

Psalm 139 (1-18, 23-24)

[1] For the Choirmaster. David's Psalm.
יהוה God, You searched me,
and You know me.
[2] You know all - whether I sit or stand,
reading my thoughts from far away.

[3] You watched my journey
and my resting-place,
familiar with all my ways.
[4] For there is not a word on my tongue
but You know it already,
through and through.
[5] You closed me in,
behind me and before me,
laying Your hand upon me.
[6] Such knowledge
is too wonderful for me,
too high, beyond my reach.

[7] Where could I go from Your spirit,
or where could I flee
from Your presence?
[8] If I climb to heaven,
You are there,
there too, if I lie in the depths.
[9] If I fly on wings to the dawn
and dwell at the sea's horizon,
[10] even there
Your hand would lead me,
Your right hand would hold me.
[11] If I ask darkness to cover me
and light to be night around me,
[12] that darkness
would not be dark to You,
but night as bright as day
and darkness like the light.

<<<

קלט (א–יח, כג–כד)

א לַמְנַצֵּחַ לְדָוִד מִזְמוֹר
יְהוָה חֲקַרְתַּנִי וַתֵּדָע:
ב אַתָּה יָדַעְתָּ שִׁבְתִּי וְקוּמִי
בַּנְתָּה לְרֵעִי מֵרָחוֹק:

ג אָרְחִי וְרִבְעִי זֵרִיתָ
וְכָל־דְּרָכַי הִסְכַּנְתָּה:
ד כִּי אֵין מִלָּה בִּלְשׁוֹנִי
הֵן יְהוָה יָדַעְתָּ כֻלָּהּ:
ה אָחוֹר וָקֶדֶם צַרְתָּנִי
וַתָּשֶׁת עָלַי כַּפֶּכָה:
ו פְּלִאָיָה דַעַת מִמֶּנִּי
נִשְׂגְּבָה לֹא־אוּכַל לָהּ:

ז אָנָה אֵלֵךְ מֵרוּחֶךָ
וְאָנָה מִפָּנֶיךָ אֶבְרָח:
ח אִם־אֶסַּק שָׁמַיִם שָׁם אָתָּה
וְאַצִּיעָה שְּׁאוֹל הִנֶּךָּ:
ט אֶשָּׂא כַנְפֵי־שָׁחַר
אֶשְׁכְּנָה בְּאַחֲרִית יָם:
י גַּם־שָׁם
יָדְךָ תַנְחֵנִי וְתֹאחֲזֵנִי יְמִינֶךָ:
יא וָאֹמַר אַךְ־חֹשֶׁךְ יְשׁוּפֵנִי
וְלַיְלָה אוֹר בַּעֲדֵנִי:
יב גַּם־חֹשֶׁךְ לֹא־יַחְשִׁיךְ מִמֶּךָּ
וְלַיְלָה כַּיּוֹם יָאִיר
כַּחֲשֵׁיכָה כָּאוֹרָה:

¹³For it is You
who created my innermost being,
knit me together in my mother's womb.
¹⁴I thank You
for the awesome wonder that I am,
for the wonder of Your works.
How well my soul knows it!
¹⁵My body was no mystery to You
when I was made in secret,
knit together deep in the earth.
¹⁶Your eyes
saw my unformed substance,
all my actions
were written down in Your book.
The days were determined
even before they had yet occurred.
¹⁷God, how precious
are Your thoughts to me,
how vast the sum of them.
¹⁸If I try to count them,
they are more than the sand
and even if I reach the end,
You would still be with me.

²³Search me, God, and know my heart,
test me, and know my thoughts.
²⁴See if the path to despair
is within me,
and lead me in the path of eternity.

Psalm 143
¹A Psalm of David.
יהוה God, hear my prayer,
listen to my pleading.
In Your faithfulness and justice
answer me
²and let not Your servant be tried,
for no one is truly just
in Your sight.

<<<

קמג

ᵃמִזְמוֹר לְדָוִד
יְהוָה שְׁמַע תְּפִלָּתִי
הַאֲזִינָה אֶל־תַּחֲנוּנַי
בֶּאֱמֻנָתְךָ עֲנֵנִי בְּצִדְקָתֶךָ׃
ᵇוְאַל־תָּבוֹא בְמִשְׁפָּט אֶת־עַבְדֶּךָ
כִּי לֹא־יִצְדַּק לְפָנֶיךָ כָל־חָי׃

ᵍכִּי־אַתָּה קָנִיתָ כִלְיֹתָי
תְּסֻכֵּנִי בְּבֶטֶן אִמִּי׃
ᵈאוֹדְךָ עַל כִּי נוֹרָאוֹת נִפְלֵיתִי
נִפְלָאִים מַעֲשֶׂיךָ
וְנַפְשִׁי יֹדַעַת מְאֹד׃
ᵗᵛלֹא־נִכְחַד עָצְמִי מִמֶּךָּ
אֲשֶׁר־עֻשֵּׂיתִי בַסֵּתֶר
רֻקַּמְתִּי בְּתַחְתִּיּוֹת אָרֶץ׃
ᵗᵘגָּלְמִי רָאוּ עֵינֶיךָ
וְעַל־סִפְרְךָ כֻּלָּם יִכָּתֵבוּ
יָמִים יֻצָּרוּ
וְלֹא אֶחָד בָּהֶם׃
ᶻוְלִי מַה־יָּקְרוּ רֵעֶיךָ אֵל
מֶה עָצְמוּ רָאשֵׁיהֶם׃
ᶜאֶסְפְּרֵם מֵחוֹל יִרְבּוּן
הֱקִיצֹתִי
וְעוֹדִי עִמָּךְ׃

ᵏᵍחָקְרֵנִי אֵל וְדַע לְבָבִי
בְּחָנֵנִי וְדַע שַׂרְעַפָּי׃
ᵏᵈוּרְאֵה אִם־דֶּרֶךְ־עֹצֶב בִּי
וּנְחֵנִי בְּדֶרֶךְ עוֹלָם׃

683 PSALM ANTHOLOGY

³For the enemy persecutes me
to crush my life into the ground.
He made me dwell in darkness
like the dead of long ago,
⁴and my spirit
was faint within me,
great fear inside my heart.

⁵I remember the days that are past,
I meditate on all You did,
I muse on the work of Your hands.
⁶I stretch out my hands to You.
My soul thirsts for You
like parched land   (selah).

⁷Make haste to answer me, God!
My spirit fails.
Do not hide Your face from me
lest I go down to the grave
like the rest.

⁸In the morning
bring tidings of Your love,
for in You I trust.
Show me the way that I should walk,
for I put my hope in You.

⁹Deliver me from my enemies, God.
I take shelter in You.

¹⁰Teach me to do Your will,
for You are my God.
Let Your good spirit guide me
on to gentle ground.

¹¹God, for Your name's sake
save my life.
In Your justice
bring my soul from trouble.
¹²In Your faithfulness
cut off my enemies
and destroy my oppressors,
for I am Your servant.

גכִּי רָדַף אוֹיֵב נַפְשִׁי
דִּכָּא לָאָרֶץ חַיָּתִי
הוֹשִׁיבַנִי בְמַחֲשַׁכִּים כְּמֵתֵי עוֹלָם:
דוַתִּתְעַטֵּף עָלַי רוּחִי
בְּתוֹכִי יִשְׁתּוֹמֵם לִבִּי:

הזָכַרְתִּי יָמִים מִקֶּדֶם
הָגִיתִי בְכָל־פָּעֳלֶךָ
בְּמַעֲשֵׂה יָדֶיךָ אֲשׂוֹחֵחַ:
וּפֵרַשְׂתִּי יָדַי אֵלֶיךָ
נַפְשִׁי כְּאֶרֶץ־עֲיֵפָה לְךָ   סֶלָה:

זמַהֵר עֲנֵנִי יְהוָה כָּלְתָה רוּחִי
אַל־תַּסְתֵּר פָּנֶיךָ מִמֶּנִּי
וְנִמְשַׁלְתִּי עִם־יֹרְדֵי בוֹר:

חהַשְׁמִיעֵנִי בַבֹּקֶר חַסְדֶּךָ
כִּי־בְךָ בָטָחְתִּי
הוֹדִיעֵנִי דֶּרֶךְ־זוּ אֵלֵךְ
כִּי־אֵלֶיךָ נָשָׂאתִי נַפְשִׁי:

טהַצִּילֵנִי מֵאֹיְבַי יְהוָה
אֵלֶיךָ כִסִּתִי:

ילַמְּדֵנִי לַעֲשׂוֹת רְצוֹנֶךָ
כִּי־אַתָּה אֱלוֹהָי
רוּחֲךָ טוֹבָה תַּנְחֵנִי בְּאֶרֶץ מִישׁוֹר:

יאלְמַעַן־שִׁמְךָ יְהוָה תְּחַיֵּנִי
בְּצִדְקָתְךָ תּוֹצִיא מִצָּרָה נַפְשִׁי:
יבוּבְחַסְדְּךָ תַּצְמִית אֹיְבָי
וְהַאֲבַדְתָּ כָּל־צֹרֲרֵי נַפְשִׁי
כִּי אֲנִי עַבְדֶּךָ:

Psalm 145 can be found on page 48.

Psalm 146

¹הַלְלוּיָהּ Praise God!
Praise God, my soul!
²I will praise God
as long as I live,
sing praise as long as I exist.

³Do not trust in human leaders,
or any people - they cannot save you!
⁴Their breath departs,
they return to the clay.
On that very day all their plans perish.

⁵Happy are they
whose help is the God of Jacob
whose hope is in the Creator,
their God;
⁶the maker of heaven and earth,
the sea and all that is in them.
It is God who keeps faith forever,
⁷who does justice for the oppressed,
who gives bread to the starving,
God who sets prisoners free.

⁸God opens the eyes of the blind,
raises up those bent low.
God loves righteous people,
⁹protects strangers,
supports the orphan and the widow,
thwarts the way of the wicked.

¹⁰God will rule forever,
your God, O Zion,
for all generations.

      Praise God!

קמו

א הַלְלוּיָהּ
הַלְלִי נַפְשִׁי אֶת־יְהוָה:
ב אֲהַלְלָה יְהוָה בְּחַיָּי
אֲזַמְּרָה לֵאלֹהַי בְּעוֹדִי:

ג אַל־תִּבְטְחוּ בִנְדִיבִים
בְּבֶן־אָדָם שֶׁאֵין לוֹ תְשׁוּעָה:
ד תֵּצֵא רוּחוֹ יָשֻׁב לְאַדְמָתוֹ
בַּיּוֹם הַהוּא אָבְדוּ עֶשְׁתֹּנֹתָיו:

ה אַשְׁרֵי שֶׁאֵל יַעֲקֹב בְּעֶזְרוֹ
שִׂבְרוֹ עַל־יְהוָה אֱלֹהָיו:
ו עֹשֶׂה שָׁמַיִם וָאָרֶץ
אֶת־הַיָּם וְאֶת־כָּל־אֲשֶׁר־בָּם
הַשֹּׁמֵר אֱמֶת לְעוֹלָם:
ז עֹשֶׂה מִשְׁפָּט לָעֲשׁוּקִים
נֹתֵן לֶחֶם לָרְעֵבִים
יְהוָה מַתִּיר אֲסוּרִים:

ח יְהוָה פֹּקֵחַ עִוְרִים
יְהוָה זֹקֵף כְּפוּפִים
יְהוָה אֹהֵב צַדִּיקִים:
ט יְהוָה שֹׁמֵר אֶת־גֵּרִים
יָתוֹם וְאַלְמָנָה יְעוֹדֵד
וְדֶרֶךְ רְשָׁעִים יְעַוֵּת:

י יִמְלֹךְ יְהוָה לְעוֹלָם
אֱלֹהַיִךְ צִיּוֹן לְדֹר וָדֹר
הַלְלוּיָהּ:

PSALM ANTHOLOGY

קמז

Psalm 147

¹ הַלְלוּיָהּ Praise God!
It is good to sing praise to our God,
  it is pleasant, and praise is right.
² God builds up Jerusalem
  and gathers up
  the outcasts of Israel,
³ healing the brokenhearted,
  binding up all their wounds.

⁴ God determines
  the number of the stars,
  giving them all their names.
⁵ Great is our God
  and mighty in power,
  whose wisdom cannot be measured.

⁶ God raises the lowly,
  humbles the wicked to the dust.
⁷ Respond to God with thanksgiving,
  sing psalms to our God
  on the harp.

⁸ God covers the heavens with clouds,
  prepares rain for the earth,
  makes grass grow on the mountains.
⁹ God gives the beasts their food,
  and young ravens
  who cry to be fed.
¹⁰ God does not delight
  in the horse's strength
  nor in a soldier's speed.
¹¹ God delights in the faithful,
  in those who wait
  on God's love.

<<<

אהַלְלוּיָהּ
כִּי־טוֹב זַמְּרָה אֱלֹהֵינוּ
כִּי־נָעִים נָאוָה תְהִלָּה:
בבּוֹנֵה יְרוּשָׁלִַם יהוה
נִדְחֵי יִשְׂרָאֵל יְכַנֵּס:
גהָרֹפֵא לִשְׁבוּרֵי לֵב
וּמְחַבֵּשׁ לְעַצְּבוֹתָם:

דמוֹנֶה מִסְפָּר לַכּוֹכָבִים
לְכֻלָּם שֵׁמוֹת יִקְרָא:
הגָּדוֹל אֲדוֹנֵינוּ וְרַב־כֹּחַ
לִתְבוּנָתוֹ אֵין מִסְפָּר:

ומְעוֹדֵד עֲנָוִים יהוה
מַשְׁפִּיל רְשָׁעִים עֲדֵי־אָרֶץ:
זעֱנוּ לַיהוה בְּתוֹדָה
זַמְּרוּ לֵאלֹהֵינוּ בְכִנּוֹר:

חהַמְכַסֶּה שָׁמַיִם בְּעָבִים
הַמֵּכִין לָאָרֶץ מָטָר
הַמַּצְמִיחַ הָרִים חָצִיר:
טנוֹתֵן לִבְהֵמָה לַחְמָהּ
לִבְנֵי עֹרֵב אֲשֶׁר יִקְרָאוּ:
ילֹא בִגְבוּרַת הַסּוּס יֶחְפָּץ
לֹא־בְשׁוֹקֵי הָאִישׁ יִרְצֶה:
יארוֹצֶה יהוה אֶת־יְרֵאָיו
אֶת־הַמְיַחֲלִים לְחַסְדּוֹ:

¹²Glorify God, Jerusalem!
Zion, praise your God!
¹³who has strengthened
the bars of your gates,
has blessed your children within you.
¹⁴God makes peace in your borders.
God fills you with the finest wheat.
¹⁵God sends out
His command on earth,
the word runs very swiftly.
¹⁶God sends snow like wool,
creates frost like ashes.
¹⁷God hurls ice like crumbs,
who can stand before that cold?
¹⁸God sends out a word
and it melts them.
God makes the wind blow
and the waters flow.

¹⁹God's word is declared to Jacob,
laws and decrees to Israel.
²⁰God has not treated
any other nation like this.
They have not known
God's judgments.

     Praise God!

יב שַׁבְּחִי יְרוּשָׁלַיִם אֶת־יהוה
הַלְלִי אֱלֹהַיִךְ צִיּוֹן:
יג כִּי־חִזַּק בְּרִיחֵי שְׁעָרָיִךְ
בֵּרַךְ בָּנַיִךְ בְּקִרְבֵּךְ:
יד הַשָּׂם־גְּבוּלֵךְ שָׁלוֹם
חֵלֶב חִטִּים יַשְׂבִּיעֵךְ:
טו הַשֹּׁלֵחַ אִמְרָתוֹ אָרֶץ
עַד־מְהֵרָה יָרוּץ דְּבָרוֹ:
טז הַנֹּתֵן שֶׁלֶג כַּצָּמֶר
כְּפוֹר כָּאֵפֶר יְפַזֵּר:
יז מַשְׁלִיךְ קַרְחוֹ כְפִתִּים
לִפְנֵי קָרָתוֹ מִי יַעֲמֹד:
יח יִשְׁלַח דְּבָרוֹ וְיַמְסֵם
יַשֵּׁב רוּחוֹ יִזְּלוּ־מָיִם:

יט מַגִּיד דְּבָרָיו לְיַעֲקֹב
חֻקָּיו וּמִשְׁפָּטָיו לְיִשְׂרָאֵל:
כ לֹא עָשָׂה כֵן לְכָל־גּוֹי
וּמִשְׁפָּטִים בַּל־יְדָעוּם

הַלְלוּיָהּ:

Psalm 148 / קמח

¹Praise God!
Praise God from heaven,
give praise in the heights.
²Praise God all you messengers,
praise God all hosts.
³Praise God, sun and moon,
praise God, shining stars.
⁴*Praise God, heaven of heavens,*
and waters above the sky.

א הַלְלוּיָהּ
הַלְלוּ אֶת־יהוה מִן־הַשָּׁמַיִם
הַלְלוּהוּ בַּמְּרוֹמִים:
ב הַלְלוּהוּ כָל־מַלְאָכָיו
הַלְלוּהוּ כָּל־צְבָאָיו:
ג הַלְלוּהוּ שֶׁמֶשׁ וְיָרֵחַ
הַלְלוּהוּ כָּל־כּוֹכְבֵי אוֹר:
ד הַלְלוּהוּ שְׁמֵי הַשָּׁמָיִם
וְהַמַּיִם אֲשֶׁר מֵעַל הַשָּׁמָיִם:

⁵Let them praise
   the name of their Creator,
   who commanded, and they were formed.
⁶God established them for ever and ever
   by unchangeable decree.

⁷Praise God from the earth,
   sea creatures and all the deeps,
⁸fire and hail, snow and mist,
   stormy winds
   that fulfil God's word.

⁹Mountains and all hills,
   fruit trees and all cedars,
¹⁰wild animals
   and all tame ones,
   reptiles and winged birds.

¹¹Earthly rulers and all peoples,
   princes and all judges of the world,
¹²both boys and girls,
   old people
   together with the young.

¹³Let them praise
   the name of the Creator,
   for God's name alone is supreme,
   whose majesty is beyond earth and heaven.
¹⁴God restored the honour of this people,
   the praise of those who love God,
   the children of Israel,
   a people so close to God.

   Praise God!

ה יְהַלְלוּ אֶת־שֵׁם יהוה
כִּי הוּא צִוָּה וְנִבְרָאוּ׃
ו וַיַּעֲמִידֵם לָעַד לְעוֹלָם
חָק־נָתַן וְלֹא יַעֲבוֹר׃

ז הַלְלוּ אֶת־יהוה מִן־הָאָרֶץ
תַּנִּינִים וְכָל־תְּהֹמוֹת׃
ח אֵשׁ וּבָרָד שֶׁלֶג וְקִיטוֹר
רוּחַ סְעָרָה עֹשָׂה דְבָרוֹ׃

ט הֶהָרִים וְכָל־גְּבָעוֹת עֵץ
פְּרִי וְכָל־אֲרָזִים׃
י הַחַיָּה וְכָל־בְּהֵמָה
רֶמֶשׂ וְצִפּוֹר כָּנָף׃

יא מַלְכֵי־אֶרֶץ וְכָל־לְאֻמִּים
שָׂרִים וְכָל־שֹׁפְטֵי אָרֶץ׃
יב בַּחוּרִים וְגַם־בְּתוּלוֹת
זְקֵנִים עִם־נְעָרִים׃

יג יְהַלְלוּ אֶת־שֵׁם יהוה
כִּי־נִשְׂגָּב שְׁמוֹ לְבַדּוֹ
הוֹדוֹ עַל־אֶרֶץ וְשָׁמָיִם׃
יד וַיָּרֶם קֶרֶן לְעַמּוֹ
תְּהִלָּה לְכָל־חֲסִידָיו
לִבְנֵי יִשְׂרָאֵל עַם־קְרֹבוֹ
הַלְלוּיָהּ׃

Psalm 150 can be found on page 180.

תהלים

שִׁיר הַמַּעֲלוֹת לְדָוִד שָׂמַחְתִּי בְּאֹמְרִים לִי
בֵּית יְהֹוָה נֵלֵךְ עֹמְדוֹת הָיוּ רַגְלֵינוּ

בִּשְׁעָרַיִךְ
יְרוּשָׁלָ͏ִם
יְרוּשָׁלַ͏ִם
הַבְּנוּיָה

כְּעִיר שֶׁחֻבְּרָה לָּהּ יַחְדָּו שֶׁשָּׁם עָלוּ שְׁבָטִים
שִׁבְטֵי יָהּ עֵדוּת לְיִשְׂרָאֵל לְהֹדוֹת לְשֵׁם יְהֹוָה
כִּי שָׁמָּה יָשְׁבוּ כִסְאוֹת לְמִשְׁפָּט כִּסְאוֹת לְבֵית דָּוִד
שַׁאֲלוּ שְׁלוֹם יְרוּשָׁלָ͏ִם יִשְׁלָיוּ אֹהֲבָיִךְ
יְהִי שָׁלוֹם בְּחֵילֵךְ שַׁלְוָה בְּאַרְמְנוֹתָיִךְ
לְמַעַן אַחַי וְרֵעָי אֲדַבְּרָה נָּא שָׁלוֹם בָּךְ
לְמַעַן בֵּית יְהֹוָה אֱלֹהֵינוּ אֲבַקְשָׁה טוֹב לָךְ

ALTERNATIVE SECOND AND THIRD PARAGRAPHS FOR THE *SH'MA*

Rabbinic teaching understands that when we recite the first paragraph of the *Sh'ma* we accept upon ourselves the 'yoke of the kingdom of heaven', the task of being God's witnesses in the world. In a similar way, by reciting the second paragraph we take on the 'yoke of the *mitsvot*', of the commandments. The third paragraph, about wearing *tsitsit*, fringes, on our garments keeps these commitments always before us. Reform Jewish liturgies have always retained the first paragraph, but sometimes removed or replaced the second and third paragraphs where the editors felt concerns about their actual content or these traditional interpretations. We have retained them within the body of the services, but offer here alternative Biblical passages with a variety of themes. They may be seen as other aspects of the words of Torah that the *Sh'ma* instructs us 'to talk about' at all times.

LIFE AND DEATH

אִם־תִּקַּח If you accept My sayings,	אִם־תִּקַּח אֲמָרָי
and set store by My commands,	וּמִצְוֺתַי תִּצְפֹּן אִתָּךְ:
turning your ear to wisdom,	לְהַקְשִׁיב לַחָכְמָה אָזְנֶךָ
and applying your heart to reason;	תַּטֶּה לִבְּךָ לַתְּבוּנָה:
if you appeal to understanding	כִּי אִם לַבִּינָה תִקְרָא
and speak out for reason;	לַתְּבוּנָה תִּתֵּן קוֹלֶךָ:
if you seek these like silver	אִם־תְּבַקְשֶׁנָּה כַכָּסֶף
and search for them like hidden treasure;	וְכַמַּטְמוֹנִים תַּחְפְּשֶׂנָּה:
then you will understand	אָז תָּבִין צֶדֶק וּמִשְׁפָּט
what is right and just,	
integrity, and every path to good.	וּמֵישָׁרִים כָּל־מַעְגַּל־טוֹב:
When wisdom comes into your heart	כִּי־תָבוֹא חָכְמָה בְלִבֶּךָ
and knowledge is a pleasure to you,	וְדַעַת לְנַפְשְׁךָ יִנְעָם:
discretion will watch over you	מְזִמָּה תִּשְׁמֹר עָלֶיךָ
and reason will guard you,	תְּבוּנָה תִּנְצְרֶכָּה:
keeping you from bad ways.	לְהַצִּילְךָ מִדֶּרֶךְ רָע
Then you will follow	לְמַעַן תֵּלֵךְ בְּדֶרֶךְ טוֹבִים
the way of good people,	
and keep the paths of the righteous.[1]	וְאָרְחוֹת צַדִּיקִים תִּשְׁמֹר:

---

[1] From Prov 2.

SH'MA ALTERNATIVE PARAGRAPHS

לֹא **The swift do not win the race,**   לֹא לַקַּלִּים הַמֵּרוֹץ
nor the strong the battle;   וְלֹא לַגִּבּוֹרִים הַמִּלְחָמָה
bread does not belong to the wise,   וְגַם לֹא לַחֲכָמִים לֶחֶם
nor wealth to the shrewd,   וְגַם לֹא לַנְּבֹנִים עֹשֶׁר
nor success to the skilful;   וְגַם לֹא לַיֹּדְעִים חֵן
for time and chance govern all.   כִּי־עֵת וָפֶגַע יִקְרֶה אֶת־כֻּלָּם:
The dust returns to earth as it was,   וְיָשֹׁב הֶעָפָר עַל־הָאָרֶץ כְּשֶׁהָיָה
but the spirit returns
to God who gave it.   וְהָרוּחַ תָּשׁוּב אֶל־הָאֱלֹהִים
This is the end of the matter,   אֲשֶׁר נְתָנָהּ:
you have heard it all: סוֹף דָּבָר הַכֹּל נִשְׁמָע
Fear God
and obey God's commands,   אֶת־הָאֱלֹהִים יְרָא
there is no more to human beings   וְאֶת־מִצְוֹתָיו שְׁמוֹר
than this.[1]   כִּי־זֶה כָּל־הָאָדָם:

The daily evening service continues with 'All this is true' on page 70,
and the erev Shabbat *service on page 135.*
The daily morning service continues with 'True is Your word' on page 58,
and the Shabbat *morning service on page 217.*

THE FUTURE

הוֹי **Come all who are thirsty,**   הוֹי כָּל־צָמֵא לְכוּ לַמַּיִם
come to the water,   וַאֲשֶׁר אֵין־לוֹ כָּסֶף
and whoever has no money,
come and buy and eat;   לְכוּ שִׁבְרוּ וֶאֱכֹלוּ
buy wine and milk with no money,   וּלְכוּ שִׁבְרוּ בְּלוֹא־כֶסֶף
with no price.   וּבְלוֹא מְחִיר יַיִן וְחָלָב:
Why spend money   לָמָּה תִשְׁקְלוּ־כֶסֶף בְּלוֹא־לֶחֶם
for what is not bread
and your labour without satisfaction?   וִיגִיעֲכֶם בְּלוֹא לְשָׂבְעָה
Listen and come to Me,   הַטּוּ אָזְנְכֶם וּלְכוּ אֵלַי
hear and your soul shall live.   שִׁמְעוּ וּתְחִי נַפְשְׁכֶם:
Seek the Eternal   דִּרְשׁוּ יְהֹוָה בְּהִמָּצְאוֹ
while God may be found,
call to God while God is near.   קְרָאֻהוּ בִּהְיוֹתוֹ קָרוֹב:

<<<

---

[1] From Ecc 9 and 12.

SH'MA ALTERNATIVE PARAGRAPHS

Let the wicked forsake their way	יַעֲזֹב רָשָׁע דַּרְכּוֹ
and those who plot harm their thoughts,	וְאִישׁ אָוֶן מַחְשְׁבֹתָיו
let them turn back to the Eternal	וְיָשֹׁב אֶל־יהוה וִירַחֲמֵהוּ
who will take pity on them,	
to our God who is generous to forgive.	וְאֶל־אֱלֹהֵינוּ כִּי־יַרְבֶּה לִסְלוֹחַ:
So the Eternal has said:	כֹּה אָמַר יהוה
Care for justice and do what is right,	שִׁמְרוּ מִשְׁפָּט וַעֲשׂוּ צְדָקָה
for My salvation is about to come	כִּי־קְרוֹבָה יְשׁוּעָתִי לָבוֹא
and My righteousness to appear.	וְצִדְקָתִי לְהִגָּלוֹת:
Happy is the person who does this	אַשְׁרֵי אֱנוֹשׁ יַעֲשֶׂה־זֹּאת
and anyone who grasps it,	וּבֶן־אָדָם יַחֲזִיק בָּהּ
caring for the Sabbath	שֹׁמֵר שַׁבָּת מֵחַלְּלוֹ
without dishonouring it,	
and keeping away from doing evil.	וְשֹׁמֵר יָדוֹ מֵעֲשׂוֹת כָּל־רָע:
Also the strangers	וּבְנֵי הַנֵּכָר הַנִּלְוִים עַל־יהוה
who join themselves to the Eternal	
to serve God and love God's name	לְשָׁרְתוֹ וּלְאַהֲבָה אֶת־שֵׁם יהוה
and to be God's workers;	לִהְיוֹת לוֹ לַעֲבָדִים
and who care for the Sabbath,	כָּל־שֹׁמֵר שַׁבָּת מֵחַלְּלוֹ
not dishonouring it,	
holding fast to My covenant.	וּמַחֲזִיקִים בִּבְרִיתִי:
I shall bring them to My holy hill	וַהֲבִיאוֹתִים אֶל־הַר קָדְשִׁי
and give them joy	וְשִׂמַּחְתִּים בְּבֵית תְּפִלָּתִי
in My house of prayer,	
for My house shall be called	כִּי בֵיתִי בֵּית־תְּפִלָּה יִקָּרֵא
a house of prayer for all peoples.[1]	לְכָל־הָעַמִּים:

---

[1] From Isa 55 and 56.

SH'MA ALTERNATIVE PARAGRAPHS

הִנֵּה **The time is coming, says the Eternal, when I will make a new covenant with Israel and Judah. It will not be like the covenant I made with their ancestors when I took them by the hand and led them out of Egypt. This covenant they broke though I was wedded to them, says the Eternal. But this is the covenant which I will make with Israel after those days, says the Eternal: I will set My Torah within them and write it on their hearts; I shall be their God and they will be My people. No longer will people teach their neighbour, or those in their family saying, 'Know the Eternal!' All of them will know Me, from the smallest of them to the greatest of them, says the Eternal.[1]**

הִנֵּה יָמִים בָּאִים נְאֻם־יְהֹוָה וְכָרַתִּי
אֶת־בֵּית יִשְׂרָאֵל וְאֶת־בֵּית יְהוּדָה
בְּרִית חֲדָשָׁה: לֹא כַבְּרִית אֲשֶׁר
כָּרַתִּי אֶת־אֲבוֹתָם בְּיוֹם הֶחֱזִיקִי
בְיָדָם לְהוֹצִיאָם מֵאֶרֶץ מִצְרָיִם
אֲשֶׁר־הֵמָּה הֵפֵרוּ אֶת־בְּרִיתִי וְאָנֹכִי
בָּעַלְתִּי בָם נְאֻם־יְהֹוָה: כִּי זֹאת
הַבְּרִית אֲשֶׁר אֶכְרֹת אֶת־בֵּית
יִשְׂרָאֵל אַחֲרֵי הַיָּמִים הָהֵם נְאֻם־
יְהֹוָה נָתַתִּי אֶת־תּוֹרָתִי בְּקִרְבָּם
וְעַל־לִבָּם אֶכְתֲּבֶנָּה וְהָיִיתִי לָהֶם
לֵאלֹהִים וְהֵמָּה יִהְיוּ־לִי לְעָם: וְלֹא
יְלַמְּדוּ עוֹד אִישׁ אֶת־רֵעֵהוּ וְאִישׁ
אֶת־אָחִיו לֵאמֹר דְּעוּ אֶת־יְהֹוָה
כִּי־כוּלָּם יֵדְעוּ אוֹתִי לְמִקְטַנָּם
וְעַד־גְּדוֹלָם נְאֻם־יְהֹוָה:

The daily evening service continues with 'All this is true' on page 70,
and the erev Shabbat *service on page 135.*
The daily morning service continues with 'True is Your word' on page 58,
and the Shabbat *morning service on page 217.*

THE JUST SOCIETY

יִשְׁאָלוּנִי **They ask Me for laws of justice,**
for they delight in approaching God.
Is it not sharing your food
with the hungry
and bringing the homeless
into your home,
clothing the destitute
when you meet them
and not evading your duty
to your own flesh and blood?

יִשְׁאָלוּנִי מִשְׁפְּטֵי־צֶדֶק
קִרְבַת אֱלֹהִים יֶחְפָּצוּן:
הֲלוֹא פָרֹס לָרָעֵב לַחְמֶךָ
וַעֲנִיִּים מְרוּדִים תָּבִיא בָיִת
כִּי־תִרְאֶה עָרֹם וְכִסִּיתוֹ
וּמִבְּשָׂרְךָ לֹא תִתְעַלָּם:

<<<

---

[1] Jer 31:30-33.

SH'MA ALTERNATIVE PARAGRAPHS

Then if you call,
the Eternal will answer;
if you call, God will say: 'Here I am!'
If you do away with the yoke,
the clenched fist, and the wicked word;
if you share what you have
with the hungry
and satisfy the needs of the wretched,
then your light will rise
like dawn out of darkness,
and your shade be like the noon,
and the Eternal will always guide you.
If you stop your foot
from doing what it wants
because of the Sabbath, My holy day;
if you call the Sabbath a day of joy,
then you shall find your joy
in the Eternal.[1]

אָז תִּקְרָא וַיהוה יַעֲנֶה
תְּשַׁוַּע וְיֹאמַר הִנֵּנִי
אִם־תָּסִיר מִתּוֹכְךָ מוֹטָה
שְׁלַח אֶצְבַּע וְדַבֶּר־אָוֶן:
וְתָפֵק לָרָעֵב נַפְשֶׁךָ
וְנֶפֶשׁ נַעֲנָה תַּשְׂבִּיעַ
וְזָרַח בַּחֹשֶׁךְ אוֹרֶךָ
וַאֲפֵלָתְךָ כַּצָּהֳרָיִם:
וְנָחֲךָ יהוה תָּמִיד
אִם־תָּשִׁיב מִשַּׁבָּת רַגְלֶךָ
עֲשׂוֹת חֲפָצֶיךָ בְּיוֹם קָדְשִׁי
וְקָרָאתָ לַשַּׁבָּת עֹנֶג
אָז תִּתְעַנַּג עַל־יהוה:

שְׂפַת־אֱמֶת Truth spoken
stands firm forever,
but lies live only for a moment.
Those who plot evil deceive themselves,
but there is joy for those
who seek the common good.
Whoever oppress the poor
insult their Maker,
those who are generous to the needy
honour God.
Righteousness raises a people to honour,
to do wrong is a disgrace to any nation.[2]

שְׂפַת־אֱמֶת תִּכּוֹן לָעַד
וְעַד־אַרְגִּיעָה לְשׁוֹן שָׁקֶר:
מִרְמָה בְּלֶב־חֹרְשֵׁי־רָע
וּלְיֹעֲצֵי שָׁלוֹם שִׂמְחָה:
עֹשֵׁק דָּל חֵרֵף עֹשֵׂהוּ
וּמְכַבְּדוֹ חֹנֵן אֶבְיוֹן:
צְדָקָה תְרוֹמֵם־גּוֹי
וְחֶסֶד לְאֻמִּים חַטָּאת:

*The daily evening service continues with 'All this is true' on page 70,
and the* erev Shabbat *service on page 135.
The daily morning service continues with 'True is Your word' on page 58,
and the* Shabbat *morning service on page 217.*

---

[1] From Isa 58. [2] From Prov 12 and 14.

SH'MA ALTERNATIVE PARAGRAPHS

THE COMMUNITY

וַיְדַבֵּר The Lord spoke to Moses:
Be holy,
for I the Eternal your God am holy!
You shall respect, each one of you,
your mother and your father.
You shall keep My Sabbaths.
I am the Eternal your God.
You shall not steal, you shall not
cheat, and you shall not deceive
- any one of you your neighbour.
You shall not swear
by My name to deceive,
and so dishonour
the name of your God.
I am the Eternal.
You shall not exploit
or rob your neighbour.
You shall not keep back a
hired-hand's wages
till the next morning.
You shall not pervert justice,
either by favouring the poor,
or by honouring the great.
You shall judge your neighbour
with justice.
You shall not go about slandering
your people.
You shall not stand by when
your neighbour's blood is shed.
I am the Eternal.
You shall not hate those near to you
in your heart,
but frankly warn them of their fault
and not share their guilt.
You shall not seek revenge nor bear
a grudge against any of your people.
You shall act with love towards
your neighbour as to yourself.
I am the Eternal.

<<<

וַיְדַבֵּר יהוה אֶל־מֹשֶׁה לֵּאמֹר:
קְדֹשִׁים תִּהְיוּ
כִּי קָדוֹשׁ אֲנִי יהוה אֱלֹהֵיכֶם:
אִישׁ אִמּוֹ וְאָבִיו תִּירָאוּ
וְאֶת־שַׁבְּתֹתַי תִּשְׁמֹרוּ
אֲנִי יהוה אֱלֹהֵיכֶם:
לֹא תִּגְנֹבוּ וְלֹא־תְכַחֲשׁוּ
וְלֹא־תְשַׁקְּרוּ אִישׁ בַּעֲמִיתוֹ:
וְלֹא־תִשָּׁבְעוּ בִשְׁמִי לַשָּׁקֶר
וְחִלַּלְתָּ אֶת־שֵׁם אֱלֹהֶיךָ
אֲנִי יהוה:
לֹא־תַעֲשֹׁק אֶת־רֵעֲךָ
וְלֹא תִגְזֹל
לֹא־תָלִין פְּעֻלַּת שָׂכִיר אִתְּךָ
עַד־בֹּקֶר:
לֹא־תַעֲשׂוּ עָוֶל בַּמִּשְׁפָּט
לֹא־תִשָּׂא פְנֵי־דָל
וְלֹא תֶהְדַּר פְּנֵי גָדוֹל
בְּצֶדֶק תִּשְׁפֹּט עֲמִיתֶךָ:
לֹא־תֵלֵךְ רָכִיל בְּעַמֶּיךָ
לֹא תַעֲמֹד עַל־דַּם רֵעֶךָ
אֲנִי יהוה:
לֹא־תִשְׂנָא אֶת־אָחִיךָ בִּלְבָבֶךָ
הוֹכֵחַ תּוֹכִיחַ אֶת־עֲמִיתֶךָ
וְלֹא־תִשָּׂא עָלָיו חֵטְא:
לֹא־תִקֹּם וְלֹא־תִטֹּר
אֶת־בְּנֵי עַמֶּךָ
וְאָהַבְתָּ לְרֵעֲךָ כָּמוֹךָ
אֲנִי יהוה:

SH'MA ALTERNATIVE PARAGRAPHS

In the presence of old age
you shall stand up,
honour the presence
of an old person, and fear your God.
I am the Eternal.
When strangers settle with you
in your land
you shall not exploit them.
The strangers who settle with you
shall be treated
as one born among you,
and you shall act with love
towards them as to yourself,
for you were strangers
in the land of Egypt.
I am the Eternal your God.
You shall not pervert justice
in measurements of length,
weight or quantity.
You shall have true scales,
true weights, true measures …
I am the Eternal.[1]

מִפְּנֵי שֵׂיבָה תָּקוּם
וְהָדַרְתָּ פְּנֵי זָקֵן
וְיָרֵאתָ מֵאֱלֹהֶיךָ
אֲנִי יהוה:
וְכִי־יָגוּר אִתְּךָ גֵּר בְּאַרְצְכֶם
לֹא תוֹנוּ אֹתוֹ:
כְּאֶזְרָח מִכֶּם יִהְיֶה לָכֶם
הַגֵּר הַגָּר אִתְּכֶם
וְאָהַבְתָּ לוֹ כָּמוֹךָ
כִּי־גֵרִים הֱיִיתֶם
בְּאֶרֶץ מִצְרָיִם
אֲנִי יהוה אֱלֹהֵיכֶם:
לֹא־תַעֲשׂוּ עָוֶל בַּמִּשְׁפָּט
בַּמִּדָּה בַּמִּשְׁקָל וּבַמְּשׂוּרָה:
מֹאזְנֵי צֶדֶק אַבְנֵי־צֶדֶק
אֵיפַת צֶדֶק וְהִין צֶדֶק יִהְיֶה לָכֶם
אֲנִי יהוה:

אַל Do not refuse any a kindness
that you owe them
if it is in your power to do it.
Do not say to your neighbour,
'Go away and come back again
and I will give it to you tomorrow' –
when you have it already.
Do not plot harm against your neighbours
while they live near you, trusting you.
Do not pick a quarrel with someone
for no reason, who has done you no harm.
Do not envy violent people
and do not model *your conduct* on theirs,
for one who is not straight
is detestable to the Eternal,
but the upright have God's confidence.[2]

אַל־תִּמְנַע־טוֹב מִבְּעָלָיו
בִּהְיוֹת לְאֵל יָדְךָ לַעֲשׂוֹת:
אַל־תֹּאמַר לְרֵעֲךָ
לֵךְ וָשׁוּב וּמָחָר אֶתֵּן
וְיֵשׁ אִתָּךְ:
אַל־תַּחֲרֹשׁ עַל־רֵעֲךָ רָעָה
וְהוּא־יוֹשֵׁב לָבֶטַח אִתָּךְ:
אַל־תָּרִיב עִם־אָדָם חִנָּם
אִם־לֹא גְמָלְךָ רָעָה:
אַל־תְּקַנֵּא בְּאִישׁ חָמָס
וְאַל־תִּבְחַר בְּכָל־דְּרָכָיו:
כִּי תוֹעֲבַת יהוה נָלוֹז
וְאֶת־יְשָׁרִים סוֹדוֹ:

---

[1] From Lev 19.   [2] Prov 3:27-32.

SH'MA ALTERNATIVE PARAGRAPHS

The daily evening service continues with 'All this is true' on page 70,
and the erev Shabbat *service on page 135.*
The daily morning service continues with 'True is Your word' on page 58,
and the Shabbat *morning service on page 217.*

THE FAMILY OF ISRAEL

וַיְדַבֵּר Now listen Jacob My servant,
and Israel whom I have chosen!
Thus says the Eternal who made you,
who formed you from the womb,
who helps you.
Do not be afraid, Jacob My servant,
Yeshurun whom I have chosen.
For I will pour out water
on the thirsty soil,
and streams on the dry ground.
I will pour out My spirit
on your descendants,
and My blessing on your offspring.
They shall spring up among the grass
like willows by running streams.
One person will say:
'I belong to the Eternal',
others will call themselves
by Jacob's name.
With his hand another will write:
'Belonging to the Lord',
and be known by the name of Israel.
Thus says the Eternal, Israel's ruler and redeemer,
the God of all creation:
'I am the first and I am the last
and besides Me there is no God.'[1]

וְעַתָּה שְׁמַע יַעֲקֹב עַבְדִּי
וְיִשְׂרָאֵל בָּחַרְתִּי בוֹ:
כֹּה־אָמַר יהוה עֹשֶׂךָ וְיֹצֶרְךָ
מִבֶּטֶן יַעְזְרֶךָ
אַל־תִּירָא עַבְדִּי יַעֲקֹב
וִישֻׁרוּן בָּחַרְתִּי בוֹ:
כִּי אֶצָּק־מַיִם עַל־צָמֵא
וְנֹזְלִים עַל־יַבָּשָׁה
אֶצֹּק רוּחִי עַל־זַרְעֶךָ
וּבִרְכָתִי עַל־צֶאֱצָאֶיךָ:
וְצָמְחוּ בְּבֵין חָצִיר
כַּעֲרָבִים עַל־יִבְלֵי־מָיִם:
זֶה יֹאמַר לַיהוה אָנִי וְזֶה
יִקְרָא בְשֵׁם־יַעֲקֹב
וְזֶה יִכְתֹּב יָדוֹ לַיהוה
וּבְשֵׁם יִשְׂרָאֵל יְכַנֶּה:
כֹּה־אָמַר יהוה מֶלֶךְ־יִשְׂרָאֵל
וְגֹאֲלוֹ יהוה צְבָאוֹת
אֲנִי רִאשׁוֹן וַאֲנִי אַחֲרוֹן
וּמִבַּלְעָדַי אֵין אֱלֹהִים:

---

[1] Isa 44:1-6.

SH'MA ALTERNATIVE PARAGRAPHS

כִּי For you are a people holy to the Eternal your God. It is you that the Eternal your God has chosen to be God's very own people out of all the peoples on the face of the earth. The Eternal did not love you and choose you because you outnumbered other peoples, for you were the least of all peoples. It was for love alone and to keep the promise which God swore to your ancestors that the Eternal brought you out with a mighty hand and rescued you from the camp of slavery, from the power of Pharaoh, king of Egypt. Listen to these judgments, be true to them and do them, and then the Eternal your God will be true to the covenant and faithful love which God promised your ancestors.[1]

כִּי עַם קָדוֹשׁ אַתָּה לַיהוה אֱלֹהֶיךָ בְּךָ בָּחַר יהוה אֱלֹהֶיךָ לִהְיוֹת לוֹ לְעַם סְגֻלָּה מִכֹּל הָעַמִּים אֲשֶׁר עַל־פְּנֵי הָאֲדָמָה: לֹא מֵרֻבְּכֶם מִכָּל־הָעַמִּים חָשַׁק יהוה בָּכֶם וַיִּבְחַר בָּכֶם כִּי־אַתֶּם הַמְעַט מִכָּל־הָעַמִּים: כִּי מֵאַהֲבַת יהוה אֶתְכֶם וּמִשָּׁמְרוֹ אֶת־הַשְּׁבֻעָה אֲשֶׁר נִשְׁבַּע לַאֲבֹתֵיכֶם הוֹצִיא יהוה אֶתְכֶם בְּיָד חֲזָקָה וַיִּפְדְּךָ מִבֵּית עֲבָדִים מִיַּד פַּרְעֹה מֶלֶךְ־מִצְרָיִם: וְהָיָה עֵקֶב תִּשְׁמְעוּן אֵת הַמִּשְׁפָּטִים הָאֵלֶּה וּשְׁמַרְתֶּם וַעֲשִׂיתֶם אֹתָם וְשָׁמַר יהוה אֱלֹהֶיךָ לְךָ אֶת־הַבְּרִית וְאֶת־הַחֶסֶד אֲשֶׁר נִשְׁבַּע לַאֲבֹתֶיךָ:

The daily evening service continues with 'All this is true' on page 70,
and the erev Shabbat *service on page 135.*
The daily morning service continues with 'True is Your word' on page 58,
and the Shabbat *morning service on page 217.*

---

[1] Deut 7:6-8,12.

קדיש תתקבל
KADDISH TITKABBAL

יִתְגַּדַּל וְיִתְקַדַּשׁ שְׁמֵהּ רַבָּא
בְּעָלְמָא דִּי־בְרָא כִרְעוּתֵהּ:
וְיַמְלִיךְ מַלְכוּתֵהּ
בְּחַיֵּיכוֹן וּבְיוֹמֵיכוֹן
וּבְחַיֵּי דִי־כָל־בֵּית יִשְׂרָאֵל
בַּעֲגָלָא וּבִזְמַן קָרִיב.
וְאִמְרוּ אָמֵן:
יְהֵא שְׁמֵהּ רַבָּא מְבָרַךְ
לְעָלַם וּלְעָלְמֵי עָלְמַיָּא:
יִתְבָּרַךְ וְיִשְׁתַּבַּח וְיִתְפָּאַר
וְיִתְרוֹמַם וְיִתְנַשֵּׂא וְיִתְהַדָּר
וְיִתְעַלֶּה וְיִתְהַלָּל שְׁמֵהּ דִּי־קֻדְשָׁא.
בְּרִיךְ הוּא.
לְעֵלָּא מִן־כָּל־בִּרְכָתָא

During the Ten Days of Penitence:
לְעֵלָּא לְעֵלָּא מִכָּל־בִּרְכָתָא

וְשִׁירָתָא תֻּשְׁבְּחָתָא וְנֶחֱמָתָא
דַּאֲמִירָן בְּעָלְמָא.
וְאִמְרוּ אָמֵן:

יִתְגַּדַּל Let us magnify
and let us sanctify in this world
the great name of God
whose will created it.
May God's reign come in your
lifetime, and in your days,
and in the lifetime of the family of
Israel - quickly and speedily
may it come.
Amen.
**May the greatness of God's being
be blessed from eternity to eternity.**
Let us bless and let us extol,
let us tell aloud and let us raise aloft,
let us set on high and let us honour,
let us exalt and
let us praise the Holy One,
Whose name is blessed,
Who is far beyond any blessing

During the Ten Days of Penitence:
Who is far above and beyond any blessing

or song, any honour
or any consolation
that can be spoken of in this world.
Amen.

<<<

KADDISH TITKABBAL

May the prayers and
supplications
of all Israel
be accepted by their
Creator in heaven.
Amen.

May great peace from heaven and
the gift of life be granted to us
and to all the family of Israel.
Amen.
May the Maker of peace
in the highest bring this peace
upon us and upon all Israel
and upon all the world.
Amen.

תִּתְקַבַּל צְלוֹתְהוֹן
וּבָעוּתְהוֹן
דִּי־כָל־יִשְׂרָאֵל
קֳדָם אֲבוּהוֹן דִּי בִשְׁמַיָּא.
וְאִמְרוּ אָמֵן:

יְהֵא שְׁלָמָא רַבָּא מִן שְׁמַיָּא
וְחַיִּים עָלֵינוּ וְעַל־כָּל־יִשְׂרָאֵל.
וְאִמְרוּ אָמֵן:
עֹשֶׂה שָׁלוֹם בִּמְרוֹמָיו
הוּא יַעֲשֶׂה שָׁלוֹם
עָלֵינוּ וְעַל כָּל־יִשְׂרָאֵל
וְעַל־כָּל־הָעוֹלָם.
וְאִמְרוּ אָמֵן:

700

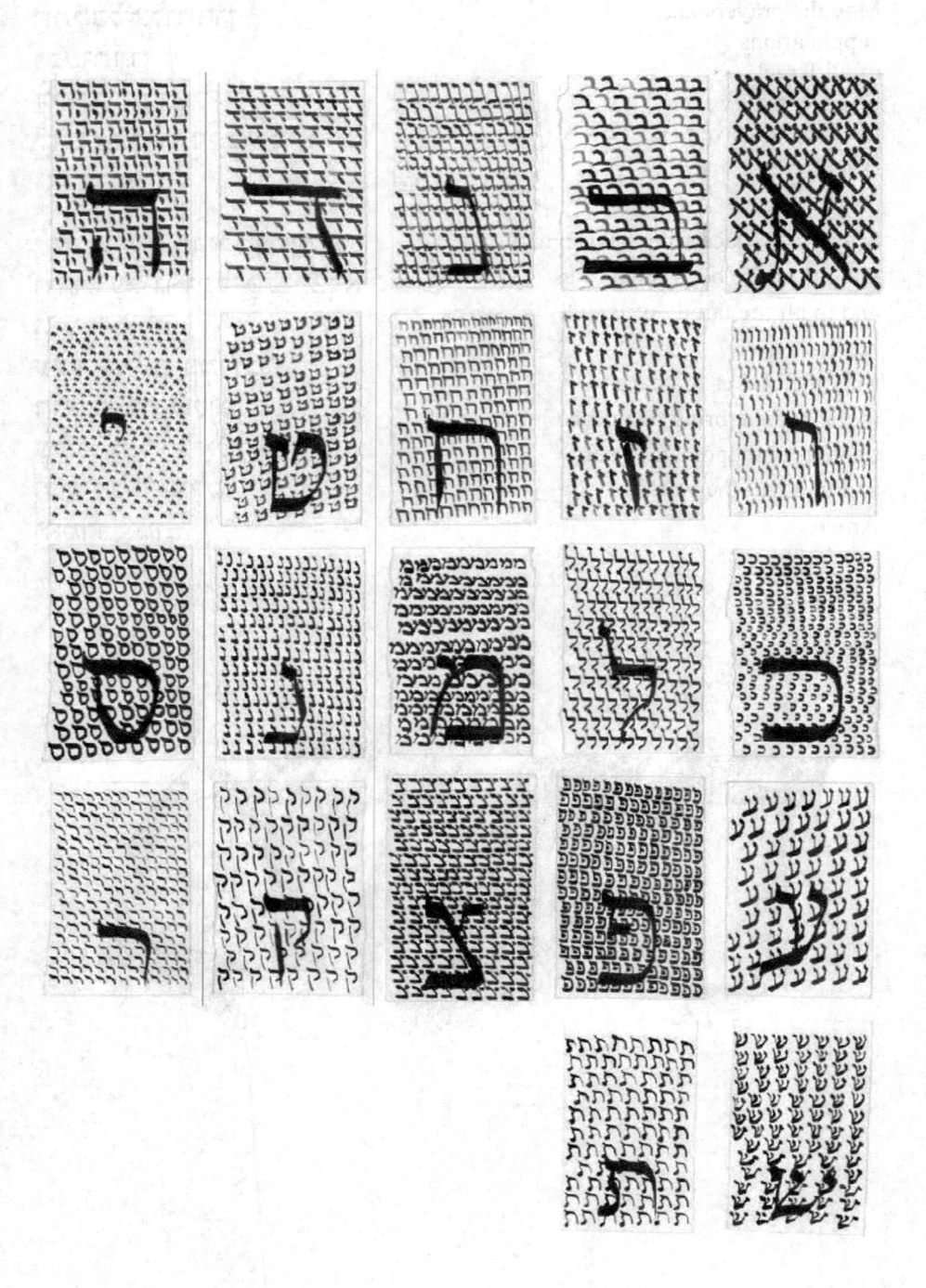

פרקי אבות

from the
Sayings of the Fathers

Pirke Avot, literally, chapters of the fathers, is a tractate of the *Mishnah* which contains ethical teachings and aphorisms of the rabbis. These were the spiritual 'fathers' of the Jewish people, which is one explanation for the title of the tractate. It was highly regarded in the rabbinic period: 'One who wishes to be pious, a *chasid*, should fulfil the words of *Pirke Avot*' (*Baba Kama* 30a). Since the period of the Gaonim (ninth century) it has been a custom to read *Pirke Avot* on Saturday afternoons, in particular on the six *Shabbatot* between *Pesach* and *Shavuot*.

The introduction traces the chain of tradition whereby the Torah given to Moses at Sinai was handed down to successive generations. In particular it emphasises the line through the prophets to the 'men of the Great Assembly', viewed by the rabbis as the source of their own authority. A recurrent theme throughout is the centrality of the study of Torah as the key to a good and successful life.

We have selected those sayings that have the most immediate impact, and also omitted the many Biblical proof texts that are quoted to support particular opinions, as these can be found in the many full editions of *Pirke Avot*.

All Israel has a share in the world to come, as it is said in the Prophets: 'And your people shall all be righteous. They shall inherit the earth forever, the branch I planted, the work of My hands to bring Me glory.'[1]

From Chapter 1

1. Moses received Torah on Sinai, and handed it on to Joshua, and Joshua to the elders, and the elders to the prophets, and the prophets handed it on to the men of the Great Assembly.
They said three things,
    Be patient and careful in judgment,
    raise up many disciples,
    and make a fence
    to protect the Torah.

2. Simon the Just was one of the last survivors of the Great Assembly. He used to say,
Civilisation is based on three things -
    on Torah,
    on service
    and on loving deeds.

3. Antigonos of Socho received tradition from Simon the Just. He used to say, Do not be like servants who serve their master in order to get a reward. Instead be like servants who serve their master with no thought of reward, and let the awe of heaven be upon you.

---

[1] *Pirke Avot* is traditionally preceded by this quotation from *Mishnah Sanhedrin* 10:1 which ends with the verse from Isaiah 60:21.

703 from the SAYINGS OF THE FATHERS — CHAPTER 1

4. Yose ben Yoezer of Tseredah and Yose ben Yochanan of Jerusalem received tradition from those who came before. The former says, Let your house be a meeting-place for the wise, sit in the dust at their feet, and drink in their words thirstily.

ד יוֹסֵי בֶּן־יוֹעֶזֶר אִישׁ צְרֵדָה וְיוֹסֵי בֶּן־יוֹחָנָן אִישׁ יְרוּשָׁלַיִם קִבְּלוּ מֵהֶם. יוֹסֵי בֶּן־יוֹעֶזֶר אִישׁ צְרֵדָה אוֹמֵר. יְהִי בֵיתְךָ בֵית וַעַד לַחֲכָמִים. וֶהֱוֵי מִתְאַבֵּק בַּעֲפַר רַגְלֵיהֶם. וֶהֱוֵי שׁוֹתֶה בַצָּמָא אֶת־דִּבְרֵיהֶם:

5. The latter says, Let your house be open wide and the poor be members of your household.

ה יוֹסֵי בֶּן־יוֹחָנָן אִישׁ יְרוּשָׁלַיִם אוֹמֵר. יְהִי בֵיתְךָ פָּתוּחַ לִרְוָחָה. וְיִהְיוּ עֲנִיִּים בְּנֵי בֵיתֶךָ:

6. Joshua ben Perachyah and Nittai the Arbelite received tradition from those who came before. The former says, Find yourself a teacher, get yourself a friend, and put the best construction on every person's conduct.

ו יְהוֹשֻׁעַ בֶּן־פְּרַחְיָה וְנִתַּי הָאַרְבֵּלִי קִבְּלוּ מֵהֶם. יְהוֹשֻׁעַ בֶּן פְּרַחְיָה אוֹמֵר. עֲשֵׂה לְךָ רַב. וּקְנֵה לְךָ חָבֵר. וֶהֱוֵי דָן אֶת־כָּל־הָאָדָם לְכַף זְכוּת:

7. The latter says, Keep away from a bad neighbour, do not associate with the wicked, and do not shrug off the thought of retribution.

ז נִתַּי הָאַרְבֵּלִי אוֹמֵר. הַרְחֵק מִשָּׁכֵן רָע. וְאַל־תִּתְחַבֵּר לָרָשָׁע. וְאַל־תִּתְיָאֵשׁ מִן־הַפֻּרְעָנוּת:

8. Judah ben Tabbai and Simon ben Shetach received tradition from those who came before. The former says, Do not be like those who influence the judges in their favour. When the parties to a dispute are standing before you, consider them both equally guilty, but as soon as they have accepted the verdict consider them both equally innocent.

ח יְהוּדָה בֶּן־טַבַּאי וְשִׁמְעוֹן בֶּן־שָׁטַח קִבְּלוּ מֵהֶם. יְהוּדָה בֶּן־טַבַּאי אוֹמֵר. אַל־תַּעַשׂ עַצְמְךָ כְּעוֹרְכֵי הַדַּיָּנִין. וּכְשֶׁיִּהְיוּ בַעֲלֵי הַדִּין עוֹמְדִים לְפָנֶיךָ יִהְיוּ בְעֵינֶיךָ כִּרְשָׁעִים. וּכְשֶׁנִּפְטָרִים מִלְּפָנֶיךָ יִהְיוּ בְעֵינֶיךָ כְּזַכָּאִים כְּשֶׁקִּבְּלוּ עֲלֵיהֶם אֶת־הַדִּין:

פרק א׳

ט שִׁמְעוֹן בֶּן־שָׁטַח אוֹמֵר. הֱוֵה מַרְבֶּה לַחְקוֹר אֶת־הָעֵדִים. וֶהֱוֵה זָהִיר בִּדְבָרֶיךָ שֶׁמָּא מִתּוֹכָם יִלְמְדוּ לְשַׁקֵּר:

י שְׁמַעְיָה וְאַבְטַלְיוֹן קִבְּלוּ מֵהֶם. שְׁמַעְיָה אוֹמֵר. אֱהוֹב אֶת־הַמְּלָאכָה. וּשְׂנָא אֶת־הָרַבָּנוּת. וְאַל־תִּתְוַדַּע לָרָשׁוּת:

יא אַבְטַלְיוֹן אוֹמֵר. חֲכָמִים. הִזָּהֲרוּ בְדִבְרֵיכֶם. שֶׁמָּא יִשְׁתּוּ הַתַּלְמִידִים הַבָּאִים אַחֲרֵיכֶם וְיָמוּתוּ. וְנִמְצָא שֵׁם שָׁמַיִם מִתְחַלֵּל:

יב הִלֵּל וְשַׁמַּאי קִבְּלוּ מֵהֶם. הִלֵּל אוֹמֵר. הֱוֵה מִתַּלְמִידָיו שֶׁל אַהֲרֹן. אוֹהֵב שָׁלוֹם וְרוֹדֵף שָׁלוֹם. אוֹהֵב אֶת־הַבְּרִיּוֹת וּמְקָרְבָן לַתּוֹרָה:

יג הוּא הָיָה אוֹמֵר. נְגִיד שְׁמָא אֲבַד שְׁמֵהּ. וּדְלָא מוֹסִיף יָסֵף. וּדְלָא יָלֵיף קְטָלָא חַיָּב. וּדְאִשְׁתַּמֵּשׁ בְּתַגָּא חֲלָף:

יד הוּא הָיָה אוֹמֵר. אִם אֵין אֲנִי לִי מִי לִי. וּכְשֶׁאֲנִי לְעַצְמִי מָה אֲנִי. וְאִם לֹא עַכְשָׁיו אֵימָתָי:

9. The latter says, Examine the witnesses thoroughly, and be careful what you say, for from your words they can learn to lie.

10. Shemayah and Avtalyon received tradition from those who came before. The former says,
    Love work,
    hate domination
    and do not get too familiar
    with a corrupt power.

11. The latter says, Wise men, watch your words! For your pupils may drink them up and die, and the name of heaven be despised.

12. Hillel and Shammai received tradition from those who came before. Hillel says, Be a disciple of Aaron, loving peace and pursuing peace, loving God's creatures and drawing them close to the Torah.

13. He used to say, A name made great is a name destroyed. Whoever does not increase his knowledge decreases it; whoever does not learn destroys his life. Whoever uses the crown of religion for his own worldly advantage must perish.

14. He used to say,
If I am not for myself,
who is for me?
But if I am only for myself,
what am I?
And if not now, when?

705 from the SAYINGS OF THE FATHERS — CHAPTER 1

15. Shammai says, Make Torah study a fixed habit. Say little and do much, and welcome everyone cheerfully.

16. Rabban Gamliel used to say, Find yourself a teacher and get rid of doubt, and do not get used to guessing your taxes.

17. Simon his son says, All my life I grew up among the wise and have found nothing better for anyone than silence. The main thing is not theory but practice, and one who talks too much causes sin.

18. Rabban Simon ben Gamliel says, Civilisation is preserved by three things:
   by truth,
   by justice
   and by peace.

טו שַׁמַּאי אוֹמֵר. עֲשֵׂה תוֹרָתְךָ קֶבַע. אֱמוֹר מְעַט וַעֲשֵׂה הַרְבֵּה. וֶהֱוֵה מְקַבֵּל אֶת־כָּל־הָאָדָם בְּסֵבֶר פָּנִים יָפוֹת:

טז רַבָּן גַּמְלִיאֵל אוֹמֵר. עֲשֵׂה לְךָ רַב וְהִסְתַּלֵּק מִן הַסָּפֵק וְאַל תַּרְבֶּה לְעַשֵּׂר אֲמָדוֹת:

יז שִׁמְעוֹן בְּנוֹ אוֹמֵר. כָּל־יָמַי גָּדַלְתִּי בֵּין הַחֲכָמִים וְלֹא מָצָאתִי לַגּוּף טוֹב מִשְּׁתִיקָה. וְלֹא הַמִּדְרָשׁ הוּא הָעִקָּר אֶלָּא הַמַּעֲשֶׂה. וְכָל־הַמַּרְבֶּה דְבָרִים מֵבִיא חֵטְא:

יח רַבָּן שִׁמְעוֹן בֶּן־גַּמְלִיאֵל אוֹמֵר. עַל־שְׁלֹשָׁה דְבָרִים הָעוֹלָם קַיָּם. עַל־הָאֱמֶת וְעַל־הַדִּין וְעַל־הַשָּׁלוֹם:

פרק שני

א רַבִּי אוֹמֵר. אֵיזוֹ הִיא דֶרֶךְ יְשָׁרָה שֶׁיָּבוֹר לוֹ הָאָדָם. כָּל־שֶׁהִיא תִפְאֶרֶת לְעוֹשֶׂיהָ וְתִפְאֶרֶת לוֹ מִן הָאָדָם. וֶהֱוֵה זָהִיר בְּמִצְוָה קַלָּה כְּבַחֲמוּרָה שֶׁאֵין אַתָּה יוֹדֵעַ מַתַּן שְׂכָרָן שֶׁל־מִצְוֹת. וֶהֱוֵי מְחַשֵּׁב הֶפְסֵד מִצְוָה כְּנֶגֶד שְׂכָרָהּ וּשְׂכַר עֲבֵרָה כְּנֶגֶד הֶפְסֵדָהּ. וְהִסְתַּכֵּל בִּשְׁלשָׁה דְבָרִים וְאֵין אַתָּה בָא לִידֵי עֲבֵרָה. דַּע מַה־לְּמַעְלָה מִמְּךָ עַיִן רוֹאָה וְאֹזֶן שׁוֹמַעַת וְכָל־מַעֲשֶׂיךָ בַּסֵּפֶר נִכְתָּבִים:

ב רַבָּן גַּמְלִיאֵל בְּנוֹ שֶׁל־רַבִּי יְהוּדָה הַנָּשִׂיא אוֹמֵר. יָפֶה תַלְמוּד תּוֹרָה עִם דֶּרֶךְ אֶרֶץ שֶׁיְּגִיעַת שְׁנֵיהֶם מְשַׁכַּחַת עָוֹן. וְכָל־תּוֹרָה שֶׁאֵין עִמָּהּ מְלָאכָה סוֹפָהּ בְּטֵלָה וְגוֹרֶרֶת עָוֹן. וְכָל־הָעוֹסְקִים עִם־הַצִּבּוּר יִהְיוּ עוֹסְקִים עִמָּהֶם לְשֵׁם שָׁמַיִם שֶׁזְּכוּת אֲבוֹתָם מְסַיַּעְתָּם וְצִדְקָתָם עוֹמֶדֶת לָעַד. וְאַתֶּם מַעֲלֶה אֲנִי עֲלֵיכֶם שָׂכָר הַרְבֵּה כְּאִלּוּ עֲשִׂיתֶם:

ג הֱווּ זְהִירִים בָּרָשׁוּת שֶׁאֵין מְקָרְבִין לוֹ לָאָדָם אֶלָּא לְצֹרֶךְ עַצְמָם. נִרְאִים כְּאוֹהֲבִים בִּשְׁעַת הֲנָאָתָן וְאֵין עוֹמְדִים לוֹ לָאָדָם בִּשְׁעַת דָּחֳקוֹ:

From Chapter 2

1. Rabbi says, What is the upright course a person should choose? That which brings honour to the one who does it, and for which one is honoured by others. Be just as careful with a light commandment as with a weighty one, for you do not know the reward given for each commandment. Reckon the loss incurred by fulfilling a commandment against the reward for it; and the profit gained by transgressing against the loss it entails. Consider three things and you will not come into the power of sin. Know what is above you - an eye that sees, an ear that hears, and that all your deeds are written in a book.

2. Rabban Gamliel, the son of Rabbi Judah the Prince, says, It is an excellent thing to combine the study of Torah with a trade or profession, for the labour necessary for both together puts sin out of mind. Study of Torah, however, which is not combined with work, ends in futility and becomes the cause of sin. Let all who work for the congregation do it for the sake of heaven. Then the merit of their ancestors will come to their aid and their righteousness will last forever. (And God will say,) 'And as for you, I credit you with a great reward, as though you had done it all yourselves.'

3. Be careful of those in power! For they draw no one near them except in their own interest. They seem like friends when it is to their own advantage, but they do not stand by people in their hour of need.

707 from the SAYINGS OF THE FATHERS — CHAPTER 2

4. He used to say, Do God's will as if it were your will, so that God may do your will as if it were the Divine will. Destroy your will for the sake of God's will, so that God may destroy the will of others for the sake of your will.

5. Hillel says, Do not separate yourself from the community. Do not trust in yourself until the day of your death. Do not judge others until you have been in their position. Do not say anything which cannot be understood at once in the hope that it will be understood in the end. And do not say 'When I have leisure I will study,' perhaps you will never have leisure.

6. He used to say, A crude person cannot fear sin, an ignorant person cannot be pious, nor can a timid person learn, nor a short-tempered person teach. Someone who is too preoccupied with business cannot grow wise. Where none take responsibility, try to take responsibility!

7. Also, when he saw a skull floating on the surface of the water, he said, Because you drowned others, they drowned you, and in the end those who drowned you shall themselves be drowned.

ד הוּא הָיָה אוֹמֵר. עֲשֵׂה רְצוֹנוֹ כִּרְצוֹנְךָ כְּדֵי שֶׁיַּעֲשֶׂה רְצוֹנְךָ כִּרְצוֹנוֹ. בַּטֵּל רְצוֹנְךָ מִפְּנֵי רְצוֹנוֹ כְּדֵי שֶׁיְּבַטֵּל רְצוֹן אֲחֵרִים מִפְּנֵי רְצוֹנֶךָ:

ה הִלֵּל אוֹמֵר. אַל־תִּפְרוֹשׁ מִן־הַצִּבּוּר. וְאַל־תַּאֲמֵן בְּעַצְמְךָ עַד יוֹם מוֹתְךָ. וְאַל־תָּדִין אֶת־חֲבֵרְךָ עַד שֶׁתַּגִּיעַ לִמְקוֹמוֹ. וְאַל־תֹּאמַר דָּבָר שֶׁאִי אֶפְשָׁר לִשְׁמוֹעַ שֶׁסּוֹפוֹ לְהִשָּׁמַע. וְאַל־תֹּאמַר לִכְשֶׁאֶפָּנֶה אֶשְׁנֶה שֶׁמָּא לֹא תִפָּנֶה:

ו הוּא הָיָה אוֹמֵר. אֵין בּוּר יְרֵא חֵטְא וְלֹא עַם הָאָרֶץ חָסִיד וְלֹא הַבַּיְשָׁן לָמֵד וְלֹא הַקַּפְּדָן מְלַמֵּד. וְלֹא כָל־הַמַּרְבֶּה בִסְחוֹרָה מַחְכִּים. וּבִמְקוֹם שֶׁאֵין אֲנָשִׁים הִשְׁתַּדֵּל לִהְיוֹת אִישׁ:

ז אַף הוּא רָאָה גֻּלְגֹּלֶת אַחַת שֶׁצָּפָה עַל־פְּנֵי הַמָּיִם. אָמַר לָהּ. עַל דְּאַטֵפְתְּ אַטְפוּךְ וְסוֹף מְטַיְּפַיִךְ יְטוּפוּן:

8. He used to say, The more flesh, the more worms; the more property, the more worry; the more slaves, the more robbery; the more Torah, the more life; the more dedicated study, the more wisdom; the more advice, the more understanding; the more justice, the more peace. Those who acquire a good reputation acquire it for themselves alone; those who acquire words of Torah, acquire eternal life.

9. Rabban Yochanan ben Zakkai received tradition from Hillel and Shammai. He used to say, If you have learnt much Torah, do not congratulate yourself, for that is why you were created.

13. He said to his disciples, Go out and see the right course a person should adopt. Rabbi Eliezer says, A kindly eye. Rabbi Joshua says, A good companion. Rabbi Yose says, A good neighbour. Rabbi Simon says, One who foresees the consequences. Rabbi Elazar says, A good heart. He said to them, I agree with the words of Elazar ben Arach, for his words include yours.

ח הוּא הָיָה אוֹמֵר. מַרְבֶּה בָשָׂר מַרְבֶּה רִמָּה. מַרְבֶּה נְכָסִים מַרְבֶּה דְאָגָה. מַרְבֶּה עֲבָדִים מַרְבֶּה גָזֵל. מַרְבֶּה תוֹרָה מַרְבֶּה חַיִּים. מַרְבֶּה יְשִׁיבָה מַרְבֶּה חָכְמָה. מַרְבֶּה עֵצָה מַרְבֶּה תְבוּנָה. מַרְבֶּה צְדָקָה מַרְבֶּה שָׁלוֹם. קָנָה שֵׁם טוֹב קָנָה לְעַצְמוֹ. קָנָה לוֹ דִבְרֵי תוֹרָה קָנָה לוֹ חַיֵּי הָעוֹלָם הַבָּא:

ט רַבָּן יוֹחָנָן בֶּן־זַכַּאי קִבֵּל מֵהִלֵּל וּמִשַּׁמַּאי. הוּא הָיָה אוֹמֵר. אִם לָמַדְתָּ תּוֹרָה הַרְבֵּה אַל־תַּחֲזִק טוֹבָה לְעַצְמְךָ כִּי לְכָךְ נוֹצָרְתָּ:

יג אָמַר לָהֶם. צְאוּ וּרְאוּ אֵיזוֹ הִיא דֶרֶךְ יְשָׁרָה שֶׁיִּדְבַּק בָּהּ הָאָדָם. רַבִּי אֱלִיעֶזֶר אוֹמֵר עַיִן טוֹבָה. רַבִּי יְהוֹשֻׁעַ אוֹמֵר חָבֵר טוֹב. רַבִּי יוֹסֵי אוֹמֵר שָׁכֵן טוֹב. רַבִּי שִׁמְעוֹן אוֹמֵר הָרוֹאֶה אֶת־הַנּוֹלָד. רַבִּי אֶלְעָזָר אוֹמֵר, לֵב טוֹב. אָמַר לָהֶם. רוֹאֶה אֲנִי אֶת־דִּבְרֵי אֶלְעָזָר בֶּן עֲרָךְ מִדִּבְרֵיכֶם שֶׁבִּכְלָל דְּבָרָיו דִּבְרֵיכֶם:

709 from the SAYINGS OF THE FATHERS — CHAPTER 2

14. He said to them, Go out and see the wrong course, one that a person should avoid. Rabbi Eliezer says, A grudging eye. Rabbi Joshua says, A bad companion. Rabbi Yose says, A bad neighbour. Rabbi Simon says, A borrower who does not pay back. It is the same whether he borrows from people or whether he borrows from God who is present everywhere. Rabbi Elazar says, A mean heart. He said to them, I agree with the words of Elazar ben Arach, for his words include yours.

15. Each of them said three things. Rabbi Eliezer says, Let the honour of others be as dear to you as your own. Do not be quick to anger. Repent even one day before your death. Warm yourself at the fire of the wise, but beware of their glowing coals lest you be scorched. For their bite is the bite of a fox, and their sting the sting of a scorpion, and their hiss the hiss of a serpent, for all their words are like coals of fire.

16. Rabbi Joshua says, A grudging eye, the impulse to evil, and hatred of people drive a person out of the world.

17. Rabbi Yose says, Let the property of others be as dear to you as your own. Train yourself to study Torah, for it is not yours by inheritance. And let all your actions be for the sake of heaven.

יד אָמַר לָהֶם. צְאוּ וּרְאוּ אֵיזוֹ הִיא דֶרֶךְ רָעָה שֶׁיִּתְרַחֵק מִמֶּנָּה הָאָדָם. רַבִּי אֱלִיעֶזֶר אוֹמֵר עַיִן רָעָה. רַבִּי יְהוֹשֻׁעַ אוֹמֵר חָבֵר רָע. רַבִּי יוֹסֵי אוֹמֵר שָׁכֵן רָע. רַבִּי שִׁמְעוֹן אוֹמֵר הַלֹּוֶה וְאֵינוֹ מְשַׁלֵּם. אֶחָד הַלֹּוֶה מִן־הָאָדָם כְּלֹוֶה מִן־הַמָּקוֹם. רַבִּי אֶלְעָזָר אוֹמֵר לֵב רָע. אָמַר לָהֶם. רוֹאֶה אֲנִי אֶת־דִּבְרֵי אֶלְעָזָר בֶּן־עֲרָךְ מִדִּבְרֵיכֶם שֶׁבִּכְלַל דְּבָרָיו דִּבְרֵיכֶם:

טו הֵם אָמְרוּ שְׁלֹשָׁה דְבָרִים. רַבִּי אֱלִיעֶזֶר אוֹמֵר. יְהִי כְבוֹד חֲבֵרְךָ חָבִיב עָלֶיךָ כְּשֶׁלָּךְ. וְאַל־תְּהִי נוֹחַ לִכְעוֹס. וְשׁוּב יוֹם אֶחָד לִפְנֵי מִיתָתְךָ. וֶהֱוֵי מִתְחַמֵּם כְּנֶגֶד אוּרָם שֶׁל חֲכָמִים וֶהֱוֵי זָהִיר בְּגַחַלְתָּם שֶׁלֹּא תִכָּוֶה. שֶׁנְּשִׁיכָתָם נְשִׁיכַת שׁוּעָל וַעֲקִיצָתָם עֲקִיצַת עַקְרָב וּלְחִישָׁתָם לְחִישַׁת שָׂרָף וְכָל־דִּבְרֵיהֶם כְּגַחֲלֵי אֵשׁ:

טז רַבִּי יְהוֹשֻׁעַ אוֹמֵר. עַיִן הָרָע. וְיֵצֶר הָרָע. וְשִׂנְאַת הַבְּרִיּוֹת. מוֹצִיאִין אֶת־הָאָדָם מִן־הָעוֹלָם:

יז רַבִּי יוֹסֵי אוֹמֵר. יְהִי מָמוֹן חֲבֵרְךָ חָבִיב עָלֶיךָ כְּשֶׁלָּךְ. וְהַתְקֵן עַצְמְךָ לִלְמוֹד תּוֹרָה שֶׁאֵינָהּ יְרֻשָּׁה־לָךְ. וְכָל־מַעֲשֶׂיךָ יִהְיוּ לְשֵׁם שָׁמָיִם:

פרק ב'

יח רַבִּי שִׁמְעוֹן אוֹמֵר. הֱוֵה זָהִיר בִּקְרִיאַת שְׁמַע וּבִתְפִלָּה. וּכְשֶׁאַתָּה מִתְפַּלֵּל אַל־תַּעַשׂ תְּפִלָּתְךָ קֶבַע אֶלָּא רַחֲמִים וְתַחֲנוּנִים לִפְנֵי הַמָּקוֹם. שֶׁנֶּאֱמַר כִּי חַנּוּן וְרַחוּם הוּא אֶרֶךְ אַפַּיִם וְרַב־חֶסֶד וְנִחָם עַל־הָרָעָה. וְאַל־תְּהִי רָשָׁע בִּפְנֵי עַצְמֶךָ:

יט רַבִּי אֶלְעָזָר אוֹמֵר. הֱוֵה שָׁקוּד לִלְמוֹד תּוֹרָה וְדַע מַה־שֶׁתָּשִׁיב לָאֶפִּיקוֹרוֹס. וְדַע לִפְנֵי מִי אַתָּה עָמֵל. וּמִי הוּא בַּעַל מְלַאכְתְּךָ שֶׁיְּשַׁלֶּם־לְךָ שְׂכַר פְּעֻלָּתֶךָ:

כ רַבִּי טַרְפוֹן אוֹמֵר. הַיּוֹם קָצֵר וְהַמְּלָאכָה מְרֻבָּה וְהַפּוֹעֲלִים עֲצֵלִים וְהַשָּׂכָר הַרְבֵּה וּבַעַל הַבַּיִת דּוֹחֵק:

כא הוּא הָיָה אוֹמֵר. לֹא עָלֶיךָ הַמְּלָאכָה לִגְמוֹר וְלֹא אַתָּה בֶּן־חוֹרִין לְהִבָּטֵל מִמֶּנָּה. אִם לָמַדְתָּ תּוֹרָה הַרְבֵּה נוֹתְנִים לְךָ שָׂכָר הַרְבֵּה. וְנֶאֱמָן הוּא בַּעַל מְלַאכְתְּךָ שֶׁיְּשַׁלֶּם־לְךָ שְׂכַר פְּעֻלָּתֶךָ. וְדַע שֶׁמַּתַּן שְׂכָרָם שֶׁל צַדִּיקִים לֶעָתִיד לָבוֹא:

18. Rabbi Simon says, Take care when you say the *Sh'ma* and the *Amidah*. When you pray, do not make your prayer a fixed formal thing, but an appeal for mercy, a supplication before God. As it is said: 'For God is gracious and merciful, long-suffering and full of love and ready to relent from threatened evil.'[1] And do not consider yourself completely wicked.

19. Rabbi Elazar says, Be diligent in the study of Torah and know how to answer an unbeliever. Also realise in whose presence you toil, and who is the Employer who will pay you the reward for your labour.

20. Rabbi Tarfon says, The day is short, and the work is great, and the labourers are sluggish, and the wages are high, and the Master of the house is insistent.

21. He used to say, It is not your duty to finish the work but you are not free to neglect it. If you learn much Torah, you will be given much reward, and faithful is your Employer to pay you the reward of your labour. But know that the reward of the righteous is in the time to come.

[1.] Joel 2:13.

from the SAYINGS OF THE FATHERS — CHAPTER 3

From Chapter 3

1. Akavya ben Mahalalel says, Keep three things in sight and you will not fall into the power of sin. Know where you come from, and where you go to, and before whom you are destined to give an account and reckoning.

2. Rabbi Chanina, the deputy High Priest says, Pray for the welfare of the government, because but for the fear it inspires people would swallow each other up alive.

3. Rabbi Chananya ben Teradion says, When two people sit together, and words of Torah pass between them, the presence of God rests between them also.

6. Rabbi Nechunya ben Hakanah says, Those who take upon themselves the yoke of Torah will find relief from the yoke of politics and worldly affairs. But those who get rid of the yoke of Torah will find the yoke of politics and worldly affairs weighing more heavily on them.

7. Rabbi Chalafta ben Dosa, of the village of Chananya, says, When ten people sit studying Torah, God's presence dwells among them, as it is said: 'God stands in the congregation of the godly.'[1] How do we know that this even applies to one person only? Because it is said: 'In every place where I cause My name to be remembered, I will come to you and bless you.'[2]

פרק שלישי

א עֲקַבְיָא בֶּן־מַהֲלַלְאֵל אוֹמֵר. הִסְתַּכֵּל בִּשְׁלֹשָׁה דְבָרִים וְאֵין אַתָּה בָא לִידֵי עֲבֵרָה. דַּע מֵאַיִן בָּאתָ. וּלְאָן אַתָּה הוֹלֵךְ. וְלִפְנֵי מִי אַתָּה עָתִיד לִתֵּן דִּין וְחֶשְׁבּוֹן:

ב רַבִּי חֲנִינָא סְגַן הַכֹּהֲנִים אוֹמֵר. הֱוֵי מִתְפַּלֵּל בִּשְׁלוֹמָהּ שֶׁל מַלְכוּת שֶׁאִלְמָלֵא מוֹרָאָהּ אִישׁ אֶת־רֵעֵהוּ חַיִּים בְּלָעוֹ:

ג רַבִּי חֲנַנְיָא בֶּן־תְּרַדְיוֹן אוֹמֵר. שְׁנַיִם שֶׁיּוֹשְׁבִים וְיֵשׁ בֵּינֵיהֶם דִּבְרֵי תוֹרָה. שְׁכִינָה שְׁרוּיָה בֵּינֵיהֶם:

ו רַבִּי נְחוּנְיָא בֶּן הַקָּנָה אוֹמֵר. כָּל־הַמְקַבֵּל עָלָיו עֹל תּוֹרָה מַעֲבִירִין מִמֶּנּוּ עֹל מַלְכוּת וְעֹל דֶּרֶךְ אֶרֶץ. וְכָל־הַפּוֹרֵק מִמֶּנּוּ עֹל תּוֹרָה נוֹתְנִין עָלָיו עֹל מַלְכוּת וְעֹל דֶּרֶךְ אֶרֶץ:

ז רַבִּי חֲלַפְתָּא בֶּן־דּוֹסָא אִישׁ כְּפַר חֲנַנְיָה אוֹמֵר עֲשָׂרָה שֶׁיּוֹשְׁבִים וְעוֹסְקִים בַּתּוֹרָה שְׁכִינָה שְׁרוּיָה בֵּינֵיהֶם. שֶׁנֶּאֱמַר אֱלֹהִים נִצָּב בַּעֲדַת אֵל. וּמִנַּיִן אֲפִילוּ אֶחָד. שֶׁנֶּאֱמַר בְּכָל־הַמָּקוֹם אֲשֶׁר אַזְכִּיר אֶת־שְׁמִי אָבוֹא אֵלֶיךָ וּבֵרַכְתִּיךָ:

---

[1] Ps 82:1.   [2] Ex 20:21.

פרק ג׳

8. Rabbi Elazar of Bertota says, Give God what is God's, for what you are and what you have are God's. Therefore David said about himself: 'For everything comes from You, and we have only given You what comes from Your hand.'[1]

9. Rabbi Jacob says, If someone is teaching by repetition as he walks along the road and interrupts his repetition and exclaims: 'How lovely is that tree! How lovely is this field!' Scripture considers that he had harmed his own soul.[2]

11. Rabbi Chanina ben Dosa says, All those whose fear of sin comes before their wisdom, their wisdom will endure. And all those whose wisdom comes before their fear of sin, their wisdom will not endure.

12. He used to say, All those whose deeds exceed their wisdom, their wisdom will endure. And all those whose wisdom exceeds their deeds, their wisdom will not endure.

13. He used to say, All those who delight their fellow-creatures, God delights in them. And all those who give no delight to their fellow-creatures, God does not delight in them.

ח רַבִּי אֶלְעָזָר אִישׁ בַּרְתּוֹתָא אוֹמֵר. תֶּן־לוֹ מִשֶּׁלּוֹ שֶׁאַתָּה וְשֶׁלָּךְ שֶׁלּוֹ. וְכֵן בְּדָוִד הוּא אוֹמֵר כִּי־מִמְּךָ הַכֹּל וּמִיָּדְךָ נָתַנּוּ לָךְ:

ט רַבִּי יַעֲקֹב אוֹמֵר. הַמְהַלֵּךְ בַּדֶּרֶךְ וְשׁוֹנֶה וּמַפְסִיק מִמִּשְׁנָתוֹ וְאוֹמֵר מַה־נָּאֶה אִילָן זֶה וּמַה־נָּאֶה נִיר זֶה מַעֲלֶה עָלָיו הַכָּתוּב כְּאִלּוּ מִתְחַיֵּב בְּנַפְשׁוֹ:

יא רַבִּי חֲנִינָא בֶּן־דּוֹסָא אוֹמֵר. כָּל שֶׁיִּרְאַת חֶטְאוֹ קוֹדֶמֶת לְחָכְמָתוֹ חָכְמָתוֹ מִתְקַיֶּמֶת. וְכֹל שֶׁחָכְמָתוֹ קוֹדֶמֶת לְיִרְאַת חֶטְאוֹ אֵין חָכְמָתוֹ מִתְקַיֶּמֶת:

יב הוּא הָיָה אוֹמֵר. כֹּל שֶׁמַּעֲשָׂיו מְרֻבִּין מֵחָכְמָתוֹ חָכְמָתוֹ מִתְקַיֶּמֶת. וְכֹל שֶׁחָכְמָתוֹ מְרֻבָּה מִמַּעֲשָׂיו אֵין חָכְמָתוֹ מִתְקַיֶּמֶת:

יג הוּא הָיָה אוֹמֵר. כֹּל שֶׁרוּחַ הַבְּרִיּוֹת נוֹחָה הֵימֶנּוּ רוּחַ הַמָּקוֹם נוֹחָה הֵימֶנּוּ. וְכֹל שֶׁאֵין רוּחַ הַבְּרִיּוֹת נוֹחָה הֵימֶנּוּ אֵין רוּחַ הַמָּקוֹם נוֹחָה הֵימֶנּוּ:

[1.] 1 Chron 29:14.
[2.] *In this period when written texts were scarce, teachers would quote and repeat texts to their students, who would in turn learn them by heart. Any extraneous* remarks made by the teacher would be assumed by the student to be part of the lesson and memorised, thus distorting the entire teaching to the next generations.

713 from the SAYINGS OF THE FATHERS — CHAPTER 3

14. Rabbi Dosa ben Horkinas says, Sleeping late, mid-day drinking, childish chatter and attending meetings of ignorant people drive a person out of the world.

יד רַבִּי דוֹסָא בֶּן־הָרְכִּינַס אוֹמֵר. שֵׁנָה שֶׁל שַׁחֲרִית וְיַיִן שֶׁל־צָהֳרַיִם וְשִׂיחַת הַיְלָדִים וִישִׁיבַת בָּתֵּי כְנֵסִיּוֹת שֶׁל־עַמֵּי הָאָרֶץ מוֹצִיאִים אֶת הָאָדָם מִן הָעוֹלָם:

16. Rabbi Ishmael says, Be respectful to your senior, and be patient with your junior, and welcome everyone cheerfully.

טז רַבִּי יִשְׁמָעֵאל אוֹמֵר. הֱוֵה קַל לְרֹאשׁ וְנוֹחַ לְתִשְׁחֹרֶת. וֶהֱוֵה מְקַבֵּל אֶת כָּל־הָאָדָם בְּשִׂמְחָה:

17. Rabbi Akiba says, joking and frivolity lead a person to immorality. Tradition is a safeguard around the Torah; giving regularly to charity is a safeguard to wealth; vows are a safeguard for self-restraint; a safeguard for wisdom is silence.

יז רַבִּי עֲקִיבָא אוֹמֵר. שְׂחוֹק וְקַלּוּת רֹאשׁ מַרְגִּילִים לְעֶרְוָה. מָסֹרֶת סְיָג לַתּוֹרָה. מַעַשְׂרוֹת סְיָג לְעוֹשֶׁר. נְדָרִים סְיָג לִפְרִישׁוּת. סְיָג לַחָכְמָה שְׁתִיקָה:

18. He used to say, Beloved are human beings for they were created in the image of God. Yet with even greater love it was revealed to them that they were so created in the image of God.

יח הוּא הָיָה אוֹמֵר. חָבִיב אָדָם שֶׁנִּבְרָא בְצֶלֶם. חִבָּה יְתֵרָה נוֹדַעַת לוֹ שֶׁנִּבְרָא בְּצֶלֶם אֱלֹהִים:

19. Everything is foreseen, yet free choice is granted. The world is judged with mercy, yet everything is according to the amount of work.

יט הַכֹּל צָפוּי וְהָרְשׁוּת נְתוּנָה וּבְטוֹב הָעוֹלָם נִדּוֹן וְהַכֹּל לְפִי רֹב הַמַּעֲשֶׂה:

20. He used to say, Everything is given on pledge, and a net is spread for all living. The shop is open, and the shopkeeper gives credit, and the account is open and the hand writes, and whoever wishes to borrow may come and borrow. But the collectors go round every day, and exact payment from people with their consent or without it, and their claims are justified, and the judgment is a judgment of truth. Yet everything is prepared for the feast!

כ הוּא הָיָה אוֹמֵר. הַכֹּל נָתוּן בָּעֵרָבוֹן וּמְצוּדָה פְרוּסָה עַל־כָּל־הַחַיִּים. הַחֲנוּת פְּתוּחָה וְהַחֶנְוָנִי מַקִּיף וְהַפִּנְקָס פָּתוּחַ וְהַיָּד כּוֹתֶבֶת וְכָל־הָרוֹצֶה לִלְווֹת יָבוֹא וְיִלְוֶה וְהַגַּבָּאִים מַחֲזִירִים תָּדִיר בְּכָל־יוֹם וְנִפְרָעִים מִן־הָאָדָם מִדַּעְתּוֹ וְשֶׁלֹּא מִדַּעְתּוֹ וְיֵשׁ לָהֶם עַל מַה שֶּׁיִּסְמְכוּ וְהַדִּין דִּין אֱמֶת. וְהַכֹּל מְתֻקָּן לַסְּעוּדָה:

21. Rabbi Elazar ben Azaryah says, Where there is no Torah there are no manners; where there are no manners there is no Torah.
   Without wisdom
     there is no fear of God;
   without the fear of God
     there is no wisdom.
   Without insight
     there is no knowledge;
   without knowledge
     there is no insight.
   Without food there is no Torah;
     without Torah there is no food.

22. He used to say, Those whose wisdom exceeds their deeds are like a tree whose branches are many, but whose roots are few. Then the wind comes and uproots it and turns it over. But those whose deeds exceed their wisdom are like a tree whose branches are few, but whose roots are many, so that even if all the winds in the world come and blow upon it, it cannot be moved from its place.

כא רַבִּי אֶלְעָזָר בֶּן־עֲזַרְיָה אוֹמֵר.
אִם אֵין תּוֹרָה אֵין דֶּרֶךְ אֶרֶץ.
אִם אֵין דֶּרֶךְ אֶרֶץ אֵין תּוֹרָה.
אִם אֵין חָכְמָה אֵין יִרְאָה.
אִם אֵין יִרְאָה אֵין חָכְמָה.
אִם אֵין דַּעַת אֵין בִּינָה.
אִם אֵין בִּינָה אֵין דָּעַת.
אִם אֵין קֶמַח אֵין תּוֹרָה.
אִם אֵין תּוֹרָה אֵין קֶמַח:

כב הוּא הָיָה אוֹמֵר. כֹּל שֶׁחָכְמָתוֹ מְרֻבָּה מִמַּעֲשָׂיו לְמָה הוּא דוֹמֶה. לְאִילָן שֶׁעֲנָפָיו מְרֻבִּים וְשָׁרָשָׁיו מוּעָטִים וְהָרוּחַ בָּאָה וְעוֹקַרְתּוֹ וְהוֹפַכְתּוֹ עַל פָּנָיו. אֲבָל כֹּל שֶׁמַּעֲשָׂיו מְרֻבִּים מֵחָכְמָתוֹ לְמָה הוּא דוֹמֶה. לְאִילָן שֶׁעֲנָפָיו מֻעָטִים וְשָׁרָשָׁיו מְרֻבִּים שֶׁאֲפִילוּ כָּל־הָרוּחוֹת שֶׁבָּעוֹלָם בָּאוֹת וְנוֹשְׁבוֹת בּוֹ אֵין מְזִיזִים אוֹתוֹ מִמְּקוֹמוֹ:

from the SAYINGS OF THE FATHERS — CHAPTER 4

From Chapter 4

1. Ben Zoma says, Who are wise? Those who learn from everyone. Who are mighty? Those who control their passions. Who are rich? Those who are happy with what they have. Who are honourable? Those who honour others.

2. Ben Azzai says, Run to do even a small *mitzvah,* but run away from doing wrong. One good deed leads to another, and one sin leads to another. Virtue is its own reward, and the wages of sin are sin.

3. Hold no people insignificant and nothing improbable, for there are no people that do not have their hour and no thing that has not its place.

4. Rabbi Levitas of Yavneh says, Be very humble, for the hope of frail human beings is the worm.

6. Rabbi Ishmael says, Those who learn in order to teach will be given the opportunity to learn and to teach. But those who learn in order to practise will be given the opportunity both to learn and teach, and to observe and practise.

פרק רביעי

א בֶּן זוֹמָא אוֹמֵר. אֵיזֶהוּ חָכָם. הַלּוֹמֵד מִכָּל־אָדָם. אֵיזֶהוּ גִבּוֹר. הַכּוֹבֵשׁ אֶת יִצְרוֹ. אֵיזֶהוּ עָשִׁיר. הַשָּׂמֵחַ בְּחֶלְקוֹ. אֵיזֶהוּ מְכֻבָּד. הַמְכַבֵּד אֶת הַבְּרִיּוֹת:

ב בֶּן עַזַּאי אוֹמֵר. הֱוֵה רָץ לְמִצְוָה קַלָּה וּבוֹרֵחַ מִן הָעֲבֵרָה. שֶׁמִּצְוָה גּוֹרֶרֶת מִצְוָה וַעֲבֵרָה גּוֹרֶרֶת עֲבֵרָה. שֶׁשְּׂכַר מִצְוָה מִצְוָה וּשְׂכַר עֲבֵרָה עֲבֵרָה:

ג הוּא הָיָה אוֹמֵר. אַל תְּהִי בָז לְכָל־אָדָם וְאַל תְּהִי מַפְלִיג לְכָל־דָּבָר שֶׁאֵין לְךָ אָדָם שֶׁאֵין לוֹ שָׁעָה וְאֵין לְךָ דָבָר שֶׁאֵין לוֹ מָקוֹם:

ד רַבִּי לְוִיטָס אִישׁ יַבְנֶה אוֹמֵר. מְאֹד מְאֹד הֱוֵה שְׁפַל רוּחַ שֶׁתִּקְוַת אֱנוֹשׁ רִמָּה:

ו רַבִּי יִשְׁמָעֵאל אוֹמֵר. הַלּוֹמֵד תּוֹרָה עַל־מְנָת לְלַמֵּד מַסְפִּיקִים בְּיָדוֹ לִלְמוֹד וּלְלַמֵּד. וְהַלּוֹמֵד עַל־מְנָת לַעֲשׂוֹת מַסְפִּיקִים בְּיָדוֹ לִלְמוֹד וּלְלַמֵּד לִשְׁמוֹר וְלַעֲשׂוֹת:

פרק ד׳

ז רַבִּי צָדוֹק אוֹמֵר. אַל תַּעֲשֵׂם עֲטָרָה לְהִתְגַּדֵּל־בָּהּ וְלֹא קַרְדּוֹם לַחְפָּר־בָּהּ. וְכַךְ הָיָה הִלֵּל אוֹמֵר. וּדְאִשְׁתַּמֵּשׁ בְּתָגָא חֳלָף. הָא לָמַדְתָּ כָּל־הַנֶּהֱנֶה מִדִּבְרֵי תוֹרָה נוֹטֵל חַיָּיו מִן־הָעוֹלָם:

י רַבִּי יִשְׁמָעֵאל בֶּן־רַבִּי יוֹסֵי הָיָה אוֹמֵר. אַל־תְּהִי דָן יְחִידִי שֶׁאֵין דָּן יְחִידִי אֶלָּא אֶחָד. וְאַל תֹּאמַר קַבְּלוּ דַעְתִּי שֶׁהֵן רַשָּׁאִים וְלֹא אָתָּה:

יב רַבִּי מֵאִיר אוֹמֵר. הֱוֵה מְמַעֵט בְּעֵסֶק וַעֲסוֹק בַּתּוֹרָה וֶהֱוֵה שְׁפַל־רוּחַ בִּפְנֵי כָל־אָדָם. וְאִם־בָּטַלְתָּ מִן הַתּוֹרָה יֶשׁ־לְךָ בְּטֵלִים הַרְבֵּה כְּנֶגְדֶּךָ. וְאִם־עָמַלְתָּ בַתּוֹרָה יֶשׁ־לוֹ שָׂכָר הַרְבֵּה לִתֶּן־לָךְ:

יג רַבִּי אֱלִיעֶזֶר בֶּן־יַעֲקֹב אוֹמֵר. הָעוֹשֶׂה מִצְוָה אַחַת קוֹנֶה לוֹ פְּרַקְלִיט אֶחָד. וְהָעוֹבֵר עֲבֵרָה אַחַת קוֹנֶה לוֹ קַטֵיגוֹר אֶחָד. תְּשׁוּבָה וּמַעֲשִׂים טוֹבִים כִּתְרִיס בִּפְנֵי הַפֻּרְעָנוּת:

יד רַבִּי יוֹחָנָן הַסַּנְדְּלָר אוֹמֵר. כָּל־כְּנֵסִיָּה שֶׁהִיא לְשֵׁם שָׁמַיִם סוֹפָהּ לְהִתְקַיֵּם. וְשֶׁאֵינָהּ לְשֵׁם שָׁמַיִם אֵין סוֹפָהּ לְהִתְקַיֵּם:

7. Rabbi Zadok says, Do not use the Torah as a crown for your own importance, or a spade to dig with. Hillel also used to say, Those who put the crown to their own use shall perish. Here you learn that those who make a profit from the words of Torah help to destroy themselves.

10. Rabbi Ishmael ben Rabbi Yose used to say, Do not judge alone, for no one judges alone except One. And do not say 'You must accept my view!' - the choice belongs to your colleagues and you have no right to compel them.

12. Rabbi Meir says, Decrease your concern for business affairs, concern yourself rather with religious affairs, and be humble before all people. If you neglect Torah, you will find many reasons for doing so, but if you labour in it, God has a great reward to give you.

13. Rabbi Eliezer ben Jacob says, Those who do one *mitzvah* acquire a counsel for the defence, and those who commit one sin acquire a counsel for the prosecution. Repentance and good deeds serve as a shield against retribution.

14. Rabbi Yochanan the sandal-maker says, Every meeting which is for the sake of heaven will endure, and every meeting which is not for the sake of heaven will not endure.

15. Rabbi Elazar ben Shammua says, Let your pupil's honour be as dear to you as your own; and your colleague's honour be as your respect for your teacher; and your teacher's respect as the awe of heaven.

טו רַבִּי אֶלְעָזָר בֶּן־שַׁמּוּעַ אוֹמֵר. יְהִי כְבוֹד תַּלְמִידְךָ חָבִיב עָלֶיךָ כְּשֶׁלָּךְ וּכְבוֹד חֲבֵרְךָ כְּמוֹרָא רַבָּךְ וּמוֹרָא רַבָּךְ כְּמוֹרָא שָׁמָיִם:

16. Rabbi Judah says, Take care when you study, for an error in teaching can do as much harm as a deliberate sin.

טז רַבִּי יְהוּדָה אוֹמֵר. הֱוֵה זָהִיר בְּתַלְמוּד שֶׁשִּׁגְגַת תַּלְמוּד עוֹלָה זָדוֹן:

17. Rabbi Simon says, There are three crowns: the crown of Torah, the crown of priesthood, and the crown of royalty. But the crown of a good reputation excels them all.

יז רַבִּי שִׁמְעוֹן אוֹמֵר. שְׁלֹשָׁה כְתָרִים הֵם. כֶּתֶר תּוֹרָה וְכֶתֶר כְּהֻנָּה וְכֶתֶר מַלְכוּת. וְכֶתֶר שֵׁם טוֹב עוֹלֶה עַל גַּבֵּיהֶם:

18. Rabbi Nehorai says, Search for a place of Torah and do not say it will search for you. For there you will find companions to help you grasp it, and you will not have to rely on your own understanding alone.

יח רַבִּי נְהוֹרַאי אוֹמֵר. הֱוֵה גוֹלֶה לִמְקוֹם תּוֹרָה וְאַל־תֹּאמַר שֶׁהִיא תָבוֹא אַחֲרֶיךָ. שֶׁחֲבֵרֶיךָ יְקַיְּמוּהָ בְיָדֶךָ. וְאֶל־בִּינָתְךָ אַל־תִּשָּׁעֵן:

19. Rabbi Yannai says, Neither the prosperity of the wicked nor even the suffering of the righteous are in our hands.

יט רַבִּי יַנַּאי אוֹמֵר. אֵין בְּיָדֵינוּ לֹא מִשַּׁלְוַת הָרְשָׁעִים וְאַף לֹא מִיִּסּוּרֵי הַצַּדִּיקִים:

20. Rabbi Mattitya ben Cheresh says, Be first to greet everyone. Be a tail to lions rather than a head to jackals.

כ רַבִּי מַתְיָא בֶן־חֶרֶשׁ אוֹמֵר. הֱוֵה מַקְדִּים בִּשְׁלוֹם כָּל־אָדָם וֶהֱוֵה זָנָב לָאֲרָיוֹת וְאַל־תְּהִי רֹאשׁ לַשּׁוּעָלִים:

21. Rabbi Jacob says, The world is like a corridor to the world to come. Prepare yourself in the corridor so that you may enter the inner chamber.

כא רַבִּי יַעֲקֹב אוֹמֵר. הָעוֹלָם הַזֶּה דּוֹמֶה לִפְרוֹזְדוֹר בִּפְנֵי הָעוֹלָם הַבָּא. הַתְקֵן עַצְמְךָ בַּפְּרוֹזְדוֹר כְּדֵי שֶׁתִּכָּנֵס לַטְּרַקְלִין:

22. He used to say, One hour of repentance and good deeds in this world is better than all the life of the world to come; and one hour of calmness of spirit in the world to come is better than all the life of this world.

23. Rabbi Simon ben Elazar says, Do not try to calm others when they are angry; do not console them when their dead lie before them; do not cross-question them when they make a vow; and do not try to see them at the time of their disgrace.

24. Samuel the younger says, 'Do not rejoice when your enemy falls and do not let your heart be glad when he stumbles:'[1] 'For God sees it and thinks it wicked and turns the Divine anger from him.'[2]

25. Elisha ben Abuyah says, If people learn as children - what do they resemble? They resemble ink written on clean paper. If people learn when old - what do they resemble? They resemble ink written on worn-out paper.

26. Rabbi Yose bar Judah of K'far ha-Bavli says, If people learn from the young, whom do they resemble? They resemble a person who eats unripe grapes, and drinks wine straight from the vat. If people learn from the old, whom do they resemble? They resemble a person who eats ripe grapes and drinks mature wine.

כב הוּא הָיָה אוֹמֵר. יָפָה שָׁעָה אַחַת בִּתְשׁוּבָה וּמַעֲשִׂים טוֹבִים בָּעוֹלָם הַזֶּה מִכָּל־חַיֵּי הָעוֹלָם הַבָּא. וְיָפָה שָׁעָה אַחַת שֶׁל קֹרַת רוּחַ בָּעוֹלָם הַבָּא מִכָּל־חַיֵּי הָעוֹלָם הַזֶּה:

כג רַבִּי שִׁמְעוֹן בֶּן אֶלְעָזָר אוֹמֵר. אַל־תְּרַצֶּה אֶת־חֲבֵרְךָ בִּשְׁעַת כַּעֲסוֹ וְאַל־תְּנַחֲמֵהוּ בְּשָׁעָה שֶׁמֵּתוֹ מֻטָּל לְפָנָיו וְאַל־תִּשְׁאַל לוֹ בִּשְׁעַת נִדְרוֹ וְאַל־תִּשְׁתַּדֵּל לִרְאוֹתוֹ בִּשְׁעַת קַלְקָלָתוֹ:

כד שְׁמוּאֵל הַקָּטָן אוֹמֵר. בִּנְפֹל אוֹיִבְךָ אַל־תִּשְׂמָח וּבִכָּשְׁלוֹ אַל־יָגֵל לִבֶּךָ. פֶּן־יִרְאֶה יְהוָה וְרַע בְּעֵינָיו וְהֵשִׁיב מֵעָלָיו אַפּוֹ:

כה אֱלִישָׁע בֶּן־אֲבוּיָה אוֹמֵר. הַלּוֹמֵד יֶלֶד לְמָה הוּא דוֹמֶה. לִדְיוֹ כְּתוּבָה עַל־נְיָר חָדָשׁ. וְהַלּוֹמֵד זָקֵן לְמָה הוּא דוֹמֶה. לִדְיוֹ כְּתוּבָה עַל־נְיָר מָחוּק:

כו רַבִּי יוֹסֵי בַּר יְהוּדָה אִישׁ כְּפַר הַבַּבְלִי אוֹמֵר. הַלּוֹמֵד מִן־הַקְּטַנִּים לְמָה הוּא דוֹמֶה. לְאוֹכֵל עֲנָבִים קֵהוֹת וְשׁוֹתֶה יַיִן מִגִּתּוֹ. וְהַלּוֹמֵד מִן־הַזְּקֵנִים לְמָה הוּא דוֹמֶה. לְאוֹכֵל עֲנָבִים בְּשׁוּלוֹת וְשׁוֹתֶה יַיִן יָשָׁן:

---

[1] Prov 24:17.   [2] Prov 24:18.

from the SAYINGS OF THE FATHERS — CHAPTER 4

27. Rabbi Meir says, Do not look at the bottle but at what it contains. You can find new bottles filled with old wine, and old ones in which there is not even new wine.

28. Rabbi Elazar Hakappar says, Envy, desire and ambition drive a person out of the world.

29. He used to say, Those who are born will die; those who are dead will live again; and those who live again will be judged, to know, to make known and to realise that God is the maker, the creator, the discerner, the judge, the witness, the plaintiff; and God will summon to judgment. Blessed be the One, in whose presence there is no fault and no forgetfulness, who shows no favour and takes no bribe, for everything is God's. Know that everything is according to the reckoning.
Do not deceive yourself that the grave will be an excuse for you,
for without your consent
you were born,
and without your consent
you live,
and without your consent
you die,
and without your consent
you will have to give an account and a reckoning before the Sovereign above all earthly rulers, the Blessed Holy One.

כז רַבִּי מֵאִיר אוֹמֵר. אַל־תִּסְתַּכֵּל בְּקַנְקַן אֶלָּא בַּמֶּה שֶׁיֶּשׁ־בּוֹ. יֵשׁ קַנְקַן חָדָשׁ מָלֵא יָשָׁן וְיָשָׁן שֶׁאֲפִילוּ חָדָשׁ אֵין בּוֹ:

כח רַבִּי אֶלְעָזָר הַקַּפָּר אוֹמֵר. הַקִּנְאָה וְהַתַּאֲוָה וְהַכָּבוֹד מוֹצִיאִים אֶת־הָאָדָם מִן הָעוֹלָם:

כט הוּא הָיָה אוֹמֵר. הַיִּלּוֹדִים לָמוּת וְהַמֵּתִים לְהֵחָיוֹת וְהַחַיִּים לִדּוֹן לֵידַע לְהוֹדִיעַ וּלְהִוָּדַע שֶׁהוּא אֵל הוּא הַיּוֹצֵר הוּא הַבּוֹרֵא הוּא הַמֵּבִין הוּא הַדַּיָּן הוּא עֵד הוּא בַּעַל דִּין וְהוּא עָתִיד לָדוּן. בָּרוּךְ הוּא שֶׁאֵין לְפָנָיו לֹא עַוְלָה וְלֹא שִׁכְחָה וְלֹא מַשּׂוֹא פָנִים וְלֹא מִקַּח שׁוֹחַד שֶׁהַכֹּל שֶׁלּוֹ. וְדַע שֶׁהַכֹּל לְפִי הַחֶשְׁבּוֹן.
וְאַל־יַבְטִיחֲךָ יִצְרְךָ שֶׁהַשְּׁאוֹל בֵּית מָנוֹס לָךְ.
שֶׁעַל כָּרְחֲךָ אַתָּה נוֹלָד
וְעַל כָּרְחֲךָ אַתָּה חַי
וְעַל כָּרְחֲךָ אַתָּה מֵת
וְעַל כָּרְחֲךָ אַתָּה עָתִיד
לִתֵּן דִּין וְחֶשְׁבּוֹן
לִפְנֵי מֶלֶךְ מַלְכֵי הַמְּלָכִים
הַקָּדוֹשׁ בָּרוּךְ הוּא:

From Chapter 5

10. There are seven characteristics of uncultured people, and seven of wise people.
    Wise people do not speak before someone greater than themselves in wisdom.
    They do not cut into another's speech.
    They do not rush to reply.
    They ask what is relevant and answer to the point.
    They speak about first things first, and about last things last.
    As to what they have not heard they say, 'I did not hear it.'
    They acknowledge the truth.
The reverse of all these applies to uncultured people.

11. The sword comes into the world because of the delay of justice or the perversion of justice.

13. There are four types of people:
    Those who say,
    What is mine is mine,
    and what is yours is yours -
    this is the average type.
    (Some say this is the selfishness of Sodom.)
    Those who say,
    What is mine is yours,
    and what is yours is mine -
    such a one is an ignoramus.
    Those who say,
    What is mine is yours,
    and what is yours is yours -
    such a one is a *chasid*.
    Those who say,
    What is yours is mine,
    and what is mine is mine -
    such a one is wicked.

פרק חמישי

י שִׁבְעָה דְבָרִים בַּגֹּלֶם וְשִׁבְעָה בֶּחָכָם. חָכָם אֵינוֹ מְדַבֵּר בִּפְנֵי מִי שֶׁהוּא גָּדוֹל מִמֶּנּוּ בְּחָכְמָה. וְאֵינוֹ נִכְנָס לְתוֹךְ דִּבְרֵי חֲבֵרוֹ. וְאֵינוֹ נִבְהָל לְהָשִׁיב. שׁוֹאֵל כָּעִנְיָן וּמֵשִׁיב כַּהֲלָכָה. וְאוֹמֵר עַל־רִאשׁוֹן רִאשׁוֹן וְעַל־אַחֲרוֹן אַחֲרוֹן. וְעַל מַה־שֶּׁלֹּא שָׁמַע אוֹמֵר לֹא שָׁמָעְתִּי. וּמוֹדֶה עַל־הָאֱמֶת. וְחִלּוּפֵיהֶם בַּגֹּלֶם:

יא חֶרֶב בָּאָה לָעוֹלָם עַל עִנּוּי הַדִּין וְעַל עִוּוּת הַדִּין:

יג אַרְבַּע מִדּוֹת בָּאָדָם. הָאוֹמֵר שֶׁלִּי שֶׁלִּי וְשֶׁלְּךָ שֶׁלָּךְ זוֹ מִדָּה בֵּינוֹנִית וְיֵשׁ אוֹמְרִים זוֹ מִדַּת סְדוֹם. שֶׁלִּי שֶׁלָּךְ וְשֶׁלְּךָ שֶׁלִּי עַם הָאָרֶץ. שֶׁלִּי שֶׁלָּךְ וְשֶׁלְּךָ שֶׁלָּךְ חָסִיד. שֶׁלִּי שֶׁלִּי וְשֶׁלְּךָ שֶׁלִּי רָשָׁע:

14. There are four kinds
of temperament:
    Easily angered, and easily pacified -
    their gain is cancelled by their loss.
    Difficult to anger,
    and difficult to pacify -
    their loss is cancelled by their gain.
    Difficult to anger, and easy to pacify -
    such a one is a *chasid*.
    Easy to anger, and difficult to pacify -
    such a one is wicked.

15. There are four kinds of students:
    Those who are quick to learn
    and quick to forget -
    their gain is cancelled by their loss.
    Those who are slow to learn
    and slow to forget -
    their loss is cancelled by their gain.
    Those who are quick to learn
    and slow to forget -
    theirs is a happy lot.
    Those who are slow to learn
    and quick to forget -
    theirs is a sad lot.

16. There are four types of people
who give to charity:
    Those who wish to give,
    but that others should not give -
    their eye begrudges
    what belongs to others.
    Those who wish others to give,
    but that they themselves should not
    give - their eye begrudges
    what belongs to them.
    Those who wish to give,
    and others to give as well -
    such a one is *a chasid*.
    Those who do not wish to give,
    nor others to give -
    such a one is wicked.

יד אַרְבַּע מִדּוֹת בַּדֵּעוֹת.
נוֹחַ לִכְעוֹס וְנוֹחַ לִרְצוֹת
יָצָא הֶפְסֵדוֹ בִּשְׂכָרוֹ.
קָשֶׁה לִכְעוֹס וְקָשֶׁה לִרְצוֹת
יָצָא שְׂכָרוֹ בְּהֶפְסֵדוֹ.
קָשֶׁה לִכְעוֹס וְנוֹחַ לִרְצוֹת
חָסִיד.
נוֹחַ לִכְעוֹס וְקָשֶׁה לִרְצוֹת
רָשָׁע:

טו אַרְבַּע מִדּוֹת בַּתַּלְמִידִים.
מַהֵר לִשְׁמוֹעַ וּמַהֵר לְאַבֵּד
יָצָא שְׂכָרוֹ בְּהֶפְסֵדוֹ.
קָשֶׁה לִשְׁמוֹעַ וְקָשֶׁה לְאַבֵּד
יָצָא הֶפְסֵדוֹ בִּשְׂכָרוֹ.
מַהֵר לִשְׁמוֹעַ וְקָשֶׁה לְאַבֵּד
חָכָם.
קָשֶׁה לִשְׁמוֹעַ וּמַהֵר לְאַבֵּד
זֶה חֵלֶק רָע:

טז אַרְבַּע מִדּוֹת
בְּנוֹתְנֵי צְדָקָה.
הָרוֹצֶה שֶׁיִּתֵּן
וְלֹא יִתְּנוּ אֲחֵרִים
עֵינוֹ רָעָה בְּשֶׁל־אֲחֵרִים.
יִתְּנוּ אֲחֵרִים
וְהוּא לֹא יִתֵּן
עֵינוֹ רָעָה בְּשֶׁלּוֹ.
יִתֵּן וְיִתְּנוּ אֲחֵרִים
חָסִיד.
לֹא יִתֵּן וְלֹא יִתְּנוּ אֲחֵרִים
רָשָׁע:

19. If love depends on some selfish cause when the cause disappears love disappears; but if love does not depend on a selfish cause it will never disappear. What love depended on a selfish cause? Amnon's love for Tamar.[1] What love did not depend on a selfish cause? David's love for Jonathan.[2]

20. Every controversy which is for the sake of heaven will in the end lead to a lasting result. But one which is not for the sake of heaven will not in the end lead to a lasting result. What was a dispute for the sake of heaven? The dispute of Hillel and Shammai! And one which was not for the sake of heaven? The dispute of Korach and all his company![3]

21. When someone leads many to goodness no sin shall come through such a person. When someone leads many to sin such a person will not even have the means to repent. Moses was worthy and made many worthy, therefore the worth of many is linked to him.[4] Jeroboam sinned and made many sin, and therefore the sin of many is linked to him.[5]

23. Judah ben Tema says, Be strong as a leopard, light as an eagle, swift as a gazelle and strong as a lion to do the will of your Creator who is in heaven.

---

[1] 2 Sam 13.
[2] 1 Sam 18.
[3] Num 16.
[4] Deut 33:21.
[5] I Kings 15:30.

723 from the SAYINGS OF THE FATHERS — CHAPTER 6

25. Ben Bag Bag says, Turn the Torah this way and turn it that way, for everything is in it. Look into it, grow old and grey over it, and do not turn away from it for you have nothing better than this.

26. Ben Hey Hey says, According to the labour is the reward.

From Chapter 6

The wise taught the following in the style of the Mishnah. Blessed be God who chose them and their Mishnah.

1. Rabbi Meir says, Those who labour in the Torah for its own sake merit many things. And not only that, the whole world is in their debt. They are called friend, beloved, those who love God. those who love humanity, those who give joy to God and humanity. The Torah clothes them in humility and awe of God and fits them to be just, saintly, upright and faithful. It keeps them far from sin and draws them to virtue, and people benefit from their advice and knowledge, their understanding and strength. It gives them a royal dignity and power. The secrets of the Torah are revealed to them, and they become like an ever-growing stream, a river that does not cease. They become modest, longsuffering and forgiving. It gives them greatness and lifts them above all things.

כה בֶּן־בַּג בַּג אוֹמֵר. הֲפָךְ־בָּהּ וַהֲפָךְ־בָּהּ דְּכֹלָּא בַהּ. וּבַהּ תֶּחֱזֵי וְסִיב וּבְלֵה בַהּ וּמִנַּהּ לָא תָזוּעַ שֶׁאֵין לְךָ מִדָּה טוֹבָה הֵימֶנָּה:

כו בֶּן־הֵא הֵא אוֹמֵר. לְפוּם צַעֲרָא אַגְרָא:

פרק ששי
שָׁנוּ חֲכָמִים בִּלְשׁוֹן הַמִּשְׁנָה בָּרוּךְ שֶׁבָּחַר בָּהֶם וּבְמִשְׁנָתָם:

א רַבִּי מֵאִיר אוֹמֵר. כָּל־הָעוֹסֵק בַּתּוֹרָה לִשְׁמָהּ זוֹכֶה לִדְבָרִים הַרְבֵּה וְלֹא עוֹד אֶלָּא שֶׁכָּל־הָעוֹלָם כֻּלּוֹ כְּדַאי הוּא לוֹ. נִקְרָא רֵעַ אָהוּב אוֹהֵב אֶת־הַמָּקוֹם אוֹהֵב אֶת־הַבְּרִיּוֹת. מְשַׂמֵּחַ אֶת הַמָּקוֹם מְשַׂמֵּחַ אֶת הַבְּרִיּוֹת וּמַלְבַּשְׁתּוֹ עֲנָוָה וְיִרְאָה וּמַכְשַׁרְתּוֹ לִהְיוֹת צַדִּיק חָסִיד יָשָׁר וְנֶאֱמָן וּמְרַחַקְתּוֹ מִן־הַחֵטְא וּמְקָרַבְתּוֹ לִידֵי זְכוּת וְנֶהֱנִין מִמֶּנּוּ עֵצָה וְתוּשִׁיָּה בִּינָה וּגְבוּרָה. וְנוֹתֶנֶת לוֹ מַלְכוּת וּמֶמְשָׁלָה וּמְגַלִּים לוֹ רָזֵי תוֹרָה וְנַעֲשֶׂה כְּמַעְיָן שֶׁאֵינוֹ פוֹסֵק וּכְנָהָר הַמִּתְגַּבֵּר וְהוֹלֵךְ וְהֹוֶה צָנוּעַ וְאֶרֶךְ רוּחַ וּמוֹחֵל עַל־עֶלְבּוֹנוֹ וּמְגַדַּלְתּוֹ וּמְרוֹמַמְתּוֹ עַל כָּל־הַמַּעֲשִׂים:

2. Rabbi Joshua ben Levi said, 'And the tables of the Law were the work of God and the writing was the writing of God engraved on the tables.'[1] Do not read 'charut' - engraved, but 'cherut' - freedom; for none are free unless they labour in Torah.

3. If we learn from others a single chapter, a single rule, a single verse, a single expression, or even a single letter, we should treat them with honour.

4. This is the way of the Torah! A piece of bread with salt you will eat, a ration of water you will drink, upon the ground you will lie, a life of hardship you will lead, and you will labour in the Torah. If you do this, 'happy shall you be'[2] - in this world. 'And it shall be well with you - in the world to come.'

5. Seek no greatness for yourself, no honours, and let your deeds be greater than your learning. Do not long for the table of kings, for your table is greater than theirs, and your crown is greater than theirs. Faithful is your Employer to pay you the reward of your labour.

ב רַבִּי יְהוֹשֻׁעַ בֶּן־לֵוִי אוֹמֵר וְהַלֻּחֹת מַעֲשֵׂה אֱלֹהִים הֵמָּה וְהַמִּכְתָּב מִכְתַּב אֱלֹהִים הוּא חָרוּת עַל־הַלֻּחֹת. אַל־תִּקְרָא חָרוּת אֶלָּא חֵרוּת שֶׁאֵין לְךָ בֶּן־חוֹרִין אֶלָּא מִי שֶׁעוֹסֵק בְּתַלְמוּד תּוֹרָה:

ג הַלּוֹמֵד מֵחֲבֵרוֹ פֶּרֶק אֶחָד אוֹ הֲלָכָה אַחַת אוֹ פָּסוּק אֶחָד אוֹ דִבּוּר אֶחָד אוֹ אֲפִילוּ אוֹת אַחַת צָרִיךְ לִנְהָג בּוֹ כָּבוֹד:

ד כָּךְ הִיא דַּרְכָּהּ שֶׁל תּוֹרָה. פַּת בְּמֶלַח תֹּאכֵל וּמַיִם בִּמְשׂוּרָה תִשְׁתֶּה וְעַל הָאָרֶץ תִּישָׁן וְחַיֵּי צַעַר תִּחְיֶה וּבַתּוֹרָה אַתָּה עָמֵל. אִם־אַתָּה עֹשֶׂה כֵּן אַשְׁרֶיךָ וְטוֹב לָךְ. אַשְׁרֶיךָ בָּעוֹלָם הַזֶּה וְטוֹב לָךְ לָעוֹלָם הַבָּא:

ה אַל־תְּבַקֵּשׁ גְּדֻלָּה לְעַצְמֶךָ וְאַל־תַּחְמוֹד כָּבוֹד. יוֹתֵר מִלִּמּוּדְךָ עֲשֵׂה. וְאַל־תִּתְאַוֶּה לְשֻׁלְחָנָם שֶׁל־מְלָכִים. שֶׁשֻּׁלְחָנְךָ גָּדוֹל מִשֻּׁלְחָנָם וְכִתְרְךָ גָּדוֹל מִכִּתְרָם. וְנֶאֱמָן הוּא בַּעַל מְלַאכְתְּךָ שֶׁיְּשַׁלֵּם לְךָ שְׂכַר פְּעֻלָּתֶךָ:

יהוה חפץ למען צדקו יגדיל תורה ויאדיר[3]

---

[1] Ex 32:16.
[2] Ps 128:2.
[3] Isa 42:21.

NOTES ON TRANSLITERATION, ICONS AND HEBREW

Key to Transliteration

All consonants have approximately the same sounds that they have in English except for 'ch' as in Scottish 'Loch Ness' or German, 'Bach'.

Vowel sounds:
- 'o' as in 'top'
- 'a' as in 'shalom'
- 'ai' as in 'aisle', 'Thailand'
- 'e' as in 'bed'
- 'ei' as in 'neighbour', 'weigh'
- 'i' as in 'machine'
- 'u' as in Ruth

The combination 'ay' represents 'a' followed by a consonantal 'y'.

The apostrophe is used for two purposes:
It separates two successive vowel sounds when they occur within a single word, as in '*Yisra'el*'.
It represents the pause when two consonants follow one another and might otherwise be a single sound, so need to be separated, as in '*sh'ma*'.

The transliteration is an approximation of the Hebrew to aid non-Hebrew readers to feel comfortable in following, or participation in, the service. It is not intended as a substitute for, or as a means for, learning Hebrew.

Special Hebrew Signs

The Hebrew vowel '*kamats*' (ָ) is usually pronounced 'a'. However the '*kamats katan*' (ָ̊) and '*chataf kamats*' (ֳ̊) are pronounced 'o', as indicated by the small circle above.

In Hebrew the stress is usually on the last syllable. Exceptions are shown by marking the stressed vowel with a '*meteg*' (ֽ) e.g. יָדַֽעְתִּי '*yada̱ti*', לָֽנוּ '*la̱nu*'.

When the consonantal name of God אֲדֹנָי appears, followed by the tetragrammaton, יהוה, the latter is pronounced 'Elohim' אֱלֹהִים, and is given the same vowels, יְהֹוִה.

Icons

🖐 The *Yad* points to where a service continues after a break e.g. when a gap is allowed for a festival insertion.

<<< The Chevrons at the foot of a page indicate that the passage continues over the page.

🕎*123* The *Menorah* followed by a page number indicates where a reflective version of a particular prayer or section of the service can be found.

The colour blue has been used throughout the services to indicate:
1. Main section headings (eg. Shabbat morning service, Opening Prayers, Morning Blessings)
2. Any additions to, or significant variations from, prayers or passages in the previous edition: e.g. the additional verses in *L'cha Dodi* or the concluding verses of Psalm 95.
3. Insertions for Festivals (eg. in the *Amidah* - for the Ten Days of Penitence)
4. Icons: The *Yad*, Chevrons and *Menorah*.
5. The header, with the exception of the page number.

Hebrew Alphabet

mem	מם	מ,ם	alef	אלף	א	
nun	נון	נ,ן	bet	בית	ב,ב	
samech	סמך	ס	gimel	גמל	ג,ג	
ayin	עין	ע	dalet	דלת	ד,ד	
pe	פא ף,פ,פ		he	הא	ה	
tsade	צדי	צ,ץ	vav	וו	ו	
kof	קוף	ק	zayin	זין	ז	
resh	ריש	ר	chet	חית	ח	
sin	שין	ש	tet	טית	ט	
shin	שין	ש	yod	יוד	י	
tav	תו	ת,ת	kaf	כף כ,כ,ך		
			lamed	למד	ל	

GLOSSARY AND INDEX

Abrahams, Israel (1858-1924). Distinguished Anglo-Jewish scholar and lecturer in Hebrew and Jewish studies. Founder member of Liberal Judaism in Britain. His many works include *Jewish Life in the Middle Ages*, **18**

Abravanel, Isaac ben Judah (1437-1508). Spanish Biblical commentator and philosopher. Finance minister in turn to kings of Portugal, Spain and Naples, **375**

Aggadah, *see* Midrash

Agnon, Shmuel Yosef (1888-1970). Hebrew writer, born in Galicia, settled in Palestine 1907. Nobel Prize for Literature 1966. Works include *The Bridal Canopy* and *Days of Awe*, **589**

Aguilar, Grace (1816-47). English novelist and Anglo-Jewish apologist of Marrano-Portuguese descent. Works include the *Spirit of Judaism: In Defence of her Faith and its Professors*, **13**

Albo, Joseph (c.1360-c.1445). Spanish philosopher and preacher. His works include *Sepher Halkkarim*, a defence of the principles and dogmas of Judaism, **576, 578**

Aleinu **prayer.** Originally in the *Rosh Hashanah* service, then a conclusion to daily services. The first paragraph emphasises the chosenness and task of Israel, the second the universal hope, **608**

Amichai, Yehudah (1924-2000). One of Israel's foremost contemporary poets, also a novelist and playwright. Born in Bavaria, settled in Palestine 1936. Developed a new style of idiomatic Hebrew poetry. Awarded the Bialik Prize 1975 and Israel Prize 1981, **566, 570**

Amos. Eighth-century BCE prophet in the Kingdom of Israel. Prophesied exile as a punishment for the people's sins, though a surviving remnant would remain, **602**

Amswych, Jenny Goldfried (b. 1978, New York). Ordained Leo Baeck College 2007. Works with Bournemouth Reform Synagogue and South Hampshire Reform Jewish Community in addition to being SW England Community Development Rabbi for the Movement for Reform Judaism, **527-8**

Amswych, Neil (b. 1974, London). Ordained Leo Baeck College 2005. Rabbi Bournemouth Reform Synagogue. Particularly interested in environmental and inter-faith issues, **527-8**

Artson, Bradley Shavit (b.1959). Ordained Jewish Theological Seminary 1988. Dean Ziegler School of Rabbinic Studies at the American Jewish University, Los Angeles. Author of several books and a widely read on-line weekly Torah commentary. Father of Jacob Shavit Artson*, **530, 562**

Artson, Jacob Shavit (b.1992), son of Rabbi Bradley and Elana Shavit Artson. Profoundly isolated by his autism, his world changed when he learned to express himself through typing and reached out to people with disabilities, **523**

Avidan, Hillel (b. 1933, London). Ordained Leo Baeck College 1966. Has served congregations in Britain and South Africa. Artist and environmentalist. Author, *Feasts and Fasts of Israel*, **607**

Avot d'Rabbi Natan (The Fathers According to Rabbi Nathan). Commentary on the Mishnaic tractate *Pirke Avot*, **573, 603**

Azikri (Azkari), Eliezer ben Moses (1533-1600). Kabbalist in Safed, **109-10**

Baal Shem Tov (Master of the Good Name, Israel ben Eliezer, 1700-60). Founder of the Chasidic* movement, **14**

Baba Batra. 'Last Gate' of the third tractate of the Mishnah*, order *Nezikin* (Damages) in the Babylonian and Jerusalem Talmuds*. Deals mainly with property, inheritance and legal documents, **548, 593**

Baba Metzia. 'Middle Gate' of the third tractate of the Mishnah*, order *Nezikin* (Damages) in the Babylonian and Jerusalem Talmuds*. Deals mainly with chattels, lost property, embezzlement, fraud, etc., **593**

Bachya, Joseph ibn Pakuda (c.1050-1120). Religious philosopher. His *Duties of the Heart* speaks of trust in God, humility and asceticism. He has a strong affinity with Arab mystics, **518, 519**

Bachya ben Asher (d. 1340). Rabbi and scholar from Saragossa, Spain, best known for the Torah commentary *Midrash Rabbenu Bachya*, into which he introduced mysticism, **553**

GLOSSARY AND INDEX 728

Bacon, Yehudah (b. 1929). Czech-born artist. Survived the concentration camps and settled in Israel in 1946. Head of the department of etching and lithography at Bezalel School of Art, Jerusalem. Art historian of the Holocaust, **534**

Baeck, Leo (1837-1956). German Reform rabbi and religious thinker. Taught at the Hochschule für die Wissenschaft des Judentums in Berlin. Leader of German Jewry before and during the Nazi period, he stayed with his congregation until he was sent to Theresienstadt. He survived and settled in England in 1945. Works include *The Essence of Judaism* and *This People Israel*, **553, 561**

Barzel, Abraham. Israeli psychologist, **529**

Bayfield, Miriam (b. 1979). Studied theology at Bristol, ordained Leo Baeck College 2006. Associate Rabbi, Finchley Reform Synagogue, daughter of Rabbi Tony and the late Linda Bayfield, **355**

Bayfield, Tony (b. 1946, Ilford). Ordained Leo Baeck College 1972. Head of the Movement for Reform Judaism. Formerly Rabbi, North West Surrey Synagogue, 1972-82 and Director of the Sternberg Centre. Lambeth Doctorate 2006. Lecturer in Personal Theology at Leo Baeck College. Author of various books, editor of *Manna*, **326, 511, 591, 606**

Becker, Lawrence (b.1951, Cleveland, Ohio). Teacher. Moved to England 1987. Ordained Leo Baeck College 2008, **563-4**

Bellow, Saul (1915-2005). American novelist whose Jewish characters search for ultimate reality in the modern world. Awarded the Nobel Prize for Literature 1976, **21-2**

Ben Amitai, Lev (b. 1901). Poet, born in Lachowitz, Russia, settled in Palestine in 1920, joining Kibbutz Deganya Bet in 1925, where he worked on the land and as a teacher, **326**

Benjamin, Walter (1892-1940). German Marxist philosopher, literary critic and translator. Collaborated with the writer Berthold Brecht. Under threat of being sent back to Nazi-occupied France he took his own life. His essays are in several collections, including *Illuminations*, **522**

Berachot (Blessings). Tractate in the Mishnah* and in the Talmud* in the order *Zeraim* (Seeds). Deals with the recitation of the daily and Sabbath prayers, **10, 14, 533, 534, 575, 599**

Berditchev, Levi Yitzchak (1740-1809). Chasidic* leader, pupil of Dow Baer of Mezritch. His central doctrine was 'love for Israel', **19**

Bergman, Samuel Hugo (1883-1975). Czech philosopher. Moved to Palestine 1920. Professor at the Hebrew University. Author of *Faith and Reason*, **594**

Berkowits, Eliezer (1908-1992). Modern Orthodox rabbi, theologian, Zionist. Born Nagyvarad, studied in Berlin where he served as a rabbi until 1939, working subsequently in England (Leeds) and Australia before settling in the United States, and from 1972 in Israel. Author of *Faith after the Holocaust*, **389**

Berlin, Isaiah (1909-1997). Political philosopher and historian of ideas, regarded as one of the leading liberal thinkers of the twentieth century. Born in Riga, came to London in 1921 and settled in Oxford. He had a distinguished academic career; his many honours included the Order of Merit, 1971, and Jerusalem Prize, 1979. Judaism and Zionism remained important to him, **555, 595**

Berlin Liberal Synagogue, Prayer Book of. A radical prayer book, published in 1848, **548**

Biale, David (b. 1949). American historian, since 1999 Emanuel Ringelblum Professor of Jewish History, University of California Davis. Publications include *Power and Powerlessness in Jewish History* and *Blood and Belief*, **564**

Bialik, Chaim Nachman (1873-1934). Hebrew poet, essayist, story writer. Born in Russia and settled in Palestine in 1924. Considered the greatest Modern Hebrew poet, **105, 462**

Billig, Michael. Professor of Social Science, Loughborough University. Interests include nationalism, psychoanalytic theory and humour. His many publications include *Rock 'n Roll Jews*. Member Nottingham Progressive Jewish Congregation, **550**

Blue, Lionel (b.1930). British Reform rabbi, graduate of Leo Baeck College, served as Convenor of the Beth Din. Co-editor of the 1977 Daily and Sabbath, High Holy Days and Pilgrim Festivals Prayer Books of the Movement for Reform Judaism, lecturer in Spirituality at Leo Baeck College. Through his broadcasting and writings he has reached millions beyond the Jewish world, **13, 587-8, 596**

Blumenthal, David R. Professor of Judaic Studies, Emory University, Atlanta, Georgia. Ordained 1964 Jewish Theological Seminary. Interests: mediaeval Jewish thought, Jewish mysticism and theology. Publications include *The Banality of Good and Evil: Moral Lessons from the Shoah* and *Jewish Tradition*, **328**

<<<

GLOSSARY AND INDEX

Boerne, Ludwig (1786-1837). German political essayist and champion of Jewish emancipation. Criticised by Heine*, **550, 605**

Bomze, Nachum (1906-54). Yiddish poet. Served with the Red Army. Emigrated to the USA, **21**

Borowitz, Eugene (b. 1924). American Reform rabbi, Professor of Education and Religious Thought, Hebrew Union College - Jewish Institute of Religion, New York. Founder editor of *Sh'ma, A Journal of Jewish Responsibility*. An influential figure in Reform Jewish thought. His many publications include *Renewing the Covenant: A Theology for the Postmodern Jew*, **574**

Bower, Ingeborg. Berlin-born poet who came to Britain on the *Kindertransport*, **524**

Brickman, Jay R. Rabbi Emeritus, Congregation Sinai (Reform), Wisconsin. Studied Jungian psychology in Zurich and Chicago and has a private practice in spiritual counselling, **531, 540**

Buber, Martin (1878-1965). Vienna-born philosopher, Bible scholar and religious thinker, best known for his books on Chasidism* and his philosophy of dialogue, expressed in his work *I and Thou*. Settled in Palestine 1938; a passionate advocate of Jewish-Arab understanding, **605**

Bunam of Pzhysha, Simcha (1765-1827). Chasidic* Rebbe with an intellectual approach who taught inwardness and stressed the search for inner truth, **519**

Celan, Paul. Most frequently used pseudonym of Paul Antschel (1920-70), poet. Born in Romania, he wrote in German and settled in France in 1948. His parents were killed in the Holocaust and he escaped death by working in a Nazi labour camp. He took his life in 1970. Nine volumes of his poetry have been published, **20**

Chabon, Michael (b. 1963). American author. Works include *The Amazing Adventure of Kavalier and Clay* and *The Yiddish Policeman's Union*. Interests include the tradition of Jewish fiction, **593**

Chafetz Chaim (Israel Meir Ha-Kohen, 1838-1933). Influential East European rabbi. Known after the name of his first book, *Chafetz Chaim*, an exposition of the laws of gossip, tale bearing and slander. His best-known work is a commentary on part of the *Shulchan Aruch*, **549**

Chasidic. Of Chasidism*, **10, 11, 13, 598**

Chasidism. A popular pietistic and mystical movement that developed in Eastern Europe in the eighteenth century.

Chicago, Judy (Judy Cohen, b. 1939, Chicago). Feminist artist, author and educator most famous for her works *The Dinner Party* and *The Holocaust Project*, **347**

Cohen, Jack (b. 1919, New York). Ordained Jewish Theological Seminary 1943. Greatly influenced by Mordecai M. Kaplan and served both Conservative and Reconstructionist movements in the US. Settled in Israel in 1961, maintaining major interest in the problems of Jewish education and religious pluralism in both Israel and the US, **584**

Cooper, Howard (b. 1953). Reform rabbi, psychotherapist and writer. Graduate of Leo Baeck College. Writes and teaches on religious, spiritual and psychological themes and their interrelationship. Author of *The Alphabet of Paradise: An A-Z of Spirituality for Everyday Life*, **24, 157, 326, 331, 332, 333-5, 336, 338, 346, 347, 371, 505, 506, 605**

Cordovero, Moses ben Jacob (1522-70). Leading Kabbalist (mystic) in Safed and author of a commentary on the Zohar*, **604**

Derrida, Jacques (1930-2004). Algerian-born French philosopher whose philosophy of deconstruction has had a very great intellectual influence. While he rarely wrote on explicitly Jewish themes, the question of his Jewishness occasioned much debate, **22**

Deuteronomy. Fifth book of the Bible, largely a repetition of the events and legislation during the 40 years since leaving Egypt, presented as a last address by Moses, **603, 608, 697**

Dubner Maggid, The (Jacob b. Wolf Kranz, 1741-1804). Popular teacher famous for his parables, **531, 579**

Dunash ben Labrat (c. 920-90). Hebrew poet and grammarian from Baghdad. He introduced Arabic metre to Hebrew poetry, **186**

Dylan, Bob (Robert Zimmerman, b. 1941). American singer, songwriter, author, musician and poet, with a particular association with the protest movement. Has had a complicated relationship with Judaism, **519**

Ecclesiastes, Book of. Late Biblical book, attributed traditionally to King Solomon, exploring a sceptical view of the goals and aspirations of life and the assurances of conventional wisdom, **690**

Ecclesiastes Rabbah. Midrashic commentary to the Book of Ecclesiastes, **519, 601**

Ecclesiasticus. Book of the Apocrypha (c. 190-170 BCE), written in Hebrew in Jerusalem by Ben Sira, largely consisting of poetic maxims in praise of wisdom and ethical conduct, **604**

Eimer, Colin (b.1945, London). Ordained Leo Baeck College 1971. Has served various communities, since 1977 Rabbi Southgate and District Reform Synagogue. Has taught Classical Hebrew and had major involvement with Vocational Studies, Leo Baeck College, **505**

Emden, Jacob (1697-1776). Halachist. Published an edition of the Siddur with his own commentary, **11**

Eruvin (Boundaries). Tractate in the Mishnah* and Talmud* in the order *Mo'ed* (Festivals). Deals specifically with restrictions on carrying, walking and cooking on Shabbat and festivals, **519, 521**

Exodus. Second book of the Bible, telling of the exodus of the Israelites from Egypt and the receiving of the divine legislation on Mount Sinai, **608**

Exodus* Rabbah. Midrashic commentary on the book of Exodus, **10, 576**

Eydoux, Emmanuel (1917-c.1999). Pen name of Roger Eisinger, French post-war author on Jewish themes, **346**

Feld, Merle (b.1947, New York). Poet, playwright, involved with Israeli/Palestinian dialogue. Author of *A Spiritual Life: A Jewish Feminist Journey*, **582**

Fleg, Edmond (1874-1963), French poet, playwright and essayist who returned to Judaism after the Dreyfus affair. Works include *Why I am a Jew* and *The Life of Moses*, **562**

Forms of Prayer. A series of prayer books of the Movement for Reform Judaism, formerly Reform Synagogues of Great Britain, **24, 25**

Frank, Anne (1929-45). Born in Germany, grew up in Holland, died in Belsen concentration camp. Her diary records the life of her family while hiding from the Nazis in Amsterdam, **389**

Frankl, Viktor (1905-97). Psychiatrist, born in Austria. Founder of Logotherapy, a school of psychotherapy concerned with finding meaning and purpose even in suffering which he developed from his experiences in Auschwitz and other concentration camps, **535**

Freedman, Paul (b. 1968, Hove). Ordained Leo Baeck College 2004. Rabbi of Radlett and Bushey Reform Synagogue. Particularly interested in liturgy, **367**

Freeman, Helen (b. 1959, Croydon). Ordained Leo Baeck College 1990, after first career as speech therapist. 1990-99 Assistant Rabbi and since 1999 Associate Rabbi, West London Synagogue, specialising in pastoral care and qualifying as a Jungian analyst, **605**

Friedman, Debbie (b. 1952, New York). American composer and singer of songs with Jewish religious content. Her *Mi Sheberach* has become part of the liturgy of many Reformed synagogues. Faculty member, Hebrew Union College – Jewish Institute of Religion's School of Sacred Music, **355**

Friedman, Edie (b. 1949, Chicago). Settled in England. In 1973 founded JCORE, the Jewish Council for Racial Equality, and remains its Director. JCORE is dedicated to challenging prejudice and racism and building bridges between the Jewish community and Asian, Black and other communities in Britain, **555**

Fromm, Erich (1900-80). Born in Frankfurt, emigrated to the US in 1933. Psychoanalyst and social philosopher concerned with Biblical ideas and twentieth-century problems. His works include *Fear of Freedom*, *The Sane Society* and *You Shall be as Gods*, **524, 580**

Fuchs, Jan (b.1912, Czechoslovakia). Settled in Manchester 1945. Jewish community worker and poet, **592**

Gelernter, David (b. 1955). Professor of Computer Science, Yale University. BA and MA from Yale in Classical Hebrew Literature. Author of many books including *Drawing Life: Surviving the Unabomber*, telling of his experience of being critically injured by opening a letter bomb from the violent opponent of technology, **578**

Genesis. First book of the Bible, tracing the origins of the world and the history of the Hebrew Patriarchs, **561, 600, 607**

Genesis* Rabbah, Midrashic commentary on the book of Genesis, **529, 533**

731 GLOSSARY AND INDEX

Ginsberg, Allen (1926-77). American poet and leader of the 'Beat Generation'. Gave hallucinatory pictures of alienation in twentieth-century US. Wrote a long poem, *Kaddish*, after the death of his mother, **539**

Glatstein, Jacob (1896-1971). Born in Lublin, emigrated to the US in 1914. Poet, novelist and critic dedicated to reviving the Yiddish language, **327-8**

Glick, Hirsch (1922-44). Poet born in Vilna, Lithuania. A partisan fighter under Nazi occupation, his song *Zog nit Keynmol* became the battle song of the Vilna partisans, **392**

Gold, Shefa. Received rabbinical ordination from the Reconstructionist Rabbinical College and Rabbi Zalman Schachter-Shalomi. Leader in Aleph, the Alliance for Jewish Renewal. Composes and performs spiritual music, **581, 582**

Goldberg, Leah (1911-70). Hebrew poet, critic and children's writer. Born Eastern Prussia, settled in Palestine 1935, **331, 540**

Goldberg, Percy Selvin (1917-81). Ordained at Jew's College and served London Orthodox congregations before changing to Reform Judaism. Minister of Manchester Reform Synagogue 1940-1975, then became Rabbi in Hot Springs, Arkansas. Author of *Karaite Liturgy and its relation to Synagogue Worship*, **587, 606**

Gordis, Daniel. Senior Vice-President/Senior Fellow, the Shalem Center Jerusalem. Received ordination from Jewish Theological Seminary. Founding Dean of Ziegler Rabbinical School at the American Jewish University, Los Angeles. Writes extensively on Israel and other matters of concern to the Jewish world, **523, 579, 590**

Gordon, Joan (b. 1920, Leeds). Writer and poet. Author of an autobiography *Tango down the Corridor* and many poems including the anthology *Picking up the Pieces*, **530, 532**

Goren, Shlomo (1917-94). Born in Poland, settled in Palestine 1926. Ashkenazi Orthodox Chief Rabbi of Israel 1973-83, **566**

Gould, Steven Jay (1941-2002). Distinguished American evolutionary biologist and historian of science. His accessible writing made him the public face of evolution, while provocative ideas stirred up academic debate, **557**

Green, Arthur (b. 1941). US rabbi, ordained at Jewish Theological Seminary, and widely-published scholar in the areas of Jewish mystical thought and contemporary theology. Since 2003 he has been the first Dean for the non-denominational rabbinical programme at Hebrew College (Massachusetts), where he is also Professor of Jewish Theology and Mysticism, **336, 502, 512, 513, 605**

Greenberg, Irving (b. 1933). US Orthodox rabbi and educator. Founding President of the National Jewish Center for Learning and Leadership (CLAL), which promotes co-operation between different Jewish religious movements. Author of many books including *The Jewish Way: Living the Holidays*, **580**

Gryn, Hugo Gabriel (1930-96). Rabbi and broadcaster. Born in Berehovo, which was then in Czechoslovakia, and transported to Auschwitz in 1944. He was ordained by Hebrew Union College, Cincinnati and served at West London Synagogue. He became a popular broadcaster on The Moral Maze. His experience as a survivor of the concentration camps is recorded in *Chasing Shadows*, edited by his daughter Naomi Gryn, **391**

Guiterman, Arthur (1871-1943). American writer, best known for his humorous poetry, **539**

Hakotun, Rabbi Moshe. Legendary Chasidic* figure to whom many sayings are attributed, **20**

Halachah *see* Midrash

Heine, Heinrich (1796-1856). German poet and essayist. Converted to Christianity in 1825 but retained a strong Jewish identity and after a serious illness in 1847 increasingly returned to Jewish themes. Exiled in France. He had a prophetic insight into the later course of German history, **521**

Heller, Arieh Leib (1745-1813). A Galician rabbi, he wrote commentaries on *Shulchan Aruch* and had an original manner of applying analytical methods to the study of halachic concepts, **576**

Herzl, Theodor (1860-1904). Journalist, founder of political Zionism after observing the Dreyfus trial. Wrote *The Jewish State* and *Altneuland*, **600**

Heschel, Abraham Joshua (1907-72) American Conservative rabbi, philosopher and theologian, Professor of Jewish Ethics and Mysticism at the Jewish Theological Seminary of America. His many books include *God in Search of Man*, **12, 13, 518, 554, 569, 577, 578, 579, 594**

<<<

GLOSSARY AND INDEX 732

Hillesum, Etty (1914-43). Dutch writer whose letters from Westerbork Transit Camp were published by the Dutch resistance. Killed in Auschwitz, **22**

Hilton, Michael (born 1951, London). Ordained Leo Baeck College 1987. Has served various communities; since 2001 Rabbi, Kol Chai Hatch End Jewish Community. Special interests are interfaith work and the history of Jewish customs. Publications include *The Christian Effect on Jewish Life*, **585**

Hirsch, Samson Raphael (1808-88). Rabbi of Frankfurt. Founder of 'modern Orthodoxy', encouraging a fusion between Western culture and traditional Jewish practices, **12**

Hoffman, Lawrence A. (b. 1942). Ordained Hebrew Union College 1969. Professor of Liturgy at HUC since 1973 and, since 2003, holds Chair in Liturgy, Worship and Ritual. Combines academic research with a passion for the spiritual renewal of American Jewry and has a major role within Synagogue 3000 as, formerly, in Synagogue 2000. Author/editor of many works, **552**

Horayot (Decisions). Tractate in the Mishnah* and Talmud*, in the order *Nezikin* (Damages). Deals with the consequences of acting according to erroneous decisions of a religious authority, **575**

Hosea. Eighth-century BCE Biblical prophet of the Kingdom of Israel in the last years before the exile. Prophesied exile because of people's corruption, while also stressing the continuance of God's love, **27**

Ibn Ezra, Abraham (1093-1167). Spanish rabbi, poet, Bible commentator, philosopher and doctor. Travelled widely throughout North Africa and Europe, **108, 184-5**

Ibn Gabirol, Solomon (c.1021-56). Spanish poet and neo-Platonic philosopher. His major work *Mekor Chayyim* (The Source of Life) was preserved in a Latin version as *Fons Vitae*. His philosophical poem *Keter Malchut* (The Kingly Crown) is part of the High Holyday liturgy, **18, 193, 599**

Ibn Verga, Solomon (fifteenth-sixteenth centuries). Spanish historian and Marrano. Wrote on persecution and a disputation *Shevet Yehudah* (Rod of Judah), **18**

Infeld, Leopold (1898-1968). Physicist, born Krakow. Collaborated with Einstein, and the success of their popular *The Evolution of Physics*, 1938, enabled him to settle in the US. In 1950 he returned to Warsaw as Professor of Theoretical Physics. Very concerned about the threat of nuclear weapons. Autobiography *Quest*, **557**

Isaiah. Prophetic book of the Hebrew Bible, now thought to be at least two separate works: First Isaiah, chapters 1-39, written in the eighth century BCE in Jerusalem, and Second Isaiah, chapters 40-66, written in the sixth century BCE during the Babylonian Exile, **601, 603, 690-1, 692-3, 696**

Jacobs, Louis (1920-2006). British Conservative rabbi, scholar and theologian. Founding Rabbi of New London Synagogue, 1964-2000. Works include *Chasidic Prayer*, *Principles of the Jewish Faith*, and *We Have Reason to Believe*, publication of which led to the 'Jacobs affair'. Lectured in Talmud at Leo Baeck College, **345, 578**

Janner, Greville (b. 1938). Lord Janner of Braunstone, Labour Member of the House of Lords, after many years as MP. Chairman of the Holocaust Education Trust. Much involved in other Jewish and national causes, **551**

Jeremiah. Seventh-century BCE Biblical prophet who warned of the destruction of the Kingdom of Judah and the Temple, but subsequently offered a message of hope to exiles, **9, 16, 548, 573, 600, 607, 608, 692**

Job. Book in the *Ketuvim* (Writings) section of the Hebrew Bible. Written in the sixth century BCE, it deals with the problem of suffering for the innocent, **533**

Jonah Ibn Janach (990-1055). Active in Cordoba and Saragossa, Spain. Philosopher, grammarian and lexicographer, whose major work was *Sefer HaShorashim*, The Book of Roots, **520**

Jonas, Hans (1903-1993). Left his native Germany in 1933 for England, then Palestine. Philosopher, best known for his influential work *The Imperative of Responsibility*, and particularly concerned with social and ethical problems created by technology. After the Second World War he taught briefly at Hebrew University, then in Canada, before settling in New York in 1955, **522**

Jonas, Regina (1902-44). Rabbi. Born in Berlin, she studied at the Hochschule für die Wissenschaft des *Judentums*, receiving private ordination by Rabbi Max Dienemann, as the first woman rabbi of modern times. She served in Berlin before being deported to Theresienstadt in 1942, where she supported people and lectured. Killed in Auschwitz in 1944, **390**

<<<

733 GLOSSARY AND INDEX

Josephus, Flavius (Joseph ben Mattiyahu HaKohen, c. 38-100). Politician, soldier and historian, Jewish apologist to the Roman world, **604**

Judah bar Ilai. Second-century CE rabbi, born in Usha, lower Galilee. Student of Akiba and Tarfon, ordained by Judah ben Baba, survived Hadrianic persecutions, **523, 574**

Judah Halevi* (c.1075-1141). Spanish Hebrew poet and philosopher and physician, author of *The Kuzari*, an exposition of Jewish life and thought in the form of a disputation before the King of the Khazars, **11, 14, 18, 414, 520**

Judah he-Chasid (1150-1217). Of Regensburg. Reputed to be a mystic. Little is known of him, **195**

Judah Loewe ben Bezalel, the Maharal of Prague (c. 1525-1609). Rabbi, Talmudist, mathematician and mystic. Associated with the legend of the Golem, **550**

Kaddish. Aramaic prayer at the conclusion of public service and of sections within it. Often recited as a memorial to the dead, it is in fact a messianic prayer in praise of life and God's greatness, **601**

Kafka, Franz (1883-1924), Czech novelist whose works express the confusion and loss of identity felt by Western man. His works include *The Trial* and *Metamorphosis*, **16**

Kahn-Harris, Deborah (b. 1968, Oklahoma). Ordained Leo Baeck College 1996. Formerly Movement for Reform Judaism University Chaplain. Associate Rabbi, Southgate and District Reform Synagogue and lecturer in Bible, Leo Baeck College, **607**

Kaleko Mascha (1907-75). Born Golda Malka Aufen in Galicia, she grew up in Berlin, where she became a literary celebrity and poet and essayist. She moved to New York in 1938, later lived in Israel, and died, alone and almost forgotten, in Zurich. Her collections of poems include *Das Lyrische Stenogrammheft*, **23**

Kanter, Shammai. American rabbi, ordained Jewish Theological Seminary. Formerly Rabbi, Temple Beth El, Rochester, New York and past editor of *Conservative Judaism*. Author of *Rabban Gamliel:The Legal Traditions*, **597**

Katz, Steven (b. 1948, London). Ordained Leo Baeck College 1975, since when he has served Hendon Reform Synagogue, first working with then succeeding his father. Chair, Siddur Editorial Committee, **515, 516, 552**

Kavvanah. Intention, the saying of prayers with spontaneity.

Keva. The saying of prayers as a fixed duty.

Kiddushin. Tractate in the Mishnah* and Talmud* in the order *Nashim* (Women). Deals with laws of betrothal and prohibited marriage, **601, 608**

Kitzur Shulchan Aruch. Simplified version of the *Shulchan Aruch*, a sixteenth-century code of Jewish law and practice by Solomon Ganzfried (1804-86), **523, 602, 605**

Klein, Zoe. Reform rabbi, ordained by Hebrew Union College 1998. Senior Rabbi, Temple Isaiah, Los Angeles. Author and poet, **537-8**

Kook, Abraham Isaac (Rav Kook). Chief Rabbi of Palestine, concerned with the religious problems of the new settlement. Poet and mystic, **13, 335, 575**

Korczak, Janusz (Henryk Goldszmidt, 1878-1942). Polish author, social worker and pioneer in children's education. He insisted on accompanying 200 orphans in his care to Treblinka extermination camp and shared their death, **524**

Kotliar, I (Koplier), Yiddish song writer, **569-70**

Kramer, Aaron (1921-97). American poet of everyday life, translator, principally of Yiddish poetry, and literary critic, **536**

Kushner, Harold (b. 1935, New York). Conservative rabbi, ordained Jewish Theological Seminary 1960. Rabbi, Temple Israel, Natick, Massachusetts. Author of many books, including *When Bad Things Happen to Good People*, **572**

Lahav-Radlemesser, Tamir (b. 1953, Jerusalem). Graduate of Bezalel Academy. Poet, photographer and owner of graphic design studio, Tel Aviv, **568**

<<<

Landau, Ezekiel (1713-93). Born in Poland. Rabbi of Prague, influential authority on halachah. Not opposed to secular knowledge, but objected to 'that culture which came from Berlin', in particular Moses Mendelssohn's translation of the Pentateuch, **558**

Leigh, Michael (1928-2000). One of the first rabbis ordained by Leo Baeck College, 1958. Rabbi Edgware Reformed Synagogue, 1963-90. Author of *Jewish Observance in the Home*, **480**

Levi, Primo (1919-87). Italian chemist and writer. Survived Auschwitz through his usefulness as a chemist. Literary works include *The Periodic Table*, *If Not Now - When* and *If This is a Man*. Committed suicide in 1987, **337, 551**

Levine, Lee I. Talmud scholar and historian of classical Judaism. Ordained 1965, Jewish Theological Seminary. Professor of Jewish History and Archaeology, Hebrew University of Jerusalem. Books include *The Ancient Synagogue: The First 100 Years*, **565**

Leviticus. Third book of the Bible, largely dealing with the laws of the priesthood, sacrifices and ritual purity, **602, 694-5**

Leviticus* Rabbah. Midrashic commentary on the Book of Leviticus, **556, 607, 608**

Levi Yitzchak of Berditchev *see* Berditchev, Levi Yitzchak

Levy, Sarah (Levy-Tanai, 1911-75). Born in Jerusalem to Yemenite parents, she trained to be a kindergarten teacher, performing in children's theatre and composing children's songs. In 1949 she founded the Inbal Dance Group. Composer of *Kol Dodi* and *El Ginot Egoz*, **379**

Lieberman, Sy, born Chicago. High School English teacher who became a noted American storyteller and has been telling stories professionally since 1982, **330**

Lipschuetz, Rabbi Israel of Danzig (1782-1860). German rabbinic scholar whose fame rests upon his commentary on the Mishnah, *Tiferet Yisrael*, **522**

Lipson, Norman. Founding Rabbi, Temple Dor Dorim, Reform Congregation of Weston, Florida, **583**

Littmann, Ellen (1900-75). First lecturer in Bible at Leo Baeck College. Wrote on Mendelssohn and translated Elbogen, **14, 526**

Lukacs, Georg (1885-1971). Hungarian Marxist philosopher and literary critic, **543-4**

Luria, Isaac ben Solomon (The 'Ari', 1534-72). Kabbalist and poet. Born in Germany, in 1569 settled in Safed where he attracted many disciples. His great contribution to Jewish thought is his amplification of the idea of *Kavvanah* (intention), **102**

Luzzatto, Moses Hayyim (RAMHAL, 1707-46). Kabbalist, Hebrew poet and writer of ethical works. Born Padua. Devoted to spiritual Zionism and a pacifist, he was a leading advocate of a bi-national state in Palestine, **590**

Magonet, Jonathan (b. 1942). Bible scholar, liturgist, interfaith activist, composer. Graduate of Leo Baeck College and its Principal (1985-2006). Co-editor of *Forms of Prayer*: Shabbat and Daily, High Holyday and Pilgrim Festival Books; editor of this edition, **15, 337, 338, 339-44, 346, 494-501, 507, 511, 560**

Maimonides (Moses ben Maimon, RaMBaM, 1135-1204). Philosopher, halachist and physician. Born in Spain, settled in Cairo c.166. Wrote the *Mishneh Torah*, a code discussing all halachic subjects, and *Guide for the Perplexed*, an exposition of Judaism's basic teachings, influenced by Aristotelian thought. One of the greatest Jewish legal authorities of all time, **11, 12, 521, 548, 556, 558, 559, 562, 573, 590, 598, 599, 600**

Malachi (c. 450 BCE). Proper name or 'my messenger'. Biblical prophet. Protested against laxity in ritual and social obligations, and prophesied the coming Day of Judgment, **601**

Marrano. Spanish word meaning 'swine', a term applied in Spain and Portugal to descendants of baptised Jews suspected of secret adherence to Judaism. The group became particularly numerous after the 1391 massacre, and the Inquisition was in part an attempt to seek them out, **18**

Marx, Karl Heinrich (1818-83). German social philosopher and economist. Born of converted Jewish parents, he was baptised aged 6. Settled in England in 1852. Chief theorist of modern socialism, **556**

<<<

735 GLOSSARY AND INDEX

Mechilta. Second-century halachic Midrashic commentary on the Book of Exodus*, attributed to Rabbi Ishmael, **608**

Mendel of Kotzk: Menachem Mendel (1787-1859). Chasidic* leader, opposed to nationalism. His slogan was 'truth', which involved the abandonment of self, and Torah study, **10, 534, 575, 600**

Micah. Eighth-century BCE Biblical prophet in the Kingdom of Judah. Spoke out against social injustice, and prophesied the exile and return of the Jewish nation, **598, 600**

Michaels, Maurice (b. 1941). Reform Rabbi, serving the South West Essex and Settlement Reform Synagogue. Having taken early retirement after a long career in industry, during which time he had been very active in communal life, he went to Leo Baeck College, where he was ordained in 1996, **500, 506**

Middleburgh, Charles H. (b. 1956, Hove). Ordained Leo Baeck College 1986. He has served various communities and is now Rabbi Cardiff Reform Synagogue and visits Dublin Progressive Jewish Congregation. He is also Lecturer and Director of Rabbinic Studies Leo Baeck College, Associate Editor *Siddur Lev Chadash* and Joint Editor, *Machzor Ruach Chadashah* and *Tefillot ve Tachanumim*, **558**

Midrash, plural Midrashim (Explanation). Rabbinic interpretation that may be either legal (Midrash Halachah) or homiletical (Midrash Aggadah), sometimes expressed in parables.

Midrash Palms. Homiletic Midrash*on the Book of Palmas, tenth century, **576, 597**

Millgram, Abraham Ezra (1908-1998). Ordained 1927. American rabbi and educationalist who settled in Israel. His many books include *Sabbath: The Day of Delight* and *Jewish Worship*, **585**

Mishnah (Learning). Legal work consisting of rabbinic decisions and interpretations of the Torah, and forming the basis of the Talmud. Compiled by Judah HaNasi in the second century CE, it is part of the 'Oral Law' as opposed to the 'Written Law'.

Mishnah Berachot *see* Berachot, **10**

Montefiore, Claude Goldsmid (1858-1938). Anglo-Jewish scholar, concerned with the New Testament period. With Lily Montagu he founded the Liberal Jewish Movement. Joint editor, with Herbert Loewe, of *A Rabbinic Anthology*, **581**

Morgan, Fred (b. 1948, New York). Ordained Leo Baeck College 1984. Rabbi, North West Surrey Synagogue and, since 1997, Temple Beth Israel, Melbourne, Australia. He has a particular interest in Midrash and modern Jewish thought, **607, 663**

Moritz, Alfred (1921-2003). Born in Munich, he was sent to England in 1937. He became Professor of Classics at the University of Cardiff and was a very active member of the Cardiff Reform Synagogue, **517**

Morris, Karen (1976-98). Karen had been very active in RSY Netzer. Her diagnosis of chronic myloid leukaemia and her death a year later touched very many. The fundraising work she began is continued in the Karen Morris Memorial Trust, **546**

Moses Chasid (d. 1927), Chasidic* leader, **608**

Mourik, Ineke van (b. 1949). Librarian University of Utrecht. Feminist author of essays, short stories and poetry, **332**.

Nachman of Bratzlav (1772-1811). Chasidic* rabbi and ascetic who used stories and parables to illustrate his mystical teachings. The great-grandson of the Baal Shem Tov*, **10, 11, 12, 14, 391, 518, 534, 539, 571, 590, 598, 601, 604**

Najara, Israel (c.1555-1615). Hebrew poet, born in Damascus, moved to Palestine. Frequently refers to Jewish suffering and redemption, **103**

Nechunya ben Hakkana. First-century Kabbalistisc rabbi quoted in *Pirke Avot*, to whom authorship of *Ana beKoach*, 'Release all captives', is attributed, **194**

Nedarim (Vows), Tractate in the Mishnah* and Talmud*, in the order *Nashim* (Women). Deals with the binding nature of spoken vows, **549**

Nuland, Sherwin B. (b. 1930). American surgeon, teacher of bioethics and medicine at Yale, author of many works including *How We Die: Reflections on Life's Final Chapter*, **541**

Numbers Rabbah: Midrashic commentary on the Book of Numbers, **549**

Ozick, Cynthia (b. 1928, New York). Writer and feminist whose fiction and essays are often about Jewish American life. Works include *The Pagan Rabbi and Other Stories*, **561**

<<<

Pesachim (Passover). Tractate in the Mishnah* and Talmud *, in the order *Mo'ed* (Seasons). Deals with the laws of Passover, **548**

Peskita d'Rav Kahana. Collection of Midrashim for the festivals and special Sabbaths of the year. Probably compiled in the fifth century, **13**

Petuchowski, Jakob Joseph (1925-1991). Reform rabbi, scholar and theologian. Born Berlin, emigrated to England 1939, settled in the US 1948. Spent his entire career at Hebrew Union College and published a great deal, particularly on aspects of liturgy, including *Prayer Book Reform in Europe* and *Understanding Jewish Prayer*, **494, 502**

Philips, Melanie. British journalist who has made the journey from the radical *Guardian* newspaper to the conservative *Daily Mail*. Writes extensively on problems facing Israel, **532**

Philo (c.20 BCE – 50 CE). Jewish philosopher living in Alexandria who sought to harmonise Greek philosophy with Judaism, **14**

Piercy, Marge (b. 1936). American poet, novelist and social activist, whose themes include feminism, social justice and treatment of the mentally ill. Writes extensively on Jewish themes, **22, 348**

Pincus, Lily (1898-1981). Came to England from Germany. Became a social worker in a family case-work agency and co-founded the Tavistock Institute for Marital Studies. Author of many books. *Death and the Family: The Importance of Mourning*, first published in 1976, became a standard text on bereavement, **533**

Pirke de Rabbi Eliezer. Aggadic work narrating events from Creation to the wanderings of the Israelites in the wilderness, **558**

Plaskow, Judith. American academic. Professor of Religious Studies at Manhattan College, specialising in feminist theology. Books including *Standing again at Sinai: Judaism from a Feminist Perspective*, **574**

Ploni Almoni. Biblical term used in the Book of Ruth (4:1) to denote an anonymous person, **509**

Plumb, Marcia (b. Houston, Texas). Ordained Hebrew Union College - Jewish Institute of Religion, New York 1988. In London since 1990, she has served various congregations before Southgate and District Reform Synagogue. She is Akiva School Rabbi and has a special interest in spirituality and spiritual direction, **585**

Proops, Marjorie (1911-96). Rebecca Marjorie Proops, *née* Israel, was born in London, started as a journalist in 1939, and became probably the UK's best-known 'Agony Aunt' through her 'Dear Marge' column in the *Daily Mirror*, **531**

Proverbs. Late Biblical book, an example of Wisdom Literature. Includes aphorisms, exhortations to seek wisdom, etc., **522, 603, 689, 693, 695**

Psalms. Biblical collection of 150 religious poems and songs used for temple worship and private meditation. Traditionally ascribed to King David as author and editor, they reflect many different periods and experiences within Biblical history, **602, 603**

Psalms, Midrash on *see* Midrash Psalms.

Rabina, Menashe (Rabinovich). Israeli composer and music critic, born in Novogrudok, Belarus, where his father was a cantor, **379**

Rabkin, Yakov. Professor of History at the University of Montreal. An Orthodox Jew, his publications include *The Threat from Within. A History of Jewish Opposition to Zionism*, **510, 565**

Radlemesser, Tamir Lahav *see* Lahav-Radlemesser, Tamir, **568**

Rashi (Rabbi Solomon ben Isaac, 1040-1105). French rabbi and leading scholar of his age. His commentary accompanied the first printed edition of the Hebrew Bible. His Talmud* commentary is still considered the standard tool for its study, **605**

Remen, Rachel Naomi, American doctor and writer, granddaughter of an Orthodox rabbi. Her personal experience of lifelong illness has led to her pioneering mind/body medicine and stressing the role of the spirit in healing. Author of *Kitchen Table Wisdom* and *My Grandfather's Blessing*, **594**

Romain, Jonathan (b.1954, London). Rabbi, writer and broadcaster. Ordained Leo Baeck College 1980, since when he has been Rabbi of Maidenhead Synagogue. Books include a work on the history of Reform Judaism and its practice. Awarded the MBE for pioneer work with mixed-faith couples, **606**

<<<

737 GLOSSARY AND INDEX

Rosen, David. Served as Orthodox rabbi in Cape Town, then as Chief Rabbi in Ireland. Since 1985 he has been in Israel, working in the area of international inter-religious understanding. In 2006 he was made Papal Knight Commander for his contribution to Catholic-Jewish reconciliation, **561**

Rosen, Michael (b.1946, London). Children's novelist, poet and author of 140 books. Works include *Carrying the Elephant: A Memoir of Love and Loss* and *Sad Book*, both following the death of his son, **547**

Rosenberg, Isaac (1889-1918). British poet and painter. Died on active service during the First World War. His powerful war poems include 'Break of Day in the Trenches', **567**

Rosenfeld, Morris (1862-1923), Yiddish poet, connected with many Jewish newspapers. Born in Poland, settled in New York 1886. His work highlighted the living conditions of East European immigrants, causing him to be known as 'poet laureate of labour'. A book of his poetry appeared in English as *Songs from the Ghetto*, **525**

Rosenzweig, Franz (1886-1929). German philosopher and Jewish educator. The deep impression made by a Yom Kippur service prevented his intended conversion to Christianity. Author of *The Star of Redemption*. With Martin Buber he translated the Bible into German, **579, 597**

Roth, Joseph (1894-1939). Austrian novelist, best known for his novel of Jewish life *Job* (1930) and his family saga *Radetsky March* (1932). He never denied his Jewish origin but was attracted by Catholicism, **557**

Rothman, Elaina (born 1948, London). Ordained Leo Baeck College 1992. Rabbi Cardiff Reform Synagogue 1992-2002. Since 2000 Chair of Siddur Steering Committee, **597**

Rothschild, Sylvia (b. Bradford). Ordained Leo Baeck College 1984, having previously trained as a psychiatric social worker. 1987-2002 Rabbi Bromley Reform Synagogue and since 2002 Rabbi Wimbledon and District Synagogue. Has written on spiritual approaches to death and dying, new liturgies and on women and illness, **422**

Rothschild, Walter (b.1954, Bradford). Ordained Leo Baeck College 1984, having previously trained as a religious studies teacher. 1984-95 Rabbi Sinai Synagogue, Leeds, and then various positions, particularly in Germany and, since 2007 Rabbi, Or Chadash, Vienna Progressive Jewish Community, **423, 509, 514, 515, 580**

Sacks, Oliver (b. 1933, London). Qualified as a doctor and since 1965 has lived in New York, where he has had clinical and academic positions in neurology. His clinical experiences have led to many books, including *Awakenings* and *The Man who Mistook his Wife for a Hat*, **538**

Sagan, Carl (1934-96). American astronomer and astrochemist. Achieved fame for writing popular science books. Dedicated to searching for intelligent life in the cosmos. Protested against the Vietnam war and nuclear weapons, **578**

Salanter, Israel Lipkin (1810-83). Founder of the Musar Movement in Lithuania, based on study of traditional Jewish ethical literature, **549**

Salida, Anouska (b. 1978). Since birth, member of Finchley Reform Synagogue. Actively involved with RSY Netzer and has done much work with young adults within the Reform Movement, **526**

Sanhedrin (Assembly). Tractate in the Mishnah* and Talmud*, in the order *Nezikin* (Damages). Deals with court procedure and criminal law, **548, 554, 573**

Sarah, Elizabeth Tikvah (b.1955). Ordained Leo Baeck College 1989. Served various congregations and as RSGB Director of Programmes before becoming Rabbi of Brighton and Hove Progressive Synagogue in 2000. Lectures in 'Liberal Judaism' at Leo Baeck College. Interested in many aspects of contemporary Jewish life and in social issues beyond the Jewish community, **606**

Sassoon, Siegfried (1886-1967). English poet and author. His father came from a well-known Jewish family. Praised for distinguished war service, though also critical of war, **355**

Sayings of the Fathers (*Pirke Avot*). Tractate in the Mishnah*, in the order *Nezikin* (Damages). A collection of ethical sayings of the Rabbis, **10, 598, 599, 603**

Schoenberg, Arnold (1874-1951). Austrian composer, protégé of Mahler. He returned to Judaism and wrote the opera *Moses and Aaron*, music to the Psalms, and a setting for *Kol Nidre*, **21**

Scholem, Gershom (1897-1982). Philosopher and historian. Born in Germany, emigrated to Palestine 1923. First Professor of Jewish Mysticism at the Hebrew University of Jerusalem. Works include *Major Trends in Jewish Mysticism*, **589**

<<<

Schonfield, Jeremy (b. 1951 to a distinguished Orthodox family). Writes and teaches on Jewish liturgy and festivals and life-cycle at Leo Baeck College and the Oxford Centre for Hebrew and Jewish studies. Author of *Undercurrents of Jewish Prayer*, **517**

Schulweis, Harold M. (b.1925). Rabbi Emeritus, Valley Beth Shalom, Encino, California, which he has served since 1970. Identified as a Conservative rabbi, he had a traditional background and is regarded as 'Reconstructionist' in his theology. Author and major contributor to renewal of twentieth/twenty-first century Jewish life, **526, 544, 559.**

Seder Eliyahu Rabbah (*Tanna d'veh Eliyahu*). Midrash in two parts. Probably from ninth-century Italy but possibly earlier, **599, 600**

Seder Eliyahu Zuta. Aggadic midrashic collection, **575**

Sefer Chasidim (Book of the Pious). Ethical teachings of the German pietist movement *Chasidei Ashkenaz*, whose leader was Judah he-Chasid* (1150-1217), **16, 582**

Senesh, Hannah (1921-44). Born in Hungary and settled in Palestine in 1939. She volunteered for a rescue mission and parachuted back into Hungary, where she was captured and shot. Some of her poems were set to music, **391**

Setel, Drorah (b. 1956). Studied at Leo Baeck College and later became the first rabbi ordained by an independent *beit din* composed solely of women. She has written, taught and organized extensively around issues of sexual and domestic violence in Jewish communities. She lives in Buffalo, NY (USA), **355**

Shabbat (Sabbath). Tractate in both the Mishnah* and the Talmud*, in the order *Mo'ed* (Seasons). Deals with the laws of Sabbath observance, **522, 581, 604**

Shemayah. First-century BCE Rabbinic sage. Quoted in *Pirke Avot*, **196**

Shapiro, Kalonymus Kalman (1889-1943). Rebbe of Piazeczna, Poland. Died in Treblinka. A manuscript of his *Divrei Torah* was found in the rubble of the Warsaw Ghetto, **535**

Sharansky, Anatholy (Natan) (b. 1948, Ukraine). Achieved fame as a Soviet dissident and symbol of the Soviet Jewry Movement. He was charged with treason and spying and imprisoned for 9 years in Siberia. On his release he went to Israel where he became a right-wing politician, **536**

Sh'ma. This comprises three Biblical passages, Deuteronomy 6: 4-8, 11: 13-21 and Numbers 15:37-41. The use of the first paragraph at least is very old and, reciting it, the Jew traditionally adopts 'the yoke of the kingdom of heaven'.

Shmuel HaNagid (993-1055). Vizier of Granada, Talmudic scholar, grammarian, philologist, poet and warrior, **519, 567**

Shneur Zalman ben Baruch of Ladi (1747-1813). Founder of the Chabad movement in Chasidism which stresses an intellectual approach, and author of the *Tanya*, **20**

Siegel, Danny. US author and poet and authority on 'microphilanthropy'. Themes are *tzedakah*, social justice, social action. In 1981 he founded the Ziv Tzedakah fund, **540-2**

Sifra (The Book). Post-fourth-century halachic Midrash on Leviticus*, **607**

Sifre (The Book). Post-fourth-century halachic Midrash on the books of Numbers and Deuteronomy, **606, 608**

Silverman, Reuven (Robert) (b. 1947, Oxford). Ordained Leo Baeck College 1975. Previously served in Curaçao and Edgware, since 1977 Rabbi, Manchester Reform Synagogue. Lectures in Counselling and Modern Jewish Thought. Author of *Baruch Spinoza: Outcast Jew, Universal Sage*, **329-30, 508**

Smith, Amnon Daniel (b. 1949, Hadera, Israel). Ordained Leo Baeck College 1977. After serving West London and Wimbledon Synagogues became Senior Rabbi of Edgware and District Reform Synagogue in 1993. Founding Chairman of the Raphael Centre, a Jewish counselling service, and teaches Pastoral Care and Community Skills at Leo Baeck College, **535**

Solomon, Norman (b. 1933, Cardiff). Orthodox rabbi, Founder and Director of the Centre for the Study of Judaism and Jewish-Christian Relations, Selly Oak College, Birmingham 1983-94, Fellow of Modern Jewish Thought, Oxford Centre for Postgraduate Hebrew Studies 1995-2001. Very active in interfaith dialogue. Publications include *Judaism and World Religion*, **560**

Sore bas Toyvim (seventeenth century, Ukraine). Probably a *firzogerin*, one who led and explained the prayers in the women's section of the synagogue. Author of *Shloshah Shearim*, Three Portals, an introduction to women's *mitzvoth* with accompanying supplicatory prayers, *t'chinot*.

<<<

739 GLOSSARY AND INDEX

Sperber, Shmuel (1904-84). Czech rabbi, Zionist and Jewish educationalist. Refugee in England. Settled in Jerusalem. Essays collected in *Ma'amarot*, **578**

Spinoza, Baruch (1632-77). Dutch philosopher from a Marrano family. Excommunicated by the Sephardic community in 1656 for unorthodox religious views, **550, 553**

Steinberg, Milton (1903-50). American Conservative rabbi. Ordained Jewish Theological Seminary 1928. Rabbi, Park Avenue Synagogue, Manhattan. His books include *The Making of the Modern Jew* and *As a Driven Leaf*, **345, 574, 577**

Summit, Jeffrey. Ordained Hebrew Union College - Jewish Institute of Religion. Executive Director of the Hillel Foundation at Tufts University, where he is also Associate Chaplain and Associate Professor in the Department of Music. Author of *The Lord's Song in a Strange Land: Music and Identity in Contemporary Jewish Worship*, **586**

Syrkin Nachman (1868-1924). Russian-born political theorist who dedicated himself to uniting Zionism and socialism, **18**

Ta'anit (Fast). Ninth tractate of the Mishnah*, in the order *Mo'ed* (Seasons). It deals with special fasts, for example at a time of drought, **13, 511**

Tabick, Jacqueline (b. 1948, Dublin). Ordained Leo Baeck College 1975 as Britain's first woman rabbi. Served West London Synagogue 1975-98 and now serves North West Surrey Synagogue. She has a major interest in areas of interfaith and social justice and chairs the World Congress of Faiths, **513**

Tabick, Larry (b.1947). Ordained Leo Baeck College 1976. Rabbi of Shir Hayim, the Hampstead Reform Jewish Community, and student/teacher of Jewish prayer and mysticism. Author of *Growing into your Soul: A Celebration of Jewish Life*, **503, 504, 510**

Talmud (Teaching). Compilation of the commentaries of the Rabbis on the Mishnah* from the second to fifth centuries CE covering both religious and civil matters. A mixture of laws, customs, discussions, stories and *obiter dicta*, it became the foundation of Jewish practice throughout the world. There are two versions, the Yerushalmi (Jerusalem), compiled in Palestine and completed in about 400 CE, and the Bavli, compiled in Babylon and completed between 500 and 800 CE. The Bavli is regarded as being authoritative, **20, 600.**

Tamaret, Aaron Samuel (1869-1931). Rabbi, writer and philosopher from Grodno. Early supporter of Zionism, but became disillusioned and led a pacifist group in the First World War, **55**

Tamid (Perpetual Offerings). Tractate in the Mishnah* and Talmud*. It deals with the daily burnt offerings and Temple organisation, **519**

Tanchuma. Midrash* attributed to R.Tanchuma bar Abba and based on the portions read from the Torah each week, usually on the opening verse, **14, 603**

Tchernikowsky, Saul (1875-1943). Hebrew poet born in Russia who emigrated to Palestine in 1931. He reacted against Diaspora Judaism and had a radical influence on Hebrew poetry, **192**

Tosefta Sotah. Sotah is the tractate relating to the ordeal of women suspected of adultery. Tosefta, meaning additional, is a second-century legal work containing discussions not included in the Mishnah*, **575**

Tucholsky, Kurt (1890-1935). German satirist and journalist. An ardent pacifist and socialist after the First World War, he wrote essays, poems and cabaret songs under many pseudonyms. Settled in Sweden in 1929, where he took his own life, **522**

Tuwim, Juljan (1894-1953). Polish poet and satirist who returned to Poland after the Second World War, **17**

Union Prayer Book. Prayer book of the American Reform Movement, first published 1894-95, **608**

Verdonk, Henriette (Sarah) (1945-2005). A Dutch primary-school teacher who later specialised in teaching the different religions of a multi-cultural society at primary-school level. Many of her poems included Jewish themes, **99**

Weiman-Kelman, Levi (b. 1955, USA). Ordained Jewish Theological Seminary 1979. In 1985 he founded the Congregation Kol HaNeshama in Jerusalem. Teaches prayer and liturgy at Hebrew Union College and Schechter Rabbinical Seminary in Jerusalem, **508**

Wieseltier, Leon (b. 1952, New York). Writer, critic and literary editor of *The New Republic*. Although distanced from his Jewish upbringing, he observed the traditional year of mourning for his father and wrote of his experiences in *Kaddish*, **589**

<<<

GLOSSARY AND INDEX 740

Wittenberg, Jonathan (b. 1957, Glasgow). Studied for the rabbinate in Jerusalem and London. Ordained Leo Baeck College 1987. Rabbi New North London Synagogue (Masorti). Involved in many interfaith and social justice projects. Publications include *The Eternal Journey. Meditations on the Jewish Year*, **606**

Wolpe, David (b. 1958). Ordained Jewish Theological Seminary 1987. Senior Rabbi, Sinai Temple, Los Angeles. Books include *The Healer of Shattered Hearts: A Jewish View of God* and *Making Loss Matter*, **584**

Wright, Alexandra (b.1956, London). Ordained Leo Baeck College 1986. Formerly Rabbi, Radlett and Bushey Reform Synagogue; in 2004 she became Senior Rabbi, Liberal Jewish Synagogue, London. Has contributed to *Hear Our Voice* and *Taking up the Timbrel*, and has special interest in the Maharal of Prague, **368, 506**

Yanchiker, Rabbi Nachum. Rabbi, Head of Slobodka Yeshivah, Lithuania, **390**

Yehuda he-Chasid *see* Judah he-Chasid, **581**

Yerushalmi Baba Metzia *see* Baba Metzia, **20**

Zephaniah. Seventh-century BCE Biblical prophet in the Kingdom of Judah. Prophecies mainly concerned the end of time and the destruction of Jerusalem, **600**

Zohar (Splendour). Major work of Kabbalah, Jewish mysticism, a commentary on the Torah and *Megillot*. While traditionally ascribed to second-century Simon bar Yohai, it is generally acknowledged to be the work of Moses de Leon in the thirteenth century, **11, 12, 608**

LIST OF ARTISTS

Althof, Rachel: b. 1949, worked as a teacher in Cologne till moving to Switzerland after her marriage, developing her work as an artist. She has exhibited internationally. Since 1982 she has worked with Hebrew and Arabic calligraphy, **401, 445, 455, 480**

Baum, Josh (b.1971, London). He studied fine art in Barcelona and lived and worked for many years in Sfat, where he painted the domed ceiling of the Abuhav Synagogue. He became a Sofer in Jerusalem, where he wrote a Torah scroll. He currently lives and works in London, **181**

Casanave, Martha: (b. 1946, USA). A graduate in Russian Language and Literature she became engaged in photography from childhood. She has been an exhibiting and working photographer and educator for thirty years. Her work is in major collections including the Bibliotheque Nationale and the J. Paul Getty Museum, **493**

Ezer, Oded (b. 1972, Israel). A graduate of Bezalel Academy of Art and Design, Jerusalem, a full-time commercial typographer and type designer, he is a lecturer at the Shenkar College of Design and Engineering, Ramat Gan, and the Wizo College of Design, Haifa. His posters and graphics have received international awards. http://www.odedezer.com, **545**

Frank, Hannah (b. 1908, Glasgow). Studied at the Glasgow School of Art and the University. Her drawings and later sculpture have been shown in the Royal Academy, the Royal Scottish Academy and the Royal Glasgow Institute as well as touring internationally, **373**

Front, Charles (b. 1930, London). He studied painting, illustration and calligraphy at the Slade School of Fine Art, London. After a number of years as an advertising art director he works as an illustrator, designer and calligrapher. He recently acquired a BA in Art History from the Open University, **175**

Games, Abram, OBE (1914-96). London-born graphic designer. His powerful works as an official war artist and as a freelance designer, including posters for the Festival of Britain and stamps for Britain, Jersey and Israel, gained him international renown. He produced designs for many Jewish causes. His design adorned the *Jewish Chronicle* supplement at the launch of the 1977 edition of *Forms of Prayer* and is reproduced with the agreement of the Estate of Abram Games, **91**

Halter, Ardyn (born London). Lives in Pardes Hanna, Israel. He is a painter, printmaker, Judaica artist and stained-glass designer and maker, with works in the Victoria and Albert Museum and the New York Public Library. Commissions include the stained-glass windows for the Rwandan Genocide Memorial in Gisozi, Rwanda and the monumental bronze sculpture 'Your Fellow Man' at Yad LaShirion, Latrun, Israel, marking the contribution of foreign volunteer soldiers to the creation of the Jewish State, **133, 215, 383**

Halter Hurn, Aviva (b. 1964). British artist and designer. Studied art at Camberwell College of Art, apprenticed with and subsequently worked with her father Roman Halter* in designing and making stained-glass windows for Beth Shalom, Nottingham. Her Holocaust prints are in the collection of the Museum of Chicago and the Imperial War Museum. She illustrated *Essential Poems for Children*, **64, 93, 159**

Halter, Roman (b. 1927, Chodecz, Poland). Artist, stained-glass designer, architect and writer. His experience in Nazi-overrun Poland as a fugitive and survivor of Auschwitz is recorded in his book *Roman's Journey*. The pictures in this edition are part of his works in the Imperial War Museum. His stained-glass windows are at Yad l'Yeled and North Western Reform Synagogue and his memorial to the victims of the Shoah, *Zachor*, is in the grounds of the Sternberg Centre. All aspects of the 'Room of Prayer' at Leo Baeck College are his work, **371, 403, 406, 564**

Horton, Mike (b. 1947, Bromley, Kent). Artist, photographer and designer. He studied art at Ravensbourne College of Art and Design before settling in Israel, where he has lived for over thirty years. A photograph he took is contracted to be on the next Israel bank note, **29, 309, 324, 365, 503**

Kempner, Gillian (*née* Holding) (b. 1959, Chester). Lives and works in Leeds. Practised as a lawyer from 1984 to 1999, when she started working full-time as an artist in a range of media from print-making to textiles, exploring the human condition and contemporary society, **434**

Kogan, Anna (b. 1985, St Petersburg). She studied at the State Academy of Art and Industry, St Petersburg, majoring in furniture design. In 2005 she attended a WUPJ seminar for mezuzah scribes in Minsk and since then Jewish calligraphy has become her major interest: she is learning Sofrut. She has exhibited in the Jewish community of St Petersburg, **220, 267, 272, 412, 572. 662**

LIST OF ARTISTS 742

Lalou, Frank (b.1958, Marmande, France). Lives in France and Belgium. Internationally known as a calligrapher, illustrator, essayist and publisher of over forty books, some originals of which are in institutions like the Bibliothèque Nationale de France and the Jerusalem Museum. His calligraphy is applied to numerous materials and through his invention of the Calamophone is linked to music. www.lalou.net, **94**

Lyskovoi, Alexander (Sasha) (b.1954, Rostov on Don). He graduated from art college in 1977, working as a designer and private teacher of painting and drawing for almost twenty years. He took up Jewish studies, being ordained as a rabbi by Leo Baeck College. He currently works as the Rabbi of the Union of Reform Congregations of Russia in Moscow, **699**

Michaels, Marc (b. 1963, Greenwich, London). He gained a Diploma in Graphic Design and Communication from Goldsmiths College and worked initially as a designer and illustrator for the Central Office of Information before moving to marketing for the Government. He studied Sofrut under Vivian Solomon. He is a *Sofer STaM* and freelance designer, author of the *Tikkun for Megillat Hashoah* and the designer of this edition of the Siddur. www.sofer.co.uk, **371, 688**

Pintor, Didac (b. 1965, Barcelona). He studied at Escola Eina, Barcelona and the Kunstakademie of Düsseldorf. He has held individual and collective exhibitions of installation and performance work in Spain and Germany. He did calligraphic drawings for the covers of *Biblioteca Judaica Catalana*. He currently lives and works in Barcelona, **591, 700**

Pludwinski, Izzy (b. 1954, Brooklyn, New York). A freelance calligrapher, *Sofer STaM* and calligraphy teacher, he now lives in Jerusalem. His commissions include work for the President's Office of Israel, the inscription of the dedication page in the Bible presented to the Pope, and the lettering of Yakar Synagogue. He has published a fine-art edition of the Song of Songs. His own calligraphic artwork involves ever-new expressive forms of Hebrew script. www.impwriter.com, **664**

Rava, Tobia (b. 1959, Padua). He obtained a degree in the Semiology of Arts at Bologna University and now works in Venice. He has exhibited in personal and collective exhibitions in Europe, South America, the US and the Far East. He deals with Hebrew iconography and is a founder member of Contemporary Art Concert. www.tobiarava.com, **60**

Reuter, Elisabeth Naomi (b. 1945, Celle). She studied graphics and fine art at WKS in Hanover. Her children's books, with her own text and illustrations, including *Judith and Lisa, Soham - eine Geschichte vom Fremdsein*, have been translated into eight languages. She has exhibited internationally and is currently working on literary works by Kafka, Kolmar and Jabes, **7**

Szlakmann, Charles (b. 1946, Lyons). He has a BA in political science. As a cartoonist he specialised in portraits, contributing for twenty years to *Le Monde* and *Les Echos*. He is the illustrator and calligrapher of a Passover Haggadah, author (text and drawings) of *Judaism for Beginners I & II* and a journalist in the field of Jewish religion and culture, **197, 277**

Van de Feer, Monique (b. 1955, Holland). Her art and writing are inspired by Jewish mysticism and Hebrew letters. Her book *Letters of Light* (2006) is about the hidden meaning of Hebrew letters. www.gingie.nl, **456, 571**

LIST OF ILLUSTRATIONS

7 '*baruch attah adonai*' by Elisabeth Reuter; **29** '*v'eirastich li be'emunah v'yadat et Adonai*' 'I betroth you to Me with faithfulness and you will know the Eternal' (Hos 2:22) by Mike Horton; **60** 'l'ascolta nel bosca' (Sh'ma in the wood) 2004 by Tobia Rava; **64** '*hashkiveinu Adonai eloheinu l'shalom*' 'Cause us to lie down in peace' by Aviva Halter Hurn; **91** 'When you call Me and come and pray to Me' by Abram Games; **93** '*eits chayim hi la-machazikim bah v'tom'cheha m'ushar*' 'It is a tree of life to all who grasp it and those who hold fast to it are happy' (Prov 3:18) by Aviva Halter Hurn; **94** '*l'chah dodi*' 'Come, my friend' by Frank Lalou; **133** 'Vines' by Ardyn Halter; **159** '*nishmat kol chai* …' 'The breath of life in every creature …' by Aviva Halter Hurn; **175** 'Psalm 92:8-10' by Charles Front; **181** 'Psalm 150' by Josh Baum; **197** '*Eil adon al kol ha-ma'asim* ...' 'God, governing all creation …' (text, page 208-209) by Charles Szlakmann; **215** 'Galilee Landscape' by Ardyn Halter; **220** '*Adonai s'fatai tiftach ufi yaggid t'hillatecha*' 'My God, open my lips and my mouth shall declare Your praise' (Ps 51:17) by Anna Kogan; **267** '*al sh'loshah d'varim ha-olam omed* ...' 'Civilisation is based on three things …' (*Pirke Avot* 1:2) by Anna Kogan; **272** '*al sh'loshah d'varim ha-olam kayyam* …' 'Civilisation is preserved by three things …' (*Pirke Avot* 1:18) by Anna Kogan; **277** '*Ha-Eil*' by Charles Szlakmann; **309** 'Omer Calendar' by Mike Horton; **324** '*b'ruchim attem b'vo'achem, uv'ruchim attem b'tseit'chem*' 'Just as you were blessed when you entered, may you be blessed as you depart' by Mike Horton; **365** '*v'nimtseiti lachem n'um Adonai*' 'I shall let you find me, says God' (Jer 29:14) by Mike Horton; Page 371 '*zachor*' 'Remember' Holocaust Memorial by Roman Halter, reproduced by Marc Michaels; **383** 'Almond Tree' by Ardyn Halter; **401** '*even ma'asu ha-bonim hay'tah l'rosh pinah*' 'A stone the builders rejected has become the corner-stone itself' (Psalm 118:22) by Rachel Althof; **403** 'Starved Faces' by Roman Halter; **406** 'Man on the Electrified Barbed-Wire' by Roman Halter; **412** '*etz chayyin hi* …' 'It is a tree of life …' by Anna Kogan; **434** '*sh'ma yisrael* …' 'Hear O Israel …' by Gillian Kempner; **445** '*sh'ma yisrael* …' 'Hear O Israel …' by Rachel Althof; **455** '… *borei p'ri ha-gafen*' '… who creates the fruit of the vine.' by Rachel Althof; **456** 'Sh'chinah' by Monique van der Feer; **480** '… *ha-motsi lechem min ha-arets*' 'who brings forth bread from the earth' by Rachel Althof; **493** selected from the collection called 'Elements' by Martha Casanave; **503** '*mashiv ha-ru'ach u'morid ha-gashem*' 'making the wind blow and the rain fall' by Mike Horton; **545** 'The Message' by Oded Ezer; **564** 'Woman Wearing Mantilla' by Roman Halter; **571** 'Intertwined Figures' by Monique van der Feer ' The holiest place is the place where people support, love, forgive and trust each other. In that place God is with us.'; **572** '*Elohai n'shamah shennatata bi t'hora hi*' 'My God, the soul You have given me is pure.' by Anna Kogan; **591** '*ha-sneh bo'eir ba-eish v'ha-sneh einenu ukal*' 'the bush burned with fire but the bush was not consumed' (Ex 3:2) by Didac Pintor; **662** '*tsaddik ka-tamar yifrach*' 'The righteous shall flourish like the palm tree' (Psalm 92:13) by Anna Kogan; **664** '*Hal'luyah*' by Izzy Pludwinski (used by permission of Efod Art Embroidery); **688** 'Psalm 122' by Marc Michaels; **699** '*mizrach*' by Alexander (Sasha) Lyskovoi; **700** '*Alef bet*' by Didac Pintor.

# SOURCES 744

SOURCES OF UNNAMED PRAYERS, MEDITATIONS AND REFLECTIONS

Unless otherwise stated, all page commentaries and introductions to sections, 'Before the Service Begins', original or revised translations, and named passages in the Study Anthology are by Jonathan Magonet (JM), as are new or amended intermediate blessings of the daily *Amidah* and *Musaf Amidah*, the new *Aleinu* and Responsive Readings. Other 'non-traditional' prayers throughout are taken from the 1977 edition of *Forms of Prayer* (FOP), composed by Lionel Blue (LB) or JM, or taken from previous editions. A number of prayers are newly composed by Howard Cooper (HC). Page numbers are as follows:

26 '*Sh'liach Tsibbur* - The Worship Service Leader' JM, **96** 'Before the Service Begins' JM, **97** 'Our Creator …' FOP (JM); 'Our God and God of our ancestors …' FOP (LB), **98** 'Creator of mercy …' FOP (LB); 'God of the spirits of all flesh' Larry Tabick; 'We bless the God who conquers strife …' FOP (LB), **99** 'On the seventh day …' JM, **154** 'Before the Service Begins' JM, **155** 'The Just Society' FOP (LB); 'The Community' FOP (LB), **156** 'The Family of Israel' FOP (LB); 'Tradition' FOP (LB); 'Life and Death' FOP (LB), **157** 'The Future' FOP (LB); 'The Covenants of God' JM; 'Our Heritage' HC, **158** 'Our Responsibility' HC; 'One Humanity' JM; 'The Gift of Women' JM, **245** Blessings for *Kuvim Haftarah* JM and Paul Freedman, **246** 'Our God whose dominion is everlasting' Michael Hilton; 'For the Sovereign …' FOP (LB), **247** 'For the State of Israel' FOP (LB); 'For Consolation'; 'For Healing' FOP, **249** Prayer for International Understanding FOP (LB), Prayer for Interfaith Understanding FOP (JM) **250** Prayer for Responsibility for Justice and the Environment HC, **258ff**. Torah Service II, Michael Hilton, **326** 'As we welcome …' Tony Bayfield; 'This is how it ends' HC, *Kabbalat Shabbat* Levi ben Amitai, **327** 'Sunset Prayer' Jacob Glatstein, **328** 'God is loving…' David Blumenthal, **329** '*Sh'ma*' Reuven Silverman, **330** 'A Short *Amidah*' Syd Lieberman, **331** 'Meditation' HC; 'Teach me, God, to pray …' Leah Goldberg, **332** 'We all have a body …', Ineke van Mourik; 'We talk of the soul …' HC, **333ff**. 'What are we? What is our life? What can we say before You?' HC, **335**, 'There are those who sing…' Abraham Isaac Kook; 'Everyone sang …' Siegfried Sassoon, **336** 'The breath of life …' HC; '*Barukh* - Blessed' Arthur Green, **337** 'The heavens declare ...' JM, 'We are in the middle …' Primo Levi, **338** 'We are a people apart …' JM; 'Pay attention, Israel …' HC, **339** '*Emet*, truth …' quoting Shmuel Sperber JM, **339-44** 'Reflections on the *Amidah*' JM, **345** 'To the Book of Deuteronomy…' based on Milton Sternberg; 'It is exceedingly difficult …' Louis Jacobs, **346** 'When the Temple stood …' JM; 'All is movement …' HC; 'To open eyes …' Emmanuel Eydoux, **347** 'We look to the future…' HC; 'And then all that has divided…' Judy Chicago; '*Yitgadal* … The old words …' HC, **348** 'Look around us …' Marge Piercy, **355** Prayers for healing: 'Hillel said …' Miriam Bayfield; 'May the source of strength …*Mi Sheberach* …' Drorah Setel and Debbie Friedman, **367** A Prayer in a Time of a Natural Disaster, Alexandra Wright, **371** A Prayer for Combating Poverty and Injustice HC, **372** A Prayer for World Peace Michael Hilton, **396** 'Eternal God, whose presence …' Sylvia Rothschild and Michael Hilton, **397** God of Abraham… JM **405** National Holocaust Memorial Day JM, **414** A Prayer on Making *Aliyah* JM; A Prayer on Leaving Home JM, **415** A Prayer for Parents when a Child Leaves Home JM, **416** A Prayer on Retirement JM; A Prayer on the Loss of a Loved One JM, **417** A Prayer During Depression, Alexandra Wright; A Prayer for Those Responsible for the Care of Others JM, **418** Prayers about Animal Companions Charles H.Middleburgh, **422** Prayers after a Miscarriage of on the Death of an Infant, 'I light this candle …' Sylvia Rothschild; 'God, full of mercy … 'Sylvia Rothschild, **423** 'Eternal One our God …' Walter Rothschild, **447** Shabbat Alone HC, **480** 'We have eaten and been satisfied …' based on Michael Leigh, **488** 'We remember…' FOP (LB), **661** Introduction to the *Hallel*, Fred Morgan.

STRUCTURE OF SHABBAT SERVICES

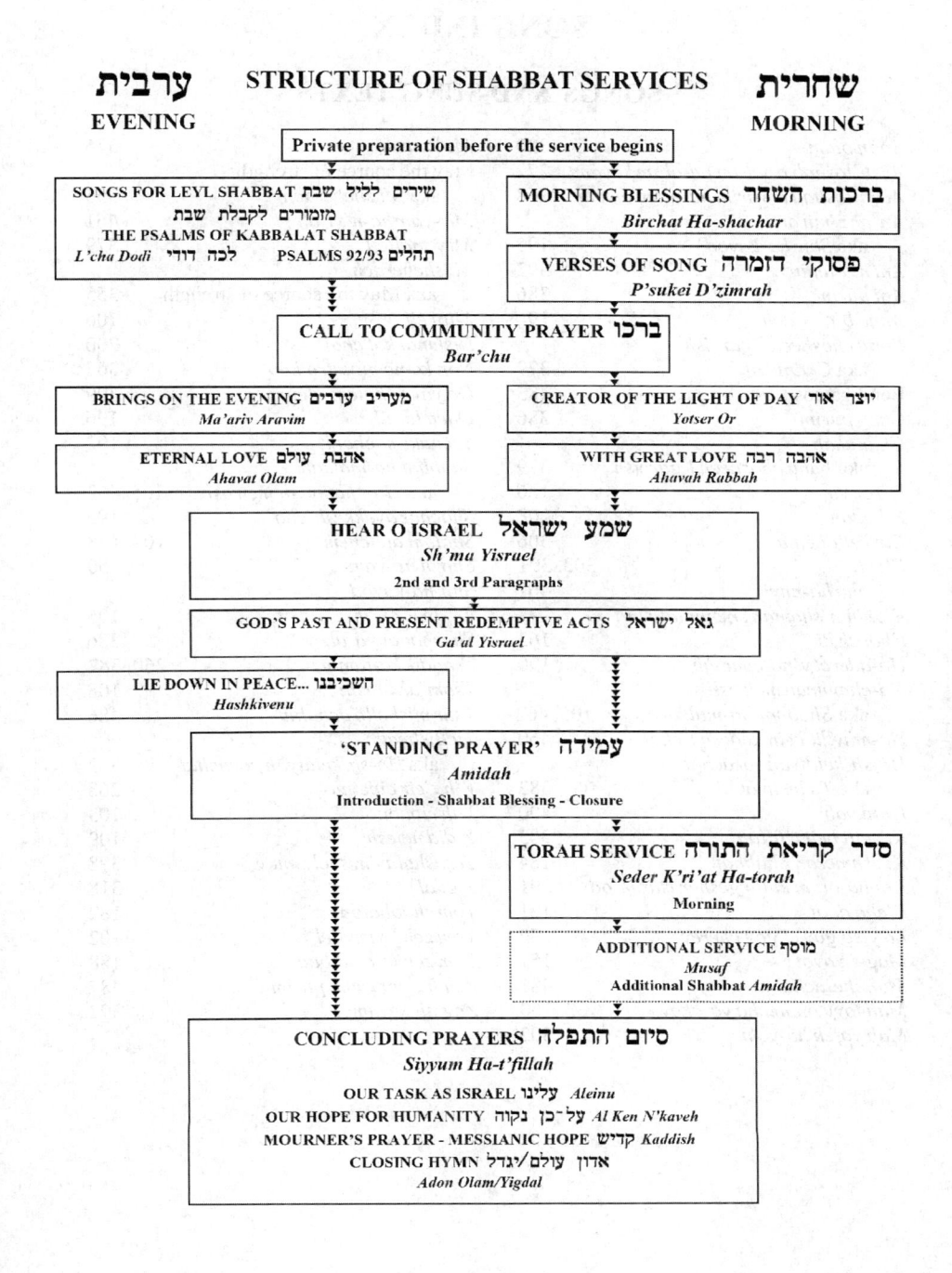

ערבית EVENING — שחרית MORNING

Private preparation before the service begins

SONGS FOR LEYL SHABBAT שירים לליל שבת
THE PSALMS OF KABBALAT SHABBAT מזמורים לקבלת שבת
L'cha Dodi לכה דודי — PSALMS 92/93 תהלים

MORNING BLESSINGS ברכות השחר
Birchat Ha-shachar

VERSES OF SONG פסוקי דזמרה
P'sukei D'zimrah

CALL TO COMMUNITY PRAYER ברכו
Bar'chu

BRINGS ON THE EVENING מעריב ערבים
Ma'ariv Aravim

CREATOR OF THE LIGHT OF DAY יוצר אור
Yotser Or

ETERNAL LOVE אהבת עולם
Ahavat Olam

WITH GREAT LOVE אהבה רבה
Ahavah Rabbah

HEAR O ISRAEL שמע ישראל
Sh'ma Yisrael
2nd and 3rd Paragraphs

GOD'S PAST AND PRESENT REDEMPTIVE ACTS גאל ישראל
Ga'al Yisrael

LIE DOWN IN PEACE... השכיבנו
Hashkivenu

'STANDING PRAYER' עמידה
Amidah
Introduction - Shabbat Blessing - Closure

TORAH SERVICE סדר קריאת התורה
Seder K'ri'at Ha-torah
Morning

ADDITIONAL SERVICE מוסף
Musaf
Additional Shabbat *Amidah*

CONCLUDING PRAYERS סיום התפלה
Siyyum Ha-t'fillah
OUR TASK AS ISRAEL עלינו *Aleinu*
OUR HOPE FOR HUMANITY על־כן נקוה *Al Ken N'kaveh*
MOURNER'S PRAYER - MESSIANIC HOPE קדיש *Kaddish*
CLOSING HYMN אדון עולם/יגדל
Adon Olam/Yigdal

SONG INDEX

SONGS AND SUNG TEXTS

Adon olam	320	Ma'oz tzur	376
Al sh'loshah d'varim ha-olam kayam	272	May the source of strength	
Al sh'loshah d'varim ha-olam omeid	268	aka *Mi sheberach*	355
An'im z'mirot		Mir-yam ha-n'vi'ah	461
aka *Shir ha-kavod*	195	Mi y'malleil	379
Ani ma'amin	392	Mi sheberach	
Ani purim	386	aka May the source of strength	355
Anna b'cho'ach	194	Mipi eil	106
Banu choshech l'gareish		Nishmat kol chai	200
aka *Chanukah*	379	Non komo maestro Dio	307
Bendigamos	485	Od yavo shalom aleinu	399
Chag purim	386	Odeh la-eil	196
Chanukah		Sachaki, sachaki	192
aka *banu choshech l'gareish*	379	Shabbat ha-malkah	
D'ror yikra	186	aka *Ha-chammah meirosh*	105, 462
Eil adon	208	Shachar avakkesh'cha	193
Ein keiloheinu	306	Shalom aleichem	104, 448
Eli eli	303, 391	Shirat ha-yam	50
Eliyahu ha-navi	461	Shir ha-kavod	
Elohai n'shamah shennatata bi		aka *An'im z'mirot*	195
t'horah hi	163	Shoshanat ya'akov	386
Ha-aderet v'ha-emunah	190	Tsaddik ka-tamar	260, 382
Ha-chammah meirosh		Tsam'ah nafshi	108
aka *Shabbat ha-malkah*	105, 462	Tsur mishello achalnu	486
Ha-mavdil bein kodesh l'chol	460	Tu Bishvat	
Ha-sh'keidiyah porachat		aka *Ha-sh'keidiyah porachat*	382
aka *Tu bishvat*	382	V'ha'eir eineinu	268
Hatikvah	400	Yah ribbon	103
Ki veiti beit t'fillah	303	Y'did nefesh	109
Ki eshmerah Shabbat	184	Yerushalayim shel zahav	398
Kol ha-olam kullo gesher tsar m'od	391	Yigdal	318
L'cha dodi	121	Yom shabbaton	182
Lo yisa goy el goy cherev	372	Yom zeh l'yisra'el	102
Magein avot	151	Yom zeh m'chubbad	188
Mah she'achalnu	481	Zeh ha-yom yom purim	387
Mah tovu ohalecha ya'akov	32, 160	Zog nit keynmol	392
Mah yafeh ha-yom	302		

PERMISSIONS AND ACKNOWLEDGEMENTS

The publishers are indebted to the following for their kind permission
to reproduce copyright material in this book

Beacon Press for extracts from *The Judaic Tradition*, edited by Nahum N. Glatzer; The Central Conference of American Rabbis for an extract from the *Union Prayer Book* II; Contemporary Books for an item by Bradley Shavit Artson from *The Bedside Torah*; Cornwall Books for a poem by Aaron Kramer from *In Illness*; Crown Publishing Group for extracts from *A Treasury of Jewish Poetry*, edited by Nathan and Marynn Ausubel, © 1957 by Nathan and Marynn Ausubel; Doubleday & Company Inc. for an extract from *The Treasury of Jewish Humour* edited by N. Ausubel, © 1951; Curtis Brown for a passage by Isaiah Berlin from *Four Essays on Liberty*; Darton, Longman and Todd for passages by A. J. Heschel quoted by Alan Ecclestone in *Night Sky of the Lord* and Marjorie Proops in *Pearls of Wisdom*; Edwin Mellen Press Ltd for an article 'Choosing a God Language' by David Blumenthal in *Problems in Contemporary Jewish Theology*, edited by Dan Cohn-Sherbok, New York 1992; Faber & Faber Ltd for passages by Lily Pincus from *Life and Death: Coming to Terms with Death in the Family* and from 'Can We Know the Universe? Reflections on a Grain of Salt' by Carl Sagan in *The Faber Book of Science*; Farrar, Straus & Giroux, Inc. for passages by A. J. Heschel from *The Sabbath* © 1951, *Moral Grandeur and Spiritual Audacity*, ed. Susannah Heschel, and *A Passion for Truth*; Fordham University Press for a passage by Jack Cohen in *Major Philosophers of Jewish Prayer in the Twentieth Century*; Joan Gordon for two passages in *If That Spoon Could Speak*; Granta Books for an item by Joseph Roth from *The Radetsky March* translated by Michael Hofmann; Gütersloher Verlagshaus for passages by Leo Baeck; *Ha'aretz* for a passage by Nachman of Bratslav, quoted by Avriel Bar-Levav in 'Guide to the Bratslav Galaxy', 24 March 2000; HarperCollins Publishers for items from *Kindred Spirits*, 1995; Harper and Row for an item by Allen Ginsberg from *White Shroud: Poems* 1980-1985; Harper SanFrancisco for a passage by Judith Plaskow from *Standing Again at Sinai: Judaism from a Feminist Perspective*, 1991; Hebrew Union College Press for a passage by Sore bas Toyvim from *The Merit of our Mothers*; Henry Holt & Co Inc for a passage by David Wolpe from *The Healer of Shattered Hearts*; Herder Verlag for two passages by Jakob J. Petuchowski from *Gottesdienst des Herzens: Eine Auswahl aus dem Gebetsschatz des Judentums*; Hodder & Stoughton Ltd for an extract from *The Gates of the Forest* by Elie Wiesel, translated by Frances Frenaye; Jason Aronson Inc for passages from *Worlds of Jewish Prayer. A Festschrift in Honour of Rabbi Zalman M. Schachter Shalomi*, ed. Shoshana Harris-Wiener and Jonathan Omerman and an item by Kalonymus Kalman Shapiro from *Esh Kodesh – the Holy Fire*, edited by Nehemia Polen; The Jewish Agency for Israel for extracts from *The Quality of Faith* by S. H. Bergman; the *Jewish Chronicle* for an article by Melanie Philips in their issue of 13 August 2004; The Jewish Council for Racial Equality for passages by Ingeborg Bower taken from *Unaccompanied Refugee Children: Have the Lessons been Learnt?* and Edie Friedman; the *Jewish Encyclopaedia* for a passage by Rabbi Israel Lipschuetz of Danzig, Vol.5, p.159; The Jewish Publication Society of America for extracts from *Post-Biblical Hebrew Literature* edited by B. Halper, for a song from *Selected Poems of Yehudah Halevi* and for a passage by Abraham Milligram from *Jewish Worship*, 1971; the *Journal of Reform Judaism* for a passage by Norman Lipson, Summer 1988; Judah Magnes Museum for a passage by Judah L. Magnes, quoted by Paul Mendes Flohr in *The Jewish Legacy and the German Conscience*; the Jüdische Gemeinde zu Berlin for a passage from their *Sefer Hamitzvot*; Rabbi Shammai Kanter for a passage by him in *World of the High Holy Days*; *Kerem* for 'The Role of the *Shaliach Tsibur*' by Jeffrey Summit, Winter 1992-93; Zoë Klein; Knopf Publishing Group for passages by Marge Piercy from *The Art of Blessing the Day, Poems on Jewish Themes* and by Harold Kushner from *Living a Life That Matters*; Ktav Publishing House for passages by Lee Levine from 'A Masorti Judaism in Israel: Challenge, Vision and Program', in *Towards the Twenty-First Century: Judaism and the Jewish People in Israel and America*, by Harold M. Schulweis from *In God's Mirror: Reflections and Essays*, and by Leila Gay Berner from *Siddur Chaverim Kol Yisrael*; Tamir Lahav-Radlmesser for his *Song of David*; Macmillan, London and Basingstoke for extracts from *The Reform Movement in Judaism* edited by D. Philipson; MANNA, *The Journal of the Sternberg Centre for Judaism* for an article by Anouska Salida, Summer 2005; Merlin Press Ltd for a passage by Georg Lukacs from *Soul and Form*; Montgomery Media Inc for two passages by Jay R. Brickman from *Reflections in a Pumpkin Field*; Oxford University Press for extracts from *A Book of Jewish Thoughts* selected and arranged by the Very Reverend J. H. Herz and for a passage by Isaiah Berlin from *Liberty 2002*; Pan Macmillan, London © Oliver Sachs, *A Leg to Stand on*; Panther Books Ltd for a quotation by

PERMISSIONS AND ACKNOWLEDGEMENTS

Bob Dylan from *Bob Dylan: Writings and Drawings*; the Penguin Group (USA) Inc for a passage by Rachel Naomi Remen in *My Grandfather's Blessings*; Penguin Group (UK) for lines by Shmuel Hanagid in *The Penguin Book of Hebrew Verse*; Picador Books for passages by Michael Chabon from *The Amazing Adventures of Kavalier and Clay* and by Leon Wieseltier from *Kaddish*; The Rabbinical Assembly and the United Synagogue of America for an extract and for songs from *The Sabbath and Festival Prayer Book*; The Rabbinical Council of America for an extract from an essay *The Lonely Man of Faith* by Rabbi Joseph B. Soloveitchik, published in *Tradition*, edited by Rabbi Walter S. Wurzburger, Vol. VII, no.2, Summer 1965; Random House Group Ltd for passages from *The Truce* by Primo Levi, published by The Bodley Head, from *I Have Landed* by Stephen Jay Gould published by Jonathan Cape and from *How We Die* by Sherwin Nuland; Readers Union Ltd for a passage by Leopold Infeld from *Quest 1942*; The Reconstructionist Press for a passage by Zelda from *Kol Haneshamah: Shabbat Eve*; Robson Books for a passage by Greville Janner from *One Hand Alone Cannot Clap*; Routledge and Kegan Paul for a passage by Franz Rosenzweig from *The Star of Redemption*, the Littmann Library of Jewish Civilisation; George Routledge and Sons for a passage by Morris Joseph from *The Message of Judaism*; Schocken Books Inc for extracts from the following: *The Essence of Judaism* by Leo Baeck © 1948; *Ten Rungs. Hasidic Sayings* by Martin Buber, © 1947, *Language of Faith* by Nahum N. Glatzer © 1947, 1967; *The Hasidic Anthology* by Louis I. Newman © 1934 by Charles Scribner's Sons, © 1963 by Schocken Books Inc., *A Jewish Reader*, edited by Nathan N, Glatzer, © 1946, 1961; *Hammer on the Rock: A Midrash Reader*, edited by Nathan N. Glatzer ©1948, 1962; *Aspects of Rabbinic Theology* by Solomon Schechter; Charles Scribner's Sons for two passages by Daniel Gordis from *God Was Not in the Fire*; Search Press Ltd for extracts from *Springs of Jewish Wisdom* © 1969; Sheep Meadow Poetry for a poem by Yehuda Amichai from *Poems of Jerusalem*; Syracuse University Press for items by Airyeh Leib Heller and Mendel of Kotsk quoted by Byron L.W. Sherwin in *In Partnership with God*; Thames & Hudson Ltd for extracts from *Tales of the Hasidim* by Martin Buber and a passage by Gershom Sholem from *Major Trends in Jewish Mysticism*; Touchstone for a passage by Irving Greenberg from *The Jewish Way*; *Tikkun Magazine* for 'A Glimmer of Hope: A State of All Its Citizens' by Yakov M. R. Fakin, July/August 2002; Union of American Hebrew Congregations for an extract from *Giants of Justice* by Rabbi Albert Vorspan; the University of Alabama Press for an extract from *Paganism, Christianity, Judaism* by Max Brod, © 1970; University of Chicago Press for 'The Philosopher of Nature and Technology' by Hans Jonas from *The Imperative of Responsibility*; Washington Square Press for two articles from *Judaism*, ed. Arthur Herzberg; Weidenfeld and Nicholson for a passage by Anatholy Sharansky from *Fear No Evil: A Memoir*; Rabbi Levi Weimar-Kelman; William Morrow Publishers for a passage by David Gelernter from *Study Talmud in How Things Are*, 1995; World Union for Progressive Judaism for extracts from *The Growth of Reform Judaism* by Walther Plaut; *The Problem of Evil* by G.Salzberger and by Yehuda Bacon from *Art and Meaning*, pamphlet no.3; *Yeshivat Hasidei Breslav* for a passage by Nachman of Bratzlav, translated by Avraham Greenbaum, in *Restore My Soul*; Ziegler School of Religious Studies for passages by Jacob Artson and Bradley Shavit Artson.

While every effort has been made to trace copyright owners of the material used,
the publishers take this opportunity of tendering apologies to any owners
whose rights may have been unwittingly infringed.

DEDICATIONS

Dedicated to the **Alyth Guild** whose members' loyalty to the Synagogue has been manifest in so many ways. Constantly remembering the lovely and irreplaceable **Linda Bayfield**, head teacher of Akiva School, wife, mother, grandma and friend. **Michael & Sue Casale and Barry Faber** remember their parents Rachel and John Casale and Sheila and Henry Faber. **Colin**: To honour all those who helped me find my way on my return to Judaism. In loving memory of our son **Bradley Marc Elster.** Barbara, Cyril and sisters, Traci, Lyssa and Dannielle. **Viv Essex** - elegant and vivacious. Adored by her loving family. An amazing lady who touched the hearts of so many. To mark the retirement of **Rabbi Simon Franses** after 21 years of dedicated service to **Middlesex New Synagogue**. **Richard Mark Freed**. Always in our thoughts and never forgotten by Gilly, Darren, Jamie, Jacqui, family and friends. **Lore and Stephen Gang**: remembered with love by Gerald and Tony Fraser. In loving memory of our parents and grandparents, **Bessie and Maurice Golby and Golda and Asher Hallé**. **Corinne and Harold Gross**, in recognition of their abiding love for books, prayer, and the Jewish people. In memory of **Student Rabbi Andreas Hinz**, ז"ל who will always inspire us. Rabbis Neil Amswych and Misha Kapustin. In loving memory of **Audrey Jacobs**. A dedicated member of Menorah synagogue. From all her family. Debbie, Andrew, Zöe and Ben Jacobs remember with love **Bubbles** who watched this inspirational *Siddur* being created from afar. With thanks to all those who have come before. Ann, Charles, Sarah, Amy and Jack **Kessler.** **Dennis Lewis** ז"ל, lovingly remembered by Ruth, Jonathan, Adam, Sarah, Gwynneth, Simon, Jennifer, Richard, Michael, Joseph and Sam. For **Natalie Masters** to celebrate her qualifying as a doctor. **Simon and Jonathan Masters**, in recognition of their IT support and help in the early days of the *Siddur*. Dedicated to **Melanie, Harry and Samuel** who have made my Jewish journey so special. In memory of **Dr Jack Morris AO and Mrs Helen Morris**. True lovers of Progressive Judaism. In loving memory of **Harvey Morris**, much loved husband of Diana, father of Anita, Simon and Barrie. **Bracha, Josh, Andie, Sam and Rabbi Jeffrey Newman** remember **Henry & Ruby** with love. On its 40th Anniversary **NWSS** is looking forward to the new *Siddur* to strengthen us seeking the Way. To the many wonderful members of Cardiff Reform community who put joy into Judaism for me. **Veronica Prescott Owen.** In appreciation of all who put so much effort into producing this Prayer Book. **Joyce & Jeffery Rose.** To commemorate our Golden Wedding and fifty years of shared Reform Judaism. **Wendy and Larry Ross.** For **Nikki Samson, Katie Balcombe, Amy Samson, William Balcombe** - how comforting - the future is in their hands. In memory of **Jon Young** ז"ל (12.6.1945 - 1.1.2007) whose generosity of spirit *inspired all who* knew him. **Jonathan Young**. A tower of support for family, his profession, wider community and world of music-making. **Hilde Weinstein** (née Davidsohn) - a survivor - much loved and missed daily by Jeannette, Jenny and David Davidson.

FAMILY RECORD

תם ונשלם שבח לאל בורא עולם